London

2

SOUTH

BY

BRIDGET CHERRY

AND

NIKOLAUS PEVSNER

D1217744

THE BUILDINGS OF ENGLAND

PENGUIN BOOKS

Penguin Books Ltd, Harmondsworth, Middlesex, England
Penguin Books, 40 West 23rd Street, New York, New York 10010, USA
Penguin Books Australia Ltd, Ringwood, Victoria, Australia
Penguin Books Canada Ltd, 2801 John Street, Markham, Ontario, Canada L3R 1B4
Penguin Books (N.Z.) Ltd, 182–190 Wairau Road, Auckland 10, New Zealand

First published 1983

ISBN 0 14 071047 7

Copyright © Bridget Cherry and Nikolaus Pevsner, 1983

Made and printed in Great Britain
by Butler & Tanner Ltd, Frome and London
Set in Linotron Plantin

TO THE MARSHES

OF CLAPHAM, BALHAM, AND TOOTING

CONTENTS

FOREWORD

BY BRIDGET CHERRY

The scope of this book needs some explanation. It covers twelve of the London boroughs created when the Greater London Council was formed in 1965 – Bexley, Bromley, Croydon, Greenwich, Kingston, Lambeth, Lewisham, Merton, Richmond, Southwark, Sutton, and Wandsworth – and also in a separate section at the end the crossings over the Thames. The Greater London boroughs north of the river will be found in the revised volumes entitled London 3: North West *and* London 4: North and North East. *Central London is covered by* London: The Cities of London and Westminster *(3rd edition, 1973). The decision to adopt the present Greater London boundaries has meant that the material in this book derives initially from four previous* Buildings of England *volumes, produced at different times and by different authors: Bexley and Bromley from John Newman's* West Kent and the Weald *(1969, revised 1976), Croydon, Kingston, Merton, and the southern part of Richmond from Ian Nairn and Nikolaus Pevsner's* Surrey *(1962, revised 1971), and the rest from two very early volumes in the series: the northern part of Richmond from* Middlesex *(1951), and the old London County Council areas (Greenwich, Lambeth, Lewisham, Southwark, and Wandsworth) from* London except the Cities of London and Westminster *(1952). All sections have been very extensively revised, added to, and brought up to date, but some disparity between the different parts is inevitable – the most obvious the variation of the subdivisions within boroughs, made necessary by the different nature of inner and outer areas. In the outer boroughs places are listed alphabetically; in the densely built up areas of the former L.C.C. such distinctions are less easy to draw, so that here, with a few exceptions, subdivisions are larger and follow the pre-1965 borough boundaries (themselves generally amalgamations of older parishes) which were used in* London except the Cities of London and Westminster, *as follows:*

L.C.C. boroughs up to 1965	Present boroughs
Greenwich, Woolwich	*Greenwich*
Lambeth and parts of Wandsworth	*Lambeth*
Deptford and Lewisham	*Lewisham*
Southwark, Bermondsey, Camberwell	*Southwark*
Battersea and most of Wandsworth	*Wandsworth*

In a very few cases topographical common sense has demanded that the present borough boundaries be ignored (though cross-references are provided). Thus Clapham is all described under Lambeth, the area of St Nicholas Deptford under Lewisham, and the south side of Blackheath also under Lewisham.

With each subdivision the arrangement follows established Buildings of England *practice: Churches (Anglican, Roman Catholic, Nonconformist, each section strictly alphabetically by name) and Cemeteries; Public Buildings;* Perambulations (divided into reasonably brief and, it is hoped, manageable itineraries). No arrangement will satisfy all users, but it is hoped that with the help of the map on pp. 2–3 (which shows the boundaries of the other London volumes and the abbreviations used for all boroughs), the borough maps,‡ the indexes of streets and buildings and of boroughs and localities, and the indexes which precede each borough, as well as the separate introductions which deal with the development of individual boroughs and point to some of their architectural highlights, readers will be able to find their way around this sprawling mass of suburban building, perhaps a little more easily than from the old 'London except' volume.*

The new general introduction to South London concentrates on the buildings mentioned in this volume, although it refers on occasion to developments north of the river. Where possible it has incorporated passages from the introduction to London except the Cities of London and Westminster, *but most of this is more relevant to North London, and so will be included in the introductions to the North London volumes. The specialist introductions which follow, on prehistoric and Roman archaeology, on timber-framed buildings, and on industrial archaeology, cover the whole of Greater London.*

A final note must be added on what is included in this book. It must be stated firmly that mention of houses or other buildings in no way implies that they are open to the public. Where a pair of dates is quoted, the first is generally for the acceptance of the design, the second for the completion, in so far as these are known to the compilers. For modern buildings the names of job architects or architects in charge have been included in addition to the name of the firm, when that information has been available. In the case of buildings by local authorities, to save repetition, the names of heads of departments are not mentioned on each occasion, but are given in the borough introductions or, in the case of the L.C.C. and G.L.C., on p. 18. The general principles on which the gazetteer is based follow those of previous Buildings of England *volumes. On churches prior*

---

*Public buildings are in the following order where possible:

1. Town hall and municipal buildings.

2. Other official buildings (law court, police station, fire station, ambulance headquarters, post office, prison).

3. Other local authority buildings (library, museum, baths, sports centres, community centre).

4. Educational buildings.

5. Medical buildings.

6. Parks.

7. Utilities (market, gasworks, power station, waterworks, sewerage).

8. Transport (railways, docks and canals, bridges).

‡It is impossible to include on the maps every street mentioned: a London street atlas is therefore recommended as a supplement. However an attempt has been made in the gazetteer to correlate every street mentioned with one shown on the map.

to c. 1830 and secular buildings of more than local interest up to around the same period information ought to be as complete as recent research makes possible, and as the space of the volume permits; the exceptions to this rule are that certain church furnishings are omitted (bells, hatchments, chests, chairs, plain fonts, and altar tables) or included only occasionally (royal arms, coffin lids with foliate crosses, brasses of post-Reformation date). Church plate, which used to be included in the gazetteers, is also left out, for plate is now very often no longer kept in the churches concerned, and in any event is not readily visible. Movable furnishings in secular buildings are not mentioned; nor are bases or stumps of crosses (although this is hardly a relevant remark for this volume). More relevant are the problems posed by buildings after 1830, which bulk so largely in Greater London. Here space demands that the traditional Buildings of England *approach of greater selectivity has to be followed. However, it will be found that much more is included and more positively appreciated than in early volumes in this series, reflecting the expanding interest in all types of nineteenth- and twentieth-century architecture and the more sympathetic eye that develops when survivals begin to have a rarity value. Information on these buildings, however, despite recent research, is still patchy, and it will be seen that there is still plenty of scope for further research here, as on earlier periods.*

As far as demolitions are concerned, the policy has been to mention, either in passing in the text, or in a brief footnote, the most important buildings that have disappeared since earlier editions. To gather all the losses together is too mammoth a task to attempt here: the copious gazetteer references to buildings of the last thirty years tell their own story. Architecturally speaking, churches have been the main disaster area (as is indicated in the separate introductions), the result of a combination of war damage, shrinking congregations, and liturgical innovations. New needs threaten other type of buildings as well – hospitals, libraries, and cinemas, for example – where conversions are not always as sympathetic as they might be. The alterations that will be most immediately noticeable to the traveller are the disappearance of acres of Victorian suburban housing, and the transformation of the South Bank of the Thames as industry has withdrawn from inner London. I have attempted to keep track of such changes (and of the research which threatened buildings generate) up to 1982, but there may well be some recent demolitions, discoveries, or worthwhile new buildings that have been overlooked. Furthermore, although I have attempted to see as much as possible for myself (exceptions are in brackets), I have been thwarted in certain cases (particularly by the time needed to cope with the almost universal London custom of locked churches). Other fields (for example the private housing of after 1918 in the outer boroughs) have so far been so little investigated that The Buildings of England *cannot yet deal with them adequately. So this foreword must end, as usual, with the familiar plea to readers for information on errors and omissions.*

ACKNOWLEDGEMENTS

Many people made the present volume possible. First to be acknowledged are those thanked in the foreword of London except the Cities of London and Westminster. *All the library work necessary for the compilation of this volume and a certain amount of preliminary fieldwork was done in the course of the years 1947–50 by Mrs K. Michaelson. She was greatly helped by the librarians and staffs of the public libraries of London, without whose interest the book could not have been written, and to whom it was dedicated. Sir Nikolaus Pevsner also had the benefit of the large photograph collection of the National Buildings Record, now National Monuments Record, and, by the courtesy of the then Ministry of Local Government and Planning, access to unpublished lists of buildings of architectural and historic interest and much other information collected by the Chief Investigator and Mr J. H. Farrar of the Historical Records Department of the London County Council. Mr H. S. Goodhart-Rendel generously placed at the disposal of* The Buildings of England *his manuscript notes on Victorian churches, and Sir Thomas Kendrick his on Victorian glass. In addition grateful thanks are expressed to Miss Darlington at the Members' Library, County Hall, Mr Stonebridge at the St Marylebone Public Library, Mr Wesencroft at the University Library, Mr Rayne Smith at the Guildhall Library, the Jewish Historical Society of London, the Public Relations Department of the London Transport Executive, and to many rectors and vicars, local historians and occupiers of houses, who went to much trouble in providing answers to written questions. The areas formerly in Surrey are likewise indebted to the preliminary extracting carried out by Miss G. Bondi and the help given by local libraries and many others, the Kentish boroughs to all those who helped John Newman with his* West Kent *volume. More detailed acknowledgement of those who gave information on individual areas is given at the end of each borough introduction.*

As for this volume, the first debt I have to acknowledge is to Sir Nikolaus Pevsner, who encouraged me to take me on the foolhardy task of bringing the Greater London area up to date; this volume is the richer for his section on the new public buildings of the South Bank, Lambeth, and the poorer for the fact that ill health prevented his further active involvement. I also am extremely grateful to John Newman, who allowed me to include the Bexley and Bromley areas from West Kent, *brought them up to date, added their borough introductions specially for this volume, and also read and commented on the new general introduction. I must also thank the specialists who have contributed. Mrs Joanna Bird, in addition to the introduction on prehistoric and Roman archaeology, provided me with geological and archaeological notes for the borough introductions, as well as gazetteer entries; Mr Malcolm Airs made available his expert knowledge of timber-framed building in the London area; and Mr Malcolm Tucker, as well as writing an informative introduction on industrial archaeology, contributed a very large number of gazetteer entries on industrial structures, as well as the whole section on Thames* crossings. The maps are the result of much painstaking work by Mr Reginald Piggott. For other illustrations we are grateful to Sir John Summerson for permission to reproduce from his Pelican History of Art *volume* Architecture in Britain: 1530–1830 *the plans of Charlton House, the Queen's House, the Royal Naval Hospital, and Eltham Lodge (Gr), St Paul Deptford (Le), and the Dulwich Art Gallery (Sk), and to the G.L.C. Historic Buildings Division which provided the drawings on pp. 45, 54, and 56.*

The inclusion of much new information has been made possible by the generosity of many who have given access to unpublished material. My major debt is to the Greater London Council. I have above all to thank Mr Ashley Barker, Surveyor of Historic Buildings, and his staff, for allowing me to consult the files of the G.L.C.'s Historic Buildings Division. Within this department I must express my especial gratitude to Mr John Earl, especially for information on theatres, to the historians Mr Frank Kelsall, Mr Neil Burton, Mr Robert Thorne, and Mr Roger White, and to three former members of their team, Dr Anthony Quiney, Miss Anne Riches, and Mrs Susan Beattie. Their thorough documentary research has enhanced the appreciation of large numbers of buildings included in this book. In addition to giving much other advice and support Messrs Kelsall, Burton, Thorne, White, and Quiney have scrutinized and improved the gazetteer. I am also grateful for help from Mr Andrew Saint, Architectural Editor of the Survey of London, Mr John Phillips of the G.L.C. map room, and Mr David Atwell and his staff in the Public Relations Office of the Department of Architecture and Civic Design, who went to considerable trouble to collect information on recent buildings by the G.L.C. The Ancient Monuments Department of the Department of the Environment allowed me to consult their files on redundant churches, and this volume has benefited (like previous ones) from the ever-growing photograph collections of the National Monuments Record. Mrs Hilary Aggett was of great help over recent alterations to churches and their furnishings in the diocese of Southwark. As usual, the willing cooperation of local libraries has been invaluable, and borough planning departments have also been extremely helpful. Our debts to these and to the numerous local organizations and individuals who have assisted over different areas, and to the specialists who have given us information on particular buildings, are more fully acknowledged at the ends of the borough introductions.

The Further Reading (p. 123) can only give a partial indication of the extent of recent research. I gratefully acknowledge here several unpublished London University theses which have been consulted: Georgina Russell, Decorated Tracery in the London Area (M.A. 1973); T. Friedman, James Gibbs (Ph.D. 1971); Christopher Monkhouse, The Station Hotel in Nineteenth-Century England (M.A. 1970); Lynne Walker, E. S. Prior (Ph.D. 1978); Roger Dixon, James Brooks (Ph.D. 1976). It is a pleasure to be able to thank many other scholars who have contributed entries or information in advance of fuller publication elsewhere. The Buildings of England is privileged in being allowed to make such work available, and is grateful to Mr W. Bonwitt (the work of Michael Searles), the *late B.F.L. Clarke, who gave me much help over churches, Mr Bruce Castle (the work of Sydney E. Castle), Mr Denis Evinson (DE), who provided long lists of Roman Catholic churches, Dr James Stevens Curl and Mr Hugh Mellor (HM), who both supplied numerous contributions on cemeteries, Mr Christopher Stell (CS) and Dr Christopher Wakeling, who patiently answered questions on Nonconformist churches, Mr H. G. D. Gibson (details on London Transport stations), Miss Hilary Grainger (the work of Ernest George), Miss Alison Kelly (lists of Coade stone), Mr Matthew Saunders (the work of Teulon), Mr Mark Swenarton (contributions on early-twentieth-century public housing), Mr Andrew Saint (the work of R. Norman Shaw), Mr T. Rory Spence (the work of Leonard Stokes), Mrs A. G. Stavridi (the work of Kempe's firm), and Mrs Sandra Wedgwood (the work of Pugin). For the entries on industrial archaeology (for North as well as South London) we have been grateful for information and other help from Mr C. Ellmers (Clerkenwell), Mr E. Sargent (West India Docks), Mr J. Yates (Kew Bridge Waterworks), Mr P. Calvocoressi and other members of the staff of the G.L.C. Historical Buildings Division, and members of the Greater London Industrial Archaeology Society, especially Mr D. A. Bayliss (Croydon, and Surrey Iron Railway), Mr W. Firth (Barnet borough), Mr and Mrs D. Hayton (Woolwich Dockyard), Mr H. D. Marks (Camden piano works), Mr S. Perrett and colleagues (South East London), Dr Denis Smith (waterworks in East London), Mr T. R. Smith (parts of Tower Hamlets), and Mr S. G. Thomas (Lambeth and Southwark). Many other people provided valuable lists of corrections and additions on a variety of subjects, answered queries, or helped in other ways. Among them must be specially mentioned Dr Malcolm Airs, Mr H. M. Colvin, Mr Alec Clifton Taylor, Mr John Newman, Dr Gavin Stamp, Mr B. J. D. Turner, Dr Christopher Wilson, and the staff of the Victorian Society.*

I have to thank Penguin Books for their support and patience during the lengthy gestation period of this volume and its companions and my colleagues in the Buildings of England office for much practical assistance; I have benefited here from stimulating discussion with Elizabeth Williamson and from the skilled help of Susan Rose-Smith, who not only assembled the photographs and plans but also undertook the thankless task of initial sorting of material. Joanna Campbell, with Judith Heaver, coped with much of the typing, and other assistance was given at various times by Tanis Hinchcliffe, Linnell McCurry, and Jeffrey West. My co-editor Judy Nairn prepared the book for the printer with her characteristic meticulousness, a task that included the laborious checking of maps and their correlation with the text, and the compilation of the indexes. The final thanks must be to my family, who for four years tolerated countless weekends disrupted by suburban detours and excursions.

17

ACKNOWLEDGEMENTS FOR THE PLATES

We are grateful to the following for permission to reproduce photographs:

Aerofilms: 41, 106
Architectural Press (photo W. J. Toomey): 99
Ashmolean Museum, University of Oxford, Department of Western Art: 16
James Austin: 8, 9, 10, 12, 19, 22, 23, 24, 25, 30, 32, 38, 40, 47, 51, 56, 67, 72, 73, 77, 81, 89, 93, 94, 95, 98
Bews & Hodge: 107
Brecht-Einzig Ltd: 108, 110
British Museum: 14
Richard Bryant: 111
Country Life: 61, 63, 66
Courtauld Institute: 26, 52
Colin Curwood: 97
Eric de Maré: 28, 78, 100, 103
Department of the Environment, Crown Copyright: 43
John Donat: 109
Greater London Council, Photographic Unit, Department of Architecture and Civic Design: 1, 2, 3, 6, 31, 35, 58, 59, 60, 79, 80, 83, 84, 85, 88, 90, 96, 101
Geoff Howard: 45, 46, 69, 71, 74
Peter R. Keen: 55
A. F. Kersting: 4, 5, 13, 34, 42, 48, 57, 62, 64, 65, 68, 70, 86, 102
Sam Lambert: 105
Ministry of Defence Procurement Executive: 37
National Monuments Record: 7, 11, 15, 17, 18, 20, 21, 29, 33, 36, 44, 50, 76, 87, 91, 92
Margaret Stern: 53
James Stevens Curl: 75
W. J. Toomey: 49, 82, 104
Victoria and Albert Museum: 27
Warburg Institute: 54

The plates are indexed in the indexes of artists, of streets and buildings, and of boroughs and localities on pp. 751 ff.

ABBREVIATIONS

AND LIST OF COUNTY COUNCIL ARCHITECTS

Area Authorities

M.B.W. Metropolitan Board of Works (1855–1888)
L.C.C. London County Council (1888–1965)
G.L.C. Greater London Council (from 1965)
I.L.E.A. Inner London Education Authority (from 1965, covering the area of the former L.C.C.)

In order to avoid repetition, chief architects of public authorities are not mentioned on every occasion in the gazetteer. Borough architects are given in introductions to individual boroughs. The chief county council architects are as follows:

Architects to the Metropolitan Board of Works, the London County Council, and the Greater London Council

Superintending Architects
Frederick Marrable 1856–61
George Vulliamy 1861–87
Thomas Blashill 1887–99
W. E. Riley 1899–1919
G. Topham Forrest 1919–35
E. P. Wheeler 1935–39
F. R. Hiorns 1939–41
J. H. Forshaw 1941–46
(Sir) Robert Matthew 1946–53
(Sir) Leslie Martin 1953–6
(Sir) Hubert Bennett 1956–71
(Sir) Roger Walters 1971–8
F. B. Pooley 1978–80
P. E. Jones 1980–

Fire Brigade Branch
Edward Cresy 1866–70
Alfred Mott 1871–89
Robert Pearsall 1889–99
Owen Fleming 1900–

Housing of the Working Classes Branch
Owen Fleming 1893–1900
John Briggs 1900–2
Rob Robertson 1902–10

Education Branch
(until 1904 architects to the School Board for London)
E. R. Robson 1871–84
T. J. Bailey 1884–1910
Rob Robertson 1910–

The Constructional Division
(Absorbed the Fire Brigade Branch and the Housing of the Working Classes Branch from 1910, and the Education Branch from 1920. Housing was placed under the Valuers Department from 1946 until 1950, when the whole of the Architect's Department was reorganized under Sir Robert Matthew, with separate heads of department for housing and education.)

Housing
H. J. Whitfield Lewis 1950–9
K. J. Campbell 1959–74
G. H. Wigglesworth 1974–80

Education
S. Howard 1950–5
M. C. L. Powell 1956–65
Schools: C. E. Hartland 1965–72
Education: M. C. L. Powell 1965–71
G. H. Wigglesworth 1972–4
P. E. Jones 1974–80

Special Works
(A separate department responsible for fire and ambulance stations, magistrates' courts, civic buildings, etc.)
G. Horsfall 1960–76
    (also senior architect Civic Design, 1965–70, and
    Thamesmead Manager from 1970)
R. A. Michelmore 1977–80
    (from 1980, principal Construction Architect)

Boroughs

See map on pp. 2–3.

Other Abbreviations (see also Acknowledgements and Borough Introductions)

DOE	Department of the Environment
NMR	National Monuments Record
N or NE London	The Buildings of England: London 4: North and North East
NW London	The Buildings of England: London 3: North West
R.C.H.M.	Royal Commission on Historical Monuments (England)
R.I.B.A.	Royal Institute of British Architects
V and A	Victoria and Albert Museum
V.C.H.	Victoria County History

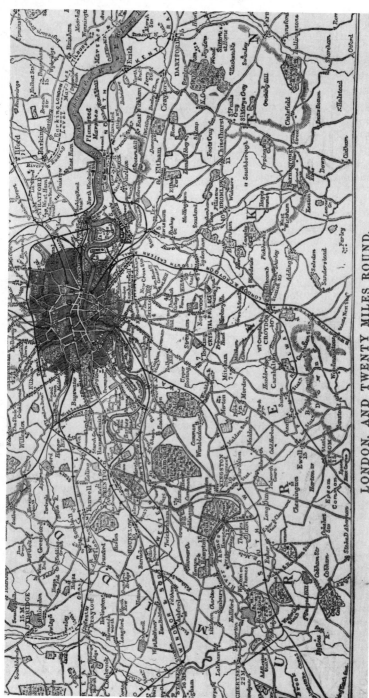

LONDON, AND TWENTY MILES ROUND.

South London c. 1850 (Copyright Guildhall Library)

INTRODUCTION

BY BRIDGET CHERRY

Greater London's population (1981) is 6,962,199. The twelve boroughs described in this book account for about a third of the total: 2,614,191 – the equivalent of Greater Manchester or of the West Midlands (each with around $2\frac{1}{2}$ million) or of the whole of Kent and Surrey added together. But this South London population is packed into an area of only about thirty by twenty-five miles, half the area of Greater Manchester and less than a fifth of that of Kent; a confederacy of towns and villages knit in a mesh of suburban growth so dense that the older centres are often hard to recognize, especially in the five boroughs which were under the sway of the old London County Council. In Lambeth the density is as high as 90.1 people per hectare; as one travels further out it dwindles to Croydon's 36.6, Kingston's 28.6, and Bromley's 19.4. It is only on those distant fringes that one can still catch glimpses of the countryside: relics of the extensive Thamesside marshes downstream to the E, the river meadows of the Cray on the Kent borders, the patches of woodland around Chislehurst or on the slopes of the Surrey Downs beyond Croydon, the flatter stretches of farmland S of Kingston and Surbiton. Such areas do not yet fully feel part of London. The heart of South London is the Thames river basin, where the London clay rises up from the once swampy riverside to the chalk hills on the southern borders, covered in places by the beds of gravel which encouraged early settlement (cf. the introduction to Prehistoric and Roman Archaeology). Within the framework of this shallow saucer the landscape has considerable variety (more so than much of North London): dramatic little hills at Woolwich, where the chalk comes down closest to the river, the flat valleys of the Thames tributaries, of the Ravensbourne running through Lewisham to Deptford Creek, and of the Wandle, traversing Merton and Wandsworth. Between them lies the natural boundary of the once wooded heights of Norwood. To the W the main landmark is Richmond Hill, rising up sharply above the upper Thames, with the high plateau of Wimbledon Common beyond it to the S. But of all this the traveller is not easily aware, for so much is covered in building.

First impressions of South London are likely to be disappointing, for the southern suburbs lack the immediate charm of country areas, or the excitement of a great city. The outer suburbs reveal their least attractive face along the arterial roads, a muddle of monotonous ribbon development, filling stations, and light

industry. Further in, slowed down by the press of traffic, the
traveller has more time to contemplate the apparently inter-
minable sequence of dingy Victorian and Edwardian shopping
parades before being whipped around the occasional bleak concrete roundabout, engineering surgery as brutal to the surrounding urban fabric as the converging C 19 railway viaducts which
still overshadow the neighbourhoods close to the Thames. From
these viaducts the railway passenger has a broader and more
intriguing perspective. From above, it can be seen that the
mantle of Victorian buildings sprawling from the Thamesside
up to the Surrey hills was never totally enveloping and is now
partially threadbare. Along the river only fragmented clusters
2 survive from the throng of warehouses built beside the docks
and quays of a busy port, and few relics remain of the factories
with their noxious effluvia which rendered the S E parts 'rather
unpleasant for human residence' (as Moggs's *New Picture of
London* mildly expressed it in 1848). Instead, glossy new towers
of offices and scruffier council flats soar above a drab C 20 medley
of derelict land and backyard industry, with only an occasional
church steeple or dignified portico as a reminder of an older past.
Beyond, in an arc roughly five miles in extent from London
Bridge, less has changed; the Welsh slate roofs of Victorian
terraces stretch in undulating waves over the gentle slopes,
broken by the hopeful ragstone towers of mid-C 19 churches, or
by the proud hips and turrets of later Board Schools and the
more frivolous curlicues of Edwardian pubs or libraries. Among
them C 20 intrusions reflect successive fashions in urban renewal: the closely packed brick apartment blocks of the 1930s,
the taller, more obtrusive post-war towers and slabs of concrete,
and the brighter tiled roofs of the tightly clustered low housing
of the 1970s. A closer look reveals underlying traces of earlier
ages; late Georgian terraces hidden behind High Street shop-
4 fronts; stretches of greenery, the residue of ancient parks and
commons, still fringed here and there by houses of a more
leisurely age. Further out, five or six miles from the city centre,
the railway cuttings become leafier, the open aspects more
noticeable (preserved by those space-consuming Victorian
necessities, cemeteries and waterworks), and the occasional
larger suburban mansion can be glimpsed, usually shorn of its
gardens, and surrounded by boxy little houses and flats of the
mid C 20. By then one is in the outer areas, and urban momentum increases again as one approaches the towns of Bromley or
Croydon, Sutton or Surbiton, with their confident brash offices
and commuters' car parks of the 1960s clustering near the
railway stations.

Such a generalized sketch does not do justice to the architectural diversity or to the individual character of so many places that
will become apparent to the persistent explorer who ventures off
the main roads. For there is much rewarding and delightful
variety embedded within the matrix of the suburbs. Buildings of
3 pre-Victorian villages and towns may be found sedulously
preserved, or tucked away in forgotten backwaters, or remain-

ing as accidental scattered survivals in those melancholy evocative areas which were swamped and then abandoned by C 19
industry. They offer telling contrasts, ranging between the extremes of simple rural styles and the most sophisticated and
up-to-date creations by kings, courtiers, and city men eager to
take advantage of the countryside convenient to London. Indeed, buildings in this book form major chapters in the history
of English C 17 and C 18 architecture, as can be demonstrated by
an excursion along the Thames, now as of old the easiest and
pleasantest route to so much of South London; to *Inigo Jones* at
Greenwich, *Wren's* Baroque splendours at Greenwich and
Hampton Court, and the scatter of elegant C 18 villas in the
neighbourhood of Twickenham and Richmond. Later periods
have their own fascination: the maritime and industrial relics of
the riverside and, inland, the subtle variety of the quieter residential neighbourhoods with their rich haul of churches, which
grew up from the late C 18 onwards, illustrating that perennial
conflict of suburban aspirations, the desire to escape from the
city and the urge to emulate it. And finally, there are the buildings of the last hundred years, when all except the outer fringes
had been built up, so that the theme becomes one of continual
and often controversial renewal, as metropolitan needs, commercial interests, or ambitious remodelling by local authorities
lay claim to the limited spaces. The varied buildings that have
resulted from all these phases of development must now be
examined in more detail.

The Middle Ages

The area now covered by the South London boroughs had
during the Middle Ages only a few major settlements: Southwark, Kingston, Croydon, and Bromley. Their past history is
still recognizable by their medieval TOWN PLANS, less so by
their buildings. Southwark, which began as a Roman suburb at
the Thames bridgehead, was independent of the City's authority
in the Middle Ages, a town in its own right, with a major priory
church (now Southwark Cathedral). The medieval past is still 8,9
just traceable in its main street with little alleys opening off.
Kingston, the ancient capital of Surrey, also owed its importance
to its riverside position. It had a medieval bridge over the
Thames, the first one upstream from London Bridge, and still
has a late C 12 bridge over a Thames tributary. Kingston declined as neighbouring Richmond grew, which no doubt
accounts for the preservation of its open market place, the best 6
example of its type in outer London. Those of Bromley and
Croydon, now built over, must once have been similar. Croydon
is a good example of how subsequent prosperity obscured the
earlier pattern. The market place on the main road, some distance from, and so perhaps subsequent to, the parish church,
was built over already by the C 16, and then almost obliterated by
the later C 19 municipal improvement that transformed this part
of the town.

Nearly all the rest of South London was until the C 18 fields, commons, and woodland, scattered with villages, farms, and manor houses. Where the river banks were not too swampy, fishing settlements were established early on. Plumstead, Woolwich, Greenwich, Deptford, Rotherhithe, Lambeth, Battersea, Wandsworth, Putney, Barnes, Sheen (the later Richmond) all appear to have begun in this way, as did the villages on the opposite side of the river (including, in this volume, Twickenham, Teddington, and Hampton). The essentially riverside nature of these villages is shown by the siting of most of the medieval parish churches close to the waterside, as is still evident, for example, at Lambeth, Battersea, Putney, and Barnes. Their parishes often stretched far S, that of Lambeth for instance as far as the natural barrier of the hills of Norwood, the North Wood of the Downs, which still form the boundary of the present borough. Inland from the Thames were other settlements with their own churches, some still in the C 18 with little more than church and manor house (Charlton, Old Malden, Lee, Morden), others rather larger: Bermondsey, Newington, Clapham, Lewisham, Merton, Mitcham, Carshalton, Beddington, Sutton, Cheam, and so on, far into Surrey where Coulsdon, Sanderstead, and Addington on the edge of the Downs, and the Kentish villages along the river Cray remained rural right into the C 20.

Some of these places became especially important in the Middle Ages because of their associations with ecclesiastical or courtly establishments. The RELIGIOUS HOUSES were St Mary Overie Southwark, a pre-Conquest foundation refounded as an Augustinian priory in 1106, the Cluniac priory of St Saviour Bermondsey, founded in 1082, the Augustinian priory of Merton, established by Gilbert, Sheriff of Surrey, in 1114–17, and Lesnes (on the Bexley border), an Augustinian priory following the Arroasian rule, founded by Richard de Lucy in 1178. Another later C 12 foundation was the Hospital of the Holy Trinity and St Thomas (the origin of the present St Thomas' Hospital), established at first within the precincts of St Mary Overie, refounded on a new site in the early C 13 by Peter des Roches, Bishop of Winchester. Southwark also had a leper hospital, and there was a further medieval hospital at Newington. There were small cells of alien monasteries at Tooting (dependent on Bec in Normandy) and at Lewisham (dependent on St Peter Ghent). In the later Middle Ages royal patronage was responsible for the Carthusians (1414) and Observant Friars (c. 1500) at Sheen, and the Observant Friars at Greenwich (1481–2).

From the C 12 there is little to see. At Bermondsey only a few carved fragments survive to show that there was early C 12 work of high quality. Lesnes, at Belvedere, is the only place where the late C 12 foundations are exposed to view; the church had a Cistercian-type plan with square-ended E chapels. Merton, whose remnants were destroyed by the railway in the C 19, is known to have had a similar E end, perhaps also late C 12, extended in the C 13. A battered late Romanesque doorway enriched with geometric ornament, formerly part of the monastic buildings, has been re-erected near the parish church. The outer walls of transepts and nave of St Mary Overie, although disguised by Gothic reconstruction and remodelling, are substantially C 12; the N transept preserves remains of an early C 12 apsidal chapel, later extended E, while the nave, as is suggested by tantalizing drawings and fragments, was probably not completed until the end of the C 12, and must have been one of the first works in London to reflect the influence of the transitional Gothic style of Canterbury choir.

With the surviving early C 13 choir and retrochoir of St Mary Overie (now Southwark Cathedral), the fully-fledged EARLY ENGLISH style is reached. The E arm of the church, with its low retrochoir with four aisles (instead of three, as at the earlier 8 Winchester), and the choir, with its well-proportioned three- 9 storey elevation with a minimum of decoration, have an unusual restraint (perhaps appropriate to Augustinians) that contrasts with the exuberance of E.E. work elsewhere. The E end of the Temple Church (*London 1*) is the nearest equivalent. The mixture of lancets with plate-tracery windows in the retrochoir indicates completion before the High Gothic phase introduced by Westminster Abbey in the 1240s. The vaulted undercroft of Lambeth Palace Chapel is simple but accomplished work of 7 similar date (i.e. a little earlier than Westminster Abbey) which makes one regret that the handsome W doorway with its trefoiled opening on Purbeck shafts is all that remains of the chapel above. The archbishop's palace of which this chapel is a part was rebuilt in subsequent centuries, and so must be mentioned later, but there are still remains to be seen of one of the many other important mansions that once fringed the south bank of the Thames. This is Winchester House, hard by St Mary Overie, the town house of the Bishop of Winchester, in whose diocese Southwark lay until the later C 19. What survives is part of a first-floor hall on the grandest scale (*c.* 79 by 31 ft), early C 14 (but on earlier foundations), with a splendid Dec rose window with a 10 distinctive design of cusped triangles and hexagons in the gable above the service end. Assisted by the Bishops of Winchester, remodelling of St Mary Overie continued throughout the Dec and Perp periods, but details have been too heavily restored and altered to be particularly enjoyable; the most interesting feature is the design of the transept clerestory windows, whose concave hexagonal lights of the end of the C 13 foreshadow the vertical mullions of later Perp windows.

For major late medieval work SECULAR BUILDINGS are more rewarding. The Archbishop of Canterbury had another palace at Croydon. This may have started, possibly in the late C 12, with a first-floor hall above an undercroft, but in the late C 14 a series of remodellings began, creating one of the best surviving examples of the sequence of state and private rooms demanded by a late medieval ecclesiastic. The large new ground-floor hall added in the late C 14 was re-roofed in the C 15 by

Archbishop Stafford († 1452), an elaborate timber construction with flying wall-plates and two sets of collar-beams. The skill of late medieval carpenters is demonstrated by other roofs in the area covered by this volume. Lambeth Palace guardroom, re-constructed in the C 19, has a re-used arch-braced roof, elaborately moulded, which is attributed to the mid C 14. Eltham
13 Palace great hall, rebuilt for Edward IV from 1475, and the similar, less well known great hall of Beddington Place, the manor house of the Carews, have variations on the hammerbeam roof, the type which became famous with Westminster Hall at the end of the C 14, with the up-to-date innovations of four-centred arched principals resting on the hammerposts, with pendants beneath them. Pendants, a type of virtuoso ornament that appears around the same time in stone vaults, continue in roofs of the early C 16. From this period this volume has two of
15 the most lavish examples, Hampton Court great hall and chapel of c. 1535, where although the construction is still in the late
17 medieval tradition, in the ornament lively Renaissance features are introduced. The tradition of the open hammerbeam roof did not end with Hampton Court. In the second half of the C 16 such roofs were used, again with Renaissance embellishments, for the hall of the remodelled Charterhouse (*see North and North East London*) and the great hall of the Middle Temple (completed
29 1570) (*London 1*), and even after 1660, for the rebuilt hall of Lambeth Palace. But this is to anticipate.

ROYAL HOUSES AND PALACES of the later Middle Ages were once numerous s of the Thames, precursors of a host of mansions of courtiers and merchants that were to spring up in the countryside within easy reach of London. Sheen (the later Richmond) was a royal palace from the time of Edward II, Edward III had a manor house at Rotherhithe, Eltham was given to the Crown in 1305, the Black Prince had an establishment at Kennington, and a century later Humphrey Duke of Gloucester had a house at Greenwich which developed into a favourite residence of the Tudor monarchs. Hampton Court, Cardinal Wolsey's show palace on the Middlesex bank of the Thames, was taken over by Henry VIII in 1525, and in Surrey, just beyond the bounds of this volume, Henry later built himself palaces at Nonsuch, near Cheam, and at Oatlands, near Weybridge. Substantial sums were spent on these buildings, as we know from the royal accounts, but little remains. Rotherhithe has entirely disappeared; parts of Kennington and more eloquent evidence for Greenwich and Nonsuch have been revealed in recent excavations, but almost nothing is visible now. At Richmond some much altered Tudor buildings of the outer court are all that are
14 left; the splendid tower block which Henry VII built by the river is known only from old views. So it is the moated site of Eltham which provides the most evocative memorial of these late medieval royal buildings, although even here all that remains of
13 an intricate complex are Edward IV's hall, already mentioned, and the adjoining footings of the privy lodgings and of the chapel rebuilt by Henry VIII. The buildings at Eltham appear to have

been a haphazard collection of different dates, replaced as need
arose, much as at the royal palace of Westminster. The special
distinction of Hampton Court, the major survival among the
early C 16 buildings, is the more orderly arrangement. One starts
with Wolsey's large outer court with lodgings, and progresses
through a series of great gate towers to the inner courts with the
state apartments. This type of layout was characteristic of the
grandest buildings of late medieval ecclesiastics (cf. the
Archbishop of Canterbury's Knole, Kent, and, on a lesser scale,
Croydon), and Henry VII's Richmond also appears to have been
laid out on these lines, but Wolsey exceeded all previous examples in magnificence. Henry VIII not to be outdone, rebuilt
the hall at Hampton Court, and provided a splendid sequence of 15
state apartments, gardens, and ancillary buildings. The full
impact of the exterior, with its exotic array of turrets and chimneys, can now be appreciated only in old views dating from 16
before the partial rebuilding of the later C 17. Inside, a little
remains to show the new taste for high-quality interior decoration of the early C 16: a few rooms of Wolsey's time with linenfold panelling and multi-ribbed ceilings, forerunners of the
ornate plasterwork that became common later in the century, 18
and, of Henry VIII's state rooms, the hall, chapel, and guard
room, with their mixture of Gothic forms and Renaissance
ornament, the 'antique' work that figures prominently in the
accounts of the 1530s. Renaissance influence was not yet an
architectural matter, as is shown equally by the terracotta medallions of 1521 by *Giovanni da Maiano*, set arbitrarily on the walls 17
of the Perp gate-towers.

One other late medieval domestic building must be specially
mentioned: Wickham Court at West Wickham, built after 1469
by Sir Henry Heydon, an exceptional compact courtyard house
whose castle overtones appear to belong to a mood of chivalric
nostalgia similar to that displayed by Tudor Richmond and
Hampton Court. The exterior of this house is of brick with stone
dressings, the earliest surviving example of brick being used for
a major building both in Kent and in the London area. In Surrey
it appears around the same time with Bishop Waynflete's buildings at Esher and Farnham of *c*. 1475 (the latter another case of a
mock fortress). Archbishop Morton's gate tower at Lambeth, of
twenty years later, is also of brick. The great hall of Eltham of 13
1475, significantly, is built of brick, but covered by a stone skin.
By the time of Hampton Court brick had clearly become an
acceptable material on the highest social level, although it was
not used universally. Hall Place Bexley, built in the 1530s by Sir
John Champeneis, a Lord Mayor of London, is in flint and
stone. It also still followed the late medieval plan of an open hall
with dais bay-window, flanked by cross-wings. Modifications to
this type of plan were characteristic of the C 16, either to achieve
architectural propriety in accordance with more classical tastes,
or simply to create more convenient living conditions. In the
1550s the exterior of Hall Place was made symmetrical, although
the open hall was retained. In other cases the open hall began to

3 be given up: this can be seen on a vernacular level at Whitehall, Cheam, of the early C 16, already with a two-storey centre.

Medieval Parish Churches

Before pursuing domestic architecture into the later C 16 it is necessary to review what remains of PARISH CHURCHES before the Reformation. This does not take long because outer London must be one of the least rewarding areas in England for this subject. In South London all the worthwhile survivors lie on the outer suburban fringes, and their character for the most part has been too heavily compromised by extensive restoration and additions to make them particularly enjoyable. Work of the PRE-CONQUEST period exists fragmentarily in some Bromley and Bexley churches, most convincingly at St Paulinus St Paul's Cray, where there is evidence for a Saxon nave and porticus, and at All Saints Orpington, which has a rare Saxon sundial with runic inscription. St Nicholas Chislehurst has a blocked pre-Conquest window, and there is walling which is possibly Saxo-Norman or later at the Lumley Chapel, Cheam, and a fragment of interlace carving at Kingston. At Kingston, however, a chapel very probably of pre-Conquest origin survived until the C 18, the reputed coronation place of the early Saxon kings. The adjoining church was by the C 12 a large aisled cruciform building, but retains no visible work of this period. In the former villages the most notable NORMAN remains are at Merton, where the chev-ron-arched N doorway with its original door, a precious survival, probably belong to the church built by the founder of Merton Priory, and so date from c. 1114–25. Addington and Erith have Norman chancels, and Crayford puzzling evidence of a Norman nave. From the later C 12 is the N arcade of Carshalton, with octagonal piers and crocket capitals, comparable to the Tran-sitional work of such Surrey churches as Banstead and Reigate. The fragments of the destroyed S arcade at Carshalton are of similar date but less accomplished, as are the robust but crude leaf and head capitals of the arcade at St Paul's Cray. On a doorway at Orpington the new Gothic crocket capitals are still mixed with traditional Norman chevron.

C 13 GOTHIC remains in a broad spectrum of buildings, frag-mentary evidence for the widespread erection or enlargement of parish churches that took place at this time. The best survivals are again in the SE, where the simple flint unaisled village chur-ches of East Wickham, Keston, and Downe have survived rela-tively unaltered. Hayes was of similar type before the C 19. Coulsdon has a small chancel of good quality, with sedilia preserved, Merton another chancel, exceptionally long, with wall arcading. The standard type of enlargement common from the late C 12 onwards, the provision of aisles, usually in the C 13–14 with circular piers with moulded capitals, can be found at Erith, Chelsfield, Bexley, Sanderstead, Beddington, St Mary Cray, and Cudham. C 14 Gothic work also remains at Crayford (early C 14 chancel), Beddington, and Sanderstead (both with chancel and tower). St Mary Cray has Dec windows with (restored) Kentish tracery, the only example in outer London. But the best C 14 church is undoubtedly St Mary Lambeth at the gates of the archbishop's palace. The tower and tall arcades on octagonal piers, with (unusually) a clerestory above, belong to a rebuilding documented to c. 1370. From the C 15 there are nave arcades at St Nicholas Plumstead (octagonal piers with hollow-chamfered arches), at West Wickham (concave octagonal piers), Chislehurst (quatrefoil piers), Crayford (a very odd single arcade dividing the church into two naves), and Kingston. Croydon, thanks to the Archbishops' patronage, had a very lavish Perp church, but only fragments of this survive in the fairly faithful rebuilding that took place after it was burnt down in the C 19. The only other late Perp work of real distinction is at St Mary Putney, where a little fan-vaulted chantry chapel was added by 11 Bishop West of Ely c. 1533, still entirely in the Gothic tradition, to the Perp church (nave arcades partly original).

By the end of the Middle Ages nearly all churches had been provided with towers. They are usually at the W end, apart from a few asymmetrically placed ones in the Kentish area (do they reflect early, pre-Conquest plans?). The most common type in the area round London cannot compete with the towers of wealthier regions of England. They are homely, quite low structures of flint or ragstone, usually having diagonal buttresses, and often a projecting stair-turret rising above the battlements. The 50 type appears already in the late C 14 (Lambeth) and goes on into the C 16 (St Mary Hornsey, NE London, datable to c. 1500). In many cases the medieval towers alone survive, sometimes heavily disguised, beside the rebuilt bodies of the churches – examples include St Nicholas Deptford, St Mary Lewisham, St Alfege Greenwich, St Leonard Streatham, St Mary Bermondsey, St Peter and St Paul Bromley.

A brief mention of MEDIEVAL FURNISHINGS will suffice. For a general ensemble, the most rewarding church is West Wickham. FONTS of the C 12 are at Bromley, Chislehurst, and Foots Cray, of the C 13 at Beddington (the last two of Purbeck marble); remains of WALL PAINTINGS of the C 13 are to be found at East Wickham, of the C 14 at Sanderstead. C 13 IRONWORK is preserved on a door at Erith. Among Perp furnishings the outstanding pieces are the noble brass eagle LECTERN at Croydon, and Bishop Fox's sumptuous but much renewed great stone REREDOS of the early C 16 at Southwark Cathedral. Otherwise the list is completed by a font at Cudham, a font cover at Orpington, some misericords at Beddington, a screen at St Mary Cray, a Nottinghamshire alabaster at Chessington, and a few fragments of stained glass – C 14 at Wimbledon, early C 16 Flemish at West Wickham. A little more can be added on MONUMENTS, although much has undoubtedly been lost. Minor brasses of c. 1400 onwards are still quite numerous, although none is spectacular, see e.g. Cheam (one of c. 1390), Carshalton, Chelsfield, Erith, St Mary Cray, Downe, West Wickham. The earliest monuments in other materials are from the C 13, both at Southwark Cathedral: a foliated coffin slab and a battered wooden effigy of a knight. (Another coffin slab also at St Paul's Cray.) A rector of Orpington has quite a showy Dec tomb recess of 1370, a rector of Chelsfield a plainer one of 1417, containing a coped tomb-chest of local marble. The most ambitious surviving tomb-chest, complete with effigy, is that of John Gower † 1408 in Southwark Cathedral. Simpler tomb-chests without effigies became popular in the later C 15, for example at Cudham, Chislehurst (1482), and Carshalton (1497). From the early C 16 are a group which must come from the same workshop: small chests with room only for three quatrefoils, with crested and panelled recess above. They are found at Beddington (1520), St Mary Lambeth (two, † 1504 and † 1524, perhaps erected together), and Croydon (c. 1536). Similar examples occur also N of the Thames, e.g. at Hackney, Norwood, and Edmonton.

Architecture and Sculpture: 1580–1630

The Reformation brought to an end the rebuilding and furnishing of churches; it also turned over to laymen the buildings of monastic houses, either for residential use, as at the Charterhouse (Is, *London N and NE*), or at Bermondsey, where Thomas Pope made himself a house on the site of the W range, or for a quarry, as happened at Merton, from where much stone was taken for Henry VIII's Nonsuch. (Henry similarly brought windows from Rewley Abbey, Oxford, for use at Hampton Court.) Pope's house at Bermondsey and Henry's Nonsuch have gone. Only Tudor outbuildings are left at Well Hall, the Ropers' house at Eltham, and the London area is equally poor in GREAT HOUSES of the ELIZABETHAN AND JACOBEAN AGE. South London is therefore not the place to chart the fluctuating progress of classical taste in the later C 16. Nothing remains of Sir Francis Walsingham's Barn Elms, nor of Thomas Cecil's Wimbledon House of 1588 onwards, which was an exceptionally interesting building, with its elaborately terraced forecourts, symmetrical front, and a plan which included the progressive feature of ground-floor hall with great chamber above. Holland House (K C) remains only as a fragment.

So one has to pass on quickly to the Jacobean continuation of this tradition, to Ham House, where the more interesting later alterations have obscured much of Sir John Vavasour's conventional H-plan house of 1610, to the quite modest Eagle House Wimbledon of 1613, and, most rewardingly, to Charlton House Greenwich, built by Prince Henry's tutor, Adam Newton, c. 1607–12. Both Eagle House and Charlton House, like Hardwick Hall in Derbyshire a little earlier, have the unconventional arrangement of a hall placed axially instead of along the front of the building, so that one enters it from one end. At Charlton the hall is the height of two floors, but has another reception room above. As for the exteriors, while Eagle House (like the much grander Holland House and many other houses of this period)

has the popular feature of shaped gables, Charlton has a more
rigorously controlled balustrade roof-line, relieved only by the
turrets projecting from the centres of each of the cross-wings,
and by an ornamental frontispiece. This has paired columns 23
with decoration derived directly from Dietterlin's pattern book
(the only known case of an exact copy). The chimneypieces 22
inside similarly display knowledge of such Netherlandish
sources, but there is also one in a more severely classical style
which can be closely associated with the work of *Nicholas Stone*.

The variants on the classical style which can be found on
chimneypieces are paralleled by the CHURCH MONUMENTS of
the period, although here again South London has not much to
offer, compared with for instance the riches of Westminster
Abbey. The number has been reduced further within the last
decade by the fires which gutted the churches of Putney and
Streatham, where two of the better collections existed. Two
interesting early Elizabethan monuments are the one to Sybil
Pen † 1562 at Hampton, a fairly early example of the wall-
monument of four-poster type, and that to the Countess of
Shrewsbury † 1568 at Erith, where the tomb-chest is confidently
classical in its detail. The tomb of Richard Humble † 1616 in
Southwark Cathedral, with figures kneeling beneath a coffered
arch with obelisks, attributed to *William Cure II*, is a characteristic example of the work of the 'Southwark School', Netherlandish carvers who had workshops on the South Bank. Another
fairly grand tomb, with a figure lying on a sarcophagus beneath
an arch, is that of Archbishop Whitgift † 1604 at Croydon; other
effigies are those of Elizabeth Lady Lumley of 1592 at Cheam,
and Sir Francis Carew † 1611 at Beddington. There is also the
one to Lancelot Andrewes † 1626 at Southwark Cathedral, but it 21
is much restored, and has lost its canopy. The Lumley Chapel at
Cheam (itself an example of refurbishing of the later C 16, with a
ribbed plaster ceiling – an interesting rarity) has a remarkable
collection of monuments, of which the best is that to Lady Jane
Lumley (1590), with delicately carved figures in shallow relief, 19
kneeling against an architectural background. The more common type of wall-monument with figures occurs quite frequently
and continues into the middle of the C 17 with kneeling figures
(Merton 1597, Wandsworth 1627, 1630, Streatham 1653), with
a more unusual seated frontal figure (at West Wickham 1608),
or, more progressively, with frontal half-figures (Southwark
Cathedral 1618, 1625, Twickenham 1642). A more interesting
phase is reached with the monuments which can be associated
with *Nicholas Stone* and his workshop. The earliest in South
London is that of the Earl of Northampton (1615) formerly in
Dover Castle, which unfortunately survives only in pieces, in the
chapel of the Trinity Hospital, Greenwich. It had a kneeling
effigy above an arched canopy, a French type, with allegorical
figures of the virtues. Southwark Cathedral has a notable later
monument, that of Lady Clerke (the Austin monument) of 1633, 20
an elaborate allegorical wall-tablet, with figures in low relief.
Quite different in character are two others by Stone, the severely

classical aedicule to Lady Newton † 1630 at Charlton, and the St
26 John monument at Battersea, also † 1630, with busts in a classical frame. The use of black and white marble for such monuments
instead of the brightly painted surfaces of Elizabethan tombs is
another sign of the new, classically-inspired taste of the early
C 17. Other monuments of this time, anonymous, but out of the
usual run, are the remarkable emblematic tablet to Grace Rowed
† 1631 at Coulsdon and the shrouded effigy of Mary Audley
† 1655 at Sanderstead, and the grand Draper monument at West
Wickham (c. 1650), a transitional type, with its kneeling children, but more relaxed reclining main figures. As a coda to the
Battersea monument the stained glass in the church should also
be mentioned. Installed by the St John family in the 1630s, it is
attributed to *Bernard van Linge* – another instance of the close
relationship that existed at this time with Flemish artists and
craftsmen.

Among other furnishings of this period, especially noteworthy are the later C 16 chest in Southwark Cathedral, exquisitely carved and inlaid, and the C 17 screen in lively Netherlandish classical taste and other fittings in Lambeth Palace
Chapel, from the time of Archbishop Laud, characteristic examples of that brief flowering of High Anglican church furnishings which was terminated by the Commonwealth. As for
the CHURCHES themselves, the only works to record are a few
cases of modest rebuilding, which shows that Gothic was still the
accepted style for village churches, even if it was now executed
mostly in brick. The three most attractive examples are the nave
and tower of St John Old Malden 1627, St Luke Charlton
c. 1630–9, and St Lawrence Morden 1636. The tower of St
Nicholas Plumstead indeed was still given battlements in 1662.

In mentioning such works one has jumped ahead of the most
progressive architectural developments. The key name of the
early C 17 is of course that of *Inigo Jones*, and his key work in
25 South London is one of national importance, the Queen's House
39 at Greenwich, begun by 1617, but not completed until the
1630s. This building and the Banqueting House in Whitehall are
the outcome of a study of Italian C 16 architecture, and especially
of the architecture of Andrea Palladio at Vicenza, far closer and
far more intelligent than that of the decorators and ornamental
carvers of the Tudor age. Now for the first time the organism of a
classical building was understood by an Englishman and sympathetically reinterpreted. Existing English custom is ignored:
the planning of the Queen's House, its central hall in the form of
a perfect cube, and a suite of rooms on the piano nobile, reached
28 by the exquisite spiral staircase, are as total a departure from
Jacobean tradition as is the stark white rectangular shape of the
exterior, so alien to the florid style of Elizabethan and Jacobean
buildings. It is not surprising that it took some time before this
severe classical villa was assimilated into the existing tradition of
country-house building, especially as the periods of Civil War
and Commonwealth were hardly propitious for a style associated
with the court. Another obstacle was that by the 1630s a lively

alternative existed, centred on the City craftsmen, particularly
the bricklayers, which drew its inspiration from the vigorous
forms of Netherlandish classicism available from pattern books.
In domestic architecture it is characterized by a combination of
the Jacobean tradition of curved gables and mullioned-and-
transomed windows with skilful exploitation of carved brick for
a display of fanciful details, among which pilasters, often in
several orders, and eared architraves were especially popular.
There are several examples of this taste remaining in the London
neighbourhood, stemming from lost precedents in or near the
City; in North London especially Cromwell House Highgate
(Hy) and Swakeleys (Hi), in South London the house now
called Kew Palace, which was built for a London merchant in   24
1631. On a lesser scale, The Presbytery, Croom's Hill, Greenwich displays similar motifs. They are also found in the woodwork of this period: the staircase hall of Ham House is one of the   27
best examples, interesting too in the way in which it uses carved
panels on the staircase instead of balusters, an early instance of
this fashion.

Churches: 1660–1815

The theme of the influence of City craftsmen on the London
countryside can be continued after the Restoration. In the case
of CHURCHES the Great Fire of 1666 provided an extra opportunity, under *Wren*'s leadership, for the evolution of new types
of plans and furnishings especially suitable for the Anglicanism
of the later C17. A decorous setting for traditional ritual focused
on the altar had to be combined with the requirement of an
auditorium around the pulpit (the arrangement which had been
developed already by the more extreme Reformed Church in
Holland). Architects, perennially fascinated by the perfection of
a central plan, had to compromise. The evolution of Wren's
plans for St Paul's is the most famous example; his City churches
provided a series of subtle and ingenious alternative solutions for
small buildings. The influence of these is reflected by St Mary
Magdalene Bermondsey (1675–9) and St Nicholas Deptford
(1697) with their interaction of longitudinal and central tenden-
cies. They were both rebuilt and probably designed by a Southwark carpenter, *Charles Stanton*. The Deptford church retains
its domestic-looking late C17 exterior, brick with stone dressings, with shaped gables, still rather Dutch. The former St
Thomas Southwark (now Southwark Cathedral chapter house)
of 1702 is of the same materials, but more correctly classical.
Other early C18 rebuildings are the charming Georgian brick St
Mary Rotherhithe, Bermondsey (1714–40 by *Dowbiggin*), and
the more austere, slightly Vanbrughian St Mary Woolwich
(1727–39).
    A new scale and a wholly urban character arrive in outer
London as a result of the New Churches Act of 1711. Most of the
twelve churches which were actually built out of fifty projected
to cope with the growth of London, are in the East End (*see*

London: North and North East), but South London has one of the
48 most splendid of them all: *Thomas Archer*'s St Paul Deptford
(1713–30), perhaps the most Roman of all Baroque churches in
London, with its handsome stone exterior, quasi central plan,
and grand semicircular portico. Hardly less impressive is
47 *Hawksmoor*'s monumental rebuilding of St Alfege Greenwich
(1711–14), the first church to be funded by the Fifty Churches
Commission. The exterior is in his very personal version of
Baroque, the plan, like those of his East End churches, has a
strong N-S as well as E-W axis, its central rectangle uninterrupted
by supports. The more conventional tower in the Wren tradition
was completed by *John James*. *James* was also responsible for the
50 rebuilding of St Mary Twickenham (another aristocratic riverside settlement). Here brick is used for the restrained but
accomplished exterior. The centres of N and S sides are again
emphasized. St Mary Magdalene Richmond (1750) is a simpler
version of the same theme. The interior at Twickenham, however, is a utilitarian preaching box with galleries (the type of plan
introduced by Wren at St James Westminster) which became the
standard arrangement for C18 rebuildings or remodellings. A
version (with balconies instead of galleries) is displayed with
exquisite neo-Grecian elegance in the chapel of Greenwich Hospital (*James Stuart* and *William Newton*, 1779–89). Simpler
imitations can be found in the parish churches rebuilt in the
expanding towns and villages: St George Southwark (*John Price*,
51 1734–6), St Mary Battersea (*Joseph Dixon*, 1775–6), Holy Trinity Clapham (*Kenton Couse*, 1774–6), All Saints Wandsworth
(1779–80), St Mary Lewisham (interior altered) (*G. Gibson*,
1774–7). The influence of the ingenuity of Wren's City churches, however, persists in the variety of steeples that were built,
especially in the first half of the C18: see in addition to that of St
Alfege Greenwich those of St Mary Rotherhithe, St George
Southwark, St Paul Deptford. That of St Mary Battersea is as
late as 1776, but by then the type was old-fashioned; Holy
Trinity Clapham has only a small tower. This church is exceptional in being built on a fresh site for the part of Clapham
growing around the common.

   Because of the legal difficulties of establishing new parish
churches the new C18 suburbs were served for the most part
only by proprietary chapels. The Ascension Dartmouth Row
Blackheath (founded 1697) began in this way, and so did St
Anne Kew (founded 1712). They retain from the C18 respectively a lavish apse of *c.* 1750 and an aisled nave of 1770. Small
proprietary chapels continued into the early C19. The type is
still demonstrated attractively by the modest classical buildings
of St John, Southend, Lewisham (1824), or Grove Chapel Camberwell (1819). Others have been enveloped in later enlargements, e.g. St Mary Balham. Early Nonconformist buildings are
similar in size and appearance; see e.g. the Congregational
Chapels at Brixton (1828) and West Norwood (1820). The neo-
Grecian portico of the Unitarian Chapel, Southwark (1821?), is
unusually grand for its date, the rare survival of the little

Friends' Meeting House at Wandsworth, of 1778, exceptionally modest.

FITTINGS and FURNISHINGS of C 17–early-C 19 churches were generally much altered in the C 19, so that the interiors of these churches rarely convey the spirit in which they were built. Galleries were particularly detested by C 19 restorers, and no C 18 pulpit survives in its original central position. Petersham has the most atmospheric Georgian village church interior, 49 complete with simple box pews, pulpit, etc. The best lafe C 17 craftsmanship is not in its original setting, but in the C 20 All Hallows Twickenham, built to accommodate the splendid fittings from *Wren*'s City church of All Hallows Lombard Street. They include an exceptional multi-pedimented reredos, and an excellent organ case, font, and font cover. St Antholin Camberwell also has a reredos from its eponymous City church. Indigenous versions of such reredoses, together with other contemporary woodwork, remain at St Nicholas Deptford and St Mary Magdalene Bermondsey. Some handsome fittings of the C 18 survive at St Mary Rotherhithe, St Mary Twickenham, and St George Southwark. Bermondsey has an C 18 font and pulpit, Dulwich College chapel a font by *Gibbs* of 1729, All Saints Carshalton C 18 communion rails, St Paul's Cray a lectern, probably foreign, in the form of a Pelican in her Piety. Finally the Greenwich Royal Hospital Chapel has a remarkable collection of furnishings, including a neo-Grecian pulpit (inspired by the Monument of Lysicrates) of oak and mahogany, with *Coade* stone medallions, an altar painting by *Benjamin West*, and much else, reflecting the new neo-classical taste of the later C 18.

The patchy distribution of MONUMENTS of the later C 17–18 indicates that, as with fittings, much must have been swept away. South London parish churches which have preserved enough to be specially recommended to the connoisseur of sculpture of this period are St Mary Battersea, St George Beckenham, All Saints Carshalton, St Luke Charlton, St Nicholas Chislehurst, St Paulinus Crayford, St Mary Lewisham, and St Mary Twickenham, but there are few major works to be discovered. The following can be singled out specially. From the later C 17 the most memorable monuments with large figures are the eloquent remains of the Atkins family memorial at St Paul 45 Clapham (1680s–1691) by *William Stanton*, and the proud com- 46 position with reclining effigy of Archbishop Sheldon (1683) by *Jasper Latham* at St John Croydon, also unfortunately not in its original condition. Examples as ambitious as this are rare; much more common are the wall-monuments with architectural surrounds embellished by cherubs, or by lively carvings of fruit and flowers (the kind of decoration which Wren was using at St Paul's Cathedral or Hampton Court). The 1680s produced an especially rich crop of these: Twickenham 1680 by *Bird* and 1686; Streatham 1686 by *Nost*; Addington 1691 attributed to *Nost*; Erith 1686; Bexley 1687; Richmond 1689, also Mortlake 1699. Cartouches with carved decoration were also popular, see

Bexley (1679), Chislehurst (1682 and other later examples), Richmond (1687), Lambeth (1692). The type continued into the C18, becoming asymmetrical and developing Rococo details: Beckenham 1718, Hampton 1738, St Mary Rotherhithe 1743
53 (to Joseph Wade, the King's carver), Carshalton 1753 (by *Rysbrack*), Richmond 1754. Busts are another perennial type: Edward Wynter 1686 at Battersea (with an enjoyable relief as well) ascribed to *Bushnell*, Richard Blisse 1703 at Southwark Cathedral, Elizabeth Thompson 1759 at Charlton. Some C18 monuments without figures adopt rather pompous compositions of funeral objects, e.g. the Shovel monument at Crayford (1732, putti and sarcophagus), or the Fellowes monument at Carshalton (1724, sarcophagus and obelisk). But there are no examples with figures on the scale or of the quality of the contemporary memorials which throng Westminster Abbey. The Richards monument of 1721 at Charlton is a late example of a free-standing figure in armour (by *Guelfi*), Sir William Scawen at Carshalton of 1722 a rare case of a reclining effigy. A simpler, often very effective C18 type was the tablet incorporating a portrait medallion. An early instance is the one to William Hewer at St Paul Clapham (1715), which interestingly is based on a Bernini design. Later portraits can be found at Chislehurst (1720), Mitcham (1727, probably by *Rysbrack*), Beckenham (1737 by *Adye*), and, most skilfully, at St Mary Battersea on the Bolingbroke monument of 1753, again by *Rysbrack*. A later example is the one of Pope at Twickenham by *Prince Hoare* (1761). There are also, from the mid C18 onwards, a number of enjoyable works on a small scale with delicately carved reliefs, for example the monument of Lord Thomas Bertie at Chislehurst, 1749 by *Cheere*, with a battle scene, the framed deathbed group at Lewisham by *Vanpook* (1787), and the figured sarcophagus at Beckenham by *Hickey* (1790). The outstanding example of this late C18 sensibility is the large, idealized retro-
55 spective monument to Thomas Guy in Guy's Hospital Chapel, carved by *John Bacon* in 1779, a highly expressive scene showing Guy rescuing a sick man, with the hospital buildings in the background.

The sculptors of the neo-classical period are fairly well represented, although mostly by minor works: *Bacon Jun.* at Twickenham (1800); *Banks* by one of his major works, another deathbed scene, at Lewisham (1791); *Flaxman* especially strik-
52 ingly at Lewisham (1797) and also at Beckenham (1801), Richmond (1806), and Streatham (1824); *Chantrey* at North Cray (1821), Chislehurst (1823), Kingston (1825), St Paul Clapham (1835), and by busts at Charlton (1817) and Lambeth (1830).

Secular Buildings: 1660–1815

From here it is appropriate to return to secular buildings and to consider their development after the Restoration. The rebuild-
29 ing of the great hall of the archbishop's palace at Lambeth in an engaging mixture of Gothic and classical was part of a conscious

revival of old traditions. In a more light-hearted vein, the turrets of *Wren*'s Royal Observatory at Greenwich (1675) perhaps hark back to the picturesque skylines of the Jacobean age. In contrast, the later Stuarts' major ROYAL BUILDINGS looked to the more recent creations of the autocratic French monarchy. The countryside around London, and especially the area covered in this volume, offers an unparalleled sequence of major examples of royal patronage of the second half of the C 17. We start with *John Webb*'s King Charles Block at Greenwich (1664), one of Charles 30 II's abortive palace schemes. With its long, heavily rusticated 39 stone façade, display of giant pilasters, and balustraded end pavilions, it must have appeared nearly as novel as the Queen's House completed by Charles I thirty years earlier. Despite the obvious influence of Webb's mentor, Inigo Jones, the forceful detailing is more mannered than most of Jones's work, and looks forward to the Baroque of the end of the century. But first came quieter episodes, in the more homely Dutch-influenced style favoured by *Wren* in the earlier part of his career. The best examples, Chelsea Hospital (1682–5) and Kensington Palace, are in NW London. The minor repairs to Richmond Palace, perhaps for James II, are in a similar style. On quite a different scale is the work at Hampton Court for William of Orange and 33 Mary Stuart, begun in 1689. Although Wren's plans for an 34 almost total rebuilding of the palace were rejected, the grounds 41 with their long avenues on the grandest scale, and the gardens embellished with *Tijou*'s exquisite ironwork, demonstrate the 42 scope of the early intentions. Inside the palace there is the equally splendid craftsmanship by *Gibbons*, *Nost*, and others, and Wren's buildings themselves are festively sumptuous in their mixture of brick and stone, even if what was finally built lacks the drama of bolder Baroque set-pieces. Before Hampton Court was complete, Wren had other opportunities to develop his interest in formal planning and grand compositions. His most impressive executed example is also in South London: the Royal Naval Hospital at Greenwich, designed from 1694 on- 39 wards, after Greenwich had been given up as a royal residence. The end result, as at Hampton Court, had to incorporate existing buildings, but here they were the more sympathetic classical creations of Webb and Jones. Another difference is that the Naval Hospital was conceived as a public monument visible from afar, a unique exploitation of the Thames river-front. So at Greenwich variety is achieved not by sculptural ornament, as at Hampton Court, which needs to be seen from close at hand, but by strictly architectural means: highly modelled surfaces in a lively rhythm of paired columns and repeated pediments, building up to the double flourish of the twin domes over hall and chapel. Among the Greenwich exteriors only the more eccentric composition of the King William Block, attributed to Wren's 40 assistant *Hawksmoor*, departs from this measured grandeur, and displays the excesses which English Baroque could reach by c. 1701–2. A similar mood is betrayed by some of the Hampton Court interiors completed a little later, the Queen's Guard

Chamber and Presence Chamber (*c.* 1716–18), for which *Vanbrugh* may have been responsible. The starker aspects of Baroque appear even more strikingly in the austere brick buildings
37 put up at the Woolwich Arsenal *c.* 1717, also in all likelihood by Vanbrugh, which set the mood for their more utilitarian successors during the C 18 in the expanding Arsenal.

The PAINTED INTERIORS of this period, on the other hand, display the sumptuous exuberance which was another facet of the Baroque. The outstanding example is *Thornhill's* magni-
43 ficent and vivacious Painted Hall at Greenwich. Hampton Court has a wider range: the King's Staircase and some of the State
44 Apartments are by Thornhill's less accomplished predecessor, *Verrio*, the Queen's State Bedchamber by *Thornhill* again, while the later decoration of the Queen's Staircase is in *Kent's* rich but more restrained manner (1734–5).

CHARITABLE BUILDINGS in the London villages are generally in a quieter style. So often financed by City merchants, it is not surprising that they display the influence of London work, that is, the tradition of the City craftsmen. A good example was the Colfe Almshouses at Lewisham, a small but handsome row of houses with central chapel built in 1664 by *Peter Mills* (now demolished). Cleaves Almshouses Kingston of 1668 in a similar style still remain, as does the tiny chapel from Boone's Alms-
35 houses at Lee (1683). Much more splendid is Bromley College, a generous foundation on a quadrangular cloistered plan, established by the Bishop of Rochester for widows of the clergy, and built in 1670–2 by *Richard Ryder*, master carpenter to the Office of Works, and West End surveyor and speculator. Morden
36 College Blackheath, exceptionally well preserved, the chapel still with its original furnishings, followed in 1695, founded by Sir John Morden, Treasurer of Bromley College, in imitation of the earlier foundation. *Wren* may have been the architect; at any rate the domestic brick and stone style which here reaches happy maturity shares features with Hampton Court: sash-windows instead of Bromley College's mullions and transoms, and a lively front range with quoined and pedimented centre framing the entrance in place of Bromley College's massive stone archway set abruptly against a brick wall. No remaining C 18 almshouses can compete with these: the most ambitious are the delightful Hopton Almshouses of 1752, a remarkable survival in inner Southwark. The Styleman Almshouses Bexley (1755) and the Houblon Almshouses Richmond (1757–8) are much simpler, for the charity which attracted wealthy benefactors in the C 18 was no longer the almshouse, but the HOSPITAL. In the late C 17 the term was still ill defined. Chelsea Hospital and the Royal Naval Hospital were designed for the old as well as the sick. It was the C 18 which saw the development of the hospital in the modern sense. The first in London to set the pattern for building on a large scale were the medieval foundations: Bethlehem Hospital was rebuilt after the Great Fire by *Robert Hooke* at Moorfields in 1675–6 (then rebuilt again in Southwark in 1812–14, *see* below). St Thomas' Southwark was given new buildings from the early

c 18 (which disappeared when the hospital had to move to Lambeth in the c 19 to make way for the railways). The earliest remaining hospital buildings in London are therefore those of the new hospital founded by Thomas Guy, to relieve the crowded St Thomas' close by. They were begun in 1721. The plan is the traditional one of wards around a cloistered quadrangle, as had been used in the grander almshouses and in the rebuilding of St Thomas', with a cour d'honneur with projecting wings in front (as on the river side of Wren's Chelsea Hospital). Guy's and St Thomas' remained the only general hospitals s of the Thames until the c 19; meanwhile in the surge of c 18 hospital building on the other bank the N fringes of the city acquired St Luke's (1751), the West End the Foundling Hospital (1742) and the Middlesex, Westminster, and St George's Hospitals, and the East End the London Hospital (founded 1746); of all these only the last preserves some of its mid c 18 buildings.

It is only the hospitals which have anything to offer in the way of major PUBLIC SCULPTURE of this period in South London. From the old St Thomas', preserved in the new building, are figures of 1682 by *Cartwright*, formerly over a gateway, a fine statue of Sir Robert Clayton by *Gibbons* of 1701–2, and a bronze figure of Edward VI by *Scheemakers* of 1737. This must reflect a special vogue of the 1730s, for there is a stone statue by Scheemakers of 1734 in the forecourt of Guy's Hospital, and one of George II of 1735, by *Rysbrack*, in front of Greenwich Hospital. At Mottingham, *Nost*'s statue of Sir Robert Geffrye, brought from the Shoreditch Almshouses, is a little earlier (1723).

There is little that need be said about other c 18 PUBLIC BUILDINGS. There are a few modest village SCHOOLS, at Rotherhithe, with pretty figures of charity children, at Morden (1731), Mitcham (1788), and, most interestingly, at Wimbledon, an octagonal one of 1758 built for fifty charity children (now William Wilberforce School). In Grove Road Richmond is a former WORKHOUSE, quite a handsome classical building of 1786 by *Kenton Couse*; in Southwark Bridge Road the remains of another of 1777, probably by *George Gwilt Sen*. The PRISONS which were such a feature of Southwark from the Middle Ages until well into the c 19 have completely disappeared. Like other institutions they were replaced during the c 19 by more extensive buildings on the fringes of suburban development (*see* below). At Woolwich, however, from the later c 18 ARMY BARRACKS AND TRAINING ESTABLISHMENTS were already heralding the scale of the c 19 and c 20. They start with *James Wyatt*'s Royal Artillery Barracks of 1775 onwards, a Roman camp in the grand manner, nearly 1,100 ft long, complete with triumphal arches. This is followed by the Royal Military Academy, moved in 1805 to *Wyatt*'s new buildings on Woolwich 69 Common from its original home in the Arsenal. Within the Arsenal is Wyatt's Grand Store of the same date, a monumental neo-classical composition facing the Thames, the only successor to Greenwich Hospital in this respect, although now obscured by inappropriate later buildings and partly derelict.

A few other building types of the C17–18 should be mentioned. The INNS which played such an important semi-public function at this time have nearly all been rebuilt or drastically altered. Of the once numerous inns of Southwark only the late C17 George in Borough High Street partially preserves the traditional arrangement of a galleried courtyard. Further out more rural types are represented by the prettified, partly weatherboarded, Greyhound at Carshalton, or the King's Head Roehampton, remarkable only because of their survival in built-up suburbia. Others, especially on the increasingly busy main roads, have polite brick or stucco fronts that would be commonplace in country towns – for example the White Hart and the former King's Head Mitcham, and the George Twickenham.

Even less remains of the other RECREATIONAL PLACES to which Londoners resorted before C19 expansion and the coming of the railways made it both desirable and possible to escape further afield. The fashion for pleasure gardens began *c.* 1660. The most famous in South London was Vauxhall Gardens in South Lambeth, frequented by all levels of society in the C17 and C18. It declined in favour as the area became less salubrious, but closed only in 1859. Its site has vanished completely. In the C18 there were diversions close to the Thames such as Cuper's Garden (near the site of the National Theatre), founded by Lord Arundel's gardener and furnished with cast-off Arundel statues. A little further off St George's Fields and Bermondsey both boasted gardens and mineral waters. The vogue for taking the waters (which began at Tunbridge Wells in the early C17) also encouraged the establishment of little spas in the hillier regions further S: the waters of Streatham Wells and Sydenham Wells were discovered in the C17; Beulah Spa in Upper Norwood was a short-lived latecomer which opened in 1831, adorned with fanciful buildings by *Decimus Burton*. The best known North London equivalents were Hampstead Wells and Bagnigge (or Sadlers) Wells, Islington. There were also numerous tea gardens attached to simple cottages or country farmhouses just the right distance for a day's excursion from town, which managed to retain their rural character until well into the C19. The only reminders of such times in South London are a house in Streatham Vale and *Burton*'s much altered lodge in cottage orné style in Upper Norwood.

Such pleasant spots were of course only the icing on the cake. The fringes of the metropolis had for long been exploited by Londoners for other purposes, particularly for activities which because of their illegal or anti-social nature were not welcome in the city. Hence the theatres and brothels of Southwark, and the industries, free from the restrictions of the City companies, which began to expand along the Thames and up the rivers, especially along the Wandle from Wandsworth to Merton. Further downstream the first docks were opened during the C17, and from then on the architectural history of the riverside is increasingly concerned with the warehouses, manufactories, and utilities that were required by a great seaport (*see* Introduction to Industrial Archaeology). Further out the open land was also cultivated for the benefit of the London consumer. The pattern is shown clearly on Thomas Milne's *Land Use Map of London and Environs* of 1800* and described in Henry Hunter's *History of London and its Environs* (1811): claypits for brickmaking on the edge of the built-up area, stretches of pasture land beyond, grazed by the cattle yielding dairy produce for the city, market gardens in the fertile flood-plain terrace gravels (especially the western stretches of the Thames, and in NE London, along the Lee Valley), hay meadows and arable farming on the higher ground further away. In the inner boroughs, the agricultural history of South London is now only faintly echoed by some street names and in the very occasional farmhouse stranded in later suburban development. But other features of Milne's map are still easily recognizable today. The cultivated land has been covered by bricks and mortar, but the wasteland and woodland which interrupted it still remains. North of the Thames the chief areas untouched were Hounslow Heath, Harrow, Harrow Weald Common, Finchley Common, and Epping Forest. On the fringes of Kent and Surrey these untilled expanses were even more numerous. They were diminished by early C19 enclosures, and somewhat municipalized in the C19, but still give an identifiable character to villages otherwise overwhelmed by the waves of C19 building that followed. Richmond Park, and the commons of Ham, Barnes, Putney, Wimbledon, Wandsworth, Clapham, Streatham, Dulwich, and Blackheath can still be found, although the commons of Teddington, Sydenham, and Penge are no more. Less remains of the main stretches of woodland, at Coombe near Kingston, at Norwood, and S and E of Croydon. The picturesque quality of such areas often acted as a magnet for the best C18 houses: Milne's map shows that by 1800 numerous small parks and estates were concentrated around the commons and heaths. It is time therefore to turn to the houses of the London countryside built by courtiers and city men from the later C17 onwards.

Domestic Buildings: 1660–1750

Starting at the top of the social scale, COURTIERS' HOUSES after the Restoration are far less ostentatious than those of the beginning of the century. The emphasis had shifted to comfort and convenience. The leading men eschewed the fancier flourishes of the City craftsmen, and adopted the more sober domestic classical style already current in Holland. *Hugh May*'s Eltham Lodge, built for Sir John Shaw in 1664, is one of the first 32 and best examples, a compact house of brick and stone dressings, very restrained in its harmoniously composed classical

*Reprinted by the London Topographical Society (publication Nos. 118–19), 1975–6.

detail. A lesser-known gentleman architect, *William Samwell*, was responsible for the additions which the Duke and Duchess of Lauderdale made to Ham House in 1672–4, which are even plainer outside, and very probably for Bushy House Teddington, which although much altered is still substantially the house built for the Ranger of Bushy Park in 1664–5. The experimental planning of these houses is of especial interest, reflecting an effort to combine the new standards of comfort and privacy with the formal ceremonial with which the exiled court had become familiar in France and Holland. The main objective was to provide conveniently accessible suites of rooms, as is demons-
25 trated at a royal level by *Webb*'s additions to the Queen's House
33 at Greenwich, and of course by *Wren*'s work at Hampton Court,
34 with a 'King's side' and a 'Queen's side', each with its own grand staircase. At Ham House the traditional Jacobean arrangement with great hall between wings was converted into a more up-to-date double-pile plan, providing a suite of apartments on each floor; at Bushy House and Eltham Lodge the suites of rooms at front and back are divided, in the first case by a continuous corridor, in the second by a specially lavish set of staircases.

These particular plans are unique, but the use of various plans based on the 'double pile', i.e. a building two rooms deep throughout, became standard for houses of the later C 17 onwards. Another contemporary trend was the more regular treatment of side elevations as well as back and front; the hipped roof and the continuous eaves cornice which helped so much to achieve this aim became a hallmark of the elegant, excellently detailed brick houses which were built from the end of the C 17 onwards. Old Battersea House is an interesting example, still a little old-fashioned in having a recessed centre, with a plan of the kind that continued to be popular in the C 18: a generous central entrance hall doubling as a staircase hall and providing access to rooms on the three other sides. There must have been many other houses of this scale and date in what are now the inner suburbs, but one now has to travel further out to find other surviving examples: York House Twickenham, much altered, but basically C 17; West Hall Mortlake; and Lewisham Old Vicarage (1692), much more modest, still preserving the mullioned-and-transomed windows that were already becoming old-fashioned. Specially handsome examples from the early C 18 are Eagle House Mitcham (1705), Marshgate House, Sheen Road, Richmond, and Wrencote and Coombe Hill, Croydon. Others can be found in the aristocratic retreats of Greenwich and Blackheath (the Manor House Croom's Hill, and the house now called Spencer and Perceval houses, Dartmouth Row (Le), of 1689) or in the little village of Petersham at the foot of Richmond Hill, especially favoured by the wealthy at the turn of the century (Rutland House, Douglas House, Montrose House).

Carshalton House (*c.* 1713), although on a rather larger scale (and with later interiors and rebuilt top floor), also belongs to this tradition of carefully detailed brick houses. It has the added advantage that despite the later school buildings attached on the

side, it still sits comfortably in spacious grounds. Roehampton
House of 1710–12, one of the few contemporary houses of 56
comparable size in the London area, has been less fortunate.
This has the more individualistic Baroque touches of the inventive *Thomas Archer*, and must have looked even more extraordinary when its considerable height was crowned by its original
broken pediment. It was also exceptional for other reasons:
according to *Vitruvius Britannicus* it was designed with quadrant
wings (now heightened), and it had a double-height upstairs
saloon (destroyed in the Second World War). Both were features
which soon afterwards were to become part of the Palladian
canon. *Gibbs*'s Sudbrook Park, Petersham, of 1726, is especially
interesting as a transitional building poised between Baroque
and Palladian, with a monumental portico and a central cube
room, a Palladian concept, but here expressed in a fully Baroque 61
manner. Equally sumptuous in miniature is *Gibbs*'s octagonal
garden room for Orleans House, Twickenham (*c.* 1720), with its
plasterwork by *Artari* and *Bagutti*.

But apart from these examples the London area is, not surprisingly, hardly a rewarding one for major country houses. The
few really grand examples of the early C 18 have all disappeared:
John James's Wricklemarsh, Blackheath, of 1721 (although
some interesting fragments of it remain at Beckenham Place,
Lewisham), *Colen Campbell*'s over-ambitious Wanstead (Re) of
1714–20, and the Duke of Chandos's equally short-lived Canons
(Hw). The metropolis was too close for large estates to remain
intact and, indeed, throughout the C 18 many of the houses built
in the neighbouring towns and villages (particularly those for the
aristocratic coteries at Richmond, Kew, and Twickenham) were
intended only as summer or occasional residences, with modest
parks or gardens of a few acres or less. The largest early C 18
private PARKS in South London (apart from the royal estates of
Richmond and Greenwich) were those of Sudbrook (now part of
Richmond Park, and partly a golf course), Ham House (mostly
built over, although the lines of the long avenues remain), and
Wricklemarsh, also built over, whose avenues appear prominently on C 18 maps.

The smaller houses fall into two main types, the villa and the
brick terrace house.* Both can be traced back to Inigo Jones and
the first half of the C 17; the prototype for the one was the
Queen's House at Greenwich, for the other the regular urban
compositions of Covent Garden and Great Queen Street (*see
London 1*). But the villa did not really find favour until the
Palladian revival of the early C 18, so it is the TERRACE HOUSE
that must be discussed first. The urban house on a narrow plot of
land, sharing its side walls with its neighbours, was nothing new.
The use of brick and stone rather than timber for the fronts of
such buildings in London goes back certainly to the earlier C 17,
as is shown by John Smythson's drawings of houses in Holborn,

---

*Or row house, as they are more logically called in America. 'Row' indeed
appears frequently in early C 18 names.

but it was *Inigo Jones*'s Covent Garden of 1630 that introduced into England the idea that a row of such houses should be treated as a single composition. The concept of the formal terrace had already spread outside London before the Restoration. A remarkable group of four dating from 1658 remain at Newington Green, Islington (Is). After 1660 more ambitious imitations of the Earl of Bedford's Covent Garden sprang up w of the City: the Duke of St Albans' St James's Square (*see London 1*), the Earl of Southampton's Bloomsbury Square, and other squares and streets laid out by the speculator Dr Nicholas Barbon (Red Lion Square, Great Ormond Street, Holborn, Ca). Meanwhile the Great Fire of 1666 and the London Building Acts which followed ensured that the narrow-fronted brick terrace house became ubiquitous in the city itself, and the Inns of Court adopted the same style for their building in the 1670s–80s (*see* the Temple, *London 1*; Grays Inn, Ca). By the 1680s, after a period of experiment, the plans of such houses were becoming standardized, and the economic and practical arrangement evolved which remained basic throughout the C18 and earlier C19 for all except the most ambitious buildings: a front and back room on each floor, the entrance on one side, leading into a narrow hall-passage with a rear staircase lit from the back of the house. Up to the 1730s there was often a closet opening off the rear room; later on there are sometimes bow windows at the back, and a service extension projecting at the end of the passage.

Outside the City and West End, houses in a formal square appear only rarely before the C19 (Kensington Square (K C), *c.* 1681, outside what later became known as Kensington Palace; Hoxton Square, Hackney (Hc), 1683), but the proliferation of terraces overlooking the Thames or beside existing greens and commons shows that an open prospect was sought when possible. An early example of such a speculative terrace outside London is Old Palace Terrace, overlooking Richmond Green, built in 1692. A little later, in more modest surroundings, although not lacking in metropolitan sophistication, is Albury 59 Street Deptford, of 1706 onwards, laid out by *Thomas Lucas*, a local bricklayer, but very up-to-date in its use of parapets instead of wooden eaves, and in its articulation of the fronts by recessed panels and brickwork of different colours. Total uniformity was not yet the aim: the lively doorcases of Albury Street show, as do others of the same period (for example Ormond Road, Richmond), that woodcarvers were still left plenty of scope for individuality. Classical forms are found only rarely at this date (e.g. at Old Town Clapham, built shortly before 1707). These houses at Clapham, Deptford, and Richmond are (or were) only two storeys above basements. Three-storey houses of the type of Old Devonshire House, Vicarage Crescent, Battersea were no doubt more common closer to London, but few survive from before the second decade of the C18.

From this time onwards three-storey parapeted terraces, by then the standard type in the City and the West End, sprang up

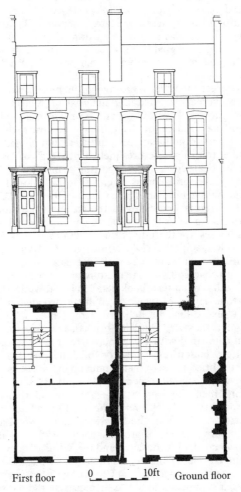

First floor   0 _____ 10ft   Ground floor

Deptford (Le), Nos. 19–21 Albury Street, 1706

in more rural settings. Particularly good examples in this volume
are Clapham Common North Side (1714–20), Montpelier Row
and Syon Row Twickenham (c. 1720–1), Nos. 7–21 Croom's
Hill Greenwich (1721), Church Row Wandsworth (1723), and
the exceptionally regular Maids of Honour Row on Richmond 57
Green (1724). There are more on the slopes of Richmond Hill,
and many others can be found in NE and NW London. They
brought a new urban formality to the villages beyond the built-
up fringes of London. The flat brick frontage was also used for
single houses, either detached in their own grounds (for example

the especially elegant Ormeley Lodge, Ham) or arranged in haphazard terrace fashion, as for instance in the charming
4 groups around Kew Green or Ham Common. This new brick urban vernacular was also used to transform the exteriors of older buildings. Frognal House Sidcup is an example of a major timber-framed and stone house that was disguised in this way.

Nevertheless for lesser buildings in the more rural parts the alternative vernacular cladding material of weatherboarding persisted into the C19. Suburban expansion has swept much away, but the outer boroughs still have survivals which show how the forms of polite architecture were assimilated into the local timber tradition. Picturesquely haphazard groups of brick and weatherboarded cottages, sporting sash-windows and the occasional Georgian doorcase, remain to be enjoyed in West Street Carshalton and Park Lane Cheam. Other good examples are Pond Cottages Dulwich and the group at the Snuff Mills Morden Hall Park; especially worthwhile individual weatherboarded houses are the one of C17 origin at Woodside Green near Croydon, and the later White House Mitcham. Picton House in Kingston High Street and a pair in Sydenham High Road have a characteristic C18 mixture of weatherboarded sides or back, with C18 pattern-book detail in front, while a house on Maidenstone Hill Greenwich even has a wooden front with imitation rustication. In Bell Hill Croydon is a house with mathematical tiles (i.e. simulated bricks), a rarity in the London area. But compared with Kent and Surrey too little survives to make outer London rewarding for this kind of study.

While the brick terraces that sprang up in the villages around London were generally speculative ventures, sometimes by professional men who lived in the neighbourhood, sometimes by local carpenters or bricklayers, the VILLAS which began to appear from c. 1720 were the conscious expression of architectural theory by a circle of architects and gentlemen-amateurs closely associated with the court and the Whig aristocracy. The twin exemplars were Palladio and Inigo Jones. The most famous is *Lord Burlington*'s own house at Chiswick (Ho) which was built c. 1723–9, a summer-time toy to demonstrate the rediscovered virtues of Palladianism. The architect of Henrietta Howard's
60 almost exactly contemporary Marble Hill Twickenham (1724– c. 1729) was *Roger Morris*, but many of the leading members of the Palladian circle were involved: Lord Herbert (the future ninth Earl of Pembroke), the Earl of Ilay, for whom Morris built a villa later at Whitton (now demolished), and possibly Colen Campbell. Marble Hill as finally built is less ambitious than Chiswick in its exterior form and interior planning, but its elegant restraint was extremely influential. With its cube room on the piano nobile and staircase *à la* Coleshill it depends as much on Jonesian precedent as on Palladio. Another villa which belongs to this early Palladian group is the White Lodge in Richmond Park, also by *Morris*, although altered and added to. Others in this neighbourhood, about which one knows too little,

have disappeared: Pope's famous villa at Twickenham, given a
new front by *Gibbs* in the 1730s; Frederick, Prince of Wales's
White House at Kew of 1730–5 by *Kent*. One distinguishing
feature of these houses, as some of their names make clear, is that
they were built of stone or faced with stucco, instead of displaying the warm red or brown brick so characteristic of the
early years of the C 18. This desire for the cool chaste exterior,
however, did not become universal until the second half of the
C 18, when, as a cheaper alternative to stone, it was generally
achieved by the use of the paler yellow-grey shades of London
stocks, or by stucco. Thus *Isaac Ware*, who particularly disliked
red brick, used yellow brick for the gallery which he added to the
older Ranger's House, Blackheath, *c.* 1749–50. The addition of
wings to earlier houses was indeed a characteristic type of improvement – other examples are Cross Deep Twickenham
(wings with bay-windows, by *Gibbs*) and Trumpeter's House
Richmond (wings and portico) – while the favourite Palladian
feature of pavilions attached by quadrant passages was used for
the extensions to the White Lodge Richmond Park by *Stephen
Wright*, 1750–2, and for those at Bushy House, where, unusually,
there are four such excrescences.

The second quarter of the C 18 also saw some more eccentric
creations, which anticipate the later interest in HISTORICAL
REVIVALS. South London has three of particular interest. The
first is *Vanbrugh*'s own house at Maze Hill, Greenwich, a mock 38
castle with turrets of 1718–26 extended soon after it was built
by an asymmetrical wing, a highly unusual procedure. It was
originally accompanied by other houses with medieval overtones
for members of his family. A little later *Kent* was playfully
experimenting with Gothic and Jacobean forms side by side with
his richly classical interiors in his alterations at Hampton Court
(1732). Then in 1749 *Horace Walpole* began the transformation
of Strawberry Hill Twickenham into a fantastic Gothic castle, 64
assisted by his Committee of Taste, chiefly *John Chute* and
Richard Bentley, for the first time basing the Gothic details of the
interiors on reasonably accurate sources. But although Straw- 63
berry Hill's influence was nationwide, and Radnor House near
by (now demolished) was gothicized before 1750, the Gothic
manner does not seem to have been much imitated in the London area in the later C 18. The surviving examples, all minor
stuccoed and castellated villas, date from *c.* 1800 or later; The
Priory Roehampton, The Priory, Bedford Hill, Balham, and in
North London Twyford Abbey (Ea) and, until recently, Berry-
meads Priory Acton. (None, needless to say, has anything to
do with medieval monasteries.) The castle style also did not have
much success. The only example that can be cited is Severndroog Castle on Shooters Hill, by *R. Jupp* of 1784, and this is
not a house but a folly, and so really belongs to the next paragraph.

If one wished to experiment with exotic architecture one did
not have to imitate Horace Walpole and live amidst Gothic
gloom; GARDEN BUILDINGS were the ideal compromise. In

the C 17 garden pavilions had simply imitated the styles current
for grander houses. South London has two such examples: the
restrained classical summer-house of Charlton House of *c.* 1630,
58 in the manner of Inigo Jones, and the charming gazebo of 1672
probably by *Robert Hooke* in the grounds of The Grange,
Croom's Hill, Greenwich. The period *c.* 1700 is represented by
Wren's work at Hampton Court, the Banqueting House, battlemented perhaps in acknowledgement of earlier buildings
here, with a grandly decorated interior, and the Bowling Green
pavilions (one much altered remaining of four) in his more
domestic style. From the 1720s we have the remains of the more
extravagantly Baroque Orangery hidden away behind Eltham
High Street, and the sterner, more Vanbrughian water tower in
the grounds of Carshalton House, designed by *Henry Joynes*.
These buildings all had a practical purpose as well as being
embellishments.

   The new approach which evolved in the Palladian circle,
where garden buildings were primarily eyecatchers at the end of
long vistas, began in the London area; first Chiswick, then
Pope's small but famous garden at Twickenham, especially
important as an early effort at picturesque naturalism. All that
remains of the latter, however, are the relics of the underground
passages beneath the house by the river, which led to the garden
beyond the road. This Pope transformed into his celebrated
grotto, decorated with minerals, which inspired so many imitations. Other grottoes in South London also are not well
preserved (two at Carshalton, one in the grounds of Hampton
Court House*). An alternative to a cave was a relic of the Middle
Ages: Walpole's Chapel in the Wood of 1772–4, late and quite
correct in its details, is the sole survivor in the grounds of
Strawberry Hill; the pretty but less authentically Gothic summer-house in Radnor Gardens is a little earlier, the only reminder now of a whole sequence of garden buildings once visible on
the Twickenham riverside. By far the best collection of garden
buildings in this volume is that in the part of Kew Gardens which
belonged to Prince Frederick's White House. Here *Chambers*
was the presiding genius. We still have his large and handsome
Orangery of 1757, and two of his little temples; also, in complete
contrast to their severe classicism, his romantic ruined arch and
65 his Chinese Pagoda, the most flamboyant (but also accurate)
example anywhere of the contemporary interest in Chinoiserie.
There were other exotic contributions at Kew which have disappeared, such as a mosque, an Alhambra, and a Chinese House
of Confucius (designed as early as 1749). The garden building
intended to celebrate famous historic personages, another
favourite C 18 type, is represented by the temple which Garrick
built in 1757 in his grounds at Hampton, to house *Roubiliac*'s
sculpture of Shakespeare. Another example of Chinoiserie is the
surprisingly bold garden building at Blackheath (Pagoda Gardens), probably of the later C 18. From the Regency period is

*Attributed to *Thomas Wright*.

Nash's oriental tent of 1814, formerly in St James's Park, re-erected as the Rotunda at Woolwich.

Domestic Buildings: 1750–1820

We must now catch up on the houses of the second half of the c 18 which accompanied these more frivolous buildings. The 1750s start with a second wave of VILLAS, inspired by the precedents of the 1720s and 30s, built for city men as well as for aristocrats. The London neighbourhood leads the country in this fashion. The area s of the Thames has a large number of survivals, even though the first and most eccentric member of this group has been demolished: Bourchier Cleeve's Foots Cray (1754), a copy of Palladio's Villa Rotonda like the earlier and more famous Mereworth, Kent. The supreme master of these later villas is *Sir Robert Taylor*, a city rather than a court architect: the three examples in this volume are Asgill House 67 Richmond of 1757–8 for his friend Sir Charles Asgill, a Lord Mayor of London, Danson Park Bexleyheath for the city merchant John Boyd (*c.* 1762), and Mount Clare Roehampton for the banker George Clive, 1770–3. Kevington at St Mary Cray is also by him, but of less interest. Taylor's forte was ingenious planning, the economic combination of different-shaped rooms within a compact space. A favourite device is the use of the canted bay-window forming part of an octagonal room inside. At Asgill House there are also oval rooms, and at Danson Park the staircase is in an elliptical central well. His other staircases are also exceptionally elegant, even when on a miniature scale. The restrained exteriors of these villas rely on a skilful balance of plain and rusticated surfaces, of bay-windows and pediments, easily disturbed by injudicious additions. Asgill House, now restored to its original form, is now the only example where these subtle harmonies can be fully appreciated. Danson Park is more on a country-house scale than the other two villas, with a piano nobile and originally with separate pavilions. A piano nobile and grand portico occur at *Chambers*'s first villa, Manresa House Roehampton (built as Parksted for Lord Bessborough), of 1760–*c.* 1768. Chambers's interiors, however, are more severe than 62 Taylor's: rectangular rooms, with fine bold plaster ceilings. Chambers also designed the fireplaces at Danson Park. As far as other INTERIORS of the mid c 18 are concerned the outstanding example is the especially sumptuous plasterwork in one room at 66 Carshalton House. Point House Blackheath has good plaster-work in the staircase hall; No. 4 Richmond Green a painted hall of *c.* 1745; Oak House Richmond Green a plaster ceiling of *c.* 1769, attributed to *Taylor*; Downshire House Roehampton a lively Rococo overmantel.

It was the early supremacy of NEO-CLASSICISM in the London area which pushed other experimental styles such as Gothic into the background. The scholarly study of classical antiquities encouraged the development of a more delicate treatment of ornament, as well as a sophisticated manipulation of rooms of

different shapes. One of the first and most influential exponents
of such ideas was *Robert Adam*. His earliest work in the London
area is at Gordon House Isleworth (1758–9) (Ho) which was
followed from the 1760s onwards by his major commissions of
Osterley, Kenwood, and Syon and by his town houses of the
West End. But there is nothing important by him in this volume
– only his somewhat unsatisfactory additions to Garrick's Villa at
Hampton (*c.* 1775) and some Gothic interiors at Strawberry
Hill. The Adam style appears to have become generally
fashionable in the 1770s. Morden Park of the 1770s is still in the
more robust tradition of the mid C 18. But the interiors of
Taylor's Mount Clare Roehampton have an Adamish lightness of
touch, and so does Plaistow Lodge (Quernmore Secondary
School) Bromley, of *c.* 1777, a large house with elegant pavilion
wings, which is attributed to *Thomas Leverton*, best known as the
architect of Bedford Square (N London). *Robert Mylne* was
another accomplished master of the style, as is shown by his
country mansion, Addington Place (1773–9), and especially by
the villa on Richmond Hill called The Wick (1775), both with
excellent original interiors, the latter including an oval drawing
room. Wandle Bank Mitcham (*c.* 1795), with an exterior similar
to The Wick, may also be by him.

   South London still has quite a scattering of lesser buildings of
the later C 18 in the compact villa tradition; tall, rather austere
three-storey houses, often with a bow-window to the garden, the
entrance front relieved by a demure centre pediment, pilasters,
or by elegant neo-classical reliefs in composition stone. Their
interiors (mostly altered) are generally simpler than those of the
earlier Palladian villas, often with a connecting suite of reception
rooms on the ground floor instead of the piano nobile. Good
examples are Lee Manor House Lewisham, probably by *Richard
Jupp* (1771), *George Gibson Jun.*'s Woodlands Greenwich (1774)
with decoration in *Liardet*'s patent stucco (both now public
libraries), Beckenham Place Lewisham (1773 and later), a rather
crude building with a lofty central hall, incongruously augmented by bits of *John James*'s Wricklemarsh, and the much
more elegant Grove House Roehampton (now the Froebel Institute), 1777 by *James Wyatt*, much added to, but with a good
original entrance hall. A maverick, dating from 1771–3, is Stone
House Upper Deptford, by *George Gibson* (*Sen.* or *Jun.*?), which
has a plan similar to Taylor's Danson Park, and an elaborate
portico. A little later are Belair at Dulwich (1780, but unsympathetically altered), and Brunswick House, Tanners Hill,
Deptford, of 1789, but so hemmed in that it is only recognizable
by its one remaining *Coade* medallion. *Coade* ornament from
another such house, Dr Lettsom's villa at Camberwell of 1779–
80, now demolished, remains on No. 86 Camberwell New Road.
The small neo-classical country seat in the villa tradition continues into the C 19 with *D. R. Roper*'s Brockwell Hall Lambeth
(1813) and Norwood Grove Upper Norwood (both now
preserved as refreshment buildings in public parks), and echoes
of the type are still apparent at Park Hill Streatham, *c.* 1830–40

by *Papworth*, which preserves its neo-classical interiors in excellent condition, and still stands overlooking its miniature picturesque grounds with a lake. Another example is The Shrubbery (begun in 1796, enlarged in 1843), a remarkable survival
tucked away in a suburban corner NW of Clapham Common.
Many others have vanished, as is clear from early maps.

The most extreme version of neo-classicism, the Grecian
style, is not well represented in South London. Its most distinguished appearance is in non-domestic work, first in a very
personal and sophisticated version, *Sir John Soane*'s Dulwich   74
Art Gallery and Mausoleum, and then in churches (*see* below).
The first fully Grecian country house in this volume is *Decimus
Burton*'s Holwood, Keston, of 1823–6. Meanwhile another   72
trend must be noted: the adoption of the picturesque composition in a classical context, achieved by the use of irregular or
oddly angled plans. *John Nash* was especially skilful at this
game. Sundridge Park Bromley, designed with *Repton c.* 1796–   73
9, has wings set at forty-five degrees; his similar Southborough
House Surbiton of 1808 is L-shaped, with a domed porch set
between the two wings. Sundridge Park also illustrates Nash's
love of the dramatic, with its boldly treated domed bow with
giant Corinthian columns; his Casina at Dulwich (demolished)
of 1797 also had a domed projection. Nash was to exploit such
grand effects soon after, in his Regent's Park terraces, just as he
made use of the irregular plan for the more whimsical delights of
the Park Villages (Ca and Wm). Both were to be of seminal
influence on later suburban housing in the London area, as was
another type of house which Nash also favoured (although he
did not invent it): the cottage orné. Few of these remain in the
London area: the best preserved is at Hanwell (Ea) and there is
another in Belsize Park (Ca). Camberwell Grove has a much
altered example, and before the Second World War had a still
better one. One of the prettiest, although really in a class by
itself, is the little Thatched House in Kew Gardens, said to have
been designed by *Queen Charlotte, c.* 1772.

Suburban Development: 1750–1820

Nash's two country houses, still on the fringes of modern built-
up London, mark a turning-point. From the early C 19 onwards,
with very few exceptions, the story of South London
architecture becomes one of suburban building. The starting-
point for a study of the suburban development of South London
is the group of maps made by John Rocque in the mid C 18.*
They show that in the mid C 18, South London was still essentially rural despite all the urban brick terraces of the early C 18
which have been mentioned. Apart from Southwark, the only
sizeable built-up areas were the industrial centres of Deptford

*John Rocque: An exact survey of Citys of London and Westminster, ye
Borough of Southwark and the county near ten miles round, begun in 1741 and
ended in 1745 (published in 1746); A topographical map of the county of
Middlesex (1754); A plan of London . . . 1762 with improvements to 1769.

and Woolwich, dependent on the Naval Dockyard and the Arsenal, and Greenwich and Richmond, where the magnets were the royal establishments. Further out Bromley, Croydon, and Kingston were still country market towns. The crucial developments of the later c 18 which led to the expansion of the villages away from the Thames was the provision of new and better river crossings and the laying out of new roads, part of the spirit of 'improvement' which was also responsible for the wider, better paved and lit thoroughfares of the City and the West End. The new road bypassing the West End (the line of Marylebone, Euston, Pentonville, and City Roads) was laid out in 1756. For South London the key events were the opening of Westminster Bridge in 1750 and the creation of Westminster Bridge Road leading to Southwark, and Kennington Road leading s. Then (more immediately important for South London's suburban growth) came the widening of London Bridge (1758–62) and the building of Blackfriars Bridge (1769). The names involved are already familiar: the well-connected city architects *Sir Robert Taylor* (together with *George Dance Jun.*) for London Bridge; *Robert Mylne* for Blackfriars Bridge. In conjunction with Black-friars Bridge, a specially ambitious layout of streets was planned where Blackfriars Bridge Road met Westminster Bridge Road. This was St George's Circus, a *rond-point* in the French manner with streets radiating off towards Lambeth and Walworth. St George's Road and New Kent Road followed soon after, con-necting the main Kent Road directly to the route to Westmins-ter, with a less well planned crossroads at the Elephant and Castle with the old Roman road from Southwark (a confusion indeed not sorted out until after the Second World War). This paved the way for the development of Walworth and Newington on either side of the New Kent Road. The next stage came with the building of Vauxhall Bridge (1818), linked by Harleyford Road to the Oval at Kennington (a grand scheme laid out a little earlier but never fully realized). From here Camberwell New Road continued s e, meeting the old Camberwell Road (already) improved by turnpiking in 1782) at Camberwell Green. Such roads both improved the ancient link between Southwark and the City, and supplemented it by direct connections with the West End, opening up new areas for the suburban housing to which we must now turn.

Suburban Housing: 1770–1850

It took some time before the new roads were built up. Rocque's map of 1762–9 already shows the main roads fringed with a few houses, but little now remains of before the 1770s in the parts of Southwark and Lambeth away from the river. These later c 18 houses took the form of ribbon development along the main 71 roads. They are urban TERRACES of similar type to those being put up at the same time in North London in the fashionable suburbs of Marylebone and Westminster, with plain, well-proportioned brick fronts, the best with delicate fanlights and

Coade stone decoration around the doors (*see* especially Kennington Park Road) or good doorcases (Nos. 154–170 New Kent Road). Further s similar terraces were built on the edge of the still secluded village of Camberwell (Camberwell Grove and Grove Lane, developed from the 1770s), and as connections with London improved more spacious groups appeared in the 1790s on the road to Peckham and elsewhere. Thomas Milne's land-use map of 1800 shows that by this time there was quite a heavily built up network of roads extending s as far as Kennington, with fringes beginning to stretch out into South Lambeth and Stockwell, down Walworth Road to Camberwell, and e from there to Peckham. But open land still separated these areas from the riverside strip of building at Rotherhithe, from the older towns of Deptford and Greenwich, and from the villages further out, where new houses were springing up down the long ribbon of Lewisham High Street and around Clapham Common.

The characteristic terrace house of *c*. 1790–1820, found equally frequently in N and E London, has a sparsely decorated brick front, often with the motif of ground- or first-floor windows set in blind arches. Examples still remain in the neighbourhood of St George's Circus and down Camberwell New Road. Occasionally groups of houses were given greater unity by the use of a central pediment, in imitation of the effect achieved by the 'palace front' terraces used from the Palladian period onwards in more fashionable areas. Nos. 140–142 Walworth Road, the remains of a development of *c*. 1790 by Henry Penton (of Pentonville, Islington, N London), is a good example; another is Nos. 309–341 Kennington Road of *c*. 1787. The most interesting architectural planning of this kind is associated with the architect *Michael Searles* (1750–1813), the son of a Greenwich surveyor. He could be described as the first local architect to make a genuinely original contribution to the architecture of South London. His buildings are of great elegance, but, alas, he cannot have been a good businessman, for almost all belong to uncompleted schemes. He was responsible for houses on the Cleaver Estate (No. 317 Kennington Road) and the houses flanking the entrance to Cleaver Square (1787–90) and, as surveyor of the Rolls Estate, for some quite ambitious work in the New Kent Road neighbourhood. His Paragon there, a crescent of 1789–90, has gone, but part of an elegant terrace in Surrey Square remains, as well as his own house and office (No. 155 New Kent Road, *c*. 1800). His best groups are at Greenwich and Blackheath: Gloucester Circus, off Croom's Hill, Greenwich, a shallow crescent of considerable sophistication, intended to form one side of an oval circus (1790–1); and the wholly admirable Paragon on the edge of Blackheath (1794–1807). This is a 70 unique composition for its date, for it is a continuous crescent made up of six separate pairs of houses and one single one, all linked by one-storey entrances within a continuous ground-floor colonnade. Colonnades, which are also found in his villas (Colonnade House close to the Paragon), clearly interested Searles, as did other devices which would unify pairs or groups of

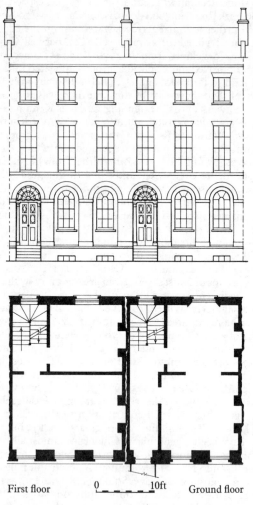

Camberwell (Sk), No. 131 Camberwell Road, *c.* 1800

buildings: for example the shared pediment which appears so
often on his drawings for semi-detached villas. It is tempting to
ascribe the frequent appearance of this feature on the fringes of
Blackheath and in Lee, in the earlier C 19, to his influence. The
centre of Greenwich, however, was given a more urban feeling
by the rebuilding for which *Joseph Kay* was responsible from
1826 onwards, when a tangle of small streets on the site of the
medieval friary were replaced by neat stucco terraces with
emphatic corner flourishes, enclosing a market, a characteristic
type of small-town improvement of the early C 19, in this case

clearly dependent in its forms on *Nash*'s work in the West End (West Strand Improvements and Lower Regent Street). Rebuilding of the other town centres had to wait until the later C 19 (*see* below); the only other significant development that should be noted is at Woolwich, where the lines of future expansion had been prepared by the laying out of new roads to link the riverside town to the military buildings on the common (Woolwich New Road 1790, Powis Street 1800).

As for the EARLY C 19 SUBURBS, one of the most ubiquitous types became the SEMI-DETACHED HOUSE, that typical English compromise between the twin Georgian legacies of the urban terrace and the villa. Apart from Searles's solutions and their progeny, another much publicized version was *John Claudius Loudon*'s own house in Porchester Terrace Bayswater (N W London) of 1823–5, a 'double detached villa' as he called it. Crescent Grove Clapham, laid out in 1824, has another variation, with pairs of houses linked by lower wings with coachhouses. This group, facing a continuous terraced crescent, is characteristic of many of the estates of this period which filled the fields between the main roads, and aimed to provide, where there was room, a hierarchy of houses of different sizes and types. The part of north Brixton around Vassall Road originally called Holland Town, laid out on Lord Holland's land in the 1820s after the opening of Camberwell New Road, similarly includes a mixture of single houses, pairs, and terraces (even the smallest being of unusually distinguished design). Regular squares are however far less common in South London than in the more fashionable western and northern suburbs, even when one takes into account those that have disappeared or have lost their original buildings (such as Nelson Square, off Blackfriars Road, of *c*. 1804–18). Chancellor listed a total of nineteen in 1907. The survivals now are fewer: West Square near St George's Circus is the oldest remaining example, with two sides of 1791–4, all that was built in place of grander schemes for this area. Trinity Church Square Walworth (1824–32), the centre of 79 the Trinity House Estate, still has four complete regular terraces, a rarity in South London. Others, such as Addington Square Camberwell, were completed more slowly, and uniformity was abandoned. Only in the 1830s–1840s do formal layouts become more common, with heavily stucco-trimmed classical terraces or villas in modest imitation of the Kensington manner. Typical examples are Walcot Square Kennington (1837–9), Stockwell Park Crescent (1830s), Albert Square, Hanover Gardens, and Lansdowne Gardens (a circus of 1843–50), all in South Lambeth, and Grafton Square Clapham and Lorrimore Square Walworth, both of the 1850s. An alternative is the quieter style of the Regency tradition which flourished especially in the 1840s. Clifton Terrace, a crescent off the New Kent Road, Camberwell, is an especially charming example (1846–52). Others worth special attention are the low bow-fronted terraces in Upper Deptford and along Shooters Hill Road, and the pedimented villas and terraces at the New Cross Road end of

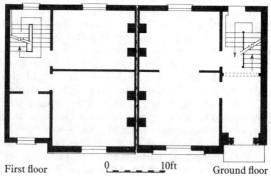

First floor   0 — — — 10ft   Ground floor

Clapham (La), Nos. 194–196 Clapham Park Road, 1822

Camberwell which have (or had) an elegant design of shallow
arches linked by pilasters, some of them with Ammonite capitals
(the type invented by Dance and later associated with Henry
Amon Wilds's developments at Brighton).

Still further out the independent Surrey towns were developing their own suburban rings. Richmond grew especially to the E
around Sheen Road. Croydon expanded in all directions after
the early arrival of the railway in 1839, the best surviving area
being the picturesque mid C19 rustic Italianate villas of The
Waldrons on the Haling Park Estate. Kingston grew little, but to

the S, the entirely new settlement of Surbiton, or Kingston-on-Railway, sprang up rapidly in the 1840s, although only a few of the stuccoed crescents and villas of those first years remain.

For the richest clientèle, however, there was enough land in South London for a different kind of SUBURBAN MANSION: the grand palazzo with its own spacious garden. *Thomas Cubitt* lined the long straight roads of his sought-after Clapham Park Estate with such houses from 1825 onwards. The Cators did likewise on a smaller scale at the same time in Blackheath Park. Further out, where land was still plentiful in the mid C 19, mansions on the grandest scale began to spring up in the neighbourhood of the Crystal Palace, on the heights of Sydenham, Penge, and Upper Norwood, and amid the greenery of Roehampton, Wimbledon, and Putney Heath. They were too tempting as prey for the C 20 developer for many to survive. The styles of such houses in the mid C 19 echoed the variety of dress of their grander country cousins. The most frequent garb was a dignified Banker's Italianate, as for example in *Burn*'s additions to Grove House Roehampton, or on a smaller scale in the suburban mansions of Nightingale Lane Balham, which have that characteristic embellishment, a picturesque campanile, as used also, for example, in some of the early development on the Dulwich Estate, and by *Laxton* at his riverside Tower House Richmond. A liking for the more rustic Italianate appears too in Laxton's Castelnau Estate Barnes. The alternative styles which survive in the early to mid C 19 suburbs such as Sydenham (see the mixture of Gothic and classical in Jews Walk) also show an increasing desire to escape from urban stereotypes. Grand houses in the London countryside which showed the way were Strawberry Hill, where *Lady Frances Waldegrave* made exten- 64 sive Gothic additions in the 1860s, and The Priory Roehampton, where *Roumieu* did much the same a little earlier. Another possibility was Elizabethan (houses of the 1850s in Queen's Road Richmond). This yearning for the picturesque is reflected in the layout of some of the better-class estates such as The Waldrons Croydon, which have winding roads and trees instead of straight grid plans.

For SMALLER HOUSES the rural traditions of the cottage orné and of the Gothic villa continued to intermingle with that of the small Regency house. Nash had shown the way at his Park Villages of the 1820s in Regent's Park. Two examples can demonstrate the variety: a bargeboarded villa of 1835 on the edge of Clapham Park, and an especially lavish mid C 19 cottage orné at Woodside, at that time still a country hamlet near Croydon. These are simply minor reflections of the stylemongering rampant among mid C 19 architects, buildings remarkable now chiefly because they provide some diversity amidst the denser suburban development of the later C 19. But before discussing the houses of this later period, it is necessary first to survey the other types of buildings that were appearing in the new residential areas.

Churches: 1815–1880

A new spurt of Anglican church building began after the
Napoleonic War when in 1818, prompted partly by the spread of
Nonconformity, partly by fear of godless mob violence, Parliament set up a Commission to give grants for the building of new
churches. The new South London suburbs were some of the first
areas to benefit. The object was quantity rather than the expensive grandeur of the 1717 Act, and the results were rapid. *Francis
Bedford*'s St John Waterloo Road Lambeth, St Luke West Nor-
76 wood, and St George Camberwell, and *Porden*'s St Matthew
Brixton all date from 1822 or 1823. They are based on the type
made popular by *Gibbs*'s St Martin-in-the-Fields of a century
earlier – the preaching box given an imposing entrance by a
temple portico, with a tower set back behind – but they are
dressed in the Grecian mode made fashionable by the Inwoods'
St Pancras (Ca) which was begun in 1819. Variations on the
theme are St Mark Kennington (*Roper & Clayton*, 1822) with
Greek Doric portico *in antis*, St Peter Walworth, with recessed
Ionic front showing the greater individuality characteristic of
Soane (1823–5), Holy Trinity Southwark, again by *Bedford*
(1823–4), making use of Hawksmoor's St George Bloomsbury
device of a side portico for an awkward site (St Luke Norwood
originally had a similar arrangement), *Savage*'s imposing St
James Bermondsey (1827–9), and *Smirke*'s St Anne Wandsworth.

By the late 1820s an alternative style was taking hold, a thin,
skimpily detailed Gothic, the type that has indeed been labelled
COMMISSIONERS' GOTHIC. The details were usually 'lancet
style' or Perp, the latter rarely understood as well as at *Savage*'s
St Luke Chelsea (NW London) of 1820–4, which was unusually
precocious. South London has plenty of examples.* For the
most part the buildings are austere, but occasionally playfulness
breaks out in the rather spindly pinnacled spires (see e.g. St John
Richmond, St Michael Stockwell, St Michael Blackheath).
Around 1840 yet a third style enjoyed a brief flowering: the
Rundbogenstil, i.e. a free interpretation of Norman, Italian,
Romanesque, or Early Christian forms. South London has one
77 of the most distinguished examples: *Wild*'s Christ Church
Streatham Hill (1840–2), paid for by the first incumbent, which
is in a free Early Christian, with polychrome brick decoration, a
very progressive feature for its date, originally with interior
decoration by *Owen Jones*. Other surviving examples are St
Peter Norbiton, on the edge of Kingston, a feeble early effort in
Norman by *Scott & Moffat*, 1841; St Thomas Charlton by *Gwilt*,

*St Michael Blackheath 1828–9 by *George Smith*; St Bartholomew Sydenham
1826–32 and St John Richmond 1831–6, both by *Vulliamy*; St John Hampton
Wick 1829–30 by *Lapidge*; All Saints Upper Norwood 1830 by *Savage*; St
Michael Stockwell 1840–1 by *Rogers*; Holy Trinity Twickenham 1839–41 by
Basevi. Contemporary rebuilding of older churches is similar: St Peter and St
Paul Mitcham 1819–21 by *George Smith*; Ham and Hampton, both 1829–31 by
Lapidge; St Nicholas Tooting 1833 by *T. W. Atkinson*; St Margaret Lee 1839–41
by *John Brown*; and Holy Trinity Bromley 1839–41 by *Hopper*.

1849–50, which has a Lombard exterior of polychrome brick, but arcades inside perversely supported on quatrefoil piers; and St Raphael Kingston, by *Charles Parker*, 1846–7, in ambiguously round-arched Italianate.

By the 1840s, although there are still a few old-fashioned examples of classical to be found (St John Clapham Road, 1840–2 by *T. Marsh Nelson*), the preferred style was undoubtedly Gothic – no longer the minimal lancet style or the simplified Perp of the Commissioners' Churches (although this still occurs occasionally: Christ Church Trafalgar Road Greenwich by *J. Brown*, 1847–9), but 'second pointed', i.e. the period of English Gothic of the later C 13–14. One of the first essays in this style was *Pugin*'s grand design for St George Southwark (now the Roman Catholic cathedral). It was built in 1841–8 in a simplified version without its intended tower, and largely rebuilt after war damage, so that it is not the best place to study Pugin's ideas, although a chantry chapel and the aisle windows survive to show 81 the quality of his detail. Pugin's principles were taken up by his pupil *Wardell* in two notable South London Roman Catholic churches, Our Lady of Victories Clapham (1849–51) and Our Lady Star of the Sea Greenwich (1851), both fine compositions with asymmetrically placed spires, typical of a new approach to Gothic, which did not treat it merely as a way of ornamenting a flat façade.

The reason why this style came to be generally adopted for Anglican churches as well was that it was vigorously espoused by the Cambridge Camden Society (later the Ecclesiological Society), and became especially associated with the liturgical reforms which they advocated. The first demonstration of these ideas in South London was the rebuilding after a fire of the old parish church of St Giles Camberwell, by *Scott & Moffat*, 1844. This has a plan of the grandest type with a long chancel, as advocated by the Ecclesiologists, and a crossing tower with spire. Appreciation and understanding of medieval work had advanced by this time – indeed *Gwilt Jun.*'s conscientious restoration of St Mary Overie, Southwark (the later Southwark Cathedral), began in 1818. St Giles was the building where *Gilbert Scott* was converted to the use of 'real' materials, insisting on stone instead of plaster for carved details. In its scale it remained exceptional for some time among suburban churches. The Perp style still lingered on occasionally, in a more full-bodied form than previously (*Ferrey*'s St John Angell Town Brixton, 1852–3, St John Blackheath Park by *Ashpitel*, 1852).

But the characteristic suburban church of the mid C 19 is represented by the numerous, rather mean imitations in Kentish ragstone of the C 13–14 Gothic village churches of the Midlands limestone belt which still dot the middle band of suburban London. Examples of above-average quality are All Saints Blackheath (1857), one of many by *Ferrey*, *Hardwick*'s St John Deptford (1863–5), and *Scott*'s exceptionally imposing St Matthias Richmond (1857–8), which boasts both clerestory and apse. All three have handsome broached spires, landmarks of

respectability for their middle-class neighbourhoods, set not in
Commissioners' fashion at the w end, but more picturesquely to
one side (a convenient arrangement, as it meant that, if necessary, the tower could be completed later as funds permitted,
without undue disturbance). At *Scott*'s St Stephen Lewisham
(1863–5), paid for by the first incumbent, the tower intended for
one of the transepts was not built, but much money obviously
went on the interior carving. Compared with these buildings,
the churches in the outer areas were still unambitious at this
time. *Ferrey*'s churches in the Croydon suburbs, or *Scott*'s extensions to St Mary Hayes, are typical.

Some of the most memorable Victorian Gothic churches are
those which departed more radically from medieval precedents.
One of the chief instigators of a more original treatment of
medieval sources, *William Butterfield*, is badly represented in
South London (St Michael Woolwich, 1888). His interest in
structural polychromy, however, is reflected in the work of
lesser architects, for example in his nephew *R. W. Drew*'s St
Peter Streatham (1870). Another original interior is *F. W. Marrable*'s St Peter Deptford (1866) which uses coloured brick to
enliven its broad nave covered by bold transverse arches. *C. L.
Luck*'s effectively colourful interior at Christ Church Surbiton of
1862–3 is more in the spirit of G. E. Street. *Street* himself was
responsible for the rebuilding of St Paul Herne Hill (1858), an
early work, praised by the Ecclesiologists, for the dull Holy
Trinity Eltham (1868–9), the rather odd Romanesque remodelling of St Luke Norwood (1870), the more assured All Saints
Putney (1878), and, most importantly, by St John the Divine,
Vassall Road, Brixton (1870–4), an urban brick church on the
noblest scale, spatially inventive inside, and with a spire that is
one of the best Victorian landmarks in South London.

The background to this burgeoning of churches in the third
quarter of the c 19, in the older urban areas as well as on the
still-expanding suburban fringes, was the growing social con-
science of bishops and clergy, stirred to greater awareness of the
urban poor. In North London Bishop Blomfield set up his
Metropolitan Churches Fund already in 1836; in South London
(in the diocese of Winchester until 1877, then in that of Rochester) the Bishop established the Southwark fund for schools and
churches in 1845; the South London extension fund followed in
1865. But it was the energy of individual patrons, both clerical
and lay, which was often responsible for some of the finest
results. Such a one is St Peter Vauxhall, *J. L. Pearson*'s first
town church (1863–4). The disappointingly penny-pinching w
front does not prepare one for the high-minded, sombre interior,
with its well-integrated mixture of details from different medieval sources – the first church in South London actually to be
built with complete brick and stone vaults throughout. With its
atmosphere enhanced by a well-preserved collection of furnishings (all too rare in Victorian churches since the Second
World War), it is one of the best places to appreciate High
Church efforts in the slums. It is still flanked by characteristic

adjuncts of enlightened Anglican paternalism: schools, orphanage, and soup kitchen. *Pearson*'s later churches in the more
comfortably off outer suburbs – St Michael Croydon (1876–83) 82
and St John Upper Norwood (1878–87) – do not have the same
intensity, but likewise show his impressive mastery of the brick
rib-vault and of the harmoniously organized interior elevation,
with which few Victorian architects could compete.

James Brooks is the name which one associates above all with
the creation of a new type of urban church especially intended to
act as a focus in poor and deprived areas. His great brick basilicas
with their austere E. E. details, lit by tall clerestories rising
triumphantly above their once squalid settings, are to be found
chiefly in the East End, at Hoxton and Shoreditch (Hc). His
major work in South London is the Ascension, Lavender Hill,
Battersea (1876), completed less ambitiously than intended, but
grand nevertheless, and with Brooks's own inventive E end, 87
with ambulatory and vaulted chapel. The Transfiguration
Lewisham, sadly, has been divided inside. The interior
remodelling of St Margaret Lee and the powerful stone-faced
Annunciation Chislehurst (1868–70) show that his work had
other aspects as well (as is shown too by his All Saints Gospel
Oak, Ca).

Good examples of what generous patronage could achieve in
poor areas are two churches promoted by Richard Foster (of the
Haggerston Churches Fund): the exceptionally lavish E. E. St
Augustine Bermondsey, somewhat in the manner of Pearson,
begun in 1875, by the elsewhere unremarkable local firm of
Henry Jarvis & Son; and the very good (and also E. E.) St
Bartholomew, Barkworth Road, Bermondsey (1866) by the
otherwise little known *E. Taprell Allen*. When a wealthy patron
and an architect of distinctive originality combined, the result
could be quite extraordinary, as is illustrated by St Mary Magdalene Addiscombe, by *E. B. Lamb*, expensively built by a
dynamic local group at loggerheads with the church authorities,
in a style no less at loggerheads with every conventional form of
Victorian Gothic. Lamb, with his fascination with capricious
timberwork, was perhaps the most extreme of the Victorian
rogue architects. *Teulon* could be similarly perverse in other
ways, but his relatively few surviving churches in South London
(Christ Church Wimbledon; All Saints Sutton) are not among
his most exciting works. The wilfully detailed work of *Bassett
Keeling* has also been depleted by war damage and demolition:
Christ Church Old Kent Road preserves only its polychrome
brick exterior unaltered; but his quieter stone St Andrew
Peckham (1863–4) survives. *George Truefitt* was another in a
similar mould, as is shown by St John Bromley (1879–80). Work
by other more straightforward architects has suffered similarly –
for example that of *William White*; the best survival among his
once numerous churches in Battersea is his bold E. E. St Mark of
1873–4.

It will already be clear that by the 1870s other styles than the
Ecclesiologists' Second Pointed had become accepted, and so

had sources other than English. The prettier ornament of the
Dec period had been ousted by the robust banded shafts and
elementary plate tracery of early Gothic, culled from both English and foreign sources. *William Knight*'s accomplished Christ
89 Church Bexleyheath (1872–7) is a good example of such a borrowing from French Gothic. One of the fascinations of South
London is the discovery of churches of this quality by less well
known architects, or by names not otherwise associated with
church building. In some cases the explanation is that the
architects lived locally. They included two Streatham residents –
the painter *Sir William Dyce*, who built the chancel of St
Leonard Streatham (1863), and, later on, *Sir Ernest George*,
architect of the more interesting brick and terracotta St Andrew
Guildersfield Road (1885–7) – and *Ernest Newton* (tower of St
George Bickley, 1905–6), who lived at Bickley; but of him more
later. Another name to look out for is *Arthur Cawston*, also a man
with local connections, who was capable of some well managed
interiors in a variety of styles: the mosaic-clad Byzantine chancel
of St Mary Balham, 1881, the late Gothic Ascension Balham,
1883–4 (where the site had been given by his father), and the
freer stone and brick St Luke Bromley, 1886–90 (also St Philip
Stepney (T H), 1888, which is in a masterly Pearson-derived
early Gothic).

Churches: 1880–1910

This wide choice of styles by a single architect is characteristic as
a whole of Late Victorian and Edwardian churches, among
which examples from practically every style from Early Christian to late Gothic can be found. In the 1880s, the soaring nobility
achieved by Brooks and Pearson was a continuing aim for some.
An unpalatably chilly French High Gothic was the mode
adopted for *W. Niven*'s huge St Alban Teddington. *G. Fellowes
Prynne* was more eclectic; his favourite device was the tall stone
rood screen which provided a dramatic focus for his lofty in-
90 teriors. It appears first at All Saints Rosendale Road Brixton
(1887–91), one of the best churches of this prolific but uneven
architect. *Shaw* included a similarly tall screen in his unfinished
St Mark Camberwell (designed 1879). Height was one way of
giving interest to the monotonously long naves that continued to
be planned (if not always completed) for the larger congregations
still so confidently anticipated.
    Another means of providing more varied spatial interest was
the treatment given to aisles. Emphasis on arcades was mini-
mized, piers became tall and slender, capitals were often omitted, and the eye is drawn instead to intriguing vistas through the
lateral spaces: passage aisles, double aisles, internal buttresses,
aisles with varying vaults and transverse arches are all recurrent
themes. Bodley and Pearson had been the pioneers of such
innovations in the 1870s (see for example Pearson's St Augustine
Kilburn, Wm). The churches of South London are not in the
forefront of these developments, but there are plenty of versions

of these themes which are rewarding to visit. Among them one can mention *Comper*'s first church, St Alban Thornton Heath (1889), *Leonard Stokes*'s Holy Ghost Balham (1891), *Tasker*'s English Martyrs Southwark (1902–3), *Pinkerton*'s St Mary, Summerstown, Wandsworth (1903–4), and *Temple Moore*'s specially impressive All Saints Tooting (1904–6). Motifs such as the arch dying into the pier are of course drawn from late Gothic, and various forms of Perp were very popular in the 1890s (for example in *Bodley*'s Holy Innocents South Norwood of 1894–5). The light and airy atmosphere of late Gothic together with a free interpretation of Perp or Flamboyant detail accorded well with the interests of the inventive Arts and Crafts architects around 1900. Good examples are *Champneys*' St Andrew and St Michael Greenwich of 1900–2, *Robson*'s St Andrew Catford of 1904, with its decidedly Art Nouveau touches, and the numerous churches by *Greenaway & Newberry* (e.g. St Hilda Lewisham, 1907).

The alternative style that produced the most interesting results was a new interpretation of *Rundbogenstil*, now Early Christian or Byzantine more frequently than Romanesque. The most intriguing example is *Beresford Pite*'s Christ Church Brix- 88 ton, designed in 1899, with its broad transepts which give it a quasi-central plan, and its complex layered surfaces both outside and in. Such a style was supremely suitable for a major church, as *Bentley* showed in a different way at the same time at Westminster Cathedral (indeed *Pite*'s later competition design for Liverpool Cathedral owed much to Christ Church). *Bentley*, however, built only in Gothic in South London (Corpus Christi Brixton 1886; extensions to Our Lady of Victories Clapham 1894–7). The Early Christian basilica was the model for *Kelly*'s grandiose All Saints Petersham (1907–8), with its quite extraordinary baptistery with immersion font, and for *Adshead & Ramsay*'s more restrained St Anselm Kennington of 1911.

The exteriors of many of these churches, so often without the towers intended by their architects, are frequently unimpressive. The churches and chapels of the Nonconformists make much more of a show, contributing more positively to the late Victorian townscape, although especially in the wealthy suburbs (e.g. Croydon) they may impress by quantity rather than quality. What helps them in their impact on the street is that for the most part architectural attention is concentrated on the façade, a legacy of the classical tradition that continued through the C 19 in defiance of Anglican Ecclesiology: see for example the proud front of the Sutherland Chapel Walworth (1842), *Pocock*'s giant portico of Spurgeon's celebrated Metropolitan Tabernacle Southwark (1859–61), and, on a lesser scale, the Baptist chapels at Peckham (1863) and Stockwell (1866). The Gothic style was not accepted widely for Nonconformist churches until the later C 19, when there was a vogue for ambitious towers and spires. One of the best in South London is that of the Congregationalists' Christ Church Kennington (1873–6 by *Paull & Bickerdike*). Until the Second World War, this church was also an interesting example of the Nonconformists' innovatory planning of this time, with a large auditorium on a central plan. Some impressive later spires are those of the Presbyterians' St Andrew (1882 by *McKissack & Rowan*) in Lewisham, *Church*'s United Reformed Churches at West Croydon (1886) and Camberwell (1890–1), and *Murray*'s Presbyterian church at Bromley (1895). Around the turn of the century a cheerfully detailed Arts and Crafts or Art Nouveau free Perp enjoyed a special popularity. The characteristic street front of this time has a large traceried w window, with a stumpy tower to one side – see for example Blackheath and Charlton Baptist Chapel of 1905 by *Dottridge & Walford*, and the numerous productions by the firms of *Gunton & Gunton* and *Baines* (Methodist Church, Fentiman Road, Lambeth, 1900).

Victorian Church Furnishings

Victorian church furnishings, especially stained glass, suffered badly during the Second World War. The best of the early work is in the R. C. churches. Only fragments from the original 81 fittings of *Pugin*'s St George Southwark have survived, but Our Lady Star of the Sea Greenwich still has interior decoration by *Pugin* and *Hardman*, and Our Lady of Victories at Clapham a Pugin window. Pugin's delicate tabernacle-work for St Augustine, Ramsgate, Kent is now in the Anglican Cathedral at Southwark. *Scott*'s earnest, correct rebuilding of St Giles Camberwell was the occasion for progressive Anglican work, a medievalizing E window by *Ward & Nixon* after designs by *Ruskin* and *Oldfield*. The builders of the new churches in the slums rarely appear to have been able to afford the rich furnishings they no doubt hoped for: the interior which best retains a High Victorian atmosphere is that of St Peter Vauxhall, with its *Clayton & Bell* stained glass and wall paintings. From St Agnes Kennington, once one of the best of the later c 19 churches in the inner boroughs, only fragments of *Temple Moore*'s elaborate woodwork of the 1880s onwards were saved for the post-war church. Complete ensembles of the end of the c 19 are more common in the wealthier outer suburbs, for example at St John Croydon, expensively refitted after the post-fire rebuilding of 1870, and at *Pearson*'s St Michael Croydon, which has more interesting turn-of-the-century furnishings in the Arts and Crafts tradition, by *Bodley* and others, as does St Nicholas Chislehurst. *Brooks*'s Annunciation Chislehurst and his refurbishing of St Margaret Lee include among their fittings notable work by the architect, and paintings by *Westlake*. In addition one can mention St Luke Ramsden Road Balham with its memorable, individualistic collection of furnishings of Renaissance inspiration; *Bentley*'s contributions to the interior of Our Lady of Victories Clapham; the chancel of St Mary Magdalene Richmond by *Bodley* (1903–4), with glass by *Burlison & Grylls*; and the Art Nouveau and other work in St John Richmond of 1904–5 by *Grove*, *Whall*, *Westlake*, and *Bainbridge Reynolds*.

Apart from these collections, some individual works deserve

special notice: among stained glass, much by *Lavers & Barraud* at All Saints Kingston and Christ Church Surbiton, a window by *Walter Crane* (1891) at Christ Church Streatham Hill, and others by *Henry Holiday* at Southwark Cathedral, St George Catford, and St Mary Wimbledon. The best collections of *William Morris* glass are at All Saints Putney, and (reset) in the chapel of Whitelands Training College Wandsworth. A delightful painted organ case by the same firm is among the Victorian fittings at St Mary Beddington. St Mary Bexley has an elaborate screen and other woodwork by *Champneys*. The mosaics by the architect *Arthur Cawston* at St Mary Balham are perhaps unusual enough to deserve a note here, as certainly does the terracotta work by the local sculptor *George Tinworth* found in St Mary Lambeth (and also outside churches, for instance in Kennington Park, and on the Doulton building at Lambeth, the firm for which he did so much work). The only monuments which need be mentioned are one by *Butterfield* of 1871 at St George Bickley, and another with an effigy by *Boehm* and *Alfred Gilbert* in St Nicholas Chislehurst, of after 1890. In a special category is the monument to the French Prince Imperial (1879) in *Clutton*'s mortuary chapel at Chislehurst intended for Louis Napoleon.

Public Buildings: 1800–1900

The public buildings and institutions of the C 19 London suburbs are of two types. In addition to those which provided for the education and welfare of the inhabitants of a particular parish, the open land on the fringes of London was exploited for large establishments designed to cater for wider sections of the metropolitan population. Older charitable foundations moved out of the crowded city to the cheaper land on the verge of the open countryside: one of the first to do so in South London was the Bethlehem Hospital, which moved to St George's Fields Southwark from Moorfields in 1811. But already a year earlier the House of Industry for the Infant Poor, for example, had found it desirable to move from built-up Kennington to still-rural West Norwood. Such moves became increasingly common, and the pattern has been repeated again in the C 20 (the Bethlehem Hospital, for example, moving out of London altogether in the 1930s). But numerous ALMSHOUSES still remain in the outer boroughs on the edge of the early C 19 built-up areas. They are often amalgamations of earlier charities, and so can be quite extensive. The City Companies were responsible for some of the most lavish layouts: the Licensed Victuallers in Asylum Road Camberwell (1827–33) by *Henry Rose*, and the Merchant Taylors at Lee (1826) by *W. Jupp*, both in a frugally detailed classical. Other classical examples are Queen Elizabeth Almshouses Greenwich (1817) and Trinity Homes Acre Lane (1822–6) by *Bailey & Willshire*, but Gothic touches appear occasionally (Chumleigh Gardens Camberwell, 1821, and in the stucco face-lifts given to the older foundations of Trinity Hospital Greenwich, 1812, and Dulwich College, 1821). The feeling

that almshouses demanded a style with national-historic overtones must account for the popularity of the Tudor and Jacobean
styles. Tudor appeared already in North London in 1825 at the
Whittington Almshouses Islington (demolished); in South London it becomes *de rigueur* from the 1830s: Hickey Almshouses
Richmond, 1832–5 by *Vulliamy*, Boot and Shoemakers' Mortlake, 1836, Aged Pilgrims Peckham, 1837, Dovedale Battersea,
80 1841, and, especially elaborate, Free Watermen and Lightermen's Penge, 1840–1 by *George Porter*. Later examples are
Hardwick's King William Naval Asylum Penge (1847), *Hesketh*'s St Clement Danes Wandsworth (1848–9), and *Daukes*'s
Freemasons North Croydon (1852), all three picturesque
compositions using diapered red brick; and *Little*'s Duppa
Almshouses Richmond (1851). The alternatives indeed echo the
current experiments in church architecture: a jolly, polychro-
matic version of *Rundbogenstil* is represented by the Thackeray
Almshouses Lewisham, 1840, and the Richmond church estate
almshouses of 1843 by *William Crawford Stow*, more seriously
Ecclesiological Gothic by *William Webbe*'s Beer and Wine
Homes Nunhead (1852–3). But after the 1850s there are no more
almshouses of any interest, although modest rebuildings with
Tudor allusions continue.

   Much greater numbers of the elderly poor were dependent for
their support on public rates, and so had to succumb to the
sterner discipline of the WORKHOUSES built by the local boards
of Poor Law Guardians set up in 1834. These catered for several
parishes together, and so were larger establishments. Their
legacy is a number of present-day hospitals which developed
around the later workhouse infirmary buildings (St John's Hospital Battersea, St Nicholas Hospital Woolwich, Lambeth Hospital Kennington). Architecturally the most memorable relic of
these unloved institutions is the quirky water tower from
Ladywell Lodge Lewisham (St Olave's Union), 1898–1900 by
Newman & Newman, who were also responsible for the same
Union's grand Jacobean offices in Tooley Street Bermondsey.

   C19 HOSPITALS are more common N of the Thames,
although the South Bank has one of the best Victorian examples
(surviving now only in part), St Thomas', rebuilt in 1868–71 by
H. Currey with splendid panache along the Lambeth waterfront,
when the railways forced it to move from Southwark. It is one of
the earliest examples of a civilian hospital built on the pavilion
principle advocated by Florence Nightingale (its precursor was
the military Royal Herbert Hospital, Woolwich). The general
hospitals were supplemented by specialist establishments, a
particular feature of C19 medical developments. One of the
earliest is the Lying-In Hospital at Lambeth, whose simple
classical building of 1828 by *H. Harrison* still remains. The care
of the insane required more space: Springfield Hospital Wandsworth, the Surrey County Lunatic Asylum, dates from 1840–2,
an extensive Tudor layout, much added to. The Royal Hospital
for Incurables, West Hill, Putney, of 1854, is in typically magni-
loquent mid Victorian classical. If one anticipates and takes the

story up to the Edwardian age, one should also mention the buildings in the less solemn styles adopted towards the end of the century, such as the Royal Hospital for Incurables at Norwood (1894 onwards), free Tudor by *Cawston* and *Hall*, the Renaissance terracotta-trimmed Royal Waterloo Hospital for Women and Children (1903–5 by *Nicholson*), and the especially engaging Belgrave Hospital for Children, Lambeth, with its Arts and Crafts elevations by *Charles Holden*, 1900–3. Outside the hospital system, outdoor care was provided by the charitable local DISPENSARIES for the poorer classes; a handsome example remains in Clapham Manor Street (1850–3 by *J. T. Knowles Sen.*).

EDUCATIONAL BUILDINGS up to 1870 were also dependent on private charity. The few early examples in South London are in a modest classical style: a dignified urban school in Stamford Street Southwark by *J. Montague*, and the smaller group of St Mark's Schools, Harleyford Road, South Lambeth, both of the 1820s. A new scale is introduced by the Licensed Victuallers' School in Kennington Lane Lambeth of 1836 (*Henry Rose*), the confident expression of middle-class aspirations, interesting to contrast with *Pearson*'s picturesque Gothic school buildings of 1860–2 behind St Peter Vauxhall (*see* above), just down the road. Gothic was, not surprisingly, popular for church schools, see e.g. the Boutcher Schools Bermondsey, by *Joseph Gale*, 1871–2. It was also used for Wimbledon College (by *Teulon*, 1860) and for the rebuilding of older foundations such as Sir Walter St John's School Battersea, by *Butterfield*, 1858–9, with many later additions. The tradition continued into the later part of the century (Aske's Haberdashers New Cross, 1875 by *Snooke*, St Dunstan's College Catford, 1888 by *E. N. Clifton*). But there were alternatives: for the British and Foreign Bible School at Sydenham, 1859 by *Dawson*, Italian Renaissance was preferred, and a very free version of this is the inspiration for Dulwich College, the most ambitious example in South London of a C19 86 public school. Its buildings, by *Charles Barry Jun.*, date from 1866–70, a long composition with the central feature of an assembly hall (rare for this date) and a skyline made picturesque by a wealth of terracotta trimmings, just as at the exactly contemporary St Thomas' Hospital. South London has no university buildings of the C19, but the urban fringes proved suitable for a number of specialized FURTHER EDUCATIONAL ESTABLISHMENTS, in much the same variety of styles that have been exemplified by other buildings. The Royal Naval School (now Goldsmiths' College) at Deptford, by *John Shaw*, 1843–5, with its smooth surfaces and widely spaced unadorned windows, is in an unusually restrained classical; the former Wesleyan Theological Training College at Richmond, 1841–3 by *A. Trimmer*, is more conventional Tudor; the Royal Military School of Music at Whitton, 1848 by *G. Mair*, is in a pompous neo-Jacobean.

Other large Victorian institutions also sprang up on the edges of built-up London. ORPHANAGES are represented by the Royal Victoria Patriotic Asylum at Wandsworth, built for orphaned daughters of servicemen. This is a particularly showy example of brash mid-century Gothic, 1857–9 by *Rhode Hawkins*, with a long symmetrical façade and central tower, the type of composition made popular by the Oxford Museum a few years earlier. The orphanage for sons of missionaries at Blackheath (1857 by *Habershon*) is more compact, but no less obtrusive. The Royal Patriotic Boys Orphanage (now Emmanuel School, Wandsworth), 1872 by *Saxon Snell*, is a little quieter. PRISONS also required plenty of space. Brixton Prison, built in 1819 by *Chawner* as a Surrey House of Correction (now much added to), and *D. R. Hill*'s Wandsworth Prison of 1849 (which like the Royal Patriotic Schools gobbled up part of Wandsworth Common) were both designed on the system of a central block with radiating wings, the type of rational plan that had been popular for workhouses and other institutions from *c.* 1880 onwards, and was used also for Millbank, Pentonville, and Holloway Prisons in North London. Wandsworth, like its exact contemporary, Holloway (now demolished), has a gatehouse in the form of a mock fortress, characteristic of the mid Victorian liking for such associations.

The crowded city made yet another demand on the open land remaining still further out. While rehousing the poor outside the inner city was impractical before the era of cheap public transport, provision for the dead was another matter. So along the southern boundaries of Lambeth, Tooting, Southwark, Wandsworth and beyond, CEMETERIES were laid out to relieve the pressure on the crowded and unwholesome churchyards of the old parish churches. One of the first was the South Metropolitan Cemetery at West Norwood, of 1836; Nunhead Cemetery followed in 1840 (laid out by *James Bunning* for the London Cemetery Company, like its more famous counterpart at Highgate). The other North London examples are Brompton (K C) (1831), Kensal Green (K C) (1833), Abney Park Stoke Newington (Is) (1840). These early examples were characterized by picturesque winding paths (an effect diminished by the later cramming of tombstones into every available space). The West Norwood Cemetery has a remarkable number of highly atmospheric monuments of excellent quality (but in poor condition), but apart from *J. O. Scott*'s chaste Grecian Ralli Chapel of 1872 in the Greek Orthodox enclosure, the C 19 chapels both here and at Nunhead have disappeared. The cemeteries of the late C 19 (erected by the parish authorities instead of by private companies) are more complete in their buildings.

75

Suburban Development: 1800–1900

While the edges of built-up London were being filled up in this way, the inner boroughs were becoming increasingly unattractive, as the older residential areas became crossed by railway lines and fragmented by industrial development (*see* Introduction to Industrial Archaeology, below). The areas in the neighbourhood of the railway stations deteriorated into slums, more

so at first in North London than south of the river. Architecturally, the consequences were twofold: there was increasing
incentive for the more respectable classes to take advantage of
the improving means of transport and settle down in the outer
suburbs, or still further out, where s of the river the neighbourhoods of e.g. Bromley, Kingston, and Croydon were easy to
reach by train; and there was growing pressure to rebuild the
inner areas. The first development proceeded much more rapidly than the second. The story is told in the population figures of
the old London boroughs of the L.C.C area:

POPULATION TABLE (IN THOUSANDS)

	1801	1821	1841	1861	1881	1901	1921	1931	1951
CENTRAL AREA									
City	128	124	123	112	51	27	14	11	5
Westminster	161	190	229	257	230	183	142	130	99
Bermondsey	46	57	69	102	135	131	119	112	61
Bethnal Green	22	46	74	105	127	130	117	108	58
Finsbury	55	86	113	129	119	101	76	70	35
Holborn	67	88	94	94	79	59	43	39	25
St Marylebone	64	96	138	162	155	133	104	98	76
St Pancras	32	72	130	199	236	235	211	198	138
Shoreditch	35	53	83	129	127	119	104	97	45
Southwark	63	100	134	174	195	206	184	172	97
Stepney	114	154	204	257	282	299	250	225	99
	787	1,066	1,391	1,720	1,743	1,623	1,364	1,260	738
INNER RING									
Battersea	3	5	7	20	107	169	168	160	117
Chelsea	12	27	40	60	73	74	64	59	51
Islington	10	22	56	155	283	335	331	322	236
Kensington	9	14	27	70	165	177	176	181	168
Lambeth	28	58	116	162	254	302	303	296	230
Paddington	2	6	25	79	126	144	144	145	125
	64	132	271	546	1,008	1,201	1,186	1,163	927
SECOND RING									
Camberwell	7	18	40	71	187	259	267	251	180
Deptford	11	14	19	38	77	110	113	107	76
Fulham	4	6	9	16	43	137	158	151	122
Greenwich	22	29	40	57	65	96	100	101	91
Hackney	13	22	38	77	164	219	222	215	171
Hammersmith	6	9	13	25	72	112	130	136	119
Hampstead	4	7	10	19	45	82	86	89	95
Lewisham	4	9	15	29	67	127	174	220	228
Poplar	8	19	31	79	157	169	163	155	74
Stoke Newington	2	3	6	11	38	51	52	51	49
Wandsworth	14	23	33	51	103	232	328	353	330
Woolwich	13	21	31	69	75	117	140	147	145
	108	180	285	542	1,093	1,601	1,933	1,976	1,683
TOTAL	959	1,378	1,947	2,808	3,844	4,425	4,483	4,399	3,348

The table shows the fluctuations in the population of the various
boroughs which constituted the County of London from 1888,
between 1801 and 1857. It will be seen that the high-water mark
of the central nucleus was reached in 1881, and that since then
there has been a progressive decrease, accelerated by the Second
World War and the bombing of London. The climax of the inner
ring was not reached until 1901 and the subsequent fall was
slower. For the second ring, increase went on until 1921, after
which a slight decrease began, followed by a drop of a million in
consequence of the Second World War. For the areas further out
which came under the Greater London Council in 1965, growth

continued for still longer. But the results of these c 20 trends must be discussed below.

Housing: 1850–1914

As for the houses built for this expanding population in the second half of the c 19, there are several types that have to be considered. The wealthy lived either in grand metropolitan mansions or, less commonly, flats, or, if they preferred more rural surroundings, built themselves houses in what are now the outer boroughs, but was then still the countryside. The less well off were catered for by the speculative builders' terraces that rapidly filled up the remaining spaces in between. The poor remained in their overcrowded slums, in which first the philanthropic societies, then at the end of the century the county council, and later still the metropolitan borough councils were able to make only very slight inroads, first by the building of model tenements and then by the provision of cheap cottages. By this period, the inner areas of South London had become too industrialized to attract much in the way of fashionable urban building of the type being put up in Westminster and Kensington (*see North West London*). The sole attempt to bring South London into the orbit of the West End was made by *James Knowles Jun.* with his luxury blocks of 1860 on the edge of Clapham Common in a bastard French Renaissance in the manner of the Grosvenor Hotel, and by his subsequent effort to develop a route thence to Westminster, through his respectable but less ambitious Park Town Estate, Battersea. The success of his Battersea development was frustrated by the multiplication of railway lines to Clapham Junction, those lines that made it so much easier and pleasanter to live outside London.

So in South London the new styles that became current in the third quarter of the century through the influence especially of Philip Webb, Eden Nesfield, and Norman Shaw are first represented in this volume by country buildings. South London has no urban houses of the 1860s–70s of the originality and quality of those of Palace Green Kensington or Cheyne Walk Chelsea (N W London). Instead one has to visit what are now the outermost
91 suburbs, to see *Philip Webb*'s Red House, built for William Morris in 1859–60 in what was then the countryside of Bexleyheath. The essence of the Red House is not easily summarized. Morris described it as being 'in the style of the c 13'.
92 Certainly the romantic medievalizing interiors and the frugally honest asymmetrical exterior reflecting the interior plan are in the spirit of Pugin, although plainer than Pugin would have made them. Webb's subtle mixture of forms, derived from lesser secular buildings, the vicarages and schools of the Ecclesiologists, included both Gothic details and homely vernacular Georgian features: sash-windows, hipped gables, and sweeping tiled roofs. The latter dominate too in two other houses by *Webb*, the Oast House Hayes (1873–4), and the smaller No. 19 Park Hill Carshalton (1868). This rediscovery of the vernacular that was

such a revelation to architects of the later C 19 could take other forms. *George Devey* in his country houses of the 1850s onwards picturesquely blended different building materials: brick, half-timbering, tiles, and roughcast. His earliest work is in Kent, but he was active also from the 1860s in the select area of Coombe Hill, Kingston, although all that remain here now from his large houses are their delightful outbuildings. Brick building of the 93 C 17 was also a potent influence. An early tribute to it was *Eden Nesfield*'s small lodge at Kew of 1866, with its steep hipped roof.

It was *Norman Shaw*, Nesfield's partner, who was the most prolific and inventive exponent of these styles, able to adopt them with equal skill for the town houses of Kensington and Chelsea, the suburbs of Hampstead, or the spreading 'old English' country mansions of Surrey. In this volume he is represented by only a few buildings: three early ones in the Bromley area (Page Heath Lane Bickley 1866, Shortlands 1868–9, and West Wickham 1870–1), by the house for the Bishop of Rochester in Kennington Park Place (1895), which is in a subdued C 18 style, and by some minor cottages in the Croydon suburbs (Sydenham Road), experimental designs of 1878–82 using *Lascelles* patent concrete slabs, prettily disguised.* The influence of Shaw and his school, however, can be found all over South London, from the eclectic picturesque compositions of the grander suburban houses, down to the way in which lesser terraces of the 1880s onwards abandoned stock brick and stucco for red brick, half-timbered gables, and white-painted wooden porches and balconies. Good suburban examples of the old English style in the grand manner are a house by *Ingress Bell* of 1879 and another by *Collcutt* of 1884, both in East Sheen, and two by *Aston Webb* in Blackheath Park (1896). They exploit the romantic mixture of half-timbering and sweeping eaves that was to inspire so many pedestrian imitations in the C 20. *Joseph Clarke*'s picturesque lodge at Beddington is in a similar spirit, the precursor of the shelters and public lavatories of later C 19 municipal parks (e.g. those outside Battersea Park). Not all later C 19 houses adopted this style: Sunnydene Sydenham (1868–70), a rare early secular work by *J. F. Bentley*, makes use of eclectic brickwork in elaboration of Webb's example, a house by *Belcher* in Kidbrooke Grove Blackheath (1889) adopts a bold individualistic form, with a tall hipped roof over a single storey with mullioned windows, while *H. V. Lanchester*'s first work, Kingswood, Dulwich (1892), is in a restrained version of Scottish Baronial with a hint of early Renaissance. A much more showy form of Renaissance was used by *Cutler* for the astronomically expensive Avery Hill, Eltham (1890).

Kingswood and Avery Hill, both built for fabulously successful businessmen, the inventor of Bovril and the 'King of Nitrate', are reminders that there was still just room for a few small country houses in their own grounds, even within what was by

---

*An earlier experimental concrete house is The Halsteads, East Sheen, by *A. W. Blomfield*, 1868.

then the territory of the London County Council. Such houses fast became white elephants; Kingswood survives as a library and community centre, Avery Hill, partly destroyed in the Second World War, as a training college, worth a visit now chiefly because of its lavish iron and glass winter garden, one of the few remaining relics of the Victorian love of enormous conservatories. The future of domestic architecture of the suburbs lay with smaller, more economically planned houses, such as those personal versions of the roughcast vernacular cottage designed by *Voysey* (represented in South London by Dixcote, Streatham, 1897, and a house in Lyford Road, Wandsworth Common, 1903), and the houses of Shaw's followers, especially *Ernest Newton*. South London has two areas rich in these, the first around Wimbledon Common, the second –
94 especially rewarding – Newton's home ground of Bickley and Chislehurst, near Bromley. Newton, who had been Shaw's chief assistant from 1876 to 1879, built in the 1880s a number of small houses in the suburban area around Bullers Wood Bickley, an older house which he enlarged in the Shaw manner in 1889, and which *Morris & Co.* decorated. Newton summed up his approach in the introduction to his *Book of Houses*, published in 1890,* which illustrated a number of these smaller houses in photographs. 'The small house', he begins, 'has not, I think, received as much attention as it deserves.' And he goes on, 'The problem presented for solution in designing a small house, is not so easy as might be supposed; a small house is in many ways more difficult to design than a large one, for while every part must be minutely schemed, nothing should be cramped or mean looking, the whole house should be conceived broadly and simply, and with an air of *repose*, the stamp of home.' Minutely schemed is just what Newton's most complete development of these houses, at Camden Park Chislehurst from 1893 to after 1916, gives the air of being. Newton's first houses imitate Shaw, with their broad gables, tile-hanging and judiciously composed chimneystacks. Other architects working in Wimbledon and the Bickley–Chislehurst area (and there were many: *Quennell*, *Ransome*, *Jackson*, *Somers Clarke*, *Niven & Wigglesworth*, *May*, and *George*) adopted versions of the Queen Anne or of the Dutch-inspired gabled style that Ernest George had made popular in his work in Kensington. Such houses continued to be built into the early years of the C 20. But by then taste was swinging, via the symmetry of *c.* 1700, towards the quieter harmonies of neo-Georgian. *E. J. May* had already experimented with this at Wimbledon (No. 2 The Grange, 1889, No. 4 South Side, 1900); *Leonard Stokes* used it very effectively for his house of 1899 in West Drive Streatham; *Reginald Blomfield* followed at Kidbrooke (1906). *George & Yeates*'s Queen Alexandra Court at Wimbledon (housing of 1904 etc. for servicemen's widows) is already a formal classical composition.

---

*I borrow this telling quotation from the introduction to John Newman's *Buildings of England: West Kent and the Weald.*

The later C 19 suburban housing of lesser rank which still
covers so much of inner South London took up these ideas more
slowly, and, as one would expect, with rather less finesse. A
debased (or enriched, depending on one's taste) form of Italianate terrace, with borrowings from other styles, prevailed in the
more urban areas (see e.g. Brixton High Road) and in the more
densely built-up suburbs such as the well laid out streets of
Brockley, Upper Deptford. An interest in Renaissance decoration was encouraged by the 1870s fashion for terracotta (see
Dulwich College, and the cultural buildings of South Kensington, N W London), but the material and style were adopted only
occasionally, for example by *Collcutt*'s speculative terraces of the
1870s in Ferndale Road Lambeth and Nightingale Road
Balham. *William Young*'s houses in Oakhill Road Wandsworth
(1879–80) are quite an early illustration of a busy display of Shaw
motifs; *Pawley*'s large houses in Auckland Road Upper Norwood of the 1880s have an unusually wild eclectic mixture of
Gothic and other features. The most enjoyable of the modest
suburban developments of this period is Merton Park, the creation of an enlightened paternalistic landlord, John Innes, from
the 1870s onwards. The styles of the houses along the generously
planted avenues illustrate the gradual shift from a cheerfully
arbitrary use of ornament *c.* 1880 by the estate architect, *H. G.
Quartermain*, to the Arts-and-Crafts-inspired cottages of after
1900 by *J. S. Brocklesby*, a similar mixture to that which is
offered by the better known Bedford Park (Ea). A version of the
garden suburb, in a more affluent and fully-fledged form,
appears near Croydon with *William Webb*'s Woodcote Village of
1901–20. These are the highlights. As one descends the social
scale the volume of building increases. From the 1860s onwards
repetitive terraces built to humdrum pattern-book recipes, the
anonymous local builders' vernacular of the later C 19, flowed
fitfully (depending on the booms and slumps of the building
industry) over the dull flat plain around the Wandle, the awkward rise up to Honor Oak, the scrubby slopes between Norwood Junction and the Croydon valley, and anywhere else where
empty land remained. Such houses – despised in the earlier C 20,
more cherished now, with their inevitable bay-window, exposed
eaves, Welsh slate roofs, and fussy composition stone doorways
– remain the predominant type in the middle ring of South
London, since most of the plainer, flimsier stuccoed terraces of
cottages of the earlier C 19 have been replaced within the last
thirty years by housing conforming to the requirements of C 20
planners. A comparison of C 19 and C 20 maps indeed shows how
the present distribution of council housing is largely explained
by the pattern of suburban development of the first half of the
C 19.

Urban Renewal: 1840–1914

Urban renewal of this kind is no new phenomenon. By the
middle of the C 19 the appalling dimensions and conditions of

the London slums had been branded as a shame for ever by Chadwick, Kay, Southwood Smith and others in their *Report on the Sanitary Conditions of the Labouring Classes*, published in 1842. The unmitigated slum stretched from the Thames through Bermondsey and Southwark on the South Bank, and on the N extended much further, through Stepney and Poplar to Bethnal Green, Shoreditch, and Finsbury. The population of Bermondsey and Southwark rose from 109,000 to 203,000 between 1801 and 1841, that of the five northern areas from 223,000 to 505,000. Together that accounted for over a third of the population in the later L.C.C. area. Pressure to do something about these conditions, particularly the hopelessly inadequate arrangements for sewerage and water supply, was increased by the alarm over the cholera outbreaks of the 1840s. But nothing permanent was achieved until the creation of the Metropolitan Board of Works in 1855, covering the area of the later county council. The Board was the first body to be given some powers over the suburban areas that were governed by a confusing variety of local boards and vestries. Its principal achievement was *Bazalgette*'s comprehensive sewerage system, designed to free the Thames from contamination, a masterpiece of engineering (*see* Introduction to Industrial Archaeology); its most visible creation the transformation of the muddy and smelly river banks into the Embankments which provided foundations for the proud riverside architecture of the later C 19 (Victoria Embankment on the N side 1860, the Albert Embankment on the S 1869, the stretch on the N from Chelsea Hospital to Battersea Bridge 1874). Direct efforts at slum clearance, however, remained ludicrously inadequate before the C 20, as they were bound to be with the limited powers that the government granted to the M. B. W. What was done in the C 19 can easily be enumerated. A few NEW STREETS were cut through some of the most congested or unsavoury areas (not a new idea: Nash's Regent Street had done much the same). In South London these were Southwark Street 1864, through the worst slums of Southwark, the widening of part of Tooley Street Bermondsey 1877–84, Creek Road Deptford 1896, Tower Bridge Road, after the completion of Tower Bridge, 1902.

The provision of PARKS was another improvement, an opportunity to provide harmless recreation for the masses away from gin palaces and from the foul air of the slums which so many believed caused the spread of contagious disease. The first examples were on a generous scale: Victoria Park (TH) in the East End, laid out in the 1840s, and Battersea Park planned at the same time but not created until 1854–61, when the featureless low-lying Battersea Fields by the Thames were transformed into an exceptionally romantic well planted landscape with a large lake and rocks. Kennington Park was made from Kennington Common in 1852; with the next phase, under the M. B. W., came Southwark Park, close to the Surrey Docks, and Finsbury Park (Hy) in North London, a long way from Finsbury where it had first been intended. By then land was scarce; the later municipal parks started as private parks donated by enlightened owners, or were snatched from potential builders by concerned public opinion: Terrace Gardens Richmond (1887), an early example by a local authority, was followed in South London for instance by Vauxhall Park and Dulwich Park, both 1890, Brockwell Park, 1891 and 1907, Ruskin Park, 1907. The move to preserve the commons came a little earlier; those of Wimbledon and Putney were safeguarded by an Act of 1871.

Such developments, however, were no solution to the housing problem of the slums. Direct attempts to tackle this began in the 1840s with the formation of the Society for Improving the Condition of the Labouring Classes, and the building of cottages (Cubitt Street near Kings Cross, Ca, 1844) and then tenements: Deal Street Stepney (TH) 1848, the flats for families in Streatham Street Bloomsbury (Ca) 1849 (the only survival of these early efforts), Portpool Lane Holborn (Ca) 1850. The Society's architect *Henry Roberts* showed model cottages at the Great Exhibition of 1851; an example of these, afterwards erected in Kennington Park, still remains. The earliest MODEL HOUSING had still been on a manageable scale; soon however it deteriorated into the grimmest multi-storeyed barracks with sunless asphalted courts between. The Great Exhibition cottages, in fact a group of four flats with communal open-well staircase, were indeed planned so that they could be multiplied on a larger scale. Only the superior artisan classes could afford the rent of such tenements, so they were no solution for the poorest. Yet they were hailed as salvation by such men as Dickens and Lord Shaftesbury. The earliest large-scale group was Columbia Square, built at the expense of Baroness Burdett Coutts in Bethnal Green (TH) in 1859–62. Meanwhile other organizations sprang up, among them the General Society for Improving the Dwellings of the Working Classes in 1852, the Peabody Trust in 1862, Sydney Waterlow's Improved Industrial Dwellings Company in 1863. In South London their work is illustrated by the I.I.D.C.'s Cromwell Buildings of 1864, on a cramped site in the notorious Red Lion Street Southwark, which like other blocks by this company was a development from Roberts's Great Exhibition model buildings, and by the Peabody Estate off Blackfriars Road, designed by *Darbishire* in 1870 in the austere brick style that became standard for their later estates. This early example, however, included the enlightened features of laundries, baths (on the ground floor), and two courtyards with trees. The Artisans, Labourers and General Dwellings Company, founded in 1867 by *Robert Austin*, a small builder, was a rather different body, which concentrated on providing modest suburban housing. Its very first estate, Shaftesbury Park Battersea begun in 1872, still appears remarkably 95 humane – small terraced houses in a variety of styles, with gardens. The later estates are further out: Queens Park Kilburn (Wm), Noel Park (Hy), and Streatham Hill (1889–94), in areas now made accessible by the advent of cheap transport. By 1895 the Company had built 6,500 dwellings, as against Peabody's

5,100 and the I.I.D.C.'s 5,350. By then there were other organizations, too many to list, among which the East End Dwellings
Company (founded 1884) and the Guinness Trust (1889) were to
be especially active.

The attitude to tenements in the inner areas fluctuated. By the
later C 19 they were seen to be far from ideal. Among their
opponents Octavia Hill, the pioneer of enlightened housing
management, was especially vociferous. Her pattern for new
working-class dwellings still survives, the deliberately picturesque cottages which she built in Redcross Way Southwark in
1887, next to a public garden and community hall. A few similar
private ventures followed (Little Suffolk Street near by, also by
Hoole), and her principles later influenced the more extensive
Southwark building projects of the Church Commissioners.
Some of the very early housing by the L.C.C. was also on a small
scale: Rushworth Street Southwark (1896), with three-storey
flats exceptionally attractively detailed in the Philip Webb tradition, by *A. M. Philips* of the L.C.C.'s Housing Branch.

But such cases were exceptional. The great backlog of sites
awaiting attention once the Housing Act of 1890 at last made it
easier for local authorities to build, as well as the relative costli-
ness of lower buildings, meant that tall tenements remained the
most usual form of public housing in the inner areas. But the
work of the L.C.C. housing branch, formed in 1893 with an
enthusiastic team nurtured on the ideals of Morris and Webb,
under the leadership of *Thomas Blashill*, was in a free style in the
tradition of Webb and Shaw, far less stark than the earlier
barrack blocks. It is illustrated best by the Boundary Street
Estate at Bethnal Green (NE London) and the Millbank Estate
behind the Tate Gallery in Westminster, both of the 1890s, in
this volume by Carrington House, a lodging house at Deptford
of 1902, and to a lesser extent by the Webber Row Estate
Southwark (1905). The Guinness Trust and other charitable
bodies (e.g. the Samuel Lewis Trust in Islington) followed suit,
so that the best of such estates of flats were no longer so different
in appearance from flats built for the wealthy in the West End or
(occasionally) in South London, for example on the s edge of
Battersea Park. The L.C.C. however could adopt an alternative
solution. The 1890 Act at last permitted the purchase of new
sites for public housing, and a further Act in 1900 allowed these
to be outside the authority's area. So on the cheaper land on the
fringe of London ESTATES OF COTTAGES were laid out; in
South London at Totterdown Fields Tooting (1903–11), and at
96 Norbury from 1905. The layout and design of the later estates
was strongly influenced by Parker & Unwin's principles of town
planning, which they had demonstrated at Hampstead Garden
Suburb (Bn, North London) from 1906 onwards. The shift
towards more picturesque villagey grouping and studious Arts
and Crafts details can be observed specially well in the development of Norbury, or in the contemporary North London estates
of White Hart Lane Tottenham (Hy) or Old Oak Hammersmith
(H F). Meanwhile an alternative, more urban type of low-rise

housing was provided by *Adshead & Ramsay*'s exceptionally appealing neo-Regency cottages and terraces for the Duchy of Cornwall's Kennington Estate (1913).

The boroughs and local councils (with the exception of Bermondsey) also built cottages, but mostly in very small quantities. The metropolitan boroughs were not allowed to build housing until after 1900, so the earliest efforts were outside the L.C.C. area. Richmond, an especially progressive-minded borough, took the lead, with its houses and cottage flats in Manor Grove of 1894–5, followed a few years later by Hornsey in North London (where *E. J. Lovegrove* the Building Surveyor of Richmond had migrated). When the metropolitan boroughs of the L.C.C. were allowed to make a start, Battersea was the pioneer with its still attractive Latchmere Estate (1903). But even the most energetic boroughs such as Battersea and Camberwell had provided only a few hundred dwellings by 1913, and some with the worst problems, for example Southwark and Lambeth, had built nothing at all.

Public and Commercial Buildings: 1890–1914

Housing is only one aspect of the architectural contribution of the boroughs at the turn of the century. A much more spectacular display was made by the municipal buildings, and to a lesser extent by the libraries, baths, and washhouses for which local authorities were responsible (provided the ratepayers were agreeable) after the Public Libraries Act of 1855 and the Baths and Washhouses Act of 1846.

The earliest remaining CIVIC BUILDING of the C19 is Kingston's jolly Market House (ex-Town Hall) of 1838–40 by *Charles 6 Henman Sen.*, an average example of provincial Italianate with two rather eccentric towers, nicely sited in the centre of the market place. The mid C19 offices of vestries or local boards elsewhere are nothing special: Woolwich 1842, Lambeth 1853 (with quite a grand classical portico), Southwark 1866 (Gothic), Wandsworth 1888 (Italianate). A new level of civic pride becomes apparent in the 1890s. Among the Surrey towns, Croydon takes the lead, with a striking municipal composition of Library and mammoth Town Hall with tower, in a mixed Franco-Flemish, by *Charles Henman Jun.* (1892–6). Richmond's Town Hall of 1893 by *W. J. Ancell* was quite a sizeable Jacobean effort but is no longer in its original state.

Within the L.C.C. Battersea has the most interesting example: *Mountford*'s Town Hall of 1892–3, indicative of the rising interest in English Baroque which *Brydon* had already demonstrated in 1885–7 in his neo-Wrenish Chelsea Town Hall (KC). The Baroque became the style *par excellence* for the public buildings of the early 1900s. South London has three such Town Halls, as sumptuous as those of many towns outside London: Deptford by *Lanchester, Stewart & Rickards*, 1902–3, Woolwich 98 by *A. B. Thomas*, 1903–6, Lambeth by *Warwick*, 1906–8, as well as the L.C.C.'s own County Hall by *Ralph Knott*, begun in 1907.

The first three make use of the accent of a tall tower (cf. Belcher's Colchester Essex), to offset the play of giant columns and pedimented windows, but the quieter roof-lines of County Hall presage future tastes; the Edwardian love of drama is confined here to the concave centre of the river front, and the Piranesian effects of the inner courtyards. Baroque exteriors of this kind provided new opportunities for architectural sculpture (used especially effectively at Deptford); the interiors too were designed to impress, as can be seen especially in the lavish circulation spaces of Battersea, Deptford, or Woolwich.

Lesser municipal buildings of this era at first occasionally used Gothic motifs (libraries at Richmond 1879–80, Kennington Lane Lambeth 1889) but more often, especially from the 1890s onwards, employed a cheerful adaptation of neo-Tudor, neo-William-and-Mary, or neo-French-Renaissance, combined with a playfulness that could sometimes be highly successful. Such buildings are still some of the most enjoyable landmarks of the suburbs. *Maurice Adams* was a skilful practitioner of a decorative neo-Wren version of this style (Camberwell Baths and Library 1902, Eltham Library 1906), but many others could play a similar game to good effect (*S. R. J. Smith*'s libraries in various parts of Lambeth, *C. Barry Jun.*'s East Dulwich Library 1896, *Wakeford*'s Carnegie Library Herne Hill 1904, *H. Cheers*'s Teddington Library 1906, to mention only a few).

Other public buildings illustrate a similar development from busy eclectic display to a spirited rendering of free Baroque by the early years of the C20. Among buildings for HIGHER EDUCATION, which multiplied rapidly at the end of the C19, Woolwich Polytechnic is a good example of the several phases from 1890 onwards, while *Maurice Adams*'s Camberwell Art School (1896–8) and *Mountford*'s Battersea Polytechnic (1890–1), and also his St Olave's School Bermondsey (1893), all show the growing fascination with Baroque forms. The story of ELEMENTARY SCHOOLS begins rather differently. These, after 1870, were the responsibility of the local School Boards, and the architects of the influential London School Board (covering the future L.C.C. area) were particularly affected by the spirit of Webb and Shaw which has already been traced in the development of suburban architecture. Therefore the early Board Schools, under the chief architect *E. R. Robson*, are neither in the Gothic associated with church schools, nor in the enriched Italianate of so many secular buildings of the time, but in a quieter 'Queen Anne' style, with sash-windows, shaped gables, and little decoration apart from the occasional stone or terracotta plaque. This style had evolved already *c.* 1872–3, in schools by *Champneys* and *Stevenson* (now demolished) as well as by Robson. Good examples are in Blackheath Road Greenwich (1874) and Wyvil Road Lambeth (1876). Under Robson's successor from 1884, *T. J. Bailey*, the buildings became a little more flamboyant. Their form was largely dictated by the need to cram on to small sites three separate establishments (Infants', Boys', and Girls'), each by the 1890s requiring an assembly hall as well as classrooms. These tall 'three-deckers', with their romantic outlines of hipped roofs flanked by cupola-topped stair-turrets, are still a prominent feature of the skyline of much of the suburbs. Their symmetrical elevations lent themselves easily to the introduction of more formal classical elements from the 1890s, and then to less dramatic and generally duller neo-Georgian forms in the early C20. The succession can be traced in most of the inner boroughs (for example: Woodhill School Woolwich, 1883; Kennington Road Lambeth, 1897; Kingswood Road Lambeth, 1898; Craigton Road Woolwich, 1904). The less restricted school sites in the outer suburbs could offer scope for more relaxed Arts-and-Crafts compositions (see for example some of the buildings by the local architects *H. Burke Downing* or *R. J. Thomson* in the borough of Merton). *W. Curtis Green*'s restrained Adult Hall at Croydon belongs in this tradition too.

The most remarkable example of the application of Arts-and-Crafts principles to public buildings is the work of the *L.C.C.'s Fire Brigade Branch*. The London Fire Brigade undoubtedly had an aura of romance. Its earliest FIRE STATIONS, under *Pearsall*, were Gothic, often picturesquely detailed (e.g. Marylebone, NW London). From 1900, however, under the leadership of *Owen Fleming* and *C. C. Winmill*, a very accomplished free style developed, strongly influenced by the work of Webb and Stokes, almost devoid of period detail, and characterized by the use of sweeping eaves above an effective juxtaposition of stone and brick to emphasize verticals and horizontals. Good examples of 1901–2 are at Greenwich and at Perry Vale Forest Hill.

In the way of CULTURAL BUILDINGS other than educational ones, South London had little to offer by the end of the century, apart from the Crystal Palace, re-erected on the hill above Sydenham after the 1851 Exhibition and burnt down in 1936. There was, however, a little more than was assumed by those who judged the suburbs by the standards of the West End. Walter Besant (who lived in Hampstead) could describe South London at this time (*South London*, 1901) as 'a city without a municipality, without a centre, without a civic history,' with 'no intellectual artistic, scientific, musical, literary centre,' its residents with 'no local patriotism or enthusiasm. One cannot imagine a man proud of New Cross.' The rise of local patriotism in the suburbs is in fact a noticeable development at the turn of the century. It can be seen in the grand town halls already mentioned, in the decoration of the occasional commercial building (see the historical allusions of the façade of Boot's at Kingston), and in some substantial benefactions by private individuals.

Architecturally the outstanding example among these is the museum given by F. J. Horniman at Forest Hill, Lewisham, begun in 1897, a forceful and original design by *Harrison Townsend*, architect of the earlier, equally progressive-minded Whitechapel Art Gallery (NE *London*) and Bishopsgate Institute (*London 1*). The powerful curved forms and the organically inspired detail successfully avoid either picturesque whimsy or

Baroque cliché. Such buildings have few imitators (the only one in this volume to display a similar spirit is *W. T. Walker*'s sweets factory in Standen Road Wandsworth of 1904). Other buildings which resulted from the generosity of local residents are not of this calibre. At Blackheath William Webster established among several institutions a Conservatoire of Music and Concert Hall in quite an impressive series of buildings busily decorated in terra-cotta by *Edmeston & Gabriel* (1894 etc.), while Upper Norwood has a Trade School and Public Halls given and designed by the local industrialist *W. F. R. Stanley* which must rank as one of the most eccentric efforts anywhere at a do-it-yourself free style.

THEATRES, in contrast, were of course wholly commercial enterprises. Suburban theatres and music halls were widespread by the end of the C 19. The earliest remaining example in South London is at Richmond, a lavish creation by *Frank Matcham* of 1899. The Grand Theatre at Clapham Junction of 1900 by *E. A. Woodrow*, at the time of writing a bingo hall, preserves its unusually exotic interior; Wimbledon Theatre of 1910 by *Massey* and *Young* is a later example, quieter inside. In the poorer areas the most famous effort to provide a 'reputable place of amusement' was the Victoria Music Hall founded by Emma Cons, the progenitor both of the Old Vic and of Morley College (the former still with its rather dull front of 1880, the latter continuing to flourish, but in later buildings). But for most people it was the PUBLIC HOUSES, so abominated by the social reformers, which provided the most accessible relief from the drabness of everyday life. In the suburban areas of the early to mid C 19, corner pubs, usually in an Italianate a little more enriched than the neighbouring terraces, had been provided as a matter of course. Stricter licensing laws from the 1870s encour-aged fewer but larger buildings, a trend encouraged by the brewers' speculations in the 1890s, when so many pubs were rebuilt. So the most memorable examples date from this decade, their exteriors a froth of turrets and gables, their bars richly enshrined in the glitter of cut glass, engraved mirrors, and glazed tiles. *W. M. Brunton*'s Kings Head Tooting of 1897 is one of the best preserved. The temperance reaction produced some drinking fountains (*see* e.g. Clapham Common), and one build-ing in South London that can be noted: *Ernest George*'s former Beehive Coffee Tavern at Streatham (1878–9). Its style (like that of his better-known Cocoa Tree at Pinner, Hw) belongs in the idealistic Webb–Shaw tradition of the Board Schools.

Pubs were designed to satisfy local needs; long-distance travellers needed larger and grander accommodation. The first STATION HOTEL in London was built near London Bridge in 1834 by *George Allen*. Its restrained classical façade alone re-mains. Once the northern railway termini were established, South London was not a good address for hotels, and the only later ones that need be mentioned here are two further out: the Queen's Hotel Upper Norwood, 1853–4 by *F. Pouget*, large and Italianate, now much altered, intended to cater for visitors to the Crystal Palace; and the former Richmond Hill (now Star and

Garter) Hotel, 1865 by *John Giles*, a debased palazzo of memorable brashness, designed to exploit the tourist attractions of Richmond.

A final paragraph on the Victorian and Edwardian periods must be devoted to COMMERCIAL ARCHITECTURE. The most interesting examples in South London were built in connection with the factories and warehouses of the industrial areas (for these *see* the Introduction to Industrial Archaeology). The Leather Market in Weston Street Bermondsey of 1833 is still in a dignified, anonymous pre-Victorian classical. The Leather Exchange near by of 1878 (*Elkington & Sons*) proudly displays its identity by thematic decoration, as does the former Hop Exchange in Southwark Street. The latter, by *R. H. Moore*, 1866, 84 although sadly altered, is particularly interesting, with an elevation with giant iron columns and an interior which had offices opening off tiers of balconies around a central hall, like the demolished Coal Exchange in the City. Southwark Street, laid out in 1862, was the show street for High Victorian commerce in South London, and still has quite a number of buildings in the opulent Venetian palazzo tradition of the 1860s–1880s (although individually most are not as good as those of Clerkenwell, NE London). Among them Kirkaldy's Testing Works by *T. R.* 83 *Smith* (1877) surprises by its round-arched severity. Tooley Street Bermondsey has the best buildings of the end of the century and beyond.

Few remain of the DEPARTMENT STORES which became the characteristic focus of such suburban shopping centres as Brixton, Streatham, or Peckham Rye. The only notable one architecturally is *Gibson*'s Arding and Hobbs, Clapham Junction (1910), with its typical Baroque corner feature. The most distinguished group of High Street premises is the especially attractive one by *Ernest Newton* at Bromley (1898), with its skilful mixture of bows, Palladian windows, and gables – a style not much employed in the inner suburbs. The National Westminster Bank at Sutton by *F. Wheeler* uses Art Nouveau motifs, rare for a bank. The most thoroughgoing late Victorian shopping centre is in the centre of Croydon, which still has a virtually complete array of busily detailed brick and terracotta frontages which sprang up in the 1890s as a result of the local council's energetic clearance of the old market area. As with the pubs, the 1890s onwards was a boom period for investment in showy shopping parades (cf. e.g. Streatham High Road, or in North London Acton, Crouch End, or Muswell Hill). A little earlier than these is Electric Avenue Brixton of 1885, an imposing but less extensive shopping street, one of the first to be lit by electricity.

The essential background without which all this architectural development would have been impossible was first the industry, above all the docks and associated manufactories, and then the development of the public utilities, services, and transport vital to the functioning of a complex built-up area. It was often in these buildings, usually the province of the engineer rather than

the architect, that new materials and techniques were introduced. The development of all these aspects is traced in Mr
Tucker's separate introduction on Industrial Archaeology. The
scale of such structures, whether they be the iron and glass roofs
78 of the Kew greenhouses and, later, of the railway stations, or the
2 towering brick walls of the riverside warehouses, or the railway
viaducts threading their way through the suburbs, cannot fail to
impress. The most interesting large early RAILWAY STATIONS
in South London have vanished (they included *Tite*'s Nine
Elms, a quiet Italianate loggia front of 1838, and *Lewis Cubitt*'s
Bricklayers Arms, with a monumental arch of 1844), although a
number of enjoyable suburban stations remain (e.g. Barnes;
Camberwell). The oldest major station front is that of Waterloo,
1 begun in 1901, the only London terminus in the Baroque style,
but too badly sited to make a successful impact.

Architectural Developments 1914–1939

This introduction must now turn to architectural developments
after 1914. Compared with the feverish activity of the preceding
decades, there is not very much in South London that need be
singled out from the inter-war years. The trends established
before the First World War continued, in more muted form and
generally without the sparkle of originality. Public buildings,
commercial buildings, and schools remained heavily under the
influence of Wren. *Sir Aston* and *Maurice Webb* had a few late
flings at Baroque (the Royal Russell Schools Addington 1924;
Kingston Guildhall 1935), as did *Sir Edwin Cooper* (Star and
Garter Homes Richmond 1921–4). More often a quieter neo-
Georgian prevailed (as in the 1939 parts of Bromley Town Hall
as compared with the original building of 1906). An alternative
was the more precise formality of the French Beaux-Arts tradition, but this was largely a prerogative of the West End. *W. E.
Riley*'s stone-faced Sessions House Newington of 1921 indicates
its influence. Watered-down medieval details were still used for
churches in a discreet but sometimes not ineffective manner (*Sir
Charles Nicholson* in south Lewisham in the 1920s, *Cyril Farey* at
St Mark Teddington 1938–9) and occasionally for other buildings (*Sir Giles Gilbert Scott*'s Training Colleges at Wandsworth
and Camberwell of *c.* 1930). The most remarkable public housing in South London was that built for munitions workers
during the First World War: *Frank Baines*'s Well Hall Estate at
Eltham of 1915 achieved surprisingly varied and picturesque
effects within a very rapid building programme; *J. Gordon
Allen*'s estate of 1915–16 at Barnes Cray, Crayford, is of interest
for its extensive use of concrete construction. After the war came
Baines's skilfully laid out Sunray Estate at Camberwell (1920–1),
part of the Homes fit for Heroes campaign. Through the 1920s
and the 1930s the L.C.C. continued with its cottagey spreads in
the Parker & Unwin manner (although without their flair), in a
friendly modernized Tudor or Georgian. They appear in the
outer suburbs at Roehampton Lane Wandsworth; strung out

more thinly at Bellingham and Downham (Lewisham) on an unparalleled scale (nearly 10,000 houses); and outside the county at St Helier on the Merton and Sutton boundary. In the inner areas lumpy walk-up flats (i.e. not over five storeys), with neo-Georgian trimmings, were the order of the day, solidly built and less grim than C19 tenements, but a far cry from the inventiveness of early L.C.C. work. The later examples tentatively introduced forms borrowed from the Modern Movement on the Continent – first long balcony bands, later on horizontal windows and flat roofs. Among the boroughs, Woolwich and Bermondsey had especially energetic housing policies, the former dispersing its cottage estates over the fields of Eltham, the latter experimenting a little more boldly than the L.C.C. in the slum areas of the Docklands.

Efforts to find a new style in the 1920s were few. All that need be noted in this volume are *Charles Holden*'s austere stone-faced underground stations from Clapham to Morden (1926), and a concrete bank in Teddington by *Randall Wells* (1929). Among major landmarks of the early 1930s was *Goodhart Rendel*'s very personal Swedish-inspired Hay's Wharf offices (1931). *Cache-maille-Day*'s St Saviour Eltham (1933), the first church in London to depart from medieval precedents, owes something to German Expressionism. His Baptist Church, Sutton (1934), is also unconventional. The most startling new building type to erupt all over the suburbs was the cinema (which, like the suburban theatre, is rapidly disappearing again). South London examples which remain to show its development range from *Stone*'s restrained Odeon Streatham (1930) to the streamlined façades of *Mather* (Camberwell 1934) and *Coles* (Balham 1938) and the Dutch-inspired brick of *Masey & Uren* (Granada Woolwich 1937). The last has one of *Komisarjevsky*'s exotic escapist interiors in the American manner of which an even better example is the staggeringly lavish Gothic fantasy of the Granada Tooting also of   101 1937.

The mixture of foreign influences which can be detected in cinemas is also apparent in the new factories fringing the arterial roads, for example Klingerit on the Sidcup bypass, of 1935–6 by *Wallis Gilbert & Partners*, another example of Dutch-inspired brickwork, instead of this firm's more usual American style (for example in the Great West Road, N W London). Public authorities generally remained resistant to innovation, so all that need be mentioned here are, among town halls, *Robert Atkinson*'s tentatively modern example at Wallington of 1935, and *Clifford Culpin*'s much bolder one at Greenwich (1939); among schools *J. W. Poltock*'s courageous Kemnal Manor Upper School Sidcup of 1938, with its long bands of glazing à la Gropius; and, among public services, *J. R. Scott*'s unadorned concrete station at Surbiton of 1937–8.

Private clients were more daring: hence the Pioneer Health Centre built for Dr Scott Williams at Peckham by *Owen Williams* in 1935, with an exterior all of concrete and glass incorporating clinics, clubs, and swimming pool, a precocious fore-

runner of the multi-purpose community buildings of forty years
later. For the same reason it was only a few private houses and
flats of the 1930s that provided an opportunity for the Corbu-
sian-influenced style that the most forward-thinking younger
architects would have liked to pursue in public housing. The
South London examples of these are *Maxwell Fry*'s Sassoon
House Peckham (1932) and Miramonte Kingston (1936–7),
102 *Harding & Tecton*'s very pure Corbusian Six Pillars Dulwich
(1933–5) and (by members of the Tecton group) *Samuel*'s By the
Links, Bromley (1935), and a terrace in Genesta Road Plumstead (1935) by *Lubetkin* and *Pilichovski*. Flats are represented
by the picturesquely grouped white blocks of Pullman Court
Streatham Hill and by Park Court Penge (1936), both by *Gibberd*. Speculative builders took little notice of these new ideas,
apart from a few cases, e.g. the Sunspan houses by *Wells Coates*
at Coombe, Kingston.

Planning since 1945

At the time of publication of *London except the Cities of London
and Westminster* (1952), architecture since the Second World
War needed only a brief paragraph in the introduction: 'Only
one big public building has so far been erected in the style of
today: the Royal Festival Hall on the South Bank (Lambeth), by
J. L. Martin (of the L.C.C. Architects Department), 1949–51,
but plenty of council estates of flats, the best being those of
Powell & Moya (Pimlico, Westminster), *Chitty* (St Pancras),
Gibberd (Hackney), *Fry & Drew* (Lewisham), *Dawbarn* (Hackney, St Pancras), *Lubetkin* (Finsbury).'
    At that time it was only possible to appreciate the very begin-
nings of the effects of the new PLANNING: Forshaw and Abercrombie's County of London Plan of 1943, and Abercrombie's
Greater London Plan of 1944, which formed the basis of the
official County Plan of 1951. Much has happened since. The
need to plan for a London which stretched beyond the boundaries of 1888 was officially recognized by the creation of the
Greater London Council in 1965 (covering an area rather smaller
than that of the Greater London plan of 1944). The Greater
London Development Plan followed in 1969, and then a public
inquiry during which many of its findings were rejected. By this
time social and economic trends hardly or not at all anticipated in
1945 had to be taken into account: for example a fall in inner-city
population even greater than expected (which has continued
since in the outer boroughs as well), the continuing demand for
better housing, especially after the scandals of privately rented
accommodation in the inner areas, the growth of car ownership,
the boom in office building in the 1960s, and the changing
pattern of London industry, notably the closure of the docks and
the shift of industry from the East End and the riverside to the
western suburbs.
    London is now a very different place from the war-scarred,
smoke-begrimed, and slum-ridden city whose rebuilding and

improvement was the subject of so much enthusiasm and idealistic discussion in the first years after the Second World War. But
the present fabric owes much to the ideas formulated then, and
to the post-war planning legislation which followed, even if it
was only much later that the physical expression of some of these
principles became noticeable.

A prime concern was to check London's unplanned growth,
that is, to prevent the continuing dispersal of the population over
the fields and market gardens of the surrounding counties which
had been such a marked feature of the 1930s. The Greater
London Plan spelt out the results up to the Second World War:

	1919	1943
City and County of London	4,540,662	2,487,100
Greater London*	4,084,923	5,892,848
TOTAL	8,624,985	8,379,948

In the parts of Greater London covered by this volume, the areas
covered approximately by the boroughs of Bexley and Bromley
expanded from c. 262,000 in 1931 to 495,000 in 1951, those of
Merton and parts of Sutton and Kingston from c. 216,000 to
393,000. The district of Sutton and Cheam was a typical case of
rapid suburbanization: c. 29,000 in 1921, c. 81,000 in 1951. Not
only speculative housing development, but the sprawling council estates (among which Croydon's New Addington became a
byword) were damned by a generation of architects and planners
eager to try out radical and more urban forms of building. The
solution adopted by the post-war plans was to prescribe densities
of development for concentric rings around central London
(settled after 1951 at 200 persons per acre for the central areas,
136 p.p.a. and below further out); to limit further suburban
expansion by a 'green belt' (the nucleus of which had been
created by an Act of 1938); and to house the surplus population
in six satellite towns beyond (later on this was extended to other
'overspill' centres such as Andover and Basingstoke). It is
largely thanks to the GREEN BELT that the present Greater
London still has stretches of countryside around its borders.
The satellite towns (Crawley in Sussex, Basildon and Harlow in
Essex, Hemel Hempstead, Hatfield, and Stevenage in Hertfordshire) do not concern us here, but the density plans (which
remained in force until superseded by the G.L.D.P.) had a
marked effect on the appearance of the suburbs in this volume.
In the northern part of the present boroughs of Lambeth and
Southwark, there was at first no choice but to build in as compact
a manner as possible, while in the middle and outer bands there
was greater freedom to experiment. In addition to the urgent
need to tackle housing (war damage having been added to the
extensive slum-clearance programme left outstanding in 1939),
the County Plan urged other priorities: the creation of more

*The larger boundaries of the 1944 plan, not of the Greater London Council of
1965.

green spaces within the built-up area, and the improvement of roads (perennial themes, as the history of C 19 London planning will have made clear). The effect of these on the appearance of South London may be mentioned briefly before the weightier matter of building is discussed.

The ROAD IMPROVEMENTS completed in South London are far less radical than the post-war proposals. Only the M 25, the outermost of the proposed concentric series of ringways, was constructed. The rest are all piecemeal improvements: the first ambitious effort was the complete replanning of the Elephant and Castle (Southwark) with new tall buildings around its double roundabout, impressive when seen at speed, but bewildering when one is a pedestrian banished to the confusing maze of underpasses. The later roundabout of the 1960s at Waterloo Road has ampler lower-level pedestrian routes, tied in quite ingeniously with the brutalist underbelly of the South Bank redevelopment (on which *see* below). But for the most part, major roadworks in the area covered by this volume (Jamaica Road Bermondsey, Vauxhall Cross, New Kent Road flyover, Rochester Way Greenwich), however necessary they may be to keep traffic moving, have been callously disruptive of the urban fabric. Only when traffic can be effectively diverted from other areas is there some visual compensation (as in the centres of Sutton and Kingston or, more recently, in the small traffic management areas in the inner parts of Lambeth).

While expensive major road proposals were dropped during the 1970s, the PARKS promised in the 1950s began at last to make an appearance, although here too large-scale plans were often abandoned in favour of smaller schemes which could be more easily realized. Southwark Park, as proposed in 1943, now extends, landscaped at last in 1982, to the Bermondsey riverside. The large 'Camberwell open space' at the southern fringe of Walworth and around the Old Kent Road, which figured so prominently in early plans, is now Burgess Park (but consists of linked areas, not a single park). In Lambeth smaller and friendlier neighbourhood parks became the aim from the 1960s. Heavier Traffic helped to kill off the early enthusiasm for main roads through parkland. But the 1940s concept of linked open spaces was eventually realized in the 1970s in two successful cases: the Lee Valley Regional Park in North London, and the well landscaped walks which now exist along many parts of the Thames riverbanks of Lambeth, Southwark, and Greenwich and which provide some of London's most enjoyable views.

Building since 1945

After this prelude, we can now turn to building since 1945. The comprehensive developments which the post-war planning legislation made possible were intended to achieve more than just the replacement of insanitary, overcrowded, or war-damaged houses; the total replanning of whole neighbourhoods was envisaged, separating industry from housing, and providing sensibly sited shops, parks, new schools, and other amenities. Lansbury in Poplar (NE London), completed hastily for the Festival of Britain in 1951, demonstrated the principle, but elsewhere the essential cooperation between different departments and authorities was rarely as effective. Furthermore, road improvements within such areas tended to dominate, as one can see if one considers some of the South London comprehensive development areas declared in the 1951 plan (Elephant and Castle, Lewisham Clock Tower, Jamaica Road Bermondsey). The two others were the special cases of old Woolwich (treated essentially as a large housing estate by the borough) and the South Bank, which was intended from the first to provide (next to County Hall) the cultural and commercial focus that South London had so long lacked.

But the prime need after the war was to provide more houses, so PUBLIC HOUSING from 1945 must be considered first. Until 1950 L.C.C. housing was undertaken by the Valuer's Department and consisted mostly of rapid building on pre-war lines: cottage estates outside the county, flats in inner London, although the latter began to incorporate improvements already mooted before the war and encouraged by the government housing manual of 1945 (more lifts, staircases instead of balcony access, maisonettes as an alternative to flats, for example). The rigidly geometrical ranks of the Woodberry Down Estate (Hackney) and the Ocean Estates (Tower Hamlets) in NE London were the show examples. The metropolitan boroughs were more adventurous. The search for original but suitably urban forms produced for example blocks of flats with a more modern appearance such as those by *Norman & Dawbarn* at Camden Road, St Pancras (Ca), *Ashley & Newman*'s low point blocks in Deptford, departing from the traditional street plan, and, especially impressive, *Powell & Moya*'s tall, elegant, tightly knit slabs at Pimlico, Westminster (*London 1*), which had to meet the challenge of the 200 p.p.a. density requirement. The re-creation of traditional London forms such as the square and the terrace had its adherents (John Summerson's *Georgian London* was published in 1945); it is seen most conservatively in Greenwich's neo-Georgian housing by *Richardson & Houfe* at Blackheath Park. At *Gibberd*'s Hackney estate in Shacklewell Lane (Hc) low flats and houses were arranged in closes, an idea which he and others also tried out, among other layouts, on the Lansbury Estate. But for those who believed in the Modern Movement, the contrasts provided by Lansbury's two- to six-storey blocks were not sufficiently dynamic, and much of the detailing was too timid. The most radical were beguiled by the powerful images of Le Corbusier's towers in parkland; others looked to the tall flats built in Scandinavia. The garden city image was no longer acceptable.

These influences began to make themselves felt once the L.C.C.'s architect's department* was reorganized under *Robert Matthew* in 1950 (succeeded by *Leslie Martin* in 1953) and given

*For further details on County Council architects *see* p. 18.

responsibility for housing. The new system included a development team which explored new types of layout, construction,
and design. The first and most famous results are in Wandsworth: the eleven-storey point blocks of the Ackroyden Estate at
106 Putney Heath, followed by those of Alton East Roehampton,
and the later more Corbusian slabs of Alton West. All these were
combined with lower blocks of flats and housing so that the same
estates included dwellings of different sizes as well as different
heights. The arrangement too was innovatory; the point blocks
in particular were laid out not in rows, but in a more random
fashion, so as to take advantage of the surrounding rolling
landscape with mature trees that remained from the gardens of
the large suburban Victorian villas of these areas. The application of these principles to the flatter and more heavily built up
inner areas was more problematic. Although a mixture of tall
flats and lower blocks was generally adopted (the proportions
varying depending on the required densities), ready-made landscape was less easy to come by. Too often, the towers were
placed close to existing (or intended) parks (see Southwark
Park), thereby diminishing the sense of spaciousness of these
limited and so very vulnerable open areas.

The two major L.C.C. estates in inner South London reflecting the new ideas of the mid 1950s were Loughborough Road
Brixton, with its centrepiece of ruthlessly Corbusian slabs
(superficially similar to Alton West, but less innovatory in their
detailed planning), and the subtler Brandon Estate Walworth
(designed under *Edward Hollamby*, then working for the
L.C.C.). It includes towers on the edge of Kennington Park, a
new square and other lower buildings in a variety of non-period
styles, and also the rehabilitation of Victorian terraces (the first
example of its kind by the L.C.C.). As a result, most of the
buildings blend successfully into the surrounding urban fabric.
Rehabilitation of at least a token number of houses and terraces
became a feature of later L.C.C. and G.L.C. estates of the
1960s–1970s (Mursell and Spurgeon Estates South Lambeth;
Gloucester Grove Estate Camberwell), but with the difference
that the older buildings often appear to be used as a quiet foil to
set off bold new architecture, instead of becoming a means of
integrating the estate with an older neighbourhood. The most
ambitious South London effort in this respect is the Pepys Estate
at Deptford (1963–6), where the forceful twenty-six-storey
towers by the Thames (one of the few settings which cannot be
overpowered by such buildings) stand close to the converted
c 18 warehouses and offices of the former Navy Victualling
Yard. The Pepys Estate and others of the early 1960s (e.g. the
Canada Estate Rotherhithe) are characterized by a deliberate
toughness, the aesthetic of exposed concrete and of chunky
outlines, which was of course not the prerogative of housing
estates alone (as the extensions to the South Bank and other
buildings show, which must be mentioned later).

There were other factors too which affected housing developments of the 1960s, in general adversely. One was the wide-

spread use of industrialized building techniques (strongly urged by the government at this time) which enforced more rigid layouts, plainer detailing, and (to be economic) larger estates and taller buildings. Morris Walk Greenwich was one of the first examples on a large scale (1963). Another problem was the provision of car-parking (after the Buchanan Report), which encouraged multi-layered three-dimensional planning separating people and vehicles, always so exciting in theory, nearly always so uninviting in reality. Roundshaw, the housing development planned on Croydon airport in 1963 (by *Clifford Culpin & Partners* for Sutton and the L.C.C.), is an early and ruthlessly diagrammatic London example, using a system of raised decks over garages. The most imaginative and visually sophisticated of such schemes is the fragment built according to the G.L.C.'s first plans for Thamesmead, the new town on the Erith marshes. This was intended as one of several spines of housing incorporating raised pedestrian walks, which were to lead to an elaborate multi-level town centre, an example of the current interest in exploring the possibilities of new urban structures of much greater complexity, and on a much grander scale, than the first post-war efforts, an interest displayed also by some of the borough housing of the mid 1960s and by such schemes as the Brunswick Centre (Camden, N London). But in the other parts of Thamesmead, and elsewhere, the G.L.C. continued building its routine mixture of low terraces and the increasingly unpopular towers. One of the few interesting examples built to a different recipe was the experimental low-density Cedars Estate Clapham (1961–8), consisting entirely of low white brick clusters of flats, presaging the abandonment of high rise which became general by the 1970s.

In the later 1960s the lead hitherto set by the County Architect's Department was no longer unchallenged; indeed even before the setting up of the new larger London boroughs in 1965, the architectural contribution of the OTHER LOCAL AUTHORITIES has to be considered. In the 1950s variations on the Roehampton patterns were predominant. The boroughs, rarely with their own architect's department, had to go to outside firms. Recurrent names in South London are *Norman & Dawbarn* (point blocks at St Mary's Woolwich) and *L. Keay & Partners* (slab blocks at Putney and, more successfully arranged, for the City Corporation in Avondale Square Southwark). In the early 1960s the search for alternatives to the loose open layouts of the L.C.C.'s mixed development produced some more interesting results. The most influential was *Darbourne & Darke*'s Lillington Gardens for Westminster. In South London one can note *Chamberlin, Powell & Bon*'s Vanbrugh Park Greenwich, begun in 1961, where the grid plan of tower and low terraces is knitted together by imaginative landscaping and gardens, and *George Trew Dunn*'s Winstanley Estate Battersea, begun in 1963, where a broad pedestrian route performs a similar function in a more urban context. Camberwell, one of the few pre-1965 boroughs with its own architect's department (under *F. O. Hayes*), produced the most consistently interesting housing. The first post-war effort on a grand scale, Sceaux Gardens, was a series of well-laid-out slab blocks, but later schemes of the early 1960s began to explore the possibilities of small, more intimate groups of houses and flats (Acorn Estate, Bonamy Estate; *see* Introduction to Southwark).

The G.L.C. reorganization of 1965 provided the occasion for the setting up of other borough architects' departments, and the undertaking of more ambitious building programmes. As it also coincided with government support for industrialized building methods, the most obtrusive buildings of this era are unfortunately the austere identical towers which so many boroughs (e.g. Greenwich) planted all over their territories, or the mammoth unloved estates of regimented concrete slabs (Southwark's Aylesbury, Wandsworth's Doddington). Less prominent, but of greater interest, are the various experimental layouts which began to be devised as an alternative to high-rise towers, for example the tightly knit courtyards (Lambeth's Stockwell Park, Southwark's North Peckham and Camden), usually of four or five storeys over garaging (and so too noisy and crowded to become popular), but occasionally lower (as in parts of the first phases of Thamesmead). *Stirling & Gowan*'s courtyard arrangement at Trafalgar Road Greenwich (for the G.L.C. 1965) is another example, unusual in its revival of severely geometric early-Modern-Movement brick detailing.

The different architectural contributions made by the individual boroughs are discussed in the borough introductions, but three must be singled out here: those of Southwark, Lambeth, and Merton. Southwark's varied achievements range from huge multi-level estates to small, low-rise groups, in the tradition initiated by Camberwell, some by the borough (under *F. O. Hayes* and later *H. P. Trenton*), others by outside architects, including some especially ingenious and original ones by *Neylan & Ungless*. Lambeth (under *Edward Hollamby*) became remarkable for the different ways in which new developments were sensitively tailored to the needs of individual sites, whether on hills (Central Hill West Norwood) or busy roads (Lambeth Towers Kennington) or suburban corners often imaginatively incorporating older buildings (Vassall Road), so that despite the volume of new work, any impression of endless repetition is avoided. Merton (under *P. J. Whittle*) is interesting because of the way in which a particular type of housing was developed: the 'perimeter plan' system of low-rise terraces around the edge of an open space, used first at Pollards Hill (1968) and then espe-107 cially attractively at Watermeads Mitcham. These, together with Southwark's small estates, and others by Lambeth (Blenheim Gardens), all demonstrated the potential of housing of only two or three storeys. The G.L.C. in the 1970s followed suit, as can be seen most dramatically in the drastic changes of plans for Thamesmead. By then, the dramatic collapse of Ronan Point (Ne) (1968) had heightened public revulsion against tower blocks and industrialized building systems.

The main change to be noted in the early 1970s is a stylistic one: the abandonment of the imagery of the Modern Movement in favour of a revival of traditional forms and materials (brick walls, pitched roofs) and picturesque cottagey layouts (helped by the abandonment of the old density levels). The move towards this style became general from around 1971–2, as can be seen in the work of *Darbourne & Darke* in N London, or by *Clifford Culpin & Partners'* D'Eynsford Estate (1971), *Neylan & Ungless's* Setchell Estate (1972) (both in Southwark), Lambeth's 111 Woodvale (completed 1975), the G.L.C.'s Ruthin Road Greenwich (1974–5), and the G.L.C.'s even more mannered mixture of new and old at Althorpe Grove Battersea. Among the very few reactions against this trend is the bold machine aesthetic and strident colouring of the groups for a housing association by *Farrell & Grimshaw* at Wimbledon, and *Rock Townsend's* old people's flats at Cavendish Road Sutton. OLD PEOPLE'S HOUSING should incidentally be noted as a special type which developed experimentally during the 1960s–1970s. The challenge to provide buildings with a non-institutional atmosphere, yet large enough to be economically viable, produced for example in the 1960s in Greenwich *Stirling & Gowan's* Perrygrove, Rectory Fields Crescent, Charlton, an inward-looking castle-like retreat, and the totally opposite solution by *Trevor Dannatt* in Langton Way, Blackheath, a pyramid with welcoming outstretched wings. Yet another version is Lambeth's intricate clusters of small courtyards behind older houses (Leigham Court Road and Garrads Road Streatham).

There is little to add about the declining role of public housing at the end of the 1970s, the final phase of this thirty-year story. Neo-vernacular forms, however attractive, were not enough to make the concept of the council estate widely acceptable, despite the example of some imaginatively planned schemes (Brockley Park Lewisham, All Saints Merton). An alternative solution increasingly adopted during the 1970s was to revitalize decaying areas by conversion and small-scale infilling. Another answer was to make council housing indistinguishable from that built for the private sector (the policy eventually adopted by the G.L.C. at Thamesmead). The gap between the two was already being bridged by the increasing volume of work by housing associations. So the housing story of the 1970s ended with the G.L.C. putting some of its houses on the market, and handing over nearly all the rest to the boroughs, which at the time of writing are able to do no more than embark on very modest schemes and attempt to put right the mistakes of the previous decades.

Public housing has done more than any other type of building to alter the face of the inner suburbs in the last fifty years; PRIVATE HOUSING could gain no foothold here, except on occasional small sites, or in a few places on the fringes of the outer boroughs. The most rewarding small groups are those built for Span by *Eric Lyons* from the late 1950s onwards at Twickenham and Petersham (Richmond) and Blackheath Park 105

(Greenwich), low, ingenious layouts of houses and flats in carefully landscaped small cul-de-sacs or set around courtyards or
communal lawns, with friendly detailing of tile-hanging or
weatherboarding, a total contrast in every respect to the council
estates of the same period. *Stirling & Gowan*'s Langham House
Close at Ham (1958) is in a dramatically opposite style, an
early demonstration of the tough brick-and-concrete exterior
favoured by many architects over the next ten years. The outer
fringes of Croydon and Coulsdon provided a more ample area for
speculative housing of the 1960s onwards. Among much
average-to-good work for *Wates*, one original experimental
group stands out: St Bernards, Park Hill, a prototype group of
stepped hill terraces by the Swiss firm of *Atelier 5* (1968–70).

The individual houses fitted into suburban streets, or tucked
away in pockets of secluded landscape in the outer boroughs, are
more personal expressions by their architects. The quiet elegance of the modern style of the fifties is represented in different
ways by the houses by *S. Buzas* and one by *L. Gooday* at Ham,
by several hidden on the wooded heights of Coombe, Kingston
(by *Kenneth Wood*, *Patrick Gwynne*, and *Tayler & Green*), and
by *Peter Moro*'s house at Blackheath Park. Close to this last
example is another later and surprisingly outré house by *Patrick
Gwynne*; other representatives of the more assertive period of the
1960s to early 70s are two by *L. Manasseh* at Petersham, one by
T. Rendle at Barnes, another by *E. Cullinan* at Eltham, and two
at Coombe, by *Kenneth Wood* and by *Vernon Gibberd*.

The outstanding examples of the 1970s do not adopt the pretty
neo-vernacular motifs of public housing, but are also in their
own very individual styles. *Derek Lovejoy*'s elegant house at
Shirley (1971) looks outward from its hillside site, and *Stout &
Litchfield*'s faceted composition at Coombe (1977) has an exterior
to be enjoyed; but the common feature of the others is the way
they avoid any outward show: *Arup Associates*' house in Drax
Avenue Wimbledon, still somewhat in the brutalist mode, *Bell
& McCormack*'s cleverly planned low building in Langton Way
Blackheath (1975–7), and *Richard Rogers*' trim high-tech boxes
hidden behind a mound at Parkside Wimbledon (1977). Finally,
one can contrast a few alternative ways of meeting the challenge
of building houses or flats on historic or otherwise prominent
sites. One solution is the pastiche, especially engagingly done at
Trumpeter's Inn Richmond Old Palace (1954) by *C. Bernard
Brown*, who was also responsible for the impeccable restoration
and additions to The Paragon, Blackheath. Near the latter is an
opposite answer, *Eric Lyons*'s Span flats in South Row (1959–
61), quiet but uncompromisingly modern. *Geoffrey Darke*'s
house in the Georgian Montpelier Row Twickenham (1967) has
a tactful front, but also refuses to play period games, and the
same is true of *Manning & Clamp*'s pleasant reticent brick
terrace facing Richmond Green (1970), and *Royston Summers*'
more forceful group in Blackheath (1969). Architects of this
calibre are, alas, rarely allowed to show their skill on the prime
sites of inner London, nor has housing had much of a chance

there. The splendid opportunities of the Thames waterfront were in the 1970s exploited in this way only by the slick luxury flats of Kings Reach, Southwark (*R. Seifert & Partners*), and then by the plainer, well grouped and well landscaped flats built by *Fitzroy Robinson & Partners* as part of the redevelopment around Blackfriars Bridge.

Houses have no obligation to be demonstrative; PUBLIC BUILDINGS have to satisfy different requirements. Among these, the cultural buildings of the South Bank are the most prominent post-war contribution to South London. The concept of revitalizing this stretch of the river goes back to the 1930s, evolved during the early post-war years (not without a good deal of controversy), and was given its first practical realization by the impetus of the Festival of Britain in 1951. The buildings took twenty-five further years to complete. First came *Sir Leslie Martin*'s Festival Hall, opened in 1951, supreme 103 among the more frivolous buildings of the Festival, demure now in comparison with what followed. The treatment of the circulation space inside is what impresses most. The 1960s added the jerky concrete antics of the G.L.C.'s Hayward Gallery and Queen Elizabeth Hall, showing off in front of the disappointingly dull Shell offices which had meanwhile reared up as a backcloth; then at last in the 1970s, jutting out at the bend of the river on the other side of Waterloo Bridge, came *Sir Denys Lasdun*'s National Theatre, a powerful and accomplished com- 109 position both outside and in. Another national building of the same era is the more ponderous Public Record Office at Kew (1967–77) by the government's *Property Services Agency*, an illustration of establishment approval of the brutalist style of the time, in marked contrast to the earlier, less demonstrative Crown Building near by. This anonymous box was built to house the first English experimental open-plan office, another example of that interest in new, less hierarchical forms of planning which, as we will see, also transformed schools and churches during the 1960s.

The creation of the outer London boroughs in 1965 called for new municipal efforts. Croydon added a glass skyscraper of offices in the 1960s behind its Town Hall (quite an early example of its kind). Sutton's Civic Centre is in the characteristic form of the 1970s, a large but compact package, incorporating library and other amenities as well as offices; Bromley has a new borough library-cum-theatre. In the Victorian suburbs the buildings produced by the flurry of municipal activity of *c.* 1900 onwards have mostly had to suffice for later needs. Town halls have been extended piecemeal rather than rebuilt. So the main buildings to note are lesser ones: some swimming pools (by *Powell & Moya* at Putney, 1968, by *L. Gooday* at Richmond, 1961, and some striking branch libraries, e.g. at Peckham (by Southwark, or rather Camberwell, 1962–7), at South Norwood (by Croydon, 1966–8) and at Upper Norwood (by Lambeth, 1969). Those of Peckham and Upper Norwood provide for other community needs as well. The Sheen Lane Centre at East Sheen

(Richmond) by the *Haworth King Partnership* (1976–8) is a particularly successful example of how even more varied functions (library, health centre, day centre, etc.) can be combined attractively on a single site. Some other prominent service buildings are not by the boroughs but by the *G.L.C. Special Works Department* (under *Geoffrey Horsfall*). Its *magnum opus* is the suave polygonal pyramid of the island extension to County Hall (1970–4), but its varied work of the 1970s is also consistently interesting and enjoyable: for instance the impressive Magistrates' Court at Richmond, and the playful Bromley Ambulance Centre and Three Rivers Centre at Lewisham, which show that sheds and garages can be fun. Even the unpromising type of a Refuse Transfer Station (Cringle Dock, Battersea) is treated with elegance. A comparable sophistication is found in the remodelling of London Bridge Station (1976–8 by *N. Wikely*, Regional Architect to *British Rail*).

Two other types of service buildings need attention; schools and hospitals. The great period for HOSPITAL REBUILDING was the 1960s. A lone precursor is the gay little outpatients' department in the Festival spirit by *Devereux & Davies* at St James Hospital Balham (1953). The next decade was less concerned with exteriors than with the need to cope with expansion and the provision of more up-to-date planning (centrally planned instead of Nightingale wards, for example). Two of the most prominent inner London examples are Guy's forbidding concrete towers (1963–75 by *Watkins Gray Woodgate*) and St Thomas's white, elegant, but impersonal deep plan monster cubes (1966–76 by *Yorke Rosenberg & Mardall*). The shift towards lower buildings is illustrated by the Greenwich Hospital, an experimental compact design by the *Department of Health and Social Security*, 1961–76, and by *Powell & Moya*'s Queen Elizabeth Military Hospital, Woolwich, of 1972–5; and the growing concern for more appealing external appearances by the Queen Mary Hospital, Sidcup.

The story of SCHOOLS begins immediately after the war. Only a few buildings can be singled out from the vast number built. The London School Plan, drawn up from 1944 to 1947, included in its ambitious programme the total reorganization of secondary education in the L.C.C. area on comprehensive lines (achieved nominally only in the 1970s, when the remaining grammar schools were compelled to become comprehensive or go independent). To achieve a balanced mix it was at first thought essential to have at least twelve-form-entry schools (for over 2,000 pupils). So the first new comprehensives were large, and visibly revelled in their scale, and in the use of modern ideas such as curtain walling and open ground floors. South London has some of the first examples: Kidbrooke (Greenwich) by *Slater Uren & Pike*, 1949–54, Dick Sheppard (Lambeth) by *Yorke Rosenberg & Mardall*, 1950–5, and Strand (Lambeth), the first built by the L.C.C., completed in 1955, with its nine-storey teaching block with classroom-sized lifts. It was soon found desirable to soften the impact of these forbidding masses; *Powell*

& *Moya*'s Mayfield at Putney (Wandsworth), ready in 1956, was a trail-blazer in this respect, in scale with its surroundings and planned so that only part of the building could be seen at a time. A more fundamental innovation (pioneered not in London but in Coventry) was subdivision of the pupils into separate 'houses', although only rarely was this given clear architectural expression, e.g. in *Chamberlin, Powell & Bon*'s delicate and attractive buildings for Trinity (later Geoffrey Chaucer) School, Southwark (1958), where the house rooms fill the angles of the pentagonal hall block. Similar motives influenced the provision of separate classroom blocks for different ages, e.g. at the later Acland Burghley School at Camden, N London. This building is one of the most extreme examples of the application of the brutalist style of the sixties to school buildings; good and less aggressive examples in South London are *James Cubitt*'s Norwood School (Lambeth), or the bold additions by *Trevor Dannatt* at Eltham Hill (Greenwich) or Furzedown, Tooting (Wandsworth).

The *Inner London Education Authority* under *Michael Powell*, followed by *C. Hartland* (1971–2), *G. Wigglesworth* (1972–4), and *P. Jones* (from 1974), which took over from the L.C.C. in 1965, produced as its *chef d'œuvre* of the later 1960s the jagged greenhouse of Pimlico School (Westminster; *see London 1*), but the inflexible planning of this building marked the end of an era; for the chief innovation which affected the appearance of schools from the later 1960s was the disappearance of the traditional classroom, reduced in numbers as smaller schools became the norm, then in importance as resource centres became popular. At the same time (in response to the Newsome Report) drama or music areas began to replace or supplement the conventional assembly hall (see e.g. Scott Lidgett, Bermondsey, Southwark). In some schools of the later 1970s there was a move to replace classrooms entirely by new types of informal teaching spaces (along the lines already established by American secondaries and English primaries), as exemplified by the deep-plan layout of Waterfield (1969–77) and the split-level clusters of Hydeburn. These two illustrate the diversity of appearance presented by schools of the 1970s: Hydeburn is a compact, elegantly set gem embedded in a nondescript suburb of Balham (Wandsworth), Waterfield an uncompromising high-tech statement in the brave new world of Thamesmead. Different again are *Powell & Moya*'s quietly distinguished additions on the confined site of Plumstead Manor, Woolwich, or the picturesquely roofed additions to John Roan, near Blackheath. The varying responses of such buildings to their different settings have as their social counterpart the movement to provide school buildings shared by the community, planned at Waterfield, achieved at the less architecturally notable Lewisham School (1971).

The L.C.C.'s post-war PRIMARY SCHOOLS, single-storey, child orientated buildings in reaction to the old Board Schools, followed the constructional lead of Hertfordshire in using a modular plan with standardized components. This could produce attractive (if repetitive) results (e.g. Heathmere Roehampton), more so than the cruder 'MACE' system used later. A few were built by other architects, e.g. the crisply designed Fairlawn Lewisham by *Peter Moro*. The major innovation of the 1960s was the introduction of open-plan teaching areas in place of classrooms, and the emphasis on better outdoor play and teaching spaces, all illustrated (at the time of the Plowden Report) by the trend-setting Evelyn Lowe School in Southwark, an experimental government design of 1967. I.L.E.A.'s contribution was the uniquely elaborate split-level Vittoria School in Islington (N London). A spate of simpler open-plan designs followed, built on a flexible rationalized system (Michael Faraday in the Aylesbury Estate Southwark is a pleasant example), the clusters of teaching areas lending themselves well to many attractive small-scale compositions. The particular needs of special schools also produced some sensitive responses – for example Clapham Park of 1967–9. Such primary and special schools are generally friendly and unassertive in appearance, one of the few exceptions being the extraordinary monumental hall added at Brunswick Hall Camberwell by *Stirling & Gowan* (1961–2).

For the buildings for FURTHER EDUCATION, which boomed with the expansion of polytechnics and training colleges in the 1960s, a tougher image was more common. Early examples are the powerful brutalist extensions to Philippa Fawcett College Streatham (Lambeth) by *John Bancroft* of the L.C.C. (1960–6) and the bold concrete and glass additions by *L. Manasseh* (1961–5) at Furzedown Training College Tooting (Wandsworth), while the London College of Printing's additions of 1969–73 at the Elephant and Castle echo the emphatic profiles of Pimlico School. The most interesting of the 1970s buildings are less flamboyant: *I.L.E.A.*'s South Bank Polytechnic, also at the Elephant, is a compact and severe red brick fortress sheltering its cunningly deployed internal spaces; *John Winter*'s additions to Morley College are contained in a smoother curtain-walled envelope.

Post-war CHURCHES need only a short note. Early rebuilding on war-damaged sites was generally distressingly mediocre. R. C. churches pursued the tired end of the Arts and Crafts tradition (*Romilly Craze*'s rebuilding of Pugin's St George's Cathedral Southwark, *Goodhart Rendel*, using an eclectic kind of Romanesque, at Most Holy Trinity Dockhead). Nonconformist churches on the other hand could be more radical (*Edward Mills*'s Methodist Church at Mitcham, 1958). Among Anglican churches the first effort at something modern was *Woodroffe Buchanan & Coulter*'s St Paul Lorrimore Square (1955–60), its interior more effective than its over-excited outside. Two churches by *Cachemaille-Day* are memorable (although not as daring as his pre-war buildings): the concrete-vaulted St James Clapham Park (1957–8) and the quieter St Philip Avondale Square (1963). The latter is octagonal, an example of the popularity of central planning in the 1960s (St Barnabas St Paul's Cray 1962, St Andrew Sidcup 1964, etc.). It is first illustrated in

South London by an early example of the liturgical movement: St Mary Camberwell of 1961–2 by *Robert Potter*, a Greek-cross plan, generously glazed. An alternative aesthetic is that of *David Bush*'s St John Peckham (1965–6), a dimly lit interior (with good stained glass by *Susan Johnson*). This church has quite a dramatic exterior profile, a feature also of the same architect's St Matthew Croydon (1965–72). From this period onwards R. C. churches also claim attention, especially two forceful, ingeniously planned buildings by *Williams & Winkley*: St Margaret 108 Twickenham (1968) and St Elphege Beddington (1971).

From churches we can turn to the temples of Mammon. There is nothing to commend among the relatively few COMMERCIAL BUILDINGS which sprang up in South London once building restrictions had been lifted in 1954. They make a poor show along the magnificent site provided by the Albert Embankment. The stodgy Shell building (by *Sir Howard Robertson*) tries harder, but fails to do justice to the South Bank, and the brasher offices which unexpectedly, a few years later, transformed Croydon almost overnight into a mini-Manhattan are not much better. The 1960s has left its mark more impressively in the other suburbs which were affected by the rush to build out-of-town offices, notably at Catford, Sutton, Bromley, and Sidcup, which all sport towers by *Owen Luder*, where the brutalist style is displayed with energy and panache. Large shopping precincts appear from the later 1960s (e.g. at Catford and the Whitgift Centre, Croydon, both pleasantly laid out, and (as part of a G.L.C. redevelopment) at Lambeth Walk); covered shopping malls a little later (undistinguished at Wandsworth, rather better done at Lewisham). The fancifully detailed red brick Bishops Palace House, Kingston (*Raymond Spratley & Partners*), completed in 1979, reflects the praiseworthy concern of the 1970s to make large offices and shops acceptable in a historic area (expressed here a little too self-consciously). Apart from these one can note two very different buildings which make original contributions: the handsome Nasmith House at Tower Bridge (*J. D. Ainsworth & Associates*, 1974), cleverly making use of the foundations of St John Horselydown; and *Foster Associates*' eye-catching warehouse in the industrial plains of Thamesmead.

A trend of the 1970s is the way in which offices of a city scale and quality began to creep from the riverside into the hinterland further s: the tall, elegant Southwark Towers at London Bridge (by *T. P. Bennett & Son*), the overpowering but well detailed cluster opposite Waterloo Station (*Fitzroy Robinson & Partners*), and, down Lambeth High Street, *L. de Soissons Partnership*'s lower Pharmaceutical Society Headquarters. The riverside itself has been almost totally transformed in the last thirty years. It is an indictment of modern methods of planning and development as much as of modern architecture that among the commercial buildings there is so little to inspire the spectator on the opposite bank. The most encouraging area, for which one can still have some hopes, is the stretch of Battersea from Vauxhall Cross to Nine Elms.

A final note on SCULPTURE IN PUBLIC PLACES. *Henry Moore*'s noble reclining figure in front of the towers of the Brandon Estate reflects the idealistic aims of the post-war L.C.C.; Lambeth Council has continued the policy in a modest way (Walcot Square, Upper Norwood Library). Outside St Thomas' Hospital is a more remote giant abstract after a design by *Naum Gabo*, on the South Bank a more mixed collection. Apart from these the parks are the most worthwhile hunting grounds: Dulwich and Greenwich with works respectively by *Hepworth* and *Moore*, and Battersea, which has another abstract by *Hepworth* and the first major piece of post-war outdoor sculpture: *Moore*'s Three Standing Figures of 1947–8.

PREHISTORIC AND ROMAN ARCHAEOLOGY

BY JOANNA BIRD

The founding of London shortly after the Roman invasion of A.D. 43 established a focus for trade, government, and general human activity which has been growing and changing almost continuously ever since. This growth has obscured much of the natural landscape of the area, and it is difficult now to see that Greater London actually incorporates parts of several distinct regions. Earlier patterns of settlement have been largely destroyed, and much of our knowledge of London's archaeology is dependent on chance finds and imprecise records, and on comparison with more fortunate areas. Even those parts – mainly in the outer boroughs – where information does survive are under constant threat from building, and modern archaeological effort is almost completely devoted to 'rescue' work.

Despite the problems, however, it is still possible to draw some general conclusions about the occupation of the area during prehistoric and Roman times from the distribution of finds and settlement sites. During the Palaeolithic and Mesolithic periods, light woodland and river banks were favoured for their game, fowl, fish, and fresh water; the presence of flint for tools may also have had an influence. From the Neolithic onwards, the need was for soils that could be easily cleared and farmed using primitive implements, with good drainage and abundant water supply: the light soils over gravels (notably in West London) and along the springline of the North Downs were consistently chosen, while the intractable and densely forested London Clay was as consistently avoided.

Several features of London's archaeology are of particular importance, and are discussed in more detail below. Briefly, they include the wealth of Lower Palaeolithic material, the presence of what must have been a major Late Bronze Age industrial centre, and the evidence for some of the earliest Saxon settlements in England; while the Thames in West London has produced a range and quantity of Bronze and Iron Age metal-work that is without parallel.

Now for GEOLOGY. The basic shape of Greater London's landscape is formed by a fold in the Chalk, which has produced ridges to N (the Chilterns) and S (the North Downs), and left a wide basin in the centre through which the Thames now flows. Much of the Chalk has been subsequently covered by later geological deposits, producing a variety of soils and surface cover. The first, consisting of a series of sand, clay, and pebble beds, which provide relatively light soils of varying utility where they reach the surface, occur mainly in SE London, and there is a springline at the junction with the Chalk. The London Clay, deposited subsequently by a warm sea, forms much of the land surface, notably in N Middlesex and across the centre of the southern portion. It is heavy and impermeable, and naturally carries dense forest. In places it is overlain by sands mixed with clay and pebbles, which form a dry light soil with springs at the junction with the clay: Hampstead and Highgate in North London are instances of this. The most recent geological deposits consist of gravels, mainly laid down during the later Ice Ages. In particular, the wanderings of the Thames have deposited a complex series of gravel terraces, forming a broad band beside the modern course of the river. Springs occur at the junction with the Clay, and light, easily worked soils are produced; the upper levels of the gravels are often a clay-like loam ('brick-earth'), naturally wooded but not difficult to clear.

The area is roughly divided by the Thames, and a major feature is the number of smaller rivers draining into it from N and S; those in the central area, such as the Fleet, have now been led into the artificial drainage system. The presence of these rivers and the flatness of the river basin has meant that much of the area bordering the Thames is naturally marshy: places such as Southwark, Lambeth, and Westminster, and large tracts of East London, would not have been habitable until relatively recently. In these areas, the river gravels are overlain by silts. Southwark was first drained during the Roman period, and the problem of securing London from flooding continues to exercise the authorities today.

The earliest traces of human activity in Greater London belong to the PALAEOLITHIC (Old Stone Age), ranging from 450,000 to 12,000 B.C. This was also the period of the later Ice Ages, and it is unlikely that the area was continuously habitable. The wide variations of climate during and between the glacia-tions are reflected in the animal remains: those of cave bear, mammoth, and reindeer bear witness to arctic and sub-arctic conditions, those of the hippopotamus to hot conditions. The archaeology of this immense period is complicated by the con-temporary geology. The course and depth of the Thames varied considerably, and a series of gravel terraces was laid down by the river: their number, sequence, and chronology are not yet fully understood, and it is from them that most of the Palaeolithic finds have come.

The Palaeolithic can be broadly divided into three phases, distinguished by the types of tools in use: they are the Lower (450,000–100,000 B.C.), with flint axes and crude flint flakes; the Middle (100,000–40,000 B.C.), with more advanced flake tools; and the Upper (40,000–12,000 B.C.), with fine flint blades (it is to this last phase that the painted caves of France and Spain belong). Almost all the material in Greater London comes from the Lower Palaeolithic; the few Middle Palaeolithic finds probably represent the debris of brief hunting sorties, while there is no certain Upper Palaeolithic material. The Upper Palaeolithic coincided with the last Ice Age, and it is probable that the area, lacking natural shelters such as caves, was uninhabitable.

Some of the most important Lower Palaeolithic sites in Europe lie along the Lower Thames Valley, and some of the richest are within Greater London: at Yiewsley–West Drayton (Hi), Ealing–Acton (Ea), Stoke Newington (Hc), and Crayford (Bx). Other concentrations occur in the West End, at Wandsworth, and along the springline of the North Downs. These sites would have been the camps of small hunting communities, and animal remains have been found with tools at Southall (Ea), Kings Cross (Ca), and Stoke Newington (Hc). Acton, Stoke Newington, and Crayford have produced evidence, in the form of flint waste, for the manufacture of implements. Other evidence is fragmentary and tantalizing: a few birch stakes woven with clematis and fern, perhaps a shelter, from Stoke Newington, and burnt stones, possibly from a hearth, at West Drayton.

The MESOLITHIC (Middle Stone Age), c. 12,000–4,000 B.C., followed the last glaciation, and for much of the period Britain was still joined to the Continent. Initial sub-arctic or tundra conditions were succeeded by forest, and the climate became warmer and wetter; arctic fauna were replaced by forest animals such as boar and deer. The typical tools of the period are small neatly worked flint 'microliths', made to be mounted in bone or wooden shafts as hunting and fishing weapons, saws, and scrapers. Heavy flint axes ('Thames picks'), antler hammers, and tools of bone (e.g. harpoons) were also produced. There are a number of known settlements where hunters and fishers had their camps, including sites where flint waste indicates working, and one site, at Twickenham (Ri), where a midden of shells and tools was found. The main areas of occupation lie beside rivers, on the less heavily wooded soils, and along the springline of the North Downs, including Hampstead Heath (Ca), Harefield Moor (Hi), Ham Fields (Ri), Wimbledon Common (Me), and Putney Heath (Ww).

The NEOLITHIC (New Stone Age), c. 4,000–1,800 B.C., saw the introduction of agriculture and pastoralism, which spread gradually from the Near East and the Balkans and reached Britain during the fourth millennium. The process must have been slow, with a considerable overlap between old hunter-gatherer and new farmer. Some at least of the Neolithic settlements would have been the permanent homes of farmers, who would for the first time have begun to change their environment by clearance and by sowing and stock-rearing. In the London area, most of the known Neolithic settlement is concentrated on easily drained and worked soils, the gravels of West London and the sands along the springline of the Downs, where water and flint were abundant. Settlements include Putney (Ww), Twickenham (Ri), Brentford (Ho), Rainham (Hv), and Baston Manor (near Hayes, Bm); some have also produced flint-working debris. Flint tools were modified to new needs (e.g. sickles), and a characteristic axe type, of polished stone or flint, was in use: some of these were traded considerable distances, and the London area has produced axes originating in the Lake District and the Alps. A further innovation at this period was pottery; despite its technical crudity – it was hand-made, and probably fired in bonfires – distinct forms and decorative styles can be recognized. A quantity of Neolithic pottery indicates a further settlement at Kingston (Ki).

In addition to settlements, there are more substantial monuments of the Neolithic, of which there are unfortunately very few traces within Greater London. The causewayed camps, of which there is a possible example at East Bedfont (Ho), were ditched enclosures with access causeways, and probably served a social and religious purpose. Another typical Neolithic monument was the cursus – a long, straight earthwork distinguished by two parallel banks and ditches – for which a ritual use is generally suggested. Part of the cursus has been identified running northwards across the western end of Heathrow (Hi); it was at least 3.6 km long. The characteristic burial rite was inhumation beneath a long, gently wedge-shaped 'long barrow': this might contain galleries, chambers, or simple burials, of considerable variety, and was normally flanked by a ditch from which the mound had been excavated. Only the Queen's Butt, on Wimbledon Common (Me), is a serious candidate for a long barrow in London, and must, if genuine, have been altered in more recent times.

The main feature of the BRONZE AGE, c. 1,800–600 B.C., was the introduction of metals, first copper and later bronze. The metals had to be imported, copper from Wales or Ireland and tin from Cornwall, and implements were made by casting in clay or stone moulds. Imports of metal objects bear witness to trade with the Continent, probably carried along the Thames. Flint and stone continued to be of importance, particularly for heavy agricultural tools for which bronze was unsuitable. Few settlement sites are known – e.g. Hayes Common (Bm) and Heathrow (Hi) – but concentrations of finds indicate a similar pattern to that of the Neolithic. A group of stone hut circles once visible on Wimbledon Common may have been of this date. Bronze Age burials were placed beneath a round barrow, one of which has been excavated at Teddington (Ri); there are a number of other possibilities, notably the mound on Parliament Hill (Ca) and King Henry VIII Mount in Richmond Park. Late Bronze Age cremations, placed in a pottery urn, were sometimes buried in a stone chest beneath a barrow or inserted (like the secondary burial at Teddington) in an older barrow. The latest rite was to bury groups of urns together, and some evidence for such urnfields comes from Yiewsley (Hi), Acton (Ea), Kingsbury (Br), Coombe (Ki), and Ham Common (Ri).

Two features of the Bronze Age in the London area are of outstanding interest. One is the high number of Late Bronze Age smiths' hoards (broken implements, copper ingots) found along the edge of the North Downs; these indicate a major metalworking industry in the area, probably trading its goods over considerable distances. The second is the enormous quantity of Middle and Late Bronze Age metalwork recovered from the Thames, mainly in West London. This cannot at present be accounted for as debris from riverside settlements: although there are very likely to be unknown sites – notably in the area of Old England, Brentford (Ho) – much of this metalwork is likely to represent ritual or funerary offerings to the river deity.

The IRON AGE, c. 600 B.C.–A.D. 43, saw the introduction of iron, a metal more easily obtained (e.g. from the Weald) and worked than bronze, and with wider uses. Another innovation, later in the period, was currency, in the form both of metal bars and of coinage. Continuing trade with the Continent is shown by imported goods, including fine wheel-made and kiln-fired pottery and Mediterranean luxury items such as wine and silverware. The most notable monuments of the period are its 'hillforts' (not necessarily on hills), some at least of which were probably first constructed in the Late Bronze Age. They were enclosed by single or multiple bank and ditch defences, and vary widely in complexity and sophistication. The best surviving examples in Greater London are the two 'Caesar's Camps', at Keston (Bm) and Wimbledon (Me); more fragmentary ones are known at Enfield (Bush Hill), Carshalton (Su) (Queen Mary's Hospital), and Hadley Wood (Bn). Settlement sites follow the pattern of preceding periods, with concentrations along the North Downs and in the w (notably at East Bedfont, Ho). The site at Heathrow Airport (Hi) included a temple, and there may also have been a shrine at Hounslow (Ho). Many settlements formerly classed as Iron Age have now been reassessed as Romano-British: the distinction is often difficult with small rural sites of the first centuries B.C./A.D., in the absence of distinctive pottery. To this group belong the sites at Charlton (Gr) and Old Malden (Ki), and a number in the Cray valley, as well as the only surviving ancient field system, on Farthing Down (Cr). As in the Bronze Age, there is a concentration of metalwork from the Thames in West London, and it includes some of the finest from Britain: the Battersea shield and the Waterloo helmet, both now in the British Museum, are among the best known pieces.

The ROMAN invasion of A.D. 43 and the founding of Londinium shortly afterwards affected the settlement pattern of the
area considerably. A system of major roads radiating from the
city to the military and civil centres of the province attracted new
villages, and there is some evidence for activity in the areas of the
London Clay, although the main rural pattern continued to
follow that of earlier periods. Apart from Londinium, there was
an important suburb at Southwark, and there must have been a
bridge across the Thames on the approximate site of Old London Bridge. Southwark began as a settlement of small clay and
timber buildings laid beside the road to the bridgehead, but was
later occupied by more spacious stone buildings, including one
beneath the cathedral. There is evidence for at least two stone
buildings at Westminster, including the abbey site. Large
cemeteries lay outside these centres, notably in Bloomsbury (Ca)
and Aldgate (*London 1*), and along the roads to the SE. Settlements include Brentford (Ho) on the Silchester road, Brockley
Hill (Bn) (possibly the Sulloniacae named in the later Roman
Antonine Itinerary) on the Verulamium (St Albans) road,
Enfield and Edmonton (En) on the Lincoln road, Old Ford (TH)
where the Colchester road crossed the Lea, and Crayford (Bx)
(probably Noviomagus) on the Dover road, with further probable sites at Croydon on the Lewes road and Merton on the
Chichester road. Settlements at Putney (Ww) and Fulham (HF)
must have served a river crossing, and many smaller roads with
farms and villages must have lain between the major routes; the
most densely occupied areas seem to have been the Cray valley
and the edge of the Downs. There is not a great deal of evidence
for villas, in the sense of large country houses with estates, but
there is some, notably at Keston (Bm), Beddington (Su),
Orpington (Bm), Wanstead (Re), and perhaps Leyton (WF). A
large building in Greenwich Park has produced a number of
fragmentary inscriptions, and was probably a temple of some
importance. A late Roman signal station, consisting of a square
stone tower within a ditched enclosure, has been excavated at
Shadwell (TH); it was probably part of the coastal defence
system of the C3 and C4. Industrial activity is represented by
two pottery sites, one at Brockley Hill (Bn) on a large scale,
exporting its wares as far as the military sites in Scotland and
Wales, and a more local one in Highgate Wood.

The earliest SAXON settlers (early C5 onwards) were probably
mercenary soldier-farmers, and their sites ring London to the S,
combining a reasonable closeness to the city with good agricultural land. No actual settlements are known, but cemeteries have
been found at Mitcham (Me), Beddington (Su), Croydon (Cr),
and Orpington (Bm). At the Battle of Crecganford (probably
Crayford, Bx), of A.D. 457, described in the Anglo-Saxon Chronicle, the Britons, officially abandoned by the Roman authorities
after A.D. 410, were defeated by the Saxons. Later (C6–7) pagan
barrows can still be seen in Greenwich Park and on Farthing
Down (Cr), and pagan settlements are also indicated in Middlesex by place-name evidence. The linear earthwork known as

Grim's Ditch, which runs across the borough of Harrow, is probably Saxon, and may be a defence against invaders from the north.

TIMBER-FRAMED BUILDINGS

BY MALCOLM AIRS

Given the lack of suitable building stone and the comparatively late exploitation of local brick earths, the vernacular or minor domestic architecture of the Greater London area (of which a surprising amount survives) is predominantly timber-framed. The carpentry traditions are those of south-eastern England, so that there is no evidence for fully cruck-framed buildings; moreover the decorative possibilities provided by the timbers of the wall-framing are discreetly observed, and – with the notable exception of the late C16 manor house at Southall (Ea) – there are none of the exuberant virtuoso displays characteristic of the western counties.

Apart from the handful of very early examples, the majority of surviving timber-framed buildings are comparatively modest in size and were built for the 'yeoman' class. The flimsier structures of their economic and social inferiors do not appear to have survived from before the C17 at the earliest and, similarly, the houses of most of their superiors are mainly represented by post-medieval buildings of brick.*

As to CARPENTRY TECHNIQUES, it is generally within the roof space that vernacular buildings have been least altered, and it is possible to follow the development of roof trusses in Greater London from about 1300 onwards. The earliest type so far identified can be reconstructed from the much-altered large barn at Manor Farm, Ruislip (Hi). All the main timbers are of uniform scantling and it originally had passing-braces with minimally jowled principal uprights. Of about the same date was the sole example of semi-base cruck construction, at Moor Hall Harefield (Hi), destroyed by fire in 1922 but recorded at the time by Sir John Summerson and identified by S. E. Rigold in a paper

*The dating of timber-framed buildings at a vernacular level is notoriously difficult and is more reliant on intuitive experience in the field than many investigators are prepared to admit. The relatively new scientific techniques of dendrochronology and radio-carbon dating have hardly been tested in the area and, consequently, it must be stressed that the dates that will be suggested are in many cases tentative and are largely based on theoretical concepts founded on the evolution of plan forms, roof trusses and joinery details. Fortunately, the combined documentary and structural research carried out by the Historic Buildings Division of the Greater London Council in the late 1960s and early 1970s has established a corpus of firmly dated buildings to give greater credence to such regional typological sequences than is often the case elsewhere.

published in 1965. Base crucks were an expensive and high-class device to clear the open hall of inconvenient aisle-posts, and an alternative method of achieving the same end can be seen at Headstone Manor House (Hw), where two massive parallel arch-braces rose from each principal post to support the tie-beam, which in turn supported the wall-plates in the position known as 'reversed assembly'. Headstone, built shortly after 1344 as the principal Middlesex residence of the Archbishop of Canterbury, contains the earliest crown-post roof so far dis-covered in the region. By 1399 this roof form had filtered suf-ficiently down the social scale to be employed by New College, Oxford, when they built a chaplain's house at Hornchurch (Hv) (demolished in 1970 following a fire; part of the framework has been preserved in the Passmore Edwards Museum), and throughout the following century it was the most common roof truss at yeoman level. Examples abound throughout the region and include East End Farm Cottage Pinner (Hw); the Cross Keys Dagenham (Bk); The Tudors and No. 33 Halfway Street Sidcup (Bx); and No. 161 Crofton Lane Orpington (Bm). In an urban context, crown-post roofs survive at No. 39 High Street Kingston (Ki) and the Church House in Romford Market Place (Hv), and a particularly majestic and plain version is preserved in the important barn attached to Upminster Hall (Hv).

The only form of longitudinal stability above wall-plate level in a crown-post roof was supplied by the central collar-plate, and the next step in the refinement of carpentry techniques, at least on the w and n w edges of the London area, seems to have been the transference of that strength to either side of the roof by means of side-purlins. Such a device was economical of timber and labour in that it was no longer necessary to provide collars for all the common rafters, yet at the same time it opened up a new area for decorative effect, with curving wind-braces rising from the principal rafters to triangulate and support the purlins. It first appears, probably in the early part of the c 15, at the great barn at Manor Farm, Harmondsworth (Hi), which was possibly built by carpenters imported from Winchester. The central post of each truss, devoid of its collar-plate, is here known as a lower king-strut, and the side-purlins are butted into the principal rafters (fig. 1). Although other examples exist in comparatively modest hall-houses in Edgware High Street (Bn), it was never widespread throughout the region, and the crown-post roof retained its popularity into the c 16.

The roof truss which superseded it and which was destined to remain the most common type until the disappearance of indige-nous carpentry traditions in Greater London was the queen-strut roof with through-purlins clasped in the angles between the collar and the principal rafters. This was a logical development from the lower king-strut roof and, similarly, first seems to appear in one of the larger barns in Middlesex, which again could well have been constructed by carpenters who came from outside the county. The barn at Headstone Manor (Hw) can be dated to shortly before 1535 and was built with arch-braced

Fig. 1. Lower king-strut with through purlins

tie-beams and queen-struts rising to the collars. It differed from the developed form of the truss only in the use of a double row of butt-purlins on each side of the roof. By the second half of the C 16, through-purlins had become the adopted norm, and the dated examples include the modest three-bay barn at Smith's Farm Northolt (Ea) of 1595 and the curiously hybrid trusses at No. 2 Bickley Road Bromley (Bm), which are almost certainly contemporary with its brick gateway dated 1599. Queen-strut roofs were almost universal in the area in the C 17 and C 18 and examples are too numerous to mention individually. Towards the end of the tradition the queen-struts tended to be set at an angle rather than on a vertical plane, and dated examples include the barn at Orange Court, Downe (Bm), with much re-used medieval timber and joggled butt-purlins, of 1779, and the demolished barn of 1809 at Coldharbour Farm, Hayes (Hi). The introduction of softwood roof trusses with king-posts and straight raking braces joined by metal straps of the types familiar from such contemporary pattern books as William Salmon's *Palladio Londinensis* (1734), Peter Nicholson's *The Carpenter's New Guide* (1792), and Batty Langley's *The City and Country Builder's and Workman's Treasury of Designs* (1745), marked the beginning of the end for local craft traditions in roof carpentry.

The earliest surviving MEDIEVAL PLAN FORM in English vernacular architecture is the aisled hall. A few examples are known from the Greater London area, albeit in a fairly fragmentary state. At the highest social level the form was already obsolete by the mid C 14; thus the Archbishop of Canterbury's manor house at Headstone (Hw) was exploring ways of liberating the hall space from aisle-posts whilst incorporating conventional aisled construction in the closed trusses in *c.* 1345. Elucidation of the complete original form of this building awaits archaeological investigation, but the two-storeyed service wing aligned at right-angles to the hall and containing the entrance passage survives intact. At Hornchurch Chaplaincy (Hv) in 1399, at what might be termed 'gentry' level, the aisled hall was still a principal feature of the building. Here, only the cross-wing at the upper end of the hall survived, but there was sufficient structural evidence left to identify the aisled form of the hall trusses.

Neither of these two c 14 houses was complete at the time of investigation, but by the c 15 hall-houses survive in increasing numbers, and it is possible to categorize them according to their original form. Many are comparatively modest yeomen houses with two-bay halls and ancillary accommodation arranged in a variety of ways. The grander examples, concentrated mainly in the E, have a central hall flanked by two-storeyed wings roofed at right-angles to the hall and with the upper storeys on the entrance front invariably jettied (fig. 2). They include the Cross Keys public house in Crown Street Dagenham (Bk); Great Tomkyns, Upminster (Hv); Turpingtons, Southborough Lane, Southborough (Bm); The Ancient House, Church Lane, Walthamstow (WF); and another public house, the Spotted Dog, No. 212 Upton Lane, Forest Gate (Ne). A slightly smaller variation on this theme was provided with only a single cross-wing, as at No. 161 Crofton Lane Orpington (Bm). But at the typically yeoman level, the accommodation of open hall, screens passage, service rooms, parlour, and two upper chambers were all neatly arranged under a single unitary roof in a form common throughout south-eastern England (fig. 3). Good examples can be seen in Sidcup (Bx) (The Tudors, with a hall of only one bay, and No. 33 Halfway Street), Pinner (Hw) (East End Farm Cottage), and West Drayton (Hi) (the King William IV public house, Sipson Road). When the upper-storey 'wings' of the unitary hall-house were jettied, the centre of the building defining the hall inevitably gave the appearance of being recessed behind the common wall-plate; there are examples of this so-called 'Wealden' type both s (Nos. 1–4 Tudor Cottages, Foots Cray High Street, Bx) and N (The Old Cottage, Cowley Road, Cowley, Hi) of the River Thames (fig. 4). Other 'Wealdens' are known to have existed closer to the centre of London, as at the corner of Clayton Road and High Street, Peckham (Sk), pulled down in 1850, and it is possible that the origins of the design should be sought in the metropolis.

The declining importance of the open hall as the dominant and principal room in the house seems to have begun early in the c 16. The initial impetus apparently came from a desire for a greater number of smaller rooms and, perhaps, a changing emphasis towards making better use of the upper storey, rather than from any great dissatisfaction with the smoke and inconvenience of the open hearth. Certainly, in a number of cases the first stage in modernizing an existing medieval house in conformity with the changed social circumstances of the c 16 involved the flooring-over of only part of the hall and the retention

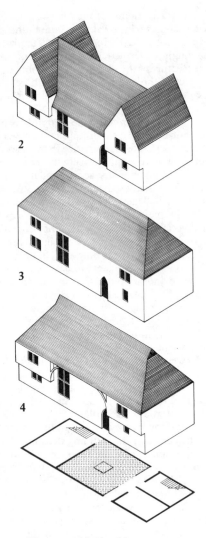

Figs. 2–4. Medieval house-types:
hall with flanking cross wings; unitary plan; Wealden type

of the open hearth in the remainder of the space. Usually, one
bay was floored over to provide an extra upper-storey room and a
gallery was contrived over the open bay, thus providing full
circulation between all the first-floor rooms for the first time.
The gallery and the new chamber over part of the hall were
protected from the infiltration of smoke by partitions, thus
effectively forming a smoke bay from the open hearth on the
ground floor up into the rafters of the roof. The arrangement is

best seen at East End Farm Cottage Pinner (Hw), where the partitions still survive for their full height and the upper part of the smoke bay has never been converted into a room. The obvious advantages of inserted brick chimneystacks to heat the house meant that the smoke bay was a fairly short-lived feature. However, innate conservatism ensured that new houses with smoke bays were being constructed as late as the end of the C 16 (No. 20A Waxwell Lane Pinner, Hw), and at No. 161 Crofton Lane Orpington (Bm) the open hearth in the partially floored-over hall was not finally abandoned until 1671. Conversely, the continuous-jettied Whitehall at Cheam (Su) appears to have been built with a chimneystack as an integral part of the design as early as *c.* 1500.

Now for POST-MEDIEVAL PLANS. With the exception of Headstone Manor House (Hw), all the medieval hall-houses in the area were fully floored-over and had had chimneystacks inserted during the course of the C 16 and C 17. And, of course, the same domestic pressures which had led to such radical alterations of existing buildings had evolved brand-new house types in the same period. As with the converted medieval houses, the basic requirement was to devise a way of providing a larger number of more specialized rooms with ease of access to the upper storeys and greater comfort in the form of heated rooms with enclosed fireplaces. The devastatingly simple answer was to put all the new service functions in a narrow bay at the centre of the house, leaving the remainder of the rectangular structure free for uncluttered domestic use. With a large chimneystack of four flues placed in the centre of the building, it was possible to heat the rooms individually on either side and on both floors, while still leaving sufficient space in the same bay to accommodate a staircase winding round the back of the stack and a small, draught-free entrance lobby at the front of the stack (fig. 5).

These lobby-entry houses – a common post-medieval type throughout lowland England – are represented in the Greater London area in substantial numbers. In their larger form they are generally asymmetrical, with a single bay to one side of the entrance stack and two bays beyond, as at Sweetman's Hall, Pinner (Hw). This meant that the rooms in the far bay were either unheated or required a separate chimneystack such as seems to be an original feature at No. 2 Bickley Road Bromley (Bm). This house can be dated to 1599, but it seems likely that the type had been established in the area for at least a generation before that. So effective was the concept that, particularly in its smaller two-bay symmetrical form with all the principal living rooms heated from a common stack, it remained a viable house design right down until the advent of central heating in the present century rendered its basic feature obsolete. Typical examples in Greater London include the three-bay vicarage in Crown Street Dagenham (Bk), dated 1665; the two-bay Maygoods Farm Cowley (Hi) of the early C 18; and the appealingly Gothick No. 25 Corkscrew Hill West Wickham

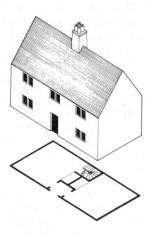

Fig. 5. Lobby entry

(Bm) of about a hundred years later. Examples in the London part of Surrey can be seen at Nos. 1 and 2 Church Road Cheam (Su) (incorporating the crown-post wing of an earlier structure) and at No. 210 Coulsdon Road Coulsdon (Cr).

Since the basic theme flourished over such a time-span, it is hardly surprising that there were a number of minor variations. Some of the early examples incorporated a porch with a small chamber above as an entrance feature, and by the late c 17 a lean-to scullery along the rear elevation had become an inevitable addition. Although the relationship between the axial chimneystack and the entrance was implicit in the definition of the design, the staircase was sometimes placed in front of the stack and opened directly onto the lobby, as at the Manor House in Manor Road Merton (Me); in other examples it was housed in a separate turret at the rear of the stack. Moreover, on a few occasions greater emphasis was placed on the principal ground-floor room by giving the bay that accommodated it the form of a cross-wing at right-angles to the remainder of the house, such as seems to have been the case at Nos. 33–35 Pinner High Street (Hw) and No. 226 Southborough Lane Southborough (Bm).

Of course, the lobby-entry plan was not the only house type that emerged in response to the changed domestic requirements of the post-medieval period, but none of the other types seems to me to have provided quite such a brilliantly simple response to the demand for draught-free warmth and comfort and first-floor bedrooms. Instead of an enclosed axial chimneystack generating radiant heat, the principal alternative plan had a chimneystack in each gable-end, similarly heating the four principal rooms, but with a certain amount of heat-loss through the outside walls and providing no structural support for the staircase (fig. 6). As a type, it seems to have evolved slightly later than the lobby-

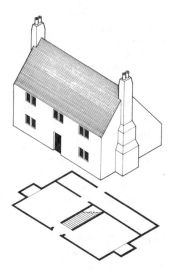

Fig. 6. Central entry with gable-end stacks and rear outshot

entrance house and was possibly inspired by a conscious desire for a fashionably symmetrical façade. At a time when brick was beginning to supersede timber, it had the advantage of integrating the stacks with the shell of the house. The staircase was invariably centrally placed in line with the entrance and was often of more generous proportions than the lobby-entry stair. Rear outshots, like that at Ashgrove Cottage, Chevening Lane, Knockholt (Kent) (just outside our area), and staircase-turrets, as at Windmill Farm, Stites Hill Road, Coulsdon Common (Cr), were common refinements. Humbler examples, such as No. 164 Sidcup Hill Foots Cray (Bx) and the Ramblers Rest public house in Chislehurst (Bm), had only a single gable-end chimneystack, leaving the bay on the opposite side of the central entrance unheated.

In form, the single gable-end stack house is identical to the true peasant cottage, one and a half storeys in height, surviving from the c 17 and c 18 elsewhere in the country, but few of the London examples seem to be small enough to postulate a direct link. Instead, the study of the housing of the vast mass of the population needs to be directed towards the lightly framed and weatherboarded buildings which survive in increasing numbers from the late c 17 onwards. They are found in most of the London boroughs and range in social stature from small, detached farmhouses, such as No. 5 Pike Lane Cranham, near Upminster (Hv) (with an interesting attached barn), through groups of semi-detached houses like those in Anglesea Road St Mary Cray (Bm), to the rows of humble terraces familiar in many of the outer suburbs. Some of them have aspirations of grandeur expressed by simple classical architectural detailing or the sham of a fashionable brick façade (Nos. 1–3 and 5–7 High Street Bexley and the imposing three-storeyed terrace dated 1737 at Nos. 4–8 Church Road, Foots Cray, Bx), but the majority are the genuine vernacular of the C 18 and C 19. They lie outside the hardwood carpentry traditions which have interested scholars over the past thirty years, but they are urgently in need of systematic investigation before their original arrangements irrevocably disappear under the heavy hand of the improver.

In a survey of this nature, it is only possible to draw attention briefly to the overall picture of timber-framing in Greater London. Limitations of space preclude any detailed analysis of the regional differences apparent in the areas N and S of the river or the effect of London itself as a source of innovation. Specialized aspects, such as the magnificent late medieval barns in what were Middlesex (Ruislip, Hi, Harmondsworth, Hi, Headstone, Hw) and Essex (Upminster, Hv), or the imposing inns on the roads out of London (for example the Golden Lion Romford, Hv, and the White Hart Edgware, Bn) can only be mentioned in passing, while recognition of the problems of interpretation attached to buildings like the long jettied row at Nos. 57–65 Stanmore Broadway (Hw) must be sought in the *North West London* text.*

INDUSTRIAL ARCHAEOLOGY

BY MALCOLM TUCKER

London‡ has been a principal centre for all kinds of manufacturing for many centuries, but it is the services sector that provides the most interest: transport and public utilities, the infrastructure of a vast conurbation, capital city, and seaport.

For 1900 years, London owed its commercial pre-eminence to the tidal Thames bringing ships forty miles inland. Extensive Roman and medieval quay walls of timber have been excavated in the City. The import trade was restricted to such riverside quays§ until intolerable congestion and theft forced the estab-

---

*I would like to acknowledge my debt to John Ashdown, who first taught me the importance of London's vernacular architecture; to J. T. Smith, who over the years has discussed a number of individual buildings with me; to Frank Kelsall, who has always been prepared to pass on his unrivalled knowledge of London's buildings; and to Anthony Quiney and Bob Weston, in whose stimulating company much of the fieldwork was carried out.

‡South London and North London are here treated together.

§The larger ships were obliged to moor in mid river, and sent their goods ashore in lighters. Wet docks had been built in the one-time shipbuilding areas downriver from the mid C 17, e.g. the Howland Great Wet Dock (*c.* 1697–9) at Rotherhithe (Sk), but these were fitting-out basins and not permitted to handle dutiable cargoes.

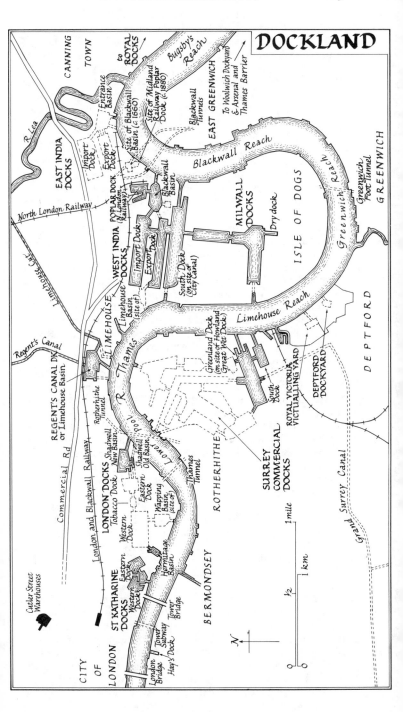

lishment of the first ENCLOSED DOCKS, the West India (1799–1806), the London (1800–5), and the East India (1803–6) (all in TH). They were enterprises of great magnitude. Rows of large, multi-storey bonded warehouses were set back behind brick-built quays, within the security of high boundary walls. Vaults for wines and spirits were provided below quay level in some cases. Ships carrying 1,000 tons could berth in water impounded at a constant level by locks and pumping engines, while entrance basins, in which the water level might vary, were provided to speed entry and exit in the busy period around high water. The St Katharine Docks (TH) (1825–8) saved space with warehouses on the edges of the quays on magnificent colonnades. Meanwhile, from 1802, on the South Bank the Surrey Docks had developed on a more open pattern for less valuable goods.

The age of railways and steamships created docks on a new scale, from the Royal Victoria (1850–5) to the King George V (1912–21). With an emphasis on rapid transit, they were no longer dominated by multi-storey warehouses. In 1909, the Port of London Authority brought public ownership and finance. But recently, trade has largely deserted London for Tilbury (established 1882) and ports nearer the sea. Most of the early docks closed in the 1960s, the West India and Millwall followed in 1980 despite considerable C20 investment, and, finally, the Royal group of docks closed in 1981. Demolitions have taken a heavy toll of warehouses, which had already suffered badly in the Second World War, and specimens of historical features are now scattered.

The riverside WHARVES have also declined dramatically since the late 1960s, when both banks of the Thames from Blackfriars to Limehouse and Rotherhithe were still lined almost continuously with warehouses, mainly of the C19. Some of their former character remains in Wapping and, on the south side, in Rotherhithe, Clink Street, Tooley Street and the neighbour-
2 hood of St Saviour's Dock and Shad Thames, the latter the most intact, with some of the densest warehousing of the late C19 at Butler's Wharf (Sk). More open wharves typify the lower river, notably at Greenwich.

Among the earliest of surviving WAREHOUSES in the port are the pair of 1795 at Free Trade Wharf Limehouse, internally gutted, and the remnant of the former G Warehouse of c. 1800 at the St Katharine Docks. They are of four storeys with steeply-pitched roofs; also the Rum Stores of 1781–9 at Deptford Vic-tualling Yard (Le) and the remaining façades (1770 and 1792) of the East India Company's great Cutler Street warehouses in the City (*London 1*). Their proportions are Georgian. More typical of riverside warehouses of the early C19 are the two- to four-storey buildings at Rotherhithe (Sk). Away from the river are some interesting buildings in the Bermondsey leather district (Sk). Slate roofs of shallow pitch soon became general, concealed behind parapets, with timber trusses sometimes of 50 ft or more span. Those of 65 ft at Whitbread's Brewery Finsbury (Is) (1784), are particularly wide. Cast-iron window frames, broader than tall, appeared at the West India Docks in 1802. A giant arcade motif of pilaster strips supporting round-headed arches was used at the St Katharine Docks in 1828 (by *Hardwick*) and became popular, often embellished with stucco after 1850 as at Hay's Wharf, Tooley Street (Sk) (1856), where two tiers of arcades are used. Gothic styles were used very occasionally, e.g. at Olivers Wharf Wapping (TH) (1870).

INTERNAL TIMBER CONSTRUCTION was usual in warehouses and related buildings in London until well past 1800, with brick external and dividing walls for the containment of fire. But bonded warehouses of four to seven storeys were found to require columns of cast iron, first seen in some of the Cutler Street warehouses around 1799 (*London 1*; demolished), the London Dock South Stacks (1806–11; demolished), and No. 2 Warehouse at West India (replacing timber stanchions in 1814). But timber columns were still used in granaries in Bermondsey (Sk) in the late C 19, and timber floors predominated until *c.* 1900, usually on wooden beams and cruciform-section cast-iron columns. Brick jack-arches were seen rarely (except in basements) before *c.* 1850, and the wholly incombustible construction of I Warehouse at St Katharine's (1858–60) is untypical, while the alternation of timber and brick floors at Hay's Wharf (1856) etc.) illustrates a delicate compromise between higher costs of construction and the risk of the spread of fire.

In other aspects of construction there has been abundant scope for new techniques. Early use was made of IRON ROOFS. The remarkable branching columns supporting the timber roofs of the London Dock Skin Floor (1811–13) mark a transitional phase. Cast-iron trusses and arched beams, and prototype wrought-iron trusses, were used in the West India Docks in 1813 (demolished). In the Woolwich Dockyard Smithery (Gr) of *c.* 1818 (dismantled), a remarkably mature truss design combined wrought and cast iron. Another early iron roof covers the riding school at Syon Park (Ho), next to *C. Fowler*'s splendid conservatory of 1827–30. Less sophisticated trusses wholly of wrought-iron flats survive at Kew Bridge Waterworks (Ho) (1837). The first iron-trussed train-shed roofs, at Euston (Ca) (1837), have gone.* Corrugated iron was developed in London *c.* 1830 for lightweight roof structures, but early examples have perished. Rolled wrought-iron I-sections were introduced by *Turner* in the remarkable Kew Palm House (Ri) (1844–8) which 78 happily survives. The Crystal Palace of 1851 (destroyed) demonstrated wholly-rectilinear multi-storey iron framing, and mass production. Of the great wrought-iron-arched train sheds, the finest architecturally is Paddington (Wm) (1854) and the largest St Pancras (Ca) (1867). Roofs of the Royal Agricultural Hall (Is) (1862), the Temperate House at Kew (Ri) (1863), the Royal

---

*Fowler's Hungerford Fish Market of 1835 (*London 1*; demolished) foreshadowed railway structures of a later era with its cast-iron 'butterfly' cantilever roofs.

Albert Hall (KC) (1871), and Olympia (HF) (1886) deserve mention.

Arch ribs of laminated TIMBER, as once used for the roofs of King's Cross Station (Ca) (1852), survive in a former gymnasium (1866) off St Pancras Road. Fabricated timber appears again in the early aircraft hangars at Hendon aerodrome (Bn) (c. 1914 and 1917). The first British building with a frame of STEEL was the Ritz Hotel (1903–6; *London 1*), though this was foreshadowed by Tower Bridge (Sk) (1886–94).

CONCRETE, made with lime mortar, was first used in quantity in 1817 by *Sir Robert Smirke*, for the foundations of the Millbank Penitentiary (*London 1*; demolished). Fireproof floors of concrete on iron joists appear in the 1840s, e.g. for model dwellings as at Streatham Street, Holborn (Ca) (1849). Concrete faced with brickwork was used for quay walls in the docks from the 1850s. Subsequent improvements in the manufacture of Portland cement allowed concrete to be exposed externally without facings of brick or stucco, in particular for the first mass-concrete bridge in Britain, near Earl's Court (KC) (1867, demolished 1873), for quay walls at the Royal Albert Dock (1875–80), for the New Church at Anerley (Bm) (1883), and for a number of domestic buildings (e.g. The Halsteads, East Sheen (Ri), 1868, and, in a pre-cast system, at Gloucester Road and Sydenham Road, Croydon (Cr), 1875).

REINFORCED CONCRETE was used as early as 1899 for a railway warehouse at Brentford Dock (Ho) (demolished), but gained ground slowly. In inner London it was hampered by building regulations until 1916. The new Port of London Authority adopted it with increasing boldness for jetties and transit sheds (London Docks 1912 (demolished), West India 1914, Royal Albert 1917, King George V 1921). The silos at Erith Oil 99 Works (Bx) (1916) and the girder bridge at New North Road, Shoreditch (Hc) (c. 1917), are mature designs. Thereafter use of reinforced concrete becomes more routine, but the Wembley Exhibition (Br) (1924), the Royal Horticultural Hall (1926; *London 1*), and the Wrigley factory at Wembley (1927) are some notable applications of the 1920s.

The C 18 and early C 19 saw a remarkable flourish of BRIDGES on the Thames (*see* section on Thames Crossings). *Labelye's* Westminster Bridge (1738–49) opened a new chapter in British masonry bridge design, and *Robert Mylne's* Blackfriars Bridge (1760–9) introduced architectural elegance. There followed, among others, *Rennie's* Waterloo Bridge (1811–17) and London Bridge (1823–31) in stone, his Southwark Bridge (1814–19) in cast iron with an immense 240 ft central span, and suspension bridges by *Tierney Clark* at Hammersmith (1824–7) and *I. K. Brunel* at Hungerford Bridge (1841–5). Alas, all of these have 68 gone. Upstream there are the handsome Richmond Bridge (1774–7) and its simpler neighbour at Kingston. At Barnes, the cast-iron-arched railway bridge is of 1846–9. The transition to wrought iron is represented on the Thames by the Westminster Bridge of 1854–62, the curiously retrospective Battersea Rail-

way Bridge, and the excellent wrought-iron-trussed railway
bridges of the 1860s at Charing Cross and Blackfriars.* Blackfriars (road), Albert, Hammersmith, and Tower Bridges are
splendid examples of Victorian elaboration. Best of the c 20 are
Kew, Twickenham, Chelsea, Waterloo, Wandsworth, and the
latest London Bridge.

The problems of crossing the Thames and the densely built-
up city have prompted major advances in the art of TUNNEL-
ING. *Sir Marc Brunel* employed the first tunneling shield for his
heroic Thames Tunnel (1825–43). At greater depth, in the
impermeable London clay, the Tower Subway (1869) proved
the worth of the Greathead shield and cast-iron segmental linings, later used so extensively for the 'tube' railways. These
techniques were combined with the use of compressed air in the
water-bearing strata of the first Blackwall Tunnel (1891–7),
while more sophisticated methods, e.g. of ground consolidation,
have been used in the c 20 where tube extensions have encoun-
tered water. The Thames–Lee Water Main Tunnel (1955–9) (*see*
Hampton, Ri) introduced the rotary drum digger and expanded
segmental linings of unreinforced concrete. In contrast, the
earlier underground railways and trunk sewers of the 1860s were
mainly of cut-and-cover construction; particularly dramatic are
the Metropolitan Railway s of King's Cross and the East London
Railway.

London is well endowed with NAVIGABLE RIVERS. The
River Lee (or Lea) was among the first in England to be artificially improved – from the c 13; not until the 1770s, however, was
its navigation reconstructed on 'modern' lines with lateral cuts
and pound locks, while the navigation weirs on the Thames, at
Teddington and Richmond (Ri), are later still. CANALS arrived
fairly late, with the Grand Junction (Grand Union) from 1796
and the Grand Surrey of 1801–10.‡ They were generally 'broad',
for river barges. The Regent's Canal (1812–20) is of special
character, passing the inner suburbs of Westminster, Camden,
and Islington, to link the Grand Junction Canal with the Docks.
It has good tunnels and bridges, particularly Macclesfield Bridge
in Regent's Park (Wm) (1816, on Doric columns) and the cast-
iron roving bridge (*c.* 1850) at Camden Town (Ca). The Grand
Union has another fine roving bridge (1820) above Brentford
(Ho), the three-level Windmill Bridge (1859) above Hanwell
locks (Ea), and the reinforced concrete aqueduct (*c.* 1933) at
Alperton (Br).

Canals suffered from the prior claims of mills to limited water
supplies. Hence the promotion of the first public RAILWAYS,
the horse-drawn Surrey Iron Railway of 1803 and its Croydon to
Merstham extension. Remains of these are now scanty. Steam-

*Earlier, more lightly constructed London examples of trussed railway bridges
have been replaced, except for the early Warren girders of 1850 under the London
Bridge Station approach (Sk).

‡London has also some of the last canals built in England, the abortive
Romford Canal (Bk) (1875), the Slough Arm (Hi) (1882), and Maypole Dock at
Southall (Ea) (1913).

STEAM RAILWAYS IN LONDON TO 1840

Company	Principal Act of Parliament	First section completed	Line completed
London & Greenwich	1833	1836	1838
London & Birmingham	1833	1837	1838
London & Southampton	1834	1838	1840
Great Western	1835	1838	1841 (to Bristol)
London & Croydon	1835	1839	1839
Eastern Counties	1836	1839	1849 (to Norwich)
Northern & Eastern	1836	1840	1845 (to Cambridge)
London & Blackwall	1836	1840	1841 (Fenchurch St)
London & Brighton	1837	1841	1841
West London (Birmingham, Bristol & Thames Junction)	1836	1844	(Willesden to Kensington)

hauled railways came to London in four phases – an early flurry in the 1830s with several trunk lines (*see* table), a period of consolidation in the 1840s and early 50s, a boom, especially s of the Thames, in the late 50s and 60s, and a culminating spread of suburban branches. No buildings survive of the first period except the Tudor station cottage at Anerley (Bm) (1839). The terminus at Euston (Ca) was demolished in 1962; its train sheds were the first with iron roofs, while its Doric entrance propy-laeum (1837) and great hall (1846) presented an unmatched monumentality. But we have three fine and individualistic early VIADUCTS, those of the London and Greenwich, the London and Blackwall, and, at Hanwell (Ea), *Isambard Kingdom Brunel's* Great Western; also Primrose Hill Tunnel, Camden, 1837 by *Robert Stephenson*, with an elaborate E portal.

Of the 1840s there are an Italianate STATION at North Wool-wich (Ne), a Tudor one at Barnes (Ri), and the iron-roofed Round House at Camden Town, of 1852 the elegant functional-ism of King's Cross Station (Ca) and a relatively intact goods station near by, and thereafter Paddington (Wm) (1854) and other termini of the first rank, and smaller stations, especially good in the 1860s s of the river. The ornate bridges of the Dulwich area (Sk) may be noted, and the architecture of the Longhedge railway works in Battersea (Ww) (1860 etc.). Multi-storeyed stables for road cartage services may be seen particu-larly at Camden Town (Ca) (*c.* 1855 etc) and Paddington (1878), and warehouses at King's Cross (1853) and Camden Town (*c.* 1900).

A parliamentary commission in 1846 decided that surface railways should not enter the central area, a policy slightly relaxed around 1860 when railways crossed the Thames from the s. The passenger termini therefore lie in a ring, linked by a circumferential UNDERGROUND RAILWAY at shallow depth (now called the Circle Line) of which the first section, the Metropolitan from Paddington to Farringdon Street, opened in 1863. The first 'tube' railway,* the City and South London, opened in 1890; the capabilities of deep tunnelling and electric traction then produced the network of deep underground lines which was effectively complete within the central area by 1914.

In the provision of services, WATER SUPPLY was the earliest concern. Conduits and wells, as at Clerkenwell (Is), served the urban area inadequately until the New River was cut from Hertfordshire, a remarkable endeavour of 1609–13. Early private supplies included those to Eltham Palace (Gr) and Hampton Court (Ri). The Duke of Northumberland's River in Hounslow (early c 16, for water power) and the Longford River (1638, for ornamental waters at Hampton Court, Ri) may also be noted. There are early reservoirs at Hampstead Heath (Ca). From 1581, an increasing proportion of London's water was pumped mechanically from the Thames; one of the earliest steam pumping stations (by *Savery*) was erected in the Strand in 1712. Filtration was developed at the Chelsea waterworks in 1823.

In the c 19, increasing river pollution began to drive the water companies up-stream, e.g. to Kew Bridge (Brentford, Ho) in 1837. All abstraction from the tidal waters below Teddington Weir was forbidden by the Metropolis Water Act of 1852, which also required filtration and the roofing of service reservoirs. This and the rapid expansion of the supply network prompted major new works in the 1850s and 1860s, as at Hampton (Ri). Under the Metropolitan Water Board (established 1903) there was further major investment, e.g. at Kempton Park and in reservoirs in the Lee valley.

Waterworks ENGINE HOUSES are among the capital's most notable industrial buildings. The earliest remaining, at New River Head, Finsbury (Is) (1767 and 1818), adapts classical conventions to functional requirements. At Kew Bridge (Ho), staid sub-Georgian of 1837 is followed by masculine Italianate of 1845. The manometer tower there (1867) is unmatched in size. More elaborate Italianate was best displayed at the demolished Lee Bridge works, Walthamstow (WF), and may be seen in the Bull engine tower (1864) at the Copper Mill Walthamstow, while further varieties survive at Hampton (Ri). The medievalism of Stoke Newington (Hc) (1856) and Shortlands (Bm) is more common in water towers. *W. B. Bryan*, the engineer to the East London Company and then, until 1914, of the M.W.B., cast aside the obligatory Italianate (e.g. of his Triples House at Lee Bridge, 1891) for a style of corbel tables, shapely roofs, and occasional half-timbering for the smaller pumping stations of the

*There had been earlier, unsuccessful schemes, particularly the Pneumatic Despatch Railway, built beneath the streets of St Pancras and Holborn, and *Peter Barlow*'s ideas for underground cable trams, for which he built the Tower Subway. The Atmospheric Railway (1844–6) at Croydon was a failure in a different context.

Lee valley. After 1900 he turned to classical mannerism, notably at Greaves, Chingford (WF) and King George V, Enfield. Croydon Corporation's Waddon (1910) follows an independent Arts-and-Crafts line. After the First World War, style degenerates, and then merges with the Georgian-modern of other public buildings.

For the MAIN DRAINAGE works of the 1860s, sewage pumping stations of exceptional grandeur were erected at Crossness, Belvedere (Bx) and Abbey Mills, Stratford (Ne), with interiors of ornate cast iron. To house the interceptor sewers along the shores of the Thames, the Victoria, Albert, and Chelsea EMBANKMENTS were created, while the Northern Outfall Sewer crosses the former marshes of Newham within an immense earthern bank. These were the foremost achievements of *Sir Joseph Bazalgette*, engineer of the Metropolitan Board of Works created in 1855 after the public health crises of the previous two decades.

HYDRAULIC POWER, i.e. the distribution of water under high pressure to work cranes, lifts, and similar equipment, was something of a speciality of London. From *c.* 1852 it spread rapidly throughout the docks and railway depots. An octagonal accumulator tower at the Regent's Canal Dock, Limehouse (TH), may be of this early date, while later, rectangular accumulator towers and pumping stations are still plentiful, although disused, e.g. at Hooper Square, Whitechapel (TH) (1886), Tower Bridge (Sk) (1894, one of the most impressive applications of hydraulic power), and several in Poplar (TH) and St Pancras (Ca). From 1883 until 1977, the London Hydraulic Power Company supplied premises throughout central London from its public mains, the world's largest system; two of its former pumping station buildings remain, at Wapping (TH) and Rotherhithe (Sk).

GASWORKS manufacturing from coal began in 1810 and thrived from the 1820s until 1970. Their masculine architecture of the C 19 has mostly vanished; there remains the vast C 20 plant 'mothballed' at Beckton (Ne). There are GASHOLDERS of special note at Fulham (HF) (*c.* 1830), St Pancras (Ca) (1860s), Bromley-by-Bow (Ne) (1870s), and East Greenwich (Gr) (1886 and 1891). Immense late C 19 iron COALING JETTIES remain at Beckton and East Greenwich.

ELECTRICITY supply started in 1878 in London, for the first electric-arc street lights, and grew rapidly in the 1890s. The earliest building surviving is at Kensington Court (KC) (1886); Ferranti's pioneering high-tension Deptford generating station (Gr) (1890) has been largely demolished. At Hoxton Square Shoreditch (Hc) (1897) is part of the first station successfully to combine electricity generation with refuse incineration. On the much larger scale of the new century, power stations for electric traction remain at Lots Road Chelsea (KC) (1902–5) and Greenwich (Gr) (1903–8). Bold architectural feeling is shown in the former L.C.C. tramways garage at Bow (TH) (1908), and its former transformer substations at Rivington Street Shoreditch

(Hc) and Upper Street Islington (Is).* A new brick style for the mid C 20 was created by *Sir Giles Gilbert Scott* at Battersea (Ww) 100 (commenced 1929), turning great bulk to architectural advantage. Fulham (HF) (1936), Croydon 'B' (Cr) (1939–50), Brunswick Wharf Poplar (TH) (1945–52), and Bankside Southwark (1950) followed. Many of these are now disused, and power stations have grown too large for urban sites; thus Belvedere (Bx) (1960) stands alone on the Erith marshes. At Edmonton (En) (1970) is Europe's largest REFUSE DESTRUCTOR.

Lastly, the 'productive' sectors of industry. Architectural evidence of former EXTRACTIVE INDUSTRIES includes chalk mines at Chislehurst (Bm) and Pinner (Hw), tile and pottery kilns preserved at Harrow Weald (Hw), North Kensington (KC), and Fulham (HF), and brick-kiln debris used decoratively for garden walls especially in Hornsey (Hy) and Southgate (En). More permanent have been products such as *Coade* stone, *Doulton* terracotta, general sanitary ware, and the ubiquitous pink or yellow London stock bricks.

SHIPBUILDING AND HEAVY ENGINEERING (in the riverside areas) were of national importance during the C 19, but have left little of architectural interest (*see* Deptford, Le, and Isle of Dogs, TH). The corresponding establishments of the NAVAL AND MILITARY authorities on the other hand were distinguished by their extensive and substantial construction. The Woolwich Arsenal (Gr) has buildings from the 1690s onwards, although much has recently been demolished; part of the former Woolwich Dockyard remains largely intact, including the great Steam Factory of 1844; rather less survives at the Deptford Dockyard and Victualling Yard (Le). The Royal Small Arms Factory at Enfield (En) (1854) is also far grander than any private enterprise of the period.

General industrial buildings from before 1850 are now scarce. The domestic scale of the C 18 is represented by the Whitechapel Bell Foundry and by the Spitalfields silk weavers' ATTIC WORKSHOPS (TH); similar C 19 provision for precision craftsmen survives in Clerkenwell (Is).

WINDMILLS are proportionately over-represented, with examples at Arkley (Bn), Upminster (Hv), Keston (Bm), Shirley (Cr), Wimbledon (Me), and Brixton (La). Of WATERMILLS, two very important survivors are the tide mills (1776 and 1817) at Three Mills on the Lee. Also of interest are the former Copper Mill at Walthamstow (WF), on the Lee, and the Snuff Mills at Morden (Me) and Calico Mill at Merton (Me), both on the Wandle. In 1805 there were thirty-eight factories within twelve miles on the Wandle. The paper and textile mill sites on the Cray (Bexley, Bx, Bromley, Bm), the gunpowder mill sites on the Crane (Hounslow, Ho, Twickenham, Ri), and former mills on the Colne (in Hillingdon borough) and other rivers are reminders of the once intense use of all available water power.‡

*The grandest power station of them all, Grove Road (Lodge Road) St John's Wood (Wm) of 1902–4 by *Peach* and *Reilly*, has been demolished.

‡The demand for flour prompted the early application of steam power to corn

Early C 19 FACTORIES were often grand, though rarely matching the scale of northern textile mills or the opulence of the Royal Mint (1811). Façades survive at No. 292 Essex Road Islington (Is) (1812), No. 201 St John's Street Clerkenwell (Is) (1828), Beaufoy's vinegar brewery, South Lambeth (La) (c. 1810), and Truman's Brewery, Spitalfields (T H) (c. 1803 and the 1830s). BREWERIES are indeed well represented, from former village breweries and maltings (as at West Drayton, Hi, or Strand on the Green, Chiswick, Ho) to Young's in Wandsworth (Ww) or Mann's in Whitechapel (T H) of the Victorian heyday. Well-composed INDUSTRIAL FAÇADES of the mid C 19 may be found occasionally in back streets untouched by redevelopment. The buildings of the leather area of central Bermondsey (Sk) and the piano factories of Camden Town (Ca) still indicate the specialized industrial character of certain parts of London at that time. Of the later C 19, there is plenty in Finsbury (Is), Shoreditch (Hc), and Southwark (Sk), where exuberant commercial architecture lined the main thoroughfares (*see* General Introduction). Light manufacturing-cum-wholesaling activities here, e.g. printing and stationery, clothing and furniture manufacture, required large window areas, often with decorated cast-iron mullions or, in a few Clerkenwell (Is) examples, façades almost wholly of iron and glass with a Gothic touch. Even of this period, the grandest, purpose-built factories have nearly all been demolished.

The C 20 has drastically reversed these C 19 specializations, so that, for instance, leather-processing in Bermondsey (Sk), hop-warehousing in Southwark (Sk), and clock-making in Clerkenwell (Is) are now virtually defunct. Some cereals are still processed in Mill Street, Bermondsey. Joinery and furniture-making, once concentrated in Shoreditch (Hc), Bethnal Green (TH), and parts of St Pancras (Ca), is now dispersed through Hackney and the Lee valley. But clothing manufacture continues in Stepney (TH) and eastern St Marylebone (Wm) and has spread to Hackney and Islington, using adapted commercial and domestic premises, while chemical-based industries still thrive on the Essex marshes, as at Stratford (Ne).

FACTORIES of after 1900 maintained architectural originality, for instance in combining Baroque embellishments and brightly-coloured engineering bricks, or glazed bricks. A freer handling may be seen in *Voysey*'s wallpaper factory in Chiswick (Ho) (1902), while the germ of Art Deco appears in the Michelin depot in Chelsea (KC) (1910).

The spread of manufacturing, especially of food and durable consumer products, through outer London along the main TRANSPORT ROUTES, already evident by 1900, was speeded by the arterial roads programme of 1919–39, while outer suburban commuters were catered for by the extensions to the under-

---

milling, recirculating water to a waterwheel at Deptford Victualling Yard (Le) in 1781 (*Smeaton*), and applied directly to rotative machinery at the great Albion Mills Southwark (Sk) in 1786 (*Watt*), both sites long obliterated.

ground lines. The restrained Scandinavian-modern of *Charles Holden*'s stations on the Piccadilly Line contrasts with the more flamboyant Art Deco factory façades of American inspiration, the 'Great West Road Style', of which *Wallis Gilbert & Partners* were the leading exponents (e.g. Firestone, Brentford, Ho (1928, demolished) and Hoover, Perivale, Ea, of 1932). Since the war, with Greater London largely built up, transport improvements have never regained their former momentum, despite some impressive motorway viaducts and flyovers and two new underground lines. Until very recently, the depletion of traditional manufacturing in the congested and expensive inner areas was encouraged by planning policies, while clean-air legislation helped to eliminate the factory chimneys which once dominated some eastern, down-wind parts of London.

The biggest changes of the 1970s have been the development of huge storage buildings and other facilities in West London to serve the expanding Heathrow Airport (Hi), while the remaining docks and their supporting warehousing and engineering services have continued to decline. The revitalization of these disused stretches of East London is one of the greatest challenges to London in the 1980s. Meanwhile work on one of the most ambitious civil engineering projects in Britain, the building of the Thames Tidal Surge Barrier, was completed in 1982.

FURTHER READING

There is no space to do more than provide some indication of the wealth of literature. The Greater London Council History Library has comprehensive, up-to-date indices arranged topographically and by subjects, for those who wish to delve further. Older books are listed in their published catalogue (*L.C.C. Members Library*, 1939). A more recent compilation, *The London Region, An Annotated Geographical Bibliography*, by P. Dolphin, E. Grant, and E. Lewis (1981), includes a section on historical patterns of growth and development and lists the public libraries holding local collections. The following notes concern general books: some of the most useful works on individual areas and buildings are listed at the end of each borough introduction.

On the Prehistoric and Roman periods the most useful recent books are R. Merrifield, *The Archaeology of London* (London, 1975); D. Collins *et al.*, *The Archaeology of the London Area: Current Knowledge and Problems* (Special Paper No. 1, London and Middlesex Archaeological Society) (London, 1976); *Time on our Side? A Survey of Archaeological Needs in Greater London* (Department of the Environment, Greater London Council, and Museum of London) (London, 1976); and R. Merrifield, *Roman London* (London, 1969). Recent discoveries are reported in *The*

London Archaeologist, published quarterly from 7 Coalecroft Road, s w 15, and in the *Kent Archaeological Review*. The journals of the county archaeological societies contain relevant articles and excavation reports: there are *Archaeologia Cantiana*, *Essex Archaeology and History*, *Surrey Archaeological Collections*, and *Transactions of the London and Middlesex Archaeological Society*. There are major collections of archaeological material in the British Museum and the Museum of London.

As the South London boroughs were once part of Kent, Surrey, or Middlesex, the older topographical books for these counties are relevant. Firstly Kent, which until the c 19 included part of the present borough of Greenwich, and until 1965 the areas of Bromley and Bexley. William Lambarde's *Perambulation of Kent*, published in 1576, is the earliest of all county histories. The county history proper however is Edward Hasted's, a mine of information, published first in a four-volume folio edition in 1778–99, and again, much revised, as twelve octavo volumes from 1797 to 1801. For churches there is Sir Stephen Glynne's *The Churches of Kent* (1877), especially useful for its many descriptions, the first as early as 1829, of churches before Victorian restoration. The drawings of churches by Henry Petrie, made *c.* 1806–10, are another valuable early source of information. The drawings themselves are lost, but a set of photographs of them is in Maidstone Museum, Kent. Later books on the subject are Dr Francis Grayling's two volumes of 1913, and V. J. Torr's *Kent Churches* of 1954, more selective, but fuller than Grayling on the chosen churches and fittings. The magazine of the county archaeological society, *Archaeologia Cantiana*, has plenty of useful articles on secular and ecclesiastical buildings alike (G. M. Livett and F. C. Elliston-Erwood, and more recently S. E. Rigold and E. W. Parkin, are the names to look for); and so do vols. LXXXVI and CXXVI of the *Archaeological Journal*. What is missing however is anything from the Royal Commission on Historical Monuments and anything beyond the first three volumes for the county (on Roman remains and the history of monastic houses) of the *Victoria County History*.

The part of Richmond across the Thames used to be Middlesex. Twickenham and Teddington have the advantage of a recent thorough volume of the *Victoria County History* (vol. 3, 1962). Hampton and Hampton Wick are included in the older vol. 2 (1911). There is also the R.C.H.M. volume on *Middlesex* (1937) which covers buildings up to 1714. In addition there is Michael Robbins's invaluable survey, *Middlesex* (1953), and the same author's compilation on churches in vol. 18 (1955) of the county periodical, the *Transactions of the London and Middlesex Archaeological Society*. Older county books are D. Lysons, *Parishes of Middlesex* (1800), the *Little Guide* by J. B. Fish (1906), and M. J. Briggs, *Middlesex Old and New* (1934).

All the other boroughs in this book belonged to Surrey. Here the chief county histories are those by Manning and Bray (3 vols., 1804–14) and Brayley and Walford (1878–81), the county periodical the *Surrey Archaeological Collections*. The V.C.H. volumes covering the area (vols. 3 and 4) are early ones, dating from 1911 and 1912. However, these can be supplemented by the topographical surveys and guides produced from the C 18 onwards, which provide a mixture of historical notes and contemporary descriptions about the neighbourhood of London. The source used by many later guides was Daniel Lysons' invaluable *Environs of London* (1795). As far as South London is concerned, most of the C 19 and later guide books limit their investigations to an account of Southwark, Lambeth Palace, and the obvious tourist attractions of Greenwich, Dulwich, Richmond, Kew, and, in C 19 guides, the Crystal Palace and Woolwich Arsenal. An exception is James Thorne's *Handbook to the Environs of London* (1876, reprinted 1970), an especially comprehensive gazetteer to the area within twenty miles of London. His elegiac comments on the retreating countryside swallowed by the *Suburban Homes of London* contrasts with W. Clarke's amusingly enthusiastic eulogy of these in his book of that name (1881). Walter Besant, in his discursive, not always reliable, but informative volumes on *South London* (1899) and *London South of the Thames* (1912) found the recent suburbs unbearably boring, but has much on the older parts of Southwark and Lambeth.

Among general histories, C. Trent's *Greater London, A History through 2000 Years* (1965) is a concise one-volume account. The two series published by Cassell and Secker & Warburg concentrate on central London, but the C 19 volumes in both include much that is relevant to the suburbs: they are Francis Shepherd's *London 1808–1870, the Infernal Wen* (1971), and Priscilla Metcalf's *Victorian London* (1972). The architectural historian of the suburbs can also learn from recent contributions made by geographers and social and economic historians to the relatively new discipline of urban history. H. J. Dyos's pioneer investigation, *Victorian Suburb: A Study of the Growth of Camberwell* (1961), has had numerous progeny: see e.g. the *Studies in Greater London* edited by J. T. Coppock and H. Prince (1964); D. A. Reeder, 'A Theatre of Suburbs, Some Patterns of Development in West London, 1801–1911', in *The Study of Urban History*, ed. H. J. Dyos (1968); F. M. L. Thompson (ed.), *The Rise of Suburbia* (1982); and on C 20 suburbs, Alan A. Jackson, *Semi-Detached London, Suburban Life and Transport, 1900–1939* (1979).

The maps that chart the expansion and development of London have been usefully catalogued by J. Howgego, *Printed Maps of London c. 1553–1850* (2nd ed., 1978) and R. Hyde, *Printed Maps of Victorian London 1851–1910* (1975). To bring them vividly to life one should look at the contemporary social investigations: Mayhew's *London Labour and the London Poor* (1851); Charles Booth's *Life and Labour of the People of London* (1902), especially series 3: Religious Influences, vols. 4, 5, and 6 (covering South London); and *The New Survey of London Life and Labour* (1934).

Working-class housing is another subject where the interests of architectural, social and economic historians overlap. Among recent studies which must be mentioned are those by J. N. Tarn, especially *Five Per Cent Philanthropy* (1973), and the Peabody Donation Fund (*Victorian Studies*, 1966), and A. S. Wohl, *The Eternal Slum: Housing and Social Policy in Victorian London* (1977). The early role of the L.C.C. is admirably dealt with by S. Beattie in *A Revolution in London Housing, L.C.C. Housing Architects and their Work, 1893–1914* (1980) and the next phase of public housing by Mark Swenarton in *Homes Fit for Heroes* (1981). The story of the county council's housing efforts is carried on more summarily up to 1975 by the G.L.C.'s *Home Sweet Home* (1976), and by the contemporary records: the L.C.C.'s *Housing* (1928), *Housing 1928–30* (1931); *Housing . . . 1945–9* (1949). *G.L.C. Architecture 1965–70* and *G.L.C. Architect's Reviews* (1974, 1975, 1976) also cover other types of building. For the county council's early schools see D. Gregory-Jones, 'The London Board Schools, E. R. Robson', in A. Service (ed.), *Edwardian Architecture*, and *The Schools of the London School Board and the L.C.C. Education Department* (G.L.C. Department of Architecture and Civic Design, typescript).

For after the Second World War the essential background books are the planning documents: Forshaw and Abercrombie's clear and attractively illustrated *County of London Plan* (1943) and Abercrombie's complementary *Greater London Plan* (1944), which describe London as it was then, and the proposals for post-war reconstruction and decentralization. These formed the basis for the official *County Development Plan* of 1951. *The London Plan, First Review* (1960) summarized the uneven progress made in the first few years. The next stage comes with the formation of the G.L.C. in 1965, and the *Greater London Development Plan* (2 vols: *Statement* and *Report of Studies* 1969) and the numerous documents emanating from the lengthy inquiry that followed. More recent social and economic trends are considered briefly in *Changing London*, edited by Hugh Clout (1978).

On industrial archaeology the pioneer survey was Ashdown, Bussell, and Carter's *Industrial Monuments of Greater London* (1969). *London's Industrial Heritage* by A. Wilson (1967) discusses selected items in greater detail. *The Industrial Archaeology of South East London* (Goldsmiths' College Industrial Archaeology Group, 1982) covers Bexley, Bromley, Greenwich, and Lewisham. On individual aspects: Sir J. G. Broodbank, *History of the Port of London* (1921, 2 vols.) and J. Pudney, *London Docks* (1975); J. Dredge, *Thames Bridges* (1897) and the London County Council's *Bridges* (1914); parts of three regional volumes in the *Canals of the British Isles* series and M. Denney, *London's Waterways* (1977); H. P. White, *Regional History of the Railways of Great Britain*, vol. 3, *Greater London* (2nd ed. 1971) and A. Jackson, *London's Termini* (1969), H. W. Dickinson, *Water Supply of Greater London* (1954) and publications of the former Metropolitan Water Board (1953, 1961, etc.); S. Everard, *History of the Gas Light and Coke Company* (1949) and the North

Thames Gas Board's *Historical Index of Gas Works* (1957); Farries and Mason's *Windmills of Surrey and Inner Lonon* (1966). P. G. Hall, *Industries of London since 1861* (1962), gives a geographical background to manufacturing. Important more specialized sudies are: A. W. Skelton, *Engineering in the Port of London, 1789–1808* and *1808–1834; Transactions of the New-comen Society*, 50 (1978–9) and 53 (1981–2). Much technical information can be found in the *Minutes of Proceedings of the Institution of Civil Engineers*; recent fieldwork is published by the Greater London Industrial Archaeology Society.

A list of specifically architectural publications can start with the two Royal Commission volumes, *East London* (1930) and *West London* (1925), which cover the old L.C.C. area, but which only deal with buildings up to 1714, and which recent research has rendered out of date in many respects. The *Survey of London* has produced only four parish volumes on South London: two on Lambeth (1951 and 1956), and two on Southwark (1950, 1955). They take the story up to around 1850 and, alas, are not as detailed as the *Survey*'s more recent productions. So for more comprehensive coverage one has to rely on the patchy Department of the Environment *Lists* (*see* borough introductions), which now include some c 20 buildings, but which are not yet all issued in revised form at the time of writing and which do not have the advantage of the *Survey*'s thorough topographical analysis. The main landmarks of architectural history, in which the London area is so rich, are of course included in the general histories of architecture, notably John Summerson's *Architecture in Britain 1530–1830* (7th ed., 1983), *Victorian Architecture* by R. Dixon and S. Muthesius (1978), and *Edwardian Architecture* by A. Service (1977). Other essential tools are *The King's Works* (H.M.S.O., 1963 onwards) for Greenwich, Eltham, Kew, Richmond, Hampton Court, and other royal buildings; H. M. Colvin's *Biographical Dictionary of British Architects 1600–1840* (1978); and the *Catalogues* of the Drawings Collection of the Royal Institute of British Architects. For contemporary accounts of c 19 buildings the *Illustrated London News*, *The Builder*, *Building News* (later the *Architect and Building News*), and *London* (later the *Municipal Journal*) are invaluable; for the c 20 the *Architectural Review*, the *Architects Journal*, *Official Architecture and Planning*, and the *London Architect* must also be mentioned. The publications of the London Topographical Society have much of interest on older buildings; the *London Journal* and *Country Life* include some articles on London architecture.

Research on individual periods and topics has multiplied fast in the last thirty years, particularly on c 19 subjects; only a sample of relevant work can be indicated here (*see also* borough introductions). Two on which this volume has leant heavily must be singled out: John Summerson's lucid account of *Georgian London*, which first appeared in 1945 (latest revised edition 1977), and B.F.L. Clarke's *Parish Churches of London* (1966) which covers all Anglican churches in the old L.C.C. area. Other illuminating studies concerned wholly or partly with buildings in the London suburbs are: D. Cruikshank and P. Wyld, *London, The Art of Georgian Building* (1975); M. Binney, 'The Villas of Sir Robert Taylor', *Country Life*, vol. 142, p. 18; M. Port, *600 New Churches, 1818–1856* (1961); John Summerson, *The London Building World of the 1860s* (1973); D. J. Olsen, *The Growth of Victorian London* (1976); Mark Girouard, *Victorian Pubs* (1975) and *Sweetness and Light, the Queen Anne Movement 1860–1900* (1977); John Summerson, 'The London Suburban Villa', *Architectural Review*, vol. 104 (August 1948); S. Muthesius, *The English Terraced House* (1982); Hugh Meller, *London Cemeteries* (1981). On theatres of 1900–1914 *Curtains!!!* (published by John Offord, Eastbourne, 1982) and on cinemas David Atwell, *Cathedrals of the Movies* (1980) both include comprehensive gazetteers.

Among recent monographs on architects and builders especially relevant for this volume are John Harris, *William Chambers* (1970), Priscilla Metcalf, *James Knowles, Victorian Editor and Architect* (1980), Hermione Hobhouse, *Thomas Cubitt* (1971), Andrew Saint, *Richard Norman Shaw* (1976), A. P. Quiney, *John Loughborough Pearson* (1979). Well illustrated anthologies include G. Stamp and C. Amery's *Victorian Buildings of London 1837–1887: An Illustrated Guide* (1980), A. Service, *London 1900* (1979), and G. Stamp (ed.), *London 1900* (*Architectural Design*, vol. 48, nos. 5–6, 1978).

For the last fifty years an adequate synthesis is lacking. Contemporary periodicals and local authority plans and brochures remain the most useful sources. Lionel Esher's *A Broken Wave, the Rebuilding of England 1940–1980* (1981) has a chapter on London; apart from this there are a number of brief guide books, one retrospective (*Battle of Styles: A Guide to Selected Buildings in the London Region of the 1914–39 Period*, R.I.B.A. London region, 1975), the others recording buildings of their time: Hugh Casson, *New Sights of London* (London Transport, 1938); Ian Nairn, *Modern Buildings in London* (London Transport, 1964); Charles McKean and Tom Jestico, *Guide to Modern Buildings in London 1965–75* (R.I.B.A., 1976).

BEXLEY

The entries in this section are by John Newman, who has revised them for this volume. They were first published in *The Buildings of England: West Kent and the Weald* (1969). The new entries on industrial buildings are by Malcolm Tucker.

INTRODUCTION

Bexley borough* forms a parallelogram extending from Erith Marshes in the N to the Sidcup Bypass in the S and bisected by the Dover Road (A2). Its E and W boundaries are ill defined, and one's general impression of the borough is of an endless sprawl of between-the-wars suburbia. Relics of the pre-suburban past take some searching out.‡ Of open country only two evocative pieces remain, Abbey Wood, Belvedere, ancient oaks and chestnuts on the escarpment falling towards the Thames-side marshes, and the park-like meadows beside the one short unspoilt stretch of the river Cray, at Foots Cray and North Cray. Nowadays it is only by rare glimpses that one can sense that the whole district consists of rolling uplands between river valleys, at East Wickham church, for instance, and at The Green, Sidcup.

Of medieval buildings, Lesnes Abbey, Belvedere, founded 1178, survives as a fairly complete set of footings. The six old

* The population in 1981 was 211,858.
‡ GEOLOGY and PREHISTORY: Erith Marshes occupy the NW corner beside the Thames, backed by a narrow outcrop of chalk; the central area is broad heathland on sand and pebble beds, with some London clay and gravel to the S. Crayford was an important Lower Palaeolithic area; later prehistoric material has been found along the river Cray and across Bexley Heath; possible Bronze Age barrows at Lesnes Abbey and West Heath to the S of it; Iron Age or Romano-British sites at Slade Green, Barnehurst, and Coldblow. Crayford was probably Noviomagus, on the Roman road to Dover. Roman remains have been found there, and along the Cray Valley and at Welling.

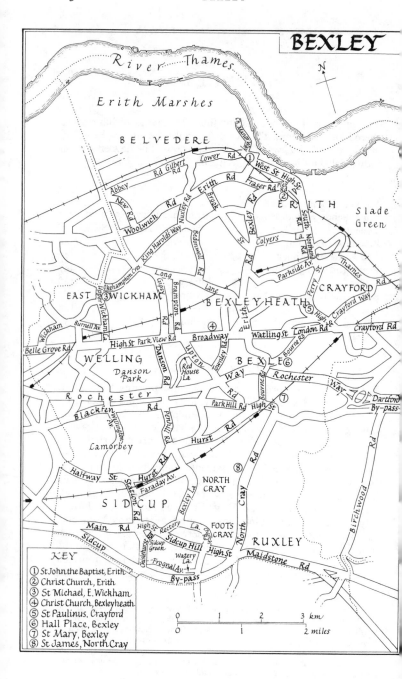

BEXLEY

River Thames

Erith Marshes

BELVEDERE

Slade Green

ERITH

CRAYFORD

EAST WICKHAM

BEXLEYHEATH

WELLING

Danson Park

BEXLEY

Lamorbey

SIDCUP

NORTH CRAY

FOOTS CRAY

RUXLEY

KEY
1. St John the Baptist, Erith
2. Christ Church, Erith
3. St Michael, E. Wickham
4. Christ Church, Bexleyheath
5. St Paulinus, Crayford
6. Hall Place, Bexley
7. St Mary, Bexley
8. St James, North Cray

0   1   2   3 km
0   1   2 miles

village churches are all, as one would expect, heavily restored, those of the three major villages – Bexley, Crayford, and Erith – quite large, and Crayford fascinating in its wayward plan; the others, East Wickham and the two Crays, Foots and North, are now of slender interest.

Between Tudor and Georgian times the area was much esteemed by those who had done well in the City. Of the dozen or so seats established here by wealthy merchants and aldermen only a few remain in good condition. Hall Place, Bexley, is now a museum of local history, and Lamorbey Park, Sidcup, is used for adult education. Frognal House, which has a complex history going back to the Middle Ages, was restored and converted to offices in 1981, while *Sir Robert Taylor*'s villa, Danson Park, architecturally the most significant, is at long last under restoration, although its stables continue to rot at the time of writing. The most serious losses occurred in the 1950s, first the Palladian Foots Cray Place, burnt down in 1950, then *Athenian Stuart*'s Belvedere, demolished in 1957.

Among Victorian buildings there is one of national importance, *Philip Webb*'s Red House, Bexleyheath, now engulfed in 91 suburban villadom but apart from that externally unscathed. 92 Otherwise c 19 housing makes little impact, and of the Victorian churches only Christ Church, Bexleyheath, lingers in the 89 memory.

As for the c 20, it is a matter of quantity not quality in churches as in houses. Barnes Cray, Crayford, is a late garden suburb of 1914–16. Contemporary with that is Erith Oil Works, 99 remarkable for precocious shuttered concrete of 1916. Otherwise it is the institutional buildings that count for something; pre-war there is Kemnal Manor Upper School, Sidcup, and more recently the Royal Alfred Seamen's Home, Belvedere, and Queen Mary's Hospital, Sidcup, which both display modern architecture favourably.

Further Reading

See p. 124.

Acknowledgements

I am grateful to Mr Edward Hollamby for help at Red House, Bexleyheath, to Mrs Ruth Hutcherson for help at Danson Park, to Mr B. N. Nunns for help at Sidcup, and to Mr P. J. Tester and Mr D. E. Wickham for information and corrections. The entries on industrial matters are indebted to the Goldsmiths' College Industrial Archaeology Group.

BELVEDERE

ALL SAINTS, Nuxley Road. 1853–61 by *W. G. & E. Haber-shon.** w tower and shingled spire. Nave and low aisles. Colossally deep transepts. Shortish chancel. That is to say, definitely not in accordance with ecclesiological ideals. Careful Dec tracery and careful knapped flint walling. The interior looks less eccentric, as the nave arcades carry straight past the transepts. Galleries in the transepts, with curvaceous balcony fronts of cast-iron foliage, part naturalistic, part palmettes. Contemporary VICARAGE next door with variegated bargeboards.

ST AUGUSTINE, Gilbert Road. Built from 1910 by *Temple Moore* to a design by *Hodgson Fowler* (B. F. L. Clarke) and consecrated in 1916. Red-brick Romanesque, better inside than out. The w front finished off in 1961.

LESNES ABBEY, New Road. Richard de Lucy laid the foundation stone of the Augustinian abbey on 11 June 1178. The abbey was suppressed by Wolsey as early as 1525, and the buildings razed. Sir Alfred Clapham excavated the site in 1909–13, but the remains were only laid bare after a second campaign in the mid 1950s. They now lie lonely and diagrammatic in a great expanse of mown grass running up to Abbey Wood at the S.

The foundations do indeed provide a useful diagram from which to learn the layout of monastic buildings. The church consisted of aisled nave, transepts with three square-ended E chapels, and aisleless chancel, which is not a normal Augustinian plan but a Cistercian one. The nave had eight bays and was 132 ft long. The bases of several shafts remain, with leaf spurs of the undercurling kind called 'waterleaf', a trademark of *c*. 1180. As the design of the church shows no development from E to W, this is dated waterleaf of 1178. Pilaster buttresses and clasping buttresses. Lady Chapel E of the S transept. It was under construction in 1371. The diagonal buttresses at once single it out as later than the rest. The monastic buildings lay on the Thamesward side of the church, as considerations of drainage dictated. On the E side of the cloisters was the rectangular chapter house, with more of the 1178 shaft bases at the doorway.‡ N of this lay the dormitory on an undercroft, with the rere-dorter at its N end. The refectory, on the N side of the cloisters, can be recognized by the steps up to the pulpit, lit from two lancets. The kitchen lay N W of the refectory, with a narrow serving-hatch through the wall. The W range was rebuilt, encroaching a little on the area of the cloisters. At its S end the only complete feature to survive, a doorway with an odd wide stopped chamfer outlined by a roll. Clapham thought it C 14. A separate infirmary block N E of the chapter

---

* The church was built as a proprietary chapel for Sir Culling Eardley but after much litigation consecrated within the Church of England.

‡ Capitals excavated from the chapter house have crocket capitals, just like those e.g. in the gallery of Canterbury Cathedral choir.

house has not been re-excavated. A few C13 TILES in a transept chapel.

ROYAL ALFRED HOME FOR AGED SEAMEN, Upper Park Road, off Erith Road to the N. 1957–9 by *Gollins, Melvin & Ward*. Long four-storeyed block facing E and W with a short central projection at the back. Curtain walling, the spandrel panels the palest of blues. Single-storey ranges snaking out at front and back. In design and colour a little insipid perhaps for the old salts.

Before 1957 the seamen occupied the eponymous BELVEDERE, the house built for Sir Sampson Gideon *c*. 1775 by *James Stuart*, author of *The Antiquities of Athens*. There was little about it that was Grecian.

BELVEDERE POWER STATION, Erith Marshes. By *Farmer & Dark* and the *British Electricity Authority*. Oil-fired. One of Farmer & Dark's crisp, no-nonsense jobs, of 1954–60. The two chimneys have an especially elegant, soaring shape. The turbine house is as severely rectangular as possible.

CROSSNESS SEWAGE WORKS, Erith Marshes, N of Thamesmead. At the outfall of the Southern Outfall Sewer (1860–2). The original sewer was 11 ft 6 in. in diameter. Two more of the same size were added in 1906. The original facilities of 1862–5 by *Bazalgette* comprised $6\frac{1}{2}$ acres of brick-roofed storage tanks and an engine house for pumping out the sewage on the falling tide. These are now disused, but the ENGINE HOUSE still contains its four beam engines by James Watt & Son, laid out on a grand scale.* Cast-iron galleries have stiff-leaf capitals and an elaborately ornamented central octagon. All was originally brightly coloured – rust now pervades. The white Gault brick exterior is a rectangular box with *Rundbogenstil* polychrome embellishments, lacking the flamboyance of the later Abbey Mills pumping station (Ne).‡ However, the BOILER HOUSE, behind, and the slightly later VALVE HOUSE, and WORKSHOP on either side, display the sculptural possibilities of round-arched brickwork. There was formerly a chimney in the form of a campanile 207 ft high. In the modern sewage treatment plant (entered service 1963), the reinforced concrete primary sludge digestion tanks are of impressive size with valve chambers dramatically corbelled out to span the roadways between the tanks.

BEXLEY

ST MARY. C13 flint church, heavily restored in 1882–3 by *Champneys*.§ Shingled spire, octagonal in the top half, pyramidal below, on a cornice with brackets; basically medieval, that is, touched up in the C18. Lancets low down in the W

---

* The engines were converted from single to twin cylinders in 1909–10.
‡ The original entrance on the N side has been obscured by a later extension.
§ The round-headed arch over the S doorway suggests that Norman walling is incorporated.

tower, one S lancet in the nave, one S, one N in the chancel, with a few old stones left in them to convince us of their genuineness. Wide, gabled N aisle continued as a chapel. There is a lancet here too. Has the aisle been widened then since the C 13? Perhaps not, for the E bay, clearly later than the rest by the tighter packed flints, has an early C 14 window in it. On the other hand an internal string-course, wholly renewed, goes round W, N, and E walls. E.E. N doorway also. E.E. S doorway. S porch of 1882. Nave arcade of four bays, round piers, arches with one large and one small chamfer. The E bay is wider than the rest, and there is no chancel arch. No doubt the nave E pier had to be rebuilt when the rood loft was introduced. The rood-loft turret* is on the S side, projecting internally, with a crocketed conical cap. Perhaps too the strangely splayed N arch in the chancel is an amalgamation of two, done at the same time. Three SEDILIA, stepping up towards the E, with continuous mouldings that look C 15 rather than anything else. – FONT. Bowl dated 1684, on a medieval stem – CHANCEL SCREEN. By *Champneys*.‡ Elaborate in itself, with a loft, and incorporating a chapel screen, stalls, and pulpit. – MONUMENTS. Thomas Sparrow † 1513. Brass of a civilian, 13 in. long. – Sir John Champeneis, 1590. Hanging monument with small kneeling figures between Corinthian columns. Entablature and three achievements on top. – Anne Traveis † 1679. Nice cartouche, of London standard. – Sir Robert Austen, 1687. Standing marble monument without figures. Vivacious architecture however; twisted composite columns, scrolly top pediment with two cartouches between the points, inscription in an oval frame. – Lady Mary Cosein. Tablet of *c.* 1700, with the inscription written on a cloth held up by two frolicking putti. – John Styleman † 1734. The monument, a large hanging one with cartouches of arms pinned to a pyramid, was erected after 1750 by *J. Annis*. – In the CHURCHYARD several neo-classical tomb-chests.

ST JOHN, Park Hill Road. By *G. Low*, 1881–2. Clerestoried nave, lower chancel, canted at the end, NE tower and stone spire towards the road. Ragstone. 'Style "Early French" not very strongly defined', was Mr Goodhart-Rendel's diagnosis. Bare, lifeless interior, in spite of stencilling all over the walls and roof of the lofty chancel.

ST JOHN FISHER (R.C.), Thanet Road, off Park Hill Road. By *Ivor Day & O'Brien* of Bristol. Opened in 1974. Welcomingly wide porch. Square-plan church under a two-stage pyramid roof ringed with a band of window.

The old parish church lies E of, and across the River Cray from, the short winding HIGH STREET. On the church side of the river two good late C 18 houses: HIGH STREET HOUSE of 1761, beside the church, and CRAY HOUSE, a little less grand, close to the river, which is straddled by a pastiche, a rebuilding of a picturesque weatherboarded mill burnt down

* Reconstructed in 1883.
‡ Information from Canon Bernard Wigan.

in 1966. On the far side, on the l., a row of shops of the late 1960s by *S. F. Everson & D. F. Searles*. Nothing special, but their yellow brick and white weatherboarding help to enliven what is otherwise a bit of a dark alleyway. On the r. Nos. 57–59, late C17, with a hipped projecting centre. Dull red brick, the date 1676 scratched on a brick. Then, on the same side, the STYLEMAN ALMSHOUSES, dated 1755, a two-storey row of twelve, with a central broken pediment. Raised brick band between the storeys, but no further ornament. Beyond them Nos. 1–7, two pairs of Georgian cottages, brick in front, timber-framed behind. A neat reminder of vernacular practice even so late. Finally, on the l., as the street broadens out into suburban roads, a gauche little ragstone UNITED REFORMED CHURCH, as late as 1890, by *G. Baines*. The spire an overgrown pinnacle. To the N, down BOURNE ROAD, the former BEXLEY NATIONAL SCHOOLS, stock brick with a pair of shaped gables, dated 1834.

HALL PLACE (Bexley Local History Museum), Bourne Road. It is a delightful surprise to come upon the house, chequered grey and white in front, healthy red brick behind, with its demure walled garden towards the road and its splendid early C18 wrought-iron GATES.* The colours immediately establish the two periods; on the S side of the C16 house a back court was built in the middle of the C17. Sir John Champeneis, Lord Mayor of London in 1534, bought the estate three years later, and the fact that a great deal of medieval carved fragments is incorporated in the walling of the present house suggests that he soon rebuilt, using the materials so plentifully supplied by the recently dissolved monasteries. Not much later, but probably after his son, Justinian, had succeeded in 1556, the N front was adapted to make it as nearly symmetrical as possible. Thus from the road one sees the hall, with long wings coming forward on either side. As left by Sir John there was only one bay-window lighting the hall, the r. one, of two–four–two lights with two transoms, the lights arched. The solar wing projected as far N as it does today, but two-storeyed for only a short way, continued by a low chapel and a narrower wing N of that. Evidence for this arrangement is in the upper half of a straight quoin half way along the W wall.‡ Chapel E window of three trefoiled lights under a segmental head. The service wing, E of the hall, projected northwards, but was lengthened to make it as long as the W wing. Quoins mark its original length on both sides. The most telling item of the remodelling was the duplication of the hall bay-window, which of course made nonsense of the original arrangement of the hall, with its upper and lower ends in the traditional way. Modern central doorway, replacing a C17 one. On the W side

* Attributed to *Thomas Robinson*.

‡ This and other modifications are confirmed by the internal dressings of the walls, chalk in the earlier work, brick in the later, discovered by Mr. P. J. Tester during alterations in the mid 1950s but now hidden.

all the larger windows are modern; the solar however did originally have a bay-window, and the turret is a rebuild of an old one. Four projections on the E wall, the S one the buttery chimneybreast, the other three communicating with the exceptionally spacious kitchen and the rooms over it. The centre of the three not a chimneybreast but a garderobe turret. Mr Tester assigns all these to the second phase, and also the chequered facing with rough flints and chalk ashlar. To complete the account of the C16 house, the internal features that belong to it are two openings above the S doorway to the hall. These Mr Tester assumes to have led from the hall gallery into a two-storeyed S porch, demolished to make way for the C17 additions. The hall ceiling is coved, with a wooden ribbed ceiling with bosses, possibly dating from the mid C16 alterations or later.* In the S wall a fireplace with a four-centred arch with leaves in the spandrels. The present arrangement of the minstrels' gallery dates from the time of Lady Limerick's occupation in the 1920s, when much woodwork and several fireplaces were imported (exact details uncertain). In the hall an organ dated 1766, formerly at Danson Park.

In its way the C17 work is equally interesting. It forms three sides of a quadrangle on the S side, two-storeyed, in red brick still largely in English bonding, with a deep hipped roof on a wooden bracket cornice. Pedimented dormers. Rusticated stone quoins and a stone string-course. Vertical laces of stone break the E front into a rhythm of 2, 7, 2. The upper windows are altered, but the wooden cross-windows survive below, set under sunk semicircular arches with stone blocks at the base and apex of the arch. That is a typical mid-C17 detail. Similar treatment of the S front, ten bays, with a big centre doorcase, a triangular pediment on carved brackets and big ears to the door surround, another mid-C17 trick. Less regular W front, with two sets of oval windows on both levels. Inside the courtyard the lower windows are set in blank arcading, originally open, and the N side is almost filled by a splendid four-storeyed staircase tower (reconstructed in 1968). It is square, the outer angles chamfered for most of their height, and the irregular fenestration following the flights of the steps. Circular window in the middle at the top, glazed ovals below it. The main windows however adapt the form of the external ones, so that the sunk arch is flattened and the keystone balances a horizontal stone bar on it, a distinctly Dutch motif. Pyramid roof growing into a picturesque two-storeyed turret with a cupola. The staircase has big bulbous balusters and ball finials on the newels. The baluster shape is repeated as a sunk pattern on the newel-post, an odd idea. In an upper room in the SW corner of the old house a fine plaster ceiling clearly of the same mid-C17 date, with big oval wreaths, in enriched rectangular frames, but distinctly Jacobean-looking foliage

* The ceiling blocks an earlier window (information from Bexley Local Studies Centre).

growing from the waists of naked figures on the sloping side parts. In the same room a stone chimneypiece with Jacobean motifs of the type more usually found in wood. Sir Robert Austen bought the house c. 1640 from the last Champeneis. The finishing touches to his building were being made a decade later: bell dated 1649, spit-rack dated 1651, 1653 found inscribed on the head of the staircase turret.*

Red-brick BARN SE of the house. It may be C16 or C17.

Hall Place is now municipally owned. The grounds run down to the river in an extremely pleasing way.

BEXLEYHEATH

CHRIST CHURCH. 1872–7 by *William Knight* of Nottingham, who had won a competition judged by Burges in 1869. The church is so grand, with such noble, soaring proportions, that one grasps at any facts that will give substance to the enigmatic Mr Knight. The materials are ragstone dressed with ashlar, and slate roofs; the plan cruciform with the central steeple, alas, barely begun. The transepts as high as the nave, the chancel not quite so high, ending in a canted apse. The style is Early French Gothic, interpreted with great freedom and originality, and makes effective use of plate tracery in the W window and the nave clerestory. Fine rose window in each transept. Internally the nave, with arcades of four wide arches on short round piers, yields to the glory of the chancel, to which the crossing space belongs, and its exceptionally lofty arches. Well-managed shafts and string-courses high up however binding all together. Interesting detailing of the crossing arch corbels. Apse arcading of elemental Norman forms that must have appealed to Burges. Only the spindly timber roofs do not satisfy – that and the total absence of worthy fittings to match the scale of the building.

TRINITY BAPTIST CHAPEL, Broadway. 1868 by *Habershon & Pite*. Classical.

The mediocre BROADWAY now has as its focus, opposite the dwarf clock tower in the market place, a massive shopping and office complex by *Fitzroy Robinson & Partners*, 1982, brick, with a steep pitched roof at either end.

DANSON PARK, 1 m. W. A crystalline villa, built from c. 1762 for John Boyd, a prominent City merchant, by *Sir Robert Taylor*, and set in a park landscaped in the later 1760s in the manner of Capability Brown. The park now looks a little bare, with its second-generation trees, and large, rather uncompromising lake. The park boundary too is now marked by all-too-visible semi-detacheds. The house consists of a *piano nobile* and half-storey above a rusticated stone basement, the walls rendered, the roofs low and slated. It has five windows on each side, but is not a square, so although the centre three are

89

* Dates reported *in litteris* by Mr Tester.

in a canted bay on the s front and at the sides, the former looks spacious, the latter taut. (Side projections originally not full-height.) The entrance is on the N side, up a grand flight of steps to a balcony as wide as the projecting, pedimented centre. Doorcase with attached Corinthian columns. The internal planning allows for a three-bay hall in the centre of the N front, rooms running the full width of the E and W fronts, with bowed projections, and an octagonal room in the centre of the s front. That leaves the core of the house for the staircase, which is elliptical, in a tight, funnel-like, top-lit well, with eight Ionic columns below the dome. Elegant wrought-iron balustrade. The decoration of the three main rooms was completed, probably *c.* 1770, with exquisite marble chimneypieces.* The octagonal room has a reticent palmette frieze and enriched ceiling (cf. Mount Clare, Roehampton, Ww). The W room has contemporary bookcases set into the walls. The organ dated 1766 has been removed to Hall Place, Bexley (Bx). The saloon is decorated with fine inset paintings of gods and goddesses between foliage panels. There is a date 1766 and the artist's name 'Pavillo' is recorded. Edward Croft-Murray accepted the suggestion that this means *Charles Pavillon*, a little-known French painter, who exhibited decorative pictures in the earliest years of the R.A. and died in Edinburgh in 1772.

Ashlar STABLES NW of the house, designed with the same lucidity, though built *c.* 1800, when the free-standing pavilions which originally flanked the house were demolished. Sadly, derelict at the time of writing.

The other Danson building to survive stands s of the A2. It is CHAPEL HOUSE, Blackfen Road, built *c.* 1760 as an eye-catcher across the park. It is just a roughcast cottage, with a lead spire at its N end, and a low flattened turret towards the road. The traceried windows look like a C19 remodelling, but an C18 drawing suggests that they are original (RW).

91 RED HOUSE, Red House Lane. 'More a poem than a house . . . but an admirable place to live in too.' That was Dante Gabriel Rossetti's verdict on the newly completed home of his friend, William Morris. The plan that Morris should have a house built for him in the country and that *Philip Webb* should design it, had been hatched during a trip to France the two took with Charles Faulkner, rowing down the Seine and visiting medieval cathedrals, in the summer of 1858. The contract was signed in April 1859, and late in the summer of the following year Morris and his bride moved in. Rossetti was not the sort of person to view Red House objectively, but his contradictory remark reflects the difficulty one finds in mak-

---

* *Chambers* was responsible for the chimneypieces, and possibly also for the main doorway, which is similar to Somerset House. (His design for the saloon chimneypiece was found in the Metropolitan Museum, New York, by John Harris.) Chambers also designed a bridge and a little Doric temple for the park, the latter now at The Bury, St Paul's Waldenbury, Hertfordshire (information from R. White).

ing a cool assessment of it as a work of architecture. One's first thought is of the imagination and boyish enthusiasm of Morris himself, Morris who wanted a house 'very medieval in spirit', who lived here with such zest for five short years. How relevant are Morris the designer and Morris the inhabitant? Then there is the fame of Red House, the status accorded it already by Lethaby as a pioneering building in which the revival of styles of the past was first abandoned, so that it became the first link in the chain that led to Gropius and modern architecture. But the recent researches of Mr Brandon-Jones and Dr Thompson have proved that Red House has been put in a false position: that the first product of Webb's independent practice leant heavily on the style of his master, G. E. Street, and even more on that of Butterfield. On the other hand Morris himself thought of it as being 'in the style of the thirteenth century'. Finally it takes a considerable effort, surrounded by a sea of suburban semi-detacheds, to remember that Morris and his friends, arriving from London at Abbey Wood station, had three miles to drive through the North Kent countryside before they reached his home in its orchard of apple and cherry trees.

What then do we see, as we turn in past the high garden wall through the heavy wooden gates? A house, substantial but not large, built of deep red brick (laid in English bond), with steeply pitched roofs covered with red tiles. Some of the gables are half-hipped, and there are half-hipped dormers too. The tall chimneystacks, at strategic points, taper by means of sloping set-offs now and then. The windows vary greatly in size and proportions, but they are all segment-headed and sashed, a Georgian shape, that is to say, not a Gothic one. Every one of these motifs had already occurred in parsonages and cottages by Butterfield, e.g. at Baldersby, in the North Riding, c. 1855. One characteristic detail Webb took from Street, the pointed tympanum, either set back or merely outlined by a relieving arch. That too comes from unpretentious buildings, like schools, where Gothic forms were reduced to the greatest simplicity. What Webb did, and it was indeed a revolutionary step to take, was to make use of this easy, informal, pared-down style in a gentleman's country house.* Webb also subscribed to the principle that roofs and windows should express the character of the rooms within. To appreciate the elevations then prior knowledge of the plan is needed. The house is two-storeyed and L-shaped. The rooms on both floors face N and W, with passages running round the S and E fronts, i.e. round the inner sides of the arms of the L. The staircase projects at the junction of the two arms. The two major rooms lie on the upper floor of the N arm, the drawing room at the W end, and Morris's study at the E.

---

* Butterfield certainly held more hierarchical views on architectural propriety. His Milton Ernest, Bedfordshire, a house comparable in size to Red House, is equipped with plenty of external shafting and window tracery.

The N front is the entrance front. The two-storeyed porch projects nearly in the centre, with a very sharp gable and a pair of windows under a pointed arch. The entrance arch repeats the shape. To the l. two windows under a hipped dormer, and then a strong, high chimneystack. To the r., a single window below, a trio above, lighting the drawing room. Thus the front is quite asymmetrical, the gables building up from l. to r., the chimneystack weighting down the l. end. The shapes all push upwards, yet the big expanses of plain wall low down give the house its solid, comfortable look. And is it too fanciful to imagine the deep eaves projected like guy ropes, tethering the roofs to the ground? Fancy certainly begins to blossom on the W side. Again, near the l. end, a chimneystack, this one of towering height, and next to it the strangest oriel, on a stem that steps out brick by brick to the full width, nearly shaving off the corner of a downstairs window on the way. The oriel windows show by their shape that they too light the drawing room. Quieter r. half, kitchen windows below, a pair of big half-dormers for bedrooms, and a long slope down to the back yard at the S end. It is typical that the upper half of the front is the more strongly characterized. Webb's contract drawings have 'roses', 'white jasmine', 'passion flower', 'bergamot' scribbled against the walls here.

From the SE, looking into the angle of the two wings, the view is far more picturesque, and the grouping apparently random. The house forms two sides of a courtyard focused on a well-head and its conical cap like a witch's hat. In Morris's time it really was a courtyard, for there were wattle fences on the S and E sides.* But this is the back of the house and Webb could relax, not bother about aligning the roof levels, let the varied fenestration create its own interest: the bulls-eye windows of the upper corridor, the long wide main-stairs windows, the long narrow one for the back stairs, and little slits for larder and pantry. The pyramidal staircase roof with its pretty lead capping, half louvre, half flèche, is enough to draw everything together to a climax. Morris's study is the only important room to look out this way. The study's E window consists of a bulls-eye over two sashes, made to read as plate tracery by the pointed blank arch that encloses them.

So we come round again at the front door. Above it a text: DOMINUS CUSTODIET EXITUM TUUM ET INTROITUM TUUM, just as Pugin would have had it, but in letters that belong to no known medieval alphabet.‡ From the far end of the spacious hall rises the main staircase, a solid piece of joinery, with tall newels that end in gawky pinnacles, and its structure frankly revealed on the undersides of the treads. The upstairs corridors run off at different levels, each through an exposed brick arch. One also notices the way the wooden

* Later, too, Morris proposed to complete the courtyard with ranges, as a home for the Burne-Joneses.

‡ No doubt Webb designed them, as he later designed the characteristic lettering on Morris glass.

window frames and door lintels are made very visible. But most remarkable of all is the decoration of the staircase vault. The flat top is painted with trios of dashes in two directions, but the concave sides have a stylized pattern in blue and green, of fans linked by loops into diagonal trails. It is highly effective and further removed from nature than any Morris pattern in other media. The design is pricked on the plaster, and week-end guests were expected to help with its execution. In fact the decoration of the whole house was the work of *Morris* and his friends, and the birth of the Morris firm in 1861 was the result of their experience here. Almost all of what they did in the rooms has alas been swept away, and the staircase is now the only ensemble.

The drawing room however, on the first floor, was original-ly the pièce de résistance. The ceiling, open to the roof, was covered with floral designs, and *Burne-Jones* began painting the walls with scenes from the medieval romance of Sir Degre-vaunt. These remain, on the S wall, and surprisingly amateur-ish they are too. In the centre of the S wall the vast settle brought from Morris's first studio, in Red Lion Square, with a loft added by Webb, to do double duty as a minstrels' gallery and a way into the roof. Today however the noble brick fireplace, with its grand hood reaching the full height of the 92 wall, is the most memorable feature. It is an astonishingly free piece: not a period detail, barely a moulding. Above it the inevitable motto: ARS LONGA VITA BREVIS. Brick fireplaces in other rooms, notably the hall and dining room, but nothing on a comparable scale. In the dining room another massive home-made piece of furniture, a chest with three gables. In the hall a cupboard, painted with scenes from the Nibelungen-lied by *Burne-Jones*. Stained glass in the lower corridor, two small experimental figures by *Morris*, and quarries with comical birds and bushes by *Burne-Jones*.

CRAYFORD

ST PAULINUS. This is a puzzle church. Not that a superficial look at the exterior rouses any suspicions. There is a nave with a Perp W tower and a N aisle as wide as the nave, a chancel with battlemented S chapel, and lean-to N chapel. All the windows are renewed (by *J. Clarke** in 1862), but one on the S side of the nave was Norman. The E window can be ignored; the others represent what was there before. Much of the flint walling has also been re-laid. The N W quoin however has not been tampered with, and in it are many blocks of tufa, with a characteristically pitted surface, a readily quarried chalk de-posit exploited by the Normans as a building stone. The lowest courses of a blocked doorway in the W wall of the N aisle are further evidence that the church is Norman in its bones.

* As Mr Geoffrey Spain kindly points out.

But this means that nave and aisle are both Norman, and together they are too wide for that to be probable; and there is a straight joint in the centre of the w wall, which means that either the nave or the aisle was once an aisleless nave. Considering the position of the blocked doorway, it must be the present N aisle which formed the original church.

That is as far as the outside can help, and a first view of the interior adds confusion to confusion. One can hardly any longer speak about 'nave' and 'aisle', but rather of two naves, for the single arcade runs down the very middle of the church and dies into the wall above the apex of the chancel arch. The complete set of Norman windows has left its mark inside, four in the N wall and four in the S. Half of them must have been reset, and, as we have seen, the evidence outside suggests that it is the N windows that are in their original places. This is confirmed by the outline of three round-headed windows in the E wall of the N nave – so the E, N, and W walls of the Norman church can be identified. That it originally had a chancel narrower than the nave and the chancel N wall later rebuilt in line with the nave's when a new chancel was built further E cannot be proved, as no N E quoin of the nave can be seen, though that is the natural assumption. One s window gives an early c 14 date for the chancel. Also a few stones of the three canopied SEDILIA. All else is Perp: chancel arch, arches to N and S chapels, and the arcade of four and a half arches on piers with four shafts in the main directions and hollows between. Square-headed Perp windows. The W tower was under construction in 1406 by *John Wells* 'cementarius'. It is stone, with diagonal buttresses and a W window that looks earlier than the rest. So the essentials of the remodelling are Perp, but the chancel aligned on the original S wall of the Norman church is Dec. Intermediate stages in the history must be missing. Probably the Norman building threw out a S aisle and S chapel, in which the S windows were reset. If this aisle and chapel were unusually wide, a new chancel further E might have been aligned on the arcade to allow a view of the high altar from all parts. This plan was perpetuated when the arcade was rebuilt. Roofs dated 1630. – PULPIT. Also c. 1630. Hexagonal, with tapering angle pilasters. – ALTAR TABLE. Designed by *James Brooks* and painted with figures of the four Evangelists; c. 1895. It was made to match the REREDOS triptych now removed and at the time of writing stored in the E chapel. – STAINED GLASS. Prominent windows in all directions by *Hugh Easton*, 1953–5. – MONUMENTS. Blaunche Marlar. Small hanging monument with a kneeling figure; c. 1600. – William Draper † 1650 and Mary † 1652. Large standing monument of black and white marble. They lie stiffly on their sides propped upon an elbow, the lady above and behind her husband. Small kneeling children, a boy at the l. and a girl at the r., and a tiny swaddled infant almost at ground level. Big double back-plate like a reredos, with an open segmental pediment on Corinthian columns. Gunnis saw

Thomas Stanton's hand in it. – Robert Mansel † 1723. Large plain standing monument of grey-veined marble. – Margaret Collins † 1732. Leathery cartouche with two putto heads. The inscription ends with the verse:

> Adam thus blest
>   (as by his Eve was crost)
> Had surely kept
>   the Paradise he lost.

– Elizabeth Shovel, widow of Admiral Sir Cloudesley, † 1732. Large and grand hanging monument. Putti hold a canopy over a black obelisk which stands on a sarcophagus balanced on a putto's head. – Henry Tucker † 1851. Remarkable as a pastiche of a late C 17 tablet. That was a period usually ignored by the mid-Victorians. The putto is too innocent, the wreath of flowers too tight and square to be quite convincing. – Several more nice tablets in the nave.

IRON AGE SETTLEMENT, just to the W of the church. The settlement was discovered during building operations and appeared to consist of a series of storage pits and gulleys (possibly hut foundations) containing Iron Age A, B, and C pottery.

Crayford was probably the Roman NOVIOMAGUS, situated on the Roman road to Kent.

BARNES CRAY, ½ m. E, was laid out from 1914 onwards as a garden village to house workers employed by Vickers to make ammunition (cf. West Street, Erith). Over half the 600 houses built in 1915–16 are constructed of concrete blocks, roughcast and colourwashed. The architect was *J. Gordon Allen*.

(INDUSTRIAL BUILDINGS. On the Cray, in London Road, a silk and calico printing works, 1800 onwards. Small pantiled brick buildings. Another in Swaisland Drive, also on the Cray, N of the town centre. The industry was established here by Huguenot refugees after 1685.)

EAST WICKHAM

ST MICHAEL. Nave and chancel without any structural division. The two N lancets are genuine evidence, those on the S are not. Traces of the three E lancets inside. The W end was rebuilt in the early C 19. W spirelet on the roof-ridge, 1897. – FONT. Dec. Hexagonal. Two ogee-ended quatrefoils on each face. – PULPIT. Jacobean. – WALL PAINTINGS. At the S end of the E wall, two large figures under arcading, C 13. – A large figure of St Michael (N wall). This looks cruder work. – TILES. Three with patterns set in the altar step. – BRASSES. John de Bladigdone, *c.* 1325. Charming and unusual, two tiny prim half-effigies in a frame of eight ogee lobes with finials. On the shaft his name in large letters. The date 1325 on the base is modern. The Arabic, not Roman, numerals show that. Total length: 44½ in. – William Payn † 1568. He wears the uniform of a Yeoman of the Guard. 12½ in. figures.

The medieval church has now been handed over to a Greek Orthodox congregation, and the brasses and other fittings removed to the modern church, of 1932 by *T. F. Ford.*

ERITH

CHRIST CHURCH, Victoria Road, off the E end of Bexley Road. 1874 by *J. P. St Aubyn.* Large and prominent, with a N W tower and stone spire. E.E. Clerestoried nave and low aisles, lower chancel with chapels and a canted apse. Stock brick with a little patterning in red brick. Short round piers with stiff-leaf capitals. Plenty of money was spent on enriching the interior. The walls of nave and chancel are entirely covered with WALL PAINTINGS, by *Ward & Hughes,* 1906–9. – REREDOS. Painted triptych of the Adoration of the Magi in a C 15 Italian style, by *A. O. Hemming,* 1904. – STAINED GLASS. The five E lancets by *Hardman & Sons,* 1875. Singing colours. C 13 style. The climax of the duskily rich interior.

ST JOHN THE BAPTIST. Largish, lowish, and not very attractive inside or out. In a heavy and silly restoration of 1877 by *Habershon & Pite,* the S porch and N chapel and aisle were added, with a blocked N doorway and a lancet among Perp windows to deceive the unwary. Flint and stone walling reshuffled, all windows renewed, W tower largely rebuilt. The S doorway is C 13, with a Purbeck marble shaft each side with narrow leaves up the waterleafy capitals. Trefoiled leaves on the stops of the hoodmould. Old, perhaps contemporary, S door, with two fine hinges. The doorway goes with the C 13 S arcade, of three short round piers and double-chamfered arches. The S E quoin of an aisleless Norman nave has been incorporated in the jamb of an arch in the S chapel. The chancel itself, though dominated by the three E lancets, shows quite a lot of its Norman features inside. It was unusually long and arcaded low down on the E wall (part of the S arch remains), and this arcading continued with one arch each on the N and S walls. One and a bit Norman windows to N and S. Traces of a doorway in the N W corner. Wide C 13 arches into N and S chapels. Blocked clerestory windows on the N side. Loose double-waterleaf capital in the S chapel. The W tower has clasping buttresses, which suggests a C 13 date at the latest. It is not bonded into the nave W wall. – SUNDIAL. Outside, on a S buttress. Only interesting as being the gift of a certain Nicholas Stone in 1643. There is no real reason to suppose that this was Nicholas Stone the sculptor. – STAINED GLASS. E window of the S chapel by *Kempe,* 1905. – BRASSES. Roger Sencler † 1425. 15 in. figure of a civilian. – John Ailemer † 1435. Civilian and his wife. Fine 33½ in. figures. – Emma Wode † 1471. Tall, thin figure in a peaked headdress. 26½ in. long. – John Mylner † 1511. 16 in. brasses. – Edward Hawte

† 1537. Armoured 14½ in. figure. (Also his wife.) – Inscription to Anne Harman † 1574, palimpsest on a fragment of a Flemish brass of c. 1500. – MONUMENTS. Elizabeth, Countess of Shrewsbury, † 1568. Recumbent effigy, still on a tomb-chest. Her head pillow lies on a half-rolled-up straw mat – a Netherlandish motif. The details of the tomb however are classical: Doric columns at the four corners and strapwork-enframed heraldic lozenges set in fine deep egg-and-dart borders. Well carved altogether. It might almost be in Westminster Abbey. – Francis Vanacker † 1686. In two parts. The inscription is on a small but lively cartouche. Below it a tomb-chest, with a plain black marble slab on top. The sides of the tomb are exceptionally finely carved with a laurel-wreath, bold drops of flowers and fruit, and, on the short end, the heads of three putti among clouds. – Lord Eardley and brother. By *Chantrey*, 1826. Large. A kneeling woman leans with bowed head on a pedestal on which stand two urns. The figure is solid and strongly carved.

(OUR LADY OF THE ANGELS (R.C.) (Capuchin Fathers), Carlton Heath, w of Bexley Road. Friary 1903, church 1963 by *Archard & Partners*. DE)

COLLEGE OF TECHNOLOGY, Tower Road, off the e end of Erith Road. By *Charles Pike & Partners*, at first in association with *E. T. Ashley-Smith*, the Kent County Architect. Workshop block 1964–6 with a bold ridge and furrow roof. The second phase, c. 1968–71, is concentrated in a thick tower block somewhat trickily detailed on the crown of the hill. Below it, confronting the approaching visitor, the domically roofed hall.

RAILWAY STATION. Still the original one, built in 1849 by *Samuel Beazley*, with staggered platforms.

OIL WORKS, Church Manor Way. In the industrial estate on 99 the riverside marshes all the factories are outfaced by the massive group of twenty-four concrete cylinders of the British Oil and Cake Mills Ltd. They were the first major work in this country of *Christiani & Nielsen*, the Danish pioneers of reinforced concrete techniques. The architect for the factory, built in 1913–17, was *Percival M. Fraser*, but the silos, for that is what the cylinders are, owed their appearance to his assistant, *S. Rowland Pierce*. And an amazing appearance it is for 1916. Here is exposed shuttered concrete, here are freestanding *pilotis*, used long before Le Corbusier exploited them. Functionally they result directly from the fact that the silos must taper at the bottom into funnels down which the nuts cascade. Thus the slim round piers carry the weight down to the ground and they, as the load-bearing members, are shuttered (with the precision of fluting rather than the roughness of *béton brut*) while the concrete faces that cover but do not carry are smooth and untextured. At the top the three wide waves of roof are equally effective, but not quite frank about the maintenance sheds behind them. Linking the silos to the riverside jetty run two concrete sheds, each spanning nearly

100 ft and over 350 ft long. The other buildings are brick-faced, with giant pilasters, not particularly well done.

The foretaste of Erith's redevelopment is in a few tower blocks, eight-storeyed at NORTHUMBERLAND HEATH, and with thirteen storeys at SLADE GREEN (strictly speaking in Crayford). The latter were complete by 1962. The town centre is largely rebuilt by *R. Seifert & Partners*, 1967 onwards. The scheme is coherent, but varied in style and inconsistent in quality. Best the RIVERSIDE BATHS, High Street, at the lowest level. 1967–8. No gimmicks. Glass N wall, to give a panorama of the river, but also providing from the road a surprising view of divers on the boards. Above and behind rises HOUSING, in particular two twelve-storey point blocks. At the back, entered from Pier Road, a SHOPPING PRE-CINCT, much less acceptable, both in its fiddling concrete facings and in the way the cars are stacked in two storeys over the shops with an access ramp trailing away down the hill.

THAMESMEAD. *See* Woolwich (Gr), Perambulation 3.

DARTFORD CREEK FLOOD BARRIER, across the mouth of the river Darent. 1974–82 by *Sir Bruce White, Wolfe Barry & Partners* (consulting engineers). Two massive reinforced con-crete piers supporting twin-leaf drop gates 100 ft wide. Around Crayford Ness, enormous earthen banks, raised in the mid 1970s for the Thames flood defences.

(Henry VIII established a large naval storehouse in WEST STREET, the NW continuation of the High Street, in 1512. More recently, the town has been distinguished by its heavy industries. In FRASER ROAD and SANDCLIFF ROAD, among old sand quarries, robustly styled brick buildings from the 1900s of the former VICKERS SON & MAXIM armaments factory, and a long steel-framed erecting shop dated 1907 from Fraser & Chalmers' engineering works.)

(In WALNUT TREE ROAD, between Bexley Road and the High Street, the former TRAM DEPOT of Erith U.D.C., 1905. Imposing frontage with tall narrow doorways. Former muni-cipal GENERATING STATION of 1903 adjacent.)

(On the riverside the modern concrete PIER replaces one of 1842, part of an unsuccessful scheme to develop a resort; cf. Gravesend, Kent.)

(In ST PAUL'S ROAD, off Mill Road, Bexley Road, 1 m. SW, the circular brick base of an early C19 TOWER MILL. Its upper storeys were of timber.)

FOOTS CRAY

ALL SAINTS, Church Road. By itself and oddly lonely beside a sweep of the ancient parkland of Foots Cray Place, consider-ing that the factories of the Sidcup Bypass are a short half-mile away. The church is virtually a new building by *Hakewill* c. 1863, though in lengthening the nave he went out of his way to keep the W spirelet, so that it now appears as a flèche. The timber W porch copies what was there before. One lancet in the chancel is old evidence, and two Perp windows in the nave are old. Also medieval the single exceedingly wide arch to the N aisle. – FONT. Purbeck marble, a good example of a common type. Square arcaded bowl, the sides slightly tapering. Four corner shafts with waterleaf capitals. Waterleaf is a motif of *c*. 1190. – GATE to the rood-loft stairs, dated 1638. Made up from the altar rails, no doubt. – PAINTINGS. Two large, round-headed panels of Moses and Aaron, done with a good deal of panache. Said to be by a Mr *Taplock*, 1709. They will have been part of an altarpiece. – MONUMENT. Recumbent effigy of a lady under a brick arch in the N aisle. Her costume is of the mid C14. Much worn down, but the carving must originally have been of good quality. Long folds falling unbroken to her feet. Headless angel to support her pillows. The loose head of a chain-mailed knight thrown in to keep her company.

FOOTS CRAY PLACE was burnt down in 1950. It was the latest of the four English Villa Rotondas, built *c*. 1756 for Bourchier Cleeve, not so much in imitation of Palladio as to outdo his friend, Lord Westmorland, at Mereworth. (Extensive gardens were created from *c*. 1902 for Samuel Waring (of Waring & Gillow) to a scheme by *T. H. Mawson*. Only fragments remain.)

CHURCH ROAD leads S from the church. At the S end, by the crossroads, the remains of the village: THE OLD HOUSE, early C19; and Nos. 4–8, an upstanding row of early C18 cottages. Three storeys. Red brick. Moulded wood cornice, the sort banned by the Act of 1709; yet the date 1737 is reported on two inaccessible bricks, so that must be the date of erection. In the HIGH STREET, TUDOR COTTAGES, a very mutilated Wealden hall house.

NORTH CRAY

ST JAMES. Rebuilt by *Edwin Nash*. Nave 1850–2, chancel 1871. Rock-faced ragstone. NW tower of 1857; shingled spire. Dec, with one or two mild surprises; e.g. the lights of the E window alternately wide and narrow, and the pretty arch to the organ recess, cusped many many times. – PULPIT. A good C17 piece. Pilasters and a bold convex cornice covered with small-scale arabesques. It has a date 1637. – CHANCEL WOODWORK, all brought in and much of it foreign, but made up into a unified whole of some splendour. The climax is the REREDOS, large panels in very high relief of the Adoration of the Magi and the Flight into Egypt. The STALLS incorporate Düreresque reliefs of the Adoration of the Magi and of the Shepherds (S) and the Visitation and Circumcision (N). Behind the stalls on the N side, a C15 RELIEF of the Seven Acts of Mercy. The end panels, with Renaissance shell-hoods, must be later. Also several pierced panels of foliage. – PAINT-

ING. A large and damaged Crucifixion. By *Gessi*, says Kelly. –
MONUMENTS. Elizabeth Buggin † 1650. Large black-and-
white-marble architectural tablet. – William Wiffin, *c.* 1652.
Small tablet with an oversized open pediment. – Octavia,
Lady Ellenborough, † 1819. By *Chantrey*, 1821. Kneeling
woman looking up, a wreath of flowers at her feet. Chantrey
used the design again at Weybridge, Surrey. – Alice Morris
† 1894, signed by *J. Nelson MacBean*. Relief of an airborne
woman in Grecian draperies, her upraised arms fully in the
round. Such allegorical females were becoming old-fashioned
in Chantrey's day.

North Cray is the most rural of the Crays. The churchyard fits
into a corner of the park of NORTH CRAY PLACE, beside the
colossal kitchen-garden walls. The walls run along the road for
quite a way, though houses hide behind them now instead of
vegetables. At the W end of the churchyard a handsome early
C 18 wrought-iron GATE leads into the park.

(In parkland, between North Cray Place and Foots Cray Place,
an ornamental five-arch BRIDGE across the Cray, of brick and
flint, 1782.)

RUXLEY

The one-time church of ST BOTOLPH seems to be at the end of
its useful life, even as a barn. It was never more than a chapel,
a simple rectangle. The flint and rubble stone walls intact.
Surviving details, e.g. the window rere-arches, and the simple
PISCINA and SEDILIA, are early C 14. Above the A 20 on a
hummock with, one is surprised to find, far-extending views
in all directions.*

FACTORIES, Sidcup Bypass. *See* Sidcup (Bx).

SIDCUP

CHRIST CHURCH, Main Road. 1900–1 by *A. R. Barker & Son*.
Ragstone banded with ashlar. Plate tracery in the tall
clerestory. Lancets in triplets in the low pent aisles. Chancel
with a canted apse. It reads like the description of a church of
the 1870s. SE tower never begun.

HOLY TRINITY, Lamorbey. Built by *Christian* in 1879 and
restored in 1949 after bomb damage. The ragstone laid crazy-
paving style gives it a C 19 texture; but the planning, nave and
gabled aisles somewhat subordinated, chancel with short
gabled chapels, is medievalizing, and the effect inside is really
remarkably like a medieval church. Dec tracery with no Victorian fancies.

ST ANDREW, Maylands Drive, E of Bexley Lane. 1964 by

---

* Excavation in 1968 revealed footings of an earlier church under the present
building. Unaisled nave and short square chancel, possibly Saxo-Norman.

Braddock, Martin-Smith & Lipley. Ingenious, fashionable, and slightly absurd. In plan an octagon, set on a slope so that the church proper, reached from the road by a glazed bridge, occupies only the roof. The walls, of charcoal brick with a band of windows above, are the walls of the parish room. The roof swoops down on four sides, and on the other four comes forward as sharp gables glazed at the ends. It makes of course a centralized building, and a very small one.

St John, Church Road, off the SE end of the High Street. 1899–1901 by *Fellowes Prynne*, incorporating a chancel and Lady Chapel of 1882 by *Withers*. Impressively big in scale, E.E., of stock brick, the dressings in red brick and stone, an artificial red stone in the chancel. The stump of a SW tower. Very long clerestoried nave, with clustered piers, the inevitable stone screen, and tiers of saints on the slant each side of it. Nobility is what Fellowes-Prynne aimed at, the nobility Pearson achieved so effortlessly. He does not achieve it for two reasons; first, there is not enough tension in the proportions, the nave especially seeming broad and spreading; and secondly, the details are largely left to look after themselves. See, e.g., the way the vaulting-shafts reach aimlessly down the wall, unrelated to the arcades; or the useless transepts, twelve inches deeper than the aisles, their sole function to create a mild diversion outside. – PULPIT. Oak. Inscribed: Antwerp 1651. Twisted columns at the angles, relief busts of the four Evangelists on the sides.

St Lawrence (R.C.), Main Road. 1906 by *Edward Goldie.*★ Stock brick. Round-arched style. Cruciform, with a shallow central dome, expressed outside by a low octagon gabled in the four main directions.

Emmanuel Church, Station Road. 1887–8 by *G. Baines*. Plate tracery with foiled openings like a series of explosions all over the building.

Kemnal Manor Upper School (formerly Cray Valley Technical School), Sidcup Bypass. 1934–8 by *John W. Poltock*, with *Christiani & Nielsen* as consultants. Not at all the normal Kent County Education Department's school design of the 1930s. A design that has worn extremely well. Concrete frame, with deep red brick facing-work and extensive glazing. The SE front is symmetrical, three-storeyed, the bands of windows turning the corners at the ends. Set back at each end two glazed staircase towers with bowed ends, *à la* Gropius. The entrance however comes at the extreme r. end, and starts the highly asymmetrical NE front, dominated by the glazed bow, and gradually dying away into the slope via a completely glazed hall block. The higher part behind is a later addition.

Holy Trinity Primary School, Burnt Oak Lane, off Wellington Avenue. 1968 by *Oliver Steer*, extended in 1971. Single-storeyed. The centre part like a pair of Ws, or rather a three-dimensional zigzag, has to be seen to be believed.

QUEEN MARY'S HOSPITAL. An impressive group, the product of a programme of reconstruction from the 1960s. At the
W end the MATERNITY DEPARTMENT, off Chislehurst
Road, 1966 by *C. F. Scott*, Regional Architect (*E. J. Wilson*,
project architect). Two-storey square block, formed on the
entrance (N) side into a symmetrical group, which recedes
from a grey-brick forebuilding, to the shiny white main block
with, again recessed, a black cube of water-tanks and other
essentials frankly revealed at the top. The NURSES' HOUS-
ING, N of Frognal House, steps gently down the hill, in series
of linked pavilions, and at the N end in flat-roofed blocks.
Completed 1965, by *W. H. Watkins, Gray & Partners*. In
between lie the ACCIDENT CENTRE and the five-storey
PRINCIPAL WARD BLOCK by the same architects, 1969–74,
forming the main range towards Frognal Avenue. Here red
brick and broad window bands predominate.

Sidcup is Chislehurst *ultra montes*, or at any rate Chislehurst N of
the A 20. Its classiness was diminished in the building boom
between the wars, and several recent office blocks and terraces of
flats are changing its character again. Yet even now the C 18
flavour of mansions in their parks is not completely lost. It will
be best to deal with these survivors first.

FROGNAL HOUSE, Frognal Avenue, behind Queen Mary's
Hospital. Large, roughly square house, early C 18 in
appearance, but certainly not in origin. The E front is the
grandest, two-storeyed like the rest, but eleven bays wide, and
the windows segment-headed and tall in their proportions.
Yellow and red brick. Top parapet. Central doorcase with
richly carved brackets. But the windows cluster together in
one place, their regularity disturbed by the pre-existing work
behind. Badeslade's print of 1719 shows the front as it is now.
Not so the S front, which in 1719 had a row of shaped gables
instead of the present parapet curving up at the ends. The
shorter windows, rougher brickwork, and moulded brick
cornice on this side all go with the mid-C 17 date that such
gables imply. Eleven bays again, nine windows and two blank
spaces at the r. The S range is however even older in origin, as
during extensive building works in 1980 it was discovered that
it incorporated a C 15 timber-framed building of two-bay hall
and storeyed wing at the E end, to which a framed W wing was
added in the C 16. The timberwork is no longer visible. Both E
and N ranges stand on stone foundations, probably of the mid
C 16; the stonework in the courtyard (now covered up) survives up to the first-floor level. The elevations of N and W
fronts are quite irregular. On the N front the stonework of the
second floor is now exposed. Fine early C 18 STAIRCASE, with
the usual carved tread-ends, one twisted and one fluted baluster per step, issuing from bulbs of foliage, and, to make it extra
grand, fluted Corinthian columns as newels.
    Early C 18 wrought-iron GATES in the long wall that follows
the road.

LAMORBEY PARK, Burnt Oak Lane, off Wellington Avenue.
Built *c.* 1744–8 for William Steele, but altered in 1784 (the
date on a rainwater head). To judge from a plan made after this
date, it was then, as now, a three-storeyed house of eight
not-quite-regular bays by five, with low wings to the W. Some
time after 1812 *John Shaw Sen.* regularized the rectangular
external outlines, making it nine bays by three, with porch-
bays to the E in bays three and seven. It is now faced with stock
brick, with Jacobean trimmings, panels of strapwork in the
parapet, and strapwork cresting to the projections. The bay-
window to the S which already existed got mullions and transoms, and curious three-dimensional strapwork finials. What
was the date of all this? Jacobeanisms as early as the second
decade of the C19 would be highly remarkable. (In the
grounds, two ICE HOUSES of 1790 and *c.* 1840.)

Visually the centre of Sidcup, in so far as it can be said to have a
centre at all, is THE GREEN. And the *clou* of The Green is the
MANOR HOUSE (now Council Offices). Late C18,* of pinky
brick laid with, for that date, remarkable roughness. Three-
storeyed, the façade to The Green of five bays, extended on
each side by the profiles of the full-grown bows on the side
façades. The three middle bays are as it were a frontispiece
pedimented, with white string-courses and the centre windows under a giant sunk arch. The porch is four very thin
Tuscan columns; the window above it vestigial Venetian.
Seven windows on the N side, all but the central one in two
full-scale bows.

SIDCUP PLACE, S of The Green, has an C18 core. This had the
remarkable plan of a square of three bays, with rectangular
projections diagonally at the corners. Only the E one stands
free now, from additions of 1853, *c.* 1896, and the 1920s. The
tradition is that it was built in imitation of a fort, in 1743.‡
(Splendid late C18 marble chimneypiece with large nymphs in
relief at the sides, and small nymphs dancing in the frieze.
NMR)

N of The Green, in STATION ROAD, are two six-storey office
blocks, not large, but as emphatic as the mid 1960s could be.
SIDCUP HOUSE, 1965 by *Bernard Engle & Partners*, has an
open ground storey on thumping great V-shaped piers, and
the OFFICES N of it grow in two directions from a tower-like
structure of exposed concrete housing the staircases. By the
Owen Luder Partnership, 1966. N again, by the station, a long,
thin, sixteen-storey slab of OFFICES, completed in 1966. The
architects were *Douglas Marriott & Partners*, and precious
little of architectural qualities they managed to infuse into it.

CHAPEL HOUSE, Blackfen Road. *See* Bexleyheath (Bx), Danson Park.

A postscript is needed on the FACTORIES beside the

---

* 1790, says Mr B. N. Nunns.

‡ But Mr Nunns notes that the house is not marked on Andrews, Dury, and
Herbert's map of 1769. *Joseph Trought* exhibited a design of a house with this plan
in 1767.

SIDCUP BYPASS, an arterial road of the 1920s, at the far SE
corner of Sidcup. KLINGERIT, 1935–6 by *Wallis Gilbert &*
Partners, shows knowledge of Dutch Expressionist brickwork. Symmetrical block. Brown brick of two shades, the
paler laid in the usual way, the reddy bricks mostly laid on
end. They add emphasis to the horizontal strips of window
and the verticals of the centrepiece. Also little windows across
angles, with projecting frames to draw attention to this feat.
The original swoopy italic lettering has been replaced. Other
modernistic details. SCHWEPPES, by the roundabout, is of
1961–2, a big-boned piece by *Tripe & Wakeham*. (Also the
former Critall metal window FACTORY, 1927.)

WELLING

ST JOHN, Roseacre Road, off the E end of the High Street. 1925
by *Evelyn Hellicar*. Brown brick, in the simplest Perp style; as
if it were something shameful to be still building a Gothic
church in the 1920s. It is indeed a shame that an architect
should build in a style he no longer believes in.

ST MARY THE VIRGIN, Wickham Street. 1954–5 by *Thomas
F. Ford*. The exterior is no more impressive than St John. Red
brick, in a sort of Georgian-Early Christian style, with a thin
Lombard s tower. Inside it is pure Soane revival, and not bad
in its way. A building like this epitomizes all that mid-C20
architecture ought not to be, yet one at least feels that Mr Ford
got a kick out of designing it. – WALL PAINTINGS. E wall,
Ascension by *Hans Feibusch*. – The rest by *Clare Dawson*, Old
and New Testament scenes arranged typologically, in accordance with common medieval practice.

DANSON PARK. *See* Bexleyheath.

Welling is almost wholly a creation of the 1920s and 30s, and its
churches match the timidity of the faceless and seemingly
endless housing around.

BROMLEY

The entries in this section are by John Newman, who has revised them for this volume. They were first published in *The Buildings of England: West Kent and the Weald* (1969). The new entries on industrial and railway architecture are by Malcolm Tucker.

INTRODUCTION

Bromley is by far the largest of the new London boroughs, but the least densely populated (296,539 in 1981). It stretches from Crystal Palace (or rather its site) on the crest of Sydenham Hill south-eastwards to the crest of the North Downs beyond Cudham thirteen miles away as the crow flies. That is right out in the country, and it is remarkable that the borough encompasses so much that has nothing to do with London. Built-up suburbia dies out around the 400-ft contour where West Wickham, Keston, Farnborough, and Orpington lie along the A232 and A21.*

---

* The GEOLOGY of Bromley is London Clay over areas of pebble beds in the N, with the chalk of the North Downs rising to the S and E, fringed by sands and capped in the S by clay with flints. From EARLY SETTLEMENTS, an extensive scatter of both prehistoric and Roman material has been found along the river Cray, which runs W of the chalk on the E side of the borough, and along the edge of the Downs. There was also a later prehistoric settlement at West Wickham. The

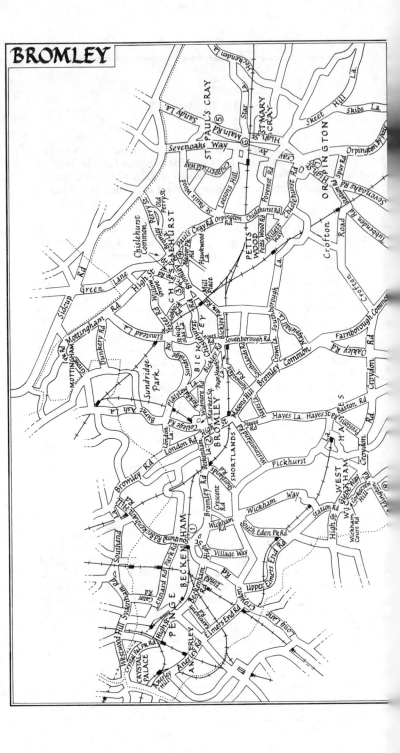

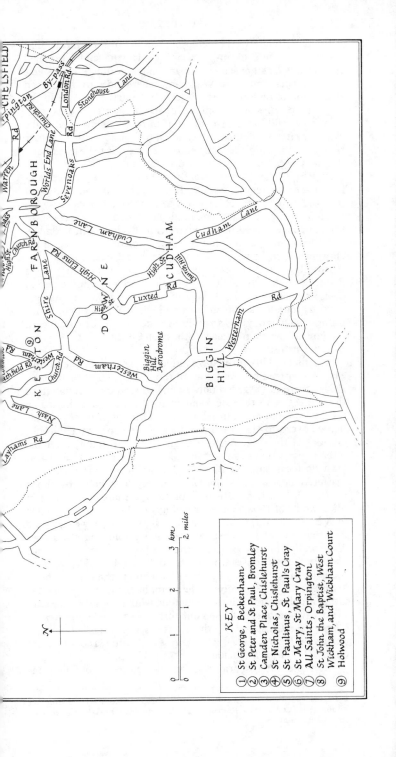

N

KEY
① St George, Beckenham
② St Peter and St Paul, Bromley
③ Camden Place, Chislehurst
④ St Nicholas, Chislehurst
⑤ St Paulinus, St Paul's Cray
⑥ St Mary, St Mary Cray
⑦ All Saints, Orpington
⑧ St John the Baptist, West
   Wickham, and Wickham Court
⑨ Holwood

In the borough twelve medieval churches or their furnishings
survive in whole or in part, and at Downe and Chelsfield
appropriate C 18 houses accompany them. A much more significant pairing is at West Wickham, where close to the church
stands the impressive brick Wickham Court, built late in the
C 15 on a progressively compact plan. Of country houses independent of village settlements, but in their generally villa-like
character not altogether independent of London, few of course
remain. Camden Place, Chislehurst, c. 1717, is the earliest, and
those by significant architects are Kevington, St Mary Cray,
c. 1767 by *Taylor*; Quernmore, Bromley, c. 1780, almost certain-
73 ly by *Leverton*; Sundridge Park, Bromley, by *Nash* and *Repton* of
72 the mid 1790s; and Holwood by the young *Decimus Burton*,
1823–6. Before London engulfed them such villas were most
thickly concentrated in the environs of Beckenham, Bromley,
and Chislehurst, as the numerous monuments surviving in the
churches of the first and last of these places bear witness.

Bromley's former character as a market town can hardly be
discerned today. Its major building to survive from the period
35 owes its existence to the Bishops of Rochester. Bromley College,
1670–2, founded as almshouses by Bishop Warner (and continuing as such today), was a building of country-wide influence in
its time. The bishop's palace (Stockwell College), of 1775, is not
so noteworthy.

Sydenham Hill formed an effective barrier to the south-
eastward spread of London until the re-erection of the Crystal
Palace there in 1852. No railway line crossed the borough until
the late 1850s: in 1858 Beckenham and Bromley were linked by
rail to London, and Chislehurst and Orpington in 1865. This
helped to create a leapfrogging effect of development in the later
decades of the C 19. Architecturally, without doubt, the most
interesting period of suburban growth in Kent is c. 1890–1914,
with its focal point in Bickley. The architect whose example
mattered most was *Norman Shaw*. A very early house by him is
in Page Heath Lane, Bickley, of 1866, a more typical one in
Shortlands, of 1868–9, and a harbinger of the Queen Anne style
in West Wickham, 1870–1. Far more significant, however, is the
fact that one of his most talented and prolific pupils, *Ernest
Newton*, lived in Bickley. Starting in 1884 and continuing until
1907 numerous houses from his hand dotted the quiet, spacious
94 roads of Bickley, Bromley, and Chislehurst, the earlier Shaw-
inspired, the later more or less emphatically neo-Georgian.
Other architects of national reputation whose houses can be seen
in goodly numbers in these same three places are *George Somers
Clarke Sen.* (Chislehurst in the late 1870s, and, especially spectacularly, at Hayes, 1882), *E. J. May* (Chislehurst, 1904–13), and
C. H. B. Quennell (Bickley, 1905–13).

After the First World War another surge of building en-

---

best surviving field monument is Caesar's Camp, Keston, a large Iron Age
hillfort. Also at Keston a Roman villa with mausolea. Other Roman remains
survive at Orpington.

veloped much of Hayes, West Wickham, and Orpington in
houses, and sacrificed the rural Cray Valley at St Mary Cray to
industry. One Corbusian house resulted, by *Godfrey Samuel* at
Bromley, of 1934–5. Meanwhile civic pride had touched Beckenham (Town Hall, 1931–2) and Bromley (Town Hall, 1906,
extended *c.* 1939). Only Chislehurst managed to preserve the
impression of *rus in urbe*.

Over the last thirty years worthwhile buildings have mostly
been in the public sector, but the dearth of central sites has sent
them flying to obscurely sequestered spots. Educational buildings come off best; there are worthwhile art colleges of 1957–62
by *George, Trew, Dunn* at Bromley and of 1972–4 by *Aneurin
John* at Chislehurst, and worthwhile schools by *Mayorcas &
Guest* (1966–9) at Beckenham and at St Mary Cray (early 1970s)
by the *G.L.C. Architect's Department*. The borough has its own
architect, *Aneurin John*, whose *magnum opus* is undoubtedly the
somewhat rebarbative, if centrally sited, Public Library and
Theatre at Bromley, 1970–5.

Further Reading

See p. 124.

Acknowledgements

Bromley Planning Department has a remarkable archive of
planning applications which document developments in the
borough since *c.* 1890. I am indebted to Mr G. King and Mr M.
Parkinson for giving access to information from this source.
Much assistance has been given by the staff of Bromley Public
Library (Local History Librarian, Miss E. Plincke). Others who
have improved the text in various places are Mr C. R. Councer,
Mr Nicholas Taylor, Mr Geoffrey Kitchener, and the Goldsmiths' College Industrial Archaeology Group.

ANERLEY

THE NEW CHURCH (Swedenborgian), Waldegrave Road.
1883 by *W. J. E. Henley*, manager of the Concrete Building
Company. Rogue Gothic in mass concrete, made using Portland cement and a pink pigment – robust material which has
weathered well. A slight deficiency of fine aggregate gives a
pleasing porous-looking texture. The workmanship appears
to have been meticulous.

ANERLEY STATION, Ridsdale Road, off Anerley Road. A
neo-Tudor station house of 1839 for the London and Croydon
Railway. The platform side remodelled later in their standard
sub-Gothic style, by the London Brighton and South Coast
Railway.

CRYSTAL PALACE. *See* separate entry, below.

BECKENHAM

CHURCHES

The churches of Beckenham are a thoroughly pedestrian lot. Even to mention some of them is to give them undue prominence.

CHRIST CHURCH, Fairfield Road, s of the High Street. 1876 by *Blashill & Hayward*. E.E. Stock brick, even the spire. Reconstructed with new roofs after bombing, by *Charles Sykes*.

The SCHOOL of 1901, by *Hooper*, and the SUNDAY SCHOOL of 1877, on the corner of the High Street, also of stock brick and of no interest except that, though similar at first sight, in every detail each is characteristic of its date.

HOLY TRINITY, Lennard Road. 1878 by *E. F. Clarke* (GR). The stunted pyramid-spire was added in 1883. Ragstone. Geometrical tracery.

ST BARNABAS, Oakhill Road, off Crescent Road. By *A. Stenning & H. Hall*, 1878 or 1884. Red brick. E.E. Brooksian, with its tall proportions, nave and apsidal chancel under one roof, and the mighty block capitals to the nave piers. The interior not however as taut and bare as Brooks could have made it. Enlarged 1912, 1933.

ST GEORGE. A humble medieval village church was replaced in 1885–7 by the present confident town church, by *W. Gibbs Bartleet*, of Beckenham. Tower completed 1902–3. The placing certainly is good, with the pinnacled s w tower closing the top of the High Street. Ragstone, with generous buff ashlar dressings. Dec. w narthex with a big rose window over it. Clerestoried nave and aisles, transepts, and canted apse to the chancel, also with pinnacles. All the proportions rather broad and low, the chancel especially broad. – STAINED GLASS. Much by *Thomas Freeth*, in the powerful vein of John Piper and Patrick Reyntiens. Apse windows and two under the tower 1963–6, N transept and N aisle 1974–5. – ALTAR CROSS and CANDLESTICKS also by *Freeth*. – MONUMENTS. Saved from the old church. None is a major work, but together they make an unusually fine collection of consistently good quality. Sir Humphrey Style † 1552. What remains of the tomb-chest and cresting is altogether Perp, without any Renaissance elements yet. Brasses of kneeling figures, 13 in. high, unusually well executed. Sir Humphrey is armoured and wears a tabard. – Margaret Damsell † 1563. A 23 in. brass, again very good and animated for its date. – James Burdett † 1710 (N aisle). Cartouche with lively mantling. – Peter Burrell † 1718 (N transept). Another cartouche, outstandingly well done. The edges of the cartouche are fantastically curled and undercut, and round it dangle luscious but tightly controlled bunches of flowers. – Hugo Raymond † 1737 (s aisle). By *Thomas Adye*. Hanging monument. Plain black pyramid on a plain black base, to show off the two vivacious white putti unveiling a medallion. Adye repeated the design at Bengeo, Herts. – Peter Burrell † 1756 (s transept). The only failure in the series. Large hanging monument in various veined marbles. In front of a pyramid with an oval medallion bust, a putto, much too small, stands disconsolately leaning on a large urn. – Stephen Holland † 1768. Again a pyramid on a hanging tablet. But note the yellow marble favoured in the mid century, and the tight, refined, up-to-date details. – Richard Acland (N transept). The monument must have been put up after his wife's death in 1771. A heavily draped woman, her hands clasped, stands by a heavily draped urn. – Amy Burrell, 1790 (s transept). Hanging monument, large but detailed with delightful delicacy, by *John Hickey*. On the sarcophagus, a relief of an old man and a woman with a baby doing homage to a languid woman by a tree. What is the subject of this scene? – Frances, Lady Hoare, † 1800 (N transept). By *Flaxman*, 1801. Grecian tablet, notably severe by comparison with the earlier monuments. Mourning members of her family, contemporarily dressed, in relief on either side of the inscription. – Catherine Vansittart † 1810 (s transept). Another large hanging monument, this time with a profile medallion on a draped altar. By *Chantrey?* asked Gunnis. – William, Lord Auckland, † 1814 (s transept). Grecian tablet with a profile medallion in very low relief. Carved in 1849 by *Henry Weekes* (Gunnis). – Jemima Wilson † 1865. Still in the pre-Chantrey tradition, with its female wreathing an urn with flowers. Signed by *Gaffin*, and poorly carved.

ST JAMES, St James's Avenue, off Croydon Road E of the station, Elmers End. The original church, of 1879–88 by *A. R. Stenning*, is hidden by the pretty Perp building of 1934 by *G. Sworder Powell*, which doubled its size. Symmetrical s elevation to the road, with two wide gables and low flanking porches on the slant. Arcade of exceedingly wide four-centred arches. – REREDOS. Painting of the Resurrection by *A. K. Lawrence*, 1955.

ST MICHAEL AND ALL ANGELS, Ravenscroft Road. 1955–6 by *W. H. Hobday & F. J. Maynard*. Neo-Byzantine, of all things.

ST PAUL, Brackley Road, N of Park Road. By *Smith & Williams*, 1872 (GR). Dec. Ragstone. – FONT. White marble. A shell held by a life-size kneeling angel. Date of death 1912, very late for such a Victorian and embarrassing piece. That is one's immediate reaction; yet of course it is a copy of *Thorwaldsen*'s font, carved in Rome in 1823.

ST EDMUND (R.C.), Village Way. By *J. O'Hanlon Hughes*. Consecrated in 1937. The only memorable church in the borough. Pale brown brick. Tall, much-windowed tower, with a curious pyramidal top of green copper. The dramatic thing is that this tower stands at the E end, over the chancel, which is thus top-lit. Wide pointed tunnel-vault in the nave, swooping down over the passage aisles. Unfortunately, not content with his effect, the architect stuck spindly ribs over it.

This and other fussinesses spoil what would otherwise be worthy of Sir Giles Scott himself.

BAPTIST CHURCH, Elm Road. 1889 by *Appleton & E. W. Mountford*. Yellow and red brick and stone. Saddleback tower with a spirelet on it.

METHODIST CHURCH, Bromley Road. 1887 by *James Weir*. Ragstone. Perp.

UNITED REFORMED CHURCH, Crescent Road. 1887–8 by *J. W. & R. F. Beaumont*. Rock-faced ragstone. Dec. Decidedly ambitious.

All three Nonconformist churches are identically planned, with a prominent tower and spire l. of the entrance front, wide, shallow transepts, and a school set across the further end.

PUBLIC BUILDINGS

TOWN HALL, Church Avenue, off the NW end of the High street. 1931–2 by *Lanchester & Lodge*. Toned down considerably in execution, compared with the published design. Tall central tower, with aedicules in all four directions high up and an octagonal top stage. Mauvish-brown brick and mauvish-grey brick.

PUBLIC HALL, Bromley Road. 1883, and unusually fresh for its date. The architect was *George Vigers*. Red and yellow brick. Tall roof with perky dormers in two rows and a lantern. Angle tourelles with lead caps. Semi-octagonal pilaster strips between the windows. Striped arches at the bottom. A loggia has been added. All done with the liveliness and freedom that mark the nineties rather than the eighties of the last century.

TELEPHONE EXCHANGE, Kelsey Park Road, s of the High Street/Manor Road junction. A gaunt Office of Works design of *c.* 1925, surprisingly effective (Nicholas Taylor).

CATOR PARK SECONDARY SCHOOL, Lennard Road. Neo-Wren with a Neo-Vanbrugh centrepiece. 1913–14 by *Wilfrid H. Robinson*.

ALEXANDRA COUNTY PRIMARY SCHOOL, Cator Road. 1952–3 by *Elie Mayorcas*.

LANGLEY PARK SCHOOL FOR BOYS, South Eden Park Road. 1966–9 by *Mayorcas & Guest*, with extensions by them completed in 1976. Much care has gone into this, to create an informally spreading, but homogeneous enclosed group sunk into a gentle slope. Muted colours: purple-brown brick and grey panels. Towards the central courtyard glazed curtain-walling and a single brilliant accent, a shiny red-tiled bow.

ST CHRISTOPHER'S SCHOOL. *See* Perambulation.

RAWLINS ALMSHOUSES, Bromley Road. In a corner of St George's churchyard. 1694, reconstructed in 1881. Of the humblest. One-storeyed plus dormers. Deep coved cornice with sunk patterns in the plaster.

OFFICES AND SHOPS, Albemarle Road, off the N end of the High Street. 1965–7 by *Derek Stephenson & Partners*. A typi-

cally thunderous affair, four-storeyed, with a castellated cresting of rectangular dormers at the top. Facing of grey aggregate
panels, in accordance with the taste of the mid 1960s.
(BECKENHAM JUNCTION STATION, at the s end of Southend
Road. Built from 1857 onwards for the Mid Kent Railway;
there are still some canopies etc. of this period. Bargeboarded
railway COTTAGES of the 1860s.)
(NEW BECKENHAM STATION, Lennard Road. 1866, with
ornamental cast-iron canopy brackets. Stationmaster's house
to the s, 1864.)

PERAMBULATION

COPERS COPE HOUSE, Southend Road, is the only remaining
pre-C 19 building in the modern borough of any architectural
pretension. The handsome early C 18 front has even quoins
and a pediment over the centre bay on giant pilasters. Brown
and red brick. Rusticated pilasters to the doorcase, and a
triangular pediment on a triglyph frieze. In the C 19 the house
was doubled in depth and given shaped end-gables.
WATERMILL, Southend Road. Two storeys, dated 1865, with
mill pond, on the river Ravensbourne.
The transformation of the village surrounded by mansions in
their small parks into a residential suburb of London began in
SOUTHEND ROAD, with large Italianate houses of c. 1850.
Just beyond are the lodges of Beckenham Place. (For Beckenham Place itself, see Lewisham (Le), Perambulation 5.) E
of this, and N of Bromley Road, lies the CATOR ESTATE, laid
out c. 1864 and still with some of its original houses. Tall and
yellow, with tentative polychromy, they are rather earnest and
stodgy.
For light relief one should go to WICKHAM ROAD, where No.
72, last survivor of a group by *Francis Hooper*, 1897, expresses
the tile-hung Norman Shaw style at its wittiest. No. 76 is also
by *Hooper*, of 1898, more relaxed but also less personal, in fact
even more like early Norman Shaw. (No. 34 appears to be by
Hooper, and so does No. 11 COURT DOWNS ROAD. N.
Taylor) Wickham Road ends with a roundabout and an
amusing cross-section of Beckenham's history. On the l.
BURRELL COTTAGE, a demure C 18 three-bay house, in
brown brick; on the far side the SOUTH LODGE of Eden
Park, a crisp white Regency job; and on the r., the servant of
suburban Beckenham, PARK LANGLEY GARAGE, in a rampant 'Road to Mandalay' style, 1928 by *Edmund B. Clarke*. On
the w side of Kelsey Park, in MANOR WAY, later run-of-the-
mill houses by *Hooper*; No. 2, of 1910, was built for himself.
In KELSEY WAY, No. 15 is by *Barry Parker*, 1929–30.*
Finally, working back further E, Nos. 124–128 BROMLEY
ROAD were built as a single house in 1884, very early but
already very assured work of *Ernest Newton*, although the way

* Information kindly provided by Mr Mervyn Miller.

the service block on the r. steps boldly forward is odd. St
Christopher's School stands opposite. Early Georgian
house, disfigured by a projecting addition on the ground floor.
Five bays and three storeys. Brown brick and fine red brick.
Spacious staircase, with one turned and two twisted balusters
to the tread. Of the new housing for which the Victorian
mansions are making way all over Beckenham only one group
deserves the highest praise. That is *Eric Lyons*'s West Oak,
The Avenue, of 1960, reached from near the E end of Bromley
Road via Downsbridge Road. Short two-storeyed terraces.
How well sited they are among the trees, and how strongly
designed, comes out very clearly by comparison with Morley Court, next door, perfectly adequate work by *Fitzroy
Robinson & Partners*, 1965–6. Further w in The Avenue some
remarkably sculptural low-rise flats of 1968–9, in buff brick
with far-projecting concrete staircase ramps. By *Derek Sharp
Associates*.

BICKLEY

St George, Bickley Park Road. 1863–5 by *F. Barnes* (GR).
Dec in a costly manner. Ragstone. Clerestoried nave, transepts, canted apse to the chancel. w tower and spire rebuilt by
Newton in 1905–6, redolent of St Mary, Oxford. Cruelly
hideous and inappropriate arcades. The interior, under the
direction of the vicar, Canon *Hugh Glaisyer*, was after bomb
damage turned from light to very mysteriously dark by blocking all the chancel windows, the clerestory, and all but single
lights of the aisle windows. – MONUMENT. The Wythes
family. Large canopied tomb-chest with side pieces, in a
straightforward Perp style. 1871 by *Butterfield*.
In 1780 John Wells built himself Bickley Hall (to the
design of *Robert Mylne*). The house was demolished only in
1963, but building on the park began as early as 1861; hence
the date of the church. What makes Bickley architecturally
interesting falls midway between the 1860s and 1960s. This is
an unusually representative group of wealthy suburban
houses that plot the progress of that sad period in English
domestic architecture when the freedom that had been won by
Norman Shaw, abandoned in a nostalgic yearning for the C18,
was buckled into the neo-Georgian straitjacket. One of the
prime bucklers was *Ernest Newton*, who lived in Bickley and
began his career in Shaw's office. Of *Shaw*'s own early work in
the neighbourhood (Stockwell College Estate) only Nos. 4–6
Page Heath Lane, of 1866, survive. Minor; altered 1974.
Beechcroft, Bickley Road, of 1885, is one of *Newton*'s first
houses. The vocabulary, tile-hanging above red brick, and a
half-timbered gable jutting forward in the centre, is Shaw's.
The desire for symmetry, and the closed outline of the hipped
roof, are too. Newton admits a playful detail or two, but the
house is noticeably crisp and spare. Westwood, Bird in
Hand Lane, N of Page Heath Lane, comes next. Also by

Newton, 1889. The same ingredients, with the same windows, rectangular but of any convenient proportion. Big off-centre chimneybreast. No. 8, next door, is by *Newton* too, built for himself in 1884, so exceptionally early. By 1902, however, to judge by LITTLE ORCHARD, Page Heath Lane, Newton has almost made the transition. All is Georgian vernacular, including the pair of canted window bays; all, that is, except the long staircase window, pushing the porch over to the left. In PINES ROAD, Nos. 2, 4, and 6 are Newton pastiche, by *Amos Faulkner*, of 1907, 1914, and 1907 respectively.

Finally, in CHISLEHURST ROAD, three fully-fledged neo-Georgian houses by *Newton*, in red brick. On the l. ENNORE (No. 35A), of 1903, a fine composition towards the garden with its unexpected central chimneybreast between two canted bays; then on the r. BICKLEY COURT, 1904, L-shaped and not entirely regularized towards the road, with canted window-bays at the back, and CROSS HAND, purely and impersonally neo-Georgian, also designed in 1904. AMAPOLA, next door, keeps up the scale, but is much more wilful, and really well out of date; 1927 by *T. Brammell Daniel*.

BULLERS WOOD, off St Nicholas Lane. *Newton*'s first major house, of 1889, famous for having been decorated internally by *Morris & Co*. In fact it was only a remodelling of an earlier house, which is left partly showing at the SE corner. The entrance front faces W and a projecting wing at the l. had to be incorporated. Newton achieved this by throwing out three more projections further r., a generous window-bay, a porch, and a bay-cum-chimneybreast. He then tied them together with a deep white egg-and-dart cornice, through which no gable breaks. Big wide windows, stone-mullioned below, wood above. The emphasis on the horizontals is very strong, and such overt Georgianisms as the cornice remarkable in 1889. Perhaps they are not hard to explain – that was the year in which Shaw, Newton's master, was rebuilding Bryanston. Even so the façade does not quite come together as a whole, and that is the measure of the architect's immaturity. Narrow N side, three-storeyed, as the land falls, with a single bay the full height. On the E side a typical sheer chimneybreast at the l. end. The rest quite informally grouped and somewhat altered. Throughout the details are fresh and original, especially the treatment of the porch, with a flat far-projecting hood, and continuous glazing above it between long wooden brackets. The interior has lost all its original Morris wallpapers and hangings, but the drawing room ceiling remains, beamed, and stencilled by *Morris* himself with a scarlet pimpernel pattern in delicate buff, green, and pink. The white woodwork however is the right colour, and one is struck by the spaciousness of Newton's planning. The setting is still superb, a steep wooded hillside plunging down below the formal terrace. The STABLES by the entrance are *Newton*'s, 1884. (His COTTAGE of the same year, at the foot of the hill, has been demolished.)

In three other areas worthwhile houses of this period are to
be found. First s of the A222, near Bickley Station. Off Southborough Road to the E, No. 5 HAWTHORNE ROAD is another
important early house by *Newton*, of 1885, showing him still
heavily dependent on Shaw. A little further s, in SOUTH-
BOROUGH ROAD, first No. 1, PARK HILL, 1899 by *Niven &
Wigglesworth*, orange brick, shaped gables, and details of a
delightful prettiness such as Newton eschewed; (then TURP-
INGTONS, an unexpected survival from much earlier – the
later C 14 – and a rarity in being a timber-framed hall-house of
the pre-Wealden type with the two-storey jettied ends separately roofed at r. angles).

N of the A222, centred on St George's church, an unusually
homogeneous and spaciously arranged suburb was developed
between 1905 and 1914. *C. H. B. Quennell* was the presiding
genius, brownish-purple brick his preferred material. The
message, of increasing formalism in the later houses, is the
same as in Newton's work. Earliest are those in DENBRIDGE
ROAD (s of Chislehurst Road just w of the railway), where No.
13 is in fact by *Newton*, of 1905. Nos. 1 and 3 are by *Quennell*,
1906, the latter for himself, quite cottagey. The similar No. 1
WELLS ROAD, alongside, is by *Evelyn Hellicar*, 1906, for
himself. Other houses by *Quennell* in Denbridge Road are
Nos. 2, 8, 10, 12, all designed in 1906–9. Progressing westwards, in WOODLANDS ROAD, No. 19 is by *Quennell*, 1907,
No. 17 by *Reginald Wheatly*, also 1907. In ST GEORGE'S
ROAD, which cuts across at this point, Nos. 19 and 21 (both
1909), 22 and 24 (both 1907) are all by *Quennell*. Latest and
most ambitious of *Quennell*'s houses are four in the w half of
Woodlands Road, ENGLEFIELD (1910) and HADLOW
(1911) on the l., DEERWOOD (1912) and ORCHARD HOUSE
(1913) on the r. The maverick here is CASTANEA, 1930–1 by
P. D. Hepworth, early flat-roofed modernistic, recently made
fit for its company by means of a pitched roof and shingle
cladding.

The last area to investigate lies N of Chislehurst Road and is more
a matter of bits and pieces. In HILL BROW off the w end of
Chislehurst Road one can single out two houses: No. 22, a
very early work of *W. Curtis Green*, 1899, roughcast, with a
pair of shallow window-bows and a Venetian motif in the
gable, and MOLESCROFT, also 1899, also roughcast, by *Newton*. More ambitious are two houses in MAVELSTONE ROAD,
off to the r. at the end of Hill Brow. THE MOUNT, 1902, with
a lodge *en suite*, is Newton-style by *Amos Faulkner*, and STOT-
FOLD, next door, 1906–7, is a more self-consciously Arts-and-
Crafts piece, by *T. P. Figgis*. Typical staircase hall inside.
Also by *Figgis* is the much coarser No. 58 HILL BROW, of
1908. The boundary towards the N is SUNDRIDGE AVENUE,
where there are further witty displays of Newtonisms, No. 26
by *W. J. Pamphilon*, and No. 28 by *F. Baxendale*, both of
1906.

BIGGIN HILL

Chaotic sprawling housing spattered all over the side of a long, steep-sided valley, a place to make the most ardent free-enterpriser admit the virtues of planning; though New Addington, next door, is unfortunately no advertisement for the latter. The shacks of the first pioneers have largely given way to cosy suburban houses and gardens. Visit the next valley westwards, over the Surrey border, to see what glorious country this once was.

ST MARK. Built in 1957–9 with materials from the demolished Victorian church of All Saints, North Peckham, and designed by *Sir Giles Gilbert Scott, Son & Partner*. Yellow brick without, red brick within. Detached, slightly tapering, NW campanile with pretty cresting. Very free neo-Gothic church, its design governed by the need to re-use the old nave roof. All the windows were engraved by the vicar the Rev. *V. Symons*, copying woodcuts from the early C15 German Biblia Pauperum. – PLATE and ALTAR CROSS. Also by Mr *Symons*.

NORHEADS FARM, ⅝ m. W. Straightforward red-brick farmhouse, dated 1715. Five bays, two storeys, and a big hipped roof.

The AERODROME, famed from the early days of the Second World War, is to the N. The most conspicuous building is the neo-Georgian OFFICERS' MESS, 1930, like a large country house.

BROMLEY

CHURCHES

HOLY TRINITY, Bromley Common. 1839 with a W tower of 1842. By *Thomas Hopper*. Still pre-archaeological, and lacking in architectural ambition. Flint, especially black on the tower. Windows with sandstone surrounds and cuspless wooden tracery. In 1884 *C. Pemberton Leach* did his best to make it more acceptable, by replacing much of the tracery with Dec designs in Bath stone (note the characteristic change from a local to a non-local stone) and by adding a stunted apse. – MONUMENT. George Norman † 1855. Signed *T. Gaffin*. Mourning soldier either side of a gravestone.

ST ANDREW, Burnt Ash Lane. 1929 by *Sir Charles Nicholson*. Really very poor. N aisle not yet built.

ST JOHN THE EVANGELIST, Park Road. 1879–80. By *George Truefitt*, who put much thought into the rebarbative design. The church lies along the road, aisled nave and apsidal chancel under a single colossal roof. S transept not projecting but carried up in a gable that develops on the E side to include a stunted octagonal spirelet. Obtrusive plate tracery. The W end done in the same take-it-or-leave-it spirit – four lancets stretched to improbable lengths between two far-projecting buttresses. The s aisle calmly continues as a lean-to against one of them. Greek cross plan to the aisle piers. The interior badly proportioned and further spoilt by whitewash and brash STAINED GLASS in the N transept window, 1951 by *Francis Spear*.

ST LUKE, Bromley Common. By *Arthur Cawston*, 1886–90. The top of the tower and the spire only completed in 1910. E.E. Red brick, with dressings of stone and yellow brick. Continuous nave and chancel. Low aisles. NW steeple. Externally it seems thoroughly conventional. Spacious interior unbroken from W to E, solid and convincing. Stone piers, brick arches, but the way the stone continues some way above the capitals is very characteristic of the date.

A short way along Southlands Road, ST LUKE'S INSTITUTE, 1891, an early work by *Ernest Newton*. Yellow brick. The end towards the road a dexterous play with geometrical shapes. Especially neat the contriving of the porches, white triangles in profile that continue the line of the roof. More ordinary side elevation with buttresses between big segmental windows.

ST MARK, Westmoreland Road. Of *Evelyn Hellicar*'s church of 1897–8 the almost detached NW tower and the arcades remain. Reconstruction (after bombing) in 1953 by *David Nye & Partners* to *T. W. G. Grant*'s design. Parabolic transverse arches support the nave roof, and conflict uneasily with Hellicar's late Perp shapes.

ST MARY PLAISTOW, College Road. Nave 1863–4 by *Waring & Blake*. Chancel added 1881 by *W. R. Mallett*. S transept and narthex 1891. N transept 1899–1900 by *Wadmore, Wadmore & Mallett*. Aisles never achieved, nor the intended SW tower. The view from the road is as confusing as the history. It takes a moment to realize that this is the S side, with a fanciful porch to the S transept. Flint, banded with Bath stone. Dec tracery. The chancel walls and roof painted in 1890, painted ORGAN CASE, ALTAR, and REREDOS (in a C15 Flemish style), all somewhat amateurishly executed, but, with the E window by *Ward & Hughes* (or should one say in spite of it?), a rich ensemble. The contrast with the wide, bare nave and transepts is extremely painful.

ST PETER AND ST PAUL. Bombing in 1941 left a tower without a church. The tower is a good example of the Kentish type. Flint. Diagonal buttresses, N turret, octagonal at the top. The new church, 1948–57 by *J. Harold Gibbons*, takes its cue from it, in materials, in scale, and in being Gothic. The relation of church to tower no longer as before. Apsidal chapel E of the tower, and N of the nave. Nave and chancel under one roof. Short, high N transept, given all the architectural emphasis. The freedom with Gothic motifs is imitated from Sir Giles Scott, but the gusto has gone out of it and so has every trace of finesse. – FONT. Norman, on a modern base that does not fit. Square marble bowl, with four shallow sunk arches per side. – DOOR. In the tower. Probably C14. A strip of blank tracery across it with quatrefoils between ogee archlets. – BRASS. Richard Thornhill † 1600. 35 in. figures. Damaged.

BAPTIST CHURCH, Widmore Road. Cheap Early Christian. 1864 by *R. H. Moore*.

PRESBYTERIAN CHURCH, Upper Park Road. 1895 by *John C. T. Murray*. Red brick and stone. Mainly E.E. It has a rather good steeple in the usual Nonconformist position, l. of the entrance front. Plain brick tower with a transparent bell stage; stone broach-spire ringed once by crisp lucarnes.

BECKENHAM CEMETERY, London Road. 1877 by *George Truefitt*, the architect of St George (*see* above) and of Tufnell Park (Ca). The complete range of ragstone chapels, lodge, and mortuary survive (HM).

PLAISTOW CEMETERY, Burnt Ash Lane. A massive lodge over the drive; ragstone E.E. chapel. 1892 by *W. R. Mallett* (HM).

PUBLIC BUILDINGS

TOWN HALL. In two independent parts, at r. angles to one another. The earlier half, in Tweedy Road, 1906 by *R. Frank Atkinson*, the later, in Widmore Road, by *C. Cowles Voysey*, completed in 1939. The contrast between them is most instructive. Both of red brick with stone dressings; both two-storeyed, consisting of a long centre and narrow, barely projecting wings. Atkinson is neo-Wren, Cowles Voysey is neo-Georgian. Atkinson's stone enrichment overdone in a typically Edwardian way. Circular domed porch, big broken pediment. Cupola. Cowles Voysey confines the stone to a plinth and a reticent centrepiece. What gives his design distinction is the subtle subordination of the wings by a slight reduction in the size of the windows, and the deftly placed chimneystacks. His is the greater discipline without any doubt.

PUBLIC LIBRARY. *See* p. 172.

ST LUKE'S INSTITUTE. *See* St Luke, above.

TECHNICAL COLLEGE AND RAVENSBOURNE COLLEGE OF ART AND DESIGN, Bromley Common. 1957–62 by *George, Trew, Dunn*.* Two colleges in one building, a long six-storey slab on a sloping site at r. angles to the main road. Detached hall block on the N, workshops by the road and at the lower end. Basically simple, the part at the top end (built first) more straightforwardly designed, but the brutalist creed of the moment required angular workshop skylights and various protruding concrete pieces, e.g. the sloping undersides of staircases and large lintels on the littlest windows.

STOCKWELL COLLEGE. *See* p. 172.

BOYS GRAMMAR SCHOOL, Hayes Lane. Designed in 1908 by *H. P. Burke Downing*, and completed in 1911. Main Block with wings. Red brick and stone. The neo-Wren style handled

* Begun under the firm's former name, *Pite, Son & Fairweather*.

with considerable panache. At the r. end a pretty little rough-cast CARETAKER'S HOUSE. Hall of 1933 at the back, also Wren-style.

QUERNMORE SECONDARY SCHOOL, London Lane. *See* p. 170.

(SUNDRIDGE PARK STATION, Plaistow Lane. 1878, a good example of a small halt with weatherboarded shelters.)

PERAMBULATION

Bromley's existence as a market town at a fashionable distance from London was challenged by the arrival of the railway in 1858. The population in 1861 was 5,505. By 1871 it had almost doubled, and continued to increase at the rate of about five thousand per decade until 1914. By then the town had become an outer suburb, a status which it retains today. What survives from pre-railway Bromley is a number of isolated buildings, mostly tucked away and not readily found, and the shape of the Market Square, on which all roads converge.

The starting place then is the MARKET SQUARE. The square itself is filled up by a miserable half-timbered block of 1933, by *T. P. Bennett & Son*. The only reason for dwelling in the square is HEAL'S (formerly Dunn's) shop, on the E side, by *Bertram Carter*, 1954–7, set back from the street line to make a much needed breathing space. Off-centre picture window on the first floor. The interior fascinatingly intricate, with subtle shifts in levels, made possible because a temporary building of 1948 was enclosed by the new shop. At the NW corner of the square one C18 brick front. Adjoining, but in the HIGH STREET, a much taller group, the ROYAL BELL HOTEL, MARTIN'S BANK, and Nos. 179–181, designed as a group by *Newton* in 1898. The three parts are clearly distinguished from each other, the first with panels of pargetted strapwork, then with Newton's favourite lead-covered bows, and the last part rising up to Tudor gables. Altogether it is a fine design. Original decoration in the hall, including a characteristic chimneypiece, and in the main first-floor room. Staircase with brass and alabaster balustrade. Newton clearly hoped that this would be the beginning of a grander High Street, but no further efforts have been made to replace the mean cottage shops on the E side. The W side mostly a no less mean rebuilding of the 1890s.

At the end of the High Street, on the r., the red brick walls of
35 BROMLEY COLLEGE. Stone gatepiers with bishop's mitres for finials, and fine wrought-iron gates dated 1666. The college is what was more often called a hospital, i.e. almshouses, founded by John Warner, Bishop of Rochester, under whose will of 1666 a college was to be built for 'twenty poore widowes (of orthodoxe & loyall clergymen)'. The land was not acquired until 1669, and an Act authorizing building passed in 1670. Work went ahead at once, to the design of *Richard Ryder*, and

was completed in 1672.* The college forms a quadrangle,
presenting a long front to the road, with the treasurer's (l.) and
chaplain's (r.) houses as moderately projecting wings. The
widows were spaciously housed, with two rooms on the
ground floor, two bedrooms, and a semi-basement kitchen.
Each was expected to be attended by one resident servant and,
if possible, by a spinster daughter. The building is of red
brick, with raised bands between the storeys. Hipped roof.
Grand stone central entrance arch, reaching right up to the
eaves.‡ Big curved pediment with the bishop's arms, supported on Doric half-columns. Triangular porch canopies in the
wings, flanked by little bulls-eye windows with little round-
headed windows on the upper level. This is the sort of
architecture popularly associated with the name of Sir Christopher Wren. But that is to place its origin considerably too
late, for the style had developed even before the Civil War,
and became the speciality of the masons and bricklayers of the
City of London both before, and even after, the Great Fire.
The college is memorable as one of the largest, one of the
soberest, and one of the earlier examples to survive. A paved
walk within the quadrangle sheltered by a lean-to roof on
correctly proportioned Doric columns of stone. A second
quandrangle, similar in design, but with wood columns, was
added in 1794–1805 for twenty more widows. The architect of
this was *Thomas Hardwick*. CHAPEL in the range between the
two quadrangles, red brick with diapering. Dec windows. By
Waring & Blake, 1863. Complete set of glass of that date by
O'Connor. It was the same architects who propped up the
external walls of the old quadrangle of the college with red-
brick buttresses, also in 1863.§

SHEPPARD'S COLLEGE is an isolated building to the NE in a
Tudor style, erected in 1840 and designed by *Joseph Shoppee*,
an Uxbridge builder, to house five spinsters made homeless by
their mothers' deaths.

There is no need to pursue the High Street northwards once it
becomes London Road, except to find an early house (1893)
by *Ernest Newton*, No. 3 GRASMERE ROAD, off Highland
Road, on the l. Tile-hanging above brick. Big half-timbered
porch bay with caryatids framing the first-floor window. No. 5
was built as the STABLES.

A route through the N and E parts of Bromley is best begun by
leaving the Market Square along WEST STREET. This continues as COLLEGE ROAD. Nothing to report, except, at the
change-over, PRIMARY SCHOOL, by *St Aubyn*, 1854–5, enlarged 1870; and the *Owen Luder Partnership*'s nine-storey
OFFICE BLOCK in Sherman Road, behind Bromley North
Station. Lift, staircases, etc. separated and stressed in towers
at one end à la Kahn. Completed 1968. No more stops before

* Mr Roger White's investigations have led to the discovery of the building
account book.
‡ Executed by *Joshua Marshall*, the King's Master Mason.
§ Mr G. McHardy kindly provided the evidence for the last sentence.

LONDON LANE, the turning on the l. after St Mary's church.
Halfway along it a notice on the right announces QUERN-
MORE SECONDARY SCHOOL. It comes as a shock to find that
the school is in reality a splendid late C18 house in excellent
condition, with no utilitarian additions obtruding on the entrance (w) side. The house was built as Plaistow Lodge for the
fabulously wealthy Peter Thellusson, the intricacies of whose
will caused so much litigation that an Act had to be passed to
prevent anyone else from making another like it. He bought
the estate in 1777. His architect is not known but the style of
the house points to *Thomas Leverton.** Yellow stock-brick
block five bays by three and two-and-a-half storeys high.
Rusticated ground floor of Portland stone. Pediment over the
centre three bays on pilasters with finely carved, idiosyncrati-
cally designed, Composite capitals. Pedimented first-floor
windows, the central one Venetian. Two-storeyed wings,
curving forward slightly, link the main block to pedimented
pavilions, which each have just one very large Venetian window with a panelled tympanum. Statues in niches and *Coade*
stone panels. Exquisite detailing throughout. Early C19 stone
porch with Greek Doric columns and entablature. The E side
unenriched brick, with the central three windows of the main
block in a wide bow. No recognizable internal features except
the back stairs, with metal balustrading characteristic of
Leverton.
The continuation of London Lane E of College Road is PLAIS-
TOW LANE. In GARDEN ROAD, a turning to the l. after
Sundridge Park Station, No. 10 is by *Niven & Wigglesworth*,
1899, No. 23 by *Newton*, 1904. Garden Road loops back as
EDWARD ROAD, where No. 18, by *Newton*, 1907, was a
mirror-image of the last before recent gross disfigurement. In
LODGE ROAD, a turning to the l. off this, just before the
entrance to Sundridge Park, first two progressive houses of
the 1950s, SILVERWOOD by *R. A. Barber*, 1958, and
BROOKLYN, 1957 by *Ivor Beresford*, both with vertical cedar
boarding and much glass; and then two houses of the International Style of the 1930s, evidence, if any is needed, that any
style at all can be handled well or badly, lightly or heavily. The
candidate for the derogatory epithets is STILLNESS, 1934 by
Gilbert Booth. Better by far the last house in the road, BY THE
LINKS, by *Godfrey Samuel*, 1934–5. The entrance side the
favourite Corbusian combination of a long horizontal slit window over a recessed ground storey carried on pilotis; the
garden side generously glazed and quite without mannerisms
of any sort.
By the Links because Sundridge Park is now a golf-course. That
it is an unusually umbrageous golf-course is due to the fact
that the park was landscaped by *Repton*.
73 SUNDRIDGE PARK, the house which the landscape setting was

* Leverton exhibited in 1780 a design for a 'gentleman's seat' in Kent 'now
building'.

to show off, still stands on its shallow s-facing slope with Elmstead Wood rising behind. It is a large, rambling mansion, with three giant porticoes, and stuccoed a dazzling white. The building history is not completely clear, which is unfortunate, as the house has a highly remarkable, not to say revolutionary, plan. Repton was first consulted by E. G. Lind, but, when in 1796 Sir Claude Scott bought the estate, his services continued to be used. *Nash* exhibited designs for the house in 1799 and Angus in his *Seats of the Nobility and Gentry*, 1804, remarks that 'the form of the house was fixed and planned on the ground at the time when Mr Repton and Mr Nash mutually assisted each other'.* Angus attributed the interiors and the stables to *Samuel Wyatt*, but his illustration shows the house without the present wings. The drive leads to the NW front, with the entrance under a four-columned Corinthian portico. Coupled giant pilasters emphasizing the angles. To the l. a one-storeyed wing coming forward at r. angles. The house itself develops towards the s, with three bays at forty-five degrees to the entrance front, and a bold domed bow encircled by six giant Corinthian columns. The continuation on the far side is a repeat, a three-bay piece going back from the bow at less than a r. angle, then an obtuse-angled turn to an attached Corinthian portico. Service wing making an L with this. To put it another way: if one ignores the wings, the plan is half a solid hexagon with a bow growing from the apex. As one sees it from the NW, however, one does not appreciate the symmetry of the plan, and in spite of the uniform height and the uniform order, the house has the picturesqueness which Nash later exploited in his castellated and Italianate houses. Whether it comes successfully through the armature of the classical orders as they are used here can be disputed.

The internal planning is remarkable for the corridors, running through the core of the house on both floors. Rooms lead off on both sides. The main staircase lies behind the domed bow, rising beyond a screen of two Ionic scagliola marble columns, first in a straight flight, then sweeping back in two arms round the wall of the circular well. Upper screen of two columns, Corinthian this time. Top-lit dome above. A great deal of typical *Wyatt* plasterwork (as typical of Samuel as of James, but somewhat out of date by c. 1800).‡ Ceilings with small inset paintings in the manner of *Angelica Kauffmann*. The best rooms are the upper of the two small circular rooms in the bow and that in the N wing. In the former the ceiling is slightly coved and decorated with plaster roundels instead of paintings. Here alone the colouring is original. The latter has a

---

* Repton in his *Theory* expresses it more strongly: 'The house, and the hill on which it stands, are exactly in due proportion to each other; and the former is so fitted to the situation and views which it commands, that I regret having shared with another the reputation of designing and adapting this very singular house to circumstances which cannot well be explained but upon the spot.' Repton lowered the hillside 30 ft perpendicularly to make a site for the house.

‡ Mr Roger White however suggests that some of this may be C 19 redecoration.

shallow segmental vault, with much-enriched ribs criss-crossing diagonally.

STABLES, NW of the house, of yellow brick. Three-storeyed central pedimented pavilion with a cupola. Long wings curving forward on each side. (Two ICE HOUSES in the grounds.)

Back in Plaistow Lane, HOLY TRINITY CONVENT, an early C18 house of three storeys, the top one treated as an attic. Seven bays in all, the end bays projecting as tiny wings. Dark red brick. No entrance on this side, or on the opposite side, which was remodelled late in the C18 with a big bow for the full height. The present entrance is modern. This description refers to the r. block; for the block that answers it and the recessed centre pinched between the two were only added in the early C20. At the farthest end of Plaistow Lane several houses on the l., roughcast not brick and tile-hung, are even so in Ernest Newton's early style. Only No. 107 is actually by *Newton*, designed in 1902.

The final outlier on the E side of the town, in BICKLEY ROAD, is THE OLD COTTAGE, behind a brick wall and gateway dated 1599. The gate arch is still straight-sided, a pre-Renaissance form, with a stretched brick hoodmould and a gable with the stumps of octagonal finials. The cottage itself also *c.* 1599. Timber-framed, with some red brick. Gabled porch open below on flat, shaped, baluster-like posts. The plan not symmetrical, but of the 'lobby-entry' type, the coming thing at that date. (In the W upper room a stone fireplace with a phoenix over it set in a roundel with Mannerist pilasters.)

Returning to the town centre via WIDMORE ROAD, one must turn l. down ST BLAISE AVENUE to reach STOCKWELL COLLEGE (Teachers' Training College). The centre of the college buildings is a red-brick block built in 1775 as the palace of the bishops of Rochester. N front of three-plus-three-plus-three bays with a central pediment. Two storeys, Victorianized roof.* Colonnade on the S side also Victorian, after 1845. No original interiors except the simple chapel immediately l. of the entrance doorway, with a deeply coved ceiling and a pedimented reredos. Far-projecting wings on the N side, of 1934–5, a wretched addition by *R. H. Turner*. In the late 1960s extensive enlargements were made under *E. T. Ashley-Smith*, the Kent County Architect. A block to the N forms the fourth side of a quadrangle. Two HOSTELS by the same architect SW of the main buildings.

S of the Market Square the HIGH STREET continues, narrow at first, but soon widening and rebuilt on both sides in the anonymous between-the-wars shopping centre style. At the junction of narrow and wide the PUBLIC LIBRARY AND CHURCHILL THEATRE, 1970–5 by *Aneurin John*, the Borough Architect. Aggressive and arbitrary, the forward-standing podium faced with green slate chips, the white slab

---

* Mr Andrew Saint has found that *Shaw* worked here in 1863, *Newton* in 1903 and 1920, and that probably both had a hand in heightening the roof.

above with windows in irregularly spaced slits. In RINGERS ROAD, a turning on the r., the extension of HARRISON GIBSON'S shop, 1960 by *Forrest & Barber*. Good fun, with good lettering. The boldly scaled ARMY AND NAVY STORE next door is by *Elsom, Pack & Roberts*, 1968–70. On the opposite side of the High Street a big shopping precinct, THE MALL, stretching back a long way, *c.* 1967–9 by the *Owen Luder Partnership*. The foot of the hill has been taken over by Bromley's first high block, TELEPHONE HOUSE, a twelve-storey slab, with a raised pedestrian shopping area behind it. The whole scheme was designed by *Alun Jones, Ward & Partners*, begun in 1962 and completed in 1967. The slab is white with black stripes on the short end and zigzagging sides. The chiaroscuro of light and shade this was meant to produce does not happen because the zigging is too gentle. Mannered treatment of the Westmoreland Road elevation, with syncopated horizontals and verticals. Much variety in the levels of the pedestrian area. A detour at this point to the r. up WEST-MORELAND ROAD soon brings one to No. 37, an undemonstrative tile-hung house by *George & Peto* of 1881.* (Further on, No. 107, by *Edward Cullinan, Brendan Wood & Sunand Prasad*, 1976–9. Rendered, with stained hard-wood details. An interesting layout, of 36 dwellings of different sizes (for a housing association), generously glazed and balconied, overlooking a large shared garden, and approached by pavements intended be a natural extension of a traditional street pattern.) Back and further on, at the top of MASONS HILL, FAIR-LAND HOUSE, commercial-looking blocks of flats, by *Trehearne & Norman, Preston & Partners*, 1966–7. Chunky concrete staircase ramps in the angles between the three blocks. If Telephone House is the highest building in Bromley, COSMOS HOUSE, on the corner of BROMLEY COMMON and Homesdale Road, is undoubtedly the longest. 1965–7 by the *Owen Luder Partnership*. Ruthlessly brutalist with a great deal of character. Of the three storeys the first and third jut rudely out under lean-to glazed roofs like greenhouses. The whole building is raised on terrifyingly thin concrete posts.

Off HAYES LANE, the turning opposite Cosmos House, housing of the 1960s like a New Town neighbourhood, HAYES-FORD PARK, approached down LETCHWORTH DRIVE. That name should be a reminder how strong an influence the Garden City tradition still exerts. The small, cosily designed detached houses are in that tradition, the communal green lawns beside the roads, the numerous culs-de-sac. The PEDESTRIAN SHOPPING CENTRE is of 1960–2 by the *Building Design Partnership*. The earlier houses are near the shopping centre, with just a few short, stepped terraces. Further building to the s in BOURNE VALE ROAD, begun in 1965, also by the *Building Design Partnership*, now introducing

* Information from Mr M. Parkinson.

bigger units, five-storeyed and seven-storeyed blocks of flats, and stronger colours, especially a deep purple brick. Back in BROMLEY COMMON, just before the Technical College, on the r. ELMFIELD, an early C18 red brick house, five bays, two storeys, and a parapet. Doorcase with bulgy Tuscan columns and a triangular pediment. Contemporary staircase. On the other side of the road three of Bromley's best recent buildings. First the AMBULANCE CENTRE, Crown Lane, by the *G.L.C. Special Works Department*, opened in 1973. A low but lively group, a prismatic clerestory over the ambulance park. Red engineering brick. Then the lighthearted PAVILION of the Blue Circle Sports Club, by *Hammett & Norton*, 1964. Finally, some way down Magpiehall Lane, ASTLEY ADULT TRAINING CENTRE, by the borough architect, *Aneurin John*, completed in 1971, all one-storeyed, a loose group unified by the quick rhythm of windows, each centred in a full-height panel of red brickwork.

(In GRAVEL ROAD, a turning to the r. after the end of Bromley Common, a large builder's workshop, timber and pantiled, probably early C19, and the stuccoed house of the proprietor.)

CHELSFIELD

Church and COURT LODGE stand alone, severed from the village by the Orpington bypass. Suburbia has so far been held off, just.

ST MARTIN OF TOURS. Early Norman nave and chancel. Herringbone laying of the flints in the chancel s wall and the nave N wall. s windows visible inside (the N lancet also in origin Norman, its sill lowered). Soon afterwards a great lengthening of the nave took place (see the N wall), and of this the w triplet partly survives. The E wall of the chancel was rebuilt early in the C13, with three tall lancets – internal shafts with shaft-rings. Also C13 the brief s aisle and the N tower. Traces of a NE annexe, i.e. the E doorway in the tower and the faint mark of a gable above it. The squint and barred window in the chancel must have opened into it. Perp s porch with C18 battlements. *E. Nash*'s restoration in 1857 replaced the chancel arch, and rebuilt the NE annexe as a vestry. – ALTAR RAILS. Stumpy turned balusters. – (STAINED GLASS. Two windows, chancel s, by *Veronica Whall*, 1925. PC) – MONUMENTS. Robert de Brun, rector, † 1417, in a recess on the N side of the chancel, coped tomb-chest of local marble, with the indents of a small Crucifixus, St Mary, and St John. In a charming way the tomb of 1668 on the opposite side of the chancel is made a pair to it, minus the brasses. – 15 in. brass of a priest, *c.* 1400 – Brasses also in the chancel to William Robroke, priest, † 1420, a lady, *c.* 1480, and Alicia Bray † 1510, each a foot and a half long. – Peter Collet † 1607. Hanging monument, with small kneeling figures better done than usual. Two babes propped up at the sides. – Peter

Heyman, a third babe, has his own inscription. – Brass Crosby † 1793. Adamish tablet, with two small mourning figures high up.

CHISLEHURST

CHURCHES

ANNUNCIATION, High Street. A fine, masculine church by *James Brooks*, 1868–70, the ragstone exposed inside as well as out, just as in his church at Perry Street, Northfleet, Kent. The simple system of a high clerestoried nave and chancel nearly as high, both with low aisles, is treated in Brooks's usual emphatic manner, exposing problems, not smoothing them away. Most surprising of all, not to say wilful, the mighty SE tower is set diagonally to the church, just touching the S chapel at one corner. The tower, left incomplete, was weakly finished off in 1930 by *E. J. May*. The W front of the church, towards the street, has a tremendous wheel window, its forms – all circles, nineteen of them – blunt and elemental. The clerestory windows of the nave however match it in scale – each a circle over two lancets. One or two strange happenings on the N side, the single flying buttress to support the chancel arch and the vestry chimney sticking out of the chancel roof. Big E window with the simplest bar tracery. The nave is full of light from the large windows high up, and the broad space satisfyingly held in by the tight curves of the roof principals. Short and thick round arcade piers (four bays) with Brooks's favourite stylized leaf capitals. The chancel is dim and lofty, a most effective contrast, heightened admittedly by the screen and wall paintings. – FONT. No doubt by *Brooks*. – PULPIT. His probably too. – CHANCEL SCREEN and LOFT. Only the base is of 1877, with figures of the apostles by *Westlake*. The rest is post-1918 in Comper's manner. – REREDOS. Vast. Designed by *Brooks*, executed in 1877 by *Westlake*. Gabled centre. Tiers of roundels l. and r. – WALL PAINTINGS. 1882 and 1892, by *Westlake*. – MOSAIC. Above the chancel arch. By *Salviati*, 1890. Designed by *Westlake*. – STAINED GLASS. E window and W window 1870 by *Hardman*, apparently to *Brooks*'s design.

ST MARY HALL, across the road, also by *Brooks*, 1878, has been demolished.

CHRIST CHURCH, Lubbock Road. 1871–2 by *Habershon & Pite*. A big church, with a conspicuous SW tower. Ragstone. Geometrical tracery. Long clerestoried nave, transepts and a canted E apse. Internally the transepts are unstressed, so the nave has seven bays altogether and the chancel seems quite remarkably small. It need hardly be said that, in spite of the revival of ritual in the C19, churches to serve the needs of Evangelical Anglican services went on being built. – STAINED GLASS. All in the E parts by *E. Frampton*, 1897 etc. It is extremely poor. One N window by *Kempe*, 1906.

St John the Baptist, Mill Place. 1886 by *E. Crutchloe*. No longer used as a church.

St Nicholas. The medieval parish church. c 15, of rough flints, enlarged and partly rebuilt in the c 19. The tower stands over the w bay of the N aisle, and bears a tall shingled spire, quite a landmark. The windows in tower and aisle segment-headed, of two lights. Four-bay arcade, besides the tower bay, on piers quatrefoil in plan. Arches with two chamfers, tower arch with three. Probably this c 15 work was undertaken by the rector of 1446–82, whose monument stands in the found-er's position on the N side of the chancel. No more of it is left. The w wall of the nave however is old, and in the gable a small blocked window rudely turned in flint may be Saxon.* In 1849 the chancel was practically rebuilt by *Ferrey*. Old PISCINA. There were lancets before the rebuilding. He also added the s aisle (with the Perp s doorway reset), copying the Perp N windows but modifying the arcade to make it approach more nearly the style of the late c 13. The spire rebuilt by *Wollaston*, after a fire in 1857, a little higher than before. The chancel lengthened eastwards, with a fancy E wall, by *Bodley & Gar-ner*, 1896. – FONT. Norman. The usual square arcaded bowl on five shafts (three renewed). – SCREENS. Chancel screen and screens in the N chapel. Basically genuine Perp. – ORGAN CASE. 1888. – REREDOS. 1896 by *Bodley & Garner*. Alabas-ter. – Of the same year the fine red and white SANCTUARY PAVEMENT by *Farmer & Brindley*. – STAINED GLASS. Sanc-tuary windows 1896 by *Burlison & Grylls*. – s aisle w window, 1894, one s window, 1900, by *Kempe*. – MONUMENTS. Alan Porter † 1482. 9 in. brass. Half-effigy of a priest. – Sir Edmond Walsingham † 1549. Early c 15 tomb-chest, the side panels with tracery of considerable complexity. In 1581 a backpiece was added with an inscription to Sir Edmond. Corinthian colonnettes and embryonic strapwork. Another inscription added in 1630. The whole repainted. – Sir Richard Betenson † 1679. Big black and white marble tablet with side scrolls and three cartouches attached to the top pediment. Mid-c 17 in feeling. The odd thing is the Tuscan pilaster that supports it, flanked by palm-scrolls. This must be an addition at the death of Lady Betenson in 1681. – Sir Philip Warwick † 1682. Large and outstandingly elegant cartouche carved with great finesse. Putto-heads and a skull among the scrolls. The scrolls themselves have a peculiar tendency to assume the shape of half-spread wings. – Thomas Farrington † 1694. Another good cartouche, but not in the same class. Note the wreathed skull at the bottom, and the bravura of its carving. – Thomas Farrington † 1712. A third cartouche. Putto-heads again around the knotted drapery. – Roland Tryon † 1720. Hanging monument, with at the top a medallion bust, and on the cornice over the tablet an urn and two reclining cherubs. Rather flabbily executed. – Sir Edward Bettenson † 1733.

* The seemingly c 12 corbel on a fat face, in the N chapel, looks ungenuine.

Large hanging monument, with more marble than ideas. Signed by *Thomas Easton*. – Lord Thomas Bertie † 1749. Hanging monument with trophies of arms at the top, and an urn. What makes it memorable is the relief at the bottom, an exquisitely carved representation of a naval battle, the ships riding on waves as stylized as rocaille work. The monument is not signed, but *Cheere*'s design for it has been recently identified. – Roger Townshend † 1760. Tablet by *Rysbrack*. – Sir Richard Adams † 1774. Large tablet in the Adam taste. – Lord Robert Bertie † 1782. Large tablet. – First Viscount Sydney † 1800. Exceedingly large tablet. – William Selwyn † 1817. Signed by *Chantrey*, 1823. Very large hanging monument. A young man stands, two young women sit pensively by a tomb. Chantrey eschews realism, for all the contemporary dress, yet he makes one accept that these really are Mr Selwyn's children and no generalized mourners. – Second Viscount Sydney. 1845 by *J. Brown*. Allegorical female too small for the substructure. – Earl Sydney † 1890. Reclining effigy in Garter robes, by *Sir E. Boehm*, completed by *Alfred Gilbert*.

St Mary (R.C.), Hawkwood Lane. 1854. The architect of this simple ragstone building was *W. W. Wardell*.* priest's house on the N side. In 1874 however *Clutton* added a mortuary chapel to the S. It was ordered by the Empress Eugénie for the body of Louis Napoleon, the home of whose exile had since 1870 been Camden Place (*see* below), although in the end he was buried in a far grander setting at Farnborough, Hants. Ashlar. The chapel's roof is sharply gabled, but rises behind a rich pierced parapet; an arrangement that echoes the chapel in the château at Amboise. Internally there is a stone rib-vault on wall-shafts with naturalistic leaf capitals. Clever Cluttonian detail. – sculpture. Christ in the Tomb. In a N recess. – monument. The Prince Imperial † 1879. He lies recumbent, fully armed.

Methodist Church, Prince Imperial Road. 1868–70. Ragstone. E.E. style, not cheaply but somewhat baldly realized.

PUBLIC BUILDINGS

Ravensbourne College of Art and Design, Walden Road, E of Elmstead Lane. 1972–4 by *Aneurin John*, Bromley borough architect. Large, low spreading group, consistently constructed with black exposed metal frames and red brick walls. Much clerestory lighting.

Girls' Technical School, Hawkwood Lane. *See* Perambulation.

Farringtons School. *See* Perambulation.

(Chislehurst Station, Bickley Park Road. Rebuilt 1900. The South Eastern Railway direct main line is of 1865, quadrupled 1900–4, with major earthworks and a tunnel.)

---

* Information received from Mr D. Evinson.

PERAMBULATION

Chislehurst is no ordinary suburb. This is because of its relationship to its common. Whereas most commons lie to one side of their towns, here the common is the very heart of the place. Chislehurst is blessed by the arrangement, and even much recent demolition of big old houses to put half-a-dozen in the place of one has not destroyed the leafy spaciousness.

St Nicholas's church is the obvious place to start, for it stands at the common's edge. From the w of the churchyard one can see quite a number of buildings more or less hidden among the trees, all of the C19 and most of them rather ugly. Turning first to the s, in MORLEY ROAD, a pretty pair of cottages, No. 2 MORLEY COTTAGES and WHIN COTTAGE, part of a larger scheme designed in 1878 by *George & Peto*.* They introduce the *leitmotif* of late C19 Chislehurst houses, wide tiled and half-timbered gables over red-brick walls. Immediately s, in HAWKWOOD LANE, the R.C. church on the r., and on the l. the buildings of the GIRL'S TECHNICAL SCHOOL, 1960 and 1967 by *E. T. Ashley-Smith*, the Kent County Architect. The last house before a lovely shaft of unspoilt hillside is COOPERS, a plain brick house of the late C18, three bays in the centre, with lower wings. It seems all of one date, although the front is yellow brick, the back red. At the back canted bays flanking the centre. The interiors however are of *c.* 1750, and the staircase has two turned balusters per step and richly carved tread-ends. So it is a matter of recasing, it seems.

Back to the church, and now E, down MANOR PARK ROAD. Here is the MANOR HOUSE, basically a gabled half-timbered house, with a two-storeyed porch; but now roughcast and greatly added to. In MANOR PARK an early house by *Sir Aston Webb*, COOKHAM DENE, *c.* 1882. He uses the Norman Shaw idiom but has nothing much to say in it. Much more personal are the five beetling Queen-Anne-style houses of the 1870s on the other side of the road by *George Somers Clarke Sen.* WALPOLE was his own house; then come PELHAM, HARLEY, MANOR PLACE, and WALSINGHAM. Back in the main road, ST PAUL'S CRAY ROAD, one should turn l. Here more Queen Anne houses by *Somers Clarke*, GRANGE COTTAGE, *c.* 1880, then a trio rising sheer from the pavement, CRAYFIELD, CLEEVELAND, and WARREN HOUSE, dated 1878. After these comes the best C18 house in Chislehurst, CHESIL HOUSE. Red brick. Only three bays and two storeys, yet all the windows have arched centres making them into simplified Venetian windows. Plain parapet with a centre pediment growing up through it. Lunette window in the pediment. Porch on fluted Ionic columns, with a broken pediment. A date *c.* 1770 would seem appropriate. Later addition at the r. side. BULL LANE runs NE, nearly opposite. Here

---

* For the staff of Charles Morley of Cooper's.

comes EASDENS, an unusually confidently handled house of
the early C20. The main shape is a familiar one, a low block
with a deep gable-ended roof and a wide nearly central gable.
Colossal chimneybreasts at each end. Shell-hood on brackets
over the front door. The architect, surprisingly, was *Sir Aston
Webb*, who built it as a church hall in 1909–11. Where Holbrook Lane joins the A222, quite a nice group of houses in the
George–Newton vein, Nos. 1–5 SHEPHERDS GREEN, 1907–
8 by *E. J. May*. A detour to the s end of Holbrook Lane brings
one to a piquant contrast in moods: on the r. HOLBROOK
END, crudely handled neo-Georgian by *Richard Creed*, 1907,
pushes forward aggressively, while *Morley Horder*'s neo-
Tudor idyll, PEASONS, of 1924, lies back on the l. in a grove
of birches.

FARRINGTON SCHOOL lies s of the A222. Symmetrical
group, rendered neo-Georgian houses of 1910–11 (by *Gordon
& Gunton*) and 1925, with the brick hall between. The hall
has pilaster strips and a little cupola. The CHAPEL is of 1935.
Brick. Cruciform, with a short octagonal crossing tower.
Romanesque in style. All but the earliest building by *Crickmer
& Foxley*. Farther on down PERRY STREET, WESTERN
MOTOR WORKS, a very early example of its type, 1909 by
E. J. May, has a high-spirited showroom of 1966–7 by *Oliver
E. Steer*. Behind, in BEAVERWOOD ROAD, Nos. 1–5 are also
of 1909 by *May*. The CEMETERY CHAPEL and LODGE at the
end are a year later, by *W. Curtis Green*.

In the other direction, i.e. further w, on the n side of the main
road, SUNNYMEAD (Bromley Borough Education Department), dated 1875 on a rainwater head. It is a typical High
Victorian medium-sized house, the sort of thing the Shaw
style was to supersede very quickly after 1875. Red brick with
black brick bands. Stone round the windows, with shafts and
foliage capitals in a few places. Polychrome tympana above the
windows. Gables and beefy bargeboards. Even a detail like the
shape of the sash-frames of the windows is worth noting. N of
this, in KEMNAL ROAD, a house on a larger scale. This is
David Brandon's FOXBURY, built in 1875–6 for H. J. Tiarks.
Stone, Jacobean; i.e. with pierced strapwork parapets and a
shaped gable over the porch. Low tower with a copper dome at
the r. of the entrance front, where the service wing begins to
branch out at the r. All in all a poor effort.

The High Street lies at the nw corner of the common, but has no
building of interest in it apart from the Annunciation Church
now its Hall has gone. Opposite the church a long block of
shops and offices of the late 1970s in reddish-mauve brick,
quite carefully detailed, with arcaded ground floor and mansarded roof, but hopelessly inappropriate in scale. Opposite
the duck-pond, in Heathfield Lane, WALLINGS, *May*'s own
house, 1913, brown brick, harbinger of a myriad between-the-
wars houses. In MEAD ROAD, which lies a short way to the N,
GOLDEN MEAD, by *Sir Ernest George*, 1881. Several other
houses in the road in the same idiom. They all have a simple

shape, usually with one large gable, and red-brick walls are hung for their top half with tile. Rectangular windows of various proportions. Moderately emphasized chimneystacks. Indeed it is a style stripped of practically all period and vernacular reminiscences. *Ernest Newton* seems to have designed them: RANDALLS and ASHTON are certainly his, for they appear in his *Book of Houses* of 1890.

The last area to be explored lies on the w side of the common. CAMDEN PLACE, off Prince Imperial Road (now Chislehurst Golf Club House). The main block, facing E, of red and yellow brick, seven bays wide, three storeys high, was built shortly before 1717 by Robert Weston. Giant pilaster strips mark bays 1, 4, and 7. In the 1860s this relatively plain edifice was decked with a one-storey pavilion l. and r., with a centrepiece displaying a big clock with sculpture round, and with a skyline of stone balustrades. The s façade, however, of austere brown brick, is clearly late C18, ending towards the w in a two-storeyed bow. What makes one eager to see inside is the knowledge that this range is the work of *George Dance Jun.* Dance was employed, to remodel the whole house, so it seems, by the first Earl Camden, the Lord Chief Justice, in the 1780s. In 1788 a room, apparently called 'the School of Athens', was completed. Another room was called 'Sir James's Grecian Room'.* Neither, unfortunately, can be identified, and nothing may have been done: what is left today is neither Raphaelesque nor Grecian. In 1807 *Dance* executed work for Camden's successor, Thomas Bonar. The breakfast room, r. of the front door, has an exquisite plaster ceiling close in feeling to Adam, but easily distinguishable from Adam's style. (In the hall, opposite the front door, a fine late C18 marble chimneypiece.) The l. pavilion, which was built by Dance, and merely cased in the 1860s, contains a remarkable Egyptian chimneypiece of polished pink granite. Could this be by Dance? The s range consisted of a suite of contrasting rooms, first an octagonal vestibule, now swallowed up by a broad corridor, then a bow-ended library, with primitivist pilasters, and finally a big, bow-ended drawing room, with, lining the bow, Ionic columns that carry spheres. The inset wall paintings in both rooms must be Victorian. All this then is disappointingly bitty; so the great spectacle of the house is the dining room in the r. pavilion, lined with fine C18 *boiseries* from a Bourbon hunting lodge.

Camden Place was bought in 1890 by William Willett Jun., the builder who had principally championed the cause of 'Pont Street Dutch' in Kensington and Hampstead, and who, after moving his own house (*see* below) to Chislehurst, invented daylight saving. He developed the Camden Place estate in two groups for high-class medium-sized commuter residences and, apart from the first few in CAMDEN PARK ROAD, *Ernest Newton* was his architect, working in conjunction with *Amos*

---

* Quoted by Mr Harold Kalman from letters in the Kent Record Office.

Faulkner, who was in Willett's office. This individualistic suburbia reveals the full range of Newton's talent before he sided with the neo-Georgians. The range is conspicuously wide, far wider than is generally supposed. One can generalize, all the same, and say that Newton uses red brick with a tile-hung top part, and proportions comfortably broad and low, with two storeys and dormers, a hipped roof, and gables for calculated effects. CEDARS, of 1893, Willett's own house opposite the entrance to Camden Place, states his case characteristically at the outset, with a sheer chimneybreast l. of the front door. The arched door-hood on columns is a special Newton favourite. One window-bay, with a flat top not a gable, at the front, the back, and the side of the house. Typical too is the garden wall. The next three houses, also of 1893–4, are the ones not by Newton, but in 1910 *Newton* made a big, immediately recognizable, addition to the second, AVONHURST. Then comes *Newton's* DERWENT HOUSE, building in 1899, with a pair of tile-hung gables in the centre of the front. Stone porch and complex window over it, in the r. bay. Dramatic chimneybreast on the downhill end. BONCHESTER HOUSE, of 1898, next door, is more broken up, with a roughcast bay coming forward on the r. It has a vertically boarded gable, not one of Newton's strong points, and a bow window under a lead dome. The next house, ELM BANK, is the smallest, but altogether too full of fun and games. Hipped l. half of the roof, gabled r. half, with a complex chimneybreast between them. Superimposed on the chimneybreast is a projecting bay, the front-door half slipping off it. One reaches the door up a flight of steps that spread out diagonally. The dormer window like a half-closed eye is as dotty as the lunette in the bottom l. hand corner of the façade. Finally, more sober, FAIRACRE, L-shaped (published in 1903). The porch bay has a chequered brick-and-stone top part, and the doorway continues the rhythm of an arched loggia at the r. end. It is a first breath of the Georgian revival.

At the bottom of the hill, in LUBBOCK ROAD, are Willett's enormous STABLES, built before 1908 (now a mixture of cottages and garages), one of *Newton's* happiest and most relaxed works. On the same side of the road are Nos. 41–45, cottages clearly by *Newton*, and opposite are Nos. 165–169 LOWER CAMDEN ROAD, 1904 by *E. J. May*.*

The second, later, group of Newton-style houses is on the other side of Camden Place, in THE WILDERNESS. On the right are MOORLANDS, 1902 by *Amos Faulkner*, with a prominent chimneystack and a circular bay-window (the house has recently been greatly extended in diluted Newton style), and THE BRAKE, by *Faulkner*, 1911, this time with a Georganiz-

* The potency of Newton's style, even after the Second World War, can be demonstrated to anyone who continues along to the end of Lubbock Road and back up the hill to Camden Place.
(To the l. off Lower Camden Road, off Old Station Hill, the CAVES, chalk workings from the C 17, converted to air raid shelters in the Second World War.)

ing porch and a weakly half-timbered gable. Opposite is
PARKMORE, also by *Faulkner*, of 1901, larger and more
formal, in purplish brick with red-brick dressings and white
plastered coving. The segmental doorway is banded in stripes
à la Lutyens. Good details include the three tall brick windows at ground level to the r., the pargetting in the gable over
the door, and some pretty leaded 'gutterstrades'. The best
94 house is COPLEY DENE, next door, by *Newton*, designed in
1904 and worthy of Lutyens in its masterly handling of asymmetry. The entrance wing, with a square roughcast porch and
a polygonal roughcast bay, three little dormers and two big
chimneys, is balanced at r. angles by a big hipped-roofed wing
with a projecting triple chimneystack. HOLNE CHASE is
quieter, with a central polygonal bay set in a roughcast gable.
It was designed in 1911 and is again by *Faulkner*.

A few final grace notes. Off YESTER ROAD, overlooking the
Newton houses in Camden Park Road, GREATWOOD, 1962
by *Norman Starratt*, one of the lamentably few good new
developments in Chislehurst. Short staggered three-storeyed
terraces on the hillside. Charcoal brickwork, white balconies
and cornice. In CAMDEN PARK ROAD itself, No. 13, 1970 by
Robert Byron, handles the steeply sloping site better than
most. On the crest of the hill, in BEECHCROFT, off the E end
of Yester Park, a pair of recent houses by *Goddard & Phillips*,
1973. Excitingly steep and complex monopitch roofs. Further
W, in Grange Drive, BABINGTON HOUSE SCHOOL, red
brick, Jacobean. 1879 by *Jarvis*. Of interest to specialists only.

CRYSTAL PALACE

The Crystal Palace, originally built in Hyde Park (KC) for the
Great Exhibition of 1851 and re-erected here in a much enlarged version in 1852–4, burnt down in 1936. Of the grand
terraced gardens in the Barry manner laid out by *Paxton* on
the hillside, only a few Italianate arcades remain (restored
1982). The sculpture was nearly all carted away except for a
gigantic head of Paxton set starkly on a pedestal (signed by
W. F. Woodington, sculptor of the Lion Brewery lion, and dated
1869) which was reinstalled in 1981 at the entrance to the
National Recreation Centre. By the lake at the foot of the hill
however the STATUES of prehistoric monsters still disport
themselves. They are of bronze, realistically painted, and
lifesize. The iguanodon was large enough for twenty-one
gentlemen to dine in its half-completed body. The statues
were suggested by Professor D. T. Ansted and made in 1854
by *B. Waterhouse Hawkins* under the direction of Professor
R. Owen. A more recent addition to the herd is the GORILLA
by *David Gwynne*, 1961. For the rest, C19 recreation has given
way to C20 recreation.

The NATIONAL RECREATION CENTRE, covering the lower
slopes, *c.* 1956–64 by the *L.C.C. Architect's Department*, is

devoted to sport. The STADIUM has sickle-shaped seating on the N side. Further E is the SPORTS HALL, a vast rectangular building, concrete-framed and with a gently zigzagging roof that results from its construction, cantilevered out from a central spine. Internally this divides the space lengthwise down the middle. On the l. the main training area, on the r. three swimming pools. Practice rooms and squash courts are cleverly slipped in under the tiered seating. The interior is very impressive, not least because there has been no attempt to impress, no contrived effects.

To the N, the HOSTEL, an isolated eleven-storey point block, planned as six hexagons round an open hexagonal well. The eye cannot analyse the complicated shape. Clad with vertical cedar boarding. Similar boarding on the STAFF HOUSES, which with their black brickwork and uncompromising butterfly roofs are extraordinarily effective. They and the hostel provide an exotic foil to the saneness of the rest.

CRYSTAL PALACE LOW LEVEL STATION. 1854 and 1875 for the London Brighton and South Coast Railway, on a monumental scale. Booking hall with cast-iron arched roof, the arch ribs perforated in foliage patterns (roof at long last refurbished in 1979). Pavilion roofs on either side. Over the four sets of stairs down to the original platforms, two huge spaces, the high walls pierced with round-arched arcades and roofed with wrought-iron trusses. Beyond was an enormous train shed with a twin arched roof, dismantled c. 1905.

Under Crystal Palace Parade (and not officially accessible), a SUBWAY from the demolished Crystal Palace High Level Station (1865, closed 1954). It is faced with red and cream brickwork. Three parallel rows of octagonal brick columns with mushroom-flared heads and diaper patterning. From the HIGH LEVEL STATION only some arcaded walls remain. A competition for low-cost energy-saving housing on this site was won in 1981 by *J. Palejowski*. The layout complements the railway remains; the houses are designed with projecting vertical glazed conservatories intended as solar collectors.

Across THICKET ROAD, a segmental-arched RAILWAY BRIDGE of 1854 on a forty-five-degree skew, with ornamental perforated parapet. Across CRYSTAL PALACE PARK ROAD, another of three segmental arches with ornamental panelled brickwork, 1854.

CUDHAM

ST PETER AND ST PAUL. Flint churches are not easy to restore without spoiling their looks, and Cudham is no exception. Yet the restorations of 1846 and 1891–2 (by *Christian*) were kinder than many round here. (The worst part is the renewal of all the Dec windows.) An interesting history can still be traced. It starts in the nave, which is Saxo-Norman, i.e. Saxon in its high, narrow proportions, Early Norman by the one small S and one small N window. Of the C13 the chancel (two N lancets are partly original) and the s tower. Chancel and tower arches similar in details, and curiously interlocked via an inner tower buttress chamfered off to become part of the chancel arch. In the C 14 the nave grew a short N aisle and the chancel a s chapel: clasping buttresses to both, an extraordinary motif to find as late as this, unless they are evidence of earlier enlargement. The Dec arcades are replacements. Low-side window at the W end of the aisle. PISCINAS in chancel, s chapel, and aisle, all in the E walls, another anomaly. In the NW corner of the chancel a corbel is half buried in the wall. What does it signify? Nave roof with moulded arch braces. In 1487 20 shillings were left 'to ye makyng of the church roffe'. – FONT. Perp. Shields in quatrefoils on the eight faces. – STAINED GLASS. One s window in the nave, 1897 by *Kempe*. – MONUMENT. Perp panelled tomb-chest in the chancel. Above its E end a canopied niche. – BRASS of Alys Waleys † 1503, 20 in. long.

MACE FARM, 1 m. NE. By *Gordon & Gunton*, 1910. Voysey-esque, with a butterfly plan, but uneasily proportioned. COTTAGES behind are by the same.

DOWNE

ST MARY THE VIRGIN, High Street. Flint. Nave and chancel under one roof. W tower E.E. with a shingled spire. One renewed lancet in the s wall of the nave, otherwise all windows late Perp. The church over-restored in 1879 by *Daniel Bell*.[*] Two vertical breaks in the s wall suggest it had a history, now beyond recall. – STAINED GLASS. Crucifixion in the E window, 1950 by *Evie Hone*. Bold in colour and design, dominating the whole church. – Sanctuary s by *Keith Coleborn*, 1973, to commemorate a voyage round the world. – MONUMENTS. Brasses to a civilian and wife, *c.* 1400. Small. – Thomas Petle, *c.* 1420. Tiny. – Jacob Verzelini, the famous Venetian glass-maker, † 1606, and wife. Large and fussy brasses.

The centre of Downe has a proper villagey feel. A timber-framed house of the Wealden sort, WALNUT TREE COTTAGES, opposite the church; but the main ingredient is the hard, unaccommodating flint cottages that one finds scattered all over the chalk uplands behind this part of the North Downs. One or two outlying houses, however, are in a softer mode:

ORANGE COURT, ½ m. E of N. The fronts of farmhouse and outbuilding diapered with alternating red and grey triangles of brick and flint. (The timber-framed barn, probably built from medieval materials, bears the date 1779.)

DOWNE COURT, ¾ m. E of s. A red-brick front of three bays. Dated 1690, but not yet achieving symmetry.

In Luxted Road on the r., first PETLEYS, early C 18, flint and red brick relieved by a white doorway and cornice; then,

---

[*] Information from Canon Bernard Wigan.

further on, DOWNE HOUSE, the large, irregular, gaunt
home of Charles Darwin.

For THE CLOCK HOUSE, High Elms Road, *see* Farnborough.

FARNBOROUGH

The village is almost submerged by oncoming suburbia. But the
church to the s on the hill among larches is still at the edge of
open country.

ST GILES THE ABBOT. In 1641 a brief was granted for rebuilding the church after a storm. The nave, flint with big, square
two-light windows with red-brick mullions, is of that date. W
tower 1838 by a certain Mr *Blackshaw**: flint and yellow brick.
Chancel 1886 by *Joseph Clarke*: flint and Bath stone. Polygonal NW vestry. The odd N projection must be a bit of the
pre-storm church. The nave roof, of 1641, still has the traditional crown-posts, only slightly modified. – FONT. Octagonal. Simple geometrical designs and panelling on the bowl.
Probably C 14. – ORGAN CASE. *c.* 1960. Pretty. High among
the rafters above the W gallery. – Bronze PLAQUE. Christ and
the Apostles. Sombre Epsteinish faces. By *Elsie March*, 1939.
– MONUMENT. Thomas Brome † 1673. Large architectural
tablet signed by *Jasper Latham*.

The stables of the demolished High Elms in High Elms Road are
now called THE CLOCK HOUSE, because of the domed clock
set high above the roofs on white posts. A pretty, informal
group. The octagonal, white-weatherboarded building
behind, formerly open at ground level, was built *c.* 1850 to
house a horizontal HORSE WHEEL, for pumping to a water
tank above. The overhead cast-iron gearing is preserved,
dismantled.

HAYES

ST MARY THE VIRGIN, Hayes Street. Flint. A crushing restoration by *Sir G. G. Scott c.* 1856–62, including a new N aisle,
and a S aisle and transept of 1878 by *J. Oldrid Scott*, have left
old walling in the chancel and one lancet in the nave W wall.‡
Inside the W tower, however, blocked original C 13 arches in
the N and S walls suggest it may have had an open ground
storey. The aisle windows are instructive – Scott *père* provides
striking plate tracery of his own invention; his son, twenty
years later, sets up replicas of the late Perp windows he is
displacing. The workmanship equally mechanical in both. –
REREDOS. 1905. Probably designed by *Sir T. G. Jackson*.
Expensive. – STAINED GLASS. The N aisle is a good place to
watch the progressive dulling of colour in Victorian glass: NE

* Mr H. M. Colvin's discovery.
‡ Old PISCINA and doorway reset in the vestry, so Mr John Armstrong kindly
tells me.

window, 1850; centre, 1866 and 1870; NW, 1880.* – MONU-
MENTS. Brasses of priests: John Osteler, *c.* 1460, demi-figure,
7 in. in length; John Andrew † 1479, 14 in.; John Heygge
† 1523, 1 ft. – The only other monument worth a glance is the
cartouche to Ann Cleaver † 1737.

HAYES GROVE, Prestons Road. The first view, of a fine Georgian front, is misleading. The centre five bays are genuinely
of, say, *c.* 1730. Two storeys. Pilaster strips at the corners, the
centre window in a raised surround. Big doorcase with a
segmental pediment. The wings however are a pastiche, and a
very clever one. The rainwater heads dated 1899. Additions
on the E front too, doubling the canted bay to approximate to
symmetry. Original staircase, with three twisted balusters per
tread. *Ernest Newton* designed the additions.

OAST HOUSE, Croydon Road, ¾ m. E of S. Built in the middle of
Hayes Common in 1873–4 by *Philip Webb* for the eccentric
Lord Sackville Cecil. Not a large house, but as independent-
minded as any by Webb and composed with a good deal more
finesse than Red House, as one would expect fourteen years
after that pioneering effort. Long and low, with a deep barn-
like roof and the chimneystacks in four massive slabs. The
materials squared ragstone blocks and red-brick dressings,
not always where expected. White window-frames and a little
white weatherboarding in the gables. The entrance (W) front
rather like an enlarged school (Webb's interest in Butterfield's
schools in the 1850s is documented), ending in gabled wings of
equal width but unequal projection. The windows are wide
and have his favourite segmental heads. (One or two window
sills lowered slightly in recent years.) In the centre three
evenly-spaced dormers of Queen Anne proportions. Low,
square porch running out the full depth of the r. wing. The E
side has the memorable feature of four wide gabled dormers in
a row starting up from the foot of the roof. They impose a
rhythm on a façade otherwise quite without symmetry. (The
bow-window at the r. end not original.) The interior has been
altered out of recognition.

THE WARREN (Metropolitan Police Sports Club), Croydon
Road. Big and gorgeously dotty late C19 mansion. 1882, by
George Somers Clarke Sen. for Walter Maximilian de Zoete.
The bit the architect loved most was the stepped gables with
ever so many steps, a terracotta scroll popped on each, and a
tiddly top pediment.

KESTON

Keston has no recognizable centre, and the church lies alone on a
lane (Church Road) below the road to Biggin Hill.

CHURCH. Nave and chancel. E.E., extended at the W in 1878 by
H. Blackwell and given a funny little bell-gable. Trefoiled N

---

* Mrs Corinne Bennett points out that they are all by *Lavers, Barraud &
Westlake.*

and s lancets in the chancel. In the nave blocked s doorway and blocked arch to a s E tower. (Cudham near by has a tower in the same position.)* – PAINTING. Of Aaron. From an c 18 altarpiece. – STAINED GLASS. Love, by *Morris & Co.*, 1909; chancel windows 1952 by *James Blackford*. – MONUMENT. George Kirkpatrick † 1838. Unsigned Grecian tablet. A bald pilgrim kneels holding a large cross, while a young woman in classical draperies holds the Bible for him to read. Confused and rather silly.

In the grounds of RAVENSBOURNE, I m. N, is a rambling single-storey house by *Howell & Killick*, 1958, the apotheosis of the Japanese-inspired style of that moment.

WINDMILL, Heathfield Road, ¾ m. NW. A post-mill in a splendid windy position, facing out over Surrey. Black and weatherboarded, on a brick roundhouse. Only the stumps of the sweeps are left. Inside is the date 1716, which makes it the oldest dated windmill in Kent.‡

In COMMONSIDE, joining Croydon Road and Heathfield Road, the former OLIVE'S MILL, a two-storey steam flour mill and outbuildings of the 1870s; now church rooms.)

HOLWOOD was the surburban estate (at that time suburban in the Roman sense) of the younger William Pitt, who as Prime Minister found his recreation in the enlargement of his house and the improving of its grounds. For the former he employed *Soane* and for the latter *Repton*. Some of Repton's planting remains to the s of the house, gloriously framing a view into Kent. Soane's house, however, was short-lived. Burnt down, it was rebuilt by *Decimus Burton*, in 1823–6, for John Ward. The new house is large (larger than Pitt's), built of expensive white brick and Portland stone, and confidently and correctly Grecian: an impressive performance for an architect in his mid twenties. Entrance (N) front fifteen bays long, the centre seven two-storeyed with lower wings ending in pedimented pavilions. (That on the r. was originally a greenhouse.) Three-bay pediment over the centre. Columns only by the doorway. The heightening of part of the wings has blurred the clarity of this arrangement. The same rhythm on the garden front, but more emphatically stressed. Four giant Ionic columns against a wide bow in the centre; low Doric columns recessed in the wings.

Inside, a small, low, square hall with Ionic half-columns and a coffered ceiling leads into the large vestibule in the centre of the house. This has now been halved in height, but was originally lit by clerestory windows above the Corinthian columns of an upper gallery. The staircase plain, but also top-lit.

* In 1950 the tower was excavated and traces of an earlier rectangular church found under the present one. Earlier foundation walls were also found under the chancel E wall, the lower possibly Roman, the Rev. Charles Gordon-Clarke points out, in view of the other Roman buildings near by.

‡ Malcolm Tucker adds: Body three storeys high, winded by a tail pole. Two pairs of under-driven stones and other machinery intact.

CAESAR'S CAMP, in Holwood Park. Iron Age hillfort of multi-vallate construction on the W and univallate on the N side. An inturned and presumably original entrance exists on the W. The best surviving field monument in Greater London.

EARTHWORK, Keston Common. Of unknown date. Possibly a cattle pound.

ROMAN VILLA, ⅓ m. NW of Keston Court Farm. A substantial villa complex built on the site of a farmstead of the C I A.D. The buildings excavated include a small corridor house 60 by 33 ft and a timber aisled building to the NE, in which three corn-drying ovens were found. Close by are several mausolea probably of the early C 3 A.D.: a circular buttressed tomb c. 29 ft (9 m.) across built of flint and tile of which only the lower part survives; a rectangular tomb c. 15 by 11 ft (4.5 by 3.4 m), with a single buttress; and a cremation tomb formed by adding a curved wall between two buttresses of the circular mausoleum.

KNOCKHOLT

See The Buildings of England: West Kent and the Weald.

MOTTINGHAM

ST ANDREW. *See* Woolwich (Gr).

ELTHAM COLLEGE, Grove Park Road. Rendered house of 1856, nine bays and two storeys with a one-storey porch on four Tuscan columns. Italianate tower behind at one corner. The chapel of 1903, towards the road, is as sprightly as the house is limp.

IRONMONGERS' ALMSHOUSES, Mottingham Road. Moved from Shoreditch in 1912* into these neo-Wren ranges by *George Hubbard*. Morden College, Blackheath, was very obviously his model. The statue of the founder, Sir Robert Geffrye, by *John Nost*, 1723, is set up on the garden side of the new buildings. Geffrye died in 1703. His monument has also migrated here, a fine Baroque cartouche with a mourning putto each side and a relief of the Lord Mayor's regalia below.

Towards Chislehurst, to the S of Mottingham Road, a large L.C.C. ESTATE of the 1930s (architect to the Council *G. Topham Forrest*; N. Taylor).

ORPINGTON

Orpington spreads and spreads, middle-class commuterland, a land of serpentine, tree-lined residential roads. The first estates for commuters were built in the 1920s. Between 1931 and 1939 the population of the Urban District nearly doubled. By 1961 the population was 80,277.

ALL SAINTS. The medieval church is small and now relegated

* The original almshouses are now the Geffrye Museum.

to be the ante-chapel to a new building three times its size, thrown out to the s. The new building of 1957–8, by *Geddes Hyslop*, uses brick and flint, i.e. local materials, but the minimal Gothic design is flimsy and unconvincing. Wide, light interior, though here too the aisle vaults, for instance, look disturbingly like cardboard. The walls of the old nave are unusually tall for its width. They suggest Saxon work, and indeed a Saxon SUNDIAL has come to light in the s wall. The sundial is inscribed in runes, one of only three Anglo-Saxon runic inscriptions so far found in South-East England, with the Roman letters OR . . . VM (i.e. *orologium viatorum*, perhaps, to show what it is); and with an Old English sentence, parts of which Mr R. L. Page has translated: '. . . to count and to hold' and 'for him who knows how to seek out how' (referring presumably to users of the sundial). At present it is upside down. N tower, W doorway, and chancel arch are all part of a remodelling of *c*. 1200. Evidence of lancets in the chancel. The tower has a rib-vaulted ground stage, once used as a chapel, see the PISCINA. (The tower rebuilt externally in the late C18 in flint and brick.) On the chancel arch keeled angle rolls and keeled shafts with little crocket capitals. Lavish W doorway of two orders of shafts with leaves on the capitals much damaged but apparently undecided whether to be waterleaf or crockets. Richly moulded pointed arch including a row of small dogtooth and big undercut zigzag. W porch built by rector Nicholas, who died in 1370 and desired to be buried there. His TOMB is beneath a big but delicately carved ogee arch with crockets and a finial and a very depressed and cuspy sub-arch. Perp N chancel chapel, which carries the Rufford arms in many places. – FONT COVER. C15. Plain ribs and a finial. – SCREEN. With a rood loft. 1916, designed by *W. D. Caröe*. – REREDOS. Large triptych by *Brian Thomas*, *c*. 1959. The C20 might never have been. – MONUMENTS. Thomas Wilkynson † 1511. Coarse brass of a priest, 37 in. long, which is bigger than usual at that date. – William Gee † 1815, Richard Carew † 1816, Richard Gee † 1817, three Grecian tablets whose only mark of distinction is that they are by *Chantrey*.

ST ANDREW, S end of Cray Avenue, South Cray. 1892–3 by *Hide & Newberry*. Oddly like a Commissioners' church outside. Romanesque interior. Recent matching W extension.

ST PAUL, Crofton Road, Crofton. By *A. B. Knapp-Fisher*, 1958. The church of 1887 is now the parish hall. Don't miss its lychgate.

THE PRIORY, near the parish church. Built before 1270, enlarged in 1393, and 'greatly improved' in 1471 by Prior Selling. It seems to have been both the clergy-house for the rector of Orpington and his numerous chaplains,* and a stopping place for the priors of Canterbury Cathedral. The medieval buildings are all of flint, but have been so renewed that they inspire little confidence. However, the E range, at the back,

---

* Until modern times St Mary Cray, Hayes, Downe, and Knockholt were all chapelries of Orpington.

shows the earliest evidence. There are traces in it of three single-light windows. In front of this, the main range consists of an open hall, with a simple Perp entrance doorway behind the porch at the s end, and one original doorway to the service wing. Bay-window at the dais end. The solar wing at the N added in 1393. In it one ground-floor room with Elizabethan plasterwork, foliage trails on the frieze and the roof-beams. Attached to the s, PUBLIC LIBRARY, by *Lord Mottistone*, 1957–60. A spirited attempt to be modern and drop historicist hints at the same time.

A long range of timber-framed OUTBUILDINGS fronts on to Church Hill Road. Weatherboarding above flint and brick towards the road, but the original framing exposed on the priory side. High central entrance for carts, with a room over it. Very well restored in 1974–5. Early C 17 queen-post roof.

THE WALNUTS, High Street, is a typical redevelopment scheme of the 1970s. First comes the shopping centre partly under cover, the usual jazzy affair, 1970–3 by *Alun Jones, Ward & Partners*. But further in things get better. The COUNCIL OFFICES are a relic of the milder post-war years, dated 1952. The SPORTS CENTRE, in purple brick, completed 1975, is by the Bromley borough architect, *Aneurin John*; and so is the COLLEGE OF FURTHER EDUCATION, 1970–3, an eleven-storey slab in red brick. Thought has clearly been given to the grouping of all these separate elements.

No. 15 STATION ROAD is a rarity, a little red-brick box of a house by *C. R. Ashbee*, 1900. Of an extraordinary directness, particularly in the detailing of the porch. Originally named, significantly no doubt, 'The Shoehorn'.

ROMAN BUILDINGS. w of the station, projecting from a bank below the council offices, flint walls, a threshold, and coarse red mosaic flooring. At FORDCROFT s of Poverest Road a Roman VILLA with a bath complex and an adjoining early Saxon CEMETERY have been found, but nothing is visible.

SE of the station, a mile-long EMBANKMENT up to 80 ft high on the South Eastern Railway. 1865–8. Large-diameter brick tunnels carry Tubbenden Lane and Sevenoaks Road beneath the embankment.

PENGE

ST JOHN THE EVANGELIST, Beckenham Road. 1850. By *Edwin Nash & J. N. Round*. *Nash* added the gabled aisles in 1861, and the transepts in 1866. Rock-faced ragstone. w tower and stone broach-spire. Geometrical tracery, treated in Nash's quirky way. The best thing inside is the open timber roofs, those in the transepts especially provocative, with beams from all four directions meeting in mid air.

CONGREGATIONAL CHURCH, Beckenham Road. 1912 by *P. Morley Horder*. Passage aisles and clerestory. Shafts on large, excellently carved corbels.

THE NEW CHURCH, Waldegrave Road. *See* Anerley.

FREE WATERMEN AND LIGHTERMEN'S ALMSHOUSES, 80
Beckenham Road. The most prominent building in Penge,
two-storeyed ranges round three sides of a quadrangle
reaching a climax in a gate-tower at the back, with battlemented turrets and ogee lead caps. Built by *George Porter* in
1840–1, when Tudor was the inevitable style for almshouses.*

KING WILLIAM NAVAL ASYLUM, St John's Road, NE end of
the High Street. Founded in 1847, designed by *Philip Hardwick* and paid for by Queen Adelaide. More Tudor almshouses round an open-ended square. Red brick and stone,
with black diaper patterns. Quite humble, but not only more
correct than Porter could manage to be, but much more
sensitively designed. Hardwick was rare in his generation, an
architect who handled all styles with equal distinction.

Penge is for most people a joke, an epitome of the dreary
suburban non-place. It is a reputation not quite deserved, and a
journey from the Crystal Palace (*see* p. 182) down the hill to the
High Street and beyond yields several buildings worth a look.

CRYSTAL PALACE PARK ROAD‡ is lined for its full length
down the r. side with tall red mansions of the 1880s. (1882 is
the date on Nos. 57 and 61.) The most self-indulgent are
towards the top end. Half way down on the l., the CHULSA
ESTATE is an especially good example of the gentle,
craftsmanly style of the 1950s. By *James & Bywater*. Yellow
brick very sparingly patterned. Shallow-pitched roofs. Five-
storey Y-shaped blocks with lower terraces further down the
hill. Near the bottom of the hill PARK COURT is a pre-war
estate typical of its time and carefully done. Brick painted
white. Flat roofs with projecting eaves. The blocks only three
storeys high, and, one notices, still carefully symmetrical.
1936 by *Frederick Gibberd*. Opposite, Nos. 1–3, a LODGE OF
Blore's Penge Place, the mansion built in 1836–8 and
demolished in 1853 to make way for the Crystal Palace.
Jacobean style.§ This interrupts a sequence of identical
Gothic mansions by *John Norton*, Nos. 5–17, and round the
corner in THICKET ROAD, Nos. 75–79.

Nothing in the High Street, but at the far end, next to the
Congregational church, KENILWORTH COURT, by *Royce,
Stephenson & Tasker*, 1961–2. Shops and a filling station,
nicely grouped and designed with excellent restraint and
firmness. Slate-hung between the windows.

PETTS WOOD

ST FRANCIS, Willett Way. 1934–5 by *Geoffrey Mullins* of
Chistlehurst. Brick. Fashionably jagged treatment of the

* Some curious details, e.g. the porter's lodge growing out of the wall, can be
attributed to the fact that the young *S. S. Teulon* was Porter's assistant (N.
Taylor).

‡ For railway bridges in Crystal Palace Park Road and Thicket Road *see* Crystal
Palace.

§ I owe this to the researches of Mr Hugh Meller.

windows. – STAINED GLASS. E window by *James Hogan*,
1946. Above average for its date, one is ashamed to say.

ST MARY CRAY

The post-war expansion in the Cray Valley has been terrific.
Many small factories in the valley W of the river, housing on the
slopes behind and also on the E side. Renewal of the old High
Street is proceeding fitfully. So it is an indictment of the planners
that St Mary Cray is no place to linger in, and an indictment of
the architects, and also it must be admitted of post-war austerity,
that there is hardly anything worthy to be mentioned in *The
Buildings of England*; not a factory, not a housing estate, and the
parish church is undistinguished.

ST MARY. Below the intimidating arches of the railway viaduct.
Flint. Outside all one sees is of the restorations of 1861–3 (*E.
Nash*), 1876, and 1895. The characteristic SE vestry is Nash's,
with needle-sharp lancets and a fantastic chimney. But the
Dec and Perp tracery was faithfully copied. Three windows
have 'Kentish' tracery, that is trefoils or quatrefoils with
split-back cusps, a device favoured in the first third of the
C14. But in essence the church is early C13. W tower and
shingled spire. Nave and aisles of three bays. Sturdy round
piers, pointed arches with a small chamfer and a keeled roll.
The arches only of the S arcade C14. The evidence at the E end
is later. C14 chancel arch. Shallow chapel at the end of the S
aisle, with a long squint. The N chapel virtually all rebuilt. –
SCREENS. Perp. Simple S chapel screen. Tower screen with
pretty intersecting tracery. – BRASSES. Richard Abery † 1508
and wives. He seems to have married identical triplets. 11 in.
figures. – Richard Manning † 1604 and wife. Civilian. 22 in.
long. – Philadelphia († 1747) and Benjamin Greenwood †
1773. The last pre-Oxford-Movement brasses, says Mrs
Esdaile. The little figures scratched rather than engraved. He
wears a wig, frock-coat, and flowered waistcoat. – Small
hanging MONUMENT to Margaret Crewes † 1602. Kneeling
figures.

ST JOSEPH (R.C.), High Street. Conspicuous brick tower with
a red and white metal construction on top, like an agricultural
exhibit. By *D. Plaskett Marshall*. Completed 1959.

(VIADUCT, at the N end of the High Street. For the London,
Chatham and Dover Railway. Nine brick arches of 1858–60,
widened 1959. To the E a chalk CUTTING 80 ft deep.)

The long, narrow High Street has lost a good many of its
houses. Of those that were left the only one of consequence,
THE ROOKERY, half-way along, burnt down in 1980.* More

---

* It was late C18, red brick, of three storeys and five bays. Everything happened in the centre bay. It projected a little; porch on Greek Doric columns,
Venetian window over, semicircular lunette window at the top.

modest early C18 houses further s, some reminder of the 'populous, handsome village' which Hasted knew.

KEVINGTON COUNTY PRIMARY SCHOOL, ¾ m. SE. Big, square, red-brick house, five bays by six. Three storeys. Wide bow the full height of the s front. Generous white window surrounds. Built *c.* 1767 by *Sir R. Taylor* (H. C. Berens). Redbrick and flint STABLES.

SHAWCROFT SCHOOL, s of the above, is a good example of the sharp informality of the early 1970s, by *Sir Roger Walters* (G.L.C. Architect's Department). Red brick. Much play with monopitch roofs.

ST PAUL'S CRAY

ST BARNABAS, Rushet Road, E of Chipperfield Road. 1962–4 by *E. F. Starling*. Greek-cross plan with the angles between the arms partly filled up. Big copper tent roof and flèche. Internal galleries on three sides and light directed on to the chancel.

ST PAULINUS. Church, school, and a row of early C19 cottages look across a loop of the river Cray (limpidly purling over sludge), to a shaggy water-meadow: memorably different from the shopping-parades and light industry around. The church has quite an interesting history. The N chapel to the chancel is separately gabled and has a NE quoin of Roman tiles. In its N wall an early lancet, in its W wall a blocked round arch with a slight chamfer. Traces of a round-headed E window (one of a triplet?) as well. High up the N wall of the nave, a blocked early window, its rere-arch visible inside, turned a little irregularly in tiles. So we seem to have evidence of a Saxon nave, a Saxon N porticus, and an early C12 N aisle made to communicate with the porticus, but later demolished.* The later parts are notable too, dating from *c.* 1200 or a very little later. W tower and shingled spire. (The convincing doorway and the unconvincing window above it are alike inventions of *c.* 1860.) Nave with blocked N arcade and s aisle. Chancel. The work is characterized by circular piers, pointed arches, and upright leaves and heads on some of the capitals. The fascinating thing is that in spite of the crude carving they are unmistakably acanthus leaves. The source for such a motif must be Canterbury Cathedral of 1175–80. The SE respond and pier have them, on the latter arranged with laborious symmetry, and the W respond of the arch to the N chapel, where some trefoil and spade-shaped leaves occur as well. In the chancel the outer jambs of a trio of E windows, and a curious large recess in the N wall. That it was never an arch to a chapel is shown by the string-course running across the back wall. There was heavy restoration in 1856–61, and the s chapel was added in 1863. Typically the Victorian restorer had to go one better and provide professional leaves and heads on the capi-

* Mr P. J. Tester has suggested to me that this is what the evidence means.

tals of his S chapel arches. Any tampering he may have done to the original work is now obscured by whitewash. He is not above suspicion. The sanctuary roof constructed after a fire in 1968.* – FONT. Octagonal. Elementary panelling of the bowl, a sunk panel and two sunk hyphens. More likely to be C 17 than C 15. – LECTERN. Charming and highly unusual. Wood, carved as a pelican in her piety, on a twisted stem. It must be foreign, C 18. – MONUMENTS. (C 13 coffin lid in the S chapel, with a very odd cross and floriated stem.) – Earl Sydney † 1890. A tablet done to look like a late C 17 one. Rather well done. – One is surprised to find that the church was redundant by 1980. It has been converted into an old people's day centre. The fittings have gone, but the tablets remain.

(NASH'S PAPER MILL, Main Road. Early C 19 onwards. Formerly water-powered, a survivor of a once extensive local industry.)

(Off HOCKENDEN LANE and off COOKHAM LANE to the N, two rows of typically Kentish hop-picker's huts, C 20, flat-roofed red brick.)

BRONZE AGE ENCLOSURE, on the site of the modern church on Broomwood Hill. It consisted of a rectangular embanked enclosure 120 ft by 60 ft with entrances in the middle of the E and W sides. Within were the foundations of at least two circular timber-built huts and a general scatter of flint-knapping debris and artefacts of Early Bronze Age character.

SHORTLANDS

ST MARY, Church Road, off Shortlands Road to the E. 1953–5 by *Ansell & Bailey*. – SCULPTURE. On the W front the Flight into Egypt, by *John Skeaping*.

In SHORTLANDS ROAD, No. 114 (at the corner of Scott's Lane) was built in 1868–9 by *Norman Shaw* as Corner House, for Mrs Craik the novelist, and extended behind in 1872. It is a very nice example of his early tile-hung style, Gothic only in its two-centred entrance arch – though Mrs Craik's reaction was, 'We shall be Gothic to within an inch of our lives.' The red brick walls with red tile-hanging above, the steep roofs and dominant chimneystacks are all meant to suggest warmth and homeliness; and a visitor to the newly-completed house reported glowing colours inside too, dull red walls and blue-grey paint in the entrance hall, scarlet serge curtains, and all the window-seats cushioned in scarlet.‡

KINGSWOOD HOUSE, Valley Road, off Shortlands Road, near the station. A comfortably designed old people's home, on a sloping site, by *Clifford Culpin & Partners*, completed 1963.

---

* Mr C. R. Councer tells me that a C 13 stiff-leaf capital was found in the rubble-filling of a vault after the fire.

‡ Dr Mark Girouard and Mr Andrew Saint are my generous informants on this house.

WATERWORKS PUMPING STATION, Valley Road. A period
piece of the 1860s, in rock-faced ragstone.*

WEST WICKHAM

Sir Henry Heydon, who died in 1504, 'buildid', in the words of
Leland, 'a right fair Manor Place, and a fair Chirche'. Church
and Court, together on a gentle hillside, are yet isolated from the
c 20 suburb in the valley by a *cordon sanitaire* of playing fields.
Real farmland to the w.

ST JOHN THE BAPTIST. Greatly restored and rebuilt. The late
c 15 windows of two cinquefoiled lights under a straight-sided
arch occur in all parts of the church. In the w part however
they are reset, for in 1847 nave, N aisle, and SW tower were
rebuilt in flint, by *Whichcord & Whichcord*. Chancel and N
chapel of ragstone rubble, the former rendered, the latter
remodelled in 1961 to take a first-floor vestry. s organ chamber
by *Sedding*, 1889, chequered in a mannered way. Leland's
'buildid' exaggerates however, for the arches to the chapel are
c 14. Simpler, slightly later, chancel arch. The arcade of 1847
simpler still, but solid and quite convincing. – WEST GAL-
LERY. – PULPIT, SCREENS, ORGAN CASE, etc. by *Sedding*.
– TILES. In the sanctuary, many with patterns. – STAINED
GLASS. Figures of the earliest c 16 in three windows of the N
chapel, reset among modern quarries. – Kneeling skeleton in
the E window, with the Heydon arms. The style and orangey
colouring characteristic of the Flemish glass painters, who
were working in London by the late c 15. – Several *Kempe*
windows: N aisle, 1896; s windows, 1899; E window, 1901. –
MONUMENTS. William de Thorp † 1407. Brass of a priest, a
foot and a half long. – John Stokton † 1515. Brass of a priest, a
foot long. – Margaret Hobbes † 1608. Alabaster hanging
monument. Small figure seated frontally, a stillborn child at
her feet. Black backing to throw up the silhouette. – Samuel
Lennard † 1618. Plain alabaster tomb-chest (used as an altar).
The mottled pattern of the material appreciated for its own
sake, something rare even among furniture-makers before the
late c 17. – Elizabeth Howell † 1838. Simple Baroque cartouche, a surprising throw-back. – Simple LYCHGATE,
medieval, but greatly restored.
WICKHAM COURT. Sir Henry Heydon bought the manor in
1469. The house he built is of brick, with renewed stone
dressings. It is not large, but even in its present mutilated state
it makes a forceful architectural impact.‡ The almost square

* Mr Malcolm Tucker adds the following: Built for the Kent Waterworks Co.
in 1866. Beams of the two former Cornish engines protrude from the engine house
(though they are now severed internally). They are unusual among c 19 engines in
London in not being fully enclosed. The early c 20 pumping station of the
Metropolitan Water Board is also ragstone.
‡ The mutilations are c 19 mullioned windows throughout, a recessed top
storey, and modern battlements and tops to the turrets.

plan with octagonal corner turrets has an unmistakably fortified character. Quatrefoil loops low down in the turrets. Yet
there is no sign that a moat ever surrounded the house, no
trace of a gatehouse, i.e. no trace of any of the preliminaries
that would make defence credible. Projecting chimneybreasts
on the N and S sides. Later low W porch, and within it the
four-centred entrance doorway with shields of arms in the
spandrels, Sir Henry's and his wife's. The interior of the
house has been greatly altered, but the arrangement of the
rooms round the four sides of a tiny courtyard, no more than
c. 16 ft square, is original. The courtyard is now covered and
takes a staircase. The C 15 timber-framed courtyard walls
however are intact, with the l. jamb of a sizeable mullioned
window on the N side. Original fireplace in the large room it
lights, which must have been the hall – one-storeyed, one
notes. The W end of this room can hardly be genuine, with an
oriel under a timber recess, and steps coming up below it.
Elaborate carved corbels. A considerable amount of armorial
GLASS of the C 16 and C 17 here and in other rooms. Where
then should one place Wickham Court in the history of house-
planning? In the line of descent from the Bodiam type of castle
certainly, for its squareness, its ranges of rooms round a
central courtyard, and for the angle turrets. But what in the
C 14 could accommodate the garrison of a castle, has by the
end of the C 15 become telescoped to house a single family,
until the courtyard is not much more than a light-well. Yet,
curiously, nothing like this recurs until White Hall, Shrewsbury, of 1578, without the turrets, and Barlborough, 1584,
combined with a new interest in a spectacular and symmetrical
exterior.

The modern suburb has its own High Street, 1 m. NW of the old
church. Little comment is called for on the efforts of the C 20.

ST FRANCIS OF ASSISI. 1935–6 by *Newberry & Fowler*. Neo-
Perp. Buff brick. SE tower. Intended N aisle not built.
ST MARK (R.C.), at the junction of High Street and Manor
Park Road. 1962–3 by *Bingham Towner Associates*. Stock
brick. The plan is a distorted octagon, with a parish room at
the E end pushing the altar into an almost central position.
Timber tent roof and hefty canopy under a skylight to emphasize this position.
Caught up in a shopping parade, at the corner of High Street and
Wickham Court Road, is WEST WICKHAM HOUSE, mainly
of 1870–1 by *Norman Shaw*, extending a house by *W. M.
Teulon*. Shaw's work is of considerable historical significance,
as one can see if one raises one's eyes above the shopfronts; for
here is the full vocabulary of the Queen Anne style, red brick,
white-framed sash windows, a deep white eaves cove,
pedimented dormers, and the teasing conflict between near
symmetry in the windows and a random placing of massive
chimneystacks (several now removed). All this a year or two

earlier than Shaw's epoch-making Lowther Lodge, Kensington (KC).

On CORKSCREW HILL, two houses deserve mention. Glebe
House has a half-H plan, the wings ending in the simplest
shaped gables. Rendered. Probably of the early c 18. No. 25 is
early c 19 Gothick, though the plan is a vernacular survival
from the c 17, with a lobby entry in front of the central
chimneystack.

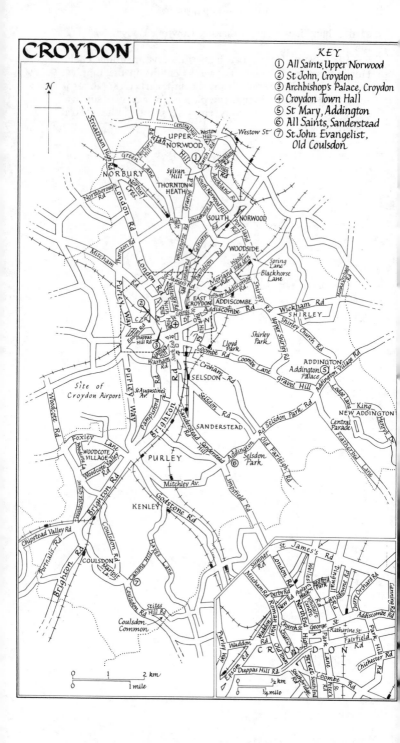

CROYDON

KEY
① All Saints, Upper Norwood
② St John, Croydon
③ Archbishop's Palace, Croydon
④ Croydon Town Hall
⑤ St Mary, Addington
⑥ All Saints, Sanderstead
⑦ St John Evangelist, Old Coulsdon

N

UPPER NORWOOD
Westow St
NORBURY
Sylvan Hill
THORNTON HEATH
SOUTH NORWOOD
WOODSIDE
Spring Lane
Blackhorse Lane
EAST CROYDON
ADDISCOMBE
Wickham Rd
SHIRLEY
CROYDON
Shirley Park
Shirley Church Rd
Upper Shirley Rd
Epsom Duppas Hill Rd
Lloyd Park
Coombe Rd
Coombe Lane
Gravel Hill
ADDINGTON
Addington Palace ⑤
ADDINGTON VILLAGE Rd
Croham Rd
SELSDON
NEW ADDINGTON
Central Parade
Site of Croydon Airport
St Augustine's Av
Selsdon Rd
SANDERSTEAD
Selsdon Park
Selsdon Park Rd
Old Farleigh Rd
Woodcote Rd
Foxley Lane
WOODCOTE VILLAGE
Woodcote Valley
PURLEY
⑥
Brighton Rd
Mitchley Av.
Limpsfield Rd
KENLEY
Godstone Rd
Coulsdon Rd
Hayes Lane
Chipstead Valley Rd
Portnalls Rd
COULSDON
⑦
Stites Hill Rd
Coulsdon Common

St James's Rd
Sumner Rd
London Rd
Mitcham Rd
Derby Rd
New Rd
North End
Church St
George St
St Katharine St
Fairfield Rd
Park Lane
Addiscombe Rd
Chichester Rd
CROYDON
Waddon
Epsom Duppas Hill Rd
Purley Way
Old Town
Coombe Rd
South End

0   1   2 km
0   1 mile

0   ½ km
0   ¼ mile

CROYDON

INTRODUCTION

The borough of Croydon fills the valley between the densely built up C19 suburbs to the N, where the land rises to the dramatic leafy heights of Upper Norwood, and the more sporadically developed settlements on the edge of the North Downs. Here, around the old villages of Addington, Sanderstead, and Coulsdon, there are still quite extensive stretches of open country and woodland, despite suburban encroachment of the last thirty years. The landscape reflects the varied geology: London Clay in the N, with some overlying gravels, higher pebble-beds around Addington Hills E of Croydon, and chalk fringed by sand and capped by clay-with-flints in the southern areas, as is evident in some of the remaining rural buildings in the S which use local materials.*

The architectural contrasts of the borough are nowhere more marked than in the town of Croydon itself, one of the most visibly prosperous and bustling centres in outer London. The brash towers which sprouted in the office boom of the 1960s jostle stranded Victorian villas in the former eastern suburbs;

---

* EARLY SETTLEMENTS: Slight Palaeolithic scatter along the Downs, then a considerable spread of later prehistoric settlement in the same area (notably at Sanderstead, Croham Hurst, and Shirley), including flint-working, and sufficient Late Bronze Age smiths' hoards to suggest a major industry. There is an Iron Age/Romano-British settlement on Farthing Down with an associated field system, and a concentration of Roman finds and burials at Croydon, on the Lewes road. Early Saxon cemetery at Croydon; C7 barrows on Farthing Down.

the old town, although renewed with the civic enthusiasm characteristic of the 1890s, still has at its central crossroads charming, incongruously low almshouses of the c 16, and, tucked away
by the church, one of the best surviving examples in England of a
medieval archbishop's palace.

The old centre of the medieval market town lay to the w of the
present one, around the church and palace, one of a string of
archbishops' palaces between Canterbury and Lambeth. The
town benefited from the connection, as is shown by the size of
the late medieval church (rebuilt after a fire in the c 19), and the
foundation by Archbishop Whitgift of the almshouses already
mentioned and a school (rebuilt in the c 19, and again in the c 20
on a new site). By the c 16 the focus had shifted away from the
church to where the sloping triangular market place lay on the
London Road, an area by then built over and turned into a
warren of narrow lanes. The town had a reputation at that time
as an unpleasant, muddy place filled with uncouth colliers (or
charcoal burners) from the surrounding woods. Defoe, however, in the c 18 called it a great corn market, and 'full of citizens
from London'. Two excellent early c 18 houses on the edge of
the town centre, Wrencote and Coombe Hill House, remain
from that time. The building of the innovatory Surrey Iron
Railway to Wandsworth (1801–3) and the Croydon Canal to
Deptford (1802–9) indicates the commercial prosperity of the
town at the beginning of the c 19.* During that century the
suburbs grew, the palace had been deserted by the archbishops,
and the centre round the markets was neglected, became slummy,
and eventually was almost entirely swept away in an ambitious
rebuilding scheme soon after the town became a borough in
1883. There had been a local health authority since 1849. Municipal pride was crowned by the lavish civic buildings of the 1890s
(by *Charles Henman Jun.*). By then Croydon had more than
100,000 inhabitants. (Population: 1801:5,743; 1831:12,447;
1851:20,355; 1871:55,652; 1891:102,697.)

Expansion was encouraged by the arrival of the steam railways
(the London and Croydon line in 1839, the London and Brighton, with its station at East Croydon, in 1841). The growth of the
town is marked by service buildings, among which the c 19
waterworks and c 20 power station provide the most notable
landmarks, and by an impressive galaxy of suburban churches.
In N Croydon: St James (1827–9 by *R. Wallace*), Christ Church
(1851–2 by *Teulon*), St Saviour (1867 by *A. R. Mullins*), St
82 Michael (planned 1875, by *Pearson*, particularly fine); to the s St
Peter (1849–51 by *Scott*), and St Andrew (1857 by *Ferrey*); to the
E St Matthew (1866 by *Blomfield*), now demolished, and the
especially eccentric St Mary Magdalene, Addiscombe (1867–70
by *E. B. Lamb*).‡ The Nonconformist churches are equally
varied. The suburban housing has survived less well. By 1870 it

* Hardly any evidence of either remains; see D. Bayliss, *Tracing the First Public
Railway* (1981).

‡The old parish church, rebuilt after a fire, by *Scott*, is also now essentially
Victorian, with a rich collection of fittings.

had spread S as far as the grounds of Haling Park (now occupied by Whitgift School), reached Addiscombe to the E, and to the N was bounded by the cemetery and workhouse in Queens Road. The most complete of the well-to-do Victorian suburbs is that around The Waldrons, built on part of the Haling Park Estate to the S. Park Hill to the E has nearly all been rebuilt; to the N and NE a little remains, including, on what was then the northern fringe, the curiosity of some early concrete cottages, with two pairs designed by *Norman Shaw*.

In the early C20 further suburban growth was encouraged by industrial expansion, especially W of the town on the edge of Croydon Airport (operating from 1915). Some rare early airport buildings remain, although the airport itself is partly built over (*see* Beddington, Su). The tradition of local employment and consequently of continuing suburban expansion, now to the S, the only available area left, was boosted after the Second World War by a growth of offices unparalleled elsewhere in outer London, and indeed in the whole country. This started after the Croydon Corporation Act of 1956, an early example of the ambitious package deal that became so popular in the 1960s, a combination of road improvements with profitable private shopping and office developments. Croydon had the advantages of closeness to yet independence of London (only 18 minutes by fast trains and a train every few minutes), lower rents than inner London, and a borough council eager to receive the large firms which the government was at that time encouraging to move out of the centre. By 1970 about six million square feet of office space had been provided in the town, with a further one and a half million elsewhere in the borough. Since then, growth has been much slower. But alas neither the offices nor the new public buildings which followed in the town centre have produced anything architecturally outstanding, nor have the new roads made Croydon enjoyable for the pedestrian, except for the small traffic-free area by the market.

The northern part of the borough all lay within the parish of Croydon until the C19. In the C18 there were small settlements at Thornton Heath, Broad Green, and Woodside (of which traces remain around the green); farms at Norbury and Selhurst. Norwood, as the name implies, was a wooded area covering the hills which form such a distinctive southern edge to the Thames basin, a natural border between the old parishes of Croydon, Lambeth, Camberwell, and Penge, perpetuated by the boundaries of the modern boroughs of Croydon, Lambeth, Southwark, and Bromley. On the lower slopes Beulah Spa opened in 1831 (cf. Sydenham Wells, Lewisham (Le), Perambulation 6). The lodge from *Decimus Burton*'s buildings remains in Beulah Hill, and several pleasant houses and cottages of this period can still be found in the same neighbourhood, notably Norwood Grove in its own grounds, and others now swamped by later housing. More intensive development came with the re-erection of the Crystal Palace on the crown of the hill further E (in Bromley); a good variety of villas and a hotel of the mid C19 remain in Church Road and Westow Street, and on the leafy hill just below the Palace, a few remarkably grand Gothic mansions of the 1880s in Auckland Road, near *Pearson*'s equally ambitious St John.

There is less to enjoy within the relentless suburban sprawl of Thornton Heath, South Norwood, and Norbury, all C 19 creations around the railway stations and continuous with Croydon by 1914. Highlights are the wonderfully eccentric Stanley Halls at South Norwood (by *W. F. Stanley*, local industrialist and 96 benefactor), 1902 etc., an early L.C.C. cottage estate at Norbury, and a few churches (St Alban Thornton Heath by *Bucknall & Comper*, 1889 etc., Holy Innocents South Norwood by *Bodley*, 1894–5).

The southern parts of the borough have a very different architectural character. Purley and Kenley are C 19 creations around their railway stations, but Addington, Sanderstead, and Coulsdon all preserve their medieval village churches (Addington with a C 12 chancel, Coulsdon with especially good C 13 work); rural buildings include a medieval hall-house at Coulsdon, a windmill at Shirley, and an C 18 country mansion at Addington (by *Robert Mylne*, with an interior remodelled by *Norman Shaw*).

After the Second World War it was still possible to build on virgin land in these areas. Development began unpromisingly in the later 1940s with the continuation of the uninspired council estate at New Addington, but since then the borough has become one of the most interesting areas in outer London for better-than-average private housing estates, mostly developed by *Wates*, for example at Coulsdon and in the Park Hill suburb of Croydon. They are largely by Wates's own architects, but at Park Hill there is also a more original scheme by an outsider, the Swiss firm *Atelier 5*, a small group of interlocking hillside terraces. Further N piecemeal renewal of the Victorian suburbs by both public and private housing began with flats, e.g. in Upper Norwood in the 1950s–60s, and continued in the later 1970s with neo-vernacular urban cottages, see the not dissimilar groups built by *Barratts* at Westow Street, Upper Norwood, and the borough housing at St Saviour's, North Croydon. Few individual recent buildings need be mentioned: St Matthew at Park Hill by *David Bush*, an enterprising angular focus for the rebuilt suburb; and an individualistic block of maisonettes at South Norwood by *Edward Cullinan*. Borough showpieces of the 1960s include the municipal offices in Croydon, the first outer London borough offices to be housed in a tower block, and a library at South Norwood. The Principal Borough Architect from 1965 to 1967 was *H. Thornley* (under the Borough Engineer, *A. F. Holt*); from 1967 there was a separate Architect's Department under *Hugh Lea*, who in 1972 became Director of Development, with *Peter G. Vincent* as Head of Architecture. The population of Croydon was 328,380 in 1965, 317,980 in 1981, the highest of all the London boroughs.

Further Reading

For publications on Surrey generally see p. 124. Current re-
search, chiefly on local history and archaeology, is reported in
the *Proceedings* of the Croydon Natural History and Scientific
Society and, for the s part of the borough, the *Local History
Records* of the Bourne Society. Good popular recent guides are
the Living History series edited by Brian J. Salter: *Central
Croydon* (2nd ed. 1978), *Coombe Shirley and Addiscombe* (1974),
Croydon's Heritage (1975). *Coulsdon, a Downland Village*, ed. U.
Broadbent and R. Latham (1976), is a useful general history.

The redevelopment of Croydon in the C19 is examined in the
very informative study by R. C. W. Cox, 'The Old Centre of
Croydon', in *Perspectives in English Urban History*, ed. A. Everitt
(1978). The *Croydon Advertiser Special* of May 1894 provides a
contemporary account. On individual buildings: J. Corbet
Anderson, *The Monuments and Antiquities of Croydon Church*
(1856 and subsequent editions), *idem*, *The Archiepiscopal Palace
at Croydon* (1879), and on the same subject P. J. Faulkner,
Archaeological Journal, 127 (1970), P. Druett, *ibid.*, 128 (1971),
and A. Oswald, *Country Life*, 8 and 15 April 1965. Also useful:
W. Godfrey, 'Whitgift Hospital', *Home Counties Magazine*, 3
(1901); H. W. Bateman, *A Short History of St John the Baptist*,
Upper Norwood (1937); J. Wright, *Addiscombe Parish Church*
(1927); and B. Learmouth, J. Nash, and D. Cluett, *The First
Croydon Airport 1915–28* (1977), also vol. II, *Croydon Airport,
The Great Days 1928–1939* (1980).

Acknowledgements

I have to thank Croydon Public Libraries, especially Mrs L. M.
Osborne, Reference Librarian, and Mrs D. Garrett, Local History Librarian, for much useful information. I am also most
grateful to Mr D. A. Bayliss (DB) for very detailed corrections
and additions, particularly on industrial matters, Dr R. C. W.
Cox for many notes on C19 buildings, Mrs J. Greenacombe for
checking the text, Mr Nicholas Taylor (NT) for notes on buildings of the 1960s, and the borough's Department of Development for information on recent events.

ADDINGTON

Still quite rural, separated from Croydon by the woodland of
Ballards Plantation around Coombe Lane and the golf course,
formerly the grounds of Addington Place.

ST EDWARD and GOOD SHEPHERD (R.C.), New Addington.
See below.

ST MARY. The exterior mostly refaced in 1876 by *St Aubyn*,
who added the N aisle and rebuilt the C18 W tower. But the
chancel, flint with ashlar dressings, is C12, with original
windows, especially a stepped triplet at the E end, of widely

spaced windows. One blocked window in the N wall looks older than the others. C13 s arcade of three bays with alternatingly round and octagonal piers, moulded capitals, and double-chamfered arches. The aisle is characteristically narrow. Lancet windows at the E end. s porch added by Archbishop Howley († 1848). Baptistery in the w tower fitted up 1913: mosaic floor, tiled walls, and alabaster FONT. – FURNISHINGS. Much contributed by or in memory of the C19 Archbishops who lived at Addington Palace. – REREDOS of alabaster, with figures of early archbishops under canopies (a memorial to Archbishop Benson † 1896). – Chancel with rich C19 stencilling and gilding. – STAINED GLASS by *Kempe*, s aisle, 1891, 1898. – MONUMENTS. Brasses to John Leigh † 1509 (and wife), 2 ft 2 in. figure in armour (chancel floor s). – Sir Olliphe Leigh † 1612, his wife, parents, and grandparents. Stiffly semi-reclining effigies one on top of the other and above them the smaller figures of the older generation, each couple kneeling and facing one another across a prayer desk. The pairs are flanked and separated by obelisks. – Two more kneeling figures of about the same period are preserved, taken out of context. – Mrs Lovell and Mrs Leigh, both † 1691. Attributed by Mrs Esdaile to *Nost*. Hanging monument without figures. Unusually severely framed inscription plate with, as its only ornament, two hanging garlands of bunches of very boldly carved flowers. – Mrs Grizzel Trecothick † 1769. Signed by *Wilton*. Tall and broad curvy pedestal and low and broad urn on it of uncommonly high quality. – Barlow Trecothick, Lord Mayor of London, † 1775. Large plain urn of white and brown marble. Very restrained. – Archbishop Howley † 1848, N of the altar. The effigy now at Canterbury. – In the churchyard an ornate cross on a very ornate pedestal erected in 1911 by Archbishop Randall Davidson to his predecessors who lived at Addington.

ADDINGTON PALACE (Royal School of Church Music). Built (as Addington Place) by *Robert Mylne* in 1773–9 for Barlow Trecothick, later acquired by Charles Manners Sutton, Archbishop of Canterbury from 1805, and then used until 1897 as an Archbishop's Palace in place of the one at Croydon (q.v.) sold in 1780. The house is of Portland stone. Originally a three-storeyed balustraded block of seven bays with wings and one-storeyed pedimented end pavilions. The centre of the house has a pediment towards the garden. No columns or pilasters at all. Many additions in the same style. Chapel, library, and other apartments of 1829–30 by *Henry Harrison*. The interior was reconstructed by *Norman Shaw* for F.A. English, a South African diamond merchant who bought the house in 1897. An extra floor was added at the same time. In the double-height hall an elaborate classical marble and alabaster chimneypiece with strapwork decoration 'reconstructed' in 1900–3 by *William Gilmour Wilson*. The splendid cedar trees and some landscaping on the edge of the golf course date from *Capability Brown*'s work for James Trecothick in 1781–2. Two good brick and stone LODGES and stone gatepiers towards GRAVEL HILL. Two more in SPOUT HILL: the LION LODGES gatepiers with lions, possibly from an earlier Addington Place: DB). (In ADDINGTON VILLAGE ROAD another LODGE, late C19 Tudor; also FLINT COTTAGE, dated 1796, and THE SMITHY, modest mid C18 brick. In BOUNDARY WAY to the N, ADDINGTON HOUSE, with a front of c. 1630; C17 timber-framed and brick C18 parts behind.)

ROYAL RUSSELL SCHOOL, Coombe Lane, completely hidden from the road. An extensive series of buildings, of 1924 and later by *Sir Aston Webb* and his son *Maurice Webb* and of c. 1964 by *Robert Matthew, Johnson-Marshall & Partners* (in charge *P. A. Newham*), an effective and uncompromising juxtaposition of formal neo-Baroque with an industrialized building system (Laingspan). The Aston Webb buildings form two and a half sides of a large quadrangle. They are of red brick with yellow stone dressings, with much brick rustica-tion. To the main wing an exterior façade with a central pediment with paired Tuscan columns, and a cloister facing the quadrangle. At r. angles, two apsidal-ended halls flanking the chapel, with a tower standing forward with an open belfry surmounted by a stumpy octagonal stone spire. Rich Baroque interior, typical of the High Church taste of the period; tunnel-vault on enormous cornice and modillions, screen of four huge columns in front of the sanctuary. The quadrangle is completed not entirely symmetrically, but harmoniously, by the additions of the 1960s, of two and three storeys, with a cloister on thin steel supports opposite the brick one; a con-siderable variety of windows and cladding materials within the rectangular framework. Separate new JUNIOR SCHOOL to the S in the same style.

ADDINGTON WELL WATERWORKS, Featherbed Lane. En-gine house of the 1880s, with two fine cast-iron A-frame beam engines by *Easton & Anderson*.

NEW ADDINGTON. A housing estate begun on the Downs S of Addington in the 1930s and taken over and enlarged by Croydon Corporation as an unofficial new town. One of the classic examples in the 1950s of 'prairie planning', or the pointless over-provision of open space, so that everything is too far apart. Some efforts to improve on amenities and visual interest were made in the 1960s. LIBRARY in Central Parade, 1964, with a zigzagging roof-line, between the poorly detailed COMMUNITY CENTRE (1955) and SWIMMING BATH (1959–63), all by the *Croydon Borough Engineer's Architects Department*. No attempt to integrate the buildings as a group. At the end of Central Parade, ST EDWARD'S CHURCH, by *Caröe & Partners*, red brick, conservative and uninspiring. Some better new buildings at the N end of the estate, where FIELDWAY leads E off Lodge Lane around cheerful tile-hung terraces and a twelve-storey block of flats (1965). In DUNLEY DRIVE near by to the S, CHURCH OF THE GOOD

SHEPHERD (R.C.), 1962 by *Tomei & Maxwell* (sanctuary reordered 1977). Detached campanile. Sheltered housing of the 1970s by the *Borough Architect's Department*.

FORESTDALE. *See* Selsdon, below.

COLENTINA. Pretty house with butterfly roofs, by *A. C. Bayley*, 1954–5.

COULSDON

The village of Old Coulsdon lies at the end of Marlpit Lane some way from the stations and their surrounding suburbs, with the church nicely placed at the E corner of the large green.

ST JOHN EVANGELIST. C15 W tower of irregular stone and flint with a later shingled spire consisting of a truncated pyramid roof with a spike. The chancel is C13: note the W lancets of the N and S aisles and, internally, the beautiful blank N and S arcading in the chancel, which rests on circular shafts. The W bay has the shafts very short and growing corbel-like out of the wall, as if taking stalls or a screen into consideration. Excellent SEDILIA with detached circular piers and richly moulded pointed trefoiled arches. The PISCINA, though small, continues the same composition. C15 arcades of two bays, with tall octagonal piers and double-chamfered arches. Double-chamfered tower arch. Big, very dominant extension on the S side, 1958 by *J. S. Comper*. This is, alas, imitation Dec. – STAINED GLASS. N aisle, by *Kempe*, *c.* 1899. – MONUMENT. Grace Rowed † 1631. A small but very remarkable tablet, in the S aisle, comparable with some Evelyn monuments at Wotton (Surrey). Diptych with segmental pediment. Between the two black inscriptions plates the small figure of a woman stands on a skull, which lies on a pedestal with pick and shovel. She looks up to heaven, which is represented by a sun and clouds in the pediment. Out of her mouth comes a scroll with writing, and there are plenty of other emblematical inscriptions. The upper half of the black inscription plate appears to be hidden by a brown cloth, also made of stone, which again is covered with inscriptions.

(ST AIDAN (R.C.), Chipstead Valley Road. Begun in 1931 by *A. Scott*, the nave completed in 1966 by *Burles, Newton & Partners*. A square plan, with seating on three sides of the sanctuary. – SCULPTURE. Crucifix by *D. Prudens*; Virgin and Child and furnishings by *X. Ruckstuhl*. – STAINED GLASS by *P. Fourmaintreaux*. DE)

(METHODIST CHURCH, Brighton Road. 1911 by *Gordon & Gunton*. Free Gothic in flint and stone, with chequered gable and battered SE tower.)

(CANE HILL HOSPITAL. Built as a lunatic asylum, 1880–3, for Surrey County Council. An imposing building on a hilltop. DB)

BRADMORE FARM, Bradmore Green. At the opposite end of the green from the parish church, towards Marlpit Lane. C18 farmhouse, roughcast; C17 timber-framed flint and brick BARN and cottage.

(TAUNTON FARMHOUSE, Taunton Lane, between Canons Hill and Stites Hill Road. Irregular flint, brick, and tile-hung exterior of various dates, but inside the remains of a timber-framed C15 hall-house with its original crown-post roof above the first floor inserted in the C17.)

(THE GRANGE, Canons Hill. Two parallel ranges, late C17 with later additions. C17 and C18 COTTAGES remain in COULSDON ROAD by COULSDON COMMON and in STITES HILL ROAD.)

(STATION APPROACH, off Brighton Road, Coulsdon North, has a group of railway houses of 1899, also continuing along the path towards the library. Picturesquely varied roof-lines with deep eaves. DB)

(GROVE WOOD HILL, W of Woodcote Grove. No. 25 is a modern house by *Edward Bank* for himself, 1936–7.)

COULSDON WOODS, N of Old Coulsdon. A large estate begun in 1967 by Messrs Wates. The most original parts are the terraces of houses running up the hill, with garages tucked away beneath gardens and footpaths. Designed by *K. Bland* of *Wates*, with elevations by *Frederick MacManus & Partners*.

FARTHING DOWN, ¾ m. S of Coulsdon South Station. Field system and Saxon barrows. The lynchets (field edges) and an ancient trackway can be seen in raking sunlight, the fields on both sides, and the track on the W side, of the road to Chaldon. The barrows, W of the road, contained inhumation burials with grave goods. A series of E–W anti-aircraft trenches dug during the Second World War are the most prominent features on the Down.

CROYDON

CHURCHES

CHRIST CHURCH, Sumner Road. By *Teulon*, 1851–2.* Paid for by Archbishop Sumner, concerned at the lack of churches in the growing town. Designed to seat 700 (transepts with galleries). The Low Church layout was much disliked by the *Ecclesiologist*. The chancel was lengthened and a W bay added to the nave in 1860, to Teulon's designs. Flint-faced, with freestone banding, the details less eccentric than in some of his other buildings, although there are several odd features such as the W 'transept' W of the S porch, and the crazy turret with spire on the E end of the nave, and some characteristic Teulonesque tracery (spherical triangles in the transepts). Vestries added 1930. – (Art Nouveau FONT, 1908. – STAINED GLASS in the apse by *Clayton & Bell*, 1891.)

EMMANUEL, Normanton Road, S of Croham Road. 1899 by *T.*

---

* Redundancy threatened (1982). I owe the details in this entry to Matthew Saunders.

Roger Smith (GR). The late H. S. Goodhart-Rendel in an unguarded moment called this the ugliest elevation he knew.

St ANDREW, Southbridge Road. 1857 by *Ferrey*, with many additions. Flint-faced, with an odd bell-turret with spirelet on a detached shaft which sprouts out of a buttress bisecting the w front.

St AUGUSTINE, St Augustine's Avenue, South Croydon. 1881–4 by *J. Oldrid Scott* (GR). Flint and yellow Bargate stone, with a crossing tower. Competent and restful interior with broad crossing arches. The detail is Dec.

St GEORGE, Waddon. 1932 by *W. Curtis Green*. A sound brick church with big gables. Whitewashed diaphragm arches inside, and complicated timber roof.

St JAMES, St James's Road. A Commissioners' church: 1827–9 by *Robert Wallace*. Yellow brick with thin lancets and a lean tower. In the tower odd triplet openings. The more robust stone chancel is of 1881 by *Charles Henman Jun.* – (FONT. Late C18 design, marble, a fluted bowl on a baluster. – Original GALLERIES with Gothic cusping beneath; the rest of the seating of 1871. – REREDOS, marble, 1884 by *Earp*, designed by *Henman*. – PULPIT. 1882. – Good brass eagle LECTERN of 1884. – STAINED GLASS. E window 1881; designed by *Henman*, made by *H. W. Lonsdale*.)

St JOHN THE BAPTIST, Church Street. The old parish church was destroyed by fire in 1867 and rebuilt, essentially to the same design although extended E by 18 ft, by *Sir G. G. Scott* in 1870. The exterior all of flint with stone dressings. Medieval the two-storeyed s porch and the tower, except for the overdone pinnacles, which are Scott's, heightened in 1915. The size and ambition of the old church, a Perp building on the grandest scale, were due to its being built at the expense of archbishops.* Nave of six bays (originally five). Tall piers of the usual moulding with four shafts and four hollows. Moulded arches. Three-light clerestory windows. Big three-light aisle windows with transom. Ceiled roof, with tie-beams on braces with traceried spandrels. Vaulted entrance below the tower; two-storeyed s porch, the lower floor vaulted. Of the old church many fragments remain, notably a late C15 tomb recess in the N aisle and two big C14 corbels (one with a head) at the W end of the s aisle. The chancel is of three bays, more overtly Victorian than the rest of the building, divided from N and s chapels by piers of polished red Devon marble. This richness is complemented by the lavish CHANCEL FURNISHINGS and DECORATION: alabaster REREDOS with much gilding, flanked by a dado of traceried arches, SEDILIA, painted N and s walls, the N with a WALL PAINTING (Feeding of the Five Thousand), 1885, elaborate SCREENS of the 1890s (given, like much else in the church, by the Eldridge family); also ORGAN CASE, TILES, and ceiled wagon roof (coloured in

* The arms of Archbishops Courtney († 1396) and Chicheley († 1443) appeared on N and W doorways.

1913) with gilded angels and bosses. – TOWER SCREEN, a First World War Memorial, by *J. Oldrid Scott*. – FONT. C 19, Perp, alabaster, with Flamboyant Gothic cover, very tall. – LECTERN. A fine, big pre-Reformation brass lectern with a sturdy stem, a foot on three small lions, and an eagle top. The same type as at St Mary Redcliffe Bristol, St Martin Salisbury, etc. – MONUMENTS. Brasses to Gabriel Silvester † 1512, a 3 ft 4 in. figure, and to William Heron † 1562 and wife, the figure only 1 ft 9 in. long (chancel arch r. and l.). – Hugh Warham of Haling Manor (a brother of the Archbishop), *c.* 1536–8(?). Tomb-chest in the s chapel with elaborately enriched quatre-foils. Canted recess with three ogee-headed niches and coarse-ly panelled arch. A similar design to tomb recesses at Bedding-ton (Su) and St Mary Lambeth (La). – Archbishop Whitgift † 1604. Alabaster; recumbent effigy in prayer lying on a bulgy sarcophagus decorated with strapwork. Background with an arch, with two allegorical figures in the spandrels and against the back wall under the arch two putti by the inscription plate. Top with obelisks and achievement. – Archbishop Sheldon † 1677. By *Jasper Latham*. Damaged and inadequately put together. Semi-reclining figure. The pillow lies on a rolled-up mat – a standard Elizabethan and Jacobean motif. Of the background the cartouche remains, but the two putti who held it have disappeared. Tomb-chest with realistic hour-glasses, bones and skulls in high relief. Fine iron railings. – J. S. Copley R.A. † 1815, signed by *Morton Edwards*. Good Grecian tablet with portrait medallion.

ST MARY MAGDALENE, Canning Road, Addiscombe. By *E. Buckton Lamb*, 1868–70, the E and W ends completed in 1906, the tower not until 1928–30. The early history of the church is as eccentric as its architecture. It started as St Paul, founded unofficially by some local residents, and paid for by Robert Parnell; the priest was his brother-in-law, a converted rabbi and theologian, the Rev. Maxwell M. Ben Oliel. But the congregation dwindled after ritualistic services were intro-duced in 1872, and two years later the church was sold to the rival official establishment of St Mary Magdalene, until then in a temporary building.

The tower stands at the N E corner, next to Lamb's apse. But this E front, with the main entrance through the tower, odd as it is, cannot be sufficient preparation for the nightmarish interior, a debauch of High Victorian inventiveness compar-able only to Lamb's other churches at West Hartlepool and Gospel Oak (Ca). The plan is roughly central, the transepts being identical and the two-bay nave corresponding to the single-bay chancel. The church is covered with the most ingenious and unexpected timberwork, big beams in all direc-tions, resting on marble columns which in their turn stand on brackets. It all works up to a small timber lantern over the centre of the crossing, supported by interior flying buttresses in the transepts. In the aisles also timbers reach up towards the nave: the whole impression is that the walls are only there on sufferance, as a necessary podium to this enormous roof. Lamb was obsessed with roofs. In this purposefully composed cacophony such anomalies will hardly be noticed as the detached columns which reach up in front of the transept ends and connect with them at the top by stonework that cuts vertically right across the oculus windows. The church deserves study particularly as a reminder of how far some Victorian church architects were from a mechanical imitation of the medieval past. This ruthless individualism is the necessary counterpart of Pearson's noble correctness. (The furnishings and fittings may reflect Ben Oliel's Hebraic interests: seven steps up to the chancel, five to the sanctuary. Around the latter emblems of the twelve apostles on marble panels. Marble and mosaic reredos by *Theodore Lloyd*.)

ST MATTHEW, Chichester Road. 1965–72 by *David Bush*. A large church for the new housing of Park Hill, East Croydon. A bold brick hexagon, windowless to the road, entered by a triangular foyer with tall, tower-like clerestory. A hall with split pitched roof incorporated to the r. – STAINED GLASS. Made up by *John Hayward* from old glass from St Matthew George Street.* In the foyer clerestory glass from St John. – SCULPTURE. Two angels from the old St Matthew.

ST MICHAEL, Poplar Walk. By *J. L. Pearson*, designed in 1876 and built in 1880–3. Big, with an incomplete S porch tower, transepts with E chapels, an apse with ambulatory, two turrets with spires on the E ends of the chancel aisles, and a flèche over the crossing. Lancets and plate tracery. The interior is one of Pearson's finest, and one of the most satisfying of its date anywhere. It is brick-vaulted throughout; the vaulting-shafts rise without interruption from the ground, crossing the string courses that define the plain brick expanse of the triforium level, a harmonious interaction of verticals and horizontals in the tradition of medieval Gothic.‡ A tiny ambulatory runs right round the E end, giving exciting cross-views. The most interesting part is the S chapel. This opens from the chancel aisle and has itself a nave and aisles, of equal height, separated by the slimmest shafts. – Lavish fittings: FONT (1904), PULPIT with canopy (1898), and richly gilded, surprisingly splendid, almost Baroque Gothic ORGAN CASE (1901) all by *Bodley*. – FONT COVER by *Frank Pearson*. – Hanging ROOD and LECTERN by *Cecil Hare*. – STALLS by *Temple Moore*. – LADY CHAPEL FITTINGS by *Comper*. – STAINED GLASS. E windows by *Clayton & Bell*; N aisle windows by *Lavers & Barraud*; others (N chapel, E, and W end) by *Kempe*, 1895 and after.

(ST MILDRED, Addiscombe. By *C. G. Hare*, 1931–2. H. V. Molesworth Roberts)

82

---

* St Matthew George Street was of 1866 by *A. W. Blomfield*; chancel 1877.
‡ Dr A. Quiney has pointed out however that Pearson achieved the classical calm of his elevation, here as in other of his churches, by the unmedieval use of the golden section (*J. L. Pearson*, 1979).

ST PETER, St Peters Road, South Croydon. A Commissioners' church: 1849–51 by *Sir G. G. Scott*. In a very prominent position, with W tower and spire, the latter not completed until 1864. Rebuilt in 1865, after a fire. Rather dull, though competent, as Scott so often is.

ST SAVIOUR, St Saviour's Road, E of London Road, North Croydon. Quite a noticeable group in the poorer end of Victorian Croydon: church of 1867 by *A. R. Mullins*, with additions of 1880, polychrome brick, lancet style, with SW tower and spire. – SCHOOL and VESTRY HALL 1892, VICARAGE in Lodge Road *c.* 1867.

OUR LADY OF THE ANNUNCIATION (R.C.),* Bingham Road, to the E off Lower Addiscombe Road, Addiscombe. 1964 by *Denny & Brian*. Separate chapel with its own entrance. Sanctuary remodelled 1975. – SCULPTURE. Crucifix and Lady Chapel reredos by *M. Clark*.

OUR LADY OF REPARATION (R.C.), Wellesley Road. 1883 by *F. A. Walters*, incorporating parts of *E. W. Pugin*'s church of 1864.

ST DOMINIC (R.C.), Violet Lane, off Warham Road, Waddon. 1961 by *Tomei & Maxwell*.

ST GERTRUDE (R.C.), Purley Road. 1903 by *F. A. Walters*. Extended E in 1922–3 by *S. Bartlett*, nave lengthened W in 1935 by *E. J. Walters*.

R.C. CHAPEL (former), Handcroft Road. *See* Perambulation 5, end.

BAPTIST CHURCH, Tamworth Road, S of New Road. 1866. Dignified classical façade.

FRIENDS MEETING HOUSE, Park Lane. The meeting house proper is by *Hubert Lidbetter*, 1959, a small friendly building of yellow brick. It is connected by a colonnade with the large, rectangular adult school hall, which has a big sweeping roof and elegantly restrained details. By *W. Curtis Green*, 1908.

PROVIDENCE BAPTIST CHURCH, West Street, off the SW end of the High Street. 1847. Three bays, with three-bay pediment. Stock brick.

ST PAUL (Presbyterian), Croham Road, South Croydon. 1905 by *Charles Henman Jun.*, the architect of the town hall. Brick with stone dressings, pretty Flamboyant details, spirelet over the crossing. – CHURCH HALL of 1909 in similar style, with bellcote.

SALVATION ARMY CITADEL, Ellis-David Road, SW of Church Street. Built *c.* 1900 in a glaring red brick, with central pediment and castellated cornice.

(UNITED REFORMED CHURCH, Aberdeen Road, between South End and St Peters Road, South Croydon. 1870 by *J. T. Barker* of Croydon. C13 Gothic; Kentish rag with Bath stone dressings.)

WEST CROYDON BAPTIST CHURCH, Whitehorse Road.

* The information on Roman Catholic churches in Croydon was provided by Denis Evinson.

1873 by *J. T. Barker*. Brick and stone classical front with quadrant colonnades to recessed wings. Founded by James Spurgeon.

WEST CROYDON UNITED REFORMED CHURCH, London Road and Campbell Road. By *Church*, 1886, Gothic, E.E., with Croydon's most ambitious spire.

CEMETERY, Queens Road, W of Whitehorse Road. Two chapels of *c.* 1880, Dec Gothic, ragstone, linked by an entrance with two arches.

ARCHBISHOP'S PALACE

ARCHBISHOP'S PALACE (Old Palace School), Old Palace Road. The manor of Croydon belonged to the Archbishops of Canterbury already at the time of Domesday Book. The house at Croydon was one of the series of palaces on the route between Canterbury and Lambeth, and became something of an administrative centre for the Archbishop's estates in Surrey, Middlesex, and Hertfordshire. The surviving buildings, although unpromising externally, form one of the best groups of their kind for appreciating the domestic arrangements of the quasi-princely late medieval ecclesiastic, achieved by successive remodelling and additions. The palace now consists of an irregular group of buildings around two small enclosed courtyards, with the hall projecting to the E. They are mostly of the C14 to C15, with later modifications, incorporating an early core, perhaps of the late C12, between the two courtyards. Except for the hall, all the principal rooms are on the first floor. After the Archbishops sold the palace in 1780 and established themselves at Addington (q.v.), the buildings fell into decay, and parts were demolished. The Duke of Newcastle rescued them and presented them to the Sisters of the Cross, who restored them from 1887 for use as a girls' school.

The palace is now approached from the E. The yard to the N of the hall is all that remains of the OUTER COURT, which originally extended further N with a gatehouse by Church Road. Around the outer court were stables and C15 brick lodgings (of two storeys, with an upper corridor, as later at Hampton Court). These have been demolished, as has the service range E of the hall.

The GREAT HALL, built probably by Archbishop Courtney, *c.* 1381–96, and remodelled by Archbishop Stafford *c.* 1443–52, is of flint rubble with stone dressings. The two-storeyed porch and some adjoining walling date from Courtney's time. The ground floor of the porch is vaulted with diagonal and ridge ribs. The end wall, with the three service doors, which collapsed in 1830, was probably of the same date. The hall is unusually broad (56 by 38 ft) and was perhaps aisled in the C14. The present windows, set high up with three stepped lights under four-centred arches, and the noble roof both date from Stafford's remodelling in the mid C15. The roof is an exceptionally complex arch-braced construction, further strengthened by Archbishop Herring's tie-beams of 1748. Above these are collar-beams at two levels. In addition there are wind-braces, and the unusual feature of flying plates in front of the purlins at the level of the first collar-beam, carrying ashlar pieces to provide support for the very long rafters. There are also short straight braces between the main arch-brace and the rafters, three to each side. The flying plates and lower collars are all splendidly moulded. The wall-posts have wooden shafts with capitals and bases, resting on angel corbels with shields (some with the Stafford arms). At the dais end of the s wall a moulded arch remains from a big bay-window. On the w wall carved royal arms of Henry VI, above a Stafford shield, now set on a curious stone plinth, but possibly originally higher up, over the Archbishop's seat on the dais. A four-centred archway in the w wall leads to a lobby, from which an early c 17 open-well staircase with robust urn-shaped balusters leads up to the GUARDROOM (now library).

The GUARDROOM, 51 by 21 ft, was remodelled as an audience chamber by Bishop Arundel (c. 1397–1414), but as the thick walls and some features in the undercroft below indicate, it may have started as a late c 12 first-floor hall. Of the late medieval roof, only the moulded principals on excellently carved angel corbels are visible below the plaster ceiling. In the e wall an early Tudor bay-window, wholly renewed in 1910, in the n wall a late c 17 fireplace with an overmantel with open segmental pediment. The balustrade of the gallery at the w end is Laud's communion rail from the chapel (symmetrically turned balusters). The guardroom lies between the two courtyards. From its w end one enters what appears to have been a suite of state apartments formed in the later c 15. The first of these (later used as a dining room) is now divided up, but still has a good ceiling with moulded beams. There is a similar one to the room above the former dining room. The suite continues on the upper floor of the c 15 brick range running n, at an angle along the churchyard wall. From this one reaches the chapel on the n side of the n court.

The CHAPEL was built probably by Bourchier (c. 1460–80), but remodelled and lengthened by Morton so as to link up with the new apartments. It is 70 by 24 ft, of brick (with some stone and flint of earlier date visible outside). Straight-headed five-light windows, the e window of seven lights, under a four-centred arch. The ceiling possibly original. – FONT. Typical of c. 1660. – SCREEN between chapel and antechapel. Late Perp, heavy, with plain rectangular one-light divisions. – STALLS. Partly c 15 (with poppyheads), partly c 17 (with arms of Laud and Juxon). – WEST GALLERY. Altered and not *in situ*. Simple geometric ornament, attributed to Laud's joiner, *Adam Brown*, who also worked at Lambeth and St John's Oxford. – STAINED GLASS. e window by *Clayton & Bell*.

The rooms around the SOUTH COURT can be reached by another staircase from the lobby between the hall and guardroom. On the N side the so called Queen Elizabeth Room, with a ceiling with moulded beams, possibly dating from a remodelling by Bourchier. At the S end a closet opens off above the porch. The windows are C 18 Georgian (as is the exterior brickwork and the porch doorway, with fanlight). Within the lower S range is the LONG GALLERY, with C 16 panelling, externally also C 18 brick, but concealing a timber-framed structure of medieval date. The short wing projecting at the W end had the timber-framing exposed. The remains in this area are not easy to interpret; there was possibly an early medieval wing on the W side of the S court, linking up with the guardroom.* The UNDERCROFT beneath the guardroom has short sturdy wooden piers down its centre, and a plain early Gothic doorway in the dividing wall towards the W end.

PUBLIC BUILDINGS

TOWN HALL AND LIBRARY, Katharine Street. 1892–6 by *Charles Henman Jun*. Not a bad design even if debased in most details. Well grouped, with the tall tower at the r. angle of the town hall and at its foot the diagonally placed porch to the library, which lies a little recessed behind a small paved piazza with a statue of Queen Victoria. The library façade is quiet in its details with a range of tall Dutch or North German pedimented windows with two transoms beneath a steep roof with spirelet. On the r. the composition is completed by the former corn exchange, with steps up to a raised loggia. The exteriors all of red brick with stone dressings. Carving on the town hall porch by *J. Wenlock Robbins*, armorial carving by *W. Aumonier*. The most notable interiors are the sumptuous marble-faced staircase hall of the town hall, and the library's large Braithwaite Hall, with open timber roof. Behind the town hall and its pleasant garden to the l., on both sides of Fell Road and fronting on Park Lane, is TABERNER HOUSE, municipal offices of 1964–7, by *H. Thornley*, architect to the Borough Engineer, a high slab on a podium, the slab narrowing towards both ends (like the Pirelli building in Milan). A bridge is provided between the blocks E and W of Fell Road.

LAW COURTS, Barclay Road, the W continuation of Fairfield Road. By *Robert Atkinson & Partners*, 1968–9. To its N, i.e. S of the E end of the technical college, is a MULTI-STOREY CAR PARK, 1961–2 by *D. H. Beaty-Pownall*.

POLICE STATION, No. 70 Park Lane, in front of the Law Courts. By *J. I. Elliott* (chief architect, Metropolitan Police),

---

* Oswald points out the remains of a newel staircase at the NW corner of the long gallery, and an early Norman window in a wall W of the guardroom. See A. Oswald, *Country Life*, 8 and 15 August 1965; also P. Faulkner, 'Some Medieval Archiepiscopal Palaces', *Archaeological Journal*, vol. 127, 1970.

planned 1967, completed 1980. Façade with horizontal brick bands.

FIRE STATION, Old Town. 1960–1 by *Riches & Blythin*. Partly three-, partly four-storeyed, an attractive composition.

POST OFFICE, High Street. *See* Perambulation 2.

POST OFFICE, Cherry Orchard Road. Large and modern in style. By *E. T. Sargent* of the *Ministry of Public Building and Works*, 1962–7.

FAIRFIELD HALLS WITH ASHCROFT THEATRE AND ARNHEM GALLERY, Park Lane. By *Robert Atkinson & Partners*. Built in 1960–2, large with symmetrical façade. Infinitely more acceptable than the same architects' technical college – *see* below. What a change of heart between 1953 and 1960.

SWIMMING POOL (former; now a garden centre), Waddon Way, off Purley Way. The good concrete diving board by *C. E. Boast*, the Borough Engineer, 1935, still remains.

TECHNICAL COLLEGE AND COLLEGE OF ART, Park Lane. By *Robert Atkinson & Partners* (*A. F. B. Anderson*), 1953–9. The largest technical college in the south of England when it was built. Brick and Portland stone over steel framing. Large, and depressingly conventional at a time when so many technical colleges went up which were fresh, light, and up-to-date. Symmetrical façade to Park Lane. Extensions of 1969–71.

RUSSELL HILL SCHOOLS. *See* Purley, below.

ARCHBISHOP TENISON'S SCHOOL, Selborne Road, s of Chichester Road. Curtain-walled building of the early 1960s by *George Lowe & Partners*.

WHITGIFT SCHOOL, Nottingham Road, off Warham Road, Haling Park. 1931 by *Leathart & Granger*. Light red brick, neo-Tudor. Music school 1966–7, with a hall to seat 300, by *George Lowe & Partners*, junior school 1979 and sports hall 1981 both by *Wilson & Womersley*.

(MAYDAY HOSPITAL, Mayday Road. Board of Guardians' hospital of 1881–5; later extensions. DB)

QUEENS HOSPITAL, Queens Road, w of Whitehorse Road. The Italianate tower with pyramid roof and fragments of the flanking façades remain from the Croydon Union Workhouse of 1865–6 by *John Berney*. The rest was destroyed in the Second World War.

WHITGIFT HOSPITAL, George Street and North End. Almshouses on a regular courtyard plan. Founded by Archbishop Whitgift and built in 1596–9 for sixteen men and sixteen women. Red brick, symmetrical street front with three gables, the middle one taller and wider, and a central archway. Small two-light windows with hoodmoulds. Flat doorway with flat open pediment. The attractive quadrangle inside with two-storeyed ranges, originally each dwelling of one room. The s range has hall and laundry, and a suite of four upstairs rooms designed originally for Whitgift himself (later used by the warden). (In the audience chamber good original panelling and furnishings.) The chapel is in the SE corner. An inscription outside records that the pretty Perp E window was given

in 1597 by a citizen of York (William Thornhill, Whitgift's
chaplain). (Inside, original simple seats, oak wainscoting,
and portraits.) The style of the almshouses is altogether as
conservative as e.g. contemporary collegiate work in the uni-
versities (Second Court, St John's College, Cambridge). The
building was restored in 1860, the date of the upper parts
of the North End front, the flint plinths, porches, and chimneystacks.

CROYDON B POWER STATION, Waddon Marsh, Beddington
Farm Road, sw of Mitcham Road. By *Robert Atkinson*, 1939–
50, never completed. Large, red, and imposing, though decidedly heavy in the details. Steel-framed, faced with brickwork of high standard. Steel lattice girder roofs and two 300 ft
chimneys. The type is similar to that created by Sir Giles G.
Scott at Battersea (Ww), but it has been handled by others
with more crispness and elegance than it is here. (Deliberately
dramatic interiors. The structure is emphasized by triangular
vertical ribs and vertical windows. Coal-handling equipment
concealed by a curtain wall on the E side. DB)

WADDON PUMPING STATION, Waddon Way, off Purley
Way. Engine house of 1911 for two horizontal steam pumping
engines. Red brick, in a free mixed C17 style. Small copper
cupola and tall chimney.

WATERWORKS, Church Road and Surrey Street. The brown
brick and stone building with the date 1851 is part of the West
Croydon engine house of the atmospheric railway, re-erected
here by the Croydon Local Board of Health.* The castellated
tower-like building was added in 1867 by *Baldwin Latham*,
engineer of the Croydon Local Board of Health. White brick
with polychrome decoration. S addition 1872 by *T. Walker*, W
addition 1912.

WATER TOWER, Park Hill Recreation Ground, between
Coombe Road and Chichester Road. 1867 by *Baldwin
Latham*. Brick, in the Norman style, 100 ft high and very
prominent. The turret was a flue for the separate engine house
(now demolished) which pumped water up to the tank. Gutted
in 1971 but preserved as a landmark.

CROYDON AIRPORT (former). The surviving buildings lie in
Purley Way. The military airport of 1915 became London's
main airport in 1920, with buildings (now demolished) in
Plough Lane, Wallington (Su). The terminal moved in 1927–8
to Purley Way (a new road constructed in 1925). AIRPORT
HOUSE, 1927–8 by the *Directorate of Works and Buildings, Air
Ministry*, incorporated a control tower with the first purpose-
built air passenger terminal in Britain. Mostly two storeys, a
steel frame clad in concrete blockwork, a rather clumsy classically inspired design. Projecting three-bay rusticated centre
with round-headed openings above. The single-storey LODGE
with pilasters, and the older neo-Georgian parts of the

---

* The Croydon Atmospheric Railway operated from 1845 to 1847 from Forest
Hill to West Croydon, along the line of the London and Croydon Railway, built in
1839.

AERODROME HOTEL next door, also date from 1928. Further s two steel-framed hangars of 1927 (now warehouses), the
s one unaltered.

EAST CROYDON STATION, George Street. One of the busiest
of suburban stations, yet still entirely c 19. Long glazed ramps
from the platforms up to the ticket office over the tracks.

PERAMBULATIONS

1. The New Croydon

During the office boom of the 1960s the area around East
Croydon Station suddenly became the most consistently mod-
ern-looking area in the whole of England. The first perambulation therefore consists almost entirely of buildings of this
date, and precedes the account of old Croydon. The impact of
the new hits the traveller at once, whether he arrives in a car
from the N by way of Wellesley Road or in a train by way of
East Croydon Station. What also hits him after the first ten
minutes is the lack of any major planning. Secure a site and
evidently you could build, four- or twelve-storeyed, pretty
well as you wished and could afford. The result looks thrilling
from a distance and from the air, rather like a chunk of inner
Johannesburg, but breaks up from near by into separate
buildings, very few of individual architectural merit. The
earliest and dullest of the office blocks are concentrated quite
densely in the stretch between Wellesley Road and East
Croydon Station, with slightly more outré followers of the
later 1960s on the fringes. Development since then has been
much slower.

Turn E from the station for a moment and you have the two
principal buildings which cannot be denied individuality,
though they may well be denied architectural merit. The first
is N.L.A. HOUSE by *R. Seifert & Partners*, 1968–70, octagonal and twenty-three storeys high, i.e. the highest building
in Croydon of its date, and, like the same architect's slightly
earlier Centre Point (New Oxford Street, Ca), squeezed on to
the middle of the roundabout. The building has a curious
rhythm of canted bays projecting in alternating positions. So
in fact no floor plan is strictly octagonal. They are square with
splayed corners, the splay of one always placed above the
middle of a side of the next lower. Behind is the building of
GENERAL ACCIDENT, FIRE AND LIFE INSURANCE,
1961–3 by *Biscoe & Stanton*, eight-storeyed, oblong, with
precast concrete elements, designed unfortunately so that the
whole looks rather like folded paper, canting forward and
backward. Even the angles do this, so that one feels like
stretching the shape straight or squashing it. The window
mullions also cant inward and outward, contradicting the
plain oblong glazing. N of this, at the corner of Cherry
Orchard Road, is the large COMMERCIAL UNION HOUSE,

one of the best of New Croydon. By the *Austin-Smith/Lord Partnership*, 1965–8. Partly twelve-storey, it has a projecting frame clad in white mosaic, with a crisp rhythm of paired uprights and strong horizontals. Recessed walling in black mosaic, with black-painted window frames. An almost detached three-storey block forms a porte-cochère. The new buildings stop abruptly at this point and ADDISCOMBE ROAD continues towards the suburb of Park Hill (*see* Perambulation 4) with some conventional stucco-trimmed villas. To pursue the rest of New Croydon one turns w.

In GEORGE STREET, opposite the station, the massive bulk of TRUST SECURITIES by *Project Design Partnership*, 1978–81, betrays its date by the use of sleek mirror glazing to the upper parts and by the sloping roof-line, a clumsy design, despite neat detailing, and without recognizable scale, because the floor heights are disguised by the insistent pattern of the red-brick verticals. There are in fact only seven storeys, plus a penthouse flat. Further on two neutral jobs on the l.: ESSEX HOUSE, a slab on a podium, and SUFFOLK HOUSE, four-storeyed throughout. Both are by *Raglan Squire & Partners*, 1960–1, i.e. among the earliest of the New Croydon. In between the two an eight-storey office block of 1980 (replacing St Matthew's church). On the N side of George Street a few reminders of earlier days: Nos. 71–79 close to the station, a quite elaborate terracotta-decorated shopping terrace of the 1890s, and No. 67, a single villa of the 1840s. New Croydon continues to the N up DINGWALL ROAD. At the corner with George Street AUSTRALIAN MUTUAL PROVIDENT SOCIETY, 1968–70 by *Fuller, Hall & Foulsham*. The broad fascia above the shops has concrete decoration not of the wild kind then fashionable. High slab above. On the E side WETTERN HOUSE, by *Ian Fraser & Associates*, 1962–3. At the corner of Lansdowne Road CAROLYN HOUSE, 1961–3 by *D. Rowswell & Partners*, and at the opposite corner No. 17 Lansdowne Road by *R. Seifert & Partners*, 1964–5, the ground floor open with pairs of raking concrete posts. Opposite this, on the E side of Dingwall Road, a MULTI-STOREY CAR PARK. After that a few large mid C19 villas still survive. CHURCHILL HOUSE, at the corner of Sydenham Road, is one of the more daring designs of the time, faced with vertically set black tiles. 1965–7 by *D. Rowswell & Partners*. Its snubnosed corner still marks the northern limit of New Croydon here.

Now through Bedford Park, past some Early Victorian houses, to Wellesley Road. This is part of the fast-traffic system constructed in the 1960s. (The underpass under George Street into Park Lane, the flyover above the High Street (*see* below), and the widening of Old Town and Church Street belong to the same period.)

In WELLESLEY ROAD the northernmost building of the 1960s is RANDOLPH HOUSE, by *William J. Harvey*, 1963–9, with wild concrete reliefs l. and r. of the entrance. PEMBROKE

HOUSE, by *Vincent & Wynn*, 1963–7, is a good example of a quieter style, a nearly square tower of nineteen floors, the top excrescences hidden by vertical concrete slabs. In BEDFORD PARK on the s side SUNLEY HOUSE, 1965–8 by *Fitzroy Robinson & Partners*, large and utilitarian, and at the corner of Wellesley Road, yet larger, of four wings in the four main directions, LUNA HOUSE by *Denis Crump & Partners*, 1967–70. On the other (s) side of SYDENHAM ROAD this job continues as APOLLO HOUSE. The entrance motifs N and s of Sydenham Road are identical. In Sydenham Road itself CANTERBURY HOUSE by *T. P. Bennett & Sons*, 1963–5.

The WHITGIFT CENTRE, 1965–70, covers eleven acres between Wellesley Road and North End.* The planner was *Anthony Minoprio*, the architects *Fitzroy Robinson & Partners*. One high tower (ROTHSCHILD HOUSE), two tall slabs, and some lower offices flank a N–S pedestrian shopping precinct on two levels, made possible by the fall of the land. To the s an open square with the polygonal FORUM restaurant in the middle; to the N a very successful smaller square, roofed over by a light glass canopy open at the sides. Most of the architectural details are banal, but the centre functions usually well as a shopping precinct. The upper level has direct entrance from Wellesley Road, the lower direct entrance from North End. Underneath is a service road for servicing the shops and offices. Access to the offices is by a special road from Wellesley Road. Further N in LONDON ROAD, the continuation of North End, is ZODIAC HOUSE, a very large development with shops, offices, and flats, by *William H. Robbins*, 1964–7. Returning s down Wellesley Road, off to the e in LANSDOWNE ROAD opposite the Whitgift Centre first the Y.M.C.A., 1958 by *E. F. Starling*, extended 1971, then on the side at the corner of the tucked-away Walpole Road, the ROYAL AUTOMOBILE CLUB offices, 1960–1, by *R. Seifert & Partners*. Opposite on the N side, RONEO VICKERS and SPILLERS, a complex by *Newman, Levinson & Partners*, 1962–4, and then on to the corner buildings of Dingwall Road – *see* above.

Futher s along the e side of WELLESLEY ROAD the PRUDENTIAL by *E. Roy Moore Associates* (*Sydney Clough, Son & Partners*, consultants), and BLACK-CLAWSON HOUSE by *Newman, Levinson & Partners*, both 1962–3. Then NORFOLK HOUSE by *Howell & Brooks* (*T. P. Bennett & Son*, consultants), 1958–9, the start of the New Croydon, a tall slab at r. angles to the street set on the usual podium. The s front of this is in Geroge Street and faces Suffolk House (*see* above). Behind Norfolk House to the N, i.e. in WALPOLE ROAD, is SOUTHERN HOUSE, by *G. & D. Crump*, 1963–7.

s of George Street Wellesley Road becomes PARK LANE. On the w side a vast development by *Ronald Ward & partners*,

* On the site of the Trinity School of John Whitgift, now at Shirley (q.v.). The buildings were of 1869–71 by *Sir A. Blomfield*.

1962–4: ST GEORGE'S HOUSE, with KATHARINE HOUSE towards the town hall, St George's Walk inside, and the w front to the High Street. It has a shopping precinct, but what an opportunity for a consistently planned whole is wasted. So close to the centre, this could have made a determining architectural contribution. As it is, it doesn't. New Croydon peters out here. At the corner of Katharine Street, further s, GAS BOARD OFFICES of 1939–42 by *William G. Newton & Partners*, an interesting compromise with modernistic horizontal ribbons over an elegant ground floor with classically moulded windows. Its neighbour in KATHARINE STREET, SEGAS HOUSE, a sympathetic extension of 1975–81 by *G. R. Toogood* of the S.E. Gas Board, uses similarly sandy-coloured materials, and also plays effectively with contrasts; an arched arcade over the pavement, chunky faceted projections in exposed aggregate above. Further s in PARK LANE, beyond the complex of public buildings on the E side (q.v.), so far just one outlying office block exists (ST CRISPIN'S HOUSE by *R. Seifert & Partners*, 1981–3), providing a typical Croydon contrast with the prettily detailed villas of the 1890s up BARCLAY ROAD.

2. The Old Croydon

The development of the old town can be traced in the street pattern, despite the intrusion of the C20 road system. OLD TOWN, CHURCH STREET, and CHURCH ROAD surround the ancient settlement with church (St John) and archbishop's palace (qq.v.). Uphill further E on the main London road, the triangle of HIGH STREET, CROWN HILL, and SURREY STREET surrounds the site of a once open market place (a lively street market still remains in Surrey Street).

Apart from the palace only a few older buildings remain near the church. In CHURCH ROAD Nos. 2–8, elaborately half-timbered, flint and brick cottages of the mid C19, on the site of the palace stables. Opposite, STELLA HOUSE, a plain industrial building, with a little polychrome brick detail, a former boot and shoe factory of *c.* 1892. Facing the w end of the church, a nice group in CHURCH STREET: Nos. 128 and 132, stuccoed, the ROSE AND CROWN, with weatherboarded back, and RAMSAY COURT (formerly Elys Davy Almshouses, founded 1447), two brick ranges dated 1875 and 1887 facing each other across a small garden.* To the s the ring road cuts by uncomfortably close, to the N CHURCH STREET winds up to Crown Hill, low in scale but bitty architecturally; the best building Nos. 61–65, C18 brick, with nine segment-headed windows and parapet; shops below. Nos. 91–93 are C17 timber-framed, heavily disguised. The s side of CROWN HILL and Bell Hill, the parallel lane behind, survived the C19

---

* The N block is possibly originally of *c.* 1700. Another similar group, SMITH'S ALMSHOUSES, in SCARBROOK ROAD near the flyover to the s: 1896 by *R. Price*.

rationalization of the market area (*see* below). Nos. 11 and 13 are C 17 timber-framed buildings, their backs to Bell Hill faced with weatherboarding and mathematical tiles, were reconstructed in 1982–3 (using the original materials where possible). A few more C 18 houses in SURREY STREET, especially handsome the red brick front of the DOG AND BULL. By the mid C 19 the network of alleys filling the former open market place had become slummy, and in the 1890s nearly everything here was swept away in a burst of civic improvement.

The W side of the widened HIGH STREET, with its multiplicity of gables, oriels, turrets, and stone and terracotta decoration so characteristic of the 1890s, is the best group of commercial buildings of its date in South London, although impressive in the aggregate rather than individually. A variety of architects were responsible, but the effect is quite coherent, and considerably more lavish than e.g. the contemporary rebuilding of the centre of Hampstead (Ca). From N to S: the GENERAL POST OFFICE by *Henry James* of the *Office of Works*, 1893–4, Tudor, and (untypically) of stone. Then No. 12, 1894 by *R. W. Price*, brick and terracotta; Nos. 14–18, 1894 by *Metcalfe & Jones*, an impressive seven-bay design with diaper decoration and central turret; Nos. 20–28, 1895 by *R. M. Chart*, with open loggias; Nos. 32–34, 1897 by *Alfred Broad*, with central bay and octagonal lantern and an archway to the arcade leading to the steep drop down to Surrey Street, the best townscape effect in Croydon; No. 36, 1895 by *Price*, the former offices of the Croydon Advertiser, with four storeys of pilasters; then a tall range with five shaped gables divided by polygonal buttresses, No. 48, 1894 by *Thomas Hepwell*; and finally Nos. 50–52 on the corner, 1896 by *Broad*, a busy façade with canted bays below three tall Flemish gables. Of the same period on the E side, Nos. 39–43, Union Bank Chambers, by *Porter & Hill*, 1893, brick and stucco, with pilasters, forming a group with the town hall buildings in Katharine Street, and No. 1 at the corner of George Street, 1889 by *W. Campbell Jones*, quite lively, brick and stone, with windows with Gibbs surrounds, and a lunette over the doorway with a bronze relief by *W. Reynolds Stephens*. The rest of GEORGE STREET also has much of the 1890s, but is less dramatic.

In NORTH END, the continuation of the High Street, Archbishop Whitgift established his foundations on what was then the edge of the town, the hospital (*see* Public Buildings) and school, whose site is now occupied by the Whitgift Centre (*see* Perambulation 1). On the edge of this, HORNES, a remarkable building of 1910 in a style reminiscent of early Charles Holden. Stone above brick, with tower and gables rising from sheer walls relieved by panels of Arts and Crafts foliage decoration, and by chequer patterns below the windows.

In the S part of the HIGH STREET and its continuation South End the impact of the New Croydon continues. S of Katharine Street DAVIS HOUSE by *G. & D. Crump*, 1960–1; then the

BRIDGE which is part of the FLYOVER and cuts the High Street in two. Just past this obstacle WRENCOTE, the finest house in Croydon, totally deprived of any visual impact by its present surroundings, dwarfed and buffeted. It dates from *c.* 1715–20 (or possibly a little earlier) and is of red and rubbed brick with wings and a recessed tripartite centre, a later C17 rather than an C18 type. Angle pilasters, an extremely richly carved frieze, and a hipped roof. Modest doorway with brackets carved as beasts' heads. Staircase with twisted balusters. The adjoining Nos. 119–121 in similar style were added by *Robert Cromie* in 1956, together with a large office extension at the back. The immediate neighbour of Wrencote to the S is GROSVENOR HOUSE, 1960–1 by *H. Hubbard Ford*, eleven-storeyed. S of this one of the best of the 1960s arrivals, LEON HOUSE, 1968–9 by *Tribich, Liefer & Starkin*, a slab of two staggered parts and a low, well set shopping plaza to its N. S of Leon House LENNIG HOUSE, by the same architects, only ten storeys high, the sill bands of the windows of reeded concrete. No. 46 is C17 altered, with a jettied front. In SOUTH END Nos. 17–19 are early C18, formally one house, red brick, set back from the road.* Near by, one of the most interesting of the C19 buildings, the Steam Boot Factory of the 1870s, was most regrettably demolished in 1981 and has been replaced by four-storey offices by *Robinson Quie Associates*.‡ Further S, cleverly angled on a corner site, the SWAN AND SUGAR LOAF, with pretty stucco decoration, dated 1896. (Further S, HALING COTTAGE and HALING PARK COTTAGE, C18, in the grounds of Whitgift School. DB)

3. *The* W *and* S *suburbs*

W of the High Street, just to the S of the ugly flyover, a pocket of modest streets of little terraces, earlier C19 in WEST STREET, of *c.* 1860 in LAUD STREET, WANDLE ROAD, etc., with a former classical pedimented chapel in Wandle Road of the same time. Further S, on the rising ground, much has been replaced by C20 flats: an early example is in DUPPAS HILL TERRACE W of Old Town, by *Riches & Blythin*, 1954, a three-ray plan, the ray to the W of ten storeys. S again, more flats have depleted the Victorian mansions of THE WALDRONS and, to its SW, BRAMLEY HILL. This was part of the Haling Park Estate (cf. Whitgift School, Public Buildings, above) which was sold for building in 1850, and laid out with winding roads and semi-detached or detached broad-eaved, stucco-trimmed Italianate mansions on the grandest scale. In The Waldrons the best remaining group is around No. 19 (distinguished by a tower), ranged in an informal crescent

---

* SOUTHEND HOUSE, Southbridge Road. Good early C19 house; entrance at the side (DB).

‡ It was the biggest industrial premises of its date in the town. Three storeys, with convex castellated centrepiece and one curved corner; finely detailed neo-Romanesque brick arcading and a heavy cornice.

facing an island with trees. In Bramley Hill, built up a little later, just one more varied group of three remains: No. 22, plain stock brick classical with Doric porch, No. 24, red brick, and No. 26, with Gothic trim, all well set back and screened by evergreen planting. At the W end of Bramley Hill a C19 red brick Jacobean estate LODGE.

Further E in PURLEY WAY a few older houses (Nos. 335–345, a Regency pair with pedimented side annexes; No. 351, early C18 with pedimented doorcase, much rebuilt) and WAYLANDS TRAINING CENTRE by *J. Thornley* (*Borough Architect's Department*), 1964–6. S of the power station in COMMERCE WAY a FACTORY for Messrs Philips by *Wallis, Gilbert & Partners*, 1955–7.

4. The E suburbs

Off the S end of the High Street to the E COOMBE HILL HOUSE (now Ruskin House) in COOMBE ROAD is early C18 and very satisfying to look at. Yellow and red brick. Five bays and two and a half storeys. Giant angle pilasters and parapet. Segment-headed windows. Pedimented doorway on Tuscan columns. Staircase with three slender balusters to each step: two twisted differently, the third columnar. Carved tread-ends. (A good wrought-iron GATE in the garden. DOE) Further E beyond the railway line, COOMBE CLIFFE, the villa built *c.* 1860 by *E. C. Robins* for John Horniman, tea merchant, stands romantically on the crest of a small wooded hill, unremarkable apart from a tower over the entrance. It had a splendid conservatory added in 1894 by his son *F. J. Horniman* (donor of the Horniman Museum, Le).*

To the N of Coombe Road, PARK HILL, an estate of mid Victorian villas laid out by the Church Commissioners, largely replaced by *Wates* housing of the 1960s–70s.‡ Much of it is pleasantly brick or tile-hung, in the Eric Lyons tradition: HILL RISE, Park Hill Rise, E of Park Hill Road, 1962–3 by *K. W. Bland*, Wates's chief architect, and HILLMERE, Brownlow Road, to the SW, by *Bland* and *Auston Vernon & Partners*. MARSHFIELD and COTELANDS in Park Hill Road are groups of flats by *Auston Vernon & Partners*, 1968–70; opposite is TURNPIKE LINK, by *F. G. MacManus & Partners*, 1966–8, two- and three-storey terraces, austerely detailed in pale brown brick with slate-grey panels and grouped excellently round landscaped courtyards (the plum-coloured tower block is by *Bland*). Further S in Park Hill Road is ST BERNARDS, twenty-one houses in three terraces of 1968–70 by the Swiss architects *Atelier 5* (partner-in-charge *Anatole du Fresne*) for Wates (originally 147 houses were planned). It is a

---

* After a scandalously long period of neglect, it was agreed in 1980 that this was to be taken down and re-erected elsewhere. The plan is cruciform, with an octagonal dome on cast-iron columns. Ironwork of standard precast panels by *MacFarlane & Co.* of Glasgow.

‡ I owe the following details to Nicholas Taylor.

224 CROYDON

group with few equals in Britain: the architects have sensitively adapted the stepped terrace system of their Siedlung Halen
at Bern (itself derived from Le Corbusier's 'Roq et Rob'
project of 1949) to the gentler suburban slopes of Surrey,
replacing rough concrete with brown stock brick and timber
stained or painted white. Each house is approached through
an enclosed garden (with an outdoor eating room under a
pergola) at an upper level, the living room having a panorama
to distant hills. The bedrooms open on to a second, lower
garden. Car parking is underground. Less demanding terraces next door by *John Bridges* of Wates, 1969–71. Further
Wates housing of the 1970s in CHICHESTER ROAD near the
new church of St Matthew (q.v.), yellow brick with tile-
hanging, pleasantly laid out. (In STANHOPE ROAD to the w,
RED LODGE, a crisp tile-hung Lutyens-style house by *W.
Curtis Green*, 1911.)

Along ADDISCOMBE ROAD towards Coombe, a few rural survivals, stranded in suburbia: No. 96, HERONS CROFT, a C17
cottage with jettied front, and No. 281, flint and brick, with
the date 1676. (HEATHFIELD, Coombe Lane, towards
Addington, is of *c.* 1800, mostly rebuilt after 1866. Entrance
front of nine bays.)

N of Addiscombe Road in HAVELOCK ROAD, now in industrial
use, a former GYMNASIUM of 1851, brown brick, round-
headed windows, the only major relic of the East India College
founded in 1809 by the East India Company and closed in
1861. The roads named after famous generals were laid out
soon after on the site (DB).

5. The N suburbs

N of the town centre, Victorian Croydon begins abruptly where
the New Croydon leaves off, around BEDFORD PARK. Along
the s part of SYDENHAM ROAD some good examples of quiet
Italianate villas, No. 34 especially grand, with six pedimented
first-floor windows. No. 56 has windows within giant brick
arches, an earlier C19 type. More large villas continued E
along LOWER ADDISCOMBE ROAD, but only scattered examples survive. The sprinkling of minor but more unusual
buildings is more rewarding. In ST JAMES'S ROAD No. 169,
a flint-faced Gothic villa, mid C19 (the former vicarage?).
Further N amidst humble late C19 terraces Nos. 237–239 and
226–228 SYDENHAM ROAD, two pairs of cottages with
projecting end gables. Designed by *Norman Shaw* (or possibly
largely by his pupils), for the contractor W. H. Lascelles. The
construction, which uses Lascelles' patent concrete slabs, is
heavily disguised in both cases. Nos. 226–228 (1881–2) is
roughcast with ornamental panels (concrete panelled ceilings
inside), Nos. 237–239 (1878) has prettier surfaces of tile-
hanging in the Surrey vernacular tradition (genuine tiles in
front, simulated ones at the back), the picturesque effect
enhanced by the careful grouping of roofs of different height,

especially when seen from the side. (Other simpler examples of Lascelles concrete cottages are in GLOUCESTER ROAD to the E, Nos. 44–50, 56–62, 72–78).* Off Lower Addiscombe Road to the S, CROSS ROAD, remnants of an older area, with a small group of artisan cottages: No. 57 'Cobden Place 1865', No. 67 etc., an earlier and simple terrace, Nos. 66–72 opposite, pre-Victorian in origin (see the pantiled roof at the back), also a battered Arts and Crafts former chapel with shell porch and dormers (ST MATTHEW'S MISSION CHURCH, 1911). N of Lower Addiscombe Road DAVIDSON LODGE at the end of FREEMASONS ROAD, built as the Freemasons' Asylum, 1852 by *S. W. Daukes*, a cheerful symmetrical composition facing a garden by the railway, beyond a lodge in the same style. Red brick with blue diapering and much stone trim. The centre is a big Dutch gable, the ends have two smaller such gables each. In between three gabled porches and three small straight gables on each side. Further E in CANNING ROAD, off to the S, *E. B. Lamb*'s vicarage to St Mary Magdalene, squared stone rubble with a variety of window types; of 1870, the time when these side streets were being built up. The development of LOWER ADDISCOMBE ROAD itself reflects the suburban expansion, with its minor centres by the stations, later C19 at ADDISCOMBE, early C20 at BINGHAM ROAD, with quite ambitious half-timbered shops of 1932 at BINGHAM CORNER. Beyond this, unremarkable C20 suburban sprawl continues to Woodside (q.v.).

By the end of the C19 the suburbs also stretched N to Thornton Heath (q.v.), the northern edge marked, as so often, by cemetery and workhouse (now Queens Hospital, q.v.). In this area much urban renewal of the later 1970s e.g. around ST SAVIOUR'S ROAD, low cottages in dark red brick with slate roofs, but, unlike the C19 artisan housing which inspired the style, pleasantly grouped around courtyards and closes. 1975–80 by *P. G. Vincent*, head of the borough's Department of Architecture.‡

(In HANDCROFT ROAD, near Croydon Grove, a former R.C. chapel, 1841, the first purpose-built R.C. church in Croydon. Very simple yellow brick, stepped gable, round-headed openings. DB)

NORBURY

A late C19 creation around the railway station on the London Road, which expanded in the 1930s and is now indistinguishable from Thornton Heath to the S, and the fringes of Streatham (La) and Mitcham (Me) to N and E.

ST STEPHEN, Warwick Road, off London Road to the E. 1908

---

* I owe the details on the work by Lascelles to Miss Helen Brooks.

‡ Other borough housing of the 1970s in ARUNDEL ROAD (W of Sydenham Road), CROYDON GROVE (W of London Road), and TAMWORTH ROAD (W of North End). In STANLEY GROVE (W of London Road) sheltered housing.

by *W. S. Weatherley*. Yellow and red brick in the Perp style. Nave and chancel in one. Nice, crisp interior with brick trim.

HEALTH CENTRE, London Road. 1976–80 by *J. H. Ingham*, chief architect of the South West Thames Regional Health Authority. Plain low group in brown brick.

NORBURY HALL, Craignish Avenue, sw of Norbury Crescent. Early C19. Grey brick, of four bays, the outer bays projecting and connected by a pretty veranda of trellis woodwork with two columns with oddly Moorish-looking capitals. The trellis is unusual because overscale.

LONDON ROAD, from Norbury to the centre of Croydon, has taken part in Croydon's expansion of offices (*see* Croydon, Perambulation 1). The largest group is just s of Norbury station: ASTRAL HOUSE is by *Ronald Ward & Partners*, 1962–5. On the e side, No. 2058 is an excellent nine-storey slab by *Riches & Blythin*, 1966–7, in cool grey precast units, set back behind a three-storey forebuilding. Set well forward by contrast is No. 2060, WATES, by *Fry, Drew & Partners*, 1962–3, a telling example of the revival of palazzo forms for prestige purposes (Maxwell Fry moving far from the International Style). Continuous bands of brown brick and of recessed windows framed in purple tiling pulled together by a roof canopy vaulted in concrete, the coving clad in bright red mosaic. Attractive courtyard inside. After some indifferent blocks (WINDSOR HOUSE by *Fuller, Hall & Foulsham*, 1963–4) comes RADNOR HOUSE, cleanly finished in ribbed concrete panels, with a black steel entrance canopy, also by *Fuller, Hall & Foulsham*, 1962–4 (NT).

NORBURY ESTATE. The first cottage estate to be built by the L.C.C. beyond its boundaries (following the Act of 1900). The hilly 30-acre site was acquired in 1901, and plans were drawn up in 1905 (main L.C.C. architects: *George Weald, P. F. Binnie, J. R. Stark, J. S. Brooks*). The layout is similar to the L.C.C.'s earlier Totterdown Fields, Tooting (Ww), or White Hart Lane, Tottenham (Hy) with a grid of roads (twenty-nine houses to the acre), and likewise with houses in a mixture of brick and roughcast with slate roofs. In NEW-LANDS ROAD n of Northborough Road four small shops of 1911–12 (no pubs were allowed). The first phase ended just before 1914 with NORTON GARDENS on the top of the hill. The later parts (1919–21) reflect the influence of Parker & Unwin's Hampstead Garden Suburb, and are more picturesquely detailed and grouped; the hillside quadrangle of cottages opening off Isham Road w of Newlands Road is an especially attractive example.

PURLEY

A C19 suburban area 2½ m. s of Croydon, which developed around the stations; no old centres.

ALL SAINTS, Church Road, e of Hayes Lane, Kenley. 1870–2

by *James Fowler*, with additions of 1897 and 1902. Gothic, ragstone, with SE tower and spire.

CHRIST CHURCH, Brighton Road, NE of Purley Station. The parish church of Purley, also by *Fowler*, 1877–8, in his usual competent but uninspired Dec.

(ST JOHN THE BAPTIST (R.C.), Dale Road, off Godstone Road s of Purley Station. Nave 1939 by *E. J. Walters*, N and s chapels 1958 by *Walters & Kerr Bate*. DE)

(UNITED REFORMED CHURCH, Brighton Road. 1903–4 by *Hampden W. Pratt*. Arts and Crafts Gothic. – STAINED GLASS. E window by *Christopher Whall*, 1920.)

RUSSELL HILL SCHOOLS (of the Warehousemen, Clerks and Drapers), Russell Hill, N of Woodcote Valley Road. 1863–4 by *John G. Bland*. Red brick, a long, symmetrical Venetian Gothic composition with plate tracery, steep roofs, gables and dormers. Raised centre with a spike; lower links to three-storey wings.

WATERWORKS, Brighton Road. Sober, round-arched design. Dated 1901, but looks fifty years earlier.

KENLEY STATION, Godstone Road. 1856 by *Richard Whittall*. Italianate cottage style with very deep gables.

PURLEY STATION and PURLEY OAKS STATION (both of 1899). Two of the London, Brighton and South Coast Railway's solid red brick buildings for improved suburban services (D. Bayliss).

In BRIGHTON ROAD, ADVERTISER HOUSE, the former water company premises, altered by *Haines, Macintosh & Kennedy* in the 1960s for the Croydon Advertiser. Long neat two-storey range with curtain-walling above the older brick wall. Opposite, on an island site, VOLKSWAGEN offices, an oval building of five storeys on stilts, with two central staircases, one cased in, one in an open well. By *Raglan Squire & Partners*, 1964–7.

SANDERSTEAD

An old village s of Croydon, its identity preserved by the surrounding golf courses and other open spaces.

ALL SAINTS. Flint with a bell-turret with spike. All windows renewed. Low arcade with octagonal piers and double-chamfered arches. C 13, built from E to w and cut into by the C 14 tower. The chancel is C 14 too, but excessively restored in 1832. The tower is very curious, decidedly oblong below, but by means of two w–E arches reduced to a square shape above. – PAINTINGS. L. and r. of the E window, King Edmund and an archbishop, two very elongated figures; C 14. – ROYAL ARMS. Of Charles I. Very large, painted, on the chancel arch. – MONUMENTS. Brass to John Atwodde † 1525 and wife. The figures are 18 in. long. – John Ownstead † 1600. Small hanging monument with kneeling figure. – Mrs Mary Audley † 1655. Black and white marble. Sarcophagus, and on it a recumbent

effigy bundled up in a shroud, but the face visible. – Tablet at
the W end of the N aisle of *c*. 1730, carrying no name or date,
only a poem. Bust with wig under an arch in an architectural
surround with an open segmental pediment. The monument
is supposed to be to the son of Mr Henry Mellish. The poem
reads as follows:

> Here lies a youth who virtue's race had run
> When scarce his yeares of manhood were begun:
> So swift a progress call'd for early rest,
> And plac'd his soul betimes among the blest.
> Another such our age despairs to find
> Of charming person and accomplish'd mind:
> Where manly sense and sweetest temper join'd.
> But fame's large volume would be fill'd to tell
> Those qualities in which he did excell:
> Then reader, drop a tear and only say
> Death saw the virtuous youth prepar'd to pay
> Great nature's debt – and call'd before its day.

St Mary, Sanderstead Hill. 1926 by *Greenaway & Newberry*.
(Gresham Primary School. Village school and schoolhouse of 1875 by *Richard Martin*; polychrome brick, bell-
turret over the schoolroom.)
In Limpsfield Road several old houses. The White
House is C 17 timber-framed, L-shaped, with closely spaced
studs. C 18 flint and brick additions behind, and later alterations. (Also No. 117, brick and tile-hung, of 1783, with
former one-storey smithy adjoining (now church hall), and
Nos. 448 etc., later C 18 brick and flint cottages.)
Selsdon Park Golf Club. Sanderstead Court, bombed in
1944, was an impressive house of 1676 with early C 18 alterations and additions. The present golf club occupies what was
the end of the N wing. Small polygonal room at the far end. To
the N the mid C 19 stables, of red and yellow brick with a
central cupola. The grounds remain, with some splendid
cedars. Good iron gates. The site of the rest of the house is
covered by two-storey terrace houses.
Selsdon Park Hotel. *See* Selsdon.

SELSDON

St John. 1935–6 by *Newberry & Fowler*. A satisfying design,
once one accepts lancet windows etc. as fitting for 1935. Red
brick, square and simple NE tower. Narrow aisles with
straight-headed seven-light windows. Nicely plain interior of
cream-coloured brick.
St Columba (R.C.), Queenhill Road, NW of Old Farleigh
Road. 1962 by *Tomei & Maxwell* (DE).
Croydon High School for Girls, Old Farleigh Road.
Very large, by *Greenwood & Abercrombie*, 1964–6. The buildings, well sited in spacious grounds, are quite hard in style, of
red brick with exposed concrete floors, some concrete roof
lights, and a considerable variety of window types.

JOHN NEWNHAM SCHOOL, Selsdon Park Road. Long ranges
of dark red brick. By *C. F. Blythin & L. C. Holbrook*, 1951–3.

Also in Selsdon Park Road, FARLEIGH VIEW, old people's
homes by the *Borough of Croydon's Architect's Department*
(*R. C. Crippen & A. F. M. Murray*), 1965, a long four-storey
building with an excessive number of contrasting surfaces and
colours, opposite one of the most deplorable 1960s housing
developments in the area. Further S, off Featherbed Lane,
and much better, FORESTDALE, a *Wates* estate begun in 1966
(chief architect *J. Bridges*). Terrace housing on a hilly site with
garages in the slopes below, as at Coulsdon.

SELSDON PARK HOTEL, Addington Road. Of a medieval core
nothing can be seen. The visible core of the present buildings
seems early C 19 and was illustrated by Neale in 1819. It was of
eleven bays, symmetrical and castellated then, and Neale says
it was chiefly designed by the owner, *George Smith* M.P. To the
same time belong apparently the outbuildings, including the
castellated tower with the higher turret. The roof of the early
C 19 building was raised and the little lantern put on some time
early in the C 20. Then, from 1925, the building was converted
into a hotel and for the purpose spectacularly enlarged by
Hugh Macintosh. All the new parts are neo-Jacobean.

SHIRLEY

ST JOHN. By *Sir G. G. Scott*, 1854–6. Flint and stone and
deliberately villagey, although not small. Bell-turret with
spike. Inside, this rests on two mighty round piers with
crocket capitals. – In the churchyard (SE corner) MONUMENT
to Ruskin's parents.

SCHOOLS. Two good ones of the fifties in the neighbourhood,
one the ST JOHN'S CHURCH OF ENGLAND SCHOOL, Shirley Church Road, by *C. T. Ayerst*, the other the JOHN RUS-
KIN GRAMMAR SCHOOL, Upper Shirley Road, by *A. G.
Gavin* (*Paul Mauger & Partners*). The new buildings of the
TRINITY SCHOOL of John Whitgift in Shirley Park, moved
from Croydon, are by *George Lowe & Partners*, 1962–5. Of
1973–7: EDENHAM HIGH SCHOOL, Orchard Way, W of
Monks Orchard Road, by the *Borough Architect's Department*.

Immediately behind the John Ruskin School rises the Shirley
WINDMILL, a tarred brick tower-mill with a boat-shaped
weatherboarded cap, complete with sails and machinery.
Built in 1854. Repaired in 1936.

In COOMBE ROAD, about ¾ m. SW of the church, COOMBE
HOUSE (now St Margaret's School), a good C 18 house of red
brick, eight bays, two storeys, with a three-bay pediment.*
Doorway with Tuscan columns and broken pediment. (The
best room inside is the library, early C 19 and somewhat

---

* According to C. Paget, *Croydon Homes of the Past*, built by James Bourdieu
after 1761 (DB).

Soanish, with a shallow coffered vault and segmental apses
DOE)

(NEW WORLD HOUSE, Bishop's Walk, N of Gravel Hill. By
Derek Lovejoy & Partners, 1971, an elegant brick and timber
house on three levels, neatly perched on the slope of a hill.)

(In SHIRLEY HILLS ROAD, No. 5 is a picturesque former
mission church of 1873, now converted to a house. DB)

(COOMBE FARM, Oaks Road. Large C16 farmhouse with
NE extension of 1844, with bell tower, and much larger extension of 1893 with half-timbered gables and weather
boarding. DB)

(On both sides of ORCHARD WAY, W of Monks Orchard Road
½ m. NE, good housing by *G. E. A. Huyton*, 1968–71, with a
lively rhythm of butterfly roofs and an ingenious layout of
houses in échelon round courtyards, set back behind three-
storey flat blocks over garages. NT)

(PARK FARM, Monks Orchard Road, in the grounds of the
Bethlem Royal Hospital near the borough boundary. Farm
house and cottage of 1843, Tudor, with older outbuildings
enclosing a farmyard. Other minor houses: No. 97 SHIRLEY
ROAD, mid C18, brick, and the WHITE LODGE, Wickham
Road, *c.* 1840, lodge with Ionic portico.)

SOUTH NORWOOD

A C19 creation which developed rapidly around the railway
station at Norwood Junction.

HOLY INNOCENTS, Selhurst Road. 1894–5 by *Bodley*. Along
the road, with nave and chancel in one and no tower. Stone.
Tall interior with slim Perp piers and no clerestory. –
STAINED GLASS. E window by *Kempe*.

ST ALBAN, Grange Road. *See* Thornton Heath, below.

ST MARK, Albert Road, NE of Portland Road. 1852 by *G. H.
Lewis*. The first church in the area, a low, capacious, apsed
building of coursed ragstone, on a corner site.

ST CHAD (R.C.), Whitworth Road, NW off Selhurst Road. 1932
by *G. Drysdale*. Brick Romanesque, apsed, with a tower at
the side.

METHODIST CHURCH, South Norwood Hill. 1873 by *Lander*.
Gothic, with tower and spire.

BRANCH LIBRARY, Selhurst Road. By *Hugh Lea*, Borough
Architect of Croydon, 1966–8. Boldly detailed; windows with
thick mullions above dark brick. The upper floor on one side
is a windowless area of ribbed concrete, with 'library' in
aggressively large letters. Attached to the library the SOUTH
NORWOOD ADULT EDUCATION CENTRE, with a tall
gabled wing of 1902 next to a plainer late C19 building.

STANLEY HALLS AND STANLEY TECHNICAL TRADE
SCHOOLS, South Norwood Hill. 1902–9. The most memorable buildings in South Norwood, endowed and designed by
the inventor and local industrialist *W. F. R. Stanley* (cf.

below), a vigorously eclectic group in red brick and stone, with two towers and a series of gabled roof-lines, adorned with the extraordinary motif of copper flowers in flowerpots. On the gable of the hall a small stone statue holding a torch. The rather ponderous free style (miles away from contemporary Arts and Crafts) relies partly on debased Italianate detail, with long oval panels and pink marble columns as recurrent motifs, but also includes eccentricities such as elliptical arches. On the clock tower a statue: 'Labor Omnia Vincit'. The trade school, at the N end of the group, was based on the German Gewerbe-schule, an experiment in technical education for 12–15-year-olds.

(CUMBERLOW LODGE (Remand Home), off Chalfont Road, E of South Norwood Hill. Stanley's home from 1878: a large, elaborate red brick house in its own grounds.)

SOUTH NORWOOD HIGH SCHOOL, Oakley Road, E of Portland Road. Built as Portland Road Board School, 1902 by *H. Carter Pegg*, a massive two-storey building in the London School Board style of the later 1890s, with symmetrical pyramid-topped stair-turrets and a steep roof with a cupola. Separate infant school; later additions.

ST MARK'S C. of E. PRIMARY SCHOOL, Albert Road, W of Portland Road. A crisp, well grouped composition in yellow brick, of the 1960s by the *Borough Architect's Department*. The former church hall in Coventry Road refurbished at the same time.

SWIMMING BATHS, Portland Road. By the Borough Architect, *Hugh Lea*, 1967–8. Well composed, with a tall wall of slate-grey glass, a plain brick wall, and a lower entrance wing on one side.

The HIGH STREET has mostly different indifferent stucco-trimmed shopping terraces of the 1870s, brightened by one cheerful landmark, the little cast-iron CLOCK TOWER at the corner of Station Road, commemorating Mr Stanley's Golden Wedding in 1907. (The STANLEY WORKS are near by in BELGRAVE ROAD, a two-storey workshop with an off-centre gable joined to a three-storey block. They produced wood-working, mathematical, and surveying instruments.) Further W along SELHURST ROAD some large and stately villas of the later C19 remain, e.g. Nos. 221–223, with polychrome brick decoration. One noticeable intruder confronts the library next door: No. 196 by *Edward Cullinan* and *Anthony Peake*, 1974–6, a stock brick cube of four maisonettes, relieved by stained timber balconies and top floor. More complete minor Victorian streets with pleasant stuccoed villas and terraces to the N, e.g. around WHITWORTH ROAD. Less survives E of South Norwood Hill, where the curving ALBERT ROAD and REGINA (formerly VICTORIA) ROAD were the first new roads in the area. A few of the first very large mid C19 Italianate houses remain in Albert Road and ELDON PARK. W. F. Stanley lived at STANLEYBURY, No. 74 Albert Road. To the NW, in LANCASTER ROAD, some more large houses at the S end, notably No. 11, mid C 19, quite elaborate, with central tower and Gothic window.

The upper slopes of SOUTH NORWOOD HILL have a few early C 19 rural villas; No. 25 is of three bays, stuccoed, and No. 30 similar, with a nice tented porch. In PORTLAND ROAD, the meaner late Victorian continuation down the hill S, nothing of note except for the pubs: the JOLLY SAILOR, tall and stuccoed at the corner of the High Street, the appropriately named SIGNAL by the railway bridge, and further S down the hill the GLADSTONE, with stucco quoins, the GREYHOUND (in Holland Road), Italianate with arched ground floor and parapet, and the PRINCE OF DENMARK, a typical jolly composition of 1898. WERNDEE, Stanger Road, N of Holland Road, is a large debased-Frenchy mansion of the late C 19.

THORNTON HEATH

A development largely of the later C 19 around the stations, spreading to 'New Thornton Heath', W of the London Road, by 1870, and continuous with northern Croydon and South Norwood by 1914.

(ST ALBAN, Grange Road. By *Bucknall & Comper*, nave 1889, chancel 1894 – in fact *Sir Ninian Comper*'s first church. Red brick; Perp. High E end over a crypt, the S chapel window corbelled out as an oriel. Six-bay nave and three bay chancel, with clerestory and hammerbeam roof throughout. The influence is clearly G. G. Scott Jun.: plain square piers and arches dying straight into them, transversely over the aisles as well as the main arcades – an austere effect, even a little papery, as Comper's glorious furnishings were never executed, except for the STAINED GLASS in the S chapel E window, 1903. NT)

(ST ANDREW (R.C.), Brook Road, W of the station. 1970 by *Broadbent, Hastings, Reid & Todd*. – STAINED GLASS. Last Supper by *Patrick Nuttgens*. DE)

(THORNTON HEATH and SELHURST STATIONS. Good examples of the red brick suburban stations built *c.* 1900 by the London, Brighton and South Coast Railway. At Thornton Heath the ticket office is on a bridge, at Selhurst it is below the line at street level. DB)

GOVERNMENT OFFICES, No. 72 High Street. Quite a good modern building. By *E. H. Banks*, 1954. Several more recent office blocks in LONDON ROAD, including CITY HOUSE, a large fourteen-storey slab by *David Stern & Partners*, designed in 1963.

UPPER NORWOOD

The heights of Norwood have some of the best views in South London. In the early C 19 the southern and western slopes attracted rural villas and some larger houses in the neighbourhood of Beulah Spa; then, in the later C 19, grander suburban mansions were built further E, close to the frequent trains from the Crystal Palace. There is no real urban centre to describe here, as the main shopping areas lie around the nearest railway stations over the borough boundary at Penge (Bm) and Gipsy Hill (La). The two churches aptly reflect the two phases of development.

ALL SAINTS, Beulah Hill. A Commissioners' church, built in 1827–9 by *James Savage*; chancel by *Edwin Nash*, 1861, W baptistery of 1952–4. Stock brick with Y-tracery and cusped lancet windows. W tower with pinnacles and recessed spire and flying buttresses against it starting from the pinnacles. Fine cast-iron Gothic gates and gatepiers to Church Road. – (The former SCHOOL next to the church is no doubt by *Savage* too. NT)

ST JOHN EVANGELIST, Sylvan Road. 1878–87 by *Pearson*. Very similar to St Michael Croydon (q.v.), and as noble. E.E. Plain red brick exterior. Façade with grouped lancets and two typically Pearsonian turrets. Transepts and straight E end. Very tall clerestory, taller than it would have been in the Middle Ages in England. Lofty stock-brick interior with arcades on clustered and quatrefoil piers, not high in comparison with the clerestory. Wall passage at clerestory level; brick rib-vaults throughout. The E chancel bay has six ribs. Aisles and outer aisles, and at the E end to the S of the chancel aisle an outer chapel with an apse. The main E window has grouped lancets (as at Pearson's St John, Red Lion Square, Ca). The S transept was meant to carry a tower, and is therefore detailed differently from the N transept. The church is 160 ft long; the spire was to have been 208 ft high. – Canted stone WEST GALLERY. – Stone ROOD SCREEN of large open arches echoing the twin sets of five lights at the E end. Well restored after war damage by *Caröe & Partners*, 1946–51. – Much good STAINED GLASS by *Clayton & Bell* was destroyed in the war; a rose window in the N transept, by *Comper*, survives.

GREEK ORTHODOX CHURCH (formerly United Reformed), Westow Street. 1878, probably by *E. Power*. Ragstone, Early Gothic.

(NORWOOD HOSPITAL, Hermitage Road. Attractive small red-brick cottage hospital of 1881. DB)

WINDERMERE HOUSE (Rehabilitation Centre), Westow Street. Built by *Sir M. D. Wyatt* as a private house, called The Mount, and converted and enlarged by *John Norton* in 1873–6 into the Royal Normal College and Academy of Music for the Blind. Stuccoed and rather dreary. Gabled centre, symmetrical sides, with the upper windows tall and reaching up into the roof. (The LODGE is by *Sextus Dyball*, 1880. G S)

VIRGO FIDELIS CONVENT (R.C.), Central Hill. Stock brick. Gothic. Several ranges of various dates. The earliest buildings, quite extensive, are by *Wardell*, 1857. Their centre is a slightly asymmetrically placed tower against which rises a canted steeply roofed bay, and in this the entrance is placed. Windows in two tiers and steep dormer windows in the roof. A steeply roofed little turret at the l. end, where, at r. angles, adjoins a range added by *George Goldie* in 1862 (St Joseph's Wing) and extended *c.* 1880 by *E. Goldie* (Bishop Grant Memorial Hall). Adjoining this, again at r. angles, i.e. opposite Wardell's wing, the convent (*E. Goldie*, 1881). The polygonal apse of the chapel projects nears its r. end. More extensions of 1904 and 1928 (opposite St Joseph's Wing and adjoining the r. end of Wardell's wing).

ST JOSEPH'S COLLEGE (R.C.), Beulah Hill. A Grecian villa of 1839 (Beulah Hill Road), enlarged in 1883 by *G. Highton*. S wing of 1910–11 and N wing with chapel and senior dormitories of 1913–28 by *B. McAdam*. Additions of 1948 and after. The style is Edwardian Classical to neo-Georgian.

BEULAH HILL winds along the SE slopes of Upper Norwood from All Saints. The site of BEULAH SPA, opened in 1831, is still marked by The Lawns, a recreation ground with stunning views S, approached past two LODGES at the fork with Spa Hill. The earlier, on the r., stuccoed, with some quatrefoil decoration and pretty bargeboarding, although much altered, is one of the buildings designed for the spa by *Decimus Burton*. The later one, Tudor red brick, dated 1864, was built after the spa had closed in 1855, unable to compete with the Crystal Palace. On the neighbouring slopes a sprinkling of C18 and early C19 villas remains among later suburbia: No. 63, a cottage with tented porch, No. 71 of *c.* 1860, Nos. 75 and 77, built *c.* 1780 (No. 75 on older foundations), each with full-height bay-windows, No. 79 of *c.* 1840. In GRANGE HILL further S two more early C19 houses: No. 10, with symmetrical three-storey front and lower wings, and GAYFERE, more irregular, with good iron porch with Greek key pattern. At the N end of Beulah Hill, off Gibsons Hill, ARNULLS ROAD, with several pretty C18–19 cottages, No. 2 brick, No. 4 stuccoed, with a nice porch. At the end a two-storey row of tiny workmen's flats of 1889. Further W down GIBSONS HILL, NORWOOD GROVE, in its own grounds (now a public park). The house faces W, early C19, stuccoed, with a central double-height bow. Along the whole of the S side a late C19 conservatory-veranda with two glazed domes. Many additions behind. Mid C19 LODGE by the drive.

The centre of Upper Norwood has a richly varied assortment of suburban villas between All Saints and Westow Street. From S to N: along CHURCH ROAD No. 207, the former vicarage, white brick with simple Tudor details, *c.* 1840. Then on the W side No. 128, Rockmount, a tall, fancifully eclectic villa of *c.* 1880, almost North American in its elaborately detailed woodwork, towering over its charming neighbour, No. 126, Westow Lodge, an early C19 stuccoed house of unusual design: a taller pedimented centre with trellised bowed veranda over a semicircular porch. No. 124, of similar date, has pretty fretted bargeboards and upper balconies. Further on, the

QUEENS HOTEL, a grand but much altered Italianate composition of 1853–4 by *F. Pouget*, built for visitors to the newly erected Crystal Palace. Originally the four-storeyed centre had low colonnaded links (now raised) to wings (the r. wing rebuilt after a fire in 1975). Opposite, two good examples of the larger Gothic suburban villa that became popular in the mid C19: Nos. 187 and 193, symmetrically laid out, each with a high and a low gabled part, on either side of a drive which led to further houses (only No. 197, much altered, remains at the end). Further N a few earlier and simpler cottages, and No. 112, the OLD HOUSE, with an early C19 stucco exterior, veranda, and glazed passage to the street. To the E, on the border with Bromley, BELVEDERE ROAD, with handsome smaller houses and a low terrace of stuccoed almshouses. In the triangle between Church Road and Westow Hill to the W, denser C19 building, partly replaced by better-than-average private housing of 1975–81 by *Clifford Davies Partnership* for *Barratts*, tightly knit, well detailed terraces of plain brick, with taller flats along Westow Street. Near by, on the site of St Aubyn's church, four-storey flats for the Croydon Churches Housing Association; elevations with very fancy coloured brickwork, 1981–2 by *Pinchin & Kellow*.

The steep wooded area between Church Road and the NE borough boundary was built up in the later C19 with amazingly sumptuous houses, mostly detached, of which many have gone. The best survivals are in AUCKLAND ROAD, near St John, where several were designed by *C. J. C. Pawley* c. 1883–4, red brick with large Gothic staircase windows as their chief feature (e.g. Nos. 134, 136, 142). Opposite, the AUCKLAND HOTEL, another large house of the same period set back behind a double drive. In SYLVAN HILL replacement began with some good housing by *Riches & Blythin*, 1956, taking advantage of the trees on the site, and much more has followed since.

WOODCOTE VILLAGE

A high-class garden suburb W of the Brighton Road, between Croydon and Purley, the houses mostly half-timbered. Very leafy, expensive, and handsome. Winding roads, and an incredibly trim triangular green at the centre with nine of the houses fronting on to it. It was laid out and partly designed in 1901–20 by *William Webb*, a Deal business man and horticulturalist, who called it the 'Garden First' system: 'The name Garden First means that the garden shall not only have prominence but that partial garden construction shall be carried out before any buildings are erected . . . the house is but the complement of the garden in a general survey of the estate'.*
No shops planned, apart from one at the corner of the green,

---

* From Webb's 'Garden First in Land Development'.

built as the Lord Roberts teetotal pub and village store.
(There was also a village smithy at No. 4, from 1904 to 1914.
DB)

(St Mark, Church Road, N of Foxley Lane. 1910 by *G. H.
Fellowes Prynne*. Kentish rag, with N W tower. The two E bays
open into shallow transepts. – STAINED GLASS. In the S aisle a
late *Morris & Co.* window of 1932 (the two Marys at the
Sepulchre) in memory of J. H. Dearle, one of the firm's
designers.)

WOODSIDE

An old hamlet swamped by Victorian expansion S from South
Norwood, and by early C 20 sprawl E from Croydon.

St Luke, Woodside Road, N W of the station. 1870 by *W. V.
Arnold*, the E end rebuilt by *W. D. Caröe*, 1949. Dull, red
brick, lancet style.

Library, Ashburton Park, S of the station. The remains of
Woodside Convent Orphanage, founded by the Rev. A.
Tooth and built in 1882. One wing of a demure Tudor cloister,
red brick, with Gothic niches at first-floor level, crowstepped
gables, and a bellcote. Recessed entrance within the cloister
walk, with a triplet of Gothic doorways. Former chapel
behind. The park, with some good trees, and the stuccoed mid
C 19 LODGE belonged to an older mansion known as Stroud
Green House before being used for the orphanage. It was
demolished in 1927.

Board Schools, Morland Road. 1891 by *R. W. Price*. Extensive (evidence of rising population), although there was
still space for the buildings to be one-storeyed.

Woodside Green is still potentially attractive, with its trees
and white posts and chains, although the few older houses
around it have mostly been submerged in mean late Victorian
development. Worth hunting out: on the N side No. 169, set
back, a charming weatherboarded house of lobby-entrance
type (see the central chimney), a taller extension to the l., a
lower one to the r.; early C 19 tended porch. Then some
stucco-trimmed villas, and more modest houses, perhaps with
old cores, in front of some minimal C 19 workers' terraces in
Dickensons Place. On the S side No. 88, a cottage orné of
the mid C 19, with very elaborate bargeboards. Further W, in a
hopelessly unsympathetic setting, No. 2, another delightful
weatherboarded house with gambrel roof and low pantiled
extension around a sturdy end chimneystack.

GREENWICH

INTRODUCTION

Greenwich is made up of the two old boroughs of Greenwich and
Woolwich (total population in 1981: 211,840). Until 1965 Woolwich included the anomaly of a strip of land on the opposite side
of the river, North Woolwich, now part of Newham. Even without this, Greenwich and Woolwich together have more of the
Thames riverside than any other London borough. Although
the main route to Kent passes through, early development was
concentrated by the river; indeed this part of London, together
with Deptford (Le), is bound up more closely than any other
with England's early naval history. Yet only the great set piece
of Greenwich Hospital exploits this position architecturally.

In the Middle Ages Greenwich, Woolwich, and Plumstead
were fishing villages, lying at the foot of the chalk hills which
come down close to the river in this part of South London. The
Anglo Saxon Chronicle mentions that the Danish fleet lay at
Greenwich in 1011. To the E lay the unfrequented scrubland of

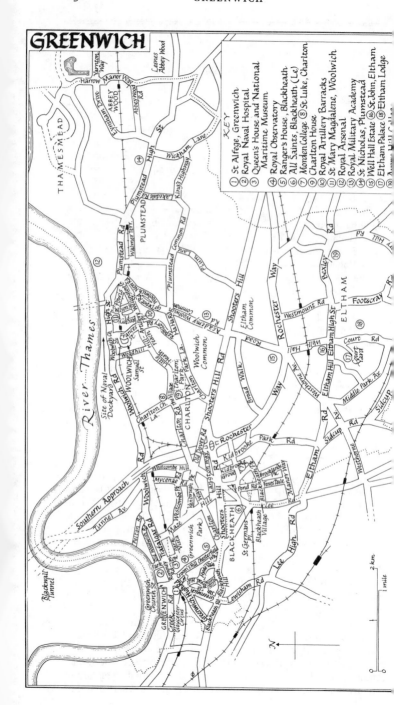

GREENWICH

KEY
① St Alfege, Greenwich
② Royal Naval Hospital
③ Queen's House and National Maritime Museum
④ Royal Observatory
⑤ Ranger's House, Blackheath
⑥ All Saints, Blackheath (Le)
⑦ Morden College ⑧ St Luke, Charlton
Charlton House
⑨ Royal Artillery Barracks
⑩ St Mary Magdalene, Woolwich
⑪ Royal Arsenal
⑫ Royal Military Academy
⑬ St Nicholas, Plumstead
⑭ Well Hall Estate ⑯ St John, Eltham
⑰ Eltham Palace ⑱ Eltham Lodge

the Erith marshes, to the s the upland plateau of Blackheath, the gateway to London. Wat Tyler camped at Blackheath in 1381, Jack Cade in 1450; Henry V was welcomed back here from Agincourt by the citizens of London; Henry VII fought the Cornish rebels here in 1497. Further E was the little village of Charlton, and Plumstead and Woolwich Commons, and further s on the higher land (clay overlain by gravel) the village of Eltham, hidden beyond the wooded slopes of Shooters Hill.* Only Plumstead among these old centres still preserves appreciable remains of its medieval church, although the c 17 group at Charlton, with the small church close to the great house (one of the few major Jacobean survivals in London), no doubt reflects 22 an older pattern. At Eltham the High Street is still just recogni- 23 zable as a former village street, and at Well Hall to the N are the minor remains of a Tudor mansion. The most important medieval monument, however, lies to the s of Eltham village: Eltham Palace, which belonged to the Crown from 1305, and was a favourite royal residence of the c 15 and early c 16. The moated site with its splendid hall built by Edward IV make it one 13 of the best preserved of the pre-Tudor royal palaces not only in London but in the whole of England.

By the time Eltham Palace was built, Greenwich also had a royal establishment, although the appearance of the large rambling brick palace of Placentia which stood by the river, between the present N wings of the Naval Hospital, is known only from excavations and from old views. It appears on Wyngaerde's drawings of 1558 as an extensive irregular structure with three courtyards. By the riverside was a five-storey brick tower and a lower range with polygonal turrets (cf. Richmond (Ri) and Eltham); the chapel projected at the E end, the hall lay behind, on the E side of the main courtyard.‡ Beyond, to the s, were Henry VIII's armouries, his tiltyard with its towers, and a gatehouse to the park, which was separated from the palace by a road. For although Greenwich, like Eltham and Richmond, had the attraction of a park for hunting (walled by James I), in addition there was for Henry VIII the appeal of the naval and military significance of the riverside. Henry built up the naval dockyards at both Deptford (Le) and Woolwich. The Great Harry was built in Woolwich in 1512, the Royal Sovereign in 1637. Further downstream the area called Woolwich Warren was used for storing arms from the c 16, the beginning of the career of the later Royal Arsenal, which by the early c 20 occupied the whole of the river bank from Woolwich to the Erith Marshes.

From the c 17 the history of Greenwich and Woolwich

---

* EARLY SETTLEMENTS: almost no prehistoric finds; an enclosed Iron Age/ Romano-British settlement at Charlton, some small barrows of uncertain date in Greenwich Park; a large Roman building in Greenwich Park, a Roman site in Eltham.

‡ Excavations have confirmed the outlines of most of the riverside range and shown that this was a Tudor rebuilding encapsulating the earlier manor houses of the c 14 and c 15 (cf. Eltham). See P. Dixon, *Excavations at Greenwich Palace 1970–71* (1972).

becomes markedly different. Both grew into towns, but while Woolwich was primarily a town of workers, dependent on local industry, Greenwich was a more aristocratic settlement on the fringes of palace and park. The palace continued as such only until the later C 17. The earliest surviving building, *Inigo Jones*'s classical villa, the Queen's House (begun 1616, completed 1632-7, enlarged 1662, and now the centre of a composition of 1807), was built on the edge of the grounds of the still-existing old palace. Seen from the river it now appears as an oddly diminutive and restrained termination to the monumental Baroque composition of the Royal Naval Hospital (now Royal Naval College) which occupies the site of the old palace. The N W wing, the King Charles Block, begun in 1664 by *Webb*, was in fact the start of a new palace for Charles II which was never completed. Its adaptation as part of a new design by *Wren* for an exceptionally grandiose almshouse for elderly seamen (the counterpart of the Royal Hospital at Chelsea, K C) dates from 1694. Work continued until the middle of the C 18, involving *Hawksmoor*, Wren's second-in-command (probably responsible for the most outré features of the King William Block), and later royal surveyors, although the most important features of the design were established by around 1700. These buildings of Greenwich therefore offer an exceptionally complete picture of the progress of the classical style as patronized by the court, over a period of more than a hundred years.

The rebuilding of Greenwich parish church, St Alfege, by *Hawksmoor* (1711–14) also belongs to this phase of confident Baroque grandeur. Woolwich has little left of this time apart from the few but remarkable early buildings at the Arsenal, especially those of *c*. 1717 probably by *Vanbrugh*, brusque, overpowering, and original, characteristics too of *Vanbrugh's* own house which remains on the E edge of Greenwich Park. Quite different is the more conventional elegance of the excellent groups of late C 17 to early C 18 brick houses which spread up Croom's Hill on the w side of the park towards Blackheath (*see also* Lewisham, Le). The most important house of this phase, however, is not at Greenwich, but at Eltham: *Hugh May*'s Dutch-influenced Eltham Lodge of 1664, one of the prototypes for the domestic style of the late C 17. The style at its maturity is illustrated most happily by the Morden Almshouses on the edge of Blackheath (1695) and by *Wren*'s delightful observatory in Greenwich Park (1675).

Although Greenwich is still rich in houses and terraces of the late C 17/early C 18, it is not a good hunting ground for C 18 mansions. The most impressive, *James*'s Wricklemarsh House, Blackheath Park, was demolished at the beginning of the C 19. By the mid C 18 the royal and aristocratic connections of Richmond and Twickenham had eclipsed the appeal of Greenwich, and good mid C 18 houses are few. The best are *G. Gibson Jun.*'s Woodlands (1774) (now a library), the Ranger's House Blackheath, of various C 18 dates, and Point House, Point Hill, with good mid C 18 interiors.

At this time Woolwich consisted only of a long street (Church Street–High Street), divided from the river first by the Dockyard, then by the Arsenal. Between them was the long ropewalk (surviving now only in name). In 1744 Woolwich had 400 ropemakers. More remains to the s, for from the later c 18 planning on a grand scale began with the arrival of the military on the common, disturbing the 'salubriousness and gentility' that had hitherto reigned undisturbed in the hills above the town. The Royal Artillery Barracks, a huge camp on the Roman model, entered by trumphal arches, was begun in 1775, the ample composition of *James Wyatt*'s Military Academy (and also   69 the equally monumental Grand Store within the Royal Arsenal) followed in 1805, and further barracks, hospitals, and attendant buildings sprang up during the earlier c 19. To reach the buildings on the common Woolwich New Road was laid out in 1790, Powis Street (now the main shopping street) in 1800. The town, however, did not emulate the well ordered layout of the military establishments, and although the expanding Arsenal attracted admiring visitors, Woolwich itself was described in 1847 as the 'dirtiest, filthiest and most thoroughly mismanaged town of its size in the Kingdom'. The town grew rapidly in the c 19, helped by the dramatic expansion of the Arsenal at the time of the Crimean War, which compensated for the decline of the Dockyard, closed in 1869. The population figures for Woolwich (without Eltham and Plumstead) are: 1801, 10,000; 1811, 17,000; 1831, 17,700; 1851, 32,000; 1861, 42,000. By then Plumstead was part of Woolwich; its population grew from 2,750 in 1831 to 8,400 in 1851, then leaped up to 25,000 in 1861 (when Eltham still had only 3,000). By 1881 the total for the three places was 75,000, in 1901 118,000, in 1921 142,000.

Although the riverside became dominated by industry during the c 19, and artisan housing sprang up (for example the streets laid out by *George Smith* N of Old Woolwich Road), Greenwich during this period had neither buildings nor population growth on the same scale as Woolwich. *Michael Searles* was responsible for an unusually elegant and ambitious urban scheme off Croom's Hill: Gloucester Circus, *c.* 1791, which remained incomplete. More successful were *Joseph Kay*'s improvements of *c.* 1830, which swept away the small streets of the old town on the site of the medieval friary which had stood close to the old palace, and replaced them by stuccoed terraces in the Nash manner. Thereafter the usual suburban expansion can be traced, e.g. in the streets off Greenwich South Street, on the slopes above Royal Hill, filling in between the more scattered c 18 houses, and around the E edges of Blackheath. Here growth was slow compared to other areas; Westcombe Park, N E of the heath, was not developed until after 1876, and Blackheath Park, although spaciously laid out by *c.* 1825, still had room for large houses towards the end of the century, as did Kidbrooke Grove further E (e.g. by *Aston Webb*, *Belcher*, and *R. Blomfield*). The population of Greenwich, 25,000 in 1831, doubled only by the 1880s, and reached 100,000 only after 1918.

It remains to mention the major architectural transformations of the last hundred years. At Woolwich the three remarkable self-help organizations that were established in the C19 have all left their mark on the town. But of the Woolwich Equitable Building Society (founded 1847), the Royal Arsenal Cooperative Society (1868), and the Woolwich Polytechnic (1890), only the last (now the Thames Polytechnic) still has its original buildings.
98 Much more impressive is the Woolwich Town Hall of 1902–6 (*A. B. Thomas*), one of the proudest examples of that era of neo-Baroque splendour. Greenwich, in contrast, has one of the more progressive town halls of the 1930s (*Clifford Culpin*, 1939), a time when many major buildings were still adorned with the trappings of Edwardian classicism (see e.g. the Woolwich Building Society Headquarters of 1934). Other buildings of the 1930s were more adventurous: the Woolwich Granada Cinema with Dudok-style exterior (*Masey & Uren*) and *Komisarjevsky* interior (1937); and St Saviour Eltham, one of the first churches in London to abandon an overtly historical style (*Cachemaille-Day, Welch & Lander*, 1932–3). There is even a full-blown example of the International Modern style (a terrace by *Lubetkin* and *Pilichowski* at Plumstead, 1934–5).

The earliest public housing in the present borough was built by the L.C.C. (Hardy Cottages, Trafalgar Road, Greenwich, 1900–1), one of the first L.C.C. slum clearance areas to have cottages instead of tenements. More interesting is the remarkably attractive instant garden suburb created by *Frank Baines* of the Office of Works at Well Hall, Eltham, in 1915, for munitions workers. Woolwich (a Labour stronghold from 1903) pursued an active housing programme on the S borders of the borough in the 1930s, but its most spectacular efforts came after the Second World War with the redevelopment of the war-damaged slum-clearance areas in the town centre. It is worth visiting the St Mary's area to see how, alas, successive experiments with different layouts (mixed development with point blocks, an ambitious scheme of linked slabs, industrialized building, and finally low-rise terraces) have failed to do justice to this dramatic hilly site. At Plumstead, too, much renewal has for the most part replaced one kind of mediocrity with another. Greenwich, less prolific in its public housing, has more memorable and diverse individual sites, ranging from the neatly ranged 1940s blocks of Fairlawn, Charlton, and *Richardson & Houfe*'s genteel Regency housing of the 1950s near Blackheath Park (*see* Lewisham) to *Chamberlin, Powell & Bon*'s exceptionally well landscaped Vanbrugh Park, Greenwich (1961–5), which is totally different in effect from *Stirling & Gowan*'s elegantly brusque Trafalgar Estate for the L.C.C. of the same decade. Old people's homes make another contrast: *Stirling & Gowan*'s Perrygrove, Charlton, 1961–4, an inward-looking plan; and *Trevor Dannatt*'s outward-facing group in Langton Way, E of Blackheath, 1975–7. More recent borough housing can be studied especially well on the edges of Woolwich Common. Before 1965 both Woolwich and Greenwich had a chief architect (*J. O. W. Jones* and *P. A.*

Kennedy) within the Engineer's Departments (Borough Engineers *R. L. Gee* and *F. H. Clinch*, respectively). After 1965 the chief architect was *J. M. Moore* (Borough Architect from 1968).

By far the largest development of the last twenty years, however, is the creation of Thamesmead on the Erith Marshes, straddling the boundary between Greenwich and Bexley. This was one of the first and most ambitious investments by the new G.L.C., the 1960s answer to Becontree and Dagenham (Bk) and to the spreading later out-county cottage estates. It was to be not just a council estate, but a new town for 60,000 people, with its own industry as well as its own town centre by the river and other amenities. The first phases of 1967–72, at the s end of the site, were splendidly impressive, as the featureless swamp was moulded into a rugged townscape with a visually (if not socially) satisfying variety of housing forms around a vast lake, complemented by *Derek Stow*'s imaginative health centre, while 110 *Foster Associates*' crisply elegant glass factory provided an original start in the new industrial area. But since then progress has been slow: the main centre has not been built, adequate local employment has not materialized, and architectural objectives changed here, as elsewhere, in the 1970s, so that the later housing, while pleasant enough, does not have the same spectacular thrill. The general impression is increasingly one of a somewhat inconveniently placed suburb rather than of an embryonic new town.

Among later public buildings are two large hospitals of the 1960s–70s (by *Powell & Moya* at Woolwich, by the *D.H.S.S.* at Greenwich), both less forbidding, and less damaging to the townscape, than hospitals elsewhere in London, and a wide range of new buildings for comprehensive schools. The changing appearance of these reflects architectural history in miniature. They start with monumental but quietly detailed examples of the 1950s – Kidbrooke (the first comprehensive in London) and Eltham Green – and are followed in the 1960s by the more brutalist additions by the L.C.C. at Eaglesfield. The 1960s extensions at Eltham Hill (then a grammar school) by *Trevor Dannatt* are also bold, but more sensitively detailed. Of the 1970s are *Powell & Moya*'s friendly, ingeniously compact additions at Plumstead, and *Stillman & Eastwick-Field*'s new Blackheath Bluecoat School, while the *G.L.C.*'s latest efforts jump from the sleek 'high tech' of Waterfield, Thamesmead (the first deep plan ILEA secondary) to the crisp, tightly knit vernacular roof-lines of the additions for John Roan, Blackheath.

Finally, private housing. A few individual houses can be singled out (notably one by *Edward Cullinan* at Eltham, another by *Bell & McCormack* E of Blackheath). But above all, the place to visit is Blackheath Park, with *Eric Lyons*'s Span estates, a 105 series of varied, sensitively landscaped developments on small sites, which began here in 1954 and still continue. They have quietly but consistently shown that there were humane and attractive alternatives both to the large domineering public housing schemes and to the indifferent speculative development of the 1950s and 60s – lessons that were learned only gradually elsewhere.

Further Reading

For general literature see p. 124. Local histories: V. D. Lipman, 'Greenwich: Palace Park and Town', *Transactions of the Ancient Monuments Society*, vol. 20, pp. 25–48; B. Platts, *A History of Greenwich* (1973); W. T. Vincent, *The Records of the Woolwich District* (1889–90). The DOE list is an early revised version dating from 1973, but there is also a well produced and informative list of *Buildings of Local Architectural and Historic Interest* published by the London Borough of Greenwich (2nd ed., 1979). The long established local periodicals, the *Greenwich and Lewisham Antiquarian Society Transactions* and the *Woolwich and District Antiquarian Society Reports*, occasionally include articles on architectural subjects.

Individual buildings: on royal buildings see *The King's Works*, *passim* (*see* p. 127); also P. Dixon, *Excavations at Greenwich Palace 1970–71* (1972). On Greenwich Hospital: *Wren Society*, vols. VI and VIII, and J. H. V. Davies, 'The Dating of Buildings at the Royal Hospital at Greenwich', *Archaeological Journal*, 112 (1956). On the Queen's House: the DOE guide by J. Charlton (1976), which corrects and amplifies the Survey of London Monograph (vol. 14, 1937). On Eltham Palace: D. E. Strong, *Eltham Palace* (DOE guide) (1958); R. Brook, *The Story of Eltham Palace* (1960); and for recent excavations, *Medieval Archaeology* (1978), p. 164. Also: *Charlton House* by A. R. Martin (1929); *The Royal Arsenal* (1963), by O. F. Hogg; *Morden College* (Survey of London Monograph, vol. 10) (1916). For Blackheath references see under Lewisham.

Acknowledgements

I am grateful to the staff of the Borough Architect's and Planning Departments for help over recent buildings, to Mr Julian Watson of the local history collection of the borough library for answering many queries, and especially to Dr Anthony Quiney, who both drove me round the borough, and improved the final text from his own investigations. The text has also benefited very considerably from the careful checking by Mr Neil Rhind (N R) and Mr Michael Kerney (M K), who have generously contributed much from their original research. I also have to thank Mr W. Bonwitt for information on Michael Searles and Mr J. Martin Robinson for details about James Wyatt. Mr Wesley Harry was of great assistance over the Royal Arsenal, Mr William Bossert of the G.L.C. likewise over Thamesmead. Mr John Jacob helped over the Ranger's House, and Mr D. E. Wickham and the Woolwich Antiquarian Society provided useful corrections on Woolwich. The entries on industrial buildings owe much to Goldsmiths' College Industrial Archaeology Group.

GREENWICH

CHURCHES

The medieval parish churches of Charlton and Greenwich, largely rebuilt in the C 17 and early C 18, instructively illustrate the changing aspirations of church builders,* from the modest brick C 17 late Gothic detail at St Luke, Charlton, to *Hawks-moor*'s monumental Baroque at St Alfege Greenwich nearly a century later, with its stone-faced exterior and giant portico. No later churches of comparable quality, except for *Wardell*'s Our Lady Star of the Sea (1851), with its *Pugin* form and decoration. The C 19 Anglican churches are of interest chiefly for their unecclesiological variety (Greenwich had an evangelical tradition). They start with the unhistorically Gothic St Michael, Blackheath Park (*Smith*, 1828), and progress via *Rundbogenstil* (St Thomas, by *J. Gwilt*, 1847) to Perp (*Brown* and *Kerr*'s Christ Church, 1847, *Ashpitel*'s St John, 1852).‡ *Champneys*' St Andrew and St Michael (1900–2) is the best of the more recent buildings.

ALL SAINTS, Blackheath. *See* Lewisham (Le).

ASCENSION, Dartmouth Row. *See* Lewisham (Le).

CHRIST CHURCH, Trafalgar Road. 1846–8 by *John Brown* of Norwich and *Robert Kerr*. Kentish rag with yellow stock brick trimmings – an odd choice. Barn-like interior with galleries (side galleries removed) and a low polygonal apse. Perp details. The spire on the tower never built.

ST ALFEGE, Greenwich High Road. A medieval foundation of venerable traditions, erected to commemorate the martyrdom of Archbishop Alfege at the hands of the Danes in 1012. The building, however, is of the C 18. The parishioners petitioned for a new church after the roof collapsed in 1710, and it was erected with money granted by the Fifty New Churches Act of 1711. The body of the building, by *Hawksmoor*, dates from 1711–14 (consecrated 1718). The old tower was recased and the steeple added in 1730 by *John James* (rebuilt in 1813). Plan and exterior are both convincingly Hawksmoor. The plan is a rectangle with a flat ceiling and towards the street a shallow E apse behind which rises the main portico, with a giant Tuscan order supporting a heavy pediment. The metope-triglyph frieze is broken in the centre to allow an arch to be thrown across which rises up into the pediment (a Late Roman motif familiar from Baalbek which was known to Hawksmoor in engravings and was also used earlier by Wren in his Great Model for St Paul's). On the N and S sides giant pilasters and big central vestibule projections with open outer staircases

---

* The third church of medieval origin, St Nicholas Deptford, although just within the borough of Greenwich, is described with the rest of Deptford under Lewisham.

‡ Demolished: *J. Wild*'s HOLY TRINITY, Blackheath Hill, 1839, E.E., stock brick, street front with two spires and an apse.

leading up to the doors. The quasi-central plan (originally emphasized inside as well by the furnishings and ceiling) is typical of Hawksmoor (Christchurch Spitalfields, TH). The tower, added inorganically to the W end with its pediment, is dependent in elevation on Gibbs and altogether much tamer than Hawksmoor's style.

Inside, too, in spite of such Hawksmoor motifs as the depressed vault of the apse and the diagonally projecting pairs of giant columns flanking the reredos and E window, there is not as much of interest as at Spitalfields or Limehouse or Wapping or Bloomsbury. The way in which the ceiling rises from corbels is decidedly weak, and the galleries do not seem to belong to the design. The gallery columns and other wood-work (for which *Grinling Gibbons* was paid £156) were, alas, mostly destroyed in the Second World War. The restoration, completed in 1953, was by *Sir Albert Richardson*. – The PUL-PIT imitates the original one. – ROYAL PEW in the S gallery. The curved supports are original. – WALL PAINTINGS. Monochrome decoration by *Thornhill*, in the apse repainted by *Glyn Jones* after war damage, on the flanking pilasters original. – Also original the excellent WROUGHT IRON-WORK. – STAINED GLASS. All by *Francis Spear*, 1953–6.

ST ANDREW AND ST MICHAEL, Tunnel Avenue. 1900–2 by *Basil Champneys*. Very pretty in its bleak setting. Yellow brick, small, with aisles, outer buttresses with a pronounced batter, free Perp tracery, and a charming wrought-iron bell-cote. An interior of originality: arcades with paired arches; a wooden barrel-vault supported by transverse arches over the nave. Future uncertain.

ST GEORGE, Kirkside Road, W of Westcombe Hill. 1890–1 by *Newman & Newman*. Tall urban red brick church in the Brooks manner standing on a steep slope; lancets, with a little tracery in the clerestory. No tower. Small apsidal sanctuary added later in place of the intended chancel.

ST JAMES, Kidbrooke Park Road. Dull Dec, by *Newman & Billing*, 1866–7. Much rebuilt after Second World War damage.

ST JOHN, St John's Park, SW of Old Dover Road. 1852–3 by *Arthur Ashpitel*. Perp, Kentish rag, with a good spire, pro-minently sited on an island in the centre of the Victorian suburb E of Blackheath. – (Later C19 furnishings: REREDOS and SCREEN by *H. S. Rogers*; STAINED GLASS by *Heaton, Butler & Bayne*.)

ST LUKE, The Village, Charlton. In its humble pre-classical C17 character a most attractive church. Rebuilt *c.* 1630, with money left by Sir Adam Newton of Charlton House. The N aisle followed in 1639. E end (new chancel and organ chamber) 1840 and 1873. The church is of brick, with even the elementary tracery of the bell-openings and the crenellations of the tower top (cf. Plumstead, Woolwich) of the same mate-rial. The window tracery of nave and N chapel is Dec (very correct for the C17). But the S porch has a typical early C17

Dutch gable, and archways set against rustication. Whitewashed interior of lowly proportions. Nave of two bays separated from the aisle by two round arches and one square pier with four slim attached shafts at the corners, quite a minor revival, inasmuch as it has no Perp precedent. The capitals are not medieval at all; nor are they classical. The s window of the old chancel (also of two bays) looks as if it might be of the preceding c 15 building. Wagon roof in the chancel c 17, in the nave reconstructed in 1925. – FONT. Stone, later c 17, handsome baluster stem and shallow round bowl with draperies and shells. – PULPIT of c. 1630. Polygonal, with eared scrolly panels and the arms of Sir David Cunningham, one of the trustees for the rebuilding. Sounding-board now in the tower. – DOOR to the s porch. Handsome early c 17, with a fan radiating from a cherub's head. – STAINED GLASS. E window by *C. F. Blakeman* replacing one of 1639 by *Isaac Oliver* destroyed in the Second World War. – One N window with c 17 heraldic glass. – MONUMENTS. Edward Wilkinson, master-cook to Queen Elizabeth, † 1568. Handsome tablet with strapwork cartouche. – Lady Newton, wife of the builder of Charlton House, † 1630. Noble black and white aedicule with broken segmental pediment: by *Nicholas Stone* under the influence of Inigo Jones. – Countess of Ardmagh † 1700, of similar type but with the broken pediment curved, the inscription on a feigned drapery, and with standing allegories outside the columns. – Brigadier Michael Richards, Surveyor-General of the Ordnance, † 1721, a very late example of the free-standing man in armour as a funeral monument. Probably by *Guelfi*. – Elizabeth Thompson † 1759, with frontal bust. – General Morrison † 1799, with the usual female figure bust over an urn: by *Regnart*. – Spencer Perceval, the Prime Minister, assassinated in 1812. Very simple, with an excellent bust by *Chantrey*. – Many minor tablets.

ST MICHAEL, Blackheath Park. By *G. Smith*, 1828–9, as part of the layout of Blackheath Park (*see* Perambulation 4). White brick and Bath stone, with aisles, clerestory, internal gallery, and a fanciful thin E spire (the 'Needle of Kent') with many pinnacles and an excessively elongated polygonal top stage. The big E window within the tower consists of a crazy assembly of motifs utterly unworried by considerations of antiquarian accuracy.

ST NICHOLAS, Deptford Green. *See* Deptford (Le).

ST PAUL, Devonshire Drive, w of Greenwich South Street. 1865–6 by *S. S. Teulon*.* Kentish rag, French Gothic, with apse. Lower part of tower with bellcote, the rest incomplete. Much rebuilt after bomb damage, although the original FONT survives.

ST THOMAS, Maryon Road, w of Woodhill, Charlton. 1849–50 by *Joseph Gwilt*. In the *Rundbogenstil*, without a tower. The external surfaces a restless pattern of red and white brick and stone.

---

* Although the *Kentish Mercury* of 3 August 1868 attributes it to *W. M. Teulon*.

Interior with N and S galleries on quatrefoil piers and with its own piers carrying the roof.

OUR LADY STAR OF THE SEA (R.C.), Croom's Hill. 1851 by *W. W. Wardell*, the same date as his church at Clapham (Ww). Fine E tower and spire with powerful polygonal turret. A simple Puginian plan with six-bay aisled nave, two-bay chancel with chapels; Dec detail. Much internal enrichment, notably the sedilia, reredos, pulpit, and stencilled ceiling of the S chancel chapel, and the open stone rood screen with rood and figure of the Virgin in a diagonally placed niche on the l. In front of the statue a silver nef lamp by *Hardman*. The decoration of the chancel and chapel of St Joseph is by *A. W. Pugin*. Founder's tomb between chancel and S chapel (Richard North † 1860) and founder's brass in the chancel floor.* Sacred Heart Chapel by *E. W. Pugin*. – (STAINED GLASS. Good E window, perhaps by *Hardman*.)

(ST JOSEPH (R.C.), Pelton Road. 1881 by *H. J. Hanson*.)

BAPTIST CHAPEL, Greenwich South Street. Front with Lombard arches, 1872 by *C. G. Searle & Son*.

BLACKHEATH AND CHARLTON BAPTIST CHURCH, Shooters Hill Road. 1905 by *S. S. Dottridge & W. J. Walford*. In the free late Gothic typical of this date; corner tower with battered buttresses.

CHURCH ARMY CHAPEL, Vanbrugh Park. 1965 by *Austin Vernon & Partners*. Curved copper-clad timber roof.

EAST GREENWICH UNITED REFORMED CHURCH (Rothbury Hall Mission), Azof Street, N of Pelton Road. Built as a Congregational mission hall in 1893 by *W. T. Hollands*. Large upper hall with a very weird and exotic roof-line (said at the time to be an adaptation of the Flemish style).

PUBLIC BUILDINGS

TOWN HALL (former), now MERIDIAN HOUSE, Greenwich High Road and Royal Hill. 1939, an early work by *Clifford Culpin*, altered by the *Rolfe Judd Practice* when the administrative section was converted to private offices. The public halls remain. A progressive building for its time, similar in style to the slightly earlier town halls of the Middlesex boroughs of Hornsey (Hy) and Wembley (Br), inspired by Scandinavian and Dutch precedents. At the time of the first edition of this book it could still be described as the only town hall in any London borough to represent the style of our time adequately. A fine, irregular composition with a tall sheer tower, with well balanced opposing elements, especially in the elevation to Royal Hill. Some of the details now with rather a period charm, especially the flat bricks and the piquant angle window high up in the tower, both Dutch (Dudok) motifs

* Richard North was the first incumbent. The church was built as a result of a vow made by his mother when she and her infant sons were rescued from drowning.

which had begun to fascinate certain English architects about 1930. The interior was much altered in 1972–4, when floors were inserted in the council chamber area. The main external changes are the addition of a third floor (allowed for in the original plans), the insertion of new windows to match the old ones in the council chamber area, and the replacement of glass blocks by windows at basement level on Royal Hill.

MAGISTRATES COURT, Blackheath Road. 1909 by *J. Dixon Butler*. Dignified stone front with semicircular domed Ionic porch.

FIRE STATION, Tunnel Avenue and Woolwich Road. 1901–2. A lively composition by the Fire Brigade section of the *L.C.C. Architect's Department*, probably designed by *H. F. T. Cooper*. The side to Tunnel Avenue is best, with stone vertical accents and big eaves. Low engine house projecting between splayed wings.

RANGER'S HOUSE, Chesterfield Walk. *See* Perambulation 1.

GREENWICH LIBRARY, Woolwich Road. A Carnegie building of 1905, by *S. R. J. Smith*, in the usual cheerful free Baroque of those years. Striped brick and stone; shell porch and pediment.

WEST GREENWICH LIBRARY, Greenwich High Road. Another Carnegie library, of 1905–7 by *H. W. Willis & J. Anderson*. Symmetrical Wrenaissance front under cupola; doorways with Gibbs surrounds. Domed reading room with corner columns.

WOODLANDS (Local History Library), Mycenae Road. Once an excellent villa, built in 1774 by *G. Gibson Jun.* for J. J. Angerstein, whose picture collection formed the first purchase for the proposed National Gallery. Much altered, but the stuccoed five-bay N front is original, with graceful frieze and medallion in *Liardet*'s patent stucco (cf. Adam's Portland Place); bow-windows added in the early C19. NE wing demolished *c*.1876 for the road; W wing largely replaced by convent buildings of the 1930s. S and E fronts refaced in Portland stone probably in the late C19. The entrance was formerly in the E front; the portico is now blocked. (Interior much altered, but the former hall retains its neo-classical ceiling and doorcases.)

BATHS, Trafalgar Road. 1927–8 by *Horth & Andrew* of Hull. Lively symmetrical composition with large brick arches and stone attic, relieved by windows with patterned glazing bars.

CHARLTON HOUSE (Community Centre). Built by Sir Adam Newton, tutor to Henry Prince of Wales, *c*.1607–12. Later owners were Sir William Ducie, who made repairs in 1659, Sir William Langhorne, East India merchant, after 1680, and in the C19 the Maryon Wilson family, for whom *Norman Shaw* restored the house and made minor additions in 1877–8. Acquired by the borough in 1925.

Charlton House is the only Jacobean mansion of the first order remaining in the precincts of London. The plan is E-shaped with four symmetrical bay-windows at the ends of

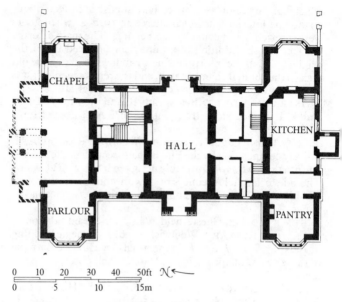

Charlton House, plan
(nineteenth-century north extensions now demolished)

the four wings and two towers in the centres of the two wings,
framing the building when seen from the W or E. The building
is of three storeys above capacious cellars, built of red brick
with stone dressings, and ends in an ornamental balustrade
with pierced open tracery. The towers have ogee roofs. It is all
plain and angular, spacious but not at all luxurious, with the
exception of the W frontispiece, that is, the door surround and
the bay-window above which suddenly breaks out into the
most exuberant and undisciplined ornament in all England
(the work of a mason probably who possessed a copy of
Wendel Dietterlin's *Architectura* of 1593 and a rare case of
close imitation).

The most remarkable feature of the interior is the position
of the HALL, just as revolutionary (though not unique in
Jacobean architecture) as Inigo Jones's at the Queen's House.
It is two-storeyed, placed at right angles to front and back, and
runs right across the building. Above it on the second floor is
the saloon reached by an elaborately carved STAIRCASE,
quadrangular with a square open well and the flights of stairs
supported by posts which between ground floor and first floor
form palm branches in vases. The sloping pilaster-balusters
progress through the three orders from ground floor to top
landing. The plasterwork is Victorian. The SALOON has an
original plaster ceiling with pendants and a marble fireplace
with restrained architectural ornament to the overmantel
above finely carved figures of Venus and Vulcan. This is very

much in the manner of Nicholas Stone.* In the bay-window
C 17 heraldic glass with the Ducie arms. On the same floor the
N wing is taken up entirely by the LONG GALLERY, also with a
good plaster ceiling. The original panelling has gone except
for pilasters by the windows. In these, more heraldic glass
with the Ducie arms. The gallery is reached from the saloon by
the WHITE DRAWING ROOM whose stone fireplace with two
tiers of caryatids, three-dimensional strapwork, and relief
scenes makes the marble one in the saloon appear very classical. The main scene shows Perseus and Pegasus; religious
subjects below (Triumph of Christ and Triumph of Death?).
Again different in style the fireplace in the SE BEDROOM on   22
the same floor, where motifs are thinner and busier. The
central scene is derived from an engraving by *Abraham de
Bruyn*. On the first floor, in the SW or DUCIE ROOM, a
fireplace of the 1660s, very sober. On the ground floor to the S
of the hall the former LIBRARY, with wooden Jacobean fireplace dated 1612, and the DINING ROOM, with a stone fireplace with curiously ambiguous quasi-terms. The NW room
was a chapel. The main alterations of 1877 involved the extension of the dining room around the projecting N tower (reduced and altered after war damage).

Of outbuildings the STABLES to the S are contemporary,
now arranged on two sides of a quadrangle. Remanagements
under Sir William Langhorne are easily discernible. In front
of the entrance on the lawn a solitary GATEWAY, plastered,
with Corinthian columns and an C 18 cresting. To the l., N W of
the house, a handsome SUMMER HOUSE of *c.* 1630, brick,
square, with Tuscan pilasters, and a concave roof. There is no
documentary confirmation of the traditional attribution to
Inigo Jones; but the complete absence of Jacobean frills at
evidently such an early date makes it quite justifiable. *Nicholas
Stone* would also be a possibility.

BLACKHEATH ART CLUB, Bennett Park, E of Blackheath
Village. 1886 by *Higgs & Rudkin*. The first of several cultural
institutions established at Blackheath by a local benefactor,
William Webster. The other three are as follows.

BLACKHEATH ART SCHOOL, Lee Road (behind the
Conservatoire). 1896 by *Edmeston & Gabriel*, with studio
block of 1911.

BLACKHEATH CONSERVATOIRE OF MUSIC, Lee Road.
1896, plain except for shell ornament over the first-floor windows; adjoining, the massive former CONCERT HALL,
1894–5. Both are again by *Edmeston & Gabriel*. Two steep
gables with much yellow terracotta artycrafty decoration and a
frieze by *Searle*. Two halls seating 1,200.

BLACKHEATH BLUECOAT SCHOOL, Old Dover Road. Transformed into a 1,000-pupil comprehensive with additions by
Stillman & Eastwick-Field, 1972–4. (Linked two-storey pavi-

* I owe this comment to Roger White, who also points out that one of the
ground-floor fireplaces is very similar to one illustrated in the *King's Arcadia*
(Nos. 277, 278).

lions grouped around paved courtyards, on a domestic scale.)

JOHN ROAN SCHOOL, Maze Hill. Large neat neo-Georgian of 1926 by *Percy B. Dannatt & Sir B. Fletcher*. The school was founded in 1644 by John Roan, Yeoman of Harriers to King Charles I.*

JOHN ROAN SCHOOL, Westcombe Park Road. Lower school for 540 children, by the G.L.C., 1977–81 (job architects *A. Webb, G. Denison*). Crisply detailed purple brick walls, tiled roof. Low but compact, with clerestory-lit laboratories angled around the library in the centre of the w block, a corresponding smaller E cluster with staffrooms etc. around hall and gymnasium, and classrooms in a staggered range along the road.

KIDBROOKE SCHOOL, Corelli Road, N of Broad Walk. By *Slater, Uren & Pike*, planned from 1949, completed 1954. The first purpose-built London comprehensive, for 2,000 girls. Huge domed copper-roofed assembly hall near the entrance (planned to seat 1,500). The hall was still required at this time as the visible expression of a school's identity. Large foyer adjoining, with circular roof-lights and elegant staircase. Delicate (perhaps deliberately feminine) detailing very different from the tougher schools of the sixties. Four-storey classroom blocks of forbidding length stretch out behind, linked by library and staffrooms above an open ground floor.

BOARD SCHOOLS. BLACKHEATH ROAD SCHOOLS (now Adult Institute). Plain, tall, and gabled, 1874, a good example of *Robson's* early school buildings for the London School Board. The style was extremely progressive for the time. To their N the Higher Elementary School of 1904 (now GREENWICH PARK SCHOOL). CHARLTON COLLEGE (formerly Charlton Park School), Woolwich Road, with a pair of ogee-topped turrets, and MERIDIAN PRIMARY SCHOOL, Old Woolwich Road, with curved cupola and pargetted gable, are typical of the more ornamental style of the 1890s.

GREENWICH NATIONAL SCHOOL OF EDUCATION AND INDUSTRY FOR GIRLS. The former school building of 1814, very modest, stands at the end of St Alfege's churchyard.

GREENWICH DISTRICT HOSPITAL, Woolwich Road. Replacing St Alfege's Hospital, the former poor house of 1843.‡ The massive new buildings (for 800 beds) are an unusually large enterprise to be undertaken by the Department of Health and Social Security (chief architect *W. E. Tatton Brown*).§ Planned from 1961, final phase completed

---

* The former boys' school building of 1807 remains in Roan Street.

‡ Described as 'the most extensive in the Kingdom and remarkable for the varied beauty of its elevations which are built in an enriched Tudor style'. The hospital also replaces the MILLER GENERAL HOSPITAL in Greenwich High Road where the early buildings, converted to other uses, remain (*see* Perambulation 1, end).

§ The development of the hospital on such a confined site was possible because the laundry and other services were offloaded to a central supply depot at Hither Green (Le), also serving other hospitals.

1976. Mostly only three storeys, with straightforward exposed concrete frame. Cheerful MURAL along Woolwich Road by *Philippa Threlfall*, pebbles and ceramics in concrete, 1972, showing the history of Greenwich riverside. Adjoining, up Vanbrugh Hill, a HEALTH CENTRE of 1976, also by the D.H.S.S., an ugly A-frame with forceful raking struts.

MORDEN COLLEGE, off St Germans Place, E of Blackheath. 36 Founded in 1695 by Sir John Morden, a Turkey merchant, on part of an estate which he had bought in 1669, as an almshouse for 'decayed Turkey merchants', each having a bedroom, a sitting room, and a half-share in a bathroom and kitchen. Defoe wrote that the intention was to let them live as gentlemen, but that funds did not permit as generous a layout as had been intended. Sir John was consciously emulating Bromley College (Bm) of which he was the treasurer. The college still functions as an almshouse. The buildings, lying in ample grounds handsomely landscaped in the C18, form a large quadrangle, the W front emphasized by two moderately projecting wings containing the treasurer's and the chaplain's quarters (cf. Bromley College). Warm brick with hard plaster quoins and dressings, not luxuriously but well and comfortably built. The mason was *Edward Strong*, one of Wren's favourite builders. Sir John Morden was on the Greenwich Hospital Commission with Wren, so it is more than likely that *Wren* designed the building, although there is no proof. It is indeed one of the best dozen or so of examples of his style in domestic as against representational architecture. Doors with hooded porches; the windows have double-hung sashes (an early example). In the centre of the W front a broad doorway with segmental pediment and, bracketing together the five middle bays, a pediment with the statues of the founder and his wife in a double niche.* An open cupola rises above the pediment. In the middle of the quadrangle, with its low straight-headed arcades on Tuscan columns and small pediments in the centres of each side, a handsome cast-iron lamp-standard in the form of a Roman Doric column with an urn on top. The CHAPEL lies on the E side, on axis with the entrance and projecting beyond the outer E front, a simple rectangle reached by two fine wood-carved doorways and itself distinguished chiefly by well carved original furnishings: reredos, three-decker pulpit in the C17 position in the centre of the E wall, pews, W gallery, and communion rails. The room is covered by a segmental vault. In the E window small stained-glass figures of *c*. 1600. To the SW of the college buildings, infirmary wing by *Banister Fletcher*, 1932–3. To the NW

* The statues were possibly added later. The will of Lady Susan Morden († 1721) included the provision of Sir John's and her effigies in stone over the great door 'in case the same shall not be done in my life time' (information from Mr W. Bonwitt). Roger White points out that the centrepiece seems to derive from an engraving of an altar recess at the Hôtel des Ardilliers, Paris, published in *The Architect's Storehouse* by Roger Pricke, 1674.

further accommodation in three blocks (1957, 1966, 1971–75) all by *Guise, Davies & Upfold*.

TRINITY HOSPITAL, Park Row. *See* Perambulation 2.

MARKET, College Approach. *See* Perambulation 1.

DEPTFORD SEWAGE PUMPING STATION, Norman Road, E of Deptford Creek. 1859–62 by *Bazalgette*. It pumps from the three main sewers of South London into the Southern Outfall Sewer. Two beam-engine houses in white brick with stone dressings, and hipped lantern roofs, joined by a boiler house. The W house extended in the same style in gault brick *c.* 1905. Electric and diesel pumps of 1934 replaced the original four beam engines. Open-sided coal sheds with arched open-web cast-iron girders, a little old-fashioned for 1859, and wrought-iron roof trusses.

EAST GREENWICH GASWORKS, E of Tunnel Avenue. Established by the South Metropolitan Gas Company, 1883–6. One of the largest in Europe. Production (latterly from naphtha) ceased in 1978. On the river, a large coal jetty of 1886, wrought and cast iron with hydraulic cranes. No. 1 gasholder (1886 by *George Livesey*) was the first in the world with four lifts (telescopic sections). The wrought-iron guide columns are 198 ft high. No. 2 (1892), 300 ft in diameter, was the world's largest, built with six lifts (the top two destroyed in 1917). The disused sulphate of ammonia bulk store is a parabolic structure of reinforced-concrete arch ribs, four storeys high.

GREENWICH POWER STATION, Old Woolwich Road. By the *L.C.C. Architect's Department*, General and Highways sections, for the L.C.C. tramways. 1902–10. Simple stock-brickwork on a monumental scale. The four tapering octagonal chimneys have been truncated at two-thirds height, destroying the sensitive proportions. They had a machicolated band below the top, of Sienese character. On the riverside, a massive coal jetty.

VICTORIA DEEPWATER TERMINAL, on the W side of the Greenwich peninsula. Prominent container-handling gantry cranes of the 1970s, the only ones on the London river front.

GREENWICH STATION, Greenwich High Road. The original terminus of London's earliest railway line, of 1840 by *G. Smith*, was re-erected on this site in 1878 in somewhat altered form. Handsome two-storey front with stone frieze and cornice on large brackets. Doorcase with Ionic columns.

THAMES BARRIER, BLACKWALL TUNNEL, GREENWICH FOOT TUNNEL. *See* Thames Crossings at end of gazetteer.

GREENWICH PALACE, QUEEN'S HOUSE, ROYAL NAVAL HOSPITAL AND RELATED PUBLIC BUILDINGS

Greenwich Palace and the Queen's House

EARLY HISTORY. In the C14 and C15 Eltham was much favoured by royalty. The manor of Greenwich, conveniently close to Eltham, was given by Henry V to Thomas Beaufort, Duke of Exeter; on his death in 1426 it passed to Humphrey Duke of Gloucester, Henry VI's uncle, and one of the most important men in England. He enlarged the estate and rebuilt the manor house (licence to crenellate 1433). His library, which formed the inspiration for the Bodleian, was housed here. The estate passed to the Crown in 1447 and was given to Margaret of Anjou, who made further improvements. She seems to have called it Plaisance or Placentia. The Tudor monarchs liked Placentia. Substantial rebuilding took place under Henry VII, c. 1500–6, as excavations have shown, and further improvements were made by Henry VIII, so that the word palace began to be applied to the group of buildings. Important royal events took place here. Greenwich was the birthplace of Henry VIII, who married here both Katherine of Aragon and Anne of Cleves, and here also his sister married the Duke of Suffolk. In 1516 Mary was born at the palace, in 1533 Elizabeth, and in 1522 the Emperor Charles V was received in state. At Greenwich also Anne Boleyn's death warrant was signed. Henry was attracted to Greenwich by his naval interests. His establishment of the Deptford and Woolwich Yards and of Trinity House are familiar. His additions to the palace included the armoury for his selected craftsmen from Milan and Germany, and the tiltyard with its romantic medievalizing towers. Minor alterations were made during the C16 and early C17, including below the timber hall an undercroft of 1605–6, the only major part of the palace to escape demolition in 1661–9; it remains below the Queen Anne Block of the Naval Hospital (*see* below).* The palace was an extensive irregular structure by the river (*see* Introduction to the borough) between the present N wings of the Royal Hospital, with a gatehouse to the park to the S. It was on this boundary that *Inigo Jones* built the Queen's House for Anne of Denmark, to whom James I had given Greenwich in 1613. The old palace must have appeared to her too large and too old-fashioned. She wanted a more livable-in and a more up-to-date house.

THE QUEEN'S HOUSE can only be described as an Italian villa. It is no more than 110 by 120 ft in size, a square two-storeyed block without any of the bay-windows, gables, and turrets which entertained the Elizabethans and Jacobeans as much as they still entertain us. Originally, however, the Queen's House was not exactly as we see it today. It possessed one feature at least as weird as any of the fanciful decorations of the usual designs of the period. A letter of 1617 rightly refers to 'some curious devise of *Inigo Jones*' in speaking of the house just begun. The device was that the villa originally consisted of two parallel ranges connected only by a bridge astride the Woolwich–Deptford Road which ran between the

* Remains of outbuildings may survive incorporated in The Chantry, Park Vista (*see* Greenwich, Perambulation 2).

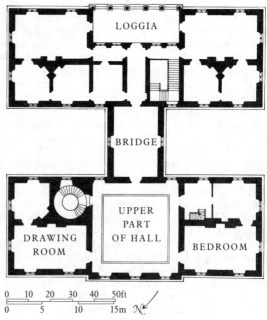

Queen's House, plan
of first floor as completed in 1637

palace and the park.* The shape was thus an H with the centre
bar in a N–S direction. The main entrance was on the N, that is,
from the old palace approached by a double flight of stairs.

Anne never lived to see her villa complete. She died in 1619
and James had not the heart to continue. Building had indeed
stopped in the previous year, and in 1619 the unfinished walls
were thatched for temporary protection. The house remained
in this state, only one storey high, until Charles I decided in
1629 to complete it for his French queen Henrietta Maria. It
was ready for occupation in 1637. From that time dates the
upper floor with its recessed loggia facing the park. The main
room was and is the HALL in the centre of the N block, 40 by 40
by 40 ft, a perfect cube, with a gallery around the upper floor.
This led to the state rooms, which were on the first floor, in the
Italian fashion, and to the bridge, a room of comfortable size,
20 ft wide, leading to the central room on the S side towards the
park. On the ground floor were the service rooms and kitchen
(removed in the C 18). The house, stripped of its furnishings
during the Civil War, was refurbished and enlarged after the
Restoration by *John Webb*, Inigo Jones's son-in-law and successor. He added two further bridges in 1662, one along the W,
the other along the E front. So the house now appeared the
perfect square which we know. The intention was to provide a

* Cf. the so-called Holbein Gate which stood between Whitehall and St James's
Park.

double sequence of state rooms for use by the King and Queen (cf. Hampton Court), but the house was never used in this way, as it was handed over to the Dowager Queen Henrietta Maria on her return to England and in 1690 became the residence of the Ranger of Greenwich Park. In 1693 Lord Romney, the holder of this post, diverted the old road further N (to the present Romney Road) so that it no longer ran beneath the building. The further minor alterations of the early C 18 (when it was intended that the house should be used for the Governor of the Naval Hospital), including the lowering of the ground-floor windows, the replacement of the casements by sashes, and the renewal of the external rendering, contribute subtly to the un-seventeenth-century appearance. Originally the upper floor was of limewashed brick, so that the window architraves projected more strongly.*

In 1807–16 the house was made the centre of a much larger composition by *Daniel Asher Alexander*. He added E and W wings, joined by open colonnades, to accommodate the naval asylums founded at Paddington in 1798 as a school for children of naval men, which was transferred to Greenwich and joined with an existing school for children of pensioners. On the W side a gymnasium and assembly hall (now the Neptune Hall) was added *c.* 1874, apparently by Colonel *Clark* of the Royal Engineers. The school left in 1933; the house was restored by the *Office of Works*, and the whole group was opened to the public as the National Maritime Museum in 1937.

The Queen's House is always regarded as one of the most important buildings in the history of English architecture. Yet its position in the place of Inigo Jones's *œuvre* is by no means clear. Jones, originally a painter and then England's most celebrated designer of masques, had revisited Italy in 1613–14. He studied architecture as well as painting, the former chiefly in Rome and in Palladio's Vicenza. He did not like the 'aboundance . . . brought in by Michill Angell' and preferred the remains of antique Rome and the 'sollid, proporsionable . . . and unaffected' style of Palladio. The latter's vocabulary is indeed clearly reflected in every detail at the Queen's House and made it to contemporary beholders, used to such fantastical buildings as Charlton House (*see* above), as novel in its chastity and bareness as any building in the new style of the C 20 can have appeared in 1925 or so to architects and laymen used to Edwardian effusiveness. Nothing like the same shock was experienced in England when Italian Renaissance forms first appeared here and there in the ornamentation of court buildings of Henry VIII a hundred years earlier.

The Queen's House is seven bays wide. It has a smoothly rusticated ground floor; the roof disappears behind a balustrade. The windows are well placed: wide apart, entirely regular, and studiously proportioned. The first-floor loggia on

---

* The cementing, however, is already visible on Hollar's engravings.

the garden side with its slim unfluted Ionic columns is espe
cially Palladian. The two-armed curved open staircase to the
terrace in front of the hall on the N side can be compared to
Sangallo's villa for Lorenzo di Medici at Poggio a Caiano. It is
difficult to tell to what extent the house completed in 1637 was
based on the designs of 1616. An undated copy of a design for a
side elevation* has a much busier composition, with rusticated surrounds to ground-floor windows of different shapes
and a Venetian window and pediment to the central bridge –
details characteristic of early Jones. Whatever the history, it
seems probable that the final restrained form of the exterior
was not conceived until the 1630s.

Although not fitted up until that decade, the most striking
feature of the INTERIOR, the central cubic HALL in the s
block, may go back to the first plans. We know that Jones was
experimenting with cubes and double cubes elsewhere by
1620 (cf. the Banqueting House, Whitehall). The consistent
symmetry must have been as bewildering to contemporaries as
the exterior. The hall was no longer the traditional hall to live
in, but frankly a vestibule, if the biggest room in the house.
The simple plaster ceiling, with a centre circle originally
decorated by paintings by *Artemisia Gentileschi* (now at Marlborough House, Westminster, and replaced by a painting in
the style of *Thornhill*), is reflected almost identically in the
black and white marble floor laid in 1637. Only the gallery is a
little narrow and its wooden balustrade looks disappointingly
cheap. The state rooms on the first floor consist of the
QUEEN'S DRAWING ROOM, E of the hall, with a carved pine
ceiling, gilded pilasters, and a frieze with monogram of
Charles and Henrietta Maria; the adjoining CABINET to the
N, also with a carved ceiling, and originally with paintings of
Cupid and Psyche by *Jordaens* (sold in 1649); and the
QUEEN'S BEDROOM to the W. This has the most sumptuous
ceiling, with a cove decorated with grotesques (attributed to *de
Critz* or *Gooderick*) and a centrepiece with an allegorical paint-
ing (Aurora dispersing the Shades of Night), a replacement for
one removed during the Commonwealth (artist unknown).
No original fireplaces remain.‡ The alterations of the 1660s
converted the Queen's bedroom into her presence chamber
and the original drawing room into the King's presence chamber and linked them to the s block by *Webb*'s two new bridges.
Both have fine plaster ceilings by *John Groves*. The one on the
E is perhaps with its quatrefoil centrepiece a little more Baroque than Jones himself would have been. But essentially
Webb's style here is not different from Jones's. All the plaster
detail of wreaths, ovolo friezes, etc., is exceptionally pure.
The rooms in the N block, subdivided by *Webb*, were restored
to their original layout in 1935. The MAIN STAIRCASE to the

* At Worcester College, Oxford.
‡ Some of the fireplaces at Chiswick House (Ho) are based on lost fireplaces
from the Queen's House. Designs also survive of fireplaces by French craftsmen
who worked for Henrietta Maria.

E of the hall is no doubt the most impressive room, circular, running up beyond the first floor to the roof, with an open well ('vacuum in ye middle' is what Jones says) and no inner supports (as Bramante, for example, still has them at the Vatican, and Vignola at Caprarola). The idea comes from Palladio (Villa Capra, Vicenza). The balustrade is of a handsome repeating wrought-iron pattern (a double scroll with a tulip-like top, hence the name Tulip Staircase). The staircase in the S block is not original; its balustrade comes from Pembroke House, Whitehall Gardens, demolished in 1936.

Royal Naval Hospital and related Public Buildings

The Tudor palace was badly treated during the Commonwealth. For a time it was a biscuit factory for the troops in Scotland; later Dutch prisoners were kept in some parts. Charles II with grander visions of royal splendour was not satisfied with a restoration of the rambling brick buildings and decided to erect a new palace for himself in an up-to-date Baroque style. The architect was to be *John Webb*. The old buildings were pulled down, and nothing now survives of them except for an UNDERCROFT built in 1605–6, and now under the QUEEN ANNE BLOCK. It has plain, very short octagonal piers and simple chamfered ribs, and was originally 70 by 30 ft. The foundation stone of the new building was laid in 1664. The plan provided for three connected ranges on three sides of a courtyard open to the river, the whole to be in line with the Queen's House. Only the W range was built. It remains as KING CHARLES BLOCK, or to be more accurate the E parts of King Charles Block; for the N W pavilion was completed only in 1712, the S front is of 1769 (*James Stuart*), and the long W front of 1811–14 (*Yenn*). Webb's work of 1664–9 is characterized by a massiveness alien to Jones. Ground floor and first floor are both rusticated. The two-storeyed front of twenty-three windows' width is articulated by a pedimented centre and by angle pavilions of three bays with an attic storey. The angle pavilions have giant pilasters, the centre attached giant columns. Giant pilasters or columns rising straight from the ground always tend to make a building appear heavy, and the attic of the angle pavilion seems to press the pilasters down yet more. There are two entrances, one in the centre and one round the corner in the S side of the end pavilion, each leading to a staircase. The central entrance passes through a vestibule with apsed ends. Apart from this the block is simply planned, with a double sequence of state rooms divided by a spine wall. But the building was never furnished for royal use.

The next stage in the development of Greenwich came when William and Mary decided against living there, preferring the healthier air of Hampton Court. Mary made over the new building to the purpose of a Naval Hospital on the pattern of the Hôtel des Invalides and Chelsea Hospital for soldiers, an idea already proposed by James II. In 1694 *Wren*

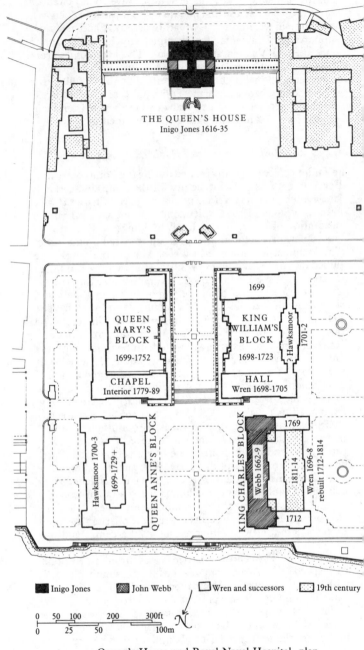

THE QUEEN'S HOUSE
Inigo Jones 1616-35

QUEEN
MARY'S
BLOCK

1699-1752

CHAPEL
Interior 1779-89

1699

KING
WILLIAM'S
BLOCK

1698-1723

Hawksmoor
1701-2

HALL
Wren 1698-1705

Hawksmoor 1700-3

1699-1729+

QUEEN ANNE'S BLOCK

KING CHARLES' BLOCK

Webb 1662-9

1769

1811-14

Wren 1696-8
rebuilt 1712-1814

1712

Inigo Jones   John Webb   Wren and successors   19th century

0 50 100   200   300ft
0   25   50   100m   N

Queen's House and Royal Naval Hospital, plan

was asked to prepare plans. The first were on a pattern similar to Webb's: a long courtyard open to the river with a central domed and porticoed structure at the s end. Then in 1699 Wren proposed something very similar to the final form: the central accent was given up, and the composition reduced to two symmetrical groups of buildings l. and r. of a long N–S axis, left entirely open and ending in the Queen's House, which was bound to appear small and distant in comparison with the Baroque scale of the new buildings. These were to consist of a block to match King Charles Block and then farther s, at right angles, connected by N–S colonnades, three parallel blocks, the southernmost to have the hall on the w, the chapel on the E, and to be crowned by tall towering domes. Hall, chapel, and colonnades were built accordingly, but the wards were arranged differently: two quadrangles were formed, each closed by the colonnades along the main axes. The quadrangles were called King William (w) and Queen Mary (E) Buildings.

The completion of the whole scheme took over fifty years, although progress was rapid at first.* Between 1696 and 1699 the foundations for all the main buildings had been dug, but by 1708 money was running out, and work stopped until 1712. The exterior of the great hall, the vestibule, and the cupola of the KING WILLIAM BLOCK, begun in 1698, had been compleated by 1705, and in 1708 *Thornhill* was starting work on the interior decoration of the hall (finished only in 1727). The w dormitory of the King William Block, built in 1701–2, was also ready internally by 1708, as was the s dormitory. The other work had advanced more slowly. The E of the QUEEN ANNE BLOCK dates from 1701–7, but the w part remained a brick carcase until given its interior in 1712 and its stone façade in 1725. The N pavilions were added only in 1725–31, the s pavilions in 1735. QUEEN MARY BLOCK was finished still later. In 1708 there were still remains of the Tudor palace in this area. The CHAPEL, vestibule, and cupola and the s and w dormitories were largely built between 1735 and 1743. Finally, to complete the story, the interior of the chapel, which had been burnt, was remodelled in 1779–89 by *Stuart*, who had in 1763 added a separate infirmary, later converted to the Dreadnought Seamen's Hospital (*see* below), and who in 1769 rebuilt the s w pavilion of the King Charles Building. The w range behind this was rebuilt in 1811–14 by *Yenn*, after a fire, replacing the more modest service block which had been added by *Wren* to Webb's palace building in 1696.

The first pensioners arrived in 1705; in 1708 there were 350, in 1755 1,550, in 1815 2,710. In the course of the c 19 more and more of the beneficiaries of the foundations were out-pensioners. The hospital closed in 1869, and in 1873 the Royal Naval College was moved from Portsmouth into the Hospital.

* For further details see J. H. V. Davies: 'The Dating of the Buildings of the Royal Hospital at Greenwich', *Archaeological Journal*, CXIII (1956).

The whole Hospital group has rightly been called 'the most
39   stately procession of buildings we possess' (Sir Charles
Reilly). The most curious thing about them, however, is that
they are indeed a procession, that is, that the space between
them is more telling than the architecture itself, in spite of
Wren's twin domes and colonnades. This independent life of
space is of course a very Baroque conception. What remains
somewhat unsatisfactory, at least when the group is viewed
from the river, is the narrowing from the two N blocks to the
two S blocks. Although this brings out the domes very
effectively, the breaking off of the colonnades below them
remains unjustified, a Baroque licence without Baroque *brio*.

Altogether Wren's buildings appear both more Baroque
and more classical than Webb's. The colonnades of coupled
columns (the motif came from Perrault's Louvre Colonnade),
the principal motif as the eye ranges along the vista and the
foot moves along the wide avenue from the river to the
Queen's House, is a static motif in its even rhythm. The walls
also are designed without disturbing motifs, and even the
domes repeat the columnar motif. Yet the outline of the domes
with clusters of columns projecting in the diagonals is
eminently Baroque and Italian (Borrominesque in origin). It
has occasionally been argued that these Baroque features are
due not to Wren himself but to his younger co-operator *Hawksmoor* (clerk of the works at Greenwich from the beginning,
and Deputy Surveyor from 1705), who might have introduced
them under the influence of Vanbrugh with whom he worked
concurrently at Castle Howard. The style of the Office of
Works about 1700 was no doubt largely one, though handled
by many executants. But the domes of Greenwich are no more
Baroque than the contemporary W towers of St Paul's, and the
colonnades and walls are far too calm in character for Vanbrugh. Vanbrugh was on the Board for Greenwich only after
1702, and was Surveyor from 1716, too late to have influenced
the main features of King William Building, which the
accounts show was well advanced by 1702. Soon after this date
there were some plans for alterations on a gigantic scale (attributed variously to both *Hawksmoor* and *Vanbrugh*). They
proposed closing the main axis towards the Queen's House by
a group of three buildings connected by oval colonnades, the
central one to house the chapel and have a huge giant portico
and a tall tower. Nothing of this seems to have been considered seriously.

The only building among the work completed by 1708
which is difficult to accept as coming from the hand of Wren is
the W range of KING WILLIAM BLOCK, which has often
(because of a misunderstanding over the date) been attributed
to Vanbrugh. But a reference in the accounts to the 'great
elliptical arch' shows that the exterior was in progress in 1702,
so that the building must have been designed at the latest by
1701. Both E and W fronts of this range are highly eccentric.
There is no proof that *Hawksmoor* was responsible, but the

style is certainly closer to him than to Wren (cf. Hawksmoor's Easton Neston). The w front is nineteen windows wide, with a bare square four-storey centre block of brick and a massive frontispiece of giant pillars and columns and a straight entablature and parapet. At the ends are three-bay, three-storey pavilions which, because they form the ends of the hall and s dormitory, are of quite different proportions. They have large round- and segment-headed windows and long curved pediments the whole width. Centre and angle pavilions are connected by only two-storeyed, that is, remarkably shrunk-looking, one-window bays which are, however, perversely over-emphasized by fantastic combined door and window surrounds crowned by open pediments. The fact that the front is of brick exposed, with stone only for the window dressings, is not to be explained by reasons of style but of economy. The E front of the same range is even more wilful. The centre of five 40 windows breaks forward, with pairs of huge giant pilasters flanking the outer windows and for the inner three a tight central one-window frontispiece with crowded pairs of columns high up on stilted bases and carrying an open much broken pediment, the whole of the three centre bays being pulled together by an arch in the upper attic storey. The window shapes are of the oddest, and rhythms clash everywhere. This E front faces the courtyard, which is closed on the opposite side by the back of the colonnade, breaking forward with a centre of six paired columns beneath a pediment flanked by blind bays with niches – features once again reminiscent of Wren at St Paul's. In the pediment sculpture commemorating Nelson, designed by *Benjamin West*, executed by *West* and *Panzetta* in 1810–12. No other parts of the Hospital share the perversity of the King William Building w range. Work by later architects on the exterior was either merely repetitive or utilitarian, e.g. the w front of the Queen Mary Building E range by *Ripley*.

The INTERIORS of the Hospital also are on the whole utilitarian, with the exception of the two main rooms: the hall and the chapel. The hall was very soon reserved for formal ceremonies only, the pensioners eating in the basement below, a room with groin-vaults supported by two rows of Tuscan columns. The PAINTED HALL is architecturally interesting 43 in that it is divided into a vestibule, a main hall, and an upper hall, each separated dramatically by steps and by fragments of cross walls narrowing the transitions. It is a theatrical and very Baroque device. Between the lower parts are giant pilasters and giant columns to form the opening. Between the upper parts the opening is narrower, lower, and arched, to add seclusion to the high table area. The central ceiling, by *Sir James Thornhill*, 1708–12, is perhaps the most effective piece of Baroque painting by any English artist, grand, abundant, and of a perfectly easy flow. It was cleaned in 1957–60, revealing a verve and brilliancy that had been obscured by fifteen coats of varnish. The main representation, framed by an oval,

shows William and Mary attended by the four cardinal vir
tues. Above the Queen hovers Concord, while Peace offers th
King an olive branch. He hands the cap of Liberty to Europe
Beneath his feet crouches Louis XIV, signifying Arbitrar
Power. Above the main group is Apollo on his chariot
beneath it Architecture with a drawing of the Hospital, an
Time exposing Truth. Farther down Pallas (Wisdom) an
Hercules (Strength) destroy the Vices. Along the border of th
oval are the signs of the zodiac. Under the arch towards th
vestibule a galley, the figure of Fame, and the English rivers
also portraits of mathematicians (N side Tycho Brahe an
Copernicus; S side Flamsteed, the first Astronomer Royal
with a scroll showing the eclipse of the sun of 1715). Under th
arch towards the upper hall is the taffrail of the 'Blenheim
with Victory flying towards her and the City of London befor
her, supported by Thames and Isis. On the side figures o
philosophers. Thornhill blocked up the N windows so as t
display the ceiling better, and filled them with paintings of th
Social Virtues (removed in 1824).

The paintings of the upper hall, done in 1718–25 by *Thorn
hill* in collaboration with *André* (who is known to hav
painted George I and his family), represent on the ceiling
Queen Anne and Prince George of Denmark, in the corner
Europe, Asia, Africa, and America, and on the walls th
family of George I and the landings of William III and George
I. In the right corner of the family group is *Thornhill*'s self
portrait. In the vestibule, whose decoration was finished i
1727, the four winds in chiaroscuro on the cupola, and wal
medallions with names of benefactors.

The CHAPEL was severely damaged by fire in 1779 an
reopened in 1789. *Athenian Stuart* was then Surveyor, bu
most of the detailed work is due to his Clerk of Works *Willian
Newton*. It is of the highest order amongst any done in the
new neo-Grecian spirit. In the octagonal vestibule four large
statues of Faith, Hope, Charity, and Humility designed b
Benjamin West and carried out in *Coade*'s artificial stone. On
the doorway into the chapel an excellent frieze by *John Bacon*.
The chapel itself has a shallow segmental vault and N and s
galleries on thin long brackets. The doors to the galleries are
set in blank arches counterfeiting coffered apses. At the w and
E ends coupled giant columns which may go back to the *Ripley*
design. In addition there is a smaller curved-out w gallery o
exquisite Ionic detail, and at the E end a vast altar painting by
West representing St Paul and the Viper, the colouring dark
and of Venetian character. In the spandrels *Coade* stone angels
by *West*. – The design of the PULPIT (formerly centrally
placed, as the top of a three-decker) is derived from the
monument to Lysicrates: circular, on Corinthian columns, o
exceptionally fine quality. The joiners were *Lawrence* and
Arrow. Oak and mahogany, with medallions of *Coade* stone
designed by *West* illustrating the life of St Paul, with scenes o
Athens including the Parthenon. – ALTAR RAIL. 1787. –

COMMUNION TABLE supported by *Coade* angels (gilded
c. 1950). – Brass CANDELABRA. – WALL PAINTINGS.
Monochrome figures between the clerestory windows by
Rebecca, De Bruyn, Catton, and *Milbourne.* The Ascension,
over the E end, also by *Rebecca.* – In the Hospital forecourt
a much weathered statue of George III as a Roman emperor
by *Rysbrack,* 1735.

Attached to the Hospital proper are the following buildings:

DREADNOUGHT HOSPITAL (originally hospital infirmary), to
the SW. By *James Stuart,* 1763–4. The W parts suffered much
in a fire of 1811. Utilitarian square block with an inner courtyard. Cemented, but no doubt originally exposed brickwork.
Interesting central arrangement of the original kitchen. No
specifically noteworthy interiors.

The NURSES' HOME, S of the Dreadnought Hospital, 1929 by
Sir Edwin Cooper, incorporates the old Hospital BOYS'
SCHOOL by *Newton,* 1783. To the l. of the Nurses' Home the
former BURIAL GROUND with a small three-bay building
recording that the first pensioner was buried here in 1749.

ENGINEERING LABORATORY, W of the Hospital. An ornate
one-storeyed building of 1875–9 with a giant order of attached
columns, rustication, and medallion decoration, somewhat in
the tradition of Cockerell.

TRAFALGAR QUARTERS, opposite the main E entrance to
the Hospital. Built in 1813 by *Yenn* for officers of the civil
administration of the Hospital. Two-storeyed, of yellow
brick, with a seven-bay one-storey Tuscan colonnade.

GREENWICH PARK. Several prehistoric remains and (between
the Observatory and Vanbrugh Castle) traces of a Roman
building (probably a Romano-British temple) have been
found of which a small part of plain red tessellated floor is
visible. The park received its brick wall under James I. Late in
the C 17 it was newly laid out with straight avenues up the hill
by the great *Le Nôtre,* Louis XIV's gardener, himself. It has
been open to the public since the C 18. Of buildings a pretty
exedra-faced C 18 CONDUIT remains;* also a neo-Georgian
REFRESHMENT PAVILION with colonnade, and a decorative
cast-iron BANDSTAND of *c.* 1880.‡ The most important building, however, is the OLD ROYAL OBSERVATORY, erected for
Flamsteed by *Christopher Wren* in 1675–6. It is of red brick
with dressings of wood made to look like stone, square in
shape, with an octagonal room on the upper floor, a top
balustrade, and two higher square turrets to the l. and r. of the
three-bay front. Wren said that the architectural features were
'a little for pompe'. In 1772–3 two pavilions were added
farther out and forward. The new building which became
necessary in 1858 is of plain brick with gables and distinguished by a bulbous dome (added in 1894 for a new 28-inch
refractor) which looks curious enough against the fantastic
skyline of the earlier structure. In 1897 a yet larger building

* Probably by *Hawksmoor,* who had special responsibility for conduits (MK).
‡ By the *Coalbrookdale Company.*

appeared, of red brick and terracotta, cruciform and with a central dome of 50 ft diameter for a 26-inch refractor. It now houses a planetarium. The more modern telescopes were removed with the Royal Greenwich Observatory to Herstmonceux, Sussex, after the Second World War.

Lower down in the park behind the Nurses' Home colossal STATUE of William IV, 1844 by *S. Nixon*, from the King William Street–Cannon Street junction in the City. E of the Observatory, bronze STATUE of General Wolfe, on a tall plinth, 1930 by *R. Tait McKenzie*. To the W a bronze casting of *Henry Moore*'s 'Standing Figure: Knife Edge'.

PERAMBULATIONS

1. W of the Hospital

Medieval Greenwich extended along GREENWICH CHURCH STREET from St Alfege to the river. Close to the river the old buildings have gone, and the Cutty Sark dominates a rather bleak plaza. Further S, on the W side, apart from a few traces of the late C17 (Nos. 15–17), brick, with wooden eaves cornice and high pitched roof) the main impression is of the C19. On the other side is a long stucco frontage, part of an improvement scheme by *Joseph Kay* of *c.* 1830 to which NELSON ROAD (built 1829) and COLLEGE APPROACH (1836), parallel turnings toward the Hospital, and KING WILLIAM WALK also belong. They are on the site of the C15 house of the Observant Friars. In Nelson Road facing terraces in a style to be compared, for example, with the contemporary West Strand Improvements in London or the building enterprises of Plymouth and Devonport: a recessed centre with Ionic columns flanked by pilasters, and rounded ends (the SW corner destroyed). College Approach is similar but a little more ornate, see especially the ends with tripartite windows. King William Walk is more eccentric, with exotic (Egyptian?) capitals. Opening off College Approach the MARKET of 1831 with a gateway on Tuscan columns. It backs on to the narrow TURNPIN LANE which winds through the centre of the site. At the S end of KING WILLIAM WALK, near the park, some older houses: No. 11, early C18, with later upper bow-window, and Nos. 12–15, early C18. By the park entrance in NEVADA STREET Nos. 10–13, four storeys, later C18, with canted upper bay-windows; further on the SPREAD EAGLE YARD, a formal stucco inn façade of the earlier C19, with central coach-way, facing the side of the THEATRE, 1871, altered and adapted in 1969 by *Brian Meeking*, with a new multi-storey exhibition-space-cum-foyer with boldly exposed concrete. (The theatre itself is long and thin, with an open stage.)

The theatre is at the foot of CROOM'S HILL, which is the pride of domestic architecture in Greenwich. There are not many streets near London which give so good and sustained an idea of the well-to-do private house from the C17 to the early C19. The street climbs upward, at first with quite urban terrace houses, and ends at Blackheath with the separate mansions of Chesterfield Walk. On the W side, first Nos. 6–12, an excellent terrace of 1721 (rainwater head); windows with keystones tied into the string course above, an unusual motif. Plain doorcases with fluted pilasters; good garden piers and railings. Then No. 14, set back, five windows wide, later C18. Nos. 16–18 are earlier – late C17, with later stucco. A varied group follows, mostly Georgian, set close to the road. No. 24 is especially pretty, with the main doorway set in a central bow-window, and a Venetian window on the first floor. No. 26, late C18, forms the return to Gloucester Circus (*see* below). No. 32 has an early C18 core with later projecting wings (the good doorcase with carved brackets brought from elsewhere). Then on the W CROOM'S HILL GROVE, a charmingly complete cul de sac, dated 1838 by the entrance, to which the next tall terrace in Croom's Hill belongs. No. 42 and Nos. 44–46, a pair with shared porch, are of 1818 (MK). No. 52 (THE GRANGE), hidden behind garden walls, is more compli-cated, with mid C17 and C18 work concealing an even older core. S front with four windows; a pedimented gable at one end with a circular window (in this corner a good upper room with coved ceiling). The W wing is mid C18. The pretty gazebo overlooking the street (restored in 1967) was built for Sir William Hooker (a later Lord Mayor) in 1672, probably by *Robert Hooke*. Brick with pyramidal roof, arched openings, one with a scrolled open pediment. Good plasterwork inside. Continuing up the hill, Nos. 54–60, a terrace built between 1766 and 1773 (MK). Now altered to flats, the central Ionic porch brought in. No. 66 is an exceptionally interesting ex-ample of a small house of the 1630s* with an exterior in the Artisan Mannerist fashion of those years (cf. the grander Cromwell House Highgate, Ca, and Kew Palace, Ri). A broad, relatively low frontage four windows wide, of brick, with pilasters on brackets, and blind panels used to articulate the upper floor. Two big gabled dormers. The plan is unambi-tious, a single pile with through passage leading to a back staircase tower. (Much altered inside; one original overmantel upstairs.) No. 68, five windows wide, after the R.C. church, was built by 1697 (MK). Higher up, between Croom's Hill and Chesterfield Walk, with its entrance front facing Blackheath, the MANOR HOUSE, built *c.* 1695 for Sir Robert Robinson, Lieutenant Governor of Greenwich Hospital, a double pile with identical front and back of exquisite doll's house sym-metry; plum brick with rubbed brick dressings. Two storeys, five narrow windows. Porch on brackets with shell cornice, steps with curved iron railings. To the SW, overlooking an

58

---

* The site was bought in 1634, according to B. Platts, *Country Life*, 17 Nov. 1966.

open green, CHESTERFIELD GARDENS, discreet neo-Georgian flats of 1937, extended in 1950 by *W. Braxton Sinclair*. (The fine stone doorcase between Nos. 10 and 11 with swan-necked open pediment came from Croom's Hill House, built 1723, demolished 1938. MK)

At the top of the hill several detached houses on the side towards the park: Hillside, Parkhall, and the White House, C 19 in appearance, but with older origins. HILLSIDE (under repair at the time of writing) incorporates a late C 17 cottage, but is now mainly C 19, cement-rendered. The land was acquired in 1716 by *John James*, who built PARKHALL to the S. Parkhall was intended (although never used as such) for his own occupation, and was completed by 1724. It was given an extra wing in 1800, and now has heavy mid C 19 stucco dressings. Inside, a good original staircase with twisted balusters, a columned screen to the entrance hall (now partitioned), and several panelled rooms. Converted to flats in 1932.* The WHITE HOUSE dates in origin from 1694, but has a mid Georgian stuccoed exterior with full-height bow probably built for Sir Harcourt Masters († 1745). Late C 17 garden walls.

Further on in CHESTERFIELD WALK two remain out of three houses built at the end of the C 17 against the edge of the park. MACARTNEY HOUSE is an irregular and confusing complex with several additions which probably incorporates one or two late C 17 buildings. Main front to the road of two storeys with an originally blind mezzanine storey in between. Six bays, three on the l. slightly recessed. *Soane* made additions in 1802 and also remodelled the interior (A small but handsome lobby with unfluted Doric columns remains.) Further extensions after 1886; conversion to flats 1925.

RANGER'S HOUSE, the second of the group, has been added to, so that it is now the most ambitious house on this side of the park. Seven bays, refronted in red brick, with a tripartite stone frontispiece, probably dating from the occupancy of Admiral Hosier (up to 1727). Doorway with Ionic columns, Venetian window above. Lower bow-fronted wings in yellow brick. In the S wing the gallery added in 1749–50, perhaps by *Isaac Ware*, for the fourth Earl of Chesterfield. The similar N wing with bow-window dates from after 1783. The gallery, later subdivided, was restored in 1959–60; since 1974 it has housed the Suffolk Collection of Tudor portraits formerly at Charlton Park, Wilts. Central stone-paved hall; good early C 18 staircase with three twisted balusters to the tread, and fluted newels. (Good panelled rooms upstairs.‡ From the corridor a spiral staircase provides access to the central cupola, which is seated inside, like a miniature gazebo.)

The third house whose origin went back to the 1690s, MONTAGUE HOUSE, was demolished in 1815. For remnants of

---

* Information from F. Kelsall.
‡ It is proposed to open these to the public.

its garden, which lay on the other side of the heath, *see* Lewisham (Le), Perambulation 1.

STREETS W OF CROOM'S HILL. The steep slopes between Croom's Hill and Greenwich South Street are covered with a delightful network of small streets. With a few exceptions, the houses are mostly of the later C 18/earlier C 19. The one grand scheme is GLOUCESTER CIRCUS, begun by *Michael Searles*, *c.* 1791 (cf. Lewisham (Le), Perambulation 1). Only the S part was built as originally planned (1791–1809), a plain crescent with three-bay houses arranged in a complex rhythm. Recessed entrances; projecting parts either four or two windows wide. Some of the two-bay parts pedimented. The terminal bays have mansards, and good end elevations with bow-windows and fanlights. The N side, completed only after 1840, was badly damaged in the Second World War. The best part is the NE corner (Nos. 1–8), of 1843. A terrace of similar date in BURNEY STREET to the N.* Minor earlier C 19 streets to the W: CIRCUS STREET, PRIOR STREET, BRAND STREET, with the later C 19 stucco-trimmed MORDEN ARMS. ROYAL HILL has at its foot some older houses, e.g. Nos. 30–36, an C 18 terrace with good doorcases; No. 38, later C 18; No. 42, altered, but with an early C 18 doorcase. Further on, also of the C 18, Nos. 50–52, 58–64, 80–82 (with early C 19 Gothic windows). HYDE VALE is on a more ambitious scale, developed from 1829, mostly with terraces of *c.* 1840 onwards (apart from one C 18 group, Nos. 56–64). HAMILTON TERRACE and its neighbours (No. 37 onwards) show the decline of classical traditions. Enjoyable minor villas and terraces can be found in ROYAL PLACE, DIAMOND TERRACE (Nos. 1–2 with good early C 19 balconies), and KING GEORGE STREET (especially complete), with small terraces on both sides of 1828–35, some of the earlier houses of the Hyde Vale estate.

At a higher level MAIDENSTONE HILL curves W from Point Hill, mid C 19‡ except for Nos. 2–8, modest early C 19, and No. 35, with a rather engaging wooden C 18 front taking advantage of the view N, five windows wide, with imitation-rustication to the ground floor. E of Point Hill is WESTGROVE LANE, with No. 1, 1789–90, three broadly spaced windows, and, further on, a purple brick house with a partly open ground floor by *Julian Sofaer*, 1963–5 (numbered as 1a Diamond Terrace). POINT HILL ends with POINT HOUSE, in WEST GROVE, the grandest of the C 18 houses, with views over Blackheath and towards the river. A house existed here by 1734 but the present appearance probably dates from the 1750s.‡ Five windows, three storeys, brick quoins, projecting pedimented centre with urns in the parapet. Unusual triangular oriel window on the top floor at back and front (the latter a

---

* Nos. 26–38 by *Richard Smirke Martyr*, 1839–40 (MK).
‡ Nos. 1–33 (College Place East) by *George Smith*, 1841; College Place West probably also by *Smith* after 1842 (MK).
§ Information from Mr Neil Rhind.

replacement). Later wings. (Good interior: panelled hall with Ionic columns; high-relief plasterwork to the staircase walls, the staircase with ornate paired balusters and carved, shaped tread-ends; projecting extension to the w with a fine plaster ceiling in the Adam style. AQ) Also in West Grove, No. 17, 1788,* No. 14, early C 18 altered, Nos. 9–12, a dominant High Victorian terrace of 1873, and Nos. 7–8, 6, 2, early C 19. At the corner with Hyde Vale a little red brick CONDUIT HEAD for the Naval Hospital, put up early in the C 18. From the top of Point Hill, the main road, BLACKHEATH HILL and its continuation Blackheath Road, leads down w to Deptford Bridge. For the s side *see* Lewisham (Le), Perambulation 1. On the N side a few C 18 houses, the best No. 89, late C 18, set back from the road, with nice fanlight and Tuscan porch. Further down in BLACKHEATH ROAD No. 31, *c.* 1776 by *Michael Searles* (MK), flanked by two groups of 1848 with pretty wooden trellised verandas, and the remains of earlier C 19 terraces: Nos. 37–45, and 72–74 (Union Place).

In the flatter, less interesting area between GREENWICH SOUTH STREET and GREENWICH HIGH ROAD there is less to note. In South Street, PENN'S ALMSHOUSES by *G. Smith*, 1884, decent red brick and stone, neo-Tudor; No. 91, early C 18 with carved brackets; and Nos. 1–11 and Nos. 13–15, an altered terrace of *c.* 1700 near the junction with the High Road. The E end of the High Road starts badly with an indeterminate wasteland, the site of an old station, redeemed only by a few buildings on the N side: the MITRE, 1831 classical, and *Trevor Dannatt*'s Greenwich Building Society extensions of 1975–6 (No. 281), neatly enfolding a C 19 building. Further w, opposite the station, QUEEN ELIZABETH'S ALMSHOUSES, founded in 1576 by William Lambarde, rebuilt in 1817 (probably by *Jesse Gibson*, surveyor to the Drapers' Company). The buildings are quite spacious, with cottages along three sides of a quadrangle, and a chapel with Ionic portico, pediment, and cupola in the centre of the s range. On the N side the better buildings are No. 141, the classical brick and stone former vestry hall of 1876 by *W. Wallen* (now a community centre); Nos. 165–169, C 18 altered; No. 189, the Prince of Orange, part of the station rebuilding (q.v.); Nos. 199–213, early C 19 pairs; No. 221, early C 18; and finally MUMFORD'S FLOUR MILLS, the last remnant of a major grain-milling centre. By *Aston Webb*, 1897, with an unusually ornate silo in Venetian style facing Deptford Creek. Opposite, the former ROYAL KENT DISPENSARY, 'instituted in 1783' as is proclaimed in bold lettering on the stucco-trimmed building by *Brandon & Ritchie* erected in 1855 after the dispensary moved here from Deptford. The building later became part of the MILLER GENERAL HOSPITAL; after the hospital closed, it was converted in 1980–1 for a Girls Regional Assessment Centre by the Borough Architect's Department (*P.*

---

* By *Michael Searles* (MK). First-floor windows in arches; Doric porch with bucrania.

Hockaday and *D. Griffin*). To the l., set back, an attractive former chapel built as the Greenwich Tabernacle in 1799–1801,* converted to a mortuary in 1980–1. Projecting three-bay centre, openings within round-headed arches. The rest of the hospital buildings were replaced in 1980–1 by borough housing, low, of yellow brick, with some Georgian allusions.‡

STREETS TO THE S. In EGERTON DRIVE, to the N off Black-heath Road, a good run of early C19 villas with large Ionic porches. In BURGOS GROVE to the W No. 2, C18, with a flat, oddly detailed doorway with pilasters and pediment, worth a look. N of the railway nothing worth a detour except, perhaps, the block of maisonettes in CREEK ROAD by *Stirling & Gowan*, 1965, a similar design to those in Trafalgar Road (*see* Perambulation 2); but because the site is to the N of the main road the projecting wings and access balconies face N, so that the street frontage is less arresting.

2. E of the Hospital

The pendant to King William Walk on the E side of the Hospital is PARK ROW, which starts with the stuccoed and pilastered TRAFALGAR TAVERN by the river, 1837 by *Joseph Kay*, its cast-iron balconies and bow-windows with canopies specially charming. Restored as a restaurant in 1968 by *S. Hendry & Smith*. Further E, shockingly squeezed in between council flats and a power station, TRINITY HOSPITAL, founded by the Earl of Northampton in 1613 but much altered. The plan is a quadrangle, like the two other almshouses founded by the Earl.§ The present battlemented and cemented exterior with an entrance tower on the N towards the river looks early C19 and belongs no doubt to the same date as the rebuilding of the chapel with its thin Gothic rib-vault, namely 1812. To the chapel projecting on the E corresponds the hall on the W, across the cloistered quadrangle. This arrangement of rooms and some details (for example the S staircase) are original. In the chapel E window Flemish early C16 stained glass representing the Crucifixion, the Agony in the Garden, and the Ascension. Monument to the Earl of Northampton by *Nicholas Stone*, unfortunately very framentary. Kneeling figure of the Earl and four smaller figures of Virtues. These are supposed to be the first English copies of antique work (presumably from Lord Arundel's marbles). The kneeling figure was originally placed above a canopy. The monument was transferred to Greenwich from Dover Castle by the Mercers' Company in 1696, to which time the Gothic Revival (very early Gothic Revival) tracery belongs. Beyond, BALLAST QUAY, a charmingly secluded corner by the river, mostly

* Information from Mr C. F. Stell.

‡ The Miller General Hospital buildings included two round wards of the later C19, and an outpatients' department, a well designed brick building in quite a progressive style, by *Pite & Fairweather*, 1927.

§ At Clun, Salop, and Castle Rising, Norfolk.

with late Georgian houses, although a few may be older (No.
10, and perhaps the core of Nos. 12–16). At the end the
HARBOURMASTER'S OFFICE, brick and stone with a bold
Italianate cornice, 1854–5. Further downstream, amidst
factories and wharves, a curiosity, ENDERBY HOUSE, built
by the famous whaling family c. 1846, with an angled bay-
window looking out over the river.

Back in Park Row, on the E side facing the Hospital, Nos. 25–26,
a large, early C19 pair, brick with stone dressings; then the
Trafalgar Quarters belonging to the Hospital (q.v. above). At
the end of Park Row, PARK VISTA skirts the edge of the
park. THE CHANTRY, backing on to it, is a rambling irregular building incorporating some C16 brickwork, the remains
of outbuildings of Henry VIII's palace of Placentia (Queen
Elizabeth's Conduit). To the street the wing on the r. is
stucco, of c. 1800, the part on the l. C20. On the building is a
carved stone replica (1975) of a lost wall plaque with the Tudor
royal arms; also an empty circular medallion with wreaths
reminiscent of the medallions at Hampton Court. On the
other side of Park Vista several good houses: Nos. 1–12, a late
Georgian terrace; No. 13 (MANOR HOUSE), a plain five-bay
two-storey early C18 front with modillioned eaves cornice, a
gazebo on the roof; No. 15, later C18 altered; and Nos. 16–18,
with Park Place 1791 under a pediment, and arched ground-
floor windows, by *James Taylor*. Off to the N in GREENWICH
PARK STREET early C19 terraces.

To the N and E of Park Row an early Victorian artisan area, with
some pleasantly complete terraces, e.g. in PELTON ROAD.
This was a planned layout by *George Smith* for Morden College, begun after 1838, completed c. 1865. *Smith* designed
many of the houses (e.g. Nos. 27–65 Pelton Road, 1842) (MK),
brick with stone or stucco dressings. A few early C19 houses
remain in OLD WOOLWICH ROAD: Nos. 122–124, with
curved end bays, No. 126, and Nos. 130–142 (Morden Place)
dated 1808. The main traffic now runs to the S of this along
TRAFALGAR ROAD. On the S side is a rare example of work
by *Stirling & Gowan* for the L.C.C. (1965–8), a quadrangle of
four-storey maisonettes with a carefully balanced, not quite
symmetrical front to the road, with the ingenious motif of
upper balconies passing through projecting wings. The
monumental expanses of plain brickwork, the rather self-
conscious corner windows, and the play of cubic volumes
recall, no doubt intentionally, the workers' housing of the
early Modern Movement on the continent. In contrast, directly opposite, HARDY COTTAGES, the remains of an unpretentious L.C.C. estate of 1900–2 on an early slum-clearance site.

The grander buildings E of the park are further up the hill,
although MAZE HILL has less than Croom's Hill on the W
side. Reminders of an earlier age are Nos. 47–49, an early C18
pair, especially well detailed. Brown brick with red brick
dressings, brick quoins and angle pilasters. The front is of six
bays, with the centre four projecting, the two entrances con-

tained within a Doric porch. Stone keystones to the narrow windows. An unusual plan, with staircases between front and back rooms: see the windows in the flank walls. (Good panelled interiors.) Nos. 53–55 are c. 1855, Tudor, diapered brick, Nos. 111–115 1750* with a carriage entrance below No. 111.

The most interesting house is at the corner of Westcombe Park Road: VANBRUGH CASTLE, *Sir John Vanbrugh*'s private house, built in 1718–26. In 1718 Vanbrugh acquired twelve acres in this area on which he built a number of houses for members of his family. His own is the only survivor; others which remained until 1910 are known from sketches.‡ Vanbrugh Castle occupies the best position, close to the park and on an eminence visible from the Hospital (Vanbrugh was the Hospital Surveyor from 1715 until his death). It is a memorable building, a private house consciously designed to arouse associations with the Middle Ages. Such ideas were not unknown among the designers of the great Elizabethan and Jacobean mansions (Wollaton, Bolsover), but this must be the first example of such a house designed by an architect for his own use. Its crenellated garden walls with turrets and its tower with conical roof conjure up dreams of a more masculine (to use one of Vanbrugh's favourite aesthetic terms), more heroic past. The house was in 1719 smaller than it is now, a symmetrical block with projecting end bays towards the entrance side and a circular stair-turret in the centre of the front. The entrance is to the side of this, the only asymmetrical element. On the N side a central bow-window overlooking the view towards the river. The first extension to the E was made probably after Vanbrugh's late marriage in 1719, and gave the house an asymmetrical shape, a revolutionary thing to do at this time. The s projection from this dates partly from the c 18, partly from after 1907. To the N there was another c 18 wing running out from the w corner, and to the w a low kitchen building (both now destroyed). The motifs of the elevations are characteristic of Vanbrugh: plain surfaces with mouldings reduced to the heavy strings which provide a strong horizontal emphasis. Narrow round-headed arches; bold chimneys. Apart from the battlements the only overt medieval detail is the use of a form of machicolation in place of a cornice. The interior (now divided up, converted by *Gordon Bowyer & Partners* c. 1979) has small rooms and narrow vaulted corridors. The gateway replaces the original one, removed for road widening c. 1906.

On the w side of Maze Hill a terrace of 1807, formerly the infirmary of the Naval Asylum School. (No. 34 has a stone staircase with octagonal well and domed ceiling; No. 38 a similar staircase around an elongated octagon.)

---

* Dates from Neil Rhind.

‡ The estate was entered by a gateway at the s end. The other houses included two battlemented towers of four storeys, the low one-storey 'nunnery' also called 'Mince Pie House', in between, and Vanbrugh House, embattled, with circular turrets.

To the E along VANBRUGH PARK by the edge of the heath. After Nos. 15–26* (good detached Victorian villas) one of the most interesting housing estates in the borough, by *Geoffrey Powell* of *Chamberlin, Powell & Bon*, 1961–5 for Greenwich Borough Council, extending N to Westcombe Park Road over nearly 7 acres (density 90 p.p.a.). Only one tall block, the concrete frame expressed boldly, the windows recessed slightly in between the uprights, the design lightened by the unexpected motifs of lunette windows in the basement and greenhouse roofs on the top. The rest of the housing is arranged in an informal grid of two storeys, unassuming, flat-roofed terraces, some with top flats approached by broad balconies over the garage roofs. Simple elevations with neat bands of upper windows. The use of distressingly unappealing cheap painted breeze blocks for the walls made it possible to be generous over the landscaping, which is exceptionally lavish, with plenty of mature trees preserved among a network of paths and communal spaces between stock brick garden walls and pergolas. From Vanbrugh Park Road the approach is between two brick piers, like a vestigial gatehouse, a faint echo perhaps of the same firm's entrance designs for the Barbican.

At the end of Vanbrugh Park mostly mid C19 terraces (Nos. 34–43). Near the junction with Old Dover Road, off to the N, BROADBRIDGE CLOSE, a cosy group of brick old people's flats for Morden College, by the College Surveyor, *Percy W. Reed*, 1951, but in the style of thirty years earlier. In WESTCOMBE PARK ROAD there are a few mid C19 stuccoed houses (Nos. 13–19 Goldsmith's College hall), but most are in a red brick Queen Anne style, of after 1876, when the estate was developed. In MYCENAE ROAD the only important earlier survival is Woodlands, now the local history library (*see* Public Buildings). No. 99 is by *E. R. Robson*, 1881–2, a large house of red brick with quite picturesque half-timbered gables (good interiors). In RUTHIN ROAD further NW, HOLYWELL CLOSE, a pleasant composition of 1974–5, pitched roofs, irregularly grouped, an early example of revival of the vernacular mode by the G.L.C. (job architect *John Hopkinson*).

3. *Blackheath and E of Blackheath*

BLACKHEATH itself is a flat, fairly featureless plain crossed by roads. Its more attractive southern edges lie in Lewisham (Le; q.v., Perambulation 1). To the E is a suburban area without much character which grew from the early C19 onwards. The best terraces face the heath: VANBRUGH TERRACE, E of the S end of Maze Hill, mid C19, Italianate; BLACKHEATH TERRACE, at the beginning of Shooters Hill Road (Nos. 7–33), 1839–41, with the shared pediments characteristic of so many houses in the Blackheath area (No. 37 dates from 1845); and to

* By *H. W. Spratt* (NR).

the s St Germans Place, facing w, with a mixture of early
c 19 houses and pairs much restored after war damage.* More
villas continue along the s side of Shooters Hill Road
(Nos. 2–20). Some way further e Nos. 141–155, of 1845, with
an unusual rhythm of rounded bays beneath deep eaves. n of
Shooters Hill Road St John's Park, a mid Victorian
suburb now truncated by the Rochester Way underpass. The
church is on an island site. Some new insertions to its s; in the
former vicarage garden, facing Langton Way, housing for
the elderly and disabled by *Trevor Dannatt & Partners*, 1975–
7, with splayed wings building up to three storeys, and many
canted windows to catch the sun. No. 4A Langton Way, by
Peter Bell & Richard McCormack, 1975, is an especially well
designed single-storey house, with garage neatly included, on
a grid plan, with interlocking indoor and outdoor spaces. s of
Shooters Hill in the neighbourhood of Morden College a few
late Victorian and Edwardian houses in Kidbrooke Grove:
No. 37 by *Reginald Blomfield*, 1906, in the style of *c.* 1700,
with eaves cornice and shell porch; No. 39 by *Belcher & Joass*,
1912; and opposite, No. 36 by *Belcher*, 1888, a large one-
storey mullioned-and-transomed villa with big hipped wings;
an unconventional design (much altered in 1922–3; n r). Central loggia on the garden side. Separate roughcast and brick
service cottage. Round the corner in Kidbrooke Gardens
No. 22 is by *Arthur M. Torrance*, 1905, again in the style of
c. 1900. A little way e in Westbrook Road Nos. 2a–c, 1971
by *Robin Simpson & Associates*, a good recent house, low, of
plum brick, stepping down to the garden. Further s in
Morden Road a few large c 19 Italianate mansions (e.g.
No. 4, 1858 by *W. G. & E. Habershon*).

4. Blackheath Park

The area e of Lee Road, now called Blackheath Park, formerly
belonged to Wricklemarsh Manor, owned in the later
c 17 by Sir John Morden, the builder of Morden College on its
e edge (*see* Public Buildings), then in the early c 18 by Sir
Gregory Page, for whom in 1723 *John James* built a very grand
Palladian mansion. The estate was sold to John Cator in 1783.
He demolished the house (re-erecting parts at his own house at
Beckenham Place, *see* Lewisham (Le), Perambulation 5) and
began to develop the grounds. The earliest new house to be
built was the present Presbytery in Cresswell Park,
just e of Blackheath Village, 1787, quite a grand three-storey
stone-faced front, five windows wide, with a Tuscan porch
approached up a double flight of steps. The Paragon on the
northern edge of the estate followed in the 1790s (*see*
Lewisham (Le), Perambulation 1). The rest of the estate is an
exceedingly handsome layout of 1806 with wide, straight,
tree-lined avenues (Blackheath Park, Pond Road, Foxes Dale)

---

* The contemporary proprietary chapel has been demolished.

which were built up slowly from *c.* 1819, mostly with detached or semi-detached villas, generously spaced. The earlier
houses are at the N end. Tucked away in the gaps are some
exceptionally interesting clusters of mid C 20 flats and houses,
mostly by *Eric Lyons* for Span (*see* below).

BLACKHEATH PARK has the best selection of C 19 houses. It
starts on the N side with No. 1, a Wrenaissance LODGE to the
estate, late C 19. Then Nos. 7–21, a plain brick late Georgian
terrace of irregular height, followed by a mixture of stuccoed
or stucco-trimmed villas. Opposite, two late Victorian houses
of 1896 by *Aston Webb*: No. 2 (Windermere), a spreading Old
English front of half-timber and roughcast over brick; and
No. 4 (The Gables), also brick and roughcast, but more
dependent on C 17 Artisan sources. Further on, No. 10, by
Patrick Gwynne, 1968, a design which sets out to shock, with
slate-hung panels and tinted glass walls, alien materials in this
area. An eyecatching spiral approach up to a central front door
flanked by projecting canted bays. No. 20, *Peter Moro*'s own
house, 1958, is a much more reticent affair, a neat rectangle
with overhanging upper floor, timberclad on the garden side;
split-level interior. More Italianate villas of *c.* 1830–40 follow,
with some especially large examples in big gardens near the
end. Varied façades: No. 99, five bays with projecting wings;
No. 101, five bays with pilasters; No. 103, pedimented wings
with tripartite windows. (BROOKLANDS in Brooklands Park
was *George Smith*'s own house, 1826, a relatively early example
of an Italianate stuccoed villa with polygonal tower and deep
projecting eaves. MK) Other survivals are more scattered.
POND ROAD has pretty stuccoed examples on a smaller scale
(Nos. 4–12). On the W edge of the estate, in LEE ROAD,
assorted villas, both modest (Nos. 51, 53, 63–69) and the
grander type with shared pediments (Nos. 71–73, 75–77 (with
nice verandas), 83–85). On the S boundary in MANOR WAY a
small colourful Italianate LODGE. To the N in PRIORY PARK,
PRIORY LODGE, with very pretty ironwork and a tall three-
storey canted bay at the back. Opposite is the battlemented
tower of the OLD PRIORY, C 19 Gothic, an exception in the
area, now sandwiched between demonstratively new parts of
yellow brick.

THE PRIORY, a group of flats S of Priory Park, is a good
introduction to the Blackheath SPAN ESTATES, the first private housing after the Second World War where as much
emphasis was laid on the surroundings as on interiors. The
earliest of these enterprising private developments, designed
by *Eric Lyons* with the architect-turned-developer *Geoffrey
Townsend*, are at Twickenham and Richmond (Ri; q.v.),
but Blackheath has the greatest number and variety. Their
specially leafy and intimate character (most have less than
forty dwellings and many under twenty) owes much to their
secluded sites, tucked away off private roads, and exempt from
the deadening effect of road engineers' requirements. Cars
are not totally excluded but their needs never appear to take

precedence over gardens and greenery.* Some groups are flats only, some a mixture of flats and low, narrow terrace houses. An important discovery was that with economical planning (e.g. open-plan interiors) houses with both private and public gardens could be built at densities hitherto reserved for flats.‡ The 1970s estates have larger three-storey houses for more affluent buyers. Their more angular style, with brick surfaces predominating, can easily be distinguished from the cosier mixture of stock brick, tile-hanging, and weatherboarding used in the 1950s and 60s.

The following tour proceeds from S W to N E. Space permits little more than a list. THE PRIORY (1954–6), like the later South Row (see Lewisham (Le), Perambulation 1), has flats only, in low blocks happily grouped around informal courtyards, with vistas through open ground-floor lobbies. Adjoining to the W, PARK ROW, Lee Road, a group of nine houses (1963). Further N, at the corner of Lee Road and Blackheath Park, SPANGATE (1964), another group of flats, pleasantly proportioned. The most extensive Span area is a little to the E, at the corner of FOXES DALE. HALLGATE, facing Blackheath Park, is another group of flats (1958) with a broad passage through to the gardens behind. Within the passage wall a SCULPTURE by *Keith Godwin* called The Architect and Society, a small oppressed figure within a square niche, commissioned to celebrate one of Eric Lyons's planning victories. Immediately to the S THE HALL, developed at different times (44 flats and 42 houses of 1957–8, a later more mannered terrace of tall houses along Foxes Dale of 1967). Along BROOKLANDS PARK to the E more houses of 1964. E again is THE LANE (1964), running S from Blackheath Park, an awkward site very tightly planned, with short rows of houses at right angles to the approach road. Jettied upper floors and split-pitched roofs. HOLM WALK opposite has taller, more formal brick terraces of 1978. Further N off Morden Mews THE KEEP (1958), like The Hall 2, is an early, quite large group of tile-hung houses. CORNER GREEN (1959), on the other side of the railway line (reached 105 from Pond Road), is memorable for its more open layout, with weatherboarded houses clustered round a green. CORNER KEEP (1979) has ten houses linking the two groups. The easternmost estates are THE PLANTATION (E of Morden Road), 1962, trim yellow brick terraces with white boarding, and PARK END to its S (at the end of Blackheath Park), 1967, with split-level roofs and, unusually, with private spaces in

---

* Maintenance of the communal gardens and exteriors was undertaken by residents' associations with Span as ground landlord, important factors in the success of the estates (nearly all the Span schemes were originally sold as leasehold properties).

‡ The densities of the schemes up to the mid 1960s were indeed slightly higher than the recommended L.C.C. figure for the area. As examples, in persons per acre, with completion dates: The Priory (flats only), 1956, 67; The Hall Phase 2 and Hallgate (houses and flats), 1958, 77; Corner Green (houses), 1959, 70; The Plantation (houses), 1962, 70; The Lane (houses), 1964, 75. Later schemes are more spacious: Park End (houses), 1967, 60; Holm Walk (houses), 1978, 50.

front as well as behind. The porches have extra rooms attached. As a moralizing postscript, the tour can end with two council estates. BROOKLANDS PARK is an L.C.C. estate of 1958, with five-storey point blocks and low terraces agreeably grouped among mature trees around an old pond and conduit house. Much L.C.C. work was still at this time comparable to Span in its concern with its setting, and in this case is barely higher in density (69 p.p.a.). Yet here in embryo are those features, point blocks freely grouped, which were to prove such a disastrous recipe a few years later. A little further S, off Weigall Road, a still less acceptable solution of the 1960s, the G.L.C.'s grim grey concrete FERRIERS ESTATE (completed 1970), an extreme example of the stark geometry produced by industrialized building methods.

5. Charlton

The old centre of the meeting of Charlton Road and Charlton Church Lane is small, and still has some village character, although it is surrounded by later C19 and C20 housing on all sides. Apart from the C17 church of St Luke, and Charlton House and its outbuildings (*see* Churches *and* Public Buildings, above), no buildings visibly of before the C19 remain in the village centre although the attractively stuccoed BUGLE HORN INN is of late C17 origin. The only rural survival now is a sweet weatherboarded cottage some way to the W in CHARLTON ROAD (No. 80). No. 103 (Kingsbury Lodge) is a white stuccoed early C19 villa. Also in the neighbourhood of Charlton Road several contrasting areas of public housing. FAIRLAWN to the S is a large council estate with the usual regular grid of walk-up flats of the 1940s onwards, enlivened by a few daring details such as inset curved concrete balconies. The earliest parts (CHERRY ORCHARD), immediately S of Charlton Road, were completed in 1947 (*Borough Engineer's Department*). Later seven-storey block by *T. P. Bennett & Son* further E. To the S, in RECTORY FIELDS CRESCENT, PERRYGROVE, an old people's home, 1961–4 by *Stirling & Gowan* for the L.C.C., an inward-looking retreat on a compact horseshoe plan, with the Louis-Kahn-inspired castellated roof-line which became popular in the 1960s. To the N, closer to the village, THORNHILL, L.C.C. point blocks of c. 1960, picturesquely grouped on a slope among trees, in the Roehampton manner. Off CHARLTON CHURCH LANE, COUTTS HOUSE, a less appealing stack of concrete boxes of c. 1970, building up to an eight-storey centre. As an antidote to all this one should look at the CHARLTON ESTATE, around Fairfield Grove and Charlton Lane, to the E of the village, straightforward pantiled and roughcast cottage housing built for Greenwich in 1920–1 by *Alfred Roberts*.

WOOLWICH

CHURCHES

The medieval parish churches were St Nicholas Plumstead, which, although much added to, alone keeps some medieval fabric; St Mary Magdalene Woolwich, rebuilt in the C 18; and St John the Baptist Eltham, rebuilt in the C 19. Little of interest among the C 19 buildings; minor works only, much altered, by *Pugin* (St Peter, R.C., 1842), *G. G. Scott* (St Barnabas, 1857–9), *Street* (Holy Trinity Eltham, 1870), and *Butterfield* (St Michael, 1887–90).* One rewarding C 20 church, however: St Saviour Eltham, by *Welch & Lander* and *Cachemaille Day*, 1932–3, the first in London to be built in a radically modern style.

(ALL SAINTS, Bercta Road, off Footscray Road w of Avery Hill Road, New Eltham. 1898 by *P. Dollar*; red brick, lancet style. Perp chancel 1930 by *T. F. Ford*.)

ALL SAINTS, Ripon Road, E of Woolwich Common, Shooters Hill. 1956 by *T. F. Ford*, replacing a bombed church begun in 1873. Brick, with a small tower with octagonal top; Greek cross plan; primly eclectic details. – MURAL by *Hans Feibusch*.

ASCENSION, Timbercroft Lane, s w of King's Highway. Begun 1903 by *A. E. Habershon*. W and E ends 1911. Brick with terracotta; polychrome interior.

(CHRIST CHURCH, Shooters Hill. 1855–6 by *Tress & Chambers*. Small, E.E.)

GARRISON CHURCH OF ST GEORGE, Grand Depot Road. Gutted in the Second World War and preserved as a fragmentary ruin. 1863 by *T. H. Wyatt*. Built when Lord Herbert was Secretary of State for War, and thus on the example of Wilton church, Wiltshire, that is, as an Early Christian–Italian Romanesque basilica. It was an ambitious, forceful building, with much structural polychromy and marble and mosaic decoration inside. Stock brick with red and blue (vitrified) brick trimmings. W rose window with spandrels in blue, red, and green stone mosaic. A Lombard porch below on Aberdeen granite columns. Open side porches in front of the recessed W wall of the aisles. Tall E apse with Lombard dwarf gallery, and small aisle apses. The aisles had galleries on iron supports, hence the two-storeyed aisle windows, the lower ones with thick gables. The clerestory windows were small, treated as a dwarf gallery.

HOLY TRINITY, Southend Crescent, s of Westmount Road, Eltham. 1868–9 by *Street*. Transept, chancel, and chancel aisles, pretty in detail, if very minor in Street's *œuvre*. Additions of 1909 by *Sir A. Blomfield & Son* (new E window, W end

---

*Demolished: ST MARGARET, Vicarage Road, Plumstead, 1858–9 by *William Rickwood*, ragstone, Perp, with a tower; chancel 1899 by *R. J. Lovell*; ST JAMES, Burrage Road, 1855, stock brick, with Italianate bell-turret; HOLY TRINITY, Beresford Square, 1833 by *J. D. Hopkins*, small, stuccoed, with a small w tower and an interior with galleries with two-storey columns.

of nave, s chapel). The chancel was extended into the nave at this time and refurnished. – (Carved REREDOS by *W. D. Caröe*; chancel panelling and decoration by *C. E. Kempe*; s chapel REREDOS and rood 1916, also by *Kempe*. – STAINED GLASS by *Kempe & Co.* and *Powell*.)

(ST ANDREW, Court Road, Mottingham.* 1878–9 by *E. F. C. Clarke*; red brick. Chancel and porch 1912 by *E. J. Gosling*.)

ST BARNABAS, Rochester Way. By *Sir G. G. Scott*, 1857–9. Built as the Naval Dockyard Church and in 1933 bodily removed to its present site. Modest size, brick with stone dressings, asymmetrical with turret. Gutted in the Second World War, and restored with a sickly Regency wedding-cake interior with tripartite Adamish arcades by *T. F. Ford & Partners*. Apse with pink and orange *Feibusch* mural.

ST JOHN THE BAPTIST, Eltham High Street. The old parish church, rebuilt in the late C 17, was replaced in 1872 by a large E.E. building by *A. W. Blomfield*. Later s w tower and spire. – (ROYAL ARMS. Early C 19. – STAINED GLASS. N aisle windows by *Burlison & Grylls*; E and W windows post-Second-World-War, E by *Comper*, W by *Barber*.)

ST LUKE, Westmount Road, Eltham. 1906–7 by *Temple Moore*. Meant to have a s w tower. Plain rectangular piers, fine wagon roof. s aisle and chapel 1933 (by *J. Tolhurst*). The N and s aisles are surprisingly different in their arcades as well as their roofs.

(ST MARK WITH ST MARGARET, Old Mill Road, W of King's Highway, Plumstead Common. Rebuilt by *David Bush*, 1976, with furnishings and glass from the demolished St Mark.‡)

ST MARY MAGDALENE, St Mary Street, Woolwich. One of the churches rebuilt with money from the Fifty New Churches Act of 1711, but begun only in 1727 and not completed until 1739. The builder was the Deptford bricklayer *Matthew Spray*, though he may not have designed it. Large, of stock brick, with two-storey arched windows and a plain W tower. Interior with galleries on crude octagonal supports and Ionic columns between these and the gently vaulted nave ceiling. The galleries and an aisle were closed off for offices and cafeteria in 1961. Chancel added in a mildly classical style by *J. O. Scott*, 1893–4. – In the s chancel chapel finely carved REREDOS with fluted Ionic columns, Creed, and Lord's Prayer. – (STAINED GLASS. A window by *H. Hendrie*, *c.* 1918. P. Cormack) – MONUMENTS, in the churchyard. To the memory of Mrs Maudslay, wife of the inventor and manufacturer, the remains of a large plain sarcophagus chest of cast iron. – Thos. Cribb, the boxer, † 1848, a lion with his paw on an urn, pathetic and a little ridiculous, inscribed 'Respect the ashes of the dead.'

(ST MARY (C. of E. and United Reformed), Greenlaw Street, NW of Rectory Place. Fittings brought from the demolished Presbyterian church in Woolwich New Road§ include ROYAL

* For Mottingham *see also* Bromley.
‡ Of 1901–2 by *C. H. M. Mileham*, Romanesque.
§ 1842, hideous Romanesque by *T. L. Donaldson*.

ARMS of George III, a rarity in Nonconformist churches. CFS)

ST MICHAEL, Borgard Road, E of Frances Street, Woolwich. Chancel begun 1875 by *J. W. Walters*, brick, E.E., with a vault; wide nave by *Butterfield*, 1887–9. Aisles and a w transept were intended; narrow aisle and SW transept added in 1955 by *T. F. Ford*. Interior with short round piers and low clerestory, with a band of coloured tiles below it, and a painted ceiling. – (REREDOS, stone and marble, by *Hems*.)

(ST MICHAEL, Abbey Wood Road. 1908 by *Blomfield & Son*.)

ST NICHOLAS, High Street, Plumstead. Of the medieval church the w and s walls of the former nave (now the s aisle) and the s transept survive, even though badly damaged in the Second World War (restored 1959 by *T. F. Ford & Partners*). They are late C12 and C13 respectively as the remains of the two-centred, arched doorways and windows show. The N aisle, added in the C15 to the medieval nave and forming the present nave (arcades with four hollow-chamfered arches on octagonal columns), was rebuilt in 1818. The church was restored in 1867–8 by *C. H. Cooke* with aggressive Dec tracery and much enlarged in 1907–8 by *Greenaway & Newberry*, with a new brick N aisle and chancel and a new chapel on the site of the old chancel in mildly Arts and Crafts Perp (reduced in size in the 1950s after war damage). The w tower, which dates from 1662–4 (not a usual date for church-building activity), has windows with elementary brick tracery, battlements, and embattled pinnacles. – STAINED GLASS. E window by *M. Travers* (P. Cormack). – (Post-war furnishings: three ALTARS by *S. Dykes Bower*; REREDOS PAINTING by *D. Towner*.)

ST SAVIOUR, Middle Park Avenue, Eltham. 1932–3 by *Welch & Lander* and *N. F. Cachemaille-Day*. A remarkably successful brick church of bold outline, one of the first in London to be built in a modern style. Short, broad, square tower at the E end (cf. Cachemaille-Day's later churches in NW London). The detail, especially inside, is derived from certain 'Expressionist' German brick mannerisms. But they come off, even the brick pulpit. The piers are set so that angles face the nave. The aisles are kept very low. Poured concrete ceiling. All windows extremely tall and narrow, at the E end filled with blue glass. Jagged, somewhat outré, REREDOS, with figure of Christ by *Donald Hastings*. The fabric not in good condition at the time of writing (1981).

CHRISTCHURCH (R.C.), Eltham High Street. 1890 by *Scoles & Raymond*. Priory buildings 1963 by *F. G. Broadbent & Partners*. – SCULPTURE of Christ in Glory on the s gable wall by *James Butler*.

(ST BENET (R.C.), Abbey Grove, N of Abbey Wood Road, Abbey Wood. 1909 by *T. Coyle*.)

(ST CATHERINE LABOURÉ (R.C.), Woolwich Road. 1961 by *Walters & Kerr Bate*.)

ST PETER (R.C.), Woolwich New Road. By *A. W. N. Pugin*, begun 1842; chancel and side chapel 1887–9 by *F. A. Walters*. Big E window between elaborate buttresses. w front with large

Dec window; the intended S W tower never built. Cheap interior with short quatrefoil piers and small two-light aisle windows. No clerestory. – STAINED GLASS. Executed by *Wailes*. – (Small presbytery next to the church 1849 by *A. W. N. Pugin*, with additions of 1870 by *E. W. Pugin*.)

SIKH TEMPLE (former Methodist Church), Calderwood Street, between Powis Street and John Wilson Street, Woolwich. 1816. Very large with two tiers of round-headed windows in recesses; Tuscan porch.

TRINITY METHODIST CHURCH, Plumstead Common Road. Polygonal church with prominent corona.

(GREENWICH CEMETERY, Well Hall Road. 1856. A spectacular site on a hillside with panoramic views. HM)

PUBLIC BUILDINGS

98 TOWN HALL, Wellington Street. By *A. B. Thomas*, 1903–6, in a florid Edwardian Baroque with plenty of broken segmental pediments and a single central broken triangular one framing another of broken segmental form. The tower asymmetrical. The composition is very reminiscent of Belcher's Town Hall at Colchester, designed in 1898. Interior mostly given over to a long entrance hall of amazing grandeur for a London borough (though cf. Deptford, Le). Three domes, a balustraded gallery all round, approached by a grand staircase at the far end which divides in two below a Venetian window. Council chambers off the gallery on one side, square, domed, with ornate plaster and woodwork. Across Wellington Street PEGGY MIDDLETON HOUSE, the first phase of new council offices of 1973–7 (Borough Architect *J. M. Moore*), displaying a sense of municipal show only in its generous exterior staircase up to the raised podium which is intended to accommodate a larger second stage.

OLD TOWN HALL, Calderwood Street, between Powis Street and John Wilson Street. 1842, and very different from the new. Small, modest, classical, with pilasters and plain pediment. Behind, in Market Street, the POLICE STATION, 1910, MAGISTRATES COURT, 1912, with a mannered steep pediment over the recessed entrance, and brick and stone PUBLIC BATHS complete the municipal centre.

FIRE STATIONS. Several by the *Fire Brigade Branch* of the *L.C.C. Architect's Department*. The one in Eaglesfield Road, at the E end of Shooters Hill, is typical of their best designs in the Arts and Crafts tradition. 1912, probably by *C. C. Winmill*. Romantic roof-line with high pitched gables and tall chimneys; façade with oriel windows. Another of similar character in Eltham Road, 1906. A third of 1913 in Plumstead High Street shows how the department has gone classical by this time.

PLUMSTEAD PUBLIC LIBRARY, with bowed windows, 1904 by the Borough Engineer *Frank Sumner* (cf. Woolwich), and

PLUMSTEAD POLICE STATION, 1893, at the corner of Riverdale Road, are the only buildings which stand out in Plumstead High Street.

WOOLWICH LIBRARY, Calderwood Street. 1901 by *Church, Quick & Whincop*. Central bow-window below a Dutch gable.

ELTHAM LIBRARY, Eltham High Street. By *Maurice Adams*, 1906, with a bold Baroque doorway.

THAMES POLYTECHNIC, created in 1970 out of the Woolwich Polytechnic. A mixed bag of different dates occupying most of the block between Calderwood Street, Thomas Street, Wellington Street, and Polytechnic Street. Founded in 1890 as the Woolwich Polytechnic Young Men's Christian Institute, the first polytechnic in London after Regent Street. The original building in Calderwood Street, 1890–1 by *H. H. Church*, has an odd façade with projecting pink terracotta piers with little Baroque caps. To the l. of this, at the corner with Thomas Street, the former main entrance, bolder Edwardian Baroque, 1915 by *Figgis & Mumby*; to the N the main hall, added by *J. C. Anderson* in 1935; round the corner in Polytechnic Street further buildings by *Church*, 1898. In Thomas Street and Wellington Street mildly brutalist post-Second-World-War additions by the *L.C.C. Architect's Department*, completed 1964. In 1979 there were over 3,500 students.

ELTHAM PALACE (Institute of Army Education). *See* Perambulation 4.

WOOLWICH COLLEGE, Villas Road, S of Walmer Terrace. Standard G.L.C. work of the 1960s (architect *Frank Kinder*) in the usual purple brick with exposed bands of concrete. Completed 1967.

AVERY HILL COLLEGE, Bexley Road, Eltham. The College of Education established here in 1906 occupies the remains of an amazingly sumptuous, mostly one-storeyed late Victorian Italianate villa in large grounds. Colonel J. T. North, who had made a fortune speculating in nitrate, engaged *T. W. Cutler* to enlarge an older house here in 1888. By 1891 Cutler had provided 'the most luxurious mansion, replete with marble staircases, picture galleries, sculpture, winter garden and every possible convenience' as it was described in the lawsuit which took place after the architect was dismissed, having spent over £100,000 instead of his estimated £65,000. The house is a spreading asymmetrical composition, whose main feature is a central steep hipped roof with cupola over the domed entrance hall which Cutler added in front of an older building. In front is a generous semicircular porte-cochère with paired Tuscan columns. To the l. was the service wing (boringly rebuilt after war damage) originally with two towers; to the r. is a tall clerestory-lit picture gallery, a rather gaunt affair looking like a squash court, relieved by a balustraded balcony in front of the roof. Inside something remains of the lavish but not very original appointments in expensive materials. Some ornate plaster ceilings and, especially in the entrance hall and former sculpture gallery leading to the picture gallery, carved and inlaid wood and marble panelling (the *British Architect* refers to Spanish mahogany, Mexican onyx, Australian Padeaux wood, and to carving by *Aumonier*, plasterwork by *Jackson's* etc.). Behind the picture gallery is the enormous WINTER GARDEN (100 ft square), flanked by fernery and conservatory, the best survival in London of such Victorian extravaganzas. Brick and stone exterior; internally of riveted steel, with Corinthian columns supporting a domed centre. In their E wing marble SCULPTURE of Galatea, 1882 by *L. Ansiglioni*. Contemporary outbuildings, also on an extravagant scale (the stables were originally panelled in teak and centrally heated), now rather overwhelmed by the extensive but undistinguished C 20 college buildings, the earlier post-Second-World-War parts with restless honeycomb-patterned brick cladding. The main LODGE on the Bexley Road (which was moved to improve the approach) is a picturesque piece with French château roof and archway.

EAGLESFIELD SCHOOL, Red Lion Lane, E of the Royal Military Academy. To the E of the buildings of 1925 the science extensions of 1961–2 are a prominent landmark. Shuttered concrete and brick, with the tough detailing typical of the L.C.C.'s work of the time.

ELTHAM GREEN SCHOOL, E of Middle Park Avenue. An early comprehensive opened in 1956 (*L.C.C. Architect's Department*). An imposing formal design, six storeys, with angled wings, the low assembly hall projecting in the centre. A little of the frivolity of the Festival era apparent in such details as the curved water towers.

ELTHAM HILL SCHOOL, Eltham Hill. Built as a girls' grammar school. In front of the buildings of 1927 a well-mannered three-storey purple brick wing added in 1974–5 when the school became a comprehensive, and a games hall with projecting clerestory glazing. To the SW a classroom pavilion with boldly contrasting layers of brick and glass; 1969 by *Trevor Dannatt*.

PLUMSTEAD MANOR SCHOOL, Old Mill Road, W of King's Highway. A comprehensive for 1,400 girls. Easily the most satisfying of the many Woolwich secondaries with post-war extensions. The original school (built as Plumstead County Secondary) has a festive neo-Wren brick front of 1913 facing Plumstead Common. Behind this a sports hall, then an admirable sequence of additions by *Powell & Moya*, 1970–3, making the best of a difficult site. The new buildings, compact yet not cramped, grouped round a variety of courtyards, are linked by a spine corridor. At the N end this ingeniously continues on two levels, the upper one forming a bridge over Heavitree Road to a final classroom block. Simple exterior details in black and white; yellow brick walls, split pitched roofs.

WATERFIELD SCHOOL, Thamesmead. By the I.L.E.A. of the G.L.C. (Education Architect *Peter Jones*), phase one completed 1977. Intended for 1,450 children. A steel-framed, mostly one-storeyed building with the image of a sleek and glossy high tech factory. Exterior with exposed blockwork and a regular grid of horizontal panels of clear or opaque glass; railings and doors in bright primary colours. The planning bristles with progressive innovations of the 1970s: purpose-built furnishings, a wing for local community use (less ambitious than intended), and, above all, in reaction to the rigid planning of such schools as Pimlico, open-plan teaching areas (the first example in a London secondary). They are achieved here by the use of deep planning and air-conditioning. The idea comes from Californian schools of the 1960s (cf. the American School in London at St John's Wood, Marylebone). The brief (originally for another, unbuilt school) goes back to 1969. These large artificially lit spaces, surrounded by special-ist teaching areas, are however less attractive than the smaller ones of primary schools, or the more interesting polygonal shapes of the American School. They open off a broad mall, intended to be the central axis when the later phases are built. By the E approach, past the canal, the tall brick wall of an old shooting range of the Arsenal, preserved as a pictur-esque feature; to the s, bleak playing fields; to the N, the unbuilt central area of Thamesmead (*see* Perambulation 3, below).

(GREENHILL SCHOOLS, Hillreach. Built as schools for the Royal Regiment of Artillery, 1856 by the *Royal Engineers Office*. The s range is the earliest part.)

ST PAUL'S R.C. SCHOOL, Wickham Lane, Plumstead. Symmetrical, with cupola. Later extensions.

PRIMARY SCHOOLS. Two good examples of large BOARD SCHOOLS: WOODHILL SCHOOL, Woodhill, 1883 by *E. R. Robson*, a picturesque roof-line with angle towers, gabled dormers and some Gothic detail; GORDON PRIMARY, Craig-ton Road, between Well Hall Road and Rochester Way, 1904 by *T. J. Bailey*, a late, more Baroque three-decker, with giant arches, steep open pediment, and yellow terracotta trim. Among smaller C19 schools: ST MARGARET'S C OF E, St Margaret's Grove, N of Plumstead Common Road, a modest village school of 1856, steep roof, tower with flèche; FOX-HILL JUNIOR, Plumstead Common Road, 1881, also one-storeyed, with cupola, Dutch gable, and terracotta ornament.

QUEEN ELIZABETH MILITARY HOSPITAL, Stadium Road, s of Repository Road. 1972–5 by *Powell & Moya*, replacing three former army hospitals.* Built on an industrial system evolved by the Oxford Regional Hospital Board; exposed concrete structure with dark panels. Not specially attractive, but less overwhelming than many contemporary hospitals of this size because entirely of two storeys. Many internal court-yards. In SHRAPNEL CLOSE the more pleasing staff accom-modation. Terraces of white concrete blockwork around

---

* Queen Alexandra, Millbank; ROYAL HERBERT, Shooters Hill; and the Military Maternity Hospital.

courtyards, one tall block of flats, and Squire House, 1911, neo-Georgian.

ROYAL HERBERT HOSPITAL, Shooters Hill Road.* The former general hospital of the Woolwich Garrison, designed by *Sir Douglas Galton*, engineer-designer, Under-Secretary of War, and nephew of Florence Nightingale. Opened 1865, with nearly 650 beds. The first large hospital completed in Britain on the pavilion principle: a long corridor with separate ward-pavilions attached at intervals. Plain Italianate, brick with stone dressings.

ST NICHOLAS HOSPITAL, Tewson Road, NE of Lakedale Road. Built as the infirmary for the workhouse of the Woolwich Union, by *Church & Rickwood*, 1871, with a wing of 1889 by *J. O. Cook*. Many additions, the latest the outpatients' wing of 1965. The original building of five bays, with a gable over the central three, is still recognizable. PLUMSTEAD HEALTH CENTRE near by is of 1977–80 by *P. Hockaday* of the Greenwich and Bexley Area Health Authority.

WOOLWICH MEMORIAL HOSPITAL, Shooters Hill. 1925–7 by *Pite & Fairweather*, genteel neo-Georgian. Outpatients' Department 1953.

ELTHAM PARK STATION, Westmount Road. Opulent platform buildings for the Bexleyheath Railway, opened in 1895.

(PLUMSTEAD BUS GARAGE. 1981 by the *London Transport Department of Architecture and Design* (Chief Architect *S. Hardy*). An ambitious complex with a space-frame roof over the parking area; diverse elevations of red brick; staff quarters with conservatory and roof gardens.)

WATER TOWER, Shooters Hill. *See* Perambulation 4, end.

NAVAL DOCKYARD (former). *See* Introduction and Perambulation 1.

THAMES BARRIER, WOOLWICH FOOT TUNNEL, WOOLWICH FREE FERRY. *See* Thames Crossings at end of gazetteer.

ROYAL ARSENAL. The name goes back to the occasion of a visit by George III in 1805, but the military history of the site began in the C16, when the area then called Woolwich Warren, conveniently close to the Naval Dockyard, was used for military stores. The Warren increased in importance after the Restoration: Prince Rupert was ordered to fortify it against the Dutch in 1667, and in 1671 the Crown bought the adjoining estate on which there was a C16 mansion called Tower Place, which became the residence of the Lieutenant General of Ordnance. Stores were transferred here from Deptford and elsewhere, and in 1695 the Royal Laboratory for the manufacture of fireworks and gunpowder moved here from Greenwich. Then in 1717 the government decided to establish its own brass foundry for the casting of guns (after a dramatic accident at the private Moorfields foundry which they had hitherto patronized). Rapid expansion followed, especially

---

* Future uncertain. I owe this entry to Peter Gotlop of the G.L.C.

during the American War of Independence and the Napoleonic Wars. *James Wyatt* was appointed Architect to the Ordnance in 1782, the first professional architect to be involved on a permanent official basis. By the C 19 the Arsenal covered 139 acres; it was increased by 114 in 1855. By the later C 19 the work force numbered 10,000, reaching its apogee of 75,000 in the First World War. After 1945 there was a rapid decline in output; in 1967 the ordnance factories were closed, and 500 of the 1,200 acres which the Arsenal then covered were handed over to the G.L.C. for housing. The Arsenal is now therefore divided into two parts, the older buildings all lying within Arsenal West. They stand, at the time of writing, isolated on the W fringe of a vast deserted area scattered with the half-used remnants of later structures, an eerie and desolate scene very different from the bustling showpiece of Victorian technology described with such gusto by contemporary guides. Knell, writing in 1865, says that it presented 'sights which stand alone and unparalleled in history, a glorious spectacle which neither Greece with her immense resources, nor Rome in her Imperial power could boast'.*

The buildings of *c.* 1717 are plausibly attributed to *Vanbrugh*, although there is no documentary proof. There were laid out on the axis of an avenue (formerly planted with trees) which led from the main entrance in Beresford Square to the river. The ROYAL BRASS FOUNDRY of 1717 is close to the entrance, of red brick with festive brick dressings, much restored when it was converted to a bookstore for Greenwich Maritime Museum in the 1970s. The centre is a bold cube with hipped roof, crowned by a lantern, originally of timber, clad in lead in the later C 18 when, under the Master Founder Jan Verbruggen, the building was extensively repaired and extended to accommodate a third furnace (1771–4). Low short wings to l. and r., brick with stone dressings, with arched windows with keystones. The interior has been altered. It had arched aisles corresponding to the windows. The mighty entrance archway is flanked by projecting piers with stripes of stone and rubbed brick. Royal arms above, within an upper arch. A little further on the remains of DIAL SQUARE, the former gun boring factory and smithy, built in 1717–20 and named from a later sundial. Only the entrance range remains. It is in such a strikingly personal Vanbrughian style that it seems more likely that *Vanbrugh* was responsible than *Andrew Jelfe* (the Clerk of the Works for the Ordnance from 1719). The building is all in brick and quite low. Central entrance with piers with an exaggerated batter flanking an arch with alternating rustication, and plain unmoulded string courses. The bronze sundial above, of 1757, is in store at the time of writing.

Directly to the W was the ROYAL LABORATORY. Two

* See also e.g. W. T. Vincent's *Warlike Woolwich*, or the entry in Thorne's *Environs* (1871).

identical pavilions remain from the original building of 1695, at the time of writing in a lamentably derelict state, exposed only since the demolition of the surrounding additions. The area between them was covered in by the C 19 (it was said to be the largest covered factory space in existence). The style of the pavilions is clearly pre-Vanbrugh; they are of brick, with stone for the quoins and for the elegant doorways and window surrounds. Each pavilion is of five bays, with a projecting centre in which there is an eared doorway; window above with keystone masks and feathery volutes. The E pavilion has lost its central pediment; the W one bears the arms of William III.

37   N of the laboratory, on the NW edge of the Arsenal, the BOARD ROOM and SALOON of *c.* 1717 on part of the site of Tower Place (*see* above). The tower which gave the house its name was demolished in 1786, and other remains have disappeared since, so the Vanbrughian addition now stands alone. The exterior, of brick apart from the stone windowsills, is a powerful, even bleak elevation, the central frontispiece with characteristically heavy rusticated piers supporting a large arch, above which is a gable treated as an open pediment. Two circular pedestals support a lion and a unicorn. On each side three bays of tall arched windows with circular windows above. At the N end a bow-window facing the river. The interior consists simply of a hall with a large room on each side. The room on the l. has an inserted floor (cutting across an C 18 grisaille wall painting of trophies); the one on the r. preserves its lofty plain coved ceiling. The bow-window is divided off by a segmental arch. Both rooms have massive stone fireplaces. The room on the l. was used after 1741 by the Royal Military Academy (q.v. below): later on it became the Model Room. The room on the r. was used by cadets for theatricals, later on as a chapel, and is now an officers' mess.

The later Arsenal buildings that remain are in a style similar to that of early barracks: strictly utilitarian stock brick, with a few austerely neo-classical embellishments: plain stone string courses, shallow arched recesses to frame windows, and an occasional cupola. Examples are: the MAIN ENTRANCE from Beresford Square, 1829 (upper part of 1897); the GUARD-ROOM N of the entrance and close to the Royal Foundry, 1788, two storeys with Greek Doric portico, designed by *James Wyatt*; the HOUSE near by built for the Master Founder, Jan Verbruggen, in 1772, four bays, with stone cornice, and ground-floor windows recessed in arches; the QUARTERS just N of this, a range of 1719 and later; and the CADETS' QUARTERS of 1752 along the S boundary wall (future uncertain). E of Dial Square the former NEW CARRIAGE STORE, built 1728, altered 1778, the present façade dating from a rebuilding by *James Wyatt* after a fire in 1802; a long symmetrical composition with central pediment and cupola. S of the laboratory, towards the river, the NEW LABORATORY EXTENSIONS, with a fifteen-bay front range and central pediment. Some way further E, near MIDDLE GATE (mid

C 19 with vermiculated gatepiers), MIDDLE GATE HOUSE, of 1809, large, three storeys over a basement, Greek Doric portico.

By the riverside, on the axis of the original avenue, the two small octagonal GUARDROOMS of 1814, one-storeyed, with windows within shallow arches. They originally flanked the water entrance. Some way to their E a much more ambitious composition, the GRAND STORE of 1806–13 by *James Wyatt* and *Lewis Wyatt*, with a large quadrangle open to the Thames, now partly filled by later buildings. Doric corner pilasters with fluted capitals. The main block (twenty-one bays long) is linked by rusticated arches to corner pavilions. The wings have projecting centres with pediments on both sides. In front, MALLET'S MORTAR, 1857, the largest in existence. Made for the Crimean War, but too late.

The buildings added after the expansion of the Arsenal in 1855 have mostly disappeared. They were in a different style, a little more ornate, making use of brick ornamentation and polychrome detail. The best example is the ARMSTRONG RIFLE FACTORY, *c.* 1858, behind the Grand Store. The major survival is the entrance to the SHELL FOUNDRY of 1856–7 by *D. Murray*, two storeys, with superimposed Doric and Ionic columns. The one-storey wings, the huge, thickly ornamented iron gate and window grilles (by *Charles Bailey*), and the factory itself have all gone.* Further S a STATUE of Wellington, 1848 by *T. Milnes*, which formerly stood in front of the Grand Store. It now rests in a trim suburban setting surrounded by plant tubs made from ironwork from the Royal Laboratory dated 1854.

OLD ROYAL MILITARY ACADEMY, Academy Road. Established inside the Arsenal, but taken to a site of its own away from the river on Woolwich Common in 1805, when *James Wyatt* erected a grand pile for it, with a N front *c.* 720 ft long, symmetrical, and consisting of a centre block and two side blocks. The centre block, with four corner turrets crowned by cupolas in imitation of the White Tower, is connected by plain one-storeyed arcades (with four-centred arches) to the side parts of nine bays' width each. Behind the centre lies the great hall. The buildings were completed in 1808. They are of yellow stock brick. Much has been added since. End pavilions of the later C 19, red brick and stone dressings, extending back around the inner buildings. Chapel of 1902 (by *Major Hemming, R.E.*), with stained glass (W window) by *Christopher Whall*, 1920 (P. Cormack). S of the Academy, MARRIED OFFICERS' QUARTERS by the *Austin-Smith Salmon Lord Partnership*, 1969. Three sets of wrought-iron GATES in Academy Road.

THE ROTUNDA (Museum of Artillery), Green Hill, off Repository Road, Woolwich Common. The Rotunda, which started

---

* The gates were removed to the Royal Ordnance Factory, Patricroft, Manchester.

life as one of the mock tents erected by *John Nash* in St James's
Park in 1814 for the celebrations of the allied sovereigns, was
re-erected as a permanent building at Woolwich in 1819–22. It
is distinguished by a festive tall Chinese concave roof of lead.
Low, polygonal yellow brick walls adorned inside by an order
of Roman Doric columns supporting thin segmental vaults.
The centre pillar was put in in 1819. Excellently restored in
1975. Also in Green Hill, OBSERVATORY MARRIED QUAR-
TERS, early C19, one-storeyed, with a central pedimented
gable.

ROYAL ARTILLERY BARRACKS, Artillery Place. The scale on
which the Artillery Barracks spread out facing the common to
the S and the front of the Military Academy in the distance can
be compared only to St Petersburg. The façade, over 1,000 ft
long, has a triumphal arch in the centre (incidentally far too
timid in the handling and inadequate in height to dominate so
long a front) and on each side a tripartite range of buildings (13
plus 21 plus 13 bays wide), the three ranges connected by
colonnades. It is immensely spacious, if not bold in grouping
or detail. Behind this façade lie enough buildings to house
4,000 men, arranged in the Roman way with a cross of main
roads ending on all sides with triumphal arches, on the S, E,
and W of one storey only. E half 1775–82, W half completed
1802. Opposite the main entrance the CRIMEAN WAR
MEMORIAL of 1860, a large bronze statue of Victory by *John
Bell*, remarkably restrained in outline and gesture. In complete contrast, the AFGHAN AND ZULU WAR MEMORIAL
further S by Repository Road, of after 1881, a pile of rough-
hewn stones with copper trophies of arms.

ROYAL ENGINEERS BARRACKS (former), Woolwich New
Road. N block of 1803, five windows wide.

CONNAUGHT (R.A.S.C.) BARRACKS, Woolwich New Road,
and ROYAL ARTILLERY BARRACKS, an addition to the
NE, formerly Grand Depot. In the same utilitarian style as
the early C19 additions to the Arsenal: yellow brick and no
decoration at all, just the motif of unmoulded arched recesses
in which the arched windows are placed. The Connaught
Barracks were originally the Royal Ordnance Hospital built
c. 1780 and enlarged in 1806. The Grand Depot Barracks
began as the Sappers' Barracks. The Corps was founded in
1787. The buildings date from *c.* 1803 with enlargements of
1814.*

---

* Two further sets of barracks were demolished *c.* 1975: CAMBRIDGE BAR-
RACKS, Frances Street. Built (as New Royal Marine Barracks) in 1847, but still in
the same Georgian utilitarian style. The barrack yard with two-storeyed arcades
was entered by a big heavy rusticated stone gateway. – RED BARRACKS, Frances
Street. Built in 1858–60 by *William Scamp* as the Royal Marine Infirmary, on the
pavilion principle: a progressive plan for its time. The style similar to that
adopted for the Arsenal buildings of the same date: red brick with prominent
yellow brick trim. Angle towers with concave spires. The main frontispiece a tall
Ionic portico with pediment.

PERAMBULATIONS

1. The Town Centre and Old Woolwich

C18 Woolwich lay close to the river, between the Naval Dockyard to the w and the Royal Arsenal to the E (*see* Introduction). WOOLWICH HIGH STREET is now an arterial road with nothing to remind one of the past apart from a few battered C19 terrace houses on the N side, and the CROWN AND ANCHOR, with a stuccoed front to the older C18 building, near the lumpy landmark of RIVERSIDE HOUSE (1962–3 by *A. Swift & Partners*).* The town began to grow up the hill after the military became established near the common. The New Road was laid out in 1790, Powis Street in 1800. The present centre stretches N and w from Beresford Square, at the w end of Plumstead Road, a bustling small town rather than a London suburb, of little architectural distinction but with plenty of character fortunately not yet destroyed by excessive mid-C20 redevelopment. POWIS STREET developed into the main shopping street of modern Woolwich in the C19. From the Victorian and modernistic throng of buildings one may single out the following (from E to w): the WILLIAM SHAKESPEARE, a tall pub of *c.* 1900 with Baroque detail; a long Victorian block of *c.* 1870, built as one composition, but spoilt by ugly shop fascias; the ROYAL ARSENAL CO-OPERATIVE STORES by *F. Bethell*, 1903, in the approved Harrod's style, that is, brick with plenty of terracotta Italian Renaissance ornament and a central dome, and with a statue of the society's treasurer Alexander McLeod in a central niche; the new R.A.C.S. stores opposite, 1938 by *S. W. Ackeroyd*, the company architect, in the modernistic taste, with imperishable materials and a tall tower; and the GRANADA CINEMA by *C. Masey & R. H. Uren*, 1937, with a more reticent Dudok-inspired brick exterior (but inside an impressionistic Gothic fantasy by *Komisarjevsky*, cf. Tooting, Ww). Opposite in JOHN WILSON STREET is the cream-faience-faced ODEON by *George Coles*, the more usual cinema type of 1937 (Art Deco interior). Between POWIS STREET and WELLINGTON STREET mostly public buildings (*see* above). The two unmissable commercial contributions are the WOOLWICH EQUITABLE BUILDING SOCIETY, Vincent Road, solid and stodgy, in a stone-faced Baroque Moderne, by *Grace & Farmer*, 1932–5, and MORGAN GRAMPIAN, Calderwood Street, Miesian utilitarian, 1970–2 by *Sir John Burnet, Tait & Partners*.

To the w of the town centre, WOOLWICH CHURCH STREET leads to the site of the NAVAL DOCKYARD. After it closed in 1869 the w part was sold in 1926 to the Royal Arsenal Cooperative Society. Several early C19 buildings remain here in industrial use, most prominent, by Woolwich Church Street,

* Demolished: GOLDSMITH'S ALMSHOUSES, Warren Lane, 1771, classical; ALMSHOUSES, Ropeyard Rails, 1843, neo-Gothic.

the STEAM FACTORY, c. 1838–44, the boiler erecting shop with massive sandstone window-heads, and a tall octagonal chimney originally over 200 ft high. To the NE, the MOULD LOFT of 1815, brick, with a tall hipped roof behind a parapet; a later building adjoins. On the riverside, two three-storey blocks of STORES, with external frames of riveted wrought iron and long bands of windows. They do not appear on a dockyard plan of 1868 and so, despite their naval appearance, may be as late as the 1880s, unless they are earlier buildings moved from another site. W of these much has been demolished.* All that remains are the granite copings of the filled-in INNER and OUTER BASINS and DRY DOCK, by the younger (Sir) *John Rennie*, 1831 and later. The central part of the Dockyard was given over to council housing in 1973 and redeveloped by 1980 by the *Borough Architect's Department*. The SUPERINTENDENT'S HOUSE and OFFICE, now a community centre, remain as a handsome centrepiece: seven bays, two storeys, with hipped roof and a central clock tower; brick, very Dutch. Despite its early C18 appearance, built in 1778–84. Apart from this only the C19 entrance gateway piers, the late C18 police building near by, with two Venetian windows on the ground floor, and two gun emplacements by the river survive. Two DRY DOCKS of 1843 have also been preserved (now filled with water and used for recreation), and a clubhouse has been added. The new formal landscaping is attractive, but the yellow brick terraces with tile-hung bay-windows are disappointingly nondescript for such a magnificent and evocative riverside site. The E part of the dockyard remains a shipyard, with two slipways still in use.

The dramatically hilly area S of Woolwich Church Street was developed from the end of the C18 and almost entirely rebuilt after Second World War damage. There were once, climbing up the hill, charming, haphazard terraces now all, alas, replaced by council flats.‡ At the E end of SAMUEL STREET the EDINBURGH CASTLE, stuccoed. At the top of the hill two more pubs, the ADMIRAL and the NAVY AND ARMY, recalling the demolished barracks opposite. A little further W the entrance to the Royal Artillery Barracks (*see* Public Buildings), and near by in RUSH GROVE STREET the Commandant's House, early C19, brick, with stone cornice and parapet. In the grounds an octagonal garden house. To the E of Samuel Street Woolwich Council's major post-war

---

* Losses include the RIGGING HOUSE, SAIL LOFT and ENGINE STORE (later used as a sugar factory), demolished in 1932, which had monumental brick wings of 1842–6 with pedimented gables, and a brick façade to the river. Between the wings on the landward side was a four-storey cast-iron-framed wall with brick infilling by *G. T. Greene*, 1856 – two years earlier than Greene's iron-framed Boat Store at Sheerness, the detailing less forthright, with bolted connections at each floor. Transverse walls gave stability. The ironfounders were *H. & M. D. Grissell*. Also demolished: the very progressive SMITHERY of c. 1814–20 by *Edward Holl* and *John Rennie*, for forging by steam. Part of the internal iron structure is to be re-erected at Ironbridge Gorge Museum, Shropshire.

‡ The last old crescent, originally 1790s, was flattened in 1982.

effort, the 62-acre ST MARY'S, the first comprehensive development area to be declared in London (1950) and the only
one of the eight post-war development areas to be carried out
by a borough and not by the L.C.C. The housing, put up
between 1952 and 1965, followed the lead of the L.C.C. in
mixing maisonettes (insensitively ignoring the curve of
Samuel Street) with four fourteen-storey point blocks. The
towers are by *Norman & Dawbarn*, on a butterfly plan (not an
L.C.C. type), with four flats to each floor. A fifth tower was
added by the borough in 1965–8. Later progress, or the
opposite, in council housing can be studied both to E and W.
Further up the hill and to the W, the disappearance of some of
the barracks (*see* Introduction *and* Public Buildings) freed
more land for borough housing in the 1960s. A grand, ruthlessly urban scheme was evolved, inspired no doubt by
Sheffield's Park Hill, but only two of the three phases were
carried out as planned. Phase one (job architects *J. M. Lakin*
and *G. Harrison*), 1966–9, and phase two (*D. J. Norris* and *E.
Sargent*), 1972–7, have as their centrepieces ingeniously
planned but clumsily detailed hexagonal horseshoes, formed
from linked slab blocks on a monumental scale, giants holding
hands, in one case around a bedraggled Congregational
church of 1859, which is too small and spindly to act as an
adequate focus. The single tall tower of flats dates from 1967–
71, one of seven in the borough produced by industrialized
building methods (*Alister MacDonald & Partners*). Phase
three (*B. Edwards* and *J. M. Shirlaw*) of 1979–83 is much
more modest: low terraces and some sheltered housing.
Further W off Maryon Road the L.C.C.'s MORRIS WALK
ESTATE, 1963–6, the first of many to use the Larsen-Nielsen
industrialized system with Taylor-Woodrow Anglian components. The large square aggregate slabs are now drearily familiar all over London. Three- and ten-storey blocks march down
the hill in parallel lines (to allow for industrialized assembly),
spaced out amidst plentiful greenery to provide a little (but not
enough) variety. To the N of Morris Walk in WOODHILL
some early C19 pairs and villas remain.

2. Plumstead and Woolwich Common

From the town centre to the E, Woolwich merges into Plumstead. It is not a rewarding area. Much council housing of the
1960s of mixed heights, e.g. S of Plumstead Road the POL-
THORNE ESTATE (*Lyons Israel & Ellis* for the G.L.C.),
1962–6; S again a much larger and more amorphous council
estate around GLYNDON ROAD, a redevelopment of 1959–81
(1,976 dwellings). Worthy environmental aims (elimination of
through roads, ten acres of open space) but visually mediocre.
To the E PLUMSTEAD HIGH STREET is reached. It has nothing of interest except for a few public buildings (q.v.). At its
E end, off ROCKMOUNT ROAD just W of Wickham Lane,
another L.C.C. estate (1962–4), the usual eleven-storey point

blocks, but strikingly sited on a slope. The topography of Woolwich, with its sudden hills and open spaces, is indeed more memorable than most of the buildings. The High Street leads towards Bostall Heath and the ample surrounding woods. Close to the N fringe of ABBEY WOOD (W of New Road) the scanty remains of LESNES ABBEY (see Belvedere, Bx). The surrounding area is covered by housing of the Royal Arsenal Co-operative Society, mostly of 1900–9, and by an L.C.C. estate begun in 1956. Thamesmead lies beyond (see below).

s of Plumstead High Street two commons, Plumstead and Winne's. On the N side of PLUMSTEAD COMMON in OLD MILL ROAD the conical brick tower of a former WINDMILL, late C18, converted to a house. In PLUMSTEAD COMMON ROAD No. 108, an early C19 villa, and the PLUME OF FEATHERS, early C18 altered. (In VICARAGE PARK to the N, the Old Vicarage, formerly BRAMBLEBURY HOUSE, c. 1765, three storeys, three windows, with later one-storey wings. Good railings.) SW of Plumstead Common in GENESTA ROAD off Plum Lane a C20 terrace of four houses worth a glance: by *Lubetkin* and *Pilichowski*, 1934–5. The projecting windowframes and curved concrete balconies are typical of Lubetkin's work (cf. Highpoint, Highgate, Ca). The living rooms are on the first floor, approached by spiral staircases.

From here further W (or from the barracks to the S) WOOL-WICH COMMON is reached. The common is divided from E to W by HA HA ROAD, no doubt recording the haha which once separated the well-kept N part from the rough S part. The haha is still visible. The military have everywhere much encroached on the common (see Public Buildings). On the E side yet another council estate on a dramatically sloping site, around NIGHTINGALE PLACE, a demonstration of changing ideals from the 1960s to the 1970s. The centrepiece is one of the twenty-four-storey towers of industrialized construction (1968–71). The earlier, lower blocks are of 1967–70 (*V. H. Hards*). The more recent phases (*R. L. Dickinson*) include a variety of buildings: stepped-back terraces facing the common (1975–82), in the style that Darbourne & Darke made popular in the late 1960s; further terraces with monopitch roofs, running with a jerky rhythm down the hill; and a yellow brick shopping parade with a community hall at one end, a pleasant building with day centre below and an upper clerestory-lit hall approached by a generous staircase (completed 1979).

3. *Thamesmead*

Thamesmead today bears but little resemblance to the ideal community visualized by its begetters. It was planned in 1965–6 as a new town on the tabula rasa of the swampy riverside marshes between Plumstead and Erith, a creation of

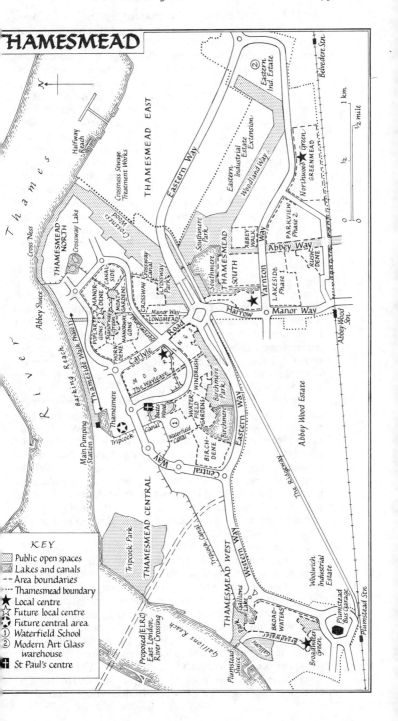

THAMESMEAD

KEY
- Public open spaces
- Lakes and canals
- Area boundaries
- Thamesmead boundary
- ★ Local centre
- ☆ Future local centre
- Future central area
- ① Waterfield School
- ② Modern Art Glass warehouse
- St Paul's centre

the G.L.C. and not directly financed by the government, although its conception owes much to official new towns elsewhere. A population of 60,000 was envisaged (later reduced to 50,000 and at the time of writing to 41–43,000). As in other new towns there was to be a proportion of private housing (at first 35 per cent), in order to avoid creating one of the pre-war single-class communities such as that at Dagenham; moreover, so that it should not become just another commuter suburb, ample industrial areas were allowed for, plus a densely developed centre close to the river of which the focus (all that is definitely going ahead at the time of writing) was to be a large lake or marina, part of the drainage essential for the waterlogged site. This formed part of the network of five lakes and canals, which is one of the most original aspects of the master plan and one of the few that has remained a constant policy. This varied waterscape, ingeniously satisfying a combination of practical, aesthetic, and recreational needs, gives Thamesmead its most distinctive sense of identity.

The original plan, and the beginnings made in 1967, belong to the Mark II phase of new towns in Britain, when planners – in reaction against the anaemic suburban atmosphere of some of the earlier essays – were aiming at emphatic contrasts between imaginatively landscaped residential areas, and tightly knit urban centres. Traffic-free streets and linear pedestrian networks were major preoccupations then, both in other new towns (Cumbernauld, for example) and in the supremely self-confident public housing of the early sixties such as Park Hill, Sheffield, and the Barbican in the City of London. Local authorities at that time were untrammelled by government spending curbs on housing. It is with these factors in mind that the master plan and the earliest phases must be reviewed.

The buildings we have now are only a fragment of the original grand design. In the early 1970s social, practical, and financial considerations dictated drastic modifications; in 1981 even the central area remained unbuilt. So a tour takes one from the first two phases, with their proud vision of three-dimensional planning, via the less flamboyant achievements of the 1970s, to the empty sites that reflect the disillusionment and stagnation of the early 1980s.

In the master plan of 1967 the waterscape was complemented by multiform buildings, dominated by tall spine blocks: continuous ranges of housing incorporating a raised pedestrian route. These wound along the river and beside the route from the southern neighbourhood towards the architectural crescendo of the central area, imposing a coherent linear urban framework on the flat landscape. The concept was derived from the L.C.C.'s plans for Hook (Hampshire) a few years earlier (never built because of local opposition). Theoretically the spine blocks had much in their favour. They were on a scale suited, it was hoped, to rapid industrial building methods, about which there was considerable optimism at the time; they were also to serve as windbreaks and noise buffers, as well as forming sheltered structures for a comprehensive upper-level pedestrian network. The deck system so popular with planners in the 1960s here neatly coincided with a local bylaw (in force before the river wall defences were built) that required all dwellings to be off the ground. But it was all too ingenious; hardly any of the advantages worked in practice, and the concept of the spine blocks was diluted after the first phases, and then, together with high-rise housing in general, disappeared completely. The striving after urbanity was replaced by the ideal of *rus in urbe*. The unifying feature became the network of green corridors around the waterways, incorporating footpaths and cycle ways, with community buildings spaced out along these routes. The low housing of the 1970s onwards is less tightly packed, at last eliminating the insidious distinction between public and private sectors.* Similarly, plans for the central area were progressively simplified, and in 1978 the intricately interwoven multi-level schemes of 1967 and 1972 were abandoned and the pedestrian areas brought down to ground level among much less complex groupings of offices, shopping, and housing.

A tour of Thamesmead should begin at the s end. To the w of HARROW MANOR WAY is the unremarkable older Abbey Wood Estate; to the E, the new town starts abruptly with LAKESIDE (1967–72), the first part to be built. The urban ideal is expressed at once by the spine block which runs alongside the road, and what remains in the mind are the contrasts between this instant linear townscape, the tower blocks further E, and the breathtaking sweep of Southmere, the largest of the five lakes. The spine block is of pale concrete slabs, relieved by wooden window-frames. Five storeys high, garaging at ground level, a central pedestrian route above. Front doors open into it from either side. The 266 dwellings range from small flats to three-bedroomed maisonettes, and this variety is reflected in the lively, well-proportioned elevations, with their change of heights, and boxed-out and stepped-back balconies. The design would seem to vindicate the decision to use an industrialized building system, until one learns that this block proved after all too complicated and costly for the Balency system adopted for the first stages elsewhere. The other disappointment is that the variety of the exterior is one of aesthetics, not of use. The spine block does not incorporate the different activities that one might expect in a traditional urban street. The end result, however cleverly designed, is simply high-density council housing. The deck admittedly has the advantage of leading directly to the local

* The rethinking is based on the *Reappraisal for Future Development* (1972), when average public sector housing densities were reduced from 100 to 80 habitable rooms per acre, and the *Review of Policy Guidelines* (1976), when a density of 80–90 h.r.a. was agreed for both sectors, subsequently reduced to a minimum of 70 h.r.a., following the recommendations of the Greater London Development Plan.

centre at TAVY BRIDGE, which has shops and community
rooms along a rather windswept plaza and, as its main landmark, the attractive angular HEALTH CENTRE by *Derek Stow
& Partners* (1970–2), dramatically jutting out on piers over the
shallow southern corner of the lake. Near by the shore
becomes a paddling pool next to a playground. In contrast to
this delightfully intimate corner the rest of the lake to the N,
stretching out to a park on the far horizon, is of an eyecatching
breadth, generous enough for sailing and boating, and of
sufficient scale to provide a serene foil to the four point blocks
on the water's edge to the S. On the N side BOAT CLUB and
restaurants, an attractive group by the *G.L.C. Parks Department*, 1977–80. Behind the towers on the S side crisp three-
storey terraces open off a tight grid of footpaths. There is a
similar housing mixture to the S of Yarnton Way, but here the
point blocks, without the advantage of a waterside setting,
appear more dour and oppressive. The point blocks account
for 42 per cent of the housing at Lakeside, the spine block for
only 19 per cent, conventional housing for 39 per cent. Further E, the second phase, PARKVIEW (1969–79; 1,251 dwellings), continues the point blocks, but the lower housing
behind is arranged around larger, more open spaces. The
spine block which forms the western boundary beside the
green finger of Abbey Way is simpler than that of Lakeside.
The contrasts have already become less dynamic. N of Yarnton
Way ABBEY WALK, a small enclave of 140 private dwellings
of 1972–80 (not by the G.L.C.). GREENMEAD, further E,
between Yarnton Way and the railway, is by the G.L.C.,
1977–82, and is an interesting example of the new policies of
the later 1970s: a mixture of public and private housing, 553
houses and flats in low broken terraces ingeniously stepped
and angled so that nearly half directly overlook the green
fingers which penetrate from the local park (a layout similar to
those developed from perimeter planning principles by the
borough of Merton, q.v.).

Farther N along Harrow Manor Way is one of the few landmarks
that preceded the new buildings; the inconvenient barrier of
the Ridgeway, the raised sewer bank leading to Crossness
Sewage Works.* Beside it the main Woolwich–Erith spine
road unfortunately cuts off the southern neighbourhood from
the rest, so that the pedestrian route has to traverse these
obstacles by an uncomfortable series of bridges. The third
phase to be built is MOORINGS (1,418 dwellings, consultant
architects *Gollins, Melvin, Ward & Partners*, 1972–7). Here
the concept of the linear spine has been considerably simplified. It still functions as a tall barrier block between the
traffic route (Carlyle Road) and the lower housing behind, but
is interrupted by the lesser roads, so that the deck becomes
merely access for the upper flats instead of a continuous route
towards the town centre. The plainer details betray the effect

* *See* Belvedere (Bx).

of cost-yardstick planning, while the curious arrangement of projecting living rooms squeezed in on the side away from the road reflects the top end of a density range of 70–140 h.r.a. then still required. The spine block is constructed of the standard precast Balency panels produced by Cubitt's site factory, but by this time the drawbacks were becoming apparent: the lengthy preparatory site engineering work and the labour available for finishing processes could not keep pace with the factory production. So the later phases of Thamesmead were developed in much smaller sections, and by 1976 the industrialized system was given up altogether. In the lower areas of Moorings, behind the spine block, the formal grid has already been abandoned in favour of more picturesque grouping, using splayed angles, around a pleasant mixture of landscaped and play areas. Towards the N end a BAPTIST CHURCH, 1975–7 by *K. C. White & Partners*, provides a minor landmark. The major one is THE MOORINGS, the local centre (1973–6 by the *G.L.C.*), which is more inviting than that of Lakeside. It faces a pedestrian terrace by a canal, a nicely varied group with an old people's centre on the r., with a secluded raised terrace, a community room over the shops, and a pub on the l., brick with monopitch roofs. Attention is focused on the whole low group, in typical new town style, by the surrounding taller L-shaped block of flats. Further W, near BUTTS CANAL, and the green corridor which runs between the as yet unbuilt central area and the W edge of Moorings, ST PAUL'S CENTRE by *Hinton Brown Langstone*, 1976–8, for use by several denominations. Not inspiring architecturally, but ingeniously planned, with two mirror-image worship areas which can be thrown into one, and further subsidiary spaces divided off by screens. The external landmark is a free-standing openwork corona. Near by is the HAWKSMOOR YOUTH CLUB, two storeys, plain purple brick, 1976–7 by the *G.L.C.*, several primary schools, and, a little further W, Waterfield Secondary School (*see* Woolwich Public Buildings). s of the school, WATERFIELD GARDENS (96 dwellings, 1977–9) and WINDRUSH (285 dwellings, 1976–80), in the pleasant, uneventful neo-vernacular modes of the later 1970s.* Similar small developments E of Carlyle Way: Longmead (1977–80), Crossway (1976–9) (the latter private housing by *New Ideal Homes*), Manorway Gardens (1978–82), and Moat Gardens (1978–81). The last two are both by the G.L.C., and are typical of planning policies of the later 1970s. Both are quite small (*c.* 200 dwellings) and are laid out around the twin foci of Manorway Green and a small lake. The brick frontages are enlivened by pretty timber details. To the N of these areas the first phase of the landscaped Thameside Walk, created in 1981.

The only other large area of housing completed is BROAD-WATERS close to the W boundary (1979–82), also low rise,

* Waterfield Gardens phase 2, private housing by *Hockaday & Allen*, was begun in 1981.

with only vestiges traceable of the original design with spine blocks. (For Plumstead bus garage to the s *see* Public Buildings.) A final expedition is however necessary in the opposite direction to where, at the far end of the Eastern Industrial Area, a vivid dragonfly alighted on the empty swamp in 1972: *Foster Associates'* warehouse for MODERN ART GLASS, in the firm's characteristic shrieking blue and green, a brilliantly simple hangar with glazed ends, the form used later for their more illustrious Sainsbury Centre at Norwich.

4. Eltham

ELTHAM PALACE (Institute of Army Education), Court Yard. The moated site of Eltham Palace, hidden away to the s of the village centre on the edge of a park, is the most evocative survival of the series of rural retreats built by the medieval monarchs in the neighbourhood of London. The manor belonged to Bishop Anthony Bek of Durham from 1295. In 1305 he gave it with the newly built manor house to Edward Prince of Wales, later Edward II. One of Edward II's sons was called John of Eltham. Edward III and Richard II frequently stayed here, and there are accounts for many royal buildings (now gone) put up in the c14. The main survival, the great hall, was begun by Edward IV in 1475; the roof was under construction in 1479, the only year for which accounts survive (when the King's chief Master Mason was *Thomas Jordan*, the Master Carpenter *Edmund Graveley*). Henry VII added further buildings (also gone); Henry VIII rebuilt the chapel (of which the foundations remain). Later in the c16, although there were still extensive buildings, as two surveys by John Thorpe show, the palace came to be used only as a hunting lodge. During the Commonwealth much was demolished. By the early c19 farm buildings covered part of the site and the hall was used as a barn. Its preservation is the result of several restoration campaigns. The first followed an antiquarian outcry after the Crown proposed to pull down the hall in 1828. Further, more thorough repairs took place in 1911–14, when the roof was taken down and rebuilt, and again in 1933–7, when the interior was made habitable at the expense of Sir Stephen Courtauld, and the hall linked to his new house to the E (by *Seely & Paget*). At the same time part of the moat was reinstated and the gardens remodelled.

The palace is approached by a stone BRIDGE over the moat which divides it from the former outer courtyards (*see* below). The bridge with four-centred arches, stone ribs, and pointed cutwaters may date from Edward IV's improvements. The drawbridge beyond has gone, as has all but a fragment of the gatehouse. Across the great court the foundations of Henry VIII's chapel lie to the r., the house built by Sir Stephen Courtauld to the l., linked at a disturbingly unhistorical angle to the much taller great hall. The house is in a vaguely French c17 style, with two splayed wings connected by a low entrance hall with arcaded porch. Some old walls and three prettily decorated bargeboarded gables of the C 15 or C 16 are incorporated. (Interior with lavish inlaid wood panelling.)

The GREAT HALL is *c.* 100 by 36 ft, smaller than the two 13 royal showpieces of Westminster and Hampton Court (Ri). Six bays, divided by stepped buttresses. In each bay a pair of windows starting high up, as was customary after tapestries had come into fashion. Simple cusped tracery; no transoms except to the longer and thinner windows of the oriels which project on each side at the dais end. The exterior surfaces are disappointing, with patched and renewed stone facing concealing the brick fabric (Reigate ashlar on the N side, less carefully squared ragstone on the more domestic S side). The splendour of the hall is now entirely that of its roof inside. It is of hammerbeam construction, not a new type (cf. Westminster Hall of the late C 14), but treated here with great sophistication. The main timbers are robust but finely moulded, and above the collars, as at Westminster, there are slender traceried mullions, a delicate effect of transparency. More up-to-date is the use of four-centred arches for the braces below both hammerbeams and collars, and the way in which the collar braces continue visually as pendants below the hammerbeams, instead of reading as part of a single arch from wall to wall (the pendants are restorations of the 1930s, carefully based on drawings of the original ones made by J. C. Buckler). The new liking for pendants can be paralleled by the exactly contemporary stone vault of the Divinity School at Oxford, and possibly a little earlier in the elaborately decorated wooden ceiling of Crosby Hall (now at Chelsea, K C). The roof of Eltham, and the very similar one at the Carew Manor House at Beddington (Su), have the first known combination of hammerbeams and pendants, an idea that was to be triumphantly developed in the C 16 carpentry of Hampton Court and elsewhere. At Eltham the ornamental effect is increased further by a double tier of curved wind-braces, arranged in opposing directions. In the centre of the roof, above the site of the open hearth, was a hexagonal louvre, its framing still visible (a later alteration to the roof). The oriel windows have little stone fan-vaults on which Edward IV's badges appear (a falcon and fetterlock). The bosses are wooden replacements of the original stone ones. The refurbishing of the hall in the 1930s included the installation of a wooden reredos at the W end (based on that in Attleborough church, Norfolk), the conversion of the E screen into a gallery, and the glazing of the windows (heraldic glass by *G. Kruger Gray*).

W of the high table end of the hall and at right angles to it lay the ROYAL APARTMENTS, three storeys high, as is known from old views, with bay-windows overlooking the moat. Their brick footings were uncovered in the 1950s. They include several projecting brick bays of the time of Henry VII, one of them polygonal (cf. Thornbury Castle). At the N W corner an older turret with gunports. To the N, projecting from this range into the great court, are the foundations of the chapel rebuilt by Henry VIII (uncovered in 1976–7), with the chaplain's house adjoining on the N, and polygonal S and N stair-turrets at the W end which led respectively to the King's and Queen's apartments. Beneath the chapel remains of an earlier vaulted undercroft (perhaps a wine cellar) were found, and near by, a room with a tiled pavement, apparently belonging to Antony Bek's manor house of the end of the C14.

The site of the palace occupies about 100 square yards, a square with an added triangle on the N. To the S of the hall Thorpe's surveys show that the whole area was covered by buildings grouped around five courts. Nothing of these remains apart from some stretches of the outer walls, partly of stone, possibly of Bek's time, and partly of brick. Thorpe shows two bridges on the S side; the footings of one remain, supporting a new timber bridge.

COURT YARD. Thorpe shows two outer courtyards to the N of the moated site, the Green Court and the Outer Court, with a gatehouse in between. Buildings around them belonged to the palace but were never arranged in any preconceived order. The gatehouse has gone, and the remaining buildings have been much restored and altered, but the ensemble, with its discreetly neo-Georgian additions, still has much charm. The most important house, Nos. 34–38, close to the palace, called the Lord Chancellor's House in the C16, is a quite large irregular timber-framed building, with a stone chimney and brick extensions at the back. Extensively restored. In the projecting S wing was the great chamber, adjoining the hall. No. 32, following to the N, was handsomely refronted in the C18: ten bays of regular composition, the sash-windows with the characteristic thick glazing bars of the early C18. On the E side the tall brick walls with brick archway enclosed the Tudor tiltyard which lay between Court Yard and Court Road. (Further E, in Southend Crescent, a small brick conduit house of c. 1600, belonging to the palace's water supply.)

32 ELTHAM LODGE (Royal Blackheath Golf Club), off Court Road. Built in 1664 by *Hugh May* for Sir John Shaw, a banker of great influence at the court of Charles II. Pepys called him 'a miracle of a man' and 'a very grave and fine gentleman'. Shaw leased the Eltham estate from the Crown in 1663, left the palace site to be used as farm buildings, and built himself a new house some way to the E. It is an outstanding example of early Restoration domestic design. May belonged, with Roger North, Sir Roger Pratt, and William Samwell, to the group of gentlemen architects patronized by the court and its circle after the Restoration. Later on May was one of the surveyors responsible for the government's negotiations with the City of London after the Fire, and for the reconstruction of Windsor Castle. Eltham Lodge and the additions to Cornbury House (Oxon) for Lord Clarendon are his first known works. They display a restrained elegance achieved through a mature

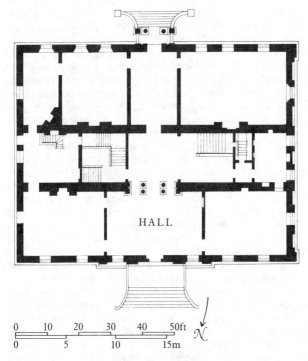

Eltham Lodge, plan

acceptance of classical forms, which owes much to Dutch precedent (the immediate result of May's journey with Lely to Holland in 1656, when he must have seen Van Campen's Mauritshuis at The Hague of 1633–5).

The house is a compact rectangular block, two storeys with basement and dormers, red brick with stone dressings. The front is seven bays wide, the three-bay centre on the entrance side distinguished by slim giant pilasters and a pediment with garlands and coat of arms, very Dutch. A simple dentilled cornice of stone runs around the pediment and is continued below the eaves of the hipped roof, early examples of these favourite features of the later C17. The garden side is less adorned; one-bay porch (probably an addition) with blank arched recesses r. and l., a motif repeated l. and r. of the central window above. The side walls also have blind arches, alternating with the windows. All now have C18 sashes.

The unexpected depth of the house is explained by the plan, a roughly symmetrically disposed triple pile, with a central entrance hall leading to the staircases which occupy nearly the whole of the middle section – an unusual arrangement (although cf. Mills's Thorpe Hall, Hunts). The screen of columns between hall and staircase hall is a later alteration. The main staircase itself rises at right angles to the hall, a fine

piece of craftsmanship, with pine panels richly carved with
foliage scrolls held by centrally placed piers, and robust
newels with urns, the type that began in the 1630s (*see* e.g.
Ham House, Ri). From the upper landing the stairs divide
into two short flights. Fine plaster ceiling in the Jones style,
with a thick oval garland framing a painting (now missing).
The house was planned with the main rooms on the first floor.
(Several on both floors have good plaster ceilings, with garlands of fruit and flowers, notably the dining room and its
annexe on the garden side and the present billiard room at the
front. Good chimneypieces in several rooms: in the front room
to the r. of the hall of wood, with Mannerist columns, in the
rear room to the r. white and pink marble with carved rams
flanking a central panel with putti shearing a sheep. The
ground-floor room to the l. of the entrance has very pretty mid
C 18 plasterwork; walls with swags and busts, ceiling with
shells, wooden chimmeypiece and overmantel with a painting
in a frame with broken pediment. Other rooms were also
redecorated in the C 18. AQ)

The village of Eltham is a shadow of what it was in the early C 20,
and hardly anything remains of the thirty houses in the parish
before 1714, mentioned by the RCHM in their volume on East
London.* ELTHAM HIGH STREET is nevertheless still
varied in scale, and has a little of the feel of an old street,
although the most interesting buildings are hidden away
behind modern frontages. From W TO E, first the GREY-
HOUND INN, much altered, but low and villagey, with an
C 18 five-window front. (Two mid C 16 fireplaces inside,
perhaps brought from Eltham Palace.) On the s side No. 90,
c. 1700, much altered. On the N side Nos. 97–101, CLIEFDEN
HOUSE, brick, with typically early C 18 windows; doorway
with a nice fanlight. More attractive from the back, where
there is another similar doorway. (Interior: barrel-vaulted
hall, and an early C 17 staircase, possibly brought in.) At the
back, at right angles to the house, a two-storey brick building
with a C 16 or C 17 diagonal chimneyshaft at one end. Near by,
at the far end of an alley off the High Street, in a derelict area at
the back of a car park, another surprise, an early C 18 former
ORANGERY, of high architectural quality. It belonged to
ELTHAM HOUSE, now demolished, and terminated the vista
at the N end of the garden. Probably built by Colonel Petit,
who extended the grounds between 1717 and 1730, it is a
single-storey building of five bays, originally with a balustraded parapet, with a taller centrepiece very much in the style
of Archer or *John James*; Corinthian angle pilasters with
excellently carved capitals and frieze, an attic with an elaborately broken pediment framing a niche. The military trophies
in the frieze must refer to Petit's profession in the Royal
Artillery, and perhaps to his appointment as major in 1727.‡

* Published in 1930. Thirteen of the houses were demolished in 1929, eight
more by 1950, and much has gone since.
‡ See Roger White, 'Eltham Orangery', *Country Life*, 13 November 1980.

Further on up the High Street the buildings with most character are the RISING SUN, with a curvaceous Victorian front
with stucco swags, No. 180, early C 19, with broadly spaced
windows and wide eaves, and the PRESBYTERY of the R.C.
church, an altered late C 18 house of brick, with partly balustraded parapet and porch with fluted Doric columns.

Little else need be sought in the surrounding C 20 suburbs to the
E, W, and S. In ELTHAM HILL, W of the High Street, No.
150, early C 18, a handsome front with the usual five segment-
headed windows, but (less commonly) with angle pilasters and
rusticated doorcase. Also the GAUMONT CINEMA, 1938 by
Andrew Mather. To the S and S W are extensive but uneventful
borough housing estates: MIDDLE PARK of 1931 onwards
(worth a visit because of St Saviour's church, q.v.), COLD-
HARBOUR, begun in 1948, with a garden-suburb layout
around Wynford Way, and a later quite ambitious SHOPPING
CENTRE with a seven-storey block of flats and a community
centre of 1961.

SOUTHEND was a small old settlement which lay SE of the High
Street. A reminder is No. 141 FOOTSCRAY ROAD
(SOUTHEND HOUSE), a regular early C 18 front five windows
wide, with earlier parts behind. Chimneys with diagonal
stacks.

E of the village in GREENHOLM ROAD, to the N off Bexley
Road, No. 1a, an interesting house by *Edward Cullinan*,
1965–6, on a narrow site, its short end to the road – a formal
composition at the end of an older street, deliberately avoiding
any period detail. Typical Cullinan features: clerestory-lit
upper living room and monopitch roof. At the back a low
garden room linked by a corridor with a transparent curved
roof. Further E, DAISY MUNNS HOUSE by the *Borough
Architect's Department* (*Everson* and *Searles*), 1976–8, displays
the current desire to fit in rather than to shock, with a carefully
designed rounded corner and hipped roof.

N of Eltham High Street, WELL HALL ROAD leads towards
Shooters Hill. On the W side, N of the railway line, TUDOR
BARN, the remains of WELL HALL, a moated manor house
which belonged in the earlier C 16 to Sir Thomas More's
daughter Margaret Roper. The house was demolished in
1733. Only part of the W side of the rectangular moat survives,
linked up with a completely surviving inner moat. To the N of
the inner moat a complete range of brick outbuildings, with
some blue brick diaper work, bearing the date 1568 (possibly
added later). The best window is at the N E end. It has six brick
mullions. Angle turrets (those at the E end restored) and a big
chimneystack. The buildings later became outbuildings of
Well Hall Farm, and were acquired by the borough and
converted to an art gallery in 1936. Inside, well restored
timber ceilings and fireplaces, two of brick, one of stone. The
bridge over the E arm of the moat also C 16.

WELL HALL ESTATE,* on either side of Well Hall Road

* This account was contributed by Mark Swenarton.

between Shooters Hill Road and Rochester Way. The first and most spectacular of the garden suburbs built by the government during the First World War to house munitions workers. The Well Hall estate was conceived, planned, and built in less than twelve months in 1915; its 1,000 houses and 200 flats provided accommodation for some of the more senior and skilled workers in the vastly expanded work force at the Woolwich Arsenal. Design was by the *Office of Works* under the young and newly appointed principal architect *Frank Baines*, a former pupil of C. R. Ashbee, and the estate was intended from the start as a showpiece solution to the emergency housing problems created by the war. Layout followed the low-density principles established by Raymond Unwin (e.g. at Hampstead Garden Suburb, Bn) and others before the war. Faced with the acute wartime problems of materials supply, Baines's approach was to make use of all and any materials that might be available; architecturally the result was a tour-de-force of picturesque design. Variety in materials and finishes (timber-framing, tile-hanging, slate-hanging, stone, brick, and rendering) was matched by complexity of shape and silhouette, and combined with period details such as the raised pavement to produce a virtuoso re-creation of the 'old English village'. This however was all costly. The general current of opinion favoured the 'simplified design' exhibited by the munitions housing schemes designed by Unwin (e.g. at Gretna near Carlisle), and it was this rather than the example of Well Hall that was endorsed by the Tudor Walters Report in 1918 and largely followed by local authorities in the 1920s.

SHOOTERS HILL, between Eltham and Woolwich, is a prominent enough elevation to have been used in the C16 as one of the beacon hills and in the C18 for semaphore operations. In spite of its relative steepness, the ancient Watling Street runs right across it. Its chief monument is SEVERNDROOG CASTLE, S of Eltham Common, a triangular Gothic tower with hexagonal corner turrets, like Lawrence Castle, Devon, of similar date, modelled on Isaac Ware's Shrub Hill, Windsor. Now wholly embedded in the trees of Castle Wood, but originally free-standing and used as a belvedere. Erected for Lady James by *R. Jupp* in 1784 to celebrate her husband Sir William's capture of the island of Severndroog off Malabar. (On the first floor, an ornamental domed plaster ceiling.) Further E the other landmark of Shooters Hill, the sturdy octagonal multi-coloured brick and stone WATER TOWER of 1910.

KINGSTON UPON THAMES

INTRODUCTION

Kingston feels less like London than most of the other areas s of
the Thames. The borough (made up of the former boroughs of
Kingston, Surbiton, and the Maldens and Coombe) stretches
from the riverside (clay and gravels) to the higher sandy heathland of Coombe Hill to the E; the southern part is clay, a long
finger of rising ground reaching into Surrey.* The town of
Kingston upon Thames has a venerable history, but one associated less with the metropolis than with Surrey (it still has the
Surrey County Council offices), and with an ancient river crossing into Middlesex. There was a bridge over the Thames by
1193, the first medieval bridge upstream from London. Kingston probably derives its name from the fact that some of the
under-kings of Surrey had their residence here. Seven West
Saxon kings, including Edward the Elder (902), Athelstan
(925), and Edward the Martyr (975), were crowned at Kingston.
The town received its first recorded charter in 1200. King John
had a residence here, and so did the Bishop of Winchester. The
bridge over the Hogsmill river dates from that time, and there
was a large C12 parish church, although what is now visible is
C14–15 and later. The borough charter dates from 1481. The old
core of the town around the Market Place, with its recognizably
medieval street plan (the best preserved of its type in outer
London), since partial pedestrianization in the 1970s is one of

---

* The few early PREHISTORIC FINDS include a Mesolithic scatter along the
Hogsmill river. There was probably a Neolithic settlement at Kingston, a Bronze
Age urnfield at Coombe, and a possibly Bronze Age barrow at the s end of
Richmond Park. From the Iron Age/Romano-British period, a settlement at Old
Malden and a building (possibly a villa) at Coombe. Concentration of finds
suggests Iron Age and Roman occupation at Kingston.

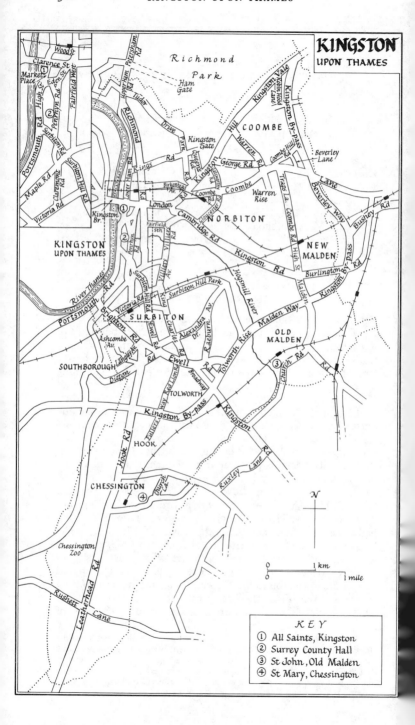

KINGSTON
UPON THAMES

Richmond Park

Ham Gate

COOMBE

Beverley Lane

KINGSTON UPON THAMES

NORBITON

NEW MALDEN

SURBITON

OLD MALDEN

SOUTHBOROUGH

TOLWORTH

HOOK

CHESSINGTON

Chessington Zoo

0   1 km
0   1 mile

N

KEY
① All Saints, Kingston
② Surrey County Hall
③ St John, Old Malden
④ St Mary, Chessington

the more enjoyable places in outer London to perambulate, even though it has nothing to compare with the Georgian urbanity of Richmond. There are indeed not many outstanding individual buildings in the borough: in the town a few C 16 urban timber-framed houses and the Cleaves Almshouses of 1668, on Coombe Hill the little C 16 conduit houses for the water supply to Hampton Court. In the southern areas, which became suburban only in the C 20, Chessington and Old Malden still have their village churches, the former partly C 13, the latter mostly delightful, modest C 17 brick, close to the manor house of *c*. 1700. The only other notable surviving country retreat is *Nash*'s Southborough House, a small villa now on the edge of Surbiton.

In the C 19 Kingston did not become a commuters' suburb, but preserved its identity, partly because it was buffered to the N by Ham Common and Richmond Park, and to the E by the wooded slopes of Kingston Hill and Coombe, but chiefly because the railway of 1840 bypassed the town and came to Surbiton (or Kingston-on-Railway as it was first called). In 1855 Surbiton became a separate local authority, setting up its own Improvement Commissioners; it was expanding fast with handsomely laid out terraces and villas with accompanying churches. The population grew from *c*. 200 in 1831 to *c*. 2,800 in 1851, *c*. 9,400 in 1881, 15,017 in 1901.* By *c*. 1870 the Portsmouth Road was built up, with streets leading off it almost as far as the present Surrey boundary at the waterworks, and suburban streets, chiefly with detached stucco-trimmed houses, filled most of the area to the S E around Ewell Road and King Charles Road. New Malden acquired its own Local Board in 1866,‡ Kingston itself remained quite small, with ribbon development only to the E to Norbiton, and there was still open land around the Hogsmill river. The 1901 population was 34,375. Remnants can still be traced of all this activity, although the Victorian character of Surbiton has been much eroded by unconsidered C 20 flat-building. Of the C 19 churches, the most interesting is St Raphael, the R.C. church built between Kingston and Surbiton in 1846 in *Charles Parker*'s idiosyncratic Italianate–Early Christian; *Scott & Moffat*'s St Peter, Norbiton 1841, is a curiosity because neo-Norman. *Luck*'s Christ Church Surbiton, of 1862–3, has a good polychrome interior and some worthwhile stained glass (as have some of the other C 19 churches, including Kingston parish church, restored by *Pearson*). Of public buildings only *Henman*'s modest provincial little Kingston Market Hall (1838–40) and *Cox*'s attractive Kingston Library and Museum (1903–4) need be mentioned.

Much more ambitious than any of this was the development

---

* Estimated figures supplied by the Borough of Kingston Heritage Service. The census figures include Surbiton with Kingston until 1901.

‡ Later administrative arrangements were as follows: in 1894 both New Malden and Surbiton became Urban Districts, Surbiton annexing Hook, Tolworth, and Southborough, while New Malden absorbed Old Malden and Coombe. Chessington was added to Surbiton in 1933. Both authorities became boroughs in 1936.

from the later c 19 of Coombe and Kingston Hill, which became
a covetable area for the grandest of mansions in their own ample
grounds. The setting for the new house in Galsworthy's *Forsyte
Saga*, it could be reached comfortably by driving from London,
yet furnished all the rural pleasures of Surrey. The largest
houses have gone, but good smaller ones remain, as well as
93 remnants of lavish outbuildings (several especially attractive
ones by *Devey*) hidden off the network of private drives. Most of
the extensive grounds have been diminished by suburban encroachment in every kind of style, including however several
outstanding c 20 private houses. *Maxwell Fry*'s Miramonte of
1936–7 demonstrates the fledgling English International Modern style at its most flamboyant and inventive; an interesting
contrast is *Dora Gordine*'s equally untraditional but more reticent house of 1935–6 in Kingston Vale to the N. Of the equally
varied post-Second-World-War houses at Coombe, the most
memorable are a group by *Patrick Gwynne* (1959); Picker One,
around a courtyard, by *Kenneth Wood* (1965–8); and Kingfishers
by *Stout & Litchfield* (1977), especially attractive with its cluster
of steep roofs by a lake.

As for other buildings of the last few decades, the only housing
that need be noted is The Keep, attractively laid out army
housing of the 1970s off Kings Road, Kingston. The out-of-
London office boom of the 1960s has left its ungainly mark in the
otherwise unmemorable suburbs of New Malden and Tolworth.
At Kingston (recommended for expansion in the Greater London Development Plan) the uninspired commercial buildings of
the 1960s and 70s were fortunately mostly concentrated around
the inner ring road, leaving the old Market Place undisturbed, so
6 that this is still on a human scale, with an enjoyable mixture of
old and demonstrably pseudo-old period pieces (see especially
Boots of 1909). By the later 1970s it was the run-down riverside
that was under threat (always a controversial area, cf. Richmond). But by then also there was timely recognition of the need
for more sensitive handling of large complexes, so that Bishops
Palace House by the *Raymond Spratley Partnership*, although
large, is detailed with some care, while the proposed development by *Ahrends Burton & Koralek* on the other side of the bridge
is even more promising.

The population of Kingston was 146,010 in 1961, 132,957 in
1981. The Borough Architects from 1965 have been *J. H. Lomas*
(1965–79) and *James Lidster* (from 1979).

Further Reading

There are no general books on architecture, and the DOE revised
list is not yet available at the time of writing, so that apart from
the general Surrey sources mentioned in the Further Reading on
p. 124, all that need be noted here are one popular account, J.
Samson, *The Story of Kingston* (1972), and one informative piece
of municipal boasting, R. W. C. Richardson, *Surbiton, Thirty
Two Years of Local Self Government*, 1888.

Acknowledgements

My main debts are to Mrs M. P. Hinton and Mr C. A. Cornish of the Kingston Heritage Service, who were able to indicate a number of fruitful sources of information as well as answering queries, and to the staff of the Borough Planning Department, who were very helpful over recent developments.

CHESSINGTON

St Mary. A kind, small old village church in a c 20 housing estate. Flint, with a straight w bell-turret with shingled broach-spire (restored by *Hesketh*, 1854 (GS); s aisle restored by *Jackson*, 1870). In nave as well as chancel early c 13 slit lancets with rere-arches still round inside. Two-light e window, probably c 17. In the chancel s wall SEDILIA, no more than two blank arches. In the back wall they have small windows of uneven sizes. – SCULPTURE. Annunciation, c 15 Nottingham alabaster (s wall). – (STAINED GLASS. s aisle easternmost window by *Morris & Co.*, 1918.)

Burnt Stub (Chessington Zoo). Partly early c 19 castellated, but mostly later Victorian in a neo-Jacobean style.

(Monk's Cottage, Chalky Lane, opposite Chessington Zoo, is later c 16, timber-framed. In Hook Road, No. 325, earlier c 19, stuccoed, and No. 435, dated 1669, brick and weather-boarding.)

HOOK

St Paul, Hook Road, ½ m. s of Kingston Bypass. By *Carpenter & Ingelow*, 1881–3. Very red. No tower. Nave and chancel in one. N aisle. Details in the style of *c.* 1310. – STAINED GLASS. e window designed by *Seddon* and executed by *S. Belham & Co.* – Chancel window by *Kempe*, 1900.

KINGSTON UPON THAMES

CHURCHES

All Saints, Church Street. A large town church, nicely hidden behind the Market Place but now entirely open to the N towards Clarence Street and Wood Street. The chief asset of the exterior is the tall crossing tower with Perp belfry windows, and a pretty brick top added by *John Yeomans* in 1708, with pineapple finials (restored to its c 18 appearance when reconstructed in 1973). The rest, flint with stone dressings, owes much to the restorations by *R. Brandon* (1862–6) and *J. L. Pearson* (1883). The building now looks predominantly late medieval, but parts of the existing fabric go back at least to the earlier c 12, when the church was rebuilt by Gilbert, Sheriff of Surrey, who gave it to his foundation of Merton Priory. To the s a small pre-Conquest chapel of St Mary stood until the C 18, possibly the coronation place of the Saxon kings. The foundations (excavated 1926) are visible in the churchyard. The w part of the existing church was its present length by the C 12. The w portal of a large Norman church was found *c.* 1865, but destroyed. The cores of the crossing piers are probably Norman too, and one piece of C 13 moulding in the E respond of the N chancel chapel betrays enlargements of the Norman church. The crossing arches with continuous double-chamfered mouldings (the E and W ones heightened by *Pearson*) look *c.* 1300. The s transept aisles (with arcades of unequal width, to accommodate the very broad nave aisle) have similar details to the four-bay nave arcades and are later. The simple octagonal piers (a little slenderer on the N) are assigned to *c.* 1400. The windows of s transept and aisles in their present (i.e. C 19) form are all Dec, as are the clerestory windows added by *Brandon*. Perp N and s chancel chapels, on the s of three bays with piers with the familiar four-shafts-four-hollows section, connected with the creation of a chantry in 1459. The church was ingeniously reordered in 1978–9 (architect *Hugh Cawdron*), when a square altar was installed beneath the central tower, serving a small congregation in the s transept or a larger one in the nave. – FONT. Of the late C 17. The pillar does not belong. – SCULPTURE. Fragment of an Anglo-Saxon cross shaft with interlace. – PAINTING. Much restored demi-figure of St Blaise on a pier of the s transept. – STAINED GLASS. Much good Victorian glass, by *Lavers & Barraud*. In the richly coloured w window God the Father in glory with apostles and prophets. (The oddly oversized heads portray local personalities. NT) – MONUMENTS. Brasses to Robert Skerne † 1437 and wife, 3 ft 3 in. figures (between chancel and s chapel). – Brass to the wife of John Hertcombe † 1488, 9 in. kneeling figure (SE crossing pier). – C 15 niche (Easter Sepulchre?) in the s chapel; quatrefoil chest front, low four-centred arch. – Another altered quatrefoil chest below a four-centred niche in the N chapel. – Sir Anthony Benn, Recorder of Kingston and London, † 1618. Recumbent effigy (s chapel). – Phillip Meadows, by *Flaxman*, 1795 (over the N door). Good monument with a boldly carved, almost detached, cherub on a cloud below an urn. – Louisa Theodosia Countess of Liverpool, 1825 by *Chantrey*. Detached figure of the Countess, seated. – Henry Davidson † 1781 by *Regnart*. Standing mourning female figure by an urn. – Henry Davidson † 1827 by *Ternouth*. Seated figure in a Grecian chair (all in the s transept). – Many minor C 17 tablets, well displayed. In the s chapel, Anthony Farre † 1643 and wife, open pediment with arms, sarcophagus and skull below. – Richard Lant † 1682, open pediment, less elaborate. – In the chancel M. Snelling † 1633, still with some Mannerist detail, strapwork and busts; Francis Wilkinson † 1681; and (w end of s aisle) Elizabeth Bate † 1607.

LOVEKYN CHAPEL (former), London Road. *See* Perambulation 1.

(ST JOHN, Springfield Road, E of Penrhyn Road. 1871–3 by *A. J. Phelps*. Ragstone, E.E., with a SE tower (upper part of 1936). Apsed E end; no clerestory. Future uncertain.)

(ST LUKE, Gibbon Road, E of Kings Road. 1888 by *Kelly & Birchall*. Brick.)

ST PAUL, Alexandra Road, between Queen's Road and Park Road. A large stone church. Nave and aisles 1878 by *F. Peck*; transepts 1924–8 by *P. Lamb*. (Lofty interior, polychrome brick.)

ST PETER, London Road and Cambridge Road, Norbiton. A Commissioners' church: 1841 by *Scott & Moffat*. Yellow and white brick, in the Norman style, with NW tower. Interior with Norman columns and still three galleries. One of Scott's first seven churches, which he afterwards called 'ignoble'; the censure not deserved in this case. Chancel and baptistery added 1909.

(ST AGATHA (R.C.), Kings Road. 1899 by *J. Kelly*. Red brick, Renaissance. DE)

(ST ANNE (R.C.), Kingston Hill. 1960 by *F. G. Broadbent*. DE)

ST RAPHAEL (R.C.), Portsmouth Road. 1846–7 by *Charles Parker*. Facing the Thames. What should one call this style? It is certainly Italian, and may be anything from Early Christian to Early Renaissance, i.e. a W tower with typically Early-Victorian-Italianate top, aisle fronts recessed behind the tower with sloping roofs, windows all round-arched with so-called Venetian tracery. The façade composition is given added prominence by further recessed N and S wings with subsidiary domestic accommodation. Interior Renaissance with Ionic arcade columns. Tall and narrow nave with clerestory. The design repeated at St Albans, Herts.

UNITED REFORMED CHURCH (formerly Congregational), Eden Street. 1855–6 by *Barnett & Birch*.* Dignified classical front. Halls rebuilt and the interior of the church altered (apse and gallery removed, new foyer and glazed vestibule formed) by *Frederick Barber* of *Barber Bundy & Greenfield*, 1963–77.

KINGSTON CEMETERY, Bonner Hill Road, E of Villiers Road. Opened 1855. Symmetrical Gothic chapels flanking a carriageway. By *Aickin & Capes* (HM).

PUBLIC BUILDINGS

GUILDHALL, High Street. By *Maurice E. Webb*, 1935, extended 1968. Brick with stone dressings; strongly forward-curving front with a centrally placed tower. Big classical aedicule motif in its middle. Not a balanced or well composed front. Inside a room with C16 linenfold panelling from the former town hall. Large additions of 1975–8 by *Ronald Ward*

* Information kindly supplied by Mr F. Barber.

& Partners and of 1979–81 by *Roy Roe Associates* and the Borough Architect, *James Lidster.*

SURREY COUNTY HALL, Penrhyn Road. 1892–3 by *C. H. Howell.* Additions of 1930 and 1938 by *E. Vincent Harris.* Stone-faced. The older part livelier, with a boldly placed tower and irregular gables. The newer ranges progressively chaster and more conventional. To the S, Surrey County Staff Club, by the *County Architect's Department,* 1972.

6 MARKET HOUSE (former TOWN HALL), Market Place. 1838–40 by *Charles Henman Sen.* A rather funny Italianate building of yellow brick (now painted grey) with four short corner towers. On the first floor facing the Market Place STATUE of Queen Anne of 1706 by *Francis Bird,* who was paid £48 for it.

COUNTY COURT, St James's Road, S of Eden Street. By *C. G. Pinfold,* completed 1961.

POST OFFICE, Eden Street. *See* Perambulation 1.

TELEPHONE EXCHANGE, Birkenhead Avenue. By *J. H. Markham,* 1937. With long window bands, but high, not low windows. Broad mullions between, faced with black glazed tiles.

KINGSTON LIBRARY, Fairfield Road, S of London Road. By *A. Cox,* 1903. Quite pretty, brick, neo-Georgian, nine bays wide, with a big portal. In front a PIER perhaps from a building in the High Street: a respond with a concave centre and triple shafts at the angles. The style looks *c.* 1300.

MUSEUM AND ART GALLERY, round the corner from the library. 1904, also by *Cox.* A handsome, small red brick building with pilasters; blind arches on the upper floor (corresponding to the gallery inside).

YOUTH CLUB, Parkfields Road, off the SE end of Tudor Drive. By *Kenneth Wood,* 1967–9.

KINGSTON POLYTECHNIC, occupying the buildings of the former College of Technology, Penrhyn Road, and the Kingston College of Art, Knights Park. Both sites have extensive but indifferent additions of 1969 onwards by the *Borough Architect's Department.*

KENRY HOUSE, Kingston Hill, formerly Gypsy Hill Training College, is also now part of Kingston Polytechnic. The old house is a minor Gothic villa, built soon after 1832 by William Ogle Hunt.* Unsympathetically extended and altered, a waste of a splendid site. To the N, hostel, communal block, and arts building by the Surrey County Architect's Department (*R. J. Ash*), completed 1966–7. To the W former STABLES, pedimented brown brick. On the E wall a relief (*Coade* stone?) of a reclining female figure. Gothic LODGE by the road.

KINGSTON ADULT EDUCATION CENTRE (formerly Norbiton School), Cambridge Road. Later C 19, Gothic, with the name in a pattern of dark brick on the gables.

* I owe this reference to Lionel Gent's research on the Coombe Estate.

KINGSTON GRAMMAR SCHOOL, London Road. By *John Loxwood King* of Surbiton, 1877–8, in 'scholastic Gothic' (*Surrey Comet*). Brick; bell-turret with a shingled spire. The E part with a lower roof was the headmaster's house.

ST JOSEPH'S SCHOOL, Fairfield South. Built as Tiffin's School, 1880, also by *J. Loxwood King*.

TIFFIN SCHOOL, London Road. *See* Perambulation 1.

MARYMOUNT INTERNATIONAL SCHOOL, George Road. *See* Perambulation 2.

ST PAUL'S C. OF E. JUNIOR SCHOOL, Alexandra Road, between Queen's Road and Park Road. 1972–3 by *Kenneth Wood*. Attractive clusters of hexagons with shallow pyramid roofs (class bases around a central work-bay). A taller cluster with clerestory lighting for the hall. The INFANTS' SCHOOL, adjoining, by the same architect, has a rectangular layout.

HOLY CROSS PREPARATORY SCHOOL. *See* Perambulation 2.

KINGSTON HOSPITAL, Galsworthy Road. Good restaurant and stores by *W. E. Tatton-Brown* of the *Ministry of Health* and *Richard Mellor* of the *South-West Metropolitan Region Hospital Board*, 1964–6.*

POWER STATION, Lower Ham Road. By *Preece, Cardew & Rider*, engineers. Opened in 1948, closed in 1980 (site to be redeveloped).

CONDUIT HOUSES. Cardinal Wolsey built a conduit stretching some three and a half miles from Kingston Hill and Coombe Hill to Hampton Court, passing under Kingston and under the Thames. Three of the conduit houses stand, and one of the intermediate inspection points. They are in the garden of the Convent of the Holy Family, George Road (Ivy Conduit), in the garden immediately to the W (Gallows Conduit – which has only one of the original twin buildings surviving, about 14 ft square, of Tudor brick wited roof), and in the grounds of a house in Lord Chancellor's Walk, Coombe Lane (Coombe Conduit, with both its original buildings, linked by an underground passage). The inspection point is Tamkins, over-restored, N of Wolsey Close off the W end of Coombe Lane in the Coombe Wood Golf Course.

KINGSTON BRIDGE. *See* Thames Crossings.

CLATTERN BRIDGE. *See* Perambulation 1.

PERAMBULATIONS

1. The Old Town, with excursions to S and E

Starting from the BRIDGE of 1828 first views give little hint of an old town. The main thoroughfare from the bridge, CLARENCE STREET, is almost entirely a C20 shopping street. On

---

* Demolished: DR BARNARDO'S HOME, Gloucester Road. Built as the Princess Louise Home or Metropolitan Convalescent Home for Young Girls in 1875. By *Saxon Snell*. Yellow brick, symmetrical, with pointed windows but an Italianate central tower.

the N side by the bridge approach, a plain early C 19 house of
three storeys. Beyond, THAMESSIDE is visible, still with a
clutter of wharves and TURK'S pleasant vernacular boat-
building premises, weatherboarded, with strip windows.*
OLD BRIDGE STREET near by marks the site of the pre-1828
bridge (medieval remains excavated 1972). To the S the riverside has been tidied up, and BISHOPS PALACE HOUSE
(*Raymond Spratley Partnership*, completed 1979), with its
shops, offices, and pub on different levels, partakes in the new
river walk. Red brick, with much artful detailing (lunette
windows, inverted arches, drum stair-turret) to enliven the
bulk of the building. The church tower just manages to peep
over the top. In Clarence Street, at the N W corner of Thames
Street, Nos. 30–32, formerly Atkins Restaurant and Bakery, a
lovingly designed half-timbered fake of 1922, with recessed
balcony and corner cupola. No. 7, much altered, was built as
the Kingston Literary and Scientific Institute by *Scott &
Moffat*, opened in 1841.‡ In THAMES STREET, leading S to
the Market Place, older houses (e.g. Nos. 18, 16), mostly
concealed behind later fronts. Nos. 3–5, another former restaurant (Nuthalls), are a flamboyant contribution of 1901; a
busy Flemish Renaissance front with shaped gable. (A banqueting hall survives inside.) At the back two riverside tea
pavilions and landing stage (restored 1982) and a new public
house (The Gazebo) and restaurant. No. 1 is a late C 16 timber-
framed house behind a plastered front (see the weatherboarded back, nicely restored, visible from Kings Passage).

6 The MARKET PLACE is dominated by the Market House
(q.v.). In front of it the SHRUBSOLE MEMORIAL, 1882 by
F. J. Williamson. High pedestal with a maiden with an urn on
her shoulder and a child by her side. Off the Market Place
there are still narrow passages, in the medieval manner. The
buildings, going clockwise from the S end, start with the
GRIFFIN HOTEL, with a friendly early Victorian façade. No.
3, the DRUIDS HEAD, has a handsome early C 18 front of five
bays, red brick with blue headers. (Good original staircase and
plaster ceilings on the first floor.) Inside Nos. 6–9 (Chiesmans,
of no architectural interest externally) a C 17 staircase from the
Castle Inn which stood on the site; a robustly rustic imitation
of the type that became popular from the 1630s (cf. Ham
House, Ri), with carved panels filled with gross foliage and
figures. No. 14, at the corner with Thames Street, is a humble
but genuine late C 16 timber-framed house, the uprights converted into pilasters in the C 18.§ Next to it Nos. 15–16
(Boot's), an ambitious creation of 1909, typical of local patriotism of that time, probably the inspiration of Dr William

---

* Redevelopment of this area planned in 1980–1 includes a large shopping area
by *Ahrends Burton & Koralek*, with glazed atrium and V-shaped terraces
projecting towards the river.
   ‡ Information from Roger White, G.L.C.
   § Both structural and documentary evidence suggests the house was built
c. 1590. It is described in a will of 1599 (information from Ian West).

Finny (local antiquary and mayor). Extended to the r. in 1929 by *Percy J. Bartlett*. Four storeys encrusted with half-timbering, plasterwork, heraldry, and kings in niches. No. 23, leading round the corner into Church Street, represents antiquarian good taste of the 1970s; a gabled and jettied C 17 timber-framed building with C 18 alterations, largely rebuilt and restored after a fire in 1973. On the E side of the Market Place No. 36, 1888 by *F. J. Brewer*, with much terracotta. No. 9 HARROW PASSAGE (formerly the Harrow Inn) has well concealed timber-framed upper parts of *c.* 1530.

The houses of CHURCH STREET, although old, are mostly too altered to be attractive. The best are Nos. 3–5, with an early C 19 upper part, and No. 2, the OLD CROWN, with C 17 timber-framing behind an early C 18 five-bay red brick front. By Crown Passage, past a shopping precinct completed in 1982, one reaches the APPLE MARKET; not with any note-worthy houses, but of a nice funnel shape. The view s from the market is closed by some stuccoed houses in EDEN STREET, but beyond the landscape abruptly disintegrates.

HIGH STREET to the W, never very grand, has suffered badly in recent years. It was West by Thames, an industrial area with passages to the river wharves, until it became a main route to the station at Surbiton (q.v.). Near the Guildhall (q.v.) the CLATTERN BRIDGE over the Hogsmill river, of the late C 12, with three semicircular slightly chamfered arches, much widened. No breakwaters. To its E the CORONATION STONE, a shapeless block of grey sandstone on which the Saxon kings are supposed to have been crowned, attractively enshrined within Victorian railings. Further s No. 17, a pretty C 18 house, low, with two canted bays (restored 1982). In the centre Venetian window and pediment; Doric porch. No. 52, PICTON HOUSE, on the W side, is of *c.* 1730, with a brick front and an unusual weatherboarded back with pilasters, lunette, and pediment. It was altered in the 1740s, when the entrance was moved to the s side, a N wing added, and the interior remodelled. (Inside on the ground floor an excellent panelled and garlanded ceiling of the 1740s; another on the first-floor landing.) Restored and converted to offices in 1979–82 (architect *Peter Jones*) after a long period of neglect and threatened demolition. Nos. 39–41 (E side), now much altered, was originally a single timber-framed and jettied house of a late medieval type once common in towns: a cross-wing (now No. 41), probably with shop and enclosed chamber above, and an open hall at the rear (smoke-blackened roof-trusses with both lower king-struts and queen-struts). Further s, No. 1 PORTSMOUTH ROAD, *c.* 1700, of five bays. No. 3 SURBITON ROAD is early C 18 with a later C 18 front; central doorway with Gibbs surround flanked by full-height canted bay-windows.

EDEN STREET, leading back from the junction of High Street and Market Place around the E edge of the old town, was little built up before the later C 19. Apart from the United

Reformed Church (q.v.) and the good purpose-built Gothic POST OFFICE of 1875 by *R. Richardson* at the corner of Brook Street, the main buildings are massive shopping precincts: to the S an L-shaped development of the 1970s, to the N another one, rather better, with a curved brick front to Eden Street and covered passages to Eden Walk, 1979. EDEN WALK itself, with staggered shopfronts below concrete panels, and a well concealed multi-storey car park above, is the first phase of this development (1968 by *Ronald Ward & Partners*). Further E the modest streets of the old town have been transformed piecemeal by office buildings of the 1970s. In FAIRFIELD, GREENLEAS, flats for old people, by *Kingston Architect's Department*, 1970–1.

The N end of the town by the station changed its scale earlier, thanks to BENTALLS. Their store, in WOOD STREET and CLARENCE STREET, largely in Hampton Court Wrenaissance, is by *Maurice Webb*, 1931–5. By the same architect and equally prominent, BENTALLS GARAGE and the stuccoed Italianate BENTALLS REMOVAL STORE.

LONDON ROAD starts from the E end of Clarence Street. Nos. 43–47 are three two-bay houses of the late C18. The brick range of CLEAVES ALMSHOUSES, 1668, consists of six houses on each side of a gabled centre with a flat door surround of rusticated blocks of alternating size and three horizontal oval windows over. *Joshua Marshall* made the coat of arms in 1670. Then the former LOVEKYN CHAPEL or Chapel of St Mary Magdalene, a chantry chapel founded in 1309, partly rebuilt in 1352, later used as a grammar school, and much renewed in 1886 after the school moved out. E end flanked by turrets; Perp tracery. Inside, two shallow recesses face one another. Their purpose is unknown. Some C18–19 houses follow: No. 105, early C18; TIFFIN SCHOOL, partly early C19, of yellow brick; No. 141, late C18; and No. 143 (Vine House) of five bays with lower two-bay wings and pilastered doorcase, early C18.*

OLD MILL HOUSE, Villiers Road, to the S by the Hogsmill river. Late C18, five bays, with an Adamish porch.

N of London Road, in QUEEN'S ROAD, the VICARAGE next to St Paul is of *c.* 1870 by *C. L. Luck*, stone, Gothic. In KINGS ROAD the former GATEHOUSE to the East Surrey Barracks, an endearingly bad toy fort designed by *Major Seddon*, 1875. THE KEEP, on the site of the barracks, is army housing of the late 1970s, a nicely grouped mixture of terraces and clusters of flats, although a little monotonous in their universal use of yellow brick. By the *Ministry of Defence Architect's Department*.

2. Coombe and Kingston Hill

Quite on its own, to the E of Kingston, is the district round

---

* Demolished: Nos. 155–157 (Snappers Castle), a pair of Gothic villas built in 1836 by *Charles M. Westmacott*, possibly incorporating part of a C17 house on the site.

COOMBE. This and KINGSTON HILL to its N were built over in the later Victorian decades with big houses in ample grounds. Few survive; as a rule only the gate lodges and traces of the drives and planting bear witness to them, and the estates have been broken up and partly covered by smaller houses (cf. Harrow Weald, Hw). One estate was that of COOMBE HOUSE, S off Coombe Lane. Two white brick mid C19 one-storeyed classical LODGES remain, in Coombe Lane and Traps Lane. On the site of the house, TURRET HOUSE, Fitzgeorge Avenue, by *F. L. Hird*, 1934, and S of converted outbuildings in Warren Rise, MIRAMONTE, 1936–7 by *Maxwell Fry*, one of the leading exponents of the modern movement in England. Concrete construction, faced with white plaster set off by blue metal trim (and kept in admirable condition). The motifs recall Fry's slightly earlier Sun House, Hampstead (Ca), but the larger site here gives greater scope for the play of open and closed elements, of different geometric shapes, and of judiciously contrasted window forms. By the road a separate garage with flat above; an open spiral staircase to an upper balcony. The L-shaped house lies further back, reached by a covered way. A tall staircase window provides the main interest on the entrance side. The S front has long window bands on two floors and a half-covered roof terrace. At the W end of the S front a projecting sun room with covered balcony over, a typical Fry motif. The horizontal emphasis of this is echoed by the curving walls uniting house and garden. In the roads to the S W a few minor examples of the infiltration of the modern style into English suburbia, e.g. the Sunspan houses by *Wells Coates & G. Pleydell Bouverie* in WOODLANDS AVENUE (Nos. 57, 65, 69). They use the device of a rounded angle to the road with the entrance recessed into it.

Further E along COOMBE LANE, on the N side, was COOMBE WARREN, one of *George Devey*'s best known houses, built *c.* 1864 for Bertrand Currie, extensively rebuilt after a fire, from 1870. The garden walls and Dutch-gabled LODGE survive. Beyond the site of Coombe Warren, COOMBE COTTAGE (now Rediffusion Engineering), also by *Devey*, built for E. C. Baring, the banker, *c.* 1863 with additions of 1870–4. A pretty composition with gables of different sizes and a low tower. Equally attractive are the L-shaped group of STABLES 93 and outbuildings in BEVERLEY LANE, which belonged to Coombe Cottage, dated 1863. Basket-arched carriageway next to a cluster of tall chimneystacks; timber cupola on one of the roofs behind. The whole group is in a remarkably mellow mixture of old brick, stone, roughcast, and tiles. Further N up Beverley Lane, EDMUNDSBURY, picturesque brick and half-timbered, *c.* 1929 by *Blunden Shadbolt*, who specialized in houses built of old materials. Circular STABLES by *Waterhouse & Ripley*. Round the corner to the W WARREN CLOSE etc. in COOMBE HILL ROAD forms part of *Devey*'s service buildings to Coombe Warren: another skilfully contrived composition with a large and small Tudor arch, a brick range curving away to the l., with overhanging roughcast gable, diapering, and grouped chimneys. Further on, SOAMES HOUSE, large, formal neo-Georgian, by *Stanley C. Ramsey*, *c.* 1930. Its projecting drawing room at the back is the former Coombe Warren PALM HOUSE, with Venetian window, Dutch gable, pilasters, pediments, and vases. In the adjoining gardens further fragments of the gates and walls of the large formal grounds. Off the N side of Coombe Hill Road COOMBE WOOD HOUSE (CEDAR COURT SCHOOL), a rambling house of timber and bricknogging, incorporates a timber-framed house from Colchester, Essex (the Perseverance Inn), taken down in 1910 and re-erected here in 1911–12 by *J. A. Sherman*. Inside, C 15 linenfold panelling and C 15–17 heraldic GLASS collected by the original owner, Walter Thornton-Smith.

Later houses at the E end of COOMBE HILL ROAD include a group of four (FAIR OAKS, etc.) by *Patrick Gwynne*, 1959, brick, excellently detailed as his work always is. Flat roofs, three houses almost level, one a little down hill, with low covered entrances neatly linked to garages, all tied into the landscape by undulating brick screen walls. ROBIN HILL by *Tayler & Green* is also of the 1950s, a simple, crisp design.

Further W Warren Road and George Road lead up to Kingston Hill. In GEORGE ROAD several substantial but not outstanding later C 19 houses remain. MARYMOUNT INTERNATIONAL SCHOOL (formerly Ballards) is of brick with tile-hanging. Near by was a group of three houses built by the father of the novelist John Galsworthy between 1866 and 1886. COOMBE COURT, a large, irregular composition of diapered brick with mullioned windows, was demolished in 1931. From the second house only the lodge (ROBIN HILL COTTAGE) remains. The grounds with their lake were the setting for Galsworthy's Forsyte House (although the house he described was imaginary). The lake survives at the end of THE DRIVE, off to the S, now surrounded by later houses including KINGFISHERS, by *Stout & Litchfield*, 1977, in this firm's distinctive style. A cluster of quarter-pyramids around a central living room, a bold geometric composition with restrained detailing – white brick, black window-frames. The third Galsworthy house is COOMBE RIDGE (Holy Cross Preparatory School), red brick with stone dressings and a tower. Off Warren Road to the E in WARREN CUTTING, COOMBE PINES, a freely grouped dignified Edwardian house by *Harold Bailey & Douglas Wood*, 1912, and PICKER ONE by *Kenneth Wood*, 1965–8, an attractive transparent composition around three sides of a courtyard. Large monopitch roofs, restrained details (white concrete, black wood). At the W end of WARREN ROAD several more large Victorian houses survive, notably WARREN HOUSE, mid C 19, with additions of 1884 and later, asymmetrical, with a variety of brick late Gothic or Tudor motifs. Entrance through a depressed arch-

way in one of the projecting wings. The straightforward VIN-
CENT HOUSE is of 1955 by *Kenneth Wood*. Timber upper
floor with a long balcony and a split-pitched roof. (BIRCH
GROVE, Coombe Park, is a large house by *Vernon Gibberd*,
c. 1970. Its special feature is a S elevation with a regular grid of
brick piers, enclosing a first-floor terrace.)

KINGSTON HILL, from SW to NE. The larger houses have
mostly gone, see e.g. the mid C 19 Gothic gatepiers and lodge
to Kingsnympton Park, whose grounds are now filled with
plain blocks of flats of the immediate post-war era by *John
Apse*, Borough Engineer of Malden and Coombe – an ambitious local authority enterprise for its date. Further on, older
survivals, especially on the W side. GALSWORTHY HOUSE
(PARKFIELD) was the birthplace of the novelist, mid C 19,
five bays, stuccoed, with prominent upper windows cutting
into the roof. FAIRLIGHT next to it, also mid C 19,
has decorated bargeboards. Then KINGSTON HILL PLACE, set
back, a large, plain, stuccoed mid C 19 house, with gatepiers.
To the S is one of the largest remaining estates, that of Kenry
House, now part of Kingston Polytechnic (*see* Public Buildings, above).

KINGSTON VALE. On the N side DORINCOURT, later C 19, an
extravagant silhouette with timber-framed bellcote and
Dutch gables. HAREWOOD is also gabled. DORICH HOUSE,
1935–6 by the sculptor *Dora Gordine* for her own use, is of
brick, three storeys, with a roof garden, and large lunette
windows (a studio on the N side). An idiosyncratic creation
slightly reminiscent of some German Expressionist buildings.
(Interior equally original, with long vistas through plain
round-arched and three-quarter-circle openings.) Near Robin
Hood Gate, PARKSIDE, early C 19, stuccoed.

HOPPINGWOOD FARM, Robin Hood Way (Kingston Bypass).
A picturesque group of farm buildings of the later C 19, round
a yard. Octagonal timber dovecote with weathervane.

MALDEN

Malden consists of the remnants of the old village away to the SW
down Church Road, and New Malden around the station, nearly
all of the C 20 and of little interest.

CHRIST CHURCH, Coombe Road. By *Freshwater & Brandon*,
1866.

ST JAMES, Bodley Road and High Street. By *Newberry &
Fowler*, 1934.

ST JOHN, Church Road, Old Malden. Chancel flintwork
medieval, the rest early C 17, built apparently at the expense of
John Goode † 1627 who, according to the inscription on the
tablet commemorating him (chancel E wall), 'hanc ecclesiam
penitus collapsam ab imis fundamentis restituit'. Brick, still
laid in English bond, with very wide joints. W tower perfectly
plain, with plain parapet. The windows here and in the body

of the church are still Perp, with lights with depressed arches. In 1875 a new nave and chancel were built by *T. G. Jackson*, reducing the former to a s aisle and s chapel (already restored by him in 1863).

ST JOSEPH (R.C.), Kingston Road. 1922–35 by *Osmund Bentley*, altered and completed by *Adrian Gilbert Scott*. Conventional Gothic; brick.

CIVIC BUILDINGS, High Street. The only notable contribution is the quite lively former FIRE STATION of *c.* 1900.

The w end of CHURCH ROAD is an oasis in this outer suburbia. Close to the church the MANOR HOUSE, *c.* 1700 and earlier, of red brick, and to the NE of the church MANOR FARM. Further E a few old cottages, an incongruous early modern house of *c.* 1935 (WOODTHORPE), a duck-pond, and the PLOUGH INN, which now looks entirely C 20 but is in fact in its core of before the Reformation.

(MALDEN GREEN FARMHOUSE. Brick, C 17, altered; weatherboarded barn.)

By the station at New Malden, two anonymous, bulky sixteen-storey office blocks flanked by five-storey car parks from the period of the office boom on the edge of London (cf. Sutton, Su). They are by *Martin Richmond* of *Planning & Development Ltd*, 1963–8. (Later offices by *Owen Luder Partnership* in Kingston Road, *c.* 1974.)

SURBITON

CHRIST CHURCH, King Charles Road. 1862–3 by *C. L. Luck*, a local architect and member of the congregation. Lengthened 1866, N chancel aisle 1864, s chancel aisle 1871. Brick with stone dressings. w front elaborate and rather 'chapelly' (GR), with a plate-tracery rose flanked by little turrets. The intended tower was never built. Interior with polychrome brick arches on columns; circular clerestory windows within round-headed arches. Elaborately painted timber roofs with tie-beams on large brackets, a reflection perhaps of Street and his interest in Italian polychromy. Remodelled by *K. White & Partners*, 1977, when the w end and the chancel were converted to meeting rooms and the altar placed in the centre of the N aisle. – STAINED GLASS. E window by *Clayton & Bell*; N aisle second from E 1865 by *Heaton, Butler & Bayne*; the rest mostly by *Lavers & Barraud*, including the triple window at the w end of the N aisle, 1871, to a design by *Burne Jones*, given by N. H. Lavers.

ST ANDREW, Maple Road. By *A. W. Blomfield*, 1871, i.e. early, and therefore more vigorous than he usually is. Yellow and red brick. With an almost separate N tower containing the porch. w front with apsed baptistery and two small doorways. Very wide nave with clerestory. Narrow aisles. Transeptal chancel chapels wide open to the chancel. Straight E end. – STAINED GLASS. By *Lavers, Westlake & Co.*

ST MARK, St Mark's Hill, off the s end of Surbiton Hill Road.

1845, completely remodelled by *P. C. Hardwick* in 1855. Destroyed in the Second World War, except for the tower and spire (completed in 1860), and rebuilt in a deplorable style by *Milner & Craze*, 1960.

ST MATTHEW, St Matthew's Avenue, N of Ditton Road, and Ewell Road. 1874–5 by *C. L. Luck*. The stateliest church in Surbiton. Big and prosperous, with a SW tower with a tall stone spire. Lancets and bar-traceried windows. Transepts, apse. (Interior remodelled 1976, with aisles closed off, by *Melhuish & Anderson*.)

ST RAPHAEL (R.C.), Portsmouth Road. *See* Kingston upon Thames.

CONGREGATIONAL CHURCH (former), Maple Road. By *James Wilson* of Bath, 1854, with stumpy twin towers. Romanesque detail.*

SCHOOLS. *See* below.

SURBITON WATERWORKS, Portsmouth Road. Moved upstream from Chelsea in 1856. Elaborate neo-Norman pumping station buildings by *James Simpson*.

SURBITON STATION. 1937–8 by *J. R. Scott* of the Southern Region Architect's Department. One of the first in England to acknowledge the existence of a modern style. Plain geometric shapes of reinforced concrete, rendered and painted. Central booking office; asymmetrical clock tower.

Surbiton was formerly Kingston New Town, or Kingston-on-Railway as it was starting to be called in 1841, when the railway had arrived (see Companion to the Almanack, 1840). In 1855 it was already a select middle-class area large enough to become a local authority independent from Kingston. The centre is now rather a mess. The chief landmarks apart from the churches are WINTHROP HOUSE, a ten-storey office block near the station by *Fitzroy Robinson & Partners*, 1959–60, the little Gothic CLOCK TOWER of 1905–6 further N, and the sumptuous terracotta ASSEMBLY ROOMS of 1882 by *A. Mason* at the corner of Maple Road and Surbiton Hill Road. The main public buildings (of no interest) are E of the station in EWELL ROAD, where there are a few older houses (No. 73, an early C19 cottage orné with trellis porch, and FISHPONDS, a plain Georgian house of 1742).

Despite unfeeling rebuilding of the 1930s onwards, the strata of respectable suburban development can still be traced, from neat stucco paired villas and terraces still in the Regency tradition, via Ruskinian eclecticism, to the more expansive outer suburbs of the 1890s. From the first phase a little remains in CLAREMONT ROAD, in THE CRESCENT (facing a pleasantly mature public garden), and in ADELAIDE ROAD, directly N of the station. All these were developed *c.* 1840 by Thomas Pooley.‡ Of the mid C19 also are the stucco or

---

* Its successor near by, of 1865 by *A. Phelps*, Gothic with tower and spire, has been demolished.

‡ He ran out of money *c.* 1842 and sold out to Coutts, whose surveyor was *P. C. Hardwick* (*see* St Mark's Church).

stucco-trimmed terraces in and around EWELL ROAD and in
BERRYLANDS, E of King Charles Road, and a few larger
houses: MANOR HOUSE CONVENT SCHOOL, The Avenue,
N of Alexandra Drive, with two curved bays, and HOLLY-
FIELD SCHOOL, Surbiton Hill Road, with four-column Ionic
porch. The later C 19 is best illustrated by ST ANDREWS
SQUARE off Maple Road to the W, tall, fussily ornamented
terraces, never completed, around a square of quite generous
size (developed by the firm of Corbett and McClymont before
1878). The more picturesque influence of the Norman Shaw
school appears in the rambling composition of HILLCROFT
COLLEGE, South Bank View, built as The Gables for Mr
Wilberforce Bryant (of Bryant & May) in 1884, in WOOD-
BURY, Kingsdowne Road, between Brighton Road and Ewell
Road, and particularly in the series of larger houses of the
1890s on the SOUTHBOROUGH ESTATE:* see especially the S
side of LANGLEY AVENUE, No. 6, 1892 by *R. P. Whellock*,
Nos. 12 and 14, 1893 by *Philip Wilkinson*, etc. No. 9
ASHCOMBE AVENUE is an atttactive C 20 house by *Ronald J.
Robson*. Opposite is SOUTHBOROUGH HOUSE, which has
survived in the middle of this development. It is of 1808 by
John Nash, L-shaped, with a pretty octagonal domed porch in
the angle. Garden front of seven bays, the middle one a canted
single-storey bay-window Stuccoed, upper windows arched,
pediment over the centre. Two-storeyed SUMMER HOUSE in
the garden.

RAVENS AIT TRAINING SCHOOL ACTIVITY CENTRE. On
the island in the Thames, a pleasant boathouse and club by
Hubbard Ford & Partners, 1971–2. White-boarded upper
floor, pitched roof of distinctive shape.

TOLWORTH

On and around the KINGSTON BYPASS, and looks it. Improvement has come from an unexpected direction, in additions to
two churches, by *Kenneth Wood*, 1957–9. Both are poor wee
things of the 1930s: now ST GEORGE has a handsomely
detailed flat-roofed church hall attached to it, and EMMAN-
UEL has been given a very successful false W front. More
prominent features of Tolworth are the underpass, completed
in 1970, and the shopping and office development by *R.
Seifert & Partners*, 1962–4, with a twenty-two-storey tower
which is the most obtrusive landmark in this part of outer
London. The most noticeable feature, though not one that is
pleasing aesthetically, is the splaying of the stilts on which the
tower rests, with the end ones tapering up to the top.

OUR LADY IMMACULATE (R.C.), Ewell Road. 1956–8 by
W. C. Mangan (DE).

TOLWORTH GIRLS' SCHOOL, Fullers Way. Three phases

---

* Disappearing fast in 1980.

typical of school architecture of the C20: pre-war neo-Georgian, post-war plain modern, and the 1970s RE-CREATIONAL CENTRE shared by the local community, with sports and arts facilities housed in a plastic-clad rectangle (*Kingston Architect's Department*, 1974–8).

TOLWORTH HOSPITAL, Red Lion Road. Geriatric ward blocks and day hospital by the *South West Metropolitan Region Hospital Board* (*Richard Mellor* and *W. B. East*), 1966–8.

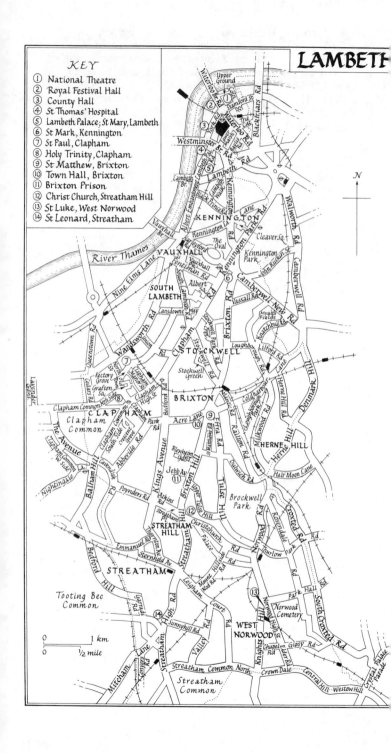

LAMBETH

INTRODUCTION

The present borough of Lambeth consists of the medieval parish, which stretched from the riverside to Norwood, with the addition of parts of Streatham and Clapham (from 1900 to 1965 included in the municipal borough of Wandsworth). For the development of these two areas see their separate introductions below.

It is only at the very N end of Lambeth that anything older than 1700 survives:* the small group of the Archbishop's Palace

* The GEOLOGY of Lambeth was formerly marshland by the river, then London Clay overlain by gravels, with higher gravels at Clapham and in the hilly areas to the S. As for PREHISTORY, there were Palaeolithic finds near the river,

and the former parish church of St Mary at the end of Lambeth
High Street, close to the river. Of the other manors in the
borough, Kennington was the most important. It was given to
the Black Prince in 1337 and has remained vested in the Princes
of Wales and Dukes of Cornwall. To this day housing development in the area is carried out chiefly by the Duchy of Cornwall
administration. Remains of the royal palace were excavated in
the 1960s. It stood between Black Prince Road and Sancroft
Street.* The main part of the manor lies in this neighbourhood,
around Kennington Lane, but there are detached parts in the N
of the borough, N of Waterloo Road.

Up to the mid C 18 the major N–S thoroughfare was the Roman
route from London Bridge along Kennington Park and Clapham
Road. Old E–W routes included Kennington Lane and Black
Prince Road, and further S Acre Lane–Coldharbour Lane. The
only coherent fringe of houses ran along the river from opposite
Westminster to Nine Elms. Inland were the pleasure gardens of
Vauxhall, of which no trace now remains. They were developed
in the C 17 as New Spring Gardens when they were frequented
by Evelyn and Pepys, and refounded in 1732 with walks, supper
boxes, the Grand Gothic Orchestra, and *Roubiliac*'s statue of
Handel. Further S along South Lambeth Road were large mansions (among them the houses of the Tradescants and Elias
Ashmole in the late C 17), and S again smaller settlements at
Stockwell and Brixton. Clapham and Streatham, now mostly in
the borough of Lambeth, were independent parishes from the
Middle Ages, and had more sizeable villages. A major change
came with the building of Westminster Bridge in 1750, and the
laying out of Westminster Bridge Road and Kennington Road.
By the time of Rocque's map in 1762 there were scattered houses
along Kennington Road. The building of Vauxhall Bridge in
1816 similarly led to the creation of Harleyford Road, leading to
the Oval, and to Camberwell New Road, and the building of new
suburban terraces in those areas. By that time Lambeth, Kennington, and Vauxhall had grown together and suburban expansion further S was beginning. New churches were built at Kennington, Brixton, and West Norwood. Allen speaks of 'neat
commodious villa residences' at Norwood, where the clearing of
the large forest had only just begun. Allen also mentions
mediocre monotonous villas on Denmark Hill, and R. Brown in
1841 recommends Herne Hill as 'a spot bespangled with suburban villas, most of which in the Italian style'.

Of the various stages of this development only fragmentary
remains can now be traced. Good stretches of the main road
ribbon development with handsome terraces typical of the later
71 C 18 remain in Kennington Park Road and Kennington Road,

and to the W a continuation of the concentration in Wandsworth (q.v.). There was
possible Roman occupation by the river on the site of Lambeth Palace, and in
Streatham. Early Saxon material has also been found at Lambeth.

* Buildings documented between 1340 and 1362 included a hall built in 1347
and another in 1355, both above vaults; also a great chamber, chapel, and minor
buildings. Foundations of the two halls, both on the same site, were found.

and of the early C19 in Kennington Lane, Camberwell New
Road, and especially in that area of Brixton Road around Vassall
Road which was known as Holland Town when it was developed
in the 1820s. A few villas of the same period survive at Brixton,
then more rural. More complete enclaves of the 1840s, the
standard mixture of terraces and semi-detached houses, modest
imitations of Belgravia or St John's Wood, remain in the streets
off the main roads in the centre of the borough, *see* especially
South Lambeth (Perambulation 3) and around Stockwell Park
Road. Grander houses of the mid to later C19 (Angell Town
Brixton, and between Brixton and Denmark Hill) have nearly all
disappeared.

By this time the N of the borough along the riverside had long
been industrialized. The Vauxhall Plate Glass Works operated
from 1670 to 1780; there were also potteries producing Delft-
ware and majolica and, later, stoneware, from the C17 to the
C19. *Coade*'s famous artificial stone factory was on the site of
County Hall from 1769 to 1840; the Lion Brewery was on that of
the Royal Festival Hall. Industry took over the old centre of
Lambeth village, with Doulton's works in Vauxhall Walk from
1815, then in Lambeth High Street. Throughout the C19 North
Lambeth became slummier and slummier. Slum clearance and
the replacement of obsolete cottages by blocks of flats became
more and more imperative. Compared with Southwark, little
was done in the C19, although churches and social centres were
built in some of the worst areas (see e.g. St Peter Kennington
Lane and its attendant buildings).* In the early C20 the Duchy
of Cornwall took the lead, and *Adshead & Ramsay*'s neo-
Regency cottages and flats in Kennington remain a model of
their kind, one which unfortunately had little impact between
the wars on the L.C.C., whose straggling amorphous estates of
dreary four- and five-storey walk-up blocks recur all over Lambeth. By 1952 it was already possible to say of North Lambeth
(in *London: except the Cities of London and Westminster*) that there
was no other area in London which showed so clearly (and not
very encouragingly) what a future inner London with everybody
living in council flats might look like. That trend has continued,
spreading S over the rest of Lambeth as well; for the last twenty-
five years acres of derelict streets awaiting demolition have been
familiar local sights, as both the L.C.C. (later G.L.C.) and the
borough of Lambeth (under *E. Hollamby*, Borough Architect
from 1963, and from 1967 to 1981 Chief Planner as well) have
pursued policies of wholesale clearance on a grand scale. By 1981
c. 42,000 households lived in council housing (out of a total of
c. 90,000 households (246,426 people) in the borough).

What then are the architectural results of thirty years of
rebuilding, which has altered Lambeth more drastically than at
any time since the spread of the C19 suburbs? The new buildings
are more varied in scale, grouping, and character than the public

---

* Some of the earliest rehousing has been demolished, e.g. the Guinness Trust
flats in Vauxhall Walk, 1893 by *Macartney*.

housing of before the Second World War. The story starts, as in most boroughs, with the introduction of the L.C.C.'s principle of mixed development (i.e. mixed sizes of dwellings as well as mixed heights of buildings), which was welcomed in the 1950s as a refreshing escape from both c 19 by-law streets and the drab and uniform five-storey walk-up flats of the 1930s–40s. Loughborough Road, Brixton, was an early example, with one of the first groups in inner London of exposed concrete slab blocks in the ruthless manner of Le Corbusier. Even more brutalist in mood are some of the later G.L.C. estates, e.g. the Mursell Estate, Stockwell, or the dour point blocks of Lambeth Walk (*Architects Co-Partnership* for the G.L.C.), typical of the 1960s also in its elaborate pedestrian and vehicle segregation. *Lambeth Council* after 1965 also experimented with the point block (see e.g. Clapham Park); theirs are the heavily profiled towers, unmistakable Lambeth landmarks repeated from Kennington to Stockwell (*see* Perambulations 1(c), 2, and 4). Tall blocks of the 1960s were not, however, always so tough in their appearance, see e.g. *Stillman & Eastwick Field*'s additions to the G.L.C. Tanswell Estate, or the borough's own Lambeth Towers, a cheerful asset to the corner of Kennington Road, while the lower housing in mixed groups, as for example at Knights Walk, Kennington, is often pleasant in scale and character.

Among the efforts to find alternatives to high-rise housing, the borough has one of the pioneering solutions of the 1960s: the G.L.C.'s Cedars Estate, Clapham, with its relatively low density white brick four-storey blocks of flats. *Lambeth*'s big medium-rise estates of maisonettes (Stockwell Park, Angell Town) have less appeal (partly because of their scale); more successful are the slightly later low-rise neighbourhoods. The first of these is Blenheim Gardens, Brixton (Lambeth, Perambulation 5), notable also for its total exclusion of vehicles; a later example is Woodvale, Norwood, typical of the 1970s in its adoption of a more cottagey style. But much Lambeth housing does not fall into such simple categories. There is no standard house-style. More often than in many other boroughs, the design responds to the challenge of a particular site, and the solutions are various. Lambeth Towers in Kennington Lane, already mentioned, is effective street architecture; Coldharbour Lane, Brixton, with its sharp contrast between overpowering barrier block and low courtyards, turns away from the main road, and so does Central Hill Estate on the slopes of Norwood, with its vistas of long slabs moulded to the contours of the hill. In contrast to these different essays on the grand scale are the old people's homes (e.g. Leigham Court Road, Streatham) or small-scale infilling among older houses. Schemes of this kind became more common from the 1970s, as the council began increasingly to recognize that it should preserve not only the best of the older buildings, but the familiar historical character of whole areas.* So in those older

---

* See the Draft Borough Development Plan, 1975. Twenty-four conservation areas had been designated by then.

streets that have survived, new buildings are generally on a small
scale, and aim at visual compatibility with what is already there
(see e.g. Clapham Manor Street). Such rehabilitation and infilling often form part of the restructuring of whole neighbourhoods to long-term (and, it must be said, frequently slow-
moving) plans, more radically conceived than in many other
boroughs. They include not only the provision of amenity buildings, but also the reduction of through traffic and the especially
welcome creation of ample new neighbourhood parks (Loughborough Park, Larkhall Park, etc.). In such improved surroundings one can enjoy the restoration or conversion and rehabilitation that has in places been done with especial sensitivity, as for example in and around Vassall Road, by *Lambeth
Council*, or sometimes by private firms (e.g. No. 167 Clapham
Road, Stockwell, by *Rock Townsend*).

Apart from the reconstruction of residential neighbourhoods,
the other main change since the war is the disappearance of most
of the industry from North Lambeth. It has been replaced by
depressingly mediocre office building along the Albert Embankment, and by the cultural precinct of the South Bank (in spirit
part of Central London rather than of Lambeth), an area which
does not live up to the hopes raised by the Festival of Britain,
although *Sir Denys Lasdun*'s National Theatre is a worthy part- 109
ner to the Royal Festival Hall. 103

All these changes have been matched by the way in which the
population of Lambeth has fallen dramatically during the last
twenty years. In 1961 it was 341,624, the highest of all the
London boroughs: in 1981 (with slightly different boundaries) it
was down to 244,143.

Further Reading

Lambeth is relatively well served by the topographical literature. The main antiquarian surveys of the old parish of Lambeth
are by J. Nichols (1786) and Thomas Allen (1826). The two
Survey of London volumes (vol. 23, 1951, and vol. 26, 1956)
cover the same area, and are useful on older buildings, even if
not up to the standard of the Survey's most recent productions.
A very full DOE list was published in 1981. Clapham has a
literature of its own, among which E. E. Smith's excellent works
must be specially mentioned: *Clapham* (1976), and *Clapham, An
Historical Tour* (1968, revised 1973); also his notes in the
Clapham Antiquarian Society's *Newsletters*, and the Clapham
Society's *Buildings of Clapham* (1978). A. R. Warwick's *The
Phoenix Suburb* is a discursive history of Norwood. Among
books on individual topics, especially informative are C. R.
Dodwell, *Lambeth Palace* (1958); G. J. Dawson, 'The Black
Prince's Palace at Kennington', *British Archaeological Reports*,
No. 26 (1976); H. W. Bromhead, *The Heritage of St Leonard's
Parish Church Streatham* (1932); K. R. Holdaway and M. D.
Lambert, *St Luke West Norwood* (1974); M. P. G. Draper,
Lambeth's Open Spaces An Historical Account (1979); David

332 LAMBETH

Hutchinson and Stephanie Williamson on the history of the
South Bank and the National Theatre (*Architectural Review*,
September 1975, p. 156, and January 1977, p. 65); and on more
recent planning matters the borough's *Draft Development Plan*
(1975). *See also* p. 124.

Acknowledgements

I am especially grateful to Mr Edward Hollamby, formerly
Director of Development for Lambeth, and his staff, who were
most helpful over recent developments. Mr E. E. Smith of the
Clapham Antiquarian Society not only contributed notes on
Clapham but generously read through and improved the
Clapham section of the text as well as other parts of Lambeth.
David Hutchison did likewise for Sir Nikolaus Pevsner's section
on the South Bank. I must also thank Mrs P. Hatfield, archivist
of the Minet Library of the borough of Lambeth, who read and
commented on the text, Mrs R. Nicholson of the Tradescant
Trust for help on St Mary, Lambeth, and Mr Andrew Saint and
Miss Hilary Grainger for letting me make use of their research
on Streatham.

LAMBETH

CHURCHES

The old parish of Lambeth extended from the river to the hills of
Norwood. In the C18 the parish church of St Mary in the
riverside village was supplemented by chapels which in the C19
became independent churches (e.g. St Andrew Stockwell, St
Anne South Lambeth Road), then by the four Commissioners'
churches which became known as the 'Waterloo' churches: St
John Waterloo Road, St Luke West Norwood, St Mark Kennington, and St Matthew Brixton, *c.* 1822. Lambeth was fortunate in its Victorian church architects: *Street* built St John the
Divine Vassall Road, *Pearson* St Peter Kennington Lane,
although *G. G. Scott Jun.*'s St Agnes Kennington, perhaps the
best church of all, has been demolished. Innovations of the later
C19 are well represented by *Beresford Pite*'s Byzantine Christ
88 Church Brixton and by *Fellowes Prynne*'s All Saints Rosendale
90 Road.* This section includes the churches within the present
borough which are within the old parish of Lambeth. For

* Demolitions: ST MARY THE LESS, Black Prince Road. 1827–8, by the same
Bedford who presents himself with so much dignity and ceremony at West
Norwood and in Waterloo Road. Here, using Gothic forms, he fell into the same
leanness which characterizes so many contemporary efforts at a medieval revival.
Stock brick with a thin bellcote, open and octagonal; inside, a broad and low hall
with exceedingly slim shafts and mean plaster ribs in a sham vault. – ST PHILIP,
Kennington Road, 1862–3 by *H. E. Coe* with s chapel by *H. S. Rogers*, 1913,
ragstone Dec. – ST SAVIOUR, Herne Hill Road. 1866–7 by *Gough*. Romanesque.
Hearty, robust, and revolting. Chancel and s transept 1870 by *W. Gibbs Bartleet*.
– ST STEPHEN, St Stephen's Terrace, 1967–8 by *N. A. Green*, replaces a church
of 1860–1 by *J. Barnett*. – PRESBYTERIAN CHURCH, Clapham Road. 1862 by
Habershon & Pite. Heavy six-column Corinthian portico and pediment.

churches in Clapham and Streatham *see* separately, below.

ALL SAINTS, Rosendale Road, Brixton. A remarkably impres- 90
sive design inside and out. By *Fellowes Prynne*, 1887–91.
Badly damaged in the Second World War, restored in 1952 by
J. B. S. Comper. The E end towers above the street with the
chancel raised above a crypt and another intermediate storey.
A picturesque outer staircase runs up S of the apse. The
material is red brick, the windows of lancet shape. The principal motif of the interior is the tall tripartite chancel screen,
Prynne's first use of this feature, derived from the medieval
screen at Great Bardfield, Essex. The church was not com-
pleted. *Comper* added a small tower. – (STAINED GLASS.
Aisle windows by *Burlison & Grylls*; one apse window by
Kempe.)

CHRIST CHURCH, Brixton Road. Built on the site of an earlier 88
chapel. Designed in 1899, completed 1902, by *Beresford Pite*
for his brother-in-law, the Rev. William Mowll. The style is
Byzantine Romanesque, like Bentley's Westminster Cathedral, an interesting departure from the free Gothic more common at the turn of the century. Cruciform, with a broad
crossing with dome on pendentives, lunettes above. Elaborate, rather fussy, W front: brick with stone dressings, with
narthex, octagonal tower, and an outdoor pulpit. The more
restrained side elevations have the layered brickwork of which
Pite was so fond; two tiers of windows within an intricate
series of arches on different planes. The interior equally original, especially in its well preserved, robust low church
furnishings. No aisles, the floor ramped to allow an easy view
of the E end. The shallow sanctuary has a semi-dome supported by a flat architrave on columns. Free-standing communion table behind a semicircular communion rail; in front
of this a large reversible lectern, flanked by pulpit and reading
desk. W gallery with openwork wooden balustrade. The crossing has an octopartite roof with patterned wood ceiling. The
bold inscriptions which cover the pendentives were designed
by *Edward Johnston*. The foundation stone is also by *Johnston*,
cut by *Eric Gill* in 1902. – MOWLL HALL, E of the church, is of
1897–8 by *Pite*, with an unusal N window.

CHRIST CHURCH, Gipsy Hill, off the W end of Westow Hill. By
John Giles, the architect of the Langham Hotel (Wm), *c.*
1850–5, large, with tall SW tower (completed 1889) and a
surfeit of plate tracery. Very odd clerestory windows.

EMMANUEL, Clive Road, W of South Croxted Road. Modest,
austerely detailed brick and concrete church and youth centre, linked by a bridge over the entrance. By *Hutchison, Locke
& Monk*, 1967–8. Compact church, with seating on three
sides, lit by a raised roof-light over the altar. Narrow vertical
windows filled with red acrylic sheet. A committee room in the
bridge doubles as a gallery. The buildings replace a church of
1876 by *E. C. Robins*. Room has even been made on the E part
of the site for a tiny open space with a footpath running
through to a group of flats designed at the same time.

HOLY TRINITY, Trinity Rise, sw of Brockwell Park, Tulse Hill. By *T. D. Barry*, 1855–6, that is at the time of the most confident tastelessness; over-adorned Dec door with twin cusped arches and a tympanum decorated with naturalistic vine foliage. Cruciform, with aisleless nave.

ST AGNES, St Agnes Place, E of Kennington Park. The church of 1874–7 by *G. G. Scott Jun.* was, alas, demolished after it had been completely ruined in the war, and replaced by a building of no significance (1956 by *R. Covell*).* Inside, some of the old furnishings have been preserved: part of the former chancel SCREEN, now below the w gallery, by *Temple Moore*, 1885–9; the carved and painted REREDOS, also by *Temple Moore*, 1891; a painted ALTARPIECE in the Lady Chapel; and parts of the PULPIT.‡

ST ANDREW, Landor Road, w of Stockwell Green. A chapel was built in 1767, extended in 1810, and remodelled in 1867 by *H. E. Coe* with Romanesque w end and tower. Vestries and chapel 1891 and 1894 by *A. J. Pilkington*. Galleries removed 1924.

ST ANDREW with ST THOMAS, Short Street, s of The Cut. 1960 by *David Nye & Partners*. A sadly dull replacement for two churches by *Teulon* damaged in the war (*see* also Perambulation 1(a)).

ST ANNE, South Lambeth Road (cf. St Andrew Stockwell). Founded as a private chapel in 1793, made into a parish church in 1869. Chancel, vestry, and tower in Romanesque style added in 1874 by *R. Parkinson*. The galleries were removed at the same time.

ST ANSELM, Kennington Road. Planned in 1911 but not completed until 1932–3. By *Adshead & Ramsay* (architects of the adjacent Duchy of Cornwall housing, *see* Perambulation 1(c)). Plain, yellow brick, Early Christian in character. Bare interior with open timber roof. Short nave (arcades with cushion capitals carved by *A. H. Gerrard*), no transept, long chancel. Baldacchino over the high altar. The original plan was for a cruciform building with central dome. – (MURAL below the clerestory. 1971 by *Norman Adams*. Abstract design.) – Adjacent VICARAGE, 1913.

ST BARNABAS, Guildford Road, N of Lansdowne Way, Kennington. 1848–50 by *Isaac Clarke & James Humphreys*. A ragstone Gothic centrepiece to the contemporary classical Lansdowne Gardens (*see* Perambulation 3).

ST BEDE (now Social and Sports Club for the Deaf), Clapham Road. 1924 by *E. Maufe*. Small, brick, with some free Gothic detail.

ST JAMES, Knatchbull Road. 1869–70 by *George Low*. Given by the estate owner, J. L. Minet. Kentish rag; late C13 detail. –

---

* Scott's church was one of the noblest Gothic Revival buildings of its date, by no means a copy of anything of the past, though in the spirit of the C14. The w front was completed (following the original drawings) and the w gallery added in 1889 by *Temple Moore*.

‡ Some of the furnishings are now in the church of the Holy Spirit, Southsea, Hants.

(STAINED GLASS. Apse and nave W by *Clayton & Bell*; aisles and transepts by *Ward & Hughes*.)

ST JOHN, Angell Town, Brixton. A good church by *B. Ferrey* of 1852–3, of Kentish rag and (unusually) in Perp style. W tower with pinnacles and chequered parapet. Arcades with octagonal piers. N transept 1876. The E end of the chancel has been divided off. – (STAINED GLASS. E window by *Hardman*.)

ST JOHN, Clapham Road. 1840–2 by *T. Marsh Nelson*. Hexastyle Ionic portico. A very late example of the classical style for the Church of England.

ST JOHN, Waterloo Road. One of the four Commissioners' churches in Lambeth known (from the site of this one) as the Waterloo churches. Designed by *Bedford* and built in 1822–4. The Greek Doric portico has a tall thin spire ending in an obelisk. 'The kind of tower', Sir John Summerson wrote, 'that Ictinus might have put on the Parthenon, if the Athenians had had the advantage of belonging to the Church of England.' The interior was mostly destroyed in the war, but restored in 1951 by *T. F. Ford*. The galleries, which also were on Greek Doric columns, were replaced by a single gallery at the W end. – FONT. Italian C18. – REREDOS. Remains of the original marble altarpiece: central panel with paintings by *Hans Feibusch*. Also by him the E window.*

ST JOHN THE DIVINE, Vassall Road. A major building by *G. E. Street*, 1870–4, one of the best Victorian churches in South London. The W tower with tall broached spire not completed until 1888–9 (under *A. E. Street*). *Bodley* decorated the interior in 1890–2. The church has a broad nave and narrow aisles with tall wide arcades (capitals carved by *Earp*); no clerestory. The E bay cants inwards toward the narrower apsed chancel (cf. St Philip and St James, Oxford), giving an oblique view of the E chapels. On the S side an apsed baptistery, with original *Street* railings. The church was gutted in 1940, but carefully restored by *Goodhart-Rendel* in 1955–8, although not precisely following Bodley's original scheme of decoration. The wooden nave roof is now pale green, with chequered ribs. – STAINED GLASS. Good new E window by *W. T. Carter Shapland*. – W window by *Kempe*.

ST JUDE, Dulwich Road. 1867–8 by *E. C. Robins*. Kentish rag, cruciform.

ST LUKE, West Norwood. Another Commissioners' church; like St John Waterloo Road (above), by *Bedford*, and also of 1822. A splendid site on rising ground at the junction of Knights Hill and Norwood High Street. It gives the Corinthian six-column portico an uplift which is missing down in Waterloo Road. The W tower above the portico very similar to Porden's contemporary St Matthew, Brixton. The interior was originally correctly orientated so that the altar was against the long E wall on the l. of the portico. In 1872–3 *G. E. Street* replaced this with a more conventional chancel at the S end,

_____

* During the 1930s there was a free-standing altar with ciborium, by *Comper*.

and divided up the nave by a Romanesque arcade, with a plaster barrel-vault above Bedford's tie-beams. – The altar BALDACCHINO dates from the redecoration of 1936 by *Sir Charles Nicholson*. – PAINTINGS above in the blind windows by *W. Christian Symons* after designs by *J. F. Bentley*, 1885. – PULPIT by *Street*, lowered in 1922. – WEST SCREEN. C 19, with round-arched arcades, brought from St Sepulchre Holborn *c.* 1926. – The reordering with nave altar dates from 1972.

ST MARK, Clapham Road, Kennington. 1822–4 by *Roper* (said to be designed by *A. B. Clayton*). Another 'Waterloo' church (*see* St John above). An interesting Greek Doric four-column portico *in antis*. The tower has a fairly solid first stage and a thin Ionic second stage with a cupola. Beneath the tower is an octagonal vestibule flanked by staircases. The interior was rudely renewed by *Teulon* in 1873–4. Teulon's work was destroyed by bombs in 1949; the more discreet restoration by *T. F. Ford* was completed in 1960. The galleries have been divided off, but the Greek columns on which they rest survive. The altar is flanked by pairs of Ionic columns. The glazed dome over the nave was introduced in 1937, and has been restored with abstract glass in blue and grey. – Carved C 17 PULPIT from St Michael Wood Street. – In the s aisle chapel a REREDOS incorporating late medieval carved panels (? Flemish), given in 1935. – (Churchyard: *Coade* stone MONUMENT to Mrs P. Bayley, 1819.)

ST MARY, Lambeth Road and Albert Embankment. The former parish church of Lambeth, nestling close to the walls and gateway of the Archbishop's Palace. Disused since 1972, but rescued in 1979 by the specially formed Tradescant Trust and enterprisingly restored as a Museum of Garden History, an appropriate use, since three generations of Tradescants are buried in the churchyard (*see* below). The elder John Tradescant († 1638) was Charles I's gardener and both he and his son were distinguished botanical travellers. They lived in South Lambeth. Elias Ashmole took over their gardens and collections and so the latter went ultimately to the Ashmolean Museum (the house and garden have entirely disappeared).

The SW tower dates from a rebuilding of 1370 and is interesting as an early example of the characteristic late medieval type of the London area. Ragstone, with diagonal buttresses, and a polygonal stair-turret (top storey renewed in 1834 by *W. Rogers*). The body of the church is also of the 1370s: the early C 16 alterations largely disappeared during the restoration by *P. C. Hardwick* in 1851–2 (surfaces all refaced, roofs renewed, and new Dec windows inserted). Nobly proportioned interior, substantially also of the 1370s. Five-bay nave. Tall octagonal piers carrying arches with wave mouldings, three-light clerestory windows, restored but original. *Hardwick*'s new aisle windows are more fancifully varied, both in their width and their tracery details. The chancel arch and probably both the broad arches between chancel and chapels are also his inventions. The chancel chapels were added in the early c 16: the Howard Chapel (N), 1522, and the Leigh Chapel (S) of the same period. The chancel projects E of the chapels, with pairs of narrow but elaborate N and S windows with rere-arches. – IMMERSION FONT, a rare example, installed as a memorial to Archbishop Benson († 1896). Semicircular, marble-faced, with a moulded kerb. – CHOIR STALLS of 1887, given by the Rector, F. G. Pelham, who is commemorated by the S chapel SCREEN (1906). – SCULPTURE. Terracotta Crucifixion panel (N aisle wall) by *Tinworth*, from the reredos designed by *J. O. Scott* and given by Sir Henry Doulton in 1887. – STAINED GLASS. Mediocre post-war glass by *F. Stephens*.*

BRASSES to Katherine Broughton, wife of Lord William Howard, † 1535, a standing figure; and to Thomas Clere † 1545. – MONUMENTS. In the chancel facing each other, two tomb-chests with shields in quatrefoils, placed in recesses with panelled reveals and voussoirs and ending in crested cornices (cf. the tomb of Hugh Warham, St John, Croydon, Cr, and the Carew tomb at Beddington, Su). The one on the N wall is to Hugh Peyntwyn † 1504, an archdeacon of Canterbury, the one on the S wall to John Mompesson † 1524, master of the Canterbury registry. – Robert Scott † 1631, a bust (in the porch). – Sir Peter Rich † 1692, oval cartouche with bold putti heads (porch). – The same motif, handled with the finesse of *c.* 1800, on two delicate ovals to Charles Carsan † 1800 and James Bryan † 1804 (N aisle). – Thomas Lett † 1830, a good life-sized bust by *Chantrey* (N chapel). – Samuel Goodbehere † 1821 by *Henry Westmacott* (porch), showing with its tendrils of ivy the coming of the loose, romantic, unarchitectural style of decoration. – John Hernaman, headmaster of Lambeth School, † 1899, and Mercy Walker, a Lambeth infants' school teacher, † 1887, two charming examples of *Tinworth*'s terracotta panels: Christ among the Elders, and Suffer Little Children (S aisle). – Herbert Lyttelton Pelham † 1914. Large coloured alabaster panel in low relief, with St George; inscription in Arts and Crafts lettering. By *E. M. Rope*, 1916. – Many minor tablets, especially in the N chapel, and good LEDGER STONES to several archbishops in the chancel floor.

The CHURCHYARD has been laid out as a garden planted with flowers introduced by the Tradescants to England and with other plants of the period. The Tradescant sarcophagus, E of the church, was erected by the widow of John the younger in 1662, repaired in 1773, and recarved in 1853 by *C. P. White*. The remarkable design has reliefs on four sides based on drawings now in the Pepys Library at Magdalene College,

---

* Furnishings removed: FONT, Perp, carved in 1852 by *C. P. White*, with pinnacled wooden canopy. – PULPIT of 1698 (from St James Kennington Park) now at St Matthew Westminster. – COMMUNION RAILS, late C 17, returned to All Saints Maidstone, from whence they came. – ORGAN CASE, 1701, added to but with some carving from the original *Harris* case, now at Milton Abbey, Dorset.

Cambridge. Trees at the angles, a crocodile, a hydra, and several ruined buildings of antiquity. The atmosphere is highly reminiscent of the *Hypnerotomachia Polifili*. – Near by, the sarcophagus of William Bligh (of the Mutiny of the 'Bounty') † 1817, with a flaming urn. – Other tombs s of the church, including, by the porch, that of *W. Sealy* † 1800, Coade's partner, a Grecian sarcophagus; on top, an urn with a snake.

ST MATTHEW, St Matthew's Road, Brixton. Yet another 'Waterloo' church, this one by *C. F. Porden*, 1822. An interesting and successful solution to the Church of England problem of the Georgian period as to how a portico and a tower can be combined. The usual solution introduced by Gibbs at St Martin-in-the-Fields is never entirely happy. Here the tower is boldly moved to the E end, and nothing interferes with the appreciation of the Greek Doric portico with four giant columns *in antis*. The tower has a tall ground floor with one window, a first upper stage with Greek Doric columns, and a second thinner and octagonal. Subsidiary entrances into the church on the l. and r. of the tower. The body of the church is of stock brick with Grecian window surrounds. The E window has two Doric columns, even inside. The church was gutted in 1976, when the first stage of its conversion into a community meeting place was completed, leaving the original organ in place in the w gallery and a chapel at the s w end of the ground floor. There were originally three galleries on piers. – Fine Grecian COMMUNION RAIL of iron. – Circular FONT with Greek-key and egg-and-tongue motifs. – Many MONUMENTS. T. Simpson † 1835 by *Sievier*; two heads in medallions. – George Brettle † 1835 by *R. Westmacott*. – Charles Kemp † 1840 and R. Gibbs by *H. Weekes*, and some other tablets. – In the former churchyard large monument to Richard Budd of Russell Square † 1824, by *R. Day*, solid neo-Greek, in three stages of decreasing size, the Grecian and Egyptian motifs of Soanian derivation.

ST MICHAEL, Stockwell Park Road. 1840–1 by *W. Rogers*. In outline and material the common Commissioners' type, but treated with deliberate naughtiness. The steeple is at the E end, hexagonal; it forms part of what became a broad porch feature of three-eighths plan when in 1880 the altar was moved from the E to the w end and the seating reversed. The original main entrance was from Stockwell Park Crescent. The clerestory has horizontal almond-shaped windows. Skinny nave with aisles and galleries on cast-iron shafts reaching up to the roof. The side chapels are also original.

ST PETER, Kennington Lane, Vauxhall. By *J. L. Pearson*, the architect of Truro Cathedral, St John Red Lion Square, and St Augustine Kilburn. This was his first major town church, planned in 1860, built (to a cheaper modified design) in 1863–4, for the Rev. Robert Gregory, together with schools, orphanage, and vicarage (*see* Perambulation 2), in the slum area that had developed on the site of Vauxhall Gardens. (The high altar stands on the site of the Neptune fountain.) The church is of stock brick with stone dressings and a little polychrome decoration. Insignificant W front with a three-bay narthex and a two-bay division above, with big projecting buttresses and a single turret (the original design was more elaborate, with a pair of turrets and a large tower and spire to one side). The interior is vaulted (a great rarity at the time). The style is an austere, well proportioned mixture of C 12 and C 13 Gothic elements combining English with French and Italian sources. The circular piers with shafts to the aisles and pointed arches are English Cistercian motifs, but the elaborately carved capitals are of Italian Gothic origin. Above is a blank wall at triforium level, and a larger plain clerestory with plate tracery. There is no chancel arch, but the E end is more ornate, with a semicircular apse with glazed triforium and shafts with shaft-rings. Exceptionally complete and unspoilt fittings. – The painted MURALS in the chancel and the STAINED GLASS in the apse triforium by *Clayton & Bell*. – Upper windows by *Lavers & Barraud*. – FONT with geometric stencilled decoration. – Good later Arts and Crafts beaten metal ALTAR FRONTAL in the Lady Chapel.

ST SAVIOUR, Lambert Road, N of Blenheim Gardens, Brixton. 1874–5 by *E. C. Robins*. Ragstone Gothic. – STAINED GLASS. E window by *Heaton, Butler & Bayne*; nave and aisles by *Powell*. – Future uncertain.

CORPUS CHRISTI (R.C.), Brixton Hill. Begun 1886; by *J. F. Bentley*. Only chancel and transepts built, very tall Gothic, striped brick and stone, in the style of *c.* 1300–30. A stone vault was intended, but there is only a pointed wagon roof.

OUR LADY OF THE ROSARY (R.C.), Brixton Road. Built as a Congregational church, by *A. J. Phelps*, 1870. E.E.; brick and vitrified headers. NE tower, formerly with a spire.

ST ANNE (R.C.), Kennington Lane. 1903–7 by *F. A. Walters*, large, with side chapels between the buttresses (cf. Stokes at Holy Ghost, Nightingale Square, Balham, Ww). (Inside, tall arcades, and an Arts and Crafts stencilled chancel.)

ST FRANCIS DE SALES AND ST GERTRUDE (R.C.), Larkhall Lane. 1902–3 by *F. W. Tasker*; Romanesque; plain W front with circular window.

ST MATTHEW (R.C.), Norwood High Street. 1905, probably by *Tasker* (Survey of London). E end 1937. W end rebuilt 1949–50 with two-storey brick front by *Plaskett & Marshall*.

BAPTIST CHURCH, Courland Grove, NW of Larkhall Lane, South Lambeth. 1840. Simple front with giant brick arches; recessed Ionic porch.

CHRIST CHURCH (Congregational), Kennington Road and Westminster Bridge Road. Only the fine tower survives of the original excellent church by *Paull & Bickerdike*, 1873–6, standing at a commanding position at the fork of two main roads. The spire is decorated with stars and stripes (as the building funds came from America).* The tower now adjoins

* The original composition was worthy of the site: spire at the corner, a cloister-gallery on the SE side leading to Hawkstone Hall; the church itself a very

an office block, with the church on the ground floor marked out by a large window behind a pierced concrete screen made up of a repeating pattern of three curving interwoven forms in high relief. The church dates from 1958–60, the halls and offices from 1972–6: architect of both: *Peter J. Darvall.*

CONGREGATIONAL CHAPEL (former), Chapel Road, West Norwood. Now Knights Hill Residents' Association. A stucco front with pediment, paired Ionic columns, and lower wings. A handsome composition, handsomely restored in 1979.

CONGREGATIONAL CHURCH, St Matthew's Road, Brixton. 1828, stock brick, with a little Greek Doric porch *in antis* and round-headed windows, matching the few older villas left amidst the recent housing estate.

METHODIST CHURCH, Fentiman Road. 1900 by *G. P. & R. P. Baines*, in the usual jolly style of the Methodists, with the usual asymmetrical turret.

METHODIST CHURCH, Coopers Yard, off Westow Hill. By *E. D. Mills & Partners*, 1964, replacing a church of 1874. Ingeniously tucked away behind a supermarket. The vestibule with STAINED GLASS serves as its advertisement.

(ROUPELL PARK METHODIST CHURCH, Norwood Road. 1879–80 by *Charles Bell*. Gothic, Kentish rag.)

(ST CUTHBERT (Presbyterian), Thurlow Park Road. 1901 by *A. O. Breeds*. Prominent building in red brick with stone dressings. N W tower.)

STOCKWELL BAPTIST CHURCH, South Lambeth Road. 1866. Classical, Corinthian portico *in antis.*

UNITARIAN CHAPEL, Stamford Street. *See* Southwark (Sk), Churches.

UNITED REFORMED CHURCH, Stockwell Green. Mostly an enlargement of 1850 by *James Wilson* of a chapel founded in 1798. Stucco front with Ionic pilasters and pediment, set back from the road, with a projecting wing on the l.

(WESLEYAN CHURCH, Mostyn Road, between Vassall Road and Loughborough Road, Brixton. 1868 by *J. Tarring.*)

(WEST NORWOOD METHODIST CHURCH, Knights Hill. 1852–3. Norman front in ragstone (Survey of London). Extended in 1894 by *F. R. N. Haswell* (CW).)

WEST NORWOOD CEMETERY, West Norwood. 39 acres. Incorporated 1836 as the South Metropolitan Cemetery, the second of the eight large cemeteries established in 1832–47 as an answer to the discoveries of social reformers regarding the shocking conditions of the city cemeteries. Typical of the enlightened, liberal attitude of the age is the fact that on the crown of the hill two CHAPELS were erected, one C of E and one Nonconformist. Both were by *Sir William Tite* (of the Royal Exchange), and both of stock brick, in a somewhat

---

well managed Greek cross with octagonal crossing; three arms filled by galleries, the fourth by communion table, pulpit, and organ. The church seated 2,500. The apse windows were by *Clayton & Bell*.

starved Tudor. The Episcopal chapel with cloisters was demolished in 1955 after war damage; the smaller Dissenters'
chapel was regrettably replaced by an indifferent pale brick
Gothic crematorium by *A. Underdown*, *c.* 1960. The cemetery
was originally laid out with paths winding up the hill between
clumps of trees. The earliest monuments and mausolea are
near the top, and include still many of the Classical Revival,
the types to be found in the older churchyards (sarcophagi,
urns, obelisks). The more ambitious Victorian Gothic monuments start in the 1850s. A hundred years later the open
landscape had been entirely and indiscriminately filled by
graves. The cemetery was acquired by the borough of Lambeth in 1966 with the ultimate intention of partially clearing it
for open space. A programme of relandscaping was begun in
the early 1970s. The intention at the time of writing is to
preserve the main monuments, and, by removing the lesser
ones, to restore something of the earlier, more open layout.

ENTRANCE, and fine cast-iron railings along Robson
Street, by *Tite*, 1836. – The most important MONUMENTS are
listed chronologically.* – Capper family, *c.* 1842. Temple-
shaped mausoleum. – Mrs Ann Joyce † 1839; by *Carlini*. A
square pier in Regency style with acanthus frieze. – Mrs Alice
Moffat † 1847 (S). Early Victorian Gothic revival with openwork trefoiled arcade (stucco on iron); vandalized. – Thomas
de la Garde Grisell † 1847 (W). Sarcophagus of cast iron and
stucco; the fine railings have been stolen. – Captain Wimble
† 1851 (W). Sarcophagus with relief of ships. – Dr Gideon
Mantell † 1852 (near W boundary). Delicately carved white
marble sarcophagus with original iron rail, perhaps by *Amon
Henry Wilds*. – Mrs Ann Farrow † 1854. Remarkable cast- and
wrought-iron structure (badly decayed) with open tracery
sides. – Thomas Cubitt † 1855 (SE). Restrained flat granite
slab. – William Crane † 1856. Pink granite cross with vine
trails (E). – Elizabeth Burges † 1855 by *William Burges* (who is
also buried here) (SE). Simple grey sarcophagus with foliated
cross in relief. – John Britton † 1857 by *George Godwin*.
Brown granite slab near the entrance. – Alexander Berens
† 1858 by *E. M. Barry* (W). Especially ambitious, in the C13
style, with figures of angels and evangelists, and twisted colonnettes, granite, black and red marble, etc. It cost £1,500. –
John Stevens † 1861 by *Anderson & McKenzie* (SE). Large grey
granite obelisk. – J. W. Gilbart ('engaged for fifty years in
advancing the science of banking') † 1863, made 1866, possibly by *Sir William Tite*. Gothic belfry with gables and spire,
prominently sited near the main entrance. – George Dodd
† 1865 by *Thomas Allom* (E). Italian Gothic pink and white
marble mausoleum with lavish cresting and pinnacles. – Edith
Harris † 1867 (S). Neo-classical mausoleum on vermiculated

* The earliest ones are at the top near the crematorium; many of the best
Victorian ones are in the neighbourhood of the Garden of Remembrance: their
direction from this is indicated by N, S, etc. Sir William Tite's memorial, once in
the Episcopal chapel, is now, with others, in the still-existing catacombs (EES).

plinth. – Dr William Marsden † 1867 (founder of the Royal Free Hospital etc.) (s). A conservative monument: a column in Regency tradition. The urn on top has disappeared. – J. W. Everidge † 1868 (near the entrance). Mixed Renaissance with segmental pediment, c. 1870. – Benjamin Colls † 1876, with a lively bust by *G. A. Carter* (NE). – John Garrett † 1881. Gothic, of wood, a curiosity. – Rev. W. M. Punshon † 1881, carved by *J. Rogerson* (s). Fine High Victorian Gothic design, with a row of arches on pink granite columns. – Rev. C. H. Spurgeon † 1892. Grey granite sarcophagus with bust, rather coarse (close to the crematorium). – Near by, Sir Henry Tate, c. 1890 by *S. R. J. Smith*. Terracotta mausoleum with Tudor windows. – Sir Henry Doulton † 1897 (E). Probably by *R. Stark Wilkinson*, architect of the Doulton works on the Albert Embankment. Red brick mausoleum with plenty of terracotta decoration. Over the door, angels in Doulton ware. – Rouyer-Guillet Mausoleum, near the entrance, in a Beaux-Arts–Neo-Grec style.

75   At the NE corner is the GREEK ORTHODOX CEMETERY, a small separate burial ground with many tombs of high quality, dominated by the admirable MORTUARY CHAPEL built to commemorate Augustus Ralli † 1872. Attributed to *John Old-rid Scott* (architect of the Greek Orthodox Cathedral, Bayswater), although unlike his other work. It is a pure Greek Doric tetrastyle temple with single-storey wings. Coffered ceiling inside. – MONUMENTS. Alexander Cassavetes †1862. Sarcophagus in the Regency tradition, with portrait bust. – John Peter Ralli † 1863 by *G. E. Street*. Large mausoleum. – T. E. Schilizzi † 1870, made 1872. Italian Gothic canopied memorial with openwork dome on cusped arches, of coloured granite and marble. – Eustratios Ralli, by *E. M. Barry* and *T. H. Vernon*, c. 1875, with sculpture by *Mabey Bros*. White marble mausoleum with Doric porch. – Another memorial, with inscription in Greek, is signed by *Cecil Thomas*, 1927.

LAMBETH PALACE

The Archbishop's Palace is the principal ancient monument of Lambeth. Londoners and strangers do not usually appreciate the fact that London possesses in this palace a complex of domestic buildings largely medieval and wholly picturesque which is of the greatest interest and merit. The archbishops owned the site from the late C12. The river front with its partly posthumously Gothic and partly classical hall between medieval towers and close to the parish church must have been eminently impressive when there was no embankment and one approached it by boat. The GATEHOUSE lies side by side with the tower of St Mary's. It was built by Archbishop Morton c. 1495, of red brick with black brick diapering. The archway has a stone vault. To the l. and r. are tall solid five-storeyed wings. There is some linenfold panelling in an upper room. Past Morton's Tower one turns l. to examine the exterior of the HALL which was rebuilt by Archbishop Juxon 29 *c.* 1660–3 after it had been destroyed during the Commonwealth. On its r. is a gateway belonging to the C 19 (*see* below), when the hall was converted into a library.

Although the hall had to be repaired after war damage, it remains one of London's most attractive buildings: red brick with stone dressings, still entirely Gothic in its structure, that is, with buttresses, two-centred pointed three-light windows with cusped lancet heads to the three lights, and a high-pitched roof covering a magnificent hammerbeam roof. Pepys called it old-fashioned, in spite of what concessions it makes to the coming classical style. These are chiefly the quoins, the main cornice with its frieze of garlands and its modillions, the two pediments to the large square projecting bays at the N and S ends of the river front, the ball finials on top of the buttresses, and the pretty hexagonal lantern with pilasters and volutes on the roof. Inside the same unworried mixture: a garland frieze at the foot of the roof, pendants with classical foliage, coffering on the walls and vaults of the bays, and a splendid very typical broad doorway with pilasters and open segmental pediment with achievement, dated 1663. The two bay-windows have coffered jambs and arches, with rather gross rosettes in the coffers. In one of the windows C 16–19 STAINED GLASS, mostly heraldic, all that was left in the palace after the war. Two tables of oak, dated 1664. The bookcases are in the neo-Jacobean of the time of Archbishop Howley's re-furnishings and enlargements: 1829–33. The projecting ones were removed after the war. The C 19 alterations were placed into the hands of that successful, if not very individual, architect *Blore*. He was responsible for rebuilding the range N of the hall, with its two-storeyed CLOISTERS. In the E cloister walk a powerful BUST of Archbishop Temple by *Epstein*, one of his last works. In the N walk a curious recess with remains of WALL PAINTING. It is flanked by two wooden Ionic columns from the W gallery of the chapel.

The range N of the cloisters is medieval and contains in fact the oldest part of the palace: the UNDERCROFT of the chapel, 7 probably dating back to Archbishop Langton's time, that is, the early C 13. It has a central row of three low Purbeck columns with moulded capitals carrying chamfered arches and ribs. The vaulting cells are carefully constructed of regular blocks laid at right angles to the ribs (i.e. in the English manner). Along the walls the ribs rest on corbels. Fragments of wall plaster with ashlar markings. The undercroft windows are plain lancets with, externally, blind trefoil arch-heads.* The CHAPEL itself was gutted during the war. The rather bland and chilly restoration by *Seely & Paget* was completed in 1955. The building dates from *c.* 1230 according to its style, and has a very good E E. doorway, round-arched with finely

---

* This unusual feature also occurs at Chipstead church, Surrey.

moulded voussoirs on three orders of stone shafts with
moulded capitals. The doorway is subdivided by a central
cluster of shafts into two openings with pointed-trefoil heads.
In the tympanum a quatrefoil. On the E side the doorway has a
segmental rere-arch resting on very short vertical pieces on
Purbeck shafts. The whole seems an earlier version of the idea
underlying the Westminster Abbey chapter house doorway.
The windows of grouped lancets with slender black Purbeck
shafts. The present vault is of plaster, replacing one put in by
Blore in 1846. This was preceded by a flat ceiling, but the
discovery of a wall rib during repairs indicates that the chapel
originally had a stone vault. – COMMUNION RAILS. Two C17
panels (formerly gates) near the altar with openwork acanthus; two now near the W end with symmetrical balusters. –
STALL ENDS. Also C17; cherubs' heads and swags in fanciful
cartouches. – The SCREEN formerly dividing off the W bay
into an antechapel, now in the room W of the chapel, bears
Laud's arms, and was part of his refitting of the chapel which
so angered the Puritans. It was probably by *Adam Brown*, who
was paid for joinery work in the chapel in 1633. Seven bays,
with a doorway with open scrollwork, upper panels with
upright oval openings with carved surrounds (an Oxford
motif), divided by tapering pilasters surmounted by busts. –
TILES. Small, C14, plain and patterned alternately. –
STAINED GLASS. 1955; coloured panels on paler quarries,
bitty. – MONUMENT. Archbishop Parker † 1575. Tomb-chest
with quatrefoil plinth, patched up after damage during the
Commonwealth.

The room W of the chapel has a boarded ceiling with
moulded ribs and pretty carved bosses. It forms the lower part
of the WATER TOWER, completed in 1435 by Archbishop
Chichele. The total cost was £291 19s. 4¼d. It is of rough
Kentish rag, four storeys high, with a higher staircase turret
on the N side, and with the windows towards the river regularly placed. The name Lollards' Tower under which it is more
usually known was in use already in the C17. It may have been
taken over from an earlier tower on the same site. (On an
upper floor are remains of a C17 prison.) Laud added to the
Water Tower a lower block of the same material. Finally,
facing N and attached to the E bay of the chapel, CRANMER'S
TOWER, brick, probably mid C16. E of the cloister is the
GUARD ROOM, a four-bay first-floor hall, which was re-
erected by *Blore* on old walls, re-using the C14 roof timbers.
The roof has moulded arched braces supported on corbels,
with tracery in the spandrels (cf. Herland's roof of 1394 at
Westminster Hall). The arched longitudinal wind braces and
wall braces also have tracery.

Beyond this is the E range, with the archbishop's residence
(now also offices etc.). Before the C19 there were two irregular
E wings with a courtyard in between. *Blore* replaced these with
a single block faced with Bath stone, in a carefully asymmetrical Tudor style. Walter Scott called it 'in the best Gothic

taste'. To the s the range has a large central tower with an oriel window above the main entrance. A wide staircase leads up in a single flight to the principal rooms. Both stair hall and oriel are vaulted. At the top one enters a broad central corridor beneath three arches; a little to the r. the upper staircase continues, lit by a very large window of five lights with two transoms. At the end of the corridor the former archbishop's STUDY (now conference room) with a big bay-window looking out over the extensive gardens to the N. Part of the N side of the building had to be rebuilt after the war. The replacement is plainer (windows without cusps) and more regular than the original.

In the courtyard N of the E range MONUMENT to Archbishop Davidson by *W. Reynolds Stephens*, 1930. Two bronze angels kneeling below a cross. To the E the former stable, also by *Blore*, with buildings on three sides, now cottages.

THE PUBLIC BUILDINGS OF THE SOUTH BANK*

The public buildings to be discussed are the Royal Festival Hall, the Hayward Gallery, the Queen Elizabeth Hall and the Purcell Room, the National Film Theatre, the National Theatre, and also the Shell Buildings, although they are not public, because they are an essential part of the rebuilding of this area after the Second World War.

The area lies between Waterloo and Westminster Bridges. In the c 17 and c 18 there were here wharves and timber-yards and waste land behind. Building started after the Waterloo Bridge had been built in 1811–17. York Road between Westminster and Waterloo Bridges was laid out about 1820 and Belvedere Road in 1814–27. The Lion Brewery on the site of the Festival Hall was built in 1826 and 1827 and the Shot Tower in 1826 too. About the middle of the century the railways came. The first Waterloo Station dated from 1848 and the complicated Waterloo Junction from 1860 to 1864. *Brunel*'s iron Hungerford Suspension Bridge was rebuilt during those years to take the railway to Charing Cross.

Plans for redeveloping the whole area in some monumental fashion began to be made in 1935. The proposal in the newspaper *The Star* dated from 1938, the Royal Academy's project from 1942. There followed in 1943 the much more realistic *Forshaw* and *Abercrombie* plan for the whole of central London. The area with which we are concerned was called 'depressing', 'derelict', and 'lacking in dignity'. When the War was over, the L.C.C. made new plans, with *Charles Holden* as a consultant. That was in 1947. It proposed offices for 10,000 civil servants, a concert hall, and a theatre. When in 1948 preparations began for the Festival of Britain, the promise was made that it would be held in 1951, and that the Festival Hall would then be ready. In fact it

* By Sir Nikolaus Pevsner.

was, except that the small hall s of the main hall was not built (and never was built).

Two years after the Festival the L.C.C. was ready with an outline plan for our area. The architect to the L.C.C. at that time was *Leslie Martin*, later Sir Leslie. It was a plan of spacious interconnecting squares and other enclosures, with views to the river and with just one high office tower.* It was an excellent plan, but in execution some of the best features were lost. On the following pages the buildings will be described and appreciated in chronological order.

THE FESTIVAL OF BRITAIN.‡ 1951, to celebrate the centenary of the first international exhibition. Director General *Sir Gerald Barry*, Director of Architecture (Sir) *Hugh Casson*. The buildings were designed by many architects, their style being throughout 'modern', i.e. without any Neo-Georgian leftovers. Within the modern style the designs differed a great deal. What they had in common, and what any exhibition buildings are bound to have in common, is a higher pitch than permanent buildings would allow themselves to display. Aesthetic quality differed, of course; gimmicky details were not excluded. As a matter of principle *The Buildings of England* do not deal with buildings which no longer exist. It is sufficient here to mention without further comment the following as of outstanding quality: Land of Britain by *H. T. Cadbury-Brown*, the display inside Countryside by *F. H. K. Henrion*, Sea and Ships by *Basil Spence & Partners*, and Lion and Unicorn by *R. D. Russell* and *R. Y. Goodden*. The most prominent buildings were the Dome of Discovery by *Ralph Tubbs*, circular, with a diameter of 365 ft, and the Skylon by *Powell & Moya*, 296 ft high.§

For the future the most important aspect of the Festival was that it was planned as a totally informal composition without axial symmetries. The principles underlying the composition were the Picturesque as created in the early c 18 for parks and gardens. The suggestion to transfer these principles from landscape gardening to urban architecture was first made by the *Architectural Review* in January 1944, January 1947, March 1948, and December 1949.‖ Thus the Festival buildings differed in height, changed in level, were loosely grouped with large and small plazas. Floorscape ranged from long slabs to cobbles, from plants in tubs and boxes to plants left to grow. All these features found their echo in the centres of the New Towns (Harlow, Stevenage, etc.) and in the proposed layout of the South Bank as worked out by the L.C.C. But when that layout was published the Festival Hall was already in full operation.

103 ROYAL FESTIVAL HALL. By (Sir) *Robert Matthew* and (Sir)

---

* See Sir J. M. Richards in *Architectural Review*, LXIV, 1953, 399.

‡ See *Architectural Review*, CX, 1951, 73–145, and more recently M. Banham and B. Hillier, *A Tonic to the Nation*, London, 1976.

§ The shaft was 256 ft long.

‖ That is, CXV, 3 f.; CI, 21 f.; CIII, 99 f.; CVI, 354 f.

Leslie Martin; group architects *Edwin Williams* and *Peter Moro*. The designing started in 1948. The building was opened in 1951. It was the first major British public building designed in the contemporary style of architecture. The concert hall seats 3,000. Plans included a smaller hall to the s; but that was never built. In addition there are of course foyers and restaurants. A remarkable amount of research has gone into such matters as acoustics, sound insulation against the neighbouring railway, seating comfort, etc. Considerable changes were made in 1962 by (Sir) *Hubert Bennett*, the then Greater London architect, group architects *N. W. Engleback* and *A. J. G. Booth*. For these changes *see* below. The description of 1953 runs as follows: Aesthetically the greatest achievement, and one which is without doubt internationally remarkable, is the management of inner space. Here, chiefly in the staircases, promenades, superimposed restaurants, etc., are a freedom and intricacy of flow, in their own way as thrilling as what we see in the Baroque churches of Germany and Austria. The various levels are nowhere placed above each other without either ingeniously contrived intermediate stages or without opening into one another by galleries, landings, or some such means. The circuits at stalls and balcony heights for instance are an experience well worth lingering over. Equally delightful is the ascent of the main stairs towards the N, where one reaches a landing from which the angles and bottom corners of the hall are visible and it seems as though the whole huge box of the hall proper were suspended without any support. Altogether, if it were not for the fact that the Hall is raised to what corresponds to second- or third-floor level and stands on retracted pillars, nothing like this spatial flux could have been obtained. This ingenious arrangement made it possible to have a large concourse right through the building below the hall. The careful choice of materials and colours also helps, much glass opening out vistas in all directions, divers timbers, slatted or reeded wooden surfaces, grey Derbyshire marble slabs, rendering in various unobtrusive colours, excellently designed carpets and textiles.

The same care has been bestowed upon the concert hall itself, though here variety of motifs is perhaps carried a little too far. The seats are arranged as stalls for 2,000, plus one balcony at the back for 600, plus four tiers of boxes on each side. These are singly cantilevered out diagonally in such a way that unobstructed view is obtained from every seat. This advantage and the acoustic advantage of broken surfaces are gained at the cost of a restless, though, it is true, highly original and lively pattern. Drawers pulled out in a hurried burglary raid, malicious critics have said. The pattern is bizarre but seemed no doubt aesthetically desirable to the architects – an indication of that reaction against the straightness and utilitarianism of 1930 which is so characteristic of 1950. The boxes are not even identical in numbers and arrangement on the l. and r. On one side there are four tiers of nine, on the other only of six, because of the differently designed royal box. The ceiling pattern also, though equally justified by acoustic considerations, appears somewhat capricious. The wavy canopy of sycamore above the orchestra for instance is there too to combine refraction towards the audience with refraction back into the orchestra. Yet to the eye it is primarily another broken instead of straight surface. Colours are rich and warm, except for the blackish-blue of the box sides and the white of the box fronts. The colour scheme succeeds in achieving intimacy in a room of whose real size one becomes aware only when looking at people at the other end. There is certainly nothing here of the circus or colosseum quality of the Albert Hall. Lighting helps a great deal also in pulling together the large room. The lit slits in the box fronts and the hovering ceiling lighting ought to be specially observed – again a deliberately diffuse effect.

The exterior of the building, on the other hand, is frankly massive. The main theme is the raised solid block of the Hall surrounded by an area of circulation rooms largely glazed on the outside. The principal façade is towards the river, sym-metrical, with much glass, an ingeniously informal asymmet-rical arrangement of the staircases, and just one motif which betrays the new urge for something decorative – the curious stone apron in the middle of the top storey. There are no sufficient structural reasons for it; it was an afterthought, quite evidently, because the smooth, dignified plainness of before was not considered enough. The problem is one of great significance with designers today. The Lubetkin flats in Finsbury tell equally eloquently. How can the bare func-tionalism of 1930 be overcome without a return to period ornament? What should modern ornament be like, granted that it has once more become a necessity? Dr Martin's answer is mauve and white tiling of one part of the side elevations, the pattern of small dark windows in the white staircase walls of another part of the side elevations, and of course the boxes in the concert hall. It is a bold, courageous answer, and it may well be old-fashioned to doubt its validity. Still, the doubt remains whether monumentality in terms of the C 20 can be achieved by building a main block and then applying busy geometrical patterns to it.

That was where the 1953 account ended. The most con-spicuous changes of 1962 were these: the river frontage was pushed forward by 30 ft towards the river, and the curious apron was eliminated. The main entrance is now on the river side. The whole of this frontage is less idiosyncratic and more neutral. The main restaurant was enlarged and replanned. The foyer was also enlarged. On the E and W sides the eleva-tion was simplified. On the s side administrative offices and dressing rooms were added.*

SHELL CENTRE. 1953–63 by *Sir Howard Robertson* and *R.*

* See *Architects Journal*, 24 February 1965, 477–87.

Maynard Smith of *Easton, Robertson, Cusdin, Preston & Smith*. In the L.C.C. master plan of 1953 one high tower was proposed. In 1954 the area to be built over by Shell was enlarged. The design for the whole centre was exhibited in 1956.* The centre consists of two buildings E and W of the railway. The E building is L-shaped and ten storeys high, the W building is U-shaped and partly ten, partly twenty-six storeys high. The high part reaches a height of 338 ft above street level. It is too broad to read as a tower. As for the structure, the tower is steel-framed, the rest is of reinforced concrete. The whole is faced with Portland stone. Below ground there is space for 400 cars, obviously not enough, if one considers that the buildings are for 5,000 employees.‡ Among its amenities there are a swimming pool, and four squash courts.

The aesthetics of the Shell Centre have been much argued. The windows are relatively small and upright in the Georgian rather than the so-called International Modern of 1930. Apart from the windows there is hardly any other relief. Robertson in a letter to the *Architects Journal* gave his reasons.§ They were that small offices call for small windows, that curtain walling is awkward to maintain, and that Portland stone weathers better.

The buildings house quite a number of works of art. In the inner hall is *Marino Marini*'s Horse and Rider. The Upstream Restaurant has murals by *Sidney Smith*. The mural in the Downstream Restaurant is by *Humphrey Spender*. In the foyer of the twenty-second floor is a mural by *Bernard Lamotte*. The auditorium of the theatre was designed by (Sir) *Cecil Beaton*. The mural of the theatre foyer is by (Sir) *Osbert Lancaster*. 'Within the tower,‖ the internal decoration of offices, board rooms and private rooms on the twenty-first, twenty-second and twenty-fourth floors was entrusted severally to a number of architect/decorators whose work was co-ordinated by *Lady Casson*. She herself was responsible for the internal design of a number of rooms on these floors. Others display the skill and taste of *H. T. Cadbury-Brown*, *Stefan Buzas*, *Roger* and *Robert Nicholson*, *Dennis Lennon*, *Raymond Schomberg*, *Ward & Austin*, *Morton Lupton*, *Design Partners*, *Cassidy Farrington*, and *Dennys*, and the French designer *Jean Royère*.' The upstream courtyard has a large fountain by *Franta Belsky*.**

NATIONAL FILM THEATRE, beneath the S arch of Waterloo Bridge. 1956–8 by the L.C.C. Architect's Department (*Leslie Martin*, completed under *Hubert Bennett*, job architect N.

---

* See *Architects Journal*, 20 May 1956.

‡ The centre incidentally has 240 telephone lines and 4,500 extensions. I owe these figures and much else to the Shell Centre brochure published in 1963.

§ See *Architects Journal*, 20 May and 5 July 1956.

‖ I am now quoting from the brochure.

** The bronze figure by *Siegfried Charoux* (The Cellist), 1958, formerly in the downstream courtyard, is in store at the time of writing, following repair, and is to be resited.

Engleback).* The auditorium is fan-shaped and has 504 seats. The dominant motif is the masking screen with its close abstract pattern mostly of rectangular motifs. The foyer lower than the auditorium.

HAYWARD GALLERY, QUEEN ELIZABETH HALL, PUR-CELL ROOM. 1965–8 by the G.L.C. Architect's Department (*Leslie Martin*, group architects *E. J. Blyth* and *N. W. Engle-back*).‡ The three parts are connected. They are mainly accessible by elevated walkways, not all at the same level. It is a thrilling experience, if the weather is fine and you are at leisure. But what if it rains, what if you are late, what if you find steps a strain? This is not the only time that I shall ask this question. The HAYWARD GALLERY§ was built for the exhibition of works of art, particularly the exhibitions of the Arts Council. It operates at three levels: storage and services, then galleries, then open-air sculpture courts and two more galleries. The main entrance is at gallery level and for pedestrians. The upper galleries have skylights appearing outside as little pyramids. The main gallery level is without windows. Where windows appear they are of arbitrary shapes and in arbitrary positions. The building is of *in situ* reinforced concrete, externally clad with pre-cast slabs, with exposed shuttering above. The reliefs are of Corbusier derivation. The concrete makes for a bleak effect in spite of the intricacies of the walkways. The nearest to the effect is Piranesi's 'Carceri'. Internally, alas, the exposed concrete fights the size, style, mood, and emotional temperature of most of the exhibits for which the gallery was built: Rothko – excellent, Jackson Pollock excellent, tribal art excellent, Picasso some excellent, some not, but Gainsborough painful and Blake could not even be tried.

The QUEEN ELIZABETH HALL has 1,106 seats, the PUR-CELL ROOM 372. These two and the Hayward Gallery form one complicated group. Walls and roof are of concrete, so that there is no break between them. The Queen Elizabeth Hall has a raking floor; so has the Purcell Room. Both are internally symmetrical. Their foyers they have in common. They are of a totally asymmetrical pincer shape. The round mushroom piers inside the foyer appear at first to be asymmetrical too, though, if one tries on paper to plot them, one will soon realize that some of the mushroom piers are parallel with the wall which has the main entrance, others should be read with the back wall of the Queen Elizabeth Hall. On the N side the piers continue and are placed again parallel with a wall of the Queen Elizabeth Hall, but now outside. The piers carry flat concrete beams. The ceiling includes rather violent shapes. The main entrance is at nearly the same level as that to the Hayward Gallery. Both entrances are for pedestrians. Some parking is

* See *Architectural Review*, CXXIV, 1958, 40.

‡ For the Hayward Gallery, the Queen Elizabeth Hall, and the Purcell Room see the *Architects Journal*, CXLV, 1967, 999–1018.

§ Sir Isaac Hayward (1894–1976) was leader of the L.C.C., later G.L.C., from 1947 to 1965.

under the Hayward Gallery; and circulation is in two single one-way loops, from a single entry in Belvedere Road. The whole group has few windows but exposed ducts. The seats are upholstered with black leather.

As for an aesthetic appreciation, this time *Peter Moro* will speak, one of the group architects for the building of the Festival Hall:* 'The old concert hall is an extrovert structure . . . the new is . . . introspective. Instead of the all-enclosing envelope, the exterior is fragmented and expresses its component parts in oddly-shaped volumes cast in concrete . . . The building is an articulated piece of sculpture with roofs and walls . . . cast in one . . . For the visual excitement . . . one has to accept a bedraggled look on a rainy day . . . If one accepts this – and the building is probably strong enough to stand it – the skilful handling of the whole complex demands nothing but admiration.'‡

NATIONAL THEATRE. By *Sir Denys Lasdun & Partners*, 1961–76.§ The prehistory of the National Theatre is complicated indeed. The Drury Lane Theatre was often called the National Theatre; so was the Shakespeare Memorial Theatre at Stratford. The Drury Lane was directed by Garrick in 1747–86. Also known as the National Theatre was the Old Vic, which was opened in 1818 as the Royal Coburg. It was bought by Emma Cons in 1880. Lilian Baylis was her niece. She died in 1937, having in 1931 built Sadler's Wells. In 1963 the National Theatre Company moved in. In 1932 the Stratford Memorial Theatre was rebuilt to designs by Elizabeth Scott. This was of brick in a blocky modern style.‖

Meanwhile, i.e. in 1913, a site in Bloomsbury had been bought, and in 1937 the awkward, roughly triangular site opposite the Victoria and Albert Museum. It was for the latter that six prominent architects, chosen by a Stratford Memorial committee, were to suggest designs. The result of this was that *Lutyens* showed his design in the Royal Academy exhibition in 1943. It was of course classical, say in the style of Lutyens's Midland Bank in Poultry. Then the L.C.C. held out hope of a site on the South Bank for whose representational development ideas were beginning to circulate. However, the site was not final. It shifted from Lutyens's on the area of part of the Festival Hall to another close by, then to immediately E of County Hall, and finally the present site. Lutyens had died in 1944, and *Sir Hubert Worthington* followed with a design with a genuine portico. This was never accepted officially. Instead,

Architects Journal, CXLV, 1967, 999–1009.

‡ For my comments on style and my appreciation, *see* above.

§ See the *Architects Journal*, CXLV, 12 January 1977, 59–88, and the *Architectural Review*, CLXI, January 1977. For the technical problems and their solutions, the issue of the *A. J.* is specially informative. For the prehistory of the National Theatre I have taken much from the articles by Iain Mackintosh, Stephanie Williams, and David Hutchinson in the *A. R.* Also in the *A. R.* are brilliant mottoes by Denys Lasdun himself.

‖ Gropius, to whom I had the pleasure of showing it, found it puzzling and certainly not modern.

in 1946 a committee was appointed to choose the architect. The members were Abercrombie, Holden, Holford, Reilly, and myself. The committee held only one meeting, a lunch at the Savoy, and chose *Brian O'Rorke*, i.e. an architect modern but not too radical.* O'Rorke made designs for the site between the Festival Hall and Waterloo Bridge, and after that site had been declared unsuitable, for the site E of County Hall. In 1949 the National Theatre Act was passed, and in 1951 the Queen (i.e. the present Queen Mother) laid the foundation stone.

The fifties meant delays, mainly for financial reasons, and in 1961 the decision was taken not to carry on. The passing idea of replacing Sadler's Wells by a National Opera House on the South Bank site was thoroughly unrealistic, given the mood of the Treasury, but interviews were held with nearly twenty eminent British 'modern' architects. *Denys Lasdun* was chosen, and his design was shown in 1965. However, this was still for the site E of County Hall. The change to the present site took place in June 1967, and we now experience Denys Lasdun's final design. The building was completed in 1976.

The building houses three theatres: the Olivier with 1,160 seats, the Lyttelton with 890, and the Cottesloe with 200 to 400 according to seating arrangements. The name Olivier needs no explanation. Lyttelton refers to Lord Chandos, chairman of the South Bank Theatre Board. Cottesloe is after Lord Cottesloe, chairman of the National Theatre Board. The plan of the whole is roughly square. The material is concrete, grey and with shuttering marks. The frontages differ totally. Towards the river, i.e. the N, the dominant motif is the terraces on three levels. To the W, about the middle, are the main entrances; below for cars to set people down, above for walkers. As one enters one is at once directed in a diagonal direction, i.e. not at right angles to the front. The S side and much of the W side are the workshops. They are almost entirely closed. Windows are only in a low strip. The material is brick, but a clerestory is faced with ribbed aluminium. Finally, most of the E side has boldly raking struts. Such struts had appeared in Denys Lasdun's Sports Centre of Liverpool University (1965–7); the general impression however is most like that of the Royal College of Physicians in Regents Park (1960–4). The terrace reminded at least one critic of Frank Lloyd Wright's Falling Water of 1938; but I consider that accident.

The most daring of the external aspects is the skyline. The highest and broadest tower is the fly-tower of the Olivier. The fly-tower of the Lyttelton is less massive and lower and starts from a lower level. Competing also are the group of square

* Reilly started the ball rolling by saying at the very beginning that he took it that nobody would want giant columns. This was agreed, and so the Worthington approach was at once eliminated. Reilly was wonderfully skilful in such situations.

turrets flanking the entrance. They serve for the lifts, and/or drainage, heating, cabling, etc., and are set diagonally. The entrance to the Cottesloe by the way is on the E side, deliberately inconspicuous between the raking struts. Seen from near or seen from far, the National Theatre refuses to be monumental (at least monumental in the sense in which I use that term). Symmetry is mostly everywhere avoided. So is any surface treatment in itself attractive. Concrete with all the shuttering marks can never be attractive. On the contrary it is a demonstration against conventional beauty. The various towers and turrets form themselves into ever-varying patterns. That, maybe, was the idea of monumentality in the seventies – 'an aesthetic of broken forms', as Mark Girouard has written. But should broken forms be the principal expression for a theatre? Should not a theatre be the envelope of the play? The only major building similarly aggressive for a similar function is Scharoun's Berlin Philharmonie of 1956–63, but the Philharmonie is entirely an interior matter. The National Theatre is in its own style outside as well as inside. Denys Lasdun's river terraces indeed link the interior to the exterior, even in the raw board-marked concrete and the egg-crate coffering of the ceilings.

The building, apart from its three theatres at different levels and apart from all the stage machinery, contains ample foyers, a restaurant for 80 diners, buffets, and of course offices etc. The restaurant was, I am told, an afterthought. The Lyttelton foyer is the most impressive, though in a gaunt way. 109 It is largely very low,* but leads to a sudden climax of considerable height. Altogether unexpected changes of level and hence equally unexpected vistas across are provided in many places. That even in the foyers the concrete is raw was to me a disappointment. Apart from the restaurants there are self-service buffets and bars (four for Olivier, three for Lyttelton, one for Cottesloe). All that seems ample; what is far from ample is the basement area for 400 cars. If all three theatres were booked up, that would be nearly 2,000 people, not counting the employees.

On the machinery and technological aspects I am not competent to pronounce. The publications referred to in the footnote give much interesting information. The details of planning on the other hand I would have liked to describe, but space does not permit more.

The Olivier Theatre has comfortable seats. All seats in Olivier and Lyttelton are in fact comfortable. The Olivier seating is in two tiers, stalls and circle, steeply rising. The mood is relaxed, or would be if it were not for the shuttering marks of the raw concrete walls and the angular fragmentary-looking suspended shapes over your head – acoustically no doubt a great asset. The stage is what one calls a thrust stage: that is, it has no proscenium and instead pushes forward so as

* It seems doubly low because of the heavy coffering of the ceilings.

to be about half-surrounded by the audience. About half – this must be emphasized, because people seem to think that it is a 'theatre in the round' like Chichester (1961), Bolton (1967), and Manchester (Royal Exchange, 1976), or in foreign terms Gropius's Total-Theater of 1927, Seattle (Penthouse, 1939), Sant' Erasmo in Milan (1952), and Washington (Arena, 1961). The earliest thrust stage seen by me was the Grosses Schauspielhaus in Berlin of 1914 (by Poelzig).

Whereas the Olivier is placed diagonally in the whole block – corner stages existed e.g. at Western Springs, Illinois, and at Dallas (by Frank Lloyd Wright, 1959–60), the Lyttelton is set parallel to the outer N and S walls. It is a much more conventional theatre, above all in that it has a proscenium arch. Seating is in two tiers, stalls and circle. Relaxing however is not as easy as in the Olivier, the reason being the ferocious concrete patterns on the side walls. The seats are a dark honey colour; in the Olivier they are mauve.

The Cottesloe is small, oblong, black, and parallel to the Lyttelton. It has three levels of balconies. It is simple, almost as if undesigned, and ideal for experimenting.

In conclusion, an attempt at comparing the National Theatre with the Hayward–Elizabeth–Purcell group. Historically the two belong together, with their confidence in raw concrete and in the diagonal, the chamfer, the bevel. But walking from the National Theatre to the Hayward area – Denys Lasdun looks positively elegant. Brutalism is a term often used for the style of the sixties and seventies. It applies without reserve to the Hayward group with its overbearing cyclopean forms and its consistent stress on horizontals. The National Theatre instead lets its horizontals be answered by the verticals of its towers.

Finally the elevated walkways. Hayward etc. and the Theatre connect their systems. They give you many varied views, and their multiplicity of levels can be a joy in itself. But they can become irritating if they are not sufficiently signposted, or if you are in a hurry to get somewhere on time, or if it rains.* Besides – where should the common users go to reach their targets in the end? From Waterloo Station one of the first signs directs you up forty-two steps ('les quarante-deux marches'), and from bus-stops you are no better off. However, signposting is not enough and access ought to be considered once more.

SCULPTURE (from W to E). On the terrace outside the Queen Elizabeth Hall, Zemran, by *William Pye*, 1972, sinuous shiny metal forms; outside the Royal Festival Hall, CHOPIN MEMORIAL, 1975 by *Marian Kubica*. Beyond Hungerford Bridge JUBILEE ORACLE, a pair of abstract bronze shapes in the Hepworth tradition, by *Alexander*, 1980. The DOLPHIN LAMPSTANDARDS along this part of the

---

* You should hear students of the University of East Anglia describing their blowy walkway.

Embankment Walk were erected in the 1960s. Like the adjacent early C20 examples in front of County Hall, they follow the design of those made in 1870 for the Victoria and Albert Embankments (which were modelled by *James Mabey*, under *George Vulliamy* as the M.B.W. Superintending Architect).

The JUBILEE GARDENS between the Embankment and the Shell Tower, occupying the site at one time destined for the National Theatre, were laid out in 1977.

OTHER PUBLIC BUILDINGS

COUNTY HALL, York Road and Westminster Bridge. The London County Council was created in 1888. Its first home was the old offices of the Metropolitan Board of Works in Spring Gardens, Westminster. The new Aldwych Crescent was at first favoured as a site for the new County Hall, but eventually the less constricted South Bank was chosen, opposite the Houses of Parliament. *Ralph Knott* (1871–1929) won the competition in 1908. Building began in 1912, but was interrupted by the First World War; the S part of the river front was completed in 1922; the N part followed in 1931–3. Behind these, facing York Road, two additional wings (North and South Blocks) were planned in 1937, by *F. R. Hiorns* of the L.C.C. (consultant: *Sir Giles G. Scott*). The first part was completed in 1939, the rest in 1950–8, apart from the block facing N, which was added, to a different design, in 1958–63. Further expansion was necessary after the L.C.C. was absorbed into the new Greater London Council in 1965. The south island block, on the roundabout in Westminster Bridge Road, dates from 1970–4 (*G.L.C. Architect's Special Works Dept*). It was planned for 1,540, to bring the total staff of County Hall up to 8,500. Additional rooms were added to the N and S sides of the members court in 1972–4 (job architect *William Whitebread* of the G.L.C.).

The building covers a trapezoidal site, with continuous perimeter blocks concealing the public rooms in the centre. The river front is 700 ft long, a symmetrical composition with a concave attached giant colonnade as its central motif. Basement and ground floor within a granite plinth; four upper floors and two attic storeys set back in the steep tiled roof. To l. and r. pavilions with the channelled rustication and the giant niches so favoured by Sir Reginald Blomfield on the strength of France, Piranesi, and Somerset House. Dance's Newgate Gaol, much in the public eye at the time of its demolition in 1902, perhaps also was an influence. The rusticated pavilions with their niches appear on the other sides as well. Knott must have had a real understanding of Piranesi, and the Edwardian mood was enterprising and melodramatic enough to allow him to do in solid stone what Piranesi had done only on paper. This mood is continued by the members' entrance off Westminster Bridge Approach, which is of a frankly operatic character, passing beneath a covered way with a circular opening in the vault, into the members' courtyard. This is the only internal court which is stone-faced; the others have utilitarian glazed tiles. Its character has been altered, not very happily, by tinted glass curtain walling, seven storeys high, on E and W sides. The later York Road blocks show the typical approach of the epigones of Edwardian Imperial glories; no change of heart, but under a willy-nilly influence of the coming Modern Movement a reduction in moulding and ornaments, and a more straightforward emphasis on verticals and horizontals. The completion of the N block is even plainer, with the concealing plinth at last abandoned in favour of exposed structural columns. The island block is more abrupt in its break with the past, as can be seen most uncomfortably where the bridge over the road enters the S block. The new building itself is ingeniously compressed on to its small site, yet makes a handsome show: an irregular hexagonal pyramid of four stepped-back storeys of open-plan offices, on a recessed sunken podium of three storeys. The lower part and subway are a brutalist experience both visually and aurally, with the heavy-handed shuttered concrete detailing familiar from the underbelly of the Hayward Gallery. The upper floors are sleeker, with smooth white bands alternating with tinted glass, enlivened on sunny days by projecting orange blinds.

SCULPTURE. Figure sculpture on the old building by *Ernest Cole* and *Alfred Hardiman*; architectural carving by *Charles Mabey*. In the members' courtyard, bronze portrait memorial plaque to Ralph Knott by *Gilbert Bayes*, 1931.

INTERIORS. The public rooms are on the first floor, approached by steps from the members' court, or from the E. The mood is more restrained than the Edwardian exuberance of the exterior, recalling the coolness of late C18 classicism, with the play of rich materials in spaces of contrasting shape. Octagonal council chamber, surrounded by a generous ambulatory, approached either from the members' court through a square lobby with Palladian openings on each wall, or up the ceremonial staircase rising in short straight flights from the E entrance. Marble everywhere (by *Farmer & Brindley*): black columns in the lobby and in the identical one on the other side, veined black columns in the ambulatory, brown columns, Doric, in pairs, around the staircase landing. In the council chamber pairs of buff Ionic columns around the walls, above a streaky grey marble dado. To the W are members' rooms around the crescent facing the riverside, refurbished after war damage. To the N passages lead first to a rectangular public room, panelled, with a barrel-vault intersected by lunettes, then to the elliptical conference hall, a more festive interior, with blue scagliola columns and a shallow dome with a little coffering. Chapel on the ground floor, made in 1955. Rail with carved panels of the Lamb, Passover symbols, Pelican, etc. Flemish C17 ceramic plaques at the chapel entrance, in the style of Della Robbia, mid C19. In several rooms, fireplaces brought from elsewhere, especially good the one in room 118, mid C 18, with a delicate carving of Aesop's fable of the Bear and the Beehives, by *William Collins*, brought from Lindsey House, Lincoln's Inn Fields.

The noble LION of *Coade* stone by Westminster Bridge, the largest of three which were on the Lion Brewery on the South Bank, is by *W. F. Woodington*, 1837.

TOWN HALL, at the corner of Brixton Hill and Acre Lane. By *Septimus Warwick* and *H. Austen Hall*, 1906–8, a cheery Edwardian brick and stone composition in an effective position. L-shaped plan, with the council chamber linking the two wings, a corner entrance, and an angle tower with muscular allegories below the top. They represent Justice, Science, Art, and Literature, as hardly one passer-by in a hundred thousand will have the wish to work out for himself. Extension and top floor by the same firm, 1938. (SCULPTURE. In the entrance hall, plaque of a wheelwright's shop, by *Tinworth*.)

LAMBETH MAGISTRATES' COURT (former), Renfrew Road. *See* Perambulation 2.

FIRE BRIGADE HEADQUARTERS, Albert Embankment. 1937 by the L.C.C. (*E. P. Wheeler*), symmetrical front of no consequence, stressing the horizontals. Practising tower behind. Sculpture on the front and memorial inside by *Gilbert Bayes*.

FIRE STATIONS (former), Waterloo Road, *see* Perambulation 1(a); Renfrew Road, *see* Perambulation 2.

KEYBRIDGE HOUSE (Post Office and Telecommunications Centre). *See* Perambulation 3.

BRIXTON PRISON, Jebb Avenue. Designed in 1819 by *Thomas Chawner*, the Surrey County Surveyor, as a Surrey House of Correction, with central polygonal block and radiating wings. Bought by the government in 1853, when it was converted and enlarged as a prison for women. Many later additions. The original small octagonal governor's house survives.

LIBRARIES. Lambeth benefited from the patronage of Sir Henry Tate, who lived at Streatham (q.v.). Many South London libraries (as well as Tate's greatest benefaction, the Tate Gallery) were designed by his protégé *S. R. J. Smith*. They are enjoyable examples of minor late Victorian municipal showmanship. The largest is the TATE CENTRAL LIBRARY, Brixton, of 1893, free Renaissance, with coffered entrance arch and pedimented end pavilions, in an important position facing the Town Hall. A bust of Sir Henry Tate († 1899) outside. The TATE LIBRARY, South Lambeth Road, of 1888 is small, with a rum curved porch with caryatids. The DURNING LIBRARY, Kennington Lane (paid for by Miss J. Durning Smith), of 1889, is in an elaborate polychrome Gothic, with arches of varied size, a gable, and a tower. A fourth library by Smith, at West Norwood, is now disused. An entrance loggia with balcony is crammed into its tiny façade. Its replacement, opposite, is the WEST NORWOOD LIBRARY AND NETTLEFOLD HALL, Norwood High Street, 1969 by *Lambeth Architect's Department*, dignified yet inviting.

Sloping roof and dark purple-red brick walls; light and spacious inside, as the library is arranged around an internal courtyard with all-glass walls. To the outside upper windows only. At the back the octagonal HALL, reached by a broad staircase of shuttered concrete. Discreetly sited in a courtyard behind, SCULPTURE by *David McFall*, 1972: Oedipus and Jocasta.

CARNEGIE LIBRARY, Herne Hill Road. 1904 by *Wakeford & Son*. Large, of picturesque design, with plenty of terracotta, a mixture of mullioned and transomed windows and Georgian motifs.

MINET LIBRARY, Knatchbull Road. The gift of the local landowner and benefactor, William Minet. The interesting octagonal building of 1890 by *George Hubbard* was alas destroyed in the war. Its meek replacement dates from 1956.

MUSEUM OF GARDEN HISTORY. *See* Churches: St Mary, Lambeth Road.

MORLEY COLLEGE, Westminster Bridge Road. Founded 1889. It developed out of the penny lectures at Emma Cons's Old Vic. The present site was developed from 1924. The buildings consist of *Maufe*'s pale brick extensions of the 1930s, and the parts of 1958 by *Brandon-Jones, Ashton & Broadbent* (to a design of *Cowles Voysey*) which replaced the original building. Wrapped around two sides of these are *John Winter*'s more spectacular additions of 1973–5, a package of air-conditioned classrooms in a smooth brown aluminium envelope. Further extensions, with meeting hall and top-floor studio, in King Edward's Walk, 1979–82. Three floors, clad in corrugated Cor-Ten steel (a material that weathers to a rusty patina).

PHILIPPA FAWCETT TRAINING COLLEGE, Leigham Court Road. *See* Streatham (La).

POLYTECHNIC OF THE SOUTH BANK AND VAUXHALL COLLEGE OF BUILDING, Wandsworth Road. 1970–4 by *Shingler Risdon Associates*. Five storeys on a plaza over a car park, with a clumsy projecting lecture theatre acting as a mammoth porch canopy.

ST GABRIEL'S COLLEGE, Cormont Road, by Myatt's Fields. 1899–1903 by *P. A. Robson*, mixed Gothic and Renaissance, the top spoilt by later additions.

SOUTH LONDON COLLEGE, Knights Hill, West Norwood. Large extensions of 1969–74 (job architect *John Bennett*, for the G.L.C./I.L.E.A.), red brick with uneven window bands.

BOARD SCHOOLS. Early examples by *Robson* are WYVIL ROAD SCHOOL, South Lambeth, of 1876, plain, gabled, with only the usual terracotta panels as modest ornament, and KINGSWOOD ROAD SCHOOL, Gipsy Road, 1880 (altered 1905), another gabled asymmetrical composition. Good examples of *T. J. Bailey*'s mature three-decker board schools with jolly Jacobean skylines are the VAUXHALL MANOR SCHOOL ANNEXE, Kennington Road (1897, s wing 1910), the similar HENRY COMPTON SCHOOL, Kingswood Road,

N of Streatham Place (1898), and the KENNINGTON SCHOOL, Cormont Road, by Myatt's Fields (1898). All have their centres flanked by staircase towers with ogee cupolas. Other good *Bailey* schools in Rosendale Road (1899) and Sunnyhill Road (1900).

BEAUFOY SCHOOL, Lambeth Walk Estate. *See* Perambulation 1(c).

BEAUFOY SCHOOL ANNEXE (formerly Beaufoy Institute), Black Prince Road. 1907 by *F. A. Powell*. Brick and terracotta with a typical free treatment of Baroque motifs.

NORWOOD SCHOOL, Crown Dale. By *James Cubitt & Partners*, 1967–72. Tough, impressive, yet not unfriendly buildings in the yellow brick and shuttered concrete so popular in the 1960s. Three-storey classroom block on two levels, with strongly projecting roof. At right angles to this is the lower gymnasium wing, with a more playful elevation: V-shaped buttresses between circular windows in giant arches.

STRAND COMPREHENSIVE SCHOOL, Upper Tulse Hill. An early I.L.E.A. comprehensive (architect in charge *J. M. Kidall*), 1956. Nine-storey teaching block (the tallest built by the L.C.C.) with chequerboard curtain wall on one side, and articulated by four large lift shafts on the other (each lift designed to hold a whole class). The school was designed for 2,210 boys. When built it was the largest in London.

DICK SHEPPARD SCHOOL, Tulse Hill. 1950–5 by *Yorke Rosenberg & Mardall* for 960 girls, one of the first post-war London schools of such a size. Four-storey classroom block behind hall, gymnasium, etc., the main circulation at first-floor level because of the sloping site overlooking Brockwell Park. The model in mind was the American university campus, but the layout had to be less generous.

LICENSED VICTUALLERS' SCHOOL (former), Kennington Lane. *See* Perambulation 1(c).

LONDON NAUTICAL SCHOOL, Stamford Street. *See* Perambulation 1(a).

ST MARK'S SCHOOLS, Harleyford Road. *See* Perambulation 3.

ST PETER'S SCHOOLS, Kennington Lane. *See* Perambulation 1(c).

SHELLEY SCHOOL, Wincott Street. *See* Perambulation 2.

PRIMARY SCHOOL, Frazier Street. *See* Perambulation 1(b).

INFANTS SCHOOL (former), Lambeth Road. *See* Perambulation 1(b).

INFANTS SCHOOL, Elder Road. *See* Perambulation 6.

CHURCH OF ENGLAND CHILDREN'S SOCIETY, Kennington Lane. 1853 by *Willshire & Parris*. Until 1908 the Lambeth Vestry Hall, i.e. one of the earliest surviving municipal buildings in South London. Clumsy but quite imposing classical front. Nine windows in groups of three divided by pilasters. Pedimented Tuscan portico.

BELGRAVE HOSPITAL FOR CHILDREN, Clapham Road. 1900–3 by *H. Percy Adams*. Cruciform plan; the elevations by his assistant *Charles Holden* when he was still under the influence of the Arts and Crafts tradition. 'The influence of Henry Wilson and Philip Webb may be recognized in the composition and the brick detail.'* The building is of brick with stone dressings; mullioned-and-transomed windows. The main feature is the entrance wing with a tall gable between two towers.

KINGS COLLEGE HOSPITAL, Denmark Hill. 1909–13 by *W. A. Pite*, the new wing by *Collcutt & Hamp*, 1937. Tall and massive, deliberately representational and almost American in scale. The later part with the entrance tower is mannered, with neo-Georgian and Cinema elements. Dental hospital and school 1965, nine-storey ward block 1965–8 by *George Trew & Dunn*. – STATUE to Sir Robert Bentley Todd † 1860. – (CHAPEL with late C 19 stained glass from the former hospital.) – Foundation stone (1909) and other inscriptions by *Eric Gill*.

LAMBETH HOSPITAL, Brook Drive, off the NE end of Kennington Road, Kennington. Developed from the infirmary buildings (1877 by *Fowler & Hill*) added to Lambeth Workhouse. (Operating theatres by *Yorke Rosenberg & Mardall*, 1967.)

ROYAL HOSPITAL FOR INCURABLES, Crown Lane, w of Crown Dale, West Norwood. 1894 by *Cawston*, 1913 by *E. T. Hall*, and more recent additions. A nice group, not at all forbidding as so many hospitals are. The style is neo-Tudor or neo-Jacobean, especially successful in the E wing with the hall. (The chapel, red brick lancet style, 1913 by *Hall*. Barrel-vault and good ironwork. DOE)

ROYAL WATERLOO HOSPITAL (former), Waterloo Road. Begun as a dispensary for children in the City of London, moved to this site in 1822. Rebuilt in 1903–5 by *M. S. Nicholson*. Detailing in the Lombardic Renaissance style, with three tiers of terracotta *logge*. *Doulton*-ware porch.

ST THOMAS' HOSPITAL, Westminster Bridge and Lambeth Palace Road. A C 12 foundation, the oldest in London after St Bartholomew's, originally connected with St Mary Overie, Southwark. In the early C 13 it moved to a site on the E side of Borough High Street, where one of the mid C 19 ward blocks, and the former church of St Thomas (with an attic used as an operating theatre), still remain (*see* Southwark (Sk), Perambulation 2 (a)). The hospital had to make way for the Charing Cross Railway Company. It was rebuilt on the present site by *Henry Currey*, 1868–71, one of the first civic hospitals in England to adopt the principle of the pavilion layout with 'Nightingale' wards (the precedent had been set by the Royal Herbert Hospital at Woolwich in 1860). The inspiration was the French Hôpital de Lariboisière which Florence Nightingale had visited. The principle was to allow maximum ventilation and dispersal of foul air. St Thomas' originally consisted of seven pavilions built on an embankment along the river-

* Letter from Sir Charles Holden to N.P., June 1955.

side, with the lower chapel near the middle. The buildings are linked by arcades. The total length was 1,666 ft. The composition is now sadly truncated: only the three s pavilions and the chapel remain. The waterfront was the only attempt on the s side of the river in the C 19 to make a civic show: rows of trimmed trees formed a promenade facing the Houses of Parliament. Each pavilion is a brick block of three wards over a service floor. The ends facing the river have two corner turrets (housing the bathrooms etc.) flanking the arcaded centres. The style is weakly Italianate. There is a profusion of ornament in *Ransome*'s concrete, and a busy skyline of pinnacles and chimneys, the expression of the complicated ventilating system.* The CHAPEL, lower than the pavilions, is also Italianate, with stone dressings and a pediment. Good interior with aisles and a coffered barrel-vault. Reredos with *Doulton* relief panels. Facing Lambeth Palace Road, the MEDICAL SCHOOL, brick with stone quoins, and a tower, in asymmetrical contrast to the formal river front.

During the Second World War the N end of the hospital was badly damaged and one pavilion completely destroyed. Total rebuilding was decided upon in 1956; the first stage, the EAST WING (outpatients etc.) facing Lambeth Palace Road, by *W. F. Howitt*, the hospital architect, was planned in 1958 and begun in 1962. It was then decided to rebuild on a much larger scale (1,250 instead of 820 beds), and in 1963 *Yorke Rosenberg & Mardall* were called in. Their plan was for two deep-plan thirteen-storey ward blocks with lower buildings, set back from Westminster Bridge Road, and approached across a piazza over a car park. Only the northern part of this plan, with one of the ward blocks, has been executed (planning permission 1966, built 1969–76). Seen from the river the huge smooth white cubes sit awkwardly next to the remaining Victorian buildings, which have been reprieved for the time being. In the centre of the formal garden on the piazza a large stainless steel FOUNTAIN, after a design by *Naum Gabo* of 1929 (made up full size after a maquette in the Tate Gallery). Flanking the main entrance, three statues from the old hospital, puny figures against a white clinical cliff. On the l. Sir Robert Clayton, marble, by *Grinling Gibbons*, 1701–2; and Edward VI (the refounder of the hospital), stone, 1682, part of a group by *Thomas Cartwright* which adorned a front gateway to the old hospital in Borough High Street. The rest of the group, two pairs of cripples, are in the main entrance hall. On the r. of the doorway another statue of Edward VI, of bronze, by *Scheemakers*, 1737. (Also in the entrance hall, six large enamel panels by *Robyn Denny*, 1976, and a mobile over the staircase by *Nechemia Azaz*. In the hall to the treatment block a *Doulton*'s tile mural of *c.* 1910, the Babes in the Wood, from one of the old wards, and a sculpture by *Antonas Brazdys*.

* See Grace Goldin, 'Building a Hospital of Air, the Victorian pavilions of St Thomas's Hospital', *Bulletin of the History of Medicine*, XLIX (1975), 512.

(Several other *Doulton* ware murals elsewhere in the building.)

LYING IN HOSPITAL (now part of St Thomas'), York Road. By *Henry Harrison*, 1828, three storeys (the top one added in 1879). Brick and stucco, with a façade of four Ionic columns *in antis*, a rare example of the small early C 19 hospital. It was founded in 1765.

BABIES' HOSTEL (now part of St Thomas'), Black Prince Road. 1913–14 by *Adshead & Ramsay*, originally a day nursery on the Duchy of Cornwall estate (*see* Perambulation 1 (c)).

KENNINGTON PARK was created from Kennington Common by the Office of Works in 1852–4. At the entrance facing Kennington Road a LODGE which is the re-erected and altered two cottages put up at the 1851 Exhibition by special request of Prince Albert to set an example of what working-class housing should be like. The detail is minimum Elizabethan, the plan has the staircase in a niche in the centre, a motif to become almost standard for mid-Victorian cheap flats. By *H. Roberts*, who designed the earliest working-class flats in existence (*see* Streatham Street, Holborn, Ca). Near by a graceful terracotta COLUMN from a fountain given by Sir Henry Doulton in 1869, modelled by *Tinworth*, once with a family group in medieval dress. Opposite the park on the W a large L.C.C. estate of 1933, to the E the Brandon Estate (*see* Southwark (Sk), Perambulation 3 (c)).

BROCKWELL PARK and RUSKIN PARK. *See* Perambulation 5.

GASWORKS, Gasholder Place, The Oval. Cast-iron framed GASHOLDER of *c.* 1870 with the emblem of the Phoenix Gas Company.

COVENT GARDEN MARKETS. *See* Battersea (Ww), Public Buildings, New Covent Garden.

1 WATERLOO STATION. 1901–22, engineer *J. W. Jacomb Hood* succeeded by *A. W. Szlumper*, the only C 20 station building in London with architectural ambitions. However, the grand Edwardian manner of the façade (by *J. R. Scott*) is badly spoiled by a hopeless position. How could anything like Helsinki or Leipzig or Stuttgart be done, where giant columns and giant sculpture stand dead against the arches of another elevated railway line? The steelwork inside is forthrightly functional, no arches, no wide spaces. The roof over platforms 16–21 is of 1885. The news cinema is of 1934 by *Alister MacDonald*. Beneath the station is an extensive system of tall brick tunnel-vaults and ramps down to the Waterloo and City Railway (*see* Thames Crossings at end of gazetteer). Rolling stock can be lifted from this line by a hydraulic hoist N of the station. W of the station, by Westminster Bridge Road, a reinforced concrete SIGNAL BOX in the International Modern style of the 1930s (cf. Surbiton, Ki).

STOCKWELL BUS GARAGE, Lansdowne Way. By *Adie Button & Partners*, 1950–4. A monumental home for 200 buses below a reinforced concrete shell roof on nine arches of considerable span (*c.* 73,000 sq. ft of uninterrupted garaging).

HERNE HILL STATION (London Chatham and Dover line).
 Booking office 1862, two storeys, polychrome brick, Gothic, a
 taller tower for the water tank. A handsome group.
STREATHAM COMMON PUMPING STATION, Conyers Road.
 See Streatham.
WATERLOO BRIDGE, CHARING CROSS (HUNGERFORD)
 RAILWAY BRIDGE, WESTMINSTER BRIDGE, LAMBETH
 BRIDGE, VAUXHALL BRIDGE. *See* Thames Crossings at
 end of gazetteer.

PERAMBULATIONS

*1. The riverside and its hinterland between Waterloo Bridge and
Vauxhall Bridge**

1 (a). Waterloo Bridge and Waterloo Road

The buildings flanking the approach to Waterloo Bridge nearly 1
 all date from after 1950: on the W the SOUTH BANK ARTS
 CENTRE and the SHELL BUILDINGS, on the E the
 NATIONAL THEATRE by the river (*see* above, Public Build-
 ings of the South Bank). Then come a few survivals: the Royal
 Waterloo Hospital and St John's church (*see* Other Public
 Buildings *and* Churches, above) at the corner of Stamford
 Street, overlooking the roundabout with its large and rather
 useless sunken pedestrian centre, 200 ft in diameter. This
 dates from 1966 (engineers *Rendel, Palmer & Tritton*, with the
 G.L.C.). STAMFORD STREET and its neighbours still mix
 warehousing with terraces in a once typically riverside way.
 CORNWALL HOUSE (H.M.S.O. store) is of 1912 by *R.
 Allison*, a surprisingly straightforward commercial structure,
 as modern in its conception as Burnet's contemporary Kodak
 House in Kingsway. Opposite, No. 127 (formerly W. H.
 Smith's printing works), the same principle but neo-Greco-
 Egyptian detail (1915 by *C. Stanley Peach*). Again on the N
 side BOOT'S offices by *H. Tanner*, 1936, an accepted pattern
 of the thirties with the staircase tower in one corner and all the
 rest long bands of windows. Then on the S side two long
 four-storey terraces, 1829, with pediments over first-floor
 windows, and ten-bay Corinthian centrepieces added *c.* 1912
 by *J. Coleridge* when the houses were converted to flats. At the
 end the LONDON NAUTICAL SCHOOL, built *c.* 1820 by *J.
 Montague* as a school for Irish children. Nine-bay brick house,
 the three central bays projecting. Entrance with Doric
 columns *in antis*. Upper storeys of the side part by *C. H.
 Townsend*, 1908–9. For the rest of Stamford Street, *see* Southwark (Sk), Perambulation 1 (b).
To the N off UPPER GROUND, where the river used to be shut
 off by wharves, KENT HOUSE, offices and studios for London Weekend Television, 1970–2 by *C. H. Elsom & Partners*,

---

* Perambulation 1 (a)–(c) can be followed as a continuous walk.

a brash mosaic-clad podium-and-tower, an unfortunate back-drop to the National Theatre. The theatre is better comp-lemented by its more recent neighbour the IB M CENTRAL MARKETING CENTRE, 1979–83 by *Denys Lasdun, Redhouse & Softley*, an asymmetrical five-storey composition around two internal courtyards with broad terraces stepping down on the E side, balancing those of the theatre when seen from the river. The entrance is on a raised podium on the W side. To the S in AQUINAS STREET pairs of pedimented cottages, 1911, part of the Duchy of Cornwall estate (cf. Kennington, Peram-bulation 1 (c), below), and very modest early C 19 workers' terraces in THEED STREET and ROUPELL STREET. Here too St Andrew's and St John's SCHOOL, plain brick Gothic, and ST ANDREW'S HOUSE, with a little more detail, 1868 by *S. S. Teulon*.* S of the railway near WOOTTON STREET blocks of L.C.C. flats (ETHELM HOUSE etc.) by *E. Arm-strong*, 1937, excellent for their date.

Back in WATERLOO ROAD loom the brown brick and bronze glazed towers of the UNION JACK CLUB and offices, a powerful composition by *Fitzroy Robinson & Partners*, 1975–6, on a transatlantic scale. Three towers of different heights, on a podium with much chamfering of angles. The club accommodation is at the back in a twenty-five-storey tower with continuous oriel windows; the office block facing Water-loo Road has a free-standing upright forming a monumental and overpowering portal.‡ On the W side a former L.C.C. FIRE STATION of 1910, more staid than earlier Arts and Crafts examples. S of The Cut the OLD VIC. It was formerly the Royal Coburg Theatre, then the Royal Victoria Hall. The side wall with large blind arches and oculi belongs to the original building by *R. Cabanel*, 1816. Remodelled 1880 by *E. Hoole*, with a Baroque stucco front; reconditioned 1950 by *Douglas Rowntree*. To the E OLD VIC WORKSHOP, by *Lyons Israel & Ellis*, 1957, with a frame of shuttered concrete, an early example of brutalism.

Further S in Waterloo Road, the stately façade of the offices built for DAVID GREIG, with three-storeyed giant columns, 1928 by *Payne Wyatt*, preserved in front of a building of 1979–80. Nos. 157–183 are the CHURCH MISSIONARY SOCIETY HEADQUARTERS, 1964–6 by *Ansell & Bailey*, five storeys, with brick bands over piers with recessed balconies in be-tween. The whole curves back, so that there is room in front for a large entrance staircase with a CHAPEL above. Bold letter-ing on the band between the two. The chapel has an E wall with rough brick panels and a plain wooden cross, and a large stained-glass window opposite the door, by *Keith New*, 1966.

---

* *Teulon* also built St Andrew's church, 1854–6, near by in Coin Street, demolished after war damage. It was of Kentish rag bands, with an asymmetrical spire, evidently influenced by Butterfield in its use of polychromy, and not as offensive as Teulon often liked to be.

‡ The original Union Jack Club was by *Cave*, 1907, tall and symmetrical, like an Edwardian hospital.

LONDON AMBULANCE HEADQUARTERS on the w side.
Similar massing, with a projecting lower wing, but clumsier.
Clad in grey mosaic. By the *G.L.C. Architect's Department*,
c. 1970. Further on, MAUDSLEY BUILDINGS, early C 20
L.C.C. flats, tall, gabled, with iron brackets beneath the eaves
as minimal ornament.

1 (b). Between Waterloo Road and Lambeth Road

Behind Waterloo Station much rebuilding. The most complete
of the older streets is LOWER MARSH, with its street market,
and the SPANISH PATRIOT, a late C 19 corner pub with lively
striped brickwork. In FRAZIER STREET a PRIMARY
SCHOOL, 1967 by *Andrew Renton & Associates*, a low red brick
building with taller hall, nicely detailed, behind matching
walls. In BAYLIS ROAD an unusually attractive cluster of
flats, eight to ten storeys, load-bearing brick, with crisply
projecting balconies. By *Stillman & Eastwick Field*, 1963 (part
of the G.L.C.'s Tanswell Estate). Further s, at the corner of
Kennington Road and Lambeth Road, LAMBETH TOWERS
is another good landmark. By *Lambeth Architect's Department*,
completed 1965, a rare example for its date of a corner site
treated with verve: ten storeys, lively elevations in black and
white with projecting windows on alternate floors.
Maisonettes, with shops, doctors' group practice, and low
projecting polygonal luncheon club neatly incorporated. The
wings are ingeniously canted to fit the site, pivoting on the lift
shaft which provides a strong central vertical feature. Opposite, off Mead Row, WELLINGTON MILLS, built by the
G.L.C. (job architect *B. Bienias*, 1970–6) but run as a housing
co-operative, 138 maisonettes pleasantly grouped in low
ranges round courtyards. The long brick balconies reminiscent of the thirties, but used here as private spaces, not for
access.

To the w down LAMBETH ROAD. At the corner, opposite
Lambeth Towers, SURREY LODGE HOSTEL, 1981, plain,
brick, with recessed windows, set back from the road. Several
terraces of *c.* 1800 on the N side. In HERCULES ROAD off to
the N Nos. 28–34, nice early C 19 cottages with iron verandas.
On the other side BLAKE HOUSE, pleasant L.C.C. flats in a
four-storey terrace on a human scale (1950s) (William Blake
lived in Hercules Road).* Nearer the historic centre of Lambeth No. 214 Lambeth Road, the former rectory, 1828–9,
altered later, with an earlier part on the r. (date stone 1778).
Then a former INFANTS' SCHOOL of 1880, an attractive
composition with a large roof with Gothic dormers, and an
attached school-house on the l. with turret. The road ends
with the parish church nearly hidden in the shadow of the

* w of the railway line, in ROYAL STREET (facing Archbishop's Park,
formerly part of the grounds of Lambeth Palace), a tough nine-storey block of
flats, by *L. Creed*, 1958, for people displaced by new buildings for St Thomas'.
Exposed concrete frame (cf. Roehampton (Ww), Alton Estate, Alton West, etc.)

Archbishop's Palace on the r. (*see* p. 342) and on the l. with the
PHARMACEUTICAL SOCIETY HEADQUARTERS, the start
of the encroachment of offices s from the Albert Embankment. Planned from 1967 (the society's former buildings were
on the proposed British Library site in Bloomsbury Square),
completed 1977. By *Louis de Soissons Partnership* (*David
Hodges*). Eight storeys on a cramped site. Sleek brown aluminium cladding over fussier lower parts. Recessed zigzagging
windows on the ground floor (lighting the library) with inset
balconies above. An assembly hall at basement level at the
back.

1 (c). Between Lambeth Road and the Oval, Kennington

Opposite the Archbishop's Palace and the former parish church
near Lambeth Bridge, only the name of LAMBETH HIGH
STREET reminds one that this was once the old village centre.
The ALBERT EMBANKMENT was built out in front of the
original shoreline in 1866–9 by *Bazalgette* to accommodate the
southern low-level sewer from Putney, with bridges beneath
for barges to reach the factories. The industry disappeared
after the Second World War, and the potential of this excellent
riverside site was frittered away from the 1950s onwards by
depressingly mediocre office building. At the E end LAM-
BETH BRIDGE HOUSE of the 1950s, brick, utilitarian, and
indifferent. The most recent contributions, replacing buildings of the 1930s,* are rather better. First DOULTON HOUSE,
by the *John S. Bonnington Partnership*, 1980–2, a tower of
fourteen storeys, breaking the pattern of the earlier post-war
offices both by its height and in its use of a vivid red brick.
Then INTERNATIONAL MARITIME ORGANIZATION, by
Douglas Marriott, Worby & Robinson, 1977–82, a well
proportioned composition with a more self-effacing four-
storey front of yellow brick, taller behind. Both buildings
display the current abhorrence of flat roofs by encasing their
lift gear in prominent steeply hipped caps. Past Black Prince
Road one can study the efforts of the 1950s onwards, bland
façades with no emphasis anywhere apart from a few attempts
to liven the roof-lines with free-standing grids. The only
exception is ALEMBIC HOUSE, by the river, which displays
the new confidence of the 1960s with its tower with boldly
projecting floors above a podium. By *Oscar Garry & Partners*,
1962.‡ The Albert Embankment ends at VAUXHALL CROSS,
one of the most unpleasant road junctions in South London,

* These were Doulton's offices, which had the German type of decoration with
emphatic verticals and some gaudy gilt and coloured decoration on the ground
floor, 1938 by *T. P. Bennett & Son* with frieze by *Gilbert Bayes* of Pottery through
the Ages; and W. H. Smith's offices, symmetrical, with a tower *à la* Great West
Road (1933).

‡ Demolished: No. 85 near Vauxhall Bridge Foot, the only reminder of an
earlier age. It was called 'modern' in 1809 and in 1823 'replete with every office
and convenience fitting for a Genteel Family'. Two storeys with two bowed
projecting wings.

and badly in need of some architectural uplift. Battles over the development of the empty sites on either side of Vauxhall Bridge raged throughout the 1970s.* In 1982 *Sebire Allsopp & Happold* won a competition with an ingenious mixture of offices and housing: a glass wall of offices to the road, stepping down from twenty-three to ten storeys, buttressed by lower housing in steps down to six storeys facing the river. On the opposite side of Vauxhall Cross at the beginning of Wandsworth Road, a sleek streamlined curved corner building completed in 1982, in Nine Elms Lane the tower attached to Covent Garden Flower Market (*see* Battersea, Ww, Public Buildings).

BLACK PRINCE ROAD. Near the river were DOULTON'S C19 premises by *R. Stark Wilkinson*, 1878, originally consisting of three buildings, all of the most self-certain High Victorian Gothic and all with plenty of *Doulton* terracotta detail. The works closed in 1956. The only survivor stands at the corner of Lambeth High Street, with corner turret corbelled out, and a tympanum below with a pleasant little relief of potters by *G. Tinworth*, the Lambeth sculptor who did so much work for Doulton's. The firm was founded in Vauxhall Walk in 1815. Farther on around Black Prince Road the old pattern of dense streets of industry and decaying old houses has been replaced almost entirely by large estates.‡

To the N the large G.L.C. LAMBETH WALK ESTATE by the *Architects Co-partnership* extends from Lambeth Walk to Kennington Road and takes in LAMBETH WALK, which has become a real walk with shops, as this is an estate with the strict traffic segregation characteristic of the 1960s. The maisonettes above have gardens on the shop roofs. But this cannot compensate for the grim total effect of the dark brown brick used throughout. The façades are relieved only by some variation in balcony shapes on the blocks farther E. Near Kennington Road three austere tower blocks loom above a bleak playground on the roof of a car park. Within the estate BEAUFOY SCHOOL, by the same firm (1961–4), for 1,665 boys. The same brown brick and the same determination to be harsh and tough, expressed here by shuttered concrete floors and beams. On the other side of Black Prince Road is the rambling and uninspired VAUXHALL GARDENS ESTATE which covers most of the area down to Kennington Lane. The usual L.C.C. blocks of the 1950s; two later point blocks (by *Lambeth*) in Vauxhall Walk. There is nothing to remind one that this was the site of VAUXHALL GARDENS, in the C18 one of London's chief open-air entertainment places (*see* Lambeth Introduction).§ It is a relief to turn further E to the

* The eastern part was the site for the notorious 'green giant', a mammoth glass tower of offices proposed in the late 1970s.

‡ Demolitions: in Vauxhall Walk: Nos. 28–42, 1768–9, some of the original houses in the street; and early Guinness Trust flats, 1893 by *Macartney*, remarkably progressive for their date.

§ The gardens covered the area between Kennington Lane, St Oswald's Place, Vauxhall Walk, Laud Street, and Goding Street.

Duchy of Cornwall housing around the site of Kennington Palace (*see* Lambeth Introduction, above). In CARDIGAN STREET, COURTENAY STREET, and COURTENAY SQUARE terraces of cottages by *Adshead & Ramsay*, 1913. They are in a neo-Regency style, something very progressive at that time. N of Courtenay Street, off NEWBURN STREET, WOODSTOCK COURT, which is an especially attractive quadrangle for old tenants with pilastered entrance and Tuscan cloister, 1914. Later work for the Duchy by the *Louis de Soissons Partnership*, e.g. in SANCROFT STREET and BLACK PRINCE ROAD Newquay and Trevose House, flats with weatherboarded bay-windows (1948), and off Cardigan Street in STABLES WAY (the site of the palace stables) houses, maisonettes, and studios (1967), in yellow brick, blending well with the older cottages.

KENNINGTON LANE. Several good houses: from W to E, by St Anne's church, ST ANNE'S HOUSE, 1824, an unusually elaborate example of Soanian neo-Greek, attributed by Sir John Summerson to Soane's pupil, *Gandy*. Note the complicated design of the entrance. Around St Peter's a group of buildings by *J. L. Pearson* for the Rev. Robert Gregory. On the l. of the church HERBERT HOUSE, three storeys with a little brick Gothic detail, built in 1860–2 as an orphanage which provided pupil-teachers for the schools behind. On the r. the VICARAGE, a late C18 house (originally that of the manager of Vauxhall Gardens) with an added gabled top floor. Behind are ST PETER'S SCHOOLS, built as schools for boys and girls and an art school (with later top storey), 1857–61 (alterations by *J. T. Knowles Jun. c.* 1873). A soup kitchen (later converted to a schoolroom) was added in 1863–4. The two-storey brick buildings are picturesquely arranged around two courtyards, with gables of varied size and an angle tower with bold pyramid roof. Further E Nos. 231–245, a terrace of *c.* 1791 excellently restored as offices and flats for the Gin Distillers' Company in 1973, and IMPERIAL COURT, the former LICENSED VICTUALLERS' SCHOOL, by *Henry Rose*, 1836, large, with a composite portico and pediment. A school would never have been so ambitious in its architecture before the C19, when higher education for the middle class became important enough to call for the monumental.*

2. *Kennington Road and streets to its* E

KENNINGTON ROAD, built up after Westminster Bridge (1750) opened up this part of Lambeth, still has a remarkably complete collection of late C18 to early C19 terraces. The best are near the entrance to Walcot Square: Nos. 121 etc. of the 1770s on the E side, with a variety of porches, Nos. 104 etc. opposite, with stuccoed ground floors; Nos. 150 etc. date from

71

* At the junction of Kennington Lane and Kennington Road, an underground gentlemen's CONVENIENCE of *c.* 1900, with original fittings (by *Finch & Co.* of Lambeth), a rare survival.

1840. WALCOT SQUARE itself is of 1837–9. Some more terraces in WALNUT TREE WALK to the W and in Kennington Road again further S: Nos. 233–291 Kennington Road, with a central pediment, and Nos. 309–341 date from *c.* 1787. No. 317 with a pediment inscribed Marlborough House is by *Michael Searles*. Nos. 155–157, in the E part of KENNINGTON LANE, with good doorcases, are of *c.* 1776–80 (Duchy of Cornwall Estate Office). In CLEAVER SQUARE, an oblong of late C 18 to mid C 19 terraces linking Kennington Road and Kennington Park Road. In the square, SCULPTURE of a recumbent figure, by *James Butler, c.* 1970. Nos. 114–132 Kennington Park Road, flanking the entrance to the square, were built in 1787–90 by *Michael Searles* for Joseph Prince (Cleaver Square was formerly Prince's Square*).

KENNINGTON PARK ROAD (part of the Roman road which runs S from London Bridge), wide and tree-planted, has some other Georgian terraces – especially good Nos. 140–162 (*c.* 1775). The rest of this area is mostly public housing, best described chronologically. In DENNY CRESCENT (N of Kennington Lane) cottages by *J. D. Coleridge*, 1913, and in CHESTER WAY later neo-Georgian housing by the *Louis de Soissons Partnership*, all for the Duchy of Cornwall. Further N three instructively different types of high-rise estates by *Lambeth*, from three decades. Around OPAL STREET a densely packed group of the 1950s, mixed heights up to nine storeys, enlivened only by some Festival-style tiled balconies and brickwork. Opposite, COTTON GARDENS, with one of the most extreme housing contrasts of the 1960s: three of Lambeth's chunky concrete towers, segregated by grass and trees from KNIGHT'S WALK, a broad paved path with crisply designed, rather Scandinavian-looking one- and two-storey houses, flat-roofed, of pale brick with dark boarding. *Lambeth's* SHELLEY SCHOOL, near by in Wincott Street, matches this mood. The third group of the 1970s, off COTTINGTON STREET, combines all the housing (and garaging) within a series of A-frame ziggurats rising to nine storeys. The internal corridors and upper level open 'streets' are rather sparsely done but there are generous upper garden balconies and nice planted walks at ground level. Along Kennington Lane Nos. 109 etc., early C 19, rehabilitated as part of the same housing scheme.

Finally, N of Cotton Gardens, some C 19 buildings worth a look in RENFREW STREET. First the polychrome brick gatepiers and lodges to Lambeth Hospital (q.v. Public Buildings), then the MAGISTRATES' COURT of 1869 by *T. C. Sorby*, brick and stone, Tudor Gothic (court room with open timber roof), and a former FIRE STATION, 1868, enlarged 1896 by a tall asymmetrical building with Jacobean gable. By the *L.C.C. Fire Brigade Department* under *Robert Pearsall*. The earlier part plainer, with slightly Gothic window details.

* Information on Michael Searles from W. Bonwitt.

3. South Lambeth: s of the Oval, Kennington, and Harleyford Road

HARLEYFORD ROAD was laid out after Vauxhall Bridge was opened in 1816, providing a direct route to Westminster from Kennington and South Lambeth. Near the Kennington end is the OVAL. It appears on maps already c. 1800, an ambitious piece of street-planning that was never fully developed. It was opened as a cricket ground in 1846, and is now surrounded by tall walls. Pavilion added by *T. Muirhead* of Manchester, 1895–7. Hobbs Gate 1934 by *L. de Soissons*. To the s, OVAL HOUSE, formerly used as a vicarage to St Mark's, of 1794–5 (much altered), with Gothic details and gabled porch. w of the Oval Harleyford Road still has modest stuccoed terraces of the 1820s. Nos. 43–59 are a symmetrical group with pediment. ST MARK'S SCHOOLS, 1824, consist of a central part of three bays and little blocks added to the l. and r. for boys and girls. Harleyford Road ends by Vauxhall Station in a desolate traffic junction created in the 1970s. To the s in BONDWAY the earliest ROWTON HOUSE of the six established by Disraeli's secretary W. L. Corry (first Baron Rowton) as cheap hostels for working men. 1892 by *Harry B. Measures*. Further w at the beginning of WANDSWORTH ROAD No. 30 (BRUNSWICK HOUSE) is a lone relic from a more respectable past. Three storeys with central pediment and a graceful semicircular porch with rams'-skull frieze of *Coade* stone. The house was built in 1758 and later occupied by the Duke of Brunswick. For the rest of Wandsworth Road *see* below.

SOUTH LAMBETH ROAD. Of the big houses that existed here in the c 17 and c 18 only the names survive, plus fragments of walls in alleyways between Meadow Place and Tradescant Road. The Tradescants and Ashmole lived in this area (*see* above, Churches: St Mary). VAUXHALL PARK at the corner of Fentiman Road was opened in 1890 on part of the grounds of the mansion of Noel de Caron. CARON'S ALMSHOUSES, founded 1618, rebuilt 1854, stand next to the park in Fentiman Road. Jacobean central gable. Behind, WHICHER AND KIFFORD'S ALMSHOUSES, 1855 by *Hunt & Stephenson*, with bargeboarded gables. The dominant building on the w side is KEYBRIDGE HOUSE (1975–6 by *G. W. Mills & Associates*), a forbiddingly huge telecommunications centre with shiny channelled aluminium projections along South Lambeth Road. For WYVIL ROAD SCHOOL, *see* Public Buildings. Down WHEATSHEAF LANE a quirkily detailed Gothic HALL of 1896, built as a Congregational mission hall; rounded ends, corbelled-out bay above the porch. On the e side of South Lambeth Road an early c 19 house of three bays, with lower wings, *Coade* stone keystones over the windows. Then SARSONS VINEGAR, the former Beaufoy Vinegar Works. Behind the offices along South Lambeth Road is preserved one of the best early industrial groups in the borough: the original buildings date from c. 1810. Of these there survive one of the lodges with columns, then on the r. the former Beaufoy Mansion (Caron Place), now offices. A ballroom extension with Venetian windows was gutted in 1941. At the end of the courtyard the dignified VAT HOUSE, three bays wide, with a cupola above the gable (altered after a fire in 1916).

On the W side Nos. 210–218 (Mawbey Place) are of *c.* 1800; after that come roads with mid-C19 stucco terraces (developed by small builders after the sale of Vauxháll Manor copyhold lands), partly replaced by post-Second-World-War estates. The C19 development includes quite varied layouts. Worth a special look are LANSDOWNE GARDENS, 1843–50, builder *John Snell*, which is a tiny circus of two-storey stuccoed terraces with heavy Doric porches, and a vista to St Barnabas. Similar terraces, also semi-detached pairs, in the surrounding streets. To the E, with the main approach off Clapham Road, ALBERT SQUARE, the grandest scheme, with four-storey urban housing on a Kensington scale, 1846–7 by an Islington builder, *John Glenn*.* Between these two, G.L.C. estates of the 1960s. The MURSELL ESTATE of 1962–6 (section leaders *Follett* and *Chapman*) has a long dog-legged six-storey range of maisonettes along CLAPHAM ROAD, a tough image, brick and shuttered concrete, with long access balconies. Behind, the usual mixture of this time, not well integrated visually: a tower block, an old people's home, two-storey terraces (the concrete details repeated here and ludicrously out of scale), and (less usual) a few C19 houses preserved at the end of Portland Grove. 432 dwellings: density 119 p.p.a. Immediately W of South Lambeth Road the SPURGEON ESTATE, 1963–7 by *S. Follett*, with 340 dwellings (136 p.p.a.), uses similar materials, and also contains a tower block, but presents a less monolithic face to the outside world. The linked maisonette blocks alternate in height between four and three storeys (top floor recessed to provide roof gardens), and the access balconies are attractively punctuated by projecting glazed staircase towers along the street. An early C19 terrace in South Lambeth Road (Nos. 282–298) has been kept as part of the estate. A little N of these the oldest house in the area, No. 274 (Beulah House) of *c.* 1798, three storeys, five bays, with lower wings. LANSDOWNE WAY has on the N side the two estates mentioned above, on the S three competing essays in concrete: the boldly functional Stockwell bus garage (*see* Other Public Buildings, above), SURREY HALL, a *Lambeth* community centre of 1971 with rather self-conscious cantilevered projections, and finally, one of Lambeth's tower blocks built of precast panels (*see* South Island Place, Perambulation 4). Further E mid-C19 stucco-trimmed houses. Others to the S in LARKHALL LANE. Here also agreeable low brick borough housing of *c.* 1982 opposite a pleasant new PARK.

* HANOVER GARDENS, nearer the Oval, is another square, but much more modest.

WANDSWORTH ROAD runs along the NW edge of the borough towards Clapham Junction, overlooking the rooftops of Battersea descending towards the Thames. Starting at Vauxhall Cross (*see* above), a few relics of decent-class earlier C19 buildings: on the W Nos. 372–376, villas with Doric porches; on the E Nos. 335–337, with Ionic porches, and further on more modest cottages (Nos. 553 etc.) of the 1820s.* In between, much council housing. On the E side, stretching up towards Larkhall Rise, the SPRINGFIELD ESTATE by the L.C.C., 1935, with large blocks of flats, and, w of Albion Avenue, housing by *L. de Soissons* and *G. Grey Wornum* (formerly a private estate), 1929–30, distinguished by rather fussy neo-Georgian trimmings (the interior courtyards better). On the W side the most interesting redevelopment is CAREY GARDENS, a G.L.C. estate of 1970–7 (*Nicholas Wood*), influenced by the March and Martin principles of perimeter planning (cf. Pollards Hill, Mitcham, Me). 403 dwellings at 136 p.p.a. Unusual layout of two irregular four-storey concentric crescents around an open space, but the grand design negated by excessive variety in the details (see the different window designs, and the complicated recessed corners of the inner crescent). Brick with exposed concrete bands. After the railway the G.L.C.'s WESTBURY ESTATE, the familiar mixed development of the 1960s, with two twenty-one-storey brutalist towers (1964–7). By Silverthorne Road Lambeth low-rise housing, 1979 by *Clifford Culpin & Partners*, and the front of the former PLOUGH BREWERY of *c.* 1870 with a big rusticated entrance arch. Good cast-iron railings in the form of twisted cables with the initial W for Thomas Woodward, owner from 1868 to 1900. (Cellar with cast-iron columns, like a crypt.) The PLOUGH INN next door occupies part of a symmetrical block of seventeen bays of very plain cottages of *c.* 1810, with a pediment over the centre five. On the E side the HIBBERT ALMSHOUSES, with crocketed centre gable and Gothic detail, 1859 by *Edward I'Anson* (EES). Nos. 827–837 are a commercial terrace of *c.* 1860 by *Knowles Jun.* Around the corner in QUEENSTOWN ROAD an elaborate three-storey Gothic terrace of the same period (for the rest of Queenstown Road and Knowles's involvement there *see* Battersea (Ww), Perambulation 2).

4. South Kennington, Stockwell, North Brixton

In CLAPHAM ROAD the largest landmark is at SOUTH ISLAND PLACE (once the S boundary of Kennington Common), a point block of 1966–7, the first of the borough's towers which form such distinctive jagged landmarks in South London (others are in Cottingham Road, Lansdowne Way, and Grantham Road). They use a Wates system to fit the design by *Lambeth Architect's Department*, and are the most extreme

---

* Demolished: Nos. 238–246, attributed to *Gandy*.

example of attempts to make the tower form visually exciting in a brutalist manner (cf. the G.L.C.'s version at the Canada Estate Rotherhithe (Bermondsey (Sk), Perambulation 3) and elsewhere). Low rehabilitation centre and luncheon club next door. In Clapham Road several terraces of the late C 18 onwards on the E side (cf. Brixton Road, Camberwell New Road below). The best group is Nos. 145–189 (soon after 1800). No. 167 on the corner of Stockwell Park Road was skilfully converted to offices, with a new back extension, by *Rock Townsend* in 1974–5. Opposite, STOCKWELL TERRACE, 1843, stucco-trimmed, on the edge of what was Stockwell Common. Next to the junction of Stockwell Road No. 209, mid C 18, i.e. an unusually early survivor, with two canted bays. Further S on the W side of Clapham Road, the STUDLEY ESTATE, quite generously laid out blocks of mixed heights, with one eleven-storey Y-plan tower and shops along Clapham Road; to the E, behind Grantham Road, a windswept cluster of three towers completed in 1969 (*see* above); their names are Arden House, Pinter House, and Beckett House. Near by however a pleasantly humane OLD PEOPLE'S HOME of re-used stock brick, two storeys, in an informal A-shape around a courtyard and garden, *c.* 1975. A similar change of heart is witnessed by the later additions by *Lambeth* to the G.L.C. SPRINGFIELD ESTATE in UNION ROAD to the W: staggered yellow brick terraces of family houses, with bay-windows and front and back gardens (car park concealed beneath), 1975–6. Towards Clapham North a good stretch of late C 18 houses again, starting with No. 355 with an excellent doorcase with large delicate fanlight. No. 369 (The Garden House) is a grander type, with two bow-windows and side entrance.

The centre of STOCKWELL lies E of Clapham Road. In Stockwell Road at first nothing but flats: STOCKWELL GARDEN ESTATE, *L.C.C.*, 1945 and 1953–65. CASSELL HOUSE on the S side, with curving frontage and glass-panelled balconies, is the most distinguished part. Then mid C 19 stucco on the N, older houses (Nos. 40–46) on the S. Between these the entrance to KING GEORGE'S HOUSE (Y.M.C.A.), 1905 by *A. T. Bolton*, cruciform plan, too tall for its board-school type domestic detailing to make a successful impact. STOCKWELL GREEN, the old village centre, is now a built-up triangle, but some good houses remain on the side near the United Reformed Church, especially No. 34 etc. and Nos. 22, 21, nearer St Andrew's. Opposite SANITAS HOUSE, built for a wine-bottling firm, 1964–8 by *Tripe & Wakeham* (on the top floor three roof gardens), and next to it a former Educational Institute of 1848 with a careful Jacobean façade (derelict at the time of writing).

Beyond Stockwell Green, Nos. 146–166 STOCKWELL ROAD (Queen's Row dated 1786), a much abused survivor of the usual late Georgian terrace housing. N of Stockwell Road Duchy of Cornwall flats by *De Soissons* in ST MICHAEL'S ROAD, 1937. Around St Michael in STOCKWELL PARK

ROAD and CRESCENT a pleasant enclave of restrained stucco villas and terraces of the 1830s onward. In GROVEWAY and LORN ROAD further E, more fanciful Gothic villas as well (especially Nos. 33–39 Lorn Road). The STOCKWELL PARK ESTATE, extending to Brixton Road, is by the *Lambeth Architect's Department*, completed 1976, a dense grid of four-storey yellow brick maisonette blocks over garages, arranged around courtyards, also incorporating shops, luncheon club, children's home, etc. Some of the upper maisonettes, in compensation for lack of access to a street, open on to a raised public walkway by which one can reach Brixton Road. Front doors are given a little extra privacy by flights of steps. But the disadvantages of overwhelming size and high density (909 dwellings at 144 p.p.a.) outweigh the amenities. Further S in STOCKWELL ROAD, the ODEON ASTORIA, by *E. A. Stone*, 1929. (Half-domed entrance, Mediterranean interior.)

E of Brixton Road ANGELL TOWN, developed in the 1850s with curving roads with tall debased Italianate houses with profuse ornament, mostly replaced in the 1970s by four-storey yellow brick maisonettes (731 dwellings, 142 p.p.a.) (cf. Stockwell Park Estate, above), although the grand scheme for linking the two areas by a pedestrian bridge over Brixton Road was not carried out. The best surviving C19 areas are the pleasant terraces at the N end of LOUGHBOROUGH ROAD, and the villas in ST JOHN'S CRESCENT facing a newly landscaped informal open space. Immediately S of this in BRIXTON ROAD Nos. 357–361, an imposing High Victorian urban terrace (restored by *Lambeth c.* 1979), four storeys, on a Kensington scale, with handsome Doric porches, and pediments to both first- and second-floor windows.

BRIXTON ROAD, linking Kennington and Brixton, formerly had plenty of decently proportioned semi-detached brick houses with occasional Ionic or Tuscan porches. Now only the better of the older terraces remain: an irregular C18 group near Groveway on the W side, and further N on the E side near Vassall Road Nos. 91–137, an especially good stretch dating from the 1820s. These and the terraces in VASSALL ROAD and FOXLEY ROAD formed a development called Holland Town, built on Lord Holland's land soon after the opening up of Camberwell New Road (1818). They were rescued from neglect in the 1970s and now make a fine show around St John's church. Nos. 105–123 Vassall Road, two blocks with large end houses, were the first to be restored (by the G.L.C. in 1973–4). No. 80 etc. opposite, formerly detached villas, were imaginatively converted to flats by *Lambeth* (1975–6) by the addition of low annexes where one might expect Victorian coach-houses. Further W a row of small shops has also been preserved, turned backwards to face an attractive little precinct with trees, with some low rehabilitated terraces beyond. Among these Nos. 11–27 COWLEY ROAD should not be missed: an unusual small terrace of 1824 composed of attached villas (also restored by *Lambeth*), two storeys high, central doorways, each bay framed by an elliptical arch, with blind arches between each house. They face typical boring inter-war L.C.C. flats (1935). The flats on the N side of Vassall Road for the Church Commissioners by *Clifford Culpin & Partners* (*R. G. Robinson*), were completed in 1971. The regular three- and four-storey terrace, although relieved by projections and recessions, also appears bland in comparison with the intricate combination of new and old opposite.

E of St John's church Nos. 92–96 are by *H. S. Goodhart-Rendel*, 1954, built as a vicarage and home for the Wantage sisters, a brick gabled group in the tradition of the domestic buildings of Butterfield or Street.

Vassall Road leads into CAMBERWELL NEW ROAD, laid out in 1818 as a route to the new Vauxhall Bridge and almost com- pletely developed *c.* 1820–30 with urban terraces and villas. On the S side they start with No. 64 (three storeys, stuccoed ground floor), with farther on linked pairs of houses and separate villas (Nos. 84–90 etc.); No. 122 onwards is a terrace again. On the N side much has been demolished until we reach Nos. 185–187. No. 189 (Clifton Cottage) is dated 1823: door- way with engaged Greek columns within rusticated stucco surround.*

To the SE around MYATT'S FIELDS is the quite different world of the Minet Estate, built up mostly in the 1890s. In KNATCHBULL ROAD, LONGFIELD HALL, 1889, bow- fronted, with corner entrances. In the park a pretty C19 bandstand. Facing the park in CORMONT ROAD, a series of large educational buildings (*see* above, Other Public Build- ings).

5. Central Brixton, Tulse Hill, Herne Hill

The centre of Brixton is the junction of Brixton Road, Acre Lane, and Coldharbour Lane, with the jolly town hall and the public library facing each other (*see* Other Public Buildings, above), the cosmopolitan bustle of the market stalls to the E, threading in and out of the railway arches, and, marooned on a roundabout to the S, the dignified old church surrounded by trees. E of the crossroads are the dominating RAILWAY VIADUCTS of the London Chatham and Dover Railway (stock brick arches of 1859–62) and the South London Railway flyover (wrought-iron girders and cast-iron piers of 1867). Some fine lattice girder trusses W of Brixton Station. Close to the brick viaduct the RAILWAY TAVERN of 1880, polychrome brickwork, with hexagonal corner clock turret. Near by, ELECTRIC AVENUE, of 1885, a tall terrace busily decorated with pedimented windows, and with glazed cano- pies over the pavement market, curving round a narrow street. It was one of the first London streets lit by electricity.

---

* At the junction of Brixton Road and Camberwell New Road, the General (now London) Cab Company, 1905 onwards. Offices and three-storey garages for 2,000 vehicles. Handsome Dutch style, yellow and red brick and terracotta.

E of the railway line, around STATION ROAD, much rebuilding of the 1970s, large, stocky red brick buildings; car park (1970 by *Lambeth Architect's Department*), offices (designed by *Edward Hollamby* for Tarmac International), and recreation centre, shops, etc., by *Lambeth* of the later 1970s onwards.

E of Brixton, the area to the s of Coldharbour Lane was laid out *c*. 1844, probably by *Henry Currey*, with some quite elegant villas, single or in pairs. Those in MOORLAND ROAD have giant pilasters; other different stucco-trimmed designs are in LOUGHBOROUGH PARK, skirting a pleasant new PARK created by *Lambeth* as part of the extensive reconstruction of the neighbourhood in the 1970s. The most obtrusive new contribution is the massive nine-storey barrier block along Coldharbour Lane (191 dwellings), intended when planned (1973) to protect the area from the later abandoned Ringway Motorway. The block was completed only in 1981. Its concrete structure is exposed in a nightmare pattern of zigzagging jetties, the scale exaggerated by the tiny windows punched in the brick walls. Behind, the rest of the new housing takes its cue from the scale of older buildings, one to three storeys (503 dwellings, 136 p.p.a.) although arranged around courtyards and not along streets. Further E is the LOUGHBOROUGH ROAD ESTATE, an early example of mixed development by the L.C.C. (*J. L. Martin*, chief architect), 1953–7. The dominant feature here is the stark geometry of the eleven-storey concrete slabs, with walls recessed behind a grid of balconies (in the manner of Corbusier's Unité d'Habitation), a similar design to that used for the slab blocks of Bentham Road Hackney, and Alton West Roehampton (Ww). To the s the Guinness Trust LOUGHBOROUGH PARK ESTATE, one of the best of its date, by *E. Armstrong*, 1938. Blocks of flats in regular rows. IVEAGH HOUSE, by *Armstrong & MacManus*, is an addition of 1954, a seven-storey block of bedsitters intended for working women, incorporating a restaurant.

RUSKIN PARK further E was opened in 1907. The porch with pairs of columns, from the C18 house which stood here, is preserved as a shelter. Ruskin grew up in this neighbourhood, and deplored its decline as it became covered with cheap housing after the opening of the suburban railways in the 1860s. Only isolated buildings are worth a note. First ST SAVIOUR'S PARISH HALL, Herne Hill Road, 1915 by *Beresford Pite* (for the demolished St Saviour's Church), an unusual design of red and yellow brick, triple-arched recessed entrance, slate-covered cupola. Nos. 106–108 DENMARK HILL are an early C19 pair of villas. In WOODQUEST AVENUE (near Herne Hill Station) one of *Lambeth*'s earlier efforts at ingenious small-scale infilling: patio houses and old people's flats on a sloping site, built across the road (*c*. 1970).

Further s BROCKWELL PARK remains from the once larger Brockwell Estate. The park was bought by Lambeth and the L.C.C. in 1891, extended in 1901–7. In the centre, on an eminence, BROCKWELL HALL, 1811–13 by *D. R. Roper*, a handsome country villa with three-bay entrance front (now used as a park restaurant). Porch with paired Ionic columns. Domed vestibule inside with nice simple plasterwork. One room is painted with rustic scenes by *Henry Strachey*, 1897. *Papworth* did repairs here in the 1820s and built a lodge, which does not survive. Good walled gardens and some out-buildings remain. TULSE HILL and UPPER TULSE HILL were laid out before 1821 on the part of the estate further w, by *Daniel Gould*. In this area good *Lambeth* housing of the late 1970s.

s and w of the centre of Brixton only scattered early C 19 surviv-als amidst C 20 council housing and late Victorian suburban development. The area declined after the coming of the subur-ban railways in the 1860s. Near St Matthew, Nos. 45–47 EFFRA ROAD are almost the sole remainder of the generously spaced early Victorian middle-class housing that used to exist along the main roads. Around the church, ST MATTHEW'S ESTATE, undistinguished G.L.C. work of the 1960s, replaced nice stuccoed cottages in Brixton Water Lane. The only worthwhile group left is in ST MATTHEW'S ROAD (Nos. 1–5), elegant villas with Greek Doric doorways, of 1825–7, near the Congregational church (q.v. Churches, above). w along ACRE LANE a little more. First TRINITY HOMES, almshouses of 1822–6 by *James Bailey & Willshire*, nine bays with raised pedimented centre and Doric porch. N range behind with former wash house, also pedimented. E range 1806 by *S. Field*. Further w some more relics of early C 19 suburban houses ranging from three-storey terraces (Nos. 46–52 etc.) to smaller villas (Nos. 53–57) and (a good way on) humbler cottages (Nos. 206–216). Opposite these a good Great-West-Road-style FACTORY of the 1930s (Pall Mall Cleaners) before one reaches Clapham Park Road and the suburban edges of Clapham.

BLENHEIM GARDENS, s of Acre Lane and E of Brixton Hill, is one of *Lambeth*'s first large low-rise redevelopments (phase one completed 1971, phase two 1974). The entirely pedestrian scheme achieves a density of as high as 112 p.p.a. because of its compact grouping, despite the fact that the buildings are no taller than the humble two- and three-storey terraces in the surrounding streets. They consist of two-storey houses and one-storey flats over garages (a total of 441 dwellings). The rigidly geometric layout is however very much a conscious piece of design, one which produces some rather bleak vistas in places, particularly around the edges where the flats are a little taller. The houses and flats are slate-hung and flat-roofed, and the only landmarks are external ones: Brixton Windmill to the E (*see* below), and the tower of St Saviour to the N. But the formality is tempered by the pleasant broad central mall with plane trees, by the smaller planted areas in the narrower alleyways, and by the way in which in some of these front doors and tiny backyards alternate. Around the edges of the estate, an OLD PEOPLE'S HOME (white-boarded upper floor) and CHILDREN'S HOME, and the WINDMILL JUNIOR TRAINING SCHOOL for handicapped children, an attractive group of two octagonal blocks, one containing a therapeutic pool, the other the hall. All by *Lambeth Architect's Department*. Overlooking the estate, in a public garden, BRIXTON WINDMILL, a brick tower mill of 1816, partly restored, with machinery from a mill at Burgh le Marsh, Lincs.

6. *Norwood*

The wooded hill of Norwood remained open country until the early C19. Development came with the sale of Lord Thurlow's estate in 1810, and the laying out of Leigham Vale and Canterbury Grove w of Norwood Road. In the same year Norwood Common was enclosed, and the development of Norwood High Street, Elder Road, Salters Hill, Gipsy Hill, etc. followed. The real building boom came after the opening of the Crystal Palace Railway in 1856. There are few older buildings of interest apart from the churches (q.v.), but several recent developments worth a look.

The centre of WEST NORWOOD at the junction of Knights Hill and Norwood High Street is notable only for its combination of church, cemetery, and public buildings on a fine hilly site. E of the High Street around DUNBAR ROAD, new and rehabilitated housing by *Lambeth Architect's Department*, 1974. In KNIGHTS HILL a Jacobean LODGE of 1861 by *Tillott & Chamberlain* survives from the Jewish orphanage moved here from Stepney (the site now occupied by Lambeth council offices). (In THORNLAW ROAD, to the w, Nos. 4 and 6 are by *George & Peto*, 1882–3.) In ELDER ROAD: INFANTS SCHOOL of 1825 and 1850, the l. part with chanelled stuccoed front and three recessed windows; MAUDSLEY COTTAGES, a very modest terrace; ELDERWOOD, a long plain yellow brick range built as a school house for the House of Industry for the Infant Poor, moved from Kennington to this rural edge of the parish in 1810.* Good railings. The other buildings replaced by WOODVALE, Lambeth housing completed in 1975, a mark II version of Blenheim Gardens (*see* above, Perambulation 5). The same type of layout, with low terraces of houses within a pedestrian precinct, surrounded by taller flats over garages, but more informal and relaxed in its grouping, with yellow brick walls and pitched roofs in the new vernacular idiom. A large green and older trees preserved in the centre. The way the old people's flatlets are squashed up along the N edge is less satisfactory. N of Woodvale in LINTON GROVE, SOUTH-VALE, an L.C.C. children's home, 1964–5, a lively composition of brick boxes on a slope; also infill housing and rehabilitation by *Shankland Cox & Partners* for Lambeth. In ELDER ROAD and GIPSY ROAD three-storeyed flats by

---

* Future uncertain.

Booth & Ledeboer, *c*. 1950. (In CROWN DALE Nos. 30 and 32 are possibly by *George & Peto*, *c*. 1885.)

Further E, off CENTRAL HILL, one of *Lambeth*'s most ambitious housing developments (1967–74). 374 dwellings, 825 p.p.a. Tiers of elegant white brick terraces stepping down a steep slope, with splendid views of London. Tinted glass balconies, floor to ceiling glazing. The smaller terrace houses solider, with enclosed yards. Stylistically still very much in the International Modern tradition and more reticent in detail than, for example, contemporary schemes on a similar scale by Camden or the G.L.C. With ingenious planning it was possible to give all the flats front doors at ground level, reached by paths along the contours of the hill, a pleasanter solution than the contrived decks and balconies used elsewhere at this time. The interlocking plans also give each living room a distant view. At the foot of the hill an open space, community buildings, and the district heating system.

CLAPHAM

INTRODUCTION

The focus of interest at Clapham is the common with the streets surrounding it on the N and the SE. It is this neighbourhood which made Thackeray wriite 'Of all the pretty suburbs that still adorn our Metropolis there are few that exceed in charm Clapham Common'. He calls it a suburb. Up to about 1830 or 1840 it was, however, quite separate from London. We can still follow its gradual growth. The core of the village was Old Town, with the parish church a little to the N. The development around the common did not begin until the C 18, with terraces, separate mansions (now nearly all gone), and a new church, Holy Trinity, which became the centre of the evangelical Clapham Sect in the early C 19. Its leaders, Wilberforce, Zachary Macaulay, and the Thorntons, all lived in the neighbourhood. Then from 1825 *Cubitt* laid out Clapham Park to the E with large mansions for rich city men (now almost entirely replaced by council flats), and in 1860 *James Knowles Jun.* began his ambitious development stretching from the N side of the common down towards Battersea. Later C 19 suburban expansion on a more modest scale and C 20 council building have swamped or replaced many of the larger houses, but there is still more of the C 18 remaining at Clapham than anywhere else in Lambeth.* Clapham only became part of Lambeth in 1965. This account includes the W part of the common, which is within the present borough of Wandsworth. For the area N of Larkhall Lane *see* above, Lambeth, Perambulation 3.

---

* This entry is much indebted to recent local research, especially E. E. Smith's excellent *Clapham* (1976) and *The Buildings of Clapham*, published by the Clapham Society in 1978.

CHURCHES

The medieval parish church of Clapham, on the site of St Paul, was replaced in the C18 by Holy Trinity, the new church on the common, which was in turn supplemented by others in the new C19 suburbs. St Paul retains some good monuments of the C16–18. The most impressive of the C19 churches, both architecturally and in its fittings, is the R.C. Our Lady of Victories, by *Wardell*.*

CHRIST CHURCH, Union Grove, off Wandsworth Road and Union Road. By *B. Ferrey*, 1861–2; Kentish rag. – VICARAGE by *G. E. Street*, with many hipped gables.

HOLY SPIRIT, Narbonne Avenue, SE of Clapham Common South Side. 1912–13 by *H. P. Burke-Downing*; Gothic, with a large wheel window and small turret as the only ornaments of the W front. Simple whitewashed interior.

HOLY TRINITY, Clapham Common. The second parish church, built in 1774–6 by *Kenton Couse* when the housing development around the common had begun. W portico enlarged in 1812 by *F. Hurlbatt*, chancel in 1903 by *Beresford Pite*. The former E window has been re-used as the S window of the Lady Chapel. The rest of the church is a plain brick rectangle, with stone quoins and two tiers of windows. A small stone clock turret with octagonal belfry over the W end. Plain interior; galleries on three sides on columns. – PULPIT. Noble simple woodwork of the original building date, originally taller. Of the same time the reredos and altar table. – ORGAN CASE. 1903 by *Beresford Pite*. – Minor MONUMENTS only: two tablets by *J. Bacon Jun.*, one to John Castell † 1804, the other to the Rev. John Venn † 1813, the zealous evangelical minister; also one with medallion bust of Bishop Jebb † 1833, by *E. H. Baily*.

ST BARNABAS, Clapham Common North Side.‡ 1879 by *W. Bassett-Smith*. Ragstone, with a tower; striped brick inside.

ST JAMES, Park Hill, Clapham Park. An interesting church of 1957–8 by *N. F. Cachemaille Day*, replacing a proprietary chapel of 1829 by *Vulliamy*, enlarged 1870–1 by *F. J. & H. Francis* and destroyed in the Second World War. The C20 building is of plain yellow brick with a slightly bowed E window and an open campanile to one side. Inside, it is similar to the architect's pre-war St Barnabas, Tuffley, Gloucester, i.e. a little more traditional than some of his other churches, not because of any historicist details, but because of the impression of a late Gothic vault given by the striking network of concrete ribs. The junction of broad, aisleless nave and aisled chancel is neatly effected by the meeting of six ribs. The low E window acts as an illuminated reredos to the altar. – FONT. A handsome bold quatrefoil of veined marble from St

---

* Demolished: ST SAVIOUR, Cedars Road, 1860, and ST STEPHEN, Weir Road, Clapham Park, 1867, both by *Knowles*; also the war-damaged CONGREGATIONAL CHURCH, Grafton Square, 1851–2 by *Tarring*.

‡ In Wandsworth. The parish was formerly part of that of St Mary Battersea.

Saviour, Ealing (Ea). – Other furnishings by *Wippell & Co.* – STAINED GLASS (conventional figured designs, colours bolder than average for their date) designed by *A. F. Erridge*.

ST JOHN, Clapham Road. *See* Lambeth (La), Churches.

ST PAUL, Rectory Grove. There was a parish church on this site at Clapham from the C12. It was demolished after Holy Trinity was built on the common. The present church was built as a chapel of ease to the new church in 1815 by *C. Edmonds*. It is of stock brick with a W pediment and no tower, a plain rectangle of three by seven bays with two tiers of windows corresponding to inner galleries of which only that on the W has survived restorations. The E end, added in a crushingly insensitive Norman or Transitional style by *Blomfield* in 1879, was converted into a community centre in 1969. The stained glass and most of the monuments are now nicely displayed in the N transept. – STAINED GLASS by *Kempe & Tower*, 1906–7, nothing special. – MONUMENTS. Bartholomew Clerke † 1589. One child remains from a larger monument. – By far the most important monument is that to the Lord of the Manor of Clapham Sir Richard Atkins † 1689, his wife and three children, by *William Stanton*. Only the 45 figures now exist; the architectural surround has gone. Sir 46 Richard erected the monument to his children before 1689, three figures, originally below a pediment on Corinthian columns. The two grown-up children are seated, the son in Roman costume; a little daughter of eight stands (Reader, survey with piteous eye/The merciless hand of destinye/Which from a tender parent's breast/With fury tore this welcome guest, etc.). The recumbent figures of the parents, Sir Richard in armour, were added in 1691. The Atkinses had been lords of the manor of Clapham since 1616. – William Hewer † 1715. A large tablet, chiefly drapery, with two cherubs high up holding a portrait medallion; also of very good quality. The design is adapted from Bernini's monument of 1643 to Maria Raggi in S. Maria sopra Minerva, Rome. Hewer was Samuel Pepys's clerk and later colleague as Commissioner of the Navy. He lived in a house on Clapham Common North Side where Pepys died. – J. B. Wilson † 1835 by *Chantrey*, an important work of its date, with a large mourning allegorical figure bending over an urn with a portrait medallion. – Rev. W. Borrows † 1852, with portrait medallion, by *J. Evan Thomas*. – BRASSES (inscription only), 1401, 1647. – Many minor tablets. – Several big sarcophagi in the churchyard, C18 and C19.

ST PETER, Clapham Manor Street. 1878–84 by *J. E. K. & J. P. Cutts*. Large, red brick, on a cramped site. Lancet windows; no tower. – (FURNISHINGS. *Kempe* glass, font, and pulpit, 1914; wrought iron screen by *W. Bainbridge Reynolds*; brass of a priest, † 1480, once in St Mary Barnes, Ri).

OUR LADY OF VICTORIES (R.C.), Clapham Park Road. One of the best Victorian churches in South London. 1849–51 by *William Wardell*; Lady Chapel 1882–6, (ritual) N transeptal chapel 1894–5, both by *Bentley* (who lived in Old Town). (Ritual) s chapel 1910 by his son *O. Bentley*, extended as an outer s aisle in 1926 by *Bernard Cox*. Wardell's work is in the best Pugin tradition and no wonder, as Wardell (who was later the most distinguished architect of Sydney) started as Pugin's pupil. An enormous advantage, moreover, of the Clapham church over, for example, Pugin's at Fulham or Southwark is that evidently at Clapham money was not too short. The broached steeple is a proud achievement in the c14 style (testifying to a newly restored Catholic equality). Inside, the six-bay nave, aisles, and chancel are as Wardell left them. The style is c14 too, with Dec window tracery, head corbels for the hoodmoulds above the arcade, and much carving. In the chancel a tierceron-vault and sedilia with rich nodding ogee arches. – A fine collection of fittings: WALL PAINTING over the chancel arch, Last Judgement, a copy by *J. Linthout*, 1926, of the one by *J. Settegast* of Koblenz, 1854. – One window has STAINED GLASS designed by *Pugin*, 1850–3; the other glass is later, that in the Lady Chapel by *Bentley*. – SANCTUARY GRILLES and LIGHT FITTINGS, also the fittings of the Lady Chapel, by *Bentley*. – Linked to the church on the s side (with a door from the (ritual) N transept) is the admirable informal L-shaped REDEMPTORIST MONASTERY, by *Bentley*, 1892–3. In the courtyard in front, entered from the road by an arch, WAR MEMORIAL CROSS, 1920 by *Giles Gilbert Scott*.

PUBLIC BUILDINGS

LIBRARY, Clapham Common North Side. By *E. B. I'Anson*, 1889, gabled, with Flemish Renaissance decoration.

FIRE STATION, Old Town. 1964 by the *L.C.C.*, purple brick and concrete, typical materials of the time.

CLAPHAM COLLEGE, Nightingale Lane, NW end of Balham Hill. Two large mansions. The older one, Hollywood, is of *c.* 1800, five bays, with *Coade* stone doorway (cf. Thurston House, Rectory Grove). The second, Broadoak, dates from 1875, built for the widow of Sir Titus Salt. Brick and stucco, with giant Ionic pilasters and Tuscan porch. Chapel, Italian Renaissance style, *c.* 1885.

LA RETRAITE CONVENT, Atkins Road. Incorporating two of *Cubitt*'s Clapham Park villas of *c.* 1860; additions by *L. Stokes*, 1908.*

HENRY THORNTON SCHOOL, Clapham Common South Side. 1965–9 by *Farmer & Dark*. The dominant motif, deliberately different from the usual run of school buildings of the 1960s, is the rapid rhythm of the narrow arched window panels in a concrete frame. Contrasting red brick staircase towers. The building has not worn well.

---

* Information from T. Rory Spence.

BOARD SCHOOLS. The most elaborately detailed is in Hasel-rigge Road, off Clapham Park Road, 1886. Other good examples: CLAPHAM MANOR SCHOOL, Stonhouse Street, s end of Larkhall Rise, 1881 with later additions; BRIXTON HILL SCHOOL, New Park Road, off Streatham Place, 1897; BONNEVILLE SCHOOL, Bonneville Gardens, SE of Abbeville Road, 1905, low with Venetian window; WIX'S LANE, w of Cedars Road, 1903, a large three-decker on the more crowded fringe of Battersea, much terracotta decoration. Two post-war schools in Clarence Avenue on the Clapham Park Estate make an interesting contrast. GLENBROOK PRIMARY is one of the standardized industrial buildings put up by I.L.E.A. immediately after the Second World War, an attractive example which has worn well: 1949–54, job architect *L. Pemberton*. CLAPHAM PARK SCHOOL for the partially sighted presents a more homely image created by a well grouped cluster of dark brick pavilions, with pyramid-roofed centre: 1967–9, job architect *Peter Banting*.

CLAPHAM NORTH B.R. STATION. Disused buildings off Voltaire Street, Gothic, with much structural polychromy.

CLAPHAM NORTH AND CLAPHAM COMMON L.T. STATIONS. The quite streamlined refurbishing by *S. A. Heaps* was carried out *c.* 1926, at the time when the line was extended s (cf. Tooting (Ww), Morden (Me), etc.).

KNIGHTS HILL TUNNEL, N of Tulse Hill. On an L.B.S.C.R. line of 1866–8 by *R. J. Hood*. Elaborate classical portals (part of the scheme for Dulwich College; *see* p. 625).

PERAMBULATION

OLD TOWN. In the centre of what was the old village the best houses are Nos. 39–43, 'recently erected' in 1707, still with wooden modillioned eaves cornices, two storeys, basements and dormers, doorways with Roman Doric pilasters and segmental pediments. Nos. 41–43 have a joint pediment for both doors. Good railings to No. 43, which was *John Bentley*'s home. He added a back extension in 1876. Next door, one much altered late C 17 house, once part of a terrace. Modest cottages opposite, then several C 18 houses: No. 16 with delicate pilastered doorway at the side and top-floor lunette; Nos. 4, 8, No. 4 with tripartite window and lunettes. On the E side again No. 23 (St Peter's Vicarage) set back, with good ironwork. At the junction with NORTH STREET the former PAROCHIAL SCHOOL, much rebuilt, but with a plain building of 1852 still remaining at the back. To the r. RECTORY GROVE winds away towards the parish church. The best older survivals: THURSTON HOUSE, five bays, late C 18, with *Coade* stone doorway *à la* Portland Place and a blocked coachway at the side, also with a *Coade* head; Nos. 51–53, a tall late Georgian pair; No. 49, a separate early C 19 villa; Nos.

55–57, c. 1850, with the same ornament as Grafton Square (*see* below).

In TURRET GROVE off to the l. (the site of the Manor House demolished in 1837) more rural villas of 1844–5 with pretty trellis porches. In the little square in front of the church Nos. 8–10, a handsome late C18 pair with projecting end bays, perhaps with an older core, and opposite, INGLETON HOUSE, the oldest parts c. 1778, rendered later, and extended for a boys' home, 1911; chapel and hall with picturesquely grouped steep roofs, overhanging eaves, and tall chimney. A few more C18–early C19 houses along LARKHALL RISE. To the r. CLAPHAM MANOR STREET, a neighbourhood mostly developed between 1837 and 1855 by local builders for Thomas Cubitt (*see* Clapham Park, below), with modest villas and terraces, some rescued from neglect and some replaced in the 1970s. The additions (planned by *Lambeth Architect's Department* from 1969) include a HEALTH CENTRE and DAY NURSERY, a low irregular brick cluster around a court with sunken play areas. The upper flats facing HICKMORE WALK to the s have independent outside staircases, exploited here to provide visual diversity. Older buildings: in Clapham Manor Street No. 42 is a former Dispensary, designed gratis by *J. T. Knowles Sen.*, 1850–3, c. 1860, grey and red brick with arched windows and stucco trim. The BOWYER ARMS, five bays, is the centre of a dignified group designed by *Cubitt* himself, 1846. In Belmont Close the ODDFELLOWS HALL, a former chapel, dated 1852, pedimented, with attached manse (Ebenezer Cottage).

Down Belmont Road to GRAFTON SQUARE, a development by Captain Thomas Ross of 1851; grand terraces on two sides, distinctive window surrounds with plant stems and corner paterae; smaller houses on the third side; the fourth was never built. Back past the fire station (*see* Public Buildings, above) to Old Town and the POLYGON. This was an irregular group of cottages built in 1792, facing outward around a polygonal site (cf. Somers Town, Ca). A few of the houses remain, facing the common, and one good shopfront (with oil jars) facing Grafton Square. Further w the OLD FIRE STATION (now a house) of 1869, a modest two-storey building with pointed arches of polychrome brick.

THE PAVEMENT continues around to the s, facing the Common. The best house is No. 17, Deane's chemists, a handsome four-bay house built in 1824, and a chemist's shop since 1839. Doorway with Ionic columns, original fittings inside.

CLAPHAM COMMON. The uneven common land, with more ponds than at present, was levelled and planted in the later C18 when this area became the most fashionable part of Clapham. Later embellishments: near The Pavement a DRINKING FOUNTAIN by *F. Muller* of Munich, showing a woman offering water to an old man, erected by the Temperance Society near London Bridge in 1884: moved here in 1895. Further w a pretty circular iron BANDSTAND from the

International Exhibition of 1862. The best houses are along
NORTH SIDE. From E to W: Nos. 5–9, a part stuccoed terrace
of 1838; No. 11, a small brick cottage close to the road,
formerly one of a pair, c. 1700, much rebuilt. Then, set back,
No. 12, c. 1730, refronted after war damage to match Nos.
13–21. These were built by *John Hutt*, carpenter, 1714–20. It
is a wholly urban terrace, as they were put up at the same time
in other villages around London: Church Row Hampstead
(Ca), Montpelier Row Twickenham (Ri), Church Row
Wandsworth (Ww), and so on. Three storeys above basements, segment-headed windows, some doorways with segment-headed pediments. The houses vary in width and detail
(partly because of later alterations) but the total effect is
uniform. Excellent iron railings to Nos. 13 and 21. No. 21 has
a coachway as well (as had No. 14 until 1955). Nos. 22–23
were replaced by painfully unsympathetic flats in 1934.
Further W were mansions in their own grounds. No. 29 (The
Hostel of God, formerly The Elms) is an excellent survivor of
these, built in 1754. Five bays, three storeys, with stone
cornice and pedimented centre with Dorich porch. Arched
ground-floor windows in arched recesses. To the garden two
full-height canted bays. (Good original staircase with turned
balusters, ground-floor rooms with marble fireplaces. Later
wings, one converted to a chapel by *W. H. R. Blacking*, 1933.)
Nos. 30–32, plain houses of 1752, are now part of the same
institution. The Elms was the home of *Charles Barry*. He or his
son *E. M. Barry* may have built the grey brick and stucco
terraces on either side of VICTORIA RISE.
The Georgian unity of the North Side is then broken with
typically mid Victorian assertiveness by *James Knowles Jun.*'s
THE CEDARS, two identical five-storey blocks flanking the
entrance to Cedars Road.* This had villas on either side, also
the church of St Saviour (destroyed in the war), all designed
by *Knowles Jun.* Cedars Road led down to *Knowles*'s less
ambitious Park Town Estate (*see* Battersea (Ww), Perambulation 2), and it seems was intended as a direct route from
Clapham to the fashionable West End. The terraces facing the
common are of considerable importance for their date: 1860.
The French pavilion roofs are amongst the first signs of that
French Renaissance Revival in London which culminated in
such buildings as the Grosvenor Hotel, also by Knowles, and
fascinated for a time America as much as England. The details
are robust and tasteless; note especially the barbarous, wholly
un-French, round-headed window surrounds with their segment-headed windows and the space between the segment and
the round top filled with gross foliage. The materials are pale
Suffolk brick dressed with cement, the contrast especially
apparent on the r. block, which has been cleaned. In No. 45,
remains of an opulent interior, with gilding, mirrors, and
scagliola columns. Of the villas in CEDARS ROAD (forty-two

* Dr P. Metcalf points out that the gateway effect of the houses is derived from
Cubitt's pair at Albert Gate, Hyde Park.

completed by 1869) only Nos. 113–119 remain. The rest is
now a G.L.C. estate of 1961–8 (*Colin Lucas*, job architect),
one of the first to mark the move away from tower blocks to a
more intimate and human scale for housing estates. 381 dwellings at 90 p.p.a., a trail-blazing example of the lower densities
adopted in inner London in the 1970s. The layout must have
been influenced by the c 19 villas: distinct three-storey blocks,
linked by balconies. The bland white brick is relieved by dark
segment-headed garage doors, in a rhythm of three and one,
which screen small communal courts in front of the flats.
There are also some small private gardens. BROADMEAD, an
old people's home, is by *Trevor Dannatt & Partners*, 1969.

Beyond Cedars Road North Side is in Wandsworth, but so
patently belongs with the rest of Clapham that it is described
here. Several c 18 houses: Nos. 58–60, stuccoed (extended for
Battersea College, 1905), No. 61, and Nos. 62–63 (much
altered). No. 80, Springwell House, is of 1819, brick later
partially refaced in stone. Nos. 111–112, Grove Mansions,
1896, brick and stone, are a prominent intrusion. Then No.
113, GILMORE HOUSE, the r. part of 1763 with polygonal
bay and pedimented window, made symmetrical by an extension. Addition at the side of 1810. At the back a CHAPEL by
Philip Webb (added for Deaconess Gilmore, William Morris's
sister), 1896–7, with fittings by *Webb* and stained glass by
Morris & Co. of 1911–13 (s window with four figures against
floral background, three roundels with angels). Hidden
behind St Barnabas, THE SHRUBBERY, No. 2 Lavender
Gardens, a remarkable surprise in this suburban setting, a
neo-classical mansion in the grand manner, although now
tightly hemmed in. Built in 1796, enlarged in 1843. Two
storeys, all stuccoed. Front of five bays, the projecting end
bays with tripartite windows between giant pilasters, and flat
Tuscan porch curved to fit against the central projecting bay.
Enriched Ionic capitals. The garden front of 1843 has the
striking feature of a projecting full-height central bow with
giant engaged Corinthian columns, flanked by three windows
on each side. (Staircase hall with circular gallery and domed
skylight, divided by columns from the entrance hall.)

WEST SIDE had in 1815 twenty large houses, of which five
remain, somewhat altered, amongst the redevelopment which
took place mostly from 1895 to 1908. They all date from
c. 1800: No. 84, three bays with large bay-window; No. 83;
Nos. 81–82, a pair with Ionic porches; No. 21, five bays.

SOUTH SIDE also once had a succession of large Georgian
mansions, but even less remains. Starting at the E end: first a
few Georgian terrace houses interrupted by the ALEXANDRA
HOTEL, 1866, with large slate-covered domed roof with cresting, and polychrome brick detail. Then CRESCENT GROVE,
a private estate laid out in 1824 by Francis Child. It is entered
between two identical houses, stuccoed, with giant pilasters.
A handsome crescent on the r., semi-detached houses with
low coach-house links on the l. Formerly there was a large

house at the end. Back along South Side there are lesser Georgian houses of different dates: Nos. 30–38 (No. 34 dated 1812), then the NOTRE DAME ESTATE, depressing L.C.C. blocks of pre-war type, built after 1945 on the site of two houses which had belonged to the Thorntons and later became a convent. Within the estate remains the façade of an ORANGERY designed by Dr *William Burgh* of York in 1793, once a handsome building with Ionic columns, *Coade* stone capitals, and pediment. No. 44 is a small villa of *c.* 1820, set back. No. 53 was once a fine three-bay house of *c.* 1780. Good Venetian window behind a garage. Further s the WINDMILL INN of *c.* 1790 forms part of a little enclave on the common. No. 78, dated 1888, is well endowed with gables, in the tile-hung Norman Shaw manner. Up LESSAR AVENUE modest flats by *W. H. Beesley*, early post-war housing for Wandsworth Council.*

CLAPHAM PARK further e was laid out with large detached mansions in their own grounds by *Thomas Cubitt*, the great builder. He bought the estate in 1825, but it was not fully built up until the 1850s–60s. It was one of the most fashionable areas in South London in the mid c 19. The main roads are Poynders Road–Atkins Road, crossed by Clarence Avenue and Kings Avenue. Cubitt's own house was in Clarence Avenue. This and most of the other houses have gone. A few survivors in KINGS AVENUE: No. 89, and No. 84 (Victoria House), of 1849, tall and stuccoed, and lesser houses in PARK HILL, at the NW end of the estate. At the SE end, No. 138 NEW PARK ROAD, a villa of 1835 in the cottage orné tradition, with bargeboarded gable and battlemented porch. Piecemeal local authority redevelopment began between the wars and still continues. As examples of changing fashions:‡ Tilson Gardens, Forster Road, neo-Georgian blocks of 1929–36 of typical L.C.C. type; Poynders Gardens, 1938, a little more daring, with curved corners and horizontal bands. Post-war buildings are more generously laid out: Nos. 96–104 Kings Avenue, monopitch-roofed terraces of 1950–5 in Swedish-influenced New Towns style; Morten Close, around a green; Nos. 42–65 Poynders Road, a quadrant of shops with flats above, *c.* 1955; Thornton Gardens and Scrutton Close, simple low housing of the late 1950s. After 1965 redevelopment by Lambeth Council, in a different mode: off Clarence Avenue three of Lambeth's earliest tower blocks, polygonal with projecting bay-windows, 1966–7. Near by a group of 'quad' houses (four back-to-back houses in a cluster), an experimental type of the 1970s; also CLIFTON, an old people's home, low patio houses and flats behind, with a doctor's surgery, a pleasantly varied group (completed in 1970) which makes use of a tiny *Cubitt* remnant (perhaps a gardener's cottage) as a warden's house. For the new schools in this area *see* Public Buildings, above.

* Others of the same date by *C. H. James* in CRESCENT LANE.
‡ I owe these examples to the Clapham Society's *Buildings of Clapham*.

CLAPHAM HIGH STREET, just like Clapham Road, Brixton
Hill, Streatham Hill, etc., consisted chiefly of C18 to early
C19 urban development in terraces. The little that is left is
obscured by the shops that began to appear from the 1830s.
No. 91 is a neat tower of offices, the first in this area, by *C. H.
Elsom & Partners*, 1968. Near by, a former Temperance and
Billiard Hall of *c.* 1900, low, with a large curved gable to the
street.* For Clapham Road *see* above, Lambeth, Perambula-
tion 4.

E of the High Street in BEDFORD ROAD and roads to the E,
especially FERNDALE ROAD, terraces and houses of *c.* 1870
designed by *T. Collcutt*, and built by *Jennings*, an enthusiast
for terracotta, as the details in a mixture of styles show (cf.
Nightingale Lane, Balham, Ww). Also in Ferndale Road,
ROGERS ALMSHOUSES, three linked late C19 pairs, and
GRESHAM ALMSHOUSES, 1882, one-storeyed, with a steep
roof with terracotta finials. In CLAPHAM PARK ROAD a little
earlier development remains, e.g. Nos. 194–196, BEDFORD
BUILDINGS, a typical tall semi-detached pair of 1822, with
ground-floor windows within segmental arches (*see* drawing
on p. 56).

STREATHAM

INTRODUCTION

For most people the C18 amenities of Streatham are connected
with the Thrales and Dr Johnson, but their home, Streatham
Park, lay to the S of Tooting Bec Common, just outside the
present Streatham (*see* Tooting, Ww). The village centre was
around the parish church of St Leonard at the junction of
Streatham High Road and Mitcham Lane. Rocque's map shows
also a smaller settlement at Lower Streatham, W of Streatham
Common. The main manor houses have disappeared. They were
Russell House, belonging to the Dukes of Bedford from 1695,
which lay near the church, and Bedford House at Lower
Streatham (rebuilt as Coventry Hall in the C18 and much altered
in the C19; demolished in 1982‡). The later C18 and C19
development followed the pattern typical of South London:
large mansions in their own grounds (especially along the N side
of Streatham Common), and ribbon development along the
main roads. By the 1840s Streatham Hill was built up and
suburban villas were beginning to appear along Sunnyhill Road
leading to Streatham Spa. Streatham Hill Station (West End of
London and Crystal Palace Railway) was opened in 1856. In

* Demolished: RUGGS FURNITURE DEPOSITORY, which began as two
Georgian houses, altered in 1834 for use as a school so as to form a four-bay block
with two projecting wings with Tuscan loggias flanking a miniature cour d'honneur.
‡ The house lay off Streatham Common North, near Streatham High Road.
Behind the front of 1877 the staircase and hall with segmental arches survived
from the house built by Lord Deerhurst (later Earl of Coventry) *c.* 1800. *Repton*
was consulted over the grounds (now covered by a council estate).

1871 Thorne could still describe Streatham as a village of mansions, villas, and genteel residences, but by the 1880s the old estates were being broken up, and the main impression now is of the late C19 houses and C20 flats which covered the gaps between and eventually the sites of the older houses.

CHURCHES

ALL SAINTS, Lyham Road, s of Blenheim Gardens. 1889 by *Talbot Bury & Hening*. Kentish rag; Dec.

CHRIST CHURCH, Christchurch Road, Streatham Hill. 1840–2 77 by *J. Wild*, a church of impressive design and historical importance, amongst the most successful in England of that *Rundbogenstil* which Gärtner and Persius cultivated in Germany and which impressed several young English architects about 1840 (cf. Wilton, Wiltshire). Stock brick with voussoirs of alternating yellow and red bricks, main entrance in a tall niche, side view with four widely spaced lower windows and thirteen closely spaced clerestory windows, a tall sheer campanile divided vertically by four pilaster strips or lesenes. All simple, but clear and concise. The interior has tall columns and a gallery between them resting on two pointed arches for each main bay. Apse without preceding chancel, in the Early Christian way. Once judiciously decorated by *Owen Jones*; his work still in the sanctuary and on the tops of the piers. – STAINED GLASS. NE and SE aisle windows to *Walter Crane*'s designs, 1891 (a rare work by this leading representative of the Arts and Crafts); E aisle windows by *John Hayward*. – Redecorated by *Arthur Henderson*, 1925–33, whitened later.

HOLY REDEEMER, Streatham Vale, in the SW corner of the borough. 1931–2 by *Martin Travers* and *T. F. W. Grant*. Perp with a cupola. Baroque fittings.

IMMANUEL CHURCH, Streatham High Road, opposite the common. A rebuilding and enlargement of 1864–5 by *B. Ferrey* of a church built in 1854 by *A. Ross*. Kentish rag. NW tower. – (STAINED GLASS. Windows by *Lavers & Barraud* commemorating the chief donors, the Leaf family of Park Hill, Streatham Common.)

ST ANDREW, Guildersfield Road, off the SW end of Streatham High Road. 1885–6 by *George & Peto*. Ernest George lived near Streatham Common, and his firm, well known for their Dutch domestic architecture, did much work in this area (*see* Perambulation). Perp, red brick and terracotta, cross-gabled aisles, NE turret. Interior with octagonal piers without capitals, broad arches dying into them, tall clerestory – an interesting and satisfying design. (Terracotta is used inside as well, e.g. for panels around the sanctuary, and for the FONT. – REREDOS, marble and mosaic, given by George in 1901–2. – ORGAN CASE. 1887 and 1897. – SCREEN. 1913 by *Jones & Willis*.) – (Good VICARAGE next door, 1886 by *George & Peto*, and CHURCH HALL, 1898 by *George & Yeates*.)

ST JAMES, Mitcham Lane. Mostly of 1910–12 by *F. Peck*, with an odd Gothic front the flying buttresses of which continue harshly the line of the pitch of the nave roof. The chancel and w spirelet added 1914–15 by *W. S. Weatherley*.

ST LEONARD. The parish church of Streatham, at the corner of Streatham High Road and Mitcham Lane, at the centre of what was the old village. Badly damaged by fire 1975, restored 1975–7 by the *Douglas Feast Partnership*, and now much more attractive than previously. The lower part of the w tower is late medieval, of knapped flint with stone dressings, with original (much restored) w doorway. Inside, C 14 tower arch, with broad continuous hollow moulding to the outer order. Star-shaped lierne-vault. The top storey of the tower and the spire were rebuilt in 1841. By then the main body of the church had been rebuilt, by *J. T. Parkinson*, 1830–1, in stuccoed brick, with windows with Dec lights and transoms, the proportions of Commissioners' type. The interior still has the wooden galleries typical of the early C 19 (completely renewed in 1976–7) supported on cast-iron columns. The chancel, of stone, with steep slated roof, was rebuilt and enlarged in 1863, to designs by *William Dyce*, the Pre-Raphaelite painter, who was a churchwarden. The work was carried out by *Ferrey*. Vestries added 1877. The detail is E. E., but almost all of Dyce's decoration was lost in the fire, as were many of the furnishings and monuments. In the refurnishing of 1976–7 the organ and choir were placed in the w gallery, the main altar brought forward, and a new chapel with central altar made at the w end of the s aisle.* – FONT. C 15 octagonal bowl with quatrefoils; stem renewed 1977. – STAINED GLASS. N aisle E by *John Hayward*, showing the history of Streatham; the first to be installed after the fire; other windows by Hayward planned. – MONUMENTS.‡ John Essifield, rector, † 1890. Inscription only. – William Mowfurth † 1513, small brass with figure in clerical garb. – William Dyce † 1865, large Gothic Revival brass with figure in front of an easel surrounded by a personal collection of saints and worthies. – Sir John Ward(?), mutilated effigy of a knight under a Dec canopy. – Edmund Tylney † 1610, Master of the Revels. Alabaster touch panel; coats of arms and ribbonwork. – John Massingberd † 1653 and wife, kneeling opposite each other between columns, the usual C 16–17 composition. – Rebecca Lynne † 1653, with clasped hands above. – John Howland † 1686. Fine large monument, attributed to *Nost* by Mrs Esdaile. Cherubs weeping beside an urn framed in a niche. Architectural surround with open segmental pediment, arms and ample draperies. – Walter Howland † 1692 and John Howland † 1674. Cartouche with cherubs' heads and wreath.

---

* Lost in the fire: the C 17 PULPIT given by Sir Matthew Howland, lord of the manor; MONUMENTS to Robert Livesey † 1607; Thomas Hobbes † 1632 (bust); Sir Matthew Howland † 1648; Cecilia Goodwin † 1664; Elizabeth Hamilton † 1746.

‡ Restoration of the monuments was carried out by *Inge Norholt*.

Good quality. – Hester Lynch Salisbury † 1773 (Mrs Thrale's mother), by *J. Wilton*. – Henry Thrale † 1781, clearly from the same workshop. Both have epitaphs by Dr Johnson. – Fredrick Howard † 1815 by *R. Westmacott*. – Elizabeth Stewart Laing † 1816 by *P. Rouw*, seated sad husband by urn. – Sophia Hoare † 1824 (a Thrale daughter), by *Flaxman*, with a relief on the top part on which husband and three daughters mourn her recumbent figure, an angel hovering above. – Many tombs in the churchyard, including one of *Coade* stone to J. Hay, 1808, with an urn.

(St MARGARET, Barcombe Avenue, in the Leigham Court Estate off Streatham Hill (*see* Perambulation, below). 1889–1907 by *Rowland Plumbe & Harvey*. Cruciform, red brick, lancet style, with a flèche over the crossing and two w turrets. – Elaborate carved REREDOS by *W. D. Caröe*, 1908, showing the early history of the church in Britain. – Lady Chapel fittings also by *Caröe*. – STAINED GLASS. E window by *Burlison & Grylls*. – Other windows by *H. Wilkinson*, 1925–30.

St PETER, Leigham Court Road. Tall polychrome brick church by *R. W. Drew*, a nephew of Butterfield, 1870. The w part of the nave and baptistery 1886–7 by *G. H. Fellowes Prynne*. Dormers added 1915. – (FONT by *Fellowes Prynne*. – ROOD by *Aymer Vallance*, 1915. – PULPIT by *F. E. Howard*, 1930. – STAINED GLASS by *L. Lee*: E and rose windows 1954, baptistery 1956.)

CHURCH OF THE ENGLISH MARTYRS (R.C.), Mitcham Lane, opposite the parish church. 1892 by *Purdie*. Big, of Kentish rag with spire; much figural carving inside. (N transeptal chapel 1962 by *T. Sibthorpe*, using thirty-three windows from the clerestory. DE)

(St SIMON AND St JUDE (R.C.), Hillside Road, Streatham Hill. 1906 by *Clement Jackson*. DE)

BAPTIST CHURCH, Mitcham Lane. 1902–3 by *G. & R. P. Baines*, the usual brick and stone façade with a NW turret and the jolly Art-Nouveau Gothic detail of the moment popular for Nonconformist churches.

METHODIST CHURCH, Riggindale Road, off Mitcham Lane N of Conyers Road. 1900 by *Wheeler & Speed*; Art-Nouveau Gothic. (Said to have the widest fibrous barrel-vaulted ceiling for its date. CFS)

(TRINITY UNITED REFORMED CHURCH, Pendennis Road. 1876–7 by *George & Peto*. Brick with stone dressings.)

UNITED REFORMED CHURCH (formerly Congregational), Streatham High Road. 1900. Large, plain, sound brick structure in the Gothic style. By *James Cubitt*.

PUBLIC BUILDINGS

POLICE STATION, Streatham High Road. 1912 by *J. Dixon Butler*.

LIBRARY, Streatham High Road. 1890, one of *S. R. J. Smith*'s efforts (*see* Lambeth, Public Buildings).

PHILIPPA FAWCETT TRAINING COLLEGE, Leigham Court Road. An interesting extension in brick and concrete of 1960–6 by *John Bancroft* (G.L.C./I.L.E.A. Architect's Department). Teaching block and communal block with assembly hall on the first floor, dining areas below. Forceful exposed concrete umbrella pier to the dining area. The structure of the assembly hall equally emphatic, with an octagonal domed roof over diagonal concrete beams. The entrance hall has a central lantern. One of the first examples of the use of the brutalist style for the L.C.C.'s educational buildings.

STREATHAM WELLS PRIMARY SCHOOL. *See* Perambulation, below.

BOARD SCHOOL, Sunnyhill Road. *See* Perambulation, below.

STREATHAM COMMON PUMPING STATION, Conyers Road. 1888 in Moorish style, with copper domes, for the Southwark and Vauxhall Water Company.

PERAMBULATION

Buildings are too scattered to make a proper perambulation. Descriptions start with the village centre, followed by the areas to its W and S (Streatham Common), then N (Streatham Hill) and E. For Streatham Park, *see* Tooting (Ww).

Little evidence of the old village centre remains near St Leonard's church, apart from the remains of the GREEN at the fork of Mitcham Lane and Streatham High Road, with its Gothic DRINKING FOUNTAIN, 1862, given and probably designed by the painter *William Dyce* (also a benefactor to St Leonard's). All around characteristic suburbia of the 1880s, the decade when Streatham boomed after the surrounding estates were broken up for building. Between Mitcham Lane and Streatham Station, Manor Park Estate, 1883 etc., W of Mitcham Lane Woodlands Estate, both largely by *Frederick Wheeler*, in a competent Queen Anne style. Along STREATHAM HIGH ROAD *Wheeler*'s more showy commercial buildings and shopping parades of the 1880s and 1890s. Further N in a slightly earlier style PRATTS, one of those Victorian suburban department stores extended in several stages, stuccoed, with arched upper-floor windows. ODEON (W side) 1930 by *E. A. Stone*. (Built as the Astoria, to seat 3,000. The Egyptian decoration inside now removed.)

E of Streatham High Road SUNNYHILL ROAD, with some modest early to mid C19 villas (Nos. 40–42, 60–78, 84–90), leads to the site of STREATHAM SPA. A little white early C19 house with a bust as centre decoration and a pretty garden marks the spot. Near by a plain gabled BOARD SCHOOL of *c.* 1900. (Further N PENDENNIS ROAD where No. 5 (COMPTON) was built by *Norman Shaw* for a painter, *G. H. Best*, in

1872–3. Tile-hung with a Gothic porch. Nice staircase inside.)
N again, LEIGHAM COURT ROAD, named after a large estate
which had a house by *Papworth* of *c.* 1820, demolished in
1908. It stood opposite Mount Nod Road. The road curves s
down to Streatham Common. No. 269, sheltered housing for
the elderly, is an especially good example of one of the many
housing schemes for old people built by *Lambeth Architects
Department.* Completed 1975. Compact clusters of one- and
two-storey flats linked by covered ways between secluded
courts and gardens. Exposed concrete blocks both outside and
in. Further s are some stately Edwardian villas near the junction with STREATHAM COMMON NORTH. This was a
fashionable area before Streatham became suburban. Of the
mansions once facing the common only one remains: Park
Hill.

PARK HILL (St Michael's Convent), despite the additions for
the convent (chiefly the plain classical chapel of 1939), is the
best older house left in Streatham. It is a late example of a
stuccoed neo-classical villa with a two-storey bow-window on
the w side, standing on top of a hill in its own grounds. It was
built for William Leaf, a London draper. Both house and
grounds were ornamented by *J. B. Papworth* (a popular
architect for South London houses), *c.* 1830–41.* The porte-
cochère on the entrance front was added in 1880 by the later
owner, Sir Henry Tate, but the main part of the house is
hardly altered. Rich plaster ceiling and original sideboard in
the dining room to the r. of the hall. The drawing room on the
w side has pilasters and a bow-window divided off by two
columns. Generous top-lit stairwell, with curved stair with
cast iron balustrade and an upper gallery with panels and
friezes with classical scenes. Similar panels in the back hall.
Beyond were *Papworth*'s lavish conservatories, aviary, and
billiard room. The huge glass roofs have, alas, been replaced
by upper floors. At the N end of the w terrace a plain Doric
summer house. The terrace overlooks the pleasant grounds
sloping down to a small lake with a grotto beyond. To the s is a
summer house of rustic branches, to the w a Gothic ruin, an
octagonal tower built no doubt as a viewpoint: all the ingredients of c 18 picturesque reduced to a suburban scale.

Facing the w end of Streatham Common, the PIED BULL and
its former rival, No. 496 Streatham High Road, built as the
Beehive Coffee House and Working Men's Lodgings; a Queen
Anne front of 1878–9 by *George & Peto.* It was intended to
benefit the workers of the neighbouring INDIA RUBBER
WORKS of P. B. Cow (of Cow Gum). The handsome chimney
added to the works in 1885 may also be by *George & Peto.* To
the s, close to the works in FACTORY SQUARE, the former
Immanuel PARISH SCHOOLS by *G. G. Scott,* 1861, extended
by *George & Peto,* 1874. Further N, Nos. 412–416 Streatham

---

* See R.I.B.A. Drawings 182/1–112. Many of these appear to be alternative
schemes not carried out.

High Road, HAMBLY MANSIONS, 1877 by *George & Peto* for P. B. Cow, tile-hung Old English Street architecture.*

STREATHAM HILL. The roads E of Streatham Hill, just N of the railway line (Downton Avenue etc.), form the fourth of the Artisans and General Dwellings Company cottage estates (*see* Battersea (Ww), Perambulation 2, Shaftesbury Park), built on part of the Leigham Court Estate in 1889–94. Nearly 1,000 houses and maisonettes, low rise (as it would be called today), with taller terraces with shops along Streatham Hill. The style is faintly Jacobean. Nos. 40–42 and 44 Streatham Hill are early C 19 villas, a reminder of the typical South London arterial pattern. Opposite, PULMAN COURT, the best of the earlier C 20 replacements.‡ Luxury flats of 1935 by *Frederick Gibberd*, a display of the motifs of picturesque modern planning and design, with old trees as part of the composition, grouping of three- and seven-storeyed parts, no symmetry of the two three-storeyed blocks, no symmetry of the balcony arrangements on the N and S of the main court, etc. The materials (white plastered walls, metal railings) equally characteristic of the modern movement. N of Pullman Court, in the neighbourhood of Christ Church, was the Roupell Park Estate, with gross and sumptuous villas of the 1850s–70s by such architects as *Banks & Barry* and *Giles & Gough*. Few survivals now: Nos. 4 and 10 CHRISTCHURCH ROAD, with cusped bargeboards and fancy brick detail, and a little more in PALACE ROAD, a good example of a select C 19 private road: e.g. Nos. 24, 28, 42, large classical villas in their own grounds, reminiscent of Cubitt's Clapham Park Estate. Halfway down is the G.L.C.'s PALACE ROAD ESTATE (352 dwellings at 90 p.p.a.), *c.* 1973–7. An interesting plan, but poorly finished and maintained at the time of writing. It starts at the w end with an appealing cluster of slate-hung hexagons (shop and Adult Education Centre). Then along Palace Road a series of irregular Y-shaped blocks with zigzagging façades to the road. Lower terraces along Christchurch Road, and between them a broad informal stretch of greenery. Curving paths and oddly angled vistas everywhere, to an extent that becomes mannered in the paved forecourts of the terraces. At the E end STREATHAM WELLS PRIMARY SCHOOL (1972–5, job architect *T. Butler*, for the G.L.C./I.L.E.A.). Next door No. 48 PALACE ROAD (Chestnut Lodge), a good house in the Voysey manner, dated 1905, hipped roof between two gables, roughcast. Further E more C 19 villas, No. 60 (dated 1883 and 1894) tile-hung *à la* Norman Shaw.

w of Streatham Hill and High Road very little. (In BELLASIS AVENUE, good housing by the *Shankland Cox Partnership* for the Coastal Counties Housing Association, 1977.) In DREWSTEAD ROAD, MAGDALEN, a plain version by Lambeth

---

* I am indebted to Andrew Saint for the details in this paragraph and for other information on George's work in Streatham.

‡ Built on the site of the Royal Asylum of St Anne, an orphanage of 1829.

Architect's Department, 1968–9, of houses on decks over garages (the A-frame type of e.g. Reporton Road, Hammersmith, H F, Brunswick Centre, Camden, Ca). The name and a C 19 LODGE recall the Magdalen Hospital originally in Whitechapel which moved here from Blackfriars in 1869. In GARRADS ROAD facing TOOTING COMMON (*see* Tooting (Ww), Perambulation) large terracotta-ornamented Edwardian houses. Behind one at the corner of Prentis Road, old people's sheltered FLATS by *Lambeth Architect's Department*, completed 1970, the same idea as in Leigham Court Road (*see* above).

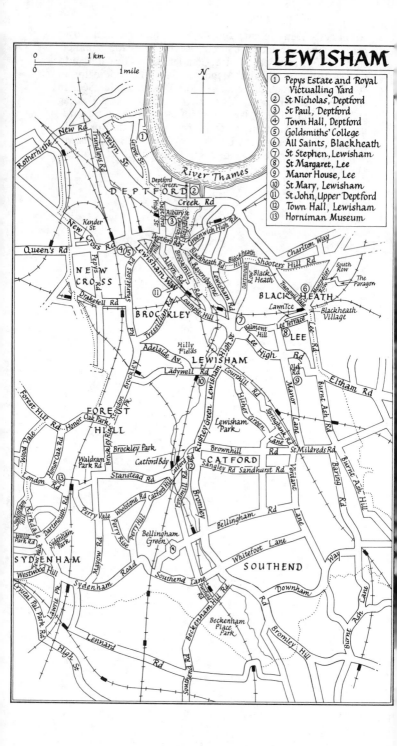

LEWISHAM

0 ___ 1 km
0 ___ 1 mile

N

River Thames

1. Pepys Estate and Royal Victualling Yard
2. St Nicholas, Deptford
3. St Paul, Deptford
4. Town Hall, Deptford
5. Goldsmiths' College
6. All Saints, Blackheath
7. St Stephen, Lewisham
8. St Margaret, Lee
9. Manor House, Lee
10. St Mary, Lewisham
11. St John, Upper Deptford
12. Town Hall, Lewisham
13. Horniman Museum

Rotherhithe
New Rd
Trundleys Rd
Evelyn St
Grove St

DEPTFORD
Deptford Green
Creek Rd
Albury St
Kender St
New Cross Rd
Queen's Rd

NEW CROSS
Pepys Rd
Deptford Bdy
Greenwich High Rd

Lewisham Way
Aldyn Rd
Brockmill Rd
Blackheath Rd
Ravensbourne
Blackheath
Blackheath Hill
Shooters Hill Rd
Charlton Way

Black Heath
South Row
The Paragon

BLACKHEATH
LawnTce
Blackheath Village

Drakefell Rd
Shardloes Rd
Tressillian Rd
Crofton Hill
Lampit Hill

BROCKLEY
Belmont Hill
Lee Terrace
LEE

Adelaide Av
Hilly Fields
LEWISHAM
Lee High
Rd
Old Rd
Manor Rd

Ladywell Rd
Brockley Rd
Stondon Pk
Lewisham High St
Courthill Rd
Rushey Green
Lewisham Park
Rither Green

Eltham Rd
Burnt Ash Rd

Forest Hill Rd
FOREST HILL
Honor Oak Park
Springbank Rd
Lane
St Mildreds Rd

Wood Vale
Honoroak Rd
Brockley Park
Waldram Park Rd
Catford Bdy
Stanstead Rd
Brownhill Rd
CATFORD
Sangley Rd Sandhurst Rd
Verdant Lane
Baring Rd
Burnt Ash Hill

London Rd
Dartmouth Rd
Wells Park Rd
Kirkdale
Sydenham Park
Perry Vale
Wooistone Rd
Catford Hill
Catford Rd
Bromley Rd
Bellingham Rd

Sydenham Hill
SYDENHAM
Mayow Rd
Perry Rise
Perry Hill
Bellingham Green
Whitefoot Lane
SOUTHEND
Downham

Westwood Hill
Sydenham Road
Southend Lane
Beckenham Hill Rd
Bromley Hill
Way

Crystal Pal. Rd
Lawrie Pk
Lennard Rd
Southend Rd
Beckenham Place Park
Bromley
High St

LEWISHAM

INTRODUCTION

Lewisham derives its name from the village which used to stretch in a long ribbon along the main road running N–S through the middle of the borough, close to the course of the Ravensbourne. Further N this river forms part of the borough boundary, and then debouches at Deptford Creek into the Thames.* Deptford, a separate borough until 1965, is now part of Lewisham, a sadly decayed and indifferently renewed area, only a shadow of its once proud past. To the NE the boundary passes through the well-heeled fringes of Blackheath, then through Lee a little further S, which was a small medieval parish absorbed into Lewisham in 1900, and continues through amorphous later suburban stretches which merge unremarkably into those of Bromley. To the SW are the more distinctive hilly Victorian

---

* The area of St Nicholas Deptford, immediately w of Deptford Creek, which is strictly speaking in the borough of Greenwich, is here included with the Deptford parts of Lewisham.

areas of Sydenham and Forest Hill. The early development of Deptford, Blackheath, and the s parts of the borough are so different that they must be treated separately.*

The glories of DEPTFORD are departed. Henry VIII's ship-yard, 'The King's Yard', the cradle of the Navy, became an army supply depot and is now used for warehousing. Pepys's Victuall-ing Yard to its N is now a council estate (albeit with some handsome remaining late c 18 buildings). John Evelyn's house, the original manor house of w Greenwich, in existence since the c 11 and in Evelyn's time called Sayes Court, 'a most beautiful place' according to Pepys, has vanished completely.‡ No trace of Peter the Great, who rented Sayes Court in 1698, remains. Deptford Green, once bordered by the mansion of Lord Howard of Effingham, Lord High Admiral against the Armada, is now a street with council flats on one side and a power station on the other. Trinity House, founded by Henry VIII in 1514, and with headquarters just behind the church by the green, moved away to Stepney in the c 17 (and to Tower Hill in 1795).

When Henry VIII started the yard, Deptford was a fishing village, with its parish church of St Nicholas at Deptford Green, close to the river. Then, like Greenwich and Woolwich, it developed into a town, long before it became a suburb. Albury
59 Street, built up from 1706, has some of the earliest terrace houses in the metropolitan style to be built outside London. Soon after (although St Nicholas had been rebuilt in the late c 17), Upper Deptford acquired its own church, *Archer*'s mag-
48 nificently Baroque St Paul. Already in 1774, when *The Ambula-tor* was published, the two parishes, Upper and Lower Dept-ford, were called 'a large and populous town'. Its population in 1800 was indeed 18,000. But of the buildings that existed at this time, apart from the two churches and the remnants of Albury Street, few remain except for some battered examples along the High Street and further s in Tanners Hill.

The c 19 trend of population is interesting. Lower Deptford, that is the parish of St Nicholas, technically in the borough of Greenwich, had 6,933 inhabitants in 1801, 7,071 in 1851, 7,267 in 1901, and 7,518 in 1921. Upper Deptford (St Paul), on the other hand, grew as other outlying suburbs did: 11,000 1801, 14,000 1831 (when the built-over area of Deptford was still, apart from the riverside, hardly more than a strip s between High Street and Church Street as far as the Broadway), 21,000 1851, 46,000 1871, 72,000 1901, 109,000 1911, 113,000 1921. After the Second World War it was reduced to 76,000, by 1965 to 68,000.

The history of BLACKHEATH is a total contrast. Without the problems of the rise and decay of riverside industry, built up too

* The GEOLOGY of Lewisham is London Clay overlain by patches of sand and gravel, with pebble beds in the E and some chalk by Deptford Creek. PREHIS-TORIC FINDS include a mesolithic scatter near Deptford Creek, and a possible Roman site at Blackheath.

‡ It lay to the N of Evelyn Street and was demolished *c*. 1728 and replaced by a workhouse. The site is now marked by a recreation ground laid out in the c 19 by one of Evelyn's descendants.

early and too densely to be much affected by later Victorian suburban growth, it has preserved its Georgian charm very effectively. Although it has the greatest concentration of older houses in Lewisham, it is not an ancient settlement. In Rocque's time, i.e. c. 1740, what is now Blackheath village was still a small cluster of houses called Dowager's Bottom, and the parish church of All Saints was built only in the mid C 19 (although there were earlier proprietary chapels in the area). The edges of the heath began to be developed in the late C 17 as newly fashionable Greenwich grew up the hill around the park.* The appeal of the Lewisham fringes of Blackheath is similar to that of parts of Hampstead, with its contrast between the polite formality of individual houses and terraces, and the disorganized manner in which the buildings encroach on parts of the heath. But Blackheath also has *Michael Searles*'s Paragon of 1794, a crescent 70 (most unusually, consisting of linked semi-detached houses), which is a masterpiece of classical composition on the grand scale. With its open outlook to the heath, it is closer to Bath or Buxton than to anything of the same date in London. The building of The Paragon on the edge of the Wricklemarsh Estate (*see* Greenwich (Gr), Perambulation 4) marks the beginning of the break-up of the larger estates in this area for suburban housing. The influence of Searles's designs can perhaps be discerned in the stuccoed sub-Palladian frontages of the 1830s onwards, which are a special feature of the area around the heath and in Lee to the S.

The SOUTHERN PARTS of the borough developed more slowly. Apart from Lewisham itself, before the C 19 the only other separate parish was Lee, a tiny settlement around a few large houses concentrated along the High Road towards Lee Green, some way away from St Margaret's church. Sydenham, a medieval settlement which became a minor spa from the C 17, remained rural until the early C 19. Other smaller centres existed at Honor Oak, Hither Green, Brockley, and Southend, but only at Southend, which still has an early C 19 chapel, and at Honor Oak, where there are a few late Georgian houses, is this past easily recognizable; the rest were submerged in the suburban flood which began in the mid C 19, although the separate patches of built-up land are still visible on maps of the 1860s. The population figures tell the story. The population of Lewisham, Sydenham, and Lee was less than 4,500 in 1801, 11,000 in 1831, 18,500 in 1851, 48,000 in 1871, 88,000 in 1891, 119,000 in 1911, and 228,000 in 1951. But even today one is struck by the plentiful open spaces and recreation grounds in the S part of the borough, especially in the neighbourhood of the Ravensbourne and its tributaries.

Worthwhile buildings earlier than the C 19 in S Lewisham are few. Apart from the tower of St Mary, nothing is visibly older than the late C 17. The highlights of this period are Lewisham

---

* For the heath itself and buildings on its N and E sides *see* Greenwich (Gr), Perambulation 3.

old vicarage and the delightful little chapel from Boone's alms-houses at Lee. From the C18 a few gentlemen's villas remain, especially the eccentric Stone House (by one of the *Gibsons*) on the Upper Deptford border, *Jupp*'s restrained Lee Manor House (now library), and, standing in its own ample grounds on the southern fringe, Beckenham Place, built by the developer of Blackheath Park, who incorporated into it parts of *John James*'s much grander mansion of Wricklemarsh which he had pulled down. A few other minor C18 discoveries await the patient explorer, but they are all few and far between.

The real speciality of Lewisham is the lesser Victorian suburban house in all its shapes and forms. Only a few can be mentioned here. They start in the second third of the C19 with a variety of types derived from Regency experiments: the Searles-inspired terraces and pairs at Lee, already mentioned; the little bow-fronted terraces in the St John's area of Upper Deptford; urban Italianate work at Hatcham; detached stucco-trimmed villas on the slopes of Forest Hill; a choice between Tudor and classical at Sydenham. From the middle of the C19 onwards, Sydenham, close to the attractions of the Crystal Palace, became a particularly classy suburb, with pretentious mansions on the grandest scale along Sydenham Hill (only a few remain). Smaller middle-class houses survive better; see for example the later C19 varieties on the Upper Deptford/Lewisham borders: on Loampit Hill, lavishly ornamented, or in Brockley, a well preserved suburb with a more coherent layout than is found in other parts of Lewisham, where commodious villas are neatly ranged along leafy streets.

By the early C20 almost all of Lewisham was one continuous suburb, equipped with its inevitable quota of churches (*see* separate introductions), railway stations (the best demolished), institutions (good examples of private benevolence at Blackheath, *see* Greenwich, Public Buildings), and educational buildings (of which the most interesting architecturally is *John Shaw*'s restrained Royal Naval School, now Goldsmiths' College, at New Cross). The open undulating hills which remained on the southern fringe were soon covered by the L.C.C.'s spreading cottage estates of Downham and Bellingham, begun in the 1920s. By then the L.C.C. had been busy for some time with the renewal of the slummier parts of Deptford, a pattern which continued vigorously after the Second World War (also pursued by the borough of Deptford), not always with aesthetically happy results. The County Council's most interesting early building is the Lodging House in Brookmill Road (1902–3), its most ambitious later effort the huge Pepys Estate on the site of the Victualling Yard (1963–9), one of their most confident pieces of brutalist showmanship, and also the only place where London's maritime historic buildings have been successfully preserved on a large scale. During the 1970s the borough of Lewisham (Borough Architects *M. H. Forward* 1964–8, *A. Sutton* 1968–73, *J. Tayler* 1973–80, *D. Butterworth* 1981–) has deliberately eschewed such display, experimenting instead with different kinds of modest housing developments on a humane and friendly scale:* especially attractive are the imaginatively grouped houses of Brockley Park in the SE of the borough.

Finally a handful of individual buildings of the last hundred years which deserve to be singled out. The two outstanding ones are from the turn of the century: *Townsend*'s Horniman Museum, Forest Hill, one of the most original Art Nouveau 97 buildings anywhere in England; and Deptford's swansong, its opulent Town Hall by *Lanchester, Stewart & Rickards*. Representatives of more recent decades are the flats by *Fry & Drew* off Bromley Road (1950s), *Owen Luder*'s Eros House, Catford, brutalism of the 1960s at its best, and for the 1970s the G.L.C.'s elegant Rivers Centre, Fordmill Road; also two good primary schools at Forest Hill (1958 and 1972) respectively by *Peter Moro* and *Michel Manser*.

The population of the whole of Lewisham was 289,130 in 1966, 231,324 in 1981, a drop of some 70,000 since 1951.

Further Reading

General accounts are N. Dews, *The History of Deptford* (1884), and L. Duncan, *History of the Borough of Lewisham* (1908). On Blackheath there is N. Rhind, *Blackheath Village and its Environs*: vol. I, *The Village and Blackheath Vale* (1976) and vol. II (1983), and W. Bonwitt, *The History of the Paragon and Paragon House and their Residents* (*c.* 1976); and on the heath itself N. Rhind, *Blackheath Centenary 1871–1971* (1971). On Albury Street, Deptford: A. Quiney, 'Thomas Lucas Bricklayer', *Archaeological Journal*, vol. 136 (1979). On Lee: E. and J. Birchenough, *The Manor House, Lee* (1971). Lewisham Local History Society *Transactions* (from 1963) have many good articles, although little that is strictly architectural. See also p. 124.

Acknowledgements

I am grateful to Mr C. Harrison and Mr J. Coulter of the borough's Archives and Local History Department for much useful information, to Mr and Mrs H. W. Eames for their advice and help, to Dr Anthony Quiney, who drove me around the borough and helped on numerous points, to Mr Neil Rhind (NR) for letting me reap the benefit of his research on the Blackheath area, to Mr W. Bonwitt for details about Michael Searles, to Mr B. D. Dance for information on St Dunstan's College, and to Mr John Marchent of the Borough Planning Department for information on recent developments.

* The rationale behind such planning can be found enticingly set out in *The Village in the City* (1973) by Nicholas Taylor (then chairman of the Borough of Lewisham Planning Committee).

402 LEWISHAM

DEPTFORD

CHURCHES

The two main churches make a telling contrast. St Nicholas, the old parish church,* is hidden away in an unworthy setting near the river, with a medieval tower, the plan and furnishings of 1697 an unostentatious demonstration of the influence of Wren's City churches. St Paul, *Archer*'s Baroque masterpiece, towers head and shoulders over the decrepit neighbourhood of the High Street. The best of the C19 suburban churches in Upper Deptford are *P. C. Hardwick*'s St John and the more individual St Peter, by *Marrable*.‡

ALL SAINTS, New Cross Road. 1869–71 by *Newman & Billing*. Kentish rag, with a large W rose window. No tower.

ST CATHERINE, Pepys Road, New Cross. 1893–4 by *H. Stock*, surveyor to the Haberdashers' Company. Large, E.E., ragstone, with brick interior. Reroofed after war damage, and reordered in the 1960s for combined church and community use.

ST JAMES, St James's Road, Hatcham, close to Goldsmiths' College. 1849–54 by *W. B. L. Granville*. A dull ragstone building notable only for its ambitious plan: cruciform with aisled transepts. Converted to the Laban Centre for Movement and Dance (Goldsmiths' College), 1979–80. – LECTERN. A good brass eagle. – Church SCHOOL by the same architect.

ST JOHN, Lewisham Way. 1855 by *P. C. Hardwick*. The typical additional parish church of a comfortably-off district growing in population. Large, with a thick Kentish rag surface, tall S W spire, and Dec tracery. Interior with tall arcades. – Stone REREDOS. – STAINED GLASS. W window by *Ward & Hughes*. – Allan MONUMENT of 1868 by *M. Noble*; an angel with a cross.

ST LUKE (with St Nicholas), Evelyn Street. 1870–2 by *T. H. Watson*. Ragstone, central tower, apsed chancel to the road. Remodelling by *Maguire & Murray* planned.

ST NICHOLAS, Deptford Green (just in Greenwich). The tower remains from a building of the Middle Ages, Kentish rag with stone dressings of *c.* 1500 (the top reconstructed in 1903–4). The body of the church, rebuilt in 1697 by *C. Stanton* and left a ruin by the Second World War, was repaired by *T. F. Ford & Partners*, 1958. The plan is similar to the earlier and less regular St Mary Magdalene, Bermondsey (Sk), that is, also developed from Wren's St Martin, Ludgate: nave of four bays with two aisles, Tuscan arcades with straight entablature, timber galleries, non-projecting transepts, and crossing at the second bay from the W. Shallow nave and transept vaults and groined vault over the crossing. The E end was divided off

* Just over the border in the borough of Greenwich, but included here.
‡ Demolished: the OLD MEETING HOUSE (Baptist), Deptford Church Street. Plain rectangle of London stock and red brick, much redone. Originally 1674; remodelled later.

after the war, so that the church is now square. Externally it is of red brick with windows of rubbed brick; stone is used sparingly, for sills, keystones, quoins, bands, and parapet. The transepts are marked by rather reactionary or provincial Dutch gables. – Excellent contemporary WOODWORK: Corinthian pedimented REREDOS, CHANCEL PANELLING, and also a PULPIT (said to be earlier). – Late C 17 CARVING of the Vision of Ezekiel in the style of *Grinling Gibbons*. – (MONUMENTS. The best, including one by *Gibbons*, were destroyed in the war. Roger Boyle † 1615 remains; alabaster, with kneeling figure and skull.) – In the churchyard many tombs and also the brick and stone-quoined three-bay CHARNEL HOUSE, built at the same time as the church. GATEPIERS with skulls.

ST PAUL, Deptford High Street. One of the most moving C 18 churches in London: large, sombre, and virile. The work of *Thomas Archer*, who also designed St John, Smith Square, Westminster, and the cathedral at Birmingham, St Paul is one of the new churches built as a result of the Act of 1711, the only one by Archer (who was a Commissioner until 1715). The petition for a second church at Deptford was accepted in the same year as the Act, no doubt helped by the fact that the Vicar of Deptford was George Stanhope, Dean of Canterbury. Archer's design dates from 1713; the steeple was an after-thought, and involved some reconstruction of the rising W end. Although the fabric and most of the decoration were ready by 1720, work continued until 1730, when the church was consecrated. Restorations: 1856 (*J. Whichcord*), 1883 (*T. Dinwiddy*), 1930s (*Eden & Marchant*), and 1970s.

The church is ingenious in plan, and equally ingenious in its solution of the eternal English W tower and W portico problem. Archer did not fancy the illogical and aesthetically pain-ful way in which Gibbs at St Martin-in-the-Fields simply let the tower ride on the Greek roof. But he did not want to dispense with a portico either. So he made his tower circular, and let it project in a semicircle at the W end (which in addition corresponded to the semicircular low apse at the E end and thus stressed a centralizing tendency welcome to Archer as it had been to Wren). Around the base of the tower is a semi-circular portico of giant columns crowned by a balustrade round the semicircle of the tower projection. Thus a structur-ally convincing and at the same time highly original solution was found (original even if one admits that the semicircular portico is derived from Wren's S transept at St Paul's or from the source of that, S. Maria della Pace, which Archer would himself have seen in Rome). The Tuscan columns of the portico are of majestic girth, contrasted against the slender upper parts of the steeple. A wide staircase fans out from it. The N and S sides of the church also have quite unnecessarily lavish staircases, each of two arms starting at right angles to the fronts and turning to end parallel with them. It is the way Palladio designed staircases for his villas, or Lord Burlington for his villa at Chiswick (and Archer himself at Heythrop, Oxfordshire). Here they lead to projecting pedimented three-bay centres emphasizing a N–S axis, another aspect of the central planning which interested English Baroque architects at this time (cf. Hawksmoor's St George Bloomsbury (Ca) and Christ Church Spitalfields (T H)). The walls are articulated by colossal pilasters with cyclopean intermittent rustication. Venetain E window bent round the curve of the apse with a bent pediment above (a very Baroque trait, no doubt indulged in by Archer on the precedent of Vanbrugh's licences).

The church, almost but not quite square, is entered through a circular entrance lobby beneath the tower. Inside, the impression is of a square within a square, the outer corners being filled by two-storey chambers (the W spaces also accommodating staircases). To the broad nave these chambers have chamfered angles, and their upper walls are opened up by large glazed round-headed windows above the projecting private pews (cf. St Martin-in-the-Fields). The rhythm of the giant Corinthian engaged columns which flank these pews and the E apse creates the illusion of an oval central space, coming closer to Borromini and the Roman Baroque than any other English church of this date. In an ambiguously Baroque fashion some of these half-columns double as responds for the short three-bay N and S aisles. Yet the aisles, and the shallow

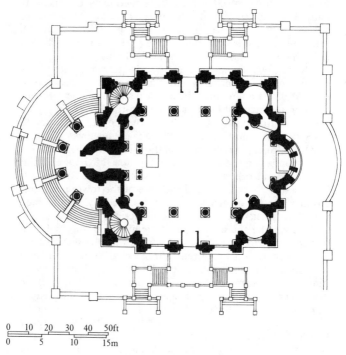

Deptford, St Paul, plan

trapezoidal chancel and apse, concur with the traditionally English emphasis on an E–W direction. Flat ceilings with splendid classical plasterwork by *James Hands*. The main galleries of wood are not organically part of the architect's design. – The FURNISHINGS cannot compete with the architecture. They were less ambitious than Archer had intended (his designs for pulpit and altarpiece were simplified by *John James* in 1721), and have been altered and rearranged. – PULPIT (cut down in 1873) of generous S-section. – Iron COMMUNION GATES and PULPIT STAIRS. – ORGAN on wooden Corinthian columns at the W end. – FONT. Neo-Norman, brought from Rochester Cathedral. – STAINED GLASS. Saint in the NW window, good mid-C18 work. – MONUMENTS. Matthew ffinch † 1745. Standing wall-monument with a bulgy sarcophagus and a large urn on top. – Maria Finch † 1745. Urn against obelisk, with Rococo decoration. – Vice-Admiral James Sayer † 1776 by *Nollekens*. Tablet with large trophy. – Dr Charles Burney, the historian of music, † 1817, with profile in medallion against an obelisk in relief. – Large CHURCHYARD, with several table-tombs and an OBELISK to the Stone family, 1807.

ST PETER, Wickham Road, W of Tressillian Road. 1866–70 by *F. Marrable*, quite interesting in plan and elevation. W tower completed 1890 by *A. W. Blomfield*. The tower is flanked by gabled vestibules. Wide nave spanned by bold transverse arches; narrow aisles, transepts, and vaulted, apsed chancel. Expensive polychrome decoration.

ASSUMPTION (R.C.), Deptford High Street. 1844. Chancel and reredos by *Canon North*, 1859. A poor building of yellow brick with skinny lancet front. (Chapel of the Sacred Heart 1886 by *F. A. Walters*.)

ZION BAPTIST CHURCH, New Cross Road. 1846.

PUBLIC BUILDINGS

TOWN HALL, New Cross Road. Only seven bays wide, but one of the most florid of Edwardian public buildings. Very Baroque central oriel window supported on caryatids overreaching themselves from the sides of the portal where they are rooted. Statues of admirals in niches on the first floor. Originally with a turret. 1902–7 by *Lanchester, Stewart & Rickards*, the firm responsible for the Cardiff Civic Centre and Westminster Central Hall. Entrance hall and grand staircase in two flights, a central one with a pair rising from it; ornate wrought-iron balustrading with foliage and anchors. Gallery with paired pink marble columns. Ornate plaster ceiling with domed lantern, swags, and putti. Council chamber with a doorway with a gilded plaster shell between Arts and Crafts figures; less grand inside, with a florid plaster ceiling.

PUBLIC BATHS AND WASHHOUSES, behind the Town Hall. 1895 by *T. Dinwiddy*.

(POLICE STATION, Amersham Vale, W of Deptford High Street. 1912, brick. Queen Anne style.)

LIBRARY, New Cross Road. By *Gerald Warren & Sydney E. Castle*, 1910–12. Edwardian Renaissance, brick with stone dressings.

LIBRARY, Lewisham Way. By *A. Brumwell Thomas*, the architect of Woolwich Town Hall (Gr). 1914. Large, Baroque, with barrel-vaulted hall and massive staircase.

SOUTH EAST LONDON TECHNICAL INSTITUTE, Lewisham Way, Brockley. Even plainer than Goldsmiths' College, but quite impressive as an unrelieved twenty-three-bay brick block. Hipped roof. The sort of effect the Danes sometimes obtained more self-consciously. Designed by *F. R. Hiorns* for the L.C.C., 1927. Extension across Breakspears Road to the W of the 1960s, with bands of windows and light grey panels, in place of the E end of the early C19 crescent. To the rear Brakspeare Building, 1973–7 by *J. Thomas* and *J. Buckrell* of the G.L.C., an uncompromising brutalist four-storey addition.

GOLDSMITHS' COLLEGE, Lewisham Way, New Cross. Built as the Royal Naval School. Badly damaged in the Second World War, and restored with a roof of different form. A plain, quite monumental block of sixteen bays with giant arched portal. It might well be a restrained Italian design of *c*. 1900 but is by *John Shaw*, 1843–5. Shaw (cf. Wellington College, Berks) is one of the most surprising architects of his generation and would deserve to be better known than he is. His sympathy with classical and Baroque forms is unique for his time. By him also the Baroque chapel (1853), brick with stone dressings. Additional block by *Sir Reginald Blomfield*, 1907–8. The great hall was formed by roofing over the parade ground.

ABBEY AND STANHOPE SCHOOLS, New Cross Road, Upper Deptford. 1898–9 by *A. B. Thomas*, the architect of Woolwich Town Hall. Dignified red brick classical.

ASKE'S HABERDASHERS' SCHOOL FOR BOYS, Pepys Road, New Cross. Founded in 1688. From the new building at Shoreditch of 1825–6 the statue of Robert Aske in the forecourt by *Croggon* of Lambeth, 1836. The present building is of 1875 by *W. Snooke*, yellow and red brick, Gothic, symmetrical, on a corner site with fine views in all directions.

ASKE'S HABERDASHERS' SCHOOL FOR GIRLS, New Cross Road. 1891 by *Stock, Page & Stock*. Quite a nice design with buttresses, plain gables, Queen Anne windows, and an asymmetrical turret with cupola, the style derived from Philip Webb.

PRIMARY SCHOOL, Hughes Fields, West Greenwich. One of the well-designed schools built *c*. 1950 by the L.C.C. Architect's Department.

VICTUALLING YARD. *See* Perambulation 2.

DEPTFORD EAST POWER STATION, Stowage, E of St Nicholas. Attached to the later building, one wall with heavy brick piers and pointed arches remains from *Sebastian de Ferranti*'s power station of 1887–9. (It transmitted power to the West End; the first electric power station to generate at high tension for transmission over a long distance.)

DEPTFORD TELEPHONE EXCHANGE, Harton Street, Upper Deptford. 1934–5 by *Christopher Bristow* of the *Office of Works*. Metal windows between plain brick bands. An early example of a modern design from the Office of Works (the effect now diluted by a later mansard roof and further large additions).

DEPTFORD WATERWORKS, Brookmill Road. Engine houses of 1811 and 1927–32. Water was taken from the river Ravensbourne from 1701; a deep well to the chalk was sunk in 1856.

DEPTFORD SEWAGE PUMPING STATION, Norman Road. *See* Greenwich (Gr), Public Buildings.

DEPTFORD STATION, on the London and Greenwich railway viaduct. The original station of 1836 had a ramped carriage approach from the S, up to viaduct level. The brick arches remain behind the High Street. The bridge across the High Street formerly rested on Doric columns.

PERAMBULATIONS

1. Central Deptford from N to S: Albury Street, High Street, Broadway, Tanners Hill

C 18 Deptford extended along the river from the Royal Victoria Victualling Yard, whose remains are now incorporated in the Pepys Estate, to Deptford Creek, the mouth of the river Ravensbourne, and inland as far S as Deptford Broadway. The only sign of the old riverside village is St Nicholas, Deptford Green, now surrounded by a power station and council flats, and separated from the area to the N by the busy Creek Road, which was cut through old streets in 1896.* DEPTFORD CHURCH STREET, which runs N, is now also a widened road of no character, but off it to the W, immediately S of Creek Road, is what used to be the gem of Deptford: Albury Street.

ALBURY STREET, formerly Union Street, was laid out and developed by *Thomas Lucas*, a local bricklayer, from 1706 (cf. p. 45). By 1717 forty houses were built. The street is a remarkable example of the early introduction of urban terrace housing in what was then a village outside the metropolis. In 1950, apart from two gaps on the S side, the terraces were still tolerably complete, with houses of two storeys, a few raised to three, plum-coloured stock brick with red brick dressings. But by 1981 only four houses (Nos. 34–40) remained on the S side. Of the larger group on the N side, only six (Nos. 21–31) are in good order at the time of writing; eleven more (Nos.

* Visible from the river, in Borthwick Street, the mid to later C 19 former boilermaker's shop of the marine engine builders John Penn & Son. Six large windows under brick and stucco arches.

13–19, 39–45) stand derelict, still awaiting their long promised restoration.* It is therefore the individual houses, and,
alas, no longer the total character of the street that can be
enjoyed. Especially good are the restored group on the N side:
Nos. 23–31 (21 is a rebuilding of 1829). The houses mostly
have segment-headed windows with sashes, and parapets, all
very up to date in 1706. Vertical lacing between the windows.
Doorcases with flat heads on brackets carved with the freedom
characteristic of the early c 18; a surprising variety of motifs
and designs, some with foliage only, one with cherubs' heads,
another (No. 27) even with whole figures of cherubs.‡ Many
of the houses have original panelled interiors and good staircases with twisted balusters too. The gaps in the s side have
been filled by G.L.C. housing of the 1970s, well-mannered
but dull groups of mottled brick, inevitably a comedown,
deliberately avoiding any effort at pastiche. They ignore the
original frontage of Albury Street, and extend s in two closes,
one with a vista of St Paul's as a marginal compensation.

59

DEPTFORD HIGH STREET, at the other end of Albury Street
from Church Street, is a decayed c 19 shopping street surviving precariously between almost wholesale clearance to E and
W.§ It became the main street only in the early c 19. There is
little that is visually rewarding, although the scruffy frontages
conceal a few remains of modest cottages of earlier days, and
one or two larger brick houses of the c 18. Examples, from N to
s: on the W side Nos. 201–203, a low, heavily disguised
timber-framed house of the c 17, and Nos. 167–169, also
modest. N of the railway bridge, behind shops, Nos. 108 (E)
and 127–129 (W), both three-storeyed, brick, c 18. A few
relics of mid-c 19 terraces (Nos. 181–195, 107–109, 111–119)
and, with more pretentious ornament, No. 18. Another low
group near the N end (Nos. 32–44); and one good late Georgian house, No. 11, with Ionic porch and bowed front.

DEPTFORD BROADWAY widens into a generous wedge shape
as it approaches the bridge over Deptford Creek. Two early
c 19 houses face down the High Street (Nos. 55–57). Further E
on the s side a good mid Victorian NATIONAL WESTMINS-
TER BANK, and the low Nos. 39–41. On the N side a few
stucco-faced houses, and the ODEON (derelict), 1938 by
George Coles. s of the Broadway CARRINGTON HOUSE, a
remarkably well designed lodging house for 800, by *J. R.
Stark* of the L.C.C. Housing Branch, 1902–3. A curving
façade, pavilion roof, and big hooded portico, shallow bows

* The story is one of appalling bureaucratic bungling by the G.L.C. Preservation was agreed in 1960, houses were emptied, and doorcases removed and stored;
but by 1973 only four houses had been repaired, and others had been demolished
(*see* C. Ward, *Vandalism*, 1973, p. 204). A further handful have been haphazardly
restored since then. All the carved brackets remaining in store with the G.L.C.
were stolen in 1982.
‡ Replaced incorrectly after restoration.
§ This has swept away other relics of c 18 Deptford, e.g. Nos. 38–44 Edward
Street and No. 170 Grove Street; also a former Wesleyan Chapel of 1803, s of
Albury Street.

and canted bays of stone. A row of pre-1914 L.C.C. cottages beyond.

TANNERS HILL continues the line of the High Street further s. Near the Broadway, Nos. 19–31, a low late C17 group of cottages around a bend. Then total rebuilding, with the Peabody VANGUARD ESTATE of the 1970s on the E, its blockwork and boarding a welcome change from the standard G.L.C. offerings, until, near the top of the hill, No. 124. Although scarcely recognizable, this is a major late C18 mansion, BRUNSWICK HOUSE, built in 1789 for Thomas Slade. The house stands sideways to the road, embedded in later additions. Originally its grounds extended s to Lewisham Way. Three storeys. The only part of the front visible is the end bay with a pretty *Coade* stone medallion, and the breaking-forward of the three centre bays, formerly pedimented. On the w side a full-height bay-window. (Two pretty fireplaces inside were extant in 1976.) w of and parallel to Tanners Hill, FLORENCE ROAD, with complete mid C19 terraces on both sides.

2. East Deptford: Evelyn Street; Victualling Yard, Pepys Estate

Lower Deptford between the High Street and the former Victualling Yard is largely a dispiriting maze of council housing of the post-Second-World-War era. The immediately pre- and post-war efforts, e.g. in EDWARD STREET, by *Ashley & Newman*, 1938–49, are a little better than average, relieved by odd angles, roughcast panels, and some Scandinavian touches such as the projecting eaves. In contrast, the MILTON COURT ESTATE further E is a typically deadening example of late 1960s mixed development with factory-built tower blocks. Belatedly, some humanity has been injected here by constructive landscaping, including the pedestrianization of WOODPECKER ROAD (*Landscape Design Group*, 1977–81). Otherwise there is just one older oasis of C18 cottages in EVELYN STREET, Nos. 212–234 (see the backs with mansarded roofs); No. 192, near St Luke's church, a solitary late Georgian terrace house; and a Fire Station. Further on a few generously ornamented late Victorian villas (Oak Villas 1881, Clare Villas).

PEPYS ESTATE, N of Evelyn Street. The site of the Victualling Yard, after 1858 called the Royal Victoria Yard (*see* Introduction), but of that one is not aware until one is close to the river. The L.C.C. began to develop the area for housing in 1963. The approach is not inviting, over a bridge past Deptford Park School, with a scrapyard on one's r., a skyscraper of flats looming on one's l., and ahead the jagged roofs of oasthouse type which mark a Youth Club on the edge of a raised shopping square. From here an upper-level walk, of the type so popular with planners in the sixties, leads past long relentless dark brick ranges of maisonettes with a rhythmic battlement

of top flats. Nearer the river, where the new buildings face the
old ones, the layout is more open, with some of the blocks on
stilts, and a generous grassy square. The maisonettes, both in
the three twenty-six-storey towers (a height unprecedented
among London flats when built) and in the lower blocks, are
of the 'scissor' or crossover type, a new, complicated form of
plan that became widely used in the sixties. Its economic
advantage was held to be the combination of single-aspect,
narrow-fronted dwellings with internal corridor access on
alternate floors. Hence the three tall slabs have separately
articulated stair and lift towers at one end. The original
scheme (completed in 1966) provides for a total of c. 5,000
people in 1,500 dwellings (density 153 p.p.a.). E of Grove
Street are uninspired G.L.C. extensions, maisonettes with
pitched roofs, in the less formal mode of c. 1980.

The buildings remaining from the VICTUALLING YARD are
some of the most imaginative conversions to be found on
G.L.C. estates. They can be approached from Grove Street by
those who wish to ignore the modern buildings. They all date
from c. 1783–8 and are by *James Arrow*, Surveyor to the
Victualling Office from 1774 to 1785.* A GATEWAY of 1788
flanked by four hefty bollards made from genuine cannon
leads first to the COLONNADE, houses and offices for the
Porter and Clerk of Cheque, converted to old people's housing
in the 1970s. Two low linked houses, five plus five plus two
bays, fronted by a covered walk with paired columns. The
colonnade leads to the corner of a square, which has on three
sides the maisonettes mentioned above, on the fourth a plain
but elegant terrace of seven three-storey houses originally for
officers of the yard, now converted to flats. The ends and centre
have pediments. S of this, facing the river, the two former
RUM WAREHOUSES, flanking the approach from the river
stairs. They are now flats, with on the ground floor at each end
premises for a sailing club and a branch library. Symmetrical,
three storeys, the far end of each building with a pediment.
The inner returns were the commandant's house and the
administrative offices. Behind the r. building, former
STABLES, low, with pediment.

The Victualling Yard was used for the storage of provisions and
clothing for the Royal Navy. The shipbuilding yard further
downstream, closed in 1869, became the City of London's
foreign cattle market (1871–1913), an army supply depot, and
then warehousing. (Much has been demolished, but a few
buildings remain off PRINCE STREET, including the C18
Master Shipbuilder's house, a few officers' houses, and a
mid C19 shipbuilding shed.

---

* The surviving buildings are all shown on a plan of the yard of 1790. Some of
the plans held by the Lewisham Archives and Local History Department are
signed by Arrow (information from Mr J. Coulter).

3. Upper Deptford: New Cross, Lewisham Way

STONE HOUSE, No. 281 Lewisham Way. The one individual house of interest in this area, built in 1771–3 either by *George Gibson Jun.*, the architect of St Mary Lewisham, or by his father *George Gibson Sen.*, a little known architect who had worked for Queen Caroline and who had travelled in Italy (according to James Elmes's memoir of his son).* The house stands in its own grounds, a square villa on an ambitious central plan, a very personal interpretation of the villa form that had been revived by Chambers and Taylor in the 1750s. Highly unconventional exterior (a characteristic of houses designed by architects for themselves), with projecting bow-windows in the centre of three sides, and on the fourth a four-column portico, two columns deep. Exterior of roughly coursed rubble. Main windows with rusticated surrounds. On the roof a cupola with concave sides. The plan, with central toplit staircase and rooms of different shapes making use of the curved projections, perhaps owes something to Taylor's villas, especially Danson Park, Bexleyheath (Bx). (On the walls of the octagonal stairwell four medallions with busts. Tripartite saloon along the whole of one side, with circular centre and groin-vaulted end compartments.)

LEWISHAM WAY has a mixture of the usual terraces: early C 19 or latest-classical stuccoed of *c.* 1840, or rows of semi-detached villas with their side entrances connected so as to form one composition (see e.g. Nos. 160–186), although the crescent between Breakspears Road and Wickham Road is rudely broken into by the extensions to the Technical Institute (q.v.). N of Lewisham Way the ST JOHN'S area, with mid C 19 terraces on quite a modest scale. An especially attractive series of bowed fronts e.g. in Albyn Road/Admiral Street. S of Lewisham Way, BROCKLEY, a later C 19 suburb, more amply laid out. Broad streets (e.g. WICKHAM ROAD, TRESSILLIAN ROAD) with tall terraces and pairs of houses of *c.* 1870, lavishly decorated. Some ingenious infilling by the *Borough of Lewisham* in TRESSILLIAN CRESCENT, 1978, with small dwellings and garages arranged in groups which respect the proportions of the Victorian houses.

At the w end of Upper Deptford is NEW CROSS, historically the manor of Hatcham, a rural area until its mid C 19 development largely by the Haberdashers' Company. The theme is C 19 housing and its replacements. A few handsome terraces remain, notably Hatcham Terrace, 1842, on the N side of NEW CROSS ROAD (Nos. 207 etc.), metropolitan Italianate, with some pediments over first-floor windows. KENDER STREET further w has No. 56, now All Saints Vicarage, of 1827 (altered in the 1850s for George England) and on one side a humbler row of the 1820s. Its modest late Georgian detail

---

* Deptford rate books indicate only one George Gibson, who owned the estate from 1766 to 1795, but was assessed for land alone up to 1771 (information from Lewisham Local History Department).

appears especially charming when compared with the
KENDER ESTATE opposite (by *F. MacManus & Partners*,
designed 1968, built early 1970s for the G.L.C.), long, anonymous terraces with flats of different sizes over garages. The
smooth white surfaces hark back to the international modern
of pre-war years (cf. the same firm's work at Kentish Town
and Tufnell Park, Ca). Along NEW CROSS ROAD close to the
borough boundary a few early C 19 villas remain (*see* Camberwell (Sk), Perambulation 3). S of New Cross Gate and Queen's
Road the SOMERVILLE ESTATE by *Howell, Killick, Partridge & Amis*, 1978. In contrast to the Kender Estate, this
takes the reaction to concrete high rise of the 1960s a stage
further with low, pantiled clusters of houses in an intricate
arrangement of cul de sacs on different levels, but all in an
unfortunately monotonous dark red brick. A community centre in the middle.

LEWISHAM

CHURCHES

The medieval parish churches were at Lewisham and Lee. A
little medieval fabric remains in the tower of St Mary Lewisham.
Nothing else is earlier than the C 18, when the rest of St Mary
was rebuilt by *George Gibson Jun*. The Ascension Dartmouth
Row may incorporate the remains of a late C 17 chapel; Southend
still preserves the rural classical chapel which belonged to the
Forster family, as a church hall. The numerous other churches
were built to cope with C 19 suburban expansion. From the
pre-ecclesiological era: *Vulliamy*'s St Bartholomew Sydenham,
and the rebuilding on a new site of St Margaret Lee, *by John
Brown*; in the more correct Gothic of the mid C 19: *Ferrey*'s All
Saints Blackheath, *Christian*'s Christ Church Forest Hill, *Scott*'s
St Stephen Lewisham.* The best of the many later churches was
St Barnabas Algernon Road (unfortunately now much altered
inside), by *Brooks*, who was also responsible for interesting
alterations and furnishings at St Margaret Lee. The inter-war
years are represented in a better way than usual by *Sir Charles
Nicholson*'s churches in the L.C.C. estates (St Barnabas, St
Dunstan, St John). Untraditional buildings begin only after the
war, with *Trevor Dannatt*'s small Congregational church at Blackheath (1957) and the Dietrich Bonhoeffer church at Forest Hill
(*G. S. Agar*, 1959). Finally, the more radical concrete style of the
later C 20 is well expressed in *Dannatt*'s Friends Meeting House
at Blackheath.

ALL SAINTS, Blackheath. Built as a new parish church for

---

* Demolished 1980: HOLY TRINITY, Sydenham Park, by *J. Emmett*, large,
correct Geometric of 1865–6. Demolished 1982: ST PHILIP, Taylor's Lane,
Sydenham, 1864–7 by *E. Nash* and *J. Round*, with S transept chapel of 1896 by
C. H. M. Mileham. Threatened 1983: ST JOHN (United Reformed, formerly
Presbyterian), Devonshire Road, Forest Hill, 1884 by *J. T. Barker*, French
Gothic, very large, pinnacled spire.

Blackheath village in 1857–67 by *Ferrey*. Puginian, with plate and Dec tracery, already rather old-fashioned. Remarkable mainly for the way in which it is placed right into the heath. Surrounded on all sides by grass, it stands as if it were a model, defying all Blackheath traditions by its Kentish rag surfaces and its spire asymmetrically placed on the s. Vestries 1890, porch 1899 by *A. W. Blomfield*.

ALL SAINTS, Trewsbury Road, off Sydenham Road. 1903 by *Fellowes Prynne*. The E end now concealed by later buildings. Only three bays of the nave were built, and a later narthex. Interior with tall octagonal brick piers and with the typical *Prynne* stone screen up to the top of the chancel arch (cf. Roehampton, Ww, and All Saints, Brixton, La).

ASCENSION, Dartmouth Row, Blackheath. The church began as a chapel of ease endowed in 1697. Modest exterior, with small cupola. The apse, richly decorated with pilasters and coffered semi-dome, dates from a rebuilding of 1750. The nave, rebuilt in 1838–9, was restored in 1950 by *Robert Potter*, after war damage. The galleries (except for the w one) have been removed. – Heraldic GLASS by *Francis Spear*.

CHRIST CHURCH, Church Rise, s of Waldram Park Road, Forest Hill. 1852–62 by *Ewan Christian*. Ragstone, Dec, sited prominently on a hilltop, with a handsome w tower with spire and corner turrets, completed 1885. (Interior altered in the 1970s by the insertion of an extra floor at the w end for meeting rooms.) – (STAINED GLASS by *Powell* and *Comper*.)

ST ANDREW, Sandhurst Road, Catford. 1904 by *P. A. Robson*. Brick; broad interior with brick piers, narrow aisles with the flying buttresses of the nave showing inside. Art Nouveau detail. The N aisle now divided off. – (Wrought-iron SCREENS. – Later STAINED GLASS by *M. Travers*, 1921–37.

(ST AUGUSTINE, Baring Road, Grove Park. E end with apse 1885–6 by *Charles Bell*, French Gothic. Kentish rag. Nave and aisles 1912 by *P. Leeds*, Perp.)

ST BARNABAS (formerly the Transfiguration), Algernon Road, s of Loampit Hill. 1881 by *James Brooks*. Impressive, austere red brick rectangle with lancet windows and a flèche between nave and chancel. The originally lofty interior now with an inserted floor, added when the church was converted to a centre for the deaf. Low aisles on low thick circular piers, with very original capitals, just four leaf spurs supporting a thin square cornice. Piers stone, arches and walls red brick. To the N a narrow outer aisle or gangway divided from the aisle by thin cloistral-looking terracotta colonnettes. Nave with large plate tracery clerestory windows; chancel differentiated by lancets instead.

ST BARNABAS, Downham Way. 1928–9 by *Sir Charles Nicholson* (cf. St Dunstan, St John). Plain Early Christian style. w front with transeptal narthex with moulded brickwork and an asymmetrical bellcote.

ST BARTHOLOMEW, Westwood Hill, Sydenham. 1827–32 by *Vulliamy*. Stock brick. w tower with thin buttresses and straight-topped diagonal pinnacles. Nave and aisles, lancet windows with Perp tracery, and battlements. Apsidal chancel 1858 by *Edwin Nash*, who widened the N aisle in 1883. – STAINED GLASS. W window by *Clayton & Bell*; two N windows by *Burlison & Grylls*.

ST DUNSTAN, Bellingham Green. 1925 by *Sir Charles Nicholson*. Only nave and aisles completed. A big sweeping roof; no clerestory.

ST GEORGE, Vancouver Road, off Perry Hill, Catford. 1878–80 by *W. C. Banks*. Built at the expense of George Parker of Lewisham House. Large and ambitious, with a NE tower (heightened 1887). Kentish rag. Polygonal apse; W front with entrances flanking an apsidal baptistery; windows with fanciful tracery; elaborate W rose window given splendid STAINED GLASS by *Henry Holiday*, 1899–1900 – Christ, cherubim, and seraphim in vivid reds and blues. (Other windows and wall decoration by *P. Bacon & R. Corbould* of Hemming & Co. Ornate stone carving: foliage capitals in the nave, FONT, and PULPIT.) Roof renewed after a fire in 1976. Good plain VICARAGE to the W, 1885, purple brick.

ST HILDA, Stondon Park, Forest Hill. 1907 by *Greenaway & Newberry*, in their rather irresponsible Arts and Crafts Gothic. Odd E end with the middle window high up above a reredos. Exterior with semicircular but traceried aisle windows and a stunted SE tower provided with an octagonal parapet decorated with brick and stone chequer.

ST JOHN, Bromley Road, Southend. The small and charming old chapel of 1824 with Tuscan porch and cupola is now used as a parish hall. New large brick church behind, never completed, by *Sir Charles Nicholson*, 1928, Gothic and not original, but sensitive in the details. (Interior reordered 1977. Furnishings and corona by *John Hayward*. – STAINED GLASS. S chapel E by *Karl Parsons* and *E. Liddall Armitage*, 1933.) – MONUMENTS to John Forster † 1834 and Elizabeth Forster † 1837, both by *Sievier* and both simple.

ST LAURENCE, Bromley Road, Catford. By *Covell Matthews & Partners*, c. 1970. Polygonal church and community rooms on a new site replacing a church of 1886–7 by *H. R. Gough* demolished for a car park. Openwork spire above the Lady Chapel.

ST MARGARET, Lee Terrace. The parish church of Lee. The old church was on the other side of the road, N of the present building. Its tower, with late medieval fabric incorporated in a rebuilding of 1813–14 by *Joseph Gwilt*, survives in ruins, surrounded by a churchyard rich in large C18 and C19 monuments, for example the Call tomb (1794, 1801) with obelisk and coat of arms. Sir Edward Halley, Astronomer Royal, and John Cocking of the early parachute accident are buried here. The new church is of 1839–41 by *John Brown* of Norwich, the Commissioners' type, with coupled lancet windows. Ornate, quite picturesque W tower, with octagonal top stage and spire. Inside, the aisles are as high as the nave; slender quatrefoil piers. Much remodelling from 1875 by *James Brooks*, to bring the church in line with more serious forms of Gothic. The chancel was lengthened and given aisles and a stone vault, the nave galleries were removed and a wooden vault added (1888), and a vaulted baptistery was inserted in the tower. – (Refurnishing of the same period: alabaster REREDOS, carved by *Earp*, painted by *Westlake*; CROSSES and CANDLESTICKS designed by *Brooks* (1875 high altar candlesticks, processional cross; 1888 Lady Chapel; 1892 high altar cross). – STAINED GLASS. Much by *Clayton & Bell*.) – BRASSES (E wall N side). Elizabeth Conhill † 1513; N. Ansley † 1593 and wife.

ST MARY, Lewisham High Street. The parish church of Lewisham. The base of the tower Perp with diagonal buttresses (recorded building dates 1498 and 1512). The tower top with handsome restrained ornamental enrichments and the body of the church 1774–7 by *George Gibson Jun*. The building is of Kentish rag with dressed stone quoins and other trim. Round-headed windows. To N and S lower transeptal-looking attachments, on the S with the unusual motif of a four-column porch with pediment. The interior poorly remodelled and the chancel equally deplorably rebuilt (by *A. Blomfield*, 1881–2). – MONUMENTS. Four of unusual weight and merit. Anne Petrie † 1787, by *Vanpook* of Brussels, simply a large, very sparingly framed relief of a woman reclining on a couch, with children at her feet and an allegorical female at her head. – Margaret Petrie † 1791, by *Banks*. The same frame and composition, the relief a dying woman on a couch with virtues around, more Grecian than the earlier one. – Mary Lushington † 1797, by *Flaxman*. The decoration also classical but 52 more restless, even if no more detailed. The two figures are melodiously composed into a tympanum shape, their bodies and draperies with the long shallow undulations of Flaxman's friends Fuseli and Blake. – John Thackeray † 1851, by Flaxman's pupil *E. H. Baily*; much more ornate, with long inscription, portrait medallion on top, a drapery pulled away from it by an angel on the l., a seated allegorical figure on the r., and reliefs of two buildings at the foot. – Many contemporary minor tablets.

ST MILDRED, St Mildreds Road, Lee. 1878–9 by *H. Elliott*. Kentish rag. Brick interior. – (STAINED GLASS. S chapel E window by *Wilhelmina Geddes*, 1952.)

(ST PAUL, Taymount Rise, S of London Road, Forest Hill. Built in 1863 as a Congregational church by *Hine* & *T. Roger Smith*; Gothic.)

(ST SAVIOUR, Brockley Rise, Forest Hill. 1865–6 by *W. Smith*, completed 1875 and 1928, truncated after war damage.)

ST STEPHEN, Lewisham High Street. 1863–5 by *Sir George Gilbert Scott*. E.E. exterior of Kentish rag. A tower was intended over the N transept. The S transept has a double gable. Exterior as well as interior competent without being at all inspiring. – Of the STAINED GLASS a few charming figured medallions by *Clayton & Bell* have survived the Second World

War. – (REREDOS by *Charles Buckeridge*, carved by *Redfern* and decorated by *Bell*, 1873, moved to the S chapel in 1875. – Chancel SCREEN by *Brooks*, 1875.)

ST SWITHUN, Hither Green Lane. 1892 by *Ernest Newton* (detailed, according to GR, by *Lethaby*). Disappointing as a building connected with these two names. Red brick with large Dec E and W windows; very tall transeptal windows. Nothing like Newton's Good Shepherd, Lee, which was, alas, badly damaged in the Second World War.

THE ANNUNCIATION AND ST AUGUSTINE (R.C.), Dunfield Road, Beckenham Hill. Red brick. Circular, centrally planned, gabled clerestory windows, lantern with copper fins, and an entrance like a barbican, with curved walls (niches inside).

(HOLY CROSS (R.C.), Sangley Road, Catford. 1904 by *Tasker*, Romanesque. Sanctuary added 1924. DE)

(OUR LADY AND ST PHILIP NERI (R.C.), Sydenham Road. 1964 by *Walters & Kerr Bate*. Large crossing with angle chapels; concrete cross arches. DE)

THE RESURRECTION (R.C.), Sydenham Park. 1974 by *Broadbent, Hastings, Reid & Todd*, pale brick, almost windowless, not inviting. – SCULPTURE. Relief of the Risen Christ over the entrance by *S. Sykes*. – Crucifix by *Elspeth Reid*.

ST SAVIOUR (R.C.), Lewisham High Street. 1909 by *Kelly & Dickie*, red brick, Italianate, with presbytery. S aisle and tall campanile added only in 1925–9. It is crowned by a figure; quite a landmark. Italian interior.

BROWNHILL ROAD BAPTIST CHURCH, Catford. 1902 by *Smee, Mence & Houchin*: the Nonconformists' typical brand of 1900 Gothic.

CHURCH OF JESUS CHRIST OF LATTER DAY SAINTS, Lee Road. By *Gareth Wright & Colin Dixie*, planned 1977, begun 1980.

CONGREGATIONAL CHURCH, Lawn Terrace, Blackheath. Within the shell of the war-damaged building of 1853 by *Brandon & Ritchie* is a small, simple church by *Trevor Dannatt*, 1957. Glazed side wall to the courtyard enclosed by the E part of the old church. In 1982 cleaned up and tactfully altered by *Watts & Partners* for their own offices.

DIETRICH BONHOEFFER CHURCH (German Evangelical), Dacres Road, S of Perry Vale, Forest Hill. (Bonhoeffer was minister of the church in 1933–5.) 1958–9 by *G. S. Agar*, in place of a church of 1883 damaged in the war. More progressive than most English churches of this date. Pale brick; nave and apsed chancel all in one. In the chancel six long thin rectangular windows of concrete and slab GLASS in bright colours, symbolizing the Evangelists, St Paul, and St Peter. By *Whitefriars Studios* after designs by the Rev. *Eberhard Bethge* and Miss *E. Wüstemann*.

FRIENDS MEETING HOUSE, Lawn Terrace. Next door to the Congregational church, also by *Trevor Dannatt*, 1973–4, much less reticent. An arresting termination to the road; a compact

1. *The Inner Boroughs:* Southwark and Lambeth,
with Waterloo Station in the foreground
2. *The Inner Boroughs:* Bermondsey (Sk), warehouses
in Shad Thames, nineteenth century

3. *The Outer Boroughs:* Cheam (Su), Whitehall,
c. 1500 with later alterations
4. *The Outer Boroughs:* Kew (Ri), Kew Green,
north side, Georgian houses
5. *The River:* The Thames at Twickenham (Ri)
6. Kingston (Ki), Market Place, with Market House
(former Town Hall), by Charles Henman Sen., 1838-40

7. Lambeth (La), Lambeth Palace, chapel
undercroft, early thirteenth century
8. Southwark (Sk), Southwark Cathedral, retrochoir,
first half of the thirteenth century
9. Southwark (Sk), Southwark Cathedral, choir,
north side, first half of the thirteenth century

10. Southwark (Sk), Winchester House, Clink Street, rose
window of the great hall, probably early fourteenth century
11. Putney (Ww), St Mary, Bishop West's chantry
chapel, early sixteenth century
12. Southwark (Sk), Southwark Cathedral,
monument to John Gower †1408
13. Woolwich (Gr), Eltham Palace, Edward IV's great hall, 1475-9

14. Richmond (Ri), Richmond Palace, Henry VII's
privy lodgings (demolished), c.1500
15. Hampton Court (Ri), Henry VIII's great hall, 1532-4
16. Hampton Court (Ri), Henry VIII's privy lodgings and gardens
(demolished) in the sixteenth century (drawing by Anthony Wyngaerde)
17. Hampton Court (Ri), terracotta medallion
by Giovanni da Maiano, 1521
18. Hampton Court (Ri), Wolsey Closet, early
sixteenth century and after 1537, ceiling

19. Cheam (Su), Lumley Chapel, monument
to Lady Jane Lumley †1577, designed 1590
20. Southwark (Sk), Southwark Cathedral, Austin (Clerke)
monument, by Nicholas Stone, 1633

21. Southwark (Sk), Southwark Cathedral, monument
to Bishop Lancelot Andrewes †1626
22. Greenwich (Gr), Charlton House, *c.*1607-12,
fireplace in the south-east bedroom
23. Greenwich (Gr), Charlton House, *c.*1607-12, frontispiece

24. Kew (Ri), Kew Palace (Dutch House), Royal Botanic Gardens, 1631
25. Greenwich (Gr), Queen's House, by Inigo Jones, 1616-37,
enlarged by John Webb, 1662
26. Battersea (Ww), St Mary, monument
to Oliver St John †1630, by Nicholas Stone

27. Ham (Ri), Ham House, staircase, c.1637-8
28. Greenwich (Gr), Queen's House, by
Inigo Jones, 1616-37, Tulip Staircase

29. Lambeth (La), Lambeth Palace, great hall (now library), *c*.1660-3
30. Greenwich (Gr), Royal Naval Hospital,
King Charles Block, by John Webb, begun 1664
31. Southwark (Sk), George Inn, Borough High Street, after 1676
32. Woolwich (Gr), Eltham Lodge, by Hugh May, 1664

33. Hampton Court (Ri), east front, by Sir Christopher Wren, 1689-94
34. Hampton Court (Ri), Fountain Court, by
Sir Christopher Wren, 1689-94
35. Bromley (Br), Bromley College, by Richard Ryder, 1670-2
36. Greenwich (Gr), Morden College, Blackheath, founded 1695

37. Woolwich (Gr), Royal Arsenal, Board Room
and Saloon, probably by Sir John Vanbrugh, *c.* 1717
38. Greenwich (Gr), Vanbrugh Castle, Maze Hill,
by Sir John Vanbrugh, 1718-26
39. Greenwich (Gr), Royal Naval Hospital, by John Webb, 1664,
and Sir Christopher Wren, 1694 onwards, and the Queen's House
by Inigo Jones, 1616-37; from the river
40. Greenwich (Gr), Royal Naval Hospital, King William Building,
east front, probably by Nicholas Hawksmoor, *c.* 1701-8

37 | 39
38 | 40

41. Hampton Court (Ri), aerial view of the palace with Bushy Park and Home Park, laid out by George London and Henry Wise from 1689
42. Hampton Court (Ri), gates designed by Jean Tijou, wrought by Huntingdon Shaw
43. Greenwich (Gr), Royal Naval Hospital, Painted Hall, by Sir James Thornhill, 1708-12
44. Hampton Court (Ri), ceiling of King's State Bedchamber (Endymion asleep in the arms of Morpheus), by Antonio Verrio, 1701

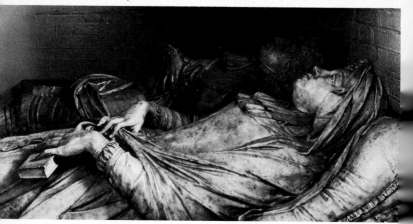

45 and 46. Clapham (La), St Paul, details from
the monument to the family of Sir Richard Atkins, by
William Stanton, before 1689 and 1691
47. Greenwich (Gr), St Alfege, east end,
by Nicholas Hawksmoor, 1711-14
48. Deptford (Le), St Paul, by Thomas Archer,
designed 1713, consecrated 1730

49. Petersham (Ri), St Peter, eighteenth-century fittings
50. Twickenham (Ri), St Mary, by John James, 1714-15,
west tower medieval
51. Battersea (Ww), St Mary, by Joseph Dixon, 1775-6

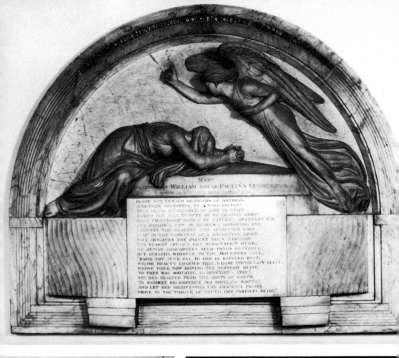

52. Lewisham (Le), St Mary, monument to Mary Lushington,
by John Flaxman, 1797
53. Bermondsey (Sk), St Mary Rotherhithe,
monument to Joseph Wade †1743
54. Greenwich (Gr), Royal Naval Hospital Chapel, pulpit, designed
by William Newton, executed by Lawrence and Arrow, *c.* 1779-80
55. Southwark (Sk), Guy's Hospital Chapel, monument
to Thomas Guy †1724, by John Bacon, 1779

52
53 54 | 55

56. Roehampton House (Ww), by Thomas Archer, 1710-12
57. Richmond (Ri), Maids of Honour Row, Richmond Green, 1724
58. Greenwich (Gr), The Grange, Croom's Hill,
gazebo, probably by Robert Hooke, 1672
59. Deptford (Le), Albury Street, c. 1706-17, doorway to No. 27

60. Twickenham (Ri), Marble Hill House,
by Roger Morris, 1724-c. 1729
61. Petersham (Ri), Sudbrook Park, by
James Gibbs, 1726, cube room
62. Roehampton (Ww), Manresa House, 1760-c. 1768,
entrance hall, detail of ceiling, by Sir William Chambers

63. Twickenham (Ri), Strawberry Hill, Holbein Chamber,
by Richard Bentley, 1758
64. Twickenham (Ri), Strawberry Hill, exterior altered
by Horace Walpole from 1749, with additions by
Lady Frances Waldegrave, 1860-2
65. Kew (Ri), Royal Botanic Gardens, Pagoda,
by Sir William Chambers, 1761

66. Carshalton (Su), Carshalton House, Blue Parlour, *c.* 1750
67. Richmond (Ri), Asgill House, by Sir Robert Taylor, 1757-8
68. Richmond (Ri), Richmond Bridge,
by Kenton Couse and James Paine, 1774-7
69. Woolwich (Gr), Old Royal Military Academy,
Academy Road, by James Wyatt, 1805

| 66 | 68 |
| 67 | 69 |

70. Lewisham (Le), The Paragon, Blackheath,
by Michael Searles, 1794-1807
71. Lambeth (La), Nos. 154-160 Kennington Road, c. 1775
72. Keston (Bm), Holwood, by Decimus Burton, 1823-6
73. Bromley (Bm), Sundridge Park, by Humphry
Repton and John Nash, c. 1796-9

70 | 72
71 | 73

74. Camberwell (Sk), Dulwich Picture Gallery (mausoleum to Noel Desenfans), by Sir John Soane, 1811-14
75. Lambeth (La), West Norwood Greek Orthodox Cemetery, monuments of the later nineteenth century
76. Camberwell (Sk), St George, by Francis Bedford, 1822-4

77. Streatham (La), Christ Church, by J. Wild, 1840-2
78. Kew (Ri), Royal Botanic Gardens, Palm House,
by Decimus Burton and Richard Turner, 1844-8
79. Southwark (Sk), Trinity Church Square, 1824-32
80. Penge (Bm), Free Watermen and Lightermen's
Almshouses, by George Porter, 1840-1

81. Southwark (Sk), St George's R.C. Cathedral, chantry chapel to Edward Petre, by A. W. N. Pugin, 1848-9
82. Croydon (Cr), St Michael, by J. L. Pearson, designed 1876, built 1880-3

81 | 82

83. Southwark (Sk), Kirkaldy's Testing Works, No. 99
Southwark Street, by T. R. Smith, 1877
84. Southwark (Sk), Central Buildings (Hop Exchange),
Southwark Street, by R. H. Moore, 1866
85. Lambeth (La), Henry Compton School, Kingswood Road,
by T. J. Bailey for the London School Board, 1898
86. Camberwell (Sk), Dulwich College, New Buildings,
by Charles Barry Jun., 1866-70

83 | 85
84 | 86

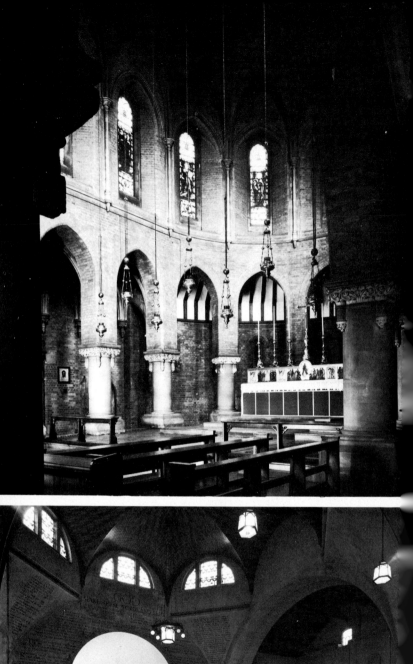

87. Battersea (Ww), Ascension, Lavender Hill, east
end, by James Brooks, begun 1876
88. Lambeth (La), Christ Church, Brixton, by
Beresford Pite, 1899-1902
89. Bexleyheath (Bx), Christ Church, by William Knight, 1872-7
90. Lambeth (La), All Saints, Brixton, by
G. Fellowes Prynne, 1887-91

<table>
<tr><td>87</td><td>89</td></tr>
<tr><td>88</td><td>90</td></tr>
</table>

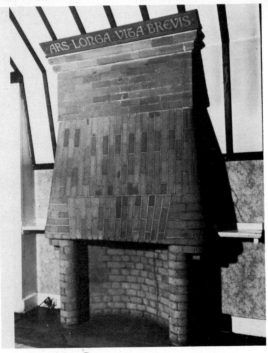

91. Bexleyheath (Bx), Red House, by Philip Webb, 1859-60
92. Bexleyheath (Bx), Red House, by Philip Webb, 1859-60,
chimneypiece in the drawing room
93. Kingston (Ki), Coombe Cottage, Beverley Lane,
stables, by George Devey, 1863
94. Chislehurst (Bm), Copley Dene, The Wilderness,
by Ernest Newton, designed 1904

95. Battersea (Ww), Shaftesbury Park Estate,
by Robert Austin, 1872-7
96. Norbury (Cr), Norton Gardens, Norbury Estate,
by the L.C.C., *c.* 1913
97. Lewisham (Le), Horniman Museum, Forest Hill,
by Harrison Townsend, 1897-1901

98. Woolwich (Gr), Woolwich Town Hall, by A. B. Thomas, 1903-6
99. Erith (Bx), Oil Works, by Christiani & Nielsen and
S. Rowland Pierce, 1913-17, interior of silos
100. Battersea (Ww), Battersea Power Station, engineers
S. L. Pearce and H. N. Allot, architects J. Theo Halliday
and Sir Giles Gilbert Scott, 1929-35

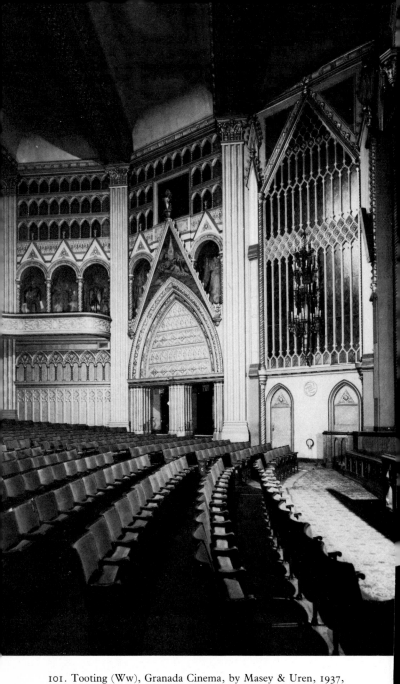

101. Tooting (Ww), Granada Cinema, by Masey & Uren, 1937,
interior by Theodore Komisarjevsky
102. Camberwell (Sk), Six Pillars, Crescent Wood Road,
Dulwich, by Harding & Tecton, 1933-5
103. Lambeth (La), Royal Festival Hall, South Bank, by (Sir) Robert
Matthew and (Sir) Leslie Martin, designed from 1948, opened 1951

104. Ham (Ri), Langham House Close, Ham Common,
by Stirling & Gowan, 1958
105. Greenwich (Gr), Corner Green, Blackheath Park,
by Eric Lyons, 1959
106. Roehampton (Ww), aerial view of the Alton Estate, by the
L.C.C. Architect's Department, Alton East (foreground), 1952-5,
and Alton West (in the distance), mostly 1954-8

107. Mitcham (Me), Watermeads, Rawnsley Avenue, by
the London Borough of Merton's Architect's Department
(R. Hodge and A. Bews), 1974-7
108. Twickenham (Ri), St Margaret (R.C.),
by Williams & Winkley, 1968
109. Lambeth (La), National Theatre, South Bank, by
Sir Denys Lasdun & Partners, completed 1976, foyer
110. Woolwich (Gr), Health Centre, Lakeside, Thamesmead,
by Derek Stow & Partners, 1970-2

111. Bermondsey (Sk), Setchell Estate, by Neylan & Ungless, 1972-8

111

polygonal building of shuttered concrete, partly on stilts, because of the change in levels. Square meeting room lit by a square central lantern; surrounding halls with roof lights.

St Andrew United Reformed Church (formerly Presbyterian), Brockley Road. 1882 by *J. McKissack & W. G. Rowan* of Glasgow (CW). E.E. sw tower with spire, a good landmark. w window with three very tall pairs of lights.

United Reformed Church, Lewisham High Street. Ragstone with tall spire. 1867 by *J. Tarring*; interior altered 1957.

(Wesleyan Chapel, Brockley Road and Harefield Road. 1876 by *Banister Fletcher*. CW)

Brockley Cemetery, Brockley Road. 1858. Chapel by *Morphew & Green*.

(Grove Park Cemetery, Marvells Lane. 1935 by *H. Morley Lawson*, very carefully landscaped in terraces incorporating viewpoints and an ornamental pool; typical of the thirties and unique in London. HM)

(Hither Green Cemetery, Verdant Lane. 1873. Nice pair of Dec ragstone chapels by *Francis Thorne*. HM)

PUBLIC BUILDINGS

Lewisham Town Hall, Catford. Undistinguished piecemeal extensions and replacements of the *Board of Works* buildings.* Facing Catford Broadway the public halls of 1931–2 by *Bradshaw, Gass & Hope*, with incongruous Gothic embellishments. Office extensions of 1958–9 and 1961–3. Facing Rushey Green the glossier Civic Suite of 1971.

The Municipal Buildings in Ladywell Road are better, a late Victorian civic cluster consisting of the old swimming baths (*Wieson, Son & Aldwinkle*, 1884) with three Gothic arches and a jolly water tower; coroner's court (*J. Carline*, Surveyor to Lewisham Board of Works, 1894), Perp; and police station, 1899, Queen Anne. Round the corner in the High Street the old fire station (*L.C.C.*, 1899), now offices, still recognizable by its practice tower.

Fire Station (former; now municipal offices), Perry Vale, Forest Hill. By the *L.C.C. Fire Brigade's Department*, 1901–2. An especially picturesque example of its type. Fanciful octagonal tower.

Telephone Exchange, Gilmore Road, w of Lee High Road. Typical *Leonard Stokes* plain early C20 Georgian. Later top storey.

Library, Manor House, Lee. *See* Perambulation 3.

Library, Lewisham High Street. 1900. Symmetrical front with terracotta trim.

Library, Forest Hill. Jacobean of *c.* 1900.

Horniman Museum, London Road, Forest Hill. Begun 97 1897, opened 1901, the gift to the L.C.C. of F. J. Horniman, a

* The original buildings, the last of which were demolished in 1982, were Gothic, of 1874–5 by *G. Elkington*, with additions of 1899–1901.

tea merchant († 1906). The museum contains his collections, which he originally opened to the public in the 1880s, in a private house. They reflect an admirably wide range of interests, with especial emphasis on anthropology and natural history. The new building by *Harrison Townsend* is no doubt one of the boldest public buildings of its date in Britain. Townsend had made his name with the Bishopsgate Institute and the Whitechapel Art Gallery; hence the choice. He added to a façade with the same emphasis on horizontal bands, angle buttressing, and a strong dominating curve as at Whitechapel a tall, massive clock tower of original and successful outline: rounded corners and round pinnacles, and with four segments of a circular cornice emerging as canopies over the clock face. If influences were at work in the architect's mind, they could perhaps have come from H. H. Richardson's work at Boston, U.S.A. The main decorative motif of the façade is a mosaic designed by *Anning Bell*: the subject is Humanity in the House of Circumstance. The curved gable of the façade expresses the glazed barrel-vaults of the museum behind. Two-storey annexe of 1911 with lecture hall (the museum from the beginning encouraged educational visits). At the back an extension of the 1930s, now used as a special exhibition hall. In the gardens a *Coade* stone group with pelican and figures of 1797 made for the pediment of the Pelican Life Insurance Company in Lombard Street. The designer was *Lady Diana Beauclerk*.

SWIMMING BATHS, Lewisham High Street. 1963–6 by the *Borough Architect's Department*.

BLACKHEATH HIGH SCHOOL, Wemyss Road, s of South Row. A girls' school (G.P.D.S.T.) opened in 1880. The buildings by *Robson*, 1879, a surprising design for this date; neo-Georgian, symmetrical, with large central portal and broken pediment. Extensions: 1882; science block 1889 by *J. Osborne Smith*; and 1907.

ST DUNSTAN'S COLLEGE, Stanstead Road, Catford. A public day school whose origins go back to a grammar school attached to St Dunstan in the East. Refounded in 1883. The new buildings in Catford are of 1888 by *E. N. Clifton*, a large, serious terracotta-trimmed Gothic front in the style of Waterhouse. Central gable flanked by turrets, prominent chimneys. The top floor was originally designed for boarders. Large hall behind (window by *Lavers, Westlake & Co.* with St Dunstan and craftsmen). On the r. the dining hall with a dramatic hyperbolic-paraboloid roof, 1961 by *Verner Rees, Laurence & Mitchell*, quite daring for its time. Other additions behind (swimming bath 1955 by *W. Fraser Granger*, library and science laboratories 1957, pavilion 1959 by *Verner Rees, Laurence & Mitchell*, music block and science laboratories 1972 by *Austin Vernon & Partners*).

LEWISHAM SCHOOL AND CROFTON LEISURE CENTRE, off Ewhurst Road, E of Stondon Park. 1971 by *Alastair Tait* of the *G.L.C. Architect's Department*, the first I.L.E.A. comprehensive purpose-built for shared community use, but unexciting architecturally. Sports buildings in mottled red brick; plain MACE classroom block with overhanging upper floors.

CATFORD SCHOOL, s of Bellingham Road. An early example of post-war secondary school buildings: 1955–6 by *G. Horsfall* and *T. Bliss* of the *L.C.C.* One big curtain-walled four-storey slab of classrooms, relieved by two recessed parts with coloured spandrel panels; low communal buildings at right angles.

SYDENHAM SCHOOL, Dartmouth Road. Large additions of 1957 by *Basil Spence & Partners*, to convert the school to a comprehensive. Six-storey classroom wing, forbidding in scale but fussy in detail, extending down the slope to the road, supported on tapering piers.

KELVIN GROVE SCHOOL, Kirkdale, Sydenham. Symmetrical arcaded Italianate front with polychrome decoration. 1859 by *Henry Dawson* for the British and Foreign Schools Society. Additions by the London School Board in 1876, 1887, and after 1902.

PRIMARY SCHOOLS. Two notable ones in Forest Hill: FAIRLAWN by *Peter Moro*, 1958, high up, overlooking Honor Oak Road. Curtain-walled classrooms with glazed hall at right angles; light, airy, and undated. HORNIMAN, Horniman Drive, w of Honor Oak Road, by *Michael Manser Associates*, 1972. Tucked into the slope of the hill, with classrooms clustered around the hall, crisply clad in ribbed plastic sheeting.

ST JOHN'S HOSPITAL, Morden Hill, E of Lewisham Road. The core is Brandon House, a nice stucco-trimmed house of 1840 with two canted bay-windows to the w. NURSES' HOME, Lewisham Hill, by *Bertram Carter*, 1938, with additions of 1948–9. Progressive for its time. Semicircular glass staircase shafts.

RIVERS CENTRE, Fordmill Road. Stylish job by the *G.L.C. General Works Department (Derek Wells)*, with echoes of James Stirling. 1977. Exterior of brown brick, red metal trim, canted angles and splayed corners. The buildings face inwards to an enclosed courtyard. The main building is simply a shed for vehicles, with glazed staff quarters at one end and stores at the other, but the whole is treated with refreshing wit and ingenuity.

LEWISHAM STATION. Single-storey round-arched booking office of 1857, neatly in the angle of two lines.

BLACKHEATH STATION. One-storey façade to the street. s bay 1849 for the North Kent Railway by *George Smith* (NR); stucco archway. The remainder *c.* 1875–8, plainer Italianate.

PERAMBULATIONS

1. Blackheath

Blackheath was not an early settlement, but one which grew up on the fringe of older parishes. The boundary is preserved by the present one between the boroughs of Greenwich and Lewisham. But as the s and w borders of the heath now form convincing entities, this account includes a few buildings just over the Greenwich border (the e parts of Blackheath village and The Paragon). For Blackheath further e, and the n and e edges of the heath, *see* Greenwich (Gr), especially Perambulations 1, 3, and 4.

The houses on the w and s fringes of the heath date from the late c 17 onwards. They are mostly haphazard groups of considerable charm, but terminate in one fine formal composition of 1794 at the e end, The Paragon by *Michael Searles*.

The tour starts at the w end, where development began in the late c 17 on the Earl of Dartmouth's estate. In DARTMOUTH HILL, climbing steeply SE off Blackheath Hill, an irregular late c 18 terrace (Nos. 98–110 BLACKHEATH HILL) and No. 2 (MONTAGUE HOUSE), mid c 18, brick, three storeys, with later Greek Doric porch. Further on Nos. 20–22, a long later c 18 house with extensions at either end; canted upper bay-windows. SHERWOOD and LYDIA HOUSE in DARTMOUTH GROVE are a grander pair, facing the heath, built in 1776. The design can plausibly be attributed to *Thomas Gayfere Sen.*, the master mason of Westminster Abbey, as the leases were to a Thomas Gayfere of Abingdon Street and to John Groves of Millbank, bricklayer.* Stuccoed, with shallow canted bays on the ground floor. Central pediment with oval window (a Diocletian window at the back), and half-pediments over the lower wings, a design of Palladian origin (cf. Sir Robert Taylor's Asgill House, Richmond, Ri). This must be one of the earliest adaptations of such a design for a semi-detached pair. The type became very popular around Blackheath and was much used by Michael Searles (cf. below). (Good cantilevered stone staircases inside.)

Now to the most rewarding road in this part of the heath, DARTMOUTH ROW, which runs s. Building began here in the 1690s, but the history of individual houses is obscure. On the w side Nos. 20–22, an irregular group, perhaps of late c 17 origin, but altered and stuccoed. Nos. 22a and 24–26 are earlier c 20 intruders, by *Leonard Hunt*, 1911, inappropriately Arts and Crafts rather than neo-Georgian. No. 28 is of 1794, L-plan, with a timber-framed weatherboarded part on the garden side (a late example of such materials, unless it is older). Then Nos. 30 and 30a (divided in 1924), a carefully designed house existing by 1753 (NR), five bays, the pedimented centre three, and the corners emphasized by brick quoins. Central door with heavy keystones, the upper window with stone surround, still quite Baroque in feeling. In No. 30 an original staircase with turned balusters and plain shaped tread ends. In No. 30a back room with a bow-window and a good Rococo plaster ceiling. The next houses may be late c 17 in origin: No. 32, four bays with later stucco; No. 34, five

---

* Information from Mr Neil Rhind.

bays, brick; Nos. 36–36a, set back, five bays with the centre three projecting, Tuscan porch. On the E side SPENCER and PERCEVAL HOUSES, originally a single house of 1689 divided c. 1890. Uncommonly good. Two storeys, nine bays, the centre five projecting. C19 extension of two further bays. Stone quoins and bracketed wooden eaves cornice, the centre formerly with stone roof balustrade. Doorway, with carved frieze, off centre. All the windows have lively keystone faces as in Queen Anne's Gate, Westminster. (In No. 21 a good staircase and two ground-floor rooms with plasterwork.) No. 25 (Dartmouth House, now owned by Southwark Diocese) is of c. 1750, three storeys, large and plain, with canted bays, and a double stair to a front door over a tall basement.

Across the heath to the encroachments on the S fringe (the area between Dartmouth Row, Shooters Hill Road, and Tranquil Vale). (THE KNOLL (now two dwellings), Eliot Hill, is of 1798 with C19 alterations (NR). Two projecting wings with pedimented gables, the wing on the l. with a projecting single-storey balustraded billiard hall added in the 1850s. Good original, rather Soanian hall. Ionic columns with a shallow arch over the entablature. The garden elevation with two full-height bay-windows to the wings, and two tented balconies in the centre.)

In the C18 there were garden buildings in this area belonging to MONTAGUE HOUSE (demolished 1815) which stood close to Ranger's House on the N side of the heath (see Greenwich (Gr), Perambulation 1). One eccentric survival of this era remains: THE PAGODA, Pagoda Gardens, a three-storey rectangular house crowned by a huge lead-clad pagoda roof with upswept corners and hooked finials of forbidding size. The top floor has a single large oval window on the main front, a circular one on the shorter side. Later additions; an early C19 wing with bow and trellised veranda, and later C19 parts behind. The date of this unusually robust Chinese extravaganza is uncertain. The earliest known view is of 1815, but a house on the site was rated in 1764 (but not in 1758), so it could have been built as early as c. 1760, when the fourth Earl of Cardigan lived in Montague House (i.e. around the same time as Chambers's quite different Chinese work at Kew, Ri). It seems more likely however that the oriental upper parts are an addition of the 1780s, the time of the Duke of Buccleuch, with whom the thistle motif in the gable could be associated.[*]

Around the Pagoda a mixed bag of later developments have filled the former gardens. To the S, a discreet L.C.C. estate of 1954–7, two- and five-storey blocks in a well wooded setting. To the N, ABERDEEN TERRACE, grand mid-Victorian brick and stucco pairs built after 1856–9. Earlier houses in ELIOT VALE (Nos. 8 and 9 built in 1805); also ELIOT VALE COTTAGE (1804), now Nos. 3–5 The Meadway. Nos. 2–3 THE

---

[*] See N. Rhind in *Greenwich Antiquarian Society Transactions*, VIII, 6 (1978), p. 246.

CLOSE (off Eliot Vale), 1881 by *W. J. Green*, behind a pretty lodge with coved bow, have blatant black and white half-timbering; Nos. 5–6 are in a quieter domestic Tudor (dated at the back 1877: NR). Nearer the heath in NORTH SEVERAL (off The Orchard), seven houses by *Royston Summers*, 1969, three storeys, all glass walls, with a strong vertical rhythm of narrowly set mullions, a prominent sight from the heath. Then to the E along ELIOT PLACE, also facing the heath, an attractive group built between 1792 and 1805 by a speculative builder, *Alexander Doull*.* The first houses (1792) are Nos. 4–5 and 7–8 (the original centrepiece, No. 9, has been replaced). Four-bay pairs, formerly with recessed side entrances, now with later wings. In the gaps houses of different design: No. 1 (HEATHFIELD HOUSE), 1795, with balustraded bow-windows flanking a central porch; Nos. 2–3, a pair of 1805; Nos. 4–5, 1793; No. 6, 1796–7, five bays with a large pediment, from 1802 the house of Stephen Groombridge, astronomer, who added a room for an observatory to the W. More early C19 houses from No. 11, followed by Nos. 1–4 GROTE'S PLACE. Grote's Place, Grote's Buildings, and Lloyds Place together make a delightful informal crescent facing the heath. The best houses are GROTE'S BUILDINGS, 1771–4 (NR), nearly symmetrical, but irregular in detail. Stock brick with red brick window heads. LLOYDS PLACE has LINDSEY HOUSE and No. 3, each of three bays, and EASTNOR HOUSE, probably of the 1750s (NR), a long front later covered in C19 stucco. To the N is an isolated cluster on the site of old gravel pits; off Talbot Place GOLFHOUSE and MILL HOUSE are a stuccoed pair of 1836, on the site of one of the Blackheath windmills.

TRANQUIL VALE leads down to BLACKHEATH VILLAGE and the station (q.v.), past ALL SAINTS CHURCH HALL, 1927–8 by *C. C. Winmill*, eclectic domestic revival with patterns of tiles, and the CROWN, old but much altered. On the SW side Nos. 45–47, a modest pair, partly weatherboarded, originally part of COLLINS SQUARE to the W, where there is a better preserved group of late C18 weatherboarded cottages (restored 1963 by *N. Macfadyen*). Further S Tranquil Vale becomes a busy shopping street, with some C18 to earlier C19 terraces behind later fronts, e.g. Nos. 23–25, late C18, and No. 23, with an especially pretty Victorian cast-iron shopfront. Nos. 25–27, VALE HOUSE, is a handsome six-bay house of 1798, with Greek Doric porch. Behind Nos. 3–9, close to the station, the remains of the BLACKHEATH LITERARY INSTITUTE of 1845 by *G. Smith*, damaged in the Second World War, sympathetically reconstructed by *Carden, Godfrey & MacFadyen* in the 1970s.

A little to the S, in INDEPENDENTS ROAD, the most obtrusive Victorian contribution to the Village, WINCHESTER HOUSE,

---

* See A. R. Martin, *No. 6 Eliot Place* (Greenwich and Lewisham Antiqu. Soc.), 1974.

1857 by *W. G. & E. Habershon*. Built as a school and home for sons and orphans of missionaries. Red brick, tall, rather coarse Gothic, with a high roof, its appearance much improved by conversion for offices in 1980. No other buildings in the Village worth a special look apart from the stuccoed former Alexandra Hall of 1863 (now LLOYDS BANK), and a few other Victorian institutions, most notably the Conservatoire further s (*see* Greenwich (Gr), Public Buildings). On the E side of Tranquil Vale a curved late Georgian terrace with shops on the ground floor continues round the corner to MONTPELIER VALE, some rebuilt in the C19 and again after war damage (Nos. 16–18, although plausibly Regency, are an entirely new design). In TRANQUIL PASSAGE to the W, the former village school, a humble building of 1851 (now library).

MONTPELIER ROW runs NE beside the heath. Terraces of the late C18 to earlier C19*: Nos. 1–4 1806–7; No. 5 by 1800; Nos. 6–14 probably 1797; Nos. 15–16, stone-fronted, 1798. No. 17 is by *U. & G. Bowyer*, 1959. Nos. 18–19 are of 1836, with shaped pediment with quadrant windows; No. 20, a similar design but with a lunette, is attributed to *Searles*, 1803–4.‡ Then No. 21, 1885 by *Benjamin Tabberer*, and Nos. 22–23, a large semi-detached pair of three storeys built by 1798. The recessed porches were heightened in the 1860s. Round the corner past the PRINCESS OF WALES (later C19, stuccoed) SOUTH ROW begins, with COLONNADE HOUSE, 'newly erected' in 1804, a fine composition of seven bays, the taller middle three bays projecting, with a Tuscan colonnade all along the front and extending beyond the house to l. and r. The architect was probably *Searles*, who was responsible for the other houses in South Row Nos. 3–6 and Bryan House (all destroyed in 1941). On their site Span flats by *Eric Lyons* of 1959–61 (cf. Blackheath Park, Greenwich (Gr), Perambulation 4). Three storeys, the front to the heath an uncompromising, well-proportioned statement of international modern principles, the back, reached through an open ground-floor lobby, with homelier Span weatherboarding.§

PARAGON HOUSE further E is of 1794 by *Searles*, three storeys with arcaded ground floor, a full-height bow on the garden side. The delightful doorway in Pond Road, installed during the post-war repairs, comes from *Adam*'s Adelphi. The restoration was by *Charles Bernard Brown*, who also painstakingly restored the much altered and damaged PARAGON to its former splendour and converted it to flats (completed 1950–8). The Paragon, marking the NE end of the grounds of Blackheath Park, was built by *Searles* in 1794–1807, a few

70

---

* We owe the following dates to Mr Neil Rhind (based on leases and rate records).

‡ See R.I.B.A. Drawings 80, built (without the s wing) probably after 1800.

§ Built only after much opposition and, finally, ministerial intervention. The L.C.C. Historic Buildings Division and the Blackheath Society supported a proposal to rebuild in pastiche.

years after his smaller Paragon in Old Kent Road. It is a crescent of unusual rhythm, six pairs and a central house, three storeys over basement, and with mansard roofs, connected by Tuscan colonnades, a favourite Searles motif. Each house is of two plus two slightly concave bays, with front door and two further windows within the colonnade on each side. The colonnades are (or were) of *Coade* stone, as is the sparing decoration. The low lodges at either end are post-war creations but entirely convincing.

To the S around FULTHORPE ROAD more post-war building, discreetly genteel council flats and houses (for Greenwich) by *Richardson & Houfe*, completed 1954 (the style required by local residents). The taller blocks of flats deliberately create the illusion of Georgian terraces; the lower houses are in the pleasant Regency cottage tradition established by Adshead & Ramsay at Kennington in the early C20. No wonder Span seemed so radical.

(In WEMYSS ROAD, WEMYSS COTTAGE, *c.* 1830 for John Sheepshanks, the art collector.)

2. Lewisham High Street and to its N and W

The old village was a long ribbon of development along the High Street, running N–S, parallel to the river Ravensbourne. Nothing of great merit at the N end of the High Street; the fussy CLOCK TOWER, a Jubilee erection of 1897, the modernistic former R.A.C.S. store of 1933 (cf. Woolwich (Gr), Perambulation 1), and the colossal brick ODEON (former Gaumont, by *W. C. Trent*)* survived the extensive war damage and now compete for attention with a mammoth covered shopping centre (1972–7 by *B.E.P. Partnership* for Grosvenor Estates). This has an attractive internal mall with bright tiled walls. Red brick entrances, multi-storey car park, more distinguished than the inevitable office tower. Linking pedestrian bridge (*Lewisham Architect's Department*, 1980–1, *J. M. Szarowcz*), a smoked glass tube supported within a tubular girder box.‡ Further S, little except for No. 270, BROOKLANDS HOUSE, 1782, five bays, much altered, with shops on the ground floor. The old village centre was at the S end at the junction with Ladywell Road. Almost the only reminders are the church and churchyard, with the open space of the recreation ground by the river further W, and the OLD VICARAGE at the corner, an excellent house of its date (1692–3), with two storeys of five bays, modillion frieze, and with windows which still have mullions and transoms of timber, a rural rather than an urban building. N extension 1879–81 by *Edwin & N. Hilton Nash*, W extension 1894–5, built of old bricks from the demolished Lewisham House opposite. (Inside, original main and service

---

* Future uncertain.
‡ I owe these details to A. Quiney.

staircases; good panelling.)* Converted to offices, 1981. s again, three prominent eighteen-storey tower blocks of the early 1960s (*Lewisham Architect's Department*), taking advantage of the small green patch of LEWISHAM PARK, where No. 78 is the sole mid C 19 stuccoed survival. THACKERAY ALMSHOUSES, Rushey Green, are pretty *Rundbogenstil* of 1840, stock brick with red brick trimmings (cf. the similar almshouses in Sheen Road, Richmond, Ri).

NW of the High Street, Victorian suburban growth links Lewisham with Upper Deptford. In LOAMPIT HILL, Nos. 60–68, mid Victorian villas with remarkably over-ornate ornamentation, swags, masks, etc. SOMERSET GARDENS off to the r. is a secluded mid C 19 close of modest houses and terraces, with nice ironwork.

NE towards Blackheath, extensive council estates. The large ORCHARD ESTATE W of Lewisham Road (partly in Greenwich) is of 1963–6, the standard L.C.C. mixture of the time, but quite generously spaced; one group of point blocks, and low stepped terraces around grassy squares. Compare, E of Lewisham Road, HEATHSIDE, the earlier L.C.C. type of walk-up flats, *c.* 1948 by *E. Armstrong*. The curved range along SPARTA STREET has a little more character than average, but the promise is not sustained by the regimented blocks behind and the taller concrete-clad additions of the 1960s to the s.

W of the High Street, off MOLESWORTH STREET by the river, a plain four-storey WATERMILL of *c.* 1830 with projecting weatherboarded hoist; an attractive survival. Tall backdrop of offices with curved staircase towers added in 1980–1 by *F. Gibberd & Partners.* s of Ladywell Road, w of the river, LADYWELL LODGE, the site of the huge St Olave's Union Workhouse of 1898–1900 by *Newman & Newman*; only the central administrative block remains, fussy, with turrets. To its r. a low brick OLD PEOPLE'S HOME of the 1960s by the G.L.C.; behind, pleasant ungimmicky housing by *Lewisham Architect's Department*, 1980, short terraces of pale brick. In their midst the WATER TOWER of the workhouse, a structure of some character, with its hefty battered base and chalet-like top with crested hipped roof.

3. Lee

A scattered settlement until the C 19. The old hamlet was at Lee Green, where little of interest remains; the church lay away up the hill to the NW (St Margaret, Lee Terrace, q.v.), the grander houses were along Lee High Road.

LEE HIGH ROAD now has only some almshouses. Of the original BOONE'S ALMSHOUSES of 1683, BOONE'S

---

* Demolished: No. 246, a more urban early C 18 house, and COLFES' ALMSHOUSES, 1664 by *Peter Mills* for the Leathersellers' Company, damaged in the Second World War. A classical one-storey group. Larger central chapel with hipped roof, rusticated quoins, oval panels l. and r. of the door.

CHAPEL is still extant, a delightful little brick rectangle with stone trimmings, two heavy round-headed windows on the front, equally heavy oval windows higher up on E, W, and S, and heavy pediments on the same sides; octagonal cupola in the centre of the roof (renewed) (cf. on a somewhat larger scale Trinity Hospital, Stepney, T H). The almshouses were rebuilt further down the road in 1875 by *E. B. l'Anson*, with a neat new Gothic chapel (now Pentecostal Church), red brick, apsed, lancet style. Behind the old chapel, the MERCHANT TAYLORS' ALMSHOUSES, 1826 by their surveyor, *William Jupp Jun*. Large, on three sides of an open quadrangle, stock brick, sparsely classical, with central feature emphasized by a pediment and cupola. The Boone mansion, Lee Place, lay near by, just to the S of the present Lee High Road, which was straightened when the house was demolished in 1825.

In OLD ROAD, curving off to the S, the only two remaining large pre-C19 houses, close together: the Manor House and Pentland House. The MANOR HOUSE (Lee Public Library), probably built for Thomas Lucas in 1771–2, by *Richard Jupp*, is an elegant five-by-three-bay structure of brick on a rusticated stone basement, and with a stone entablature. Projecting taller three-bay centre. Four-column one-storey porch, now glazed; a full-height bow in the centre of the garden side. Inside, the original staircase was removed *c.* 1932, but the large staircase hall still has a screen of columns to the l., and on the landing above a smaller screen carrying groin-vaults. Medallions with putti. Pretty plasterwork in other rooms, especially a ceiling of Adamish design in the ground-floor room with the bow-window. The grounds with a lake are now a public park; an ice house survives in a private garden. PENTLAND HOUSE (Goldsmiths' College Hall of Residence) is an irregular composition of different dates, now all stuccoed. The centre is the original house of *c.* 1685, five bays, projecting eaves, double-span roof. Additions of the C18–20 to l., r., and behind. (Inside, a staircase with late C17 carved newel-heads, said to come from Lee Place.)

In Manor Lane, LOCHABER HALL, a simple former church hall by *Ernest Newton*, 1910. HURST LODGE in Lee High Road to the N is a detached villa of 1819, now the centre of a factory, much altered.

Between the High Road and Lee Terrace there were only scattered large houses until the rapid growth of stuccoed suburban terraces and villas in the second quarter of the C19. The tithe map of 1839 shows the development just beginning, with the earliest stretches at the E end of LEE TERRACE (Nos. 22–32, 47–61) and individual villas further W (Nos. 3–5). Nos. 47–61, of 1834–5, are of the Searles type (cf. Blackheath, Perambulation 1), with shared pediments, half-lunettes in the attics, and doorways in the linking wings. Later versions are a little more spacious and ornate, see e.g. DACRE PARK to the S, where they have a variety of porches. Another type has windows carried up between prominently bracketed eaves (Nos. 22–32

Lee Terrace and Nos. 1–8 and 9–16 CHURCH TERRACE). By the 1860s development was nearly complete (see first Ordnance Survey map). (Later additions are Nos. 7–9, of 1869 by *William Webster*, and Nos. 40–42, 1868, partly by *G. L. Taylor* and partly by *E. I'Anson*. NR) Further W in BELMONT HILL, SACRED HEART CONVENT, a large, rambling, asymmetrical composition with a belvedere tower, possibly an old house much disguised (previous names: Lee Grove; The Cedars; there was a house on the site before 1640). The present exterior is probably the result of alterations for John Penn, the engineer († 1878), after 1855. To its W the remains of a stable block, now a garage. Also in Belmont Hill No. 24, THE PRIORY, Gothic, and some plainer villas. In THE GLEBE, N of Lee Terrace, laid out *c*. 1849, a few survivals of more picturesque Italianate or Gothic villas. Finally, LEE PARK, a long straight route back from the E end of Lee Terrace to the High Road, with on the W side a shallow crescent (Nos. 119–148), 1842–52, tall pairs of houses, the centre ones with pediments and half-lunettes, the outer ones with the odd feature of top windows jammed up under the eaves.

4. Catford

The junction of Rushey Green, Catford Road, and Bromley Road is the modern administrative centre of the borough. But the main landmark is not the town hall (q.v.) but EROS HOUSE, offices over shops and car park, by *Owen Luder*, 1962, one of the earliest and best of the brutalist towers which mushroomed around the fringes of London in the 1960s (cf. Croydon and Sutton). Nine storeys, a powerful design with an intricate rhythm; pairs of windows beneath projecting concrete hoods, a Japanese touch, set in a pattern of different planes. Separate stair-tower boldly expressed in glass and concrete. Further S No. 167 RUSHEY GREEN, the BLACK HORSE, a jolly pub of 1897 with recessed arcaded balcony and corner turret, and No. 61 BROMLEY ROAD, formerly Sangley Farm, early C19 with Greek Doric porch. To the W, CATFORD BROADWAY, a mean creation of 1927 concealing ELMWOOD, a three-bay mid C18 house, much added to. The tough urbanity of Eros House is echoed by MILLFIELD TOWERS opposite, a lofty cluster of council flats, with drum staircases of yellow brick. At their foot, a SHOPPING CENTRE, a plain but pleasant combination of open and covered spaces. All by the *Owen Luder Partnership*, 1969–74. Lewisham's less monumental, friendlier public housing of the 1970s is illustrated by two schemes near by: to the W in VINEYARD CLOSE, off Catford Hill, low staggered terraces of 1972 (their pitched roofs are later additions); to the E in REDFERN ROAD, off Brownhill Road, three-storey terraces of twenty-nine flats, linked by glazed staircases. Their special feature is partial solar heating, one of its first large-scale applications.

Planned from 1973, built in 1978–81 by *Royston Summers Associates* for Lewisham.

N W of the Broadway the area around R A V E N S B O U R N E P A R K was laid out as a high-class estate from 1825, spaciously planned (cf. Blackheath Park, Greenwich (Gr), Perambulation 4). Little remains of this time apart from Nos. 60–62, built in 1825–30, a stuccoed pair with lower wings in arched recesses, and doorways with Ionic columns, and Nos. 3–7 and 11–15, built by 1835.*

5. S E *Lewisham*

The S fringe of the borough was completely rural until the C 20. The former hamlet of S O U T H E N D in B R O M L E Y R O A D is recalled by the former chapel (*see* St John) and the rural Victorian Gothic S C H O O L and S C H O O L H O U S E. To the W and E extensive L.C.C. cottage estates of the 1920s–30s, mostly nicely laid out, with quite pleasant houses. B E L L I N G H A M, begun in 1921 (2,674 houses), has a semi-formal plan, with six roads converging on B E L L I N G H A M G R E E N, but the buildings there are not sufficiently tightly knit to impress. Recent additions by *Shepheard & Epstein*. D O W N H A M (1924–38, over 7,000 houses) is more diffuse, with long winding roads.

P A S S F I E L D S, Daneswood Avenue, E of Bromley Road, is one of the most interesting groups of flats to be built immediately after the Second World War in London. By *Maxwell Fry & Jane Drew*. Curved five-storeyed range, a shorter projecting wing again 'breaking' at right angles and returning with the former direction. To the S W three three-storeyed blocks. The five-storeyed part is of concrete box-framed construction, partly rendered; the three-storeyed ranges are in weight-bearing brick. In style the difference from earlier work by Maxwell Fry is the greater diversity of small motifs, for example the balconies of alternating depth and the scattered loggias – a jerky, typical 1950 rhythm. At the N W corner it gets even more complex and less regular and achieves much interest. Extremely good minor details, such as light fittings and lamp standards.

(B R O M L E Y C O U R T H O T E L, Coniston Road, W of Bromley Hill. The origin of the house is a villa built in 1767, rebuilt and remodelled *c.* 1801–11 by Charles Long, later Baron Farnborough. Large and rambling, with many additions.)

B E C K E N H A M P L A C E. The only large mansion in ample grounds to remain in the area. The grounds, now a public park and golf course, are mostly in Lewisham; the house actually lies just over the boundary, in Bromley. The estate was bought by John Cator, the developer of Blackheath Park (*see* Greenwich (Gr), Perambulation 4), in 1773 from the trustees of the second Earl of Bolingbroke. The main house is a restrained

* Information from John Coulter, Lewisham Archives and Local History Department.

Palladian block, stone, seven by four bays, two storeys over a tall basement, with a curved feature on the garden side, the only ornament here an iron balcony and rusticated basement quoins. On the entrance side a projecting wing with giant four-column Ionic portico, of quite different character. The explanation is that this is an addition, built from materials brought from Wricklemarsh House at Blackheath Park, the Palladian mansion by *John James* of 1721 which Cator demolished in 1787. The additions have been made so crudely that it seems unlikely that the same patron could have commissioned both of them and the original villa. So was the house already in existence in 1773? The re-used parts must include not only the columns but the stonework of the projecting wing. The side walls have a heavy rusticated basement, attic windows with stone surrounds, and excellently detailed tripartite Venetian windows with pediments and engaged columns. They are visible on an old view of Wricklemarsh House. The wall within the portico has two empty niches. The entrance is at first-floor level (i.e. the rooms of the original villa are at *piano nobile* level), but because of the rise of the ground, the columns stand awkwardly without a plinth. A mean pediment is formed by the gable of the projecting wing. (An architect could hardly have been responsible.) In the pediment the Cator arms and palm fronds of *Coade* stone.* Inside, a groin-vaulted passage with pretty plaster ornament leads through the projecting wing to a bare central roof-lit hall, with balconies on four sides. Two small staircases behind doors in the far wall. To the N, plain late C18 brick STABLES, symmetrical, with clock turret. Two nice pairs of stone LODGES, one-storeyed, at the W corner of Foxgrove Road, and in BECKENHAM HILL ROAD, one of the latter heightened later by a Jacobean gable. RED HOUSE, Beckenham Hill Road, is good early C20 neo-Georgian.

6. *Sydenham, Forest Hill, and* SW *Lewisham*

The hilly region of Sydenham has a character quite different from the rest of Lewisham. A sizeable hamlet existed by the C16 along Sydenham Road. Uphill to the W were the 500 acres of Sydenham Common, of which WELLS PARK is now the only reminder. Springs were discovered there *c.* 1640 and Sydenham became a minor spa, but did not develop much until the common was enclosed in 1819. In the later C19, after the opening of the Crystal Palace at Upper Norwood, Upper Sydenham became a suburb of large wealthy mansions. Many directors and officials of the palace lived in the neighbourhood, including Paxton, Owen Jones, its secretary Sir George Grove, and Samuel Phillips, author of the catalogues.

In SYDENHAM ROAD there is little to remind one of the old hamlet apart from Nos. 32–34, a pair with old tiled, hipped

* The portico at Wricklemarsh was without a pediment.

mansard roofs, rendered fronts with Gibbs-surround front doors, but weatherboarded sides. Weatherboarded timber-framed cottages were once characteristic of the area. Several altered c 18 houses further E. (No. 122 is a well preserved plain house of c. 1800.) The next stage of Sydenham, of the early to mid c 19, can be enjoyed best in Jews Walk and Kirkdale. At the corner of the two, FARNBOROUGH HOUSE, a three-bay early c 19 villa.* In SYDENHAM PARK to the E more urban stuccoed terraces. Down JEWS WALK three further classical villas, all slightly different, and contrasting Tudor Gothic pairs opposite (Nos. 1–15), some plain stock brick, others with diapering. Similar houses continue in WESTWOOD HILL (Nos. 14–28) towards St Bartholomew (q.v.). On the s side of Westwood Hill, THE OLD CEDARS, large, with a Victorian front (but from the back visibly a house built c. 1780–90, with two full-height bow-windows, and with contemporary STABLES at the side). Few remain of the lavish later Victorian mansions in every style, standing in large wooded gardens, which used to cover the upper slopes.‡ The most interesting survival is SUNNYDENE (No. 108) at the corner of Sydenham Hill, 1868–70 by *J. F. Bentley* for W. R. Sutton, founder of the Sutton housing trust. Eclectic Queen Anne mixture, with elaborate brickwork. The adjoining house, ELLERSLIE, although much altered, was also built for Sutton by *Bentley*.

In SYDENHAM HILL, No. 16, THE WOOD, c 19 Tudor, low and irregular, built c. 1840, extended in the 1850s. Towards the N end the Victorian flavour is maintained by a few more ponderous and presumptuous examples, of no great aesthetic merit: No. 36, The Cedars, debased classical; No. 34, Sydenham Hill House, with entrance tower and Jacobean roofline; and the Frenchy No. 46, Castlebar. Two with rather more charm are Eliot Lodge, KIRKDALE, a picturesque Gothic composition in the style of Devey, c. 1857, doubled in size c. 1870 (the earlier part near the road), and Phoenix House, ELIOT BANK, Jacobean. From here a steep drop N towards Forest Hill, a dramatic site for some low early L.C.C. point blocks (1957–8).

FOREST HILL did not develop much until after the railway came in 1839. On the s side of LONDON ROAD a few mid c 19 classical terraces; in the roads to the N Italianate villas of the same period, especially in HONOR OAK ROAD, where there are also a few older houses: HILL HOUSE, of the late 1790s, ASHBERRY COTTAGE, probably c. 1809 (with a royal coat of arms over the back door), and, just behind, in WESTWOOD PARK, THE WHITE HOUSE of the 1780s.

Finally, items in the Forest Hill area too isolated to fit into a perambulation. Older buildings: THE ELMS, Elm Lane, off the NE end of Perry Hill. A surprising relic: a later c 18

---

* Future uncertain.

‡ Demolished: WESTWOOD, remodelled by *Pearson* in 1881 in the style of Chambord, with exceptionally lavish detail in hand-cut red bricks.

farmhouse, hemmed in but genuine apart from the later bay-windows. Three windows wide; delicate Doric porch. In PERRY VALE, Nos. 101–103, a mid C 19 cottage orné. STANSTEAD LODGE, Stanstead Road, is a large Tudor villa of c. 1840, stuccoed, with crowstepped gable. Curiosities: in ROUND HILL, W of Dartmouth Road, the upper part of the octagonal spire from *Wren*'s City church of St Antholin, formerly in a garden. In the garden of No. 23 LIPHOOK CRESCENT, N of the Horniman Museum, a FOLLY TOWER, late C 19, octagonal, of rubble. This was a garden building of Tewkesbury Lodge (demolished c. 1930) which stood in Honour Oak Road. Two houses of c. 1900 built by the last owner, Mr Beyer, for his son and daughter also survive at the extremities of the former estate. They are HAVELOCK HOUSE, Honor Oak Road (now part of the Metropolitan Police complex) and HAMILTON LODGE (now Euro-centre).*

Recent public housing is plentiful but mostly unmemorable. A good representative is the L.C.C. DACRES ESTATE on the N edge of MAYOW PARK W of Mayow Road, five towers of 1962 and a SCULPTURE ('Pacific') from the Crystal Palace grounds. Crisp low yellow brick terraces of the 1970s to the S off SILVERDALE. BROCKLEY PARK, N of Stanstead Road, is an interesting example of more recent trends. Homely timber-framed, partly weatherboarded clusters of imaginatively grouped houses, around a secluded green, with more to the S. A special feature is the flexible planning which allows for an additional front room or garage. By the *Borough of Lewisham Architect's Department* (*Geoffrey Wigfall*), 1978–80.

* Information from Mr H. W. Eames.

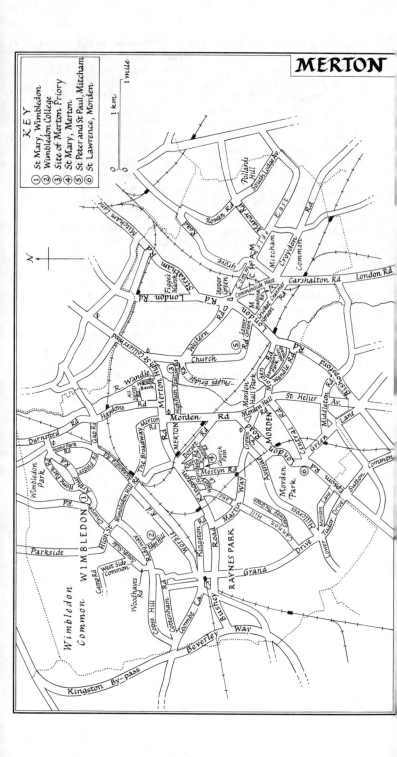

MERTON

KEY
1. St Mary, Wimbledon
2. Wimbledon College
3. Site of Merton Priory
4. St Mary, Merton
5. St Peter and St Paul, Mitcham
6. St Lawrence, Morden

0 1 km
0 1 mile

N

MERTON

INTRODUCTION

Merton has four distinct characters: the plateau of Wimbledon at the N W corner of the borough (gravel overlying clay), the low-lying, much-built-over valley of the Wandle close to the Wandsworth border, the suburban stretches around Mitcham further s (also gravel over clay), and Morden (low clay hills). The last two areas were rural until the C 20.* Before 1965 there were three local authorities.‡ The population in 1965 was 184,190, in 1981 166,100.

On the higher ground to the w the village of Wimbledon perches on the S E corner of the vast common. An isolated settlement in the Middle Ages, from the C 16 onwards it received a decided social cachet from the succession of Cecil and Spencer manor houses (now gone). A few good houses of the C 17 onwards survive, however, especially on the prime sites on the S E edge of the common, and the village character of the High Street and other picturesque enclaves of cottages has been zealously if a little self-consciously preserved. But the predominant character of Wimbledon is that of an affluent suburb of the C 19 and later, when the surrounding fields were transformed by an informal

* The EARLY SETTLEMENTS were on the gravel areas: a large group of Palaeolithic finds at Mitcham, and a scatter of later prehistoric material on Wimbledon Common, where hut circles also used to be visible (a Bronze Age village?). The Queen's Butt Wimbledon Common may have been a Neolithic long barrow. Caesar's Camp Wimbledon is an Iron Age hillfort. Roman finds indicate a settlement beside Stane Street in both Merton and Morden and a probable site at Mitcham. A large mound in Morden Park may be a Roman barrow. Around Morden Road, N E of Ravensbury Park, Mitcham, was the site of an early Saxon cemetery.

‡ Wimbledon had a local board from 1866, a U.D.C. from 1894, and became a borough in 1905. Merton was a U.D.C. from 1907, to which Morden was attached in 1911. Mitcham was a U.D.C. from 1915, a borough from 1934.

scatter of wealthy houses, especially in the neighbourhood of the common and along Ridgway further s. They include all shades of architecture, from the late classical villa with drive and shrubbery to the detached Arts and Crafts or neo-Georgian house of the turn of the century and after. Earlier Victorian architects to be found here include *Roumieu, Ransome*, and *Penrose*; later ones *E. J. May, George & Yeates, T. G. Jackson, Baillie Scott*, and the local firm *Hubbard & Moore*. C 20 developments have regrettably diminished their number and replaced them with tightly packed town houses and blocks of flats (the latter even more prevalent over the border in Putney, Ww).

The most attractive features of the E part of Merton are less immediately apparent. The northern stretch, low-lying clay traversed by the river Wandle, is densely covered by late Victorian housing similar to that in the adjacent parts of Tooting and Wandsworth (Ww) and by industry, which grew up early along the river. Some of the leading English c 18 calico-printing mills were at Merton, and the tradition was continued in the c 19 by William Morris's workshop on the same site and by Liberty's printworks; all this has alas obliterated nearly every trace of Merton's most important medieval building, the Augustinian priory founded in 1114. The Statute of Merton was enacted here, and Walter de Merton, founder of Merton College Oxford, came from here. The village developed some way to the w, around the parish church (with good c 12 and c 13 work), which now stands in delightful leafy seclusion amidst the late Victorian middle-class suburb of Merton Park created by the architects *Quartermain* and *Brocklesby* for the eccentric self-made local landowner John Innes. Meanwhile the humbler streets of 'New Wimbledon' filled the area between Wimbledon Broadway and Kingston Road, and more suburban development spread s with the railways (stations: Lower Merton (later Merton Park) 1855, Merton 'Abbey' 1868, Raynes Park 1870).

Further s the village of Mitcham and the scattered settlement of Morden remained rural until the c 20, only to be engulfed by the miles of suburban sprawl encouraged by the extension of the Northern Line to Morden in 1926. Yet there is still much to enjoy. At Morden there is a c 17 church, still rural in feeling, on the edge of Morden Park, which, complete with its c 18 mansion, survives as a reminder of that feature so typical of northern Surrey from the c 17 onwards: the house of the gentleman merchant, or professional man, set in its own grounds and enjoying a country outlook, yet within easy reach of London. Not far off are two other parks of older origin: Morden Hall Park and Ravensbury Park, both with the Wandle running through their grounds, while the special charm of Mitcham lies in the interlocking greens, the urban Upper Green at the hub of an ancient road network, Lower Green and Cricket Greens further s along the London Road, the latter still quite rural, with some good houses. All the greens connect with the much larger Mitcham Common to the SE. A secondary village centre is still traceable between Lower Green and the church further w. Some other older houses survive scattered along the London Road and by the river Wandle to the s, along with sporadic remnants of the late C 18 and early C 19 ribbon development which Cobbett disliked so much.

Of the best individual buildings in the borough, apart from the churches, the earliest are in Wimbledon: the rectory, partly medieval, and the early Jacobean Eagle House in the High Street. There are two good examples in Mitcham of the compact brick classical house of the later C 17 type: another Eagle House (1705) (now handsomely restored) and The Canons of 1680 (altered), nicely set in its own grounds, with an early C 16 dovecote behind. The Manor House, Merton, is also of the C 17, though less ambitious. Morden Hall preserves some mid C 18 features; Morden Park is an excellent house of 1770. Wandle Villa of 1790 in Phipps Bridge Road, the small but accomplished Wandle House Mitcham, attributed to *Robert Mylne*, and the Regency Morden Lodge should also be mentioned. The way in which these houses and their grounds alternate with industry along the Wandle is one of the special characteristics of the area (which indeed is one of the best hunting grounds for early industrial buildings in London). Lately the *Borough Architect's Department* have made their own distinguished contribution to this diversity, with their exceptionally attractive Watermeads housing development on the site of Mitcham Grove, which overlooks a landscaped opening off the Wandle close to Ravensbury Park.

Watermeads is one of a series of borough housing schemes 107 which deserves a special note, together with its predecessor at Pollards Hill, and its successor, All Saints Merton. They neatly encapsulate three phases in the history of low-rise housing. The development at the foot of Pollards Hill, planned in 1968, was one of the first large-scale demonstrations of the possibilities of building to a relatively high density (100 p.p.a., i.e. rather lower than in inner London, cf. contemporary work in Southwark) without using tall flats. The special contribution of Pollards Hill is its 'perimeter planning', with terraces compactly zigzagging around the edge of a generously large open space (on the principle that houses can be closer to open space than to each other). Watermeads (1974–7) is a development from this, looser and less

WATERMEADS

POLLARDS HILL

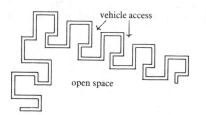

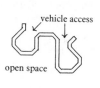

dogmatic, with special account taken of residents' needs,* and greater sensitivity in the landscaping of both the hard and grass areas. All Saints Merton (1978) is at first sight very different; low fragmented groups, whose final plan derives only very remotely from the earlier schemes and exchanges their smooth international modern idiom for a modest urban vernacular, designed to blend with the surrounding late Victorian suburb. There could hardly be a better symbol of the changing aims (or some would say of the loss of self-confidence) of public housing. More diverse are the neighbourhoods s of Merton High Street, at Phipps Bridge, and N of Lower Green Mitcham, which provide interesting contrasts between the mid sixties and the seventies, while the picturesque detailing of the housing at Grand Drive, Lower Morden, is a good example of the new aesthetic aims of the later 1970s. Alas, after this brief golden age of experiment (under *Philip J. Whittle* 1965–70 and *Bernard V. Ward* from 1970), the Borough Architect's Department was closed down in 1980.

Three other recent buildings are worth a special visit: the sympathetic addition by *Dry Halasz Dixon* to the unique octagonal C18 school at Wimbledon; and two highly individual private houses also in Wimbledon, one of concrete by *Arup Associates*, and one of glass and steel by *Richard Rogers*.

Further Reading

General accounts are: E. M. Jowett (ed.), *An Illustrated History of Merton and Morden* (1951); K. Denbigh, *History and Heroes of Old Merton* (1975); and W. A. Bartlett, *The History and Antiquities of the Parish of Wimbledon* (1865) (reissued 1971). Among a number of good recent pamphlets are *Eagle House Mitcham* (1974), *The Canons* (1977), and *Morden Park* (1977), all published by the Merton Historical Society; N. Plaistow, *Wimbledon Windmill* (1977); R. Milward, *A Short History of Wimbledon* (John Evelyn Society) (1977); and *Merton Park, The Original Garden Suburb* (John Innes Society) (1979). The revised DOE list is not yet available at the time of writing. *See also* p. 124.

Acknowledgements

I gratefully acknowledge the help of a number of local experts who have contributed much to the text: The John Innes Society and Mr Anthony Woolfenden on Merton Park, Mr E. N. Montague on Mitcham, Mr W. J. Rudd on Morden. The Borough Library, Planning Department, and former staff of the Architect's Department also went to considerable trouble in answering my questions.

* Related to an inquiry into user reaction at Pollards Hill, a surprisingly rare kind of investigation at this time.

MERTON

CHURCHES

MERTON PRIORY. Founded by Gilbert, Sheriff of Surrey, for the Augustinians in 1114, established on a new site in 1117, and given a foundation charter in 1121–2. After the Dissolution building materials were sent to Nonsuch and to St Mary Battersea (Ww). The church lay on the site and to the s of Station Road. Its plan is known from excavations.* The most interesting survival is the doorway now re-erected in St Mary's churchyard (*see* below), possibly part of the guest house discovered during the demolition of Abbey House in 1914. Along Station Road some walling, an apparently Jacobean gateway made up from medieval stones, and a small enclosure showing one area of the foundations. More of the precinct wall remains behind flats in Windsor Avenue.

ALL SAINTS, All Saints Road. By *Micklethwaite & Somers Clarke*, 1891–3. Brick, with a big bellcote over the w end. Nave and wide N aisle. Octagonal piers with arches dying into them.

CHRIST CHURCH, Christchurch Road, N of Church Road, Colliers Wood. 1874 by Messrs *Francis*. A rural design in stock brick, with timber belfry and spire (AW).

(ST JAMES, Beaford Grove, N of Martin Way. By *T. Ford & Partners*, 1957. – WALL PAINTING of the Resurrection by *Hans Feibusch*. – STAINED GLASS. Shapland memorial window and w window by *John Hayward*.)

ST JOHN THE DIVINE, High Path. 1914 by *C. H. Gage*. (Light and spacious interior. – STAINED GLASS. Lady Chapel E window by *Morris & Co.*, 1919.)

ST MARY, Church Lane. According to the Merton cartulary, rebuilt by Gilbert, the founder of the priory, i.e. between 1114 and 1125. Much restored (the exterior all refaced in flint), but the fabric of the nave Norman, see a window in the N wall near the W end. Norman N door with zigzag, badly rebuilt when *Benjamin Ferrey* added the N aisle in 1866. s aisle of 1856 by *F. Digweed* and the w arch from 1897 by *H. G. Quartermain*. Early C 13 chancel, unusually long (four bays), divided inside by fine tall blank arcading, a Surrey feature. Slightly chamfered arches on slender chamfered supports. Lancet windows remain in three bays, one on the S, two on the N. Hammerbeam chancel roof with ceiled coving between the wall and the hammerbeams. Excellent C 15 timber porch with traceried panels and bargeboards. – REREDOS. 1889 by *Ewan Christian*. – DOOR within the Norman N doorway, apparently con-

---

* It was of Cistercian type: an aisled nave, transepts each with four straight-ended E chapels, and a larger straight-ended chancel. In the C 13 the E end was enlarged, the chancel received aisles, and a straight-ended Lady Chapel was added to the E of the big new chancel. The W end had a stepped porch. The cloister lay to the s; the chapter house was apsed. An outer chapel of *c.* 1300 to the W of the priory, with a fine six-light window, survived until the early C 19.

temporary. Good simple ironwork with C-shape hinges. – STAINED GLASS. S aisle, four two-light windows commemorating John Innes, a late *Morris & Co.* work of 1907, not specially good. – S aisle E, a delicate design with a small panel with groups of figures, 1876. – MONUMENTS. Gregory Lovell † 1597 and wives. Good hanging wall-monument of alabaster, with kneeling figures. – Smith family, erected by the widow of Captain Cook. Grecian relief with kneeling figure. By *R. J. Wyatt*, signed Rome 1832. – Re-erected in the churchyard the sumptuous DOORWAY of *c.* 1175 from the priory (*see* above), of three orders, with a number of elaborate boldly three-dimensional geometrical motifs. – Some other medieval fragments are built into the side of the archway facing the vicarage garden.

(St JOHN FISHER (R.C.), Cannon Hill Lane. 1962 by *F. G. Broadbent & Partners.* DE)

(St JOSEPH (R.C.), Merton High Street. 1966 by *Conor P. Fahy.* DE)

METHODIST CHURCH, Colliers Wood High Street. By *E. D. Mills*, 1936. Modern for its date.

PUBLIC BUILDINGS

MANOR CLUB AND MERTON PUBLIC HALL, Kingston Road. Two of John Innes's establishments, by *H. G. Quartermain*, the first (1890–1) founded as a working men's club, the second (1900) as a masonic lodge.

MELROSE SCHOOL, Melrose Road. A low, irregular gabled range, close to the old church, appropriately villagey in scale. Original parts 1870, picturesque but tough Gothic, by *Aldridge & Willis*; several additions, including an extensive one dated 1901, by *H. G. Quartermain* (AW).

SINGLEGATE SCHOOL, Christchurch Road, N of Church Road, Colliers Wood. 1897 by *H. Burke-Downing.* Exuberant and eclectic. One-storeyed, with pilasters, steep gables, and some half-timbered and Gothic detail.

RUTLISH SCHOOL, Watery Lane. The late Victorian part is the former manor house of John Innes, the creator of Merton Park. A total rebuilding *c.* 1870–1900 of a former farmhouse, most of it by *H. G. Quartermain*: an eclectically picturesque composition with Tudor doorway, oriel window, and gables and bargeboards (good panelling and plasterwork inside). Undistinguished school buildings of 1957 next to it. Also part of Rutlish School, the former John Innes Horticultural Institute, Mostyn Road, established with money left by John Innes. It was opened in 1910 and moved from Merton in 1953. Buildings of *c.* 1910 and later.

JOHN INNES PARK, Mostyn Road. Originally the grounds of the manor house, little altered. The secluded evergreen walks give it a delightfully intimate character. Entrance lodge, cottage, and archway by *H. G. Quartermain*, probably *c.* 1890.

The wooden bandstand, handsome brick walls, and a rustic cricket pavilion (Aylward Road) date from the park's opening in 1909 (AW).

COLLIERS WOOD AND SOUTH WIMBLEDON STATIONS. By *Charles Holden*, 1926. Two of the standard type of the s extension of the Northern Line (cf. also Tooting Common and Tooting Bec, Ww), the first to abjure period suggestions, albeit not as radical as Holden's later Piccadilly Line stations. The character is decidedly that of concrete (although stone-faced) and the forms are heavy and cubic, with reminiscences however of Holden's earlier more classical office buildings (e.g. in High Holborn). Corner entrances with the principal window subdivided not by columns but by square piers carrying balls, the L.T. motif in the round.

PERAMBULATION

In the pleasantly secluded area round the church, traces of the old village blend happily with varied late C19 suburban development. The chief remains of the village are along CHURCH PATH: a fine wrought-iron gate to No. 10 (formerly to a C17 house) facing the church, some contemporary brick walling, the plain vicarage of *c.* 1800, a small terrace of cottages, and Merton Cottage, Georgian with a Victorian refronting. Interwoven with the old roads (Church Path, Church Lane, Watery Lane) are the new roads of the suburb called MERTON PARK created by John Innes, a property developer who turned local landowner and benefactor (*see* Public Buildings). He settled at Merton in 1867 and remained until his death in 1904.* DORSET ROAD, SHERIDAN ROAD, and MOSTYN ROAD are the main thoroughfares of the new estate, broad, generously planted avenues laid out *c.* 1870. The earliest development, very plain, yellow brick, of *c.* 1870–5, can be found for example in MOSTYN ROAD, DORSET ROAD, and KINGSWOOD ROAD. It contrasts sharply with what followed: the deliberate creation of a garden suburb, with generous planting of trees and holly hedges (a distinguishing feature of the area), allied to picturesque and artistic houses in the up-to-date Domestic Revival style by the estate architect *H. G. Quartermain*. Examples can be found in and around Mostyn Road, Sheridan Road, and Dorset Road, dating from *c.* 1880 to just after 1900 – tile-hanging, half-timbering, Queen Anne windows, gables and bargeboards, and much else. A simpler red brick, roughcast, and terracotta style appears in his last buildings *c.* 1897–1904 – WILTON CRESCENT for example, or his own house, No. 18 DORSET ROAD, 1902. As Merton Park was also a farming estate, cottages designed by Quartermain for farm and estate workers

* The account of Merton Park (and much other information on Merton) was contributed by Anthony Woolfenden.

are just round the corner from City men's homes. Pretty ones
are in CHURCH LANE facing the churchyard, 1881, and in
WATERY LANE (Nos. 8–12, c. 1895–8). The result is great
diversity both of scale and size, far more so than in the more
famous Bedford Park, for example.

The next estate architect, *J. S. Brocklesby*, added some sensitive
and attractive Arts and Crafts houses. Nos. 2–30 MELROSE
ROAD, c. 1906–11, include a range of pretty whitewashed
cottages, with low-pitched roofs and angled bays. More by
him in WATERY LANE; he lived briefly in No. 15 (1907),
then designed and moved into No. 17, STEEP ROOF (c. 1908)
– a steep roof indeed, with minute dormers high up. Among
his later work is a group of flint-walled and pantiled houses of
the mid 1920s: Nos. 19, 38, and 40 SHERIDAN ROAD and
THE FLINT BARN, No. 35 MOSTYN ROAD, impressive,
barn-like, and allegedly constructed from materials from old
farm buildings. Innes laid out more roads further s, but
development was slow, and CIRCLE GARDENS, intended to
have a church as its focus, was not built up until c. 1930.

KINGSTON ROAD and its continuation MERTON HIGH
STREET, the main road to London, were built up by the time
of Rocque's map, but only a few older buildings remain. The
mediocre redevelopment has been redeemed a little by recent
housing schemes. From w to E, first No. 180, ALMSHOUSES,
dated 1797, modest. Then LONG LODGE, later C 18, with a
brown brick front and a pediment with blind oculus, once the
home of Frederick Shields, the Pre-Raphaelite painter. Then
DORSET HALL, also later C 18, brown brick with red brick
dressings. At the corner of Rutlish Road, pleasantly grouped
two-storey housing by the *Borough Architect's Department* (*A.
Jadhar, D. Nicklin*), 1975–81. No. 120, MANOR HOUSE (so
called only after the C 17), is timber-framed, probably of
c. 1700 with a later brick front; five bays, small central pediment with lunette. Further on, the NELSON ARMS on the s
side of the High Street, a brash, jolly turn-of-the-century pub
with bold lettering, marks the site of the entrance to Merton
Place, where Nelson lived with the Hamiltons in 1801–5. The
grounds were sold for building in 1823, and the C 19 artisans'
cottages that followed were gradually replaced between 1951
and 1977 by the amorphous HIGH PATH ESTATE. The
earliest parts, near St John's church, are four-storey flats
round courtyards, 1951–7 by *A. J. Thomas*; the later stages,
with three unlovable high rise towers *en échelon*, are by
William Ryder, 1964 and 1968–70, built according to a
master plan of 1956 by *Clifford Culpin & Partners* and *A. J.
Thomas*. The more attractive final phase, 1975–7 by *William
Ryder & Partners*, has low terraces pleasantly set back from
the High Street.

N of the High Street around ALL SAINTS ROAD some housing
worth a detour: one of the last major works by the *Borough
Architect's Department* (*R. Hodge* and *A. Bews*), begun in 1978
(the department was disbanded in 1980). Low terraces, two

and three storeys, in scale with the surrounding late C19 streets. The planning derives from the 'perimeter' principles first used at Pollards Hill and then developed for Watermeads (*see* Mitcham, below), here interpreted much more loosely, so that at first sight the result looks very different. The open spaces flow informally between the outer three-storey terraces and the centrepiece, a lower pink-walled two-storey horseshoe terrace, quite a formal design, with hard standing areas for cars in the centre. The terraces are a mixture of houses and flats, with an interesting variety of dwelling types in the curved angles (cf. Watermeads). Unlike the earlier estates, the ranges do not form a single ribbon. Early plans for the area indeed had more continuous terraces, which disappeared as plans progressed and the integration of old and new buildings and routes became an important aim. In appearance, too, there is a world of difference between the friendly but slightly clumsy neo-vernacular forms used here – with their mansard roofs and slate-hanging – and the immaculate enamelled surfaces of the earlier schemes. Near by, along WANDLE BANK, a few late Georgian terrace houses face the river and Wandle Park.*

The landmarks of COLLIERS WOOD at the E end of Merton High Street are the underground station (*see* Public Buildings) and LYON TOWER, 1966 by *Bader & Miller*, an outlier of the rash that spread over Croydon at that time: quite well proportioned, with strongly projecting mullions, but all in a grim dark grey.

Alongside the river Wandle industrial buildings. The most interesting are in STATION ROAD, near the site of Merton Priory (*see* Churches), where in 1881 William Morris established his workshops in a former calico factory by the Wandle, of which nothing remains. Liberty's workshop followed, and to the S part of the former LIBERTY PRINTWORKS survives, mostly rebuilt since 1910. An old colour house, dated 1742, of brick, flint, and re-used stone, with a pantiled roof, was partly altered in the late C19. Late C19 block printing rooms adjoin. C18 brick wheel house, with a fine C19 undershot waterwheel (four sets of seven cast-iron arms originally on a timber shaft).

PHIPPS BRIDGE ROAD. *See* Mitcham.

MORDEN HALL. *See* Morden.

MITCHAM

CHURCHES

ST BARNABAS, Gorringe Park Avenue, N of Figge's Marsh. Big, thoughtful neo-Bodley by *H. P. Burke-Downing*, 1914. A hall-church with huge arcades, lacking its intended N aisle.

---

* Further N, in COPPERMILL LANE, an early C19 mill cottage with an early to mid C19 three-storey range, formerly a tannery, but possibly built for the Garratt Copper Mills.

Quite sensitive. – CHURCH HALL of 1908 by the same architect, in a cheerful free neo-Georgian, well detailed.

ST PETER AND ST PAUL, Church Road. The parish church, rebuilt in 1819–21 by *George Smith*. Large, and still of the Commissioners' type, stuccoed, with bald Perp detail. The only anomaly is the tower in a SE position; its base is medieval. Tall interior with very pretty tierceron- and lierne-vaults. – MONUMENTS. Sir Ambrose Crowley † 1713 and Lady Crowley † 1727. Good, with two profile portraits in a medallion within an architectural frame, with putti on the pediment. Designed by *Gibbs* (drawing, not quite identical, in the V and A), probably carved by *Rysbrack*, c. 1727. – Mrs Tate. 1821 by *Westmacott*. Woman holding a chalice. – Several late C18 tablets, e.g. Sophia Tate † 1780 by *C. Harris*.

ST PETER AND ST PAUL (R.C.), Cranmer Road, Cricket Green. Undistinguished. 1889 by *F. A. Walters*.

METHODIST CHURCH, Cricket Green. By *Edward Mills*, 1958. Big-boned, modern, honest, but unfortunately clumsily detailed. Zigzag timber roof, steel-framed, on Y-shaped columns, the wall set back to form a loggia on the N side. The wall behind the altar is of rough-cut slabs of York stone. Church hall on the N.

ZION CHAPEL (former). *See* Perambulation 1.

PUBLIC BUILDINGS

VESTRY HALL (former), with FIRE STATION behind, Lower Green. 1887 by *R. M. Chart*. Red brick, ugly.

THE CANONS (Community Centre), Madeira Road. One of the manors of Mitcham, once a possession of the canons of St Mary Overie, Southwark. The present house was built by John Odway, who was granted a building lease in 1680. It stands in its own grounds (now a public park) between Cricket Green and Mitcham Common: a good late C17 house, stuccoed later. Five-window front, two storeys above a tall basement, with projecting one-bay centre. Three windows deep. Dentilled cornice and hipped roof. Two-bay addition on the l. Staircase inside, centre-back, with strong twisted balusters. Behind the house an older DOVECOTE, C16, square, of coursed stone with some flint and brick, much patched. To the N, beside the bowling green, a handsome one-storey building, the first phase of a SPORTS CENTRE, by *A. Jadhar, L. Drake, G. Capper* of the *Borough Architect's Department*, 1978. Behind the house, old garden walls (tablet 1761), now enclosing car parks.

LIBRARY, London Road. By *Chart, Son & Reading*, 1933, neo-Georgian, the first expression of Mitcham's pride in its new borough status.

LIBRARY AND COMMUNITY CENTRE, South Lodge Avenue, Pollards Hill. 1969–70 and 1970–2 by *M. Kitchen* of the *Borough Architect's Department*. One-storeyed, with emphatically projecting flat roofs, handsome complements to the housing estate around (*see* Perambulation 2).

EAGLE HOUSE (Adult Education Institute), London Road, just N of Upper Green. The finest house in Mitcham. Built in 1705 for Fernandez Mendez, physician of Queen Catherine of Braganza. His initials are on the rainwater heads. In 1711 he leased it to Sir James Dolliffe, a director of the South Sea Company. The house is of yellow and red brick, five bays wide and four deep, two storeys high over a basement, with a three-bay projection and pediment, a hipped roof, dormers with segmental gables, and a balustrade and a cupola or belvedere on the roof. In spite of its noble and elegant composition it is decidedly conservative; if it were not for the slenderer windows one might mistake it for a building of 1650–60 of the school of Roger Pratt. The curiously humble doorway – a plain apsidal hood on small carved brackets – leads into a passage through to the back door. In this rises the staircase, with three twisted balusters to each tread, and shaped but not carved tread-ends. (A second staircase at a right angle on the l.) Excellent wrought-iron GATES with Dolliffe's initials. The Southwark Board of Guardians leased the estate in 1855 and added a large school building to the N, since demolished.

WILLIAM MORRIS MIDDLE SCHOOL, South Lodge Avenue, Pollards Hill. 1970–2 by the *Borough Architect's Department* (*S. de Grey, R. Padovan*), planned for 600 children. The first new middle school in Merton, one of the few London boroughs to adopt a three-tier education system. A low rectangle with flexibly planned teaching areas with movable partitions on either side of a service core. The poor natural lighting that results from the deep plan is improved only by the central botanical court with glazed pyramid roof. MACE structure, as usual not specially attractive externally.

MITCHAM STATION, London Road. Three-bay house of *c.* 1800, stock brick, with three-bay pediment. Wide elliptical entrance arch. Converted to a station later.*

PERAMBULATIONS

1. The Village and the Greens

The old village lay around the church and Lower Greens. In CHURCH ROAD, still a narrow lane with a village flavour, some old cottages, and Nos. 60–64, an eight-bay mid C18 house with double roof, stuccoed. The VICARAGE is plain early C19. Further E, on the site of Hall Place, a medieval house demolished in 1870, a small rubble archway from the chapel of 1348, repaired with stones from Merton Priory. On

---

* There is no evidence that it was built for the horse-drawn Surrey Iron Railway of 1803, whose alignment the steam railway of 1852–3 approximately followed. But does the archway suggest commercial premises served by the line?

the s side of LOWER GREEN WEST the pretty former SUN-
DAY SCHOOLS, founded 1788, clock turret 1792, enlarged
1812, retaining the turret. Nine bays with a raised centre. In
LONDON ROAD the WHITE HART INN, refaced in 1747, of
seven bays, with a Doric porch. Next door Nos. 346–348,
timber-framed with a Georgian front, and opposite, BURN
BULLOCK, the former Kings Head, a good C18 five-bay,
three-storey house with a Tuscan porch, dummy windows,
and a modillioned cornice of 1911; the back older (timber-
framed, with tile-hanging). The green on the E side of London
Road, known as CRICKET GREEN, still has a pleasantly
semi-rural atmosphere, with the TATE ALMSHOUSES on the
s, stock brick, one-storeyed with a central gable, 1829 by J. C.
Buckler, and some spaced-out gabled Victorian villas. Nos.
8–10 were built in 1838 as the school house of the infants'
school. No. 46, a tiny one-storey building, was a Wesleyan
preaching house of 1789. On the N side ELM LODGE, early
C19, then MITCHAM COURT, set back, stuccoed. Three-bay
centre of 1840, with an Ionic porch and top-heavy lunette
dormers. Later wings of irregular height. Then the WHITE
HOUSE, C18, with a Regency exterior of 1826 (three storeys
with a semicircular entrance bow with two Greek Doric
columns), and CHESTNUT COTTAGE, C18 altered. Further
E, near where Cricket Green meets Mitcham Common, an
OBELISK of 1822 with the inscription 'In grateful recollection
of the goodness of GOD through whose favour water has been
provided for this neighbourhood'.* To the N are the grounds
of The Canons (see Public Buildings), approached from
MADEIRA ROAD. In COMMONSIDE WEST, PARK PLACE,
plain late Georgian. Four-window front with doorway with
engaged Ionic columns, facing away from the road. Later
additions. Towards the N end of Commonside West and along
COMMONSIDE EAST opposite, modest cottages and houses
in a mixture of brick and weatherboarding, the type once to be
found all over Mitcham. On the E side, PROSPECT HOUSE,
C18 (reconstructed), with bay-windows, and No. 17, early
C19, with pediment over a single bay, a little grander than the
others. The two roads meet at the E end of UPPER GREEN,
straddling the London Road and transformed into a suburban
centre at the end of the C19, with a prim little Victorian
CLOCK TOWER (or rather clock column) and two pubs, the
brashly striped QUEENS HEAD, and the half-timbered
KINGS ARMS (1906).

w of Upper Green, WESTERN ROAD, with the former ZION
CHAPEL of 1818 (now industrial), stock brick, with
pedimented gable. Further w a dreary area of gasometers and
factories. A detour can take in LOVE LANE to the sw with its
tiny mid C19 cottages characteristic of the haphazard development of the waste land on the fringes of London, and some

* Further E, on the common, near Windmill Road, the round house of a
POSTMILL of 1808. The hollow post contains a driveshaft (cf. Wimbledon,
below).

borough housing equally characteristic of the vacillating policies of the 1960s–70s: bulky red brick ziggurats on the N side
of Western Road (1972–6); low pale brick terraces further W in
FOUNTAINS PLACE (1966–9), agreeably planned around
pedestrian routes, but starkly detailed.

2. The peripheral buildings

These are too scattered to make a consecutive perambulation
(except for those along the river Wandle).

N of Upper Green in LONDON ROAD, FIGGE'S MARSH,
another open space, with a mid C18 three-storey pair near the
SE corner and on the W side DENNIS REEVE CLOSE,
pleasant old people's housing of 1976–9 (A. Smith and R.
Burkmar of the Borough Architect's Department).

S of Lower Green near the station, Nos. 470–472 and 482–484,
two dignified pairs of four-storey houses built c. 1840 by a
local builder, Thomas Finden, the S one with a neat extension
with brick arches added 1981.

Further S the mixture of houses, industrial relics, and parks
along the RIVER WANDLE make an interesting sequence,
described from E to W, starting from London Road. In
RIVERSIDE DRIVE, E of the N end of Bishopsford Road,
WANDLE HOUSE, a small but handsome stock brick house of
c. 1795,* three by two bays, parapet with intermittent balustrading, ground-floor windows in blind arches, a bow-window
facing the river. Ascribed to Robert Mylne (DOE) on account
of its similarity to The Wick, Richmond (Ri). Now
unsympathetically surrounded by suburban housing, and
itself an adjunct of a drab office block of 1963 to which it is
connected by a glazed link. The additions replace earlier
extensions. There was formerly a door in the l. bay facing the
road. Near by, up a lane before Mitcham Bridge, GROVE
MILL, quite handsome two-storey yellow brick industrial
buildings of 1863. On the E side of London Road, close to the
bridge, a picturesque group of weatherboarded cottages,
1750–1850, adjoining the sites of some of the Mitcham mills
now obliterated.

WATERMEADS, off Rawnsley Avenue, W of Bishopsford Road. 107
One of the most attractive council developments of the 1970s
in London. 1974–7 by R. Hodge and A. Bews of the Borough
Architect's Department, 186 houses and flats arranged in a
meandering three-storey ribbon overlooking delightfully
landscaped grounds, with a cedar tree surviving from a former
house on the site (Mitcham Grove) and a new lake created
alongside the river to the S. Ravensbury Park adjoins to the W,
so that in these directions there are continuous vistas of trees
and water (and easily accessible play areas as well). The form
of the housing was developed from Pollards Hill (see below),

---

* The earliest date at which the building appears in the land tax records (E. N.
Montague).

but took into account the less successful aspects of that estate; so here the featureless open area was avoided, and splayed corners afford better views for the flats at the angles of the terrace. The plan, more relaxed than the rigid rectilinear geometry of Pollards Hill, sets off admirably the trim, functional surfaces. As at Pollards Hill, vitreous enamel panels are used on the upper floors (here buff, not white); the ground floor has pale rendered walls. The N sides of the meander form two polygonal closes, instead of dull garage courts (cf. the later All Saints, Merton). Integral garages, slightly projecting, with balconies above. The main living rooms are on the first floor.

RAVENSBURY PARK, off Wandle Road. In the pleasant park by the river is the site of the ancient Ravensbury Manor House which belonged to the Throgmorton family in the C 16, then to the Carews of Beddington (Su). It was demolished c. 1860. Some brick walls of later extensions remain. By the road, No. 162, the former Ravensbury farmhouse. THE GABLES, No. 2 MORTON ROAD, are the former stables and garage block to Ravensbury House; c. 1910 by H. Porter and Percy Newton in a Lutyens-inspired neo-Georgian (AW). Further on, at the junction of Wandle Road and Morden Road, Whiteley Products, the former RAVENSBURY SNUFF MILL, later C 19, with two cast-iron low-breast-shot wheels inside. Near by on the Wandle were the Ravensbury Print Works, like those of Merton (see Merton: Perambulation) an important C 18 industry in this area. Further N up MORDEN ROAD, WHITE COTTAGE, a handsome three-storeyed weatherboarded house of the C 18.

The Wandle continues through Morden Hall Park (see Morden), then runs beside PHIPPS BRIDGE ROAD towards Merton. Towards the S end, CHERRY ORCHARD ESTATE, borough housing of c. 1979, grouped around two greens opening off two spine roads, an informal type of perimeter plan derived from Watermeads (see above). Further N, surrounded by the less appealing PHIPPS BRIDGE ESTATE, fifteen-storey flats of the late 1960s, No. 98, WANDLE VILLA, a modest house of the later C 18, said to have been built by J. A. Rucker, calico manufacturer. Five windows wide, pedimented doorcase. Restored 1981. Small stuccoed Gothic lodge. No. 84, at the end of an early C 19 terrace, is a FOLLY, a small tower of c. 1875 said to have been made from stones from London Bridge.

MITCHAM GARDEN VILLAGE, off Carshalton Road S of Cranmer Road. 1929–32 by Chart & Reading. A keyhole-shaped close with houses facing inwards, all different. The spirit of Blaise Hamlet over a century late. Pleasant layout; poor half-timbered houses.

POLLARDS HILL, South Lodge Avenue, on the E fringe of the borough. 1968–71 by the Borough Architect's Department (M. Kitchen project architect, with R. McCormack, P. Bell, D. Lea, N. Alexander). A locus classicus of the high-density, low-rise housing that began to be developed in the 1960s as an alternative to the high-rise schemes of the previous decade. A brilliantly concise layout of three-storey houses and flats (100 p.p.a.) in an ingenious rectilinear Greek-key meander around the edges of the 41-acre site (a development from Sir Leslie Martin and Lionel March's theories of perimeter planning*). Three types of open space are provided: tiny private back-yards, small grassy squares partly enclosed by the inner sides of each meander, and a park along South Lodge Avenue unusually generous in scale but disappointingly flat and featureless. On this side a library and community centre (*see* Public Buildings). The outer sides of the terraces have integral garages and face rather monotonous garage courts. The single-aspect flats at the corners also have disadvantages. But the total impression is strikingly humane in comparison with so much other housing of the same period, and ten years later, there were few overt signs of dissatisfaction. The pristine appearance is due to the crisp contrast between the dark wooden window frames and the gleaming white stove-enamel panels which enclose the prefabricated concrete framework, their starkness reduced by much lush planting around the backyards.

EASTFIELDS, Acacia Road, off the SE end of Grove Road. A smaller scheme, completed 1974, by the same team as Pollards Hill, and designed on the same principles. The terraces here enclose a rectangular space, with smaller squares opening off it.

MORDEN

A scattered village S of Merton, until overwhelmed by suburban expansion after the underground extension opened in 1926. The Morden shopping centre lies around the underground station at the junction of Crown Lane and London Road. E of this Morden Hall with its park, on the site of the old manor house; to the S another old centre, with the parish church of St Lawrence and Morden Park with its C18 house. The L.C.C. St Helier Estate of the 1930s straddles the SE borough boundary (*see* Sutton).

(EMMANUEL, Dudley Drive, SE off Tudor Drive. 1962 by *K. C. White*.)

ST GEORGE, Central Road. The present church was built of brick in 1932 as a two-purpose church hall; wooden hall to its E added as a temporary church in 1938; low link in between, 1976.

ST LAWRENCE (Morden parish church), London Road. Of 1636, an interesting and rare date for churches. Red brick, mainly in English bond with wide joints, probably a refacing of an older building (see the stone plinth and thick walls). Nave and chancel in one, N vestry 1805, S porch, embattled W tower with two set-offs, in darker brick with stone quoins,

* L. Martin and L. March, *Land Use and Built Form*, 1966.

restored in 1887. Windows in c 14 style, those to N and S of two cusped lights with elongated quatrefoils. These, and especially the four-light E window with its large straggly tracery heads of early Perp form, may date from 1636 (or are they later restorations, associated with the Flemish bond brickwork below the windows?). Simple whitewashed interior. Roof with tie-beams and kingposts, purely utilitarian. – PULPIT. Formerly a three-decker, with original stair and sounding board, 1720. – COMMUNION RAIL. Three-sided, with twisted balusters, also 1720. – WEST GALLERY. 1792. – STAINED GLASS. E window largely c 17, with figures of Moses and Aaron with the Tablets of the Law; kneeling donors beneath. Partly renewed (including the painted dove in the tracery) in 1828. – MONUMENTS. Mrs Elizabeth Gardiner † 1719 (benefactress of the parish and donor of pulpit and communion rail). Inscription on feigned drapery within a Corinthian aedicule. – Sir P. Leheup † 1777. Bust before a black triangle. – Mrs Leheup † 1775. Good, large, simple tablet. No figures. – Many good minor tablets to the Garth family of Morden Hall, and others. – CHURCHYARD with several bulgy sarcophagi.

(ST TERESA (R.C.), Bishopsford Road, St Helier. 1930 by *W. C. Mangan*. DE)*

BATTERSEA CEMETERY, Lower Morden Lane. Half-timbered lodge, good railings. Formal drive leading to the chapel (1891 by *W. C. Poole*).

(MERTON AND SUTTON CEMETERY, Green Lane, Lower Morden. Stripped classical chapel by *Albert Thomas*, 1947. HM)

MORDEN HALL (council offices), Morden Hall Road, and MORDEN HALL PARK. The manor was acquired in the mid c 16 by the Garths, who lived at Morden Hall until the later c 18. In 1872 the estate was bought by the Hatfield family, proprietors of the Snuff Mills in the grounds. They gave the park to the National Trust. The Garths rebuilt (or re-modelled?) the house in the mid c 18. The exterior has been deprived of its attraction by later stucco and alterations of *c.* 1840. The house lies close to the road, hidden by a tall wall and trees. Three storeys, the N front nine windows wide, the S front with four-window centre, and two long projecting wings flanking a courtyard. An old view shows the centre with one-storey portico between full-height re-entrant projections (now disguised by later additions). (Large entrance hall with mid c 18 fireplace; Palladian staircase around a well; staircase ceiling with mid c 18 plasterwork.) Good wrought-iron entrance gates; c 18 STATUES of Neptune and Venus. Along Morden Hall Road the long red brick wall (much repaired) is probably older than the house. Within the grounds, various cottages and outbuildings including STABLES, up a drive to the S of the house, later c 19 one-storey ranges around a

---

* For other churches of the St Helier estate *see* St Helier (Su).

courtyard, entered by a bold archway of red and yellow brick
surmounted by a clock turret; and, s of the drive, a WALLED
GARDEN (now a car park) with a clairvoyée section on the s
side with cast-iron railings with vertical Greek key pattern.
Within the grounds, the E parts of which are a public park,
various cottages and outbuildings. The most interesting lie by
the mill stream. Light cast-iron bridges of early C19 type over
the mill stream.

SNUFF MILLS, Morden Hall Park, close to the stables. C18 and
C19, mainly of brick, with some weatherboarding, formerly
with two waterwheels of cast iron facing each other across the
mill stream (one removed 1968). Brick-roofed tobacco-drying
oven. To the W of the stream, adjoining the mills, MILL
COTTAGE, weatherboarded. To the E the larger MORDEN
COTTAGE, irregular and picturesque, partly weatherboarded, with a two-bay centre with castellations and obelisks, and Tudor dripstones over the windows.

IVY LODGE, Morden Hall Road. Apparently an C18 garden
building or lodge, later converted to a two-storey cottage.
Simple three-bay stuccoed W front; s side with tall central
segmental archway below modillioned eaves; E side with
another full-height arch, now blocked except for a lunette
window at the top. Smaller arches in the N wall visible inside.

MORDEN LODGE, Morden Hall Road. Handsome Regency
villa, set back from the road in its own grounds. Two storeys,
stuccoed, Greek Doric porch.

LODGES, Morden Hall Park. Grey brick, c. 1840, one-storeyed.
One in Morden Road, another at the N end of Morden Hall
Road.

MORDEN PARK (council offices). Close to the parish church, W
of London Road. A fine house of 1770 set in extensive
grounds. Built by John Ewart, merchant and distiller, on part
of the Morden Hall estate. Five-window front of two storeys
with a parapet; brown brick. Arched ground-floor windows in
yellow brick-arched recesses. Venetian doorway with Tuscan
demi-columns and pediment, linked to the pedimented window above by a balustrade and scrolls. The N and S sides of
seven bays, with symmetrical one-storey canted bay-windows
at either end (the SW one heightened in the later C19). Large
two-storey bow-window at the back. The front door leads to
an entrance hall connected by a screen of two Ionic columns
with a staircase of imperial type, starting in one flight and
continuing in two. (From the half-landing one enters the
saloon with the bow-window. On the S side on the ground floor
are the drawing room and library, with a half-domed recess
with columns. On the N side dining room and kitchen.) At the
back of the house a courtyard with two small round houses and
the remains of a crinkle-crankle wall. (In the park SW of the
house a MOUND, possibly a Roman barrow later used as a
garden feature.)

MERTON TECHNICAL COLLEGE, London Road. Pleasantly
sited on the edge of Morden Park. 1971–2 by the *Borough*

Architect's Department (*A. Jadhar, R. Poole*). Long, neat curtain-walled range with projecting middle storey; unsightly one-storey workshop and dustbin excrescences.

SWIMMING POOL, Morden Park. 1962–7 by *George Lowe & Partners*. Rather a clumsy design.

MORDEN L. T. STATION, London Road and Crown Lane. 1926. The southernmost of *Charles Holden*'s stations on the City and South London Railway extension (later Northern Line). Yet another variation on a theme (cf. South Wimbledon (Me), Tooting Bec (Ww), etc.). Three-storey office block added above in 1960.

MORDEN ROAD STATION (Wimbledon and Croydon Railway). 1855 by *G. P. Bidder*. Hipped roof, central chimney.

The character of the old centre around St Lawrence's church has suffered from road widening. S of the church the MANOR HOUSE, with a late C18 three-bay brick front, late C19 tile-hung in parts behind. Further S in Epsom Road the stuccoed GEORGE INN, with an early C19 E elevation masked by extensive alterations of 1931. N of the church, CHURCH FARM COTTAGE, a small rural weatherboarded survival, restored. Across the busy London Road at the beginning of CENTRAL ROAD, OLD SCHOOL HOUSE, 1731, a simple brick cottage with an inscribed tablet; later C19 additions behind. To the rear, enclosed by a boundary wall, yellow brick flats with mansard roofs built by the Housing Association for Officers' Families, *c.* 1928 and later. Further N and E, the less institutional EARL HAIG HOMES, by *Grey Wornum* and *Louis de Soissons*, 1931 onwards. Neo-Georgian ranges of two and three storeys around large grassed quadrangles. On the N side of Central Road HATFEILD MEAD, borough housing by *A. J. Thomas* of the 1950s, and a PRIMARY SCHOOL of 1910.

At LOWER MORDEN a large area of borough housing (219 dwellings), W of Grand Drive near the entrance to Battersea Cemetery. 1977–80; *A. Jadhar* and *L. Drake* of the *Borough Architect's Department*. Three pleasant clusters of two- and three-storey terraces arranged around a cul-de-sac access road. In total contrast to the style of Pollards Hill or Watermeads (*see* Mitcham), the houses are differentiated by a deliberately picturesque variety of materials and motifs (slatted balconies, oriels, tile-hanging, even diapered brickwork).

CROWN LANE. The mediocre shopping centre around the L.T. station has as its focus CROWN HOUSE by *A. Green*, 1959–61, a curved slab of twelve storeys on a two-storey podium with shops on the ground floor (quite an early example of the type in outer London). Further W a modest curiosity, Nos. 23–37, NORTH'S COTTAGES, a two-storey late C19 terrace built by Thomas North, owner of a local sheet-metal works. Brick ground floor, upper floor and roof originally all clad with corrugated iron. Most of the houses altered. No. 31 is the best preserved, with tiny corrugated iron dormers as well. No. 33 has a neat porch in the same material.

WIMBLEDON

INTRODUCTION

In the Middle Ages Wimbledon was one of several small settlements on the fringes of the area of wasteland which partially survives as Wimbledon Common, still the wildest open space in London. The parish was exceptionally large, including the small hamlet of Roehampton (now in the borough of Wandsworth), as well as the riverside villages of Putney (Ww) and Mortlake (Ri). The church lies a little to the NE of the old village centre. The rectory close to it was leased by William Cecil, the later Lord Burghley, as a country retreat c. 1550. After 1558 it became the residence of his eldest son, Thomas Cecil, first Earl of Exeter, who acquired further land at Wimbledon and in 1588 began to build a new manor house on a magnificent scale close to the church, the first of a sequence of great mansions which have all disappeared. By a splendid piece of detective work, the late Mr C. S. S. Higham showed that Cecil's house stood approximately astride Home Park Road, facing N downhill over a series of terraced forecourts. It was altered in the 1640s for Queen Henrietta Maria, by *Inigo Jones* and *Nicholas Stone*. To the W of the church a house was begun c. 1720 by *Colen Campbell* and *Lord Burlington* for Sir Theodore Janssen, but never completed. When in 1732 Sarah, Duchess of Marlborough, built a house (burnt in 1785) to the SW, designed by *Henry Herbert*, ninth Earl of Pembroke, and *Roger Morris*, the Tudor building was cleared away to provide a northern vista. The next on the site, Wimbledon Park House, built by *Henry Holland* for Earl Spencer in 1799–1802 on the foundations of the Marlborough stables and sold in 1846 to a developer, J. A. Beaumont, survived, hemmed in by later streets, until 1949. Fragments of the park (landscaped by *Capability Brown* in 1765) remain as a golf course, public park, and the All England Tennis Club.

CHURCHES

CHRIST CHURCH, Copse Hill. By *S. S. Teulon*, 1859–60, enlarged 1881. A powerful composition, with a sturdy stone tower above the chancel, capped by a pyramid roof and steeply gabled dormers. The circular stair-turret to one side may date from 1875, when *F. C. Penrose* added the choir vestry. The tower is picturesquely buttressed by adjuncts of different heights: twin-gabled organ chamber, tall S transept, and short sanctuary with Dec E window. Long nave without clerestory; very quirky capitals. The W bay and W wall added 1881 by *Charles Maylard*. – REREDOS. 1907–12 by *E. C. Shearman*. – SEDILIA made up of arcading formerly against the E wall. – STAINED GLASS. N aisle window by *Hugh Arnold*, 1908 (P C). – VICARAGE by *David Rock & Robert Smart*, 1964–6. Dark brick, monopitched roof, with garage and parish room projecting in front.

HOLY TRINITY, Merton Road. 1862 by *J. Johnson*, early Dec, with a bell-turret. (Interior altered 1979. – STAINED GLASS by *Mayer* of Munich, 1975.)

ST JOHN, Spencer Hill, NE of Edge Hill. 1875 by *T. G. Jackson*. Red brick without a tower. Dec detail. Between nave and chancel an odd bellcote on a buttress with many set-offs. (Interior now whitewashed. – STAINED GLASS. One *Morris & Co.* window, 1926, in the S aisle. – Another by *Hugh Arnold*, 1914 (PC).)

ST LUKE, Ryfold Road, W of Durnsford Road. 1909 by *T. G. Jackson*. Brick, with a half-timbered porch. Lofty Dec chancel. E window with two strong mullions *à la* Seddon. Plainer plate-traceried nave but still on a grand scale: brick arches dying into stone piers, emphatic wooden roof trusses to the broad aisles. W end unfinished.

ST MARK, St Mark's Place, Worple Road. The original church by *C. G. Maylard* of 1880, extended in 1888, burnt down in 1966. Its replacement is by *Humphreys & Hurst* and *David Nye & Partners*, 1968–9. Brick, clerestory-lit, with a top lantern, lower meeting rooms, and foyer to S and W.

ST MARY, Church Road. The ancient parish church. Chancel masonry of the later Middle Ages, including a low-side window. The rest rebuilt first by *John Johnson* of Leicester in 1788, then again in 1843 by *G. G. Scott & Moffat*. Chancel largely rebuilt by *Scott* in 1860. Flint with stone dressings. W tower with spire. Perp details. Interior with three galleries. To the S of the chancel the Cecil Chapel, built in 1626–36 and containing the simple black marble MONUMENT to Sir Edward Cecil, Viscount Wimbledon, † 1638. No figures, nor any figural relief. The chapel is of brick with small windows below the roof and a simple rib-vault. – ARMOUR. In the Cecil Chapel. – STAINED GLASS. Also in the Cecil Chapel, a handsome C14 figure of St George and heraldic glass of the C17. – In one S window three figures designed by *Henry Holiday*, executed by *Morris & Co.*, 1923. – Three panels in a window further E also by *Morris & Co.*, 1925. – MONUMENTS. James Perry † 1821, erected by the Fox Club. Seated figure below a bust of Charles James Fox. – (John Miland † 1877. Bust by *W. Calder Marshall*. – Sir Joseph Bazalgette † 1891 by *Gaffin*. NT) – In the churchyard many large monuments, notably Gerard de Visme † 1797, a pyramid of blocks of vermiculated rustication with corner acroteria to the base.

(ST MATTHEW, Wimbledon Park. By *E. C. Shearman*, c. 1910, rebuilt after the war by *J. S. Comper*. NT)

ST PETER, Haydons Road. 1911–12 by *Greenaway & Newberry*. Only the E part completed, a tall E.E. design; spacious interior; vaulted S chapel. The W part (now church hall) still the mission church built in 1901.

(CHRIST THE KING (R.C.), The Crescent, E of Wimbledon Park Station. 1928 by *A. G. Scott*. DE)

SACRED HEART (R.C.) Edge Hill. 1886–1901 by *F. A. Walters*. Large, tall, and long, without any special vertical accent. Flint and stone. Nave and aisles and polygonal apse. Dec, with pinnacles on the buttresses. Flying buttresses for the apse. Interior with much figural stone decoration. – (PRESBYTERY, attached to the parish hall to the N; 1981–2 by *W. Evans*.)

(ST WINEFRIDE (R.C.), Latimer Road, NE of Merton Road. 1905 by *F. A. Walters*. DE)

WAT BUDDHA PRATEEP (Thai Buddhist Temple), Calonne Road. By *Sidney Kaye, Firmin Partnership*, c. 1978–82, with traditional Thai details (curved roof tiles, carved teak doorframes).

(WESLEYAN CHURCH, Griffiths Road, S of The Broadway. 1903 by *R. J. Thomson*.)

CEMETERY, Gap Road. Late C19 chapels; broached spire.

PUBLIC BUILDINGS

TOWN HALL, Wimbledon Hill Road and The Broadway. Stone-faced, symmetrical, and dull. By *A. J. Hope (Bradshaw, Gass & Hope)*, 1931. Behind the Town Hall in Queens Road jollier municipal buildings in the stripy style of the turn of the century: MAGISTRATES' COURT 1895, POLICE STATION (opposite) 1900, FIRE STATION 1904.

SWIMMING BATHS, Latimer Road, NE of Merton Road. 1900 by *R. J. Thomson*.

WIMBLEDON COLLEGE, Edge Hill. Founded in 1860 by the Rev. John Brackenbury as an Anglican Preparatory Military Academy. From 1894 a boys' school run by the Jesuits, from 1944 a grammar school, from 1969 a comprehensive. Extensive buildings from all four phases on the crest of the hill. The original ones of 1860 by *Teulon* consist of the schoolhouse, a picturesque brick Gothic mansion to the r. of the hall, and behind this and to the N, a long, rather gaunt three-storey gabled range with projecting wings, built as dormitories. The hall itself was burnt down in 1977. Its replacement of 1980 by *W. Evans* makes quite a handsome show, with its splayed plinth and its red brick walls in sympathy with the older buildings, although the abrupt horizontal roof-line is at odds with the rest of the skyline. The wings of the dormitory building were extended NW in 1865–7 by *Teulon*, NE (in a less spiky Gothic) in 1896–8. The Perp CHAPEL to the SW was added by *F. A. Walters* in 1910. The courtyard behind completed by utilitarian classrooms and laboratories of 1951 by *Hudson & Hammond* and by further additions of 1965 by *H. Cullerne Pratt*. In the NE corner of the courtyard the old gymnasium of 1883, converted to a library in 1980; to the S technical and arts building of 1968–72 by *W. Evans*.

KING'S COLLEGE SCHOOL, South Side. Transferred from Somerset House in 1897. A plain rendered Georgian house

(Cooke: 1750) with a Tuscan porch and, attached to it, the broad chapel-like brick front of a neo-Perp range by *Sir B. Fletcher*, 1899. More buildings of the C19 and C20.

RICARDS LODGE SCHOOL, etc., in the area between Leopold Road, Arthur Road, and Home Park Road. PARK HOUSE SCHOOL, the Middle School of 1972–4, occupies the site of Wimbledon Park House (*see* Wimbledon Introduction), which survived until 1949. In the SW corner of the grounds, BISHOP GILPIN PRIMARY SCHOOL, 1966, nicely detailed. RICARDS LODGE SCHOOL partly occupies the Victorian Gothic mansion built by *John Nicholls* in 1875–7 for Percy Mortimer, the developer of the surrounding roads. Red brick with stone dressings; gables and a tower.

WILLIAM WILBERFORCE SCHOOL, Camp Road. A most engaging building. A simple two-storey octagonal brick schoolhouse of 1758–61, built as a charity school for fifty poor children, originally containing both schoolroom and master's accommodation. Extended in 1834 to the SE, and altered and added to after 1870. Restored in 1974–6 by *Dry Halasz Dixon* with the *Borough Architect's Department*, when it was converted as an E.S.N. school, with a low NW polygonal extension sympathetically detailed. Brown brick with pantiled roofs.

(BOARD SCHOOLS. DUNDONALD ROAD SCHOOLS SE of Worple Road. 1904 by the local architect *R. J. Thomson*. Nice domestic detailing. – PELHAM HIGH SCHOOL, Pelham Road. 1909 by *H. P. Burke-Downing*. An accomplished formal neo-Georgian composition. AW)

ATKINSON MORLEY HOSPITAL, Copse Hill. Established 1869. It incorporates Cottenham House, an older building.

VILLAGE CLUB AND HALL, Lingfield Road, close to the outlying part of the village NW of Ridgway. 1858 by *S. S. Teulon*. Picturesque small group enlivened by coloured brick and a varied roof-line, the hall with an eccentric traceried window; tower adjoining. Enlarged 1879.

(LABOUR HALL AND WILLIAM MORRIS HALL, Merton Road. Two roundels of *Morris & Co.* glass of *c.* 1881, with Chaucer and Helen of Troy, given in 1931.)

TELEPHONE MANAGER'S OFFICE, Worple Road. By *W. S. Frost* of the *Ministry of Public Building and Works*, 1958–62. Neat curtain-walling.

ALL ENGLAND LAWN TENNIS AND CROQUET CLUB, Church Road, Wimbledon Park. The first championships were held at the old grounds in Worple Road in 1877. The present club in Church Road dates from 1922. A short way from the championship courts a covered tennis court by *C. J. Pell & Partners* (engineers), 1958. A shell-concrete vault of 175 by 175 ft covers two existing courts. The vault is only 3 in. thick. Shallow segmental lunettes on all four sides. Centre with a 14-ft dome of glass-fibre laminate. In addition two hundred 21-in. glass domes for daylighting and a system of tubes for artificial lighting.

SOUTH WIMBLEDON UNDERGROUND STATION. *See* Merton.

PERAMBULATION

The church lies some way to the NE of the pre-Victorian village, which preserves something of its character in the High Street and around the E end of the Ridgway. Downhill to the E is the undistinguished commercial centre around the station; to the W, the desirable residential streets in the neighbourhood of the common, with houses of the C 18 especially along West Side Common, and of the C 19 and early C 20 along Parkside and South Side and in the streets off them.

The perambulation starts with the High Street and then describes buildings to its NE, SE, W, and N.

The HIGH STREET, a broad road with irregular frontages, still has pleasant echoes of a village street, with its small closes running off the s side, between a mixture of cottages, inns and prosperous small shops of the type that wealthy suburbs can afford (cf. Highgate, Ca, NE London). Mostly modest later Georgian frontages, especially on the s side, some the result of tactful early C 20 improvements (e.g. Nos. 38–39, altered by *Thomson & Pomeroy* in 1907). ASHFORD HOUSE dates from 1720 (later shops in front). CLAREMONT HOUSE (Nos. 44–45) is a nice simple L-shaped late C 17 brick house with Georgian alterations and possibly earlier parts behind. The only important house is EAGLE HOUSE, set back on the N side, built in 1613 for Robert Bell, one of the founders of the East India company, a façade of three widely spaced bays with three big shaped gables. Brick, now mostly rendered. Three canted bay-windows; central entrance leading into the middle of one short side of the hall, which runs at r. angles to the front through to the back of the house, still an unusual arrangement at that time (but cf. e.g. Hardwick, Derbyshire, and Charlton, Gr). Original three plaster ceilings on the first floor and one on the ground floor, the hall overmantel on the ground floor, and the panelling of the former dining room (1730). The house was bought by the architect *Sir T. G. Jackson* and restored in 1887. He rebuilt the back centre wing. Further E on the same side some minor former municipal buildings, including a FIRE STATION, tile-hung, with a pretty bell-turret of 1890. E again, a taller late Victorian shopping parade ending with the NATIONAL WESTMINSTER BANK by *Cheston & Perkin*, 1895; domed corner turret with Franco-Flemish carving.

CHURCH ROAD leads NE from here towards the parish church, and the sites of the Cecil and Spencer mansions (*see* Wimbledon Introduction). Immediately N of the church is the OLD RECTORY of *c.* 1500, the house taken by William Cecil, later Lord Burghley, as his country retreat in 1549. Considerable additions, especially of 1846 and after, when it was bought by J. A. Beaumont, the developer who laid out the surrounding roads on the Spencer Estate. Original one range with specially thick walls, two stair-turrets, and some interior features, including a pointed arch in the former chapel. Also good panelling of *c.* 1600, probably brought in. Near the church in ARTHUR ROAD (running N E) a stuccoed early C 19 LODGE formerly of Wimbledon Park House (*see* Wimbledon Introduction) which stood on the site to the E now occupied by Park House Middle School (q.v.). Also in Arthur Road a WELL HOUSE (the well is 563 ft deep) built by Earl Spencer in 1798 in order to raise water for his house. Octagonal with a dome. Converted to a house in 1975, with windows in the former recesses.

S E from the High Street WIMBLEDON HILL ROAD leads down towards the station. Few notable buildings apart from Nos. 100–102, BYRON HOUSE, an unusually handsome stuccoed villa of *c.* 1860; two wings with gables treated as pediments, with a recessed entrance in between with Ionic columns, and a Venetian loggia above. A little way uphill from this on the opposite side, BELVEDERE DRIVE, where No. 1 is by *Ernest George & Yeates*, 1901; a nearly symmetrical Queen Anne front. E from here between St Mary's Road and Lake Road QUEEN ALEXANDRA'S COURT (Royal Homes for Widows and Daughters of Naval and Military Officers), 1904–5, 1908, 1912, by *Ernest George & Yeates* with *C. E. L. Parkinson.* A formal layout of four tall blocks around three sides of a quadrangle. Brick, Georgian sashes, hipped roofs, but the plain stone panels in which the doors are set, with their circular and arched windows above, still with Arts-and-Crafts leanings. They are crowned by little pediments. On the fourth side of the quadrangle balustraded terraces with urns, and a low garden pavilion as centrepiece, with pediment, bold hipped roof, and tall clock tower.

At the send of WIMBLEDON HILL ROAD, BANK BUILDINGS, a tall late Victorian parade in hot pink terracotta with shaped gables. At the opposite end of THE BROADWAY (otherwise a much rebuilt muddle) the WIMBLEDON THEATRE, 1910 by *Cecil Massey* and *Roy Young* with *Frank J. Jones.* One of the few remaining London suburban theatres. Corner entrance with a dome. (Eclectic Adamish interior, unaltered.)

The RIDGWAY, an old road, runs S W from the junction of Wimbledon Hill Road and the High Street. Near this end a few modest late Georgian terraces and cottages, also in the streets off, especially OLDFIELD ROAD; also the Village Hall (*see* Public Buildings). Further on and in the surrounding roads a few remaining examples of substantial later C 19 mansions, and rather more of the compact houses of *c.* 1900 which followed. Several of the first type in THE DOWNS, e.g. No. 17 (Adult Education Centre), *c.* 1890, large and eclectic, with some Gothic detail and a polygonal turret over the entrance. A more original house is No. 13 BERKELEY PLACE, 1894 by *James Ransome*, now sadly hemmed in, a nice, freely detailed building with shaped gable to the road and a side elevation with a large archway. In RIDGWAY No. 54 is by *T. G. Jackson*, 1908, a good example of the quieter Queen Anne style by then fashionable for smaller houses. The streets between Ridgway and South Side are especially rich in such houses.

In LAURISTON ROAD No. 1 is also by *Jackson*, again with details of *c.* 1700: two colours of brick, big dormers, egg and dart below the eaves. No. 6 is by *P. B. Freeman*, unusually of grey brick, with narrow Queen Anne windows, and a projection with canted bay and segmental gable on one side. No. 9 is a very handsome house by *Sir Ernest George*, 1892–4; a long front with wooden mullion-and-transom windows, bracketed eaves below a big hipped roof, and a porch with bulgy balusters, entered from one side. The avoidance of total symmetry is again noticeable. Nos. 15 and 17 are by *Ransome*, with irregular Dutch gables. Before this, HEREFORD HOUSE, a solitary Italianate stucco example from an earlier generation. More in the parallel road, THE GRANGE. This is entered from South Side between two presumptuous turreted mansions of the 1890s, but afterwards smaller houses again predominate. No. 1 is by *Aston Webb*, late C 19, with Dutch features, No. 2 1889 by *E. J. May*, another very attractive, not quite regular composition. Ground floor with mullion-and-transom windows, but upper floor with sashes; a big hipped roof with swept-up eaves and little twin-gabled dormers, an early example of the tentative move towards neo-Georgian motifs. No. 4 is of 1908 by *Hubbard & Moore*, a very successful local firm (*see also* below), roughcast, with their characteristic two large gables with egg and dart frieze, and two-storey bay-windows with tile-hanging. No. 7 is by *Ernest Newton*, a picturesque asymmetrical tile-hung composition with large staircase window, bow-window, and gable. No. 18 on the opposite side is a rum house by *Arthur Cawston*, tall, with an enormous half-hipped roof with two levels of dormers, quite un-English in feeling. Other lesser houses of the same period in LINGFIELD ROAD, e.g. Nos. 42 and 43, with three-bay neo-Georgian fronts. In SOUTH SIDE, No. 4 is of 1900 by *E. J. May*, but too much altered to be enjoyable (window-frames all replaced). Further along South Side some older houses: SOUTH LODGE (No. 7), with a simple brick and stucco front of 1840, and RUSHMERE, an C 18 farmhouse, three-bay front with brick bands, much altered and extended in the C 19.

From the s w end of South Side one can continue to the N along WEST SIDE COMMON. Here there are also Georgian houses on a considerable scale, mostly altered. CHESTER HOUSE (much altered) was built *c.* 1670 and owned in the C 18 by Horne Tooke, who built himself a tomb in the garden. WEST SIDE HOUSE is of the 1760s, two storeys, five bays, hipped roof, and outbuildings. In HANFORD ROW to the w, late C 18 cottages. Then, set back, CANNIZARO HOUSE, named from the Duke of Cannizaro who lived there in the early C 19. Owned in the later C 18 by the politician Henry Dundas,

Viscount Melville, the house was much enlarged in the later
C 19 and rebuilt or repaired after a fire in 1900 in a lavish,
rather Baroque neo-Georgian. Thirteen bays wide, the centre
with two orders of columns and a big pediment. The grounds
laid out in the later C 18 are now a public park. Then STAM-
FORD HOUSE, dated by Cooke 1720. Three storeys, five bays.
Finally THE KEIR, built in 1789, stuccoed, with a Grecian
porch with closed sides. In the grounds the remains of a small
R.C. chapel built in 1838. The surviving parts were the
priest's living quarters. The N continuation of West Side
Common is WEST PLACE, a nice humble, unified early C 19
road. Round the corner CAMP ROAD with a few more houses
and the octagonal William Wilberforce School (q.v.), and
CAMP VIEW, a picturesque terrace in the Norman Shaw
New-Zealand-Chambers manner with wooden upper bay-
windows overlooking the common. (For Caesar's Camp, see
Wimbledon Common, below.) Back now to the S end of this
intrusion into the common to where a delightfully haphazard
collection of C 18 and C 19 cottages along CROOKED BILLET
face a small green.

WOODHAYES ROAD leads SW from here. (SOUTHSIDE
HOUSE has a façade of 1687 incorporating an earlier building,
extended and altered in 1776.) Nos. 2 and 4 are a pair of C 18
five-bay houses, each with a slightly projecting, pedimented
three-bay centre. Brick and rubbed brick. Tuscan doorways.
No. 4 has its original glazing bars. No. 6, called GOTHIC
LODGE, is indeed in Gothick style, with pretty ogee-arched
and crocketed heads to the upper windows. The date 1763 on a
lead pump-head. Original staircase and some chimneypieces.
The house was much enlarged c. 1880–90. Further W, among
later suburban development, one recent house worth a detour:
No. 2a DRAX AVENUE, 1972 by Arup Associates, an elegant
L-shaped composition. Concrete blockwork. Projecting
upper floor. A carport to the road, a secluded raised garden to
the l. A detour to the S can take in LOUIE BLACK HOUSE in
ELM GROVE, a pleasant example of a small housing association scheme by Dry Halasz Dixon Partnership, 1974–7.

The final Wimbledon excursion is along PARKSIDE, along the E
edge of the common towards the borough boundary, where
most of the grander mansions were built in the C 19 and early
C 20. The styles ranged from late classical to Voysey, Lutyens,
and beyond. The sequence is now much depleted, especially
at the N end, where houses have been replaced by mediocre
private and model L.C.C. housing (see Putney (Ww), Perambulation). Starting at the W end of the High Street first an
uncompromising yet discreet interloper, No. 22, 1977 by
Richard Rogers. Two transparent one-storey boxes with yel-
low-painted steel frames, hidden by a mound from the road.
Then several turn-of-the-century houses by Hubbard & Moore
(Nos. 23, 25 (Old Pound House, by Moore), and 28) with
gables or pediments; others include No. 26 by Stanley J. May,
1906, Voyseyish Art and Crafts, and No. 33 by F. Wheeler Son

& Searle, with mullioned bay-windows. Further on, slightly earlier styles: No. 49 (BEECHHOLME), mid C 19, and Nos. 54 and 56, both later C 19. More houses of *c.* 1900 in the roads to the E: see e.g. MARRYAT ROAD and PEEK CRESCENT, especially No. 2 with giant Ionic corner pilasters, and No. 5 (by *Hubbard & Moore*, 1905), with round-headed centrepiece above pilasters. In CALONNE ROAD No. 21 (ROSEMALL) is by *M. H. Baillie Scott*, 1910, gabled and tile-hung, with the obligatory bit of half-timbering in the centre. The later houses in this area of ample winding roads also espouse the Arts and Crafts tradition rather than neo-Georgian. A travesty of the latter style reappears in the terraces of town houses of the 1960s–70s which are depressingly numerous in Wimbledon, e.g. further N in SOMERSET ROAD. The subtleties of fifty years earlier appear to have been entirely ignored. So it is a refreshing change to come upon CEDAR COURT and OAKFIELD, plain staggered terraces in dark brick, and two eleven-storey towers of private flats and some linked three-storey blocks, all by the *Building Design Partnership*, 1966. Architectural details excellent, but layout poor, with too many internal roads. QUEENSMERE, Queensmere Road, further N again, is mid Victorian neo-Tudor. For the G.L.C. housing in this area *see* Putney (Ww), Perambulation.

WIMBLEDON COMMON has few buildings apart from the enclave by West Side Common. The Lords of the Manor, the Spencers, threatened to encroach on it in the C 19, but were prevented by the Commons Preservation Society, confirmed by Act of Parliament in 1871. In WINDMILL ROAD, on the borough boundary off Parkside to the W, a few houses, including HEATHFIELD HOUSE, early C 19, with shallow bow-windows, and MANOR COTTAGE, both stuccoed. Also the early C 19 MILL HOUSE, close to the well-known WIND-MILL, built in 1817–18, altered in 1893 on reconstruction as a landmark. A composite type uncommon in England. It was formerly a hollow postmill with a small body turning on a vertical post encasing a driveshaft to machinery in the round-house below. The post was enclosed in a conical wooden tower. In 1893 the post was removed, the conical tower heightened, and the body made still smaller. Very large two-storeyed octagonal roundhouse (faced in brick in the 1860s on conversion to cottages). Further N the common becomes Putney Heath (*see* Putney, Ww). SW of the windmill is CAESAR'S CAMP, W of Camp Road, a circular Iron Age HILLFORT with a straight section on the N side, and a single ditch and bank; the W entrance may be original. It was reduced in the C 19 by a speculative builder who, for once in Surrey, didn't succeed. Excavations in more recent times have shown that the bank lay behind a ditch 35 ft wide and over 12 ft deep, and faced with timber on both sides. Pottery suggests a first occupation in the C 3 B.C. 600 yds N of Caesar's Camp the QUEENS BUTT, Wimbledon Golf Course, possibly a Neolithic long barrow, but without ditches. Later used as a firing butt.

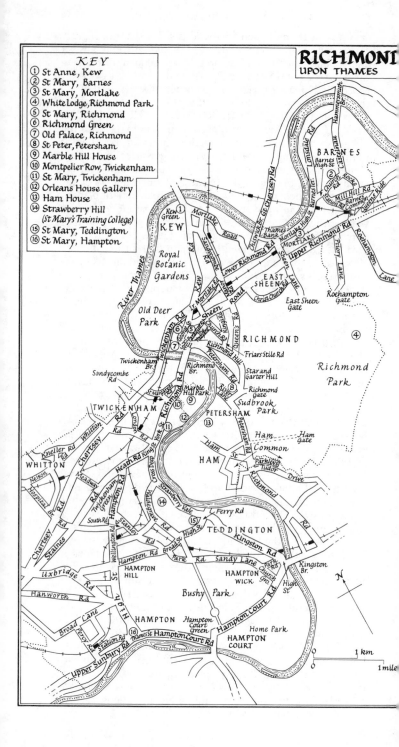

RICHMOND
UPON THAMES

KEY
1. St Anne, Kew
2. St Mary, Barnes
3. St Mary, Mortlake
4. White Lodge, Richmond Park
5. St Mary, Richmond
6. Richmond Green
7. Old Palace, Richmond
8. St Peter, Petersham
9. Marble Hill House
10. Montpelier Row, Twickenham
11. St Mary, Twickenham
12. Orleans House Gallery
13. Ham House
14. Strawberry Hill
    (St Mary's Training College)
15. St Mary, Teddington
16. St Mary, Hampton

RICHMOND UPON THAMES

INTRODUCTION

No other London borough except Westminster has a greater wealth of major palaces and mansions than Richmond upon Thames, created in 1965 from the Surrey Boroughs of Barnes and Richmond and the Middlesex Borough of Twickenham. The two areas have indeed long been linked socially and geographically by the Thames, a major thoroughfare from early on, when it bore the medieval kings to their palace at Sheen, then the Tudor monarchs to Hampton Court. The riverside park at Richmond attracted the Hanoverians, and the picturesque Thames scenery invited not only C18 aristocrats, but businessmen, literati, and artists, to build their villas along its banks. Pope laid out his famous gardens at Twickenham, Garrick built a house (which still survives) further upstream at Hampton, Thomas Gainsborough is buried at Kew, James Thomson, George Thomson Sen., and Sir Joshua Reynolds lived in Richmond, to mention only a few names. Enough remains still to convey an impression of that time portrayed in the letters which Horace Walpole wrote from Strawberry Hill at Twickenham, when Georgian high society divided its time between the mansions on the Twickenham riverside, the social gatherings in the town of Richmond, and the great houses of the more secluded villages of Ham and Petersham.

Evidence for earlier ages is now thin. The river attracted prehistoric settlement,* and there were medieval villages with their own churches at Barnes, Mortlake, Twickenham, Teddington, and Hampton, although little more than a few church towers remain to show this.

By the end of the Middle Ages RICHMOND, or Sheen, as it was then known, was the most important centre. It grew around Sheen Palace, one of the most favoured royal palaces under Edward III, who died there, and Richard II, who ordered it to be demolished after his Queen, Anne of Bohemia, died there, then under Henry V, who rebuilt it, then under Henry VII, who rebuilt it again after a disastrous fire in 1497 and called it Richmond Palace after his own title. Queen Elizabeth I died at Richmond Palace, and Henry Prince of Wales as well as Charles I as Prince of Wales lived there. Charles I enclosed Richmond Park, the 'New Park', as a royal hunting ground. During the Commonwealth all the main buildings of the palace were demolished, and what was left of subsidiary buildings was leased out to various tenants, by whom some parts were restored, some neglected, and some rebuilt. Plans for its restoration by *Wren* in the 1680s for James II were interrupted by the King's departure in 1688; but most of the surviving buildings had remained in the hands of tenants. By the early C18 these buildings were being altered and rebuilt as private houses for court officials, attracted to Richmond by the residences of the royal family in and near the Home Park further N (*see* Kew, Introduction to Royal Botanic Gardens).

The appearance of the Tudor palace is known superficially from Wyngaerde's drawings of 1562, Hollar's engravings of 1638, and other illustrations. On the internal planning a description by Lancaster Herald of 1502 and the Parliamentary Survey of 1649 help, but only a little. Next to nothing is known of the architectural details, tellingly compared by John Aubrey to those of Henry VII's chapel at Westminster. All this is highly frustrating because the scanty evidence suggests that Henry VII's Richmond was an early and influential example of those show Tudor palaces of which the Duke of Buckingham's Thornbury Castle is a reflection, and Henry VIII's Hampton Court a later flowering. The palace had three courts, with a gateway to

---

* PREHISTORIC SITES: finds from Ham Fields; an important Neolithic site at Twickenham; an axe hoard at Teddington; possible Bronze Age burials in Richmond Park; Roman burials at Barnes, indicate the importance of the area.

Richmond Green, a side gate by the kitchen premises, and an entrance from the river. Closest to the river was the almost square block of the privy lodgings, three-storeyed around a 14 small central court, with tiers of mullioned windows in polygonal projections (cf. Thornbury) and a picturesque skyline with ornamental chimneys and fourteen turrets capped with little lead cupolas with wind vanes (cf. Hampton Court). On the NE side, away from the river, was a large four-storeyed staircase tower, and beyond this lay the middle court, 66 ft square, with two-storeyed galleries (built or rebuilt by *Inigo Jones*) on the SW, the hall on the NW, the chapel (above an undercroft) on the SE, and the 'Middle Gate' building on the NE side, leading into the outer or base court. The hall had a roof with pendants, and a central hearth (cf. the earlier hall at Eltham Palace (Gr) and the later Hampton Court). Attached to the hall was a clock tower, and beyond it, to the NW, was an extensive range of kitchen buildings, pantries, and other domestic offices. The principal kitchen had a large octagonal pointed roof which shows clearly in the old prints. The outer courtyard was 200 ft square, surrounded by two-storeyed brick buildings, of which something survives (see Perambulation 1). To the SE Wyngaerde shows a garden enclosed by two-storeyed galleries (cf. Thornbury and Hampton Court). On the other side of the privy lodgings, between the kitchens and the river, was a large walled orchard. The Green was the jousting place outside the palace gates. The original small park lay in a triangle between the river and the NW side of the palace and the green. It was incorporated, with much of the demesne land of the manor (and a small part of the common fields), into a larger park (now the Old Deer Park and the western part of Kew Gardens, q.v. Kew) by James I at the beginning of his reign. On a part of the demesne land, close to the river N of the palace, Henry V had founded a Carthusian monastery in 1417 (at the same time as the Bridgettine house across the river, *see* Syon Park, Ho). Its remains and those of subsequent mansions on the site were cleared away for a new palace projected by George III, but this was hardly started before it was abandoned, the only completed building being the Observatory in what is now the Old Deer Park. Another religious house, the Observant Friars, was established by Henry VII in 1501 in the palace grounds. Its chapel was probably the building shown by Wyngaerde to the S of the gardens.

Although occupation of the palace ceased in the later C17, royal interest in Richmond revived with the Hanoverians, beginning with the use of Ormonde Lodge in the Old Deer Park by the Prince of Wales from 1719 (*see* Kew, Royal Botanic Gardens, Introduction). The progress of Richmond's development as a fashionable town is shown in Overton and Hook's delightful panorama of 1726 called 'The Prospect of Richmond'. By then the buildings of the Tudor palace had been reduced to little more than the outer court, and were eclipsed by neat brick terraces facing the Green: Maids of Honour Row, just completed, and 57 Old Palace Terrace of 1692 (one of the first of its type outside

London). The street later called George Street was already built up, with scattered houses continuing along Sheen Road to the E. Others dotted the slopes above the church, and quite a lot of buildings already stood beside the riverside road to Petersham and on the slope of Richmond Hill, towards the new park enclosed by Charles I. Plenty of handsome early C18 houses remain, e.g. in the streets off Richmond Hill, to give an impression of those years. Later Georgian houses followed on the fringes, exploiting the views of the river: notable examples are
67 *Taylor*'s Asgill House by the river (1757) and the houses of the 1770s at the top of Richmond Hill by *Chambers* and *Mylne*, villas now rather than terrace houses (although an accomplished, very urban house possibly by *Taylor* on The Terrace, Richmond Hill, also dates from this time). As one might expect, the parish church was rebuilt in the C18; there was a concert hall on the
68 Green by 1722, a theatre in 1766. The bridge over the river replaced the ferry in 1774–7 and linked Richmond with equally fashionable Twickenham.

With such riches of the C18, later architectural contributions tend to be overlooked or unappreciated. Richmond was a favourite place for excursions in the C19. The railway came in 1846. The Victorians provided new hotels, by or overlooking the river, including an ambitious one by *John Giles*, which stands close to the delightful Terrace Gardens laid out by the local authority in 1887. By then the town had expanded: Lower Richmond around Kew Road with its own church (St John, by *Vulliamy*, 1831) was quite a populous suburb, although this area was fragmented by the building of the 1930s bypass. Better preserved are the more modest stuccoed terraces which filled the lower ground around Sheen Road, giving way to villas further out where they are interspersed with the inevitable almshouses on the urban fringe (of 1757, 1842, 1853, etc.). The eastern slopes of the hill were filled by larger, respectable suburban villas of the 1850s (some survivals e.g. in Queen's Road), around *Scott*'s imposing new church of St Matthias (1857). The population of Richmond was in 1801 4,628; 1841 7,760; 1861 10,962; 1881 19,066. The area became a Borough in 1890 (including Kew, Petersham, and part of Mortlake). Early municipal efforts were enterprising: they included the first library in outer London (1879–81), and some of the earliest council housing (Manor Grove, begun 1894). A flamboyant new theatre appeared on the Green in 1899 (by *Matcham*), but apart from this and the commercial development of George Street (continued, with little distinction, in the C20), the older parts of the town centre were left largely unspoilt. Since the Second World War vacillating official policies on this area have been responsible for decay and demolition of some good houses (most notoriously on the river front by the bridge), although local vigilance has prevented further disasters. There have been some noteworthy restorations (that of Asgill House the most outstanding), and some imaginative church conversions (St John, St Matthias).

The development of other places in the parts of the borough E

of the river can be traced more briefly. The history of KEW is
intimately bound up with that of Richmond. It began as a
riverside settlement by the ferry to Brentford (replaced by a
bridge in the C 18), and flourished especially when the green
became the prelude to the royal residences in what is now Kew
Gardens (for these *see* Royal Botanic Gardens, Introduction).
Only the C 18 garden buildings from this time survive, but Kew
itself still has its church, begun as a chapel in 1710, and the
spacious green retains a comfortable, informal Georgian atmos-   4
phere despite the main road running through it. Even before the
C 18 the area was a favoured one for country residences, as is
shown by the house later called Kew Palace now within the   24
gardens which was built for a London merchant, one of the best
examples of the 'artisan' style of the London bricklayers in the
1630s. Further downstream other major houses have disappeared, notably Sir Francis Walsingham's Barn Elms, but the
attractions of the riverside are still illustrated by the Georgian
terraces of Barnes and Mortlake, modest versions of what one
can find at Chiswick across the river. Both BARNES and MORT-
LAKE are now engulfed by developments of the C 19 onwards,
although they have kept more of their pre-Victorian character
than the former villages of Putney and Battersea (Ww) closer to
London. The neighbourhood of Barnes Green is still specially
pleasant. Mortlake became an industrial centre already in the
C 17, with Sir Francis Crane's short-lived tapestry works established in 1619. Inland, EAST SHEEN (the counterpart to West
Sheen alias Richmond) remained a tiny settlement on the edge of
Sheen Common, with some wealthier houses growing up on the
fringes of Richmond Park.

The stretches between these old centres, filled up from the
C 19 onwards, have little to single out. Worthy of note are the
elegantly Italianate villas of the Castelnau area of Barnes (by
Laxton, from 1842), the large, romantically picturesque houses
of the late C 19 onwards at East Sheen (by *Collcutt*, *Ingress Bell*
and others), and the railway stations at Barnes and Kew Gardens. By far the most exciting C 19 buildings are those at Kew for
the Royal Botanic Gardens, beginning with *Burton* and *Turner's*
magnificent Palm House of 1844–8. The later C 20 can offer only   78
the impressive but much less lovable Public Record Office of
1973–7, and some pleasing minor contributions such as the
Sheen Lane Centre.

W of Richmond Park and S of Richmond Hill lies the most
secluded part of Richmond, deceptively rural because of the
continuous stretch of Richmond Park, Sudbrook Park, and
HAM COMMON. The focus here is another great mansion by the
river, Ham House, begun in the early C 17, but with much of the
1630s and 1670s, when it belonged to the Lauderdales. It can be   27
approached from Ham Common which, like Kew Green, is
charmingly fringed by predominantly C 18 buildings. Further N,
near the other entrance to Ham House, is the little village of
PETERSHAM, still with its medieval and Georgian church, and   49
with a group of excellent stately detached brick houses of the late

C 17 onwards, mostly lying quite close to the road. The grandest
61 mansion remaining in this area is *Gibbs*'s Sudbrook Park of
1726, standing in its own grounds. The aristocratic atmosphere
is surprisingly little disturbed by Victorian or Edwardian developments (although the eccentric All Saints Petersham should
not be missed), or by the quite extensive housing built after the
Second World War, which is (with a few exceptions) discreetly
sited, and not without interest. Highlights from the 1950s are
the quiet and cheerful groups by *Eric Lyons*, and the very
104 different early brutalist Langham House Close by *Stirling &
Gowan*, each influential in their own way (all at Ham); from the
1960s a pair of houses by *Leonard Manasseh*, from the 1970s an
attractive one-storeyed group by *Manning & Clamp* (both at
Petersham).

The w side of the Thames is without the unmatched landscape
of Richmond Hill and Richmond Park, and (with the important
exception of Hampton Court and its parks) has been more
intensively built over in the c 19 and c 20. Architectural interest
5 is therefore largely confined to stretches by the river. At T W I C K -
E N H A M the centre of what was the village has suffered badly,
first from unfeeling development, then from thoughtless demolition of the small-scale buildings that remained close to the
river. But a memorable aristocratic stretch lies to the E, near the
50 church (a fine rebuilding by *John James* of 1714–15). The houses
range in style from the mid c 17 York House to *James Gibbs*'s
small but splendid Baroque Octagon, all that remains of Orleans
House, which stands close to one of the first of the c 18 English
60 Palladian villas, *Roger Morris*'s Marble Hill, now restored to its
pristine elegance, in its own park close to the river. In between
are handsome examples (Montpelier Row, Syon Row) of the
type of brick terraces becoming fashionable by the early c 18 (cf.
Richmond). Upstream the Georgian scene is more fragmentary;
Pope's villa has gone, and Walpole's delightful Gothic Straw-
63 berry Hill, although excellently preserved, lies hidden within
64 the grounds of a college. Away from the river other c 18 houses
have vanished, for example at the former hamlet of W H I T T O N,
where Sir Godfrey Kneller had a villa, and *Morris* built Whitton
Park for the Earl of Ilay, a house later owned by Chambers. A
few former rural havens survive amid suburbia, including the
charming house which the artist *Turner* built for himself at East
Twickenham. This part of Twickenham is indeed a good hunting ground for suburban types, starting with the 1820s villas
built by *Lloyd* on the Twickenham Park estate, and continuing
with the denser streets of solid Gothic houses of the mid c 19.
Twickenham Green to the w, although with its own church from
1839 (by *Basevi*), grew more slowly; the main interest here is
c 20, some of *Eric Lyons*'s earliest Span estates of the 1950s (as
well as more recent ones) (cf. Ham and Blackheath Park, Gr).
The only other c 20 buildings that need be noted specially are
108 two churches: St Margaret East Twickenham, a distinguished
modern design by *Williams & Winkley* (1968), and All Hallows,
built for the growing suburb around the new Chertsey Road in

1939 by *Robert Atkinson*, incorporating the tower and the splendid furnishings from *Wren*'s All Hallows, Lombard Street, a notable piece of rescue work for its date.

Continuing upstream, TEDDINGTON is a disappointment after Twickenham, with little apart from the tiny, mostly C18 church as a reminder of its earlier history. The larger C18 houses have been replaced by indifferent industrial and commercial development as well as suburbia. The exception is Bushy House (1660s and later) on the edge of Bushy Park, one of the extensive parks insulating Hampton Court from the surrounding villages. The history of HAMPTON COURT is too well known to be repeated here. The parks, as well as its decline as a royal residence in the C18 in favour of Richmond, explain why the neighbourhood is less densely populated with C18 mansions than other riverside areas. Minor C18 work can be found along Hampton Court Road, and rather more at Hampton Court Green, where the houses of royal officials were built at the entrance to the palace. Hampton itself, further E, retained its identity as a separate village, and still has a good number of lesser houses of the C17 onwards, most notably Garrick's villa, with its little Shakespeare temple by the river. Similar minor C18 houses grew up along the river at HAMPTON WICK, a hamlet which obtained its own church only in 1829 (by *Lapidge*, who also rebuilt the church at Hampton). Of the later buildings in this area the most spectacular are the ambitious church of St Alban at Teddington (by *Niven*, 1889) and the extensive Hampton waterworks of 1853 onwards.

The population of the whole borough was 180,200 in 1966, 159,693 in 1981. The local authority has not made its presence felt as obviously as in some other boroughs (which has its good and its bad side). The Borough Architects since 1965 have been *H. S. Gardiner* (1965–9) and *M. J. C. Edwards* (from 1969).

Further Reading

There are plenty of popular guides, but no comprehensive account of the immense architectural riches of this borough. The revised DOE list is not yet available at the time of writing. By far the most useful of recent books are *Images of Richmond* by B. Gascoigne (1978) and *Images of Twickenham* by B. Gascoigne and J. Ditchburn (1981), which are copiously illustrated catalogues of topographical prints with informative historical introductions. An older source is R. S. Cobbett, *Memorial of Twickenham* 1872). Richmond Library has published notes on buildings by the Richmond and Twickenham riverside. On a few individual buildings thorough recent studies exist: M. P. G. Draper and W. A. Eden, *Marble Hill House* (1970); P. K. Thornton and M. F. Tomlin, *The Furnishings and Decoration of Ham House* (1980); P. Foster and E. S. Pyatt, *Bushy House* (1976). For Hampton Court there are the volumes of the *King's Works* (*see* p. 127), but the C19 works by E. F. Law are still useful.

Acknowledgements

In view of the inadequacies indicated above, I am particularly indebted to the many people who have allowed me to make use of their unpublished research. On Hampton Court I had the benefit of help and advice from Miss Juliet Allan of the Inspectorate of Ancient Monuments, and from the knowledgeable local historian Mr Gerald Heath; I am also grateful to Mr H. M. Colvin for letting me see prior to publication the text on Hampton Court in vol. IV of *The King's Works*. Mr Heath also provided me with much information on Hampton. Mr John Cloake was very helpful over Richmond Palace, likewise Mr Fred Hauptfuhrer over Asgill House and Mr Maurice Tomlin of the Victoria and Albert Museum over Ham House. Mr Michael Snodin and Mr Clive Wainwright, also of the V and A, gave me the benefit of their recent research on Strawberry Hill. Mr Paul Velluet (P V) of the Richmond Society supplied me with copious notes on the buildings of the town, Mr G. E. Cassidy provided information on Kew. Miss Diana Howard, Principal Reference Librarian of the Borough Library, answered numerous queries, and Mr Graham King of the borough's Department of Technical Services (DTS) provided me with much detail on both old and new buildings all over the borough.

BARNES

The area to visit in Barnes lies just W of the S end of Castelnau – Church Road, with the church, and on to Barnes Green and Barnes Terrace by the river.

HOLY TRINITY, Castelnau. By *Thomas Allom*, 1868.*
Coursed ragstone, in a free Dec, a turret to the l. of the W gable. Adjacent VICARAGE (No. 162), austere stock brick, red brick trim (unlike the rest of Castelnau).

ST MARY, Church Road. Gutted by fire in 1978. Only the outer walls survived, making complete rebuilding necessary. The W tower, brick, of the Thames valley type of the C 16 and C 17, remains, with a turret on the S side; also the medieval chancel (which later became the E end of the S aisle). In its E wall three C 13 stepped lancets below a vesica window. In the S wall of the former nave a blocked Norman doorway was discovered after the fire. In 1980 it was decided to replace the later additions (nave, chancel, and N aisle of 1904–8 by *Charles Innes*) by a radical new building by *Edward Cullinan*, retaining the medieval form when seen from the S, but housing the altar in a N wing projecting from the old church.‡ – CHURCHYARD with good C 18 and C 19 tombs.

---

* Information from Mr R. C. Gill.

‡ Destroyed in the fire: S aisle window by *Wailes* 1853. Badly damaged: two small brasses to the young girls of the Wyld family † 1787, and the monument to Sir Richard Hoare of Barn Elms † 1787, a seated mourning woman and child by an urn, by *J. Hickey*.

(ST MICHAEL, Elm Bank Gardens, off Barnes Terrace. By *Charles Innes*, 1891–3.*)

ST OSMUND (R.C.), Castelnau. 1958 by *Ronald Hardy* (DE). Brick, with a large plain pointed w window.

METHODIST CHURCH, Station Road. 1906, conventional Dec, red brick on an ambitious scale. Unfinished sw tower.

ST PAUL'S SCHOOL, Lonsdale Road. Founded by Dean Colet in 1509, moved to Barnes in 1969. By *Feilden & Mawson* (in charge *B. Feilden* and *R. Thompson*), 1966–8, a large, low, industrialized structure (CLASP Mark IV) by the river. (SOUTH AFRICAN WAR MEMORIAL. Elegant tempietto of Portland stone with ribbed copper dome, 1906 by *F. S. Chesterton*. JOHN COLET MEMORIAL. Bronze group of Dean Colet and two kneeling scholars by *Hamo Thornycroft*, below an open bronze canopy, 1902. One of Thornycroft's most appealing works. Brought from the school's former home in West Kensington. PV)

BARN ELMS WATERWORKS, E of Castelnau. Established by the West Middlesex Water Company in 1838, initially with two settlement reservoirs.

BARNES STATION. An engaging small Tudor building on the edge of the common; red brick with diapering, very tall chimneys. 1846 by *Tite*, one of the earliest station buildings remaining in Greater London.

HAMMERSMITH BRIDGE, BARNES RAILWAY BRIDGE. *See* Thames Crossings at end of gazetteer.

PERAMBULATION To the E of the church is HOMESTEAD HOUSE, early C18, five bays, two storeys, modillioned eaves cornice, yellow and red brick. Weatherboarded wing to the l. In front of the house a good iron gate and a row of pollarded lime trees. To the w STRAWBERRY HOUSE (formerly the rectory), early C18, with added second floor and parapet. Plain exterior, but a good staircase with three twisted balusters to each tread and carved tread-ends. Further w facing BARNES GREEN, THE GRANGE, also early C18, but altered and added to. Good early C19 railings and overthrow. To its l. the CONVENT OF THE SACRED HEART, partly C18 and partly Early Victorian Tudor Gothic. On BARNES GREEN, close to the pond, a former village school of 1850 (now day centre) with pretty bargeboards. BARCLAYS BANK lies opposite in Church Road, two-thirds of a towering Edwardian Wrenaissance frontage, the start of redevelopment that one is grateful did not proceed further. To the w there are still some small cottages, then in STATION ROAD, facing the green, first a low stuccoed villa with pedimented windows (now health centre), then MILBOURNE HOUSE, with an irregular C18 front but older behind. Inside an Elizabethan or Jacobean fireplace in the entrance hall (not *in situ*) and the remains of a Jacobean staircase. Further s, off Station Road in WILLOW AVENUE, No. 14, approached by a bridge over Beverley

---

* Information from Mr R. C. Gill.

Brook, a small single-storey house by *Timothy Rendle*, 1967–8, of brick and timber, with an emphatic horizontal roof-line. No window to the road. At the corner of Station Road and MILL HILL ROAD, THE CEDARS, late C18, with later roughcast Doric porch. BARNES COMMON begins here, a pleasantly informal area of trees and scrub, although too much broken up by roads. Off Mill Hill Road further E an island of houses including some weatherboarding. At the boundary with Putney Common a one-storey early C19 TOLL HOUSE

BARNES HIGH STREET continues W from Barnes Green, with little of interest until one reaches BARNES TERRACE with its pleasant stretches of houses lying alongside the river: Nos. 3–14 and 28–31, all C18, and mostly with cheerful iron verandas or balconies. Especially handsome No. 3 with a Tuscan porch and a balcony with wooden trelliswork over, and No. 7 with a very broad bow.* No. 11a, a former factory site, has houses in Georgian style, 1981–2 by *E. Hill* (DTS). At the W end THE WHITE HART, a jolly turn-of-the-century pub with corner turret.

CASTELNAU was developed after the opening of Hammersmith Bridge in 1827. It has much friendly, remarkably standardized early Victorian villa architecture, mostly semi-detached with typical arched windows with continuous mouldings. The estate was designed by *William Laxton*, from 1842, for the Boileau family of Castelnau House. The public house called THE BOILEAU is in the same style. It lies in a good position at the junction with Lonsdale Road. Tuscan porch.

In DYERS LANE N of Upper Richmond Road, pleasantly laid out low red brick houses and flats by *Richmond upon Thames DTS* (*James Wood, Carlos Pyres*), 1978.

BARN ELMS, the mansion of Sir Francis Walsingham, Secretary of State to Queen Elizabeth from 1579 to his death in 1590, was rebuilt by Thomas Cartwright in 1694, remodelled by Richard Hoare in 1771, and demolished in 1954. It stood E of Rocks Lane, near the river. Nothing remains, except the ornamental pond and the ICE HOUSE on an artificial mound into which its pit extended, and a LODGE and AVENUE in Lower Richmond Road. The area which was famous as that of the Ranelagh Polo Club has been converted into an L.C.C. playing area with CHANGING ACCOMMODATION, etc., in the excellent L.C.C. style of the 1950s.

EAST SHEEN

ALL SAINTS, East Sheen Avenue, E of Sheen Lane. 1929 by *Newberry & Fowler* (R. C. Gill). Red brick, with lancet windows and a flèche. (Rebuilt after destruction by fire, 1965.)

CHRIST CHURCH, Christ Church Road. 1862–4 by *Sir Arthur Blomfield*. Stone. SE tower with pyramid roof, which collapsed

* The river view has been regrettably obscured by the flood defences built in the 1970s.

the day after it was completed, and had to be rebuilt. Cross-gabled s aisle. Plate tracery. N aisle of 1887.

(ST PHILIP, Marksbury Avenue, E of Sandycombe Road, North Sheen. 1928–9 by *Edward A. Swan*, insignificant outside but with a genuine C16 timber interior, bodily removed from Woodhall Farm, Oxted, Surrey.)

(EAST SHEEN CEMETERY, Sheen Road. Small Gothic chapel with flèche, by *Reginald Rowell*, 1903. One outstanding MONUMENT, the Lancaster tomb (1920), with magnificent bronze angel. HM)

SHEEN LANE CENTRE. 1976–8 by the *Haworth King Partnership*. Attractive, enterprising mixture of public and commercial buildings around an irregular pedestrian square, ranging in height from the one-storey LIBRARY and DAY CENTRE on the l. to the two-storey HEALTH CENTRE and three-storey offices on the r. Unifying details in the idiom of the mid seventies; mottled red brick, canted angles, and sloping roof-lines, neatly echoed by the hard landscaping.

What is worth looking at lies mainly in the roads around the N edge of SHEEN COMMON. In SHEEN LANE, No. 173 is the former stables of Sheen House (demolished 1907), symmetrical, yellow brick, seven bays with clock turret. 1788 (rain-water heard). The chief pre-Victorian survival is in CHRIST CHURCH ROAD: PERCY LODGE, mid Georgian, of three bays, with Venetian windows (wooden mullions). Big bow-window to the garden. In the principal living room a good mid Georgian fireplace. Good gatepiers and wrought-iron gates. The house and grounds owe much to the careful restoration in the 1920s by *Robert Atkinson*, whose home it was. (THE MALL, in the former grounds, has houses designed by *Atkinson* in 1924. DTS) To the r. of Percy Lodge WEST LODGE, the former stables of Percy Lodge. Opposite, MERTON COTTAGE, brick, with a double gable and segment-headed windows, early C18, and some minor cottages. A little further NW early C19 iron GATES, perhaps brought from elsewhere, to the former Sheen Wood.

In the Late Victorian decades a number of big houses were built at East Sheen by architects such as Collcutt, Aston Webb, and Ingress Bell. They have now nearly all been replaced by more modest C20 detached villas. There are two major survivors. First OAKDENE, No. 105 Christ Church Road, by *T. E. Collcutt*, 1884, in the picturesque old English style. A long wing with close-set half timbering over brick; clustered chimneystack. Then LONGFIELD, off Christ Church Road, by *Ingress Bell*, illustrated in 1879. Two tile-hung gables of different sizes and mullioned windows. Off to the s in FIFE ROAD, THE HALSTEADS by *A. W. Blomfield*, 1868, one of the first houses in England to be built of concrete. The contractor was *Joseph Tall*, the inventor of standardized concrete shuttering. Gabled, stuccoed exterior, somewhat altered. In Fife Road also early C20 houses in a wide variety of styles, see e.g. THE ANGLES, with butterfly wings and tile-hanging; and, especially large, SHEEN GATE at the corner of Sheen Lane, half-timbered, by *Sydney E. Castle*, 1924, additions 1935.* In its grounds, INWOOD by *Garner, Preston & Strebel*, with a dramatic broken gable, 1979–80. THE RED HOUSE, at the corner of Sheen Lane and Richmond Park Road, is of 1904 by *Arthur Young*, formal early Georgian, with a central arched window over the porch, but a weatherboarded bay on the side elevation.

(Further N, off ST LEONARD'S ROAD, an attractive group of mid C19 stock brick cottages, served by a central footpath. DTS)

HAM

The chief interest of Ham is Ham House, which lies away from the main road, close to the river. Ham Common, ½ m. to its S, on the fringe of Richmond Park, was a sufficiently aristocratic neighbourhood to attract some wealthy Georgian houses, and remains especially attractive.

ST ANDREW, Church Road, N of Parkleys. 1830–1 by *E. Lapidge*, with a dull S aisle (with rose window) of 1860 by *R. Brandon* and a chancel by *Bodley & Garner*, 1900–1. Lapidge's work is of grey brick, Bodley's of red. Lapidge's front has two polygonal turrets, incorrectly detailed, and lancet-shaped Perp two-light windows.

PERAMBULATION. In the neighbourhood of the common a variety of interesting and enjoyable buildings, old and new. To the E of Petersham Road HAM GATE AVENUE, with SUDBROOK LODGE, late C17, of five bays and two and a half storeys with hipped roof, and then ORMELEY LODGE, an exquisite early C18 house of five bays and two and a half storeys, the five-bay width composed in a nice rhythm with a narrow central bay in red rubbed brick. Slender segment-headed windows. At the angles giant pilasters. Beautiful doorway with Corinthian pilasters and a frieze carved with cherubs' heads and palm leaves. The windows above the door-way singled out by brick ears and an apron. Lower wings. Out-standingly fine wrought-iron gatepiers, gates, and railings. Through the doorway one enters at once the staircase hall, which cuts through the house to the garden entrance. The staircase has delicate balusters, for each step two twisted and one ornamentally turned, and carved tread-ends. Continuing to the E towards the Ham Gate of Richmond Park (*see* Rich-mond, Perambulation 5), the last house on the r. is PARK GATE HOUSE, of yellow brick, 1768, three storeys with lower wings, rusticated ground floor. Pedimented stables. In LATCHMERE LANE to the S, pleasant borough housing by *Brewer, Smith & Brewer*, 1972 (DTS).

* Also by *Sydney E. Castle*, 300 houses on the Barker Estate near North Sheen station (i.e. part of Clifford Avenue, Warren Avenue, etc.), 1923–8; No. 33 Fife Road, 1923–4; and No. 46 Sheen Common Drive (Little Heath), 1922–4, a pleasant, less flamboyant design.

Then to the w of Petersham Road, HAM COMMON, N side: first SOUTH LODGE, built in 1862–72 as the National Orphan Home for Girls. Yellow brick, late classical, with a central turret in the Italianate style. Tall centre and lower wings. Then ORFORD HALL, early C18, with later wings, and after that the two lodges to Ham House, three bays, the middle one projecting and crowned by a Dutch gable. Then SELBY HOUSE, of five bays and two and a half storeys, red and rubbed brick. Arched ground-floor windows, parapet.

In HAM STREET, leading N from the common, on the w side, Nos. 57 and 59, two excellent, crisply designed, one-storeyed flat-roofed houses of 1952–4 by *Stefan Buzas*. Off to the E in SANDPITS ROAD a terrace of five houses by *Eric Lyons*, 1955, yellow brick and tile-hung, as precisely and attractively drawn as his Parkleys Estate (*see* below). In SANDY LANE a modern house by *M. Howard-Radley*, 1957, rather outré, with an overhanging weatherboarded upper storey of trapezoidal section, and another more recent one by *Colin Stansfield-Smith*.

Then back to Ham Street and into the past with BEAUFORT HOUSE, C18, GREY COURT, late C18, pedimented, and then, behind long walls with brick piers and stone vases, the MANOR HOUSE, yellow and red brick, earlier C18, the wings rebuilt. Three-bay pediment. (Additions on the garden side 1908 by *J. Compton-Hall*. Houses in the grounds 1980–1 by *Colin Bottomley*.) After that the grounds of Ham House.

HAM COMMON, w side. From N to s: ENDSLEIGH LODGE, a cottage of *c.* 1800, with lower wings with a double-curved top to reach the walls of the cottage, and two solid wood fanlights. GORDON HOUSE is C18, of five bays, grey brick, with canted bays in the two end elevations. Then some cottages, and after that FORBES HOUSE, by *Oswald P. Milne*, 1936, an unusually good piece of neo-Georgian design. LANGHAM HOUSE is again C18, simple, of grey brick, with Tuscan porch; below it LANGHAM HOUSE CLOSE, by *Stirling & Gowan*, 1958, a landmark in the emerging style of the late 1950s in England, in reaction against all-glass façades and thin, precise detailing: two- and three-storey with exposed concrete floors, a lot of yellow brick, and thick white-painted trim to the windows. Finally, CASSEL HOUSE, early C19 and especially good. Five bays and broad one-bay wings with tripartite windows with fan-lunettes. Roman Doric porch. Arched ground-floor windows. Nice entrance hall with at its back the staircase curving up in a bow. Thin iron balustrade. 104

Further E by the river, RIVERSIDE, a large, dull Wates estate of 1961–8. In the centre shops and flats by *M. McQuisten* of *Wates*; church and school by *Covell, Matthews & Partners*.

PARKLEYS, E of Upper Ham Road. 1953–6, the largest of *Eric Lyons*'s excellent early SPAN ESTATES, cf. Twickenham (Ri), Blackheath Park, Greenwich (Gr). 169 flats and six shops, in two- and three-storeyed blocks, all crisply and quite light-heartedly treated. The shopping terrace faces Upper Ham Road, its middle floor projecting, with a band of balconies.

Behind, two-storeyed terraces grouped in closes with vistas through (cf. The Priory, Blackheath Park), and small H-shaped three-storeyed blocks all of the same plan. Centre with glazed front reached by a long narrow canopied passage. Lobby and staircase behind the glass wall. In each wing two flats on each floor. All flat-roofed, the cladding materials a pleasant mixture of yellow brick, tile-hanging, and odd coloured surfaces. Opposite, the huge reactionary brick and stone front to the HAWKER AIRCRAFT COMPANY, by *Sir Hubert Worthington* and *Norman & Dawbarn*, 1958. The style was an odd choice to house the manufacture of modern jet aircraft. Close to Parkleys, in HAM FARM ROAD, a good house by *L. Gooday*, 1956, with a low roof of uneven pitch.

HAM HOUSE, ½ m. N of Ham Common. One of the largest early C17 houses remaining in the Greater London area, externally perhaps not as attractive as other houses of this period, but internally of high architectural and decorative interest. The present approach from Ham Street is not right. The approach laid out in the 1670s was by two avenues, one from the E, from Petersham Road (*see* Petersham), and one from the S from Ham Common (*see* above). Their lodges remain. The avenues meet on the axis of the formal gardens to the S of the house. The three gateways on the S front (two with original gates) date from 1675–6. They are based on the N gateway (*see* below).

The main entrance is from the N. Forecourt with side walls decorated with niches for busts. The gatepiers to the river Thames (across which, at Twickenham, Marble Hill is, and Orleans House was, visible) were designed by the architect *William Bruce* in 1671. Original gates. In the middle of the forecourt a *Coade* stone figure of Father Thames by *John Bacon*.[*]

The plan of the house is roughly an oblong, with two wings projecting not quite at the end, to the N. But this is not the original scheme. The house as first built by Sir Thomas Vavasour in 1610 had, as we know from one of John Smythson's drawings, an H-plan of the usual Elizabethan and Jacobean type. About 1630 it came into the hands of William Murray, first Earl of Dysart, who was responsible for some remarkable internal alterations in 1637–8. But Ham is equally notable for the additions and refurbishings made for his daughter, the Countess of Dysart, and her husband the Duke of Lauderdale, in 1672–4. They consulted *William Bruce* (cf. above; a cousin of the Countess), but the work was carried out by *William Samwell*, one of the less well-known of those gentlemen-amateurs of the generation of Pratt and May. He filled in the space between the S arms of the Jacobean H-plan house and lengthened the S front a little at either end. The work undertaken in both the 1630s and the 1670s is unusually well-documented.

EXTERIOR. Much of the carcase of the building is Vava-

* For another cast *see* Terrace Gardens, Richmond, Perambulation 4.

sour's, but with alterations of 1672–4 and the C 18. It is of brick with stone dressings, three storeys high, with a hipped roof. The five-bay centre of the N front is twice recessed. The first step is of two bays' depth and one bay width, open on the ground floor in arches. Originally there were turrets here, ending in ogee caps. The second, outer step has at its front a canted bay-window. The principal doorway in the middle, with attached Tuscan columns and a metope frieze, is not a specially impressive piece. Originally it was the entrance to a square porch continued above by a two-storeyed bay. Windows of the cross type, except for the canted bays, where they have been given C 18 shapes. In the C 17 they were mullioned and transomed. Busts were placed in oval niches below the first-floor windows when the front sections of the forecourt wall, from which they came, were demolished c. 1800. The S front is entirely *Samwell*'s plain regular composition of 1673–5, except for the canted bay-windows of the H-wings of 1610 and the Venetian windows above them which, like the sashing of all other windows, are C 18.

The INTERIOR PLANNING is of special interest in showing how a Jacobean house was brought in line with the new standards of comfort, privacy, and courtly ceremonial adopted after the Restoration. Roger North, in his essay *On Building*, described the alterations as the best he had seen. The great hall and the position of the staircase in the inner hall to its E go back to Vavasour's house, as Smythson's plan shows, as does the long gallery occupying the whole of the upper floor of the W wing. William Murray's alterations of the 1630s appear to have been chiefly concerned with refurbishing existing rooms in a more up-to-date style, but the new S range of the 1670s provided more lavish accommodation: on the ground floor a suite of rooms each for the duke and duchess – withdrawing room, bedchamber, and closet, arranged symmetrically on either side of a central dining room. The bedchambers occupy the projecting S arms of the original house; the closets are in the corner additions. On the first floor the arrangements of the 1670s are less easy to appreciate because of later alterations. A sequence of state rooms was contrived, starting with the dining hall above the ground-floor hall, and ending with the queen's bedchamber in the centre of the S front, with her closet adjoining. The special feature of Ham is that much of the furniture provided in the 1670s also survives, although it lies outside the scope of this book.*

A tour of the house can follow more or less the route prescribed in the guidebook. The GREAT HALL is, in accordance with its date, 1610, in the asymmetrical position which was the English Gothic and Tudor tradition. All its motifs, however, are later. The S windows of 1610 were blocked when the S rooms were added. The marbled white of the walls is

* For further details see the excellent guidebook, *Ham House*, published by the Victoria and Albert Museum, 4th ed. 1976 by Maurice Tomlin; also P. Thornton and M. Tomlin: *The Furnishing and Decoration of Ham House*, 1980.

based on the original decoration. The room above, originally
the dining room, was thrown into one with it at the end of the
C 17, when the gallery with its pretty balusters was put in. The
plaster ceiling however, the first instance of the remarkably
progressive style adopted by William Murray in his alterations, is of 1637 or 1638 by *Joseph Kinsman* and entirely in the
new Inigo Jones style of e.g. the Queen's House at Greenwich,
with panels, oblong, oval, and otherwise, framed by wreaths,
guilloche, etc.

27   Adjacent on the E is the STAIRCASE, also rebuilt about
1637–8. Of wood, rising through two storeys with a spacious
open well, it is as progressive as the hall ceiling, for instead of
the usual balusters and the usual strapwork decoration it has a
balustrade with oblong openwork panels decorated with rich
trophies. The newel-posts, similarly decorated, carry very
handsome baskets of fruit. All this clearly heralds the type of
staircase which became popular for greater houses about 1660.
The plaster ceiling (again by *Kinsman*) is in the most restrained style of Inigo. The doorcases on the other hand are in
the curious mannered style current among some architects
and craftsmen in and near the City of London, especially from
around 1630 (cf. Kew Palace, Ri; also Swakeleys, Hi). The
somewhat fantastic ears and broken pediments are unmistakable. They are by *Thomas Carter*, a joiner; it seems a little
doubtful whether he should be regarded as the designer of the
stair balustrade as well.

In the South Apartments the most interesting feature is the
ceiling painting in the WHITE CLOSET, attributed convincingly to *Antonio Verrio*, who came to England from Paris about
1672.

One of the most important lessons to be learnt at Ham
House is the difference between plasterwork of the 1630s at its
most progressive and plasterwork of the 1670s in the then
accepted style. To make these comparisons one ought to study
the rooms on the first floor. Of William Murray's time are the
NORTH DRAWING ROOM, immediately W of the hall gallery,
and the LONG GALLERY which runs through the whole W
arm of the H of 1610, its most remarkable motif the extremely
refined Ionic pilasters (by *Carter*), decorated between the
volutes of the capitals with dainty garlands. In the North
Drawing Room another Jonesian plaster ceiling by *Kinsman*,
doorcases similar to those of the staircase (by *Carter*), and a
boldly Baroque fireplace surround with twisted and spiral-
fluted columns of stucco, *à la* Bernini's recent baldacchino at
St Peter's, or rather *à la* Raphael's Cartoon with the Healing of
the Lame Man. Inorganically above these columns big, fat
scrolls. In addition playful putti, nearly full-round, clamber-
ing about the frame of the picture over the mantelshelf – a
surprisingly merry *tour de force*. Of the same date also the small
GREEN CLOSET next to the North Drawing Room, the coving
and ceiling painted by *Francis Cleyn*, who also did the inset
pictures in the North Drawing Room.

In the South Apartments on the first floor plaster ceilings of
c. 1674, still essentially dependent on Inigo Jones's innovations of 1620–30, but treated much more lightly. The detail
is busier and finer than in the work of 1638. There are also
big acanthus scrolls in some places, a motif not to be found in
the earlier work. The examples to be studied are in the
ANTECHAMBER to the queen's bedchamber, and the
QUEEN'S CLOSET. In the queen's closet the fireplace is of
scagliola, that is stucco treated to look like marble – one of the
earliest uses in England. The technique had been introduced
in Italy early in the C17, and John Evelyn says in 1664 that it
was still unknown over here.* In the same rooms excellent
woodwork, too, notably the overmantel in the antechamber to
the queen's bedchamber.

STABLES. To the w of the house, probably basically C17,
but extended or altered in 1787, the date that appears at the
back. Converted for housing in 1979–80 by *Colin Bottomley*,
retaining one original unit with its C18 fittings.

The GARDENS, landscaped by *Repton*, as he says in his
'Fragments' of 1816, were restored in the 1970s by the National Trust to the formal layout of the 1670s.

HAMPTON

The village lies by the river beyond Hampton Court, separated
from the palace by the large green which in character and
function is so much an appendage of the palace that it is treated
under Hampton Court. The church stands high up in the village
centre, in the middle of the triangle formed by Church Street,
High Street, and Thames Street. The area became a fashionable
retreat from the later C17 onwards, and several good houses
remain, although the village is spoilt by incessant traffic.‡

ALL SAINTS, The Avenue, N of Broad Lane. 1908 by *Greenaway & Newberry*, completed later.

ST MARY, the parish church, was rebuilt in 1831 by *E. Lapidge*,
the architect of several churches in the neighbourhood. The
usual plain white brick building with lean lancet windows and
a w tower without unnecessary adornment. Inside, s and n
galleries and tall quatrefoil piers reaching right up to the roof.
Nothing mysterious, nothing enthusiastic. In 1888 *Sir Arthur
Blomfield* added a sumptuous but hard short sanctuary at the
E. Tracery in the nave windows added after 1907. – MONU-
MENTS. In the SW porch, Sibel Pen † 1562, a standing wall-
monument of the four-poster type, the lower part of the
columns and the tomb-chest with strapwork decoration. Recumbent effigy, the body hardly modelled at all. Long inscription ('Pen here is brought to home, the place of long abode/

* See R. B. Wragg, *Country Life*, vol. 122, p. 718.
‡ Historical details on Hampton houses are based on the research which Mr
Gerald Heath kindly made available.

Whose vertu guided hath her shippe, in to the quyet rode',
etc.) on a tablet under a simple, unadorned (that is early)
pediment; strapwork scrolls to l. and r. – In the s aisle Mrs
Thomas † 1731, designed by *Archer* and signed by *W. Powell*.
A noble composition, though the figures of the semi-reclining
mother and seated daughter are not very sensitive. Behind
them a grey obelisk, the whole in an altar framing. – George
Tilson † 1738 (s w porch), with above the long inscription an
enterprising putto on a highly asymmetrical cartouche. –
Captain A. Ellice, Comptroller General of the Coastguards,
† 1853, by *Bedford*, with a coastguard mourning by the Captain's coffin. – Many more tablets of similar dates on the
galleries. – In the churchyard a clumsy bare pyramid to John
Greg of Dominica † 1795.

ROSEHILL (library and flats), Upper Sunbury Road. A later
C 18 house of three storeys, three windows wide, with additions. (Original staircase.)

HAMPTON PRIMARY SCHOOLS: JUNIOR SCHOOL, Percy
Road, 1905 by *G. E. S. Laurence*, a typical blend of Arts and
Crafts with neo-Georgian; INFANT SCHOOL, Ripley Road, to
the w, c. 1969 by *Manning & Clamp*. Concrete blockwork.
Teaching areas in three half-gabled clusters around the hall.
An early example of a post-Plowden open-plan primary school
Another is BUCKINGHAM PRIMARY, Buckingham Road, s
of Hanworth Road, 1974 by *John Spence & Partners*.

GENERAL ROY'S SURVEY BASE, Roy Grove, off Hanworth
Road. A cannon with a plaque commemorates the Ordnance
Survey set up by General Roy († 1790).

HAMPTON WATERWORKS, Upper Sunbury Road. Following
the 1852 Metropolis Water Act, three water companies moved
their intakes upriver to Hampton, with three nearly identical
pumping stations by *Joseph Quick*. The buildings now standing on Upper Sunbury Road, empty of machinery, can be
described from w to E. The West Middlesex Company's buildings have gone. The Grand Junction Company's station has, at
its E end, Quick's engine house of 1853–5, in a dainty Italianate with large round-arched upper windows and perforated
parapet, built for two Bull engines. The projection at the front
is the base of a former chimney-cum-standpipe tower. The
boiler house at the side has blank arcading. At its w end, a
beam engine house of 1881–2 by *Alexander Frazer*, rather
plain. Adjacent, semi-detached waterworks cottages of the
1850s and a simple sub-Italianate gate office. Then on the
corner, the Southwark and Vauxhall Company's engine house
of 1853–5,* to the same design as the Grand Junction's.
One-storey extensions to the s in the same style, including a
broad chimney embellished with pilasters and relieving
arches. E of Lower Sunbury Road, later buildings for the
Southwark and Vauxhall Company. The MORELANDS building has two large and heavy-looking Italianate engine houses

* Later known as the RUSTON house.

at either end of a blank-arcaded boiler house fifteen bays long, the W house, with ornamental lozenge-pattern window frames, of 1867–70 by *Joseph Quick* (for two 80 inch. beam engines), the E house of 1885–6 by *J. W. Restler*. A central standpipe tower, Italianate with prominent cornices, was demolished in 1970. To the E, the RIVERDALE building of 1897–1900 (for three triple expansion engines). Engine house with a quasi-Elizabethan E-plan, boiler house with aisles and clerestory, all with tall, round-headed windows. Finally, the gatehouse and clock tower, mixed Italian-cum-Elizabethan, late C19. The filter beds behind are from 1867 onwards. (The old steam plant was scrapped in 1943.) The STILGOE engine house, 1935–43 by *A. J. Johnson*, houses eight steam turbines driving centrifugal pumps and generators. Brick on a steel frame; two chimneys arranged symmetrically. The DAVIDSON primary filter house to the W is of 1936–47.

THAMES-LEE WATER MAIN TUNNEL. From Hampton Waterworks to the King George V Reservoir at Chingford, running 160 ft below St Mary's church. Constructed 1955–9, in use 1966, *Sir William Halcrow & Partners* consulting engineers. 19 miles long, 102 in. in internal diameter, mostly tunnelled through the London Clay. The longest tunnel in Europe, and the longest in the world through soft strata.*

PERAMBULATION. CHURCH STREET starts by the church with No. 9, built between 1791 and 1802, with C19 projecting wings. Opposite No. 2, THE OLD GRANGE, pebbledashed, with two gables of the 1630 type, with concave curves carrying straight pediments. A fireplace inside appears if anything older than 1630. Then ORME HOUSE, probably built *c.* 1698, three storeys, five windows wide, with a contemporary pediment and door hood both brought in (*c.* 1929) from other places. Minor stuccoed houses follow. At the junction with HIGH STREET a small C18 terrace (Nos. 62–68), two storeys with a central niche, and one old shopfront. Then continuing along the E side several quite ambitious Georgian houses, mostly altered. No. 78 (Ivy House) has a curious front with shaped gables flanking a centrepiece with a cupola added *c.* 1900. The core of the house goes back to the C17. Then some C18 houses (Nos. 80–84), including Hope Cottage, built as a coach house by *c.* 1780. No. 90 is early C18 or older, with a first-floor bay on thin columns. No. 100, GROVE HOUSE, built *c.* 1726–7 by Lady Mary Downing, has a substantial, five-window centre with quoins, extended to the l. by two bays; early C19 porch. (Good original staircase with twisted balusters. At the NE corner, behind the extension, a spectacular room in Moorish style added apparently as a music room *c.* 1906 by Colonel C. J. Stutfield. Domed, with columns with carved capitals supporting cusped arches, tiled walls, stained glass, all surfaces richly ornamented with abstract patterns.)

* It was also the first tunnel to use an expanding lining of unreinforced concrete tapered segments and the first to use successfully a rotary drum digger. The tunnelling was carried out in 1955–9.

After that small cottages trailing away towards Hampton Hill. On the w side of the High Street, from N to S: No. 101, ELMGROVE HOUSE, C18, three storeys, with Doric porch; No. 87, a small plain C18 house right on the road; No. 81, c. 1780, with a pretty trellis porch, set back; and No. 67, THE OLD FARMHOUSE (formerly Park Brook), L-shaped, with an early C19 exterior (perhaps older). The grandest house on this side is BEVEREE, set in its own grounds. Five-window centre with wings; pedimented porch. Erected in the early C19 near the site of a house built by Dr John Blow c. 1691 (demolished 1799); much rebuilt after a fire in 1867. Nos. 33–35 are a terrace of c. 1720 with later stucco trim; rusticated angle pilasters. On the other side of the High Street the central triangle has a few more cottages and the JOLLY COOPERS, all modest C18.

Up STATION ROAD some tough but not unattractive red brick terraces by *Hutchison Locke & Monk*, c. 1978. Then No. 30 at an angle to the road, later C18, with canted bays and open pedimented doorway, followed by a sweet creeper-clad cottage and a humble terrace (Nos. 46–54) of c. 1710–20. Back along THAMES STREET (reached via Plevna Road and Upper Sunbury Road with the extensive waterworks, *see* above). Several minor C18 street fronts, especially on the N side (Nos. 54–56, 38, 22–26, 20), with a few on the s (No. 15, derelict, and No. 3). The best is No. 1, RIVERDALE, brown brick with red dressings, four windows, 'newly erected' in 1772, with a w extension probably of the mid C19.

HAMPTON COURT ROAD continues along the riverside towards Hampton Court. On the edge of the village GARRICK'S VILLA, on the N side. Garrick bought a house here in 1754. Major alterations were made c. 1775 by *Adam*, who added a new front with central upper portico of four wooden columns over arches, and paired pilasters at the ends. The result is aesthetically unsatisfactory; the details, especially the attenuated pilasters, are Adam's, but no unity of composition is achieved. The wing on the l. is of 1864. The house, converted to flats in 1922, is now the centre of a select neo-Georgian estate of the 1960s, incorporating Garrick's ORANGERY (much altered, with upper floor of 1922). Close to the river and separated from the house by the road* is Garrick's SHAKESPEARE TEMPLE, a little octagon with a deep Ionic portico, built to house Roubiliac's Shakespeare of 1758 (the sculpture is now in the British Museum). It seems likely that *Roubiliac* himself designed the building.‡ It was restored by *D. W. Insall* for Richmond Council. Further on, a house by the river called GARRICK'S HOUSE, with a long thin C18 front to the road, and WHITE LODGE, C18, with pedimented centre, looking towards the Diana Fountain in Bushy Park.§

* But linked by a tunnel with grotto entrance at the s end.
‡ See T. Murdoch, *Burlington Magazine*, January 1980.
§ St Albans, an C18 house with C17 features installed in 1922–3, given to the borough in 1964, was demolished in 1972.

Then more recent riverside houses among which the Swiss chalet of Messrs. Hucks and Son, Marine Engineers, deserves mention. It was brought over *c.* 1899 and looks wonderfully incongruous. Past the chalet the Green is soon reached (*see* Hampton Court, end of entry).

HAMPTON COURT*

INTRODUCTION

The manor belonged to the Order of the Knights Hospitallers of St John of Jerusalem until 1514, when it was leased by Wolsey. He was the coming man in English politics, just under forty years old. His King, Henry VIII, was twenty-three. Wolsey's father had been a butcher at Ipswich. The boy had unbounded ambition and exceptional ability. He went into the Church, found patronage with several noblemen, and in 1507 became a Chaplain to Henry VII. Henry VIII took him over and made him Almoner. Then in 1513 he was elected Dean of York. From that day his rise was unparalleled: Bishop of Lincoln in 1514, Bishop of Tournai in 1514, Archbishop of York in 1514, Lord Chancellor in 1515, Cardinal in 1515, Papal Legate in 1518, Abbot of St Albans in 1521, and Bishop of Winchester in 1528. He also farmed three more English bishoprics for foreign occupants. Where at a great royal pageant the Archbishop of Canterbury appeared with 70 servants, Wolsey brought along 300. When the King's sister had a household of 44 and his eldest daughter of 65, Wolsey's numbered 429. As Archbishop of York he had a sumptuous town house, north of the Palace of Westminster, which Henry VIII later converted into the Palace of Whitehall. He founded a school at Ipswich (which never developed) and Cardinal College at Oxford (which became the celebrated Christ Church), and built or remodelled three country seats of which the Manor of the More, Herts, was the most luxurious, but Hampton Court infinitely the biggest.

'Why come ye not to Court?' wrote the satirist Skelton.

> To wyche court?
> To the Kynges Courte?
> Or to Hampton Court?
> Nay, to the Kynges Courte,
> The Kynges Courte should have the excellence
> But Hampton Court
> Hath the preemynence.

Wolsey's Hampton Court was the greatest of all houses built in England at the time, the only building that could compare in scale with the contemporary Chambord of François I. This

---

* I am grateful for much help over this account to Miss Juliet Allan of the Inspectorate of Ancient Monuments, to Mr Gerald Heath, who allowed me to make use of his unpublished research, especially on the houses of Hampton Court Green, and to Mr H. M. Colvin, who let me see the account of Hampton Court before its publication in vol. IV of the *King's Works*.

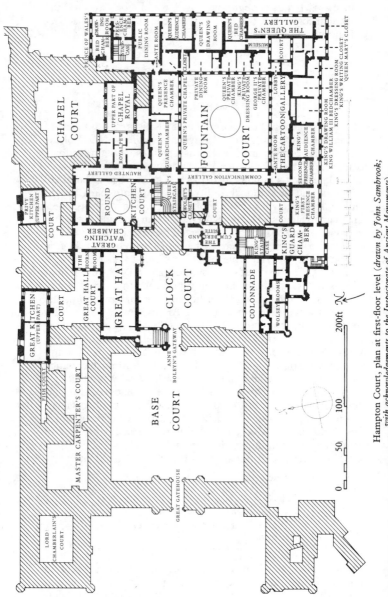

Hampton Court, plan at first-floor level (*drawn by John Sambrook; with acknowledgements to the Inspectorate of Ancient Monuments*)

unashamed display was one of the many things that irritated the king, and when Wolsey in 1525 decided to make a present of the house and its furnishings to Henry VIII it was too late. In 1529 he was deprived of all his lands and belongings, and in the next year he died after his arrest for high treason.

The exact form of Wolsey's palace at the time when it was taken over by the King is unclear. Wolsey's complete building accounts do not survive, although it is known that in 1515 the master mason was *John Lebons*, who later worked at Cardinal College. The palace seems to have started as a courtyard house, around part of what is now called Clock Court; the surviving work shows that it was soon enlarged piecemeal, probably in Wolsey's time. Base Court was added to the W (at first without its projecting wings), the W range of Clock Court was extended S, the S range rebuilt, and the E range remodelled as a tower block with royal suites on different floors. In 1531 the King's lodgings were mentioned as being on the principal floor, those of the Queen above, those of Princess Mary on the ground floor. The court called Round Kitchen Court was added to the E, and possibly other buildings in this area. It seems therefore that it was Wolsey who was responsible for much of the general outline of the palace as it now stands.

Henry VIII spent more on Hampton Court than on any other of his palaces, except perhaps Greenwich. His queens spent much time there and it was the birthplace of Edward VI. Henry's chief works were the rebuilding of the great hall in 1532-4 on the site of Wolsey's hall, on the N side of the Clock Court, the completion of the chapel, and the creation of new royal lodgings around the court later rebuilt as Fountain Court. He also extended the offices along the N side of the palace. His chief workmen were *John Moulton*, master mason; *Christopher Dickinson*, in charge of bricklayers; *James Nedeham*, master carpenter, and from 1522 Surveyor of the King's works; and *William Clements*, master carpenter from 1532. It has been calculated that between 1529 and 1538 *c.* £35,000 was spent. A considerable amount went on elaborate interior decoration, including 'antique' ornament, of which much was carried out by foreigners, notably *John Maynard*.* The great hall, Watching Chamber, and chapel roof are the chief survivors of this taste, but the accounts show that there was originally much more, for example in the new separate suites of apartments built for the King and Queen in 1533-5. Of these only the Watching Chamber remains, which had the function of a guardroom, at the beginning of the sequence of King's apartments. They lay between the present Clock Court and Fountain Court. There was also a long gallery around part of the Cloister Court. The King's apartments ended in a projecting feature with octagonal turrets overlooking the Privy Garden. The Queen's apartments occu-

---

* Other workmen employed on the 'antique' ornament included the foreigners James Mercaden and Robert Sande, Richard 'Frencheman' and Henry Blankston; also the English(?) John Hethe, and Robert Skyngke of London ('moulder of antyk').

pied the E range and terminated in another long gallery. Wyngaerde's view from the river shows the romantic profusion of the
16 ornamental chimneys and cupolas which were a particular feature of Tudor palaces in the early C 16 (cf. Richmond). To the w
Henry added a covered tennis court (converted into lodgings in
1670–4), which survives, and to the N an open tennis court
(perhaps on the site of the present one), and a bowling alley (now
gone) lit by windows brought from Rewley Abbey, Oxon, spoils
of Henry's dissolution of the monasteries.

The palace was used by subsequent monarchs; James I held
his Hampton Court Conference here in 1604 to settle controversial church matters. But of building little was done apart from
minor improvements and repairs. A new privy kitchen and some
outbuildings were added c. 1570. The present tennis court was
built c. 1625. Under the Commonwealth the palace was kept for
Cromwell's use. Charles II busied himself on the layout of the
park. The additions he made to the palace, apart from the
remodelling of the tennis court, disappeared in the rebuilding
that followed soon after.

William and Mary, who did not like Whitehall, decided to
make Hampton Court their Versailles. *Wren* started work in
1689. The final results however were not as ambitious as had at
first been intended. Henry VIII's royal lodgings were demolished, and new state apartments for the King and Queen
were planned around three sides of the new Fountain Court. By
the time William died the structural work was complete on the
new court, with its regular E and S frontages to the gardens, and
on the new colonnade on the S side of Clock Court, which formed
the approach to the King's apartments. The Banqueting House
in the Privy Gardens was built c. 1700.

Under Queen Anne and the first two Georges the state rooms
continued to be painted and furnished; the chapel was redecorated in 1711. The rooms on the N side of Fountain Court, (the
uncompleted Queen's side) were decorated c. 1716 (displaying
the influence of *Vanbrugh*) and, together with the remainder of
the Queen's suite and the small rooms in the N E corner, were
adapted for the family of the Prince of Wales. Further rooms
followed in the remodelled range on the E side of Clock Court,
together with the gateway from Clock Court to Fountain Court
dated 1732 and designed by *Kent*. At about the same time part of
the N front towards Tennis Court Lane was heightened.

George III did not use Hampton Court, and since then no
monarch has resided there. Former lodgings were granted 'by
grace and favour' to servants of the Crown. The state apartments
were opened to the public in 1838, soon after Victoria, young
and public-spirited, had ascended the throne. From then on
there was a more energetic programme of repairs and renovation
with the object increasingly of restoring the palace exterior to its
Tudor appearance. From 1832 the work was in the charge of
Edward Jesse, with *Blore* as consultant and *Inman* as executive
architect. From c. 1882 onwards, under the influence of the
Hampton Court historian Ernest Law, there was widespread

reinstatement of mullioned windows and decorative chimneys:
among the most important transformations were the lengthening of the octagonal buttresses to the outer gateway and the
rebuilding of its vault to disguise the restoration that had taken
place in the C 18, the rescue of the discarded gates and of the
astronomical clock, and finally the digging out of the Tudor
bridge over the moat, which took place in 1909–10.

EXTERIORS

Described in the following order: W front, Base Court, Clock
Court, N front, service courts including interiors of cellars and
kitchens, Chapel Court, Fountain Court and E and S fronts
(including the Orangery and the Vine).

The main approach is from the W, that is Hampton Court Green 41
(see end of entry), through the TROPHY GATES built for
William III (altered to take George II's coat of arms). Four
plain gatepiers with trophies and lion and unicorn (renewed
1780) lead into the outer Green Court, with the river on the r.
and the CAVALRY BARRACKS of 1662, enlarged in 1713, on
the l. Other buildings were cleared away in the C 19 to provide
a more dignified approach.

The front of Wolsey's building, with its Great Gatehouse, originally two storeys higher, is reached across a moat (filled in by
Charles II and William and Mary) by a BRIDGE built by
Henry VIII and dug out in 1909. The King's Beasts on the
parapet, added in 1909–10 to replace the missing originals,
were renewed in 1950. The façade, nearly 400 ft wide, is the
grandest of its date in Britain. Its perfect symmetry seems to
belong wholly to the Renaissance, just then entering England
in the learning of Erasmus, More, Grotius, Colet, and in the
art of Torrigiani at Westminster Abbey.* The wings that lie
across the moat at either end were afterthoughts, as the brickwork shows, but may belong to Wolsey's time.

Wolsey indeed began to build almost exactly when François I
started on Chambord. But to remember Chambord makes it at
once clear that Hampton Court still holds fast to the Gothic
style. Not only is every detail Perpendicular (with the exception of the two terracotta medallions which were not originally
here; on them see Anne Boleyn's Gateway, below), but the
conception of an outer range with a tall symmetrical gatehouse
also needed no Italian introduction to England. It existed
already in the mighty front of Harlech before 1300. Bodiam is
a well-known example of c. 1400. There are many late medieval buildings of a more domestic character which show how
the gatehouse continued as the main feature of a show front
(archbishops' palaces such as Knole, Kent; or Oxburgh,

---

* The symmetry was originally less perfect. The Tudor gatehouse had a large
and a small entrance, with oriel windows placed over the larger non-central
entrance.

Norfolk, 1482). The St Aldate's façade of Wolsey's Cardinal
College in Oxford, now Christ Church, also exhibits the same
scheme. The French C 14 was familiar with it too (see, for
example, Charles V's Louvre). So the composition of the
Hampton Court front cannot be taken as a sign of the coming
of Italian principles; it is rather one of many northern parallels
to the new sense of order which in the South chose antiquity as
its ally. The shape of the gatehouse, the oriel window set into it
(with a panel with the arms of Henry VIII), the texture of the
dark red brick to its l. and r. with its diapering of vitrified
brick (the gatehouse itself is unfortunately of a harsh red
colour), the free spacing of the windows, and the fantastic
shapes of the chimneys (renewed without exception) can all be
regarded as typically Perpendicular and typically English.
The C 18 appearance of the GREAT GATEHOUSE (it had
largely been rebuilt in 1771–2) was disguised in 1882 by the
lengthening of the octagonal buttresses on the entrance side
and by a stone vault which replaced the flat C 18 ceiling (the
vault derived from two original corbels and springers).

The BASE COURT, entered through the two contemporary
doors of the gatehouse (replaced here after 1882), is perfectly
square and surrounded on the N, S, and W by ranges of
two-storeyed battlemented 'lodgings' for members of the
household. Each lodging had its own chimney and garderobe,
and was approached not by a staircase, but by the more new-
fangled corridor or gallery (as e.g. at the earlier Archbishop's
Palace, Croydon). The upper corridors were reached by
the gatehouse stair-turrets, renewed by Queen Elizabeth in
1566. The gatehouse opposite, known as ANNE BOLEYN'S
GATEWAY, possibly because it was altered while she was
queen, is actually part of Wolsey's original work which extended around Clock Court and to the E and NE of it. It is
crowned by a pretty C 18 cupola with a bell of 1480. Below is a
clock brought by William IV from St James's Palace as a
replacement for the astronomical clock (see below). The gateway has an oriel window like the great gatehouse and two
17 terracotta medallions. They have busts of Roman Emperors in
surrounds with egg-and-dart, lions' heads, and trophies, and
are part of a set of eight for which *Giovanni da Majano* was
paid £2 6s. in 1521. Two more are on the other side of this
gateway, and four on the E gateway of Clock Court. The two
similar ones on the great gatehouse (see above) were brought
from Windsor* and may originally have come from the so-
called Holbein Gate at Whitehall. There are two more (reset,
without surrounds) at Hanworth (Ho), and a similar surround
(without a bust) at Greenwich (Gr). The medallions are, except for the tomb of Henry VII in Westminster Abbey, the
earliest manifestations of the Italian Renaissance in England,
although (as with the interior decoration of Wolsey's and
Henry VIII's Hampton Court) Renaissance here means

* *Gentleman's Magazine*, 1845, ii, 594.

ornamental devices, not yet any understanding of classical architecture. The Base Court is 168 by 166 ft as against, for example, the 264 by 261 ft of Tom Quad at Christ Church. The uniformity is broken by the bold W front of Henry VIII's Great Hall with its large Perpendicular window appearing on the l. of Anne Boleyn's Gateway.

After this, the CLOCK COURT delights with its variety of heights and forms. The W side carries on the motifs as before. The E side of the GATEHOUSE is the same as the W except that instead of the oriel window there is the ASTRONOMICAL CLOCK made by *Nicholas Oursian* in 1540. It shows the hour, the day, the month, the number of days since New Year, the phases of the moon, and (an eminently characteristic addition) the times of high water at London Bridge. The sun is shown revolving round the earth. The face on the other side of the tower was lost when the inner works were removed in 1835. The astronomical face, removed later, was replaced in 1881, and new works were installed. Below is a terracotta panel with Wolsey's arms (partly defaced). Very different from the W range is the view to the N, where the sheer wall of the GREAT 15 HALL rises with its cellars with small windows, then a large expanse of unbroken brickwork, and then the five four-light transomed windows with four-centred heads, separated by narrow buttresses rising in three steps. The hall was built by Henry VIII in 1532–4 on the site of Wolsey's hall, but on a larger scale. In the E bay a vast oriel window with a pair of windows each with five transoms. As it abuts rather awkwardly and has buttresses of different proportions, the oriel was perhaps re-used from Wolsey's hall (cf. the similar hall window at Christ Church, Oxford).*

The S side of the Clock Court has undergone many changes. Laid out in the paving is the line of Wolsey's original range, uncovered by excavations. The W range shows the original join. S of this line the later Wolsey range, now hidden by the spectacular, somewhat operatic appearance of *Wren*'s entrance to the King's apartments. He kept the Tudor brick wall with its windows, turret, and bay-windows (which is therefore uncommonly well preserved) and placed in front of it a colonnade of Portland stone with coupled columns (*à la* Perrault's Louvre Colonnade) and a weighty entablature with cornice and balustrade. Two trophies raise the horizontal line of the balustrade and end in vases. The large round-headed windows above the colonnade on the l. are, like the brickwork around them, of course also of Wren's period. Between colonnade and hall stretches the E side of the court, several times remodelled, although still with fabric of Wolsey's time. The entrance feature (the approach to the Queen's apartments) is of 1732 by *Kent* (remodelled in 1844), an exceedingly early example of the Gothic revival of the C 18.‡ The pretty tablet and window

* We owe this suggestion to the *King's Works*, vol. IV.

‡ According to Horace Walpole it was Sir Robert Walpole who insisted that the new work should match the old.

above the doorway are part of Kent's design. Most of the
brickwork is of the same period.

The NORTH FRONT, nearly 700 ft long, faces Tennis Court
Lane. The buildings on the N of the lane are of no architectural
importance, but the palace itself here is almost entirely of the
C 16, an outstanding example of the Tudor style where it had
no reason to give up utilitarian freedom of composition. First
come the gabled parts N of the Master Carpenter's Court, then
the kitchens with their projecting clusters of chimneys, and
after a while the E kitchen, probably an Elizabethan addition,
with the same feature. From the turret soon after that the N
range of Chapel Court starts, higher and duller (heightened
in the C 18, with windows of the C 19). The only later parts are
the W end, remodelled in the C 18, and some easily recognizable C 19 reconstructions.

Between this irregular frontage and the more formal courts
already discussed lie, as can be guessed from the N front, a
series of smaller courtyards surrounded by the extensive SER-
VICE BUILDINGS needed by such a large establishment.
They can be entered from the NE corner of the Base Court,
although they cannot all be visited: from W to E, the Lord
Chamberlain's Court, the Master Carpenter's Court, Fish
Court, Great Hall Court, Round Kitchen Court. Beneath the
Great Hall (entered from Base Court), the KING'S BEER
CELLARS. (A large household in the C 16, that is before the
introduction of coffee, tea, or cocoa, consumed an amount of
beer inconceivable today.) In the centre of the cross wall is a
stone pier which supports the central hearth in the hall above
(*see* below). The cellars (total length 100 ft) are divided into
nave and aisles by two rows of octagonal oak posts.

N of the Great Hall and its court, NORTH CLOISTER leads to the
SERVING PLACE by the side of the great kitchens. Several oak
hatches open into it. The food was taken from here up the
stairs to the Horn Room, the serving place for the high table
end of the great hall and the King's apartments beyond. The
GREAT KITCHENS are an object lesson in large-scale Tudor
catering. The E kitchen, built by Wolsey, 37 by 27 ft, has three
huge fireplaces (one later reduced in width). To the W is the
new kitchen added by Henry VIII in 1529, now divided by a
C 17 partition wall with ovens. There are three large open
fireplaces in the E part, and in the W part two stone hatches
(one made into a doorway in the C 17) from which food was
taken up to the lower end of the great hall. The present
kitchen roof dates from c. 1840, but stone corbels of the
original high roof remain, together with traces of later inserted
floors and partitions. A PRIVY KITCHEN (not open to the
public) was added by Elizabeth I further E; its serving place
(altered in the C 19) can be seen towards the E end of the North
Cloister. NORTH CLOISTER runs along the N side of ROUND
KITCHEN COURT, which owes its name to the circular building in its centre, built as a public lavatory c. 1700. This court
was a creation of Wolsey's, and when built was not merely a

service court. There is some evidence that the cloister formerly continued around all four sides: the rebuilding of the Great
Watching Chamber on a larger scale encroached upon the w,
while the s side was reconstructed as part of the Queen's
apartments in the later c 17. The two remaining cloister
walks, North Cloister and Chapel Cloister (along the E side,
with the entrance to the chapel), are two-storeyed, with
straight-headed four-light windows. (For the chapel *see*
below, end of section on Interiors.)

CHAPEL COURT, E of Round Kitchen Court, has Tudor brickwork on the ground floor, and in the N E corner a turret with a
(restored) lead cupola; otherwise there are many c 17, c 18,
and c 19 alterations. The E range, built as Henry VIII's
covered tennis court, was heightened and rewindowed as
lodgings for the Duchess of York in 1670–4; of this time two
rusticated doorways and windows with scrolled surrounds.

The next section is almost entirely concerned with the transformation of Hampton Court under William and Mary. *Wren*
began work in 1689. His first proposals were for a radical
rebuilding, sweeping away the whole of the Tudor palace
apart from the Great Hall, which was to remain as the focal
point of a grand approach from the N through Bushy Park (the
layout of Bushy Park still reflects this intention). s of the hall
was to have been a new w front, with a central dome on axis
with the E–W line of the Long Water of Home Park, and
behind it a large courtyard with two projecting staircases to
the King's and Queen's state apartments (cf. Bernini's first
plan for the Louvre). In the end the only part of the old palace
to be pulled down was the Tudor predecessor to Fountain
Court. Building proceeded rapidly at first; the carcases of the s
and E ranges and some of the interior fittings of the King's side
were complete by 1694, the year when Queen Mary's death
interrupted operations. They were resumed in 1698, and the
King was in residence by 1700, but work on the Queen's side
continued until *c.* 1718.

FOUNTAIN COURT is much smaller than the court which 34
Wren had first planned. The grand staircases had to be
accommodated rather awkwardly at either end of the existing
Tudor w range. This side, lower than the others, has plenty of
jagged Tudor excrescences looking down on to the serenity of
the work of 1689–*c.* 1702. The court is only 117 by 101 ft, as
against, for example, the (about) 290 by 150 ft of Schlüter's
Court at Berlin, the (about) 300 by 300 ft of the Louvre Court,
and the (about) 300 by 230 ft of Stockholm. With its brick on
the stone arcade and stone trim to the windows it is cheerful, a
little busy, and anything but grand and courtly. The piers of
the arcade are square and squat, and above the long, noble
windows of the main floor is a row of circular panels and then
an attic storey above – no firm subordination of everything to
one ruling effect, but instead a comfortable spreading out of
little effects. The circular features contain windows on three
sides: on the s they have grisaille panels with the Labours of

Hercules, painted by *Laguerre*. The surrounding decoration of orange wreaths and lion skins (carved by *William Emmett* in 1691) is an allusion to Hercules, the classical hero with whom William liked to identify himself, and who reappears elsewhere in the building. The likely inspiration was Poussin's roundels with the same subjects in the Louvre Grande Galerie. The ground-floor arcades incidentally have semicircular arches, but the cross-vaults behind them are depressed, and this shows outside. The reason is that the floor level of the first floor inside is lower than the apex of the arches of the arcade (a typically Baroque discrepancy between what appears and what is real). Wren had originally intended to give the arches solid lunettes, the same device that he had used at Trinity College Library, Cambridge, twenty years before, but he had to change them during construction in 1689, at the request of the King, who considered the cloister too low.

The E walk of the cloister round Fountain Court has two symmetrical apsidal recesses, the N one opening into the main entrance hall from the E side. This hall, plain with four Tuscan columns, is in the centre of the E front, and the duplication of the recesses is therefore a clever way (similar to many used before in France) to achieve symmetry when two opposite fronts of the same room have two different axes.

33 The EAST FRONT is twenty-three windows wide. It has a low ground floor with boldly segment-headed windows (an early example in England), a main floor and small round windows above, and an attic storey topped by a balustrade (as in the fronts towards the court, rather a scattering than a pulling together of effects). The corners have quoins but no other emphasis. In the centre is a seven-bay projection, and in the centre of this a further projection of three bays. So there is a convincing *crescendo* from the plain brickwork of the walls to pilasters and then attached columns. Also the wall of the whole projection is ashlar-faced. But while the *crescendo* works from the outer ends towards the centre, it fails in the development from bottom to top, for the main pediment is not the crowning motif of the whole; the attic storey continues behind it, and the top balustrade runs all the way through, keeping the pediment under. From the point of view of the Grand Manner Hampton Court is infinitely inferior to Versailles or the Louvre Colonnade. The English have never been able to carry off that autocratic grandeur, and William III could do it less and wanted less to do it than almost any other British monarch. (Although cf. Greenwich, which is, significantly perhaps, not a royal palace; Charles II's gardens are another matter, *see* below). To be successful in the Versailles style, the largest scale is necessary, as imitators at Schleissheim, Ludwigsburg, Caserta, Stupinigi, La Granja, etc., knew only too well. With a mere 300 ft, Louis le Grand cannot be emulated.

The same qualities and shortcomings are apparent on the SOUTH FRONT. Here again the centre with its four columns and no pediment is weak (especially since the removal of the balustrade statues), and the subcentres in the middle of the recessed parts are a little restless. The balustrade seems more than anything to crush all impetus. As far as the details are concerned, the magnificent ironwork of the entrances compensates for much else that is missing. The sash-windows here and in other places at Hampton Court are among the earliest in England. The sculptural decoration is of high quality. The pilasters and columns of the projecting centre on the s are linked by garlands of fruit and flowers with trumpets, sceptres, and crowns over the central window. In the pediment above is a lively relief of Hercules triumphing over Envy, by *Cibber*, 1694–6. In front of the E façade two statues of Mars and Hercules, by an unknown sculptor. The statues on the top balustrade have been removed. As for the relationship between exterior and interior, the external symmetry disguises rooms of various shapes and heights (as will be found inside), and some of the circular windows are blind. They were originally painted with the four seasons. The centre of the ground floor of the s front was designed as an orangery.

To finish the walk round the outside, one should continue w along the s front. Beyond the William and Mary work is an earlier projecting structure with a corner turret. The date it bears – 1568 – applies only to the tall stone bay-window (possibly a replacement of a wooden oriel); this projection appears in Wyngaerde's view and must belong to the new lodgings added by Wolsey (*see* Introduction). After that the exterior of Wolsey's Base Court appears again, largely hidden by the ORANGERY, built by *Wren* under William III, a very plain utilitarian building which now houses the *Mantegna* cartoons of the Triumph of Caesar. Past the Orangery one is faced with the E side of the wing projecting from Wolsey's w façade.* The buildings here are partly c 17 and partly late c 19. The VINE in its Vinery was planted in 1769 by *Capability Brown*. The main branch is now over 100 ft long.

INTERIORS

This account follows the usual visitor's route, which is confusing, historically speaking. It starts with the state apartments begun by William and Mary, taking in on the way some rooms remaining from Wolsey's Hampton Court; continues with the c 17 and c 18 interiors around Fountain Court and further N; and ends with Tudor remains (including Wolsey's Closet to the E) in the w range of Clock Court and Henry VIII's Watching Chamber and Great Hall. The chapel is described at the end.

The KING'S SIDE and QUEEN'S SIDE of FOUNTAIN COURT are both approached from Clock Court. The visitor enters the King's side first, through *Wren's* colonnade on the s side of

---

* In this wing offices for a Conservation Centre, converted by *Weston-Lewis, Clarke & Arnold*, 1979.

Clock Court. The KING'S STAIRCASE is of the type specially popular at the time, with flights of stairs and landings occupying three sides of a square or rectangle. The centre remains free as a wide open well. The airiness of this Baroque arrangement is emphasized by *Tijou's* lovely wrought-iron balustrade instead of heavy stone balusters. The paintings by *Verrio* of 1701–2 are dull in comparison: the compositions spill insensitively over the cove and the rounded corners without any articulation. On the ceiling a Banquet of the Gods; on the E wall the King in the guise of Alexander being introduced by Hercules; on the other walls elaborate political allegories based on Julian the Apostate's *Satire of the Caesars*, with the emperors as the last of the Stuarts.

Steps lead down from the King's Guardroom, the start of the state rooms on the first floor at the corner of the Wren s front, to the three remaining WOLSEY ROOMS on the s side of Clock Court (the easternmost is divided into two). They have some plain stone Tudor doorcases and fireplaces, some linenfold panelling, and original ceilings (all much restored) of great importance, for they seem to be the earliest examples of a type that was to develop so prodigiously in Elizabethan and Jacobean days. Here for the first time do we find these fine ribs interlaced with stars, lozenges, and bands. There are no pendants, only knobs at the junctions of the ribs. In the w room a ceiling with Wolsey's badges, and also a picture of *c.* 1640 showing the palace before Wren's alterations. One returns now to the state rooms.

In the large panelled KING'S GUARDROOM 3,000 pieces of arms neatly arranged during the time of William III. The KING'S SIDE then continues with the First Presence Chamber, Second Presence Chamber, Audience Chamber (formerly Privy Chamber) (in the centre of the s front), and King's Drawing Room. Preparations for their decoration were already in hand by 1694; the completion after 1698 (under *William Talman*) was less ornate than *Grinling Gibbons's* first drawings. There is much excellent woodwork, all by *Gibbons* (with the exception of two panels by *John Le Sage* over the fireplace in the First Presence Chamber), including exquisitely carved overmantels, picture frames, cornices, and doorcases. The walls were intended to be hung with tapestries. Overdoors painted by *Jacques Rousseau* (presence chambers) and *Bogdany* (bedchamber and the smaller rooms beyond). In the FIRST PRESENCE CHAMBER a large painting of William III landing at Margate, by *Kneller*, 1697, made for this position, but typical of the helplessness of English court artists when it came to celebrating the glories and triumphs of royalty. In the STATE BEDCHAMBER the *Verrio* ceiling paintings begin, characteristically English in their tempering of Baroque ideals. The Italian artist schooled in France has done in his far from masterly way what Wren did in architecture: he has made the sweeping compositions of southern Baroque palatable in our climate by freezing all individual figures.

Thus they appear as firm and fixed as a Wren column. The colours are dismally lacking in fire. The subject in the bedchamber is Endymion asleep in the arms of Morpheus, in the KING'S DRESSING ROOM Mars asleep in the lap of Venus. They were painted in 1701. At the SE corner of the building the small private rooms of the King and Queen adjoin. A private staircase at this point leads down to the tiny CHOCOLATE COURT and to other private apartments on the ground floor.*

44

The public tour continues on the first floor through the Queen's state rooms along the E front (visited here in reverse order to the intended sequence). In the QUEEN'S GALLERY what is perhaps the most attractive fireplace in the palace, by *John Nost*, with a scrolled pediment, two cupids, two doves, and a bust of Venus, very free and playful as a composition. It was made for the King's Bedchamber and moved here in 1701. The tapestries are *Le Brun* designs. The Queen's Gallery formerly housed the Mantegna cartoons now in the Orangery. The ceiling of 1715 (Verrio had died in 1707) in the QUEEN'S STATE BEDCHAMBER shows how *Thornhill* was the only man in England capable of some Baroque *brio* (cf. Greenwich Royal Hospital). The subject here is Leucothöe restraining Apollo. Below the cornice are medallions of George I, the Prince of Wales, Princess Caroline, and their son Frederick. Much of the furniture, made in 1715–16 for the Prince of Wales, is a good example of the comfort and 'middle-class' commodiousness of English cabinet-making and upholstery at the time of Richardson, even when done for the court. The Prince of Wales and his family took over the Queen's side after 1714, and lived at Hampton Court until they quarrelled with the King in 1717. In the QUEEN'S DRAWING ROOM (completed under Queen Anne) ceiling and wall paintings by *Verrio* of 1702–5 glorifying the Queen's justice, the Queen's power over the four quarters of the globe, and the Fleet (in the background of the scenes with Prince George of Denmark as Lord High Admiral and with Cupid drawn by sea-horses).

After the QUEEN'S AUDIENCE CHAMBER come the rooms left unfinished until after 1714, when they were made into the Prince of Wales Suite. Before entering them it is convenient to mention the other rooms around Fountain Court. It should be noted that the Queen's side includes, parallel to the state rooms, a series of small rooms facing Fountain Court (Queen's private chapel, closet, private dining room, private chamber, etc.). It is important to remember that Wren provided such cabinets for the comfort of the royal families: not the whole of their daily lives was spent in the larger and chilly saloons. Among the seven small rooms the first, the QUEEN'S PRIVATE CHAPEL, partly fitted up *c.* 1717 and completed for Queen Caroline, wife of George II, is distinguished by an

---

* Some of these have *Gibbons* carvings above the fireplaces as surrounds for pictures.

octagonal dome and skylight (necessary as the room has no outside walls). The CLOSET next to the chapel and the QUEEN'S PRIVATE CHAMBER have marble wash-basins in the walls. In the KING'S PRIVATE DRESSING ROOM an excellent *Gibbons* overmantel.

All the windows on the S side of Fountain Court belong to the CARTOON GALLERY, completed in 1695 for the celebrated seven *Raphael* cartoons bought by Charles I in 1623 which are now at the Victoria and Albert Museum. The tapestries made from them and now hanging in their place are of the C 17. On the chimneypiece a charming, oddly Rococo-looking relief of the Triumph of Venus, by *Nost*. Panelling with paired giant pilasters and splendid carved pendants by *Gibbons*. The COMMUNICATION GALLERY runs along the W range of Fountain Court. To its W are C 16 parts (Wolsey Closet; *see* below). The gallery leads to the landing at the top of the QUEEN'S STAIRCASE which fills the corner between the N and W ranges of Fountain Court. Constructed within the fabric of the C 16 range already in 1692, it is in plan like the King's staircase, and has, like it, an iron balustrade by *Tijou*. The decoration, not completed until 1734–5, is by *Kent*, the ceiling with a festive dome with blue and white coffering, the walls painted with reliefs against gold mosaic. On the W wall an earlier framed painting by *Honthorst* of the Arts and Sciences introduced to Charles I and Henrietta Maria in the guise of Apollo and Diana.

Along the N range of Fountain Court two large state rooms intended as the first of the Queen's suite, but decorated only in 1716–18 for her son: the QUEEN'S GUARD CHAMBER and PRESENCE CHAMBER. The robust and overpowering details are very different from the elegance of the earlier rooms, and *Vanbrugh* appears to be the most likely designer.* Gargantuan marble chimneypieces, in the Guard Chamber with lifesize terms in the form of Yeomen of the Guard, in the Presence Chamber with gross upper brackets. Doors with broken pediments. The Guard Chamber has large scrolly brackets on the walls, and both rooms have coved ceilings on equally bold brackets. From this room one can enter the PRINCE OF WALES SUITE at the end of the S range, fitted up for the Prince and his family in 1716–18. The marble chimneypieces in the Music Room (later called the PUBLIC DINING ROOM) and in the other rooms are perhaps also by *Vanbrugh*. The achievement of arms is by *Gibbons*. The W end of the Music Room was divided off to provide access to the family rooms beyond along the N side of Chapel Court (i.e. in the tennis court range remodelled in the late C 17).

The CUMBERLAND SUITE of three small rooms along the E range of CLOCK COURT (together with the entrance from the court and the completion of the Queen's staircase, *see* above)

---

* To him also is attributed a contemporary project for reviving Wren's idea of a grand N entrance to Hampton Court.

belongs to the time of George II (after 1731). Just as Kent had used Gothic forms for the entrance, so do the elaborate plaster ceilings of this suite include a remarkable one with the deliberately historicist motif of Jacobean pendants. The bedchamber, in contrast, is embellished with sumptuous classical cornices. In it a bed recess with paired Ionic columns and shallow segmental pediment; flanking closets with lunettes.

The E range of Clock Court, despite the reconstruction by *Kent*, still retains much C16 fabric, and within it is one of the most interesting of the Tudor interiors, the WOLSEY CLOSET (accessible from the Communication Gallery). The date of this room is a puzzle. It is only about 12 ft square, but possesses the most perfect Early Renaissance ceiling in England, made of wooden ribs with papier-mâché panels. The pattern of interlaced octagons with inset squares of gold on blue, mostly with Tudor roses and the Prince of Wales feathers, would suggest a date after the birth of Prince Edward in 1537, but this may only have been a remodelling, as the frieze bears Wolsey's motto. On the upper part of the walls two layers of painting (of the Passion and Resurrection): the earlier one, perhaps of the beginning of the C15, was painted over later (after 1537?) in the heavy, somewhat coarse style of Leonardesque (Last Supper), Michelangelesque (Scourging of Christ) Romanism in the Netherlands. The linenfold panelling below incorporates old panels sold to the Board of Works in 1886 by Ernest Law.*

The tour of the palace now continues with the Tudor parts further N and passes along the upper level of the cloisters to the E and N of the Round Kitchen Court. A door leads to the Chapel Royal (*see* below). At this level were the King's and Queen's Holyday Closets, overlooking the chapel (see the remains of the ceilings at the sides, interrupted by the later central entrance).

In the GREAT WATCHING CHAMBER, which dates from 1535 and 1536, a ceiling with a wooden rib design similar to those of Wolsey's rooms S of Clock Court (*see* above), but with pendants (carved by *Richard Rydge*). In some of the panels papiermâché bosses. Early C16 Flemish tapestry on the walls, and in the grand curved bay-window with three sets of mullions, glass made by *Willement* in 1846. This room was Henry VIII's Guard Chamber at the entrance to his state rooms (no longer in existence; *see* Introduction). The scale of magnificence of Henry VIII's Hampton Court can now only be judged by the GREAT HALL, erected in 1532–4 in the place of Wolsey's more modest hall. It is 106 by 40 by 60 ft, as compared with the 100 by 36 ft of Edward IV's Eltham, the 115 by 40 ft of the contemporary hall of Christ Church, and the 244 by 70 ft of Westminster Hall. The bay-window (possibly re-used from Wolsey's hall, *see* Exteriors, above) has a little fan-vault high up and two long slim three-light windows. As at Eltham there

---

* Information from Mr Gerald Heath. (In a room on the second floor of the Clock Court E range a fireplace with Wolsey's motto.)

was originally a central hearth, now marked by a stone slab. The elaborate louvre above, shown by Wyngaerde, was removed in 1663. The magnificent hammerbeam roof was designed by the King's Master Carpenter *James Nedeham*. The hammerbeam roof was used at Westminster Hall late in the C 14, and hammerbeams with pendants appear at Eltham in 1479; the still more elaborate roofs of Christ Church and Hampton Court are among the proudest descendants of the type. The technique is wholly Gothic, but the detail has the same Renaissance finesse as Wolsey's Cabinet. The lantern-shaped roof pendants were carved by *Richard Rydge*. The braces for the hammerbeams spring from carved corbels at the level of the window mullions. There is carving on the spandrels above the braces as well, and the arms of Henry, Anne Boleyn, and Jane Seymour. The screen on the other hand is still medieval throughout. As in all English medieval halls, it hides a servants' passage. The stair to its s is the main entrance from Anne Boleyn's Gateway. Communication between kitchen and high-table (that is, E) end of the hall is by the stair ending in the HORN ROOM, to the NE, which was the serving place for both the High Table and the King's apartments beyond. The tapestries against the walls are by *van Orley*, woven by *Pannemaker* of Brussels, *c.* 1540. The roof, originally painted, was scraped during restoration in the 1920s.

The CHAPEL ROYAL, whose plan belongs to Wolsey, was completed by Henry VIII in 1535–6. At the w is a wider antechapel (the scheme familiar from such earlier Oxford college chapels as New College or Magdalen) with a doorway with two early Renaissance panels in which Wolsey's arms have been replaced by Henry's impaling Seymour. The gallery of dark wood, the columns supporting it, the staircase leading up to it, and the royal pew above (with ceiling painted by *Thornhill*) are all of the early C 18 – the time when the chapel was thoroughly overhauled. Rainwater heads outside bear the date 1711. Of the same period are the panelling of the chapel itself and the splendid REREDOS with coupled fluted Corinthian giant columns supporting a wide broken segmental pediment. The carving is by *Grinling Gibbons*. The painted decoration along the top parts of the walls by *Thomas Highmore*, completed before 1712, makes a very poor show compared with Gibbons's uncanny skill. The broad mighty curve of the reredos pediment is in strong contrast to the roof; with its stars of lierne-vaulting and its exuberant pendants, as typical an example of English work of the 1530s as can be found anywhere in the palace. The fact that it is of timber and not of stone (like the Divinity School or the cathedral choir in Oxford or Henry VII's Chapel in Westminster Abbey) will disappoint only those who know it. The windows were altered *c.* 1711, when the one beyond the organ was blocked by a *trompe l'oeil* by *Thornhill*. The other windows were restored to their Tudor form in 1894 (based on the old window remaining behind the *trompe l'oeil*). The COMMUNION TABLE and BENCHES belong to the Wren period, the ORGAN was made by *Christopher Schrider*, Father Smith's son-in-law (cf. Westminster Abbey).

THE GARDENS, PARKS AND THEIR BUILDINGS

Wolsey is said to have enclosed about 2,000 acres around his palace. The main parts of this vast park are now Home Park to the E and Bushy Park to the N of the palace and gardens, divided from them by Hampton Court Road. The Tudor gardens lay between the palace and the river. Henry VIII did much to them, and his three main gardens appear on Wyngaerde's view: the 16 Pond Garden, the walled Privy Garden, and the Mount Garden. The Privy Garden had a formal geometrical arrangement and was embellished by an array of sundials and standards with the King's beasts holding revolving vanes, the first major example of this characteristic Tudor formula. By the end of the C 16, and perhaps earlier, the Privy Garden included topiary figures. The Pond Garden had ponds surrounded by low brick walls with the King's beasts. The ponds (dug in 1536) acted as reservoirs for a fountain in what is now Clock Court. The main feature of the smaller Mount Garden was the mound built up against the E wall in 1533–4, surmounted by a tall arbour with a large lead cupola. There were also numerous other arbours and 'banqueting houses' of various shapes in the grounds, several of them attached to the covered gallery which led from the royal apartments to the Watergate. On the N side of the palace was the Privy Orchard, with two more banqueting houses, and Henry VIII's tiltyard, surrounded by walls and viewing towers.

In the 1540s work was carried out on the elaborate conduit which brought water from Coombe Hill across the Thames (*see* Kingston, Ki). The conduit (usually ascribed to Wolsey though it may have been made at this time) supplied drinking water for the palace until the C 19.

Little new work was carried out in the grounds until the time of Charles I. The additional water supply created in his reign by the diversion of the Longford River through the grounds of Bushy Park was presumably intended for the magnificent fountain designed by *Francesco Fanelli*, put up in the Privy Garden but later moved to Bushy Park. Then after the Restoration came the works which transformed the grounds into what is still their present layout: Charles II's *patte d'oie*, possibly designed by *André Mollet* and referred to by Evelyn already in 1662, laid out in front of the E side of the palace, with its Long Water extending through Home Park, followed by William III's still more ambitious schemes. William's revolution was in this case indeed so unbloody that it was no revolution at all. He followed the *Roi Soleil* just as wholeheartedly as his more autocratic predecessor Charles II had done. As a result the present appearance of both parks is, in spite of all later alterations, that of the late C 17 and the earliest C 18, that is the period of the greatest influence on all Europe of Versailles and Le Nôtre's immortal work there.

41   It is due to William III and his gardeners *George London* and *Henry Wise* that the Home Park and Bushy Park are now the best places in England to remember the grandeur of Versailles. The scheme was approved in 1689 and planting began immediately. N of the palace a mile-long avenue was laid out through Bushy Park, ending in a 'wilderness' geometrically planted about 1714 on the N side of the palace (the site where Wren at first hoped to have his *cour d'honneur*). On the E side a garden was planned to complement Wren's new E wing. Charles II's Long Water was completed *c.* 1710 with a semicircular canal, and within the semicircle an intricate garden with box scrollwork was planted, probably designed by *Daniel Marot*, with thirteen fountains and yew trees clipped into obelisks. The garden was later simplified by Queen Anne. *Tijou*'s exquisite iron screens were made at the same time, either to enclose this garden, or for their present site at the end of the Privy Garden. On the S side the Tudor gardens at first remained, with the Water Gallery by the river, a Tudor structure altered and furnished for Queen Mary's use while Fountain Court was under construction. After her untimely death William had it demolished. Around the same time, *c.* 1700, the Mound was levelled, a new Banqueting House built, and the Privy Gardens replanted, with a raised terrace leading beside the Thames to the oval bowling green between four *Wren* pavilions. *Talman* proposed a Trianon in the French manner, but nothing came of this.

TOUR. The tour begins on the S side; then the E side, the N side, and Bushy Park.

On the S side of the palace the FLOWER GARDENS occupy the site of Henry VIII's Privy Gardens, of which nothing remains apart from some walling outlining the original enclosures. At the W end, near the Lower Orangery (now housing the Mantegna cartoons) and the Vinery (*see* Exteriors), the POND GARDENS, of which the SUNK GARDEN, lying within Tudor walls, was laid out in the 1920s in formal C 17 style. Beyond is William III's BANQUETING HOUSE, *c.* 1700, possibly on the site of a Tudor building; a plain exterior with battlements, which suggests that *Wren* felt here the same necessity as when completing Tom Tower in Oxford of some harmony between a new building and a large and important set of pre-existing old ones. Inside it is richly decorated with wall and ceiling paintings by *Verrio* and enriched doorcases by *Gibbons* (the latter possibly re-used from the Water Gallery). The little KNOT GARDEN, an imitation of Tudor gardening, was created in 1924. In front of the Wren S front, William's PRIVY GARDEN, originally a formal parterre, now with trees too tall for this to be appreciated. Along its side a raised walk leading to the exedra by the Thames, where are displayed ten of the

42   twelve magnificent GATES designed by *Tijou* for which he was paid the colossal sum of £2,160. The smith who assisted him was *Huntingdon Shaw*. The gates are perhaps the most spectacular individual piece of craftsmanship at Hampton Court,

though of a skill so excessive as to hurt the feelings of any
Ruskinian or Morrisite. In fact, however, there is a deliberate
contrast between the broad luxuriant curves of the centrepieces with lush three-dimensionally curling leaves and garlands and the plain sensible uprights in between.

Along the E front of the palace is the BROAD WALK, continuing S
to the riverside, its width at this end diminished by one of
England's most gorgeous herbaceous borders. On the axis of
the E front, William III's semicircular Fountain Garden, laid
out by *London* and *Wise*, now only a shadow of the original, its
thirteen fountains reduced to a single central pool, its intricate
box hedges replaced by plain lawns. The main feature is the
three radiating avenues of dwarf yew trees, following the lines
of Charles I's *patte d'oie*, which continue as three avenues far
across the HOME PARK with the LONG WATER along the
centre one, divided off from the semicircle by a *Tijou* screen. It
is worth walking some way along Long Water, as from the
Home Park one gains the best view of the Versaillean
approach to the palace. In the SW corner of the park was the
BOWLING GREEN which had four corner pavilions by *Wren*.
Two were converted to a residence in the C18, but all were
demolished in 1852 except the S one; this has two canted
bay-windows and other additions disguising Wren's rectangular box with stone quoins and hipped roof. Also in Home Park
the STUD HOUSE, a neat exterior with stalls divided off by
wooden arcades with Tuscan columns. The house is chiefly of
1817–18.

On the N side, near the NE corner of the palace, the TENNIS
COURT, built *c.* 1625, refitted by Charles II, but now with a
series of close-set large C18 windows, which makes it as
light-looking as any sports building of the present day. At the
far N end of the Broad Walk FLOWER POT GATE, one of the
entrances to the palace grounds from Hampton Court Road. It
dates from 1699 and has putti with baskets of fruit and flowers
by *Nost*. To the W of the N parts of Broad Walk the WILDER-
NESS, made *c.* 1714,* a set piece in French late C17 gardens.
Its present landscaping is, of course, later; but the MAZE,
probably of the same time, retains its original layout. It was
originally of hornbeams (now mostly yew and privet). Immediately N of the Maze the LION GATE, the chief N entrance
to the palace, where Wren planned to have his grand entrance
from the Bushy Park avenue. As it is, the Lion Gate is something of an anti-climax, compared with the scale of Bushy
Park, a feeble echo of Wren's dreams. The stonework bears
Queen Anne's monogram. The lions are seated upon massive
stone piers with engaged Tuscan columns on bulgy Baroque
bases. The gates, of excellent workmanship, but dispropor-
tionately small, have the monogram of George I.

The TILTYARD GARDENS to the NW end the tour of the
grounds. It is here that in Henry VIII's time tournaments

* Information from Mr Gerald Heath.

were held. Spectators sat on towers placed at intervals along the high brick walls. Only one remains. The tiltyard became a kitchen garden under William III, an ornamental garden in 1924. In the garden a sundial of 1765 from Garrick's villa at Hampton. Restaurant by the *Ministry of Public Building and Works*, 1965.

BUSHY PARK covers 1,100 acres. Opposite the Lion Gate the Grand Avenue by *London and Wise* begins, leading to the Diana Fountain. The avenue has two central rows of chestnut trees 168 ft from each other, and outside them four rows of lime trees on each side. The chestnut trees are 42 ft apart, another 42 ft separates them from the first line of lime trees, and another 42 ft lies between rows one and two of these. Rows two and three have 66 ft in between, rows three and four again 42 ft. Two more lime avenues run towards the paddock and Hampton village. The main avenue is interrupted about three-quarters down its length by a large circular pond in which in 1713 a bronze statue of Diana was placed on a high (but not high enough) rusticated pedestal. The basin, its pedestal decorated with frostwork, was made *c.* 1699. A statue by *Nost* was intended, but after William's death it was decided to re-use the fountain which Charles I had erected in the Privy Garden. This was an elaborate affair with bronze sea monsters and putti, surmounted by a figure of Arethusa, designed, according to Evelyn, by *Fanelli*. It had been much altered in 1689–94 by *Edward Pierce*, when some of the figures were recast, and was further rearranged when it was re-erected in Bushy Park by *Wren*. The figures of the boys were recast at this time. The size of the figures may have been right for their original position; in Bushy Park they are far too small and the elegant, smooth workmanship can only be appreciated by those provided with field-glasses. It is uncertain whether the misnamed figure of Diana reflects Fanelli's original. The only important buildings inside the park were UPPER LODGE, rebuilt in the early C18, of which only the stables and brewhouse survive, a neat utilitarian structure in the late Wren style; and BUSHY HOUSE (now the National Physical Laboratory), built as the Ranger's House in the 1660s (*see* Teddington).

In the Woodland Gardens, Waterhouse Pond, where the course of the LONGFORD RIVER made by Charles I divides. On the overflow a decorative brick stucco house, rebuilt in the C19. An attractive brick bridge with three arches ½ m. N.

The ROYAL MEWS on Hampton Court Green were built as the King's New Stables in 1536–8, extended in 1567–70 by the new barns and a coach house, and have been much altered since. The main survivals are the magnificent barn dated 1570 with two rows of small round-headed windows in the refaced front wall and a kingpost roof (the building is now divided into two storeys); and a square block of somewhat earlier date, built around a courtyard. Most of the detail is renewed, but the Tuscan arcade opening out into the stalls remains inside the NW range.

OUTSIDE THE PALACE GROUNDS

HAMPTON COURT GREEN has an exceptionally fine group of houses on the s side, close to the E end and turning s toward the bridge, many of them built or repaired for court officials in the late C 17 or early C 18. The MITRE HOTEL (an inn from 1666) makes a stately start, with an early C 19 front. Then THE GREEN and PALACE GATE HOUSE, the Keeper's House, rebuilt in 1716, divided in two in 1734. OLD COURT HOUSE was the official residence of the Surveyor General, probably rebuilt by *Wren* after 1708, much altered since (later upper floor, canted bay-window, rebuilt rear elevation). Note the enormous tulip tree in the garden. PAPER HOUSE, next door, was the Royal Gardener's house (front rebuilt 1713). COURT COTTAGE, the Master Carpenter's lodgings, was much rebuilt in 1703; early C 18 front of five bays. Then FARADAY HOUSE, with a central canted bay, originally one with CARDINAL'S HOUSE, the Masons' New Lodge, rebuilt in 1713–15. ROTARY COURT (the New Toy Inn of 1839, an unsuccessful venture converted to three houses in 1856) is the largest house on the s side of the Green: eleven bays. Later a hospital, since the 1970s flats for the elderly. On the N side the most ambitious of the houses closer to the palace is HAMPTON COURT HOUSE, now a children's home. Built in 1757 for the mistress of the Earl of Halifax, with additions and alterations of the mid C 19 for a classical scholar, Marmaduke Blake Sampson, remodelled further in the 1890s and after 1914. Seven-bay front with low curved galleries leading to square little wings. Mansard roof with central dome. s front after 1895. (Much altered inside, with a galleried hall of after 1914.*) C 19 picture gallery (later a theatre), built for Sampson. Pleasing grounds‡ with some C 18 features: a small lake, an octagonal summer house (former ice house?), and a GROTTO, which existed by 1769, derelict at the time of writing. It had an interior with lateral apses and a central recess, and a plaster vault decorated with plenty of ammonites. Further E PRESTBURY HOUSE, early C 18, five bays with wings, the WHITE HOUSE, three bays, probably of 1751, CHETWYND HOUSE, c. 1790, and CRAVEN HOUSE, built soon after 1784, altered in 1869. Along HAMPTON COURT ROAD on the r. several TEA HOUSES with verandas, some of them as fanciful as if they stood at New Orleans. On the l. facing them WILDERNESS HOUSE, a noble, plain, five-bay house of c. 1700. Its neighbour is the KINGS ARMS, late C 18 with an early C 19 porch. Further on towards Hampton Wick a number of good houses skirt the grounds of the palace. The best are IVY HOUSE, rebuilt after 1776, with a central window

---

* Some plasterwork here and in the entrance hall perhaps of the C 18 (R. White).

‡ The garden layout and buildings have been attributed to *Thomas Wright*; see E. Harris, *Country Life*, 5 August 1982. The grotto was intended to simulate a starry firmament, reflecting Wright's astronomical interests.

with pilastered surround; GLYCINE HOUSE, late C 17, with old iron railings and gate; PARK HOUSE, C 18 (built by 1721); SUNDIAL COTTAGE, half-timbered, possibly made up from old material; and LANCASTER LODGE of *c.* 1700.

BRIDGE. *See* Thames Crossings at end of gazetteer.

HAMPTON HILL

ST JAMES, St James's Road and Park Road. 1864 by *Wigginton*. N aisle 1874, chancel enlarged 1877, S aisle 1879. Exceedingly ugly, but not without the punch of which the sixties were capable. W tower with pinnacles and spire added by *Romaine-Walker & Tanner*, 1887.

ST FRANCIS DE SALES (R.C.), Wellington Road. 1966 by *Burles, Newton & Partners*. Large brick rectangle with slit windows with coloured glass. Campanile.

In HAMPTON HILL HIGH STREET very little to see: No. 114, *c.* 1800, with a pair of battlemented bow-windows; Nos. 165–167, the remains of a terrace of *c.* 1827; and Nos. 157–159, Prospect Place, early C 19 cottages.

HAMPTON WICK

By Kingston Bridge, to the E of Hampton Court, the counterpart of Hampton further W, but of less interest.

ST JOHN THE BAPTIST, St John's Road, off Church Grove. A Commissioners' church of 1829–30 by *E. Lapidge* (cf. Hampton). The usual rather starved yellow stock brick building of the period, with lancet windows, W turret, and galleries on three sides. Chancel added 1887; restorations 1880 and 1911. – (VICARAGE by *Teulon*, *c.* 1854, deliberately picturesque.)

(COUNCIL OFFICES (former), High Street. Tall tile-hung building of 1887. DTS)

(LIBRARY, off School Lane. By *Richmond upon Thames DTS* (*M. J. Landolt*), *c.* 1979.)

KINGSTON BRIDGE. *See* Thames Crossings.

The best houses are in the High Street and Lower Teddington Road. On the E side of the HIGH STREET Nos. 2–8 and 16, and on the W side No. 9, mostly of the early C 18; further on No. 60, C 18, weatherboarded, with canted bays and gabled porch. (Interior with chinoiserie staircase and some early panelling. DTS). In LOWER TEDDINGTON ROAD, which branches off towards the river, No. 2, early C 18, five bays, with a C 19 oriel window (C 18 staircase). No. 4, two storeys, is of late C 16 origin (RCHM), the N cross-wing formerly taller. (Reset mullion and transom window of *c.* 1600; some panelling and a fireplace with carved overmantel of the same date.) Then No. 6, early C 19, of five bays; No. 8 (RIVERSIDE), early C 18 altered; and Nos. 20–20b (WALNUT TREE

HOUSE), early C 18, with a good doorcase with segmental pediment and Corinthian pilasters. (Garden down to the river with a GAZEBO.)

(Off OLD BRIDGE STREET on the riverside Messrs Gridley Miskin, metal-framed storage buildings, c. 1900 in origin. DTS) In PARK ROAD, leading W towards Bushy Park (see Teddington), Nos. 24–30, mid C 19 Gothic, with castellated gables, and No. 40, c. 1800, a villa with a good tented balcony. At the corner with Sandy Lane, terracotta OBELISK of 1900 commemorating T. Brown, a shoemaker, preserver of a public footpath across Bushy Park. In SANDY LANE, BUSHY HOUSE and the THATCHED HOUSE, a pretty pair, originally a single cottage orné, later roughcast, with Gothic glazing.

HOMEPARK HOUSE, Hampton Court Road. Close to the Hampton Wick entrance to Hampton Court. C. 18, of good proportions. Five windows wide; later addition. Adjoining LODGE of c. 1800. THE GATEHOUSE is grey brick, late C 18. For houses further along Hampton Court Road, see Hampton Court.

KEW

CHURCHES

ST ANNE, Kew Green. Built in 1710–14 as a chapel, originally only a nave with twenty-four pews. Yellow brick with arched red brick windows. Lengthened in 1768 by *J. J. Kirby*, Gainsborough's friend, who also added the N aisle. The W façade, with a one-storey four-column portico, and a S aisle were added in 1805 by *Robert Browne*. Also at the W end a polygonal clock turret. Is this the work of *Sir Jeffry Wyatville*, who altered the W end in 1837–8? The MAUSOLEUM added E of the E end for the Duke and Duchess of Cambridge in 1850–1 by *Ferrey* appears externally with a lead-covered half dome. Italian Renaissance niches in the walls. In 1884 the S aisle was rebuilt and the church received its present E end (replacing one of 1827 by *T. Hardwick*), with the odd octagonal cupola and the odd Venetian tracery of the windows. It is to this that the church owes its peculiar character. The design was by *Henry Stock*. N vestries 1902. Extended by a parish room to the N in matching style by *Rex Johnson*, 1979, with a pedimented N front.

Inside, five-bay arcades with Tuscan columns of timber; vaulted ceiling. The crossing has brown and pink scagliola columns, the apse white and gold columns. Dome on squinches, with gold stars on a blue ground. Redecorated 1906 by *Sir Ninian Comper*. – WEST GALLERY. 1805. On cast-iron columns. – STAINED GLASS. E window by *Kempe*, 1893, with figures between Renaissance candelabra. – S chapel E window by *Mayer & Co.* of Munich in a sentimental German Renaissance style. – MONUMENTS. Many, but none of major importance. The following deserve mention. Lady Capel † 1721.

Urn between pilasters under a baldacchino. Weeping putti l. and r. – Francis Bauer, the botanical draughtsman, † 1840. By *Westmacott Jun.* Portrait medallion at the top, pretty palette arrangement at the foot. The inscription plate is framed by thick garlands of flowers. – Sir W. J. Hooker, director of the Botanic Gardens, and author of the standard work on ferns, † 1865, with *Wedgwood* medallion and panels of ferns. By *Woolner & Palgrave.* – Sir J. D. Hooker, the son of the former and also a director of the Gardens, † 1911, also with ceramic panels of plants. – In the churchyard monument to Clementina Jacobi Sobieski Schell † 1842 or 1843, called after Clementina Sobieski, wife of James III, the Old Pretender. The design in imitation of the Stuart monument by Canova in St Peter's, Rome.

ST LUKE, The Avenue, w of Sandycombe Road. 1888 by *Goldie, Child & Goldie*, in their characteristic irregularly coursed ragstone. Large towerless nave, and chancel of equal height. Conversion and extension of the nave for a day centre, with an inserted upper floor, planned 1980 (architects *Hutchison, Locke & Monk*).

OUR LADY OF LORETO AND ST WINIFRIDE (R.C.), Leyborne Park, off the N E end of Sandycombe Road. 1906 by *Scoles & Raymond.* Severe Italianate front with pedimented centre; red brick with stone dressings. Good parish hall, low and pantiled, by *Maguire & Murray*, 1978–9.

PUBLIC BUILDINGS

PUBLIC RECORD OFFICE, Ruskin Avenue, off Mortlake Road. The Public Record Office was established in 1838; its C 19 buildings are in Chancery Lane in the City of Westminster. The huge new building at Kew by the *Property Services Agency (H. J. McMaster, J. C. Clavering, G. O. Miller)*, planned from 1969 and built in 1973–7, designed to house modern records (mostly from *c.* 1800), is on a scale unprecedented among archive repositories open to the public. It covers 6,300 square metres, with 360,000 linear feet of storage (over three times the capacity of Chancery Lane), and space for 500 readers. Five storeys and a basement, a square, forbidding, concrete-clad exterior with boldly oversailing chamfered upper floors, the style of the late sixties. The three floors of repositories are recognizable by their minimal horizontal slit windows; the deep-plan, air-conditioned search rooms, offices, and workshops below have broader bands of glazing, sloped inwards to reduce harmful sunlight. Inside, the brutalist treatment is carried through to the shuttered concrete main staircases. The rest is more neutral. The two search rooms and the reference room occupy about half of the first floor. Furniture in the search rooms by the *P.S.A.*, generously spaced centrally planned tables for eight instead of the usual parallel lines of desks. Pioneering technological devices include the use of computers for ordering documents, which arrive by means of conveyor belts and a paternoster in the central service core.

CROWN BUILDING, Ruskin Avenue, to the N of the P.R.O. By *J. C. Clavering*, superintendent architect under *W. S. Bryant* of the *Whitehall Development Group* of the *Ministry of Public Building and Works*, 1967–9. Square single-storey block on stilts, overlooking the Thames. The first purpose-built open-plan office in this country (following the German practice of *Bürolandschaft*), an experimental design intended as a possible prototype for future government offices.

KEW SEWAGE TREATMENT WORKS, E of Mortlake Road, S of the P.R.O. 1887–9 and later, dominated by the heavily-modelled rusticated brick chimney of the power house.

KEW GARDENS STATION, off Sandycombe Road. Built by the London and South Western Railway, 1868–9, and one of the few remaining C19 stations on the North London line. Two storeys, lower wings, yellow brick, with nicely detailed round-headed openings.

KEW RAILWAY BRIDGE, KEW ROAD BRIDGE. *See* Thames Crossings at end of gazetteer.

PERAMBULATION

KEW GREEN. The parish church lies on the green, asymmetrical and very effectively placed. The green is triangular, as they so often are. Two of the three sides are lined with worthwhile 4 houses, mostly Georgian; the entrance to the Botanic Gardens lies in the angle between them. Along the SW side from the E, first a nice brick group, Nos. 17–25, two- and three-storeyed, then some more varied frontages (Nos. 29–31). No. 33, set back, early C18, was the Earl of Bute's study; No. 37 further on was his residence, a long rambling house, approached by a Greek Doric porte cochère of 1838–40 extending over the pavement. Then Nos. 39–45, THE GABLES, remodelled, but the shape of the gables genuine C17. Then lesser things until one reaches ROYAL COTTAGE, plain late Georgian, and HERBARIUM HOUSE (No. 55), early C18 with red brick lacing and handsome Corinthian doorcase, next to the main gates. On the N side first the HERBARIUM, a big building with an eight-bay centre with giant pilasters, attached to a good seven-bay Georgian house of three storeys with projecting corner bays, a doorway with Ionic columns and a pediment, windows with feathery keystones, and an original staircase. The additions for use as a herbarium date from 1877 (at the back), 1902 (S), 1932 (parallel to the original building), and 1969 (library extension). Then, starting with ABINGDON HOUSE (No. 61), a long group of square C18 houses with canted bays and iron balconies. The best is No. 71, late C18, of five bays, the middle three a little projecting and on the ground floor blank-arched. The group ends with No. 73.

Other houses of note are No. 77, C 18 red brick, altered, and No. 83, the dower house of Lady Capel (*see* Introduction, Royal Botanic Gardens). Early C 18, five windows wide, with carved wooden cornice. Across the main road the green continues with more modest houses; WATERLOO PLACE, 1816, and a few others. On the E side there is only a small Georgian group, Nos. 18–22; the largest is No. 20, five bays and three storeys. At the S end Nos. 2–4, BANK HOUSE, where the Palace Guard lodged in George III's time, five bays, with projecting balustraded ground floor and two pedimented Doric doorways.

Along KEW ROAD a few more C 18 houses, brick or stucco, No. 352 with a pretty Adamish doorcase; then smaller cottages of the earlier C 19 (Cumberland Place 1831) and a grander one with two shallow bows (No. 294). Further S in the neighbourhood of Kew Gardens Station streets of pleasant gabled later Victorian villas of middling size; and one minor interloper, No. 11 BROOMFIELD ROAD, to the W, a small detached roughcast house in the Arts and Crafts tradition, 1931 by *Smith & Brewer*.

ROYAL BOTANIC GARDENS

INTRODUCTION. The Royal Botanic Gardens originated as the grounds of three different establishments: Kew Palace or the Dutch House, built as a London merchant's country house in 1631, at the N end near Kew Green; a house near by later known as the White House, whose gardens, first planted by Sir Henry Capel († 1696) and Lady Capel, were praised e.g. by Evelyn; and the old park of Richmond Palace, extending N along the river from Richmond. During the C 18 the whole area became a favourite retreat for members of the royal family, who took over and added to the existing buildings, and improved the grounds. This phase ended in the early C 19, and in 1841 the gardens, united since 1802, became a national institution. The surviving buildings at Kew therefore fall into three groups: the C 17 Kew Palace, the garden buildings, which are all that survive from the C 18 royal occupation, and the greenhouses and the museums etc. put up after 1841.

HISTORY. The royal development of Richmond Park begins in the C 17, when a lodge on its outskirts was enlarged for William III; partly rebuilt by the Duke of Ormonde, who leased the building from *c.* 1702 (hence its name ORMONDE LODGE), it was bought by the Prince of Wales as a summer residence in 1719. The house stood towards the N edge of what is now the Old Dear Park. Several plans were made for a large palace in the park during the reign of George II, but nothing came of them.* The lodge remained the favourite residence of the King and Queen Caroline, who did much for

* A model for one by *Kent*, of *c.* 1735, is in Kew Palace.

the gardens, which stretched out to the W and N along the river. The dividing line was roughly along the present Holly Walk. Her gardener was *Charles Bridgeman*, the leading exponent of the transition from formal to informal, her architect *William Kent*. He put up, among other garden buildings, a Hermitage with busts of philosophers, and that celebrated folly Merlin's Cave, a tripartite structure with thatched bee-hive roofs and a Gothick ogee-arched entrance. Inside were wax figures of Merlin and his secretary, of Queen Elizabeth and her nurse, of Elizabeth Tudor, the queen of Henry VII, and of the Goddess Minerva. Built in 1735, and hence very early Gothick, like Esher. When *Capability Brown* remodelled the gardens for George III in 1765 he swept this delicious toy away. This landscaping was planned in conjunction with a new palace, for which *Chambers* made several designs, but it seems that only the foundations were begun.

Meanwhile the eldest son of George II, Frederick Prince of Wales, and Princess Augusta had settled at Kew, asking *William Kent* to remodel or rather rebuild for them Sir Henry Capel's house. The result was the WHITE HOUSE, built in 1730–5 to the SE of the Dutch House, separated from it by the road to Brentford Ferry; the centre of its site is now marked by a SUNDIAL put up in 1832. It was a plain classical structure with a pedimented five-bay centre of two and a half storeys, pedimented two-bay and two-storey wings, and one-storeyed outer wings. Alterations were made by *Chambers* for George III in 1772–3, after the schemes for a new palace had come to nothing. The house was demolished in 1822. All that remains is the separate kitchen. Ormonde Lodge was demolished in the 1770s, and so the only other survivals of the royal building activities of the C18 are the garden structures (*see* below) and the Royal Observatory and three obelisks in the Old Deer Park (*see* Richmond, Public Buildings).

After the Prince of Wales had died in 1751, his widow, the Dowager Princess Augusta, took a special interest in the gardens, and in 1759 laid the foundation of the present Botanic Gardens by dedicating about nine acres to botanical purposes. She was advised by William Aiton. After her death, Sir Joseph Banks, trusted by George III, her son, worked on their development. The White House remained the country residence of George III and Queen Charlotte until in 1801 they decided to build, just W of the Dutch House, a more ambitious and showy, if no more comfortable palace. This, designed by *James Wyatt*, was a generously crenellated and turreted castle with a central keep of four storeys. It had cast-iron supports following Samuel Wyatt's incombustible system patented in 1800, and cast-iron window tracery. The interiors were never completed. George IV had it blown up in 1827–8.

KEW PALACE, or the DUTCH HOUSE, built in 1631 by Samuel 24 Fortrey (a London merchant of Dutch descent) as a country house close to the river, is of the moderate size of 70 ft length and 50 ft depth. On its site had stood a C16 house of which part of the basement, a fireplace on the second floor, and some re-used linenfold panelling (library anteroom) remain. The palace is of brick, laid with supreme skill and artistry in Flemish not English bond, something of an innovation at the time. Three storeys, with to the main fronts three gables with double-curved sides and crowning pediments alternately triangular and segmental – also still an innovation in 1630. The windows originally had brick crosses of a mullion and a transom, and that was a relatively novel motif too.

The style of Kew Palace seems to have appealed to only a limited stratum of civilization: the connoisseurs and virtuosi appreciated the classicity of Inigo Jones, but the wealth of the provinces still went into buildings in the Tudor tradition, of stone in the North, timber-framed in the West. In and around London however there was a class, chiefly merchants, who scorned the Tudor tradition as old-fashioned, but could not make themselves accept the restraint of the Palladian style. For them such brick houses were built, their gables demonstrating by their crowning pediments their awareness of the Renaissance. The chief survivals of this style in the London area are Cromwell House, Highgate (Ca) (c. 1637–40) and Swakeleys (Hi) (c. 1630–8). Broome Park, Kent (1635–8), is another contemporary example. Kew Palace is the oldest firmly dated survival (although the style appears to have been introduced to London somewhat earlier, see the pedimented gable of Lady Cooke's house in Holborn, drawn by John Smythson in 1619).

One of the most characteristic features of the house is the evident delight in play with brickwork, such as the rustication round all windows. The centre bay is enriched by superimposed pilasters and, on the top floor, by columns – the pilasters on the ground floor have been removed – and by arched windows. The interior is very simply arranged, with a cross passage through from the present doorway to the river doorway and two main rooms to its l., two to its r., on each floor. The details date mostly from the mid and later C18, when the house was occupied by the royal family, see e.g. the staircase with three turned balusters to the tread and carved tread-ends. Specially interesting are the ceiling of one room on the first floor (queen's boudoir) with an original plaster ceiling of c. 1631 – still in the Jacobean tradition – and the overdoors of a room on the ground floor (king's dining room), an C18 imitation of this Jacobean style, due in all probability to *Kent*, who was working at the White House c. 1730 and doing similar bits of Jacobean Revival at Hampton Court in 1732. The delightful formal garden on the river side of Kew Palace was laid out in C17 style in 1975.

THE GARDENS. Kew Gardens, nearly 300 acres in size, cannot be compared with any of the other older botanic gardens in the world: the combination of botanical interest and beauty of landscape is unmatched. It is the consecutive work of two ages, the mid C18 and the mid C19. In the mid C18 Princess

Augusta's gardens assumed their shape under *Chambers*, George III and Queen Charlotte's gardens at Ormonde Lodge (*c*. 1764) under *Capability Brown*. Of Chambers's work it is mostly the small buildings which still exist. The principal alterations in the layout, after the gardens had been passed on to the State – of the buildings the Perambulation will treat – are due to Sir William and Sir Joseph Hooker (*see* St Anne, above), directors in 1841–65 and 1865–85. When Sir William was appointed in 1841, the garden was 11 acres in size. He increased it to 76 in five years. The picturesque lake was excavated in 1845 and later enlarged; the pond in front of the Palm House, of 1847, and the four main vistas, Broad Walk, Holly Walk, Pagoda Vista, and Cedar Vista, were designed by *W. A. Nesfield*.

PERAMBULATION from N to S. The main ENTRANCE GATES from Kew Green are of 1845–6 by *Decimus Burton*. The thick, scrolly iron gates were made by *Walker* of Rotherham, the equally thick garlands on the stone piers by *J. Heming Jun*. In one of the two outer niches a statue of a child by *John Bell*, 1863. The vases come from earlier gates to Kew Palace. On entering one has at once on the r. the small house called AROID HOUSE NO. 1, by *John Nash*, originally one of two pavilions flanking the garden façade of Buckingham Palace, re-erected here in 1836. Its companion is still *in situ*. It has glass walls with Tuscan pilasters along the sides and six Ionic columns *in antis* along the fronts. Even the pediments are mostly glazed. The structure is of cast iron. To its W 'The Sower', a STATUE by *Sir Hamo Thornycroft*, 1886, on a later base by *Lutyens*. Near by, the site for the REFERENCE COLLECTION BUILDING, with glazed public concourse, exhibition space, and library, designed by *Manning & Clamp* in 1982. S of this the ORANGERY, built by *Sir William Chambers* and dated 1761 (although built in 1757), for a long time England's largest hothouse. Chambers, then thirty-eight years old, was Princess Augusta's favourite architect and taught her son, the future George III, the art of drawing. The orangery stood SE of her house, the White House. It is seven bays long with rusticated walls and arched openings, the first and last bays pedimented, of brick, still stuccoed with Chambers's secret form of stucco.

W of the orangery, in the NW corner of the gardens, the BOTANICAL BUILDINGS of the later C19 and C20, mostly not of architectural interest. The latest newcomer is the ALPINE HOUSE, a 46-ft-square pyramid whose outline can be transformed by jagged opening roof flaps. There are only four internal supports. By *R. H. Partnership* and the *Property Services Agency*, 1979. By Kew Road the JODRELL LABORATORY AND LECTURE THEATRE, by *C. G. Pinfold* of the *Ministry of Public Building and Works*, 1965. The VICTORIA GATES in Kew Road were cast by the *Coalbrookdale Company*.

The most important botanical buildings lie quite close to the Victoria Gates, or can be reached by following the Broad

Walk from the orangery to the pond. The pond lies between the Palm House and Museum No. 1, two buildings equally characteristic of the sound and enterprising spirit of the gardens in the 1840s and 50s. The PALM HOUSE, one of the boldest pieces of C19 functionalism in existence – much bolder indeed, and hence aesthetically much more satisfying, than the Crystal Palace ever was – was designed by *Decimus Burton*, with *Richard Turner* the engineer. Burton had previously been involved with Paxton over the conservatories at Chatsworth. The splendid uncluttered external form of the building is due originally to Burton, not to Turner (whose first proposals were for a building with 'ecclesiastical' detail). The wide uninterrupted internal spaces now appear to have been the result of subsequent collaboration between Burton and Turner, who, as ironfounder, was also responsible for many of the details. The most notable of Turner's contributions was the use of wrought iron instead of the clumsier cast iron for the frame. The wrought-iron ribs are the earliest examples of substantial rolled I-section beams to be used outside shipbuilding.* Building took from 1844 to 1848. The Palm House, 362 ft long, and in its centre 62 ft, in its wings 33 ft high, consists entirely of iron and glass and has curved roofs throughout. The rise of the roofs up the wings and then up the centre is unforgettable. The vertical walls and the vertical strip at the foot of the centre roof are too low to interfere with the strong rhythm of the indentical curves. A short distance to the N is the WATER LILY HOUSE, built in 1852 for the recently introduced Victoria Regia, with delicate roof-trusses in a roundel pattern, by *Turner*. Opposite the Palm House across the pond is MUSEUM NUMBER ONE, built as such in 1856–7. Designed by *Burton*, it is as straightforward a job as the Palm House – stock brick, eleven bays long, the detail in a utilitarian minimum-classical. Also connected with this mid-C19 moment is the Italianate CAMPANILE, S of the pond. Of 1847, also of stock brick, it is also by *Burton*, built as a chimney for the furnaces beneath the Palm House. In front and facing the pond the set of QUEEN'S BEASTS, stone replicas of the plaster originals carved by *James Woodford* for the Coronation of Queen Elizabeth II and displayed outside the W annexe to Westminster Abbey.

Near the pond also begins the chain of C18 GARDEN BUILDINGS with which *Chambers* and others embellished Princess Augusta's gardens. Chambers's temples, all dating from *c.* 1760–3, were published by him in 1763. The first, the TEMPLE OF AEOLUS, to the NE on a little hill, a domed rotunda with Tuscan columns, was rebuilt by *Burton* in 1845. The second, the TEMPLE OF ARETHUSA, SE of the pond and N of the campanile, is of 1758. Front with two Ionic columns

---

* For two different views on the role of Turner see *The King's Works*, vol. VI, and E. J. Diestelkamp in *Journal of Garden History*, vol. 2, No. 3 (1982), and *Transactions of the Newcomen Society* (forthcoming, 1982–3).

between two pillars and a pediment. s of the campanile and the Victoria Gate the TEMPLE OF BELLONA (1760). Façade with a portico of two pairs of Tuscan columns; metope frieze; shallow dome on a drum behind. Inside, a room with an oval-domed centre. On the walls garlands and medallions with the names and numbers of British and Hanoverian regiments connected with the Seven Years' War.

Some 800 ft W is KING WILLIAM'S TEMPLE or the Pantheon, built in 1837 to the design of *Sir Jeffry Wyatville*. Four Tuscan columns with a metope frieze at the front as well as at the back. On the long sides the metopes are replaced by windows. Inside a number of finely shaped and finely lettered cast-iron tablets commemorating British victories from Minden to Waterloo.

s of King William's Temple the bulky and unmistakably clumsy shape of the TEMPERATE HOUSE, known originally as the Winter Garden, 628 ft long, designed by *Burton* in 1859–62. It consists of a long rectangular greenhouse, extended in 1898–9 by lower N and s wings which are linked to the main building by octagonal vestibules. The construction is of light wrought-iron lattice arches, but, unlike the Palm House, the sashes are of wood, and are straight, not curved, designed (according to Hooker's instructions) so that the roof could be opened up on hot days. It was also Hooker who specified that the roof should be hidden by a stone cornice.* As a result it is an anti-climax after the naked beauty of the Palm House. The Temperate House was restored, after long neglect, by *Manning, Clamp & Partners* from *c.* 1978–82. The glazing was entirely renewed, panes with thin aluminium bars replacing the original wooden frames.

Opposite the N end of the Temperate House to the E is the FLAGSTAFF, the trunk of a Douglas Fir, 225 ft long, erected on a mound in 1959. To the s is the NORTH GALLERY (which houses – by hook or by crook – 848 flower paintings of 1872–85 by *Marianne North*), built by the architectural historian *James Fergusson* to illustrate his theory of lighting temples.‡ Further s is a LODGE designed by *Eden Nesfield* and built in 1866. This is historically speaking an extremely important work, as it is in the style made popular by Nesfield's former partner Norman Shaw about six years later. Red brick, walls with short pilasters, tall truncated pyramid roof with central chimneystack. Dormer windows with segmental pediments. The style was later wrongly called Queen Anne. Its sources are in the English brick architecture of *c.* 1630–60, itself influenced by Holland. Kew Palace no doubt inspired Nesfield. s of this, *Chambers*'s RUINED ARCH (1759–60), picturesquely overgrown at the time of writing. To its sw the REFRESHMENT PAVILION, a nice straightforward piece of building, light, generously glazed, and with a raised centre, 1920 by the

---

* We owe these details to Robert Thorne.
‡ Information from David Watkin.

Ministry of Works (*R. D. Allison*). Its predecessor had been burnt in 1913 by Suffragettes.

65   Here one joins the avenue called Pagoda Vista and can walk straight to *Chambers's* PAGODA. This supreme example of chinoiserie, built of stock brick in 1761, is 163 ft high and of ten storeys. On each of the upper storeys is a balcony with a pretty Chippendale railing all round, and on the top there were originally eighty enamelled dragons. Wooden spiral staircase inside. Although Chambers is best known as an academic Palladian and co-founder of the Royal Academy, there was a strain of fantasy in him which comes out very occasionally in details of his Palladian buildings – the Piranesian arches of Somerset House, the plan of the Casino at Marino – but to which he could give free rein only at Kew. Chambers had seen China as a young man, had written about Chinese architecture in 1757, and later published some wild theories on Chinese landscape gardening and the role of terror in it. Of the necessity of the latter he does not seem to have been able to convince Princess Augusta, but his desire to design exotic buildings was not satisfied with the Pagoda. In the wilderness, which was the part of the garden entered by the ruined arch (*see* above), there were, as well as the Pagoda, a Moorish Alhambra (1758), based on a design by *Muntz* of 1750, and a Turkish Mosque, remarkably early examples of a somewhat indiscriminate historicism.*

To the S E of the Pagoda, in the S E corner of the gardens, is the LION GATE.

To the W of the Pagoda only two more buildings need attention. The CHOKUSHI MON, or Gate of the Imperial Messenger, is a replica of the famous gateway made for an exhibition in London in 1910 and presented to the gardens. A little over ¼ m. W, the QUEEN'S COTTAGE, built and, it is said, designed by *Queen Charlotte*. It dates from *c.* 1772 and belongs to the part of Kew Gardens which was the grounds of Ormonde Lodge, at that time rearranged by *Capability Brown*. This dear little cottage, oblong, of timber-framing and brick with a thatched roof, has across the middle on both sides a gabled projection flanked by lower porches. The centre room downstairs is papered with Hogarth prints. On either side is an elegant staircase leading to the upstairs room, which is painted in the guise of a floral arbour. The work is attributed for good reasons by Mr Croft Murray to the *Princess Elizabeth* (cf. Frogmore, Windsor Great Park, Berkshire).

* Other buildings which have disappeared included a Chinese House of Confucius, probably built *c.* 1750, by *Chambers*; a Gothic Cathedral, very gimcrack and very pretty, designed by *Muntz c.* 1759; several more classical temples by Chambers: to Pan (1758), Victory (1759), Solitude (1760), the Sun (1761), and Peace (1763); the Gallery of Antiques, Menagerie, and Aviary; and the Theatre of Augusta, which was a colonnade for the Princess's theatrical parties (1760).

MORTLAKE

Mortlake was once a handsome riverside village. By the church one can still get the old flavour. But nowadays the most prominent building from the river is the brewery.

ST MARY, Mortlake High Street. Mostly by *Sir A. Blomfield*, chancel 1885, nave (by his firm) 1905, replacing a rebuilding of 1840 by *S. Beachcroft*. Parish room, rector's office, and choir vestry 1980 by *Maguire & Murray*. What remains from an earlier time is the Perp w tower of 1543, built by order of Henry VIII. The inscription is bogus. Top storey probably of 1694. A pretty open lantern and part of the N wall, brick with plain round-arched windows, of 1815. Inside a Perp w doorway (probably re-used) instead of a tower arch. Spandrels with blank tracery. – FONT. Simple, Perp, octagonal. – (STAINED GLASS. In the tower window a single light (Annunciation), an attractive simple design by *Holiday*, made by *Powell's*, 1866. M. Harrison) – MONUMENTS. Francis Coventry †1699 by *William Kidwell*. Hanging wall-monument with inscription plate flanked by two young standing figures carrying the scrolly entablature and an open pediment with an urn in the middle. A fine, rich, luxuriant piece. – Nicholas Godschall † 1748. Good, with a group of three cherubs' heads in the 'predella'. – Viscountess Sidmouth † 1811, by *Westmacott*. Relief with the dying young woman on a couch held by an allegorical figure. Faith stands on the l. The relief is flanked by Greek Doric quarter-columns. – In the churchyard an ARCH erected about 1865 out of the materials of the tower doorway then being rebuilt. – Adjoining the church the pretty VESTRY HOUSE of *c*. 1660–70. Brick. Doorway with a straight hood on carved brackets.

ST MARY MAGDALEN (R.C.), North Worple Way, s of Mortlake High Street. By *G. R. Blount*, 1852. – In the nearby R.C. CEMETERY the MAUSOLEUM designed by *Lady Burton* to Sir R. F. Burton † 1890, the explorer and translator of the *Arabian Nights*, a life-size stone tent with a crucifix above the place where the entrance seems to be. The tomb is visible through a window. – (Several modest tomb slabs by *Leonard Stokes* to his relatives. HM)

In the HIGH STREET, w of the church, depressing flats by *E. Colley*. To the E the best houses, especially No. 123, a later Georgian façade with a porch of four Tuscan columns. Gate-piers and interior of *c*. 1720. Good entrance hall and staircase. The house and garden were painted by Turner (Frick Collection, New York, and National Gallery, Washington). Now flanked by depot buildings (conversion for workspace by *Arup Associates* proposed 1981). Other houses worth a look are No. 119 (L-shaped), No. 117 (with bow and tented balcony to the river), No. 115, and Nos. 103–105, all Georgian. MORTLAKE BREWERY now dominates the riverside. The High Street frontage was built in 1869 as an extension to Messrs Phillips and Wogan's Brewery after the closure of Thames Street, which ran down to the river from Lower Richmond Road. The other parts of the brewery, mid C19 and later, were mostly demolished in the 1970s and replaced by a modern brewing plant of frankly industrial character (*Douglas Marriott Worby & Robinson*, 1979–81).

Further W the following buildings deserve record. First the BOOT AND SHOE MAKERS' BENEVOLENT INSTITUTION, W of the station between two blocks of flats. Built in 1836. Imitation Tudor brick. In AYNSCOMBE LANE, between Lower Richmond Road and Thames Bank, the GATEPIERS of the former Cromwell House, rusticated, with a niche in the street fronts. The gate is C18 wrought iron. Another big house was Tapestry House, now also demolished. Mortlake was the seat of the English tapestry workshops, founded in 1619, which flourished until the Civil War.

In THAMES BANK an extremely pleasant group of houses facing the river, especially THAMES COTTAGE, THAMES BANK HOUSE, and LEYDEN HOUSE, all of C18 appearance. The road continues as a towpath to the NW under CHISWICK BRIDGE (*see* Thames Crossings at end of gazetteer).

In WESTHALL ROAD, N of Mortlake Road E of the railway, WEST HALL, a good house of the late C17, three by four bays, with a hipped roof with a tiny lantern. Doorway with attached Tuscan columns.

S of the railway, in FITZGERALD AVENUE, N of Upper Richmond Road and W of Priory Lane, the COACH HOUSE, an engaging folly. It incorporates old fragments, including a big Wren-type doorcase dated 1696 and several attached Ionic columns.

PETERSHAM

ALL SAINTS, Bute Avenue, W of Sudbrook Park. 1907–8 by *John Kelly*, the gift of Mrs Lionel Warde. A large, very red church of brick and terracotta. The mixture is Waterhouseish, the style emphatically Italian Early Christian or Romanesque. Round-arched windows etc. and a tall S campanile. Very lavish interior, the sanctuary up a high flight of steps, with marble floor, screen, and seats, and carved REREDOS. N of the nave a quite exceptional BAPTISTERY with its own ambulatory around a vaulted immersion font and, on the upper level, a small font supported by big angels. Separate church hall and institute.

ST PETER. A church of uncommon charm, lying along a path leading N from the main road. Chancel of the late C13 (one N window a cusped lancet). The rest rebuilt in the early C16; transepts and tower added in the early C17, extended later. Nave and W tower of red brick, the tower with battlements and a pretty octagonal lantern added in 1790. S transept enlarged, and galleries added, in 1840 by one *Meakin*. Brick with arched windows. The interior is well preserved in its

pre-Victorian state. – FONT on a baluster stem, 1740. – BOX
PEWS, GALLERIES in the transepts. – Two-decker PULPIT,
made in 1796, with iron handrail to the steps. – READING
DESK, raised and corresponding to the pulpit. – MONUMENT.
George Cole † 1624 and his wife and their grandson George
Cole. Stiffly reclining effigies. Recess flanked by columns, its
shallow arch coffered. In the 'predella' the small reclining
figure of the grandson. – (In the churchyard, gravestone of
Albert Henry Scott † 1864 by his father *Sir G. G. Scott*, who
lived at the Manor House, Ham.)

Petersham, for its small size, is unusually rich in fine houses of
the late C 17 and C 18 whose dates and ownership require
further investigation. They lie close together at a sharp bend
of PETERSHAM ROAD and traffic makes it almost impossible
to see them. The best are on the N side. From E to W:
PARKGATE (No. 137), late C 18, with an Ionic porch. Then
the path to the church with CHURCH HOUSE, early C 19,
with big projecting eaves. PETERSHAM HOUSE has a late
C 17 front with a charming semicircular domed early C 19
porch with Ionic columns. Of the same time the top storey.
Excellent staircases with strong twisted balusters and mytho-
logical wall paintings of *c.* 1710 by *Laguerre*. Three excellent
fireplaces of *c.* 1775. Excellent wrought-iron gates and railings. On the S side some mediocre C 20 housing, but also
RESTON LODGE, with an early C 19 front of five bays, two
and a half storeys, stuccoed, with a porch of two pairs of
Tuscan columns; probably earlier behind. Cast-iron gates
with thick ornament. Then MONTROSE HOUSE. Of early
C 18 appearance, although said to have been built in the later
C 17 by Sir Thomas Jenner, a Catholic lawyer who owned
much property in Petersham. Yellow and red brick. The
original centre five bays wide. Brick quoins. Segment-headed,
slender windows. Aprons below the first-floor windows. Two-
storeyed attachments. Roman Doric porch. Iron gates at the
corner. Opposite is RUTLAND LODGE, an exquisite example
of the style of the later C 17, possibly also built by Sir Thomas
Jenner († 1707). Seven bays and two storeys plus an attic
storey above the cornice. Slender windows vertically laced
together. Beautiful doorway, broad, with a segmental pediment on Roman Doric pilasters against a rusticated background. The railings of the front garden form a semicircle.
Fine gates. Converted into flats after the interior was destroyed by fire in 1967.*

Rutland Lodge is at the corner of RIVER LANE, which bends
down to the river. On the W side the MANOR HOUSE, early
C 18, five bays and two storeys, with segment-headed frieze,
and a segmental pediment (a later introduction). Set back
from the road, two modern houses by *L. Manasseh*, 1964–7.
The smaller one, COURTYARDS, has an internal court; the

---

* The staircase had a coved ceiling and noble plasterwork of *c.* 1740, slender
balusters, three to the tread, and carved tread-ends. In the drawing room was a
glorious big Rococo cartouche above the fireplace.

larger, DRUM HOUSE, is of one and two storeys, L-shaped, with roof terraces. Large semicircular projection at one end (containing a swimming pool). Further on a pretty C 17 timber-framed cottage. Then PETERSHAM LODGE, close to the river, an irregular stuccoed front to the road with a large wing projecting forward. The original house of six bays was built *c.* 1740 and occupied by Robert Ord († 1778). To the garden a fine pediment with Rococo decoration. The present entrance in the angle of the main house and the wing leads to a staircase with a bulbous dome, and flattened segmental upper windows, clearly a later alteration. In the garden a ROTUNDA.

Back to the part of PETERSHAM ROAD which runs s towards Ham. On the w side first some small houses: an early C 19 terrace (Nos. 136–142) and a single C 18 house (No. 147). Behind is DOUGLAS HOUSE, which overlooks the former E drive to Ham House. Built *c.* 1700, yellow and red brick, five bays and two storeys, with hipped roof and one-bay pediment. The doorway frieze curving up in the middle and a segmental pediment on brackets. Big stable block on the r., with projecting wings, a hipped roof, and a pedimented one-bay centre. The buildings are now part of the GERMAN SCHOOL. Additional school buildings by the German firm *Kersten Mertinoff & Struhk*, designed 1972, completed 1981 (executive architects *W. H. Marmorek* and *Clifford Culpin & Partners*). The landscaping is by *R. Hermes*.

The GATEHOUSE to the drive to Ham House is in a spectacular Jacobean of *c.* 1900, outdoing the house to which it was intended to be an introduction. Near by, TREE CLOSE, by *Manning & Clamp*, 1976, delightful intimate groups of one-storey sheltered housing for single people, arranged around small gravelled courts opening off a central square. Crisply detailed, with pantiled roofs.

The E side of PETERSHAM ROAD has towards the s end some more C 18 houses (Nos. 250, 230), and, returning N, the former LODGES to Petersham Park.* GORT HOUSE was originally one house with GORT LODGE in SUDBROOK LANE. Early C 18, with a two-storey front to the main road, seven bays wide, and a doorway to Sudbrook Lane with a charming frieze curving up in the middle. In the same lane one or two more good if less spectacular houses, particularly HARRINGTON LODGE of *c.* 1700 with a segmental pediment. Off the s end in HAZEL LANE, WHORNES PLACE, a nostalgic creation by *Blunden Shadbolt*, 1925, with materials brought from Sir William Whorne's timber-framed house of 1487 at Cuxton, Kent.

SUDBROOK PARK, s of Sudbrook Lane. The enviable clubhouse of the golf course is the house by *James Gibbs* built in

---

* PETERSHAM PARK, also, confusingly, called Petersham Lodge, was a house (replacing an earlier one) built by *Lord Burlington* for William Stanhope, first Viscount Petersham, to which additions were made for the first Lord Camelford. It was demolished in the early C 19, when the grounds were thrown together with Richmond Park.

1726 for the Duke of Argyll and Greenwich (the grandson of the Duchess of Lauderdale of Ham House, q.v.). Nine bays, brick and stone dressings. Basement, main and upper storey. Slender segment-headed windows with aprons. Brick quoins, parapet. The main accent on the garden as well as the entrance side a giant portico of Corinthian columns with frieze and raised balustrade, projecting only slightly in front of the façade, so that the space behind the columns is actually a loggia. On the entrance side the effect has been spoiled by a tall extension forward of the portico. On the garden side a splendid open stair towards the entrance, starting in two flights parallel with the façade and then joining up into one. The plan is typically Palladian. The centre is a cube room 61 which runs through from front to back portico. The other rooms open out from it, and on the upper floor have to be reached from the small staircases. The cube room is luxuriously decorated: giant coupled pilasters, coved ceiling, marble fireplace, doorways with very finely designed heads and pediment – Gibbs at his most Baroque.

RICHMOND

CHURCHES

CHRIST CHURCH, Kew Road. By *A. Blomfield*, 1893.

HOLY TRINITY, Townshend Road, N of Sheen Road. 1870 by *R. Brandon*. (Tower by *Luck*, 1880, demolished *c.* 1970.)

ST JOHN THE DIVINE, Kew Road. 1831–6 by *Lewis Vulliamy*: a Commissioners' church. It cost £5,633. Chancel, S chapel, and vestries added 1904–5 by *A. Grove*. Vulliamy's façade is of grey brick, with the craziest W spire and senseless flying buttresses from the W porches up to the nave. Grove's E end is a fine composition in free Gothic, with thin lancets flanking a sturdy buttress with a Crucifixion beneath its gable. On the N side, sympathetically designed flats above the vestries, part of the alterations of 1980–1 by *Dry Hastwell Butlin Bicknell* which include a new hall on the N side of the church. Aisleless nave with a flat ceiling. Pretty W balconies above the W gallery, their parapets projecting on a ribbed coving. The area beneath was partitioned off by an attractive wood and glass screen in 1980–1 when other facilities were added to make the church usable as an occasional concert hall. At the E end an excellent collection of Anglo-Catholic furnishings, mostly by *Grove*, including woodwork (especially in the Lady Chapel) with decidedly Art Nouveau touches. – Of the copious PAINTED DECORATION by *N. H. J. Westlake*, only the ceiling of the chancel, the upper part of the E wall, and the large painted TRIPTYCH (1909) remain. – IRON SCREEN and GATES to the Lady Chapel by *Bainbridge Reynolds*; simple reticulated patterns. – Good STAINED GLASS of 1912 in the Lady Chapel E window by *Christopher Whall*, figured panels on clear glass. –

Two-light s window by *Mabel Esplin* (PC). – STATIONS OF
THE CROSS by *Freda Skinner*, 1955–70, in the tradition of
Eric Gill's work at Westminster Cathedral. – To the E of the
church, across St John's Road, CHURCH HALL by *Grove*,
1910–11, brick, with an Art Nouveau carved stone doorway
reminiscent of Harrison Townsend.

ST MARY MAGDALENE, Paradise Road. The old parish
church. Perp w tower of *c.* 1507, faced with flint and stone in
1903–4. The body of the church of 1750; N and s fronts earlier.
Yellow and red brick. Five bays, arched windows. On the s
side a pediment over the three middle windows, a cross-
accent, not in harmony with medieval principles. It was originally balanced by a projecting porch in the centre of the N side,
removed in 1864. Higher chancel of flint and stone, with
chapel and vestry, 1903–4 by *G. F. Bodley*. Inside, arcades of
five bays with slender Tuscan columns, a straight entablature,
a clerestory, and an inappropriate open timber roof of 1866
(by *A. W. Blomfield*). Tower arch of *c.* 1507. – FONT. An c 18
fluted bowl on a new stem. – PULPIT. A nice c 18 piece,
hexagonal, on twisted columns. – Good chancel furnishings
and decoration: STAINED GLASS by *Burlison & Grylls*, COM-
MUNION RAILS and HIGH ALTAR 1932 by *W. Randoll
Blacking*. Ceiling painting 1976 in pretty Gothic colours.

   MONUMENTS. A worthwhile collection with rewarding
inscriptions. Several c 17 monuments with kneeling figures
and without figures. Artistically the most interesting are the
following: Robert Cotton † 1591. Brass plate with kneeling
figures. – John Bentley † 1660, and his wife and daughter,
with three busts in a thin architectural frame (not the original
arrangement). Attributed to *T. Burman*. – Viscount Broun-
cker † 1687, a vigorous Baroque cartouche in an architectural
frame. – Sophia Chaworth † 1689. Another good architectural
tablet, stone and black marble. – Randolph Greenway † 1754.
Very fine hanging monument; Rococo decoration in the Kent
style. – William Rowan † 1767. Bust before obelisk. – Major
Bean † 1815, by *John Bacon Jun*. With a kneeling desperate
woman by an urn on a pedestal. – Barbara Lowther † 1806, by
Flaxman. Exactly the same ingredients, but handled with
much greater restraint, indeed just a little coldly. – Edmund
Kean. 1839 by *Loft* (Kelly). Draperies with attached profile
medallion. – Mrs Holland † 1844, by *E. W. Wyon*. A weeping
female by an urn. The urn bears just the one word, 'Holland'.
– J. Lever † 1870. Brass with canopies, two saints, and inscription. – Mary Elizabeth Maxwell † 1915. Bronze relief
with portrait bust by *J. E. Hyett*. – In the CHURCHYARD,
besides many table tombs, Sir Matthew Decker, 1759 by
Scheemakers. Sarcophagus and obelisk.*

ST MATTHIAS, Friars Stile Road. 1857–8 by *Sir G. G. Scott*.
The grandest church in Richmond. NW tower with tall spire

---

* In the former churchyard extension, Vineyard Passage, the large Grecian
tomb of T. Cundy † 1825, 'architect of Pimlico', and his family.

(195 ft), completed 1861–2. Nave and aisles, chancel, apse. Choir vestry 1884 by *J. O. Scott*; All Saints Chapel 1915 by *Cecil Hare*. Clerestory with lancets, arcaded on the outside (as at All Saints Stamford and other Lincs churches). Other windows with geometrical tracery. Tall interior; arcades with foliage capitals. Pretty painted ceiling to the chancel roof, *c.* 1890. Nave roof ceiled 1914 (nave and aisles). The w end was divided off in an especially sympathetic conversion by *Hutchison, Locke & Monk*, 1975–8. Two E bays of the nave remain. The w end now has rooms in the aisles on two levels, and a w gallery. The partitions are ingeniously faced with timber from the former pews. – Well preserved FUR-NISHINGS. SANCTUARY FITTINGS 1908–9 by *Hare* (panelling completed and stalls added by *D. Pearce*, 1934). – Openwork traceried SCREEN and ORGAN CASE by *Sir A. Blomfield*, 1896. – Good STAINED GLASS. Apse windows *c.* 1861 and w rose 1868 by *Wailes*; some N and S aisle windows by *Hardman*; All Saints Chapel windows, 1916.

ST ELIZABETH (R.C.), The Vineyard. 1824. Chancel, presbytery, and tower rebuilt by *F. A. Walters*, 1903. Yellow and red brick, with a w tower carrying a Baroque cap.

OUR LADY OF PEACE (R.C.), Sheen Road. By *Goodhart-Rendel, Broadbent & Curtis*, 1953–4.

BETHLEHEM CHAPEL, Church Terrace, off Paradise Road. 1797. Nice stuccoed façade. Three bays with blank arcading. To the l. and r. one-bay, one-storeyed entrance attachments.

CONGREGATIONAL CHURCH, The Vineyard. 1831 by *John Davies*. Grey brick, Norman. Porch with a remarkably elaborate tympanum. All the ornamental work is of brick.

FIRST CHURCH OF CHRIST SCIENTIST, Sheen Road. 1939–53 by *Braxton, Sinclair & Barton*. Heavily modelled red brickwork, with some free Baroque details.

(UNITARIAN CHURCH, Ormond Road, N of The Vineyard. Apse with five STAINED GLASS lancets by *Morris & Co.*, 1912.)

UNITED REFORMED CHURCH, Little Green. 1884–5 by *W. Wallace*.

(RICHMOND CEMETERY, Grove Road, E of Queen's Road. 1861. Two Gothic chapels of imaginative design, with plate tracery. HM)

PUBLIC BUILDINGS

MUNICIPAL OFFICES (former Town Hall), Hill Street. 1893 by *W. J. Ancell*; mixed Renaissance. Originally with an ornate gabled skyline, destroyed in the Second World War. Remodelled by *Gordon Jeeves*, 1952. Interior rebuilding planned 1981 (*see* Perambulation 2).

MAGISTRATES COURT, Parkshot, NE of Richmond Green. 1975 by the *G.L.C. Architect's Department*. A well proportioned building of white concrete blockwork and tinted glass, housing five clerestory-lit courtrooms. Attractively designed, but an overpowering neighbour in a Georgian street.

POST OFFICE, George Street. *See* Perambulation 3.

PUBLIC LIBRARY, The Green. 1879–81 by *F. S. Brunton*. Gothic. Richmond was the earliest local authority in the outer London area to adopt the Libraries Act.

RICHMOND BATHS, Old Deer Park. By *Leslie Gooday*, 1966. Good, straightforward buildings of dark brick. The main block with the pool has a large window facing the park, with strongly projecting mullions. Lower flanking ranges and long brick walls successfully tie the group into its surroundings.

THEATRE, The Green. 1899 by *Frank Matcham*. A remarkably self-assured contribution to the Green, designed in total neglect of any Georgian responsibilities. Red brick and brown terracotta. Plenty of ornament. Two symmetrical turrets with copper-covered cupolas.

OLD OBSERVATORY, Old Deer Park. Built for George III in the park of Richmond Palace by *Sir William Chambers (see also* Kew, Royal Botanic Gardens). Complete at the time of the transit of Venus in 1769. Now a block of five by three bays, the building originally took the form of a villa with a central block with basement and two upper storeys flanked by one-storey wings (raised in the c 19). The observatory proper on the roof, like a cupola or belvedere, an idea derived from Swedish observatories built in the 1740s–50s at Uppsala and Stockholm, which were the first to house instruments in a turret instead of on an open tower. The long sides have a canted central bay. Inside, an octagonal room corresponds to each of them. The two octagons have one side in common – an ingenious plan. Nice, somewhat Chippendale-Chinese woodwork inside (by *James Arrow*), especially the gallery in one of the octagons. The three OBELISKS close to the observatory, a reminder of the era when it measured London's official time, were paid for in 1778, and are by *Edward Anderson*. The building was used by the Meteorological Office until 1981.*

RICHMOND COLLEGE, Richmond Hill, off Queen's Road. Built as the Wesleyan Theological Institution in 1841–3 by *A. Trimmer*, large and prosperous neo-Tudor, with a symmetrical front of fine ashlar stone with projecting wings. Four-storeyed, in the recessed centre the two lower storeys taken as one. In the middle the familiar gatehouse motif. A corridor leads to the LIBRARY (now subdivided) added by *Sir E. Maufe* in 1931.

ROYAL BALLET SCHOOL (WHITE LODGE), Richmond Park. *See* Perambulation 5.

HOLY TRINITY C. OF E. PRIMARY SCHOOL, Upper Richmond Road. 1976 by *Green, Lloyd & Adams*, a pleasant single-storey brick building with an eccentric hall lantern (PV).

ST JOHN'S SCHOOLS (former), Clarence Street. *See* Perambulation 3.

* Use as offices and museum proposed 1981 (architects *Clifford Culpin & Partners*) (DTS).

ROYAL STAR AND GARTER HOME, Richmond Hill. 1921–4 by *Sir Edwin Cooper* for invalid and incurable servicemen, a large neo-Georgian–Imperial building of brick with ample stone trim, the chief accents pairs of recessed giant columns. Large hipped roof. The style and the position, with its view across the plain, are like those of a Swiss or American luxury hotel of the early C20. Memorial hall of marble with Ionic columns.

ROYAL HOSPITAL, Kew Foot Road, off the NE end of Twickenham Road. The core is a house of *c.* 1750 (ROSENDALE HOUSE), the home of the writer James Thomson. Inside a stately staircase. Additions of 1896 by *Smith & Brewer*; rehabilitation unit in Evelyn Road by *Hutchison, Locke & Monk*, 1980.

NORTH THAMES GASWORKS, Manor Road. Offices and restaurant by *Tripe & Wakeham*, 1968–9.

RICHMOND STATION, Kew Road. 1936–7 (Southern Railway). Portland stone, with some Scandinavian features. Lofty booking hall.

RICHMOND HALF-TIDE WEIR AND FOOTBRIDGE, TWICKENHAM BRIDGE, RICHMOND RAILWAY BRIDGE, RICHMOND BRIDGE. *See* Thames Crossings at 68 end of gazetteer.

PERAMBULATIONS

1. Richmond Green and Richmond Palace

RICHMOND GREEN is one of the most beautiful urban greens surviving anywhere in England. After the first shock of the theatre all is quiet happiness: No. 1, C17 with later rendering and Roman Doric porch; No. 2, C18 with similar porch; No. 3, Gothick, stuccoed and embattled; No. 4, mid C18, set back; No. 6* with a blank-arched ground floor and a recessed Roman Doric doorway; Nos. 8–9 of eight bays, with a pedimented four-bay centre; No. 10, a fine three-bay early C18 house of three storeys; No. 11 of the same time with an outstandingly good carved doorcase and good wrought-iron work outside; No. 12, again of the same time, with a carved doorcase and good staircase; and so on to Nos. 21–22 with doorways with Roman Doric pilasters and friezes, where the s corner is reached.‡ The Green extends here to the s and forms a square. On its E side OLD PALACE TERRACE, an identical group of seven with identical doorways (straight hoods on carved brackets). In the middle pairs the doorways adjoin. Each house of three bays, with two storeys over a basement.

---

* Rebuilt as their own offices by *Darbourne & Darke*, 1981; No. 2 restored and extended by the same firm.

‡ Nos. 21–22 repaired and converted by *Manning & Clamp* as part of a larger development behind; *see* Perambulation 3.

They are known to have been built in 1692,* which makes them a very early example of an urban brick terrace outside London. The house at the NE corner is of the same date, with the doorway moved to face the Green. No. 18 King Street at the other end is slightly later. Behind this square and the E side of the Green towards George Street several lanes, e.g. PAVED COURT with houses also built in the 1690s. No. 1 has an excellent early C19 bowed shopfront. Along the SW side of the square three noteworthy houses on the site of the house of Franciscan Observant Friars founded by Henry VII *c.* 1500. First OAK HOUSE, attributed to *Robert Taylor c.* 1769, of three bays with a broad Tuscan porch. In the principal room on the first floor a sumptuous classical plaster ceiling. The second, OLD PALACE PLACE of *c.* 1700, is seven bays wide. Pedimented doorcase with carved brackets. Remains of Tudor wall paintings have been discovered, so the house must incorporate older fabric. The house was restored for Sir Kenneth Clark by *Wellesley & Wills* in 1928, after having been divided in two, and subdivided again in 1982–3. Thirdly OLD FRIARS, dated 1687 on a rainwater head. Cellars of *c.* 1500 survive. The house is of two and a half storeys, five and a half bays wide. The first windows on the l. on all floors are extremely slender, a motif typical of *c.* 1700–10. Excellent wrought-iron gate. Attached on the r. and a little recessed an addition of *c.* 1735–40 which was used as an assembly room. Rusticated Venetian window to the back and to the front that anomaly, a Venetian window which is quadripartite, not tripartite, by having the arched middle part doubled.

Then follows the SW side of the Green, first with TUDOR HOUSE and TUDOR PLACE, C18 altered, and then with
57   MAIDS OF HONOUR ROW, built in 1724 for the maids of honour of Caroline of Anspach Princess of Wales, who lived at Richmond (or Ormonde) Lodge (*see* Kew, Royal Botanic Gardens). An excellent, entirely uniform terrace of three-storeyed five-bay houses. Brick aprons, vertical lacing between the windows. Doorcases with Roman pilasters and metope friezes. Fine wrought-iron gates and railings, and brick piers topped by balls. No. 4 belonged in 1744–9 to J. J. Heidegger, manager of the King's Theatre in the Haymarket. For him, probably in 1745, his scene painter *Antonio Jolli* decorated the entrance hall with topographical landscapes taken from Zeiler's *Topographia Helvetiae* (Heidegger was Swiss), Merian's *Topographia Italiae*, and, for the more exotic subjects, Fischer von Erlach's *Historische Architektur*. Above the door leading to the staircase a painted score open at the beginning of an aria from an opera performed at the Haymarket in February 1745.

At the end of this terrace are the remains of RICHMOND PALACE (*see* below). Beyond the gateway only the OLD

---

* The terrace was a speculation by Vertue Radford, a barrister. The builder was a local carpenter, *William Wollings*. We owe this information to Mrs E. Horsfall Turner.

COURT HOUSE, again early C 18 with additions. Good large later C 18 fanlight. The house formed a pair with WENT-WORTH HOUSE, which was drastically modernized by *Laxton c.* 1858. The NW side starts with CEDAR GROVE (now called The Virginals) of 1813, with giant pilasters on the garden front. The rest of this side is mostly Italianate villas, semi-detached and otherwise, built after the demolition of Pembroke House, previously Fitzwilliam House, about 1854. On the NE side first an admirably reticent terrace by *Manning & Clamp,* 1970, dark brown brick, with high front-garden walls forming part of the composition; then PORTLAND TERRACE, two palatial Italianate stucco pairs. Further E LITTLE GREEN, another extension of the Green, with three more C 18 houses, the theatre (*see* Public Buildings), and ONSLOW HALL, brick and stucco Italianate, with a round-arched ground floor, built in 1857 as a Cavalry College by *Broadbridge.*

RICHMOND PALACE and OLD PALACE YARD. Little now remains to recall Henry VII's splendid building (*see* Introduction to the borough). Facing the green is a simple GATEWAY of Henry VII's time with a large and a small stone arch, with his arms (recently renewed) over the larger archway. The gateway led into the outer courtyard of the palace, now Old Palace Yard. Attached on the l. the range containing OLD PALACE and PALACE GATE HOUSE. Here a part of the Tudor brick buildings which formed the outer wall of the palace remains, notably in the large canted bay nearest to the gate and the lower part of the smaller bay and adjoining flat wall in the centre of the front facing the Green. The building has been many times repaired and altered during its life as a private dwelling, the second large bay (on Old Palace), for instance, having been introduced for the sake of symmetry in the mid C 18 when adjoining and projecting parts of the old structure were finally pulled down. In Palace Gate House a C 17 staircase with cut-out balusters. At the back, a small stair-turret is probably original. Within the secluded square of OLD PALACE YARD two further buildings incorporating remains of the palace. On the l. THE WARDROBE, with much of the Tudor brickwork (with blue diapering) and interior timber-framing surviving later alterations. The NW front, facing the Court, shows at ground level Tudor arches of an arcade probably bricked up at the same time that a linking block was built to join the Wardrobe to the gatehouse (late C 17). These two sections of the palace, together with the range where Maids of Honour Row now stands, were all that was retained directly in royal hands in the latter part of the C 17 – no doubt because they were the least dilapidated. Repairs had been carried out by the last tenant before the Restoration in 1660, and more appear to have been done about the time that the manor and palace building were granted to James Duke of York (the future James II) in 1664. James, who commissioned, but never proceeded with, plans for a complete rebuilding, used the premises mainly as a nursery for his children. After the birth of Prince James Edward (the Old Pretender) in 1688 further renovations were put in hand under the supervision of *Christopher Wren*. The SE (garden) front of the Wardrobe, of thirteen bays, has a three-bay pedimented central projection. The general appearance and details suggest a date in the 1680s (cf. Wren's work at Kensington and Hampton Court), but documentary evidence points to a date about 1708. Inside, panelling and corner fireplaces (with some good carved mantelpieces) and a nice staircase in No. 2 with Jacobean-looking twisted balusters, but an open string, and so probably early C 18 in its present form.*

TRUMPETER'S HOUSE is on the site of the middle gate of the palace, on the SW side of the courtyard. It was formerly Trumpeting House, named from the stone figures which stood on either side of the portico. When the house was converted into flats by *C. Bernard Brown* in 1950–2, Tudor fabric was discovered, but is no longer visible.‡ A lease was granted to the diplomat Richard Hill in 1700, and the brick-layer *John Yeomans* was working here for him *c.* 1703–4. The back, facing Old Palace Yard, has a curious gabled centre with angle piers topped by little caps, which looks early C 19, but existed already in the early C 18. On either side plain brick wings, set back, and not in line with each other. The main front, of eleven bays, faces the river across a lawn (the site of the Privy Lodgings of the Tudor palace). This front is of outstanding quality, although not all of the same date. In the centre a giant portico of two pairs of Tuscan columns with pediment, described as a recent addition in 1722.§ The separately roofed pavilions at the ends, with pediments above Venetian windows and tripartite lunettes, are later additions, as they do not appear on a plan of 1736 but are shown on one of 1756. In one room a delightful Rococo ceiling with profile busts of Milton and Pope. In the gardens a copper beech planted in 1813, and close to the river a castellated SUMMER HOUSE. Back in the Old Palace Yard, lying back to the N, TRUMPETERS' INN, a skilful Georgian pastiche of 1954–6 by *C. Bernard Brown* (who was also the restorer of Blackheath Paragon, Le). Portico and lantern are both his.

2. *The Riverside*

OLD PALACE LANE runs down toward the river with a nice terrace of humble early C 19 cottages. At the SE corner, facing
67 the Thames, ASGILL HOUSE, a Palladian villa of great charm, the most perfect of *Sir Robert Taylor's* surviving houses in the London area since its restoration in 1969–70.

* I owe the above paragraph to Mr John Cloake.
‡ See K. Courlander, *Richmond*, 1953, and C. Bernard Brown, *The Conversion of Old Buildings into New Homes*, 1955.
§ Information from H. M. Colvin.

Built in 1757–8 as a summer residence for his friend Sir
Charles Asgill, a merchant banker who was Lord Mayor of
London in 1761–2, illustrated in *Vitruvius Britannicus* volume
IV in 1767. The site is that of the palace brewhouse, just
outside the main walls. The house stands close to the river, so
that it can exploit the admirable views both across and along
the Thames.

The river front is of three wide bays, the centre with a broad
canted bay-window of full height, a typical Taylor feature,
ending in a hipped roof. The wings are lower, with Palladian
half-pediments, happily restored to their original form in
1969–70 (the work carried out by *Donald Insall & Associates*).
One-storey canted bays to the side elevations, a slightly
projecting flat centre to the entrance side away from the river
(before 1969 concealed by Victorian extensions). The exterior
is of golden stone, exquisitely detailed (originally Bath stone,
refaced with Doulting stone in the 1950s). Rusticated ground
floor, each stone delicately fluted; vermiculation around the
central arched doorways at back and front. The exterior
ornament is otherwise very restrained: blind balustrades below
the first-floor windows, a continuous string course at their sill
level just to hint at the classical proportions of the whole,
pediments over the central windows, exceptionally deep boldly
modelled eaves supported on brackets.

The interior is an excellent example of how Taylor enjoyed
fitting rooms of varied shapes into a compact plan: Asgill
House is indeed the smallest and most ingenious of his London countryside villas. The service rooms (now disused) were
in a concealed basement. The central room on the river side on
both ground and first floors is octagonal, taking in the canted
bay facing the river (cf. Mount Clare, Roehampton, Ww;
Danson Park, Bexleyheath, Bx). Flanking the octagon are
rectangular rooms on the ground floor, enlarged by the side
bays (which are rounded on the inside). On the entrance front,
away from the river, there were originally two small oval
rooms, one containing the staircase, flanking a narrow groin-
vaulted entrance corridor. This arrangement was altered in
the C19 when an outer hall (now demolished) was added. One
now enters a square hall, made from part of the corridor and
part of the oval room to its l. On the r. a tall archway to the
stair-hall. Before 1969 there was only a low doorway in this
position, so Taylor must have wanted the miniature tour de
force of the staircase to come as a surprise. It is cunningly
fitted into the tiny oval space: a half landing on the long side,
the angle of the flight calculated so that it neatly clears the
arched window. At the curved ends there is room only for a
single turned baluster to each tread. The small first-floor
landing is treated with surprising panache. Two Venetian
arches with guilloche bands, on Ionic columns, one to the
groin-vaulted central corridor, the other to the upper staircase
which continues in the N wing. There is so little room that the
vista through the arches has to be interrupted by the elegantly

curved balustrade of the stairwell. In the octagonal room on
the first floor c 18 panel paintings by *Casali*, oval and round-
ended, placed here in the c 19. They were formerly in the
dining room downstairs. The Victorian surrounds were simplified in the 1969–70 restoration. In the adjoining room to the
s a handsome bed recess, the details similar to those of the
landing arches. Beside it an opening (enlarged) to a dressing
room (now divided up, with a new groin-vault over the central
part). The special feature of the top floor, where only the
central rooms have windows, is the two delightful oval rooms
above the octagon, connected by a tiny lobby in the left-over
space within the central bay, from which one has unparalleled
views over the river. Taylor used the same arrangement later
at Sharpham, Devon. The oval rooms have coved ceilings, as
do the square rooms behind them on this floor. As for fittings
in the rest of the house, there are good cornices and overdoors
in the ground-floor s room and octagon (the N room is now a
kitchen) and two excellent Rococo fireplaces to Taylor's designs, which, alas, have lost their overmantels. The one in the
s room is of veined red marble, the other of stone painted to
look like marble. This, formerly in the N room, is now in the
octagon facing the window, in place of the original arrangements of two fireplaces in the angles of the room. The garden,
never very large, has a pleasant winding path, made after
1969, which provides a more suitable approach than the former Victorian entrance closer to the house.

Now along CHOLMONDELEY WALK by the Thames, past the
grounds of Trumpeters House (*see* above) to Nos. 1–3, built
soon after 1760, altered later. After Friars Lane, ST HELENA
HOUSE and ST HELENA TERRACE, built *c.* 1835, high up
on a terrace over boathouses, followed by the WHITE CROSS
HOTEL, with a Greek Doric porch, of about the same date
(top storey *c.* 1865). Then the ASSEMBLY ROOMS, a long
wing of 1836–7 stretching towards the river (previously
attached to the Castle Hotel, which stood in Hill Street on the
site of the Town Hall and Whittaker Avenue). After this came
several wealthy c 18 houses with garden fronts overlooking
the river, a fine group on an outstanding site, which was
scandalously allowed to decay for more than twenty years
while redevelopment was debated. Hotham House, at the N
end, was demolished in 1960. Plans for rebuilding behind
those façades that survived, replacement by replica façades,
and the filling of the gaps in between were at last agreed in
1981 (architects *Brewer, Smith & Brewer*). In the centre,
HERON HOUSE, a handsome five-bay house of 1693 converted by *Henry Laxton* in 1858 as part of the ROYAL (later
PALM COURT) HOTEL which later also occupied the buildings further s.* TOWER HOUSE at the SE end, also by
Laxton, 'of considerable pretensions' (*Building News* 1858),

* The roof structure of Heron House includes some re-used moulded timbers,
possibly from Richmond Palace (DTS). The royal mews were on this site.

with its tall Italian-villa tower next to the bridge, was re-prieved from proposed demolition and restored in 1968. The redevelopment scheme agreed in 1981 (for a mixture of offices, flats, and shops) includes a square with offices and shops between Heron House and Hill Street, and rebuilding behind replica frontages in Bridge Street and Hill Street. The façade of the former Town Hall (q.v. above) is also to be incorporated.

3. The Town Centre and Streets to the E

This is the part of the town most affected by C 20 development, and is rewarding only in patches.

Starting from the Town Hall in HILL STREET, the most con-spicuous building is the NATIONAL WESTMINSTER BANK, c. 1960, a traditional Bankers' Classical façade with blind pedimented upper storey over rusticated ground floor, an elevation reminiscent of that of the Literary and Scientific Institute which used to stand on this site. No. 5 (crudely altered for the Gaumont Cinema) was once a good five-bay red-brick house of the early C 18. Detail of high quality: windows with moulded brick surrounds, segmental heads with stone keystones, projecting aprons. Inside, the staircase and some panelled rooms survive.* A few other minor Georgian remains in Hill Street, and rather more in KING STREET, which leads to Richmond Green (see Perambulation 1); e.g. THE OLD SHIP, with a late C 17 core and later additions, and some modest C 18 terrace houses. Nos. 10–12 have a wooden eaves cornice. The old scale is disagreeably disrupted by Dickins & Jones' store at the corner of King Street and GEORGE STREET, the main shopping street. Little to note here apart from a few stuccoed fronts, e.g. Nos. 23–24, the former Greyhound Hotel, now GREYHOUND HOUSE, with a well restored entrance passage, and a tall red sandstone-trimmed POST OFFICE of 1886, although the small alleyways off on either side are more enjoyable.‡ On the s side CHURCH COURT leads to St Mary, the parish church (q.v.), with CHURCH WALK on the E: a group of pleasant cottages in-cluding the CHURCH ROOMS (with the Refectory restaurant below), a weatherboarded range set back. s of the church PARADISE ROAD, with the former Magistrates Courts (now Citizens Advice Bureau and Vestry Hall), 1895 by *W. J. Ancell*, small, informal, with shallow bow-windows; and on the N side HOGARTH HOUSE (Nos. 3–4) (the home of the Woolfs' Hogarth Press in 1915–24), a much restored, very plain early C 18 front, five bays wide. Venetian window at the back. The character of the rest of the street has been destroyed by C 20 demolitions and new building, which began with

* Proposals were made in 1981 to restore the house and build an office block behind, by the *Oxford Architects Partnership*.

‡ The Post Office was converted as part of a redevelopment behind extending to Richmond Green (q.v., Perambulation 1) by *Manning & Clamp*, 1982.

BAYER HOUSE (*R. Seifert & Partners*, 1963–4). Neat white and grey details, better than some of this firm's later work, but too large for the site. Further E some attractive late C18 three-storey pairs remain on the S side (Spring Terrace, Nos. 1–8).

THE SQUARE is the irregular widening at the E end of George Street, where the two roads from the N and E, Kew Road and Sheen Road, converge. The poor end of the town, with some minor but quite engaging buildings. At the fork, DOME BUILDINGS sports a prominent slated dome of *c.* 1907–8, but has an older origin. The ground floor was built as a Mechanics Institute in 1843, by *Wardell & Littlewood*; hall converted to a swimming pool in 1855, when baths and wash houses were added around the outside (now shops). Upper floor 1867 by *R. Brewer*. Behind, in SHEEN ROAD, a cheerful little former FIRE STATION-cum-CLOCK TOWER, 1870 by *R. Brewer*, in a picturesque free Gothic, and WATERLOO PLACE, a tiny early C19 terrace of cottages leading N to the beginning of Kew Road, from the 1890s grandly named THE QUADRANT. Mostly indifferent C19. The haphazard S side, although much rebuilt, is still on a small-town scale (the only C18 houses, Nos. 36–37, have alas been demolished). Little else here apart from No. 23a, C19 auction rooms which resemble a jolly Gothic chapel, and the RAILWAY HOTEL, 1888, with restrained terracotta trim. Beyond the station, next to St John's church, offices by *Dry Hastwell Butlin Bicknell Partnership*, a cluster of polygonal bays with mansard roofs, under construction 1981–2.

PARKSHOT, which runs parallel to The Quadrant and can also be reached from Richmond Green, has one excellent terrace (restored 1979–80), now dwarfed by the new Court House (*see* Public Buildings). It consists of No. 3 (early C19) and Nos. 4–6 (built in 1734). Segment-headed windows, rubbed red brick. Doorways with rusticated wooden surrounds. Opposite, MARCAR HOUSE, an elegant refronting of an older factory, purple brick and stained timber, 1976 by *Garner, Preston & Strebel*. At the corner of Parkshot and CLARENCE STREET a group of minor late C18 buildings, and in Clarence Street the former ST JOHN'S SCHOOLS, 1867 and probably by *A. W. Blomfield*, once a picturesque Victorian Gothic group, all derelict at the time of writing. A bold turn-of-the-century pub, the ORANGE TREE, facing Kew Road.

Between the Old Deer Park and Kew Road, in the ambience of the royal palaces, a few more good houses, cut off from the town centre since 1933 by the bypass. They start with ST JOHN'S GROVE, a mid C19 terrace, and No. 11, a more individual cottage orné of *c.* 1840 with decorated bargeboards and a quatrefoil in the gable. From here KEW FOOT ROAD runs N with No. 12 on the W side, another early C19 cottage, castellated. Nos. 19–23 is an admirable early C18 group, brown brick with red dressings, doors with flat hoods on brackets carved with cherubs (cf. Ormond Road, Perambulation 4). Further on No. 39, late C18, four bays, and another C18 house incorporated in the Royal Hospital (*see* Public Buildings). In the OLD DEER PARK, the only relic of its royal past, the former Observatory (*see* Public Buildings); and a GRANDSTAND for the Richmond Athletic Association by *Manning & Clamp*, 1960s.

LOWER MORTLAKE ROAD. At the W end Nos. 5–7, Tudor, dated 1853, adjacent to the Kew Road roundabout. At the corner of Crofton Terrace, laboratories built for ELECTRONIC INSTRUMENTS by *Llewelyn Smith & Waters*, 1954–5, a tall modern block, visible from afar.

In SHEEN ROAD a good cross-section of those buildings characteristic of a main road running out of a town, isolated Georgian houses and fragments of C18 terraces now surrounded by denser Victorian and later developments (see especially the streets off, e.g. Dunstable Road, Sydney Road, with mid C19 stuccoed houses), and further out a few cottages and some almshouses built when land on the rural fringe was still cheap. Examples, from W to E. On the edge of the town, quite out of scale with their surroundings, LICHFIELD COURT, two huge blocks of flats with streamlined balconies, 1935 by *Bertram Carter*.* On the S side two pairs of late C18 houses with recessed entrances, and a short terrace. On the N, No. 34, built by 1771, a three-bay house with tripartite first-floor windows below shallow arches and a blind centre roundel. Then No. 36, MARSHGATE HOUSE, a very good example of the five-bay house typical of *c.* 1700; built by a London merchant, John Knapp. Red brick with rubbed dressings, eaves cornice. Restored 1979 by *J. N. G. Sherwen*. (Good interiors; a later plaster ceiling on the first floor in high relief, with some Rococo elements, probably mid C18.) Fine wrought-iron gate with the Knapp monogram. A mixture of C18 houses and cottages follows, notably, on the S side, No. 41 with an early C19 four-storey bow-window, and Nos. 43–45, early C18, with good pilastered doorcases and vertical brick lacing. HOUBLON ALMSHOUSES (to the S in Worple Way), with the dates 1757 and 1758, consists of three separate blocks around a lawn, very plain. No. 95, DUNSTABLE HOUSE, is large, late C18, of five bays plus lower wings. Some way further on some modest early C19 terraces and villas on the S side (Nos. 131 etc.), and on the N side quite a colony of almshouses. HICKEY'S ALMSHOUSES are of 1832–5 by *Lewis Vulliamy*. Grey brick, three big multi-chimneyed neo-Tudor blocks linked by angled walls. Many later additions. Front railings and enlargement to porter's lodge 1850–3 (upper floor to lodge 1934). Chapel enlarged by *A. W. Blomfield* 1863. At the back a further range with eight houses, 1850–1 by Mr *Long*, and twelve one-storey houses of 1973 by *Manning, Clamp & Partners*. E of the Hickey Almshouses, the RICHMOND CHURCH ESTATE ALMSHOUSES, 1843 by *William Crawford Stow*, a

---

* Information from Miss Anne Churcher.

lively neo-Norman design in polychrome brick (cf. Thackeray Almshouses, Lewisham, (Le), Perambulation 2). Facing the additions to the Hickey Almshouses in St Mary's Grove an enclave of mid C 19 small stuccoed villas, with pub to match (The Mitre). A little to the N in Manor Grove, off Manor Road to the E, an interesting early housing scheme of the 1890s, probably designed by the Richmond Borough Surveyor *E. J. Lovegrove*. Richmond was the first local authority to adopt the new powers introduced by the Housing Act of 1890, which permitted local authorities to build independently of slum clearance or demolition. Nos. 1–62 Manor Grove (fifty cottages with parlour, scullery, two or four bedrooms, and twelve cottage flats) were built in 1894–5, Nos. 63–135 were added in 1898–9. The treatment of the elevations, brown brick with red dressings, square bays, clearly derives from the work of the philanthropic dwellings companies (cf. especially the Artisans, Labourers and General Dwellings Company estates at Noel Park, Wood Green, Hy, and, earlier, at Shaftesbury Park, Battersea, Ww).*

4. The Slopes of Richmond Hill

HILL RISE, the main road S from the bridge, has some plain C 18/early C 19 terraces on either side. At the corner of Bridge Street, CHRISTIES, formerly the KINGS HEAD, stuccoed, late Georgian. Opposite, at the corner of Ormond Road, the ODEON by *Leathart & Granger*, with exotic Spanish interior (much altered inside). No. 6, early C 18 (original staircase), set back behind a shop, adjoins LISSOY in ORMOND ROAD, with an excellent doorcase on carved brackets with cherubs' heads. This street and others on the slopes of Richmond Hill abound in delightful early C 18 houses. ORMOND TERRACE follows, C 18, all the windows straight-headed, of rubbed brick, but the houses not identical. Bracketed doorcase to No. 6. No. 7 has a later C 18 front (good fanlight). Then ORMOND HOUSE, five bays, windows with recessed aprons. Later alterations; C 19 doorway, perhaps not in the original position. On the N side THE ROSARY and THE HOLLIES, a pair built *c.* 1699–1700 back to back by Nathaniel Rawlins, the London merchant and local building speculator who built Clarence House in The Vineyard (*see* below). Each front of five bays; three side bays to the street beneath a double roof. Later bow-windows. The cornice to The Rosary is a restoration of 1967–8. (Good original staircase with closed string in each house.) On the N again, set back, the early C 19 stock brick VICARAGE, three bays with Tudor porch.

CHURCH TERRACE forks S from Ormond Road: on the E side another much altered terrace of *c.* 1730. No. 2 with doorcase with carved brackets. HERMITAGE HOUSE adjoins, with a

---

* We owe these details to Mark Swenarton. Later council dwellings, in the form of cottage flats, 1908–9 by *J. H. Brierley*, are in Victoria Place, off Red Lion Street.

broad canted bay to the N, two windows wide, perhaps added
to an earlier house. Fine wall piers with urns. E past the
church, HALFORD ROAD leads to HALFORD HOUSE: C18,
the earliest part of 1710, the rest 1745. Additions of 1867
behind (JC). Near by, further up the hill, THE VINEYARD,
an irregular curving road. At the E end the former British
Schools, white brick, austere Tudor, 1867 extended 1908.
Then, returning towards Hill Rise, VINEYARD HOUSE (No.
26), early C18 with late C18 doorway in a projecting wing to
the garden. Wrought-iron gate. Further W earlier C19 villas
on the S side, opposite the QUEEN ELIZABETH ALMS-
HOUSES, an uninspired C20 rebuilding of a foundation of
1767,* and BISHOP DUPPA ALMSHOUSES, 1851 by *Thomas
Little*, white brick, Jacobean, with elaborate roof cresting.
The classical garden entrance with original tablet may come
from the old almshouses of 1661 which stood further up the hill
on the main road. On the opposite side, NEWARK HOUSE,
c. 1750, with a doorway with Gibbs surround and a broken
pediment on carved brackets, and MICHEL'S PLACE, a small
early C19 terrace encroaching on to the land in front of
MICHEL'S ALMSHOUSES, a modest range of 1811 with a
three-bay pediment and slightly projecting wings. On the r. a
range of 1858. On the N side CLARENCE HOUSE (No. 2),
built by Nathaniel Rawlins *c.* 1696, an irregular front of seven
plus two windows. (Good interior features.) In LANCASTER
PARK off to the S some attractive late Georgian cottages.
The Vineyard leads back to HILL RISE. A little way downhill
Nos. 24–32, an early C18 pair concealed by projecting shops,
and Nos. 34–42, formerly a large Georgian house, now divided up as offices. C18 centre, with porch, a bow-fronted
addition to the l., and a far-projecting addition to the r., also
bow-fronted, spoiling the original proportions. Several nicely
varied shopfronts up the hill. In RICHMOND HILL itself No.
28 etc., a plain early Victorian terrace with a first-floor veranda, and No. 48, OLD VICARAGE HOUSE, symmetrical,
castellated and turreted. The castellations date from 1809 but
there is a mid C18 core (JC). On the other side a block of flats,
alas, replacing CARDIGAN HOUSE.‡ To the E in CARDIGAN
ROAD, a block of flats by *Eric Lyons*, 1953–4, a good, lively
composition, if perhaps a little too varied in its surfacing
materials (including tile-hanging, and yellow and blue corrugated perspex). Round the corner in FRIARS STILE ROAD
Nos. 19–23, another smaller job by the same architect, with
shops on the ground floor. In the neighbouring streets focus-
ing on St Matthias' church (q.v.) some large mid C19 villas
remain.

---

* Replacing early Victorian stucco Tudor buildings.
  ‡ Of 1777 by *William Eves*, seven bays and two and a half storeys, grey brick.
  Towards the street a Venetian window in the middle with an oval window over
  and a relief of two crossed cornucopias below the raised pediment. To the river a
  central canted bay-window; Greek Doric lodge. In the grounds were Richmond
  Wells, popular in the C18.

Back in Richmond Hill, TERRACE GARDENS, sloping down the hill with a splendid view of the river, covering the grounds of Buccleuch House and Lansdowne House which were acquired by the local vestry and laid out in 1887. Here in the lower part, at the opposite corner of the lawn by the Petersham Road entrance, STATUE of Father Thames by *Bacon*, of *Coade* stone (cf. Ham House). In the upper part Aphrodite, a sturdy girl in a pond, by *Allan Howes*, 1952. On the E side Stuart Terrace, 1872, long and four-storeyed, then No. 114, yellow brick with balconies; No. 116 (Downe House), *c.* 1771 (JC), with lunettes on the top floor; and Nos. 118–120, similar to No. 114 but altered. Nos. 124–126, set forward from the previous house, large and plain yellow brick probably of the 1770s, is the beginning of THE TERRACE. The best house here, No. 3 The Terrace, is a fine, ambitious, three-bay house built in 1769 for Christopher Blanchard, playing-card manufacturer. Attributed to *Sir Robert Taylor* (cf. Ely House, Dover Street, London of 1772). Rusticated ground floor, frieze above it. On the first floor only two windows, with Ionic half-columns and pediments, standing on a common plinth. An attic storey above, and pediment. Inside, plaster ceilings, fireplaces, and a staircase with wrought-iron balustrade. No. 4, with a brick front restored in 1974, is a less ambitious house of the 1730s. Four bays, with ground-floor bow and balustraded parapet added in the late C18. Next door, DOUGHTY HOUSE, *c.* 1769, but much altered and enlarged *c.* 1790, and again in the early C20 for the Cook family. They added an art gallery behind, for their private collection, an impressive imperial classical stone front by *Brewer, Smith & Brewer*, 1915 (JC). Then two houses on the opposite side, the pair standing on their own in this enviable position. First THE WICK, by *Robert Mylne*, 1775 for Lady St Aubyn, a delicately decorated front with a charming porch and a broad bow to the river. Fine interiors, especially the oval drawing room with its decoration by widely spaced stucco garlands. In front of the house a good arched iron lamp-holder. Garden walls with urns. In the garden a SUMMER HOUSE with Tuscan columns. The neighbour is WICK HOUSE, built in 1772 for Sir Joshua Reynolds by *Sir William Chambers*. The exterior not specially attractive. Enlarged in the late C19, and further altered as a nurses' home, 1950. The view over the river Thames at its bend is famous. It even inspired Reynolds to paint it; no wonder – he had, as we have seen, a proprietary interest in it. Since the mid C19 the view has had to take in as well a self-confident High Victorian pile further down the slope: the PETERSHAM HOTEL (built as Richmond Hill Hotel, later called the Star and Garter after the old hotel of that name at the top of the hill had been replaced by the Star and Garter Home). 1865 by *John Giles*, the architect of the Langham Hotel, Marylebone (Wm). Of crude proportions, but with excellent detail (brought out nicely by a recent cleaning). Pale stock brick with red brick dressings, carved capitals. Iron balconies on two levels. The *Building News* commented on the 'verandahs well adapted for the serene pleasures of post prandial nicotine enjoyment'. Inside, a sumptuous staircase round a well, rising to the fourth floor, almost comparable in scale to the grand hotels of seaside resorts. Ceiling with painted medallions by *Galli* (others in the second-floor banqueting hall have been painted over). The rest of the interior much altered.

From here one can either return to Richmond Hill and continue as far as the park (*see* below) or return to the centre of the town by PETERSHAM ROAD, where there are a number of good C 18 houses on the W side: No. 63, *c.* 1760; Nos. 55–61, *c.* 1720; IVY HALL HOTEL, late C 18, with canted bays, a Venetian window, a handsome porch, and early C 19 additions; Nos. 43–47, early C 18; and BELLEVUE, No. 39, late C 18, facing s, with a medallion with a figure playing a lyre in the central pediment.

At the top of RICHMOND HILL on the E side a delightful long late C 18/early C 19 group lying back from the road, all different heights and sizes, with balconies and verandas, bows and bays. The end is punctuated by ANCASTER HOUSE, at the corner of Queen's Road and the park gate. Built in 1772, yellow brick with later additions. Elegant porch to the street and two full-height bays; another on the side near the park gate. Front to the park, where there is a similar porch. The house has been attributed to *Adam*. Between it and the Star and Garter Home (*see* Public Buildings), a FOUNTAIN of red granite, a memorial to the Duchess of Teck, 1901 by *Williamson* of Esher.* Another FOUNTAIN at the top of Queen's Road, with an iron cage or arbour, by *T. E. Collcutt*, 1891. QUEEN'S ROAD, starting on the NW side of the park, has some palatial mid C 19 villas, stuccoed Italianate or red brick Tudor, the latter probably by *John Blore*, who was designing villas in the Elizabethan style here in 1858.‡ On the park side, clusters of houses and flats for a housing association, by *Darbourne & Darke*, planned 1978, sensitively grouped and detailed, as one expects from this firm. At the N end borough housing of 1981 (*O. Karel, Richmond Technical Services*). To the N of these, in GROVE ROAD, a former workhouse, 1786 by *Kenton Couse*. The core is a nice plain brick building with projecting wings and a cupola. Many additions.

5. Richmond Park

Richmond Park is more than 2,000 acres in size, stretching from Richmond Hill s to Ham and E to Wimbledon Common. The new park (so called to distinguish it from the Old Deer Park by the river, closer to Richmond Palace) was first enclosed by Charles I. The building of the tall wall was complete in 1637.

---

* The bronze bas reliefs have been replaced by marble panels.

‡ *Building News* 22 October 1858.

The park was stocked with deer and remained a favourite hunting ground right into the C 19. Private shooting ceased only in 1904.

LODGES. At HAM GATE a plain brick cottage of 1742. At RICHMOND GATE the gate and stuccoed lodges are of 1798, by *Capability Brown*.

WHITE LODGE (Royal Ballet School). The centre, begun by George I and built *c*. 1727–9, is by *Roger Morris*. The pavilions, linked by quadrant tunnels, added by *Stephen Wright* in 1751–2, were completed with the upper parts of the quadrants only in the early C 19, when Lord Sidmouth occupied the house. The building, like Morris's Marble Hill, Twickenham, begun a few years earlier, is a very early monument to the Palladian Revival, much influenced by Lord Burlington. Fine ashlar stone. Five bays, one and a half storeys towards the entrance, basement plus one and a half storeys towards the garden. Towards the garden rustication below, then a four-column attached portico of Doric three-quarter columns and a pediment. Central Venetian window. The large open staircase leading up to the portico, starting in one flight and then opening into two, is C 20. Towards the entrance a corridor and porte-cochère added in 1801 by *James Wyatt*. *Repton* made some alterations in 1816, when he laid out the grounds. Inside, brought in, an excellent staircase with a wrought-iron balustrade. Some good original features remain: saloon with a high coved ceiling, former library with a Corinthian-columned screen with a segmental arch, and Palladian ceilings to several rooms on the piano nobile (RW). STABLES 1846 by *John Phipps*. Many extensions for the Royal Ballet School. The sunken Ashton Studio is by *Tanner & Partners*, 1970s.

PEMBROKE LODGE. Mid C 18 with later additions. Porch of two pairs of Tuscan columns. Some good fireplaces inside.

THATCHED HOUSE LODGE. Built originally for Sir Robert Walpole *c*. 1727, perhaps by *Kent*. Core of white brick, three windows wide, with a canted bay in the middle. W wing of 1872. In the garden the THATCHED HOUSE, a delightful little summer house with a thatched roof and a balcony towards the valley. The two principal rooms inside painted *c*. 1769–85 for General Medows, attributed by Croft Murray to *A. M. Borgnis* and *Zucchi*. Etruscan motifs (cf. Osterley, Ho).

(WHITE ASH LODGE and HOLLY LODGE. Both mid C 18, two storeys. DOE)

TEDDINGTON

The architectural pleasures of Teddington are considerably fewer than those of the villages preceding and following it along the Thames. What remains in one's mind of a suburb now as much built over as Twickenham further N is the historically more than aesthetically impressive contrast between the two churches of St

Mary and St Alban standing side by side in Ferry Road. There could be no more poignant memento of the natural and intimate role of the church in the village of the C 16, C 17, C 18, and its ambitious yet so much less convincing role in the C 19. The C 20 sequel is no less characteristic: the Victorian church has been made redundant, and its modest neighbour is back in use.

ST ALBAN, Ferry Road. 1889 (consecrated 1896) by *W. Niven*.*
Incomplete at the W. Yet, as it is, its size is bewildering: aisles and ambulatory in the French Gothic manner, with tall clerestory and flying buttresses, chancel of three vaulted bays, and unvaulted nave of five, all of ashlar stone, very high, very correct, and rather cold. – The FITTINGS were by *A. H. Skipworth*.

ST MARK, St Mark's Road, to the S W off Kingston Road, South Teddington. 1938–9 by *Cyril Farey*. Blocky brick exterior with low crossing tower; rudimentary Romanesque with narrow aisles.

ST MARY, Ferry Road. A tiny brick building with a S aisle with brickwork in a diaper pattern of dark vitrified headers, perhaps C 16. The rest (except for the C 19 chancel) dates from 1753–4, a miniature copy of John James's design at Twickenham with one of those sweet battlemented towers of which provincial Georgian church-builders were so fond, and a N front with round-headed windows and even a pediment. The interior is curious, with its Gothic piers dating from the alterations of 1833 by *R. Willshire*, and its three parallel plastered pointed tunnel-vaults. – (STAINED GLASS of 1960 by *M. A. E. Buss*.) – LECTERN from St Alban (*see* above). – BRASS to John Goodyere † 1506 and wife. – MONUMENTS to Sir Orlando Bridgman † 1674, and to W. T. Stratton † 1814, the latter, with a kneeling woman under an altar overhung by a branch of weeping willow, by *Sir Richard Westmacott*.‡

(SACRED HEART (R.C.), Kingston Road. 1893 by *J. Kelly*.)

(CEMETERY, Shacklegate Lane, W of Waldegrave Road. 1879. A model Victorian example, with bargeboarded lodges and two Gothic chapels with crocketed spires, by *T. Goodchild*. HM)

PUBLIC LIBRARY, Waldegrave Road. 1906 by *Henry Cheers*. Jolly Baroque with two scrolly gables.

(NORMANSFIELD HOSPITAL, Kingston Road. Founded by Dr J. H. Langdon-Down, who in 1868 acquired an unfinished private house and converted it as a home for mongol children. Many additions, notably an amusement hall added in 1874 by *Rowland Plumbe* as multi-purpose theatre and entertainments hall, a progressive concept for its time. Proscenium arch with Gothic decoration, elaborate stage and scenery. GLC)

TEDDINGTON WEIR. *See* Thames Crossings at end of gazetteer.

---

* Future uncertain at the time of writing.
‡ Demolished: ST PETER AND ST PAUL, Church Road. 1863–73 by *G. E. Street*. Yellow and red brick, no steeple.

A perambulation of Teddington is not very rewarding. Starting from the churches in Ferry Road, the HIGH STREET has a few houses that pre-date the railway age: a pretty terrace of brick cottages of 1759 near the E end, and further W a few worthwhile houses: e.g. Nos. 159, 119, C 18; No. 83, probably timber-framed, of C 16 or C 17 origin; and Nos. 79–81. No. 23, LLOYDS BANK, is an interesting building with a distinctive concrete façade, 1929 by *Randall Wells*.* At the W end ELMFIELD HOUSE (council offices), dignified C 18, five bays, with Greek Doric porch added later. An incongruous office block next door, and another, still larger, across the road by the station (Barclays Bank Trading Centre), distinguished by external supports, have not improved the scene. Over the railway further redevelopment on the site of St Peter and St Paul by *Biscoe & Stanton c.* 1978. A little more to see down PARK ROAD. First the CLARENCE HOTEL, mid C 19, only two storeys, but with very elaborate stucco decoration. Opposite, ADELAIDE HOUSE and CLARENCE HOUSE, C 18 stuccoed, three and two windows wide. Further S a good group: THE ELMS, *c.* 1700, five windows, brick bands with Doric doorcase of *c.* 1720, and OLD MANOR COTTAGE and NORFOLK LODGE, both C 18. THE CEDARS is a group of Span houses by *Eric Lyons*, 1958.

BUSHY HOUSE (National Physical Laboratory), Bushy Park.‡ A plain but substantial house with an interesting history.§ Built as an official residence by Edward Proger, Ranger of Middle Park (part of Bushy Park), *c.* 1664–5, remodelled by a later Ranger, George Montagu, Earl of Halifax, *c.* 1720, with additions of the C 18 and of *c.* 1820 when it was occupied by the Duke of Clarence, the future William IV.

The main house is an almost square block seven by seven bays, three storeys over basements (the top storey added some time before 1797). The centre three bays on the E and W sides slightly recessed, the centre five on the N and S slightly projecting. A larger central arched window on the garden side. The present exterior of unadorned brick probably dates from the time of the second Earl of Halifax († 1737). Around this time, or a little later, four one-storey pavilions were added, connected to the main block by quadrant corridors (formerly colonnaded but now closed in, and partly disguised by later additions), cf. the White Lodge, Richmond Park (Richmond, Perambulation 5). Porch on the W side, with plain Doric columns, possibly re-used from the colonnade. On the E side the pavilions were enlarged by bow-fronted additions with verandas, probably *c.* 1820.

The chief interest of the interior is that it preserves the plan of the house of 1664–5, plausibly attributed to *William Samwell* (*see* Ham House) because of its similarity to Samwell's

---

* Information from Graham King, DTS.

‡ For Bushy Park *see also* Hampton Court, The Gardens.

§ Admirably investigated by P. Foster and E. S. Pyatt in *Bushy House* (1976), on which this account is based.

(demolished) Eaton Hall, Cheshire. The rectangular hall, entered at its short w side, has at its opposite end a triple archway to a central N–S corridor leading to the N entrance. This central corridor, a progressive innovation, is repeated through the whole width of the building on the other floors. The staircase is tucked away in a stair hall in the angle of hall and corridor. On the s side a single large room made after 1792 out of a dining room and a smaller room. The central columns have been removed. One ceiling of the 1660s remains in a cabinet in the S E corner, with thick plaster flowers and fruit; putti heads in the spandrels around the central oval.

In the grounds a charming CLOCK HOUSE, a small pavilion with octagonal cupola, built for a walled Dutch garden, probably in the 1660s, restored in 1977 by *Manning, Clamp & Partners*, an ORANGERY of the 1830s, and a ROTUNDA with six plain Doric columns, probably from the quadrant links. (Also a BREW HOUSE, late C 17, two storeys, brown brick, with modillioned eaves cornice.)

In the National Physical Laboratory the Alfred Yarrow ship-towing tank of 1911, 500 ft long under a north-light roof, the first such testing facility for commercial ship models in Britain. The cafeteria and conference centre of 1961 at Glazebrook Hall has a mezzanine floor in gay 1950s spirit, with tapered columns and a cantilevered staircase, within the brick shell of a former wind-tunnel house.

TWICKENHAM

CHURCHES

ALL HALLOWS, Chertsey Road. The tower, a notable landmark on a dull road out of London, is that of *Wren*'s All Hallows, Lombard Street, rebuilt here by *Robert Atkinson*, 1939–40, after the City church had been demolished in 1938. Portland stone, with pierced parapet. Entrance on the E side with porch with Corinthian columns and richly carved festoons. A short cloister links the tower to the body of the church. Minimally Wrenish exterior, brick with stone dressings. The interior, more daring for its date, with narrow aisles, unadorned round arches, and plain surfaces relieved only by the restless pattern of the concrete lozenge coffering of the ceiling, forms an austere and over-large setting for the excellent FURNISHINGS brought from All Hallows and some other City churches. – FONT. From St Benet Gracechurch. Baluster type, with a bowl charmingly carved with cherubs' heads and flowers. Wooden FONT COVER similarly decorated and crowned by a figure of Charity and children. – From All Hallows: PULPIT, hexagonal, on a slim pillar, with carved tester and REREDOS, richly decorated, a rather naive Baroque composition with a large triangular pediment enclosing smaller ones, and painted panels below of 1880. – ORGAN

CASE and other woodwork now at the W end of 1694, of high quality; also other paraphernalia characteristic of City churches: SWORD RESTS (c. 1800 and c. 1831), BREAD SHELVES (S aisle), carved ROYAL ARMS of Charles II (in the ringing chamber). – CANDELABRA. In the nave, one by *J. N. Comper* from St John Red Lion Square. – Beneath the tower another of 1764 made by *John Townsend* (arms replaced). – MONUMENTS from All Hallows and St Dionis Backchurch, displayed in the cloister and tower. The best is a bust of Edward Tyson † 1708 by *Edward Stanton*. – Also within the tower a remarkable carved wooden GATEWAY, formerly to All Hallows churchyard, decorated with bones, skulls, hourglasses, etc.

(ALL SAINTS, Campbell Road, N of Staines Road W of Meadway, East Twickenham. 1914 by *J. S. Alder*. Brick with stone dressings. – C19 PULPIT and SEDILIA from St Gabriel Poplar. – STAINED GLASS. W window with the Good Shepherd by *Morris & Co.*, designed by *Burne Jones*, 1890, formerly in the Haweis chapel of St James, Westmoreland Street, Marylebone.)

HOLY TRINITY, Twickenham Green. 1839–41 by *Basevi*, with a W tower imitating crisply and thinly in white brick the local C15 tower type. Inside, slim tall piers without capitals supporting four-centred arches. Aisles with lean-to roofs, no clerestory. Interior altered in the 1970s. The chaste, somewhat brittle character of the Gothic Revival of the Commissioners' churches. An instructive contrast to the vulgar and thick chancel and transepts added by *F. T. Dolman*, 1863.

50 ST MARY, Church Street. The parish church lies close to the river in a churchyard with good tombs. The W tower remains from the medieval church, a typical Middlesex design, late C14, Kentish rag, with diagonal buttresses and a stair-turret reaching up higher than the battlemented top of the tower. The body of the church was redesigned by *John James* and rebuilt in 1714–15. James was one of the surveyors to Queen Anne's Fifty New Churches, and author and translator of several books on the theory of architecture. His chief work in London is St George, Hanover Square. The Twickenham church has a plan wisely emphasizing the N and S sides, that is the sides visible from village and river. The nave has five bays, the chancel projects. Bays two to four also project (one can hardly say transeptwise, because the projecting part is wider than the rest). They have big pediments on broad, robust brick Tuscan pilasters, with something of the vigour of Vanbrugh and Hawksmoor. The rubbed and gauged brickwork is superb. At the E end a circular window and a straight segmental pediment. The whole is obviously an architect's not a local mason's work. Galleries inside (altered 1859), disappointingly taking no notice of the exterior projections. The extensive interior restorations of 1859–71 were largely removed from 1955 onwards, when the sanctuary was remodelled, and the nave ceiling redesigned, with rather anaemic pastel-coloured

Adamish plasterwork, by *Sir Albert Richardson*. Other enrichments added in keeping (nave CANDELABRA, PULPIT
TESTER). – The PULPIT itself dates from 1772. – Original
wooden REREDOS and metal ALTAR RAILS. – C17 COM-
MUNION TABLE. – STAINED GLASS. E window by *Bryan
Thomas*. – Heraldic glass by *Jane Gray*. – Many fine MONU-
MENTS, now well restored and displayed. The connections of
the church with Pope are familiar. Here is the monument to
his parents and himself, by *Francis Bird* (N gallery), and the
tablet (on the outer wall of the chancel) to Mary Beach, his
nurse, also put up by him, in a Gibbsian frame of intermittent
rustication. A larger monument to Pope was erected by
Bishop Warburton in 1761, a plain broad obelisk in relif with
portrait medallion, very restrained, by *Prince Hoare* (N gallery). – Other noteworthy monuments: Francis Poulton and
wife † 1642, two frontal demi-figures of terracotta, their hands
crossed on a skull. The whole of the top part of the monument
has disappeared. – M. Harvey (SE corner of the chancel), a
flaming urn in the round, ascribed by Mrs Esdaile to *Bushnell*.
– Sir W. Humble † 1680 and son, attributed by Esdaile to
Bird, and Sir Joseph Ashe † 1686 (tower),* both with well
carved architectural frames and putti. – Nathaniel Piggott
† 1737, by *Scheemakers*, with inscription by Pope (s gallery). –
Chaloner Ogle, signed by *Rysbrack*, 1751, with a putto amid
trophies against a short obelisk (N gallery). – George and Anne
Gostling, signed by *John Bacon Jun.*, 1800, with a mourning
figure seated in front of a tall pedestal supporting an urn. Good
and genuine, not at all mawkish (s gallery). – Lady Mary
Wildman † 1825, draped urn by *R. Westmacott*.

(St MICHAEL AND St GEORGE, Wilcox Road, s of South
Road, Fulwell. 1913 by *J. S. Adkins*. – PULPIT and LEC-
TERN from St Thomas Bethnal Green.)

St STEPHEN, Cambridge Park, N of Marble Hill Park, East
Twickenham. 1874 by *Lockwood & Mawson*. Kentish rag;
Dec. Chancel 1885; tower completed 1907.

St JAMES (R.C.), Popes Grove, w of Cross Deep. 1885 by *J. S.
Hansom*. Respectable Early Gothic, brick with stone dressings. No tower.

St MARGARET (R.C.), St Margarets Road, East Twickenham. By *Williams & Winkley*, 1968. One of the best recent
churches in London. An ingeniously compact plan, based,
like the same architects' church in Wallington (*see* Beddington, Su), on a series of rectangles with cut-off corners. On the
r. the weekday chapel, on the l. a hall which can be opened up
to the main church at the back. Vestries tucked away beneath.
The chief features externally are the self-conscious projecting
angle of the appendage to the hall (containing only a reading
room, cloakroom, and stores) and a rather uneasy porch. The
interior is more satisfying: the main church is spacious yet 108

---

* Similar to the monument to his son-in-law (William Windham) at Felbrigg,
Norfolk, which is by *Gibbons*.

intimate, because of its two ceiling heights, with clerestory-lit sections over the diagonally opposed baptistery and larger sanctuary space. Each has an excellent STAINED GLASS window by *Patrick Reyntiens*. Otherwise, ruthlessly simple surfaces: obscured glass, concrete blockwork, carpeted floors, so that all depends on the handling of space and light.

PUBLIC BUILDINGS

POST OFFICE, London Road. *See* Perambulation 1.

PUBLIC LIBRARY, Garfield Road, off York Street. 1907 by *Howard Goadby*, Baroque, with busts of Pope and Tennyson and a Jacobean staircase around the entrance hall.

RUGBY UNION HEADQUARTERS, Whitton Road. Opened 1909, with two covered stands (E and W) and terraces; N stand added 1924, E stand raised, W stand rebuilt in two tiers 1931–3, all overtopped in 1980 by the chunky concrete S stand of precast concrete, with three tiers for 11,751 spectators. It has an impressive canopy of twelve shallow p.v.c.-filled shallow arches, anchored by six slim pylons. Architects *Howard Lobb Partnership*, engineers *Jan Brobowski & Partners*. Over the Rowland Hill Memorial Gate (1929) a *Coade* stone lion from the Lion Brewery Lambeth, a brother of the one now outside County Hall, installed here in 1972.

FOOTBRIDGE to Eel Pie Island. 1957. Sinuous ribbon of prestressed concrete.

TWICKENHAM BRIDGE. *See* Thames Crossings at end of gazetteer.

Twickenham's exceptionally rich collection of wealthy riverside mansions are now nearly all in public or institutional ownership. They are described below from E to W, instead of in the usual order of their present functions.

60 MARBLE HILL HOUSE. An exquisite Palladian villa built for Henrietta Howard, the mistress of George II, later Countess of Suffolk, impeccably restored to its C18 state by the *G.L.C.* in 1965–6. Begun in 1724, completed *c.* 1729. The site was purchased for Mrs Howard by Lord Ilay, who had an estate at Whitton near by, and the house was built by *Roger Morris*, Ilay's own architect, with the advice of *Lord Herbert* (the later ninth Earl of Pembroke), one of the leading aristocratic champions of the Palladian revival. *Colen Campbell* may also have been involved in the initial design, as is shown by an unnamed sketch attributed to him, now at Wilton House, which shows the house with low pavilions omitted in the final design, as was the grand double staircase shown in the drawing of Marble Hill published in *Vitruvius Britannicus*. The result is an exterior exceptionally chaste and restrained, depending for its effect on the harmonious balance between plain surfaces and openings.* The principles look back to Inigo Jones's Queen's

* The windows, later altered, were restored to their original proportions in 1965–6.

House, Greenwich (Gr), and were taken up again in the villas of the 1750s, for which Marble Hill was an important prototype (*see* e.g. Roehampton, Ww). The house is stuccoed, with stone dressings. Slightly projecting three-bay centre to N and S with a pediment with cartouche. The centre of the N side is further emphasized by giant Ionic pilasters above a rusticated basement. Pedimented central window on each side. Otherwise there are only the simplest of mouldings and plain horizontal stone bands. Pyramidal roof behind a modillion cornice.

The plan is straightforward. The centre is occupied by a major and a minor staircase on the N side, and on the S by a typical English Palladian low hall, with four Ionic columns. Above this, on the piano nobile, the Great Room, a cube extending into the attic. On the E side of the attic floor a long gallery.

INTERIORS. Handsome mahogany STAIRCASE leading to the piano nobile, with a closed string, carved square newels, and sturdy turned balusters, a conscious revival of C 17 forms, derived, it has been suggested, from Coleshill, Berkshire, then thought to be by Inigo Jones. The upper walls with pedimented frames and some sparse ornament. The chief showpiece, the GREAT ROOM, white and gilt, inspired by Inigo's single cube at Wilton, is an accomplished exercise in symmetry; 24 ft in each direction, the walls divided into three, with central pedimented doorcase and chimneypiece (the latter crowned by reclining putti) flanked by picture frames which originally contained copies of Van Dycks (*à la* Wilton). Enriched architrave with plain coved ceiling above. Woodcarving by *James Richards*, George I's master carver. E of the Great Room LADY SUFFOLK'S BEDCHAMBER, with a bed alcove defined by a pair of Ionic columns, and a coved ceiling. Simple C 18 chimneypiece brought from No. 29 Clapton Common, Hackney. On the ground floor the BREAKFAST PARLOUR also has an alcove, with arches and decorative garlands. On the other side of the hall the DINING PARLOUR, made from two rooms by *Matthew Brettingham* in 1750–1, and next to it the PAPER ROOM, square with groined vault. The other rooms very plain.

The GROUNDS, now a public park, were laid out by *Charles Bridgeman* from 1724. *Pope* was also involved, as his correspondence shows. C 18 views show an open lawn to the river, flanked by chestnut groves. STABLES early C 19, two storeys, with pediment and cupola. ICEHOUSE, W of the house.

ORLEANS HOUSE GALLERY, Riverside. A relic of Orleans House, named after Louis Philippe Duc d'Orleans, who lived here in 1800–14 and 1815–17. The original house was a plain brick building with stone dressings, built in 1710 by *John James* for James Johnson, Queen Anne's Secretary of State. The main surviving feature is the OCTAGON, a small but sumptuous garden room added *c.* 1720, but perhaps designed earlier, by *James Gibbs*, which soon provided a suitable setting for the reception of the new queen, Caroline of Ansbach. When the rest of the house was demolished in 1927, the octagon and its plain adjoining service wings were rescued by Mrs Ionides, who bequeathed the building to Twickenham as a public art gallery in 1962. The octagon has a lively exterior, of stone and yellow and red brick, with tall round-headed windows with typical Gibbs surrounds, and rubbed brick pilasters. Parapet, originally with urns (see Gibbs's *Book of Architecture*, 1728, plate 71). Domed interior, with almost all the wall surfaces enriched with splendid plasterwork by *Artari* and *Bagutti*. Their characteristic reclining figures and energetic putti adorn the pediments of both doorways and chimneypiece. There are also busts in lunettes higher up, and medallions on the walls, depicting King George II and Queen Caroline; a third medallion, a later addition, may be of Louis Philippe. The whole is a telling illustration of the effects of Gibbs's Roman Baroque training.*

YORK HOUSE (Municipal Offices), York Street. A handsome house on an H-plan, with shallow projections, 2 plus 3 plus 2 bays, plain and dignified. Three storeys, brick with stone quoins; cemented rusticated ground floor, hipped roof. The date is uncertain: it appears to be mid C17, probably built by the second Earl of Manchester in the 1650s, and remodelled in the early C18 (to which the exterior details and perhaps the separately roofed centre on the garden side must belong). There is no firm evidence to associate the work of either period with the Earl of Clarendon, who appears to have owned the house in the later C17. The only decorative element outside is the N door, with a steep broken pediment of S-curves ending in thick scrolls. Interior much altered; a mid C17 staircase, spoilt by a lift, remains, however, in the wing to the l. of the entrance hall. Balusters with tapering Ionic pilasters. Later, lower extensions to l. and r., including a conservatory said to have been added by Anne Damer, as her studio, in the later C18. Later eminent residents included the family of the Comte de Paris in the C19. In the grounds near the river (erected to screen a now demolished warehouse) a colossal fountain and over-life-size Italian statuary, an amazing spectacle installed by the Indian merchant prince Sir Ratan J. Tata in 1906. (It had been acquired in 1904 for Whitaker Wright's Witley Court, Surrey, but was never unpacked.)

ST JOHN'S HOSPITAL, Amyand Park Road, off London Road to the NE. The core is a late C18 house with a pediment.

ST CATHERINE'S SCHOOL, Cross Deep. In the grounds of POPE'S VILLA, demolished in the early C19. The school occupies a neo-Tudor house by *H. E. Kendall Jun.*, built for Thomas Young, a tea merchant, with later enlargements. Brick chapel by the river, 1935 by *Brewer, Smith & Brewer*; C20 buildings on the other side of the road, on the site of Pope's garden (classrooms 1960–2 etc. by *Dodge & Reid*,

* We owe these comments to Dr Terry Friedman.

multi-purpose hall 1978 by *E. G. V. Hives & Son*). The site of Pope's villa was approximately in line with the chapel, but closer to the road. Pope took a lease of house and grounds in 1718, and *Gibbs* remodelled the house for him the following year, giving the river front the tripartite Palladian arrangement with tall three-storey centre which is familiar from many C18 paintings and engravings. A first-floor portico was added in the 1730s on the advice of *Kent* and *Burlington*. Beneath this a broad arch led to a passage which passed beneath the house and road to the garden beyond. This passage was Pope's celebrated GROTTO, which still survives, although it has lost most of its decoration. It started with a single chamber with a porch at either end, and was enlarged by an additional chamber in the 1730s when, with the help of a geologist, the Rev. William Borlaze, it was adorned with minerals, to give the impression of a subterranean mine or quarry, the equivalent of the 'naturalistic' effect aimed at in the garden itself. Of the garden nothing remains. The passage led to a 'wilderness', and to a shell temple (completed 1725, rebuilt after it had collapsed ten years later). Nearby was a mound from whose summit one could enjoy a prospect of the Thames. The formal vistas down the centre of the garden leading to Pope's monument to his mother were framed by densely planted trees to give the impression of a forest. The whole was on a miniature scale, and no doubt would now appear very artificial in comparison with later C18 landscaping; but at the time it was a most influential example in the transition from the stiff formality of the Dutch and French garden tradition to more naturalistic picturesque effects.

STRAWBERRY HILL* (St Mary's College) is by far the most 64 important and rewarding of the monuments of Twickenham, preserved in an excellent state, owing to the care and appreciation of the college which it now houses. It was of all early Gothic Revival buildings of Britain the most influential and appears still as charming and convincing as it must have been when it was new.

Horace Walpole was thirty when he leased 'a little plaything house' close to the river in 1747 (letter of 8 June 1747). In 1749 he bought it, made some minor alterations, and began to landscape the grounds, but only in September 1749 does he mention his 'future battlements'. So the idea of converting the cottage into a Gothic castle seems to belong to that year. After that he never looked back. He consulted a few friends and a number of folios of engravings of medieval work and started on addition after addition, until by 1766 the house was complete. Apart from a few C19 modifications it remains little altered. To the S is the office wing designed by *Essex* in 1779 but built by *Wyatt* only in 1790. The Waldegrave wing of 1860–2 lies between this and the original house on the site of

* We are grateful to Mr Michael Snodin and Mr Clive Wainwright of the V and A for much help with this account.

Walpole's stables. Further s the buildings added for the college in the c 20, which now cover much of the grounds, are fortunately screened by trees, so that when seen from the e Walpole's bijou can still be appreciated very much in pristine form. He could indeed be proud of his castle, a place equally suited to writing *The Castle of Otranto* and the gossipy letters which poured forth from it in such unparalleled numbers, a place, that is, both aweful and amusing, both romantic and Rococo. The first alterations of 1748, by *William Robinson* of the Office of Works, were considered inadequately Gothic. He was therefore demoted to Clerk of the Works and the actual designing was done by a 'Committee on Taste' whose main members were *Walpole* himself, his friend *John Chute* of The Vyne, Hampshire, and *Richard Bentley*, son of the great philologist. Others involved were *J. H. Muntz*, who had worked as painter and draughtsman for Chute at The Vyne; after 1761, *Thomas Pitt*, later Lord Camelford; and, also in the 1760s, *Robert Adam*. Later still designs were provided by *James Essex* and (for a garden building) by *John Carter*, and *Thomas Gayfere*, master mason of Westminster Abbey, was employed to execute the chapel in the wood designed by *Chute*. The last three already mark the transition to the more serious archaeologizing work which was to characterize the Gothic revival of the earlier c 19.

The Gothic style for domestic purposes was not as absolutely new in 1750 as is often presumed, and as it seemed to those from Germany and France who were aware of what the Prime Minister's son did, but not of what had been done before. Even if one forgets about Vanbrugh's appreciation of the virile Middle Ages and about Hawksmoor's fantastic towers of All Souls College, Oxford, there remain such things as Gibbs's Gothic Temple at Stowe (which Walpole called 'pure and beautiful and venerable', 4 August 1753); Sanderson Miller's Gothic buildings; Batty Langley's naive efforts at a Gothic columnar order; Kent's Esher Place, praised by Walpole as 'kentissime'; and at Twickenham itself Radnor House, engraved with its Gothic front as early as 1754 and probably built in the thirties, and (also not far from Twickenham) Kent's Gothic doorway and windows of 1732 at Hampton Court (q.v.). Of Kent Walpole says he never knew 'how to enter into the true Gothic taste' (September 1753). What then did he mean by the true Gothic taste? If one looks up his letters, one finds a very odd, illogical mixture of meanings. 'The charming venerable Gothic' is what he calls it (25 July 1748). Other words of description for genuine or imitation Gothic buildings are 'pretty', 'neat', and so on. 'Venerable barbarism' also occurs (27 April 1753). His enthusiasm for Gothic forms is undoubted, though he liked to conceal it and playfully to pretend only to be 'grave about trifles' (6 October 1753). But he was grave, at least in one way: he insisted on many details about the house being accurate copies of existing and published Gothic work.

That attitude was new, and became two generations later the attitude of a more archaeologically minded epoch. In Walpole there is still vacillation between tracery as an alternative to Chinese fretwork and as a motif belonging to a venerable past age. Still, even when he copied he copied in a spirit very different from that of the c 19. For he did not mind in the least whether a tomb became a fireplace or a bookcase. Accuracy mattered, but any feeling for a work of the c 13 or c 14 as an organic whole not to be separated from its genuine setting was still absent. Even with its exact copies here and there, the whole of Strawberry Hill remains make-believe, and it is that very ambiguity of it that makes it so much more attractive than the heavy-handed exactness of c 19 period imitation. Walpole was as far from Ruskin's or Morris's ideals of purity as Roubiliac with the naturalistic rocks of his tombs or Robert Adam with his use of artificial stone, or the sham bridge in the grounds of Ken Wood. In fact *Essex* designed a sham Gothic bridge for Strawberry Hill in 1778, which was made in 1792, and garden gates of lithodipra were designed in 1769 and made in 1771. The windows of this early part, with their ogee heads and quatrefoils, are still exactly as fanciful and unarchaeological as Gothic work by Kent.

EXTERIOR. As one approaches from the s one sees on the r. a bay and one window each side. This part, with the possible exception of the bay, represents the original toy-house of 1698; the visible s front was designed by *Chute c.* 1752, as was the E front (the centre, with a first-floor bay, was added in 1748 by *Robinson*); and the rooms to the r. were completed in 1754. The long gallery wing with its buttresses, uniform in contrast to the variety of the older group, was completed by *Chute* in 1762; the rooms behind it sticking out in a rather untidy way to the N were added in 1758–9 (Holbein Chamber with little cloister below); 1762 (oratory); 1758–63 (quatrefoil cabinet now used as a chapel*); and 1771–2 (Great North Bed Chamber). The exterior of the round W tower by *Chute* is of 1760; the Beauclerk turret N of it by *James Essex* was projected in 1798. To build a house on this scale completely asymmetrically was perhaps Walpole's most important single innovation,‡ an application of the principles established for picturesque gardening in the 1720s (*see* Chiswick, Ho) which seems to belong entirely to Walpole; he probably knew it when he wrote as early as 25 February 1750: 'I am almost as fond of the Sharawaggi, or Chinese want of symmetry, in buildings, as in grounds or gardens.' The irregular roof-line was also important to him. The Beauclerk tower, he wrote after its completion in 1776, has 'an exceedingly pretty effect breaking the long line of the house picturesquely and looking very ancient'. The grouping of the whole in the final state in which it

* When built, visible as an almost detached tower.
‡ The asymmetry was at least partly dictated by the site. The road originally touched the house: its course was altered for the gallery wing and was moved again probably in the C 19.

appears, for instance in engravings of 1784, is indeed most felicitous, neither overcrowded with fancy detail nor uniform as classical Georgian architecture of 1750/60 deliberately was.

The present appearance of the exterior, however, is not as Walpole left it. The house formerly had pinnacles. The present Tudor chimneys and the heightening of the round tower and the Beauclerk tower are C 19 alterations; the pebbledash also is not original. The whole gallery wing, tower, and Beauclerk turret were refaced by Lady Waldegrave. The bay of the S front was raised by one storey, incorporating windows originally in the wall behind, as part of the extensive restorations by *Sir Albert Richardson* after the Second World War. Compared with the house, the offices of 1790 are competent but dull, similar to so much college work done about 1800. The large and ornate mid Victorian wing in between was added in 1860–2 by *Lady Frances Waldegrave* (apparently without an architect), one of the most famous of Victorian political hostesses. She inherited Strawberry Hill through her marriage into the Waldegrave family, who were distantly related to Walpole, and reopened the house in 1856, after years of neglect. By this time Walpole's collections had been dispersed in the great sale of 1842.*

The GARDENS are no longer what they were. 'Riant', Walpole wanted them to be. He began landscaping at once in 1748. Part of the spacious lawn which lay between house and river still remains, but only a few bands of trees survive from the serpentine wood which framed the lawn to the S, and just one of the many garden buildings (*see* below); the rustic cottage, the sham bridge, the shell bench have all gone.

INTERIOR. The house can be entered from the N by the little cloister, or from the garden. Coming from the garden the first room is the LITTLE PARLOUR on the S side, with a Gothic chimneypiece by *Bentley* (1753) modelled on Bishop Ruthall's tomb at Westminster. In the window lights (as in nearly all the rooms) fragments of heraldic glass and C 17 medallions, possibly Walpolian, but certainly rearranged since the Second World War, like most of the glass in the house. To the r. is the former CHINA CLOSET (now cloakroom) with another Gothic fireplace (possibly by *Chute*). To the l. the former YELLOW BEDCHAMBER, with a curious Rococo chimneypiece by *Bentley* (now incomplete, formerly painted black and yellow). The STAIRCASE HALL constructed in 1753–4 is in the spirit of Walpole, although much of the detail is not original. The two thin lancets on either side of the door, with heraldic glass, belong to *Richardson*'s postwar reconstruction. The paper 'painted' in perspective to imitate Gothic fretwork is an imitation (not completely accurate) of the 1960s.‡ Walpole himself wavered in his descrip-

---

* There is a large collection of furniture from Strawberry Hill, as well as original drawings, in the Lewis Walpole Library, Farmington, Conn., U.S.A.

‡ The original design was repainted in 1793–4 by *Cornelius Dixon* and covered up in the C 19.

tions of the staircase between 'the most venerable gloom . . . that ever was since the days of Abelard' and 'so pretty and so small that I am inclined to wrap it up and send it to you in my letter' (letters of March and June 1753). By the approach to the hall from the N is the LITTLE CLOISTER added by *Chute* in 1758–61, a small arcade incorporated into an outer hall in the C 19 and opened up again by *Richardson*, who also rebuilt the N wall and carried out much refacing, and the ORATORY of 1762. (In the former Prior's Garden adjacent is a reproduction of Horace Walpole's screen copied from Bishop Niger's tomb in Old St Paul's.) Also on the N is the great parlour or REFECTORY (1754), a large room with a fanciful Rococo Gothic chimneypiece by *Bentley*, with tall pinnacles and much cusping. The window was enlarged in 1774. The ground floor of the W extension added by *Chute* beyond the little cloister was more substantially altered in the C 19, when the GREAT CLOISTER facing the garden was converted to servants' rooms. On the N side the former PANTRY now houses 'Virgilia', a white marble relief, 1871 by *Woolner*, who had once been a Pre-Raphaelite. The adjacent PASSAGE is almost certainly Walpole's 'winding cloister', set with Roman reliefs and medieval alabasters probably placed there in his time. On a wall here, formerly external, the only survival of the original roughcast plaster finish of the house.

UPSTAIRS. In the original house, the former BLUE BED-CHAMBER (over the little parlour) has another of *Bentley*'s Rococo Gothic chimneypieces (1754) and some reset stained glass. The former BREAKFAST ROOM with bay-windows to the E was remodelled in 1856–8 as that favourite Victorian fantasy, a Turkish boudoir, with velvet tented ceiling, fretwork panelling, and chimneypiece with Moorish allusions. The mirror and upper part are by *Lady Waldegrave*, the lower is *Robinson*'s original of 1748 (almost identical to an example by Kent for Mr Pelham at Esher, which Horace Walpole described as 'not truly Gothic'). Window lights with C 17 scenes and blue glass. Over the boudoir MR WALPOLE'S BEDCHAMBER, with a Gothic chimneypiece by *Chute* with panelled sides, the original cresting missing. The ARMOURY, with triple Gothic arches and fleur-de-lys studding the vaults (the latter decoration, and the cusping over the doors, added by *Lady Waldegrave*), forms a small anteroom to the LIBRARY (over the refectory). Whereas the staircase was by *Bentley*, the library, of 1754, is by *Chute*. Most of Bentley's suggestions were rejected by Walpole although the Jacobean doors and doorcases belong to his scheme. It is the first room with serious medieval imitations. The elaborate Gothic bookcases were copies from the side doors to the screen of Old St Paul's. The multiplication of the motif and its translation into wood, needless to say, alter their character completely. The chimneypiece imitates John of Eltham's tomb in Westminster Abbey. Walpole and his friends knew these works from engravings by Hollar and others in the books by Dart, Dugdale, and other antiquarians. The painted heraldic ceiling, designed by *Walpole* himself (but redrawn by *Bentley* and executed by *Clement*), is inspired by C16 plasterwork, but the central rosette is of course a classical C17–18 idea.

One passes to the W extension through the STAR CHAMBER (ready by 1754), a small room with a window (rebuilt by *Richardson*) completely filled by coloured glass, and the TRUNK CEILED PASSAGE (extended in the C19). The HOLBEIN CHAMBER above the little cloister, by *Bentley*, 1758, is divided by a screen with fantastic Gothic detail – as imaginative as anything by Rococo decorators on the Continent. The gates to the choir at Rouen were Bentley's chief source of inspiration. The large chimneypiece with pinnacled niches on either side was (according to Gray) inspired by Rouen high altar and (according to Walpole) by Archbishop Wareham's tomb at Canterbury; the ribbed ceiling again imitates Tudor plasterwork (Queen's Dressing Room, Windsor). Beyond, the GREAT NORTH BED CHAMBER of 1771–3 by *Chute*, with a Portland stone chimneypiece by *Gayfere* designed by *Walpole*, based rather loosely on the tomb of Bishop Dudley at Westminster Abbey, a ribbed ceiling, and doorcases with Gothic tracery and pinnacles. The E doorway is C19. In the windows armorial GLASS, probably that supplied by *Peckitt* of York. The ceiling is taken from one of *c.* 1520 at The Vyne.

The GALLERY, designed by *Chute* and *Thomas Pitt* after Walpole's final quarrel with Bentley and built with the cloister below in 1761–3, reveals more than anything in the house how close the spirit of that gothicizing of 1760 is to the Rococo on the one hand and to Robert Adam's classicizing on the other. Looking at this gilt fretwork, at the ever-changing reflections in the bits of mirror glass in the niches and the small panels of the papier-mâché fan-vault (by *Bromwich*), it seems difficult to understand why Walpole should have been so disgusted with Adam's 'gingerbread and sippets of embroidery'. But then Walpole's judgement was always easily swayed by personal animosity, rancour, or gossip. All is glitter and *gaîté* in the gallery (no venerable gloom, no pedantic copistry). Yet the big door (now renewed), taken from a drawing by *Muntz*, did indeed come from the N door at St Albans, the vault from the aisles of Henry VII's Chapel in Westminster Abbey, and the arrangement of niches from Archbishop Bouchier's tomb at Canterbury. N of the gallery the CHAPEL (or tribune or cabinet), built in 1761–3, mostly to *Chute*'s design, quatrefoil, and with the most entertaining of Rococo-Gothic vaults, said to be derived from the York chapter house: this however must be taken with several pinches of salt, not only because one would look in vain there for the star of yellow glass* which terminates Walpole's vault, but also because of the intricate flowing traceries, in fact derived from the W window of York. The walls were originally covered with bric-a-brac, a collec-

* Renewed by *Richardson*.

tor's cabinet with eighteen ivories let into its front, paintings, statuettes, vases, and so on. The room was formerly very dark, with lurid glass by *William Price II*. Openwork Gothic door by *Pitt*, niches by *Muntz* (derived from the N door of St Albans).

At the far end of the gallery the ROUND TOWER, designed by *Chute* in 1759, housed the kitchen on the ground floor. In the ROUND ROOM above a scagliola chimneypiece which comes from no less a monument than Edward the Confessor's shrine, however 'improved by Mr *Adam*' (with whom Walpole was not yet cross in 1766). The ceiling pattern is inspired by the rose window tracery of Old St Paul's, the Gothic panelling of the bay-window based on the tomb of Eleanor of Castile. The armorial stained glass was inserted by Lady Waldegrave. The adjoining tiny room in the BEAUCLERK TURRET has a decorated plaster ceiling. The turret, projected by *Chute* in 1758, was built in 1778 to designs by *Essex*. It reminded Walpole of Thornbury, Gloucestershire. The adjacent back staircase, with a simple Gothic balustrade and two blocked windows, leads to a servants' corridor which reveals the originally separate nature of the tribune tower. S of the round tower comes the WALDEGRAVE WING of 1860–2, built by *Lady Frances Waldegrave* without an architect, and apparently to her own designs.* It is in an excellent and not at all pedestrian neo-Gothic. Apart from the change of scale, it is the profusion of naturalistic foliage among the tracery patterns that gives away the Victorian date, but the overall feeling is of the 1820s or 30s. The main rooms are an anteroom, the vast DRAWING ROOM with a tall bay-window to the garden and a lush chimneypiece, and on the other side of the central corridor the DINING ROOM and BILLIARD ROOM. Beyond this is the wing added as offices in 1790, and converted to guest bedrooms in the C19, which now links up with the C20 buildings.

The COLLEGE BUILDINGS, serving 1,200 students (1979), started with plain Tudor ranges by *Pugin & Pugin*, 1925. Further additions by *Sir Albert Richardson*, of which the chief is the CHAPEL, 1962, tall, pale brick, parapeted, Gothic only in its tracery and in the general form, which is inspired by Albi Cathedral: see the narrow aisles forming passages through the buttresses, with galleries above. Excellent stained glass in rich colours by *Gabriel Loire* of Chartres: semi-abstract designs based on the mysteries of the Rosary. The ground floor forms one wing of the LIBRARY, which encloses a small cloister to the W. In front of the chapel a landscaped forecourt, made in the 1970s by the *Architectural and Planning Partnership*. By them also the later buildings around the playing fields further W. Near the porter's lodge one incongruous Walpole survival now without its protective vegetation: the CHAPEL IN THE WOOD, a garden building designed by *Chute* in 1772, finished in 1774 (executed by *Gayfere*), and refurbished in the 1950s as

* The plans were drawn out by her clerk of the works, *Ritchie*. Her builder was *Kelk*, the carver *Plows* (J. M. Crook).

a real chapel with new murals and stained glass (by *Harry Clarke*). It is small (8 ft wide), built to make a nice show of Walpole's stained glass (now at Bexhill Church, Sussex) and to house a C 13 shrine which he had brought from Rome (now at Wilton Church, Wilts). The exterior is precisely copied from the Audley tombs at Salisbury; the interior had pretty blue and gold fan-vaulting and blue and yellow tiles. The fan-vaulting (designed by *Chute*) survives, but the (ritual) E apse and skylight were apparently added by *Lady Waldegrave*, who kept her statue in the chapel.

PERAMBULATIONS

1. The Village Centre, from Marble Hill Park to Cross Deep

MONTPELIER ROW, facing E across Marble Hill Park, is one of the best examples near London of well-mannered, well-proportioned early Georgian terrace development. Built soon after 1720 as a speculative development by Captain John Grey, perhaps by the same builders as Syon Row (*see* below). First Nos. 1–15, then some Victorian houses and one modern one, No. 25, by *Geoffrey Darke*, 1967, tactful yet original, with its brown brick and matching window levels (but casements, not sashes, and quite a different treatment at the back). Then a terrace of three C 18 houses (Nos. 26–28) and MONTPELIER HOUSE and SOUTH END HOUSE, of three and five bays, grander than the rest. South End House has a very pretty early Gothic revival addition to the SW. The C 18 houses are of three storeys, mostly of three bays, of brownish stock brick with rubbed red brick dressings, absolutely flat except for the doors. These also are without porches. The various motifs of the surrounds are a good study in detail of the 1720s. Only one house on the other side, No. 33, C 18, double-fronted but quite modest. ORLEANS ROAD, parallel to the W, is a mews lane with cottages, a former small school of 1856, Gothic, and SOUTHEND COTTAGE and WHITE COTTAGE, a formal arrangement with facing pedimented gables, presumably service buildings for South End House.

The main charm of Twickenham village lies in the short stretch between Marble Hill Park and the church. The river is un-embanked here (hence the plots of garden between street and water), and appears narrow with the leafy Eel Pie Island opposite. RIVERSIDE winds between high garden walls. From E to W: close to Orleans House Gallery (*see* Public Buildings), RIVERSIDE HOUSE, *c.* 1810, with bow-windows and a later colonnaded porch at the side. FERRY HOUSE is later C 18, big, stuccoed, with a canted bay on brackets over-looking the river. Then FERRYSIDE, set back, C 18, unfortunately roughcast. The WHITE SWAN INN, C 18 with later balconies etc., is followed by an irregular terrace of white Georgian houses of any height, shape of doorway and porch, and position of bay-window. At the corner of SYON ROW the plaque 'SION ROW 1721'; two C18 houses; then Nos. 3–12, an orderly terrace with varied doorways ranging from leaf-scroll decoration characteristic of *c*. 1700 to the Gibbs type with intermittent rustication. The effect is similar to Montpelier Row, but less grand. The small cottages in FERRY ROAD behind make a nice contrast. Riverside continues past the gardens of York House (*see* Public Buildings) to DIAL HOUSE (vicarage), with a sundial of 1726 from the house built by *John James*. The exterior otherwise is of 1890, yellow and red brick.

After the churchyard, a few more good houses in THE EMBANKMENT, especially No. 5, C17, timber-framed and brick, with a half-hipped roof with gable to the road, a unique survival in the neighbourhood, Nos. 3 and 2, both handsome early C18, and Nos. 22–25, also early C18, stock brick. Behind these a MISSION HALL of *c*. 1871 by *Edis*. The rest of this area, pitted with car parks on the sites of cottages cleared away in the 1950s, cries out for sympathetic small-scale infilling. Only tantalizing fragments of lanes and alleys remain. In CHURCH STREET, No. 9, with the rebuilt ST GEORGE'S PLACE behind (by *Biscoe & Stanton*, 1977), shows more positively what can be done. Opposite, Nos. 44–46 are a 1980 refurbishment of two C18 buildings, by *Manning, Clamp & Partners*. The rest of Church Street remains pleasantly unspoilt in scale, although with little to single out. One remembers THE FOX, stuccoed C18, and bits of weatherboarding (No. 47) and old brickwork.

The central street of the village is KING STREET, fine and broad, but of no architectural interest apart from a few houses on the N side: Nos. 10–12, C18 altered; the GEORGE, C17, with later stucco and canted bays; and Nos. 58–60, C18. At one end a conservatively Italianate Edwardian BANK, stone-faced, with pediment; at the other a showy cinema. Still less to see to the N. Off London Road, opposite the festively Wren-aissance POST OFFICE (1908 by *S. Rutherford*), GROSVENOR ROAD, with one good C18 house, much rebuilt, between office blocks and cottages. Beyond a churchyard, around RAILWAY APPROACH, pleasant yellow brick terrace houses of 1977 by *Wates*, and old people's housing by *Richmond upon Thames*, 1981. By the railway the only large-scale commercial development so far, REGAL HOUSE (partly municipal offices), 1966 by *Bernard Gold*. Another four-storey office block opposite (*P. Bermingham* of Messrs *Arunbridge*, 1981). In LONDON ROAD No. 137, nice mid C18, and, further N, HEATHAM HOUSE, Whitton Road, also mid C18, with a plastered two-storey centrepiece and a good iron gate.

The riverside W of the village centre was also fringed by wealthy C18 houses, but fewer remain. (In the grounds of Thames Eyot is a Tuscan loggia of Portland stone leading to a small shellwork grotto, and a long riverside balustrade with vases and steps down to the water, surviving from Poulett Lodge, a house of the 1730s altered in the 1870s by *F. Chancellor* and demolished *c.* 1930.) Then in CROSS DEEP first the house called CROSSDEEP, perhaps of *c.* 1700, with later alterations. Five bays, three storeys, red brick. The charming Gothic wood detail of the windows must be later C 18. Doorway with an entablature curved up in the middle, a motif typical of *c.* 1720–40, perhaps of the time when *Gibbs* remodelled the house, adding the side wings with full-height bay-windows facing the river. (Good original staircase and woodwork.) Fine iron gates and piers with pineapples. Then after St Catherine's School (*see* Public Buildings), RYAN HOUSE, the remaining half of a house built in 1807 by Baroness Howe near the site of Pope's villa. Three storeys, stucco. RADNOR HOUSE, which followed, was destroyed in the Second World War. All that remains is the Rococo Gothic octagonal SUMMER HOUSE in RADNOR GARDENS. Trefoil arches and ogee windows. The inspiration for this must have been its famous neighbour, Strawberry Hill (*see* Public Buildings). Radnor House itself had been given a Gothick exterior at a very early date, *c.* 1749, and there was also, by the river, a chinoiserie gazebo.

2. *Twickenham Green*

TWICKENHAM GREEN, W of the village centre, is an attractive large wedge-shaped open space, the N and W sides still quite cottagey. In COLNE ROAD, parallel to the present N side, two good houses, Nos. 74 and 78, the latter with projecting centre with Venetian window and lunette. Along the S side of the Green stuccoed villas of the earlier C 19, then GIFFORD HOUSE, an old people's home by *Buxton, Truscott & Wall*, 1975, Holy Trinity (q.v.), and some informal housing behind, pleasantly done, 1979 by *Manning Clamp & Partners*. Other modest villas of the C 19 to the S down POPES AVENUE, as well as a few good C 20 houses (No. 69a by *Kenneth Wood*, low, hidden away, and No. 45 by *Dry Halasz & Associates*, 1968, of re-used stock brick). Near by, Ajanta, in WALPOLE GAR-DENS, is a single house of 1954 by *Eric Lyons*, who is better known for his Span estates (q.v. Blackheath Park, Greenwich, Gr, and Ham, Ri).

The SPAN ESTATES which should be seen here are THURNBY COURT (corner of Wellesley Road and Spencer Road), 1958, a compact tile-hung quadrangle of twenty-seven flats, similar to some of the early groups at Blackheath, and FIELDEND, off WALDEGRAVE ROAD, completed 1961. Fieldend is a more generously laid out group of fifty-one weatherboarded terrace houses (only forty rooms per acre), with private back gardens, arranged informally around an idyllic secluded area thickly planted with silver birch trees, now the most sylvan of all Span developments in London. A perimeter road for cars.* Further

* Other early Span groups W of Twickenham Green: BOX CORNER (Second and Third Crossroads), six flats (1951) and six houses (1954); and in CAMPBELL ROAD twenty houses (1955).

w, off STRAWBERRY VALE, MALLARD PLACE, 1978–80 by the *Eric Lyons Cunningham Partnership*, forty-five houses and fifty-seven flats, a denser but more affluent development than the earlier Span schemes. Attractive three-storey groups with pitched roofs, with their own mooring places at the riverside.

(Further s, off Twickenham Road, towards Teddington, GROVE GARDENS, a 1920s cottage estate built by the Royal Dutch Shell Company, planned on garden city principles. DTS)

3. East Twickenham

SANDYCOMBE LODGE, Sandycombe Road. A symmetrical cottage, with central gable and lower wings with prettily rounded corners, designed and built for himself by *Turner* the painter in 1812; he was his own 'architect, contractor, surveyor, foreman and clerk of the works'.

East Twickenham was a part of Twickenham Park, a large estate which originally extended into Isleworth (Ho, *London 3: North West*). Part of it was taken by Joseph Todd, for whom in 1828 *Leonard Lloyd* built Park House (demolished 1923) on a site near Park House Gardens. A one-storey lodge remains (No. 90 RICHMOND ROAD). The grounds in between were filled with large suburban villas, e.g. those in ROSSLYN ROAD and adjoining streets built just at that time in the C 19 when taste was shifting from Italianate to Gothic. In RIVERDALE ROAD an especially complete sequence of five huge Ruskinian Gothic houses, polychrome brick, with towers over the porches. Further N in Richmond Road No. 397 (RYDE HOUSE, incorporated in a housing, shopping, and office development by *Thomas Saunders*, 1979. This and Bute Lodge, in PARK ROAD to the N, survive from another part of the Todd estate which *Lloyd* developed with villas already in the 1820s. BUTE LODGE has a pretty centrepiece with gable and pilastered bow-window; lower wings with rounded corners, which must have been inspired by Turner's Sandycombe Lodge. In WILLOUGHBY ROAD, No. 1, of similar date, a small villa with an extra tall campanile, refurbished for offices as part of a larger complex by *Manning Clamp & Partners*, 1981.

Further N up ST MARGARETS ROAD, No. 134, stuccoed, *c.* 1830, with gable treated with pediment, and a porch with Ionic columns, a good contrast to the R.C. church next door. The tile-hung flats in the front garden are a less happy neighbour. s of St Margarets Road, CAMBRIDGE PARK, another C 19 suburb, of less interest, which replaced the house and grounds named after its early C 19 owner, the writer R. O. Cambridge. (There is another Span group of 1958 here, also called THE CEDARS. HAVERSHAM GRANGE, Haversham Close, is by *Rosenberg & Gentle*, 1980.)

WHITTON

Once a small hamlet w of Twickenham, now drowned by suburban expansion.

ST PHILIP AND ST JAMES, Kneller Road and Hounslow Road. 1862 by *F. H. Pownall*, small and clumsily picturesque, with a bell-turret. Kentish rag outside, yellow and red brick inside. N aisle and N chapel. – SCULPTURE. C 15 carved alabaster panel, *c.* 2 ft high, of Christ with symbols of the Passion, found near Valle Crucis Abbey, Wales, and given in 1913. – STAINED GLASS. E windows by *Clayton & Bell*, 1862; w window by *C. E. Kempe*, 1892.

(ST EDMUND (R.C.), Nelson Road. 1961–3, designed by *F. X. Velarde*, completed by *R. O'Mahony*. An elongated plan on a narrow site. – FONT and AUMBRY by *David John.* DE)

KNELLER HALL (Royal Military School of Music), Kneller Road. An extraordinary affair which has replaced the villa called Whitton House which Kneller, the painter, built for himself in 1709–11. The house, enlarged by two wings by *Philip Hardwick*, became a teacher training college in 1847. What we now see is a vast neo-Jacobean pile with a frontispiece with two turrets, and in front of them an arcaded stone screen linking the projecting wings. The date is 1848, the architect *George Mair*. The walls of Hardwick's wings were incorporated, but *Kneller*'s original house was demolished.* Nice gatepiers with wreaths and shallow urns, late C 18.

MURRAY PARK, further w off Kneller Road, marks part of the grounds of WHITTON PARK (demolished *c.* 1847), built for the Earl of Ilay by *Roger Morris*, with additions by *Gibbs*, and later altered by *Chambers* for himself.

POWDER MILLS, in Crane Park, w of Chertsey Road. Part of the site of HOUNSLOW POWDER MILLS, which ceased production in 1920. Gunpowder had been made at sites along the river Crane since C 16 if not much earlier. There remain various mill streams, wheel pits and machine bases, and high earthen mounds which partly enclosed the small sheds where the powder was ground. The so-called 'Shot Tower', a conical brick tower 80 ft high, formerly had a shallow conical lead roof surmounted by a timber bellcote. A date 1828 above the doorway is no longer visible. It is most unlikely to have been used for casting lead shot; it may have been a water tower for fire-fighting or hydraulic equipment.

* It was of five bays with a central cupola and the unusual feature of concave domed corner cupolas.

SOUTHWARK

INTRODUCTION

Modern Southwark is made up of three boroughs formed in 1899: Southwark, consisting of the parishes of St Saviour, St George the Martyr, St Mary Newington, and Christ Church; Bermondsey, a medieval parish augmented by the riverside

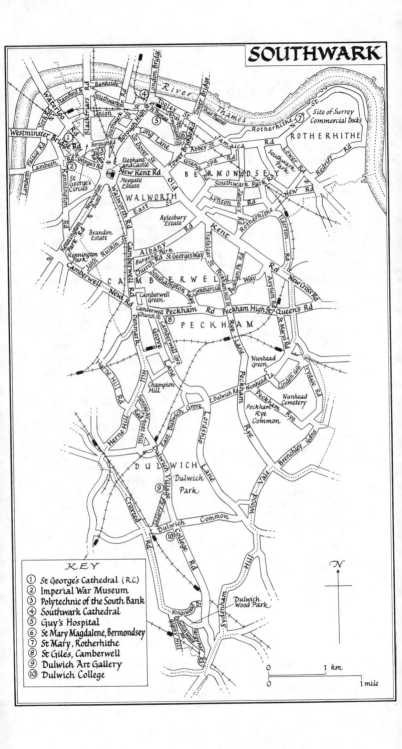

SOUTHWARK

River Thames

Site of Surrey Commercial Docks

ROTHERHITHE

BERMONDSEY

WALWORTH

CAMBERWELL

PECKHAM

DULWICH

Dulwich Park

Dulwich Wood Park

KEY

1. St George's Cathedral (R.C.)
2. Imperial War Museum
3. Polytechnic of the South Bank
4. Southwark Cathedral
5. Guy's Hospital
6. St Mary Magdalene, Bermondsey
7. St Mary, Rotherhithe
8. St Giles, Camberwell
9. Dulwich Art Gallery
10. Dulwich College

N

0   1 km
0   1 mile

parishes of Rotherhithe, St John Horselydown, St Olave, and St Thomas; and Camberwell, a large parish of medieval origin further s. The gazetteer maintains the pre-1965 divisions of Southwark, Bermondsey, and Camberwell, with churches and public buildings at the beginning of each section.

The geology is London Clay, mainly overlain by sands and gravels; with former marshland in the N, especially to the E. The slight prehistoric scatter, mainly close to the river, was perhaps left by fishers and fowlers.

Roman Southwark was an important suburb of Londinium, to which it must have been connected by a bridge. The settlement spread s along Borough High Street, the approximate line of a Roman road which unites several important roads from the s. Early clay and timber structures were later replaced by stone buildings with mosaic floors, usually of plain red tesserae. A cemetery and agricultural area has been found to the SE. From the Middle Ages, Southwark was more intimately London than any other area outside the City and Westminster. It was the bridgehead of London Bridge, which was rebuilt in stone about 1200 and remained the only bridge across the Thames until the mid C 18, and the only major settlement on the southern side of the river. It was a burh as early as the C 10, it sent its own representative to Parliament from 1295, it was granted to the City by various charters in the course of the C 14, and it became Bridge Ward Without in 1550.

As long as inns to accommodate travellers have existed at all they must have existed at Southwark, and Chaucer's Tabard is only an accidental early mention. Stow in 1598 writes of the 'Spurre, Christopher, Bull, Queen's Head, Tabard, George, Hart, King's Head, etc.'. The Hart comes into Shakespeare's *Henry VI* (and of course the *Pickwick Papers*), and the sale of the Queen's Head provided John Harvard with some of the money bequeathed to the college which became Harvard University. But all these inns, except for a fragment of the George, have 31 disappeared. Their heyday was the C 18 and early C 19 with their rapid improvements of coaches and roads and their ever faster and more frequent traffic.

Another Southwark speciality, which, like the inns, extended E into Bermondsey, was the town houses of the church dignitaries of southern England. These have also all but disappeared. Only of Winchester House, the grandest of these, is anything 10 left. The houses of the Bishops of Rochester, the Abbots of St Augustine Canterbury and of Battle and Hyde and Beaulieu, and of the Priors of Lewes and St Swithun's Winchester, have all gone.

To the palace of the Bishops of Winchester belonged a liberty, known as the Clink, and it was this liberty which attracted theatres into Southwark. The first building in London erected specially as a theatre stood, it is true, in Shoreditch. But this was followed after only ten years by the Rose, Rose Alley, near Bankside, which was put up for Henslowe in 1587. In 1595 appeared the Swan in another liberty, Paris Garden, and in 1599 the Globe on the s side of Park Street, near Bankside. This was established by the Lord Chamberlain's Men, until in 1603 the warrant was renewed by James I for the King's Men including William Shakespeare, who no doubt at that time lived in Southwark, just as we know for certain that Henslowe did (and Fletcher and Massinger amongst authors). Henslowe in 1613, when the Globe had been burned down and before it was rebuilt the following year, built yet another theatre, the Hope. The theatrical managers were by no means averse to light entertainment. Henslowe and Alleyn in 1594 became Masters of the Sport, that is, of bear-baiting, which, for example, at the Swan and the Hope alternated with theatrical performances. Bearbaiting was popular in Southwark in the c 16 before theatres existed, and remained popular till the Commonwealth. There were special bear rings which can be seen near the sites of the theatres on c 16 and c 17 views and maps (for example, Agas's of c. 1560).

Besides the inns and the theatres Southwark possessed a third speciality now no longer visible: the prisons. There were seven of them, the Clink burnt down by the Gordon rioters in 1780, the Compter close to the n end of Borough High Street, the King's Bench and the Marshalsea, of venerable and gruesome medieval traditions, the White Lion, situated like the King's Bench and Marshalsea near St George's church (a little n and nw of it). Dickens's father was imprisoned in the second Marshalsea (established in 1811). The new c 18 King's Bench was at the e end of Borough Road, and the Horsemonger Lane Gaol was in Harper Road, a model prison of 1791–8, where Leigh Hunt had a comfortable time.

While all these sights of Southwark can no longer be seen, the borough preserves one of the most important of the many large and wealthy priory and monastery churches which London once possessed (the others are St Bartholomew Smithfield and Westminster Abbey). Gone, or all but gone, are the priory of St Saviour at Bermondsey, the priory of St John at Clerkenwell, the Charterhouse, the priory of Holy Trinity, Aldgate, the Holywell nunnery at Shoreditch, the Cistercian abbey of St Mary Graces at Stepney, and so on. But St Mary Overie, which became
8   Southwark Cathedral in 1905, still remains with much c 13 and
9   c 14 work in it, and is apart from Lambeth Palace the most important medieval monument in South London.

Down to the middle of the c 18 Southwark remained Bankside along the river, the High Street from the bridge to St George's with a few streets branching off it, and ribbons on the two main coaching roads fanning out s of the church, that is, the road to the Elephant and Castle (and Croydon) and the Dover road (Kent Street, later renamed Tabard Street). Then in 1739–50 Westminster Bridge was built, and in 1760–9 Blackfriars Bridge. This opened up for development the area between the bridge and Newington Butts, which was laid out by *Robert Mylne* according to the boldest plan then carried out in London (but with less ambitious buildings than those which *George*

Dance proposed for the area). The plan is clearly indebted to Parisian precedent. It draws a completely straight N–S line from Blackfriars Bridge and lets it meet the road from Westminster Bridge at a circus, a proper French *rond-point* from which, apart from these two, three more roads radiate: Lambeth Road, London Road, and Borough Road. There is no Arc de Triomphe de l'Étoile to mark the enterprise, but an obelisk was erected in the circus in 1771. Only a little later came St George's Road. New Kent Road dates from 1751; then in 1815 Great Dover Street was made as a bypass to improve conditions in the narrow Tabard Street, until then the chief exit into Kent. Industrial enterprises on a large scale also began at this time. The most famous was the Albion Mill built close to Blackfriars Bridge by *Samuel Wyatt* in 1786, the first corn mill to use Watt's rotative steam engine. It burnt down in 1791. By then another type of improvement had appeared: the philanthropic institution. Southwark has two well preserved C18 examples, a large and a small: Guy's Hospital and the Hopton Almshouses.

By the later C18 the neighbouring parts of Bermondsey were also heavily built up, and Bermondsey Street was already within this wholly urban setting. At its S end lay in the Middle Ages the priory of Bermondsey (Abbey Street), founded from La Charité-sur-Loire in 1089 and soon one of the richest alien houses in the country. The glory of the church was the miracle-working Rood of Grace. To the E of the priory in the open country was a grange. The priory was pulled down at the Reformation (except for fragments of a gatehouse, *see* Grange Walk, Bermondsey Perambulation 2), and by 1559 a mansion had been erected in its stead which belonged to Sir Thomas Pope, the founder of Trinity College, Oxford. The grange, however, still stood in the C18, about where the Library and Town Hall now are. Even as late as 1800 there was plenty of open country to the E and also the SW of the parish church, which incidentally had been built (as was often the case) immediately adjoining the priory. Spa Road close to the grange was called thus because of a chalybeate spring discovered in the second half of the C18 and developed into a spa by the painter Thomas Keyse. It flourished for but a short time towards the end of the century.

Rotherhithe (or Redriff, as it was also called) was something quite separate, a village with its church close to the river, and in addition one long intermittent ribbon of wharves and cottages behind them, reaching from West Lane all round the bend of the Thames almost to the border of Deptford, that is, to the Naval Victualling Yard. It is a ribbon well over two miles long. C18 houses were built at intervals along it (only one now remains). All the land inside the bend was marshy and in no way made use of, except that at the far SE end a dry dock had been built as early as 1599, and a wet dock in 1696–1700.

The C19 commercial development of Rotherhithe was wholly conditioned by the building of docks which were developed during the C19, amalgamating as the Surrey Commercial Docks in 1864. They grew to cover an area of 460 acres. The Surrey

Canal (never completed), crossing the s of Bermondsey and coming out into the docks, had been built in 1801–10. The first project of a Thames Tunnel at Rotherhithe dates from 1805. It was finally built (a great engineering feat) by the elder *Brunel* in 1825–43 and restricted to railway use in 1865. For a passenger, lorry, and car tunnel Rotherhithe had to wait until 1908. The population of Bermondsey was 46,000 in 1801. It grew to 102,000 in 1861 and 122,000 in 1871,* and living conditions were among the worst in London. Dickens describes in *Oliver Twist* what living in Jacob's Island, that is, the area s of Bermondsey Wall, meant: 'tottering house fronts projecting over the pavement, dismantled walls that seem to totter, chimneys half crushed hesitating to fall . . . windows broken and patched, with poles thrust out to dry the linen that is never there, rooms so small, so filthy, so confined that the air would seem to be tainted even for the dirt and squalor which they shelter . . . every repulsive lineament of poverty . . . and every imaginable sign of desolation and neglect'. Kingsley in *Alton Locke* is even more outspoken on Bermondsey slums and the rooms 'without a single article of furniture. . . . Through the broad chinks of the floor shone up, as if it were ugly staring eyes . . . the reflexions of the rush-light in the sewer below'. That was in 1850. Then gradually these slums were replaced, first by 'model dwellings', that is, such huge and callously designed blocks of tenements as can still be seen (now cleaned and renovated) in Fair Street. Similar improvements took place in Southwark. One can trace the progression from e.g. Cromwell Buildings in Redcross Way (1864) to the more generously laid out Peabody Estate in Black-friars Road (1870), then to the more revolutionary solution (in an urban setting) of cottages, under the leadership of Octavia Hill (Redcross Way, 1887 etc.), and so to some of the earliest and most attractive *L.C.C.* flats off Blackfriars Road (1896). The housing had to be squeezed in between the railway viaducts and bridges which by then cut across Southwark and Bermondsey in all directions (London Bridge Station was opened in 1836), and between the commercial buildings. These, despite all the war damage and the more recent clearance, provide the most poignant reminders in London of Victorian and Edwardian commerce and industry; see especially the gaunt riverside
2 warehouses of Tooley Street and Shad Thames (Clink Street and Rotherhithe are shadows of their former selves), the area of the leather trade around Weston Street in central Bermondsey,
83 and the more presumptuous commercial façades of Southwark
84 Street, cut through slums in 1865 (an improvement which, like Tower Bridge Road of 1902, was clearly dependent on Hauss-mann's Paris).

The population of the old borough of Southwark was already 66,000 in 1801; 91,000 in 1831. Its climax was reached in 1901 with 206,000. The figure for Bermondsey in 1901 was 131,000.

---

* The main jumps were in the parish of St Mary Magdalene from 58,000 in 1861 to 80,000 in 1871 and in the parish of St Mary Rotherhithe from 18,000 in 1851 to 24,000 in 1861.

After that the numbers began to drop; in Bermondsey, partly because of an especially active programme of slum clearance by the borough, it was down to 97,000 in 1939. The trend was accelerated by the Second World War and then by the decline of the docks. In 1951 the figures for Bermondsey were 61,000, for Southwark, 97,000. By this time ambitious redevelopment plans had been conceived by the L.C.C. The Forshaw and Abercrombie plan of 1943 envisaged the rebuilding of almost the whole of Bermondsey between Old Kent Road and the river, and the riverside extension of Southwark Park. Road improvements, such as the widening of Jamaica Road and the total reconstruction of the Elephant and Castle junction, were among the first schemes to be put into effect, but the architectural trailblazer was the L.C.C.'s Brandon Estate by Kennington Park (1955–8), one of the first in inner London to demonstrate not only the mixing of tower blocks with lower buildings, but also the preservation and conversion of older houses.

The development of Camberwell is a different story. At the time of Rocque's map, that is in 1744, Camberwell, Peckham, and Dulwich, which are now hardly recognizable nuclei within one large urban area, were still villages separated from each other by ample fields. Between them a few hamlets such as Peckham Rye and Nunhead were scattered. Even as late as on a map of 1867 the land s of Champion Hill and Peckham Rye was all open, and Dulwich at the census of 1871 had only 700 houses. Peckham Rye Park still had its farmhouses after 1900 and Dog-kennel Hill its hedgerows on the l. and r. Population figures grew from 7,000 in 1801 to 18,000 in 1821, 28,000 in 1831, and 40,000 in 1841. The borough had 111,000 inhabitants in 1871 and 260,000 in 1901. In 1931 the recession had just started (251,000), that is people had begun to move farther out. In 1951 there was a population of 180,000.

The earliest urban areas were along the main roads from London, that is the Camberwell and Old Kent Roads, and also along Peckham High Street. Almost nothing remains older than the later C18. At this time Camberwell became quite a fashionable country retreat; the later Georgian terraces of Camberwell Grove are still evidence of this. But the northern parts of Camberwell remained unbuilt; when the Surrey Canal was made in 1801–10 it still ran through fields, and so did the Camberwell New Road when first laid out in 1815 to connect Camberwell with Kennington, Lambeth, and Westminster. The main building in these areas started c. 1820–30. Alport in 1841 speaks of 'the level portion' of Camberwell as an area 'not affected by the building mania' and still 'affording rich pasturage'. Most of the land was used for growing vegetables for the London market. On the hills farther s building went on briskly in the forties and after, and even more rapidly from the 1870s, when better public transport was available. The nature of this development, for the most part piecemeal speculation by small builders, has been analysed in the late Professor Dyos's classic book.* By 1900 only

* H. J. Dyos, *Victorian Suburb: a study of the growth of Camberwell*, 1966.

Dulwich Village, protected through its possession by Dulwich College, retained its pre-Victorian character. Despite post-Second-World-War buildings on the southern fringe, Dulwich still preserves a semi-rural atmosphere of exceptional charm as a setting for its C18 houses, old college buildings, gallery by Soane, and grandiloquent Victorian college.

74
86
In the rest of Camberwell much earlier Victorian development has been replaced since 1945 by great swathes of council housing (Camberwell had the highest housing construction figures of all London boroughs between 1945 and 1962). The variety of solutions developed by both the Borough Architect's Department under *F. O. Hayes* (later Borough Architect of Southwark, 1965–9) and by the outside architects employed by the borough make this one of the most interesting areas in London for the study of post-war housing. The large schemes, with the exception of Sceaux Gardens, elegantly restrained mixed development off Peckham Road of the late 1950s, are less rewarding than the varied small estates which explore courtyard layouts and where, even at 136 p.p.a., high buildings were kept to a minimum (Acorn Estate) or omitted altogether (Bonamy Estate, planned 1963; East Dulwich Estate, planned 1965). North Peckham Estate, also planned 1965, does not use above five storeys, but is unappealingly huge in scale, and has the elaborate pedestrian segregation encouraged in the 1960s, trends that were to be carried to extremes after 1965 on the new London Borough of Southwark's Aylesbury and Heygate Estates, some of the most notorious products of industrialized building. These estates were attempts to solve at one stroke the problems of the long neglected Walworth area of old Southwark (for from 1964 the Architect's Department had to deal with all three areas of Bermondsey, Southwark, and Camberwell). Yet meanwhile small and ingenious low-rise schemes continued (often by outside architects for the borough), long before this type became universally popular; good examples are the outstanding work by *Neylan & Ungless*, starting with Linden Grove, 1966; or by *Higgins Ney & Partners*, *Peter Moro & Partners*, and others (*see* Perambulations). The first large low-rise estate distinctively in the neo-vernacular fashion was D'Eynsford (*Clifford Culpin & Partners*, planned 1971), the second the especially attractive
111 Setchell Estate (by *Neylan & Ungless*, planned 1972). Borough architects since 1969 have been *H. P. Trenton*, succeeded in 1977 by *K. L. Robinson* (since 1972 under *C. Griffiths* and from 1980 *R. C. Maxwell* as Director of Development). By 1977 63.7 per cent of Southwark homes were council owned; the highest figure after Tower Hamlets and Barking. As in other inner boroughs, the population has declined rapidly since 1951 (borough figures: 1961, 313,413; 1981, 211,858 – a drop of over 100,000 in twenty years).

As for other recent buildings, the office towers around the Elephant and by London Bridge represent commercial developments of the 1960s and 1970s respectively; London Bridge Station itself is the most up-to-date of all the major London termini. The C 20 has not yet quite overtaken the whole of the riverside. But along the waterfront only ghosts of the Victorian past remain. Wharves, warehouses, and factories stand empty, most of the Surrey Docks have been filled in. Occasionally new uses are found, and a picturesque semblance of the industrial Thames-side intermittently maintained. A positive gain is that the river is more approachable than before, since the creation of riverside walks and open spaces (especially well done around Bankside, E of Blackfriars Bridge). Elsewhere (e.g. Kings Reach, W of Blackfriars Bridge) all has been flattened for offices and luxury flats. The hotly debated issue whether this trend should be allowed to swamp the whole riverside was still unresolved in 1981.

Further Reading

There is copious older literature on the ancient borough, e.g. M. Concannen and A. Morgan, *The History and Antiquities of the Parish of St Saviour's Southwark* (1795), and W. Rendle, *Old Southwark and its People* (1878). The best architectural coverage for the northern part of the present borough is provided by the Survey of London volumes No. 22 Bankside (1950) and No. 25 St George's Fields (1955), although both are inadequate by present standards. Useful introductory pamphlets on different neighbourhoods have been published by Southwark Library (1972–82). For further information on other areas one has to go to older books: E. J. Beck, *A History of Rotherhithe* (1907); G. W. Phillips, *The History and Antiquities of the Parish of Bermondsey* (1841); E. T. Clarke, *Bermondsey: Its Historic Memories and Associations* (1901); W. H. Blanch, *Ye parish of Camerwell* (1875); and P. M. Johnson, 'Old Camberwell', in *Trans. London and Middlesex Arch. Soc.*, vols. 3 and 4. The revised DOE list dates from 1973, an early production and so not as thorough as those for some other boroughs (although there are some later additions). The C 19 development of Camberwell is discussed in H. J. Dyos's pioneer study of suburban development: *Victorian Suburb* (1961). On individual buildings: F. T. Dollman, *The Priory of St Marie Overie Southwark* (1881); Bernard Bogan, *The Great Link* (1948) (on St George R.C. Cathedral). The Camberwell Society's publications include views of old Camberwell published by Stephen Marks, and some notes on architectural subjects.
    See also p. 124.

Acknowledgements

I am much indebted to Mr M. J. Stocker of the Borough Architect's Department, who went to great trouble to gather together information on recent buildings, and to Miss Mary Boast, lately the librarian of the borough's local studies collection (one of the best organized in Greater London), for help on older buildings. Mr S. C. Humphrey and Mr B. Nurse, archivist and librarian of the local studies collection, are also gratefully acknowledged. On Guy's Hospital I am grateful for help to the archivist Mr T. H. Orde and to Professor Cawson. On Camberwell Mr Stephen Marks's researches were especially useful; Mr Justin Howes helped on Dulwich. Mr Jonathan Ouvry kindly let me see Octavia Hill's correspondence relating to buildings in Southwark. On the Anglican cathedral I am particularly indebted to Dr Priscilla Metcalf, who allowed me to use the section on furnishings and monuments prepared for her forthcoming edition of the Buildings of England Cathedrals volume. I have benefited also from discussion with Dr Christopher Wilson and Miss Christie Arno on the cathedral. On the R.C. cathedral I am grateful for help to Mrs Sandra Wedgwood and Mr Rory O'Donnell.

SOUTHWARK

CATHEDRALS

ST SAVIOUR AND ST MARY OVERIE, London Bridge. An Anglican cathedral since 1905, but in the Middle Ages the Augustinian priory of St Mary Overie. The priory founded in the early C12 had been preceded by a pre-Conquest foundation. The C12 church was damaged by fire c. 1212. Rebuilding took place during the C13: the precise dates are not known. In 1260 a new bishop of London was consecrated in the church, but there was still an indulgence for contributions to the church fabric in 1273, and in 1303 the church was called 'for thirty years a ruin'. That leaves the dating of the individual parts of the church much in doubt. At the end of the C14 the W front and central tower were rebuilt, and during the C15 the C13 parochial chapel E of the S transept was reconstructed, and the nave and N transept were given wooden vaults. What one sees today, however, owes much to the C19 restorers. Work began in 1818–23 with the choir and tower, conscientiously restored by *George Gwilt Jun.*, and continued in a less satisfactory way with the transepts, much altered in 1830 by *Robert Wallace*. The parochial chapel was pulled down in 1822 and the chapel E of the retrochoir removed for road widening in 1830, but proposed demolition of the retrochoir itself was halted, and *Gwilt* restored it 'gratuitously' in 1833. Meanwhile the nave had become ruinous and, despite antiquarian protests, was deprived of its roof in 1831, and pulled down in 1838. Its replacement of 1839–40 by *Henry Rose* (in a feeble Gothic caricatured by Pugin) was itself swept away for *Sir A. W. Blomfield*'s nave of 1890–7.

EXTERIOR. First impressions are not rewarding. Seen from the E the four gables of the retrochoir huddle in a cramped position below the approach to London Bridge. Beyond rises the five-bay E arm with its clerestory and E window rebuilt by *Gwilt*, and behind this the tall central tower

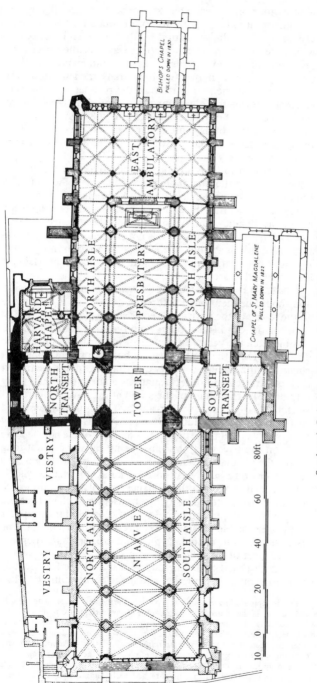

Southwark Cathedral, plan (*from R.C.H.M. East London*)

with its four pinnacles. The exterior surfaces are all visually and unappealingly C 19, mostly of knapped flint with stone dressings, with the exception of the tower and transepts, which are of ashlar. The two upper stages of the tower (the lower one attributed to *Henry Yevele* by John Harvey) are late C 14–C 15, each with two two-light transomed windows on each face. The chequer pattern of the parapet is a renewed original feature; the big pinnacles, restored by *Gwilt*, were replacements of pinnacles altered in 1689. A spire was projected, but nothing more than a start was ever made. The flying buttresses to the E arm were added in the C 14 and rebuilt by *Gwilt*.

The main entrance is now on the S side. The C 14 W door was not replaced by Blomfield. On the N side, where the domestic buildings of the canons lay, the C 19 warehouses have been cleared away, so that the church can once again be seen from across the Thames. On this side just a little evidence remains to show that the C 12 church was not entirely destroyed in the fire: some rubble walling in the N wall of the N transept, and the curve of a former apse to the N transept chapel, overlaid by an early Gothic arch.

INTERIOR. A few further C 12 remains can be seen inside and should be mentioned before the C 13 design is discussed. In the N wall of the nave are a recess and two doorways: the W door for the canons is a plain round-headed arch; the E one (visible from the vestry entrance) for the prior was once more elaborate. Only the jambs survive, but the presence of shaft-rings (and the evidence of early C 19 drawings of the destroyed arch of three carved orders) suggests a late rather than early C 12 date. At the W end of the S wall of the nave is a battered stretch of early Gothic wall arcading. This is usually assigned to the post-fire rebuilding, but its capitals (of Canterbury type) suggest that these details too could be of the late C 12. So work on the nave was, it seems, being carried out not long before the fire made rebuilding necessary.* In the N transept a few earlier C 12 survivals, corresponding to what is visible outside, can be seen in the E chapel: two plain round-headed arches (much restored) between transept and chapel rest on piers with scalloped imposts. In the N E corner of the chapel, E of the apse visible outside and so presumably belonging to an extension to the chapel, a puzzling corner shaft (perhaps re-used), set diagonally, as if for a vault.

THE C 13 CHURCH. The C 12 remains are too fragmentary to permit much speculation about the earlier church. Their

* This is supported by drawings and plans of the medieval nave made before it was destroyed in the 1830s. The design of the W bays differed from the rest of the seven-bay nave. The responds (reproduced in *Blomfield*'s nave), with grouped shafts with acanthus foliage, must have been derived from the Trinity Chapel at Canterbury (completed 1184) and are important evidence of the spread of early Gothic ideas to London. The second pair of piers from the W were exceptionally large and appear to have been giant columns extending through the middle storey. Drawings show them with attached early Gothic shafts. Was this a recasing of an older elevation?

survival suggests that the older building dictated the dimensions of at least the ground plan of transepts, crossing, and nave. But it is for the existing C 13 choir and retrochoir that Southwark is famous. They are designs to be respected, for they are both interesting and well balanced in the way in which the classic Gothic style demanded balance. The CHOIR (or 9 rather the part of the building E of the crossing, for the liturgical choir extended also W of the crossing) has a three-storey elevation of comfortably English, not French, proportions.* The relatively low arcade has alternating circular and octagonal piers (cf. Canterbury and earlier English Romanesque buildings), but this is not very noticeable because of their attached shafts: three towards the nave and aisles, one towards the arches (in the N arcade). The S arcade differs by having three also towards the arches (but corbelled off just below the capitals). The triple shafts facing the nave run right up to the springing of the vaults, although the imposts of the arcade capitals and the sill course of the triforium are carried round them.‡ This taking down of the vaulting shafts right to the ground instead of resting them on corbels above the piers recalls French rather than English practice, although it can be paralleled by the contemporary E end of Rochester. Equally untypical of English Gothic is the neat way in which the vault springs from the clerestory sill level, instead of from just above or below it. Between arcade and clerestory there is not a gallery or tribune (as e.g. at Lincoln, or later at Westminster Abbey), but an arcaded wall passage of four even arches (not a continuous passage, as it is interrupted by solid wall over the piers). The replacement of the first-floor gallery by such a passage was something which the most progressive French cathedrals were then doing (Chartres, Reims). But one can also point to the paired arches of the Trinity Chapel at Canterbury as a possible English source, so the extent to which the Southwark choir design can be derived directly from France is open to debate. What is clear is that it is a deliberately austere design, moulded capitals throughout, the minimum of decoration (a little dogtooth in the N triforium), a tidy interlocking of horizontals and verticals, the opposite to the effect achieved by, for example, Lincoln Cathedral. The clerestory has single lancet windows and a wall passage behind a stepped triplet arch, i.e. a wholly English design. The vaults (like the clerestory, rebuilt by *Gwilt*, with cast-iron roof trusses above) are quadripartite (i.e. French rather than English), but with the cells filled with masonry on the English, not the French principle. The grouped lancets of the E wall are an invention by *Gwilt*, replacing a late Gothic window (an interestingly early example of 'correct' C 19 antiquarianism).

* Was this also determined by the C 12 elevation? See the crossing arches discussed below.

‡ This is not strictly true of the S arcade, where the shaft-rings and imposts are of different profiles; one of several minor differences which suggests some difference in date between N and S arcades (cf. also pier shapes and bases).

8   The liking for plainness and evenness displayed in the choir is reflected also in the RETROCHOIR: this has four aisles, not three as Winchester and the Temple have. The six piers have four shafts *en délit* in the cardinal directions and four hollows in the diagonals – not a characteristic early C13 type (the use of diagonal hollows is difficult to parallel until the C14).* The inner aisles are slightly taller than the outer ones. When was the retrochoir begun? To try to answer this question one must look at some of the details. The bases have a double roll, like those of the choir S arcade, and unlike those of the choir aisle responds and the N arcade. The E lancets have dogtooth like the N choir triforium. So one could argue for a chronology that runs: lower walls of choir aisles and N arcade, then retrochoir and S arcade (and upper part of N arcade). The important conclusion from this is that the retrochoir cannot be the earliest part of the C13 rebuilding. The retrochoir vaulting ribs have transverse arches and ribs of the same thickness but slightly different profiles, the same type as those of the S aisle, which argues for completion of retrochoir and choir together,‡ perhaps not long before the consecration by the Bishop of London in 1260. The differences between N and S sides of the choir already mentioned suggest that building progress may not have been rapid. Another significant feature is that while the E wall of the retrochoir has lancet windows, in the choir aisles and N and S retrochoir walls windows with bar tracery appear in alternation with lancets. The tracery windows are of three lights, the central one taller, with three unfoiled circles above, a motif that can hardly be earlier than the mid C13. These windows were restored by *Gwilt*, but apparently faithfully. They have nook-shafts with stiff-leaf foliage of Westminster Abbey type. The easternmost window of the N side of the retrochoir has Dec tracery and is a C14 replacement. Similar flowing tracery occurs in the W wall of the retrochoir between the arches behind the high altar (filled in probably when the early C16 reredos was installed).

The CROSSING is odd in its detail. The crossing piers towards the nave and the E arm are completely unmoulded, as if they were the remaining parts of a plain wall. The outer orders of the E and W arches die into this wall, the middle order (with flat soffit and angle rolls, a Canterbury Gothic type) rests on corbels supported by crocket capitals (E) or by carved heads (W). These crossing arches perhaps pre-date the fire; if so, they must have dictated the height of the new choir. The later N and S arches rest on grouped shafts which on the S side run nearly down to the ground, and on the N side stop some way above it. Above the crossing arches an arcaded passage of the later C14 on all four sides. Set in the ceiling are some of the late

* Were the hollows intended for free-standing shafts (cf. Lincoln)? The bases have clearly been altered, but the capitals make no allowances for such extra shafts.

‡ The N aisle vaulting ribs have more varied profiles – experimental and earlier?

medieval nave bosses, gilded (q.v., furnishings). The work was done by *George Pace*.

The N and S TRANSEPTS differ greatly. The visible C 12 remains in the N transept and N transept chapel have already been noted. The thickness of the N transept N and W walls indicates that the C 12 walls were simply concealed in the later C 13 by blank pointed recesses with arches on Purbeck marble shafts. The vaulting shafts are also of Purbeck. The transept is two-storeyed, with no triforium and a clerestory with wall passage and windows of one or two lights. The arch to the N choir aisle, next to the crossing pier, is awkwardly stilted, probably a C 14 modification when the crossing piers were strengthened. The four-light N window *à la* Salisbury chapter house is of 1830 by *Wallace*, who also rebuilt the vaults. The E CHAPEL or HARVARD CHAPEL, apart from the C 12 work, is largely by *Blomfield*, 1907. The S TRANSEPT is entirely Dec. The system of elevation resembles that on the N, and the differences in detail are instructive for the change of taste (for example no Purbeck marble). The vaults and S window are by *Blomfield*. The three-light clerestory windows (renewed but original in their design) have as the main motif of their upper lights a concave-sided hexagon, i.e. Dec with Perp leanings (cf. Gloucester S transept).* To the E of the transept was the parochial chapel of St Mary Magdalene, given by Bishop Peter de Roches in the C 13, and rebuilt by Cardinal Beaufort in the C 15. His arms are on the E wall of the transept. The chapel was destroyed in 1822.

The NAVE is wholly of 1890–7, except for the C 12 remains already mentioned, and the E responds. *Blomfield*'s design, competent but dull, was inspired by the choir, but is a little more ornate.‡

CHAPTER HOUSE. *See* St Thomas's church, Perambulation 2(a) below.

FURNISHINGS, W to E.§ The accumulated monuments and other furnishings, though not like Westminster Abbey's in quality or quantity, and giving only a slight idea of the rich deposits silted up in London's churches before the Reformation, do suggest that St Saviour's in its time was no mean parish.

NAVE. To the l. of the S door, marble FONT with towering wooden cover, by *George Bodley* with all the stops out. – On the high sill of the W window, spirited FIGURES in carved wood of King David with a harp and a pair of trumpeting angels, from the organ of 1703. – STAINED GLASS. W, Creation window by *Henry Holiday*, 1893; N aisle 1900–9 by

---

* Christopher Wilson suggests a date in the 1290s on the basis of comparisons with details at St Etheldreda Holborn and St Stephen Westminster. That would make the work at Southwark very progressive.

‡ The medieval nave, finally destroyed in 1838 but known from drawings, was similar in proportion but with details which suggested a later date than the choir (e.g. a trefoil-headed blind triforium arcade in all except the last two W bays), and stiff-leaf decoration in the aisles.

§ Revised by Dr Priscilla Metcalf.

Kempe, whose s aisle glass went in the last war. – At the w end of the N aisle, a display of oaken BOSSES from the nave's timber vaults of 1469, carved with symbols and foliage and showing how such bosses looked before being plugged in, rather like champagne-corks except that each stump has slots for ribs. – MONUMENTS. Near the bosses a C15(?) *memento mori* or *gisant*, the effigy of an emaciated corpse, probably from the lower deck of a more worldly memorial. – Near the E end of the N aisle, John Gower, *Anglorum Poeta celeberrimus*, † 1408, a recumbent figure on a tomb-chest in a recess with a canopy of three cusped ogee arches, his head resting on his books, *Vox Clamantis*, *Speculum Meditantis*, and *Confessio Amantis*: carving not of high quality and much repainted. – At the E end of the s aisle, Shakespeare Memorial, 1911 by *H. W. McCarthy*, with a reclining figure in gelatinous brown alabaster and a background relief showing old Southwark, celebrating the neighbourhood of the Globe Theatre. (The poet's younger brother Edmond, 'player', was buried in the church in 1607, as were the playwrights John Fletcher † 1625 and Philip Massinger † 1640, in graves no longer marked.)

CROSSING. C20 portable ALTAR, with BISHOP'S THRONE and other mobile sedilia, placed here for services and removed for concerts, in keeping with the new liturgical scene. – The three-tiered brass CHANDELIER of 1680, on an elaborate chain with a crown and mitre, represents continuity.

N TRANSEPT. On the w wall the Austin MONUMENT, the most rewarding in the cathedral, by *Nicholas Stone* (Whinney), erected by a literary-minded lawyer, William Austin, in 1633, and also commemorating his mother, a benefactress of the church, who had become Lady Clerke. It is based on the parable of the sower and related themes, with a (now brightly gilded) angel of the Resurrection pointing to the sun of righteousness and supported by the rock of Christ, from which issue a stream and a serpent. Standing corn below, bound by a scroll lettered *Si non moriatur, non reviviscit*, between two resting figures with haying implements and sun hats, and below them a winnowing fan with inscription: in short, Stone was gracefully expressing an allegorical epigram in the manner of the metaphysical poets. – Near by (but mobile) an early C17 ALTAR TABLE with carved frontispiece and twisted legs, gift of the same Lady Clerke. – On the N wall, MONUMENT to Lionel Lockyer † 1672, reclining gawkily to the tune of a claim that 'His virtues & his PILLS are soe well known / That envy can't confine them under stone / . . . his PILL Embalmes him safe / To future times without an Epitaph'. – Also, for Richard Blisse † 1703 a lively full-wigged bust under looped drapery inside an aedicule with curved pediment, all skilfully designed. – Lord Mayor's SWORD REST, 1674, from St Olave, a demolished church downstream of the bridge, proof of ritual visits from the City to Bridge Ward Without.

HARVARD CHAPEL. Oddly enough, its treasure is a spired TABERNACLE by *A. W. N. Pugin*, of painted and gilded stone and plaster enshrining a brass door set with gems: shown in his Medieval Court at the Exhibition of 1851 and then given to his church of St Augustine Ramsgate; translated here in 1971. – PAINTING. Pietà by the C16 Ferrarese *Garofalo*, small, but with whole figures. – STAINED GLASS of *c.* 1907 designed late in the career of *John Lafarge*, the American pioneer of modern pictorial glass technique.

N CHOIR AISLE. MONUMENTS. Wall-monument to John Trehearne † 1618, 'Gentleman Portar to James I', and wife, two frontal half-figures and offspring below. – Oaken effigy of a recumbent cross-legged knight, possibly of the Warenne family, *c.* 1275 but considerably restored, especially and saccharinely in the face. – Free-standing tomb, in a prime spot doubtless cleared in the mid C16 between aisle and high altar, of Alderman Richard Humble † 1616, kneeling with two wives under a coffered arch with obelisks and achievements on top. Probably by *William Cure II* (Esdaile). – STAINED GLASS in two lancets 1856 and 1867 by *Powell* of Whitefriars.

CHOIR AND SANCTUARY. Filling the E wall, the progressively restored remains of the early C16 stone REREDOS given by Bishop Fox † 1528, tiers of canopied niches with figures in the richly packed manner of the Henry VII Chapel walls at Westminster or the reredos at Winchester. As much as survived the Reformation here was hidden after 1703 by a carved wood altarpiece (very like the one at St Magnus just over the bridge), removed during or after Gwilt's work on the choir. By then, of the C16 reredos no figures, no canopies, and only two carved string courses remained. In 1833 canopies, friezes, and demi-angels only were restored to it by *Wallace*.* Statues by *Nicholls* of Kennington were added in 1905.

RETROCHOIR. By the N wall, Elizabethan CHEST with much intricate architectural and heraldic detail in woodcarving and inlay, given by a treasurer of St Thomas's Hospital, Alderman Hugh Offley, *c.* 1588, the year he was elected sheriff. It incorporates with his own the arms and initials of his father-in-law Robert Harding † 1568, so it probably dates from the years when they were in business together: a museum piece. – C20 ALTARS and SCREENS by *Comper*. – STAINED GLASS. At the E end of the N wall, Martyrs' Window, 1890s by *Ward & Hughes* of Frith Street, Soho. – On the S, window of the 1920s to Thomas Francis Rider, Blomfield's builder.

S CHOIR AISLE. MONUMENTS. Between aisle and sanctuary, free-standing tomb of the great Bishop Lancelot 21 Andrewes † 1626, the last to live at Winchester House. The tomb was placed first in the now-gone Bishop's Chapel E of the retrochoir and moved to the W side of the retrochoir after the fire of 1676, when the canopy was lost (the present canopy is by *Comper*). Well modelled draperies, but the face much restored. – W of it, Edward Talbot † 1934, first Bishop of Southwark (1905–11), afterward of Winchester, by *Cecil*

* See the Dollman plates based on Wallace's before-and-after drawings.

Thomas. – On the s wall, chaste Greek tablet to Abraham Newland † 1807, chief cashier for thirty years to the Bank of England, by *John Soane* when architect to the Bank. – Set in the floor at the steps to the s transept, fragment of a ROMAN MOSAIC found in the churchyard.

S TRANSEPT. MONUMENTS. On the w side a slightly hallucinatory wall-monument to William Emerson † 1575: miniature emaciated corpse on a mat rolled under his head. – Above it, John Bingham † 1625, saddler to Elizabeth I and to James I, a half-figure in an arched recess. – Below, part of a C 13 coffin lid, tapered, with foliated cross. – Skied on the w wall, tablet to Richard Benefeld with bust in mid-C 17 dress. – On the s, the Rev. Thomas Jones † 1770 by *William Tyler*, one of the founders of the Royal Academy. – To the l., two early C 18 wall-monuments translated in 1901 from St Thomas's, one to Thomas Cole † 1715 with charming cherub heads. – Between the E wall arches, Bishop Beaufort's arms with cardinal's hat (conferred 1426), set up perhaps to celebrate both the hat and building work in St Mary Magdalene chapel, then entered through those arches; he may also have presided over the finishing of the tower. – ORGAN CASE. Free-Renaissance design by *Blomfield*.

CHURCHYARD. The only remaining tomb is George Gwilt Jun.'s † 1856, between the buttresses of the s choir aisle, beside the cathedral's eastern arm that he made safe.

ST GEORGE'S CATHEDRAL (R.C.),* St George's Road. This is, in ecclesiastical terms, *A. W. Pugin*'s most important church in London, and as such has always attracted much criticism, notably from Ruskin. It was built with great financial difficulties between 1841 and 1848 and was from the outset a compromise. In Pugin's own words, 'St George's was spoilt by the very instructions laid down by the Committee that it was to hold 3,000 people on the floor at a limited price: in consequence, height, proportion, everything was sacrificed to meet these conditions.' The E end, the lowest part of the w tower, the long yellow brick aisle walls, and a few details inside are all that now remains of Pugin's church. The rest is rebuilding and extension by *Romilly Craze* after damage in the Second World War. The result, although essentially a C 20 Gothic revival building, still depends on Pugin's original plans. In 1838 Pugin was introduced by his patron, the Earl of Shrewsbury, to the church committee then discussing the replacement of the inadequate R.C. chapel in London Road. He produced an ambitious design for a major church with a three-storey elevation, stone vaults, and a huge central crossing tower, a splendid expression of Catholic hopes after Emancipation. It was always intended to be an important church, though not envisaged as a cathedral (the R.C. hierarchy was established only in 1850). The scheme, however, was rejected as too expensive and a competition was held in 1839.

* We are grateful to Mrs A. Wedgwood for contributing to this entry.

On 14 December Pugin was declared the winner. This new, much more modest plan, with a chancel, N and S chapels, a very long nave with gabled aisles, and a W tower, was dictated by the restricted site (there was formerly a built-up road immediately to the N). The rather dull grouping of the exterior was to have been redeemed by a magnificent tower and spire, which takes pride of place in the frontispiece to *An Apology for Christian Architecture*, published in 1843. St George was one of three major churches that Pugin designed between 1839 and 1840, the other two being his more famous St Giles, Cheadle, and the now replaced St Oswald, Liverpool. After the variety of his earliest buildings, they form a related group and mark the emergence of his first mature style, which is characterized by the use of the Decorated or Second Pointed style and a centrally placed W tower. Of these three churches, St George, because of its size, is the least successful. Moreover the great W tower and spire, intended both in the C 19 and the C 20 to be its most impressive feature, have never been built. The cathedral was restored and redecorated in 1888–1905 by *F. A. Walters*, who reassembled many dispersed Pugin fittings.

Inside, it is easy to pick out the remains of Pugin's work: see the large Dec E windows, (liturgical) N aisle windows, all to a different pattern, and the carefully accurate medievalizing of the Perp Petre Chantry of 1848–9 complete with its original 81 furnishings (apart from the stained glass) off the S aisle. The Honourable Edward Petre († 1848) was one of the main bene-factors of the church. His chantry is a tiny enclosed chapel with table tomb, carved altarpiece with Virgin and child, angels, and its own stone vault. The addition of the new Lady Chapel beyond has effectively made the chapel free-standing, like those little medieval chantries at, say, Gloucester or Win-chester. At the E end of the N aisle the Blessed Sacrament Chapel with original fittings (*see* Furnishings, below). Oppo-site, within the N aisle, the Knill Chantry of 1856–7, to relatives of Pugin's third wife, designed after Pugin's death in 1852 by his son *E. W. Pugin*, in a delicately refined Gothic, with a vault supported by thin internal piers linked to the outer walls by transoms. It is based on a design by him for a chapel at Ushaw, Durham, of 1855. Well carved capitals with birds and frieze; stone reredos. W of the Petre Chapel, St Patrick's Chapel, begun in 1845 as a chantry for George Talbot, completed as a relics chapel in 1905, and largely reconstructed after the war. St Joseph's Chapel, with a stone vault, has been converted from the Weld Chantry of 1890.

After relishing the C 19 work, any medievalist will wince at the details of the C 20 rebuilding, with its effort to marry the desiccated traditions of Arts and Crafts free Gothic to Pugin's fragments. Yet the scale is noble, the long nave is undoubtedly improved in proportion by the addition of a clerestory, and the pseudo-transepts created by heightening the E bays of the aisles add a spatial interest lacking in the original building. *Romilly Craze* was clearly influenced by Pugin's first design.

His early proposals (1943) already suggested the addition of a clerestory. Those of 1949 envisaged an elaborate stone vault with liernes and bosses over the nave. This was still intended when final plans were accepted in 1953 and rebuilding began, which explains the massive nature of the piers which replaced Pugin's original ones (although these had survived the bombing). The aisles were built as planned, with the illusion of a vault created by flying ribs à la Bristol, but the upper parts were completed to a simpler design, so that the piers support only stone transverse arches with a boarded ceiling in between (a failure of intent not uncommon in the Middle Ages as well).

A chronological pursuit of the rest of the new building is rather like tracing the decline of Perp in the C 16–17. The very peculiar clerestory windows of 1956–8 with their semicircular transom (an echo of the curved rood beam in Pugin's first design?) are also a post-1953 modification, as is the design of the equally unmedieval W window. The Lady Chapel, with yawning rectangular openings with uncusped lights, dates from 1961–3. The baptistery at the W end, with its faintly C 20 exterior N of the entrance, was completed in 1966. The extension of the chancel into one bay of the nave dates from the 1953 designs; the reorientation of the Lady Chapel is an experiment of 1977.

FURNISHINGS. In the Blessed Sacrament Chapel original *Pugin* fittings: gates (by *Hardman*), encaustic tiles, altar, and reredos. – STAINED GLASS. E and W windows by *Henry Clarke Studios* of Dublin. Brilliant colours, dull drawing, best seen from a distance. – SCULPTURE. Virgin and Child (Lady Chapel), small, Flemish, C 18. – MONUMENTS. Two table-tombs with effigies. – Thomas Provost Doyle † 1879 (who was chiefly responsible for the building of the C 19 church); Archbishop Amigo † 1949. The contrast in quality of detail echoes the building history.

Next to the cathedral the Archbishop Amigo Hall, 1940 by *Robert Sharp*. Beyond the E end bishop's and clergy houses fill the apex of the triangular site. Their rebuilding by *F. A. Walters* (1886–7) to a uniform battlemented height destroyed the picturesque variety of roof-line achieved by Pugin's original group of clergy house and schools.

CHURCHES

Nothing remains of the medieval fabric of the two surviving parish churches of medieval Southwark: St George Southwark and St Mary Newington.* The oldest building is now the rebuilt St George of 1734. Then come the churches of the 1820s, the era of the Commissioners: St Peter Walworth by *Soane* and Holy Trinity by *Bedford*. The best of the numerous Victorian chur-

* Other medieval churches were St Margaret and St Mary Magdalen Overy (redundant after their parishes were united in 1540 to form that of St Saviour, with the present cathedral as the parish church).

ches were lost during the Second World War; the only replacement of any interest is St Paul Lorrimore Square.*

ALL HALLOWS, Pepper Street, s of Union Street, w of South-wark Bridge Road. Of the church by *G. G. Scott Jun.* of 1879–80, gutted in the Second World War, only one chapel and a few fragments survive, incorporated into a new building by *T. F. Ford*, 1957, no longer in use as a church.

ALL SAINTS, Surrey Square, off Old Kent Road s of East Street. Now Church of the Lord (Aladura). 1959 by *N. F. Cachemaille Day*, replacing a church of 1864–5 by *Parris & Field*, damaged in the Second World War. Some of *Cachemaille Day*'s fittings now in St Peter, Liverpool Grove (*see* below).

CHRIST CHURCH, Blackfriars Road. 1960 by *R. Paxton Watson & B. Costin*, a feeble little replacement of the church damaged in the Second World War.‡

HOLY TRINITY (Henry Wood Hall), Trinity Church Square, NW of Great Dover Street. A Commissioners' church of 1823–4 by *F. Bedford*, the site given by Trinity House, which developed the surrounding estate at the same time (*see* Perambulation 3(e)). Bedford built several impressive Greek Revival churches in South London at this time (cf. St Luke Norwood; St John Waterloo Road; St George Camberwell). Holy Trinity has a curious plan. The portico of six giant Corinthian columns is on the N and a porch opposite on the S, but the altar was as usual at the E end. Externally the dominant accent is the tower above the N pediment. Its top storey is octagonal *à la* Tower of the Winds. The church was closed in 1960, and the interior gutted by fire in 1973. The conversion, by *Arup Associates*, 1973–5, to an orchestral recording and rehearsal hall, was a happy solution. The brick-vaulted crypt was given a lower floor, and became a cafeteria and stores; the church itself (whose original three galleries and flat ceiling had been destroyed in the fire) is now an open hall with a new w gallery for choir and organ. The walls retain their pilasters and cornice. Good gatepiers and railings (replicas of those destroyed in the Second World War).

* Churches demolished since 1950 include, in addition to those mentioned below: ST ANDREW, New Kent Road, by *Newman & Billing*, 1882; ST MARK, East Street, by *Jarvis*, 1874; ST MARY MAGDALENE Congreve Street by *Ferrey*, 1842; ST PAUL, Wesminster Bridge Road, by *W. Rogers*, 1857; ST STEPHEN Manciple Street by *Teulon*, 1850 (a Greek cross interior with Rhenish tower roof); ST STEPHEN, Walworth Common, by *Jarvis*, 1871; WALWORTH ROAD BAPTIST CHURCH, 1863–4 (six giant attached Corinthian columns); CROSSWAY CONGREGATIONAL UNION New Kent Road, 1905 by *Hugh Mackintosh* (a tall playful asymmetrical tower); SURREY TABERNACLE (later Borough Synagogue), 1865 (six giant Ionic columns); UPTON BAPTIST CHAPEL, Lambeth Road, late classical, 1813–14; BROWNING HALL (originally Lock's Field Meeting House, then York Street Chapel, 1790, with alterations of 1840 and 1875).

‡ The original church dated from 1671; it was rebuilt in 1738–41, probably by *James Horne*, remodelled and given a Romanesque chancel by *C. R. Baker King*, 1890–1. The church was of brick with stone quoins and other trim, long sides with two tiers of windows with Gibbs surrounds, square w tower.

LADY MARGARET CHURCH, Chatham Street, between New Kent Road and East Street. Now closed. 1888–9 by *Ewan Christian*. Brick, E.E. A large building on a small site. (Brick arcades with narrow aisles, shallow transepts. Apse with glass by *Clayton & Bell*.)

PEMBROKE COLLEGE MISSION, Barlow Street, NE of East Street. The lower part by *E. S. Prior*, 1891–2, the church above completed *c.* 1908 by *H. Passmore*, not to Prior's original design. Remodelled as church and hall by *Williams & Winkley*, 1976.

ST AGNES, St Agnes Place. *See* Lambeth (La).

(ST ALPHEGE, Lancaster Street. 1880–2 by *Robert Willey*. Red brick, aisleless, minimal E.E., famous for its extreme Anglo-Catholicism.

ST GEORGE, Borough High Street. 1734–6 by *John Price*, in replacement of a medieval church. A sound, sturdy church, uncommonly well sited, so that from N as well as S its tower appears to advantage. Square white W tower, two octagonal upper stages, and octagonal spire, nothing too transparent, all massive and trustworthy. The body of the church red brick; two tiers of windows in composition derived from Wren's St James, Piccadilly. E window Venetian with cartouche and garlands above. Interior altered by *William Hedger*, 1807–8. The usual three galleries. Flat plaster ceiling with graceful cherubs designed by *Basil Champneys* (1897), restored by *T. F. Ford* after damage in the Second World War. – Fine PULPIT, free-standing on four slim Ionic columns. – PAINTINGS. Moses and Aaron from the reredos, now on the W gallery. – Low BOX PEWS. – Graceful iron COMMUNION RAILS. – ROYAL ARMS (Stuart), excellently carved, against the parapet of the W gallery. This and the paintings came from St Michael Wood Street in the City of London. – Many minor TABLETS.

ST JOHN, Larcom Street. A ragstone church with gabled clerestory and SW tower formerly with a saddleback top, tucked away behind the Town Hall in Walworth Road. 1859–60 by *H. Jarvis*. Vestry 1912 by *Greenaway & Newberry*. – (FITTINGS by *Comper*: altar and rails 1928, reredos 1938.)

ST JUDE, St George's Road. Now closed. 1897–9 by *W. J. H. Leverton*, replacing the Philanthropic Society's Chapel. Simple red brick, E.E.

ST MARY, Kennington Park Road. Facing the road a fragment of the stone W front and tower by *J. Fowler*, 1876, sheltering the church of 1957–8 by *A. Llewelyn Smith*. The church is the successor to the medieval parish church of Newington which stood by the burial ground on the E side of Newington Butts.

ST MATTHEW, New Kent Road. 1855–7 by *H. Jarvis*. Ragstone front with tower and spire to one side. (Interior remodelled 1926–7 by *M. Travers*. The arcade columns were encased by Tuscan plaster columns, the clerestory windows added, and the apse closed off by a screen with reredos.)

ST PAUL, Lorrimore Square, between Kennington Park Road

and John Ruskin Street. 1955–60 by *Woodroffe Buchanan & Coulter*. One of the most ambitious post-war churches in Southwark, designed as a focal point within the Brandon Estate (*see* Perambulation 3(c)). It replaces a church by *H. Jarvis* of 1854–6, destroyed in 1941. A restless, somewhat self-consciously modern exterior, with spiky gables and dormers in the copper roof, and a zigzagging band of honeycomb-patterned aisle windows. The church hall and vestries lie beneath, recessed behind an open chapel. The interior is pleasantly calm, with subdued lighting and a boarded ceiling of interesting shape. The planning is still traditional: long nave, transepts, and E Lady Chapel – SCULPTURE. Risen Christ, by *Freda Skinner*; coloured GLASS by *Goddard & Gibbs*.

ST PETER, Liverpool Grove, E of Walworth Road, S of East Street, Walworth. A Commissioners' church of 1823–5 by *Soane*, and though not as interesting as the Soane church at Bethnal Green, yet characteristic of his sense of clean-cut line. The design is close to his later Holy Trinity, Marylebone Road. The church is of yellow stock brick with much emphasis on the straight top entablature. The windows tall and arched in arched brick recesses; a stone transom shows that a gallery exists inside. The W front exhibits four giant Ionic columns set back to keep the integrity of the block shape of the building. They carry a balustrade above the common entablature, and on this the somewhat attenuated W tower can safely stand. It has a square lower part below a circular stage with composite columns, and a small dome. Within the tower a vestibule with elegant arches to N and S staircases with thin iron balustrades. Between the bellringers' chamber and the stairs recesses with Ionic columns. The interior of the church restored in 1953 after war damage, in pastel shades, by *T. Ford*. Galleries on unfluted Doric columns and a flat ceiling. The W bay and the chancel are separated from the nave by typically Soanian paper-thin segmental arches. E end altered by *E. Christian* in 1888 and again in 1953. – Original plain Soanian REREDOS. – (Some FITTINGS by *N. Cachemaille Day*, brought from his church of All Saints, Surrey Square.) – STAINED GLASS. Violently coloured post-war E window by *Claire Dawson*. – FONT. 1839 by *Garland & Fieldwick*. An elegantly decorated bowl on a fluted column.

ST THOMAS, St Thomas Street. *See* Perambulation 2(a).

ENGLISH MARTYRS (R.C.), Rodney Road, S of New Kent Road. 1902–3 by *F. W. Tasker*. Insignificant yellow brick exterior, but interior worth looking at. Lofty nave with lofty side chapels, the latter with transverse pointed tunnel-vaults and low passageways from chapel to chapel. – (Altar and reredos etc. 1961 by *F. G. Broadbent & Partners*.)

MOST PRECIOUS BLOOD (R.C.), O'Meara Street, between the E ends of Southwark Street and Union Street. 1891–2 by *F. A. Walters*. Romanesque, apsed, with large circular W window.

ST WILFRID (R.C.), Lorrimore Road. 1915 by *F. A. Walters*, a mean late Perp exterior, red brick (but with notable furnishings and Lady Chapel).

BOROUGH WELSH CONGREGATIONAL CHAPEL, Southwark Bridge Road. 1872–3, debased classical, by *Thomas Thomas* of Swansea.

METROPOLITAN (or SPURGEON'S) TABERNACLE, Newington Butts. The giant Corinthian six-column portico survives from *W. W. Pocock*'s building of 1859–61, put up for the popular preacher C. H. Spurgeon. The rest was destroyed by fire in 1898, replaced by a structure by *Searles & Hayes* (largely of iron), and rebuilt again *c.* 1959 after damage in the Second World War.

STAMFORD STREET UNITARIAN CHAPEL. Only the severe Greek Doric hexastyle portico remains of the chapel of 1823 by *Charles Parker*. The rest was demolished in 1964.

SUTHERLAND CHAPEL, Walworth Road. 1842; built for the popular Congregational preacher Dr Edward Andrews. A monumental classical front with two giant Tuscan columns *in antis*, now mostly concealed by shops and used as a theatre store.

PUBLIC BUILDINGS*

The MUNICIPAL BUILDINGS of the former borough of Southwark are in Walworth Road. TOWN HALL, sadly Gothic in red brick, by *Jarvis*, 1866; CENTRAL LIBRARY, adjoining the Town Hall, equally insignificant, by *I'Anson*, 1893; HEALTH CENTRE, adjoining the Library, by *P. Stuart*, 1937.

SESSIONS HOUSE, Newington Causeway, s continuation of Borough High Street. 1921 by *W. E. Riley*. Large, all stone, very restrained classical. Plain stone-faced extensions behind (1967–9), and a large, bolder s wing with bronze windows at the side and a plain wall to the street (1977), by the *G.L.C. Architect's Department*. (Inside in the Justices' Room a chimneypiece of 1612 from Hicks Hall Finsbury.)

HARPER ROAD LIBRARY, sw of Great Dover Street. A pleasant one-storey glazed box by the Borough of Southwark's Architect's Department (job architect *R. Stuke*), 1968–71.

PASSMORE EDWARDS LIBRARY, Borough Road. 1898 by *C. J. Phipps*. The decoration in the Arts and Crafts manner.

JOHN HARVARD LIBRARY, No. 211 Borough High Street. Part of a red brick commercial development by *Ronald Fielding Partnership* in association with *Southwark Architect's Department*, 1977.

PUBLIC LIBRARY (former), Southwark Bridge Road. *See* Perambulation 2(c).

---

* Demolished since 1950: LIBRARY, Old and New Kent Road, by *C. Batley*, 1907, neo-Gothic (mosaic panels preserved at the Livesey Museum, Camberwell); NEWINGTON INSTITUTE, Westmoreland Road, with original nucleus of 1850, utilitarian but of considerable size.

IMPERIAL WAR MUSEUM, Lambeth Road. This is what remains of BETHLEHEM HOSPITAL after the patients' wings had been demolished to enlarge the Geraldine Mary Harmsworth Park. The hospital dates back to 1246. It had specialized in the care of the insane by 1400. It was transferred after the Fire of London from Bishopsgate to Moorfields, where a grand new building was erected by *Robert Hooke*. The transfer to Southwark took place in 1812. The existing building with giant portico with six Ionic columns is by *James Lewis* and dates from 1811–14. Later enlargements by *P. Hardwick* and by *Sydney Smirke*, who added wings (since removed) and the tall copper dome (replacing a small cupola), in 1844–6 (the dome rebuilt in the 1970s after a fire). The octagonal drum of the dome contained the hospital chapel with galleries on cast-iron supports on five of the eight sides. The interiors all now much altered. The hospital moved to Eden Park, Beckenham (Bm), in 1926. In Lambeth Road a small stucco LODGE dated 1837.

LEISURE CENTRE, Newington Butts, Elephant and Castle. Large, low complex incorporating swimming pool, sports centre, etc. By *Southwark Architect's Department*, 1978–80.

SOUTH BANK POLYTECHNIC (incorporating the Borough Polytechnic and College of Commerce). The new buildings in London Road are by the G.L.C. Architect's Department (Education Architect *Peter Jones*, job architect *John Weller*), 1976. Four storeys, the lowest below road level. A single inward-looking block covering a large site, with exterior glazing in the Stirling tradition, punctured by red-brick pylons. Some of these have staircases, but the ones flanking the entrance are there only to create the feeling of a gatehouse shutting out the unpleasant whirl of traffic around the Elephant and Castle. The main interior feature is a three-storey 'street' reminiscent of a covered shopping mall, with offices, students' rooms, etc. on one side (connected by internal light wells), and on the other sports hall, library, and auditorium, the first two with glazed space-frame roofs. Around them and overlooking them upper floors with classrooms. Earlier buildings for the Borough Polytechnic in Borough Road: a bad front by *Le Maître* (1930); the older buildings behind originally belonged to the British and Foreign School Society. Later additions off Thomas Doyle Street (1953) and in Southwark Bridge Road (1960–2) by *Norman & Dawbarn*.

LONDON COLLEGE OF PRINTING, Elephant and Castle. The earlier parts (completed 1964), two neutral curtain-walled blocks of four and fourteen storeys, by the *L.C.C. Architect's Department*, form part of the Elephant and Castle redevelopment. The extension of 1969–73 is more idiosyncratic, in the tradition of the Pimlico School, with its receding profile with sloping-back windows on third and fifth floors, topped by a penthouse studio.

GEOFFREY CHAUCER (formerly TRINITY HOUSE) SCHOOL,

Harper Road, N off New Kent Road. 1958 by *Chamberlin, Powell & Bon*. One of the more original of the new comprehensives of the 1950s. Not too large, with the individual elements easily recognizable. The school is shielded by walls and grass mounds from the New Kent Road, and approached along a quiet tree-lined avenue from Harper Road. On its axis a courtyard with a pool. To the r. the pentagonal hall block, covered by a folded star roof of hyperbolic parabolas separated by roof lights. The inclusion of house rooms in the angles of this block was one of the first efforts to break up large comprehensives into smaller, more friendly units. The group of gymnasia to the l. also have a roof of unusual form, sloping down in the centre. At the sides four-storey classroom blocks.

St Saviour and St Olave's School for Girls, New Kent Road. 1903 by *Campbell Jones* (later wing 1928).

(English Martyrs School, Rodney Road, S of New Kent Road. By *L. Stokes*, 1904.)

Aspen House School for delicate children, Kennington Park Gardens. By *Stillman & Eastwick Field*, completed 1977. A neat low red-brick building looking inwards to courtyards.

Michael Faraday School, Aylesbury Estate. By the *G.L.C. Architect's Department*. A good example of the open-plan primary school as developed by I.L.E.A. in the 1960s. Cheerful exterior with blue cladding and low pitched roofs.

Paragon School, New Kent Road. *See* Perambulation 3(e).

Bacon's School, Old Kent Road. *See* Perambulation 3(e).

Guy's Hospital, St Thomas Street.* Thomas Guy founded his hospital right opposite St Thomas', of which he had been a governor from 1704, to remedy the overcrowding at the older hospital. He was the son of a wharfinger but had made an immense amount of money as a stationer and publisher, and later by successful speculation in South Sea stock. He began building in 1721 and died in 1724, leaving £200,000 for the endowment of the hospital. His intention was that it should be for 'incurables' (for whom St Thomas' could not cater), as his will makes clear,‡ although the new hospital very soon took on the role of a general hospital. The old part is a large symmetrical building with two inner cloistered courtyards (cf. St Bartholomew's and the old hospital of St Thomas) and two far-projecting wings forming a *cour d'honneur*. The size is considerable, thirteen bays for the centre and fifteen for the wings. The original design was by *Thomas Dance* (no known relation to George Dance) who died in 1733. The ranges around the courtyards were built in 1721–5; E wing added in 1738–41 by *James Steere*, Dance's successor as surveyor. The w wing was not built until 1774–7 by *R. Jupp Jun.*, although a

* I have to thank Mr T. H. E. Orde, archivist of Guy's Hospital, and Professor R. A. Cawston for help with the revision of this account.

‡ 'Two new Squares of Building in Southwark . . . for reception of . . . Four hundred poor Persons or upwards labouring under any Distempers, Infirmities or Disorders who . . . are adjudged or called Incurable, and as such not proper Objects to be received into, or continued in the present Hospital of St Thomas or other Hospitals . . .'

view of 1739 and other evidence shows that both wings had been planned in Guy's lifetime. The centrepiece was transformed by *Jupp* in 1774 by means of a Palladian stone-faced frontispiece with two outer giant pilasters and four inner attached giant columns, all Ionic, and with sculpture by *Bacon*: two niches with statues of Aesculapius and Hygeia on the first floor, three bas reliefs, and allegorical figures in the pediment. The ground floor is rusticated and arcaded; the rest of the building is stock brick. The E wing, containing the most impressive interior, the Court Room, as a central feature, was destroyed in the Second World War, but the exterior has been rebuilt in facsimile of the original. The w wing contains the CHAPEL, a unique survival. This has groined vaulted galleries on three sides, and houses the monument to Guy by *Bacon*, 55 1779, one of the noblest and most sensitive of its date in England. It still has the compositional flourish and technical mastery of the Baroque and Roubiliac, yet shows the genuine warm feeling of the new age. The sanctuary of the chapel was remodelled in 1956. Marble arch over the altar by *Louis Osman*. The two inner courtyards are separated by a block with an open arcade. Originally the courtyards also had open arcades. They were glazed in 1788, to provide additional ward space. The wards remained in use until 1962. In one courtyard is preserved an alcove from the London Bridge of 1758–62, removed during widening in 1902–4. In the other a statue of Lord Nuffield by *Maurice Lambert* (1944). A statue of Guy by *Scheemakers*, 1734, stands in the forecourt, a fine, humble figure, with religious reliefs against two sides of the pedestal. The iron railings to St Thomas Street date from 1741.

To the s of the c 18 buildings, on the l. a big Victorian block, with angle turrets and a tall tower (Hunt's House) by *Rhode Hawkins*, 1852 (N wing 1871). On the r., c 20 additions by *J. H. T. Wood* and *W. J. Walford*. The York Clinic is by *W. J. Walford* and *Murray Easton* (1939). Further to the E the post-war extensions. Rebuilding was being discussed already before the war. In the end the results were New Guy's House, a surgical block, 1957–61 by *Alexander Gray* of *Watkins, Gray & Partners*, a plain eleven-storey range with two cross wings, and the much more dominant thirty-storey GUY'S TOWER, 1963–75 by the same firm (*Watkins Gray Woodgate International UK Group 3*). This is one of the highest hospital buildings in the world. It houses, *inter alia*, maternity wards, children's wards, research departments, and at the top the dental hospital and school. The tower consists of two parts: a plain rectangle with continuous window bands shielded by solid balconies, and the ribbed-concrete-faced service tower with the lumpy projection of the lecture theatre near the top. Wolfson House, a hostel for medical students, was completed in 1977. The final stage of reconstruction, comprising a six-storey podium integrated with the base of the tower, will house the medical wards and outpatients' services.

Also part of the hospital, GREENWOOD THEATRE, at the

corner of Snowsfields, with proscenium stage and auditorium to seat 460. By *Athony Cox* (*Architects Co-Partnership*), completed 1975.

ST THOMAS' HOSPITAL (former), St Thomas Street. *See* Perambulation 2(a).

BANKSIDE POWER STATION. 1957–60 by *Mott, Hay & Anderson* (engineers) and *Sir Giles Gilbert Scott* (consultant architect). The last of the huge brick power stations which began with Battersea (*see* Battersea (Ww), Public Buildings), this was built to burn oil, not coke. Symmetrical, with central square tower-like chimney 325 ft high. Large windows to E, W, and N, a smaller horizontal band to the S. But the main impression is of the stunning scale of the bare walls of immaculate brickwork, excellently set off by the smooth greensward beside the new riverside walk.

RAILWAYS. The extension by (*Sir*) *John Hawkshaw* of the SOUTH EASTERN RAILWAY from London Bridge to Waterloo and Charing Cross (1859–64) and Cannon Street (1861–6) was very disruptive (prompting St Thomas' Hospital to move to Lambeth). The viaduct includes a gargantuan 180-ft-span box-girder bridge over the London Bridge Station approach, 1863. – The LONDON, CHATHAM AND DOVER RAILWAY by *Joseph Cubitt*, 1860–4, takes an uneventful course on viaduct from Herne Hill to Blackfriars. Across the junction of Borough Road and Southwark Bridge Road, an eyecatching steel truss, an ingenious strengthening of the original box-girder bridge.

LONDON BRIDGE, CANNON STREET RAILWAY BRIDGE, SOUTHWARK BRIDGE, BLACKFRIARS RAILWAY BRIDGES, BLACKFRIARS BRIDGE. *See* Thames Crossings at end of gazetteer.

PERAMBULATIONS

1(a). The Riverside from London Bridge W *to the borough boundary*

The Thameside has three distinct characters: pre-Victorian, Victorian, and later C20. The way in which they are often incongruously interlarded is still one of the chief attractions of Southwark, although the area has lost much of its Victorian industrial flavour over the last twenty-five years. Starting at LONDON BRIDGE there are first of all two levels (dating from the rebuilding of London Bridge of 1823–31; *see* Thames Crossings), the bridge approach, and the canyon down below, which was once filled with impressively bare and sheer Victorian warehouses. At the lower level, crossing Tooley Street, a single land span of *Rennie*'s bridge remains, in granite, the joints of paper-thin precision. The buildings on the W side of the bridge belong to both levels. No. 2, HIBERNIA CHAMBERS, is staid Italianate, built in 1850 by *William Cubitt*. Two storeys above a rusticated basement. Until reconstructed in 1976, the two storeys below street level were warehouses. No. 4, BRIDGE HOUSE, earlier and plainer, by *George Allen*, 1834, was one of the first grand hotels in London, serving the new railway terminus opposite.* The new lower-level, quite thoughtfully designed offices are by *Holford Associates* (N) and *Renton Howard Wood* (S). Across the new paved square, MINERVA HOUSE, pleasantly undulating brick offices and flats, by *Twigg, Brown & Partners*, 1979–83. Narrow windows with U-shaped sills. In between, the cathedral reveals its blackened and much restored flank to the river.

Now into CLINK STREET, past the ancient landing-place of St Mary Overy's dock. Here one can still thread one's way between warehouses up to six storeys tall: St Mary Overy Wharf, 1882 by *G. A. Dunnage*, with arched gables above the loading doors; Pickford's Wharf, mid C19, with giant pilasters to the river, and the smaller-scale Winchester Wharf.‡ In their midst are the remains of WINCHESTER HOUSE, the town residence of the Bishops of Winchester from the C12 to the C17. To visualize what it once was like one must remember the Archbishops of Canterbury's Lambeth Palace. Winchester Square was the courtyard. On its N side lay the great hall, 80 ft by 36 ft over an undercroft. Its remains, visible from Clink Street, date from the C14, but stand on earlier foundations. Parts of the S and W walls survive, with a doorway of two orders in the S wall, and three less distinguished doorways in the W gable wall, leading to the offices. Above these the remains of a gorgeous rose window (restored in 1972), a unique design, made up of an inserted hexagon with eighteen cusped triangles around a smaller hexagon filled with radiating daggers of alternating widths. A date in the early C14 seems likely, when these motifs were fashionable in London (cf. the interest in curved triangles at Old St Paul's, especially the E window, and a window (with double curved triangles) in the cloister at Westminster Abbey).§

Inland from here, S of Winchester Square, one can make a diversion to take in a few domestic survivals: in STONEY STREET, opposite the back of the MARKET with its open iron arcading, the WHEATSHEAF, with a C19 front, No. 5, a good early C18 red brick house, and the C18 MARKET PORTER. Down PARK STREET a simple terrace rebuilt by *Henry Rose*, 1831 (Nos. 1–13), and further on Nos. 21–23, an C18 pair, and Nos. 22–26, an early C19 terrace (derelict). (Another terrace of the same period near by in THRALE STREET.) At

---

* Its excellent interiors were destroyed in 1971. They included a stone staircase with Ionic columns and a reception room on the top floor with apsed ends, pilasters, elaborate frieze, and coffered plaster ceiling.
‡ Clink Wharf (*c.* 1896–9) was demolished in 1982.
§ I owe these comparisons to Georgina Russell. Christopher Wilson also draws attention to another circular window using triangles and hexagons, at Bridgwater, Somerset.

the N end of REDCROSS WAY, on a cramped site, CROM-
WELL BUILDINGS, early flats by the Improved Industrial
Dwellings Company, 1864, with typical cast-iron galleries.
BANKSIDE, with its theatrical memories (*see* Introduction,
above), continues the riverside walk W of Southwark Bridge.
The C19 commercial character of the area has now nearly
disappeared. The walk starts with a happy surprise: No. 1,
THE ANCHOR, a low, much rebuilt late C18 pub, at the edge
of the Bishop of Winchester's Clink territory (note the iron
posts defining this, dated 1812). The RED LION WHARF
follows, a Venetian Gothic warehouse of 1865, refurbished
1981; but after that much has gone.* Further on (away from
the river) the low stock brick UNION WORKS at the corner of
Emerson Street. The next old enclave comes after Southwark
Bridge: Nos. 49–52 Bankside, facing the river. Nos. 50–52
(restored), dated 1712, have doorways with carved brackets.
No. 49, CARDINAL'S WHARF, is taller and thinner. In front
is a pleasant little paved square, made in the late 1970s when
the flood barrier made it necessary to raise the river wall. New
landscaping on a larger scale has also transformed the next
part of the river bank, where the sheer brickwork of the
mammoth power station (*see* Public Buildings), directly opposite St Paul's, is effectively set off by a swathe of verdure. This
gives way to the harder but not unattractive brick surfaces of
the EDGER DEVELOPMENT close to Blackfriars Bridge
(1974–80). By the river a low, free-standing pub, the FOUND-
ERS ARMS, polygonal, with a rather heavy roof-line, and flats
of six to eight storeys (for Southwark Council), whose austere
geometry of inset balconies is relieved on the S side by a paved
plaza with trees. Behind is the monster of the group, LLOYDS
COMPUTER CENTRE (*Fitzroy Robinson & Partners*), with
cyclopic channelled concrete lift shafts, and sleek stepped-
back upper floors looking curiously like superimposed
streamlined train carriages. The building is on the site of the
Blackfriars Road Railway Goods Depot (1863 by *J. Taylor*) of
which some of the substructure remains on the W side.
Past the bridge the even less democratic package of the KINGS
REACH development (*R. Seifert & Partners*; project architect
Ivan Starkin, begun 1970), with luxury flats and hotel, offices,
and a pub next to the bridge. The arrogantly jagged pile of flats
and hotel, with their smooth cream-faced surfaces, continuous window bands, and sharp right angles, are now one of the
most conspicuous landmarks of the South Bank when seen
from the river. Further W BARGE HOUSE STREET, the site
of the sheds for the royal barges. This neighbourhood, apart
from one unexpected survivor, Nos. 69–70 UPPER GROUND,
still at the time of writing consists of tall warehouses of the
earlier C20, the most eyecatching the showy modernistic

---

* Demolitions include CEYLON WHARF, extending back to Park Street; other
good warehouses in PARK STREET of 1827 (rainwater head), with later alterations. Four low storeys in plain stock brick, paired pilasters, Doric columns to the
entrance of No. 42.

tower of the OXO WAREHOUSE (by *A. W. Moore*, 1928), which does not fail to advertise O X O from wherever one looks across the river to Southwark. w of this, on the borough boundary, the largely empty site around COIN STREET, whose future has long been in dispute.

I(b). *Stamford Street and Southwark Street from W to E*

S of the riverbank the main thoroughfares W–E are Stamford Street and Southwark Street. The w part of STAMFORD STREET is in Lambeth (*see* Lambeth (La), Perambulation 1). It was laid out *c.* 1790, built up by *c.* 1815. Of this period nothing now except the façade of the surprisingly severe portico of the former Unitarian Chapel (*see* Churches, above). Among the commercial buildings one can contrast the various offices now occupied by I.P.C. – DORSET HOUSE by *L. A. Culliford*, 1931–3, and the KINGS REACH offices (*see* above) with a street range with its structure expressed as projecting fins, and a tower behind with the same motif around a curved end. On the s side, No. 17, with a sheer glass and marble wall of the 1970s in front of RENNIE HOUSE, the former Sainsbury's factory, 1935 by *Sir Owen Williams*. This was a bold, honest reinforced concrete structure six storeys high, the first in London to be built on the flat slab principle, i.e. with the main weight of the floors supported by two internal rows of massive columns (their mushroom heads now concealed, except in the basement, by suspended ceilings). Much altered in 1972–5 when the building was remodelled as offices and laboratories, with a new top floor, by *Scott, Brownrigg & Partners*. On the N side of Stamford Street at the corner of Rennie Street (whose name recalls the engineering works of John Rennie & Son) STAMFORD HOUSE, formerly Sainsbury's warehouse and office, 1912 by *Sykes*, also of reinforced concrete; but, as was then the practice, the structure is completely concealed by brick with stone dressings. Corinthian pilasters to the upper floors. N extension 1928. Remodelled as offices by *Denis Lennon & Partners*, 1971–3, with two new top storeys replacing additions of 1939.

SOUTHWARK STREET, linking Blackfriars Road to Borough High Street, was cut through in 1862 by *Bazalgette*, but according to older and bolder plans by *Pennethorne*. It was the first street in London where a special duct for water, gas, and telegraph services was provided in the centre of the roadway. The older streets run off at angles. In HOPTON STREET, to the N, in poignant contrast to the architecture of Southwark Street, the HOPTON ALMSHOUSES, 1752, happily restored after war damage. A pretty group of two-storeyed cottages, birck with stone quoins. The principal block has a pedimented committee room as its centre. The projecting wings are separate from the central block, and two more blocks project further towards the street, each again with its own projecting (but attached) wings. A little further on No.

61, a tiny survivor of c. 1702, four windows wide, doorway with carved brackets.

The architecture of Southwark Street itself represents High Victorian Southwark and included some of the most consistent stretches of that period still remaining in London. Of noteworthy quality No. 99 on the s side, KIRKALDY'S TESTING WORKS, four storeys, very subdued *Rundbogenstil*, 1877 by *T. R. Smith* (a pupil of Hardwick). The ground floor accommodates David Kirkaldy's 350-ton-force materials-testing machine made in 1864 by *Greenwood & Batley* of Leeds (preserved *in situ*); the upper floor had a museum. His motto 'Facts, not opinions' over the doorway.* On the other side Nos. 124–126, Venetian Gothic with thin colonnettes, with a tactful extension of the 1970s keeping to the same proportions. Still of the c19 on the s side, the buildings framing Great Suffolk Street, both with rounded corners (No. 89 with more elaborate detail). The N side is ruined by ST CHRISTOPHER'S HOUSE, 1959 by *Morris de Metz* (called, when built, 'the largest office block under one roof in Europe'). No. 59½ (Barclay Trust) is of 1890 by *T. M. Lockwood*, with three orders of pilasters and a florid doorcase with the bell-buoy motif of the Bell Asbestos Company. Then, after Southwark Bridge Road, quite a complete late Victorian stretch on the N side (ground floors altered). Opposite, No. 49, one of the first buildings in the street (1867 by *E. Bates*). Nos. 51–53 are similarly ornate but a little taller. CENTRAL BUILDINGS on the N side, once the most magnificent building in Southwark Street, was erected as the Hop Exchange in 1866 by *R. H. Moore*. Southwark was a centre of the hop industry. It is an interesting attempt at pulling a six-storey front together with three super-storeys: giant iron columns for ground and first floor and long narrow blank arches for the upper floors. The top floors were demolished after a fire in 1920. The entrance, with pediment with hop and harvesting scenes and florid iron gates (with hop decoration), leads to an open vestibule with marble columns (now painted). The splendid exchange hall, 75 ft high, with offices opening off decorative balconies on four levels (cf. the Coal Exchange), still survives, although the ground floor has been covered over, and the original glass and iron roof replaced after the fire.

2(a). Borough High Street

s from London Bridge we follow the BOROUGH HIGH STREET and explore its turnings. This area has the longest urban tradition of the inner areas of South London. It was built up by the early c17, and although almost nothing remains of this date, the medieval and Tudor pattern of tall narrow buildings

---

* Kirkaldy pioneered the scientific and independent testing of materials used in civil engineering.

with courts and alleys opening off is still easily recognizable. N
of ST THOMAS STREET, next to ALAM HOUSE (1974–6 by
Igal Yawetz Associates, brown brick), the remains of the former ST THOMAS' HOSPITAL (strictly speaking in Bermondsey). The hospital was founded in the C12, and with the
coming of the railway moved to a new site in Lambeth (*see*
Lambeth (La), Public Buildings). What remains is chiefly ST
THOMAS'S CHURCH, now the chapter house of Southwark
Cathedral. It was built as the parish church in 1702–3, but
once formed part of the S side of the courtyard of the hospital.
It looks like a minor City church, red brick with stone quoins
and dressings and with houses to its r. The square tower
stands out into the street. The church itself has four tall arched
windows and a pediment to stress the two middle ones. The
interior is simple, with N and W galleries, and a finely moulded
cornice. (Pulpit of 1704, five-sided.) In the roof an attic used
as a herb garret, then converted in 1821 as an operating theatre
(rediscovered in 1957 and restored as a medical museum). It
adjoins a dignified stone ward block, three storeys, with a high
basement, nine bays long. The W end (now containing a post
office) is exposed to the High Street, set back from the other
frontages. The building dates from 1842–4 and formed the S
wing of the hospital front court, rebuilt by *Samuel Robinson*
and *James Field* as part of the new approach to London
Bridge.* E of the chapter house the treasurer's apartments
(now called Collegiate House) with two pedimented doorways, one unusually broad. The N front of the church and
house (visible, with the ward block, from behind London
Bridge Street) has giant pilasters and is with its brickwork
with rubbed bricks for the window surrounds an exceptionally
characteristic piece of domestic architecture of *c.* 1700. Back
in St Thomas Street, yet further E a plainer early C19 terrace
(Nos. 11–15) opposite Guy's Hospital, and to its W more
Georgian terrace houses (Nos. 2–16, 1819). A somewhat strident contrast is *Newman & Billing*'s opulently Italianate
building, Nos. 24–26 of 1862, built for Guy's Hospital medical staff with carvings by Mr *Seal* of Walworth. Now incorporated in NEW CITY COURT, with offices and hospital
staff accommodation, extending back to George Yard and the
High Street, begun in 1982, by *Halpern Partnership*. (No. 43
is a bank by *George Hubbard*, 1910.)
In KING'S HEAD YARD, S of St Thomas Street, the KING'S
HEAD of 1881, the successor of one of the famous Southwark
inns. It now carries a robustly carved late C17 bust of Henry
VIII. Back in Borough High Street No. 67 (W. H. LeMay
Hop Factors), late C19, with a decorative panel of hop gather-
ers above. No. 71 is the celebrated GEORGE INN, only a 31
shadow of what it was still a hundred years ago, for in 1889 the
Great Northern Railway who owned the premises decided to

---

* Dr P. Metcalf points out that it is the only remaining evidence of the extent of
road widening intended in *Smirke*'s overall plans.

demolish the N wing and centre. So now only a fragment of the typical galleried design remains, the design which conditioned early English theatres and figures so prominently in so many C 18 and C 19 novels. The galleries have plain balusters, not as elegant as they would have been for a less homely job. The George was built only after the Southwark fire of 1676. To the E of the galleried part is a larger plain brick part with horizontal and a few vertical and segment-headed windows. Some ground-floor rooms still have C 18–early C 19 fittings, e.g. a sash-windowed bar.

On the W side of the High Street BOROUGH MARKET, behind a mediocre brick front of 1932. The older market place was where the High Street broadens around the island on which formerly stood St Margaret's church and later the town hall. It now has some stately Italianate banks. On the W side are older buildings: Nos. 38–42, earlier C 18 restored, and No. 50, which has in its yard the only remaining example in the area of a timber-framed house with overhanging upper floor (Calvert's Buildings). Opposite, Nos. 91, C 18 with good staircase, 93–95, 101 (the former Boot and Flogger Inn), late C 17 altered, and 141–143, with traces of late C 18 *Coade* stone decoration. In NEWCOMEN STREET off to the E the KINGS ARMS of 1890 exhibits the sumptuously carved ROYAL ARMS from the gatehouse to the remodelled London Bridge. The date must be *c.* 1730–40. Opposite, No. 9, MARSHALL'S CHARITY, four-storey Tudor offices of 1853, with carved stone heads. In the High Street further S much rebuilding of the 1970s.

2(b). Union Street

UNION STREET runs W from the Borough High Street. No. 14 (Price Waterhouse Training Centre) is a nicely refurbished hop warehouse of *c.* 1853, with giant arches (alterations by *T. P. Bennett & Son*, 1973–5). Nos. 31–37 are early C 19. Nos. 59–61 have a good early C 19 shopfront and gated archway. Then the former ST SAVIOUR'S PAROCHIAL AND NATIONAL SCHOOLS, 1908, in a cheerful neo-Georgian, two storeys with playground on the roof. To the S of Union Street lay the once notorious Mint Rookery, with Marshalsea Road as its main thoroughfare. It was outside the city jurisdiction; a paradise for criminals and prostitutes, and consequently entirely rebuilt from the later C 19 onwards. On the N fringe of this area just S of Union Street in REDCROSS WAY a specially interesting group: two sets of cottages, a hall and a garden, planned by Octavia Hill and embodying her belief that the working classes deserved a civilized environment instead of the tenements common at the time. REDCROSS COTTAGES, overlooking REDCROSS GARDENS, were built in 1887, WHITECROSS COTTAGES, behind, in AYRES STREET, in 1890. The architect was *Elijah Hoole*. The earlier cottages have a picturesque variety of different-sized gables and upper bay-windows, the later ones are tile-hung with an end gable. The style is more enjoyable than that of Hoole's socially progressive institutional buildings (Toynbee Hall, TH). The garden was laid out at the same time, but the original landscaping (by *Emmeline Sieveking* for the Kyrle Society) does not survive. Reset on a wall a mosaic roundel, The Sower, by *James Powell* after a sketch by *Lady Waterford*, 1896. At the end of the cottages the former RED CROSS HALL, 1887–8 by *Hoole*, completes the group. Simple lancet windows. The interior was decorated by *Walter Crane* in 1889, with 'Deeds of heroism in the daily life of ordinary people'. Ten panels were planned, but only three executed.*

The cottage experiment was repeated in SUDREY STREET, a little to the S, where *Hoole* designed GABLE COTTAGES for the Rev. T. Bastow in 1889. These are of an even more fanciful design, arranged almshouse-fashion, on three sides of a courtyard, but with further tiny spaces opening off the corners, and with a wealth of half-timbering, plasterwork, tile-hanging, and angled gables, all on a toytown scale. The Ecclesiastical Commissioners (who had adopted Octavia Hill's methods of housing management) followed with WINCHESTER COTTAGES, built by *Cluttons* in 1893–5, in COPPERFIELD STREET, just W of Southwark Bridge Road. (Compare WINCHESTER BUILDINGS, 1885, near by.) Round the corner in SAWYER STREET, WHITEHILL HOUSES are a small block of flats, built in 1889 by *L. Ambler* for the Countess of Selborne, one of Octavia Hill's associates. For later flats, one can look at a group at the corner of Union Street and GREAT GUILDFORD STREET, 1937–8 for the Ecclesiastical Commissioners by *E. Armstrong*, more generous in their internal planning than most contemporary local authority housing, and unusual for their date in the way in which the lower N range is stepped back along the line of the road. Behind it are parallel higher E and W ranges.

Further W, GREAT SUFFOLK STREET, crossed by the Piranesian arched bridges of the South Eastern Railway. To the S, No. 55, a gaunt late C 19 five-storey warehouse, and No. 59 of the same period, yellow and blue brick, a bacon-curer's premises, with stoves in a range behind.

2(c). Southwark Bridge Road

SOUTHWARK BRIDGE ROAD, from S to N. Little of interest at the S end apart from the Fire Brigade Training Centre (Winchester House). The tall back parts are still recognizable as the workhouse built in 1777 for St Saviour's parish, probably by *G. Gwilt. Sen.* The front has a handsome façade with Ionic pilasters and Doric porches. Extensions for the Fire Brigade of 1878 (Gothic detail) and 1911 (bay-windows). Nos. 68–86

* See *The Builder*, 9 November 1889; Crane's *Reminiscences* (1907), pp. 359–60.

form a modest early C19 terrace. At the corner of Union Street
the former PUBLIC LIBRARY, weak Italianate by *John Johnson*, 1893. Near the river, the former ANCHOR BREWERY,
owned by Henry Thrale in the C18. The parts behind all
rebuilt. To the street a three-storey C19 building, not very
thoughtful additions of 1932 and 1938 by *O. Faber*, and
ANCHOR TERRACE, a large, symmetrical composition of
1834. Projecting ends and centre with stone balustrades, iron
balconies in between. On the W side undistinguished offices of
the 1960s, replacing *Joseph Emberton*'s Universal House of
1933.*

2(d). Blackfriars Road and streets off

BLACKFRIARS ROAD, from N to S. Much rebuilt, especially at
the N end.‡ On the W side WEDGE HOUSE, 1963–7 by *Hugh
V. Sprince*. Strong horizontal bands, recessed ground floor.
More of interest in the side streets. In NICHOLSON STREET
low-rise housing by *Richard Sheppard, Robson & Partners*,
completed in 1975 (but designed in 1967–8, and so an early
example of the reaction against high rise). Parallel terraces of
two to three storeys, broken frontages with stepped-back
pitched roofs, with an emphatic use of bold red tiles. Pedestrian approaches alongside sunken back gardens.§ NELSON
SQUARE, S of Union Street (where Shelley lodged), once of
1804–18, has (apart from Nos. 44–47) been entirely replaced
since the Second World War with dull eight- to nine-storey
blocks of flats by *Southwark Borough Council*.
Back in BLACKFRIARS ROAD, on the W side, remains of Georgian terraces, Nos. 74–86. To the E again at the corner of
POCOCK STREET and GLASSHILL STREET the DRAPERS'
ALMSHOUSES of 1820, not big, and made Gothic only by the
wooden casements of the windows. At the corner of Pocock
Street and RUSHWORTH STREET, ST ALPHEGE HOUSE,
1910 by *William Bucknall*. Near by, the (former) CONVENT
OF THE REPARATION, a well detailed house in the style of
the early C18, by *Walter Tapper*, 1911–12. CHAPEL behind, in
simple Renaissance style, with a pedimented centre to King's

---

* This was one of the first buildings in England to follow the continental
precedent and show rounded corners without any visible supports. The walls
divided into horizontal strips of window glass and opaque pale green glass as a
wall covering. Demolished in 1981–2: the former Petty, Wood & Co. warehouse
N of Thrale Street by *Roumieu*, 1878, a gargantuan free Renaissance extravaganza
with seven-storey tower, and Grey and Marten's leadworks, 1880, with a tall
chimney close to the river.

‡ Losses include No. 3, James Parkinson's Natural History Museum of 1788,
later the Surrey Institution, which had as its centre a handsome rotunda with
Tuscan columns originally carrying a gallery, and smaller domed rooms with
skylight. (*Coade* vases and plaques from the demolished No. 7 are rebuilt into a
garage wall behind. A K)

§ Also in Nicholas Street the Edward Edwards ALMSHOUSES, rebuilt 1973,
part of a redevelopment including a new pub and an office block in Blackfriars
Road.

Bench Street. Panelled interior, with wooden barrel-vault. Then, between Rushworth Street and King's Bench Street, some noteworthy early L.C.C. housing of 1896–7 (by *R. M. Taylor* of the L.C.C.'s Housing Branch). Two blocks (MERROW and RIPLEY), only three storeys high, with quirky Arts and Crafts details to the street (see the angular chimney, gables, and big eaves), and on the inside a small friendly court. Plain central staircases and short access balconies. Two similar blocks (ALBURY and CLANDON) a little further s, on either side of BOYFIELD STREET. Staircases with Tudor details. The scale of these early flats should be compared with what the L.C.C. put up shortly afterwards: see in KING JAMES STREET the more traditional tenements by *Joseph, Son & Smithem*, of 1899, relieved only by Jacobean trimmings. More housing contrasts across Blackfriars Road. PEABODY SQUARE is an early Peabody Estate of 1870–1 by *Darbishire*, not as tall and crowded as the later estates. Sixteen four-storey blocks around two courtyards with trees. Separate laundries. The flats had the usual shared sculleries, but staircase access, not corridors as in the earliest Peabody examples. In WEBBER ROW recent housing by the *Peabody Trust's Architects Department*, 1976, and, further on, L.C.C. work of 1905 by *J. R. Stark* (of the L.C.C. Architect's Department), tall blocks with nicely detailed eaves.

3(a). *St George's Circus and the area to its s and* W

ST GEORGE'S CIRCUS is the hub of SW Southwark and NE Lambeth. Before it became the meeting point of Blackfriars Road and Westminster Bridge Road, with Lambeth Road, London Road, and Borough Road radiating from it, the district had been St George's Fields, where Gerard of the Herbal collected wild flowers, where the Wilkes and Liberty meetings were held, the Gordon Rioters assembled, Methodist preachers roused the deepest feelings of thousands of listeners, and Lunardi's balloon ascended in 1785. The route from Blackfriars Bridge to Newington Butts was laid out in 1769 by *Robert Mylne* (surveyor to the Blackfriars Bridge Committee). In the centre of the Circus, where this road crossed the turnpike road, was an OBELISK, dated 1771 (now removed to the N apex of the Geraldine Mary Harmsworth Park). Little building took place along the main roads until after 1812, and the Circus does not today convey anything like the conviction of a French *rond-point*. The main landmarks are the ROYAL EYE HOSPITAL of 1890–1 and *Douglas Marriott Worby & Robinson*'s own offices, a good corner building, brown brick, with bronze projecting bay-windows on three sides, 1973–5. In LONDON ROAD some modest terraces of the 1820s survive; further s, in and around ST GEORGE'S ROAD, some earlier development – Nos. 63–83, 1794, and, especially attractive, WEST SQUARE, W and E sides of 1791–4, s side *c.* 1800–10. The much more ambitious schemes by *George Dance* for this

area were not carried out. (N of St George's Road ALBERT
TERRACE, Gladstone Street, of 1849.)

In BOROUGH ROAD a former Presbyterian chapel (No. 189);
plastered front with giant pilasters and entrance in a
French-looking niche with banded rustication. Opened in
1846. Later part of Hoe's printing-press manufactory next
door (which was demolished in 1983). Further on, Nos.
47–60, a large factory, originally Day & Martin, blacking
manufacturers, c. 1889. Fifteen bays and five storeys, still
essentially in the classical tradition (with pilasters and
pediment), but the curved roof is of corrugated iron. An
ostentatious chimney behind. Little else to note here apart
from an early much altered BOARD SCHOOL (1874) tucked
away in BELVEDERE PLACE, and No. 83 (now BARCLAYS
BANK) in a mixture of Gothic and Scottish Baronial, built for
the South London Institute for the Blind by *C. Ashby Lean*,
1906. At the junction of Borough Road and Borough High
Street the SCOVELL ESTATE, a low-rise villagey group by
Southwark Architect's Department, 1978.

3(b). Elephant and Castle

ELEPHANT AND CASTLE. In 1950 this could still be described
as 'the most unselfconscious muddle of buildings and traffic,
so much so that although it is a circus of six converging roads,
it has not even a proper name'.* By then, redevelopment was
imminent. A comprehensive development area was proposed
in the L.C.C. plan of 1951; clearance began in 1956. The
result is one of the least loved creations of the London post-
war planners, or rather, of the road engineers, because it is
clear that the comfort of pedestrians had very low priority. On
foot one is first bewildered by the tortuous subways beneath
the double roundabout, then, on emerging, deafened by
traffic and crushed by the ruthless scale of the surrounding
towers, confusingly similar at first sight. The few pre-war
survivals are welcome landmarks: the portico of Spurgeon's
Tabernacle to the W (*see* Churches, above) and the scruffy
South London Press building over the underground at the N
apex. The largest of the new buildings demonstrate the confidently tough aesthetic of exposed concrete of the early 1960s.
Clockwise from the N: ALEXANDER FLEMING HOUSE
(government offices), blocks of different heights around service cores; a rather dark internal court with a pool. Next door
is a CINEMA, quite small, with fussy concrete and tiled surfaces (auditorium seating 1,050 with roof ingeniously cantilevered from diagonal beams). All by *E. Goldfinger*, 1962–7.
Opposite is a ten-storey office tower and the three-acre multi-
level covered shopping centre, by *Boissevain & Osmond*, an
early depressing example of the species, unsuccessful, no

---

* The name came from a public house which became, as so often in the suburbs, a
terminus for public transport.

doubt partly because of the uncivilized access. Converted to offices and conference centre in 1978 by the *Percy Thomas Partnership* and much improved in appearance. The original drab almost windowless exterior was refaced with more cheerful green g.r.c. panels and bands of glazing. To the s the *L.C.C.*'s DRAPER ESTATE (1962–5), high-rise flats over shops, with one twenty-five-storey tower. On the w side lower public buildings (Southwark Leisure Centre, London School of Printing; *see* Public Buildings, above), then PERRONET HOUSE, another block of flats with a three-storey wing along St George's Road. In the centre of one of the roundabouts just one inspired touch: a GENERATING STATION clad in shiny aluminium panels, doubling as a monument to Michael Faraday, the pioneer of electricity. Especially effective at night.

3(c). Newington Butts, Kennington Park Road, and the area to the E

NEWINGTON BUTTS, from N to S. On the w St Mary's churchyard, which became a public garden when the church was rebuilt on a site further S. In CHURCHYARD ROW the third of the big Rowton Houses (now LONDON PARK HOTEL), 1896 by *H. B. Measures* (*see* Lambeth (La), Perambulation 3). Opposite, G.L.C. housing of 1982–3, then *Southwark Borough Council's* NEWINGTON ESTATE of 1971–7; low yellow-brick terraces. On PULLEN'S ESTATE N of Manor Place, older tenement blocks with workshops.

KENNINGTON PARK ROAD continues S with on either side some of the prettiest late Georgian terraces in South London. For the w side *see* Lambeth (La), Perambulation 2. On the E side, Nos. 61–167 date from 1789–93. Various designs, some with especially nice fanlights (Nos. 95, 101, 125, 131), some with *Coade* stone decoration (Nos. 75, 127, 133). Later buildings: No. 59, the former vicarage of St Mary's, Gothic, 1873, and KENNINGTON STATION, 1890, one of the original stations on the first tube line (City and South London Railway). The dome housed the head-gear of a hydraulic lift.

Off to the E down KENNINGTON PARK PLACE. No. 5, built for the Bishop of Rochester (now a day nursery), is by *Norman Shaw*, 1895. A very subdued Queen Anne façade of six bays. At the back the former chapel, with lunette windows and big eaves. Then some older houses around the edge of Kennington Park: No. 9, early C19 altered, stuccoed, with Soanian incised pilasters and recessed entrance; No. 11, late Georgian; and ST AGNES PLACE, Nos. 1–7, an early C19 terrace with bow-windows at the back.

The BRANDON ESTATE begins E of St Agnes Place, its unmistakable cluster of white towers the symbol in the late 1950s for the regeneration of South London. The original scheme which was drawn up in 1955 by the L.C.C. Architect's Department (architect in charge *Edward Hollamby*) included five eleven-storey towers overlooking an extended

Kennington Park. In the end six eighteen-storey towers were built (1957–8), the estate was extended to the s in the 1960s, with five still taller towers (twenty-six storeys high), and the park was not enlarged as intended. So the present rather bleak appearance of the w part of the estate is very different from the original conception, which was much closer to Roehampton (Ww) (q.v., Alton Estate). The early towers try hard not to be too monolithic. They have recessed centres, and each group of four storeys is set back within a concrete frame. On top are curved sloping structures housing the services (cf. Golden Lane on the N edge of the City of London a little earlier). Forlornly stranded on a grass mound near the towers is a noble sculpture by *Henry Moore*, Reclining Figure, set up as part of the idealistic post-war L.C.C.'s policy of modern sculpture in public places (cf. Battersea Park, Ww, and Stifford Estate, TH). On the far side of the towers a long seven-storey range with projecting centrepiece and a passage through to the SHOPPING PRECINCT.

This E part of the estate deserves to be explored further, for the aspect of the Brandon Estate which is still relevant twenty-five years later is not the towers (although they were the feature immediately imitated) but the relaxed mixture of different types of housing and enclosing spaces, and especially the retention of older terraces among the new buildings, not a common practice in the 1950s, when a clean sweep was all the rage among planners.* The shopping centre has a BRANCH LIBRARY with clubroom above, and a mural and other decoration by *Anthony Holloway*. Round the corner to the l. one reaches FORSYTH GARDENS, a large new square, a revival of Georgian planning traditions, but with four-storey maisonettes in a neutral c 20 style instead of terrace houses. The well cared for tiny front gardens, compared with the tatty no man's land around the towers, make it clear where people prefer to live. (Contrast the gardens also with the present unkempt state of the public space of the square itself.) Up LORRIMORE ROAD, with a nicely restored terrace dated 1852, and with all kinds of new houses round about (e.g. GREIG TERRACE, with boarded upper floor and gables), to LORRIMORE SQUARE, with St Paul's church as its strident centrepiece (*see* Churches, above). The s side of the square is mid c 19 (plain stuccoed ground floors), the N and W sides are new. More variety further E, with original terraces on both sides of CARTER STREET, new cottagey bungalows in LORRIMORE ROAD, and another garden, partly enclosed by three-storey flats. Here one can leave the estate by a passage through to PENROSE STREET, but the transition is hardly noticeable. To the E SUTHERLAND SQUARE, a narrow

---

* The Brandon Estate was the first L.C.C. development to incorporate older houses. It was argued that the low density of these parts made the towers necessary if both additional parkland and the prescribed 136 p.p.a. density were to be achieved.

rectangle with earlier C 19 houses with pairs of heavy
Roman Doric porches, leads one into Walworth Road.

3(d). Walworth Road and the area to the E

WALWORTH ROAD has just one part of a late C 18 terrace which
enables one to visualize how happy and unadventurous the
road once looked: Nos. 140–152, near the N end, built c. 1790
by *Francis Hurlblatt* for Henry Penton (of Pentonville). The former centre (Nos. 140–142) was distinguished by a pediment
with a figure in a medallion (formerly between garlands).
The second pediment, ingeniously added at the other end to
make the remains of the terrace symmetrical, and the portico
date from 1978, when the building was converted as Labour
Party Headquarters by *Russell Diplock Associates*. In CAM-
BERWELL ROAD, the continuation of Walworth Road, more
terraces remain (*see* below, Camberwell, Perambulation 1). In
between, Edwardian shopping parades (dated 1906–8) and
much C 20 rebuilding. Opposite Sutherland Square (where
the previous perambulation ends) LIVERPOOL GROVE leads
E to St Peter's church (*see* Churches, above). To the S the
modest PEACOCK TERRACE, dated 1842. Beyond, a large
area rebuilt by the Ecclesiastical Commissioners, mostly from
1903–9 (LIVERPOOL GROVE, PORTLAND STREET, etc.).
Three-storey 'cottage flats', an unusual type, influenced by
the earlier cottage housing, built by *Cluttons* for the Commissioners under the guidance of Octavia Hill (*see* above, Perambulation 2(b)).* Each group of flats is entered by a central
doorway, and the homely atmosphere is underlined by bay-
windows, half-timbered gables, and some variety of grouping,
although not yet following the low-density garden-city principles which were adopted soon after for the L.C.C. cottage
estates.

There could hardly be a greater contrast between these streets
and what follows to the E. Southwark's AYLESBURY ESTATE,
designed in 1967, completed 1977, the most ambitious post-
war development by any London borough, covers 64 acres
(Borough Architect *F. O. Hayes*, succeeded by *H. P. Trenton*). Like the Brandon Estate further W, it was intended as an
improvement on the small scruffy streets in the hinterland
between the main roads, and, also like the Brandon Estate, it
was planned to be on the edge of a park which never came to
fruition quite as intended (for Burgess Park *see* below, Camberwell, Perambulation 3). There the similarity ends, for
there is no acceptable variety here. An exploration can be
recommended only for those who enjoy being stunned by the
impersonal megalomaniac creations of the mid C 20. The
estate has 2,434 dwellings, for c. 8,000 people (density: 136
p.p.a), 100 per cent garaging, and complete segregation of
pedestrians. This means that to traverse the area one must

---

* Octavia Hill managed the Commissioners' Walworth estates from 1884.

ascend to a third-floor walkway. The preferred form is not the tower, but the slab, which does not make for recognizable landmarks. The blocks are four, five, eight, ten, or fourteen storeys high; the lower ones are grouped alternately round garage courts and grassed areas. The only visual relief from the repetitive industrialized building system (Jespersen 12M) comes from the low MICHAEL FARADAY SCHOOL (*see* Public Buildings), the red-brick flats of an older estate (dull, but quite friendly by comparison) enclosed within the new development, and from the tall chimney next to the drab community centre. Along THURLOW STREET the largest slab of all (the longest block in Europe built to an industrialized system, according to the *Guinness Book of Records*). At the N end of this some shops and a health centre at walkway level, but the deck here is not wide or interesting enough to be an adequate substitute for a real street.

The back streets between the Aylesbury Estate and New Kent Road have little of interest. A few remnants of early C19 development (DAWES STREET). In BRANDON STREET and LARCOM STREET, WALTER'S CLOSE, pretty almshouses round two quadrangles, 1961 by *Berry Webber & Son*, for the Drapers' Company. One court is open to the street, with a rather Swedish clock turret over the centre block, the other has an arcade to the street of three shallow segment-headed arches. Lovingly detailed, in two shades of brown brick. The N end of Brandon Street dissolves into the HEYGATE ESTATE, which was planned from 1968–9 and built in 1970–4, with 1,194 dwellings. The scale and style are already familiar from the Aylesbury Estate, but here there are also a few lower terraces squeezed in N of Heygate Road. The tall slabs, with their long glazed balconies, make an impressive sight from a distance, an extension visually of the cluster of towers around the Elephant and Castle, but that is all one can say in their favour.

3(e). New Kent Road, Old Kent Road, Great Dover Street

The first part of this final segment of Southwark has too much traffic to make a pleasant walk. In NEW KENT ROAD the original type of housing only visible in Nos. 154–170. Late C18, with unusual doorcases. Of the more ambitious developments built from 1788 by *Michael Searles*, surveyor to the Rolls Estate, only the name of the PARAGON is preserved in the road and large SCHOOL of 1898. But opposite, BARTHOLOMEW STREET has a complete frontage of late Georgian houses of 1818–19. Continuity is then disturbed by the FLYOVER of 1970. In OLD KENT ROAD, on the E side first BACON'S SCHOOL, 1896, a long symmetrical composition typical of the Board Schools of the 1890s. Then, after the Industrial Dwellings, No. 155, *Michael Searles*'s own house and office, 1800, a plain four-bay two-storeyed villa with a big hipped roof. Opposite, Nos. 218–250 incorporating *Searles* houses of 1784 onwards, much altered. Nos. 215–231, a C 19 stuccoed terrace, is worth a look because of the former premises of CARTER'S the Hatters, now a tyre shop; two jolly mural paintings and a hatted bust over a clock. Carter's former warehouse (note the lettering) is opposite, at the entrance to SURREY SQUARE. This was another Rolls Estate development. On the N side part of a long terrace of 1793–4 by *Searles*. The centrepiece has a pediment decorated with a fan motif. Some arched windows on the ground floor. The W end ruthlessly replaced by another Board School.

From the flyover back N via GREAT DOVER STREET, laid out as a bypass to avoid the area to the N as early as 1815, now a district of extensive county council housing replacing C 19 slums. A revealing sequence: the most recent contribution (1977) around REPHIDIM STREET, a little inward-looking group by the G.L.C. The brown brick walls and sloping roofs proclaim its allegiance to the new vernacular, in contrast to the concrete towers next door of 1961–3. W of Great Dover Street some mixed development characteristic of the friendly, prebrutalist work sometimes favoured by the L.C.C. in the 1950s; by *Sir John Burnet, Tait & Partners*, 1953–6. A string of eleven-storey three-pronged towers, and some cosy staggered terraces of cottages (Burbage Close and Chettle Close). Then after No. 165, an imposing red-brick and terracotta pile of 1891, TABARD GARDENS, just to the N, one of the *L.C.C.*'s most ambitious early C 20 slum clearance estates: planned in 1910 for 2,450 people, opened in 1916. Later extensions. The flats are grouped round a garden, but have none of the lively detail of earlier L.C.C. work (cf. Boundary Estate, Bethnal Green (T H), and the Millbank Estate, Westminster).

S and W of Great Dover Street the more respectable early–mid C 19 development around Trinity Street, mostly on land belonging to Trinity House. In TRINITY STREET itself, terraces with stuccoed ground floors and stuccoed window surrounds of 1827 onwards. Some plainer terraces in FALMOUTH ROAD (*c*. 1837). MERRICK SQUARE is visibly a little later, see the proportions (1853–6). The cornices were removed in 1947. TRINITY CHURCH SQUARE of 1824–32 is 79 an admirably complete composition, with houses on all four sides; of the same type as those in Trinity Street. In the centre the church of the same date, now a rehearsal hall (*see* Churches, above). In the gardens in front an important piece of statuary, a more than life-size figure of a king said to come from Richard II's Westminster Hall. The upper part and back are heavily restored, but the rest is in the style characteristic of the late C 14. It ought to be protected by a canopy.

Other early C 19 developments disappeared during and after the last war (Dickens Square 1844) and at the time of writing have still been only partially replaced by the L.C.C. maisonettes (*c*. 1960) around the LIBRARY and SCHOOL in Harper Road (*see* above, Public Buildings). HARPER ROAD leads W into

NEWINGTON CAUSEWAY, where there are still a few simple early C19 terraces (Nos. 32–38, 52–54) similar to those in London Road and around St George's Circus (*see* above, Perambulation 3(a)); also Nos. 48–50, the former Atlas Paperworks, 1880 by *Chambers* of Queen Street, with three stone heads of Atlas, and globes as capitals.

BERMONDSEY

CHURCHES

Two existing churches have medieval origins: St Mary Magdalene Bermondsey and St Mary Rotherhithe. They are both buildings of considerable charm, now substantially of the late C17 and earlier C18 respectively. The first Commissioners' period is nobly represented by *Savage*'s St James, the late Victorian most notably by *Jarvis & Son*'s St Augustine. The foreign seamen's churches in Rotherhithe make an interesting C20 group.*

CLARE COLLEGE MISSION (disused), Dilston Grove, SW edge of Southwark Park. 1911 by *Simpson & Ayrton*. Nice simple sunny building, roughcast, with somewhat Italian roof and tall segment-headed windows. Aisleless.

HOLY TRINITY, Rotherhithe Street. 1960 by *T. F. Ford*, replacing a Second Commissioners' Church of 1837–8 by *S. Kempthorne*. Mural by *H. Feibusch*.

ST ANNE, Thorburn Square, S of Southwark Park Road, W of St James's Road. 1869–70 by *J. Porter*. Brick, with SW tower and spire.

ST AUGUSTINE, Lynton Road.‡ Ambitious urban red brick, lancet style. Established in a poor area by Richard Foster. The architects were *Henry Jarvis & Son*, builders of many South London churches. This is their most notable building. E parts 1875–8, W end 1882–3. The tower was never built. The church stands on a concrete vaulted undercroft. Lofty interior with vaulted chancel of three bays and straight-ended ambulatory (cf. Southwark Cathedral). The nave is architecturally more elaborate, with carved capitals on stone columns, richly moulded arches, and a layer of arcading in front of the clerestory windows. Vestries added by *Hesketh & Stokes*, 1907 (on the site of the N chapel).

ST BARTHOLOMEW, Barkworth Road. 1866–7 by *E. Taprell Allen*. Red brick on an ambitious scale. The tower was never built. Impressive interior with a five-bay arcade of red and yellow brick, plate tracery between chancel and S chapel, and a

---

* Churches demolished since 1950 (in addition to those mentioned below): ST BARNABAS, Plough Way, 1873 by *Butterfield*; CHRIST CHURCH, Jamaica Road, 1838–9 by *L. Vulliamy*, brick, E. E.; CHRIST CHURCH, Parker's Row, 1848 by *W. B. Hays* and *G. Allen*, neo-Norman; ST LUKE, 1885 by *J. Gale* and *F. Baggaly*; ST PAUL, Kipling Street, 1848 by *Teulon*.
‡ Threatened with demolition.

clerestory. The nave partly filled with temporary classrooms at the time of writing. – STAINED GLASS. In the N aisle, four good windows by *Heaton, Butler & Bayne* with figures of saints, 1897–1903.

(ST CRISPIN, Southwark Park Road. 1958–9 by *T. F. Ford*, replacing a church of 1879–80 by *Coe & Robinson*. Mural by *Hans Feibusch*, 1959.)

ST HUGH (Charterhouse Mission), Crosby Row, NW off Long Lane. 1892–8 by *Carpenter & Ingelow*.

ST JAMES, St James's Road and Thurland Road. 1827–9 by *James Savage*. The grandest church in Bermondsey, and the most expensive of the London Commissioners' churches (they gave £17,666). Front with a deep portico of unfluted Ionic giant columns and pediment. The W tower slim with a rather Baroque, very transparent top part excessively divided horizontally into smaller and smaller sections; Grecian detail. The N and S sides of the church eight bays long with straight-headed windows and (which is exceptional) a clerestory. The interior was altered in 1965: the W end and aisles have been divided off. It has been tactfully done; the galleries with their big unfluted Ionic columns remain. Flat coffered ceiling. Projecting arched chancel with an enormous PAINTING of the Ascension of Christ by *John Wood*, 1844. – Heavy cast-iron COMMUNION RAILS of S-curved section. – CURIOSUM. In the playground in the former churchyard a splendid covered SLIDE with a half-timbered tower, given to 'the little children of Bermondsey' in 1921.

ST JOHN HORSELYDOWN, Fair Street and Tower Bridge Road. The church by *Hawksmoor* and *John James* of 1727 was destroyed in the Second World War. The lower parts of the walls are incorporated in an office block (*see* Perambulation 1, below).*

ST KATHERINE, Eugenia Road, SE of Rotherhithe New Road. By *Covell Matthews & Partners*, 1960, replacing a church of 1884 by *W. O. Milne*. Timid exterior of pale brick, with zigzagging walls and triangular-headed windows with concrete tracery. The interior rather better, with ashlar-faced chancel, and abstract coloured GLASS by *W. T. Carter Shapland*. A large corona over the altar. More could have been made of this site on the edge of the central square of the Silwood Estate (*see* Perambulation 3, below).

ST MARY MAGDALENE, Bermondsey Street. The medieval parish church of Bermondsey was established just to the N of the Cluniac priory of which almost nothing now remains (*see* Southwark Introduction, above, and Perambulation 2, below). The lower stages of the W tower and perhaps some of the N aisle may be C15; the rest was rebuilt in 1675–9 by

---

* The church of 1727–33, probably designed together by *John James* and *Hawksmoor*, was a landmark of South London with its silly but lovable spire in the shape of an oddly tapered column. It was a stately building, all stone-faced, the W front severely bare, without a portico, the N side symmetrical with two outer slightly projecting bays and a big central Venetian window.

Charles Stanton. There is a nave plus two aisles of different widths. The exterior has large round-headed windows and the s transept an odd semicircular s gable. The whole exterior was stuccoed in 1830, and it was then also that *George Porter* remodelled the w front in a gimcrack but charming, wholly unscholarly Gothic Revival. The aisles project as far w as the w tower and end in castellated lean-to roofs. The tower has pinnacles and a top stage with four gables and a tiny lantern. The interior retains its late c 17 character. It is modelled on Wren's St Martin, Ludgate (begun in 1677): nave of one oblong groin-vaulted bay, then a groin-vaulted crossing, then two oblong groin-vaulted bays and a chancel with a depressed coffered barrel-vault. From the crossing transepts reach out to N and S also with depressed vaults. The s transept projecting beyond the s aisle wall originally had a door. The arcades have giant Tuscan columns with straight entablatures, returning N and s into the transepts. The result is the mixture of longitudinal and central elements so much favoured by Wren. The chancel was lengthened in 1883. N, S, and w galleries run on regardless of the transepts. The s gallery was added in 1794. The w gallery was much restored after a fire in 1971. – FONT. Marble bowl with cherubs' heads, on a stem of 1808. – Good late c 17 to c 18 WOODWORK: PULPIT (remodelled), ORGAN CASE (made in 1750), REREDOS (reassembled), carved festoons over panels with the Lord's Prayer, etc., flanked by wall paintings of Moses and Aaron; PANELLING, DOOR, CUPBOARDS at the w end. – Two brass CANDELABRA in the nave, of Dutch type, inscribed 1699 and 1703. – STAINED GLASS. E window with pictorial glass of 1883. – CAPITAL. No doubt from the c 12 priory. An ornate example perhaps from the cloister. A sunken trefoil on each face, with beasts at the corners. Abacus with crowstepped ornament. – MONUMENTS. William Casteil † 1687, dignified largish epitaph. – William Steavens † 1713. – Many minor tablets.

ST MARY ROTHERHITHE, St Marychurch Street, near Rotherhithe Station. The rebuilding of the medieval church began in 1714, but was still incomplete in 1737. The w tower has an inscription of 1747 and the chancel is possibly also as late as that. The architect of the tower was *L. Dowbiggin* (of St Mary, Islington) although *B. Glanville* was also involved.* Yellow brick with rubbed red brick and stone trim. Quoins and arched windows in two tiers; the whole simple and friendly, amid old trees (the church of a busy riverside village). Spire with thin circular top stage of detached Corinthian columns, and octagonal obelisk spire, rebuilt in 1861. Interior of three unequal bays with tall Ionic columns and shallow vaulted ceiling. The galleries were removed in 1876 during a restoration by *Butterfield*, who added wrought-iron rails around the chancel. – REREDOS and chancel PANELLING, fragments in LECTERN, COMMUNION RAILS, STAIRCASE to w gallery

---

* £45 was also paid to *John James.*

and SEATING, all nice C 18 work. The reredos panels were painted in the later C 19 by *Florence T. Nicholson*. W gallery with fine ORGAN CASE with Doric ertablature, erected 1764. – Brass CANDELABRA in the nave.* – MONUMENTS. Captain Anthony Wood † 1625, with proud relief of a merchantman. – Joseph Wade, King's Carver in His Majesty's Yards at Dept-   53 ford and Woolwich, † 1743, delicious quite asymmetrical Rococo cartouche, first-class workmanship. – Christopher Jones, master of the Mayflower, † 1622, erected 1965.

MOST HOLY TRINITY (R.C.), Dockhead and Jamaica Road. An eclectic rebuilding of 1960 by *Goodhart-Rendel*, replacing the church of 1834–8 by *Kempthorne* destroyed in 1940. Curious two-tower W front of patterned brickwork, with triangular-headed windows. Shallow arched clerestory windows. Whitewashed concrete barrel-vaulted interior with narrow aisles and a wide crossing. The adjoining Convent of Mercy by *Pugin*, of 1838, destroyed in the war, was also rebuilt.

ST GERTRUDE (R.C.), Debnams Road, SE off Rotherhithe New Road after the railways. 1902 by *F. W. Tasker*. Greek-cross plan; plain classical detail with groined timber vault.

ST PETER AND THE GUARDIAN ANGELS (R.C.), Paradise Street, N of Jamaica Road and Southwark Park. 1902 by *F. W. Tasker*.

BERMONDSEY CENTRAL HALL, South London Mission (Methodist), S end of Bermondsey Street. Rebuilt 1968, but retaining the front of 1900 by *Charles Bell*, with Tudor gatehouse motif, red brick and terracotta.

FINNISH SEAMEN'S CHURCH, Albion Street, off the N end of Lower Road. 1958 by *Yorke Rosenberg & Mardall* (cf. Perambulation 3).

ST OLAVE (Norwegian Seamen's Church), Lower Road. 1927 by *John L. Seaton Dahl*. Neo-C 18 domestic-looking building with typically Danish spire.

SWEDISH SEAMEN'S CHURCH, Lower Road. Neat additions in a well-mannered Scandinavian style, by *Elkington Smithers* and *Bent Jorgen Jorgenson*, 1967. A plain brick house in front of an open concrete belfry with slated spire and large weathercock. An older church lies behind.

PUBLIC BUILDINGS

MUNICIPAL BUILDINGS, Spa Road. A group of two, the more recent one on the r. in an oddly pure neo-Greek Revival (1928 by *H. Tansley*). The PUBLIC LIBRARY (1890 by *John Johnson*) has little to recommend it.‡

CROWN COURT, English Grounds, N of Tooley Street. 1979–82 by *P. S. A. Architects*; brown brick.

* The small allegorical late C 17 PAINTING of King Charles the Martyr has been stolen.

‡ The oldest member of the group, the old Town Hall, 1880 by *Elkington*, the Borough Surveyor, has been demolished.

POLICE STATION AND MAGISTRATES' COURT, Tooley Street. By *J. D. Butler*, 1904, quite spectacular of its date, with a large broken curved pediment and an outward-curving balcony, and a doorway with a curved hood on elongated brackets.

SWIMMING BATHS, Lower Road. By *W. S. A. Williams* of *Sir F. Snow & Partners*, 1965. Baths, assembly hall, and cafeteria in a U around a sunbathing area.

ROTHERHITHE CIVIC CENTRE AND LIBRARY, Albion Street, r. off the N end of Lower Road. By *Yorke Rosenberg & Mardall*. Unadorned red brick. To the E, by the Finnish Seamen's Mission (*see* Churches, above), a paved plaza with SCULPTURE: Bermondsey Boy by *Tommy Steele*, of curiosity value only.

SOUTH LONDON COLLEGE (Tower Bridge Branch) (formerly ST OLAVE'S GRAMMAR SCHOOL), Tooley Street. 1893 by *Mountford*, the architect of the Old Bailey, the Battersea Polytechnic, the Northampton Institute in Finsbury, etc. A handsome red-brick building with white stone dressings. The hall with large windows forms the centre and is distinguished by a centrepiece with broken pediment, and a Georgian lantern. To the l. a wing formerly open on the ground floor, with a projecting polygonal stair-turret. The school founded in 1561 has moved to Orpington (Bm), where the statue of Queen Elizabeth from the original building is preserved in the headmaster's garden.

(AYLWIN SCHOOL, Southwark Park Road. 1965 by *Mayorcas & Guest*, for 975 girls. A ten-storey teaching block and lower buildings.)

SCOTT LIDGETT SCHOOL, Keeton's Road, off Jamaica Road E of St James's Road. 1968–71 by the G.L.C. Architect's Department (job architect *Eric Classey*, Education Architect *Michael Powell*). A comprehensive school for 1,380 boys. Designed at the same time as Pimlico School, but a complete contrast to it in appearance: no architectural bravado here, just pleasant, well grouped, concrete and red-brick buildings with generous provision for non-academic activities, a direct response to the Newsome Report of 1963. The plan is a grid of linked pavilions (intended, somewhat rigidly, for different faculties), with covered ways in between and with an avenue of plane trees preserved along the line of Keeton's Road, an especially happy touch. The only hint of grandeur is the large entrance court facing Drummond Road with a staircase up to the hall. The sloping windows of the hall roof and of the art block on the r. add a little variety to the rectangular outlines. The courtyards of different size include one with a sunken area for an open-air theatre.

BACON'S FREE SCHOOL and BOUTCHER SCHOOL. *See* Perambulation 3.

PETER HILLS SCHOOL (former), Rotherhithe. *See* Perambulation 2.

BERMONDSEY HEALTH CENTRE, Grange Road. 1936 by *H.*

Tansley. Modernistic symmetrical brick front with angular corner windows. Unlike town halls (*see* above), health centres had to be up to date.

SOUTHWARK PARK. Laid out in 1865–9. Designed, like Finsbury Park in North London, by *A. McKenzie*. The centre, with its secluded pond and island, is still quite pleasant. After the Second World War most of the lake was filled in because of bomb damage, and the original park of 65 acres gradually extended N to the riverside (q.v., Perambulation 3).

LONDON BRIDGE STATION. The earliest London railway station, opened in 1836 as the terminus of the London and Greenwich railway but rebuilt many times since. From 1847 the site was divided between the South Eastern Railway and the London Brighton and South Coast Railway. Much of the Brighton train shed of 1866 remains on the S side. The present station by *British Rail Architects* (regional architect *N. Wikely*), 1976–8, replaces a haphazard collection of C19 buildings much damaged in 1940.* The rebuilding includes a tower block of offices (*see* Perambulation 1), an opportunity at first missed at Euston. The awkward site on top of the C19 viaduct dictated an informal but efficient plan. This is the first major station in London where, at long last, bus, rail, and underground are united beneath one roof. The roof is a two-layer space-frame structure painted a dramatic yellow, and crowned by little pyramidal roof lights *à la* Hayward Gallery. An elegant curved wall of tinted glass and brown tiles divides the bus area from the station concourse, which covers a large triangular space between platforms and buffet. The noise is muted by black rubber floors, the lighting restrained – very different from the bright glossiness of Euston.

The expansion of the mid-C19 station converted the roads beneath to long tunnels. Rusticated archways indicate the original part, where the present wine vaults were once arcades. Across the N end of Joiner Street, by Tooley Street, a rare survival: six early Warren truss girders by *P. W. Barlow*, 1850, illustrating composite cast- and wrought-iron construction.‡ Overhead, the extension of 1859–64.

LONDON AND GREENWICH RAILWAY. *See* Bermondsey, Perambulation 2, Spa Road.

BRICKLAYERS ARMS STATION, Pages Walk, off Old Kent Road, E of Tower Bridge Road. The sole remaining architectural features are four sandstone gatepiers at the main entrance, and a tripartite brick gateway in Hendre Road. In Pages Walk railway housing of the 1840s, and the blank arcaded wall of former stables, mid C19. The monumental arch has disappeared. The station was originally built in 1844 for passengers and freight by *Lewis Cubitt* (cf. Kings Cross

* The original buildings of 1836 by *George Smith* and of 1840 by *L. Cubitt, J. V. Rastrick*, and *H. Roberts* were rebuilt in 1851 by *J. Beazley*. *Henry Currey* added a terminus hotel in 1861–2.

‡ Cast-iron triangular frames are bolted together, with bottom chords of pin-jointed wrought-iron tension bars.

Station) for the Croydon and S.E. Railways, which declined to pay the charges demanded by the Greenwich Railway for the use of the London Bridge terminus.

SURREY DOCKS. The Howland Great Wet Dock was a very early fitting-out basin of about 10 acres, *c.* 1697–1699 by *John Wells*. Later it was renamed the Greenland Dock and used by the whaling trade. From 1804 through to the C 20 the Surrey Docks grew in an irregular manner, initially under three separate companies, and the system extended eventually to 460 acres of land and water. The deepwater Quebec Dock of 1923–6 was the last to be constructed in London. The docks maintained associations with the northern seas, as the names (Norway Dock, Russia Dock, Canada Dock) imply, and the N parts were devoted principally to the softwood timber trade, with large ponds for the storage of timber afloat. Multi-storey warehouses were confined to the S parts and do not survive. The docks closed in 1969, and have mostly been filled in for redevelopment. S of Redriff Road, and intended to be kept as open water, there remain the GREENLAND DOCKS, reconstructed (for the third time) and enlarged to 22 acres in 1894–1904 by *Sir John Wolfe Barry*, succeeding *J. A. McConnochie*, and the SOUTH DOCK, a rebuilding of 1851–5 by *James Walker*. Across both entrance locks, contemporary swing footbridges. Across the connecting passage, a swing footbridge of interesting stayed-cantilever design, 1862 by *Henry Grissell*, originally situated in the N part of the docks. At the Russia Dock passage, in Redriff Road, the preserved substructure of a hydraulic swing bridge, *c.* 1900. N of Redriff Road, the eerie desolation of the 1970s is beginning to be replaced by low-rise public housing and light industry. On the site of the Canada Dock, a shallow LAKE has been created, and a FOREST has been laid out on the site of the Russia Dock. Off Lower Road, the former DOCK OFFICES of 1892 (derelict) with a tall thin clock tower, grey and red brick.

ROTHERHITHE TUNNEL, THAMES TUNNEL, TOWER BRIDGE, TOWER SUBWAY, CITY AND SOUTH LONDON RAILWAY TUNNEL. *See* Thames Crossings at end of gazetteer.

PERAMBULATIONS

1. The Riverside, from London Bridge E to Southwark Park

Starting in the plaza in front of the new London Bridge Station, the transformation of this part of the South Bank to a C 20 extension of the City seems almost total. Only Southwark Cathedral and Guy's Hospital peeping out between the tower blocks remind one of the past. On the W side LONDON BRIDGE HOUSE (by *R. Seifert & Partners*, 1962), on the E, built as part of the redevelopment of the station (*see* Public Buildings, above), the more distinguished SOUTHWARK

TOWERS (by *T. P. Bennett & Son*, 1977–9), the headquarters of the chartered accountants Price Waterhouse, with three twenty-three-storey wings of small offices around a central service tower. Screens of reflecting glass break up the surfaces and give the building a glitteringly elegant but secretive face. Beyond is yet another tower which is part of Guy's Hospital (*see* Southwark (Sk), Public Buildings).

From the plaza one must descend to the lower level of TOOLEY STREET. The Victorian warehouses at the W end have gone,* and *H. S. Goodhart-Rendel*'s ST OLAVE'S HOUSE, offices of the HAY'S WHARF COMPANY, 1931, stands alone, its shock effect now diminished by another concrete building opposite. It is on the site of *Flitcroft*'s St Olave, Tooley Street. The building was a milestone in the introduction of the Continental modern style into England. The sources, with its dainty drawn outline figure of St Olaf at the SW corner, and the graceful if somewhat preciously sharp and angular forms of the river front, are no doubt Swedish. The reliefs are by *Frank Dobson*. CHAMBERLAIN'S WHARF, immediately E, 1860s, seven storeys, dwarfing a three-storeyed office on the landward side, has a particularly fine Doric pilastered river frontage. Back in Tooley Street, No. 15, DENMARK HOUSE, 1908 by *S. D. Adshead* for the Bennett Steamship Company, is lushly ornamented in artificial stone. Nos. 17–25, COLONIAL HOUSE, is by *C. Stanley Peach*, 1903. Further E a continuous line of warehouses remains between Tooley Street and the river – note especially Nos. 47–49, 1860s, particularly handsome, six storeys, the lower four within giant arches, by *W. Snooke & H. Stock*. The same arrangement is used in the warehouses of HAY'S WHARF proper, ranged round Hay's Dock, and reached through an archway under Nos. 51–67 of 1887. These were built *c.* 1856, also by *Snooke & Stock*, rebuilt to similar designs after the great Tooley Street fire of 1861. The internal structure mostly timber floors on cruciform cast-iron columns, but interspersed with some brick jack-arched floors (as fire barriers). In the basement a portion of chalk rubble wall from the medieval Abbot of Battle's Inn. On the river front, replacing war damage, six-storey cold stores of 1947, horizontally striped in concrete and pink brick with cantilevered balconies and no windows; an effective style.‡ To the E, Symons Wharf, 1936–9 by *Hay's Wharf Estates Department*.§ In Tooley Street again, Nos. 71–73, a stationer's warehouse, 1870, large windows with cast-iron colonnettes; Nos. 75–81, an early Victorian wholesaler's warehouse, small Egyptian pediment and cast-iron window frames; No. 84, late

---

* Fennings Wharf, by London Bridge, is externally C 20, but incorporates a timber-stanchioned warehouse of 1836 by *George Allen*.

‡ The wall-mounted cranes have been removed, as the riverside is no longer used for delivery. The warehouses in the Tooley Street area were used for wines, spirits, groceries, and cold storage. New Zealand dairy produce first reached Hay's Wharf in 1867.

§ In ABBOTS LANE a four-storey warehouse, 1856, with unusual circular ground-floor windows.

C 19 South Eastern Railway offices, with monumental porch; and the SHIPWRIGHT, with an oriel on a plaster figurehead. From here eastwards Tooley Street was widened in 1877–84. At the time of writing there are gaps with views of the river on the N side. Nos. 115–121 are a jolly building of New Scotland Yard type, c. 1902.

Near Tower Bridge, opposite the former Grammar School (see above, Public Buildings, South London College), a statue of S. B. Bevington, first mayor of Bermondsey (†1907), by *Sydney March*, and a bust of Ernest Bevin (†1951). TOWER BRIDGE ROAD was made in 1902. To the S is the older FAIR STREET, and behind tall C 19 tenements (now modernized and a little less bleak than previously) the former churchyard of St John Horselydown. The church (see Churches, above) was gutted in the war, but its foundations have been re-used most successfully for NASMITH HOUSE (London City Mission). The new building (by *John D. Ainsworth & Associates*, 1972–6) is three storeys high above a basement formed within the walls of the old church. Recessed glazed ground floor, making a neutral break between the stone below and brick above. The pitched roof is broken in the centre, so that the gable end with its central stairs neatly echoes the shape of the end wall of the former early C 18 VICARAGE next door. The vicarage is of brown brick with red dressings, and has a projecting centrepiece with a small pediment. In the former churchyard, a one-storeyed stuccoed WATCH HOUSE (not in good repair), and a FOUNTAIN with a stem of twisted dolphins probably dating from when the churchyard became a public garden in 1882. S of the churchyard ST OLAVE'S ESTATE, which can serve as a typical example of the type of housing put up as part of Bermondsey's energetic slum clearance programme between the wars. The splayed layout and modernistic details are a little more adventurous than most contemporary work by the L.C.C. Further E, ST JOHN'S ESTATE, of the same period, extended by a paved square, a raw red-brick block of flats (with private gardens) and a boys' club, by *Peter Moro & Partners*, 1969. Back in TOOLEY STREET, No. 283 (Southwark Social Services), by *Newman & Newman*, 1898, built as St Olave's Union office: quite a grand Jacobean building with three shaped gables.

2 N of Tooley Street the riverside streets, notably SHAD THAMES, the most dramatic industrial street surviving in London. The towering warehouses and lattice wrought-iron bridges crossing at all heights still remain much in their Victorian state. Doré has immortalized the Dante-cum-Piranesi appearance of such areas. At the W end COURAGE'S ANCHOR BREWERY, founded 1789, much rebuilt after a fire in 1891, closed 1982. Part of the street façade appears mid C 19. The street then runs in a canyon between the late C 19 six- to eight-storey BUTLER'S WHARF warehouses, which extend 150 yards inland in this block. Opposite the quay entrance, a clock with an ornamental setting dated 1891–2. At the corner of Maguire

Street, a very large four-and-a-half-storey granary, earlier
C19, the street frontages refaced later in grey brick. SHAD
THAMES PUMPING STATION for storm drainage, 1906–8
by the *L.C.C.*, is of glazed brick and terracotta. Then tall
concrete-framed warehouses from between the two wars,
some bridging the street. Shad Thames turns S here to skirt
the 300-yard-long tidal inlet of St Saviour's Dock (the one-
time mouth of the River Neckinger, which led towards Bermondsey Abbey), which is surrounded by grain and pea and
spice mills. Mainly of the second half of the C19, these follow
the narrow plots of earlier wharves, and a variegated succession of façades from four to seven storeys twists towards
Dockhead. Several buildings have small wooden mullioned
windows and timber interiors, a characteristic of mills and
granaries of this area, while No. 1 Wharf and Shuter's Wharf
have distinctive flat tops to their broad gabled roofs. St
George's Wharf has discrete bands of blue brick and a cornice,
and very small cast-iron windows. Lime Wharf, dated 1883, is
untypical, in red brick with a gabled sack hoist. The landside
mill of St Andrew's Wharf (Butler's Grinders) has a prominent water tower, for fire protection, and a mid-C19 cast-iron
footbridge across the street. More mills and granaries down
the E side of the dock in MILL STREET, including Unity
Wharf and Mill Wharf. The six-storeyed St Saviour's Wharf is
more in the general warehouse style, as are the warehouses
round the yard of New Concordia Wharf. They formed part of
the St Saviour's Flour Mill, established in 1882 and reconstructed in 1894–8 after a series of fires. Still with timber floors
and beams on circular cast-iron columns. The mill itself is
marked by its water tower and chimney, truncated in 1979.*
Reed's Wharf with wooden windows terminates the sequence.
Spiller's biscuit works, opposite, on a more extensive scale
from 1905 onwards.

Jacob's Island was the site of some of the worst mid-C19 slums.
The area was first built over around 1700, but the evidence for
that period has now vanished.‡ The most interesting result of
slum clearance is a little further on, around WILSON GROVE,
an oasis of garden-city cottages of 1928 by *Culpin & Bowers*,
built in reaction to the tenement tradition of the area (cf. Fair
Street) at the instigation of the local M.P., Dr Alfred Salter.
At Chambers Wharf in BERMONDSEY WALL WEST,
another granary-style warehouse of *c.* 1865. Then the large
Chambers Wharf Cold Stores of the 1930s, with decorative
brickwork on the street side. In FARNCOMBE STREET, the
DUFFIELD SLUICE, on a former drainage outfall, a small
puritan building of 1822 for the local Commissioners of
Sewers.

* New Concordia Wharf was converted to workshops, offices, and flats in
1981–3 by *Pollard Thomas Edwards & Associates* in succession to *Nicholas Lacey
& Associates.*

‡ Until 1950 there survived a row of houses in East Lane, and one delightfully
wealthy house at the N end of George Row, dated 1706, but still with curved
gables of the mid C17, and a very fine shell hood over the door.

Once densely and evocatively packed with riverside warehouses and mills, BERMONDSEY WALL EAST from here to Rotherhithe is now a desert, with two solitary warehouses and the lonely ANGEL INN with a picturesque, partly weatherboarded river front. The buildings have been replaced by a riverside park (*see* below, Rotherhithe, Perambulation 3).

2. *Central Bermondsey*

For the centre of Bermondsey one must start again in ST THOMAS STREET from the old border with Southwark. The change from borough to borough used to be a change of industry (from hops to leather), reflected in a change of smell. The traditional centre of the Bermondsey leather trade is the former LEATHER MARKET in WESTON STREET, established in 1833, a dignified building of stock brick with giant pilasters in the centre, and arched doorways at the ends (one surviving) for the vans to drive in. Next door the LEATHER HIDE AND WOOL EXCHANGE of 1878 by *George Elkington & Sons*, with a big porch with atlas figures and delightful roundels showing leather industry scenes. The W side of Weston Street is all new, but down LEATHERMARKET STREET there are still plenty of older industrial buildings. Nos. 1–5 and 2–4 are mid C19, with boldly modelled brick façades and circular corner towers topped by chimneypots. Other warehouses in TYERS GATE (diamond pattern window grilles) and MOROCCO STREET. Back in WESTON STREET, MESSRS VOS, leather merchants, brick and stucco offices of the mid C19.

BERMONDSEY STREET, the old High Street connecting the riverside with the parish church, still has a recognizably village character, even though the older houses are interrupted by C19 warehouses and factories and by C20 lorry forecourts in front of even bigger buildings. The S end near the church is the most coherent part, but the best house is at the N end: No. 78, late C17, with a pretty oriel window, and a double overhang; the top floor weatherboarded. Around it, an irregular C18 group with stuccoed fronts (Nos. 68–72, 74–76). Further S a plain terrace dated 1828 (Nos. 124–130) and No. 191, set back next to the church, also early C19, a grey-brick house of three bays with a gable treated as a pediment. The best of the commercial buildings are No. 103, a single bay with a three-centred arch below a gable; No. 173, earlier C19, four storeys with fine Tuscan cornice and giant pilasters; and Nos. 180–182 with Gothic wrought-iron grilles and cast-iron colonnette mullions. In TANNER STREET, SARSONS MALT VINEGAR WORKS, with oak vats standing in the open, and more good small late C19 industrial buildings further E.

At the S end of Bermondsey Street near the parish church, in the large former churchyard, an early C19 stuccoed WATCH HOUSE. The church lay just to the N of the ABBEY, but of the great abbey church itself no trace is left. Abbey Street, laid out in 1820, is on the site of the nave. The crossing was near the junction with Tower Bridge Road, which in 1905 was cut diagonally across the site of the cloister and the C16 mansion of Sir Thomas Pope to the S. BERMONDSEY SQUARE is on the site of the inner court, which lay W of the cloister. In its S W corner some plain early C19 terraces. The only medieval remnant *in situ* is in GRANGE WALK off to the E, which led to the Priory Grange. Nos. 5, 6, and 7 are a group with gables to the road and, although much remodelled, are recognizably one side of a late medieval GATEHOUSE.* The chamfered order on the l. of No. 6 was the S jamb of the gateway. Nos. 8–11, a nice group with mostly segment-headed windows and two doors with carved bracket, date from *c.* 1700. At the corner of Griggs Place a former CHARITY SCHOOL FOR GIRLS, dated 1830, brick, with round-headed windows on the upper floor. (No. 67 is early C18, five bays and two storeys.) Parallel with Grange Walk GRANGE ROAD, with only scrappy Georgian bits: Nos. 8–11 at the beginning – BACON'S FREE SCHOOL, rebuilt in 1891;‡ No. 44, *c.* 1800, formerly one of a pair, two storeys with big Ionic porch; and Nos. 170–174 opposite, earlier C19 (porches with wreaths on the lintels). Then the ALASKA FACTORY with a gateway with a seal, dated 1869, and MARTIN'S 1930s-modern factory behind. Further on, set back from the main road, BOUT-CHER SCHOOL, 1871–2 by *Joseph Gale* of Bermondsey, a picturesque group of an L-shaped school building of two storeys with gabled upper windows with plate tracery, a tower over the porch, and a schoolmaster's house on the r., also with a tower.

The SETCHELL ESTATE begins behind Boutcher School. By 111 *Neylan & Ungless*, for Southwark, 1972–8, one of the most deliberately villagey groups of low-rise housing to be built in inner London in the 1970s. Nothing over three storeys (312 dwellings at 136 p.p.a.). The houses are loosely grouped in terraces of different heights. They have steeply pitched tiled roofs and pale brick walls, with upper parts rendered or tile-hung (an echo perhaps of Bermondsey's pre-war housing, cf. Wilson Grove above). The layout follows the old street

* The priory has never been properly excavated. Evidence for the buildings depends chiefly on a few fragments, and on drawings made by J. C. Buckler before 1820. Surviving carved pieces (a capital in the church (q.v.) and other fragments in the Cuming Museum Southwark) show that there was lavish decoration of the earlier C12 (perhaps in the cloister). Documentary evidence indicates much rebuilding of the E end in the C13 to C14 (choir altar dedicated 1206, building indulgences 1286, further consecrations 1338). The chapel of the Holy Cross, for the miracle-working rood, was being built *c.* 1230. Cloister and refectory were rebuilt in 1380. Sir Thomas Pope's house was built in the mid C16 on the site of the cloister W range, with a garden on the site of the church. A late medieval gatehouse between the outer and inner courtyards (at the N entrance to Bermondsey Square) survived until 1820. See A. R. Martin, 'On the topography of the Cluniac Abbey of St Saviour at Bermondsey', *Journal Brit. Arch. Ass.*, no. 32 (1927).

‡ The bust of Josiah Bacon by *William Cox* is now in Bacon's Comprehensive School, Delaford Road.

pattern, but with cul-de-sacs for cars alternating with pedestrian walks. The spine is a broad gravelled way planted with trees. At one end of this is the TENANTS' HALL, with a very steep, rather mannered, roof. The details everywhere have been given above-average attention: note the decorative ridge tiles (even on garage roofs), the ingenious variety of private spaces, and the subtle changes in the widths of the pathways.

SPA ROAD leads NE from Grange Road, with public buildings (q.v.). At its N end it is crossed by an early viaduct* for the London and Greenwich Railway, 1833–6 by *G. Landmann*. The bridge here, and another in Abbey Street, is on Greek Doric cast-iron columns. Nothing else in this area except for an early C 19 group in ABBEY STREET (Nos. 140–148). From Bermondsey Square one can return W along LONG LANE, connecting the parish churches of Bermondsey and St George, Southwark. A bitty street, much renewed, with C 19 industrial buildings. No. 239, a large warehouse used by fur dressers, has a lively façade of *c.* 1875, with cast-iron colonnettes dividing the windows. No. 217, former multi-storey stables over cart sheds, is of 1886 by *J. Butterworth*. Internal ramps beneath the belfry-cum-ventilator at the gable end. Also some handsome older houses, including Nos. 135–145, early C 19, and Nos. 142–152, incorporating an early C 18 pair, each of three bays. No. 148 has a fine doorway with curly broken pediment on Corinthian pilasters, and a good interior (in one room a marble chimneypiece with scenes of the leather trade).

3. Rotherhithe

The essential walk is along ROTHERHITHE STREET, all round the Thames bend from the W to the E end of the street. The chief features used to be the impressive relation of street to tall warehouses and of warehouses to damp alleyways leading to river stairs. This survives now only in a few places, and the houses that remained to indicate a still older past have also nearly all gone.‡ At the beginning of the walk all has given way to the extended Southwark Park. S of this and its Jubilee boulder monument, No. 23 PARADISE STREET, a plain three-bay, three-storey villa of stock brick, built in 1814 and later used as a police station. Nice ironwork lampholder; on the l. a four-bay addition.

After Elephant Lane the group around St Mary's church preserves something of the atmosphere of Victorian Rotherhithe, with tall mid-C 19 warehouses crowding around the few remaining older buildings of the riverside village,

---

* The whole viaduct is 3¾ miles long, a quite remarkable length.

‡ Among the older houses lost in the mid-C 20 transformation of Rotherhithe: No. 41 Cherry Garden Street, late C 18 with simple but graceful door surrounds; Nos. 6 and 26–34 Mayflower Street, terraces of 1721–6; and No. 49 Rotherhithe Street, *c.* 1700. Among the warehouses: No. 141 Rotherhithe Street (Cumberland Wharf), *c.* 1800. Also Park Buildings, Rotherhithe Street (early Bermondsey council flats), by *Marchment & East*, 1903.

although the bustle of riverside industry has gone. At the time of writing some of the warehouses are derelict, others have new uses (printers, theatre, craft workshops in Hope Sufferance Wharf). The remaining warehouses include: EAST INDIA WHARF, extensive four-storey granaries; HOPE SUFFERANCE WHARF, a variegated group including a long three-storey early C19 granary with a hipped roof; THAMES TUNNEL MILLS, various dates, up to seven storeys (to be) converted to flats); and GRICES WHARF (four storeys) and GRANARY (c. 1797, three storeys, rounded corners). Facing the s side of the church in this quiet backwater, the former PETER HILLS SCHOOL, a three-storey, three-bay house with quoin strips. It must date from c. 1700, though the school moved into it only in 1797; the two pretty little figures of schoolchildren on the first floor also c. 1700. In the former churchyard to the w of the school, WATCH HOUSE and ENGINE HOUSE, both dated 1821. Back in Rotherhithe Street the MAYFLOWER INN, a picturesque pastiche, and a little further on, after the early C20 L.C.C. flats, *Sir Marc Brunel*'s ENGINE HOUSE for his Thames tunnel of 1825–53, a small building with a square battered chimney built probably in 1842 and altered several times. Restored in 1976, when the raised brick paved piazza was added. Near by is the original tunnel access shaft (*see* Thames Crossings). In REN-FORTH STREET a large PUMPING STATION of the London Hydraulic Power Company, 1902–3, with chimney, roof-top tanks, and accumulator tower with fancy brickwork.*

Further on are a lock entrance and the vast vacant stretches of the SURREY DOCKS now under redevelopment (*see* Public Buildings), a fringe of C20 council houses and industry by the river, and a good way on at GLOBE WHARF (No. 205) the THAMES RICE MILLS, built c. 1883 as a grain warehouse, a vast six-storey block with giant pilasters. Further again NEL-SON DOCK HOUSE (No. 265), which affords the one possibility on the river of visualizing the comfortable life of a well-to-do C18 shipbuilder. A mansion of five bays with a cupola on the roof, and a handsome front with good iron gate, tripartite entrance up a stone stair, Venetian window on the first floor, and an ornamental circular window on the floor above, all in a stone surround. Next to Nelson Dock at Columbia Wharf a late C19 brick granary in an unusual Moorish style.

Inland very little of note except for those interested in post-war council housing. Hardly anything older remains, apart from some minor early C19 terraces in JAMAICA ROAD (Nos. 124 etc.) and at the s end of LOWER ROAD. The chief landmarks are the county council estates, dating from the most domineering period of the *L.C.C.* and *G.L.C.*'s *Architect's Department*. E of Lower Road first the CANADA ESTATE, 1962–4, with the

* At HORSEFERRY WHARF, a large riverside warehouse with shuttered concrete walls and mushroom-pier construction. By *Joseph Hill*, 1937, for the Vitrea Drawn Sheet Glass Company.

tough concrete detailing typical of that time (perhaps thought suitable for a tough dockland area). Low maisonettes and two lumpy twenty-one-storey towers with every fourth floor recessed (two-room flats between the three-room ones). Further s in a smoother idiom the five-storey slabs of the OSPREY ESTATE (*Yorke, Rosenberg & Mardall*, 1946–9). s of ROTHERHITHE NEW ROAD a sad, confused jumble of flats and industry, chiefly the L.C.C.'s SILWOOD ESTATE (*c.* 1955 onwards). The earlier part still has some of the idealism of the post-war L.C.C., with its effort at a public space (SCULPTURE by *U. Nimptsch*) opposite St Katherine's church, surrounded by plain blocks with painted concrete frames, and one eleven-storey slab on stilts. The hefty sixteen-storey towers further N are an addition of 1958–66. Even more insensitive than these is the twenty-six-storey tower of the ABBEYFIELD ESTATE (1965–7), whose afternoon shadow stretches halfway across Southwark Park, a typical example of how existing open spaces were used to justify, and then were spoilt by, high-rise flats on their borders. For SOUTHWARK PARK itself *see* Public Buildings, above. Contributions by *Southwark Borough Council* to this area need only brief mention: N of Southwark Park Road the bleak ROUEL ROAD ESTATE (1970–5), three to seven storeys, with its barrier block along the railway line (relieved by miniature upper gardens by *Maurice Pickering*), to the s, THORBURN SQUARE, rebuilt as a pedestrian precinct around the Victorian church of St Anne, and, near the Silwood Estate, SILVERLOCK, six-storey flats with projecting balconies in a watered-down Lillington Gardens style (by *Stock Page & Stock*, 1977–8).

Back near Jamaica Road, the development between KEETONS ROAD and St James's church by *Neylan & Ungless*, begun in 1981, adopts a friendlier style: low, well detailed terraces, brick with white plastered upper floors, arranged round a variety of closes and courtyards (cf. the same firm's Setchell Estate, Perambulation 2, above).

CAMBERWELL

CHURCHES

The medieval parish church of St Giles was supplemented by several proprietary chapels in the late Georgian period. Only the one in Camberwell Grove remains. There have been demolitions, but fewer than in Southwark or Bermondsey.* Apart from

* Demolished since 1950: ST CHRYSOSTOM, Hill Street. Built as a proprietary chapel in 1813, nice stuccoed 'Commissioners' Gothic front, thin intersected tracery. The interior with three galleries on thin iron shafts. – CAMDEN CHURCH, Peckham Road. Built in 1795 for the Countess of Huntingdon's Connexion, much enlarged 1814. Chancel 1854 by *Scott* in a Byzantine style said to be the outcome of consultation with *Ruskin*.

Bedford's neo-classical St George, Wells Way, of 1822, and *Scott*'s serious Gothic rebuilding of St Giles of 1844, Camberwell churches are chiefly interesting for two reasons. The first is the vast number of the minor later Victorian churches built to serve the expanding suburbs. They include interesting works by lesser known architects (St Barnabas by *W. H. Wood*, St Bartholomew by *E. Taprell Allen*) as well as churches by more familiar names such as *Bassett Keeling* (Christ Church, St Andrew), *Banks & Barry* (St Stephen), *Barry Jun.* (St Peter), *Street* (St Paul), and *Norman Shaw* (St Mark). The remains of the ambitious Catholic Apostolic Church (now Greek Orthodox Cathedral), an early work by *Belcher*, deserves special mention. The second group of interest is the post-Second-World-War replacements. The hesitant progress of modern church design from the early fifties to mid sixties is charted by St Luke, St Faith, St Mary, St Philip, and St John.

ALL SAINTS, Blenheim Grove, w of Rye Lane, s of the station. 1870–2 by *H. E. Coe*. A humble building of ragstone, with apse and a wide aisled nave.

CHRIST CHURCH, Old Kent Road. By *E. Bassett Keeling*, 1867–8, replacing a church across the road of 1837. Polychrome brick, with a SE tower and a big Dec chancel window facing the road. The interior remodelled after war damage by *T. F. Ford*.

ST ANDREW, Glengall Road, NE continuation of Peckham Hill Street. Now the Celestial Church of Christ (Nigeria). 1864–5, also by *E. Bassett Keeling*. Ragstone, with a low, oddly de-tailed NW tower which has lost its spire, w narthex, and large w window. Irregular plan: N aisle and transept, but on the s side only a narrow passage. Wilful plate tracery. (Arcades with short granite columns; carved capitals dated 1872, 1876, 1884. Roof with decorative notched arch braces, dimly lit chancel (a Keeling feature), and apsed sanctuary. – PULPIT. Elaborate five-sided piece of different woods, with marquetry panels with figures.)

ST ANTHOLIN, Nunhead Lane. 1877–8 by *Ewan Christian*. Red brick, lancet style. The w end demolished after war damage and replaced by a single-storey vicarage with an enclosed garden. The restoration, completed in 1957, was by *Laurence King*. – REREDOS from *Wren*'s St Antholin, Watling Street, also damaged, but skilfully restored. A noble composition with the decalogue in the centre, and in the side-pieces, flanked by Corinthian demi-columns and crowned by seg-mental pediments, the Lord's Prayer and the Creed.

(ST AUGUSTINE, Honor Oak Park, SE of Brenchley Gardens. 1872–3 by *William Oakley*. Ragstone. Tower completed 1888; N aisle enlarged 1900 by *Grose*. – STAINED GLASS. w window and one s window by *Heaton, Butler & Bayne*.)

ST BARNABAS, Calton Avenue, between Dulwich Village and East Dulwich Grove. 1892–5 by *W. H. Wood* of *Oliver, Leeson & Wood* of Newcastle. The big square tower was added in

1908. The church is of very red brick with Perp tracery of North English character. Interior with tall octagonal piers without capitals and no division between nave and chancel. Lean-to aisle roofs and small clerestory windows. – FURNISHINGS. Much woodwork of 1895 onwards by *F. E. Day*. – STAINED GLASS. E window by *E. B. Powell*, 1922, quite good.

ST BARTHOLOMEW, Barkworth Road. *See* Bermondsey.

ST FAITH, Sunray Avenue, Herne Hill. 1958–9 by *David Nye & Partners*. Red-brick exterior in a debased Gothic. The surprise inside is the elaboration of the E end: a polygonal Lady Chapel behind an apsed sanctuary, reached by a minute ambulatory, but glimpsed from the nave through an open screen behind the altar. – Narrow lancets in the Lady Chapel with STAINED GLASS.

The CHURCH HALL (previously used, although not intended, as a church) was more progressive for its date: 1907–8 by *Greenaway & Newberry*. Small, with a big dormered slate roof starting low down, and a low arched W window between stumpy turrets.

76 ST GEORGE, Wells Way, corner of St George's Way. The oldest Anglican church in Camberwell, disused since 1970, and since gutted by fire and vandalism. 1822–4 by *Bedford*, who also built the 'Waterloo Churches' at Norwood and in Waterloo Road. St George is more or less a replica of St John, Waterloo Road: hexastyle Greek Doric giant portico and W tower of two stages behind. The interior had three galleries inside on Greek Doric columns; flat ceiling. Apse added by *Basil Champneys*, 1893, when the choir was raised; much internal embellishment 1909. The position of the church originally had much charm. It stood alongside the Surrey Canal close to a bridge in what must have been a handsome neighbourhood. It is now on the edge of the new Burgess Park.

ST GILES, Camberwell Church Street. The parish church of Camberwell was destroyed by fire in 1841. *Scott & Moffat* won the competition for the rebuilding. The executed structure was simpler than the first design, which had included a vault in terracotta. During building Scott was converted to the use of 'real' materials, and the details were all in stone. It was completed in 1844. The style is a rather raw E.E., not yet as refined and competent as Scott was to be later. Yet the *Ecclesiologist* said of it: 'On the whole a magnificent work', and Eastlake in his *Gothic Revival*: 'In the neighbourhood of London no church was considered in purer style'. Large, with spire of restless yet heavy detail over the crossing. The tracery is cut by machine. – Inside, the C 14 SEDILIA and PISCINA of the old church preserved. – STAINED GLASS. W window with late C 13 grisaille said to come from Trier. – E window by *Ward & Nixon*, based on designs by *Ruskin* and *Edmund Oldfield*, a splendid composition of rich purple and red medallions, obviously inspired by Chartres. – Chancel windows: angels in foiled circles, all that remains from windows by *Lavers & Barraud*. – Transepts: depressingly crude glass by *Comper* replacing two excellent *Morris* windows destroyed in the war. – MONUMENTS. Little of interest. On the S wall of the S transept a number of late BRASSES, including a C15 knight and several kneeling couples with children, e.g. John Bowyer † 1570, wife and eleven children. – Nothing else to note except the Masterman monument († 1927) with good plain lettering by *Eric Gill* (moved from St George), and a tablet to Captain A. Nairne († 1866), Gothic, with a ship, by *Gaffin*.

ST GILES CENTRE, across the road on the site of the vicarage, was built in 1967.

ST JOHN, Meeting House Lane, between Peckham High Street and Asylum Road. By *David Bush*, 1965–6. One of the most interesting of the borough's post-war churches. It stands on the site of the bombed church of St Jude by *Blomfield* of 1875–6. The exterior is dominated by the big sloping roof, which breaks upward at the end to give the impression of a tower. Inside is a generous foyer, the small chapel of St Jude opening off a corridor, and the large, dimly lit rectangular space of the church itself. Plain interior with exposed brick walls embellished only by a bronze Crucifixion (from the former church of St Chrysostom). The altar is fixed on a platform in one corner (an old-fashioned arrangement). – On the other side a brilliantly coloured semi-abstract STAINED GLASS window with the Creation, by *Susan Johnson*. – Also by her the window with the Crucifixion in the corridor, and one inspired by the design of the church in the chapel of St Jude. – SCULPTURE. Mother and Child, fibreglass, by *Ron Hinton*.

ST JOHN, East Dulwich Road. 1863–5 by *Charles Bailey*. Ragstone, with a tower with broach-spire. Vestries added 1883 and 1914. Reconstructed after war damage by *J. B. S. Comper*, 1951, with a new clerestory, concrete vault, and simpler details. – CIBORIUM and STAINED GLASS also by *Comper*.

ST LUKE, Farnborough Way, between St George's Way and Commercial Way. 1953–4, begun by *A. C. Martin*, completed by *Milner & Craze*. Large, brick, neo-Byzantine, with central crossing tower and apse.

ST MARK, Cobourg Road, off Old Kent Road between Albany Road and Trafalgar Street. The chancel and part of the nave 1879–80, S chancel aisle 1883–4, designed by *Norman Shaw*. The rest not completed until 1932. Not a very inspired work, nothing like, for example, St Michael, Bedford Park (Ho). Hall-church with octagonal brick piers and wooden vaults, decidedly Dutch in feeling. Stone screen wall of Perp detail between nave and chancel, carried right up to the chancel arch. The W baptistery also as tall as the nave and chancel. The woodwork was of pine, stained green. The church is now used as a store.

ST MARY, St Mary's Road. 1961–2 by *Robert Potter* of *Potter & Hare*. One of the first new churches in London designed for the liturgical movement (cf. St. Paul, Bow Common, TH).*

* Early examples by this firm are the Ascension, Crown Hill, Plymouth, and St George, Oakdale Park.

Centrally planned, cruciform, and very light and transparent, with the interior on view to the outside world (in contrast to most churches of the later 1960s; cf. St John, Peckham). The four big gables are all glazed with clear glass. There are roof lights as well, rising to a small central flèche. The w gable cants outwards. The church replaces a bombed building of 1839–41.

ST PAUL, Herne Hill. A rebuilding by *Street*, 1858, of a church of 1843–4 by *G. Alexander* which had been damaged by fire. The w tower, spire, and long outer nave walls of the typical Commissioners' church were kept, but *Street* enlarged the chancel and embellished the interior with carving by *Earp* and stained glass by *Hardman*. The result was much praised by Ruskin. The nave columns have lusciously carved crocket capitals; the clerestory has trefoil arcading on short marble shafts in front of the quatrefoil windows. The chancel has more marble, and a large Dec E window. – FONT and PULPIT, pinkish sandstone and marble, clearly of the same date. – ROOD SCREEN of 1921. – REREDOS. Alabaster and marble, with carved heads, in the same style as the MONUMENT to Captain James Horsbach († 1836 but obviously erected later), navigator and hydrographer, with a relief of a ship. – John Ruskin † 1900, a tablet recording his early life at Denmark Hill, rather surprisingly, a profile medallion in a Renaissance aedicule with medieval foliage. – STAINED GLASS. Mostly lost in the Second World War. The excellent w windows of the aisles survive, also some small upper lights elsewhere. – VICARAGE, E of the church, an excellent *Street* design with projecting porch, hipped gable, and a little Gothic detail.

ST PETER, Lordship Lane, Dulwich. 1873–4 by *Charles Barry Jun*. The tower with its slated broach-spire not completed until 1885; the w part of the nave begun 1885. Kentish rag with remarkably lavish polychrome interior. Marble columns, coloured brickwork, and terracotta diapering *à la* Westminster Abbey. – STAINED GLASS. w window with pictorial scenes of *c.* 1891.

ST PHILIP, Avondale Square, off Old Kent Road w of Rotherhithe New Road. 1963 by *N. F. Cachemaille Day*, replacing a bombed church of 1875. A modest brick building which makes a pleasant group with the older church hall and vicarage in an area otherwise entirely rebuilt. The plan is an octagon within a square. Chapel, porch, and vestry neatly fitted into the triangular corners. Simple white interior with icon-like PAINTING of a Crucifixion above the altar, and a delicate CEILING PAINTING with angels, both by *John Hayward*.

ST SAVIOUR (now also United Reformed Church), Copleston Road, NW of East Dulwich Road off Grove Vale. 1880–1 by *Weeks & Hughes*. Of brick, aisled. Converted into the COPLESTONE CENTRE, with small church, large hall, and offices, in 1978 by *T. F. Ford & Partners*.

St Silas, Ivydale Road, Nunhead. 1902–13 by *J. E. K. & J. P. Cutts*. Ragstone, Dec.

St Stephen, College Road, Dulwich. 1867–75 by *Banks & Barry*. Ragstone with a slated spire (cf. St Peter) and gabled clerestory. Inside, PAINTINGS of the trial and stoning of St Stephen by *Sir E. Poynter*, 1872. – (STAINED GLASS. E windows by *Kempe*; w window by *M. Forsyth*, 1952.)

Our Lady of Sorrows (R.C.), Bird in Bush Road, E of N end of Peckham Hill Street. 1864–6 by *E. W. Pugin*. A large church of stock brick with stone dressings, lancet and Dec windows, and a cheap whitewashed interior.

Sacred Heart (R.C.), Camberwell New Road. Brick, rebuilt in 1953 by *D. Plaskett Marshall*, but looking like a building of the 1930s.* The nave is stepped in narrowing sections to baffle noise from the railway.

(St Alban (R.C.), Herring Street. 1903 by *F. W. Tasker*. Romanesque. DE)

(St Thomas More (R.C.), Lordship Lane. 1929 by *J. Goldie*. Restored after war damage 1953. Lady Chapel 1970. – STAINED GLASS by *Patrick Pye*. DE)

St Mary, Camberwell New Road. Cathedral (since 1977) of the Greek Orthodox Church, which in 1963 took over the building put up in 1873 for the Catholic Apostolic Church. The architects were *J. & J. Belcher*. Brick with plate tracery. Facing the road a tiny cloister and numerous church rooms as required by the Catholic Apostolic church (cf. their former church in Bloomsbury, now Christ the King, Ca). The church behind is on quite an ambitious scale, with apse and transepts, but was truncated after war damage, so that the western part of the nave now forms a small open courtyard.

Baptist Chapel, Rye Lane. 1863 by *Bland*. An imposing front with projecting central pediment and Tuscan columns.

Calvary Temple (United Pentecostal Church), Councillor Street, NE off Camberwell New Road just w of the railway. Dated 1891 – a late example of the use of Italianate details. Arcaded porch and tower with open belfry in front of a brick church with an apse.

Clubland Church (Methodist), Camberwell Road. Bland post-war rebuilding has replaced *E. Maufe*'s somewhat modernistic façade of 1928–30. This was built together with a hostel on the site of a chapel put up by *Michael Searles* in 1813.

Emmanuel United Reformed Church, Lordship Lane. A large ragstone Dec building with a prominent spire terminating the view down Barry Road. By *W. D. Church*, 1890–1. It could be mistaken for a C of E church were it not for the huge Sunday Schools next door of 1898.

Friends' Meeting House (former), Highshore Road, w off the N end of Rye Lane, Peckham. 1826, enlarged 1843. Stock brick, extremely simple and yet distinguished, owing

* It replaces a church of 1863 by *C. A. Buckler*, destroyed in the Second World War.

mainly to the one subtle detail that the two wings projecting from a pedimented centre with a one-storey Tuscan colonnade have their corners rounded.

GROVE CHAPEL, Camberwell Grove. Pretty, late Georgian chapel with a five-bay, two-storey front, very modest. *Coade* stone date plaque. Built in 1819 by *David Roper*.

PECKHAM METHODIST CHURCH, Woods Road, s of the w end of Queen's Road. Low, with a half-gable and clerestory along one side. By *Gordon Bowyer & Partners*, 1972–4. With the housing near by, it replaces the chapel in Queen's Road.*

NUNHEAD CEMETERY.‡ The fifty-one acres of the cemetery of All Saints, Nunhead, in a picturesquely hilly position, were consecrated in 1840. This cemetery, like Highgate, was laid out by the London Cemetery Company to designs by *James Bunning*, architect to the company. A formal drive approaches the ruined Anglican chapel through noble cast-iron entrance gates and classical piers of Portland stone. Just inside are two charming lodges of exquisite neo-classical design. Bunning designed both gates and lodges. The paths through the cemetery are circuitous and winding, apart from the main axial drive and a subsidiary path at right angles to this main avenue. These serpentine paths recall Bunning's layout at Highgate. The monuments in Nunhead are not as distinguished as those in many other London cemeteries, perhaps reflecting the less socially elite classes buried there. Among the most impressive is the high granite obelisk erected in 1851 to commemorate the Scots martyrs to the cause of Parliamentary Reform. *Thomas Little* won a competition to build the chapels in 1844. His designs (which survive) were in the Decorated style of Gothic; the materials were Kentish rag with freestone dressings. The Dissenters' chapel has been demolished, and the Anglican chapel is in ruins. The shaft catacomb has been filled in, and the rectangular catacomb sealed up. Nunhead Cemetery was purchased in 1976 by the borough of Southwark. Part will be retained as a cemetery, while other parts will be laid out for recreation.

CAMBERWELL NEW CEMETERY, Brenchley Gardens. Chapel, quite impressively neo-Gothic, by *Sir Aston Webb & Sons*, 1930; brick, Italianate crematoria by *W. Bell* and *Maurice Webb*, 1939.

PUBLIC BUILDINGS

SOUTHWARK TOWN HALL, Peckham Road. Built as Camberwell Town Hall in 1934 by *E. C. Culpin & Bowers*. Singularly undistinguished. Adjoining buildings are also used as council offices (*see* St Giles Hospital and Perambulation 2).

MAGISTRATES' COURT, D'Eynsford Road, facing a plaza off

* This was a monstrously ugly building of 1864 by *Hoole*, with a demonstratively asymmetrical and crazily detailed NW turret.

‡ This entry was contributed by James Stevens Curl.

Camberwell Green. 1965–9. Large, dull, stone-faced building with green tinted windows.

POLICE STATION, Camberwell Church Street. 1898. Arts and Crafts style, with a bold stone hood over the doorway.

FIRE STATION (now Ambulance Station), Old Kent Road and Shorncliffe Road. *L.C.C.* work of 1903.

NORTH PECKHAM CIVIC CENTRE (library and public rooms), Old Kent Road and Peckham Park Road. By the Southwark Borough Architect's Department (*F. O. Hayes*), 1962–7. Three plain yellow-brick storeys over a recessed ground floor with ceramic mural by *A. Kossowski*. In the LIBRARY a steel MOBILE of the Camberwell Beauty Butterfly by *Brian Kneale*.

KINGSWOOD HOUSE, Bowen Drive, off Kingswood Drive, Dulwich. Now a library and community centre for the post-war L.C.C. estate that fills the grounds. A substantial villa built in the form of a rambling stone-faced baronial castle by *H. V. Lanchester* for L. J. Johnstone, the founder of Bovril, in 1892. It cost £20,000. Additions on the w side 1897 (rainwater head). It was apparently constructed around an older house, although little evidence of this remains apart from some cornices upstairs. It was Lanchester's first building, and is without the exuberant decoration characteristic of the firm after Rickards joined it (*see* Deptford (Le) Town Hall). Plain, quite austere exterior with mullioned windows and battlements, reminiscent of Shaw's most severe country-house style (Flete, Devon, and the plainer parts of Cragside) and with not a whiff of half-timbering. Decoration is confined to some delicate Renaissance panels around the l. bay-window, and to the bold segment-headed door arches. To the l. of the projecting porches, the great hall (now library) on the ground floor only, but quite tall, with the unusual feature of a gallery over an ingle-nook fireplace, and a separate room opening off in the corner bay-window. Behind the hall a room with a lavish plaster ceiling in the Jacobean manner. Modest staircase. The upper floor is on two levels, because of the height of the hall, divided by an E–W corridor. In the main front room an C18 fireplace. On the garden side on the ground floor two projecting rooms, the E one domed; the W one (the former billiard room) is now the children's library.

LIBRARY and BATHS, Wells Way, between Albany Road and Southampton Way. 1902 by *Maurice Adams*, a picturesque group with Baroque porch, Gothic gable, Tudor windows, and a Queen Anne bay-window, and yet quite successful and typical of 1900. (Inside, mosaic of the Camberwell Beauty butterfly (*c.* 1920), moved from Samuel Jones's factory in Southampton Way.)

EAST DULWICH LIBRARY, Lordship Lane and Woodwarde Road. A pretty corner building of 1896 by *Charles Barry Jun.*, with canted porch with semi-dome set at an angle.

LIVESEY MUSEUM, Old Kent Road. By *R. P. Whellock*, 1890. Built as a library, damaged in the war, repaired and converted to a museum in 1974 (by *M. & D. Dove*). (Mosaic panels from the demolished library of 1907 in Old and New Kent Road.)

CAMBERWELL PUBLIC BATHS, Artichoke Lane, N of Camberwell Church Street. With a big striped brick and stone shaped gable. 1891 by *Spalding & Cross*.

ST BARNABAS PARISH HALL, Dulwich Village. 1910, Arts and Crafts style, with big sweeping roofs, tile-hung gable, and cupola.

CAMBERWELL SCHOOL OF ARTS AND CRAFTS and PASS-MORE EDWARDS SOUTH LONDON ART GALLERY, Peckham Road. 1896–8, with baroque caryatids at the portal and baroque window pediments. By *Maurice Adams*. By the entrance to the gallery a SCULPTURE, bronze nude, by *Karel Vogel*. On the l. of the Art School, totally unsympathetic large concrete extension by *Murray, Ward & Partners*, c. 1960. Two long bands of windows with others of irregular shape in between.

WILLIAM BOOTH MEMORIAL TRAINING COLLEGE, Champion Park, between Denmark Hill and Grove Lane. By *Sir Giles Gilbert Scott*, 1932, with a symmetrical front centred on a massive tower similar to that of Scott's Cambridge University Library. Brick with Gothic stone detail, somewhat American Collegiate in flavour. In front of the building two bronze statues by *G. Wade* representing William Booth and Mrs Booth, 'promoted to glory'.

DULWICH COLLEGE, College Road. A complex of buildings all connected with the College of God's Gift, founded by Edward Alleyn, the actor who played Tamburlaine, Dr Faustus, and Barabbas in 'The Jew of Malta'. The old buildings are at the N end of College Road; the C19 college lies further S. Alleyn bought the land in 1605. The gift comprised a chapel, a school for twelve poor scholars, and twelve almshouses, all now called the OLD COLLEGE. The building contract was made in 1613 and makes it clear that the bricklayer-contractor *John Benson* designed the buildings. The almshouses (of which the E wing is now called EDWARD ALLEYN HOUSE) were opened in 1619. The college extends along three sides of a quadrangle, enclosed until 1866, when the excellent iron gates (by *G. Buncker*, 1728) were moved to their present position on the N side. The W range is now offices. The chapel is in the centre. The N front of chapel and schoolhouse originally had an order of giant Doric pilasters, a very remarkable feature for its date. The design is no longer easily recognizable, as the building has been much repaired and altered. The central tower fell in 1631, the W range had to be repaired after 1661, the E range was rebuilt (with pilasters and pediment) in 1738–9. Then in 1821 the college surveyor *George Tappen* (succeeded by *Sir Charles Barry* in 1831) covered the building in stucco and remodelled the E range. *Charles Barry Jun.* added the cloister and rebuilt the tower with a château roof in 1866. So the impression is now of a C19 building, stuccoed and with crudely sham-Tudor windows, but not lacking in appeal. The CHAPEL was remodelled and given a S aisle in 1823. The font is of 1729, designed by *Gibbs* and made by *Van Spangen*: a handsome marble bowl on a baluster; the inscription in Greek and reversible. Reredos of 1911 by *W. D. Caröe*. The OLD GRAMMAR SCHOOL, a small stuccoed building all on its own, standing opposite the W wing of the Old College at the corner of Gallery Road and Burbage Road, is also Tudor in style. It was built in 1841–2 by *Sir Charles Barry*.

DULWICH COLLEGE, NEW BUILDINGS. The old founda- 86 tion was reformed in 1857, and new, very much larger premises were provided for the school, ½ m. S down College Road. The architect was the younger *Charles Barry*, and the date 1866–70. It was one of the most ambitious school rebuildings of the period, made possible by the £100,000 provided as compensation by the railway lines which ran through the college estate. The new buildings planned for 600 boys consist of a symmetrical group of three large blocks connected by one-storey arcaded links (now glazed). The N and S blocks were intended for lower and upper schools respectively, each with classrooms behind a master's residence. The central block had lecture theatre and laboratory below an assembly hall (all progressive features for their time). The style is ornate North Italian Renaissance, with very elaborate multi-coloured decoration including much terracotta (one of the first places where it was employed as a building material on a large scale), and a fancifully exotic roofscape ('Chinese pagodas are temperate in comparison' said the *Building News* in 1869). The HALL has free Perp windows at either end, an open timber roof of hammerbeam type, and a central lantern. The corbels rest on marble columns. To its N the MASTERS' LIBRARY, with original shelves, and an early C17 overmantel with paintings of Pietas and Liberalitas, brought from the old school (acquired by Alleyn from a barge, it is said). To the N W the later library, by *E. T. Hall*, a small, rather jolly Baroque building of 1902, in brick and stone, typical of its date. To the S are two BOARDING HOUSES of 1932–3 (the school did not originally take boarders) by *Beresford Pite*, with big hipped roofs, and buildings of the 1950s onwards (the present number of pupils is *c.* 1,400). From N–S: SCIENCE BLOCK, *c.* 1950, then across the playground the small LOWER SCHOOL, 1948 and 1961, and to its W a group composed of REFECTORY and ARTS ROOMS around a small quadrangle open to the E. Concrete and dark brick in the tough idiom of the 1960s, with the exposed concrete frame coming forward as hoodmoulds over the upper windows, as deep projecting eaves over the glazed side walls of the refectory, and even repeated as part of the staircase structure within the foyer. E of College Road, GYMNASIUM, 1966, and behind this, the EDWARD ALLEYN HALL, 1981 by *Tim Foster* and *Theatre Projects Consultants*.

DULWICH PICTURE GALLERY, S of the Old College. By *John* 74 *Soane*, 1811–14, one of his most severely original works, badly damaged in the Second World War but repaired and reopened

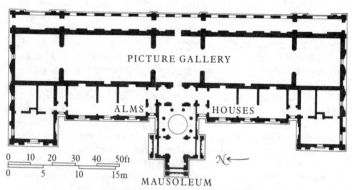

PICTURE GALLERY

ALMS   HOUSES

0 10 20 30 40 50ft
0   5   10   15m

MAUSOLEUM

Dulwich Picture Gallery, plan

in 1953, and redecorated (according to Soane's original schemes) in 1980–1. The almshouses on the w side were converted into galleries in the later c 19. Additional galleries on the e side. The gallery contains, apart from pictures left by Alleyn to the college, the Cartwright Collection (bequeathed 1686) and the collection brought together by the art-dealer Noel Desenfans for King Stanislas of Poland but in the end not sold to him. Desenfans left the paintings to Sir Francis Bourgeois, who in his turn left them to the college. Soane's building had to be an art gallery principally, but also to house a small mausoleum to Desenfans flanked by small almshouses. (Soane had already designed a mausoleum for Desenfans in his house in Charlotte Street in 1807.) Soane produced several ambitious schemes, but was restricted by lack of money. The total cost was under £10,000. The building is of stock brick, with stone dressings. One cannot do better than quote Sir John Summerson on gallery and mausoleum: 'Look first at the plan. The main element is the sequence of five galleries, three square and two oblong. Joined to this, at right angles, are two wings with lower buildings between them while in the centre of these is the mausoleum. Observe how carefully each element is given quasi-independence of its neighbour, chiefly by the device of making slight recessions in the plan where small entrance lobbies are introduced. This produces a curious tension throughout the design, each part bearing a distinct and intense relationship to the whole. The mausoleum is inset in the plan, but retains its identity entire. The low forebuildings are lodged between the mausoleum and wings without making direct contact with either . . . In the handling of the mausoleum (probably inspired by that of an Alexandrian catacomb . . . published 1809) the same quasi-detachment is noticeable. The portals in the open arches do not touch the jambs; and the frieze is recessed so that the cornice seems suspended over the piers instead of resting on them. The resulting composition is a quintessence. Inertia has been drained away; and yet further to increase the feeling of tension, the masonry of the lantern is delicately grooved – a "cat's cradle" of lines in tension. The interior of the mausoleum is a wonderful study of intersection and the building as a whole reaches a level of emotional eloquence and technical performance rare in English, or indeed in European architecture.' Attention may be drawn to a few more features. Soane uses the sturdy Greek Doric order inside the entrance room of the mausoleum, yet it carries merely a thin shallow dome. Yellow glass is used to create a different atmosphere from the galleries. The lantern rises above the 'chancel' behind the entrance room, supported only by equally thin-looking arcades without any articulation by capitals. The detail is everywhere highly personal. Soane never uses motifs because they were familiar or popular or academically welcome. The lantern especially is as original in its treatment of antique precedent as any by the boldest c 20 classicists, say Lutyens, and has indeed a distinct c 20 flavour.

Two further schools were established by Dulwich College Governors in the c 19: ALLEYN'S SCHOOL, Townley Road, a formal late c 19 Jacobean front with cupola (later additions); and JAMES ALLEN SCHOOL, East Dulwich Road, for girls, with early c 20 neo-Georgian buildings.

KINGSDALE SCHOOL, Alleyn Park, s of Gallery Road. 1959, one of the *L.C.C.*'s early comprehensives. Plain, symmetrical, curtain-walled three-storey classroom blocks around two courtyards, one paved, one grassed, visible to the road through an open ground floor. The hall (with sunken well) in the centre.

WILSON'S GRAMMAR SCHOOL (former), Camberwell Church Street. Founded in 1615. The present buildings 1882 by *E. R. Robson*; irregular gabled front, red brick with stone dressings.

BACON'S COMPREHENSIVE SCHOOL, Delaford Road. *See* Perambulation 3.

ARCHBISHOP MICHAEL RAMSEY C OF E SECONDARY SCHOOL, Wyndham Road, off Camberwell Road s of John Ruskin Street. 1971–5 by *T. Ford & Partners*. Notable only for the fact that it includes the rebuilt parish church of ST MICHAEL as part of the school buildings. The small brick church stands near the road, and has a rather frivolous spire-cum-lantern filled with coloured glass. (In the entrance hall a *Coade* stone Charity Boy of 1785, originally from Lambeth Ragged Schools. AK)

BRUNSWICK PARK SCHOOL, Benhill Road, N E of Camberwell Green. Notable for its extraordinary eyecatching dining and assembly hall, by *Stirling & Gowan*, 1961–2, white brick with three huge windows, rearing up out of a green lawn, like a waterworks gone berserk, as Ian Nairn has put it. The building is a square (the flat-roofed quarter with kitchens etc.). The windows are at clerestory level; inside, the light falls dramatically through raking roof-beams.

PECKHAM SCHOOL, Peckham Road. Well detailed curtain-walled ranges around a hall, pleasantly set back from the road behind trees. By *Lyons Israel & Ellis*, 1956–8.

SACRED HEART R.C. SECONDARY SCHOOL, Camberwell New Road. Neat red-brick-faced buildings with black painted floor bands, by *Hudson & Hammond*, 1959.

ELFRIDA RATHBONE SPECIAL SCHOOL, off Glengall Road, NE continuation of Peckham Hill Street. 1959–60 by I.L.E.A. (Education Architect *John Bancroft*). The assembly hall is a glazed box, with heavy concrete beams; contrasting brick corner pavilions. One of the first I.L.E.A. schools to experiment with large areas of patent glazing.

IVEDALE SCHOOL. A good, bold example of the three-decker type of Board School in Ivydale Road, near Nunhead Cemetery, 1891, generously decorated. Battlemented centre with tall turreted roof.

BESSEMER SCHOOL, Denmark Hill. A good example of work of the *L.C.C. c.* 1950. Another is LANGBOURNE PRIMARY, Lyall Avenue, off Kingswood Drive. 1952, light and airy, two storeys, pre-cast horizontal concrete cladding panels. Just down the road the NURSERY SCHOOL, by *Stillman & Eastwick Field*, 1967, illustrates a favourite later form of plan: a cluster of hexagons, attractively grouped, white brick with pitched roofs.

ST JOSEPH'S PRIMARY SCHOOL, Pitman Street. *See* Perambulation 1.

EVELYN LOWE PRIMARY SCHOOL, Marlborough Grove, off Old Kent Road w of Rotherhithe New Road. An influential experimental design by the *Department of Education and Science*, 1967, discussed in the Plowden Report of the same year which stressed the importance of informal teaching. The open-plan classrooms are housed in linked pavilions of domestic appearance shielding the playground from the road.

CRAWFORD PRIMARY SCHOOL, Crawford Road, of 1972–5 (*Roger Wilkes*) and BELLENDEN PRIMARY SCHOOL, off Peckham High Street, 1980–1 by *Linda Suggate* are good examples of later schools by the *I.L.E.A. Architect's Department*.

ST GILES HOSPITAL, Peckham Road and St Giles Road. The older buildings dull, by *W. S. Cross*, except for the five-storey circular ward block of the late C 19 (no longer in use); a rare survival (facing Havil Street). The newer ones quite cheerful, in a chunky Arts and Crafts style, 1904 by *E. T. Hall* (partly now used as Southwark council offices).

SOUTH LONDON DOCTORS' CENTRE and SOUTHWARK ADULT EDUCATION INSTITUTE, St Mary's Road, Peckham. Built as the Pioneer Health Centre in 1934–5, by *Sir Owen Williams*. The place of a famous medico-social experiment, initiated by Doctors Scott Williams and Innes Pearse. The area was chosen because its population provided a cross-section of low, middle, and upper middle income groups. The idea was that instead of medical services being called upon only when people feel sick, they should be available to every-body at regular intervals, regardless of their state of health, because health overhauls would detect disorders early and could remove them not only by strictly medical means but also by altering environmental conditions. Thus the health centre was worked out as a combination of club and clinic. It was designed as such to Dr Scott Williams's requirements. Pioneer work indeed, socially as well as architecturally. The centre also provided for the district a kindergarten, gymna-sium, swimming pool, theatre, indoor sports, etc. The centre of the building is the swimming pool on the first floor sur-rounded by cafés and other rooms for spending one's leisure in. The pool is separated from them by glass walls. The only space shut off from circulation is the consultation block on the top floor. The front has a centre with six gently out-curved bays. All concrete and glass.

RAILWAY STRUCTURES. The unusually ornate examples around Dulwich were designed by *Charles Barry Jun.*, at the stipulation of the landowners, the governors of Dulwich Col-lege. On the LONDON CHATHAM AND DOVER main line of 1860–3, at Turney Road, a BRIDGE with a three-span ornamental cast-iron façade, with monogram AC and date 1863. The façade is largely independent of the wrought-iron girder structure behind. Other good BRIDGES on the Tulse Hill branch, 1869, across Croxted Road and Rosendale Road,* the latter three-arched with heavily modelled red and cream brickwork. The N entrance to the 1¼ m. long PENGE TUNNEL has an elliptical portal with Gibbs surround, side piers, and a bracketed cornice. By *Joseph Cubitt*, 1860–3. In the deep and leafy approach cutting, the wooden buildings of SYDENHAM HILL STATION.

On the LONDON BRIGHTON AND SOUTH COAST RAILWAY of 1864–8 between East Dulwich and Tulse Hill, cast-iron ornamental plates on the bridge abutments 'AC 1866'. NORTH DULWICH STATION is by *Charles Barry Jun.*, remarkably fine. Red brick with cream pilasters, stone dress-ings, and a loggia in stone. Contemporary timber and corru-gated iron platform canopies. Either side of Burbage Road a VIADUCT faced in red brick with a perforated parapet, and 'AC' alternating with '1866' on concrete medallions in the spandrels. On the lattice girder BRIDGE over the London Chatham and Dover Railway here, the abutments have sand-stone caps with the arms of Dulwich College.

PECKHAM RYE STATION (L.B.S.C.R.), Rye Lane. Tall booking office between two viaducts, 1866, in an ornate Italian Renaissance characteristic of the South London line.

DENMARK HILL STATION (L.B.S.C.R.). 1864–6. Two storeys, heavily modelled Italianate, but with French pavilion roofs, straddling the leafy cutting. Gutted by fire in 1980.

GASWORKS, Old Kent Road. Gasholders of 1867, 1872, 1875,

---

* The latter just inside the borough of Lambeth.

and 1881, the latter two with tank walls of mass concrete, an early use of the material for this purpose, by *George Livesey*, engineer.

PERAMBULATIONS

1. *Camberwell Green and its surroundings*

The centre of old Camberwell is Camberwell Green, with Camberwell Church Street running E towards Peckham. It can be approached from the Elephant by Camberwell Road, or from Kennington by Camberwell New Road (laid out after Vauxhall Bridge opened in 1818). Both have remains of late Georgian terraces. In CAMBERWELL NEW ROAD, continuous stretches on both sides (*see also* Lambeth (La), Perambulation 4), especially good those S of and opposite County Grove (Nos. 226 etc., 257 etc.). In CAMBERWELL ROAD there is an elegant group on the E side with some nice fanlights, and opposite, something more special, No. 86, a former stonemason's premises, with stuccoed front, pilasters, and three *Coade* stone medallions (should a mason advertise cast stone?). They came from Dr Lettsom's house in Camberwell Grove. Behind the respectable terraces came later piecemeal development, now largely replaced. Between the two main roads the G.L.C.'s WYNDHAM and COMBER ESTATES cover the area of what was one of Camberwell's worst C19 slums, the lumpy tower blocks of 1962–4 marking the shift to the brutalist style in the *L.C.C.'s Architect's Department* (cf. Canada Estate, Rotherhithe). To their N in Pitman Street ST JOSEPH'S PRIMARY SCHOOL, exceedingly plain Queen Anne, by *Leonard Stokes*, 1909. A different housing formula back in Camberwell Road: No. 134 (Churchmead, Bishopsmead), some of *Neylan & Ungless*'s plain but ingenious low-rise housing for Southwark (1967–71), making the best of a bad site. Two parallel three- and four-storey ranges facing some grass, with well hidden upper private patios.

E of Camberwell Road the only older survivals worth a look are the pleasant irregular early C19 houses and terraces around ADDINGTON SQUARE. Further S are miscellaneous results of slum clearance: the tall Four Per Cent Industrial Dwellings of 1900, and the still taller series of slabs along PICTON STREET of 1956, part of the *G.L.C.*'s straggly ELMINGTON ESTATE, worth exploring for the curious assembly hall of the BRUNSWICK PARK SCHOOL (*see* Public Buildings, above). S again, Peabody housing of 1974 in Lomond Grove (*M. de St Croix*), and finally, S of Elmington Road, the D'EYNSFORD ESTATE, by *Clifford Culpin & Partners*, 1971–8, one of Southwark's first large low-rise estates of the 1970s (365 dwellings), almost aggressive in its use of vernacular motifs. Rugged tiled roofs with big projecting eaves, generous balconies, and intricate pathways between tiny walled back gardens.

CAMBERWELL GREEN still has its green, but little else of note except for some houses on the W side (No. 15, C 18 with big top window with fan motif, and Nos. 7–13, an early C 19 terrace). The most conspicuous building is the NATIONAL WEST-MINSTER BANK of 1899 by *A. Williams*, in the Edwardian Baroque style with a corner tower as if it were a town hall. Nothing much in Camberwell Church Street, which runs E from the Green, but from it a street leads S in which the best domestic architecture of Camberwell proper can be seen: CAMBERWELL GROVE, a straight, thickly planted avenue, with well preserved late Georgian terraces and semi-detached houses connected by one-storey entrance bays. The street began as a private avenue behind the mansion house of the Cock family near Church Street (cf. Bruce Grove, Tottenham, Hy) and was built up after this house was demolished and the grounds split up (sale of 1776). The houses towards the N end date from the 1770s–80s (Nos. 33–45, 1785; Nos. 79–85, c. 1778). The most elaborate house was that built by Dr John Coakley Lettsom in 1779–80 (demolished in the 1890s). It stood in its own grounds to the E of Camberwell Grove. (Some of its *Coade* stone decoration survives at No. 86 Camberwell Road; *see* above.) *Riches & Blythin's* LETTSOM ESTATE of 1970 stands in part of the grounds. Higher up in Camberwell Grove, stuccoed houses built on part of the Lettsom Estate in the earlier C 19: notably GROVE CRESCENT (Nos. 169–183), alternate pairs with large pediments, and the beginning of GROVE PARK, a development begun by the railway engineer and speculator William Chadwick (according to Blanch's *Camberwell*) with a tiny stuccoed lodge at the corner. No. 8 Grove Park is an older detached three-bay house, much altered, built by Lettsom's friend Henry Smith c. 1776–80. In its former grounds a long low DAY NURSERY by *Neylan & Ungless*, 1971–3. On the other side of Camberwell Grove GROVE CHAPEL (*see* Churches, above) fits perfectly into the late Georgian atmosphere. S of Grove Park come continuous stucco terraces, some with Greek Doric porches, ending with No. 220, The Hermitage, a late C 18 or early C 19 rustic cottage with tree-trunk columns supporting the eaves, but suburban-ized by pebbledash.*

One can return to the centre of Camberwell either by Champion Hill and Denmark Hill, or by Grove Lane. CHAMPION HILL formed part of the De Crespigny Estate and was de-veloped around Champion Lodge on Denmark Hill (de-molished 1841) from c. 1840. Despite later intrusions it re-tains the leafy, secluded atmosphere of select suburban villas in their own grounds. The best survivors are (from S to N) No. 47 and No. 29, plain early C 19, and the older No. 23 of 1791, with a three-bay, three-storey centre with long colonnaded porch, and later wings. It has been attributed to *M. Searles* (*see* Blackheath, Le). (Good staircase inside.) The N end of Cham-

---

* A much better cottage orné (No. 94, opposite the chapel) was destroyed in the last war.

pion Hill is taken up by flats and by the William Booth College in Champion Park (*see* Public Buildings), but at the bottom of DENMARK HILL, after the hospitals (*see* Lambeth (La), Public Buildings), there are still some nice early C19 detached villas (Nos. 93–99). Nearer Camberwell Green an ODEON CINEMA (disused), a streamlined corner building of 1934 by *Andrew Mather*.

GROVE LANE developed similarly to Camberwell Grove but is now more bitty. Towards the s end CHAMPION GROVE, also on part of the De Crespigny Estate, stuccoed pairs of *c.* 1840, of varying size. HAREFIELD GARDENS opposite is a crisply detailed terrace of flats, not too large, by *Stillman & Eastwick Field* for the G.L.C., 1966–70, brown brick with black boarding. Further down the hill stuccoed houses again: Nos. 139–161, Nos. 103–109 with bowed windows, and Nos. 83 and 65a, distinguished by Gothic details. No. 72 opposite is an intrusion of *c.* 1970 in mottled brown brick, scaled to fit in with the grander mid-C19 houses in DE CRESPIGNY PARK rather than with Grove Lane. At the bottom of Grove Lane, Nos. 49–55, early C19 brick, and finally Nos. 18–62, an excellent terrace of the late C18.

SUNRAY ESTATE (Casino Avenue Estate),* on the s slopes of Herne Hill, is one of the most celebrated products of the 'Homes fit for Heroes' campaign. Built in 1920–1 on a unique combination of direct labour and building guild principles, organized by the Office of Works under its director, *Sir Frank Baines*, and widely admired not only for the speed and efficiency of its operations but also for the quality of its architecture. Baines abandoned here the picturesque flamboyance of his earlier Well Hall and Roe Green schemes and relied for effect on careful site planning and the contrast of steeply pitched tile roofs with plain rendered walls. The s end of HERNE HILL is a typical late Victorian area near the station (over the borough boundary; *see* Lambeth (La), Public Buildings), dominated by the HALF MOON in Half Moon Lane, a cheerful corner pub of 1896, generously decked out with bay-windows, balconies, and marble columns.

2. Peckham: Peckham Road to Queen's Road, with excursions N and S

PECKHAM ROAD, connecting the old villages of Peckham and Camberwell, is mostly an accumulation of public buildings (q.v.) and L.C.C. flats. The exception is the late Georgian group around the town hall (all now municipal offices). On the s side, set back, a group of three houses, two identical ones of five bays, linked up later, and one of three bays, with good doorways with fanlights. Opposite are some more late Georgian houses, altered. Behind these, SCEAUX GARDENS, the

---

* This entry has been contributed by Mark Swenarton. The name 'Casino' comes from the casino built in 1797 by *Nash* or *Repton*, demolished in 1906.

first of a whole series of council estates N of Peckham Road. This one was Camberwell's showpiece of 1955–9 (Borough Architect *F. O. Hayes*). Two fourteen-storey slabs of cross-over maisonettes, and lower blocks (one and six storeys), pleasantly grouped in mature gardens, not yet complicated by the 1960s rage for massive car parks (403 dwellings at 136 p.p.a.). Further N in SEDGMOOR PLACE, hidden among low 1970s terraces (by *Stock Page & Stock*), the AGED PILGRIMS' HOME, completed in 1837, two storeys, brick, with embattled gatehouse motif. Inside is a quadrangle with a monument to the founder, William Peacock, in the centre. Behind, in HAVIL STREET, the much plainer BETHEL ASYLUM for aged women, also built by William Peacock in 1837.

Continuing E along Peckham Road, Sceaux Gardens is followed by the CAMDEN ESTATE with the NORTH PECKHAM ESTATE immediately to its N, two ambitious pieces of re-development by *Camberwell* (later Southwark) council, designed respectively in 1969 and 1965, and instructive to compare. Both are built on a deck system with car parking beneath, and are linked by a bridge across COMMERCIAL WAY. The earlier scheme, completed in 1972, was considered enlightened for its date in avoiding tall slabs, but the monotonous upper walkways and cramped courtyards surrounded by the five-storey dark brick maisonettes are not inviting. 1,433 dwellings (the largest estate after Aylesbury). The Camden Estate (completed 1976), built in a more cheerful yellow brick, has more variety and is not so large (874 dwellings). Once one has found one's way up the busy broad central walk, CHEPSTOW WAY is quite attractive. At one end it widens into a little square overlooked by a taller block of flats with shops below, and with a health centre opposite.

The centre of Peckham is the junction of Peckham High Street with Peckham Hill Street and Rye Lane. In PECKHAM HILL STREET a few remnants of early C19 terraces.* In the HIGH STREET the last remaining survivors of the village past disappeared in the war (cf. R.C.H.M.), although a few old houses can still be glimpsed above and behind shopfronts. At the junction of RYE LANE the pompous 1930s cornerpiece built for JONES AND HIGGINS, the former local department store which grew along Rye Lane (see the dates). It started at No. 3 in 1867. Off Rye Lane early to mid-C19 terraces, but nothing special except the former Friends' Meeting House in Highshore Road (*see* Churches, above), the very modest GIRDLERS' ALMSHOUSES in CHOUMERT ROAD, by Mr *Woodthorpe*, architect, 1852, and a curiosity: Nos. 48–54 ELM GROVE, built in Bath stone cut and laid to look like stock brick. Further E just a few old buildings remain in QUEEN'S ROAD, leading away from the village to New Cross: No. 4 probably of the time of George II, and Nos. 6–10 c. 1700, an

* (Further N, E of Peckham Park Road, COMMUNITY CENTRE, in a G.L.C. estate, by *F. MacManus & Partners*, c. 1978.)

attractive group. Nos. 30–54, a late Georgian terrace, and Nos. 142–148, two early C19 pairs at an angle to the road, stand isolated among redevelopment.* N of Queen's Road recent buildings predominate: off CARLTON GROVE Camberwell Borough Council's ACORN ESTATE, 1957–63 (*F. O. Hayes*), an interesting attempt for its date at low-rise housing, one seven-storey slab on stilts with two- and three-storey houses behind round pedestrian courtyards (cf. North Peckham, above). The E side of Carlton Grove demonstrates the return to favour of the street terrace – a range of four-storey flats by *Higgins & Ney*, 1970–6 – while MONTPELIER ROAD should be visited for Nos. 76–78, a discreet piece of infilling in an older street, by *Peter Moro & Partners*, 1969–73. More by the same firm further E, between YORK GROVE and POMEROY STREET, 1976, a three-storeyed gabled frontage with upper-level deck behind, private yards, and a communal garden, around two squares.

Finally, s of Queen's Road. E of Lausanne Road late 1970s housing by *H.K.P.A.* In ST MARY'S ROAD, past the Health Centre (*see* Public Buildings, above), SASSOON HOUSE (opposite the church), a well designed block of flats by *Adams, Thompson & Fry*, or rather *Maxwell Fry*, 1932. Between St Mary's Road and Rye Lane much new building of the late 1970s, e.g. around Consort Road, by *Clifford Culpin & Partners*, 1978.

3. The N and E edges of Camberwell: Albany Road, Old Kent Road

ALBANY ROAD was laid out through fields soon after the GRAND SURREY CANAL was made in 1801–10.‡ The canal closed in 1971. Around it a large park was proposed already in Forshaw and Abercrombie's County of London plan of 1943, which conditioned the planning of the area for the next twenty years. Hence the dense estates N and s of the intended open space. For the Aylesbury Estate to the N *see* Southwark (Sk), Perambulation 3(d). Its counterpart to the s, along St George's Way, after the church and library in Wells Way (*see* above, Churches and Public Buildings), is GLOUCESTER GROVE ESTATE (*G.L.C. Architect's Department*, 1971–7; 1,210 dwellings at 142 p.p.a.), a fortress-like chain of six-storey slabs linked by yellow-brick staircase drums. They shield an enclave of restored early C19 white stucco villas around NEWENT CLOSE. The new park, now called BURGESS PARK, for long consisted only of fragmented pieces of green; these were at last linked up in 1980–2. An eight-acre boating lake

---

* Redevelopment has accounted for a terrace of weatherboarded cottages in Consort Road.

‡ The canal was an ambitious conception by *Ralph Dodd* (replaced as engineer by *John Rowe* in 1802). Only three miles were built (the promoters diverted their attention to the Surrey Docks). A short branch to Peckham was added in 1825–6. Two ornamental wrought-iron BRIDGES survive over this, at Willowbrook Road (1870) and Commercial Way (1872); another in Old Kent Road.

was opened in 1982, and a formal brick-paved park entrance created in the New Kent Road. In the neighbourhood a number of early C 19 buildings, previously threatened by the park, but now likely to survive. They comprise the following. In ALBANY ROAD, s side, very modest terraces of *c.* 1810–20. CHUMLEIGH GARDENS are former almshouses of the Female Friendly Society, a charming W range of plain stock brick with Gothic windows, 1821, separate flanking wings of 1844 and 1847. Some stark late Georgian houses (Rosetta Place 1822) in COBOURG ROAD. GLENGALL ROAD is especially worthwhile. It has pairs of stuccoed villas with giant pilasters linked by shallow arches, two storeys above basements. The same motifs occur on GLENGALL TERRACE. The date is *c.* 1843–5, and the design very similar to houses in New Cross Road (*see* below).

In OLD KENT ROAD little of interest apart from a few remnants of early C 19 ribbon development (cf. Nos. 464–470, 543–549) and two housing estates on the E side worth a look. WESSEX HOUSE (No. 375) is by *Peter Moro & Partners*, 1971–4, somewhat in the idiom of James Stirling, bright red brick, three storeys, with much canting and recessing of bays and balconies to shield flats from the traffic. AVONDALE SQUARE, by *Sir Lancelot Keay, Basil Duckett & Partners* for the City Corporation (on Bridge House Estates land), makes a surprisingly successful self-contained composition (surprising because the same ingredients elsewhere have so often proved unsatisfactory). The tall buildings date from 1958–62. An L-shaped shopping precinct off a service road, and a quiet green space beyond, bounded by a ten-storey slab, and by three eighteen-storey point blocks which look across to the rebuilt St Philip (*see* Churches, above) and its older hall and vicarage. The lower Harman Close and terraces near by were added in 1962–7. Further E, on either side of ROTHERHITHE NEW ROAD, the BONAMY ESTATE, planned 1963, by Camberwell Architect's Department (*F. O. Hayes*), completed 1970. One of their efforts to avoid tall blocks and to create more intimate enclosed spaces (cf. Acorn Estate and North Peckham, Perambulation 2, above). Nothing over four storeys, plenty of private patios at different levels, staircase links instead of access galleries, but good intentions spoilt by unappealing, drab surfaces.* Returning to Old Kent Road the main landmarks further s are the plain ASTORIA CINEMA, 1930 by *E. A. Stone* (derelict), the North Peckham Civic Centre opposite, and further s the Livesey Museum and Christ Church (qq.v.)

At the corner of COMMERCIAL WAY the KENTISH DROVERS, a low pub of *c.* 1840 with a huge painted sign curving round the corner, and good late C 19 fittings. Next to it in Commercial Way some houses of the same date: Elizabeth Place 1844,

---

* In DELAFORD ROAD, BACON'S COMPREHENSIVE SCHOOL preserves a bust of Josiah Bacon, 1703 by *William Cox*, from Bacon's School, Grange Road, Bermondsey.

Doddington Place 1833, with pilasters and pediment, and another pair of the same design, although called Doddington Cottages, 1836. Further s, beyond the *G.L.C.*'s TUSTIN ESTATE (1964–9, the usual mixed development with three towers), Old Kent Road becomes NEW CROSS ROAD. Around the railway bridge by the borough boundary the relics of an interesting group: a few early c19 three-storey houses and some villas, all with the distinctive decoration of pilasters with ammonite capitals supporting segmental arches. The ammonite capital was a motif popularized by *Amon Wilds* at Brighton. Its only other surviving occurrence in London is in Rotherfield Street, Islington.*

Finally, s of Old Kent Road, two particularly rewarding diversions. CLIFTON TERRACE is a single composition of 1846–52 but still in the Regency tradition, two storeys, with taller ends and centre. Red brick, an unusual material for that date, very restrained details, nice cast-iron porches. The whole terrace excellently restored by *Southwark* (1977) as the *pièce de résistance* of a redevelopment area. ASYLUM ROAD has another restoration: CAROLINE GARDENS, the former almshouses of the Licensed Victuallers' Benevolent Institution, 1827–33 by *Henry Rose*, the only grand composition amongst the many almshouses of Camberwell. Exceptionally large. Long double ranges (houses both back and front with courts in between); two far-projecting wings. Brick, of two storeys, embellished only by a central portico of six giant Ionic columns screening the E end of the chapel (interior destroyed in the war). Further ranges behind (1849, 1858, 1866) in the same style brought the total up to 176 dwellings.

4. SE *Camberwell: Nunhead and Peckham Rye*

The main impression is of a sea of small late Victorian houses spreading relentlessly over the hills, broken by Peckham Rye Common and by the open land of the cemeteries and waterworks further E. The following exceptions are too scattered to make a proper perambulation.

The old centre of Nunhead, NUNHEAD GREEN, is a pathetic scrap of grass and asphalt, redeemed only by the BEER AND WINE HOMES on the N side, 1852–3 by *William Webbe*, a gabled yellow-brick Gothic front of some character, the centre with oddly angled chimneys. Well restored, with new housing added behind, by *M. & D. Dove*. Round the corner in CONSORT ROAD the slightly older almshouses (1834) of the Girdlers' Company (BEESTON HOUSE) make a good contrast: a terrace of five stuccoed Tudor houses in a garden, with a separate one-storey range on either side, tactfully added since the Second World War. In NUNHEAD LANE the older

---

* The Ammonite order was invented by *G. Dance Jun.* and used by him in designs for Alderman Boydell's Shakespeare Gallery, Pall Mall, 1789 (D. Stroud: *George Dance*).

houses have nearly all disappeared. To the s the modest suburban scale of the area is continued in the work of the *Design Research Unit* (for Habinteg housing association from 1978) around TAPPESFIELD ROAD, but not by the pompous pre- and post-war *L.C.C.* flats in LINDEN GROVE. Off Linden Grove LIMEWALK is worth exploring, one of *Neylan & Ungless's* small developments for Southwark, 1966, an original solution for a long narrow site. It begins as a broad paved walk, entered by a passage beneath a bridge. On the l. an old people's home, on the r. terrace houses, with gardens at the back over garages. Then comes a subtle change of access, and a narrow alley continues beneath slate-hung bridges (containing bathrooms). The windowless walls here are slightly eerie, but the whole has a strong sense of identity, and the attention to well organized public and private spaces that is characteristic of this firm's work (cf. Harlow New Town). s of Linden Grove Nunhead Cemetery (*see* Churches, above). (Opposite the cemetery entrance, the oddly gaunt and earnest Gothic edifice of Messrs DANIELS, monumental masons.)

Opposite St Silas (*see* Churches) Nos. 300–302 IVYDALE ROAD, a children's home by *Southwark Architect's Department*, 1971–3. The concrete blocks and tough iron railings, fashionable architect's materials of *c.* 1970 (cf. Camden), immediately mark it as a 'council' building even though it is unnamed. Much the same can be said of the even weirder children's home in UNDERHILL ROAD (1969–72).

PECKHAM RYE COMMON has on its E the *L.C.C.* RYE HILL ESTATE (1939–64). The pleasantest parts are the low-density terraces (54 p.p.a.) around TORRIDGE GARDENS, hidden behind the dull pre-war blocks and the 1960s towers. On the w side early c 19 villas and houses, and on the corner of EAST DULWICH ROAD, KING'S (the former KING'S ARMS), by *Westwood Sons & Partners*, 1957, which makes an effort to be interesting, with its pierced screens and sun terraces at different levels. Finally DAWSON'S HEIGHTS, Overhill Road, chiefly worth the climb because of the splendid views in all directions. The two twelve-storey brick ziggurats with their chunky bands of balconies and access galleries are disappointing close up, although they now form one of the most dramatic features of the Southwark horizon. They face each other grimly across a drab stretch of green. By Southwark Architect's Department (*F.O. Hayes*), 1966–72 (initial design by *Kate Macintosh*).

5. Dulwich

The centre of old Dulwich lies to the N of the college (*see* Public Buildings) along the road called DULWICH VILLAGE which runs s from Red Post Hill, a wide, tree-planted street with some good Georgian brick houses on its E side. First at the corner of COURT LANE the old BURIAL GROUND, with its excellent early c 18 iron gates, flanked on the l. by No. 1b

Court Lane, a cottage of 1814, and on the r. by a pair of C 19 stucco villas with windows framed in giant arches. The larger houses, set back from the road, start after the burial ground: No. 57, yellow brick, built in 1793; No. 59, plainer C 18 (altered 1938), also of three storeys, brown brick with red dressings; and Nos. 61–67, post-Second-World-War neo-Georgian. The CROWN AND GREYHOUND, a cheerfully gross gabled pub of c. 1895, marks the centre of the old village (it replaced two early C 18 inns). Small C 18–19 cottages and shops on either side, close to the road, then some more large houses on the E side, starting with Nos. 93–95, a clever neo-Georgian pastiche of 1934. No. 97 is of 1796, tall, five windows wide, with ground-floor windows within arches, and Ionic doorcase. No. 101, 1760, has canted bay-windows; then an irregular group with a six-bay centre of 1759–60. On the l. (No. 103) an addition with a door with a broad fanlight; on the r. a more substantial wing built in 1794, projecting forward, with Ionic porch.* The rest is C 20 Tudor, as is most of the w side.

Around this nucleus larger detached houses. To the N, at the E corner of VILLAGE WAY, LYNDENHURST, early C 18, five windows wide, red-brick dressings, and further w, POND HOUSE (now flats, with the grounds built up). Much altered and added to. A small but grand C 18 centre, tall, with pediment and Venetian window. Lower two-storey wings, each one window wide. On the flank of the r. wing a semicircular porch with Tuscan columns, on the l. an early C 19 wing; later additions behind. To the w, in GALLERY ROAD, BELAIR, standing back in its own grounds (now a public park). A villa of 1785, of handsome proportions, but with cement rendering (much rebuilt in 1964 by *Southwark Borough Council*). Entrance front with giant pilasters and a broad arched doorway. Full height bow-window to the garden with a screen of Ionic columns around the ground-floor window. (Interior with circular staircase.)

The N side of DULWICH COMMON was also a favourite spot for Georgian houses. From w to E, the survivors are: ELM LAWN, mid C 18 (but reduced in size and altered), an irregular stuccoed and bay-windowed front; OLD BLEW HOUSE, early C 18, rendered; and THE WILLOWS and NORTHCROFT, a stuccoed pair with projecting eaves, 1810 by *George Tappen*, the college surveyor. Then, E of College Road, GLENLEA, a pretty stuccoed villa of 1803 also by *George Tappen*. Five bays, battlemented parapet, bow-windows, and Ionic pedimented portico. In COLLEGE ROAD, the continuation of Dulwich Village, a few more C 18 houses N of the Common: Nos. 11–15, opposite Old College; No. 23, BELL COTTAGE, weatherboarded, with Doric doorcase; BELL HOUSE of 1767 (altered by *Lutyens*), a long, brown-brick, two-storey house with taller centre with Venetian window and a bell tower

* I owe these dates to Mr Justin Howes.

flanked by a pair; and No. 41, 1721, altered. Behind these houses DULWICH PARK, given by Dulwich College to the L.C.C. and opened in 1890. Good gatepiers in College Road and Dulwich Common. Near the lake, SCULPTURE by *Barbara Hepworth*, 1970: Two Forms (Divided Circle).

Further S, opposite the C19 college buildings, a delightful spot, POND COTTAGES, some weatherboarded, one (No. 3) tiny five-bay two-storey brick. They face the charmingly landscaped millpond.* The surrounding playing fields and golf course maintain the rural atmosphere, but S of them the southern tip of Dulwich is now mostly of after 1950. Around KINGSWOOD DRIVE, W of College Road, first an early post-Second-World-War *L.C.C.* estate, large but uninteresting, built in the grounds of Kingswood House (now a library; *see* Public Buildings). The roads S of this, between Sydenham Hill and Gipsy Hill Stations, were laid out by the Dulwich College estate from 1860, with detached villas and large gardens. Nos. 24–28 DULWICH WOOD AVENUE, well detailed Italianate by the College Surveyor, *Charles Barry Jun.*, were the first to be built and, with the later No. 22 and THE PAXTON, a dignified Italianate pub at the corner of Gipsy Hill, are now the only remnants of that era. The rest has been replaced by private housing of the 1950s onwards, either in terraces or flats; see for the former e.g. Woodland Drive and Great Brownings E of College Road, for the latter, Dulwich Wood Park near Tylney Avenue, all *Wates* developments (architects *Austin Vernon & Partners*) which exploit the hilly wooded landscape better than most. Off Sydenham Hill, CRESCENT WOOD ROAD has a few more C19 villas remaining, and also one early modern house worth examining: SIX PILLARS, by *Harding & Tecton*, 1933–5. Concrete, plastered. 102 Two storeys, rectangular, with a smaller structure rising above the upper floor and giving access to a roof terrace hidden from the street by a tall parapet. Only a balcony of typical Tecton shape opens in the parapet. The brick drum of the staircase is visible behind. On the same front the ground floor is partly replaced by the six pillars which give the house its name. A wing of odd shape (conditioned by the site) stands at right angles to the main block. The living room shares a curved interior wall with the staircase lobby. DULWICH WOOD HOUSE on SYDENHAM HILL‡ is another handsome Italianate house, now a pub, with a *villa rustica* air.

EAST DULWICH, which mostly lay outside the Dulwich College estate, is dull late C19 surburban. The old centre was a small hamlet around GOOSE GREEN, a widening of East Dulwich Road, with St John's church on its N side. Two small-scale Southwark housing schemes worth a look: to the W the EAST DULWICH GROVE estate, with small pedestrian terraces at right angles to the main road, only one and two

* They were originally associated with the claypits and brick kiln whose site lay near the present gymnasium (J. Howes).
‡ For the other side of Sydenham Hill, *see* Lewisham (Le), Perambulation 6.

storeys high, 1965–7, an early example in London of its type; to the s, No. 524 LORDSHIP LANE, one of *Neylan & Ungless*'s intricate inward-looking little schemes on a tight site, 1969–74. The exterior, facing the main road next to St Peter's church, is unrevealing. Beneath an archway one enters a minute, well planned oblong courtyard with small flats on two sides. One feels one is trespassing, and that is no doubt a good thing.

SUTTON

INTRODUCTION

The borough of Sutton (total population 169,343 in 1981) is
largely C 20 suburban, especially in its monotonous northern
stretches, yet still contains some places of great charm. The river
Wandle runs through the N E part where the gravel overlies the
London Clay; as in Merton, it attracted both early industry and
rural retreats (see the northern part of Wallington). The old
settlements lie further S on higher ground, along the springline
of the chalk on the N edge of the Surrey downs, in a line running
roughly from E to W.*

The range of worthwhile buildings which remain is wide.
Medieval churches, or parts of them, survive at Cheam, Carshalton, and Beddington, with excellent monuments of all periods; a 19
major late medieval hall roof hidden within the much rebuilt
manor house at Beddington; and there are well preserved vernacular survivals at Cheam, notably Whitehall, the most accessible timber-framed house in Greater London. The many large 3
C 18 houses that once existed, especially in the neighbourhood of
Carshalton, have for the most part left little trace except for a few
garden structures and parts of their parks. The exception is
Carshalton House, which, although extended by school buildings, is still recognizably a substantial early C 18 mansion, with
good interior features, especially one mid C 18 room of outstand- 66
ing quality, and grounds which include *Henry Joynes*'s memorably Vanbrughian water tower. Camden House, The Brandries,
is another C 19 survival at Beddington. There is less to single out
from the C 19: a *Teulon* church at Sutton, C 19 redecoration and a

---

* PREHISTORIC SITES: a series, notably at Carshalton, Beddington, and
Cheam, from the Mesolithic onwards, including settlements, flint-working, and
bronze-smithing; a possible Bronze Age barrow at Carshalton, an Iron Age
hillfort at Queen Mary's Hospital site, Carshalton, an Iron Age/Romano-British
settlement on the E at Waddon, a Roman bath house at Beddington sewage farm,
Roman burials at Beddington and Bandon Hill, an early Saxon cemetery at
Beddington.

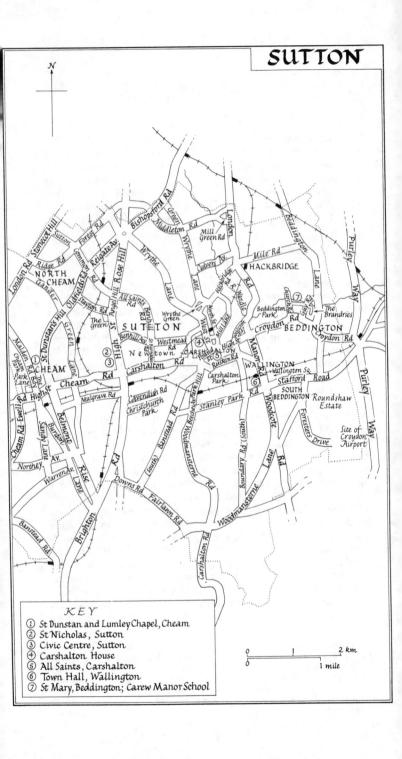

SUTTON

N

KEY
1. St Dunstan and Lumley Chapel, Cheam
2. St Nicholas, Sutton
3. Civic Centre, Sutton
4. Carshalton House
5. All Saints, Carshalton
6. Town Hall, Wallington
7. St Mary, Beddington; Carew Manor School

0   1   2 km
0   1 mile

BEDDINGTON AND WALLINGTON

BEDDINGTON AND WALLINGTON

639

Morris & Co. organ gallery in Beddington church, a minor house
by *Webb* at Carshalton, and also there, *Frank Dickinson*'s home,
Little Holland House, a remarkable Arts and Crafts survival. As
for the C20, *Atkinson*'s Wallington Town Hall and *Cachemaille-
Day*'s Sutton Baptist Church represent the tentative search for
new forms before the Second World War; the centre of Sutton
the brasher conflict of styles in commercial architecture of the
1960s; and Roundshaw, Wallington, the most dogmatic type of
public housing of the same period. Later buildings for the
borough (cf. Cheam, Carshalton) have been on a progressively
more tactful scale, in accord with a constructive conservation
policy (*see* Whitehall and Little Holland House). The most
interesting new building of the 1970s is *Williams & Winkley*'s
R.C. St Elphege, South Beddington.

Further Reading

The DOE list dates from 1974. Useful recent general histories are:
D. Cluett, *Sutton Scene, A Brief History of the London Borough of
Sutton* (1975), and A. E. Jones's illustrated directory of *Old
Carshalton* (1973). On individual buildings: A. E. Jones, *Car-
shalton House* (1980), and pamphlets published by the Sutton
Libraries and Arts Services on two buildings which the borough
enterprisingly took into its care: *Whitehall* (1978) by C. Bradley
and *Little Holland House* (1974) ed. D. Cluett. On Carew
Manor, *London Archaeologist*, Spring 1983, a first summary of
investigations by the Carew Manor Group by B. Weston,
D. Cluett, and J. Phillips. On industrial subjects: *The River
Wandle* (London Borough of Sutton, 1974). See also p. 124.

Acknowledgements

My chief acknowledgement is to the Principal Reference
Librarian Mr Douglas Cluett, who supplied me with very
informative notes and corrections on both old and new
buildings, and went to great trouble to arrange visits. I am also
grateful to Mr K. Mercer, Senior Borough Planner, who helped
over new buildings, to Mr D. J. Turner for information on
Beddington, and to the Rev. T. Surtees for details about St
Dunstan, Cheam.

BEDDINGTON AND WALLINGTON

The two places are confusing. Beddington was the old village, of
which St Mary's church and the Carew Manor House (now
school) next to it on the edge of Beddington Park are the main
survivors. Wallington was a hamlet further S which developed
along Manor Road and Woodcote Road only after the railway
came in 1847, but which has now given its name to most of the
area.

(ALL SAINTS, London Road, Hackbridge. 1931 by *H. P.
Burke-Downing*. Rodney Hubbuck)

HOLY TRINITY, Manor Road. 1867 by *Habershon & Brock* (GR). Flint and stone, with a W tower and spire, and a broad, low apse.

ST MARY, Church Road, Beddington. Quite a big church for what was a village when it was built, pleasantly sited next to the manor house on the edge of the park. There are late C11–C13 fragments. Nave arcades with octagonal piers, probably early C14, as shown by the N aisle window and the original S aisle one (now W window of the Carew Chapel) with curvilinear tracery. Tower and porch, and possibly chancel, probably of *c.* 1390, when Sir Nicholas Carew left money for the rebuilding; the Carew Chapel S of the chancel a little later. Flint and stone, with a W tower, nave and aisles, chancel and higher S chapel. An outer N aisle was added when the church was restored. Interior with tall tower arch, arcades with very odd piers – octagonal with short fronts and long diagonals, which are however in the middle stop-grooved in a rather unlikely way. The S chapel is of two bays, and the arcade here has a pier of the familiar four-shafts-and-four-hollows section and complicatedly moulded arches. Nave roof, chancel arch, chancel roof, and decoration date from the restoration of 1867–9 by *Joseph Clarke*, who also added the W vestries at this time. The work was done for the Rev. A. H. Bridges, rector from 1864 to 1891, a very wealthy man who also acquired much of the adjoining park. The dormer windows are by *H. P. Burke-Downing, c.* 1913.* – FONT. C13, square on five supports of Purbeck marble, the usual type with shallow blank arcading. – PULPIT. 1611, but still with linenfold panels though separated by posts with arabesque decoration. – Former REREDOS, in nine painted parts (Last Judgement), now in the N aisle (W wall). By *Clayton & Bell*, given in 1869 by Bridges, as was the ORGAN GALLERY by *Morris & Co.* This is a delightful piece. The player's space is screened like a minstrels' gallery. Painted dado with floral ornament and a tier of small figures. – CHANCEL STALLS. Seven on the S side and two on the N have MISERICORDS with shields, foliage, and two heads. – MONUMENTS. Brasses in the chancel, three hidden by the stalls. The other two are of Nicholas Carew † 1432 and his wife. The figures measure 4 ft 7 in. They lie under cusped round arches. – Also Katheryn Berecroft and her sister † 1507. The figures here are only 10 in. long. – Sir Richard Carew † 1520 and wife. Fine Perp recess in the Carew Chapel, similar to tomb recesses at St Mary Lambeth (La) and Croydon (Cr). Chest front with elaborate quatrefoils. On it brasses 20 in. long. Back recess with coarse panelling up the jambs and along the depressed arch. Cresting. – Sir Francis Carew † 1611. Alabaster. Recumbent effigy, the head on a rolled-up mat. Kneeling family in relief against the front of the tomb-chest. Back wall with two columns, but no arch. Obelisks and achievement at the top. – LYCHGATE. Probably also

* Details kindly supplied by the late H. V. Molesworth Roberts.

c. 1868 by *Clarke.* – Good CHURCHYARD WALLS. Red brick; the part adjoining the Manor House C 17 or earlier.

(ST MICHAEL, Milton Road, s off Stafford Road, South Beddington. By *W. D. Caröe*, 1906. Later additions. Nave altar by *Covell Matthews*, installed in the 1970s.)

(SACRED HEART (R.C.), Guy Road. 1963–5 by *Tomei & Maxwell.*)

ST ELPHEGE (R.C.), Stafford Road, South Beddington. The original church of 1908 (by *J. H. Beart Foss* and Father *Benedict Williamson*) is now used as a hall. Next to it the church by *Williams & Winkley*, 1971, one of the best examples in London of progressive R.C. churches (cf. St Margaret, East Twickenham (Ri), by the same firm). Plain brick exterior with central roof-light, the interior spare but interesting, with its prominent roof supports and canted angles. The main church is a large square minus a corner, the separate chapel a smaller one. The main altar is in a deliberately accessible position near the entrance, with slightly raked seats on three sides. The vestibule is incomplete. The intention is to link it with the old church.

(CONGREGATIONAL CHURCH, Stanley Park Road. By *P. W. Meredith*, 1928.)

(METHODIST CHURCH, Beddington Gardens, w of Boundary Road (N). By *Frank Windsor*, *c.* 1908.)

(PRESBYTERIAN CHURCH, Stafford Road. By *J. Wills*, 1887. Red brick. GS)

CROWN COURT (former TOWN HALL), Woodcote Road. 1935 by *Robert Atkinson.* A decidedly pretty design, though if compared say with Dudok's work at Hilversum very minor and still very traditional. Still, this is not Georgian, as all other municipal buildings of those years were in England. Brick and stone. Nine bays, the middle ones more widely spaced. Central turret. Much fluting of the stone verticals. Behind the town hall, COURT HOUSE, by *Robert Atkinson & Partners*, 1962; LIBRARY,* 1936, altered in 1962–3 by *Robert Atkinson & Partners*; and CLINIC, by the *Surrey County Architect's Department*, 1964 – not progressive for their dates.

CAREW MANOR SCHOOL (Beddington Place). In the buildings extending to the NE of St Mary's church, part of the Carew mansion of the C 15–16 survives. Rebuildings or extensive alterations have been attributed to Sir Nicholas Carew († 1539), Sir Francis Carew († 1611), and Sir Nicholas Carew († 1727). The hall is preserved between the later projecting wings. It is over 60 ft long and over 30 ft wide, and very tall. Two tiers of two-light windows to the E (C 19 replacements of Georgian windows). Splendid hammerbeam and arch-braced roof with tracery over the collar-beams and two tiers of double-curved wind-braces. Hammerbeams with short pendants. Bosses with Tudor roses. The details are similar to

---

* In the grounds a length of characteristic L-shaped plate rail and sleeper blocks from the Merstham extension to the SURREY IRON RAILWAY.

Eltham Palace (Gr) and suggest a late C 15 rather than mid C 16 date.* At one end a large trophy of arms, of plaster. There are extensive cellars of both brick and stone, partly contemporary with the hall. Little is known of the rest of the Tudor house. The moat and drawbridge were repaired in the Civil War (account book in the Surrey Record Office). Evelyn described the house as decaying, but 'a noble old structure, capacious . . . and proper for the old English Hospitality'. It was rebuilt in 1702–14 on a half-H plan, with the old hall in the centre disguised by giant Corinthian pilasters and central entrance; further alterations were made in 1818 by *D. A. Alexander*. None of these appear to have survived the drastic rebuilding of 1865–6 by *Joseph Clarke* for the Lambeth Female Orphan Asylum, although the present projecting wings must stand on the site of the C 18 ones, and possibly on those of the earlier house. They are now linked by a lower corridor. Red brick with stone dressings, gables, Tudor detail.

In the later C 19 the Rev. Mr Bridges acquired much of the grounds and outbuildings. He laid out the PARK to the W of the house, and probably built (for his own use?) the very pretty LODGE to the N, dated 1877, an elaborately picturesque half-timbered design by *Joseph Clarke*. N W of the house a fine brick octagonal DOVECOTE, early C 18. The handsome iron GATES and SCREEN at the entrance to the house are C 20 facsimiles.

The GARDENS of Sir Francis Carew were famous in the C 17, and included both waterworks and orangery (the latter preserved in winter by a temporary shed). John Evelyn described it as the first orange gardens in England. Several C 17 to C 18 walls survive, including a remarkable one nearly 200 ft long, with blank arcading divided into pairs by simple pilasters on the N face. This may date from the improvement to the gardens by Sir Nicholas Carew (1707–12). The S side of the wall (laid in English bond) would appear to be older, but there is no evidence to associate it definitely with the orangery. BEDDINGTON PARK COTTAGES are a much altered group of outbuildings of the late C 16-early C 19.

WILSON'S SCHOOL, Stafford Road and Mollison Drive. By *Sheppard Robson & Partners*, 1974. Crisply handsome buildings of yellow brick with brown boarded fascia.

For other schools at Roundshaw, *see* Perambulation.

PERAMBULATION. The centre of C 19 and C 20 Wallington is around the town hall, S of the station in WOODCOTE ROAD. Opposite the town hall, WALLINGTON SQUARE, a well designed shopping centre by *Robert J. Wood & Partners*, 1962–5. The street façade has two storeys of curtain-walling

---

* Recent examination of the roof, however, has shown that the construction is not identical to Eltham. The arch braces are tenoned into the principal rafters, a separate piece of timber continuing the line of the arch-brace down to the hammerpost, thus giving the illusion of a true hammerbeam roof. The joints are masked by applied mouldings. Does this suggest a modernization of an earlier roof?

above shops, neatly taking in the slope of the road. The centre shops step back towards a passage leading to an open precinct with more shops, a pub, and, at the far end, a thirteen-storey block of flats in dark brick with exposed concrete floors. Further s, Woodcote Road is fringed by many recent flats, like so many of the main roads in this area (cf. Sutton). A few older houses further N. In MANOR ROAD around the mid C19 DUKE'S HEAD some earlier C19 cottages, Nos. 8–16 (perhaps incorporating older work) and Nos. 32–40. The best buildings lie around the river Wandle. In LONDON ROAD, WALLINGTON BRIDGE is early C19. Near by, No. 258 (Willsmer Engineering), a C19 two-storey weatherboarded mill (formerly a cotton mill for a calico printing works). No. 282 is late C18, five windows wide, with arched ground-floor windows and an Adamish porch. No. 284, WANDLE BANK, was the home of the Pre-Raphaelite painter Arthur Hughes. Early C18 brick, five bays, angle pilasters. The back older, with two rendered gabled wings. A little further N on the r. the GRANGE RESTAURANT, 1967 by the *Borough of Sutton*, replacing The Grange, which was destroyed by fire in 1960.* Opposite, two blocks of flats placed at right angles, with a fully glazed connecting link (Borough Engineer *A. W. Poynor*). At HACKBRIDGE GREEN, two groups of C18 cottages and the OLD RED LION, early C18. At the corner of MILL GREEN ROAD an example of one of the good estates of flats designed in the 1950s for the borough of Wallington, by *Pite, Son & Fairweather*. In Mill Green Road, towards Mitcham, once again near the river, three mid C19 stuccoed villas (Crieff Villas), and further on to the w in MIDDLETON ROAD, Riverside, a former mill house, earlier C19, two storeys with two canted bay-windows.

E of the old parish church of Beddington, in The Brandries, CAMDEN HOUSE (Brandries Hill House), the only survivor of several C18 and C19 mansions in this riverside neighbourhood. Probably early C18 with a late C18 rendered front; five bays with giant Ionic pilasters, smaller pilasters to the top floor. This work was probably done for Francis Baring, who bought the house in 1790 and spent £2,400 on it. *Richard Jupp* (Surveyor to the East India Company, of which Baring was a director) has been suggested as architect. Garden walls and wrought-iron gate in GUY ROAD; also BRANDRIES COTTAGE, C17. To the w of London Road in WANDLE ROAD a late C19 mill, tall and narrow, and low buildings with tiled roofs, probably early C19. Across the river a row of weatherboarded one-storey cottages.

ROUNDSHAW (entrance from Foresters Drive or Stafford Road). Croydon airport closed down in 1959. The plan for redeveloping part of the site (377 acres) with housing for c. 7,600 people was published in 1963 (architects *Clifford*

* The Grange was a rich house of 1879–80, picturesquely grouped, with gables and much tile-hanging.

Culpin & Partners, for the Borough of Sutton and the G.L.C.).
It is an early example in London of those ambitious multi-level
vehicle-segregated schemes which began with Park Hill
Sheffield and Cumbernauld New Town, became popular
during the 1960s, and fell out of favour once they had been
tried out. The general plan is a grid, with buildings of varied
heights, mostly two-storey terrace houses and four-storey
maisonettes and flats, with, at the far end, one very large
eleven-storey block. The dominant feature of the plan is the
strict segregation of traffic and pedestrians, particularly elaborate for the larger blocks. These are built in pairs, linked by a
wide deck or platform above garages (the plan allows for the
garaging of *c.* 2,000 cars, i.e. one car per dwelling). Both
upper maisonettes have doors opening on to this deck, from
which one can reach bridges over the roads, play spaces, etc. –
a much more humane system than the old-fashioned type of
narrow access balconies. The colours are kept neutral. The
larger blocks are of concrete slabs with a ribbed surface, the
smaller houses of purple brick with grey, white, or black
details. The layout suffers from the drawback common to
housing on the deck principle: the discrepancy of scale between the small conventional terraces and the large blocks
with their gaping car ports below the decks (cf. Reporton
Road, Hammersmith, H F). At the S E corner of the site the first
PRIMARY SCHOOL to be built on the site, a simple single-
storey building in dark brick with white boarding; next to it
the BOILER HOUSE of the district heating system, with an
enormous white chimney and the machinery visible through
all-glass walls. A later primary school in REDFORD AVENUE,
and in MOLLISON DRIVE a third, and also a youth club and a
SECONDARY SCHOOL. Also in Mollison Drive a small COM-
MUNITY CENTRE, built in the 1970s. The housing added in
the later 1970s, although still contained within the ruthless
geometry of the grid plan, makes some concession to neo-
vernacular fashion (brown brick and tiled roofs). To the S and
E the rest of the airport remains as open space and sports
grounds, apart from an industrial estate off Imperial Way near
the old airport terminal (*see* Croydon (Cr), Public Buildings).
In the distance a splendid view of the Croydon skyscrapers,
that unplanned brave new world of the 1960s which twenty
years later seems to be as brief an episode as the grandiose
housing schemes of the same decade.

WOODCOTE. *See* Croydon.

CARSHALTON

The centre of Carshalton is still a delightful spot. There is plenty
of water, of which good use is made, and there are plenty of
enjoyable buildings large and small. The only aesthetically
major one is of course Carshalton House.

ALL SAINTS.* The church lies in a slightly elevated position, above the High Street and the pond. From here it is entirely the work of the *Blomfields*, uncle and nephew, in 1893–1914. It is big, and, with the little polygonal turret by the vestry in addition to the old tower with its spike (which replaced a cupola in 1830), it makes quite a lively composition. But behind, to the S, the medieval church appears, externally only in the former chancel, with blocked lancet windows‡ and a C 15 E window of three lights, and the lower part of the former S aisle wall. The upper parts are an alteration of the early C 18 – cf. the arched windows and their surrounds. (The S aisle was raised in 1723 and the church 'beautified'. B. F. L. Clarke) Medieval also the lower parts of the tower, which was an axial tower. Inside, the church of 1893 has at the W end a half-octagonal baptistery, and wide nave and aisles. The medieval N aisle, which was Norman, was destroyed, but some capitals from it survive in store. The present S aisle was the nave of the medieval church; its S aisle is now an outer S aisle. The arcade survives here, with its octagonal piers and leaf-crocket capitals and its double-chamfered pointed arches, a good and typical work of the late C 12. The tower arches are also pointed, possibly inserted in earlier walls. The W arch rests on moulded capitals. In the old chancel, now Lady Chapel, rounded-trefoil PISCINA. Late medieval kingpost roof. – REREDOS designed by *Bodley c.* 1900 and painted in panels by *Comper* in 1931–2. – REREDOS in the Lady Chapel. Good early C 18 work with pilasters and a segmental pediment, gilded and painted by *Comper* in 1936. – SCREEN with ROOD also designed by *Bodley*, *c.* 1914, and also decorated by *Comper* (1931). – ORGAN PROSPECT with an amazingly lavish organ (W end), by *Comper*, 1931–8. – PULPIT. Georgian, with *Comper* additions (1946). – Fine wrought-iron COMMUNION RAIL (Lady Chapel); early C 18. – STAINED GLASS. In the Lady Chapel by *Kempe*, 1895 and 1900. Also other windows by him. – Large ALTAR CROSS by *Reginald Blomfield*, illustrated in 1892, still entirely in the Arts and Crafts style, with heart-shapes and thorn-trails. – MONUMENTS. Tomb-chest to Nicholas Gaynesford † 1497 (S chapel, N wall). Above it kneeling brass figures. The brasses were originally enamelled. The work was done before his death. – Brass to Thomas Ellingbridge and wife. She died in 1497 (S chapel, floor). Mutilated; large figures under canopies and between shafts. – Brass to a cleric, late C 15, fragmentary (S chapel floor). – Brass to Joanna Burton † 1524 (nave floor). – Tablet to Dorothy Burrish † 1685. With cherubs and drapery (S chapel, S wall). – Henry Herringman † 1703, by *W. Kidwell* (S chapel, S wall). Lively scrolly tablet with putti and putti heads. The putti keep a curtain open. No effigy. – Sir John Fellowes † 1724. Tall

* For further details on the church see the excellent guidebook by H. V. Molesworth-Roberts, revised edition 1966.
‡ Now obliterated.

standing wall-monument without figures. Big, heavily fluted
sarcophagus. On it two vases and a tall obelisk on a pedestal. –
Sir William Scawen † 1722 (outer s aisle, e end). Reclining
effigy. Above it sarcophagus with a weeping cherub standing
on it. Big Corinthian columns l. and r. carrying urns. A
disjointed composition. – John Braddyll, by *Rysbrack*, 1753.
Tablet with pediment and Rococo cartouche at the foot (s aisle
e end). – Sir George Amyand † 1766. Fine plain urn in a fine
plain niche. – Michael Shepley † 1837, by *E. J. Physick*
(chancel n wall). With a woman kneeling by the dead man.
The group is placed under a baldacchino niche.

GOOD SHEPHERD, Queen Mary's Avenue, Carshalton
Beeches. 1930 by *Martin Travers & T. F. W. Grant*. Stock
brick; a Spanish Mission gable, a copper clerestory, and a
Baroque interior.

(HOLY CROSS (R.C.), North Street. 1933 by *W. C. Mangan*.
DE)

(BAPTIST CHURCH, Strawberry Lane, n of Mill Lane. The
church hall is a former c 18 house called Strawberry Lodge.
Five windows wide, early c 18 doorway with plain shell hood,
later rendering. c 19 extension. DOE)

(METHODIST CHURCH, Ruskin Road. 1926 by *Andrew
Mather*. Round-arched Georgian; porch with antefixes. H. V.
Molesworth Roberts)

LIBRARY, The Square, e of the parish church. Built as the
council offices, 1908 by *R. Frank Atkinson* and *W. Willis Gale*.
In an ornate early c 18 style with Baroque pediment, brick
quoins, and red and blue brick chequering.

SPORTS AND LEISURE CENTRE, Westcroft Road. 1977 by
Module 2 Ltd and the *Borough Architect*.

CARSHALTON HOUSE (Daughters of the Cross). A large mansion within its own grounds at the w end of the village, hidden
behind high walls, and now adjoining extensive school buildings. It was built in the early c 18 by Edward Carleton, a
tobacco merchant who went bankrupt in 1713. The house was
sold in 1714 to Dr Radcliffe and in 1716 to Sir John Fellowes
of the South Sea Company, who in 1720 also went bankrupt.
Both Radcliffe and Fellowes made improvements to the
property, but there were also several later remodellings of the
interior which are undocumented. Most of the present interior
does not tally with the two inventories made in 1714 and 1720.
The later owners were, from 1730, Sir Philip Yorke, later
Lord Chancellor and first Earl of Hardwicke, who between
1749 and 1752 let it to his son-in-law Admiral Lord Anson;
from 1754 to 1766 George Amyand, a Hamburg merchant;
from 1767 to 1782 the Hon. Thomas Walpole.

The house is a large solid block of nine by seven bays, of
yellow and red brick, with two storeys on a basement, an attic
storey above the cornice, and a hipped roof. The top floor has
been altered, as a roof-line discovered during the alterations in
the 1970s indicates that the third-floor rooms (which are
mentioned in the early inventories) were formerly within

sloping attics. To the s the first and last bays and the three centre bays project a little. The accents on all three floors are marked by pilaster strips of rubbed red brick. In the centre a porch with Corinthian columns and pediment, added probably c. 1750. The E side facing the garden has a slight central projection of three bays and an early C 18 richly carved doorway with segmental pediment on brackets. Wrought-iron rails flank the steps up to both s and E doorways. The N side is not entirely regular. The central projection may be a later tidying up.* The present entrance is through a passage on the w side which now links the house with the school. This is a colonnade with stone Tuscan columns (now glazed in and with a C 19 upper storey) which may also be C 18.

The colonnade leads to the ENTRANCE HALL, which is probably an C 18 alteration. The original entrance may have been on the s side. The hall is a small room with a low groin-vaulted centre resting on four attached columns and continued to w and E by short tunnel-vaults. To the r. in the sw corner is the BLUE PARLOUR, the finest room in the 66 house. Its decoration, in a very personal taste, looks a little later than the hall, and perhaps dates from c. 1750. Glorious arcading against the wall, the arches alternating with coupled fluted Ionic pilasters, carrying short stretches of straight entablature crisply decorated with foliage and interlacing. Chimneypiece with figures in medallions. To the w the corners are divided off and the space in between is made into a lower groin-vaulted alcove, screened from the room by two fluted Ionic columns, which here take the place of pilasters, and an arch. The groins are decorated with delicate trails of fruit and flowers, the arches with enriched guilloche bands. What was the purpose of this room? There is now a window in the alcove, but if it was originally blind (as is the one in the identically planned room above) it could have been intended as a bed recess. The partitioned-off corner to the s w is a closet; behind the other one is a back staircase of early C 18 type, which leads from basement to attic. It seems likely that the mid C 18 decoration was therefore applied to an already existing alcove.

The MAIN STAIRCASE, in a narrow space to the N of the hall, of early C 18 character with all balusters twisted, enriched mouldings, and carved tread-ends, is almost certainly not in its original position. (The Carleton inventory refers to a great staircase and hall under a single heading.) The central room, now LIBRARY, has early C 18 oak panelling, an overmantel with a painted panel of Neptune and Amphitrite, and a fine doorcase with columns and pediment. The room to the N is very plain, with a simple Greek-key cornice. In the OAK

---

* Facing bricks found within the central N room during restoration work, and the Rocque plan of c. 1768, support the possibility of a former recessed centre on this side. The irregular N w corner could possibly incorporate an older building. The walls of the s rooms include re-used building material, including clunch rubble.

PARLOUR in the middle of the s side, panelling and a doorcase of similar character to the library, and an overmantel with excellent carving in the Gibbons tradition, with the Fellowes arms, around a painting of a landscape. The Rococo fireplace with masks and the pretty ceiling with sunburst and foliage must be mid c 18. The only other notable room is the small one in the N E corner, with landscapes painted on the tall main sections of the panelling and other scenes (not all of the same date) on the dado beneath.* Croft Murray attributed the main panels (and also the Oak Parlour and library overmantels) to *Robert Robinson* who died in 1706, which would suggest they were brought from elsewhere. This room must be the PAINTED PARLOUR mentioned in the Carleton inventory. The plan of the rest of the ground floor at that time is however difficult to establish. Both 1714 and 1720 inventories imply that there were four main rooms on the ground floor apart from staircase and hall. The most likely ones are those along the s and E fronts, perhaps with a s entrance leading into a staircase hall in the space occupied now by the library and part of the room to its N. On the first floor there is a central E–W corridor. The s W and s E corner rooms repeat the plan of the Blue Parlour, with alcoves flanked by closets. Their simple decoration, with pilasters supporting arches with plain guilloche bands, is close to that of the entrance hall. In the central room on the N a pretty Victorian fireplace with painted scenes behind glass.

The GROUNDS were laid out by Sir John Fellowes, who employed *Charles Bridgeman* and bought trees from Joseph Carpenter, a partner of Henry Wise. The present layout, which is informal and picturesque, is however probably the result of later modifications. Rocque's map of *c.* 1768 still shows a formal arrangement, but by 1783 Watts's *Seats* shows the present irregular LAKE (now usually dry) and the GROTTO at the s end. This has chambers and passages (now mostly blocked up) behind a stone façade of five bays. The outer bays have small segment-headed windows, the slightly projecting centre rusticated arches and pilasters. Beyond the lake on the E boundary rises the curious and impressive WATER HOUSE, with a tower reminiscent of Vanbrugh. It must have been built by Fellowes in 1719–20. Payments are recorded both to *Richard Cole*, a waterworks engineer, and to *Henry Joynes* (who was Comptroller of Works at Blenheim in 1705–15, under Vanbrugh). The building is of red and yellow brick, five by five bays, with a tower rising above the centre of the far (E) side. Arched windows, broad pilasters, with free capitals with a kind of fluting or gadrooning. The ground floor has coved rooms, the middle one with an oval centre, the l. (N W) one with a marble bath with a sunk basin and blue and white Delft wall tiles. The long room on the other side was an orangery. In

* The paintings were damaged by a burst radiator in 1978 but have been restored.

the tower was a pumping engine to lift the water from the springhead of the lake to a cistern which supplied the house. Remnants of the lower part of the waterwheel survive. Externally the upper storey of the tower has large open arches, buttresses with bases rising to the level of the sills of these arched openings, and a top with typically Vanbrughian fancy battlements and pinnacles. At the main W entrance a handsome pair of GATEPIERS with crowned lions'-heads from the Fellowes arms. W of the school buildings the CHAPEL, 1899–1900 by *E. Ingress Bell*. Brick with dressings of stone and knapped flint. Tower with octagonal lantern and spire. (Interior with mosaics in Byzantine style.)

PERAMBULATION. Carshalton reveals itself most dramatically to the traveller arriving from Sutton. The road skirts the S wall of the grounds of Carshalton House, turns sharp l., meets the gates, sharp r., and arrives at the wide and varied ponds and their bridges, which form the centre of the village. Meanwhile to the l. WEST STREET, modest, but the least spoilt of the old village streets. It starts with the Water House (*see* above), looking doubly imposing from here. Then on the E side a few nice houses (Nos. 2–12), all or partly weatherboarded, of varied shape and size, of the early C 18 onwards. Nos. 20–24 is a long rendered range, perhaps basically C 17. More cottages down WEST STREET LANE (especially No. 25, C 18, weatherboarded). On the other side of West Street old people's housing added discreetly in a close behind (*London Borough of Sutton*, 1979–80). Further on No. 42, C 18 altered, with a C 19 shop canopy, and near the railway bridge No. 80, ROSE COTTAGE, five windows wide, with an early C 19 front (deeds of 1809) added to an older house. Doorcase with Corinthian columns and pediment brought from elsewhere.

Back in the centre, FESTIVAL WALK runs beside the course of the stream (often dry) which flows from Carshalton House to Carshalton Ponds. In this attractive setting stands the OLD RECTORY, a red brick house of the early C 18, with a front of four windows and blue brick chequering, wooden eaves cornice, and doorcase with carved brackets. The W part is a later addition. Festival Walk continues as HONEYWOOD WALK between later houses (THE LODGE, 1866, quite grand) and the ponds to NORTH STREET, where No. 21 is perhaps C 17, four windows wide, with carriage entrance; later rendered front. To the E of North Street THE GROVE, a public garden, once the grounds of a private house, with a fine if small stone BRIDGE of one segmental arch called for no good reason the Leoni Bridge (for *Leoni*'s connections with Carshalton *see* below). (Also in the grounds a fragment of a large waterwheel now set in cement.)

North Street leads back to the church and the beginning of the HIGH STREET. The main building at the W end is the GREYHOUND INN, predominantly C 19 Jacobean, but with earlier parts, the most attractive the projecting weatherboarded wing with two upper canted bay-windows overlooking the ponds. E of this, pleasant OLD PEOPLE'S HOMES in a friendly vernacular style. Brick and weatherboarding, with overhanging gables. By *Thompson & Gardner* for the London Borough of Sutton, 1967. W of the church, set back, pretty brick cottages (ST MARY'S) and a few more to the E: No. 4, incorporating an old flint and masonry wall, and No. 6 (now a wine bar), with a former C19 butcher's shop set in a late C16 timber-framed building with plastered front. C17 rear wing. The rest of the High Street has less of interest. (Nos. 16–20, timber-framed, are perhaps C17.) On the N side a SHOPPING PRECINCT and flats, running back to The Grove, by *Robert J. Wood & Partners*, 1967–8. Further E, the FOX AND HOUNDS, C18 but much altered. NE of the High Street WESTCROFT ROAD, with C18–19 outbuildings, cottages, and garden walls, most of them survivals from two demolished mansions, Parkfields and Bramblehaw. NW of The Grove, MILL LANE, mostly industrial, with offices and laboratories of VINYL PRODUCTS, a neat two-storey curtain-walled block with royal blue spandrels, 1964, and later fussier additions of *c.* 1970 (*Norman Bailey, Samuels & Partners*). STONECOURT is C18, altered.

s of the High Street was yet another large house, CARSHALTON PLACE, demolished in 1927. It was possibly a late C18 rebuilding of an older house called Mascalls. A design made by *Leoni* for a house on this site for Thomas Scawen, *c.* 1723–7, was never carried out. All that remains are two garden buildings. In THE SQUARE near by a nine-bay stuccoed structure with a central four-column Tuscan portico, possibly derived from plans by Leoni for a more elaborate building, converted to offices in 1980–1. In CARSHALTON PARK, which survives from the grounds of the house, a large GROTTO at the head of a long canal-like sheet of water (usually dry). Centre of three arches and four broad piers, the central arch taller and wider than the others. To the l. and r. of the centre, bays with segment-headed alcoves. Inside, a vestibule with niches at the ends, and an octagon room behind with a coved ceiling.

s of the village centre, No. 19 PARK HILL, a minor house by *Philip Webb*, 1868, built for the novelist W. H. White (Mark Rutherford). Brick, with hipped roof and tile-hanging. Back addition 1896 for a billiard room, faced with *Lascelles'* patent concrete panels. Other houses in a similar style followed, e.g. No. 11 (built for White's brother-in-law). Continuing s to BEECHES AVENUE, No. 40, LITTLE HOLLAND HOUSE, is a unique period piece, a testimony to the impact of the Arts and Crafts movement on a self-taught artist and craftsman. *Frank R. Dickinson* (1874–1961) designed and built the house in 1903–4, and himself made all the fittings and furnishings. It is small, with an unassuming roughcast exterior, and unremarkable in plan apart from the staircase rising from the living room *à la* Voysey. Exposed beams, carved with animals and the inscription 'Serve humanity, the Gods we know not'; panelling with painted scenes and family portraits; robust

Arts and Crafts furniture. Dickinson was a versatile craftsman who also worked in metal: see the hammered copper panel over the hearth and the Art Nouveau door fittings. In the bedroom upstairs a charming frieze. Many of his paintings are also preserved here. The house and contents, unaltered, remained in the family until 1972, when with remarkable enterprise it was bought and restored by the London Borough of Sutton.

BRITISH INDUSTRIAL BIOLOGICAL RESEARCH ASSOCIATION, E of Woodmansterne Road, 1 m. S of Carshalton. Good buildings on a hill, by *B. & N. Westwood, Piet & Partners*, 1962–4.*

To the N of the village, at WRYTHE GREEN, WOODCOTE HOUSE, timber-framed, with unusual diagonally laid weatherboarding and a semi-octagonal canted bay, probably built in 1861–7. Much restored.‡

CHEAM

The remains of the old village lie along Malden Road, to the E of Cheam Park, which adjoins the Little Park of Nonsuch just over the present Surrey boundary (*see The Buildings of England: Surrey*). The area of Worcester Park further N derives its name from Worcester Park Farm, which stood on land formerly in Nonsuch Great Park. It was developed from 1865 after the railway arrived in 1859.

ST ALBAN, Gander Green Lane. Built in 1930 from barns from Cheam Court Farm, by *A. J. Marshall & E. A. Swan* (in imitation of St Philip, North Sheen, Ri). Nave with tie-beams and queenposts.

ST DUNSTAN, Church Road. The church of 1862–4 by *Pownall*, replacing an C18 building, is large and dull, with a NW tower with broach-spire added by *Carpenter & Ingelow* in 1870. Lancet windows, quatrefoil windows in the clerestory, apse. Interior with arcades with crocket capitals and polychrome brick walls. – STAINED GLASS. Good W lancets and rose with medallions with the life of St John the Baptist, 1872 by *Clayton & Bell*. – N transept, N and S aisles, four windows with saints, by *Kempe & Co.*, 1909–28.

The LUMLEY CHAPEL, in the churchyard, is the chancel remaining from the medieval parish church. Of flint with

---

* THE OAKS, demolished 1957–60, lay 1½ m. S of the village. It was an C18 house in the grounds of which was erected the magnificent temporary supper pavilion designed in 1774 by *Robert Adam* (and illustrated in his *Works*) for the betrothal feast for the future twelfth Earl of Derby. The house was large and irregular, with turreted and castellated additions possibly by *Adam*, and interiors of the highest quality, including a room with segmental apses and Corinthian wall arcading, attributed to *Sir Robert Taylor*.

‡ During restoration it was found that the house had originally been one-storeyed, giving some support to the claim that it began as a tollhouse, moved to this site and rebuilt after the Kennington to Sutton turnpike was abolished in 1865 (information from D. Cluett).

stone dressings, possibly C 12, with some remains of round-arched, blocked windows. Renewed early Perp E window. Octagonal pier and double-chamfered arch. The roof inside is a delightful remodelling of 1592 (date on one of the pendants). Along the top of the walls a plaster frieze; the tie-beams also plastered with a fruit trail. Ceiling above tunnel-vaulted, with the typical pattern of thin ribs. – BRASSES. Civilian, c. 1390, c. 3 ft 6 in. (a piece in the middle missing). – Civilian, c. 1390, demi-figure, c. 12 in. – John Yerde † 1449 and wife, made c. 1475, less than 7 in. figures. – John Compton and wife, 1458, demi-figures, 9½ in. – William Woodward † 1459, demi-figure, c. 7 in. – Thomas Fromonde † 1542 and wife. Palimpsest of kneeling figures and St John Evangelist of c. 1420 and a scroll, heart, etc., dated 1500. – MONUMENTS. Jane Lady Lumley † 1577, designed in 1590. Incomplete. Three alabaster panels with kneeling figures. Quaint architectural backgrounds said to be representations of the Nonsuch Palace interiors. Two of the panels are placed on the front of a tomb-chest, the third above, against the back wall. – Elizabeth Lady Lumley † 1603. Alabaster of good quality. Recumbent effigy, well carved clothes. The monument was made in 1592, before her death. – John Lord Lumley † 1609. Large inscription plate flanked by two black columns, and carved shields. Strapwork and arms at the top. No figures. – Philip Antrobus † 1816. By *Henry Westmacott*. Grecian with two flanking Greek Doric columns. – Many minor tablets.

St MARY, The Avenue, between Sandy Lane and Burdon Lane, Cuddington. 1895 by *A. Thomas* (*Whitfield & Thomas*). Flint and not brick, with a polygonal apse and a flèche. – (STAINED GLASS. W window by *L. Lee*, 1959.)

St CECILIA (R.C.), Stonecot Hill, North Cheam. 1957 by *H. S. Goodhart-Rendel*.

St CHRISTOPHER (R.C.), Dallas Road, S of High Street. The E end is the chapel built in 1867–8 for Cheam School by *Slater & Carpenter* (house demolished 1935). A handsome building with Geometric Gothic windows and a rather roguish double wagon roof with chamfered collar-beams. A dull new nave has been added at a right angle.

(St MATTHIAS (R.C.), Brinkley Road, Worcester Park. 1965 by *Tomei & Maxwell*. Romanesque with NW campanile. DE)

BAPTIST CHURCH. *See* Perambulation.

St ANDREW PRESBYTERIAN CHURCH, Northey Avenue and The Avenue. The older part (red brick and terracotta with a flèche) is the church hall, by *Matley, Brotherton & Mills*, 1924–7. The larger new part, 'moderne' in style, without a tower, is by *Maxwell Ayrton*, 1931–3. An addition of 1956.*

LIBRARY, Church Road, W of Malden Road. 1962 by *P. Masters & A. Pereira*. A good neat building, although rather large for its site in the centre of the old village.

---

* Demolished 1978: St PHILIP, Cheam Common Road. 1873–4 by *Carpenter*. Red brick, lancet windows, bellcote on E end of nave.

ST ANTHONY'S HOSPITAL, London Road, North Cheam. By
 Anthony Jones (of *John Laing Design Associates*), 1973–5. Extensive low buildings with pitched roofs.

SUTTON DISTRICT WATER COMPANY, Gander Green Lane.
 Well grouped, crisply detailed one- and two-storey buildings
 of the 1970s.

PERAMBULATION. Near the church, in and around MALDEN
 ROAD, just a little survives of the old village, although it is a
 pity that to the S the effect is spoilt by the adjoining mock-
 Tudor shopping parades of between the wars, and the BAP-
 TIST CHURCH of 1907 (with hall of 1920 and extension of
 1938). The HIGH STREET was entirely spoilt by road widening in the 1920s.

Starting from the churchyard and the LYCHGATE of 1891,
 bargeboarded with three archways, Nos. 1–2, OLD FARM
 HOUSE (formerly Church Cottages), makes a good beginning, a timber-framed house with rendered front and old tiled
 roof, well restored. The front part (central chimneystack,
 lobby-entrance plan) is probably of *c.* 1600, the E bay and the
 back wing older (crown-post roof). THE COTTAGE and some
 weatherboarded outbuildings follow. In MALDEN ROAD,
 THE RECTORY, a substantial house of brick and mathematical tiles with double-gabled end to the road, and a five-bay
 garden front, an C18 remodelling of an older core. To the S a
 row of weatherboarded cottages, Nos. 5–9 Georgian, No. 3
 with two gables and small windows, C17.

WHITEHALL, No. 1, is the most interesting house in Cheam,   3
 excellently restored (by *John West & Partners*, 1975–6) and
 maintained by the borough as a museum piece. Timber-
 framed, three bays, of *c.* 1500, with continuous jetties to front
 and back. The two attic gables, projecting porch with upper
 room, back staircase tower, and S chimneystack are additions
 probably of the mid to later C16. The attractive weatherboarding that covers the whole building was added in the C18.
 The original close studding and curved braces of the back wall
 can be studied inside, as can the crown-post roof. It is an early
 example of a two-storeyed hall house, i.e. a house with the
 main living area no longer open to the roof as had been the
 medieval practice. It is one of the best preserved examples of
 the type, and certainly the most accessible in the London
 area. There are two brick chimneystacks; on the N side of the N
 stack two curious recesses. The S stack has ovens, and so by
 the time it was added this must have been the service end. At
 the back a wing added in the C17 when the house is believed to
 have been used by Cheam School. In the downstairs room a
 plain marble C18 fireplace brought from West Cheam Manor.

N of Whitehall Nos. 45–47 THE BROADWAY, a low C17 range,
 weatherboarded and roughcast, much altered by shops. In
 between PARK LANE leads down towards Cheam Park; the S
 side, a happily picturesque sequence of weatherboarded cottages of different sizes and dates, is one of the best groups of its
 kind in London. The oldest houses are Nos. 7–11 (Oak

Cottage) and No. 25 (both C 17). The N side, weatherboarded old people's homes of the 1970s, does not jar too acutely. At the end a small one-storey LODGE to the park, stuccoed, with pedimented porch and rounded corners, c. 1820.

Other survivals are isolated. In THE BROADWAY, OLD COTTAGE, a timber-framed jettied house of c. 1500, with gable to the road, moved from a site near by in 1922. To the E in PARK ROAD Nos. 3–5, C 18 brick, with an Adamish doorcase; the OLDE RED LION, low, c. 1600, much altered; and No. 38, a late C 18 front with fanlight and two bow-windows, older behind. CHURCH FARM LANE, with some old walls and an outbuilding (of West Cheam Manor House), leads to CHURCH FARM HOUSE; early C 19 stucco front, C 17 timber-framed part behind. Extension (for nurses' home) by *Thompson & Gardner*, 1970s. Towards the N end of MALDEN ROAD Nos. 89–91, weatherboarded cottages.

EWELL ROAD has a little more opposite the entrance to Nonsuch Park – a weatherboarded group called PARK COTTAGES, some earlier C 19 villas round the corner, and the FARMER MEMORIAL of 1895, a cross over a drinking fountain.

WARREN AVENUE, WILBURY AVENUE, ONSLOW AVENUE, 1 m. S. Front-garden walls incorporate red brick walling from a C 17 HARE WARREN.

ST HELIER ESTATE

An L.C.C. estate on the Merton and Sutton boundary, designed in its extensive original parts in 1928–36 under the L.C.C. Architect, *G. Topham Forrest*. Pleasant streets in the Parker & Unwin cottage tradition around CENTRAL AVENUE.

On the estate ST PETER, Middleton Road, a disappointing church of 1932 by *Sir C. Nicholson* (GR), and BISHOP ANDREWES'S CHURCH, Wigmore Road, 1933 by *Geddes Hyslop*, rather modernistic, small, with a big, broad, short crossing tower and roofs over the other parts reaching very low down. Several tricks of brick ornamentation. For ST TERESA, Bishopsford Road, *see* Morden (Me).

ST HELIER HOSPITAL. Big, tall and broad, symmetrical composition, in a utilitarian modern idiom. 1938 by *Saxon Snell & Phillips*.

SUTTON

The village, which lay between The Green at the N end of the High Street and the parish church further S, was transformed during the period when the main Brighton road passed along the High Street (1775–1809), then grew into a town after the railway came in 1847 (population 1841: 1,304; 1881: 10,334).* In the

---

* Growth was especially rapid after the Sutton Water Company (incorporated 1863) made water supplies easily available on the hitherto undeveloped chalk areas.

1960s there was an outburst of commercial development which promised to turn the town into a second Croydon, but which has since fizzled out except for the area near the station. The two new soulless back streets for the traffic, and the partial pedestrianization of the High Street, are the results of the development plan of 1968. The High Street itself is disappointingly mediocre architecturally, but remains on a human scale, because the tall blocks of the 1960s–70s have nearly all been set back from it.

ALL SAINTS, Benhilton. By *S. S. Teulon*, 1863–6. Large and very prominently placed at the foot of Angel Hill. Big broad w tower. Dec details. Broad nave, cruciform piers with chamfered corners. Circular clerestory windows. None of the more obtrusive mannerisms of Teulon. – (STAINED GLASS. 1965, outstandingly good. E window by *J. & M. Kettlewell*, s aisle windows by *John Hayward*. A. Clifton-Taylor)

CHRIST CHURCH, Christchurch Park. 1888 by *Newman & Jacques*. Red brick, with polygonal apse. No tower. Lancet windows. The w end with the quite separate porch with doorways in three directions and the baptistery between two low bays is of *c*. 1910–12 (by *J. D. Round*). Inside, spectacular ROOD SCREEN with the rood supported on an openwork crown.

ST BARNABAS, St Barnabas Road, Newtown. 1884–91 by *Carpenter & Ingelow*. Red brick. – STAINED GLASS. E window by *Morris & Co.*, the Sermon on the Mount, a pictorial design across five lights, a good example of the firm's late work, if a long way from Morris.

ST JOHN BAPTIST, Avenue Road, Belmont. 1915 by *Greenaway & Newberry* (GR).

ST NICHOLAS, St Nicholas Road. The old parish church was rebuilt by *Edwin Nash* in 1862–4. Flint with broach-spire, not attractive. – (MONUMENT. Concealed behind the organ, Dorothy Lady Brownlow †1700, an elaborate wall-monument by *William Stanton*; reclining figure with mourning putti.*) – In the churchyard (now truncated and overshadowed by the civic centre) many good tombs including a MAUSOLEUM of 1777, with pyramid roof, rusticated quoins, and rusticated door surround. It is to James Gibson, citizen and merchant of London, and his family. – RECTORY and CHURCH HALL to the w, by *Devereux & Partners*, 1975.

OUR LADY OF THE ROSARY (R.C.), St Barnabas Road. Converted from a school into a church by *E. Ingress Bell* in 1887 (GR). His is the tall polygonal roof over the chancel, which has a domical vault inside.

Just s of St Nicholas in CHEAM ROAD two more remarkable churches. One is the TRINITY METHODIST CHURCH, 1907 by *Gordon & Gunton*, with a bold tower carrying a 'crown' like Newcastle and Edinburgh Cathedrals. Ragstone polygonal

---

* Drawing in the V and A: see J. Physick, *Designs for English Sculpture 1680–1860* (1969), p. 52.

apse. Church hall attached to the 'E' end. The other is the
BAPTIST CHURCH, 1934 by *Cachemaille-Day*. Red brick
with 'moderne' details; the secular parts well grouped. (Striking interior with the windows framed by dramatic, steeply
pointed wall arches.)

CIVIC CENTRE, St Nicholas Way. 1973–8 by the *Borough
Architect's Department* (*J. Trevor Jobling*, Director of Technical Services; *Peter Hirst*, Borough Architect). A monolith
containing Civic Offices, Library, Advice Bureau, and
College of the Liberal Arts, an imaginative mixture. Plain
brick exterior, not enhanced by its cramped position between
service road and car park. The main approach is on two levels,
the lower one via a subway from the High Street leading into a
courtyard, with the information office at ground level and the
informal foyer to library, exhibition gallery, and coffee area on
the floor above.

HEALTH CENTRE, Robin Hood Lane, W of the High Street. By
the *Borough Architect's Department*, 1969. Two storeys, white
brick.

ROYAL MARSDEN HOSPITAL, Brighton Road. Big blocks by
Lanchester & Lodge, 1960–2.

HIGH STREET, from N to S. The High Street starts by The
Green with the new and the old: HELENA HOUSE by *Morgan
& Branch*, 1962, curtain-walling with green spandrel panels,
and THE CRICKETERS, with weatherboarded part obscured
by later additions. At the bend EAGLE STAR HOUSE, a
composition in concrete by the *Owen Luder Partnership*, 1963–
7. A nine-storey office block above two projecting storeys with
shops. The line of shops follows the curve of the road, then
turns back along two sides of a little precinct. In front of this is
a free-standing building with glazed upper floor on concrete
stilts, linked (with the main block) by wilfully complicated
stairs to a car park behind. The tall block has horizontal bands
of concrete with a rough surface, and round-ended lift-shafts
and stairs of concrete with the shuttering marks exposed. The
group looks best from the N, making an emphatic statement at
the entrance to the High Street, but closer up there are too
many tricky details (e.g. the low concrete lintels of the shop
doorways).

Then little to note until MARSHALL'S ROAD is reached. Off to
the l. housing of 1978–9 by the *Borough Architect's Department*;
demure terraces, apparently of purple-brown brick (in fact
timber-framed with brick cladding). At the corner of Benhill
Avenue, THE GRAPES, later C 19, debased Italianate. Further s a few modern buildings of 1957–8: LILLEY & SKINNER
by *M. Egan*, and, much better detailed, WILLERBYS by *C. J.
Epril*, small fry compared with what was built in the 1960s,
e.g. BOOTS and SAINSBURYS opposite, with large upper
blind wall, 1969 by *Basil Whiting*. Further up the hill on the E
side is W. H. SMITH, with a good plain front of concrete and
glass bands, in scale with the older shops. Hiding behind this,
but very prominent from a distance, is a nine-storey block on

stilts, with the entrance in Throwley Way. The whole complex is by the *Owen Luder Partnership*, 1961–4. The tall block is a forceful, boldly profiled rectangular building with canted corners. There is a staircase tower at either end, the one nearer the High Street projecting well above the main building. The towers have continuous vertical bands of rough concrete, the office block has chamfered horizontal bands, projecting forward from the window plane. Both the Sutton buildings by this firm are an instructive illustration of the shift from the use of glass curtain-walling in the Miesian tradition to the more expressionistic use of reinforced concrete that was gaining ground in the early 1960s.

In ST NICHOLAS ROAD, off the other side of the High Street, the most interesting shopfront in Sutton, the extension built for AMOS REYNOLDS (now Skinners) by *Michael Manser Associates*, 1965–6. Brilliantly simple. A plain wall faced with narrow white unbonded tiles, laid vertically, cut through by two tiers of cantilevered steel-framed glass boxes which act as miniature rooms for furniture display. Opposite, ST NICHOLAS HOUSE, by *Riches & Blythin*, 1965. Three-storey block, grey curtain-walling above shops, interlocking with a seven-storey block above. Back in the High Street on the E side a shopping precinct with bridge to the car park in Throwley Way (begun 1979), then SURREY HOUSE, another large block with a tower of offices at the back. Projecting mullions. 1975 by *R. J. Wood & Partners*. At the top of the hill the crossing with Carshalton Road and Cheam Road, marked by the old inn sign of the COCK above a central signpost. The successor to the building demolished in 1961 is sadly characterless, a waste of a focal point.* As a compensation there is BARCLAYS opposite, a good late C19 corner building with lavish French Renaissance ornament, and further on the more unusual NATIONAL WESTMINSTER BANK in Brighton Road at the corner of Sutton Court Road, 1902 by *Frederick Wheeler*, with nice Art Nouveau carving around the windows.

In SUTTON COURT ROAD near the railway the biggest group of offices. The first to come was VIGILANT HOUSE by *Robert J. Wood & Partners*, 1961–6, still in the Miesian tradition with its seventeen storeys of curtain-walling. The structure is of reinforced concrete, cantilevered out on two sides, so that, as one approaches, the building seems to float above a void (in fact a sunken car park). Spandrel panels are in a neutral pale green; the top floor is finished off neatly by a broad black band. The companion building, SENTINEL HOUSE, is of four storeys, with the same details, but on stilts. The two are linked by an ingenious T-shaped entrance bridge over the car park. Opposite, WATERMEAD HOUSE, by the same firm, 1975, faced with unbonded white tiles, and BANK MANSIONS, only four storeys high, by *Trehearne, Norman, Preston*

---

* The COCK of 1897 had a pretty façade with a round angle bay and two shallow minor bays, all three with scrolly ornament.

& *Partners*, 1979, white tiles and bronze windows. Next to the station, tallest of all, two linked slab blocks faced in pink granite, by *Brewer, Smith & Brewer*, 1979–80. In BRIGHTON ROAD, SUTHERLAND HOUSE, by *Robert J. Wood & Partners*, 1961–6, eleven storeys with bands of white mosaic.

Further s along the Brighton Road and the roads off it was an area of large Victorian villas (with Christ Church, q.v.), now almost entirely replaced by flats. Exceptions are STOWFORD, mid C 19, and No. 139, a pretty C 18 house of three bays, with a circular window over the door and lower wings. In CAVEN-DISH ROAD the new scale is used even for old people's flats (FISKE COURT), with some originality. By *Rock Townsend*, 1978. Two four-storey blocks linked by a greenhouse-type projecting gallery at third-floor level. The lift to the gallery in a separate tower. Four staircases painted in bright primary colours. Whether this high-technology approach appeals to the residents is another matter.

Back to the N, E of the High Street, around LIND ROAD, ST BARNABAS ROAD, etc., SUTTON NEW TOWN, a modest late C 19 artisan area with numerous pubs.

WANDSWORTH

INTRODUCTION

The London Borough of Wandsworth extends from the industrial riverside of Battersea as far w as some of the most extensive
open spaces in London: Wimbledon Common and Richmond
Park.* In the Middle Ages Battersea and Wandsworth were
separate parishes with their own churches; so was Tooting further s. Putney and Roehampton lay within the huge parish of
Wimbledon which also embraced the wasteland of Putney Heath
and Wimbledon Common. By the C18 the main settlements
were the villages of Battersea, Wandsworth, and Putney, close to
the river, and further s, the villages or hamlets of Clapham,
Balham, and Upper and Lower Tooting. w of Putney the area
called Putney Park, or Roehampton, was by then studded with
aristocratic mansions and villas on the fringes of Richmond
Park. The whole area, together with Streatham (since 1965
mostly in Lambeth), was already united under Wandsworth
Local Board of Works in 1855, although Battersea was an independent (and energetic) local authority between 1887 and 1965.

* PREHISTORIC SITES. There was dense Palaeolithic concentration across
Wandsworth, and a scatter of later finds, including possible Bronze Age barrows,
on Putney Heath. Neolithic settlement and flint-working at Putney; a possible
Bronze Age barrow at Tooting. There was a ROMAN SETTLEMENT beside a
probable river crossing at Putney, with burials to the w, and further Roman
burials at Battersea.

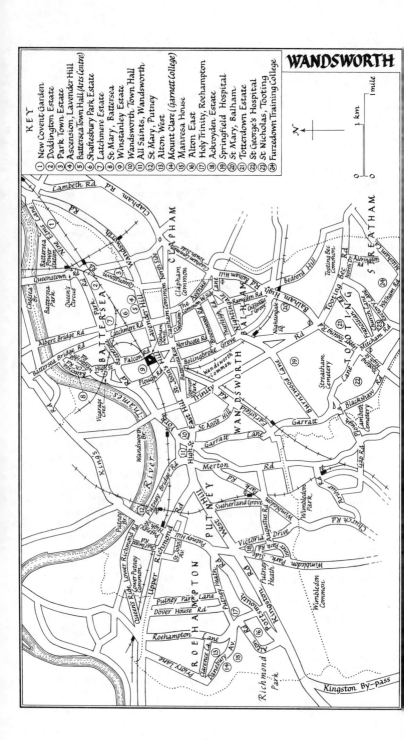

WANDSWORTH

KEY

1. New Covent Garden
2. Doddington Estate
3. Park Town Estate
4. Ascension, Lavender Hill
5. Battersea Town Hall (Arts Centre)
6. Shaftesbury Park Estate
7. Latchmere Estate
8. St Mary, Battersea
9. Winstanley Estate
10. Wandsworth Town Hall
11. All Saints, Wandsworth
12. St Mary, Putney
13. Alton West
14. Mount Clare (Garnett College)
15. Manresa House
16. Alton East
17. Holy Trinity, Roehampton
18. Ackroyden Estate
19. Springfield Hospital
20. St Mary, Balham
21. Totterdown Estate
22. St George's Hospital
23. St Nicholas, Tooting
24. Furzedown Training College

Wandsworth was the largest of all the L.C.C. boroughs (population in 1951 330,000).

The total population for the whole of the present borough is 254,898 (1981). The whole area is too large and has monuments too scattered to be treated under one heading. It is therefore described here under the following areas: Balham, Battersea, Putney, Roehampton, Tooting with Streatham Park, and Wandsworth. Clapham, most of which is in Lambeth, is all described under that borough, as is the eastern part of Streatham. It is not easy to draw the boundaries between these areas. Battersea, Putney, and Wandsworth especially merge into one amorphous Victorian suburb, and the buildings worth hunting out are for the most part isolated.* The following architectural highlights can be singled out here.

Most of the old centres are still identifiable (in some cases only just) by a sprinkling of pre-Victorian buildings: a few good riverside houses at Battersea (especially Old Battersea House), C18 terrace houses at Wandsworth, small villas or country houses at Balham (The Priory), Streatham Park (Furzedown), Putney, and Tooting. The richest by far is Roehampton, where in settings now largely of the post-Second-World-War era, the surviving country mansions run the whole gamut of styles from Baroque to Gothic Revival: *Archer*'s Roehampton House, *Chambers*'s house for Lord Bessborough (now Manresa House), *Robert Taylor*'s Palladian villa, Mount Clare (Garnett College), *Wyatt*'s neo-classical Upper Grove House (Froebel Institute), The Priory (early and mid C19 Gothic). The rest of the story is the usual one of C19 expansion and of C20 replacement. In the mid C19 the unbuilt areas were exploited for the extensive hospitals, cemeteries, and other institutions needed by the growing metropolis (see especially Tooting and Wandsworth for hospitals, Wandsworth for schools and almshouses). The southern part of Battersea is especially rewarding for the study of urban housing and public buildings of the mid C19 onwards, including both *James Knowles Jun.*'s speculative development, the Park Town Estate, and some of the earliest planned artisan housing in London (Shaftesbury Park), followed by Battersea Borough Council's own Latchmere Estate (1903). The theme of planned housing can be pursued at Tooting and Roehampton (early C20 L.C.C. cottage estates) and then at Roehampton and Putney, which have some of the most influential work of the L.C.C. of the mid C20, the first important demonstration of the principle of combining tower blocks and lower housing with generous open spaces. This has to be contrasted with the more depressing local authority rebuilding which transformed much of Wandsworth and Battersea during the 1960s/early 1970s. In 1977 34 per cent of Wandsworth households were in council

* For the purposes of this volume the s part of Battersea excludes the areas immediately around Clapham Common, which are described under Clapham (La). Wandsworth includes East Hill and the area w of Wandsworth Common, as far s as Garratt Green and Summerstown; Putney includes West Hill and Putney Heath.

housing. That is, however, a low figure when compared with other inner boroughs, and indeed the only memorable borough efforts of this time are *Battersea*'s (later *Wandsworth*'s) Wilberforce Estate (*George Trew Dunn*), a medium- and high-rise estate laid out around pedestrian courtyards, the earlier parts of 1963–6 pleasanter than many other developments of this date; and, as an extreme example of the worst excesses of industrialized building of the 1960s, the Doddington Estate in Battersea Park Road. Interesting examples of the 1970s return to low-rise housing are the small groups built by the G.L.C. and by or for Wandsworth on Putney Heath;* also *Wandsworth*'s Maysoule Road, Battersea (*Phippen Randall & Parkes*). Many of Wandsworth's estates of the later 1970s, although low, are still ruthlessly large (e.g. Kambala Road, Battersea). However, the *G.L.C.*'s Althorpe Grove, Battersea, at long last displays a sense of appropriate scale in its approach to redevelopment of an old area in contrast to the earlier estates in Battersea, and to the hideous Arndale Centre at Wandsworth of the previous decade.

Further Reading

There is little older literature of use to architectural historians and no DOE revised list yet available, but a considerable quantity of recent research on c 19 Battersea. On pre-Victorian matters, J. G. Taylor's very thorough *Our Lady of Batersey* (1925) deals with more than the history of the church. Simmond's *All about Battersea* (1882) is informative on developments of the time. J. Roebuck, *Urban Development in* c 19 *London: Lambeth, Battersea and Wandsworth 1838–1888* (1979) is chiefly administrative history; P. Metcalf, 'The Park Town Estate and the Battersea Tangle', *London Topographical Society*, 121 (1978), has much of interest on planning and architecture. The *Wandsworth Papers* published by the Wandsworth Historical Society include two on urban development: *South Battersea, the Formative Years* by R. Logan (1977), and *Battersea New Town 1790–1870* by Keith Bailey (1980). This society has also published some well researched Heritage Walks (1977 onwards). Apart from these there is very little on other areas. D. R. Young, *The Church on the High Road* (typescript, n.d.; copy available in the Greater London History Library) is a thorough history of St Mary Balham; Joan P. Alcock, *Where Generations Have Trod* (typescript, Polytechnic of the South Bank, 1979), and *Surrey Archaeological Collections* (1981) deal with Manresa House Roehampton.
See also p. 124.

Acknowledgements

I am grateful to Mr Keith Bailey of the Wandsworth Historical Society, and to Mr Richard Shaw, the borough's local history librarian, for answering many questions; to Mr Vernon Gibberd

---

* The Borough Architect from 1965 to 1980 was *L. Phillips.*

for help on Old Battersea House; to Mr P. R. Gilfillan for information on Roehampton; to Mr John Partridge for discussing with me the L.C.C. estates at Putney and Roehampton; to Dr Priscilla Metcalf, Mr Nicholas Boulting, and Mr E. E. Smith, who read all or parts of the text and offered useful corrections and comments; and to the staff of the Planning Department for details on recent developments.

BALHAM

CHURCHES

THE ASCENSION, Malwood Road, W of Balham Hill. 1883–90 by *Arthur Cawston* (the architect of St Philip, Stepney, T H), quite an original interior, with an arcade worth noting: slender octagonal piers without capitals, and pierced spandrels. Large transepts, narrow E aisle with tile mosaic of 1888. – (STAINED GLASS. E window by *Clayton & Bell*, baptistery and N transept by *Lavers & Westlake*.)

ST JOHN, Bedford Hill. Chancel 1883 by *R. J. Withers*, nave 1899 by *E. H. Elphick*, stock brick.

ST LUKE, Ramsden Road. An impressive red brick Lombard Romanesque exterior, 1883–9 by *F. W. Hunt*. Short chancel with apse, NW campanile 1892; W apsed baptistery 1899. An Early Christian church was intended, and the interior is indeed basilican, with no chancel arch, although the arcades are pointed, and rest on Early Gothic capitals. – Notable FURNISHINGS: a successful amalgam of Early Christian, Renaissance, and other sources. Low marble SCREEN of Early Christian type (1894), marble PULPIT, and LECTERN supported by large marble angel (1901), all made by *Farmer & Brindley*, designed by *William White*. – Carved SEDILIA (1896), STALLS, PULPIT TESTER, by *Harry Hems*. – Apse MOSAIC (1902–7) and STAINED GLASS by *Powell's*: deep colours filling the small apse windows above the mosaic and in the aisles. – Festive ELECTROLIERS, 1903. Those of the nave are based on a Cellini pendant, those of the chancel have Fra Angelico angels. – Bronze CANDELABRA, cast from originals by Giovanni da Bologna. – S Lady Chapel refitted by *Martin Travers*, 1924–7, the pale STAINED GLASS window of St David added at the same time. – Tall FONT COVER also by *Travers*.

ST MARY, Balham High Road. The church began as a proprietary chapel in 1805, and became parochial in 1855. The W front is a showy Wrenian confection, with a pediment between twin towers (only one completed) and a projecting domed baptistery, by *William Newton Dunn*, 1903. Behind it is the plain preaching box built by *F. Hurlbatt* in 1807, to which transepts were added in 1824, also by *Hurlbatt*, and a vaguely Byzantine apsed chancel in 1882, by *A. Cawston*. Spacious interior (the side galleries were removed in 1891). Chancel lavishly decorated with marble and mosaic panels in the 1890s; painted ceiling, alabaster PULPIT. – Sculptured PANEL of the Raising of Lazarus, N chapel, 1886. – STAINED GLASS. Apse clerestory windows by *Clayton & Bell*. – Baptistery windows by *Heaton, Butler & Bayne*, figures in suitably Mannerist frames. The bulgy columns of the baptistery itself are typical of its turn-of-the-century date. – Glass SCREEN, creating a W narthex, 1973. – CHURCH SCHOOLS, E of the church. Modest; 1859, 1884, etc.

HOLY GHOST (R.C.), Nightingale Square. 1897 by *Leonard Stokes*. Very cheap, with an unassuming brick exterior, but an interior which shows the spatial imagination of its designer. This was especially evident in the narrow N aisle before it was opened up to the Lady Chapel beyond. Originally there were shallow pointed side chapels between the buttresses, creating an interesting ambiguity. They could be seen either as chapels behind the polygonal, capital-less piers, or as bays of a continuous aisle.

CHURCH OF JESUS CHRIST OF LATTER DAY SAINTS, Nightingale Lane. 1966 by *David M. Rae*. Zigzagging gables and a slim open campanile. Alterations 1979–80 by *L. Gooday & Associates*.

PUBLIC BUILDINGS

LIBRARY, Ramsden Road. 1898 by *S. R. J. Smith* (cf. Lambeth (La), Public Buildings: Libraries), a pretty example of the free Tudor and Georgian mixture of *c.* 1900. One-storeyed, with a bow-window.

CLAPHAM COLLEGE, Nightingale Lane. *See* Clapham (La), Public Buildings.

HYDEBURN SCHOOL, Chestnut Grove. A comprehensive school for 900 children. One of the more interesting I.L.E.A. buildings of the 1970s. A telling contrast of images: in Hearnville Road the original Board School of 1905, a plain Queen Anne mansion; behind it the additions of 1973–7 (*P. Reynolds* and *B. Wilson* of the *G.L.C. Architect's Department Education Branch*), a compact two-storey polygonal cluster which, apart from the games hall, is almost entirely clad in tinted glass, like the sleekest of 1970s industrial buildings. Library, music, and drama areas in the central core surrounded by classrooms grouped in split-level open-plan clusters off roof-lit corridors. The school is surrounded by grass, despite the small site, which does much to soften its impact on a brick suburban setting.

ST JAMES' HOSPITAL, St James's Drive, off the SE end of Trinity Road. Modernization of the C19 hospital buildings, which originated as the St James's Industrial Schools, began with the new OUTPATIENTS' DEPARTMENT, 1953 by *Devereux & Davies*, progressive for its date: three storeys, flexibly planned, with cheerful, deliberately non-institutional interiors using bright colours. The main exterior ornament is the gay undulating roof-line of porch and waiting room, projecting slightly from the main block. Further improvements to the hospital from 1954 by the same firm, notably the new central facility block, 1969, with dining rooms, operating theatres, etc. On the lawn outside the outpatients' department a sculpture, bronze nude by *Douglas Wain-Hobson*, 1954.

LONDON TRANSPORT STATIONS. BALHAM and CLAPHAM SOUTH on the Morden extension of the Northern Line of 1926 have stations by *Holden*, with good entrance halls (cf. Tooting, below).

PERAMBULATION

Balham was never a proper village, just a settlement on the main road between Clapham and Tooting, before it became absorbed in the growth of London in the C19. On BALHAM HILL nothing of interest except the ODEON (now LIBERTY) cinema, one of *George Coles*'s symmetrical streamlined exteriors in cream faience (1938). BALHAM HIGH ROAD continues S with a few early C19 terrace houses, and some way S a few larger detached villas of the same period. The best is No. 207, MANSBRIDGE HOUSE, stuccoed, with central doorway with Doric columns *in antis*. Two similar houses further on, much altered (HAMILTON HOUSE, OAK LODGE). In BALHAM GROVE to the W some smaller villas with Doric porches (Nos. 5–15), and in OLD DEVONSHIRE ROAD to the E some more individualistic examples (Nos. 24–26 classical, No. 22 Tudor Gothic; also GOTHIC LODGE at the SE corner).

THE PRIORY, Bedford Hill. On the edge of Tooting Bec Common. One of the few remaining Regency Gothic villas in outer London (cf. The Priory Roehampton, Ww). Built in 1822; restored and converted to flats, after long neglect, in 1981–2. Stuccoed brick, battlemented, with spindly corner pinnacles. In the grounds somewhat harsh red brick housing of the 1970s.

On the opposite side of BEDFORD HILL, large red brick houses of the 1880s–90s with much ornamental brickwork in the Shaw or Ernest George tradition, part of the estate developed by Alfred and George Heaver.

NIGHTINGALE LANE, which divides Balham from Clapham to the N, has rather more character. By ENDLESHAM ROAD W of Ramsden Road a group of three pairs of tall semi-detached houses by *T. E. Collcutt*, 1879, extravagantly decorated with French Renaissance motifs in terracotta. A shopping parade to match follows; also smaller houses in Endlesham Road. In contrast, THE NIGHTINGALE and the mid C19 cottages behind in WESTERN LANE still have a rural air. Opposite, No. 74 Nightingale Lane, one of the few surviving examples of the wealthy mansions built here *c*. 1850–60, extended and heightened, but still with its Italianate tower. Another further on: NIGHTINGALE HOUSE (No. 105), 1871 by *R. Richard-*

son (large extensions *c*. 1904 and further additions 1973–6 for the Homes for Aged Jews).

BATTERSEA

INTRODUCTION

Of the old village of Battersea only a shadow is left: the C 18 church and a few houses worth examining. The manor had belonged to the Abbey of Westminster, then after the Dissolution for a while to the Crown, and from 1627 to 1763 to the St John family. Their manor house lay E of the church, later the site of flour mills. It was mostly pulled own in 1793, and the last remaining interiors seem to have left Battersea well into the C 20. The industrialization of the riverside came only after the arrival of the railways. Until then Battersea had been chiefly a market-gardening area. Down to Elizabethan times lower Battersea was marshy and boggy. Then a marsh wall was built and the land reclaimed. On a map of 1838 there were still no more houses than the village round the church and a cluster along Falcon Road; a sub-manor, York House, in York Road (where Price's candle factory now stands); and another group of houses in Bolingbroke Grove (the site of one of them absorbed by a hospital). Carlyle coming over from Chelsea could take exercise in fine weather on Lavender Hill, and Kingsley's Alton Locke remembers the 'flowery dykes of Battersea Fields' as they were in his youth. Then in 1838 the Southampton Railway opened its London depot at Nine Elms, and in the 1840s–60s the railways grew rapidly. Clapham Junction Station was opened in 1863. Battersea Park with its romantic lake was laid out in 1854. The population, 5,540 in 1831, rose to 10,560 in 1851, 19,600 in 1861, 54,016 in 1871, 107,262 in 1881, 168,905 in 1901, and then remained more or less stationary until the Second World War reduced it to 117,000. More recently much of the industry has disappeared, and is beginning to be replaced by offices and warehouses, especially around Nine Elms.

CHURCHES

The parish church of St Mary, close to the river, is still a simple C 18 preaching box, with one of the best collections of monuments in South London. Of the many C 19 churches built to supplement it only *James Brooks*'s outstanding Ascension, Lavender Hill (1876), and perhaps St Mark, Battersea Rise (1873–4), the first among several Battersea churches by *William White*, deserve special mention.*

---

* Demolitions: ST GEORGE, Nine Elms Lane. 1827–8 by *Blore*, modest with lancet windows, chancel of 1874, W bellcote of 1913. – ST MARY-LE-PARC, Albert Bridge Road. 1883 by *William White*. Only the eastern part of the church, apsed with chapels, was built. – CONGREGATIONAL CHURCH, Battersea Bridge Road. By *H. Fuller*, 1866, crude Norman with plate tracery.

ALL SAINTS, Prince of Wales Drive, w of Queen's Circus.
1976–8 by *David Gill*, replacing a church of 1882–3 by *F. W.
Hunt*. An ingenious multi-purpose space, the sanctuary separated by folding doors and lit by a higher roof with clerestory,
which defines the special function of the building from the
outside. Against the lower windows STAINED GLASS from
the old church. A projecting upper floor is divided off for
offices.

ASCENSION, Lavender Hill. Begun in 1876 by *James Brooks*,
completed by *J. T. Micklethwaite & Somers Clarke*, who took
over *c.* 1882. The E end of the nave was begun to a modified
design in 1883, the upper part and W end not completed until
1893–8. The church is a noble design of great simplicity, along
the lines of Brooks's earlier churches in Hackney. Exterior of
brick with lancet windows to the clerestory; no aisle windows.
Unbroken lines of nave, aisle, and ambulatory roofs (like a
Cistercian church). In the original design these were countered by a bellcote over the crossing and by a S W tower outside
the S aisle, which were not built. Interior with short, round
piers, square capitals, in the nave left uncarved, in the chancel
carved with stiff-leaf foliage not at all in period imitation. The
upper walls have the red brickwork exposed. The nave has a
wagon roof, the aisles lean-to roofs, the chancel a wooden
vault resting on stone shafts. The Morning Chapel to the N of
the chancel, built in 1876–7, has a genuine stone vault on
clustered piers, an extremely convincing bit of medieval
Gothic. Around the E end a very narrow ambulatory with a 87
lean-to roof. The spacing of the ambulatory piers creates an
illusion of greater size. Octagonal S W porch inside the tower
stump. The bellcote, designed by *Micklethwaite*, was demolished after a fire, *c.* 1978. – ROOD SCREEN. Large and
ambitious, by *George Wallace*, 1914. A distraction from the
original design of the church. – STAINED GLASS by *C. E.
Kempe & W. E. Tower* (E window Christ in Glory 1881,
Presentation in the Temple 1891, Christ, Virgin, Elizabeth
1896, Daniel and Malachi 1897, Visitation 1900, Annunciation 1904).

CHRIST CHURCH, Battersea Park Road. 1959 by *T. F. Ford*,
on the site of a church of 1849 by *C. Lee* and *T. T. Bury*
destroyed in the Second World War. – (FITTINGS by *M.
Travers* brought from St Stephen, Battersea. – MURAL by
Hans Feibusch.)

CHURCH OF THE NAZARENE, Winstanley Estate. *See* end of
Perambulation 2.

ST BARNABAS, Clapham Common N side. *See* Clapham (La).

ST BARTHOLOMEW, Wycliffe Road, S of Eversleigh Road.
Now Greek Orthodox. 1900 by *G. H. Fellowes Prynne*, stock
brick, tall nave with narrower chancel of the same height, rose
window in the W gable.

ST LUKE, Ramsden Road. *See* Balham, above.

ST MARK, Battersea Rise. 1872–4 by *William White*, the first of
his Battersea churches. Large, E.E., on an ambitious scale.

Small w tower, now covered by a shingled timber spire of picturesque Continental castle type. The church lies on a slope, so that the E end stands on a large vaulted crypt. The canted apse is picturesquely flanked by the low, half-hipped SCHOOLS dated 1866, and the church hall. The church is of concrete, with a brick skin. Plate-tracery windows of moulded brick; exterior walls with some diaper decoration. Nave with stone columns, E end apsed, with brick piers to the ambulatory.

ST MARY, Battersea Church Road. The parish church of Battersea is mentioned in 1157. The present building dates from 1775–6, designed by *Joseph Dixon*, a homely dark brick box with a square tower, stone quoins and trimmings, and two tiers of windows, the main, upper ones round-headed. Onestoreyed w porch with Tuscan columns with a pediment, with incongruous but charming small oriel behind the columns. Inside, timber galleries on three sides and a flat ceiling with a large central star or rosette motif of the same classical style as the capitals of the columns which carry the galleries. Restored 1876–8 by *A. W. Blomfield*, when new stalls and seating were installed. – STAINED GLASS. The E window was preserved from the old church. The predominantly yellow glass, probably given *c.* 1631, can be attributed to *Bernard van Linge*. It celebrates the St John family of Battersea, with coats of arms, and portrait medallions below of their antecedents Henry VII, Margaret Beauchamp, and Elizabeth I. – In the circular window to l. and r. painted glass with a lamb and a dove, 1796 by *James Pearson*. – (Several post-war windows, replacing Victorian windows destroyed in the Second World War, including one commemorating Benedict Arnold, by *John Hayward*.)

MONUMENTS. A fine collection at gallery level, and many minor tablets as well. – Sir Oliver St John, Viscount Grandison, † 1630. Commissioned before his death from *Nicholas Stone*. Two frontal busts, not of high quality, against a background with columns l. and r. and heavy segmental pediment, that is, classical at a remarkably early moment and no longer Jacobean at all. – Edward Wynter † 1686, in the style of *Bushnell* (Mrs Esdaile), with bust and a relief on the apron showing two of Mr Wynter's chief feats:

> Alone unarmed a Tigre he opprest
> And crushed to death ye Monster of a Beast.
> Thrice-twenty mounted Moors he overthrew
> Singly on foot, some wounded, some he slew
> Dispers'd ye rest; what more could Samson do!

Sir John Fleet † 1712, James Bull † 1713, wall-tablets with rich floral and foliage carving and cherubs' heads, by the same craftsman. – Holles St John † 1738. Sarcophagus and urns. – Henry St John, Viscount Bolingbroke, the politician (in the Harley Cabinet), philosopher, and admirer of Voltaire and in his turn admired by Pope, married to Mary Clara des Champs de Marcilly, a niece of Madame de Maintenon, † 1751. The monument is by *Roubiliac*, modest yet of excellent quality, with two delicately carved portrait medallions to the l. and r. of the apron, and above an urn under heavy drapery in a frame of odd, somewhat lava-like Rococo shape. – John Camden and his daughter Elizabeth Nield, signed by *Coade* of Lambeth, 1792, a young woman *c*. 5 ft high, standing by a pedestal with an urn, all of *Coade* stone.

ST MICHAEL, Cobham Close, off Bolingbroke Grove. 1881 by *William White*. Brick, with wide gabled aisles and aisled apsidal E end over an undercroft. Crowstepped gables, brick diapering. – (STAINED GLASS by *Lavers, Barraud & Westlake*.)

ST PAUL, St John's Hill. Minor ragstone church of 1868 by H. E. *Coe*; SW tower and spire. Now used partly as a community centre. – STAINED GLASS. N aisle window by *W. Geddes* and *C. Blakeman*, 1955. PC)

ST PETER, Plough Road. Only the sturdy tower with short spire remains. It was added in 1911 to a church of 1875–6 by *William White*, apparently to his original design. – (In the CHURCH HALL and COMMUNITY CENTRE near by, lively MURALS of New Testament scenes by *John Lessore*, 1960–1.)

ST PHILIP, Queenstown Road. In the centre of the Park Town Estate (*see* Perambulation 2), by the estate's architect, *James Knowles Jun.*, 1869–70. Ragstone, with a short tower with tall belfry windows and pinnacles. Apse with Dec tracery.

ST SAVIOUR, Battersea Park Road. 1870–1 by *E. C. Robins* (or *G. R. Roper*; GR). Undistinguished ragstone; no tower.

ST STEPHEN (now Assemblies of the First Born), Battersea Park Road. 1886–7 by *William White*. Polychrome brick, meagre NE tower with short broach-spire.

OUR LADY OF MOUNT CARMEL AND ST JOSEPH (R.C.), Battersea Park Road. Lady Chapel 1868 by *C. A. Buckler*, nave and apsidal sanctuary 1879 by *J. Adams* (DE).

SACRED HEART (R.C.), Trott Street, E of Battersea High Street. 1892 by *F. A. Walters*, in the late Norman style, with a commanding spire. Red brick. St John Bosco Chapel added and sanctuary reordered 1970 by *Greenhalgh & Williams* (DE).

ST VINCENT DE PAUL (R.C.), Altenburg Gardens, between Lavender Hill and Clapham Common (E end). 1906–7 by *Kelly & Dickie*. Brick with stone dressings in a Romano-Romanesque style, with mosaic in the tympanum. Campanile and baptistery at the end of the aisle.

BAPTIST CHAPEL, Northcote Road. 1887–9 by *E. W. Mountford*; round-arched Renaissance. Red brick. Tower on the l. corner.

(CONGREGATIONAL CHAPEL, York Road. 1870 by *E. C. Robins*. Crude Norman exterior, incorporating part of the church of 1736 built for the Baptists. CW)

METHODIST CHURCH, Broomwood Road. 1899 by *Read & Macdonald*; Arts and Crafts.

METHODIST CHURCH (former), Westbridge Road. *See* Perambulation 1.

ST ANDREW (formerly Presbyterian, now Dutch Reformed

Church). 1886 by *Henry Stone*. The curious tower, with shingled storey on columns and tall spire above, collapsed in 1977.

PUBLIC BUILDINGS

TOWN HALL (Battersea Arts Centre). 1892–3 by *E. W. Mountford*, the architect of the (later) Old Bailey. The development
of his style can be studied well at Battersea. The town hall has
a long symmetrical front with central cupola and a semicircular porch. Ample figure sculpture in pediment and spandrels,
designed and carved by *Paul R. Montford*, clearly a foretaste
of Edwardian things to come. (On the pediment: Labour and
Progress, Art and Literature, instructing the youthful figure
of Battersea.) The interior is equally lavish. A low entrance
hall precedes the spacious STAIRCASE HALL, spanning the
whole width of the building, with stairs starting in one flight,
then dividing to lead in leisurely fashion to the gallery at
first-floor level. Roof-light above figured plaster coving (by
Gilbert Seale), marble balustrades. The former council chamber, along the street front on the first floor, has a large segmental barrel-vault. – SCULPTURE, on the staircase. Eurydice by
W. Calder Marshall, 1893. – Behind, approached by a separate
side entrance, a large public hall (seating 1140); ceiling with
good plasterwork. Splendid octagonal foyer with glazed dome
and much marble.
LIBRARIES. Battersea adopted the Libraries Acts in 1887, the
same year that the new borough of Battersea was formed. The
CENTRAL LIBRARY, Lavender Hill, is of 1888–90 by
Mountford, still entirely in the domestic Pont-Street-Dutch
tradition. Red brick Jacobean trimmings. Connected to it at
the back the REFERENCE LIBRARY, Altenburg Gardens, by
the Borough Engineer, *T. W. A. Hayward*, a belated example
of the Arts and Crafts fancifulness which sometimes had such
pleasant results about 1902. Built as late as 1924 (although
designed so an upper floor could be added). One-storeyed, with
attractive glass-roofed interior. Much emblematic decoration.
The former SOUTHLANDS BRANCH LIBRARY, High Street
(now a training centre for South Thames College), with a wing
to the street of 1906, is an example of the pretty irregularity
with oriel windows at different levels which minor official
architecture in those years achieved under the stimulus of
Voysey. By *Withers & Meredith*.
LATCHMERE LEISURE POOL, Latchmere Road. 1982–3, replacing the Latchmere Baths, which was another example of
early municipal enterprise (*see* Perambulation 2): 1889 by
Rowland Plumbe, H. T. Bonner, and *Charles Jones*.
WESTMINSTER COLLEGE (former Battersea Polytechnic),
Battersea Park Road. 1890–1 by *Mountford* (cf. library and
town hall), a long, symmetrical façade of two and a half
storeys, end wings with bows and gables. Brick and stone
dressings, considerably freer in the mixing of motifs than the

public library: for example, circular windows with attic storey, aedicules, curved broken pediments, intermittent rustication of voussoirs on the ground floor; like the town hall, already a design of Edwardian flavour. Double-height entrance hall with arcaded gallery on two sides, and a nice plastered ceiling. To the w the LIBRARY, added 1909, in the form of a handsome Wrenian chapel. E end with curved walls and stone centrepiece with open segmental pediment. Good library fittings inside. To the N, additions by *F. D. Clapham*, 1912.

SIR WALTER ST JOHN SCHOOL, Battersea High Street. Founded in 1700. The original buildings replaced in 1858–9 by the new ones by *Butterfield*, since then much altered and added to. The surviving Butterfield part is the centre of the present range along the street, two-storeyed, the upper floor with tall gabled dormers with cusped lights. Diapered brick with stone dressings, a vigorous masculine design. The entrance is through a double archway. The classrooms (originally five) were formerly reached by an external staircase from the playground. Adjoining was Butterfield's headmaster's house, replaced in 1913 by the great hall and gymnasium by *A. H. Ryan Tennison*, still in the Gothic tradition but less forceful. The hall is an upper room with an elaborate open timber roof with cusping below the tie-beams. The stage belongs to a tactful extension by *T. Denny* of 1937–8, at which time a N wing was added and other alterations made. A S wing completed in 1951 replaced the one of 1913 destroyed in the war; a science block (in L.C.C. purple brick and concrete) of 1961 completes the quadrangle. In the library (formerly classrooms) a large Gothic window in the gable to the street, with STAINED GLASS by *Lawrence Lee*, 1968, a bold, semi-abstract design with figures symbolizing learning and the brotherhood of man. The school also occupies Devonshire House in Vicarage Crescent by the Thames (*see* Perambulation 1 below).

BOARD SCHOOLS. HEATHFIELD PRIMARY, St Rule Street, off Wandsworth Road. An altered but still picturesque skyline of shaped gables, steeply pitched roof, and cupola. HIGHVIEW PRIMARY, Plough Road, is another example (1890). – ELTRINGHAM PRIMARY, Eltringham Street, opposite Wandsworth Bridge. A late *Robson* single-storey asymmetrical infants' school, dated 1885. – LAVENDER HILL, Latchmere Road. 1888–91 by *T. J. Bailey*, with a separate building for pupil-teachers.

ST JOHN'S HOSPITAL, St John's Hill. The gaunt older buildings began as the infirmary and casual wards added by *Beeston Son & Brereton* in 1868 to the Wandsworth and Clapham Union workhouse (now demolished).

BATTERSEA PARK. A park on the site of Battersea Fields was proposed in 1844, when Victoria Park was being created (*see* Tower Hamlets, Volume 4). Plans were made by *Pennethorne* but nothing was done until 1854, when the park was laid out together with the surrounding streets. The flat site was landscaped with earth from the docks; the river was embanked only after 1861. The 15-acre BOATING LAKE, surrounded by dense plantations, is the most extensive and romantic of those created in the London municipal parks of the C 19. The ambitious original layout included the subtropical garden, dramatic rocks, and alpine garden, probably designed by *John Gibson*, the superintendent. The small PUMPING STATION of 1861 was built to supply water to the lake. CAFÉ by *H. A. Rowbotham*, 1939. – Notable SCULPTURE. Three standing figures by *Henry Moore*, 1947–8; the first important open-air statuary in London to be set up after the Second World War. – Single Form by *Barbara Hepworth*. – War memorial group, 1924 by *E. Kennington*.

NEW COVENT GARDEN, Nine Elms Lane. The market moved from Covent Garden in 1974. The new buildings by *Gollins, Melvin, Ward & Partners*, 1970–5, are spacious, hygienic, practical, planned for motorized transport and surrounded by ample parking and unloading areas, all advantages notoriously absent in the old buildings in central London. They occupy 65 acres as opposed to the old market's 12 acres. But they lack both the charm of Fowler's market and, alas, the crisp elegance of the best recent industrial buildings (cf. the Flower Market, Cranford, Ho), which could have been an asset in this desolate area. The smaller, more accessible part is the brick-faced office tower by Vauxhall Cross, with covered shops at podium level, linked by a bridge to the FLOWER MARKET, 100 yds square, with a lumpy eaves profile formed by the space-frame diagrid roof masked by a white g.r.p. insulating skin. Internally its potentially impressive expanse of coffering-in-reverse is spoilt by clumsy strip-lighting. Further S, well barricaded from the road, the FRUIT AND VEGETABLE MARKET, two parallel blocks each 375 ft long, each arranged with small showrooms off a spine corridor (not unlike the plan of the old market) and double-height areas behind for storage. Concrete blockwork, the unloading areas shielded by canopies with vertical glazed strips. Well detailed perimeter walls with some railings to break the monotony.

100 BATTERSEA POWER STATION, Chelsea Bridge. The W half (disused since 1974) was built first, in 1929–35, by *S. L. Pearce*, engineer-in-chief, with *H. N. Allot* as consultant engineer. *J. Theo Halliday* was the architect of the brick exterior, and of the extraordinarily elaborate interior with giant pilasters faced in faience, marble-lined walls, and bronze doors with sculptured panels. *Sir Giles Gilbert Scott* was brought in as consultant on the exterior when the building was already under construction. He was responsible for the details, such as the elaborate parapet and the bases to the fluted chimneys. The building is one of the first examples in England of frankly contemporary industrial architecture, and set the pattern for the power stations of the next two decades. The outline is square and bold, what there is of symmetry is functionally justified, and granted that the fluting on the

chimneys and walls is a decorative motif, it is at least not a period motif, but one that goes well with the general verticality of the composition. The E half, added in 1944–55 (and closed in 1983), was anticipated in the original design. Innovating technical features were, in the earlier part, water sprays to clean the chimneys, and, in the post-war part, the supplying of district heating to the Churchill Gardens Estate across the river.

WATERWORKS PUMPING STATION, Kirtling Street, off the s end of Nine Elms Lane. Sub-Georgian beam-engine house of *c.* 1840.

CRINGLE DOCK REFUSE TRANSFER STATION, near the pumping station off Nine Elms Lane. By the *G.L.C. Special Works Department*, 1969–71. Hygienic, enclosed and mechanized installation for loading refuse barges. A concrete core surrounded by lower parts with a varied roof-line, neatly clad in cheerfully coloured corrugated sheeting.

RAILWAYS. In the rush hours, the railway lines E of CLAPHAM JUNCTION are the busiest in the world. Most are on stockbrick viaducts, with the earlier low-level lines serving railway yards, making a vigorous landscape. Their history is complicated.*

BATTERSEA PARK STATION, in Battersea Park Road, sandwiched between two viaducts, was built for the London Brighton and South Coast Railway in 1865–7. Lush Italianate, the tall booking hall with a central arcade on pairs of leafy cast-iron columns, and female heads in roundels in the spandrels. On platforms 2 and 3, original high-backed wooden seats, and elaborate railings round the stairwell. An adjacent RAILWAY BRIDGE has a cast-iron arched ornamental fascia of 1865, with arms of the L.B.S.C.R.

NINE ELMS STATION, damaged in the Second World War, has been replaced by the New Covent Garden Market (*see* above).‡

* The first line to be built was the London and Southampton, 1834–8 by *Joseph Locke*, in succession to *Francis Giles*, running S W to N E to a terminus originally at Nine Elms, and from 1848 to Waterloo. This became the London and South Western Railway in 1839 and reached Southampton in 1840. To the W, the L.S.W.R. line from Clapham Junction via Barnes to Richmond and later Windsor, 1846 by *Locke*. From the s via Balham and Clapham Junction, the western leg of the London Brighton and South Coast Railway, originally the independent West End and Crystal Palace Railway, 1853–6. This runs E alongside the L.S.W.R., and to the N across the river (by Grosvenor Bridge) to Victoria, the last stretch built as the Victoria Station and Pimlico Railway, 1859–60 by *John Fowler*. Converging on the same bridge, from the S E via Brixton, the West-End leg of the London Chatham and Dover Railway, 1860–2 by *Joseph Cubitt*. This was realigned through Battersea on a high-level line in 1866–7. Alongside the L.C.D.R. on the W, the Brighton Company's South London line via Brixton to London Bridge, 1867, again on the high level, to which their line via Clapham Junction was also raised. Lastly, to the N W, the West London Extension Railway, 1859–63 by *William Baker*, crossing the river to Kensington and the main lines to the west and north.

‡ It was a very early station, built for the London and Southampton line in 1838 by *Tite*, a quietly Italian front of seven bays, the centre five opened up in a giant loggia of pillars and arches beneath a straight attic; a sound job, without the dramatization of Euston.

E of Silverthorne Road (off Queenstown Road) the former LONGHEDGE LOCOMOTIVE AND CARRIAGE WORKS of the Chatham and Dover Railway, 1860 onwards by *Joseph Cubitt*. Several buildings remain, with distinctive round-headed lancet-like windows used to particular effect in the broad eaved gable ends.

GROSVENOR (VICTORIA) RAILWAY BRIDGE, CHELSEA BRIDGE, ALBERT BRIDGE, BATTERSEA BRIDGE, WEST LONDON EXTENSION (BATTERSEA) RAILWAY BRIDGE. *See* Thames Crossings at end of gazetteer.

PERAMBULATIONS

1. The Riverside Village

The centre of the former village lies S of the church, at the irregular square where Battersea Church Road, Westbridge Road, the High Street, and Vicarage Crescent converge. The HIGH STREET has little of note apart from the public buildings, No. 108 (Katherine Low Settlement, earlier C18), and the carved inn sign of THE CASTLE, said to be late Tudor. The other streets all have some good houses, although mostly too scattered to make up a coherent picture. BATTERSEA CHURCH ROAD starts with the RAVEN INN, an original little structure of the mid C17, with top-heavy curved Dutch gables and quoins, then continues with a low, irregular curving terrace of cottages. This has been incorporated in the G.L.C.'s ALTHORPE GROVE redevelopment of 1976–80. The C18 and C19 structures are embedded amidst some whimsical novelties (though with less zany results than at the OLD SWAN opposite). Round-headed arches appear as a recurrent motif. What is important is that the scale and line of the old frontages are respected with a sensitivity seldom found in earlier housing developments. Behind are new buildings around an open space which is to have a shallow stream intended for paddling (a miniature echo of Thamesmead?). A regular crescent W of Westbridge Road, a staggered group to the E framing a view of the church, with nothing over four storeys. There is also a club room and a nursery school. In WESTBRIDGE ROAD Nos. 129–133, a plain three-storey house and cottages of the second quarter of the C18, altered *c.* 1818, fit in happily. There are no felicities of this kind further S, where the G.L.C.'s SOMERSET ESTATE, of the later 1960s, and Wandsworth's SURREY LANE ESTATE (*R. Seifert & Partners*, 1970–4) are predictably unlovable representatives of 'mixed development' public housing with tall towers. In between, a few C19 cottages and villas survive along the E side of WESTBRIDGE ROAD; also the former METHODIST CHURCH, plain mid C19 classical. Beyond it Nos. 2–4 stand out, a semi-detached pair of 1845, flint with stone dressings, elaborately Gothic, with statues in niches in the gables.

In BATTERSEA BRIDGE ROAD nothing left except a few mid C19 terraces and the more lavishly stuccoed EARL SPENCER. CHURCH ROAD has humbler houses to the S, to the N an industrial area where the most striking building is a late C19 FLOUR MILL (Hovis), of stock brick embellished with pilasters and a little terracotta.*

VICARAGE CRESCENT, close to the river, has the best houses. No. 42 is the former vicarage, probably c. 1800, three storeys, five windows. No. 44, DEVONSHIRE HOUSE (now part of Sir Walter St John School; see Public Buildings) is of c. 1700. Three storeys and five bays, modillioned eaves cornice and Doric porch. The stucco and the pretty balconies added later. Fine C18 gate with overthrow. Good panelling inside; narrow hall leading to a stair-hall at the back; staircase with twisted balusters. Behind is the ROYAL ACADEMY OF DANCING, in a C19 four-storey warehouse with cast-iron windows, remodelled in 1974.

A little further W, now rather hemmed in, is the best house, OLD BATTERSEA HOUSE, later C17, plain but substantial, a good example of a London builder's version of the Dutch-inspired type introduced at the Restoration by May and Pratt (cf. Eltham Lodge, Woolwich (Gr), Perambulation 4). Restored, after long neglect, by *Vernon Gibberd*, 1972–4. A half-H plan; two storeys, with dormers in a hipped roof above a broad coved cornice. The W front, facing the river, is of nine bays, a flat front, but with the seven windows divided up by two blind half-windows flanking the central three. The centre window on the first floor emphasized by a moulded eared brick surround. The windows all now have C18 sashes; the original effect, with casements or perhaps sashes with thick glazing bars, would have been less delicate. Central doorway flanked by tapering brick pilasters carrying brackets and a heavy pediment. The carved frieze with globe and instruments may refer to Samuel Pett, Controller of Victualling to the Navy, who lived here in the later C17 and was perhaps the builder. Similar doorway and central window on the E front, here flanked by two shallow projecting wings each of two bays. The N front has been altered; the S one has six regularly spaced windows, with a pair of narrow blind windows in the centre; sundial with the date 1699 above. Despite the apparent regularity the N wing is oddly angled (were there older buildings on the site?). The best feature of the interior is the broad oak staircase with closed string and robust twisted balusters, rising in three stages around the hall which fills the whole of the centre of the E side. The gate at the stairhead, with thick bars, appears to be contemporary. Original panelling in the central W room and the SW room on the ground floor, plain apart from

---

* The future of this area was debated throughout the 1970s. Plans for undulating terraces of riverside housing and offices by *Chapman Taylor Partners* were approved in 1980.

fluted Corinthian pilasters and a little carving around the entrance to the staircase hall. The other rooms refurbished in the 1970s. The SE room is made from two smaller rooms. Upstairs, bedrooms with closets adjoining; in the central W room dado panelling with remnants of C18 chinoiserie decoration.

A little further on the C20 takes over again – ST JOHN'S ESTATE, 1931–4 by *W. J. Dresden* for Battersea Borough Council, five-storey blocks of the L.C.C. between-the-wars type, crowding out the scale of the old buildings.

2. The Rest of Battersea

The following, described in a rough zigzag from E to W, are worth looking at. A continuous perambulation is possible, but is recommended only for the determined.

QUEENSTOWN ROAD. The PARK TOWN ESTATE, developed by Philip Flower and designed in 1863–4 by *James Knowles Jun.*, was a humbler version of Knowles's Cedars Estate (*see* Clapham (La), Perambulation), part of a grandiose scheme to link Clapham with Pimlico and Belgravia by the new Chelsea Bridge (opened 1858). Success was limited by the simultaneous multiplication of the railway lines of the London Chatham and Dover and the London Brighton and South Coast Railway Companies, causing Queenstown Road to weave its way beneath a gloomy series of bridges before reaching Queen's Circus and Battersea Park.* Plain grey brick terraces of the 1860s remain in the main kite-shaped area of the estate around ST PHILIP SQUARE, in STANLEY GROVE, BROUGHTON STREET, and ST PHILIP STREET. The ornament, of a lushly gross kind (cf. Clapham), is mostly confined to the tympana over first-floor windows. The houses in the square itself are a little grander, with porches. Most of QUEENSTOWN ROAD itself and the other parts not built until the 1870s have red-brick terraces with flat bays, an undistinguished design, interrupted only by a few individual houses near the square which are closer to the ideals of Webb or Shaw: Nos. 102–112, three pairs by *T. J. Bailey* (the London School Board's Architect), 1879–81, and Nos. 114–120, two pairs by *Thomas Jekyll*, 1875.

QUEEN'S CIRCUS AND PRINCE OF WALES DRIVE. Queen's Circus, laid out in the 1860s, never fulfilled its promise of West End sophistication. The chief accent now is the remarkably ornate Old English composition of the PUBLIC LAVATORIES of 1899 by the park entrance. On the W side was All Saints, replaced by flats ignoring the curve of the circus (*Sir L. Keay & Partners*, 1979). The plain but handsome red-brick VICARAGE of 1890 remains in PRINCE OF WALES DRIVE,

---

* The complicated story has been deftly unravelled by Priscilla Metcalf in *The Park Town Estate and the Battersea Tangle* (London Topographical Society, no. 121, 1978).

linked to the new, more modest church (q.v.). Then follow
colossal mansion blocks, overlooking the park, with the hearty brick and stone stripes typical of their date (1899 etc.).

NINE ELMS, the area around Nine Elms Lane, between Battersea Park and Vauxhall, was for long a desolate expanse of
disused railway land, gasworks, and declining industry. It
began to be transformed in the 1970s. The New Covent
Garden Market, opened in 1974, was one of the first arrivals
(see Public Buildings). The most striking newcomer among
the later, quite trim offices and warehouses that are filling the
remaining spaces is the STATIONERY OFFICE BUILDING
by *PSA Architects* (*A. Henocq*), completed 1982, a decidedly
formal three-sided arrangement of offices splayed around a
courtyard, each of the four glazed floors stepping slightly
back, a little in the manner of James Stirling's Florey Building
at Oxford. Warehouses and packaging departments behind,
clad in grey corrugated steel. The whole is raised on an angular
plinth of re-used granite setts, and, set off by some yellow
paintwork, makes a prominant display when seen from the
other side of the river.

BATTERSEA PARK ROAD, formerly Lower Wandsworth Road,
the old route from Nine Elms to Battersea village, was already
built up by the middle of the C 19, but of that little evidence
remains. The whole of the s side is now post-Second-World-
War council housing, chiefly Wandsworth's disastrous mistake of the 1960s, the DODDINGTON ESTATE, 1967–71 by
Emberton, Frank & Tardrew; 970 dwellings (136 p.p.a.). The
grey chequered concrete slab blocks marching beside the
railway are a chilling monument to that mistaken era of high-
rise and industrialized building: the system used here is Jespersen 12M (as at Southwark's Aylesbury Estate). The homely brick details of the low shops, library, and health centre,
loosely grouped around a pedestrian square off Battersea Park
Road, cannot compensate for the arid, empty spaces over the
car parks, the bleak upper access ways, and the inhuman scale
of the whole conception. Further w, more of the C 19 remains:
on the N side the DOVEDALE ALMSHOUSES, and two lodges,
Tudor detail, 1841, with a one-storey range (BLUNDEN
ALMSHOUSES) added in 1974. On the s Nos. 445–447,
Shakespeare and Byron Villas, an eccentric mid-C 19 pair
with Lombard arches around a common gable, and the
LATCHMERE, a grand Italianate corner pub at the junction
of Latchmere Road.

LATCHMERE ROAD and the LATCHMERE ESTATE. On the w
side, just N of the railway, the two symmetrically disposed red
brick LODGES with shaped and crowstepped gables belonged
to the Wandsworth and Clapham Union's Dispensary and
relief station behind (now demolished) of 1886 by *T. W.
Aldwinkle*. There was until recently another welfare building
of the 1880s opposite, the Latchmere Baths (see Public Buildings). Behind this is Battersea Borough Council's LATCH-
MERE ESTATE, exemplary municipal housing of 1903 (the

first to be built by an L.C.C. borough). Nearly 300 simple yellow- and red-brick two-storey cottage flats (all built as self-contained units each with access to a garden and with electric light) in terraces along a grid of roads with suitably progressive names: Reform Street, Freedom Street, Burns Road (after the local M.P. John Burns, who had pressed for the legislation needed to allow the borough councils to adopt the relevant part of the 1890 Housing Act). The designs of the houses appear to have been drawn up by *W. Eaton*, architectural assistant to the borough surveyor *J. T. Pilditch*, inspired by several winning competition designs. To the W a generous recreation ground, and N of this some other houses to a different design. Further S, between the railway lines, unplanned mid-C19 stucco artisan cottages (Knowsley Road etc.) make an interesting contrast.

95 SHAFTESBURY PARK ESTATE, off Latchmere Road S of the main railway lines, was built on the site of Poupart's market gardens in 1872–7 by the Artisans, Labourers and General Dwellings Company, the earliest of this philanthropic enterprise's estates of cottages. It was pioneer work, earlier than any local authority housing. The architect was *Robert Austin*; 1,135 cottages, one block of flats, an institute, and thirty shops were planned (the institute was not built). No pubs were allowed. There was originally an open space (Brassey Square) in the centre, later built over when the company was in financial difficulties. The entrance to the estate in Grayshott Road is emphasized by two corner turrets. By the square the taller buildings, a block with shops, and a block of flats, both with miniature corner turrets and some Gothic detail. The way in which the edges and centre of the estate are emphasized architecturally is reminiscent of earlier artisan housing such as Swindon railway village. The cottages fall into a few classes (three types, with five to eight rooms) with a moderate amount of variety between them, stock brick and red and black brick, a little Gothic ornament.

LAVENDER HILL and ST JOHN'S HILL, by Clapham Junction, are the heart of Victorian and Edwardian Battersea. Apart from the public buildings (*see* above) only the following need to be singled out. ARDING & HOBBS, a large suburban department store (founded in Wandsworth in 1876). A baroque corner cupola at the corner of St John's Hill, and large display windows at first-floor level. 1910 by *James Gibson*, displaying a similar Edwardian magniloquence to that found in central London stores (the only such example in South London). The rebuilding was the result of a fire in 1909. FALCON HOTEL, 1887, debased Italianate, with an excellent interior with much engraved glass and a delightful window showing the present building and its predecessors. GRAND THEATRE (now bingo club), St John's Hill, 1900 by *E. A. Woodrow*, one of the few surviving suburban examples of its kind, rather a gaunt façade, with two squat towers adorned with Italo-Romanesque arcading. The auditorium, although altered, preserves its exotic boxes with pagoda canopies and plaster fronts with Chinese dragons. A false ceiling obscures the upper balcony and shallow dome. Further up the hill, No. 92, L.C.C. education offices of 1909 (*T. J. Bailey*) masquerading as a dignified Queen Anne house of nine bays with bold segmental pediment, and some once-prosperous mid C19 stucco villas and terraces (see e.g. St John's Hill Grove, w side, built 1848–9).

Further s BOLINGBROKE GROVE runs along the e side of Wandsworth Common past the hospital on the site of an older house. The area between Wandsworth and Clapham Common was developed from the 1860s.* Nos. 23–26 Bolingbroke Grove, more generously set back than the rest, are by *E. R. Robson*, 1876; red brick with shaped gables. The streets off have smaller terraces, for example in HONEYWELL ROAD, with characteristically elaborate brickwork and bargeboarded gables. COBHAM CLOSE, a *Wandsworth* estate of the 1970s, keeps nicely in scale, with pedestrian ways replacing some of the roads.

Finally PLOUGH ROAD leads n from St John's Hill down to the less salubrious area nearer the river, a ragbag of post-Second-World-War council housing. In MAYSOULE ROAD, three-storey yellow-brick terraces (171 dwellings at 100 p.p.a.) by *Phippen Randall & Parkes*, 1976–80, the best example of Wandsworth's belated rediscovery of low rise. The special features are the front extensions incorporating garages and staircases to upper flats. To the w another low-rise group of the same date, this time by the G.L.C.; less well detailed. To the n the older and grimmer blocks of the L.C.C.'s WILBER-FORCE ESTATE (*Burnet, Tait & Partners*), designed in 1939 (as the details show) but not built until 1946. E of Plough Road the more interesting WINSTANLEY ESTATE, an ambitious enterprise begun well by Battersea, finished badly by Wandsworth. Architect: *George Trew Dunn*. The first phases (1963–6, 816 dwellings at 136 p.p.a.), which mix four- to five-storey maisonette blocks with several point blocks and a single tall slab, are memorable for the spine route, LIVINGSTONE WALK, leading past a nicely varied sequence of small open spaces enclosed on three sides by the lower blocks, an interesting attempt at a new type of urban pattern. It ends with HUITT SQUARE, a larger area with some shops and a doctor's surgery (formerly a junior library) within one of the tall blocks. The later parts to the e (the Livingstone Road Estate, 1969–72, 342 dwellings and an old people's home) are much less successful. The pedestrian route meanders confusingly across a soulless podium over a giant garage. The dull factory-made cladding panels of these buildings are less appealing than the earlier dark-grey brick and boarding. At the edge near the railway, the small circular CHURCH OF THE NAZARENE, 1968–70 by *Green, Lloyd & Son*, makes a brave effort with a boldly lettered chunky ramp spiralling around it.

* For the w side of Clapham Common *see* Clapham (La), Perambulation.

FALCON ROAD. On the W side the MEYRICK ARMS remains from the Conservative Land Society's development of the area in the 1860s. Further N a few other C19 remnants: the QUEEN'S HEAD and some stuccoed houses opposite. The rest nearly all council housing. On the E side the L.C.C.'s FALCON ESTATE, 1959–63, still quite modest and friendly, with its three six-storey point blocks with angled balconies and lower terraces. To the W the *Borough Architect's Department*'s KAMBALA ESTATE (1975 onwards), neo-vernacular on the grand scale (629 dwellings, 133 p.p.a.), with maisonette blocks disguised by steep pantiled roofs. This is at least an improvement on the borough's large and unappealing YORK ROAD ESTATE further W, with its twenty-four-storey tower (1967–72 by *Howes Jackman & Partners* and *William Ryder & Associates*; a total of 828 dwellings).

PUTNEY

CHURCHES

ALL SAINTS, Lower Common, S of Queen's Ride. 1873–4 by *G. E. Street*. Yellow brick exterior, red and black brick inside. Painted wagon roofs, vaulted baptistery at the W end of the N aisle, iron screens. – REREDOS by *Street*, decorated by *R. Spencer Stanhope*. – STAINED GLASS. An unusually large number of *Morris & Co.* windows, one of the best groups in London, ranging in date from 1877 to 1930. – Baptistery: two circles with choirs of boy angels, surrounded by smaller foliage roundels, 1877, designed by *Burne Jones*; the most attractive windows in the church. – Organ chamber E wall, 1877, three lights with angels (designed by *Morris*). – E window 1878. Three lights with saints in two tiers, white and gold on deep patterned grounds (all designed by *Burne Jones*, except for St Catherine by *Morris*). – W window 1883, figures in three tiers, by *Burne Jones*. – Nave N fourth from W, 1884; third from W, 1898; second from W, 1929; westernmost, 1910. – Nave S, easternmost, 1889; second from E, 1903; third from E, 1922; all these windows of two lights with figures designed by *Burne Jones*. – Small lights beside the organ. Angels by *Morris*, 1898. – S transept, three tall lights with one figure by *Morris* (St Mary Magdalene), the others by *Burne Jones*, 1890.

HOLY TRINITY, West Hill. 1863 by *J. M. K. Hähn*; ragstone, Dec; spire 1888 by *G. Patrick*.

ST JOHN, St John's Avenue. A suburban Dec Gothic centrepiece, 1858–9 by *Charles Lee*, NW tower 1865, chancel and aisles 1888, S chancel chapel 1910.

ST MARY, Putney Bridge, the parish church, looking across the river to Fulham church. The manor belonged to the See of Canterbury from William the Conqueror till 1535. The church was originally a chapel-of-ease to Wimbledon. The chief C17 event in its history was the Council of War held by

Cromwell, Fairfax, Fleetwood, Ireton, and Rich in 1647. They sat round the communion table with their hats on. The w tower survives from a rebuilding of the C15; three stages with battlements and NE stair-turret, grossly restored. The rest of the church was much rebuilt by *E. Lapidge* in 1836–7, and radically restored and reordered by *Ronald Sims* in 1980–2, after it had been gutted by fire in 1973. The result is a most successful interior of the later C20, making use of what could be preserved from the older building. The most complete survival is the CHANTRY CHAPEL built by Bishop West of Ely (†1533), who was born in Putney. It is one of the very few examples of expensive late medieval patronage in the village churches of the London area. Lapidge moved it from the S to the N side of the chancel. The chapel dates from the very early C16, and has two bays, gracefully fan-vaulted, and two panelled arches open to the chancel. Pre-restoration drawings show that it was originally closed off from the aisle with a door and windows, with a larger opening above (the latter restored after the fire). The fine Perp nave arcades, four bays, four-centred arches on piers with shafts and hollows, angel busts over the piers, are also at least partly medieval (investigations after the fire showed that the footings of the S arcade belonged with the medieval foundations). The outer walls of the broad aisles were rebuilt by Lapidge in a lean Perp, stock brick with stone dressings. They were left unplastered inside after the fire. In the new reordering the altar has been placed in the N aisle, with seats facing it in a half-hexagon. – Effective FITTINGS by *Ronald Sims*, in the tradition of George Pace. Quite elaborate black metal hanging lamps, a corona over the altar supported by the beams remaining from the C19 gallery. Simple wooden sanctuary furniture. – STAINED GLASS. Pale abstract patterns against clear glass, by *Alan Younger*, allowing a view of the trees N of the church. – The new roof has deep pyramidal coffering over the nave; the same motif is used in reverse beneath the organ gallery. The former chancel is divided off by a glazed screen, the S aisle partitioned for church offices, all handsomely detailed. They are approached by a neat internal passage formed in the gap between the aisle and the church hall of 1959. The new angled porch at the SW corner of the building provides access to both church and offices.

MONUMENTS. In the w tower: Richard Lussher †1615, architectural surround: a broken segmental pediment bearing allegories, over a frame with strapwork and ribbon work. Obelisks at the sides. – Catherine Palmer †1619. Inscription framed by a very good strapwork cartouche and two columns with broken pediment. – Sir Thomas Dawes †1655, just a skull on a bracket. – Leicester Burdet †1691, and Thomas Payne †1698, two lively cartouches. – Several further minor monuments; others were lost or badly damaged in the fire. – LEDGER STONES, rediscovered after the fire, reset around the altar.

ST MARY, Keble Street, Summerstown. *See* Wandsworth.

ST MICHAEL, Granville Road and Wimbledon Park Road. 1896–7 by *E. W. Mountford*; E end 1905. The tower unbuilt. Red brick, 'large and handsome with a somewhat Caröeish west window' (B.F.L. Clarke). (Panelled piers without capitals. – STAINED GLASS by *Burlison & Grylls*.)

ST PAUL, Augustus Road, Wimbledon Park. Nave 1877, chancel 1888, by *Micklethwaite & Somers Clarke*. Dull exterior of red brick with a flèche; Dec windows. Wide nave, light in character, with octagonal piers of elongated section. Wagon roof. – STAINED GLASS by *Kempe*, 1893–1901. – REREDOS by Kempe's partner and successor *Tower*. – PANELLING and SCREEN also contemporary.

OUR LADY AND ST PETER (R.C.), Victoria Drive. 1971 by *Tomei Mackley & Pound*. Central square block surrounded by lower passages and vestries. The steep roof is carried on eight lattice beams which continue upward to form a central lantern-cum-flèche. – STAINED GLASS in the sanctuary clerestory by *Whitefriars Studios*.

PUTNEY BURIAL GROUND, Upper Richmond Road (behind Nos. 205–213). Opened 1763. (Monument to Harriet Thomson; *Coade* tomb-chest with medallion with a mourning woman. AK) (Other good table tombs, e.g. to Robert Wood and Stratford Canning.)

PUTNEY CEMETERY, Lower Richmond Road. A walled enclosure on the edge of Putney Common. Ragstone chapels and lodge by *Barnett & Birch*, 1855.

PUTNEY VALE CEMETERY, Kingston Road. 1891 by the Borough Engineer *E. J. Elford*. Monuments in every imaginable style (HM).

PUBLIC BUILDINGS

NEWNES LIBRARY, Disraeli Road, off Putney High Street. 1899. Tall, florid Jacobean.

SOUTHLANDS COLLEGE, Wimbledon Park Side and Queensmere Road. The original house, BELMONT HOUSE, was built for Daniel Meinertzhagen in 1864. The college moved from Battersea in 1930. New buildings by *Yorke, Rosenberg & Mardall*. Hall at the SW end completed 1953; exterior faced with Yorkshire slabs, brick, and ornamental tiles by *Peggy Angus*. Block with lecture rooms E of the old building completed 1957. This has sunbreaks over the windows and a bold exposed outer staircase against the end wall. Another block with lecture rooms and gymnasium 1959–62. (Further extensions by *P. Whiting*: amenities block 1966, students' union 1968, library 1972.) – S of Queensmere Road, in the grounds of a neo-Tudor house of c. 1900, an extension, with student refectory, and five small residential blocks by *Yorke, Rosenberg & Mardall*, 1961–3.

WHITELANDS COLLEGE, Sutherland Grove. Built as a teacher training college by *Sir Giles Gilbert Scott*, 1929–31. A free, mainly utilitarian grouping with a few genteel neo-Gothic forms, a striking contrast with the coarse and pompous style popular for institutional buildings of the C 19 (cf. the former Royal Victoria Patriotic School, Wandsworth Common). – CHAPEL with outstanding *Morris & Co.* STAINED GLASS brought from the former college chapel at Chelsea. The windows were adapted to fit the round-headed forms in the new chapel. – E window 1886, three lights with the Virgin, Christ, and St Mary Magdalene above smaller scenes, designed by *Burne Jones.* – Also by him the N and S windows, with female saints, originally designed for single lights. Those on the N side of 1885–7, on the S of 1891–3. – Chapel of St Ursula: St Ursula with three girls, 1885. – The iron gates to the college also come from Chelsea.

MAYFIELD SCHOOL, West Hill. Large but compactly grouped comprehensive school for over 2,000 girls, by *Powell & Moya*, 1956. The buildings are attached to an old school, do not exceed three storeys, and are not all visible at once – the first deliberate reaction in London against those early comprehensives of blatantly intimidating scale. Classroom blocks with neatly detailed exteriors, the internal planning (long central corridors) less satisfactory. Impressive, plain assembly hall, the roof supported by four steel columns, with subsidiary halls which can be opened up to seat the whole school at once.

LINDEN LODGE SCHOOLS (for the Blind), Princes Way, E of Victoria Drive. NORTH HOUSE is of 1933, built as a private house by *Sir Edwin Lutyens*.

BRANDLEHOW PRIMARY SCHOOL, Brandlehow Road, to the S off Putney Bridge Road. A progressive period piece of 1951 by *E. Goldfinger*; low, L-shaped.

SOUTHMEAD PRIMARY SCHOOL, Princes Way. *See* Perambulation.

ROYAL HOSPITAL FOR INCURABLES, West Hill. Founded in 1854. A very large, grand Italianate affair, by *W. P. Griffith*, 1864, built around an C 18 core. Three linked blocks, the end ones with pediments and engaged columns, the centre with a screen of two Corinthian columns. Behind are some attractive additions by *Hammett, Norton & Drew*: the Chatsworth Wing of 1976, an attractive cluster of one-storey homes for the disabled, staggered frontages with good views to the S; and an octagonal hydrotherapy pool with glazed roof and cupola, 1981.

SWIMMING BATHS AND DRYBURGH HALL, Dryburgh Road and Upper Richmond Road. By *Powell & Moya*, 1968. Informal buildings of different heights around older trees, the cheerful blue and white detail of the exterior suggestive of the function. L-shaped pool with a bold roof with V-shaped beams.

OBELISK, Putney Heath. 1788 by *George Dance*. Brick, formerly cased in stucco. It commemorates the experimental 'fireproof house' erected here in 1776 by David Hartley, which had iron and copper plates between the floors.

PUTNEY RAILWAY BRIDGE, PUTNEY (FULHAM) BRIDGE.
See Thames Crossings at end of gazetteer.

PERAMBULATION

In 1792 Putney had only 2,294 inhabitants. The old parish
church by Putney Bridge, now dwarfed by the office blocks
that began to appear from the 1960s, is almost the only indication that this was the village centre. A little more of pre-
Victorian Putney remains in LOWER RICHMOND ROAD off
to the W; the best survival is WINCHESTER HOUSE (Putney
Constitutional Club), the oldest part of *c.* 1730, five bays with
small pediment, lunette over Venetian window. W wing *c.*
1760. Bay-windows on the garden side, perhaps later. The
DUKE'S HEAD, by the river, is very modest in comparison
with the STAR AND GARTER HOTEL, with its late C19
iron-trimmed bulbous Frenchy roof. On the S side Nos. 37–
41, early C19 cottages, remain near LOCKYER HOUSE, council flats around a courtyard, 1971–4, an addition to the
borough's PLATTS ESTATE whose main landmark is an
obtrusive tower with sculptural roof excrescences (*Diamond,
Redfern & Partners,* 1964–5). Between Lower Richmond
Road and the river, the EMBANKMENT, made up as a road in
1887, with a picturesque succession of Victorian boathouses.
Further S between Lower and Upper Richmond Roads, an
attractive irregular network of small streets, developed from
the 1840s onwards. Especially good stuccoed villas of *c.* 1850
in CHARLWOOD ROAD, others in QUILL LANE and
STRATFORD GROVE to the E. Off REDGRAVE ROAD is
PUTNEY DAY NURSERY, a larger detached villa, a little
earlier than the surrounding streets. Other mid C19 examples
remain further W on the S side of Upper Richmond Road.
PUTNEY HIGH STREET is a busy shopping street with little of
architectural interest, although the variety of frontages and
the survival of old passageways indicate its past history.* The
only buildings worth a passing glance are LILLEY AND
SKINNER, with generous Arts and Crafts roughcast gable of
c. 1900; LLOYDS BANK by *Maufe, c.* 1927–8;‡ the WHITE
LION of 1887, which with its neighbours was rebuilt when
the street was widened for the new Putney Bridge; and THE
RAILWAY, a big jolly corner pub at the junction of Upper
Richmond Road. The golden age of Putney was the middle of
the C19, when villas rose l. and r. along Putney Hill and
Putney Heath. A few grand Italianate examples remain on
PUTNEY HILL, and one solitary Gothic survival in ST
JOHN'S AVENUE (No. 18). Further S around WEST HILL
more complete Edwardian areas and, towards Wandsworth,
some C18 houses (Nos. 23–37), an irregular group, much

---

* See *Wandsworth Heritage Walks I* (1975), ed. K. Bailey.
‡ Information from Nikolaus Boulting.

altered.* Otherwise all haphazard, anonymous C 20 blocks
of private flats, with only a few exceptions. The GREEN
MAN, Wildcroft Road, on the heath between Portsmouth
Road and Kingston Road, is basically C 18.‡

PUTNEY HEATH. The area between Putney Heath and Wimbledon Park was developed with large houses and villas in
spacious grounds from the early C 19, a less aristocratic version of Roehampton (q.v.). Like Roehampton, it was exploited for council housing after the Second World War, but
redevelopment here has been more piecemeal and there is no
grand design as at Alton West.

Along WIMBLEDON PARK SIDE a number of C 19 houses
remain: at the N end No. 89, FAIRLAWN, by *Rawlinson
Parkinson*, 1853, for Edwin Saunders, surgeon dentist to
Queen Victoria. Large, late classical, with two wings with
heavy pediments on giant pilasters, and a screen of Ionic
columns in front of the entrance. Further S No. 83,
BROADHEATH, Italianate, grey brick and stucco; No. 80,
stuccoed; and the stuccoed LODGE to Albemarles, one of
several relics of houses now demolished. Behind Fairlawn is
TUDOR LODGE, *c.* 1860, with ample stone dressings and a
turret. In the gardens between the two the ACKROYDEN
ESTATE begins. This dates from 1950–4. It was the first of
the post-Second-World-War developments by the *L.C.C.
Architect's Department* (newly re-established in 1950 under *Sir
Robert Matthew*) to demonstrate the principle of mixed development, the mixture of low and high housing and of dwellings of different sizes on a single estate.‡ The idea had already
been used, to good effect, at Powell & Moya's Churchill
Gardens, Pimlico, but the Ackroyden Estate and the bigger
Alton Estate which followed at Roehampton (q.v.) are very
different in their mood from Powell & Moya's essentially
urban development. The W part of the Ackroyden Estate (the
first part to be completed and so the most well known) has just
one tower (designed by *Colin Lucas*), a point block of eleven
storeys called OATLAND COURT. T-shaped (three flats to a
floor), the end walls brick and the sides cement-rendered,
with a simple pattern provided by generous balconies. No
fussiness, no applied pattern-making. A good roof shape enclosing the top of the lift shaft. To the S lower buildings of two
to five storeys, the blocks of maisonettes fanning out off
Windlesham Grove, avoiding a rigid grid, and at the SW
corner a group of flats neatly turning the corner with a lower
link containing laundry and stores. The materials are brick
with rendering, the flat roofs project slightly in the Swedish

---

* For Oakhill Road *see* Wandsworth, Perambulation, below.

‡ Further along the old line of the PORTSMOUTH ROAD across Putney
Heath, SCIO HOUSE, a battlemented and gabled Tudor Gothic villa of *c.* 1843
for the speculative builder John Elger, possibly by his friend *Harvey Lonsdale
Elmes*, was demolished in 1982.

§ The team for Ackroyden included: architect in charge *H. G. Gillett*, with
A. W. C. Barr, E. Moholi, A. P. Roach, J. Partridge.

manner, there are plenty of humane details at ground level. The keynote is the intimate and informal grouping, much enhanced by the mature landscaping of the old gardens. E of Victoria Drive the other half of the estate (the total is 488 dwellings): a more open layout, less satisfying, with a shopping centre, three more towers, and groups of maisonettes, some with flatter, more characterless elevations, with large windows and spandrel panels, a type much used later on by the L.C.C. and more prone to shabbiness. SOUTHMEAD PRIMARY SCHOOL, Princes Way, E of Victoria Drive, was built at the same time, one of the many post-war primaries built along Hertfordshire lines (planned on an 8 ft 3 in. grid and faced with horizontal concrete slabs).

The impact of the new type of L.C.C. estates can be seen in two large enterprises of the Wandsworth Borough Council E of Princes Way: SOUTHMEAD, by *Lancelot Keay, Basil Duckett & Partners*, and EDGECOMBE HALL around Beaumont Road, by *Clifford Culpin & Partners*, both planned 1957, and applying the principles of mixed development with less happy results. The towers (eight and ten storeys respectively) are more numerous, the lower buildings more fussy. Further S the L.C.C.'s ARGYLE ESTATE (1956 etc.) straggles amorphously around Wimbledon Park Road and along Kingsmere Road. The best part is the group of flats and maisonettes around Winterfold Close off the end of Albert Drive. The gaps between the large estates have been filled up with pockets of low-rise housing. They provide some interesting contrasts. From S to N: QUEENSMERE,* at the S end of Victoria Drive, attractive but rather cramped brown brick terraces and clusters using split-level planning on the steep slope (*G.L.C. Architect's Department*, 1971–7, *c*. 100 p.p.a.). N of this several quite low-density small developments built as public housing but mostly sold off by Wandsworth: FULWOOD WALK and FULWOOD SQUARE, an extension to the Ackroyden Estate with folksy pantiled roofs (*Leonard Vincent, Raymond Gorbing & Partners*, 1976–8, 91 p.p.a.); TIBBETTS CLOSE, a charming, intimate arrangement of terraces along alleys and around a tiny square, excellently detailed (*Andrews, Emerson & Sherlock*, 1958–61); and immediately N of this a pleasantly informal group of pantiled houses on two sides of a courtyard W of Inner Park Road, by *Wandsworth's Architect's Department*, 1977–9. The cheerful cuckoo in the low-rise nest is the four-storey block of flats in CLAUDIA PLACE, by *Farrell Grimshaw*, 1974, with the firm's characteristic horizontal corrugated cladding, projecting glazed staircase, and flamboyant bright green and yellow paintwork. The same style is used for their ingeniously designed terrace houses opposite, with stepped-back roof gardens.

* For Queensmere Road *see* Wimbledon (Me), Perambulation.

ROEHAMPTON

INTRODUCTION

There are three main strata of Roehampton; the old village around Roehampton High Street and the s end of Roehampton Lane, the large mansions and aristocratic villas remaining from the Georgian and Victorian eras (all now in institutional use), and the C 20 housing estates in their grounds, which in the 106 1950s–60s made the name of Roehampton famous among architects and planners all over the world. Roehampton began as part of the parish of Putney: in the C 16 Putney Park was a deer park between Putney Park Lane and Priory Lane. s of this, off Clarence Lane, was the first Roehampton House, built in the earlier C 17 by Sir Richard Weston and rebuilt as Grove House in the C 18, which survives as the Froebel Institute. A second Roehampton House (now a hospital) was built in the early C 18 56 on the w side of Roehampton Lane. Other houses followed; the position of Roehampton was highly desirable, close to both Wimbledon House and Richmond Park. Despite the disappearance of some of these houses in the earlier C 20, and the buildings in the grounds of the survivors, there is still nothing like Roehampton anywhere in London to get an impression of the aristocratic Georgian country villa. The major houses are described roughly from s to N, after the account of the village, and of the mid-C 20 developments.

CHURCHES

HOLY TRINITY, Roehampton Lane. 1896–8 by *G. H. Fellowes Prynne*. Corsham stone exterior with Early Dec detail and a spire 200 ft high. Interior with one of Prynne's successful rood screens, or, to be more accurate, a tripartite traceried opening filling the whole height of the chancel arch. Prynne got the idea from the medieval screen at Great Bardfield, Essex, and used it first at All Saints, West Dulwich, Lambeth (La). – PAINTED ALTAR PANELS also by *Prynne*.

ST MARGARET, Putney Park Lane. Built in the mid C 19 as an undistinguished Baptist chapel; Kentish rag, Gothic. Much altered after it became C. of E., c. 1912 by *A. G. Humphrey*, and in 1925 by *Forsyth & Maule*, who added the brick Gothic E end.

ST JOSEPH (R.C.), Roehampton Lane. 1881 by *F. A. Walters*. E extension 1958. Presbytery, porches, and baptistery 1963 by *Tomei & Maxwell*.

PERAMBULATION

ROEHAMPTON VILLAGE. Holy Trinity is out of keeping with the remains of the village (it replaced a church by *Ferrey* of 1842; before that there was only a chapel in the grounds of the first Roehampton House). Opposite the church, at the corner of Alton Road, the late C 19 VICARAGE, with tile-hung gable, and a formal early C 20 Queen Anne CHURCH HALL. But to the N of the church enough survives around the narrow HIGH STREET to visualize the Georgian appearance of the village, especially the KING'S HEAD, with projecting weather-boarded wing (a little dolled up). This faces ROEHAMPTON LANE, now a busy road which acts as frontier between the huge council estate to the W and the modest remains of the village.

To the N of the village, after the major houses along Roehampton Lane (*see* below), FAIRACRES, on the W side, one of the first blocks of private flats to break the spell of Georgian Roehampton. 1936 by *Minoprio & Spencely*. In itself a very commendable design, a crescent facing away from the road; slightly modish 1930s motifs. E of Roehampton Lane, around DOVER HOUSE ROAD, the L.C.C.'s ROEHAMPTON ESTATE, 1920 onwards; pleasant houses in a mixture of brick and roughcast, with some closes and set-back groups in the Parker & Unwin manner, although lacking the flair of some of the other early cottage estates (cf. Norbury, Cr, Old Oak Hammersmith, H F). In the middle, PUTNEY PARK HOUSE, a stuccoed Regency villa with a full-height bow-window on the garden side and a huge, rather ungainly enclosed porch; preserved as a community building, but in a disappointingly cramped position. The edge of the estate is PUTNEY PARK LANE. On the W side, GRANARD LODGE, white stuccoed Italianate, a relic of the demolished Granard House. W of Roehampton Lane, around PRIORY LANE, public housing of the 1970s: *Wandsworth*'s WOKING CLOSE (*Emberton, Tardrew & Partners*, 1968–70) and the LENNOX ESTATE, for the G.L.C. by *Gollins, Melvin, Ward & Partners*, once again in the form of low brick terraces, although with harsher, more mechanical details than the cosy early cottage estates. It is as if the Alton Estate had never existed. Near the entrance to the Lennox Estate, more overtly C 20 flats partly for the staff of the Priory Hospital (*see* Major Houses, below), by *D. Y. Davies Associates*, 1975–7. Four three-storey blocks, white concrete blockwork and neat black details, crisply echoing the colours, if not the materials, of The Priory itself. Further S, the BANK OF ENGLAND SPORTS GROUND (the site of Clarence House), with pavilion by *Thorp*, and archives building 1908–10 by *Blomfield*, wings 1939, large, tall neo-Georgian Utilitarian. Then TEMPLETON, plain brick late Georgian, six-window centre with lower wings (interior: staircase with wrought-iron balustrade).

ALTON ESTATE

106 The Alton Estate at Roehampton, planned from 1951 by the newly established *L.C.C. Architect's Department* under (*Sir*) *Robert Matthew*, was one of their first and most famous ven-

tures in grouping buildings of different heights and sizes on one estate (the principle called mixed development), so that a relatively high density could be achieved (100 p.p.a.), together with open spaces and some private gardens. Hitherto almost all L.C.C. housing had been either cottage estates on the edge of London (*see* e.g. Roehampton Estate, Dover House Road, Perambulation above) or inner city tenement blocks. The sites were large (the only undeveloped area on this scale in London available to the L.C.C. at this time), *c.* 130 acres, later increased by further additions, and were planned for a total of *c.* 9,500 people, the equivalent of a new town neighbourhood. Schools, community buildings, and shops were necessary, and were planned from the beginning, although not in an especially distinguished way, and there is no single focus. The object however was more than just the provision of decent housing; Roehampton exemplifies better than anywhere else in London that idealism that characterized so much post-war planning, the marriage of economic, rational buildings with sensitive grouping and generous landscaping, of social purpose with aesthetics. By now it is a familiar story that in pursuing the grand ideal some of the realities of everyday living were not considered closely enough (distance from shops, families off the ground, etc.). The drawbacks became especially noticeable in the imitations of Roehampton that soon sprang up, for these were without the compensation of the unique landscape that this estate was able to exploit.

The nature of the sites demanded a different treatment for the two parts of the estate, which were planned by separate teams of architects.* A tour should begin with ALTON EAST, the earlier design, built in 1952–5 apart from some later additions. It is the immediate successor to Ackroyden (*see* above, Putney (Ww), Perambulation), which was the very first of the L.C.C.'s mixed developments. Alton East occupies the area between Portsmouth Road, Bessborough Road, and Alton Road. The ten eleven-storey point blocks (square, with four flats to each floor and so clumpier but more economical than the T-shaped blocks at Ackroyden), scattered over the bosky slope which had been covered by large Victorian gardens, contain about three-fifths of the dwellings; the rest are in lower terraces of houses and maisonettes, some with staggered frontages, set at right angles to the roads and reached by paths. The effect is of picturesque informality. The terraces have shallow pitched roofs, i.e. are not stridently modern in idiom. (The curious bite in some of the roofs is to allow lighting to internal bathrooms, an innovation that made narrower frontages possible – a significant move toward more compact urban planning.) Near the top of the hill is a small shopping

---

* The team for Alton East under *R. Stjernstedt* (architect in charge) included (at different times) *A. W. C. Barr, O. J. Cox, A. R. Garrod, J. Partridge, B. Adams, H. Gravensen, P. Nevill, J. N. Wall, H. P. Harrison*. The team for Alton West under *Colin Lucas* consisted at first of *J. Partridge, W. G. Howell, J. Killick, J. F. Amis*, later joined by *J. R. Gallery, R. Stout, G. F. Bailey*.

centre; at the bottom HEATHMERE, a delicately designed primary school, one of the best of the early post-war schools by the L.C.C. (job architect *H. Smith*, 1953), making good use of colour. Opposite, No. 66, a single relic of the Victorian Alton Road. The later groups of houses and flats near by, which include the red brick terraces by *Howell, Killick, Partridge & Amis*, 1966–9 for the G.L.C., are not part of the original L.C.C. design, nor are the crude concrete maisonette blocks with upper links which were added by the *G.L.C.* in the 1970s to the w of Bessborough Road. (No. 26 Bessborough Road is earlier, by *Connell, Ward & Lucas*, 1938.)

ALTON WEST is best approached along Danebury Avenue, which starts opposite Roehampton High Street. It is a much larger area than Alton East, extending along the edge of Richmond Park, consisting of the grounds of the mansions of Mount Clare, Downshire House, and Manresa House, which were all preserved (*see* Major Houses, below). It was decided to build on only 66 out of a total of nearly 100 acres, and it was the preservation of the open space of the Downshire Field, and of the maximum number of trees, that conditioned the layout. The planning took several years. Designs were finally approved in 1954, although there were later additions.*

The impression at the beginning of Danebury Avenue is quite urban, with a shopping parade and a ten-storey tower standing sentinel over a playful little library with a series of saucer domes.‡ Further N are rather rigid lines of maisonette blocks and terrace houses, less informal than the groups at Alton East but not quite urban enough to make an impressive promenade. Then come the first of several groups of point blocks, set among trees, and lower flat-roofed terraces, more uncompromising than those at Alton East, and less attractive, especially when seen from above. Beyond is the surprise which made Alton West famous, the noble sweep of the Downshire Field with its array of five mighty concrete slabs on stilts. The slabs, built in 1954–8, are the most important innovation of the estate. They are related to the slabs at Bentham Road, Hackney (Hc), designed at the same time (*see London 4*),§ and are composed of narrow-fronted maisonettes, whose two-storey outer walls are recessed within the frame of the balcony and cross walls, creating a powerful, dynamic pattern of large squares over the whole block, most effective from a distance when their impact is set off by the undulating greenery. The field was deliberately landscaped, and a valley made in the centre, to enhance the setting of the buildings. The slabs are placed quite far apart and turn their short blind

* A total of 1,872 dwellings was planned in 1953. A further 470 were added between 1956 and 1966, as neighbouring sites became available. The largest of these additions are the group of six point blocks near Manresa House, of 1966.

‡ This group was intended from the beginning, but not planned and built until 1959–61. The tower was originally to have been only eight storeys high.

§ The architects chiefly responsible for the development of this design in the L.C.C. were *W. J. Howell* and *C. St J. Wilson*.

ends of shuttered concrete towards Richmond Park.* The composition changes according to one's position (the point blocks do not have this excitement); the ideal vantage point is the terrace in front of Mount Clare, a suitable place to reflect upon the Palladian precedent of geometric forms in a picturesque landscape, and on how difficult it is for C20 architecture to provide satisfying counterparts. The more immediate sources for the Alton Estate are Le Corbusier's high-rise projects of the pre-war years, and in particular for the slabs, with their surfaces of concrete shuttering and grid balconies, his Unité d'Habitation at Marseilles, completed in 1952. But the informal grouping of tall blocks at Roehampton also owes something to Swedish precedent, which had an important influence on some of the L.C.C. architects.‡

The application of the principles of the picturesque tradition to public housing helped to make Roehampton internationally famous. Within a London context other innovations are equally significant. The technical achievements at Alton West included for example a district heating system (as had been done already at Churchill Gardens, Pimlico, by Powell & Moya), the building of the slab blocks without scaffolding, and also the provision within them of mechanically ventilated bathrooms, all principles that were to be taken up during the era of industrialized building that followed. Visually the slabs are harbingers of the tougher, more ruthless use of concrete construction derived from Le Corbusier that was to pervade the L.C.C. Architect's Department and much English architecture elsewhere over the next decade.

MAJOR HOUSES

DIGBY STUART COLLEGE AND CONVENT OF THE SACRED HEART, Roehampton Lane. On the site of an C18 mansion, ELM GROVE, of which nothing now remains.§ The present convent buildings are extensive but undistinguished (architects: *Hadfield* and *Hungerford Pollen*), with the exception of the remains of *William Wardell*'s chapel of 1853 close to the road, now encapsulated in post-war buildings by *Lawrence H. Shattock* (1952–60). The chapel consisted originally of nave, transeptal chapel, and chancel with rose window. The nave has been destroyed. Windows with Dec tracery on one side, a

* The reduction of the impact on the park was the deciding factor in the siting, and the result of government intervention. The original plans sited the slabs at right angles to their present positions, so that the flats had splendid views, but made up a wall of building facing the park.

‡ The unexecuted plans of 1935 by *Gropius* and *Maxwell Fry* for an estate near Windsor with tall blocks in a landscape setting can also be compared. For a fuller discussion of these ideas see N. Pevsner: 'Roehampton, Housing and the Picturesque Tradition', *Architectural Review*, July 1959.

§ The original Elm Grove, to which *Gibbs* added a room *c.* 1725, was burnt down *c.* 1790. Its replacement, by *James Spiller* for Benjamin Goldsmid, was destroyed in the Second World War.

graceful tracery arch dividing off the chapel on the other side.

DOWNSHIRE HOUSE (Garnett College), Roehampton Lane. Built in the 1770s and much altered since. The first occupier was General Cholmondeley († 1775).* The house stands close to the road, with a rather dull exterior of red brick, much restored, especially on the s side following the demolition of the s wing after the Second World War. (This may have been by *Robert Brettingham*, who worked on the house for the Marquess of Downshire possibly *c*. 1795.) The existing building is of three storeys, six bays plus a N wing with bay-window, probably an addition. Doorcases with segmental pediments. The most notable interior is the central hall with black and white marble floor and Rococo plaster frame over the fireplace. The stair-hall to the l. is all c 20, but in the s w room is a fine later c 18 frieze. The long narrow central room facing the garden has shallow early c 20 bow-windows flanked by two shell niches of early c 18 character (re-used?). The owner from 1912 to 1920 was Sir Stephen Herbert Gatty. In his time extensive formal gardens were laid out, of which a small part survives to the N. Brick walls, stone balustrades with pineapples, a hipped-roof summerhouse with paired columns, by *Oswald P. Milne*. CEDARS COTTAGES, nine bays, one and a half storeys, with parapet, also of brick with rubbed brick dressings, is probably the N service wing of Cedars Court, another late c 18 house demolished before the Second World War.

GROVE HOUSE (Froebel Institute), Clarence Lane, stands near the site of the first Roehampton House of the earlier c 17. It was replaced by the present building, by *James Wyatt* for Sir Joshua Vanneck in 1777, with its delicate nine-bay front consisting of a projecting three-bay centre with pediment, Venetian window, and one-storey porch with paired columns. Two-storey wings with balustrades. To the l. the extensive Italianate additions for Pauline Duvernet, the ballet dancer, later Mrs Stephens, 1851 by *William Burn*. In the original house a good entrance hall: walls with pilasters and elegant plasterwork, and a room to the l. with Adamish ceiling and fine chimneypiece. A rather cramped roof-lit staircase behind. The c 19 rooms have sumptuous panelling both in the large front room and the smaller back room facing the garden. Beyond are additions by *Norman & Dawbarn* for the Froebel Institute: communal block close to the house, and education block further s, 1959–61, brick with exposed concrete frame. (In the grounds in 1862 *Burn* built a mausoleum to Mrs Stephens, close to the site of the Roehampton Chapel.)

MANRESA HOUSE, w of Danebury Avenue, within the Alton West Estate. Like Mount Clare (*see* below), now part of Garnett College (teachers' training college). While Mount Clare displays itself proudly on the crest of the hill, Manresa House is hidden away behind high walls, its c 18 core further

---

* We owe this and other Roehampton details to Mr P. R. Gilfillan.

concealed from the entrance by the additions made when it was in Jesuit ownership from 1860 to the 1960s. The original house (called PARKSTED), designed in 1760 by *Sir William Chambers* for Lord Bessborough, was nearly complete by 1768. Ceiling drawings dated 1761 and 1763 survive. It was the first of several Palladian villas designed by Chambers in the early 1760s. They belong to the second generation of Palladian houses in England, forty years after Colen Campbell's Stourhead, Lord Burlington's Chiswick (Ho), and Roger Morris's Marble Hill, Richmond (Ri). The main front faces w across Richmond Park, five bays with rusticated ground floor and quoins, stone centrepiece, with six-column Ionic portico and pediment at the level of the *piano nobile* approached by two curving staircases. The prototype for the façade appears to have been Bourchier Cleeve's Foots Cray (Bx) (q.v.), built in imitation of the Villa Rotonda *c.* 1756; but the obvious inspiration for a villa in the London countryside, that is a relatively modest rural retreat rather than a full-scale country house, was of course Chiswick House. Behind the house, hidden from the park, Chambers planned two stable wings (see *Vitruvius Britannicus*), which were replaced by extensions for the Jesuits by *H. Clutton*, of after 1860. The central doorways to the inner courtyard may be re-used C18 work. Across the back of the house, at basement level, the wings are linked by a broad corridor with Tuscan columns; the other side of the courtyard is closed by a clumsy four-storey block of the 1950s. Further ranges were added in 1877–80 (s) and 1885–6 (N) by *F. A. Walters*. The C19 wings, of brick and stucco, carefully repeat the original rustication.

The plan of the C18 house does not have the complexity of Chiswick and other Palladian imitations. The portico leads to a large hall, with the stair-hall behind, flanked by four corner rooms of different sizes. The only exceptional feature of the plan has disappeared. According to *Vitruvius Britannicus* the main staircase, which now rises around three sides of an open well, enclosed a smaller servants' staircase (cf. Webb's Amesbury, Wilts). This was apparently destroyed by a fire in the C19, and its only indication is some minor breaks in the balustrading. In the entrance hall a monumental stone fireplace by *Joseph Wilton*, with raised centre, swags, and trophies of the arts (similar to others by him at Chambers's Peper Harow, Surrey). The main rooms all have noteworthy plaster ceilings in Chambers's early style, powerful, individualistic, and rather cramped geometric arrangements containing not always very suitable shaped classical motifs. In the dining room (NE) they include hounds and wreaths, with winged female figures at the corners, and a loose vine scroll. The two lobbies in this room were probably added when the wings were built in the C19, although the elaborate doorcases may be re-used. The large library (sw) has a ceiling with trophies of the arts, owls, and sphinxes. The centre window was originally a niche. In the SE room a coved ceiling with candlesticks and wreaths at the corners, in high relief. On the top floor (much altered), a skylight with medallions with heads and prows above the site of the central corridor. In the basement below the portico a small vaulted passage with charming floral plasterwork, perhaps intended as a loggia. In the additions the only notable interior is the CHAPEL on the s side (now disused), begun by *J. J. Scoles*, completed after his death in 1864 by *Nicholl*, elaborate Italian Renaissance, with marble pilasters, barrel-vaults penetrated by clerestory windows, and arches with top-lit domes decorated by bizarre coffering in different patterns. Apses to the sanctuary and N aisle. In the adjoining room a coloured marble fireplace with fluted Ionic columns, presumably from the C18 house. In the garden to the E of the chapel a circular entablature from the portico of an C18 garden temple (the rest in store). (Another temple from Manresa House is in the grounds of the principal's house at Mount Clare.)

MARYFIELD CONVENT, w of Danebury Avenue. 1939 by *Scoles & Raymond*, in convincing early C18 idiom; red brick with giant pilasters and large doorcases. Many additions.

MOUNT CLARE, w of Danebury Avenue. Built for George Clive, a banker and cousin of Lord Clive, by *Robert Taylor*, 1770–3.* The wooden Doric portico was added by *P. Columbani* after the house was bought in 1780 by Sir John Dick, British Consul at Leghorn. It is approached by a curved double staircase and shaded by an enormous cedar tree. The large portico sits rather uneasily against the projecting centre of Taylor's neat Palladian villa. Rusticated ground floor of stone, stucco above (the contrast lost since all is now painted white). The front is of five bays; the sides of three bays have centre windows accented by pediments. Facing the garden a half-octagonal centre projection, a favourite Taylor motif. Also typical of Taylor is the ingeniously compact planning using rooms of different shapes (cf. Asgill House, Richmond (Ri), Perambulation 2) and the delicate interior plasterwork, so much daintier in effect than Chambers's work at Manresa House of a few years earlier. The entrance hall has a coffered transverse barrel-vault. On the walls two portrait plaques signed *F. Shubin*, Rome 1772. They have been identified as the Counts Orlov, and were probably given to Dick by the Duke of Gloucester at Leghorn.‡ Some of the other plaster decoration, e.g. the festoons with husks, may have been added by *Columbani* at the same time. In the SW corner of the house is the staircase, with elegant iron balustrades, fitted into a curved space. In the centre of the garden side an octagon room, with big niches with mirrors in two of the walls and a coved ceiling with delicate swags and foliage. The SW room also has a coved ceiling, Chippendale bookcases recessed in niches (one with trompe l'œil books), and an elaborate door-

---

* This was discovered by Anne Riches. Payments were made to Taylor; there is no evidence to support the previous attribution to *Henry Holland*.

‡ See A. Kelly, *Burlington Magazine*, April 1970, pp. 224–8.

case. The large N room was remodelled in the C 19, but like the other rooms has a good C 18 marble fireplace, with a medallion with wreath and figures. Upstairs the best room is the octagonal one to the garden, with Corinthian columns in the angles. *Capability Brown* was paid for work on the grounds in 1774–5, but the surroundings have been much altered. C 19 additions were removed when the house was taken over by the G.L.C. in 1954 and converted into common rooms for Garnett College. The separate two-storey painted white brick ranges of the college (1960s) do not interfere with the main view of the house, but come a little too close. (In the grounds of the principal's house a small TEMPLE moved here from Manresa House. Greek Doric portico and tapering entrance door; a pretty painted ceiling inside.)

THE PRIORY (Priory Hospital), Priory Lane. A rambling, battlemented sham-Tudor complex, of which the earliest part is a stuccoed Gothic villa of *c.* 1800, with two canted bay-windows flanking a triple-arched entrance. Much extended from *c.* 1840–1 for Sir James Knight-Bruce by *R. L. Roumieu*, and again in the 1860s, when it became a private mental hospital. (An elaborate *Roumieu* chimneypiece remains inside.)

ROEHAMPTON HOUSE (Queen Mary's Hospital), Roehampton Lane. The second house of this name at Roehampton, built by *Thomas Archer* in 1710–12 for Thomas Cary. Much enlarged by *Lutyens* in 1911–13 for A. M. Grenfell; later converted to a hospital. The original house (now used as a nurses' home) consists of the seven central bays. Red brick; basement, two and a half storeys, and a top parapet. The details have the wilfulness typical of Archer. Rusticated brick quoins to emphasize the corners and angles of the three-bay projecting centre. The middle bay, on the E as well as the W side, has door, main upper window (a niche on the E side), and top balustrade all connected, and all of dressed stone. The doorway has pilasters carrying a broken pediment, with a tall arched opening above on a scale quite different from the other windows. These are embellished only by tall brick keystones, moulded surrounds, and aprons. To the l. and r. of the entablature of the main window circular openings, further breaking the symmetry of the composition. The whole was originally crowned by a gargantuan cleft pediment, similar to Archer's St John Smith Square and his demolished Monmouth House, Soho. *Vitruvius Britannicus* shows the main block with low curved links to pavilions (which may never have been built). *Lutyens* heightened the links to two storeys, and added three-storey wings. The interior has been altered. The main room was the saloon on the first floor over the entrance hall, extending through two storeys and completely decorated with paintings by *Sir James Thornhill*: landscapes on the walls, and the Feast of the Gods on the coved ceiling. These were destroyed in the Second World War and the room has since been divided up. The main and subsidiary staircases,

56

in the centres of N and S fronts, were removed when the wings were added. In the present N wing a staircase apparently made from a combination of the two (RCHM). Open string (an early example), turned and twisted balusters. The upper part has moulded soffits and marquetry decoration.

TOOTING AND STREATHAM PARK

INTRODUCTION

There are two parts of Tooting: Upper Tooting or Tooting Bec; and Lower Tooting or Tooting Graveney. In the Domesday Book Tooting appears as held by the Abbey of Bec in Normandy; hence the name Tooting Bec. It was part of the manor of Streatham, and so belonged to the Howlands in the C17, to the Dukes of Bedford in the C18. Tooting parish church is at Tooting Graveney, which derives its name from the Gravenel family which held the manor from Chertsey Abbey in the C12 and C13. In the C17 it belonged to the Maynards. In 1871 Thorne described this area as 'a region of villas and nursery gardens . . . very pleasant and apart from the common, very commonplace'. It remained quite distinct from Upper Tooting until the later C19, when the open land in between was filled up by houses and hospitals and cemeteries. The main centre of Lower Tooting is now at Tooting Broadway Station, away from the old church. S of Tooting Bec Common is the area called Streatham Park, the site of Streatham Place, the house of the Thrales frequented by Dr Johnson. The rest of Streatham, with the parish church and site of the manor house, lies within the borough of Lambeth (*see* Streatham, La).

CHURCHES

ALL SAINTS, Franciscan Road. 1904–6 by *Temple Moore*. Built through a bequest from Lady Charles Brudenell-Bruce in memory of her husband, the first Marquess of Ailesbury. The church is the centrepiece of the L.C.C.'s Totterdown Fields Estate (*see* Perambulation, below). It is large, and of honest design, stock brick outside, with a N tower; tracery of *c.* 1300. Double-aisled interior, the aisles vaulted in timber so that the arches of the shafts separate the aisle bays not longitudinally but transversely. E Lady Chapel with three arches to the chancel. – Italian FURNISHINGS, collected by the first vicar, Canon Stephens, adapted by *Walter Tapper*. Temple Moore did not like them. – REREDOS, Baroque, from Bologna, with a late C17 copy of a Velázquez. – CANDLESTICKS from Florence, CHOIR STALLS, CREDENCE, TESTER CANON, PREACHER'S CHAIR, and IRON GRILLE from a church near Como. – ALTARPIECE, Lady Chapel. French C16. – FONT, PULPIT, ORGAN CASE, and memorial to the founder by *Tapper*. – STAINED GLASS. E window by *V. Milner*.

HOLY TRINITY, Trinity Road, Upper Tooting. At an angle to the road. Ragstone, with a short W tower, now rather dwarfed by later extensions. The original building 1854–5 by *Salvin*; tower 1860 by *Ferrey*, who also added the N transept and widened the N aisle in 1889. The S aisle, widened in 1893, was divided off as a church hall in 1976. Plain interior, once embellished with many large WALL PAINTINGS in a Pre-Raphaelite style, 1906–13 by *Richard Castle*, a member of the choir. The survivors are: St Agnes (N chapel), St Oswald (W wall), and three on the tower walls around the font. – Much C19 STAINED GLASS, the N aisle windows and the window to the founder, Henry Browse († 1897), especially good.

ST ALBAN, Aldrington Road, Streatham Park. 1888–93 by *E. H. Martineau*. Byzantine. The *Morris & Co.* glass of *c.* 1893 was mostly destroyed in a fire in 1947. Rebuilt by *J. S. Comper*.

ST AUGUSTINE, Broadwater Road, W of Upper Tooting Road. By *H. P. Burke Downing*, 1929–31; Gothic.

ST JAMES, Mitcham Lane. 1910 by *F. Peck*, with an odd Gothic front with flying buttresses harshly continuing the line of the pitch of the nave roof.

ST NICHOLAS, Church Lane. The old parish church, which had the remarkable feature of a circular tower on its N side, was replaced by a new church on a site a little further W. It is in a Commissioners' Gothic, 1833 by *T. W. Atkinson*. Stock brick, with a thin façade with a W tower typical of the date. Lancet windows in odd shallow niches, with fancy Dec tracery. Chancel, vestry, and organ chamber 1873–5; transepts 1889. Originally three galleries as usual. – MONUMENTS. Brass to Elizabeth Fitzwilliam † 1582 and her husband † 1597, kneeling in a freestone surround with pilasters. – Lady Bateman † 1709. Large cartouche with drapes and cherub's head, flaming urn in the centre with two seated cherubs, the whole against a black marble background. Attributed by Mrs Esdaile to *Francis Bird*.

ST ANSELM (R.C.), Balham High Road. 1933. An eclectic mixture of Gothic and classical. Dome over the crossing.

ST BONIFACE (R.C.), Mitcham Road. 1907 by *Williamson & Foss*. Interior based on SS. Vicenzo ed Anastasia, Rome. Ostentatious Venetian Romanesque W front of 1927 with Egyptianizing capitals and a bell-tower.

BAPTIST CHURCH, Mitcham Lane. 1902–3 by *G. & R. P. Baines*, the usual brick and stone façade with a NW turret and the jolly Nonconformist Art-Nouveau Gothic detail of the moment.

UNITED REFORMED CHURCH, Mitcham Road. 1904–5 by *Gordon & Gunton*, an austere, minimally Gothic exterior with a huge octagonal slate roof and cupola. An example of the centralized planning popular with Nonconformists from the later C19.

LAMBETH CEMETERY, Blackshaw Road. Brick Gothic

LODGES and CHAPELS 1854 by *F. K. Wehnert* and *J. Ashdown*.

STREATHAM CEMETERY, Garratt Lane. Stone LODGES and two CHAPELS by *W. Newton Dunn*, Gothic, opened 1893.

PUBLIC BUILDINGS

FIRE STATION, Trinity Road. 1907. One of the *L.C.C. Fire Brigade Department*'s free, asymmetrical stone and brick compositions.

LIBRARY, Mitcham Road. 1902 by *William Hunt*; top floor added 1908. Much terracotta decoration.

FURZEDOWN TRAINING COLLEGE, Furzedown Drive. The core is a large plain mansion of *c.* 1800 which once stood in its own grounds to the S of Tooting Common. It was bought in 1862 by Philip Flower (developer of the Park Town Estate; *see* Battersea (Ww), Perambulation 2), and altered by *James Knowles Sen.* in 1862–7. Five-bay front with heavy cornice and parapet. On the W side an excellent conservatory of *c.* 1865 with barrel-vaulted glass roof. Additions for the college crowd around, leaving just a little of the exotic C19 planting. The new buildings are by *L. Manasseh and Partners*, 1961–5. The eleven-storey residential block has rather ugly concrete cladding panels; the communal buildings to the S, a bold mixture of glass and concrete, are more attractive.

BOARD SCHOOLS. Notable examples of the symmetrical, three-decker turreted type: PENWORTHY PRIMARY, Welham Road, SMALLWOOD PRIMARY, Smallwood Road, opposite Streatham Cemetery, 1898, and ENSHAM SCHOOL, Franciscan Road, a later design, with giant arches in terracotta (cf. Woolwich (Gr), Public Buildings). – FURZEDOWN SECONDARY, Welham Road, has a big Baroque centrepiece of *c.* 1910, with rusticated brick surround to a large window. Good additions (gymnasium and science blocks) by *Trevor Dannatt & Partners*, 1965–7.

ST BENEDICT'S HOSPITAL (former), Church Lane. A stately brick neo-Georgian front on a grand scale. Built as Tooting College (for St Joseph's R.C. College, Clapham) in 1887–8 by *William Harvey*; later used as an old people's home before becoming a hospital. It was built in the grounds of Hill House, a mid C18 country house which survived in Rectory Lane until replaced by a nurses' home *c.* 1961.

ST GEORGE'S HOSPITAL, between Coverton Road and Blackshaw Road. The N part of the site, called the Fountain Hospital, was opened as a fever hospital in 1893 (temporary buildings by *T. W. Aldwinkle*); the S part, known as the Grove Hospital, had buildings by *A. Hessell Tiltman*, 1894–9, of which a few remain next to the expanding new complex by *Watkins Gray Woodgate International*, planned from the later 1960s for the move of St George's Hospital here from Hyde Park Corner. Phase one of the medical school was completed in 1977, phase

one of the hospital in 1977–9. Rebuilding is intended to
continue during the 1980s, to accommodate 1,201 beds, with
2,100 staff and 400 medical students. Unlike the architects'
other London hospitals (Guy's, Royal Free), the ward blocks
here are not higher than six storeys.

TOOTING BEC HOSPITAL, Tooting Bec Road. Built as Tooting Bec Asylum, before 1916. Forbidding brick blocks; good
iron railings with Art Nouveau touches.

SPRINGFIELD HOSPITAL, Beechcroft Road. *See* below,
Wandsworth, Public Buildings.

STATIONS. TOOTING BEC and TOOTING BROADWAY, like
Clapham South and Balham, are on the extension to Morden
(later the Northern Line), opened 1926. They were designed
by *S. A. Heaps*, who was probably responsible for much of the
interior detail, and *Charles Holden*, who designed the chaste,
stone-faced, stripped classical exteriors (with inventive details
such as the London Transport signs for capitals). They relate
to Holden's earlier work, rather than to his later Piccadilly
Line stations.

PERAMBULATION

TOOTING COMMON (made up of the three commons of Tooting Bec, Tooting Graveney, and Streatham) is the remains of
common land which once stretched as far as Mitcham. It
became a metropolitan open space in 1873. There is a pretty
LODGE, dated 1879, by Dr Johnson's Avenue.

LOWER TOOTING. MITCHAM ROAD runs from the church
to the High Street, with a simple pump of 1823 at one end,
and a florid lamp post and statue of Edward VII at the other,
neatly summing up the shift from village to suburban centre.
The former DEFOE CHAPEL (now a shop) was built in
1776 for congregation established in 1688. Two-storey
pedimented classical front. The main landmarks are the
octagonal roof of the United Reformed Church (q.v.) and
the GRANADA CINEMA (now bingo hall). Behind its prosaic
classical façade (*Masey & Uren*, 1937) is a breathtakingly
palatial interior designed by *Theodore Komisarjevsky*, the best 101
example in London of the American-inspired escapist extravaganzas of the 1930s. Huge foyer: a baronial hall with vaguely Byzantine columns and grand staircase, a more intimate
Hall of Mirrors with Gothic arcading, and a vast auditorium
(seating over 3,000), with Gothic coffered ceiling, wall
arcades, and canopies over the proscenium arch. The colours
chiefly cream, green, red, and brown. The bright lighting
necessary for bingo dispels something of the magic. TOOT-
ING HIGH STREET has a few C18 houses: No. 93, incorporated in a school, and, more worthwhile, Nos. 99 and
101, early C18, with segmented-headed windows. Further s,
WATERFALL HOUSE, set back, at the corner of Langley
Road, of *c.* 1800; three-storey centre, lower wings, arched

windows on ground and first floors. The simple terrace houses in keeping near by are by *Forsyth & Colley*, 1980.

UPPER TOOTING. The oldest house is LA RETRAITE (convent school), in Tooting Bec Road, with a dignified C18 front, five-bay centre with projecting wings with Venetian windows below lunettes, the glazing all unfortunately altered. In UPPER TOOTING ROAD a few more C18 houses, altered (Nos. 68–72), but the chief focus is the KINGS HEAD, 1896 by *W. M. Brunton*, with a gross and jolly mansarded, balconied centre, and lavish use of engraved glass inside. Further N, TRINITY CRESCENT, by Holy Trinity, has large mid C19 stucco houses. FLOWERSMEAD, Upper Tooting Park, is progressive early post-Second-World-War housing for Wandsworth (87 dwellings, 77 p.p.a.) by *Covell & Matthews*, 1949–54, with a curving block reminiscent of Tecton's Spa Fields, Islington (Is).

TOTTERDOWN ESTATE, Lessingham Avenue, Franciscan Road, etc. The L.C.C. bought Totterdown Fields in 1900, and laid it out with a grid of streets of two-storey terraces, built in 1903–11 (the earliest at the W end) – a total of 1,229 houses and four shops. The drawings are mostly signed by *E. Stone Collins* of the L.C.C. (S. Beattie). No variety of layout, but some in the mixture of roughcast, tile-hanging, gables, and bay-windows.

STREATHAM PARK. The Streatham Park Estate is on the site of the house and grounds of the Thrales. The house was demolished in 1863. The select villas have now nearly all been replaced by council housing. The most important survivors are close to the common, hemmed in by the G.L.C.'s Fayland Estate of the 1960s. No. 2 WEST DRIVE is by *Leonard Stokes*, 1899, excellently proportioned, sober early neo-Georgian, with a fine grouping of chimneys on the hipped roof. DIXCOTE, NORTH DRIVE, of 1897 for R. W. Essex, was designed by *Voysey* but executed by *Walter Cave*. It is Voysey's largest London house, a little crammed in, but of the happy rambling composition characteristic of the great architect; also with one of his typical massive, trustworthy chimneys. (Good staircase.) Further W, FURZEDOWN LODGE, one-storeyed, with a prettily decorated cove, the former entrance lodge to Furzedown (*see* Public Buildings, above), by *J. K. Knowles Sen.*

WANDSWORTH

INTRODUCTION

Wandsworth was once really on the river Wandle, which can still be followed from close behind the church and the houses of Wandsworth Plain, then where it is crossed by the High Street by means of a bridge of 1820, and then up S. But it does not make itself much noticed in the old village centre, and it is a far cry now from Izaak Walton's remark on the 'fishful qualities' of the river. The fast-flowing Wandle had ground flour for London already from the Middle Ages, and by the mid C18 it was extensively exploited by water-powered industry. Parallel to the river the Surrey Iron Railway, built in 1801–3 by *William Jessop*, has left hardly any visible remains.* It was closed in 1846, when the steam railway arrived. Up to that point the industry was in a rural setting. Until 1891 the manor house, rebuilt in the later C17, stood near Wandsworth Bridge, and Harrison in 1776 wrote of the 'many handsome seats in this village belonging to the gentry and to those citizens who have retired from the fatigues of business', and the Railway Guide of 1851 still mentions its 'countless elegant villas', though now side by side with 'numerous manufactories . . . worked by water power'. The population in 1851 was 9,611 as against 4,455 in 1801. By 1881 it had grown to 28,000, by 1901 to 68,332 (that is, the parish, not the whole borough), encouraged by the opening of the suburban railway stations.* By then streets of small late Victorian terraces had filled the whole of the uninspiring low-lying area E of the Wandle, and stretched S and E of the remnants of Wandsworth Common to join up with those of Balham and Upper Tooting.

CHURCHES

ALL SAINTS, Wandsworth High Street. Nothing is visible of the medieval church on the site. Modest brick w tower, the lower part of 1630, the upper storey, crowned by urns, added in 1841 and restored in 1955 after war damage. The body of the church, rebuilt in 1779–80 by *William Jupp*, was altered in 1841 and 1859. Simple classical S porch. *E. W. Mountford* added a new roof and a classical chancel in 1899–1900. Interior tunnel-vaulted on painted wooden columns; the galleries keep behind them. – PULPIT. Good, of the building period, on baluster shaft. – Marble FONT and large churchwarden's PEW of the same date. – MONUMENTS. Brass to Nicholas Maudyt, 1420, in armour, head missing. – Henry Smith † 1627, kneeling in profile against a niche flanked by columns. – Susanna Powell † 1630, same composition.

ST ANDREW, Garratt Lane. 1889–90 by *E. W. Mountford*. Gothic, i.e. before Mountford turned classical (cf. above and

---

* It was the first publicly promoted railway, independent of a canal undertaking, and the first railway in south-east England. It ran for eight miles from Wandsworth up the E side of the Wandle valley to Mitcham (Me) (q.v.) and thence to Croydon, with a short branch to Hackbridge near Sutton (*see* Beddington (Su), Town Hall). The water supply of the intensively industrialized river Wandle was already wholly committed to driving waterwheels, ruling out a canal. The railway, horse-drawn, used L-section cast-iron plate rails, popular at the time, on stone sleeper blocks, with a gauge of 4 ft 2 in. At Wandsworth there was a quarter-mile-long canal or linear dock for transhipment of Thames barges, which remained in use until 1932. Its blocked-off entrance remains at Feathers Wharf. Other remains are stone sleeper blocks built into a wall on the w side of York Road, and others inside the Ram Brewery.

‡ Wandsworth Station, Battersea Rise, 1841, replaced in 1863 by Clapham Junction; Wandsworth Common 1853 and 1869; Earlsfield 1884 etc.

Battersea, Public Buildings). Red brick, two w turrets instead of a tower, nave and chancel under one roof, tall clerestory. (Interior of diapered brick. – *Doulton* FONT by *Tinworth*. – STAINED GLASS. E window by *Heaton, Butler & Bayne*, s aisle w by *M. Travers*.)

ST ANNE, St Ann's Hill. A Commissioners' church of 1820–4, by *Robert Smirke*. The only classical early C19 church in the borough, of unhappy outer proportions, with an Ionic giant portico and circular tower behind it, exactly twice as high as it should be. The design of the tower is very close to Smirke's St Mary Wyndham Place Marylebone (Wm). The rest of the building plain stock brick with large round-headed windows above smaller ones. Alterations by *William White*, 1891, chancel added by *Mountford*, 1896, with neo-Wren detail. When the church was first built it stood right on the edge of the new suburbs spreading up the hill from the High Street.

ST BARNABAS, Lavenham Road and Merton Road. 1906–8 by *C. Ford Whitcombe*. Large, red brick, Perp, with chancel raised over an undercroft.

ST MARY, Keble Street and Wimbledon Road, near the N end of Plough Lane. 1903–4 by *G. Pinkerton*, replacing the earlier C19 chapel of the hamlet of Summerstown. Red brick with free, rather coarse tracery; SE tower not completed. (An unconventional interior: alternate aisle bays with barrel-vaults. – STAINED GLASS. 1928 by *Morris & Co.* to *Burne Jones* designs.)

ST MARY MAGDALENE, Trinity Road. 1887–8 by *B. E. Ferrey*, brick, E. E. Chancel of 1900 and N aisle of 1906 added by *Cole & Adams*.

ST MICHAEL, Granville Road and Wimbledon Park Road. *See* Putney.

ST THOMAS A BECKET (R.C.), West Hill. Nave and s transept 1893–5 by *E. Goldie*, chancel and Lady Chapel 1897–9, s aisle and porch 1901, N aisle and transept 1912, tower 1926–7 by *Goldie* and *J. P. Conlan* (DE).

FRIENDS MEETING HOUSE, No. 59 Wandsworth High Street. 1778, a humble brick rectangle. The rear, overlooking the burial ground, of intimate charm. (Interior restored to its original condition *c.* 1980.)

HUGUENOT BURIAL GROUND, Mount Nod, between East Hill and Wandsworth Common North Side. Monuments of 1687 and after, including table tombs to Peter Paggen † 1720 of Wandsworth Manor House and John Gilham † 1728.

WANDSWORTH CEMETERY. Opened 1878. Gothic entrance in Magdalen Road.

PUBLIC BUILDINGS

TOWN HALL AND MUNICIPAL OFFICES, Wandsworth High Street. Three phases, none distinguished. The centre 1926 by *E. L. Elford*; the part to the r. 1935–7 by *E. A. Hunt*, grand, stone-faced, with carved frieze, but of no merit; the part to the l. of 1973–5 by *Clifford Culpin & Partners*, red brick bands, on a splayed plinth, tactfully low to the High Street, taller behind.

WANDSWORTH PRISON, Heathfield Road, between Earlsfield Road and Trinity Road. 1849 by *D. R. Hill* of Birmingham. Built as an additional Surrey House of Correction, to supplement what is now Brixton Prison. An outer brick wall of the 1970s unfortunately now encloses the bold GATEHOUSE, an Italianate mock fortress with a pair of three-storey towers, embellished by quoins and tapering rusticated pilasters (cf. Hill's Winson Green Prison, Birmingham). The more utilitarian prison buildings behind have wings radiating from a taller central tower (cf. the original plan for Brixton, and Pentonville, Islington). Staff housing of the C19 is tidily ranged around the perimeter walls.

SPORTS PAVILION, King George's Park, Burr Road, off Merton Road to the E. 1966 by the *Borough Architect's Department*. One-storeyed around a courtyard.

SOUTH THAMES COLLEGE, Wandsworth High Street. Built as a technical institute by the L.C.C. (*G. Topham Forrest*), 1926. Dark brick neo-Tudor.

ROYAL VICTORIA PATRIOTIC ASYLUM (later Spencer Park School), Trinity Road, Wandsworth Common.* Built as a school for orphaned daughters of servicemen, 1857–9 by *Rhode Hawkins*. A typically pompous Victorian symmetrical composition of yellow brick, with coarsely robust Gothic detail. Three storeys with entrance below a central tower; lower towers at the ends, corbelled-out turrets and bow-windows. Statue of St George and the Dragon in a central niche. Separate chapel. Low concrete additions of the 1960s to the N.

EMMANUEL SCHOOL, on the adjoining site to the N, but approached past a LODGE from Battersea Rise, built as the boys' school of the same institution, was taken over by the present school in 1881. It is a similar composition on a slightly smaller scale, red brick, less grandiose in its Gothic detail, with herringbone brick decoration. 1872 by *H. Saxon Snell*. Additions behind of 1896 and of the mid C20. – (In the CHAPEL, PAINTINGS of Moses and Aaron, and COMMUNION TABLE, said to come from St Benet Fink in the City.)

GARRATT GREEN SCHOOL, Aboyne Road, W of Streatham Cemetery. 1959 by the *L.C.C. Architect's Department*, for 2,200 girls. One of the first London comprehensives where the buildings were divided up to avoid too massive a scale (cf. Mayfield, Putney). Nothing over four storeys. The school had the advantage of a pleasantly open site with trees‡ formerly occupied by the farm of Springfield Hospital.

BOARD SCHOOLS. RIVERSIDE PRIMARY, Merton Road.

---

* To be converted to an arts centre.
‡ Since reduced for sports grounds.

1890–1 by *T. J. Bailey*. Picturesquely asymmetrical three-decker with gables and turret. – Other examples in Broadwater Road (*c.* 1900 and 1905) and Honeywell Road (1891).

SPRINGFIELD HOSPITAL, Beechcroft Road. Built as the Surrey County Lunatic Asylum, 1840–2 by *E. Lapidge*. Brick with stone dressings, Tudor detail, battlements. Long wings projecting forward. (Many extensions from 1863 onwards. New chapel 1881, superintendent's house 1881–2, large hospital block 1898, etc.) COMPUTER CENTRE in the grounds by *Andrews, Sherlock & Partners*, 1979.

WANDSWORTH BRIDGE. *See* Thames Crossings at end of gazetteer.

PERAMBULATION

WANDSWORTH HIGH STREET, running downhill to the crossing over the Wandle, has little to offer. Its focal point is the ugly, overpowering ARNDALE CENTRE, a mammoth package of covered shopping area, 516 flats, car park, slipper baths, etc., by *Seymour Harris & Partners*, 1967–74. Apart from the unassuming parish church and the late C 19 SPREAD EAGLE (good interior) the only buildings of interest are those of the RAM BREWERY at the corner of York Road (Messrs Young since 1831). The main process building of five storeys, L-shaped, functional C 19 yellow brickwork topped by a cooling tank. In front, a later extension, in yellow brick and Portland stone, with segment-headed giant arcade. W of this, a five-bay mid-Georgian red brick house with Gibbs-surround doorway in yellow brick. (In the old board room two C 18 plaster portrait medallions of Inigo Jones and Andrea Palladio. The style suggests Italian craftsmanship.) On the E corner the extensive Brewery Tap public house, 1883, brick and stucco. At the rear of the site, a C 19 stable block. Plant includes two beam engines on cast-iron A-frames, by Wentworth & Sons of Wandsworth, one of 1835, remodelled 1863, the other of 1867, still in use.

In WANDSWORTH PLAIN, just N of the High Street, the best surviving early Georgian houses in the area, Nos. 1–6 CHURCH ROW, three storeys over basements, doors with Corinthian pilasters, five-bay centre with pediment. The centre house with a sundial dated 1723. Nos. 7–9 are a later C 18 addition. Little else remains in this area of before the C 20, apart from a stuccoed terrace in ARMOURY WAY and the CRANE public house. Further N a few good houses, too scattered to make a consistent perambulation.

First WENTWORTH HOUSE in DORMAY STREET, early C 18, two storeys, five bays. In PUTNEY BRIDGE ROAD Nos. 22 and 24, early C 18, and a few early C 19 terrace houses, messed up by the railway line. To the W in OAKHILL ROAD, Nos. 155–171, 1906 by *Edward G. Hunt*, Arts and Crafts cottages with big stacks, hipped gables, and crowstepped party walls. Some way further W Nos. 23 and 25, 1879 and 1880 by *William*

Young (who worked on the Cadogan Estate and wrote a book on town houses). No. 23 was his own house, an enjoyable piece of propaganda for the style of the moment among its more retiring Italianate and Gothic neighbours: a picturesque composition, crammed full of fashionable decorative motifs (tile-hanging, sgraffito, terracotta, stained glass). In POINT PLEASANT, to the N off Putney Bridge Road, PROSPECT HOUSE, a surprising gem in an unprepossessing industrial area by the river – a stuccoed two-storey Regency villa of three bays, with giant Soanian incised pilasters and a semicircular porch with Ionic columns. Probably built *c*. 1805 for Joseph Gatty, owner of the vinegar works near by. Restored in 1975.

Wandsworth s of the High Street also has only isolated buildings worth a mention. Roughly from W to E: first in MERTON ROAD, DOWN LODGE, later C18 altered, three storeys, wooden Doric porch, and the LORD PALMERSTON, a nice later C19 stuccoed pub. In STANDEN ROAD, further s, off Merton Road and Wimbledon Park Road, BENHAM & SONS, a remarkable Art Nouveau former confectionery works, 1904 by *W. T. Walker*, a bold, symmetrical composition in green, white, and blue glazed brick, with decorative roundels. A tower with a copper dome at either end, doorways with pronounced hoods. At SUMMERSTOWN, a former hamlet to the E, ST CLEMENT DANES ALMSHOUSES, Garratt Lane, 1848–9 by *R. Hesketh*, an unusually large composition, low, long, Tudor, of brick with diaper patterns of black headers. Lodge to match. The almshouses were out in the country when built. They are now surrounded unsympathetically by an estate of 1969–72; slabs with angular brutalist end staircases.

WANDSWORTH COMMON is extensive, but was encroached upon in the C19 and divided in two by the railway. The remains were preserved by the Wandsworth Commons Act of 1871 (cf. Wimbledon, Me). On the W side near the N end HEATHFIELD GARDENS, a small group of pretty houses of the early C19. Further s LYFORD ROAD, a good area for Edwardian houses, many by *Hubert East* of *Wimperis & East*. The most interesting is No. 68 (The White Cottage), a minor work of 1903 by *Voysey*. Its special feature is the projecting centre rising to a third-storey belvedere. (Inside, a large central hall with staircase, original fireplace and fittings.) On the common itself the curiously villagey hexagonal weatherboarded WINDPUMP (now without sails and with a cap of the 1970s), at the junction of Earlsfield Road and Windmill Road. It was built in 1837 to restore a water supply disrupted by the adjacent railway cutting. Off TRINITY ROAD, just s of the railway on the edge of the common and close to the Royal Patriotic Schools (*see* Public Buildings), the FITZHUGH ESTATE, 1953–5 by the *L.C.C.* (job architect *Oliver Cox*), an extreme example of the Roehampton principle of retaining the maximum amount of trees and views: five eleven-storey point blocks of Alton East type, i.e. of the humane, pre-brutalist period, no low buildings at all.

Along EAST HILL, which links Wandsworth to Battersea, a few
C 18 houses, including No. 123, early C 18 with carved wooden
doorcase with open pediment, No. 174 of *c.* 1736, and No.
178, mid C 18. At the fork, in front of the Huguenot burial
ground, BOOK HOUSE, the former Board of Works offices,
1888 by *J. Newton Dunn*, symmetrical Italianate. To the N, E
of Trinity Road, a large area of low-rise yellow brick housing
by *Diamond, Redfern & Partners* for Wandsworth, of 1975
onwards (478 dwellings, 70 p.p.a.) with a DAY CENTRE at the
corner, one-storeyed with three big hipped roofs, by the
Borough Architect's Department.

THAMES CROSSINGS

BY MALCOLM TUCKER

The river which was the reason for London's existence and a highway in its own right was also a barrier, and to some extent is still. There were no bridges between London Bridge and Kingston, above the limit of tides, until the construction of Fulham (Putney) Bridge in 1729, and the City of London and its suburb of Southwark enjoyed almost a monopoly of cross-river traffic other than by ferry. The congestion of the medieval London Bridge was less enjoyed, although its encumbering houses were demolished in 1758.

When bridges came to be built, the great breadth of the Thames produced some of the finest in the land (*see* Introduction to Industrial Archaeology). Westminster Bridge of 1750 was the first substantial 'modern' bridge; the City countered in 1769 with Blackfriars Bridge. The spread of development on the Surrey side, and increased financial and engineering capabilities, led in the early C19 to the construction of Southwark, Waterloo, Vauxhall, and Hammersmith Bridges and a new London Bridge – others had already appeared at Battersea and across the narrower reaches at Kew, Richmond, and Hampton Court. 68

Further bridges, road and rail, were added by the Victorians, but from *c.* 1860 rebuilding assumed a growing importance. Scour of foundations was a special problem, resulting in part from the lowering of the river level and greater tidal movement after the constricting piers of Old London Bridge were removed in 1831. Ever-increasing traffic flows were another problem. London Bridge and other bridges in the City were and are financed and maintained from medieval endowments, the Bridge House Estates, with no burden on the rates. Westminster Bridge was government-financed. Most others were the promotions of private companies charging tolls. After 1877 the Metropolitan Board of Works, its sewerage tasks completed, brought the private bridges within its jurisdiction (Hammersmith and below), freed them from toll, and set about the rebuilding of those of inadequate capacity or strength, a task that continued until the Second World War under the L.C.C. Other authorities did likewise. Some bridges have been replaced two or three times.

London Bridge is the head of navigation for large vessels: below it, the required navigation clearances and the great width of the Thames are major obstacles to fixed crossings. Tower Bridge illustrated the complications, and at Woolwich trunk road traffic still crosses by ferry. *Sir Marc Brunel*'s Thames Tunnel was an early and heroic solution. Other tunnels had to await the improved techniques and more liberal public finance of the end of the century, when the London County Council, successors to the M.B.W., provided two road tunnels and two pedestrian subways. These costly works and the Woolwich Ferry were provided and are maintained toll free in acknowledgement of the natural handicap of East London in its cross-river communications and to balance politically the public expenditure on bridges in the west.

Though bridges have been rebuilt and widened, the motor age has seen remarkably few additions to the c 19 river crossings – only Chiswick and Twickenham Bridges on the Great Chertsey Road of the 1930s, and a duplicate Blackwall Tunnel* – although new facilities are projected for the Docklands. Recent investment has been in other directions, such as the Victoria Line and the immense Thames flood barrier.

The bridges and other works which join the banks of the Thames are here described from E to W. The buildings which line the river, and the Thames Embankments, are dealt with under the appropriate boroughs.

GREENWICH

WOOLWICH FOOT TUNNEL. By *Sir Maurice Fitzmaurice*, for the L.C.C., 1909–12. Similar to the Greenwich Foot Tunnel (*see* below). An earlier subway here, begun in 1876 by *J. H. Greathead*, was not completed.

WOOLWICH FREE FERRY. Provided and maintained free of toll by the L.C.C. and its successor the G.L.C. The terminals designed by *Husband & Co.*, 1964–6, with steel-trussed ramps adjustable to a 30-ft tidal range, replace floating landing-stages first installed in 1889.

THE THAMES BARRIER (Charlton to Silvertown), Greenwich. Necessitated by the increasing height of surge tides in the Thames estuary, to protect London from catastrophic flooding. It is a most ambitious civil engineering work, mostly hidden below water. Designed by *Rendel, Palmer & Tritton* for the G.L.C. Department of Public Health Engineering, under the Act of 1972. Construction began in 1974 and was effectively completed in 1982. There are four navigation openings each of 200 ft,‡ two subsidiary openings of 103 ft, and four side spans also of 103 ft. While the side spans have radial gates which fall from above, the navigation openings have rising sector gates, a novel feature. Of a narrow D-shape in section, and pivoted at each end, they will rotate into a vertical position when a flood warning is given, but normally lie flat in the river bed. Beneath the gates and shaped to their curve, cellular pre-cast concrete sills span from pier to pier. Dimensions are huge. The main gates, of welded steel, are 66 ft tall in the

* The Dartford Tunnels, away downstream, are beyond the limits of this volume.
‡ The same width of opening as Tower Bridge.

vertical position, designed for a differential head of 28 ft, and each weighs 1,300 tons without the counterweights. The concrete piers, supporting the gates and their hydraulic operating machinery, are founded on the underlying chalk, requiring excavations some 90 ft below water level. The piers are capped with boat-shaped roofs of laminated timber clad with stainless steel. On the s bank a tall control building with sculpted roof and viewing galleries, by the *G.L.C. Architect's Department*. The river walls and banks for many miles downstream have also been extensively raised.

BLACKWALL TUNNEL, Greenwich. The NORTHBOUND TUNNEL, by *Sir Alexander Binnie* of the L.C.C., 1891–7, is 4,410 ft long excluding the approach cuttings. 3,115 ft were driven through mixed water-bearing strata using a 'Greathead' shield and compressed air; it was the first time that these techniques had been combined, representing a major advance in sub-aqueous soft-ground tunnelling. A temporary sealing layer of clay was laid on the river bed. The lining, of cast-iron segments filled with concrete, is faced with white glazed bricks. The pattern was followed for the L.C.C.'s other tunnels at Greenwich, Rotherhithe, and Woolwich. The internal diameter is 24 ft, with a carriageway only 16 ft wide, and sharp bends. Astride the s approach, the SOUTHERN TUNNEL HOUSE, of red sandstone, an ambitious building with steep pavilion roofs and angle turrets of characteristic Art Nouveau outline. Pretty and progressive. By *Thomas Blashill*, architect to the L.C.C.

The SOUTHBOUND TUNNEL (1960–7) is by the *G.L.C. Directorate of Highways and Transportation*, the 2,870-ft bored section by *Mott, Hay & Anderson*. Internal diameter 27 ft; driven under compressed air with the ground consolidated by grouting from two pilot tunnels. The ventilation stacks, of eyecatching streamlined shape, are by the *G.L.C. Architect's Department*.

GREENWICH FOOT TUNNEL. By *Sir Alexander Binnie*, 1897–1902. 11 ft internal diameter. Circular shafts for lifts and stairs, with domed glass roofs.

SOUTHWARK

ROTHERHITHE TUNNEL (Rotherhithe to Limehouse), Bermondsey. By *Sir Maurice Fitzmaurice*, 1904–8. 4,860 feet long, excluding the approach cuttings, with 3,740 ft of driven tunnel. Generally similar to the Blackwall Tunnel; 27 ft internal diameter.

THAMES TUNNEL (Rotherhithe to Wapping), Bermondsey. The first tunnel to be built underwater through soft ground,[*] it passes within a few feet of the bed of the Thames. The Cornish engineer *Robert Vazie*, who in 1805 began construc-

---

[*] Ralph Dodd had suggested a tunnel from Gravesend to Tilbury in 1798.

tion from Rotherhithe towards Limehouse, was replaced by *Richard Trevithick*, who completed 1,000 ft of timbered pilot tunnel by 1808, when an inundation and an adverse opinion from Jessop caused the proprietors to abandon the project. In 1825 (Act of 1824) a revised scheme on a new line was begun by *(Sir) Marc Brunel*, using a tunnelling shield he had patented in 1818, the first of its kind. It had twelve rectangular cast-iron frames placed side by side and 22 ft high, supporting three working platforms and the roof. Tiers of boards supporting the earth face in front were strutted from the frames by screw jacks. Each board in turn was removed, excavated behind, and screwed forward by $4\frac{1}{2}$ in., until a frame could be jacked forward by that amount and the process repeated. The brick-work of the permanent structure was constructed at the rear at the same slow rate. Without such a device, the project would have been impossible. There were five major inundations, counteracted by dumping clay on the river bed, and from 1828 to 1835 work was suspended for lack of finance. With government assistance and remarkable perseverance, the tunnel was opened in 1843. It is 1,200 ft long. Two parallel vaults, of horseshoe section, 14 ft wide and 16 ft high and joined at intervals by cross arches, form the interior of a brick box 38 ft wide and 22 ft high externally. At the ends are access shafts 50 ft across. Spiral ramps for carriages were never constructed, and it remained a foot tunnel until converted in 1865–9 for the East London Railway. It now carries underground trains, and its elegant brickwork can no longer be appreciated. For the engine house, *see* Bermondsey (Sk), Perambulation 3.

TOWER BRIDGE, Southwark. 1886–94 (Act of 1885) by *Sir John Wolfe Barry*, engineer, and *Sir Horace Jones*, architect. The lowest bridge on the Thames, its form was governed by navigational requirements: the Pool of London was still inten-sively used by ships and barge-trains, and a clear passage was stipulated of 200 ft width and 135 ft headroom,* to remain unobstructed for two hours at each high tide. This was relaxed after the bridge was built. The towers contain passenger lifts and support two high-level footbridges, for use when the bascules were raised. In the architect's words, they are 'steel skeletons clothed with stone'. The Gothic style was required by Parliament, in deference to the neighbouring Tower of London; the barren detailing was performed after Jones's death, however. The side spans are hung from curved lattice girders. The use of the suspension principle follows here from the provision of towers (needed for the high-level footbridge), rather than vice versa. The stiffening by trussing of the sus-pension members rather than the suspended deck is unusual. The bascules were electrified in 1976, but some of the magni-ficent hydraulic machinery by *Armstrong Mitchell & Co.* is preserved, including the tandem cross-compound steam pumping engines under the S approach viaduct. Yellow brick

---

* The as-built dimensions are slightly larger.

boiler chimney and accumulator tower, stern and sentinel-like, alongside.

TOWER SUBWAY (Vine Lane, off Tooley Street, to Tower Hill), Southwark. 1869 by *P. W. Barlow*; *J. H. Greathead*, contractor. This small tunnel, 6 ft 8 in. internal diameter and 1,340 ft long, introduced three features with a profound effect on later tunnelling under London, paving the way for the tube railway network: it was dug in the dry, deep in the London Clay; it was lined with cast-iron segments; and it used the cylindrical 'Greathead' shield, developed from patents by Barlow. Originally conveying a cable-hauled tramcar, part of a system of underground transport envisaged by Barlow, it was soon converted to a foot tunnel, and closed in 1896 after Tower Bridge was opened. Now carrying water mains, it is marked by a small round entrance building of 1926 in Tower Hill.

CITY AND SOUTH LONDON RAILWAY TUNNEL, Southwark. By *J. H. Greathead* (with *Sir John Fowler* and *Sir Benjamin Baker*, consultants), 1886–90. The first deep tube railway, using electric traction, although cable haulage was originally intended. Twin tunnels, of internal diameter only 10 ft 2 in. The section under the river, from Borough to King William Street, was abandoned when the line was realigned and extended northwards in 1900, and it remains disused in its original form. Its successor, subsequently enlarged, is the City Branch of the Northern Line.*

LONDON BRIDGE, Southwark. The wooden Roman bridge was near the site of the medieval one, about 200 ft E of the modern structure.‡ The stone bridge of *c.* 1176–1209, succeeding earlier timber ones, had nineteen arches and a drawbridge. Its picturesque houses were removed in 1758–62 by *Robert Taylor* and the younger *Dance*, who made a central navigation span and built stone alcoves on each pier; examples are preserved in Guy's Hospital (Sk) and at Victoria Park, Hackney (Hc). From 1581 to 1828 some of the arches housed waterwheels which pumped drinking water from the Thames. Rebuilt to the W in 1823–31 to *Rennie*'s design by his son, *John*, the bridge was widened in 1903–4 by cantilevering the footways. Five elliptical masonry arches of up to 152 ft span (quite ambitious) rested on slightly troublesome timber-piled foundations. Sir John Summerson commented, 'It lacks the engineering excitement of Southwark and the architectural grandeur of Waterloo.' On its demolition in 1968, the granite facework was sold and re-erected at Lake Havasu City, Arizona. The latest bridge is of 1967–72 by *Mott, Hay & Anderson*,

* Other tube railways under the Thames are the Waterloo and City (1893–8 by *J. H. Greathead*, *W. R. Galbraith* and *R. F. Church*), the Charing Cross branch of the Northern Line (S extension of 1923–6), the Bakerloo Line (1897–1906, delayed by financial problems), and the Victoria Line (S extension of 1967–71).

‡ The Roman bridge may have been rebuilt on a slightly different site in the early C2. Investigation of the Pudding Lane site in the City of London has revealed a possible pier for an early bridge lying in front of a C1 quay.

with *Lord Holford* as architectural adviser. Prestressed concrete cantilevers form three slender spans, founded on concrete piers dug deep into the clay.

CANNON STREET RAILWAY BRIDGE, Southwark. By *(Sir) John Hawkshaw*, 1863–6 (Act of 1861), widened in 1886–93. Five spans, up to 136 ft, of quite shallow plate girders on fluted Doric cast-iron piers. Ornamental brackets or modillions, giving a bold cornice effect, were regrettably removed in 1979, as were the Doric capitals, and the heads of the piers were encased in concrete during strengthening works in 1981.

SOUTHWARK BRIDGE. *Rennie*'s Southwark Bridge of 1814–19 (Act of 1811) had only three spans, of 210 ft, 240 ft, and 210 ft, to reduce the obstruction of a narrow part of the river. The piers were of granite on piled footings, the arches of cast iron, with solid ribs and triangulated open spandrels. The central span was the largest ever achieved in cast iron.* The ironfounders, *Walkers* of Rotherham, were almost bankrupted by the work. The present bridge, of 1912–21, is by *Mott & Hay*, engineers, and *Sir Ernest George*, architect, with five steel arches on granite piers.

BLACKFRIARS RAILWAY BRIDGES, Southwark. The W bridge, now disused, is of 1862–4 (Act of 1860) by *Joseph Cubitt* and *F. T. Turner*, with five lattice girder spans up to 185 ft clear. Piers treated architecturally, with four-shafted Romanesque columns and, at the abutments, magnificent cast-iron pylons bearing the insignia of the London, Chatham and Dover Railway. The E bridge (St Paul's Railway Bridge), of 1884–6 by *J. Wolfe Barry* and *H. M. Brunel*, has five wrought-iron arches.

BLACKFRIARS BRIDGE, Southwark. Architectural style came to the Thames with *Robert Mylne*'s bridge of 1760–9, its nine slightly elliptical arches in Portland stone embellished at the piers with twin Doric columns. It suffered from scour around the footings, however, and was replaced in 1860–9 by *Joseph Cubitt* and *H. Carr* with five wrought-iron arches faced with cast iron, on granite piers but founded on caissons. The decoration involved enormous attached columns in red granite with leafy Portland stone capitals which were kept when the bridge was widened on the W in 1907–10.

LAMBETH

WATERLOO BRIDGE, Lambeth. *Rennie*'s bridge of 1811–17 was a design of great strength and directness, with similarities to his earlier Lune Aqueduct and Kelso Bridge. There were nine elliptical arches of 120 ft span, entirely uniform, giving a level parapet. Coupled Greek Doric columns attached to the piers. The granite masonry was meticulously cut, with vous-

---

* *Telford* and *Douglass*'s proposed 600-ft span for London Bridge (1800) was unrealistically ambitious. Burdon's bridge at Sunderland of 1793–6 had a 236 ft span.

soirs 9 ft deep at the haunches. Inverted arches internally carried the thrust across the piers. The shallow spread-footings on piled foundations were less substantial, however, and severe settlement of two piers in 1923 led in 1936 to the bridge's controversial demolition. The new bridge of 1937–42 by *Rendel, Palmer & Tritton*, with *Sir Giles Gilbert Scott* as collaborating architect, is also of high architectural merit, resilient and elegant in the shallow arcs of its five spans, each of nearly 240 ft. They are reinforced concrete box girders, cantilevering, not arching. Spandrels faced with Portland stone, with exposed aggregate concrete around the rim of the arch. The cutwaters are concrete shells encasing the relatively flexible structural piers.

CHARING CROSS (HUNGERFORD) RAILWAY BRIDGE, Lambeth. By (*Sir*) *John Hawkshaw*, 1860–4 (Act of 1859), widened on the w in 1882–8. There is a total of nine spans, the six river spans of 154 ft. Pin-jointed trusses, a fine example of the technique of the period.* The structure makes use of the brick piers of *I. K. Brunel*'s Hungerford Footbridge of 1841–5, a suspension bridge which had a 660 ft centre span. Its chains were incorporated in the Clifton Suspension Bridge at Bristol, completed in 1864 as a memorial to Brunel.

WESTMINSTER BRIDGE, Lambeth. In his bridge of 1738–50, *Charles Labelye* introduced scientific expertise to British bridge design, for instance in confirming mathematically the equilibrium of the arches. It had fifteen semicircular spans, 76 ft clear at the centre and diminishing evenly towards the sides. The foundations were prefabricated in timber caissons, sunk into dredged excavations and pre-loaded. A notable settlement failure of one pier was overcome by making the affected spandrels hollow for lightness. Scour of the shallow foundations subsequently dogged this, as it did other Thames bridges. The present bridge of 1854–62, by *Thomas Page*, with *Sir Charles Barry* as architectural consultant, consists of seven arches of unambitious span, the shape 'drawn parallel to an ellipse' for greater navigation clearance. Cast-iron fascias and parapets gothicized with quatrefoils. Structural ribs with cast-iron haunches and wrought-iron crowns, a transitional design. The 84 ft width between parapets was exceptional for the period.

LAMBETH BRIDGE. One of four new river crossings recommended by a select committee in 1854, constructed originally in 1861–2 by *P. W. Barlow*, on his principle of the lattice-stiffened suspension bridge, with three equal spans of 268 ft. Cheaply built, it suffered severely from corrosion. The present bridge of 1929–32, slightly upstream, is by the L.C.C.'s engineer *Sir George Humphreys*, with *Sir Reginald Blomfield* as consultant architect. Five steel arches, the approaches flanked by obelisks.

VAUXHALL BRIDGE, Lambeth. Begun in 1811 by *Rennie*, as a

* Cross-girders renewed in 1979 in a major overhaul.

stone-arched bridge. After construction of the N abutment in 1813 the proprietors switched to a cheaper design in iron by *James Walker*, opened in 1816 as the 'Regent Bridge', and demolished in 1898. It had nine cast-iron arches with vertical-ribbed spandrels, of only 78 ft span. The present bridge of 1895–1906 by *Sir Alexander Binnie* is of five steel two-pinned arches, re-using the piled footings of the earlier abutments. Piers with bronze figures by *Alfred Drury* and *F. W. Pomeroy*.

WANDSWORTH

GROSVENOR (VICTORIA) RAILWAY BRIDGE (Battersea to Victoria), Battersea. Rebuilt in 1963–7 by *Freeman, Fox & Partners*; five open-spandrel steel arches ten tracks wide, the ribs of welded box section. The previous bridge, similarly arranged, was of wrought iron. The original two-track bridge of 1859–60 by *(Sir) John Fowler* was widened on the Chatham (E) side in 1865–6 by *Sir Charles Fox* and on the Brighton (W) side in 1901–5.

CHELSEA BRIDGE, Battersea. *Thomas Page*'s suspension bridge of 1851–8 had elaborate cast-iron-clad towers. Its concise and functional replacement, by *Rendel, Palmer & Tritton*, 1934–7, with *G. Topham Forrest* of the L.C.C. as architect, is technically interesting as a self-anchored suspension bridge, the pull at the ends of the cables being taken by a thrust through the stiffening girders, which are also an early use of high-tensile steel. The 352 ft main span, small for a modern suspension bridge, is determined by the nature of the site.

ALBERT BRIDGE, Battersea. 1871–3 (Act of 1864) by *R. M. Ordish*, on his rigid suspension principle, with diagonal stays of wrought iron radiating from the towers. The light suspension chains merely take the weight of the stays. In 1971–3, to allow heavier traffic loads, the main span, of 400 ft, was propped in the middle by the G.L.C.

BATTERSEA BRIDGE. The old wooden bridge familiar from Whistler's painting, by *Henry Holland*, 1771–2 (Act of 1766), originally with nineteen short spans, was replaced in 1886–90 by *Sir Joseph Bazalgette*, with five cast-iron ribbed arches. It has a cast-iron ornamental fascia to a flatter curve than the structural arches; a not very agreeable effect.

WEST LONDON EXTENSION (BATTERSEA) RAILWAY BRIDGE. 1861–3 by *William Baker* of the London and North Western Railway. Five 144-ft river spans of wrought-iron arches on a slight skew, the open spandrels diagonally braced with a resemblance to old Southwark Bridge.*

WANDSWORTH BRIDGE. 1936–40 by *Sir T. Pierson Frank*, with *E. P. Wheeler* and *F. R. Hiorns* of the L.C.C. as

* Countersunk riverheads on the external faces reinforce the illusion of an earlier cast-iron design.

architects. Steel plate girders cantilever in sweeping curves from two river piers, replacing five utilitarian lattice trusses of 1870–3. The central span is 300 ft.

PUTNEY RAILWAY BRIDGE. 1887–9 for the London and South Western Railway. Five lattice-girder river spans of 153 ft by *William Jacomb*.

PUTNEY (FULHAM) BRIDGE. A bridge was proposed here in 1671 and built in 1727–9 by *John Phillips*, the King's Carpenter, to the designs of *Sir Jacob Ackworth*, as a wooden viaduct of some twenty-six spans, its heavy beams resting on narrow timber piers.* The present bridge by *Sir J. Bazalgette*, 1882–6 (Act of 1881), has five segmental arches of granite, up to 144 ft in span. Three-branched cast-iron lampstandards at the centre of each arch. Widened on the E in 1933.

RICHMOND UPON THAMES

HAMMERSMITH BRIDGE, Barnes. *William Tierney Clark*'s suspension bridge of 1824–7 had a 422 ft main span, with masonry towers of great solidity embellished by the Tuscan order. It was replaced in 1883–7 by *Sir Joseph Bazalgette*, who re-used the piers and abutments. Iron-framed towers clad in cast iron, partly gilt, with little Frenchy pavilion tops, and elephantine ornament at the approaches. Eyebar chains of forged steel. The deck stiffening girders were replaced in a major overhaul in 1973–6.

BARNES RAILWAY BRIDGE. The upstream (disused) half by *Joseph Locke* and *J. E. Errington*, 1846–9, the oldest bridge remaining below Richmond, consisting of three cast-iron arches of 120 ft span with vertical-ribbed open spandrels, was duplicated in 1891–5 with wrought-iron bowstring trusses – an unfortunate choice visually.

CHISWICK BRIDGE, Mortlake. 1933, for the Great Chertsey Road. Three concrete arches faced with Portland stone. By *A. Dryland*, the art supplied by *Sir Herbert Baker*.

KEW RAILWAY BRIDGE. 1864–9 by *W. R. Galbraith*; five spans of lattice girders and ornate cast-iron piers.

KEW ROAD BRIDGE. 1903 by *Sir John Wolfe Barry* and *Cuthbert Bereton*. Three handsome elliptical arches in grey granite with rock-faced voussoirs and bold bracketed cornice, replacing a stone arched bridge of 1784–9 by *James Paine*, which itself followed a bridge with seven timber arches of 1758–9 by *John Barnard*.

RICHMOND HALF-TIDE WEIR AND FOOTBRIDGE. Three sluice gates 66 ft wide are lowered on the falling tide to maintain 5 ft depth of water for navigation upstream; a barge lock and boat rollers are provided. At other times, the sluice gates rotate into a horizontal position in the steel-arched

* There was also an aqueduct here for the Chelsea Waterworks Company, 1853–82.

superstructure, allowing an uninterrupted passage. 1892–4 by *James More* and *F. G. M. Stoney.*

TWICKENHAM BRIDGE, Richmond and Twickenham. By *Alfred Dryland*, engineer, and *Maxwell Ayrton*, architect, 1928–33. Three main arches of reinforced concrete, the central span 113 ft. The first large concrete bridge on the three-pin principle in this country, the articulated joints deliberately, if clumsily, expressed. Art-Deco detail.

RICHMOND RAILWAY BRIDGE. Three 100-ft span open-spandrel steel arches of 1908 by *J. W. Jacomb Hood*, replacing a cast-iron bridge of similar appearance by *Joseph Locke* and *J. E. Errington*, opened in 1848 (cf. Barnes, above).

68   RICHMOND BRIDGE. 1774–7 by *Kenton Couse* and *James Paine.* Widened in 1937. Beautiful design of five arches, in Portland stone.

TEDDINGTON WEIR. 1811, one of several built on Rennie's recommendation to improve the navigation, which had been notoriously bad. It is at the limit of tides. The Old Lock, rebuilt in 1857 and again in 1950, is supplemented by the 650-ft-long Barge Lock and the diminutive Skiff Lock. Suspension FOOTBRIDGE below the weir by *G. Pooley*, 1888, with steel towers, now protected with concrete.

See also Hampton Court Bridge, below.

KINGSTON

KINGSTON RAILWAY BRIDGE. Five steel arches of 1907 by *J. W. Jacomb Hood* replacing cast-iron ones of similar form of 1860–3 by *J. E. Errington.*

KINGSTON BRIDGE. 1825–8 by *Edward Lapidge*, widened on the upstream side in 1914. Five elliptical arches of brick, faced with Portland stone. There had been a bridge at Kingston ever since the early C13, if not earlier.

RICHMOND UPON THAMES

HAMPTON COURT BRIDGE.* By *W. P. Robinson* (engineer) and *Sir Edwin Lutyens*, 1930–3. Three elliptical spans, the arches themselves of fairfaced concrete, the rest brick and Portland stone, inevitably in Hampton Court Wrenaissance style. This is the fourth bridge on the site since 1750: the first had seven 'Chinese'-style wooden arches.

See also above for Richmond crossings.

---

* The N bridgehead is in the former Middlesex part of the borough of Richmond upon Thames, the S one is in Surrey. The W bridgeheads of the Kingston bridges are in Richmond borough.

GLOSSARY

Particular types of an architectural element are often defined under the name of the element itself; e.g. for 'dog-leg stair' see STAIR. Literal meanings, where specially relevant, are indicated by the abbreviation *lit*.

For further reference (especially for style terms) the following are a selection of books that can be consulted: *A Dictionary of Architecture* (N. Pevsner, J. Fleming, H. Honour, 1975); *The Illustrated Glossary of Architecture* (J. Harris and J. Lever, 1966); *Recording a Church: An Illustrated Glossary* (T. Cocke, D. Findlay, R. Halsey, E. Williamson, Council of British Archaeology, 1982); *Encyclopedia of Modern Architecture* (edited by Wolfgang Pehnt, 1963); *The Classical Language of Architecture* (J. Summerson, 1964); *The Dictionary of Ornament* (M. Stafford and D. Ware, 1974); *Illustrated Handbook of Vernacular Architecture* (R. W. Brunskill, 1976); *English Brickwork* (A. Clifton Taylor and R. W. Brunskill, 1977); *A Pattern of English Building* (A. Clifton Taylor, 1972).

ABACUS (*lit*. tablet): flat slab forming the top of a capital; *see* Orders (fig. 19).

ABUTMENT: the meeting of an arch or vault with its solid lateral support, or the support itself.

ACANTHUS: formalized leaf ornament with thick veins and frilled edge, e.g. on a Corinthian capital.

ACCUMULATOR TOWER: *see* Hydraulic Power.

ACHIEVEMENT OF ARMS: in heraldry, a complete display of armorial bearings.

ACROTERION (*lit*. peak): plinth for a statue or ornament placed at the apex or ends of a pediment; also, loosely and more usually, both the plinths and what stands on them.

ADDORSED: description of two figures placed symmetrically back to back.

AEDICULE (*lit*. little building): architectural surround, consisting usually of two columns or pilasters supporting a pediment, framing a niche or opening. *See also* Tabernacle.

AFFRONTED: description of two figures placed symmetrically face to face.

AGGER (*lit*. rampart): Latin term for the built-up foundations of Roman roads; also sometimes applied to the ramparts of hillforts or other earthworks.

AGGREGATE: small stones added to a binding material, e.g. in concrete. In modern architecture used alone to describe concrete with an aggregate of stone chippings, e.g. granite, quartz, etc.

AISLE (*lit*. wing): subsidiary space alongside the nave, choir, or transept of a church, or the main body of some other building, separated from it by columns, piers, or posts.

ALTAR: elevated slab consecrated for the celebration of the Eucharist; cf. Communion Table.

ALTARPIECE: *see* Retable.

AMBULATORY (*lit*. walkway): aisle around the sanctuary, sometimes surrounding an apse and therefore semicircular or polygonal in plan.

AMORINI: *see* Putto.

ANGLE ROLL: roll moulding in the angle between two planes, e.g. between the orders of an arch.

ANNULET (*lit.* ring): shaft-ring (*see* Shaft).

ANSE DE PANIER (*lit.* basket handle): basket arch (*see* Arch).

ANTAE: flat pilasters with capitals different from the order they accompany, placed at the ends of the short projecting walls of a portico or of a colonnade which is then called *In Antis.*

ANTEFIXAE: ornaments projecting at regular intervals above a classical cornice, originally to conceal the ends of roof tiles.

ANTEPENDIUM: *see* Frontal.

ANTHEMION (*lit.* honeysuckle): classical ornament like a honeysuckle flower (*see* fig. 1).

A   P   A   P   A

Fig. 1. Anthemion and Palmette Frieze

APRON: raised panel below a window or at the base of a wall monument or tablet, sometimes shaped and decorated.

A.P.S.D.: Architectural Publications Society Dictionary.

APSE: semicircular (i.e. apsidal) extension of an apartment: *see also* Exedra. A term first used of the magistrate's end of a Roman basilica, and thence especially of the vaulted semicircular or polygonal end of a chancel or a chapel.

ARABESQUE: type of painted or carved surface decoration consisting of flowing lines and intertwined foliage scrolls etc., generally based on geometrical patterns. Cf. Grotesque.

ARCADE: (1) series of arches supported by piers or columns. *Blind Arcade* or *Arcading*: the same applied to the surface of a wall. *Wall Arcade*: in medieval churches, a blind arcade forming a dado below windows. (2) a covered shopping street.

ARCH: for the various forms *see* fig. 2. The term *Basket Arch* refers to a basket handle and is sometimes applied to a three-centred or depressed arch as well as to the type with a flat middle. A *Transverse Arch* runs across the main axis of an interior space. The term is used especially for the arches between the compartments of tunnel- or groin-vaulting. *Diaphragm Arch:* transverse arch with solid spandrels spanning an otherwise wooden-roofed interior. *Chancel Arch:* w opening from the chancel into the nave. *Nodding Arch:* an ogee arch curving forward from the plane of the wall. *Relieving* (or *Discharging*) *Arch:* incorporated in a wall, to carry some of its weight, some way above an opening. *Skew Arch:* spanning responds not diametrically opposed to one another. *Strainer Arch:* inserted across an opening to resist any inward pressure of the side members. *See also* Jack Arch; Triumphal Arch.

ARCHITRAVE: (1) formalized lintel, the lowest member of the classical entablature (*see* Orders, fig. 19); (2) moulded frame of a door or window (often borrowing the profile of an architrave in the strict sense). Also *Lugged Architrave*, where the top is prolonged into lugs (*lit.* ears) at the sides; *Shouldered*, where the frame rises vertically at the top angles and returns horizontally at the sides forming shoulders (*see* fig. 3).

ARCHIVOLT: architrave moulding when it follows the line of an arch.

ARCUATED: dependent structurally on the use of arches or the arch principle; cf. Trabeated.

ARRIS (*lit.* stop): sharp edge where two surfaces meet at an angle.

ASHLAR: masonry of large blocks wrought to even faces and square edges.

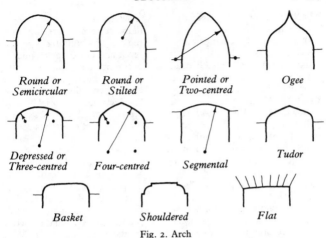

Round or Semicircular

Round or Stilted

Pointed or Two-centred

Ogee

Depressed or Three-centred

Four-centred

Segmental

Tudor

Basket

Shouldered

Flat

Fig. 2. Arch

Lugged

Shouldered

Fig. 3. Architrave

ASTRAGAL (*lit.* knuckle): moulding of semicircular section often with bead-and-reel enrichment (q.v.).

ASTYLAR: term used for an elevation that has no columns or similar vertical features.

ATLANTES (*lit.* Atlas figures, from the god Atlas carrying the globe): male counterparts of caryatids (q.v.), often in a more demonstrative attitude of support.

ATRIUM: inner court of a Roman house; also open court in front of a church.

ATTACHED COLUMN: *see* Engaged Column.

ATTIC: (I) small top storey, especially within a sloping roof; (2) in classical architecture, a storey above the main entablature of the façade, as in a triumphal arch (q.v.).

AUMBRY: recess or cupboard to hold sacred vessels for the Mass.

BAILEY: area around the motte or keep (qq.v.) of a castle, defended by a wall and ditch.

BALANCE BEAM: *see* Canals.

BALDACCHINO: free-standing canopy, properly of or representing fabric, over an altar supported by columns. Cf. Ciborium.

BALLFLOWER: globular flower of three petals enclosing a small ball. Typical of the Decorated style.

BALUSTER (*lit.* pomegranate): a pillar or pedestal of bellied form. *Balusters:* vertical supports of this or any other form, for a handrail or coping, the whole being called a *Balustrade*. *Blind Balustrade:* the same applied to the surface of a wall.

BARBICAN: outwork defending the entrance to a castle.

BARGEBOARDS: corruption of vergeboards. Boards, often carved or fretted, fixed beneath the eaves of a gable to cover and protect the rafters.

BARROW: burial mound; *see* Bell, Bowl, Disc, Long, and Pond Barrow.

BARTIZAN (*lit.* battlement): corbelled turret, square or round, frequently at a corner, hence *Corner Bartizan*.

BASCULE: hinged part of a lighting bridge.

BASE: moulded foot of a column or other order. For its use in classical architecture *see* Orders (fig. 19).

BASEMENT: lowest, subordinate storey of a building, and hence the lowest part of an elevation, below the main floor.

BASILICA (*lit.* royal building): a Roman public hall; hence an aisled building with a clerestory, most often a church.

BASTION: one of a series of semicircular or polygonal projections from the main wall of a fortress or city, placed at intervals in such a manner as to enable the garrison to cover the intervening stretches of the wall.

BATTER: intentional inward inclination of a wall face.

BATTLEMENT: fortified parapet, indented or crenellated so that archers could shoot through the indentations (crenels or embrasures) between the projecting solid portions (merlons). Also used decoratively.

BAY LEAF: classical ornament of formalized overlapping bay leaves; *see* fig. 4.

Fig. 4. Bay Leaf

BAYS: divisions of an elevation or interior space as defined by any regular vertical features such as arches, columns, windows, etc.

BAY-WINDOW: window of one or more storeys projecting from the face of a building at ground level, and either rectangular or polygonal on plan. A *Canted Bay-window* has a straight front and angled sides. A *Bow Window* is curved. An *Oriel Window* rests on corbels or brackets and does not start from the ground.

BEAD-AND-REEL: *see* Enrichments.

BEAKER FOLK: late Neolithic settlers from western Europe named after a distinctive type of pottery vessel found in their funerary monuments (often round barrows) and their settlements. The Beaker period saw a wider dissemination of metal implements in Britain.

BEAKHEAD: Norman ornamental motif consisting of a row of bird or beast heads with beaks, usually biting into a roll moulding.

BELFRY: (1) bell-turret set on a roof or gable (*see also* Bellcote); (2) chamber or stage in a tower where bells are hung; (3) belltower in a general sense.

BELGAE: Iron Age tribes living in north-eastern Gaul, from which settlers came into Britain between 100 and 55 B.C. and later. These immigrants may not have been numerous, but their impact on material culture in southern Britain was marked.

BELL BARROW: early Bronze Age round barrow in which the mound is separated from its encircling ditch by a flat platform or berm (q.v.).

BELL CAPITAL: *see* fig. 8.

BELLCOTE: belfry as (1) above, usually in the form of a small gabled or roofed housing for the bell(s).

BERM: level area separating ditch from bank on a hill-fort or barrow.

BILLET (*lit.* log or block) FRIEZE: Norman ornament

Fig. 5. Billet Frieze

English

Flemish

Fig. 6. Bond

consisting of small half-cylindrical or rectangular blocks placed at regular intervals (*see* fig. 5).

BIVALLATE: (of a hill-fort) defended by two concentric banks and ditches.

BLIND: *see* Arcade, Balustrade, Portico.

BLOCK CAPITAL: *see* fig. 8.

BLOCKED: term applied to columns etc. that are interrupted by regular projecting blocks, e.g. the sides of a Gibbs surround (*see* fig. 13).

BLOCKING COURSE: plain course of stones, or equivalent, on top of a cornice and crowning the wall.

BOLECTION MOULDING: curved moulding covering the joint between two different planes and overlapping the higher as well as the lower one, used especially in the late C 17 and early C 18.

BOND: in brickwork, the pattern of long sides (stretchers) and short ends (headers) produced on the face of a wall by laying bricks in a particular way. For the two most common bonds *see* fig. 6.

BOSS: knob or projection usually placed at the intersection of ribs in a vault.

BOW WINDOW: *see* Bay-window.

BOWL BARROW: round barrow surrounded by a quarry ditch. Introduced in late Neolithic times, the form continued until the Saxon period.

BOWSTRING BRIDGE: with arch ribs rising above the roadway, which is suspended from them.

BOX FRAME: (1) timber-framed construction in which vertical and horizontal wall members support the roof. (2) in modern architecture, a box-like form of concrete construction where the loads are taken on cross

walls, suitable only for buildings consisting of repetitive small cells. Also called *Cross-wall Construction*.

BOX PEW: *see* Pew.

BRACE: subsidiary timber set diagonally to strengthen a timber frame. It can be curved or straight. *See also* Roofs (3) and figs. 24–8.

BRACKET: small supporting piece of stone, etc., to carry a projecting horizontal member. *See also* Console.

BRATTISHING: ornamental cresting on a wall, usually formed of leaves or Tudor flowers or miniature battlements.

BRESSUMER (*lit.* breast-beam): big horizontal beam, usually set forward from the lower part of a building, supporting the wall above.

BROACH: *see* Spire.

BRONZE AGE: in Britain, the period from *c.* 2000 to 600 B.C.

BUCRANIUM: ox skull used decoratively in classical friezes.

BULLSEYE WINDOW: small oval window, set horizontally, cf. Oculus. Also called *Œil de Bœuf*.

BUTTRESS: vertical member projecting from a wall to stabilize it or to resist the lateral thrust of an arch, roof, or vault. For different types used at the corners of a building, especially a tower, *see* fig. 7. A *Flying Buttress* transmits the thrust to a heavy abutment by means of an arch or half-arch.

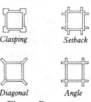

Clasping   *Setback*

Diagonal   *Angle*

Fig. 7. Buttresses

CABLE MOULDING: originally a Norman moulding, imitating the twisted strands of a rope. Also called *Rope Moulding*.

CAIRN: a mound of stones usually covering a burial.

CALEFACTORY: room in a monastery where a fire burned for the comfort of the monks. Also called *Warming Room*.

CAMBER: slight rise or upward curve in place of a horizontal line or plane.

CAMES: *see* Quarries.

CAMPANILE: free-standing bell-tower.

CANALS: *Pound Lock*: chamber with gates at each end allowing boats to float from one level to another. *Flash Lock*: removable weir or similar device through which boats pass on a flush of water. Predecessor of the pound lock. *Tidal Doors*: single pair of lock gates allowing vessels to pass when the tide makes a level. *Balance Beam*: beam projecting horizontally for opening and closing lock gates. *Roving Bridge*: carrying a canal towing path from one bank to the other.

CANOPY: projection or hood usually over an altar, pulpit, niche, statue, etc.

CANTED: tilted, generally on a vertical axis to produce an obtuse angle on plan, e.g. of a canted bay-window.

CANTILEVER: horizontal projection (e.g. step, canopy) supported by a downward force behind the fulcrum. It is without external bracing and thus appears to be self-supporting.

CAPITAL: head or crowning feature of a column or pilaster; for classical types *see* Orders (fig. 19); for medieval types *see* fig. 8.

CARREL: (1) niche in a cloister where a monk could sit to work or read; (2) similar feature in open-plan offices and libraries.

CARTOUCHE: tablet with ornate frame, usually of elliptical shape and bearing a coat of arms or inscription.

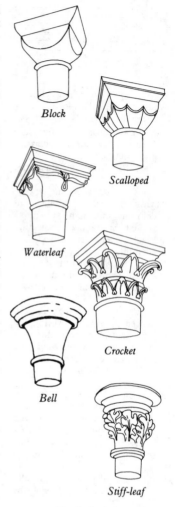

Block

Scalloped

Waterleaf

Crocket

Bell

Stiff-leaf

Fig. 8. Capitals

CARYATIDS (*lit.* daughters of the village of Caryae): female figures supporting an entablature, counterparts of Atlantes (q.v.).

CASEMATE: in military architecture, a vaulted chamber, with embrasures for defence, built into the thickness of the wall of a castle or fortress or projecting from it.

CASEMENT: (1) window hinged at the side; (2) in Gothic architecture, a concave moulding framing a window.

CAST IRON: hard and brittle, cast in a mould to the required shape. *Wrought Iron* is ductile, strong in tension, forged into decorative patterns or forged and rolled into e.g. bars, joists, boiler plates. *Mild Steel* is a modern equivalent, similar but stronger.

CASTELLATED: battlemented.

CAVETTO: concave moulding of quarter-round section.

CELURE OR CEILURE: enriched area of a roof above the rood or the altar.

CENOTAPH (*lit.* empty tomb): funerary monument which is not a burying place.

CENTERING: wooden support for the building of an arch or vault, removed after completion.

CHAMBERED TOMB: Neolithic burial mound with a stone-built chamber and entrance passage covered by an earthen barrow or stone cairn.

CHAMFER (*lit.* corner-break): surface formed by cutting off a square edge, usually at an angle of forty-five degrees. When the plane is concave it is termed a *Hollow Chamfer*. *Double-Chamfer*: applied to each of two recessed arches.

CHANCEL (*lit.* enclosure): E arm or that part of the E end of a church set apart for the use of the officiating clergy, except in cathedrals or monastic churches; cf. Choir.

CHANTRY CHAPEL: chapel, often attached to or inside a church, endowed for the celebration of masses principally for the soul of the founder.

CHEVET (*lit.* head): French term for the E end of a church (chancel and ambulatory with radiating chapels).

CHEVRON: V-shaped motif used in series to decorate a moulding: also (especially when on a single plane) called *Zigzag*.

CHOIR: the part of a church where services are sung. In monastic churches this can occupy the crossing and/or the easternmost bays of the nave.

Also used to describe, more loosely, the E arm of a cruciform church.

CIBORIUM: (1) a fixed canopy of stone or wood over an altar, usually vaulted and supported on four columns, cf. Baldacchino. (2) canopied shrine for the reserved sacrament.

CINQUEFOIL: *see* Foil.

CIST: stone-lined or slab-built grave. If below ground, covered with a protective barrow. It first appears in late Neolithic times and was also used in the Early Christian period in West Britain.

CLADDING: external covering or skin applied to a structure, especially framed buildings (q.v.), for aesthetic or protective purposes.

CLAPPER BRIDGE: bridge made of large slabs of stone, some making rough piers, with longer ones laid on top to make the roadway.

CLASP: *see* Industrialized Building.

CLASSIC: term for the moment of highest achievement of a style.

CLASSICAL: term for Greek and Roman architecture and any subsequent styles derived from it.

CLERESTORY: uppermost storey of the nave walls of a church, pierced by windows. Also applied to high-level windows in domestic architecture.

CLUSTER BLOCK: multi-storey building in which individual blocks of flats cluster round a central service core.

COADE STONE: a ceramic artificial stone made in Lambeth from 1769 to *c.* 1840 by Eleanor Coade († 1821) and her associates.

COB: walling material of clay mixed with straw.

COFFER DAM: a temporary structure to keep out water from an excavation in a river, dock, etc.

COFFERING: arrangement of sunken panels (coffers), square or polygonal, decorating a ceiling, vault, or arch.

COGGING: a decorative course of bricks laid diagonally as an alternative to dentilation (q.v.). Also called *Dogtooth Brickwork*.

COLLAR: *see* Roofs (3) and figs. 25–8.

COLLEGIATE CHURCH: church endowed for the support of a college of priests.

COLONNADE: range of columns supporting an entablature; cf. Arcade.

COLONNETTE: in medieval architecture, a small column or shaft.

COLOSSAL ORDER: *see* Order.

COLUMN: in classical architecture, an upright structural member of round section with a shaft, a capital, and usually a base. *See* Orders (fig. 19).

COLUMN FIGURE: in medieval architecture, carved figure attached to a column or shaft flanking a doorway.

COMMUNION TABLE: unconsecrated table used in Protestant churches in place of an altar (q.v.) for the celebration of Holy Communion.

COMPOSITE: *see* Orders.

COMPOUND PIER: grouped shafts (q.v.), or a solid core surrounded by attached or detached shafts.

CONSOLE: ornamented bracket of compound curved outline (*see* fig. 9).

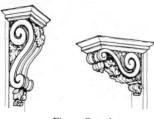

Fig. 9. Consoles

COPING (*lit.* capping): protective capping course of masonry or brickwork on top of a wall.

CORBEL: projecting block of stone or timber supporting something above. *Corbel Course:* continuous course of projecting stones or bricks fulfilling the same function. *Corbel Table:* series of corbels to carry a parapet or a wall-plate; for the latter *see* Roofs (3) and figs. 24–7. *Corbelling:* brick or masonry courses built out beyond one another like a series of corbels to support a chimneystack, window, etc.

CORINTHIAN: *see* Orders (fig. 19).

CORNICE: (1) moulded ledge, projecting along the top of a building or feature, especially as the highest member of the classical entablature (*see* Orders, fig. 19); (2) decorative moulding in the angle between wall and ceiling.

CORPS-DE-LOGIS: French term for the main building(s) as distinct from the wings or pavilions.

COTTAGE ORNÉ: an artfully rustic building usually of asymmetrical plan. A product of the late C 18/early C 19 Picturesque.

COUNTERSCARP BANK: small bank on the downhill or outer side of a hill-fort ditch.

COUR D'HONNEUR: entrance court before a house in the French manner, usually with wings enclosing the sides and a screen wall or low range of buildings across the front.

COURSE: continuous layer of stones etc. in a wall.

COVE: a concave moulding on a large scale, e.g. to mask the eaves of a roof or in a *Coved Ceiling*, which has a pronounced cove joining the walls to a flat central panel smaller than the area of the whole ceiling.

CRADLE ROOF: *see* Wagon Roof.

CREDENCE: in a church or chapel, a shelf within or beside a piscina, or for the sacramental elements and vessels.

CRENELLATION: *see* Battlement.

CREST, CRESTING: ornamental finish along the top of a screen, etc.

CRINKLE-CRANKLE WALL: wall undulating in a series of serpentine curves.

CROCKETS (*lit.* hooks), CROCK-ETING: in Gothic architecture, leafy knobs on the edges of any sloping feature. *Crocket Capital: see* Capital (fig. 8).

CROMLECH: word of Celtic origin still occasionally used of single free-standing stones ascribed to the Neolithic or Bronze Age.

CROSSING: in a church, central space at the junction of the nave, chancel, and transepts. *Crossing Tower:* tower above a crossing.

CROSS-WINDOWS: windows with one mullion and one transom (qq.v.).

CROWSTEPS: squared stones set like steps e.g. on a gable or gateway; *see* Gable (fig. 12).

CRUCKS (*lit.* crooked): pairs of inclined timbers, usually curved, which are set at bay-length intervals in a building and support the timbers of the roof (q.v.). The individual cruck is known as a blade. *Base:* blades which rise from ground level to a tie- or collar-beam upon which the roof truss is carried; in timber buildings they support the walls. *Full:* blades rising from ground level to the apex of a building; they serve as the main members of a roof truss and in timber buildings they support the walls. *Jointed:* blades formed from more than one timber; the lower member normally rises from ground level and acts as a wall-post; it is usually elbowed at wall-plate level and jointed just above. *Middle:* blades rising from half-way up the walls to a tie- or collar-beam upon which the roof truss is supported. *Raised:* blades rising from half-way up the walls to the apex. *Upper:* blades supported on a tie-beam and rising to the apex.

CRYPT: underground or half-underground room usually below the E end of a church. *Ring Crypt:* early medieval semicircular or polygonal corridor crypt surrounding the apse of a church, often associated with chambers for relics.

CUPOLA (*lit.* dome): especially a small dome on a circular or polygonal base crowning a larger dome, roof, or turret.

CURTAIN WALL: (1) connecting wall between the towers of a castle; (2) in modern building, a non-load-bearing external wall composed of repeating modular elements applied to a steel-framed structure.

CURVILINEAR: *see* Tracery.

CUSP: projecting point defining the foils in Gothic tracery, also used as a decorative edging to the soffits of the Gothic arches of tomb recesses, sedilia, etc. When used decoratively within tracery patterns called *Sub-cusps.*

CYCLOPEAN MASONRY: built with large irregular polygonal stones, but smooth and finely jointed.

CYMA RECTA and CYMA RE-VERSA: *see* Ogee.

DADO: the finishing of the lower part of an interior wall (sometimes used to support an applied order, i.e. a formalized continuous pedestal). *Dado Rail:* the moulding along the top of the dado.

DAGGER: *see* Tracery.

DAIS: raised platform at one end of a room.

DEC (DECORATED): historical division of English Gothic architecture covering the period from *c.* 1290 to *c.* 1350. The name is derived from the type of window tracery used during the period (*see also* Tracery).

DEMI-COLUMNS: engaged columns (q.v.) only half of whose circumference projects from the wall. Also called *Half-Columns.*

DENTIL: small square block used in series in classical cornices, rarely in Doric. In brickwork *dentilation* is produced by the projection of alternating headers or blocks along cornices or string courses.

DIAPER (*lit.* figured cloth): repetitive surface decoration of lozenges or squares either flat or in relief. Achieved in brickwork with bricks of two colours.

DIOCLETIAN WINDOW: semicircular window with two mullions, so-called because of its use in the Baths of Diocletian in Rome. Also called a *Thermae Window*.

DISC BARROW: Bronze Age round barrow with an inconspicuous central mound surrounded by a bank and ditch.

DISTYLE: having two columns.

DOGTOOTH: typical E.E. decoration of a moulding, consisting of a series of small pyramids formed by four leaves meeting at a point (*see* fig. 10). *See also* Cogging.

Fig. 10. Dogtooth

DOME: vault of even curvature erected on a circular base. The section can be segmental (e.g. saucer dome), semicircular, pointed, or bulbous (onion dome).

DONJON: *see* Keep.

DORIC: *see* Orders (fig. 19).

DORMER WINDOW: window projecting from the slope of a roof, having a roof of its own and lighting a room within it. *Dormer Head:* gable above this window, often formed as a pediment.

DORTER: dormitory; sleeping quarters of a monastery.

DOUBLE CHAMFER: *see* Chamfer.

DOUBLE PILE: *see* Pile.

DRAGON BEAM: *see* Jetty.

DRESSINGS: the stone or brickwork used about an angle, opening, or other feature worked to a finished face.

DRIPSTONE: moulded stone projecting from a wall to protect the lower parts from water; *see also* Hoodmould.

DRUM: (1) circular or polygonal stage supporting a dome or cupola; (2) one of the stones forming the shaft of a column.

DRYSTONE: stone construction without mortar.

DUTCH GABLE: *see* Gable (fig. 12).

EASTER SEPULCHRE: recess, usually in the N wall of a chancel, with a tomb-chest thought to have been for an effigy of Christ for Easter celebrations.

EAVES: overhanging edge of a roof; hence *Eaves Cornice* in this position.

ECHINUS (*lit.* sea-urchin): ovolo moulding (q.v.) below the abacus of a Greek Doric capital; *see* Orders (fig. 19).

EDGE RAIL: *see* Railways.

E.E. (EARLY ENGLISH): historical division of English Gothic architecture covering the period *c.* 1190–1250.

EGG-AND-DART: *see* Enrichments.

ELEVATION: (1) any side of a building: (2) in a drawing, the same or any part of it, accurately represented in two dimensions.

EMBATTLED: furnished with battlements.

EMBRASURE (*lit.* splay): small splayed opening in the wall or battlement of a fortified building.

ENCAUSTIC TILES: glazed and decorated earthenware tiles used mainly for paving.

EN DELIT (*lit.* in error): term used in Gothic architecture to describe stone shafts whose grain runs vertically instead of horizontally, against normal building practice.

ENGAGED COLUMN: one that is partly merged into a wall or pier. Also called *Attached Column*.

ENGINEERING BRICKS: dense bricks of uniform size, high crushing strength, and low porosity. Originally used mostly for railway viaducts etc.

ENRICHMENTS: in classical architecture, the carved decoration of certain mouldings, e.g. the ovolo (q.v.) with *Egg-and-Dart*, the cyma reversa (q.v.) with *Waterleaf*, the astragal (q.v.) with *Bead-and-Reel*; see fig. 11.

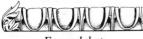

Egg-and-dart

Waterleaf

Bead-and-reel

Fig. 11. Enrichments

ENTABLATURE: in classical architecture, collective name for the three horizontal members (architrave, frieze, and cornice) carried by a wall or a column; *see* Orders (fig. 19).

ENTASIS: very slight convex deviation from a straight line; used on classical columns and sometimes on spires to prevent an optical illusion of concavity.

ENTRESOL: mezzanine storey within or above the ground storey.

EPITAPH (*lit.* on a tomb): inscription in that position.

ESCUTCHEON: shield for armorial bearings.

EXEDRA: apsidal end of an apartment; *see* Apse.

EXTRADOS: outer curved face of an arch or vault.

EXTRUDED CORNER: right-angled (or circular) projection from the inner angle of a building with advancing wings, usually in C16 or C17 plans.

EYECATCHER: decorative building (often a sham ruin) usually on an eminence to terminate a vista in a park or garden layout.

FASCIA: plain horizontal band, e.g. in an architrave (q.v.) or on a shopfront.

FENESTRATION: the arrangement of windows in a building.

FERETORY: place behind the high altar where the chief shrine of a church is kept.

FESTOON: ornament, usually in relief, in the form of a garland of flowers and/or fruit, suspended from both ends; *see also* Swag.

FIBREGLASS (or glass-reinforced polyester (GRP)): synthetic resin reinforced with glass fibre, formed in moulds, often simulating the appearance of traditional materials. GRC glass-reinforced concrete) is also formed in moulds and used for components (cladding etc.) in industrialized building.

FIELDED: *see* Raised and Fielded.

FILLET: in medieval architecture, a narrow flat band running down a shaft or along a roll moulding. In classical architecture it separates larger curved mouldings in cornices or bases.

FINIAL: decorative topmost feature, e.g. above a gable, spire, or cupola.

FLAMBOYANT: properly the latest phase of French Gothic architecture where the window tracery takes on undulating lines, based on the use of flowing curves.

FLASH LOCK: *see* Canals.

FLÈCHE (*lit.* arrow): slender spire on the centre of a roof. Also called *Spirelet*.

FLEUR-DE-LYS: in heraldry, a formalized lily, as in the royal arms of France.

FLEURON: decorative carved flower or leaf, often rectilinear.

FLOWING: *see* Tracery (Curvilinear).

FLUSHWORK: flint used decoratively in conjunction with dressed stone so as to form patterns: tracery, initials, etc.

FLUTING: series of concave grooves, their common edges sharp (arris) or blunt (fillet).

FOIL (*lit.* leaf): lobe formed by the cusping of a circular or other shape in tracery. *Trefoil* (three), *quatrefoil* (four), *cinquefoil* (five), and *multifoil* express the number of lobes in a shape. *See also* Tracery.

FOLIATE: decorated, especially carved, with leaves.

FORMWORK: commonly called shuttering; the temporary frame of braced timber or metal into which wet concrete is poured. The texture of the framework material depends on the imprint required.

FRAMED BUILDING: where the structure is carried by the framework – e.g. of steel, reinforced concrete, timber – instead of by load-bearing walls.

FRATER: *see* Refectory.

FREESTONE: stone that is cut, or can be cut, in all directions, usually fine-grained sandstone or limestone.

FRESCO: *al fresco:* painting executed on wet plaster. *Fresco secco:* painting executed on dry plaster, more common in Britain.

FRIEZE: (1) the middle member of the classical entablature, sometimes ornamented; *see* Orders (fig. 19). *Pulvinated Frieze* (*lit.* cushioned): frieze of bold convex profile. (2) horizontal band of ornament.

FRONTAL: covering for the front of an altar. When solid called *Antependium*.

FRONTISPIECE: in C16 and C17 buildings the central feature of doorway and windows above it linked in one composition.

GABLE: (1) area of wall, often triangular, at the end of a double-pitch roof; *Dutch Gable*, characteristic of *c.* 1580–1680: *Shaped Gable*, characteristic of *c.* 1620–80 (*see* fig. 12). *Gablet:* small gable. *See also* Roofs.

GADROONING: ribbed ornament, e.g. on the lid or base of an urn, flowing into a lobed edge.

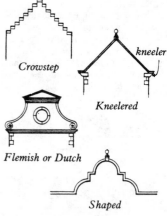

Fig. 12. Gables

GALILEE: chapel or vestibule usually at the W end of a church enclosing the main portal(s).

GALLERY: balcony or passage, but with certain special meanings, e.g. (1) upper storey above the aisle of a church, looking through arches to the nave; also called tribune and often erroneously triforium (q.v.); (2) balcony or mezzanine, often with seats, overlooking the main interior space of a building; (3) external walkway, often projecting from a wall.

GALLERY GRAVE: chambered tomb (q.v.) in which there is little or no differentiation between the entrance passage and the actual burial chamber(s).

GALLETING: decorative use of small stones in a mortar course.

GARDEROBE (*lit.* wardrobe): medieval privy.

GARGOYLE: water spout projecting from the parapet of a wall or tower, often carved into human or animal shape.

GAUGED BRICKWORK: soft brick sawn roughly, then rubbed to a smooth, precise (gauged) surface with a stone or another brick. Mostly used for door or window openings. Also called *Rubbed Brickwork*.

GAZEBO (jocular Latin, 'I shall gaze'): lookout tower or raised summer house usually in a park or garden.

GEOMETRIC: historical division of English Gothic architecture covering the period *c.* 1250–90. *See also* Tracery. For another meaning, *see* Stair.

GIANT ORDER: *see* Order.

GIBBS SURROUND: C18 treatment of a door or window surround, seen particularly in the work of James Gibbs (1682–1754) (*see* fig. 13).

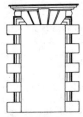

Fig. 13. Gibbs Surround

GIRDER: a large beam. *Box Girder*: of hollow-box section. *Bowed Girder*: with its top rising in a curve. *Plate Girder*: of I-section, made from iron or steel plates. *Lattice Girder*: with braced framework.

GLAZING BARS: wooden or sometimes metal bars separating and supporting window panes.

GOTHIC: the period of medieval architecture characterized by the use of the pointed arch. For its subdivisions *see* E.E., Geometric, Dec, Perp, Flamboyant.

GRANGE (monastic): farm owned and run by members of a religious order.

GRC and GRP: *see* Fibreglass.

GRISAILLE: monochrome painting on walls or glass.

GROIN: sharp edge at the meeting of two cells of a cross-vault; *see* Vault (fig. 35).

GROTESQUE (*lit.* grotto-esque): classical wall decoration in paint or stucco adopted from Roman examples, particularly by Raphael. Its foliage scrolls, unlike arabesque, incorporate ornaments and human figures.

GROTTO: artificial cavern usually decorated with rock- or shell-work, especially popular in the late C17 and C18.

GUILLOCHE: running classical ornament of interlaced bands forming a plait (*see* fig. 14).

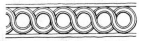

Fig. 14. Guilloche

GUNLOOP: opening for a firearm.

GUTTAE: *see* Orders (fig. 19).

HAGIOSCOPE: *see* Squint.

HALF-TIMBERING: archaic term for timber-framing (q.v.). Sometimes used for non-structural decorative timberwork, e.g. in gables etc. of the late C19.

HALL CHURCH: medieval or Gothic Revival church whose nave and aisles are of equal height or approximately so.

HAMMERBEAM: *see* Roofs (fig. 28).

HEADER: *see* Bond.

HENGE: ritual earthwork with a surrounding bank and ditch, the bank being on the outer side.

HERM (*lit.* the god Hermes): male head or bust on a pedestal.

HERRINGBONE WORK: masonry or brickwork in zigzag courses.

HEXASTYLE: *see* Portico.

HILL-FORT: later Bronze Age and Iron Age earthwork enclosed by a ditch and bank system; in the later part of the period the defences multiplied in size and complexity. Varying from about an acre to over fifty acres in area, they are usually built with careful regard to natural elevations or promontories and range in character from powerful strongholds to protected farmsteads.

HIPPED ROOF: *see* Roofs (1) (fig. 23).

HOODMOULD: projecting moulding shown above an arch or lintel to throw off water. When the moulding is horizontal it is often called a *Label. See also* Label Stop.

HUSK GARLAND: festoon of nut-shells diminishing towards the ends.

HYDRAULIC POWER: use of water under high pressure to work machinery. *Accumulator Tower:* to house a hydraulic accumulator which accommodates fluctuations in the flow through hydraulic mains.

HYPOCAUST (*lit.* under-burning): Roman underfloor heating system. The floor is supported on pillars and the space thus formed is connected to a flue.

ICONOGRAPHY: interpretation of the subject matter of works of the visual arts.

IMPOST (*lit.* imposition): horizontal moulding at the springing of an arch.

IMPOST BLOCK: block with splayed sides between abacus and capital.

IN ANTIS: *see* Antae.

INDENT: shape chiselled out of a stone to match and receive a brass.

INDUSTRIALIZED BUILDING (system building): the use of a system of manufactured units assembled on site. One of the most popular is the CLASP (Consortium Local Authorities Special Programme) system of light steel framing suitable for schools etc.

INGLENOOK (*lit.* fire-corner): recess for a hearth with provision for seating.

INTARSIA: *see* Marquetry.

INTERCOLUMNIATION: interval between columns.

INTERLACE: decoration in relief simulating woven or entwined stems or bands.

INTRADOS: *see* Soffit.

IONIC: *see* Orders (fig. 19).

IRON AGE: in Britain, the period from *c.* 600 B.C. to the coming

of the Romans. The term is also used for those un-Romanized native communities which survived until the Saxon incursions especially beyond the Roman frontiers.

JACK ARCH: shallow segmental vault springing from beams, used for fireproof floors, bridge decks etc.

JAMB (*lit.* leg): one of the vertical sides of an opening.

JETTY: in a timber-framed building, the projection of an upper storey beyond the storey below, made by the beams and joists of the lower storey oversailing the external wall. On their outer ends is placed the sill of the walling for the storey above. Buildings can be jettied on several sides, in which case a *Dragon Beam* is set diagonally at the corner to carry the joists to either side.

JOGGLE: mason's term for joining two stones to prevent them slipping or sliding by means of a notch in one and a corresponding projection in the other.

KEEL MOULDING: moulding whose outline is in section like that of the keel of a ship (fig. 15).

Fig. 15. Keel Moulding

KEEP: principal tower of a castle. Also called *Donjon*.

KENTISH CUSP: *see* Tracery.

KEY PATTERN: *see* fig. 16.

KEYSTONE: central stone in an arch or vault.

Fig. 16. Key Pattern

KINGPOST: *see* Roofs (3) and fig. 24.

KNEELER: horizontal projecting stone at the base of each side of a gable on which the inclined coping stones rest. *See* Gable (fig. 12).

LABEL: *see* Hoodmould.

LACED WINDOWS: windows pulled visually together by strips of brickwork, usually of a different colour, which continue vertically the lines of the vertical parts of the window surround. Typical of *c*. 1720.

LACING COURSE: one or more bricks serving as horizontal reinforcement to flint, cobble, etc., walls.

LADY CHAPEL: chapel dedicated to the Virgin Mary (Our Lady).

LANCET WINDOW: slender single-light pointed-arched window.

LANTERN: (1) circular or polygonal turret with windows all round crowning a roof or a dome. (2) windowed stage of a crossing tower lighting the interior of a church.

LANTERN CROSS: churchyard cross with lantern-shaped top usually with sculptured representations on the sides of the top.

LAVATORIUM: in a monastery, a washing place adjacent to the refectory.

LEAN-TO: *see* Roofs (1).

LESENE (*lit.* a mean thing): pilaster without base or capital. Also called *Pilaster Strip*.

LIERNE: *see* Vault (fig. 36).

LIFT: in a gasholder, one of the telescopic sections.

LIGHT: compartment of a window defined by the mullions.

LINENFOLD: Tudor panelling where each panel is ornamented with a conventional representation of a piece of linen laid in vertical folds.

LINTEL: horizontal beam or stone bridging an opening.

LOGGIA: gallery open along one side of a building, usually arcaded or colonnaded. It may be a separate structure, usually in a garden.

LONG BARROW: unchambered Neolithic communal burial mound, often wedge-shaped in plan, with the burial and occasional other structures massed at the broader end, from which the mound itself tapers in height; quarry ditches flank the mound.

LONG-AND-SHORT WORK: quoins consisting of stones placed with the long side alternately upright and horizontal, especially in Saxon building.

LOUVRE: (1) opening, often with lantern over, in the roof of a building to let the smoke from a central hearth escape; (2) one of a series of overlapping boards or panes of glass placed in an opening to allow ventilation but keep the rain out.

LOWER PALAEOLITHIC: *see* Palaeolithic.

LOWSIDE WINDOW: window set lower than the others in a chancel side wall, usually towards its w end.

LOZENGE: diamond shape.

LUCARNE (*lit.* dormer): small gabled opening in a roof or spire.

LUGGED: *see* Architrave.

LUNETTE (*lit.* half or crescent moon): (1) semicircular window; (2) semicircular or crescent-shaped area of wall.

LYCHGATE (*lit.* corpse-gate): roofed wooden gateway at the entrance to a churchyard for the reception of a coffin.

LYNCHET: long terraced strip of soil accumulating on the downward side of prehistoric and medieval fields due to soil creep from continuous ploughing along the contours.

MACHICOLATIONS (*lit.* mashing devices): in medieval military architecture, a series of openings under a projecting parapet between the corbels that support it, through which missiles can be dropped.

MAJOLICA: ornamented glazed earthenware.

MANOMETER or STANDPIPE TOWER: containing a column of water to regulate pressure in water mains.

MANSARD: *see* Roofs (1) (fig. 23).

MARQUETRY: inlay in various woods. Also called *Intarsia*.

MATHEMATICAL TILES: facing tiles with one face moulded to look like a header or stretcher, most often hung on laths applied to timber-framed walls to make them appear brick-built.

MAUSOLEUM: monumental building or chamber usually intended for the burial of members of one family.

MEGALITHIC (*lit.* of large stones): archaeological term referring to the use of such stones, singly or together.

MEGALITHIC TOMB: massive stone-built Neolithic burial chamber covered by an earth or stone mound.

MERLON: *see* Battlement.

MESOLITHIC: 'Middle Stone' Age; the post-glacial period of hunting and fishing communities dating in Britain from *c.* 8000 B.C. to the arrival of the Neolithic (q.v.) communities, with whom they must have considerably overlapped in many areas.

METOPES: spaces between the triglyphs in a Doric frieze; *see* Orders (fig. 19).

MEZZANINE: (1) low storey between two higher ones; (2) low upper storey within the height of a high one, not extending over its whole area. *See also* Entresol.

MILD STEEL: *see* Cast Iron.

MISERERE: *see* Misericord.

MISERICORD (*lit.* mercy): shelf placed on the underside of a hinged choir stall seat which,

when turned up, supported the occupant during long periods of standing. Also called *Miserere*.

MODILLIONS: small consoles (q.v.) at regular intervals along the underside of the cornice of the Corinthian or Composite orders.

MODULE: in industrialized building (q.v.), a predetermined standard size for co-ordinating the dimensions of components of a building with the spaces into which they have to fit.

MOTTE: steep mound forming the main feature of C11 and C12 castles.

MOTTE-AND-BAILEY: post-Roman and Norman defence system consisting of an earthen mound (motte) topped with a wooden tower within a bailey, with enclosure ditch and palisade, and with the rare addition of an internal bank.

MOUCHETTE: *see* Tracery (fig. 33).

MOULDING: ornament of continuous section; *see* e.g. Cavetto, Ogee, Ovolo, Roll.

MULLION: vertical member between the lights in a window opening.

MULTI-STOREY: modern term denoting five or more storeys. *See* Cluster, Slab, and Point Blocks.

MULTIVALLATE: (of a hill-fort) defended by three or more concentric banks and ditches.

MUNTIN: vertical part in the framing of a door, screen, panelling, etc., butting into or stopped by the horizontal rails.

NAILHEAD MOULDING: E.E. ornamental motif consisting of small pyramids regularly repeated (*see* fig. 17).

NARTHEX: enclosed vestibule or

Fig. 17. Nailhead Moulding

covered porch at the main entrance to a church.

NAVE: the body of a church W of the crossing or chancel which may be flanked by aisles (q.v.).

NECESSARIUM: *see* Reredorter.

NEOLITHIC: term applied to the New Stone Age, dating in Britain from the appearance of the first settled farming communities from the continent *c.* 4000–3500 B.C. until the beginning of the Bronze Age. *See also* Mesolithic.

NEWEL: central post in a circular or winding staircase; also the principal post where a flight of stairs meets a landing. *See* Stair (fig. 30).

NICHE (*lit.* shell): vertical recess in a wall, sometimes for a statue.

NIGHT STAIR: stair by which monks entered the transept of their church from their dormitory to celebrate night services.

NOGGING: *see* Timber-framing.

NOOK-SHAFT: shaft set in the angle of a pier or respond or wall, or the angle of the jamb of a window or doorway.

NORMAN: *see* Romanesque.

NOSING: projection of the tread of a step. A *Bottle Nosing* is half-round in section.

NUTMEG MOULDING: consisting of a chain of tiny triangles placed obliquely.

OBELISK: tapering pillar of square section at the top and ending pyramidally.

OCULUS: circular opening or window in a wall or vault; cf. Bullseye Window.

ŒIL DE BŒUF: *see* Bullseye Window.

OGEE: double curve, bending first one way and then the other. Applied to mouldings, also called *Cyma Recta*. A reverse ogee moulding with a double curve also called *Cyma Reversa* (*see* fig. 18). *Ogee* or *Ogival Arch*: *see* fig. 2.

ORATORY: (1) small private

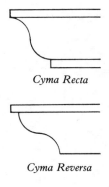

Cyma Recta

Cyma Reversa

Fig. 18. Ogee Mouldings

chapel in a church or a house; (2) church of the Oratorian Order.

ORDER: (1) upright structural member formally related to others, e.g. in classical architecture a column, pilaster, or anta; (2) especially in medieval architecture, one of a series of recessed arches and jambs forming a splayed opening. *Giant* or *Colossal Order*: classical order whose height is that of two or more storeys of a building.

ORDERS: in classical architecture, the differently formalized versions of the basic post-and-lintel (column and entablature) structure, each having its own rules for design and proportion. For examples of the main types *see* fig. 19. In the *Composite*, the capital combines Ionic volutes with Corinthian foliage. *Superimposed Orders*: term for the use of Orders on successive levels, usually in the upward sequence of Tuscan, Doric, Ionic, Corinthian.

ORIEL: *see* Bay-window.

OVERDOOR: *see* Sopraporta.

OVERHANG: *see* Jetty.

OVERSAILING COURSES: *see* Corbel (Corbelling).

OVERTHROW: decorative fixed arch between two gatepiers or above a wrought-iron gate.

OVOLO MOULDING: wide convex moulding.

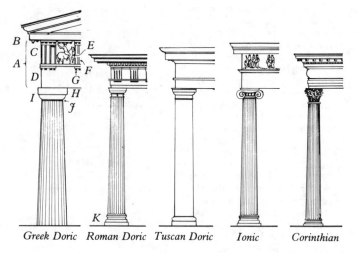

Fig. 19. Orders: A Entablature; B Cornice; C Frieze; D Architrave; E Metope;
F Triglyph; G Guttae; H Abacus; I Capital; J Echinus; K Base

PALAEOLITHIC: 'Old Stone'
Age; the first period of human
culture, commencing in the Ice
Age and immediately prior to
the Mesolithic; the Lower
Palaeolithic is the older phase,
the Upper Palaeolithic the later.

PALIMPSEST (*lit.* erased work):
re-use of a surface. (1) of a
brass: where a metal plate has
been re-used by turning over
and engraving on the back; (2)
of a wall painting: where one
overlaps and partly obscures an
earlier one.

PALLADIAN: architecture following the examples and principles
of Andrea Palladio (1508–80).

PALMETTE: classical ornament
like a symmetrical palm shoot;
for illustration *see* fig. 1.

PANELLING: wooden lining to
interior walls, made up of vertical members (muntins q.v.)
and horizontals (rails) framing
panels (*see* linenfold; raised and
fielded). Also called *Wainscot.*

PANTILE: roof tile of curved S-
shaped section.

PARAPET: wall for protection at
any sudden drop, e.g. on a
bridge or at the wall-head of a
castle; in the latter case it
protects the *Parapet Walk* or

wall walk. Also used to conceal
a roof.

PARCLOSE: *see* Screen.

PARGETTING (*lit.* plastering): in
timber-framed buildings, plasterwork with patterns and ornaments either moulded in relief
or incised on it.

PARLOUR: in a monastery, room
where monks were permitted to
talk to visitors.

PARTERRE: level space in a garden laid out with low, formal
beds of plants.

PATERA (*lit.* plate): round or oval
ornament in shallow relief,
especially in classical architecture.

PAVILION: (1) ornamental building for occasional use in a garden, park, sports ground, etc.;
(2) projecting subdivision of
some larger building, often at
an angle or terminating wings.

PEBBLEDASHING: *see* Rendering.

PEDESTAL: in classical architecture, a tall block carrying an
order, statue, vase, etc.

PEDIMENT: in classical architecture, a formalized gable derived from that of a temple, also
used over doors, windows, etc.
For variations of type *see* fig. 20.

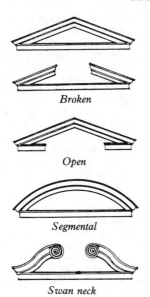

Broken

Open

Segmental

Swan neck

Fig. 20. Pediments

PEEL (*lit.* palisade): stone tower, e.g. near the Scottish–English border.

PENDANT: decorative feature hanging from a vault or ceiling, usually ending in a boss.

PENDENTIVE: spandrel formed as part of a hemisphere between arches meeting at an angle, supporting a drum or dome (*see* fig. 21).

PENTHOUSE: subsidiary structure with a lean-to roof; in modern architecture, a separately roofed structure on top of a multi-storey block.

Fig. 21. Pendentive

PERISTYLE: in classical architecture, a range of columns all round a building, e.g. a temple, or an interior space, e.g. a courtyard.

PERP (PERPENDICULAR): historical division of English Gothic architecture covering the period from *c.* 1335–50 to *c.* 1530. The name is derived from the upright tracery panels then used (*see* Tracery).

PERRON: *see* Stair.

PEW: loosely, seating for the laity outside the chancel. Strictly an enclosed seat. *Box Pew*: with equal high sides, entered by a door.

PIANO NOBILE: principal floor, usually with a ground floor or basement underneath and a lesser storey overhead.

PIAZZA: open space surrounded by buildings; in the C 17 and C 18 used erroneously to mean an arcaded ground floor, especially adjoining or around an open space.

PIER: large masonry or brick support, usually for an arch. *See also* Compound Pier.

PIETRA DURA: ornamental or pictorial inlay by means of thin slabs of stone.

PILASTER: flat representation of a classical column in shallow relief against a wall. *Pilastrade*: series of pilasters, equivalent to a colonnade. *Pilaster Strip: see* Lesene.

PILE: row of rooms. The important use of the term is in *Double Pile*, describing a house that is two rows thick.

PILLAR: free-standing upright member of any section, not conforming to one of the Orders.

PILLAR PISCINA: free-standing piscina on a pillar.

PILOTIS: French term used in modern architecture for pillars or stilts that carry a building to first-floor level leaving the ground floor open.

PINNACLE: tapering finial, e.g. on a buttress or the corner of a tower, sometimes decorated with crockets.

PISCINA: basin for washing the communion or mass vessels, provided with a drain; generally set in or against the wall to the s of an altar.

PLAISANCE: summer house, pleasure house near a mansion.

PLATE RAIL: see Railways.

PLATEWAY: see Railways.

PLINTH: projecting courses at the foot of a wall or column, generally chamfered or moulded at the top.

PODIUM: continuous raised platform supporting a building. In modern architecture often a large block of two or three storeys beneath a multi-storey block covering a smaller area.

POINT BLOCK: high block of housing in which the flats fan out from a central core of lifts, staircases, etc.

POINTING: exposed mortar jointing of masonry or brickwork. The finished form is of various types, e.g. *Flush Pointing, Recessed Pointing.*

POND BARROW: rare Bronze Age barrow type consisting of a circular depression, usually paved, and containing a number of cremation burials.

POPPYHEAD: carved ornament of leaves and flowers, generally in the form of a fleur-de-lys, as a finial for the end of a bench or stall.

PORCH: covered projecting entrance to a building.

PORTAL FRAME: in modern architecture a basic form of construction in which a series of precast concrete beams, placed in pairs to form 'portals', support the walls and roof. The upper part of each beam is angled up to where they meet at the roof ridge.

PORTCULLIS: gate constructed to rise and fall in vertical grooves at the entry to a castle.

PORTICO: a porch, open on one side at least, and enclosed by a row of columns which also support the roof and frequently a pediment. When the front of it is on the same plane as the front of the building it is described as a *Portico in Antis* (Antae q.v.). Porticoes are described by the number of the front columns, e.g. Tetrastyle (four), Hexastyle (six). *Blind Portico:* the front features of a portico applied to a wall.

PORTICUS (plural porticūs): in pre-Conquest architecture, a subsidiary cell opening from the main body of a church.

POSTERN: small gateway at the back of a building.

POUND LOCK: see Canals.

PRECAST CONCRETE: concrete components cast before being placed in position.

PREDELLA: (1) step or platform on which an altar stands; hence (2) in an altarpiece or stained glass window, the row of subsidiary scenes beneath the main representation.

PREFABRICATION: manufacture of buildings or components off-site for assembly on-site. *See also* Industrialized Building.

PRESBYTERY: (1) part of a church lying E of the choir where the main altar is placed; (2) a priest's residence.

PRESTRESSED CONCRETE: see Reinforced Concrete.

PRINCIPAL: see Roofs (3) and figs. 24, 27.

PRIORY: religious house whose head is a prior or prioress, not an abbot or abbess.

PROSTYLE: with a free-standing row of columns in front.

PULPIT: raised and enclosed platform used for the preaching of sermons. *Three-decker pulpit:* with reading desk below and clerk's desk below the reading desk. *Two-decker pulpit:* as above, but without the clerk's stall.

PULPITUM: stone screen in a major church provided to shut off the choir from the nave and also as a backing for the return choir stalls.

PULVINATED: see Frieze.

PURLIN: see Roofs (3) and figs. 24–7.

PUTHOLES		or		PUTLOCK

HOLES: in the wall to receive putlocks, the horizontal timbers on which scaffolding boards rest. They are often not filled in after construction is complete.

PUTTO: small naked boy (plural: putti. Also called *Amorini*.)

QUADRANGLE: rectangular inner courtyard in a large building.

QUARRIES (*lit.* squares): (1) square (or diamond-shaped) panes of glass supported by lead strips which are called *Cames*; (2) square floor-slabs or tiles.

QUATREFOIL: *see* Foil.

QUEENPOSTS: *see* Roofs (3) and fig. 26.

QUIRK: sharp groove to one side of a convex moulding, e.g. beside a roll moulding, which is then said to be quirked.

QUOINS: dressed stones at the angles of a building. They may be alternately long and short, especially when rusticated.

RADIATING CHAPELS: chapels projecting radially from an ambulatory or an apse; *see* Chevet.

RAFTER: *see* Roofs (3) and figs. 24–8.

RAGGLE: groove cut in masonry, especially to receive the edge of glass or roof-covering.

RAIL: *see* Muntin.

RAILWAYS: *Edge Rail:* rail on which flanged wheels can run, as in modern railways. *Plate Rail:* L-section rail for plain unflanged wheels, guidance being provided by the upstanding flange on the rail. *Plateway:* early railway using plate rails. *Sleeper Block:* stone block to support rail in lieu of timber sleeper.

RAISED AND FIELDED: of a wooden panel with a raised square or rectangular central area (field) surrounded by a narrow moulding.

RAKE: slope or pitch.

RAMPART: wall of stone or earth surrounding a hill-fort, castle, fortress, or fortified town. *Rampart Walk:* path along the inner face of a rampart.

REBATE: rectangular section cut out of a masonry edge to receive a shutter, door, window, etc.

REBUS: a heraldic pun, e.g. a fiery cock as a badge for Cockburn.

REEDING: series of convex mouldings; the reverse of fluting.

REFECTORY: dining hall of a monastery or similar establishment. Also called *Frater*.

REINFORCED CONCRETE: concrete reinforced with steel rods to take the tensile stress. A later development is *Prestressed Concrete*, which incorporates artificially-tensioned steel tendons.

RENDERING: the process of covering outside walls with a uniform surface or skin for protection from the weather. *Stucco*, originally a fine lime plaster worked to a smooth surface, is the finest rendered external finish, characteristic of many late C18 and C19 classical buildings. It is usually painted. *Cement Rendering* is a cheaper and more recent substitute for stucco, usually with a grainy texture and often left unpainted. In more simple buildings the wall surface may be roughly *Lime-plastered* (and then whitewashed), or covered with plaster mixed with a coarse aggregate such as gravel. This latter is known as *Roughcast*. A variant, fashionable in the early C20, is *Pebbledashing:* here the stones of the aggregate are kept separate and are thrown at the wet plastered wall to create a textured effect.

REPOUSSÉ: decoration of metalwork by relief designs, formed by beating the metal from the back.

REREDORTER (*lit.* behind the dormitory): medieval euphemism for latrines in a monastery. Also called *Necessarium*.

REREDOS: painted and/or sculptured screen behind and above an altar.

RESPOND: half-pier or half-column bonded into a wall and carrying one end of an arch. It usually terminates an arcade.

RETABLE: a picture or piece of carving standing at the back of an altar, usually attached to it. Also called an *Altarpiece*.

RETROCHOIR: in a major church, the space between the high altar and an E chapel, like a square ambulatory.

REVEAL: the inward plane of a jamb, between the edge of an external wall and the frame of a door or window that is set in it.

RIB-VAULT: *see* Vault.

RINCEAU (*lit.* little branch) or ANTIQUE FOLIAGE: classical ornament, usually on a frieze, of leafy scrolls branching alternately to left and right (*see* fig. 22).

Fig. 22. Rinceau

RISER: vertical face of a step.

ROCK-FACED: term used to describe masonry which is cleft to produce a natural rugged appearance.

ROCOCO (*lit.* rocky): latest phase of the Baroque style, current in most Continental countries between *c.* 1720 and *c.* 1760, and showing itself in Britain mainly in playful, scrolled decoration, especially plasterwork.

ROLL MOULDING: moulding of part-circular section used in medieval architecture.

ROMANESQUE: that style in architecture (in England often called Norman) which was current in the C 11 and C 12 and preceded the Gothic style. (Some scholars extend the use of the term Romanesque back to the C 10 or C 9.) *See also* Saxo-Norman.

ROMANO-BRITISH: general term applied to the period and cultural features of Britain affected by the Roman occupation of the C 1–5 A.D.

ROOD: cross or crucifix flanked by the Virgin and St John, usually over the entry into the chancel, on a beam (*Rood Beam*) or painted. The *Rood Screen* beneath it may have a *Rood Loft* along the top, reached by a *Rood Stair*.

ROOFS: (1) *Shape:* for the external shapes and terms used to describe them *see* fig. 23. *Helm:* roof with four inclined faces joined at the top, with a gable at the foot of each. *Hipped* (fig. 23): roof with sloped instead of vertical ends. *Lean-to:* roof with one slope only, built against a vertical wall: term also applied to the part of the building such a roof covers. *Mansard* (fig. 23): roof with a double slope, the lower one larger and steeper than the upper. *Saddleback:* the name given to a normal pitched roof when used over a tower. *See also* Wagon Roof.

(2) *Construction:* Roofs are generally called after the principal structural component, e.g. *crown-post, hammerbeam, king-post*, etc. See below under *Elements* and figs. 24–8.

A *single-framed* roof is constructed with no main trusses. The rafters may be fixed to a wall-plate or ridge, or longitudinal timbers may be absent altogether. A *common rafter* roof is one in which pairs of rafters are not connected by a collar-beam. A *coupled rafter* roof is one in which the rafters are connected by collar-beams.

A *double-framed* roof is constructed with longitudinal members such as purlins. Generally there are principals or principal rafters supporting the longitudinal members and dividing the length of the roof into bays.

(3) *Elements: Ashlar piece.* A short vertical timber connecting an inner wall-plate or timber pad to a rafter above.

Braces. Subsidiary timbers set diagonally to strengthen the frame. *Arched braces:* a pair of

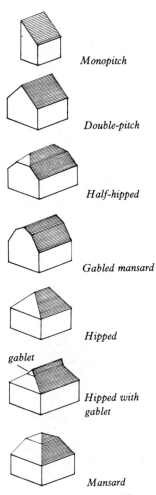

Monopitch

Double-pitch

Half-hipped

Gabled mansard

Hipped

gablet

Hipped with gablet

Mansard

Fig. 23. Roofs: external forms

curved braces forming an arch, usually connecting the wall or post below with the tie- or collar-beam above. *Passing braces:* straight braces of considerable length, passing across other members of the truss. *Scissor braces:* a pair of braces which cross diagonally between pairs of rafters or principals. *Windbraces:* short, usually curved braces connecting side purlins with principals. They are sometimes decorated with cusping.

Collar-beam. A horizontal transverse timber connecting a pair of rafters or principals at a height between the apex and the wall-plate.

Crown-post. A vertical timber standing centrally on a tie-beam and supporting a collar purlin. Longitudinal braces usually rise from the crown-post to the collar purlin. When the truss is open lateral braces generally rise to the collar-beam, and when the truss is closed they go down to the tie-beam.

Hammerbeams. Horizontal brackets projecting at wall-plate level on opposite sides of the wall like a tie-beam with the centre cut away. The inner ends carry vertical timbers called hammerposts and braces to a collar-beam.

Hammerpost. A vertical timber set on the inner end of a hammer-beam to support a purlin; it is braced to a collar-beam above.

Kingpost. A vertical timber standing centrally on a tie- or collar-beam and rising to the apex of the roof where it supports a ridge.

Principals. The pair of inclined lateral timbers of a truss which carry common rafters. Usually they support side purlins and their position corresponds to the main bay division of the space below.

Purlin. A horizontal longitudinal timber. *Collar purlin:* a single central timber which carries collar-beams and is itself supported by crown-posts. *Side purlins:* pairs of timbers occurring some way up the slope of the roof. They carry the common rafters and are supported in a number of ways: *butt purlins* are tenoned into either side of the principals; *clasped purlins* rest on queenposts or are carried in the angles between the principals and the collar; *laid-on purlins* lie on the backs of the principals; *trenched purlins* are trenched into the backs of the principals.

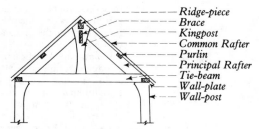

Fig. 24. Kingpost Roof

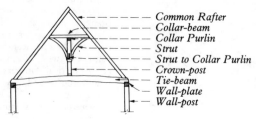

Fig. 25. Crown-post Roof

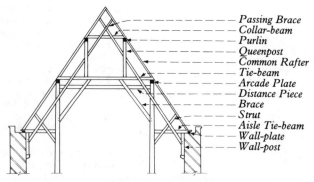

Fig. 26. Queenpost Roof

Queenposts. A pair of vertical, or near-vertical, timbers placed symmetrically on a tie-beam and supporting side purlins.

Rafters. Inclined lateral timbers sloping from wall-top to apex and supporting the roof covering. *Common rafters:* rafters of equal scantling found along the length of a roof or sometimes interrupted by main trusses containing principal rafters. *Principal rafters:* rafters

which act as principals but also serve as common rafters.

Ridge, ridge-piece. A horizontal, longitudinal timber at the apex of a roof supporting the ends of the rafters.

Sprocket. A short timber placed on the back and at the foot of a rafter to form projecting eaves.

Strut. A vertical or oblique timber which runs between two members of a roof truss but

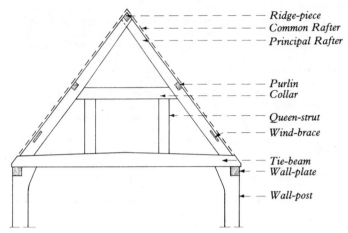

Fig. 27. Queen-strut Roof

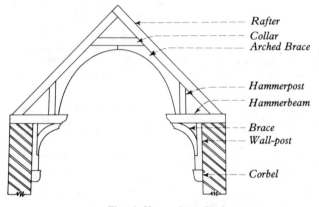

Fig. 28. Hammerbeam Roof

does not directly support longitudinal timbers.

Tie-beam. The main horizontal, transverse timber which carries the feet of the principals at wall-plate level.

Truss. A rigid framework of timbers which is placed laterally across the building to carry the longitudinal roof timbers which support the common rafters.

Wall-plate. A timber laid longitudinally on the top of a wall to receive the ends of the rafters. In a timber-framed building the

posts and studs of the wall below are tenoned into it.

ROPE MOULDING: *see* Cable Moulding.

ROSE WINDOW: circular window with tracery radiating from the centre; cf. Wheel Window.

ROTUNDA: building circular in plan.

ROUGHCAST: *see* Rendering.

ROVING BRIDGE: *see* Canals.

RUBBLE: masonry whose stones are wholly or partly in a rough state. *Coursed Rubble:* of coursed stones with rough

faces. *Random Rubble:* of un-
coursed stones in a random
pattern. *Snecked Rubble* has
courses frequently broken by
smaller stones (snecks).

RUSTICATION: exaggerated
treatment of masonry to give an
effect of strength. In the most
usual kind the joints are recessed by V-section chamfering
or square-section channelling.
Banded Rustication has only the
horizontal joints emphasized in
this way. The faces may be flat,
but there are many other forms,
e.g. *Diamond-faced*, like shallow pyramids, *Vermiculated*,
with a stylized texture like
worm-casts, and *Glacial* (frostwork) like icicles or stalactites.
Rusticated Columns may have
their joints and drums treated
in any of these ways.

SACRISTY: room in a church for
sacred vessels and vestments.
SADDLEBACK: *see* Roofs (1).
SALTIRE CROSS: with diagonal
limbs.
SANCTUARY: (1) area around the
main altar of a church (*see* Presbytery); (2) sacred site consisting of wood or stone up-
rights enclosed by a circular
bank and ditch. Beginning in
the Neolithic, they were elabo-
rated in the succeeding Bronze
Age. The best known examples
are Stonehenge and Avebury.
SARCOPHAGUS   (*lit.*   flesh-
consuming): coffin of stone or
other durable material.
SAUCER DOME: *see* Dome.
SAXO-NORMAN: transitional
Romanesque style combining
Anglo-Saxon and Norman features, current *c.* 1060–1100.
SCAGLIOLA: composition imitating marble.
SCALLOPED CAPITAL: *see* fig. 8.
SCARP: artificial cutting away of
the ground to form a steep
slope.
SCOTIA: a hollow moulding,
especially between tori (q.v.) on
a column base.

SCREEN: in a church, structure
usually at the entry to the chancel; *see* Rood (Screen) *and* Pulpitum. A *Parclose Screen* separates a chapel from the rest of
the church.
SCREENS or SCREENS PASSAGE:
screened-off entrance passage
between the hall and the service
rooms of a medieval, C16, or
early C17 house.
SECTION: two-dimensional representation of a building,
moulding, etc., revealed by
cutting across it.
SEDILIA (singular *sedile*): seats
for the priests (usually three) on
the S side of the chancel of a
church.
SET-OFF: *see* Weathering.
SGRAFFITO: scratched pattern,
often in plaster.
SHAFT: vertical member of round
or polygonal section, especially
the main part of a classical
column. *Shaft-ring:* ring like a
belt round a circular pier or a
circular shaft attached to a pier,
characteristic of the C12 and
C13.
SHARAWAGGI: a term, first used
c. 1685 in Sir William Temple's
Essay on Gardening, which describes an irregular or asymmetrical composition.
SHEILA-NA-GIG: female fertility
figure, usually with legs wide
open.
SHOULDERED: *see* Arch (fig. 2),
Architrave (fig. 3).
SHUTTERED   CONCRETE: *see*
Formwork.
SILL: (1) horizontal member at
the bottom of a window- or
door-frame; (2) the horizontal
member at the base of a timber-
framed wall into which the
posts and studs (q.v.) are
tenoned.
SLAB BLOCK: rectangular multi-
storey block of housing or
offices.
SLATE-HANGING: covering of
overlapping slates on a wall,
which is then said to be *slate-
hung. Tile-hanging* is similar.
SLEEPER BLOCK: *see* Railways.
SLYPE: covered way or passage,

especially in a cathedral or monastic church, leading E from the cloisters between transept and chapter house.

SNECKED: see Rubble.

SOFFIT: (lit. ceiling): underside of an arch (also called *Intrados*), lintel, etc. *Soffit Roll:* roll moulding on a soffit.

SOLAR (lit. sun-room): upper living room or withdrawing room of a medieval house, accessible from the high table end of the hall.

SOPRAPORTA (lit. over door): painting or relief above the door of a room, usual in the C17 and C18.

SOUNDING-BOARD: horizontal board or canopy over a pulpit; also called *Tester.*

SOUTERRAIN: underground stone-lined passage and chamber.

S.P.A.B.: Society for the Protection of Ancient Buildings.

SPANDRELS: roughly triangular spaces between an arch and its containing rectangle, or between adjacent arches. In modern architecture the non-structural panels under the windows in a framed building.

SPERE: a fixed structure which serves as a screen at the lower end of an open medieval hall between the hall proper and the screens passage. It has a wide central opening, often with a movable screen, between posts and short screen walls. The top member is often the tie-beam of the roof truss above; screen and truss are then called a *Speretruss.*

SPIRE: tall pyramidal or conical feature built on a tower or turret. *Broach Spire:* starting from a square base, then carried into an octagonal section by means of triangular faces. The *Splayed-foot Spire* is a variation of the broach form, found principally in the south-eastern counties, in which the four cardinal faces are splayed out near their base, to cover the corners, while oblique (or intermediate)

faces taper away to a point. *Needle Spire:* thin spire rising from the centre of a tower roof, well inside the parapet: when of timber and lead often called a *Spike.*

SPIRELET: see Flèche.

SPLAY: chamfer, usually of a reveal.

SPRING or SPRINGING: level at which an arch or vault rises from its supports. *Springers:* the first stones of an arch or vaulting-rib above the spring.

SQUINCH: arch or series of arches thrown across an angle between two walls to support a superstructure of polygonal or round plan over a rectangular space, e.g. a dome, a spire (*see* fig. 29).

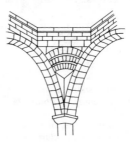

Fig. 29. Squinch

SQUINT: an aperture in a wall or through a pier usually to allow a view of an altar of a church otherwise obscured. Also called *Hagioscope.*

STAIRS: *see* fig. 30. A *Dog-leg Stair* has parallel flights rising alternately in opposite directions, without an open well. *Newel Stair:* ascending round a central supporting newel (q.v.), called a *Spiral Stair* or *Vice* when in a circular shaft. *Well Stair:* term applied to any stair contained in an open well, but generally to one that climbs up three sides of a well with corner landings, e.g. the *timber-framed newel stair,* common from the C17 on. *Flying Stair:* cantilevered from the wall of a stairwell, without newels. *Geometric Stair:* flying stair whose inner edge describes a curve. *Perron* (lit. of stone):

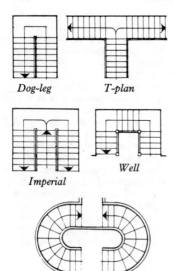

Dog-leg   T-plan

Imperial   Well

Perron

Fig. 30. Stairs

external stair leading to a doorway, usually of double-curved plan.

STALL: fixed seat in the choir or chancel for the clergy or choir (cf. Pew). Usually with arm rests. Often framed together like a bench.

STANCHION: upright structural member, of iron or steel or reinforced concrete.

STANDPIPE TOWER: see Manometer.

STEAM ENGINES: *Atmospheric*: the earliest type, worked by the vacuum created when low pressure steam was condensed in the cylinder, as developed by Thomas Newcomen. *Beam Engine:* with a large pivoted beam moved in an oscillating fashion by the piston. It may drive a fly wheel or be *Non-rotative*. Different types are the *Watt* and *Cornish* engines (single-cylinder), the *Compound* (two cylinder) or *Triple Expansion* (three cylinders). The cylinders may be mounted in various ways.

STEEPLE: tower together with a spire, lantern or belfry.

STIFF-LEAF: type of E.E. foliage decoration. *Stiff-leaf Capital: see* fig. 8.

STOP: plain or decorated blocks terminating mouldings or chamfers in stone or wood, or at the end of labels, hoodmoulds, or string courses.

STOUP: vessel for the reception of holy water, usually placed near a door.

STRAINER: *see* Arch.

STRAPWORK: late C16 and C17 decoration, resembling straplike interlaced bands of leather.

STRETCHER: *see* Bond.

STRING COURSE: horizontal stone course or moulding projecting from the surface of a wall.

STRINGS: two sloping members which carry the ends of the treads and risers of a staircase. Closed strings enclose the treads and risers; in the later open string staircase the steps project above the strings.

STUCCO (*lit.* plaster): *see* Rendering.

STUDS: subsidiary vertical timbers of a timber-framed wall or partition.

STYLOBATE: solid platform on which a colonnade stands.

SUSPENSION BRIDGE: bridge suspended from cables or chains draped from towers. *Stay-suspension* or *Stayed-cantilever Bridge:* supported by diagonal stays from towers or pylons.

SWAG (*lit.* bundle): ornament suspended like a festoon (q.v.), but usually representing cloth.

SYSTEM BUILDING: *see* Industrialized Building.

TABERNACLE (*lit.* tent): (1) canopied structure, especially on a small scale, to contain the reserved sacrament or a relic; (2) architectural frame, e.g. of a statue on a wall or free-standing, with flanking orders. In classical architecture also called an *Aedicule*.

TABLE TOMB: a memorial slab raised on free-standing legs.

TABLET FLOWER: medieval ornament of a four-leaved flower with a raised or sunk centre.

TAS-DE-CHARGE: the lower courses of a vault or arch laid horizontally.

TERMINAL FIGURE: pedestal or pilaster which tapers towards the bottom, usually with the upper part of a human figure growing out of it. Also called *Term*.

TERRACOTTA: moulded and fired clay ornament or cladding, usually unglazed.

TESSELLATED PAVEMENT: mosaic flooring, particularly Roman, consisting of small *Tesserae*, i.e. cubes of glass, stone, or brick.

TESTER (*lit.* head): flat canopy over a tomb and especially over a pulpit, where it is also called a *Sounding-board*.

TESTER TOMB: C 16 or C 17 type with effigies on a tomb-chest beneath a tester, either free-standing (tester with four or more columns), or attached to a wall (half tester) with columns on one side only.

TETRASTYLE: *see* Portico.

THERMAE WINDOW (*lit.* of a Roman bath); *see* Diocletian Window.

THREE-DECKER PULPIT: *see* Pulpit.

TIDAL DOORS: *see* Canals.

TIE-BEAM: *see* Roofs (3) and figs. 24–7.

TIERCERON: *see* Vault (fig. 36).

TILE-HANGING: *see* Slate-hanging.

TIMBER-FRAMING: method of construction where walls are built of interlocking vertical and horizontal timbers. The spaces are filled with non-structural walling of wattle and daub, lath and plaster, brick-work (known as nogging), etc. Sometimes the timber is covered over by plaster, boarding laid horizontally (weather-boarding q.v.), or tiles.

TOMB-CHEST: chest-shaped stone coffin. *See also* Table Tomb, Tester Tomb.

TORUS: large convex moulding usually used on a column base.

TOUCH: soft black marble quarried near Tournai.

TOURELLE: turret corbelled out from the wall.

TOWER HOUSE: compact medieval fortified house with the main hall raised above the ground and at least one more storey above it. The type survives in odd examples into the C 16 and C 17.

TRABEATED: depends structurally on the use of the post and lintel; cf. Arcuated.

TRACERY: intersecting ribwork in the upper part of a window, or used decoratively in blank arches, on vaults, etc. (1) *Plate tracery: see* fig. 31(*a*). Early form of tracery where decoratively shaped openings are cut through the solid stone infilling in a window head. (2) *Bar tracery:* a form introduced into England *c.* 1250. Intersecting ribwork made up of slender shafts, continuing the lines of the mullions of windows up to a decorative mesh in the head of the win-

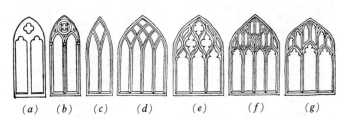

(*a*)   (*b*)   (*c*)   (*d*)   (*e*)   (*f*)   (*g*)

Fig. 31. Tracery

dow. The types of bar tracery are: *Geometrical tracery: see* fig. 31(*b*). Tracery characteristic of *c.* 1250–1310 consisting chiefly of circles or foiled circles. *Y-tracery: see* fig. 31(*c*). Tracery consisting of a mullion which branches into two forming a Y shape; typical of *c.* 1300. *Intersecting tracery: see* fig. 31(*d*). Tracery in which each mullion of a window branches out into two curved bars in such a way that every one of them is drawn with the same radius from a different centre. The result is that every light of the window is a lancet and every two, three, four, etc., lights together form a pointed arch. This also is typical of *c.* 1300. *Reticulated tracery: see* fig. 31(*e*). Tracery typical of the early C 14 consisting entirely of circles drawn at top and bottom into ogee shapes so that a net-like appearance results. *Panel tracery: see* fig. 31 (*f*) and (*g*). Perp tracery, which is formed of upright straight-sided panels above lights of a window. *Dagger:* Dec tracery motif; *see* fig. 32. *Kentish* or *Split Cusp:* cusp split into a fork. *Mouchette:* curved version of the dagger form, especially popular in the early C 14; *see* fig. 33.

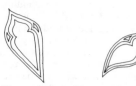

Fig. 32. Dagger   Fig. 33. Mouchette

TRANSEPT (*lit.* cross-enclosure): transverse portion of a cross-shaped church.

TRANSITIONAL: transitional phase between two styles, used most often for the phase between Romanesque and Early English (*c.* 1175–*c.* 1200).

TRANSOM: horizontal member between the lights in a window opening.

TREAD: horizontal part of the step of a staircase. The *Tread End* may be carved.

TREFOIL: *see* Foil.

TRIBUNE: *see* Gallery (1).

TRIFORIUM (*lit.* three openings): middle storey of a church treated as an arcaded wall passage or blind arcade, its height corresponding to that of the aisle roof.

TRIGLYPHS (*lit.* three-grooved tablets): stylized beam-ends in the Doric frieze, with metopes between; *see* Orders (fig. 19).

TRIUMPHAL ARCH: type of Imperial Roman monument whose elevation supplied a motif for many later classical compositions (*see* fig. 34).

Fig. 34. Triumphal Arch

TROPHY: sculptured group of arms or armour as a memorial of victory.

TRUMEAU: central stone mullion supporting the tympanum of a wide doorway. *Trumeau Figure:* carved figure attached to a trumeau (cf. Column Figure).

TRUSS: braced framework, spanning between supports. *See also* Roofs.

TUDOR FLOWER: late Gothic ornament of a flower with square flat petals or foliage.

TUMBLING or TUMBLING-IN: term used to describe courses of brickwork laid at right angles to the slope of a gable and forming triangles by tapering into horizontal courses.

TUMULUS (*lit.* mound): barrow.

TURRET: small tower, usually attached to a building.

TUSCAN: *see* Orders (fig. 19).

TWO-DECKER PULPIT: *see* Pulpit.

TYMPANUM (*lit.* drum): as of a drum-skin, the surface between a lintel and the arch above it or within a pediment.

UNDERCROFT: vaulted room, sometimes underground, below the main upper room.

UNIVALLATE: (of a hill-fort) defended by a single bank and ditch.

UPPER PALAEOLITHIC: *see* Palaeolithic.

VAULT: ceiling of stone formed like arches (sometimes imitated in timber or plaster); *see* fig. 35. *Tunnel-* or *Barrel-Vault:* the simplest kind of vault, in effect a continuous semicircular arch. *Groin-Vaults* (which are usually called *Cross-Vaults* in classical architecture) have four curving

Cross- or Groin-Vault   *Tunnel- or Barrel-Vault*   *Pointed Barrel-Vault*

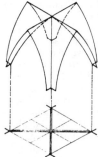 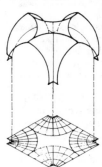

Fig. 35. Vaults

Quadripartite Rib-Vault   *Fan-Vault*

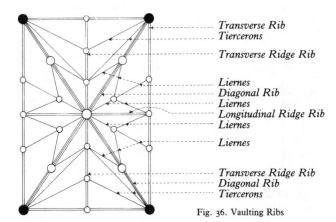

Transverse Rib
Tiercerons
Transverse Ridge Rib

Liernes
Diagonal Rib
Liernes
Longitudinal Ridge Rib
Liernes

Liernes

Transverse Ridge Rib
Diagonal Rib
Tiercerons

Fig. 36. Vaulting Ribs

triangular surfaces produced by the intersection of two tunnel-vaults at right angles. The curved lines at the intersections are called groins. In *Quadripartite Rib-Vaults* the four sections are divided by their arches or ribs springing from the corners of the bay. *Sexpartite Rib-Vaults*, most often used over paired bays, have an extra pair of ribs which spring from between the bays and meet the other four ribs at the crown of the vault. The main types of rib are shown in fig. 36: *transverse ribs, wall ribs, diagonal ribs,* and *ridge ribs. Tiercerons* are extra, decorative ribs springing from the corners of a bay. *Liernes* are decorative ribs in the crown of a vault which are not linked to any of the springing points. In a *Stellar Vault* the liernes are arranged in a star formation as in fig. 36. *Fan-Vaults* are peculiar to English Perpendicular architecture in consisting not of ribs and infilling but of halved concave cones with decorative blind tracery carved on their surfaces.

VAULTING-SHAFT: shaft leading up to the springer of a vault.

VENETIAN WINDOW: a form derived from an invention by Serlio, also called a Serlian or Palladian window. The same motif is used for other openings (*see* fig. 37).

VERANDA(H): shelter or gallery against a building, its roof supported by thin vertical members.

VERMICULATION: *see* Rustication.

VERNACULAR ARCHITECTURE: design by one without any training in design, guided by a series of conventions built up in a locality (Brunskill).

VESICA: oval with pointed head and foot, usually of a window or tracery.

VESTIBULE: anteroom or entrance hall.

VICE: *see* Stair.

VILLA: originally (1) a Romano-British farm or country house. The term is one of convenience and covers a wide spectrum of sites, ranging from humble farmsteads to sumptuous mansions associated with large estates. Various architectural traditions, including both classical and vernacular, are evident in villas, but all display some pretension towards fundamental Roman standards. (2) the C16 Venetian type with office wings, derived from Roman models and made grander by Palladio's varied application of a central portico. It became an important type in C18 Britain, often with the special meaning of (3) a country house which is not a principal residence. Gwilt (1842) defined the villa as 'a country house for the residence of opulent persons'. But devaluation had already begun, and the term also implied, as now, (4) a more or less pretentious suburban house.

VITRIFIED: bricks or tiles fired to produce a darkened glassy surface.

VITRUVIAN OPENING: door or window which diminishes towards the top, as advocated by Vitruvius, book IV, chapter VI.

VITRUVIAN SCROLL: classical running ornament of curly waves (*see* fig. 38).

Fig. 37. Venetian Window

Fig. 38. Vitruvian Scroll

VOLUTES: spiral scrolls on the front and back of a Greek Ionic capital, also on the sides of a Roman one. *Angle Volute:* pair of volutes turned outwards to meet at the corner of a capital. Volutes were also used individually as decoration in C17 and C18 architecture.

VOUSSOIRS: wedge-shaped stones forming an arch.

WAGON ROOF: roof in which closely set rafters with arched braces give the appearance of the inside of a canvas tilt over a wagon. Wagon roofs can be panelled or plastered (ceiled) or left uncovered. Also called *Cradle Roof*.

WAINSCOT: *see* Panelling.

WALL MONUMENT: substantial monument attached to the wall and often standing on the floor. *Wall Tablets* are smaller in scale with the inscription as the major element.

WALL-PLATE: *see* Roofs (3) and figs. 24–7.

WARMING ROOM: *see* Calefactory.

WATERHOLDING BASE: type of early Gothic base in which the upper and lower mouldings are separated by a hollow so deep as to be capable of retaining water.

WATERLEAF CAPITAL: *see* fig. 8.

WATER WHEELS: described by the way the water is fed on to the wheel. *Overshot:* over the top. *Pitchback:* on to the top but falling backwards. *Breastshot:* mid-height, falling and passing beneath. An *undershot* wheel is turned by the momentum of the water passing beneath. In a *Water Turbine* water is fed under pressure through a vaned wheel within a casing.

WEALDEN HOUSE: medieval timber-framed house of distinctive form. It has a central open hall flanked by bays of two storeys. The end bays are jettied to the front, but a single roof covers the whole building, thus producing an exceptionally wide overhang to the eaves in front of the hall.

WEATHERBOARDING: overlapping horizontal boards, covering a timber-framed wall, most common after the mid C18.

WEATHERING: inclined, projecting surface to keep water away from wall and joints below. Also called *Set-off*.

WEEPERS: small figures placed in niches along the sides of some medieval tombs. Also called *Mourners*.

WHEEL WINDOW: circular window with radiating shafts like the spokes of a wheel. *See also* Rose Window.

WROUGHT IRON: *see* Cast Iron.

INDEX OF ARTISTS

INDEX OF STREETS AND BUILDINGS

This index has entries for all major buildings mentioned by name in the introduction and gazetteer (all churches and public buildings, and the most important buildings included in the perambulations) and for all streets mentioned in the gazetteer. For place names see separate index of boroughs and localities.

References in **bold** type are to the page of the gazetteer on which the street or building receives its principal discussion. References in *italic* type are to buildings which no longer stand. References in roman type within an italic entry are to remaining parts or furnishings of a vanished building.

Broadways and High Streets are indexed together, followed by their individual names. The following types of buildings are indexed under the appropriate main heading: Board Schools, Cemeteries, Civic Centres, County Courts, Fire Stations, Friends' Meeting Houses, Health Centres, Magistrates' Courts, Manor Houses, Municipal Offices, Police Stations, Post Offices, Power Stations, Public Baths and Swimming Pools, Public Libraries, Pumping Stations, Telephone Exchanges, Town Halls, Underground Stations, Water Towers, Waterworks, Windmills.

The following abbreviations are employed for boroughs:

Bm	Bromley	Le	Lewisham
Bx	Bexley	Me	Merton
Cr	Croydon	Ri	Richmond
Gr	Greenwich	Sk	Southwark
Ki	Kingston	Su	Sutton
La	Lambeth	Ww	Wandsworth

INDEX OF BOROUGHS AND LOCALITIES